FROM THE LIBRARY OF

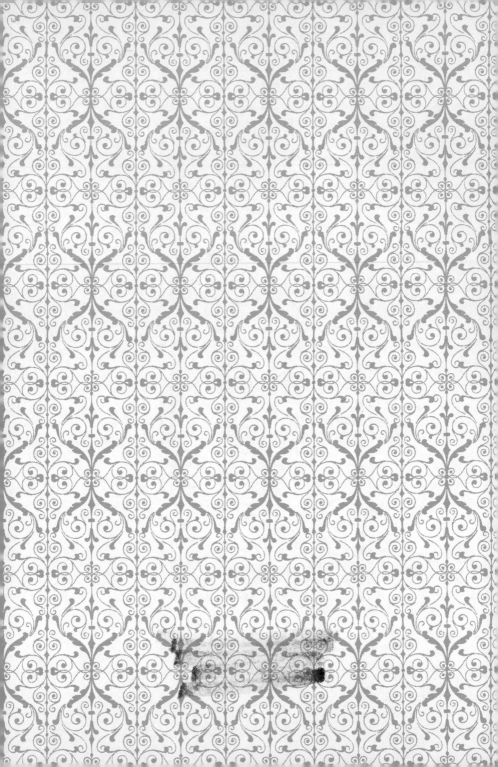

· CASTLE WAITING ·

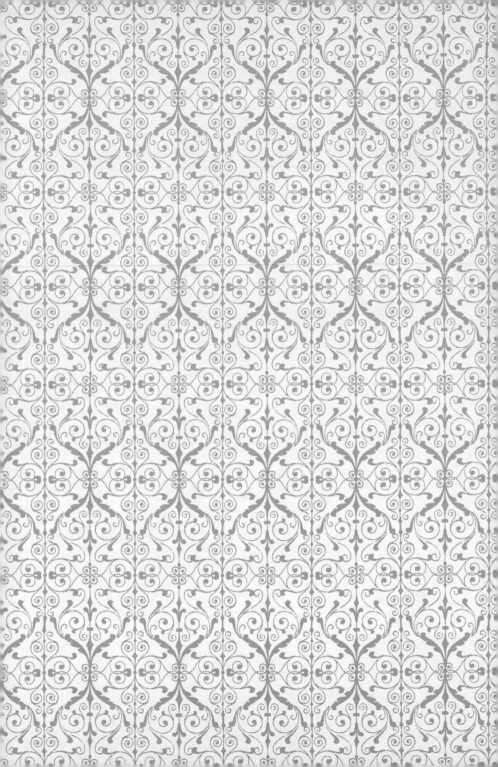

Castle Waiting

· BY LINDA MEDLEY ·

With an introduction by Jane Yolen

SANCTUM
OMNIUM · GATHERUM

FANTAGRAPHICS BOOKS

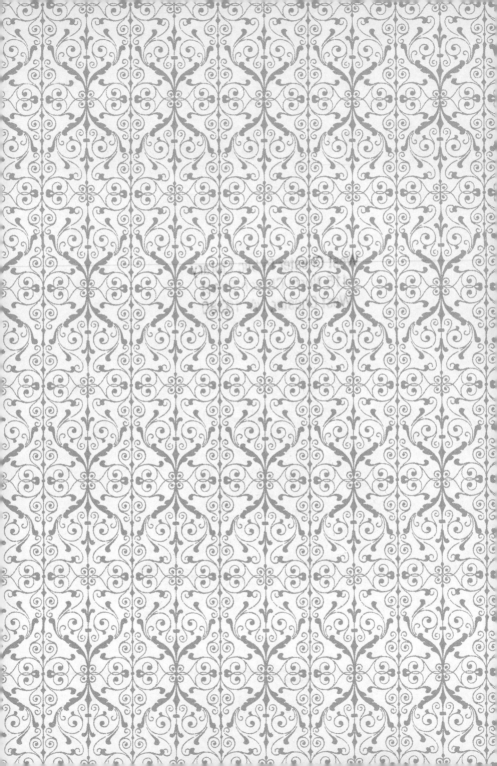

Introduction.

Waiting for the Castle
· BY JANE YOLEN ·

ONCE UPON A TIME, which is how all good fairy tales begin (if you grew up within the Western culture), a child was born in the rural Salinas area of California. Or Califunny as those of us who live 3000 miles away like to call it. Which, if one were writing a fairy tale, would be prophetic. If one were drawing a comic, it would come with a banner: *Here is born Linda Medley*. Then an arrow to a group of trees, Rackham trees. A child sits with her back against the heavy bark, in her lap a drawing pad. There is a newspaper, folded to the comics page by her side, a copy of Grimm Tales on her lap. Under this picture it says: "She drew from the age of three. She didn't see a city until she left for college."

Comics. Funnies. Like Linda, I grew up with them. But the serious comics of today, the Neil Gaiman/Dave McKean/Charles Vess/Jeff Smith kind of comic that mixes faerie and magic and morbidity, referencing literature and art and history, pulling in myth and symbol and cultural appropriations, those are a far cry from the Archie comics that I grew up with. They have more to do with classic storytelling and classic book illustration than Dagwood and Blondie.

So once after that time, Linda Medley headed off to art school, studying in the illustration program at the Academy of Art College in San Francisco. Picture her at a drawing board, the Bay Bridge outside her window (though she may have looked out on another view, this is magic, remember.) A long shot, repeated three and a half times, for the three and a half years she took to get a BFA. There is a computer to one side of the drawing table with BROKEN NOT IN USE DO NOT TOUCH THIS MACHINE EATS ART scribbled all over in red paint.

In high school one year I sneaked a friend's copies of the Tales from the Crypt. *To this day I can remember the panels in Bradbury's "The October Game" with horrific awe. But I came to those comics too late. By 1954 the media attack on horror comics pulled the plug on the E.C. line. I'd read all that my friend had to lend me and there were no more.*

Right out of college, Linda was so good, she landed lots of different illustration jobs, some even drawing comics. Picture all those doors opening, labeled *Dragon Magazine, Dungeon Adventures Magazine*, Gift Wrap Designer. Doors that open onto inviting fields where we see gamboling fauns in one, gambling tables in another, and an endless pile of Christmas presents in the third.

But what I really loved were not comics but fairy tales and fantasy books. The artwork of Arthur Rackham, H. A. Ford, Kai Nielsen, Heath and Charles Robinson. (We actually own a large original Charles Robinson painting, only slightly eaten by rats, a water scene with an infant and fish swimming about, though as far as we know, he never illustrated The Waterbabies.*) As a child I had eaten up every Andrew Lang Colour Fairy book. As an adult I was in love with Isak Dinesen, Angela Carter, Alice Hoffman, Tanith Lee. My new illustration heroes were Trina Schart Hyman, Charles Mikolaycak, the Dillons, Brian Froud, Terri Windling, and Alan Lee.*

Picture this, at a con, the young—still very young at 25—Linda Medley showing ten pages of superheroes she and her brother Greg had made up when they were kids to a DC editor. He is flipping through the pages. FLIP FLIP FLIP. And then FLIPFLIPFLIPFLIPFLIP-FLIPFLIP. He turns to Linda who is standing diffidently by his side, expecting nothing. "These are pretty good. Send them to DC."

Another arrow, in gold, with sun rays as the package goes to the offices of DC. A door like the three doors above. Only closed. With a heavy metal slot in the door. With the package slipping through the slot. Close up through the slot: DC offices with manuscripts and art work cascading off of desks onto the floor. A man on phone is saying, "Linda, you want to do something for us?" I told you, this is a fairy tale. But unlike most fairy tales, this one is true. I will argue the difference between True and true with you some other time, when we are sitting comfortably, drinks between us.

It took me years to rediscover comics. X-Men when my son's band, "Cats Laughing," was referenced in several. Then at Will Shetterly and Emma Bull's Minneapolis house one weekend, I was the only one awake and I found Will's Captain Confederacy *stuff. And then* Sandman *written by Neil Gaiman. Was this the same eager young man who I met at World Fantasy Con in London where he was dancing attendance on the Queen of British children's fantasy, the irrepressible Diana Wynne Jones? Astonishing.* Sandman *was what I would have wanted to write if I did comics. Which of course I don't do. Didn't do. Then.*

So once after that other time, this time, Linda Medley walked through the D.C. door. Super-heroes escort her in. Justice League, Wonder Woman, Batman, Superman, Green Lantern, Doom Patrol all crowding around her. They lean over her shoulder, open bottles of ink, nearly push her off the chair. They follow her into the bathroom. Offer her toilet paper. Wash her hands. She cannot get them to leave her alone.

I was alone in my family reading comics. Even as a child. And not till my oldest son, Adam, a musician, a fanatic reader of fantasy and sf, grew up enough did we share that secret pleasure. But we only share "Sandman" and, after that, Books of Magic. *I even got to write an intro to* Books of Magic. *I met Linda Medley there, didn't realize it. Got called one of the fantasy witches by Gaiman. Adam produced his spoken word records. Neil and I write songs for The Flash Girls, Folk Underground, hangers-on in the garage band world. Suddenly there are circles within circles.*

So once finally a time, Linda Medley got to do exactly what she wanted to do all along, write and draw her own comics. *Castle Waiting* was the result. It had everything in it that she'd been born to do: Comics, Grimms, Rackham, faeries, magic, potions, notions, pregnancy, birth, death, jokes, truth. Rather, Truth. How can I argue with you over a glass of something unless I get my own terms right.

And then I got to do two comics for Charles Vess for his Book of Ballads, *which made me realize how hard they are to write. That is where I saw a preview of* Castle Waiting.

So when I look at the whole of *Castle Waiting*, with its arcing storyline, its in-jokes, and outtakes, the fully realized place and the three-dimensional characters—and I am just talking script here—I can marvel at how polished and secure the writer is. But she's also the illustrator and her work is the same: polished, secure, fully realized, with quickly identifiable characters who remain "in character" whether they are speaking or standing to the side.

And then there are those wonderful sudden "I get it!" moments: the three pigs waving goodby to Jain who is off to seek her fortune (as well as hide out from an angry husband). When Jain gets called the daughter of the wealthy Count of Carabas—I think: a Puss in Boots reference? And Iron Henry/Iron John. And Rackham, who doubles as the stork. And... and... and... LADIES WITH BEARDS! I who do pucker and plucker every day, am in love.

In other words, what I adore about Castle Waiting *is that while it is a fully realized world, a world that any ordinary reader can enjoy, it is also a world for which I have special knowledge. Knowledge I have been years amassing. So I feel as if Linda Medley is an old friend who has written* Castle Waiting *just for me — a feminist fairy tale with attitude, heart, imagination, laughter, love and truth. Er, Truth.*

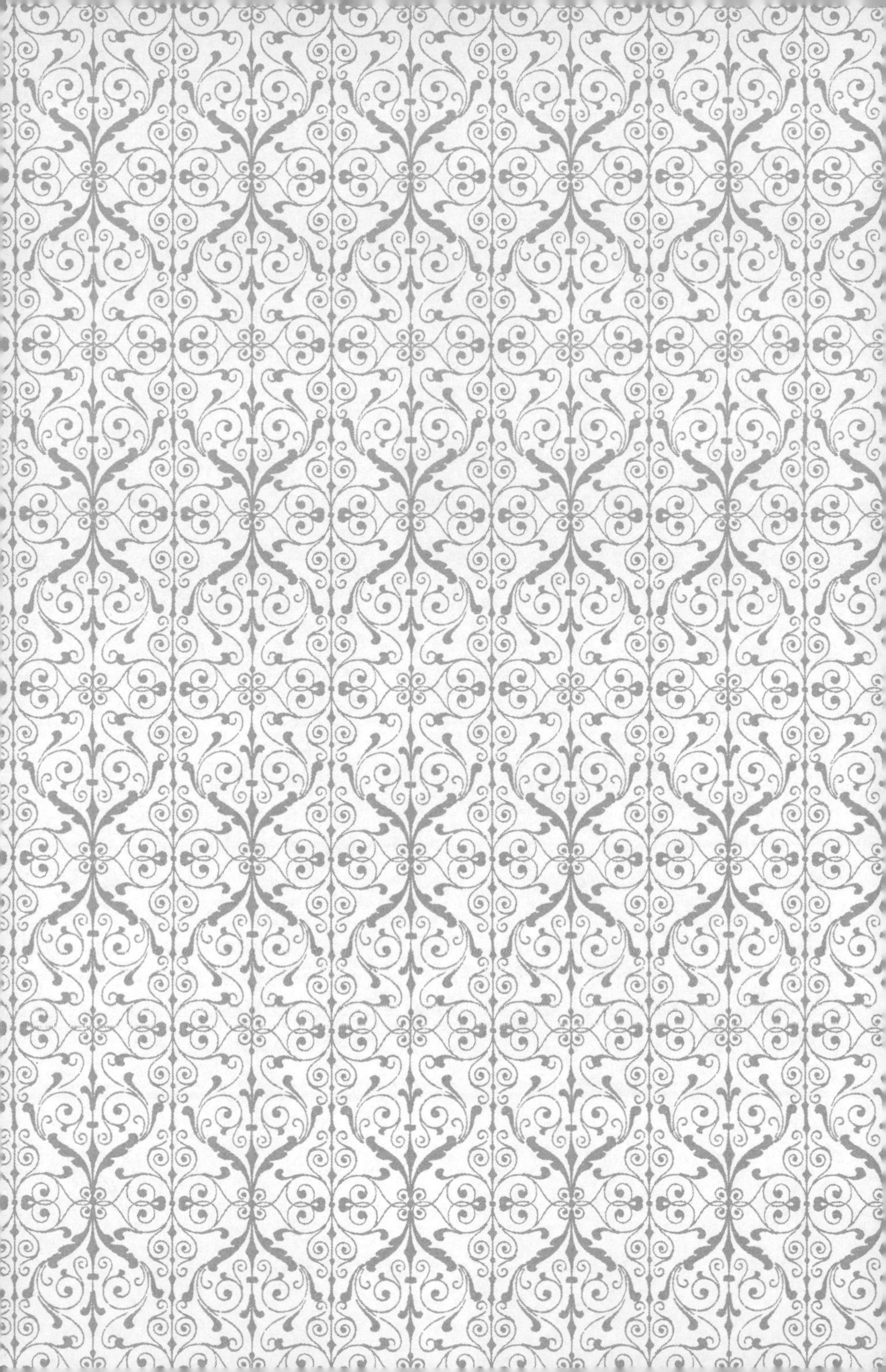

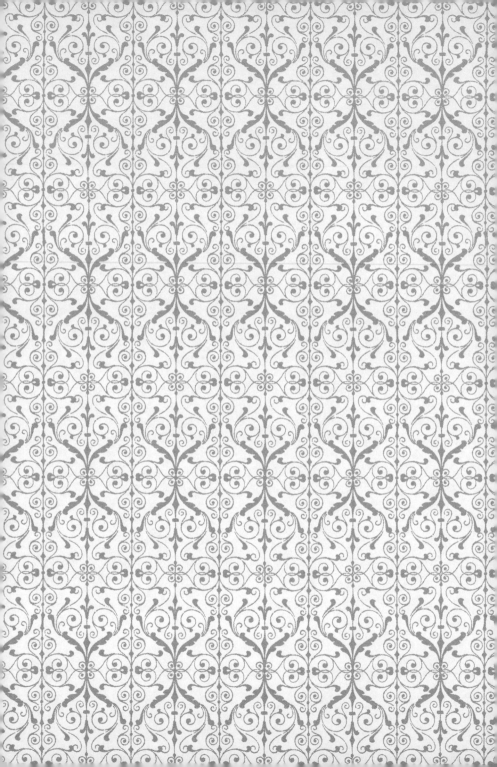

Chapter 1.

· THE CURSE OF BRAMBLY HEDGE PT. I ·

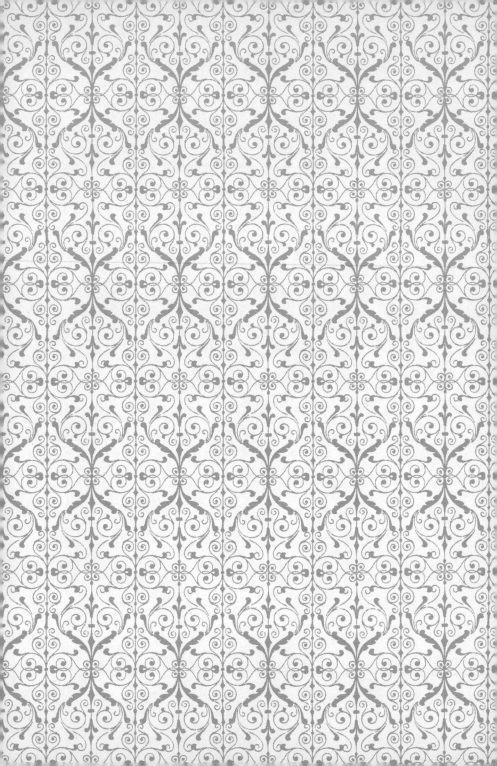

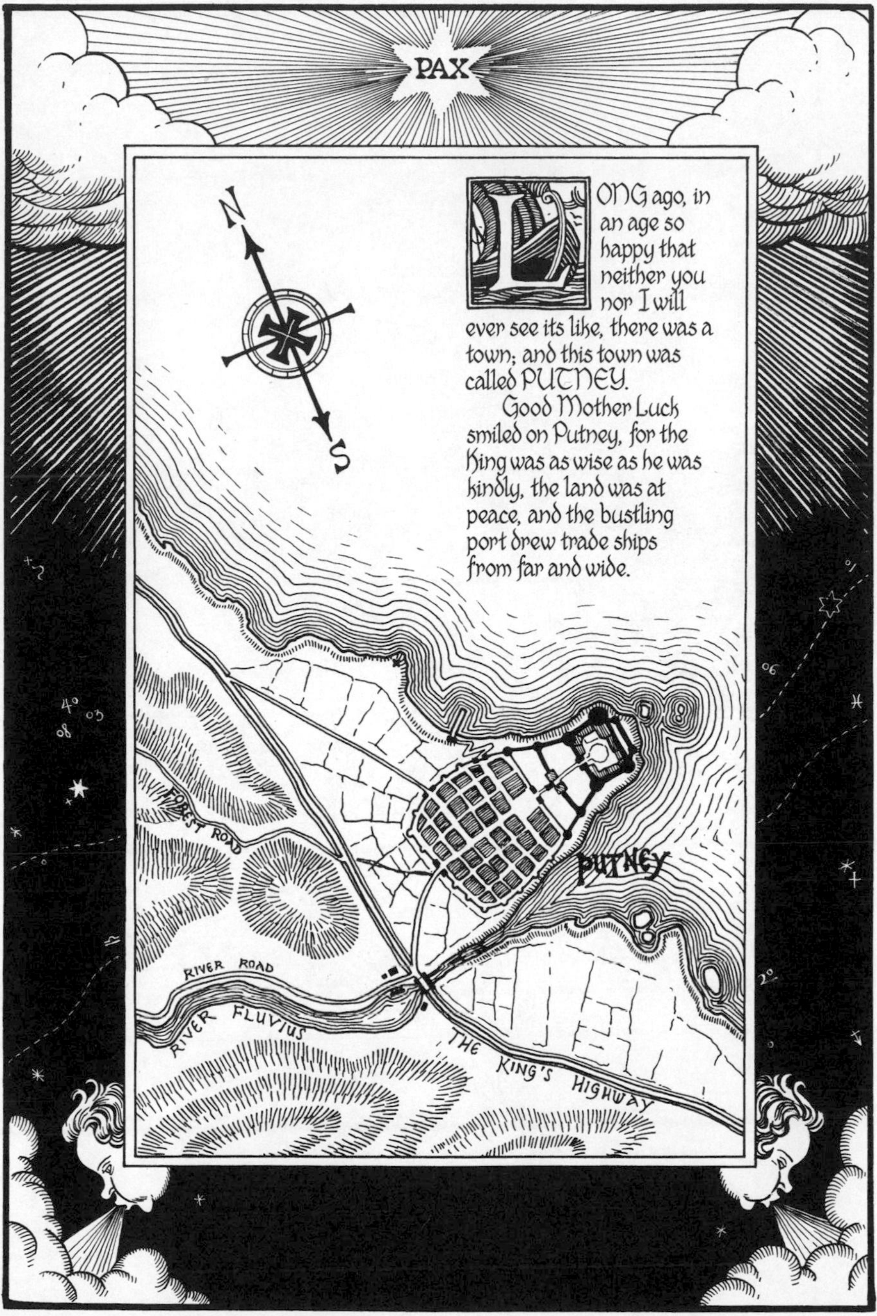
PAX
N
S
FOREST ROAD
PUTNEY
RIVER ROAD
RIVER FLUVIUS
THE KING'S HIGHWAY

LONG ago, in an age so happy that neither you nor I will ever see its like, there was a town; and this town was called PUTNEY.

Good Mother Luck smiled on Putney, for the King was as wise as he was kindly, the land was at peace, and the bustling port drew trade ships from far and wide.

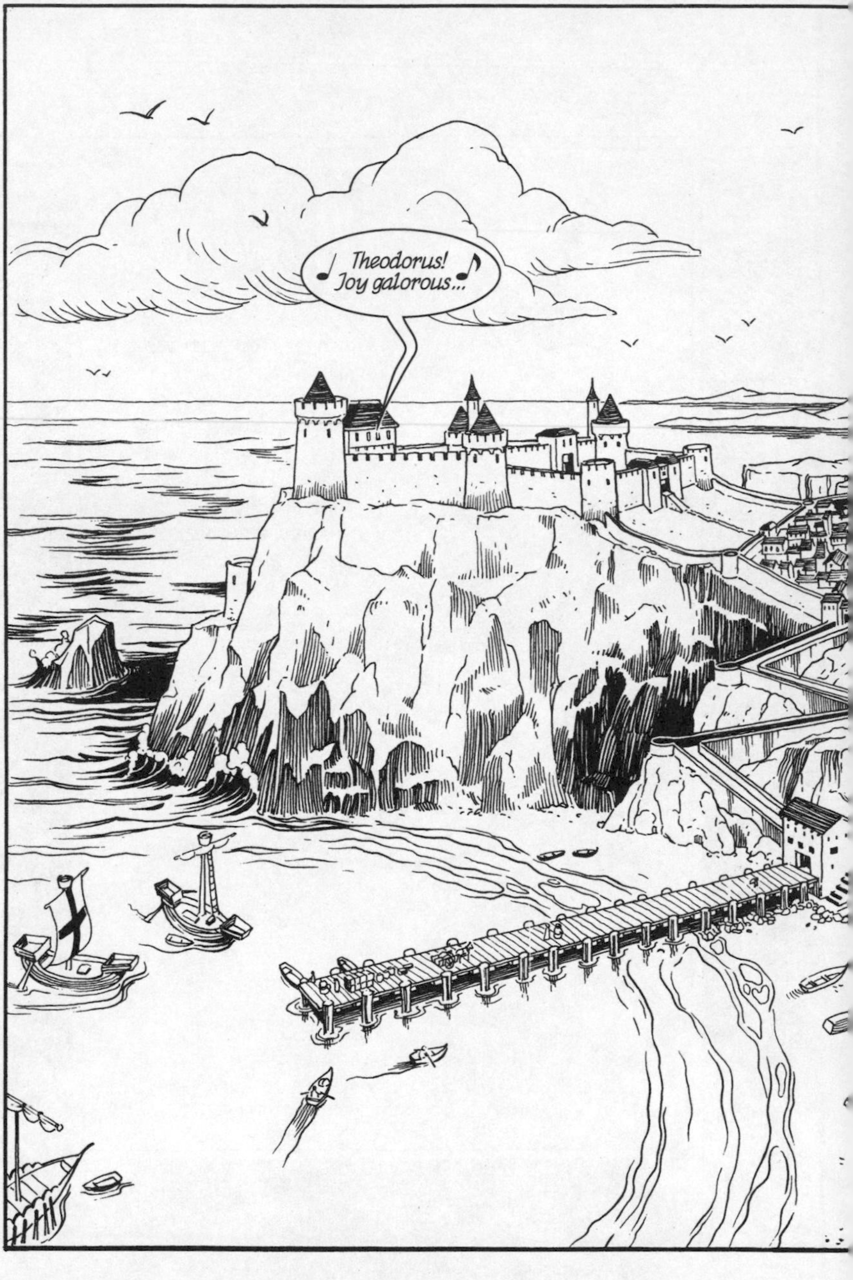
♩ Theodorus! Joy galorous... ♪

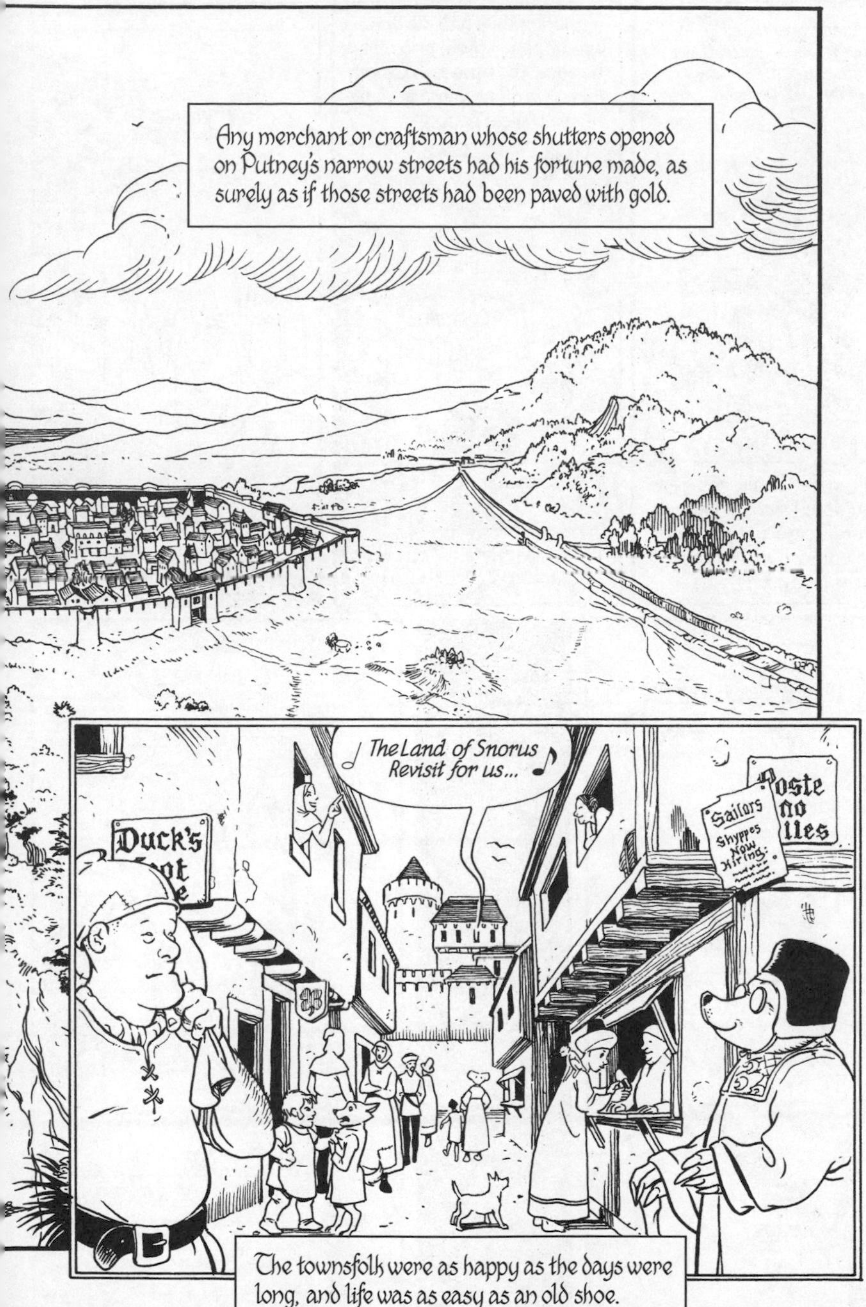
Any merchant or craftsman whose shutters opened on Putney's narrow streets had his fortune made, as surely as if those streets had been paved with gold.
The Land of Snorus Revisit for us...
Duck's
Sailors
Shyppes Now Hiring
The townsfolk were as happy as the days were long, and life was as easy as an old shoe.

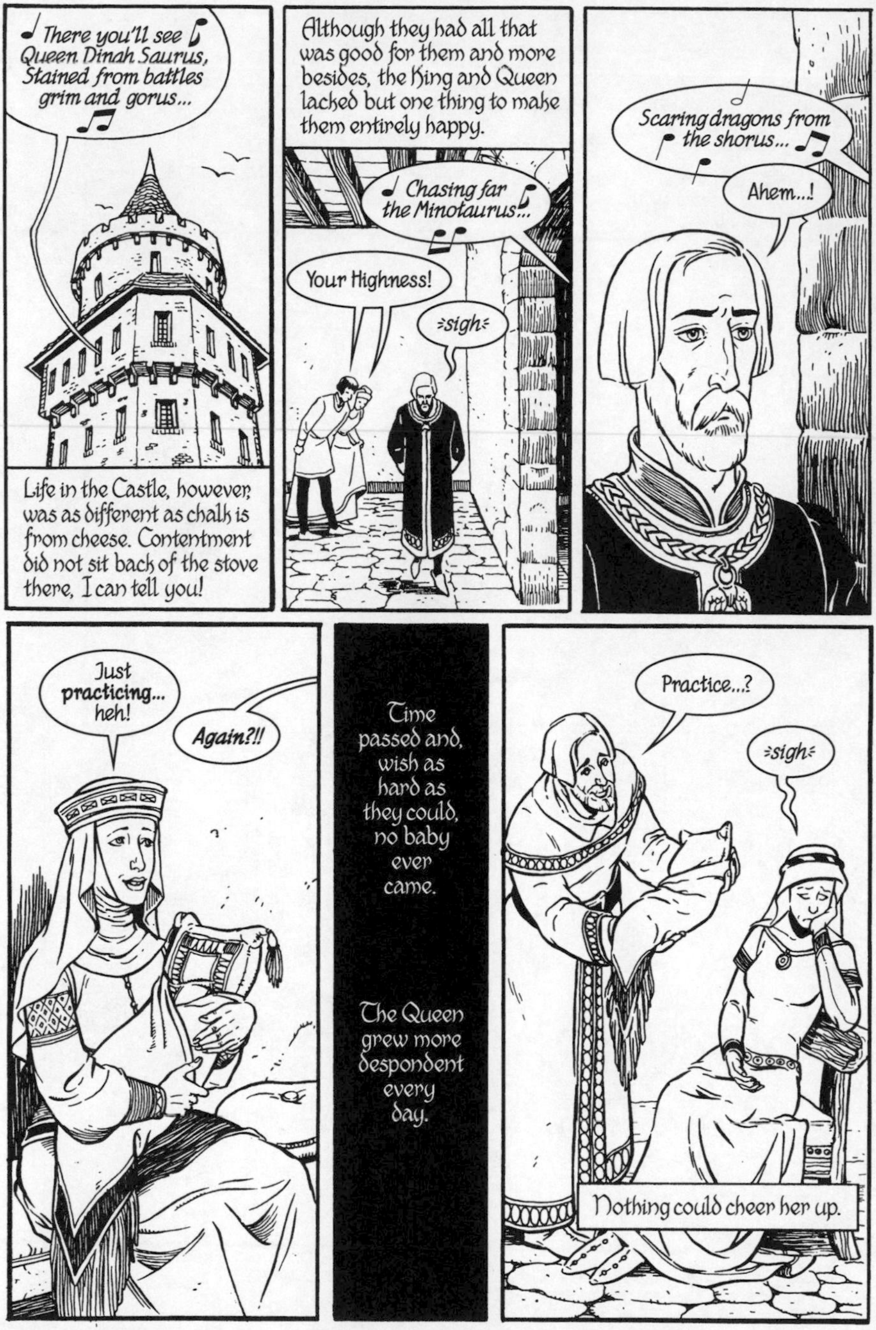
There you'll see Queen Dinah Saurus, Stained from battles grim and gorus...
Life in the Castle, however, was as different as chalk is from cheese. Contentment did not sit back of the stove there, I can tell you!
Although they had all that was good for them and more besides, the King and Queen lacked but one thing to make them entirely happy.
Chasing far the Minotaurus...
Your Highness!
sigh
Scaring dragons from the shorus...
Ahem...!
Just practicing... heh!
Again?!!
Time passed and, wish as hard as they could, no baby ever came.
The Queen grew more despondent every day.
Practice...?
sigh
Nothing could cheer her up.

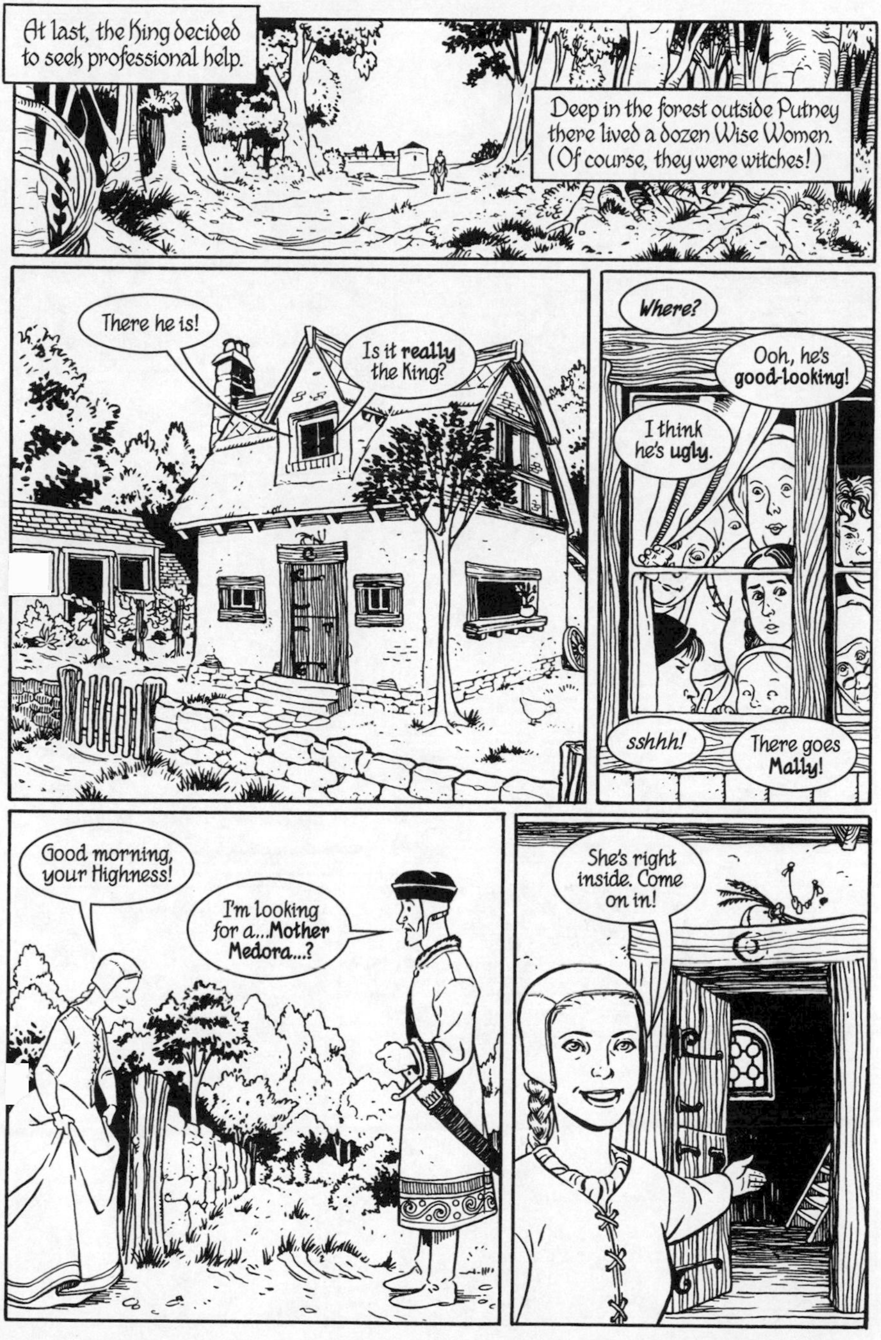
At last, the King decided to seek professional help.
Deep in the forest outside Putney there lived a dozen Wise Women. (Of course, they were witches!)
There he is!
Is it **really** the King?
Where?
Ooh, he's **good-looking!**
I think he's **ugly.**
sshhh!
There goes **Mally!**
Good morning, your Highness!
I'm looking for a... **Mother Medora...?**
She's right inside. Come on in!

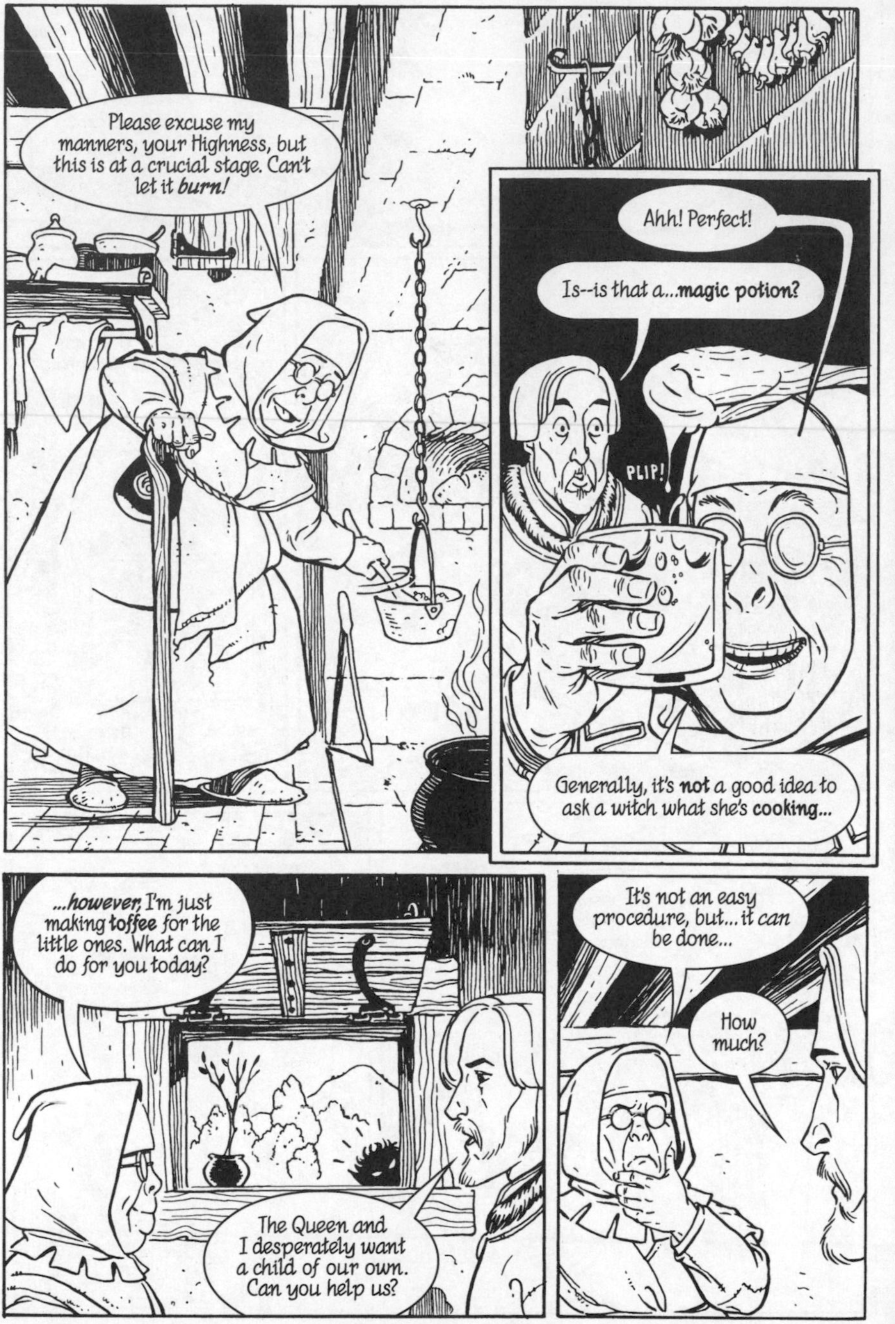
Please excuse my manners, your Highness, but this is at a crucial stage. Can't let it *burn!*
Ahh! Perfect!
Is--is that a...**magic potion?**
PLIP!
Generally, it's **not** a good idea to ask a witch what she's **cooking...**
...however, I'm just making **toffee** for the little ones. What can I do for you today?
The Queen and I desperately want a child of our own. Can you help us?
It's not an easy procedure, but... it can be done...
How much?

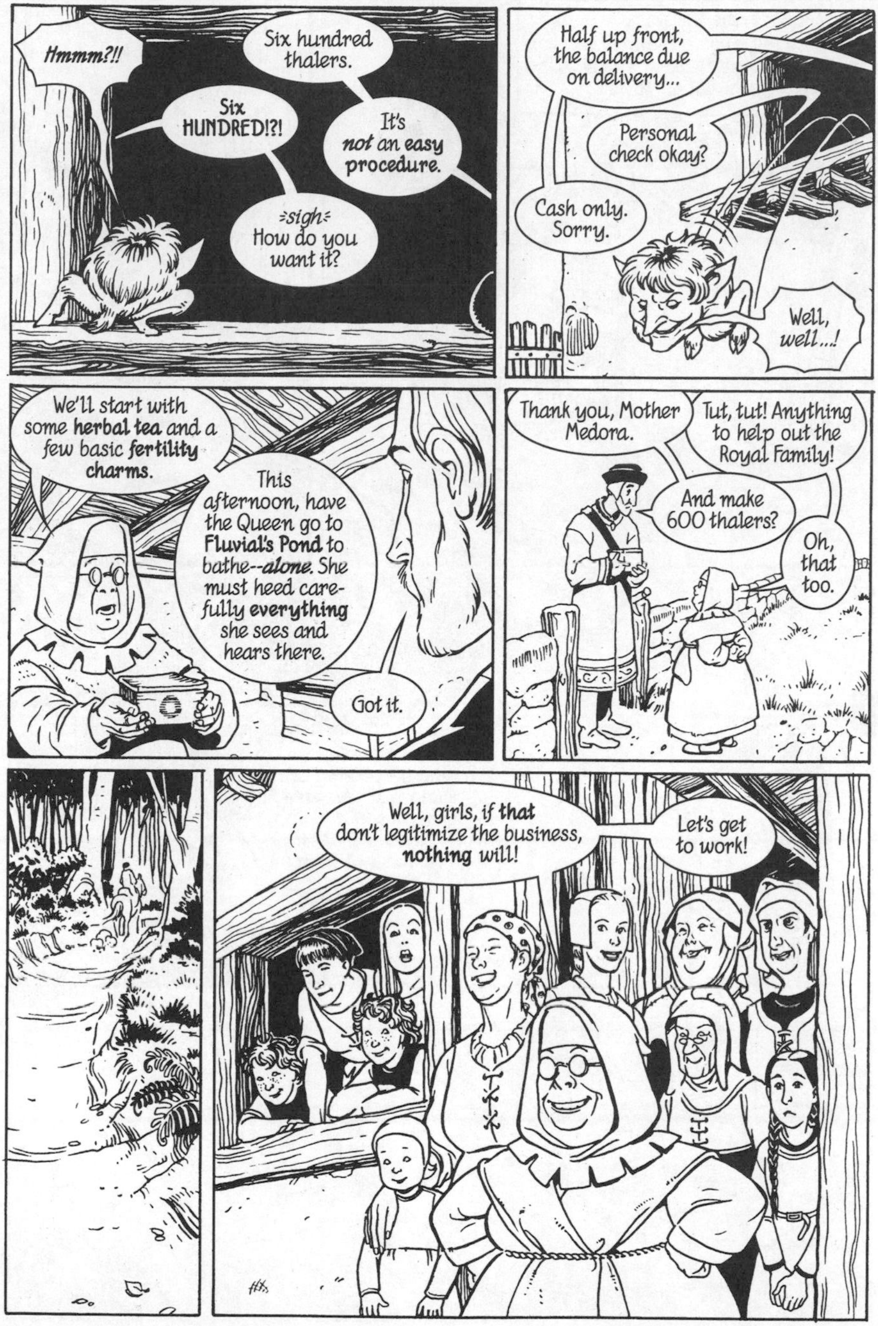
Hmmm?!!
Six hundred thalers.
Six HUNDRED!?!
It's not an easy procedure.
≈sigh≈ How do you want it?
Half up front, the balance due on delivery...
Personal check okay?
Cash only. Sorry.
Well, well...!
We'll start with some herbal tea and a few basic fertility charms.
This afternoon, have the Queen go to Fluvial's Pond to bathe--alone. She must heed carefully everything she sees and hears there.
Got it.
Thank you, Mother Medora.
Tut, tut! Anything to help out the Royal Family!
And make 600 thalers?
Oh, that too.
Well, girls, if that don't legitimize the business, nothing will!
Let's get to work!

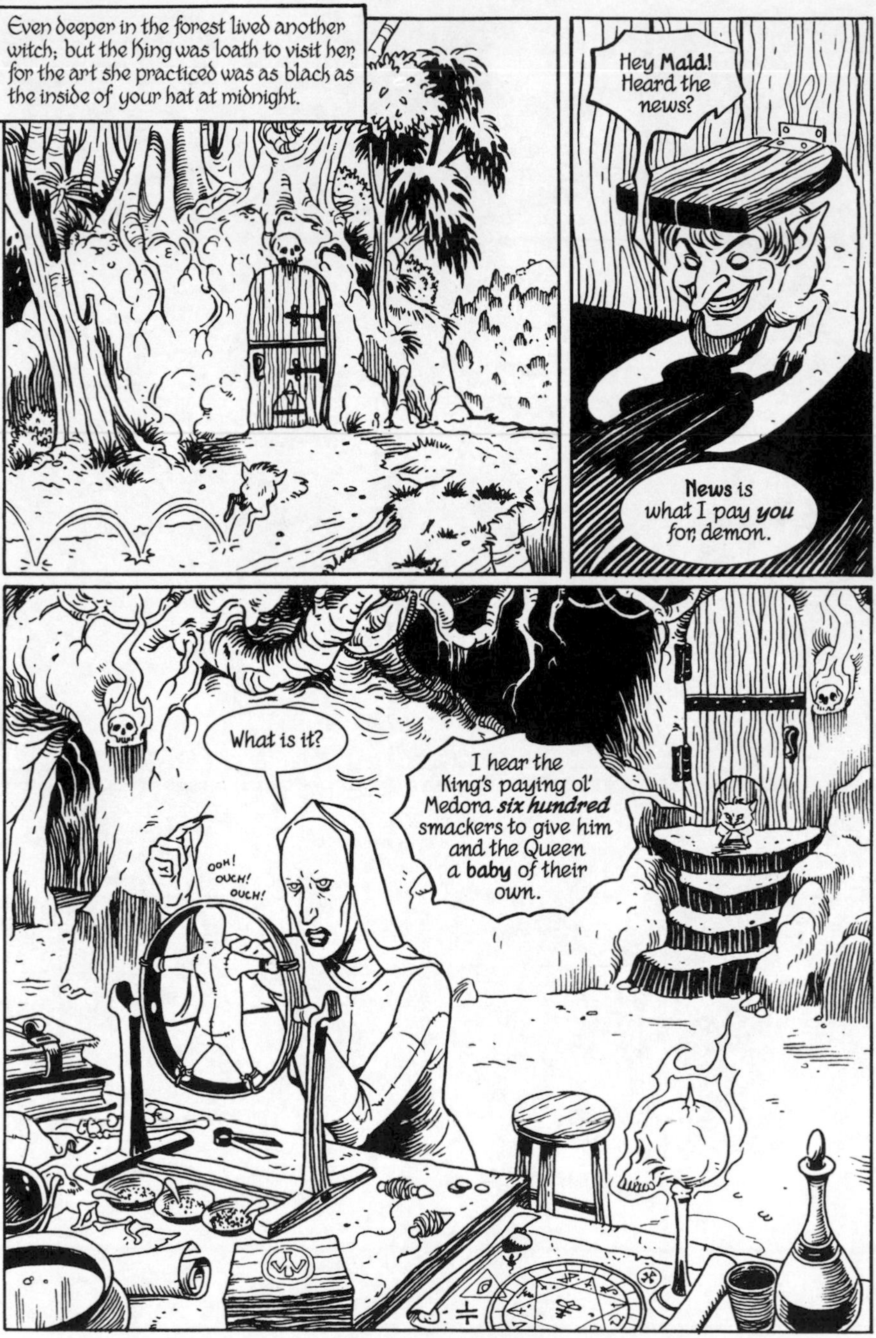
Even deeper in the forest lived another witch; but the King was loath to visit her, for the art she practiced was as black as the inside of your hat at midnight.
Hey Mald! Heard the news?
News is what I pay you for, demon.
What is it?
I hear the King's paying ol' Medora six hundred smackers to give him and the Queen a baby of their own.
OOH! OUCH! OUCH!

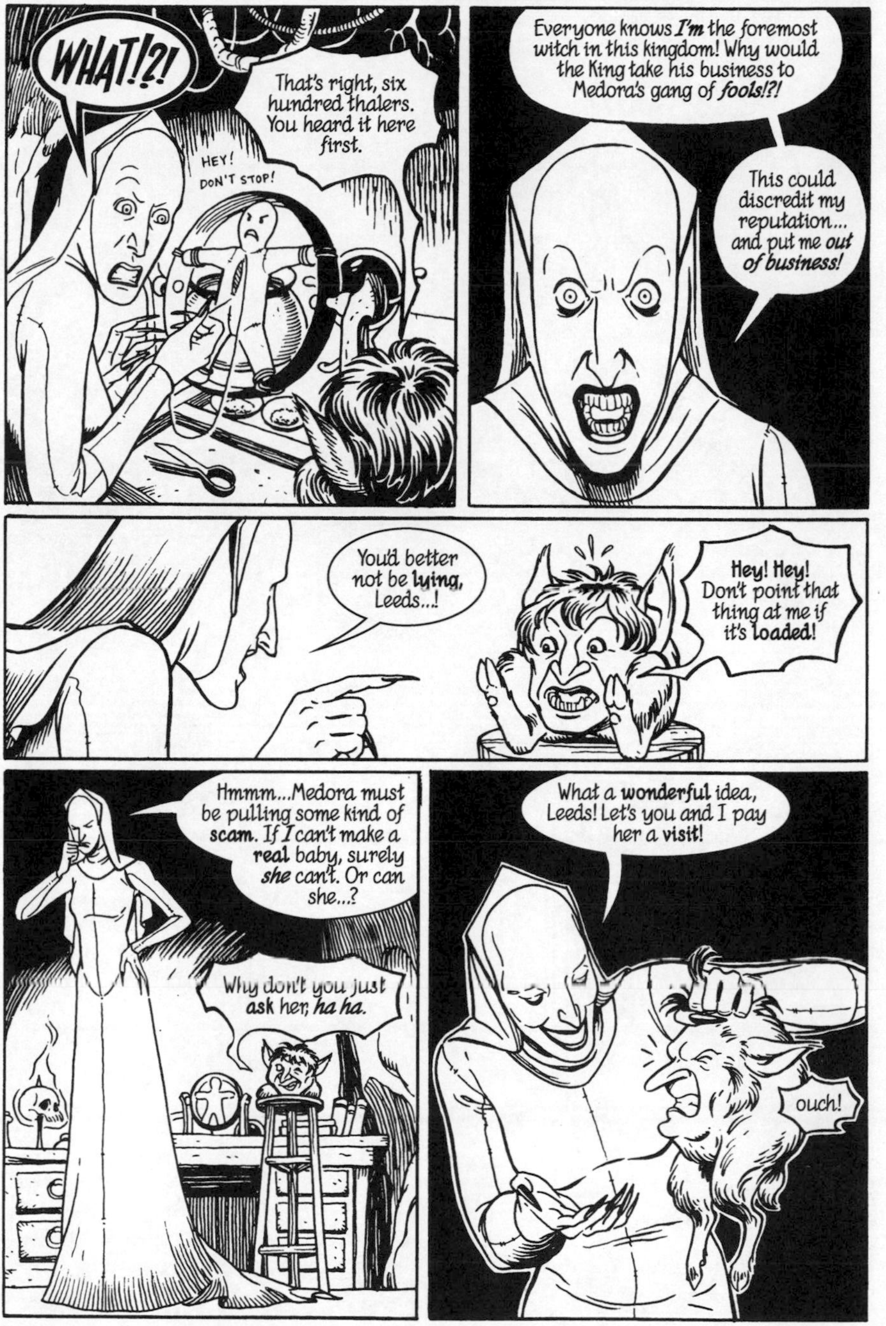
WHAT!?!
That's right, six hundred thalers. You heard it here first.
HEY! DON'T STOP!
Everyone knows I'm the foremost witch in this kingdom! Why would the King take his business to Medora's gang of fools!?!
This could discredit my reputation... and put me out of business!
You'd better not be lying, Leeds...!
Hey! Hey! Don't point that thing at me if it's loaded!
Hmmm...Medora must be pulling some kind of scam. If I can't make a real baby, surely she can't. Or can she...?
Why don't you just ask her, ha ha.
What a wonderful idea, Leeds! Let's you and I pay her a visit!
ouch!

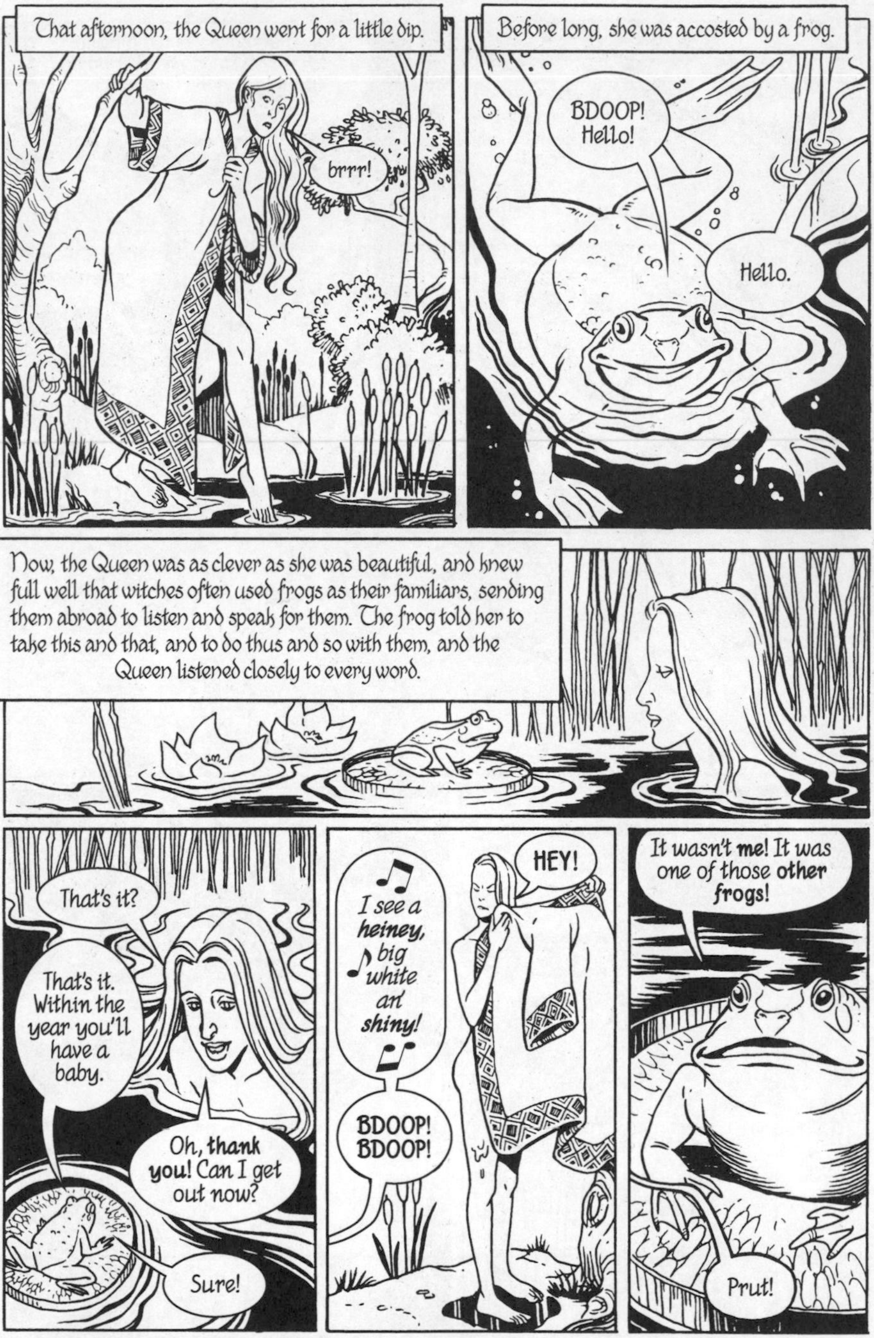
That afternoon, the Queen went for a little dip.
brrr!
Before long, she was accosted by a frog.
BDOOP! Hello!
Hello.
Now, the Queen was as clever as she was beautiful, and knew full well that witches often used frogs as their familiars, sending them abroad to listen and speak for them. The frog told her to take this and that, and to do thus and so with them, and the Queen listened closely to every word.
That's it?
That's it. Within the year you'll have a baby.
Oh, thank you! Can I get out now?
Sure!
I see a heiney, big white an' shiny!
BDOOP! BDOOP!
HEY!
It wasn't me! It was one of those other frogs!
Prut!

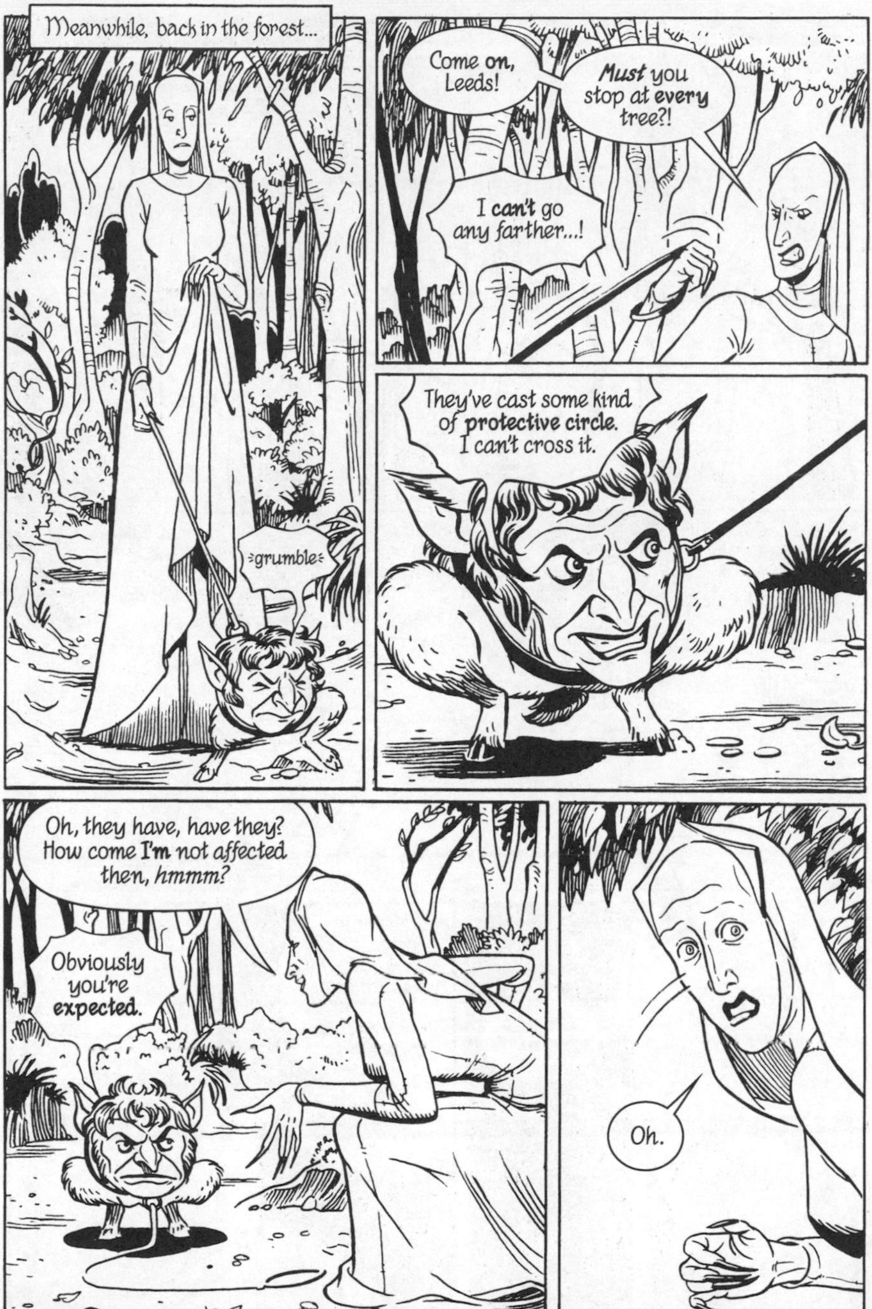
Meanwhile, back in the forest...
grumble
Come on, Leeds!
Must you stop at every tree?!
I can't go any farther...!
They've cast some kind of protective circle. I can't cross it.
Oh, they have, have they? How come I'm not affected then, hmmm?
Obviously you're expected.
Oh.

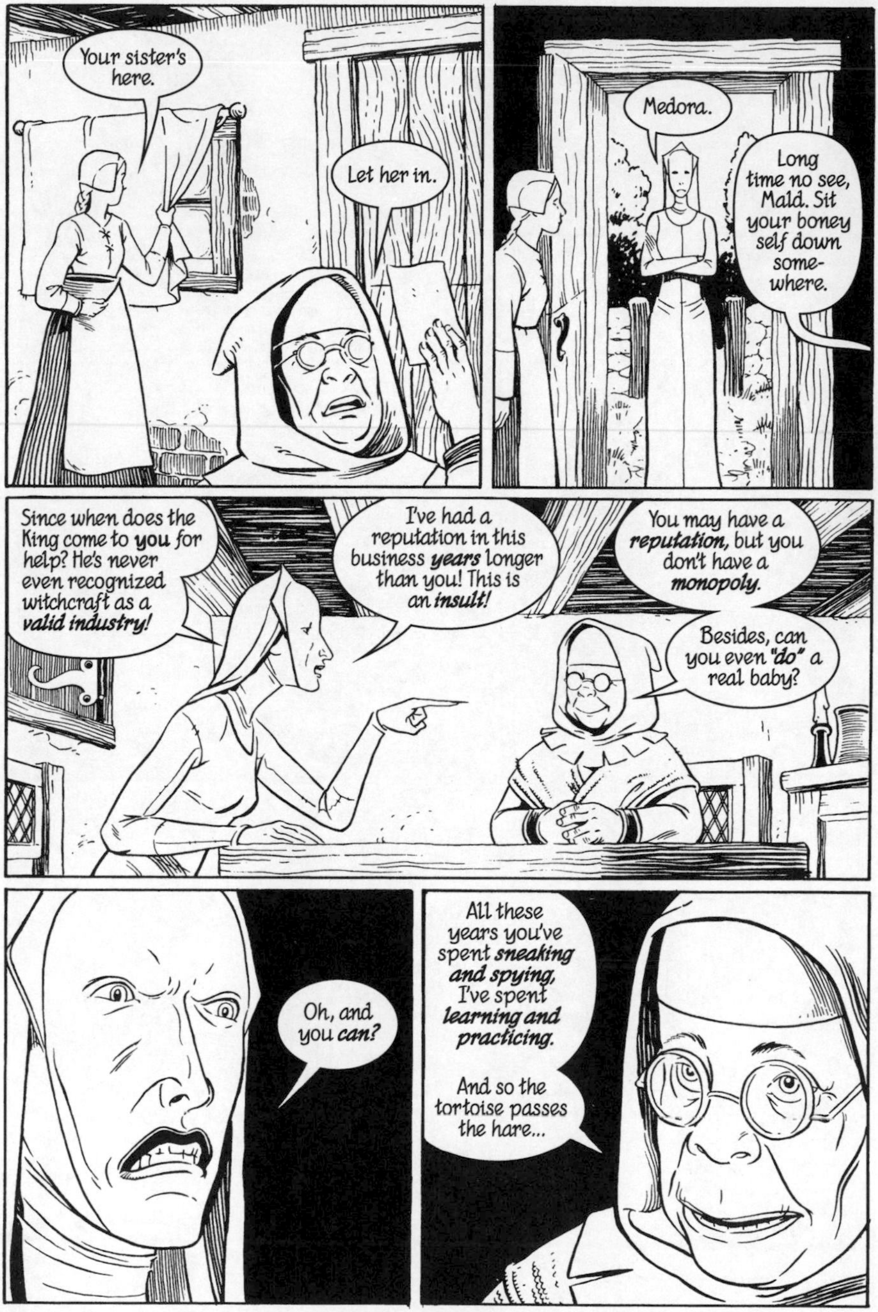
Your sister's here.
Let her in.
Medora.
Long time no see, Mald. Sit your boney self down some-where.
Since when does the King come to **you** for help? He's never even recognized witchcraft as a ***valid industry!***
I've had a reputation in this business ***years*** longer than you! This is an ***insult!***
You may have a ***reputation,*** but you don't have a ***monopoly.***
Besides, can you even ***"do"*** a real baby?
Oh, and you ***can?***
All these years you've spent ***sneaking and spying,*** I've spent ***learning and practicing.***
And so the tortoise passes the hare...

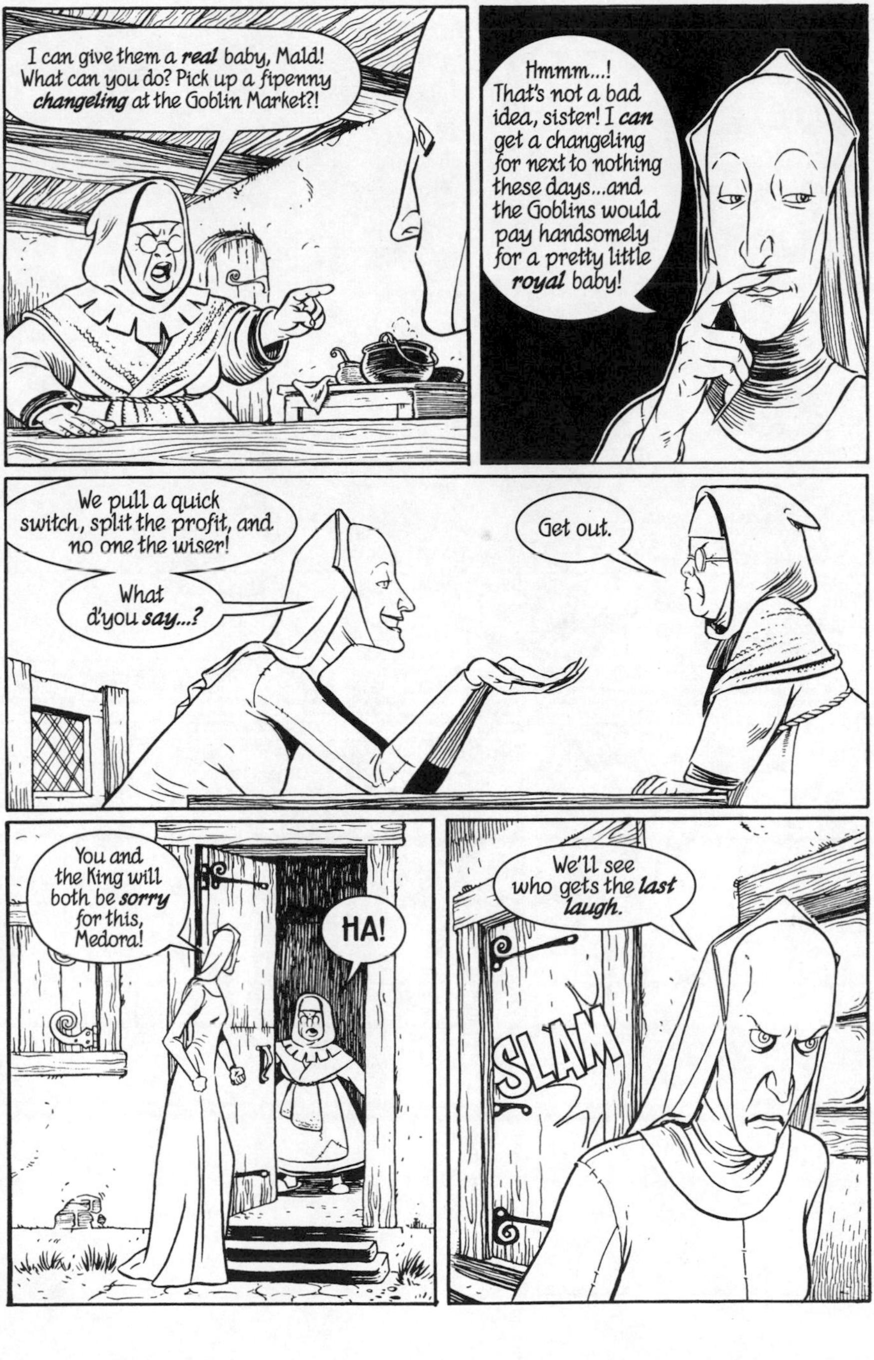
I can give them a real baby, Mald! What can you do? Pick up a fipenny changeling at the Goblin Market?!
Hmmm...! That's not a bad idea, sister! I can get a changeling for next to nothing these days...and the Goblins would pay handsomely for a pretty little royal baby!
We pull a quick switch, split the profit, and no one the wiser!
What d'you say...?
Get out.
You and the King will both be sorry for this, Medora!
HA!
We'll see who gets the last laugh.
SLAM

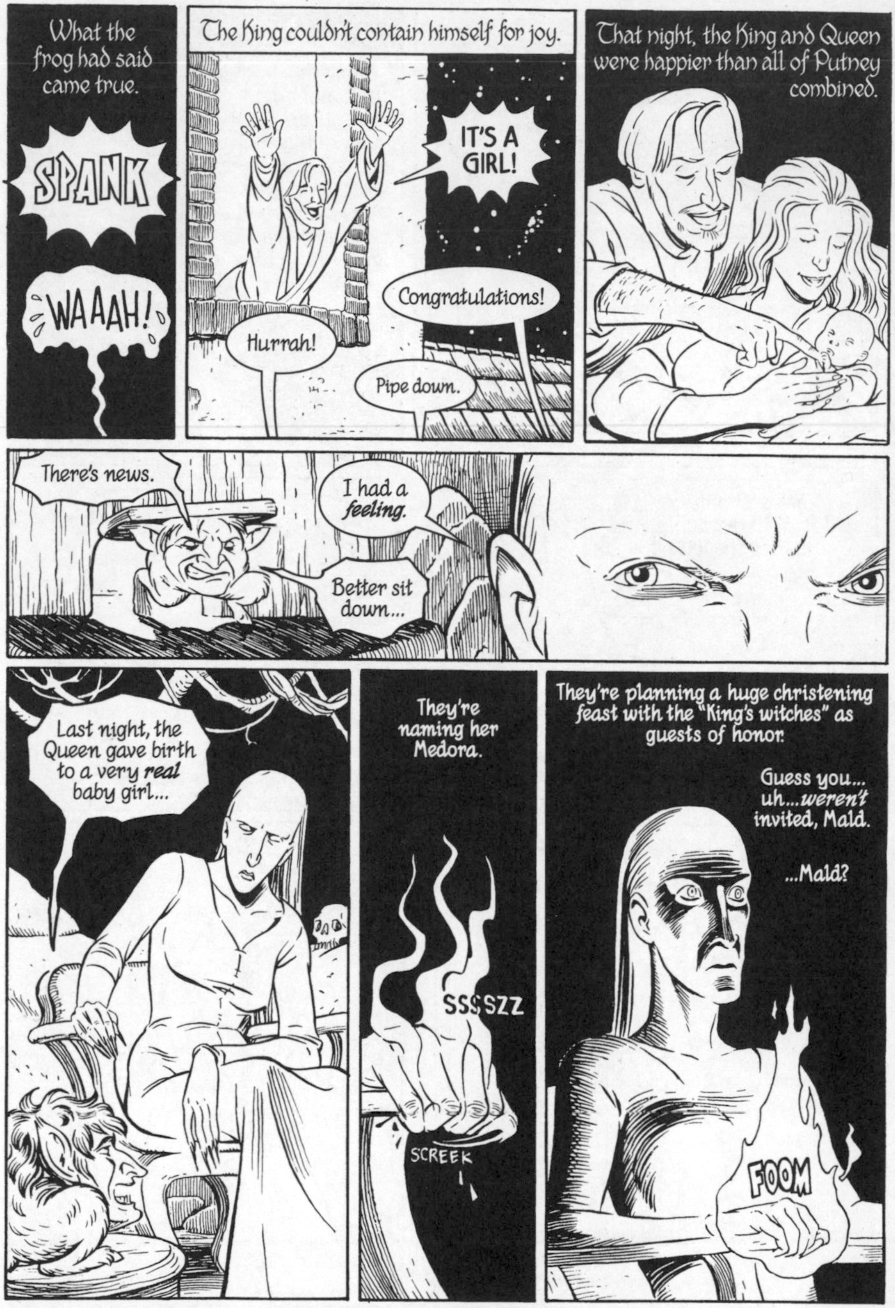
What the frog had said came true.
SPANK
WAAAH!
The King couldn't contain himself for joy.
IT'S A GIRL!
Congratulations!
Hurrah!
Pipe down.
That night, the King and Queen were happier than all of Putney combined.
There's news.
I had a *feeling*.
Better sit down....
Last night, the Queen gave birth to a very *real* baby girl...
They're naming her Medora.
SSSSZZ
SCREEK
They're planning a huge christening feast with the "King's witches" as guests of honor.
Guess you... uh...*weren't* invited, Mald.
...Mald?
FOOM

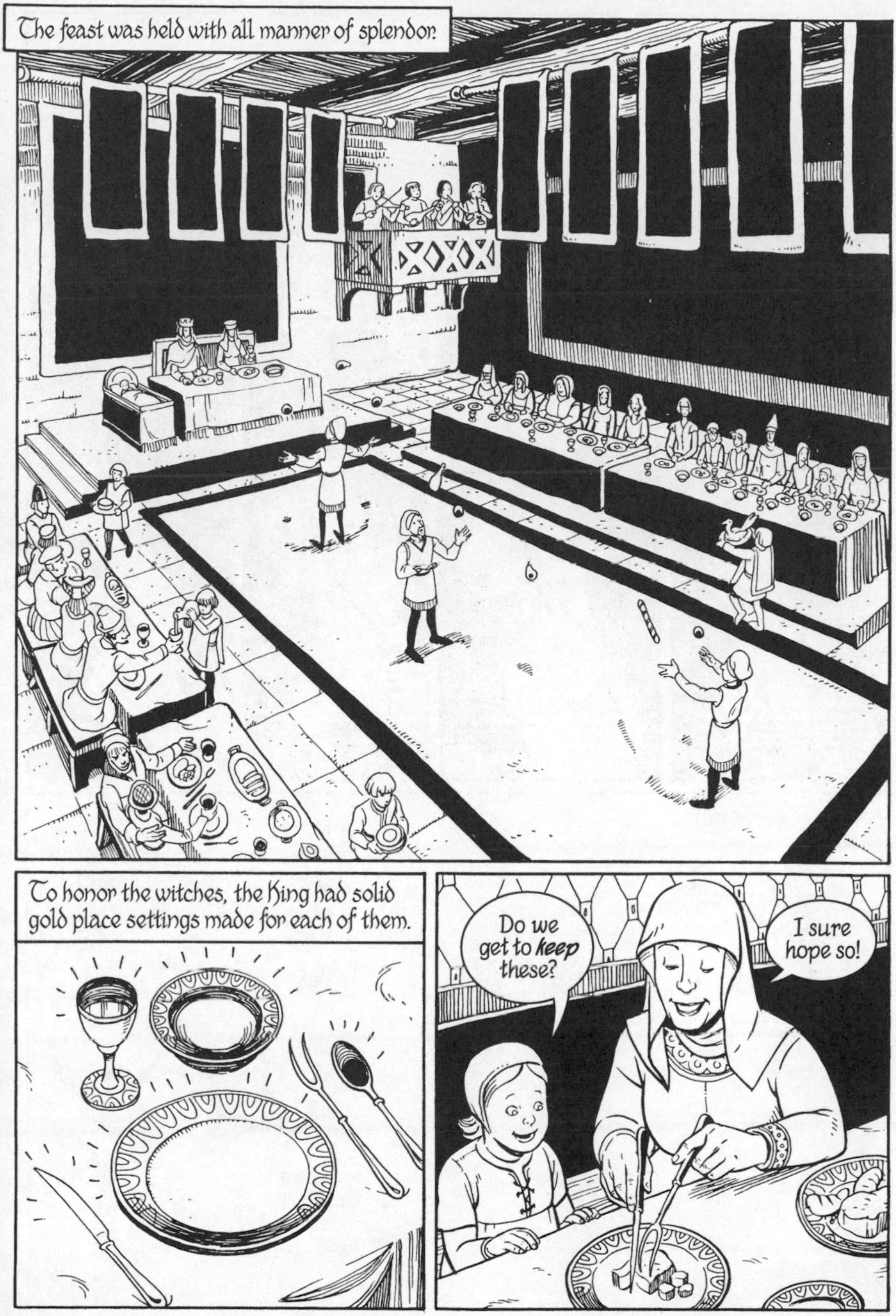
The feast was held with all manner of splendor.
To honor the witches, the King had solid gold place settings made for each of them.
Do we get to *keep* these?
I sure hope so!

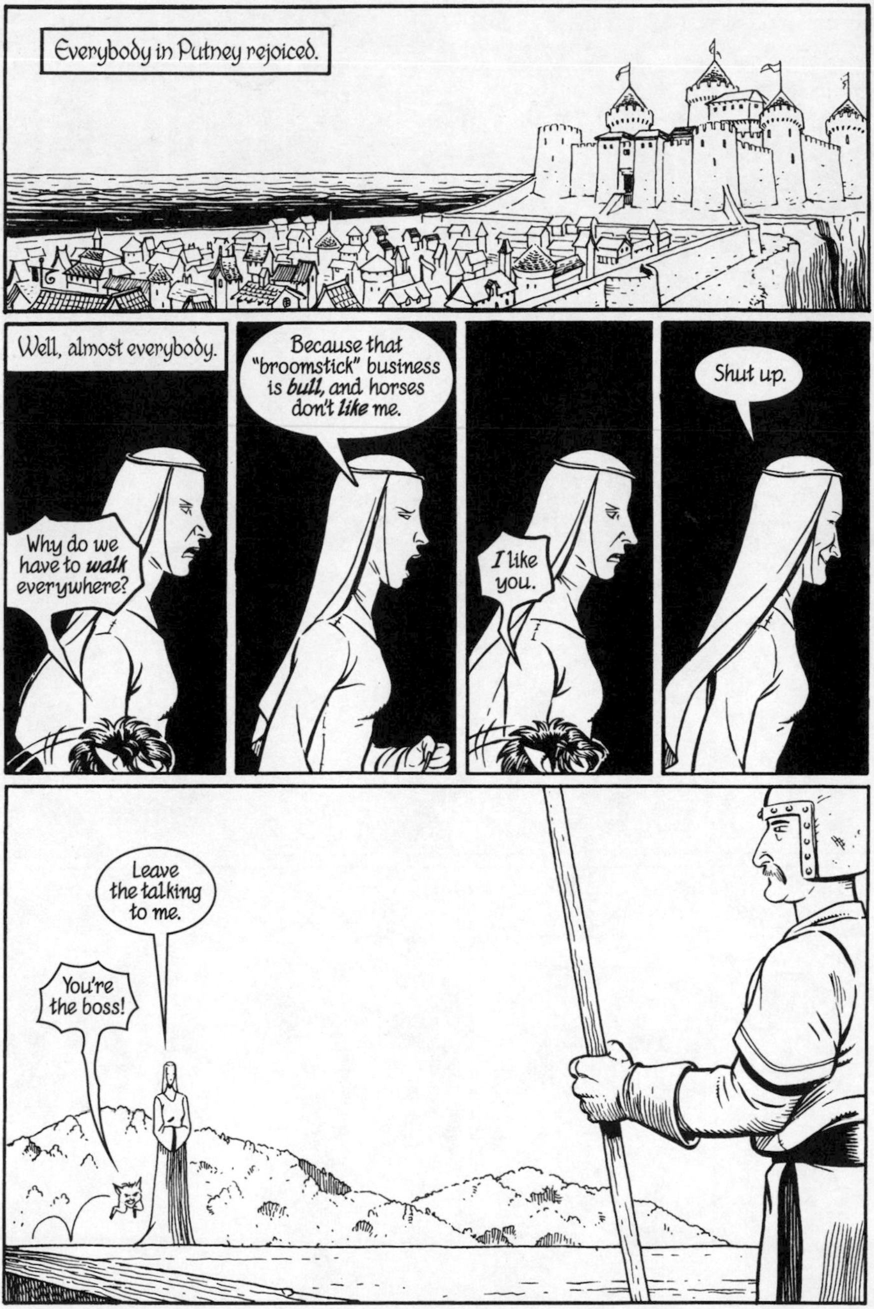
Everybody in Putney rejoiced.
Well, almost everybody.
Why do we have to *walk* everywhere?
Because that "broomstick" business is *bull*, and horses don't *like* me.
I like you.
Shut up.
Leave the talking to me.
You're the boss!

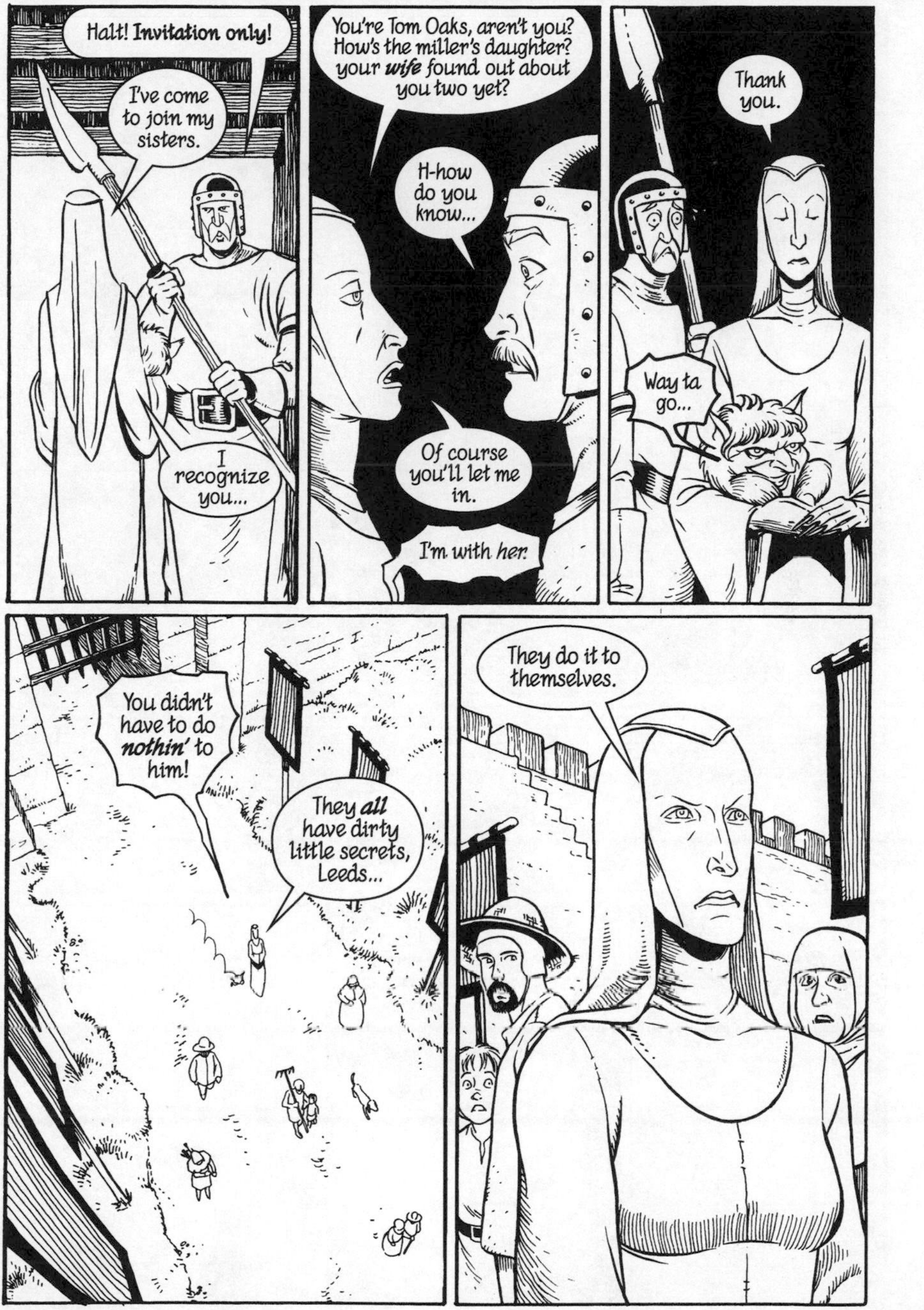
Halt! **Invitation only!**
I've come to join my sisters.
I recognize you...
You're Tom Oaks, aren't you? How's the miller's daughter? your ***wife*** found out about you two yet?
H-how do you know...
Of course you'll let me in.
I'm with *her.*
Thank you.
Way ta go...
You didn't have to do ***nothin'*** to him!
They ***all*** have dirty little secrets, Leeds...
They do it to themselves.

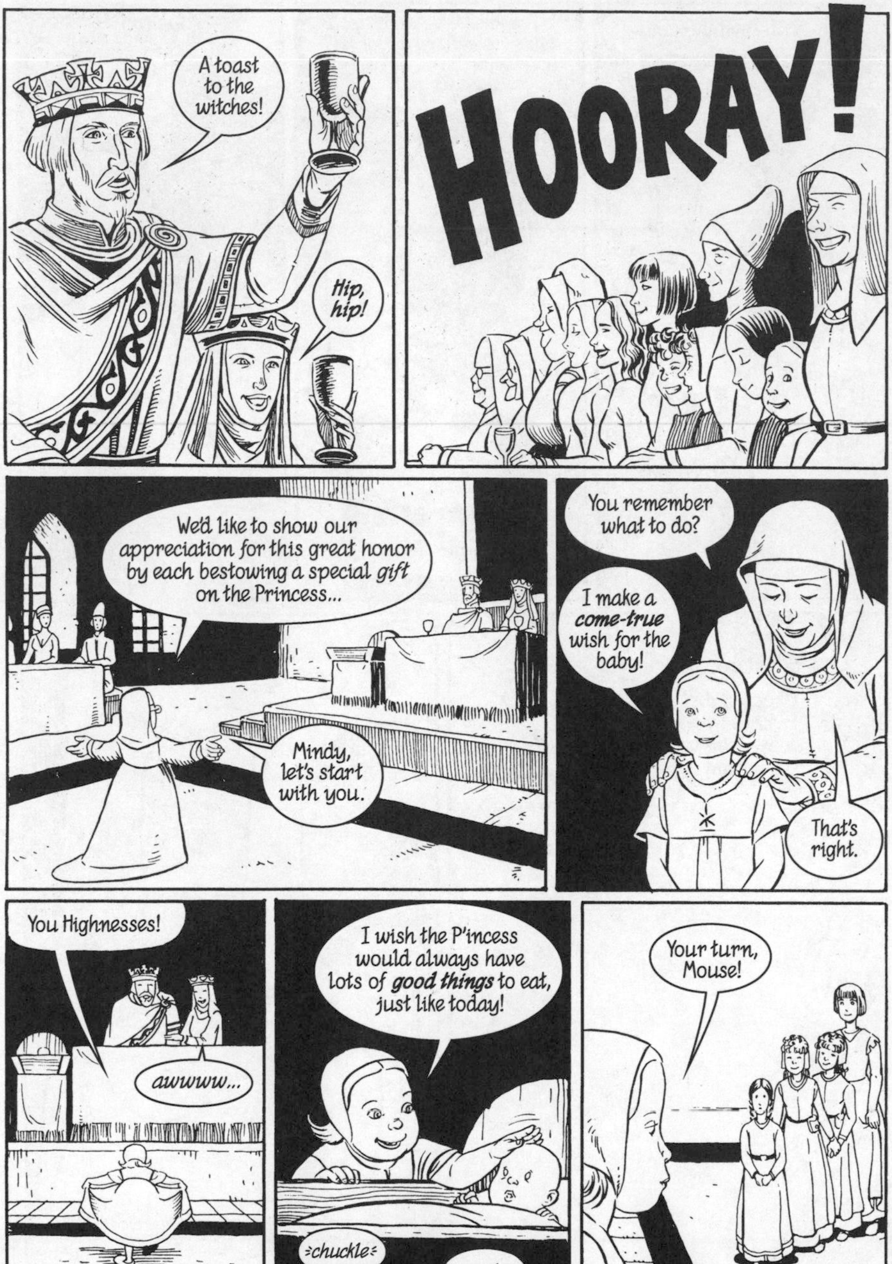
A toast to the witches!
Hip, hip!
HOORAY!
We'd like to show our appreciation for this great honor by each bestowing a special *gift* on the Princess...
Mindy, let's start with you.
You remember what to do?
I make a **come-true** wish for the baby!
That's right.
You Highnesses!
awwww...
I wish the P'incess would always have lots of **good things** to eat, just like today!
chuckle
giggle
Your turn, Mouse!

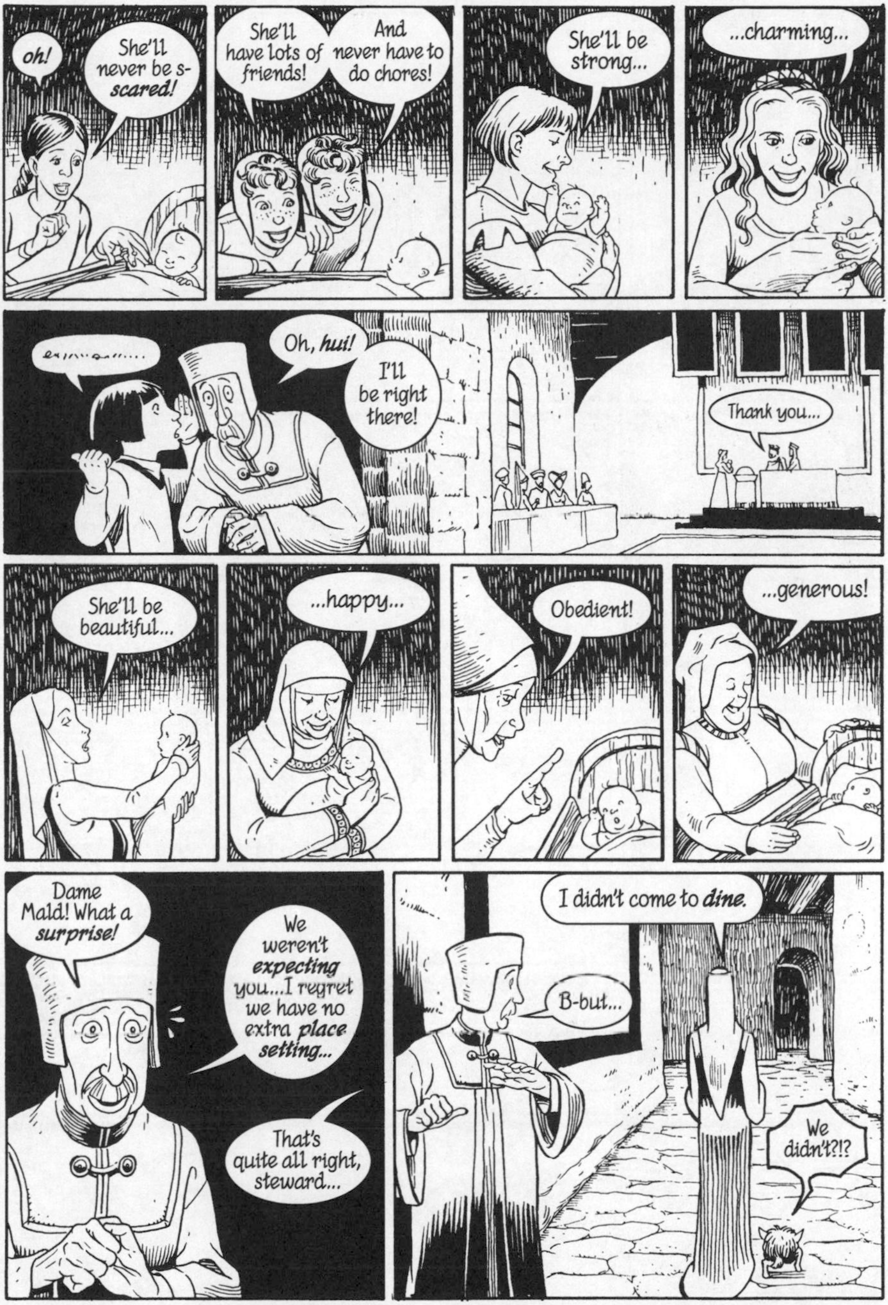
oh!
She'll never be s-*scared!*
She'll have lots of friends!
And never have to do chores!
She'll be strong...
...charming...
Oh, *hui!*
I'll be right there!
Thank you...
She'll be beautiful...
...happy...
Obedient!
...generous!
Dame Mald! What a *surprise!*
We weren't *expecting* you...I regret we have no extra *place setting...*
That's quite all right, steward...
I didn't come to *dine.*
B-but...
We didn't?!?

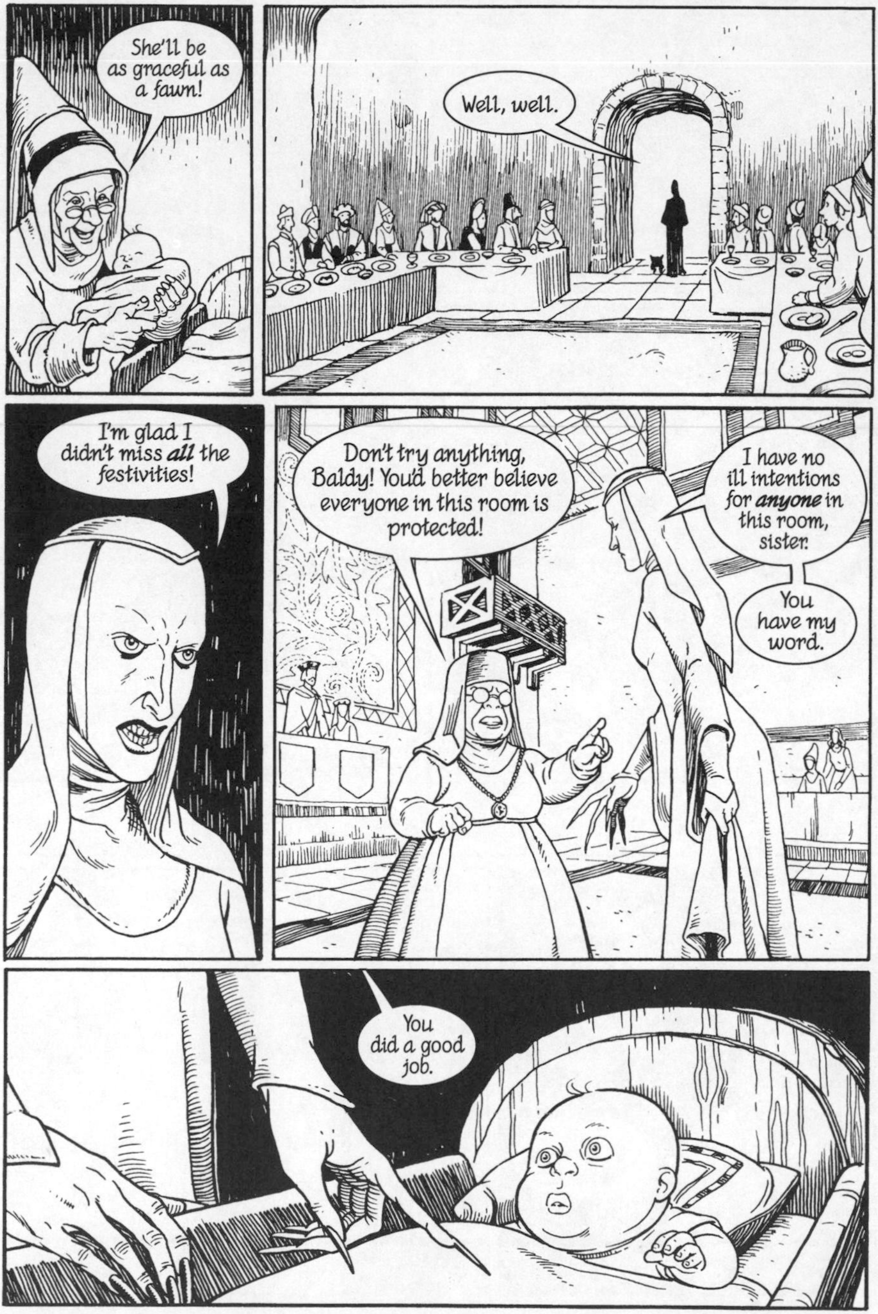
She'll be as graceful as a fawn!
Well, well.
I'm glad I didn't miss *all* the festivities!
Don't try anything, Baldy! You'd better believe everyone in this room is protected!
I have no ill intentions for *anyone* in this room, sister.
You have my word.
You did a good job.

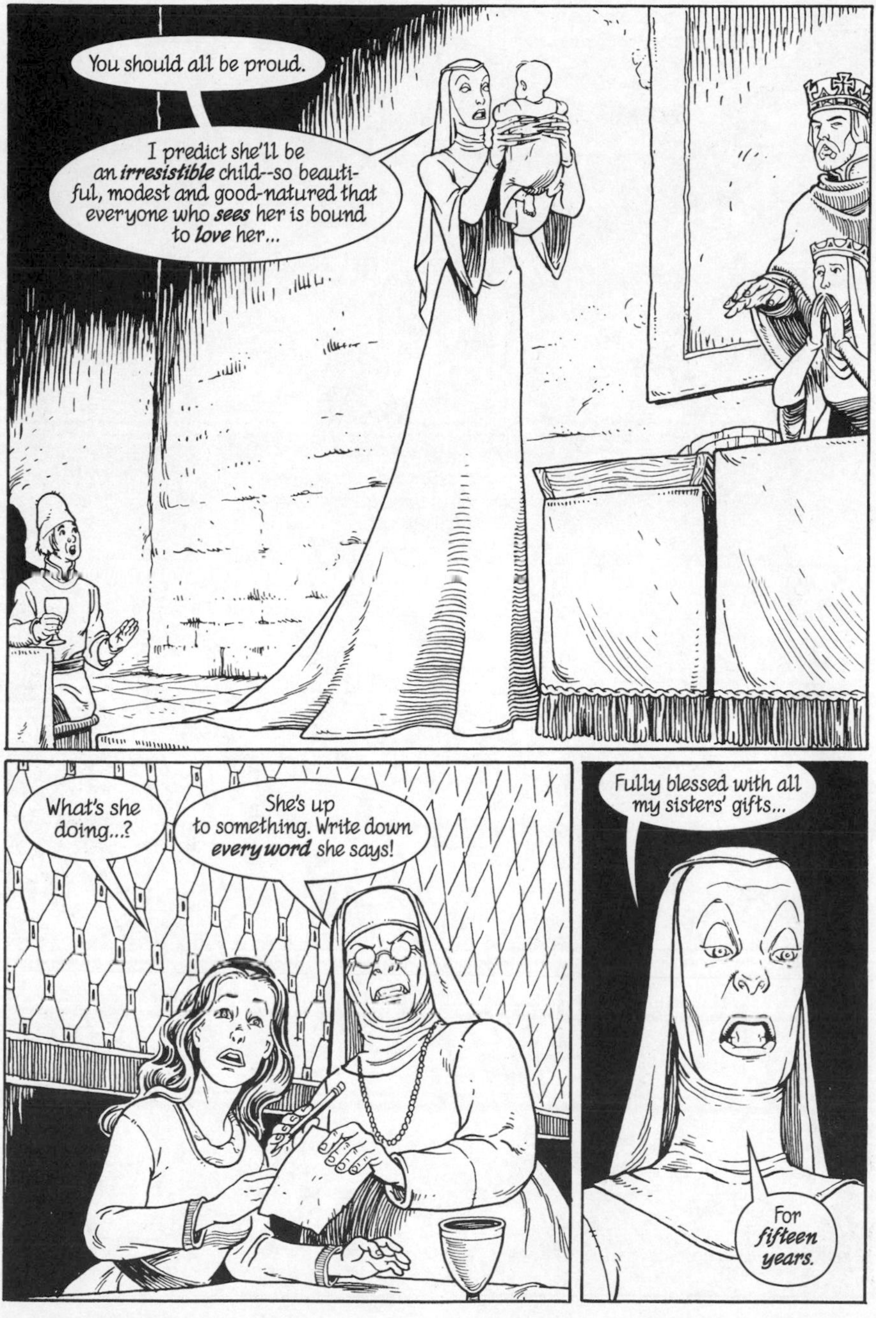
You should all be proud.
I predict she'll be an *irresistible* child--so beautiful, modest and good-natured that everyone who *sees* her is bound to *love* her...
What's she doing...?
She's up to something. Write down *every word* she says!
Fully blessed with all my sisters' gifts...
For *fifteen years.*

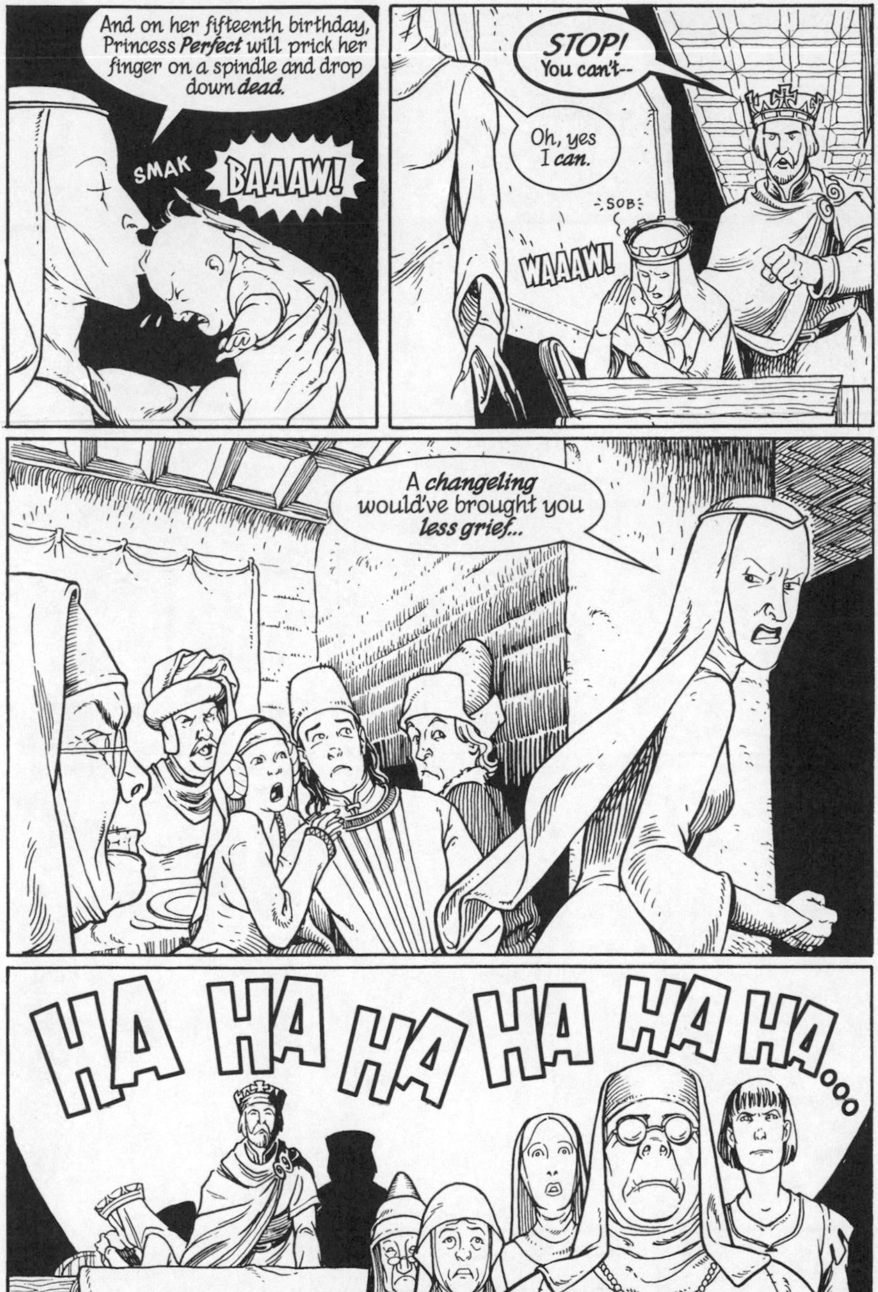
And on her fifteenth birthday, Princess *Perfect* will prick her finger on a spindle and drop down *dead*.
SMAK
BAAAW!
STOP! You can't--
Oh, yes I *can*.
SOB
WAAAW!
A *changeling* would've brought you *less grief*...
HA HA HA HA HA HA...

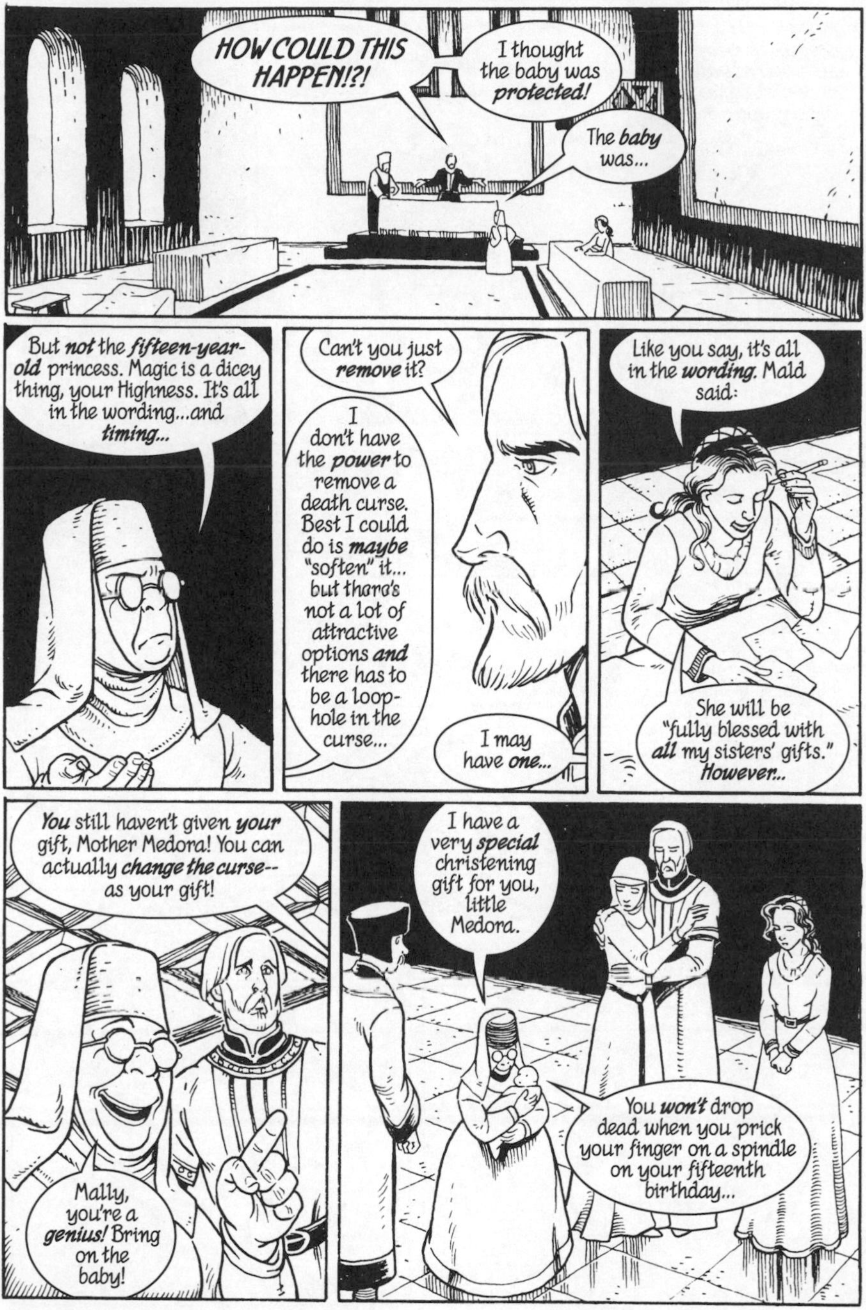
HOW COULD THIS HAPPEN!?!
I thought the baby was protected!
The baby was...
But not the fifteen-year-old princess. Magic is a dicey thing, your Highness. It's all in the wording...and timing...
Can't you just remove it?
I don't have the power to remove a death curse. Best I could do is maybe "soften" it... but there's not a lot of attractive options and there has to be a loop-hole in the curse...
I may have one...
Like you say, it's all in the wording. Mald said:
She will be "fully blessed with all my sisters' gifts." However...
You still haven't given your gift, Mother Medora! You can actually change the curse--as your gift!
Mally, you're a genius! Bring on the baby!
I have a very special christening gift for you, little Medora.
You won't drop dead when you prick your finger on a spindle on your fifteenth birthday...

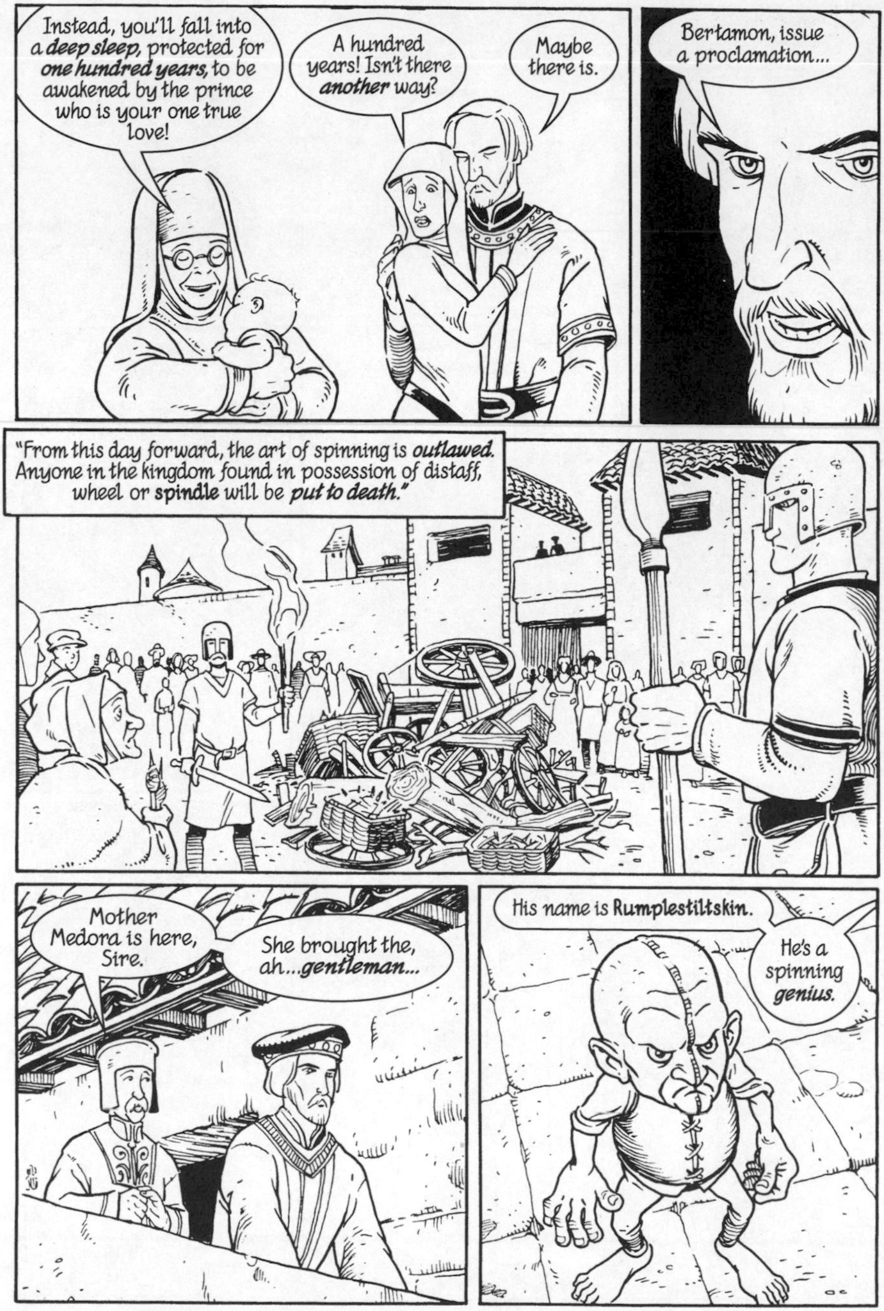
Instead, you'll fall into a **deep sleep**, protected for **one hundred years**, to be awakened by the prince who is your one true love!
A hundred years! Isn't there **another** way?
Maybe there is.
Bertamon, issue a proclamation...
"From this day forward, the art of spinning is **outlawed**. Anyone in the kingdom found in possession of distaff, wheel or **spindle** will be **put to death**."
Mother Medora is here, Sire.
She brought the, ah...**gentleman**...
His name is **Rumplestiltskin**.
He's a spinning **genius**.

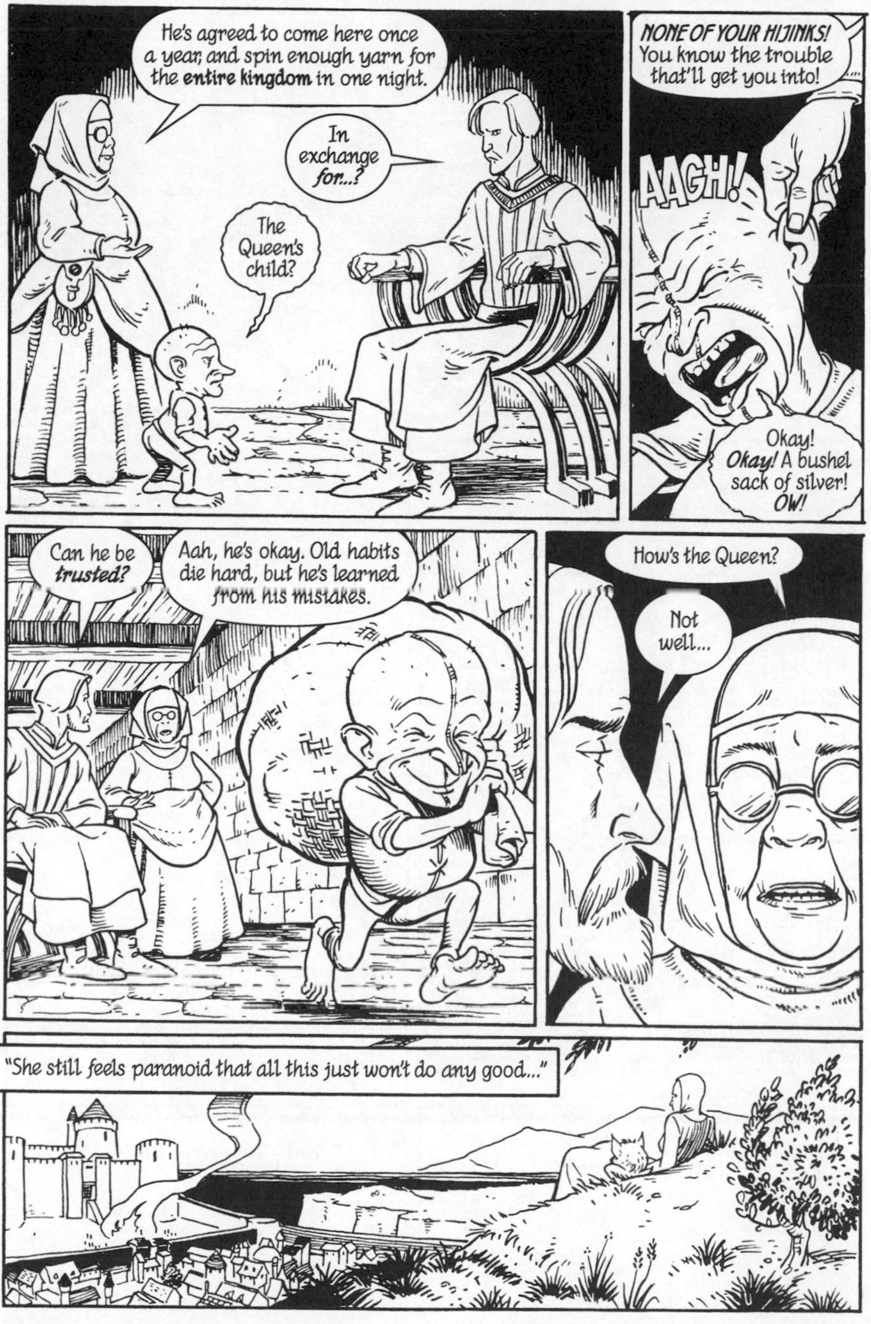
He's agreed to come here once a year, and spin enough yarn for the **entire kingdom** in one night.
In exchange *for...?*
The Queen's child?
NONE OF YOUR HIJINKS! You know the trouble that'll get you into!
AAGH!
Okay! *Okay!* A bushel sack of silver! *OW!*
Can he be *trusted?*
Aah, he's okay. Old habits die hard, but he's learned from his mistakes.
How's the Queen?
Not well...
"She still feels paranoid that all this just won't do any good..."

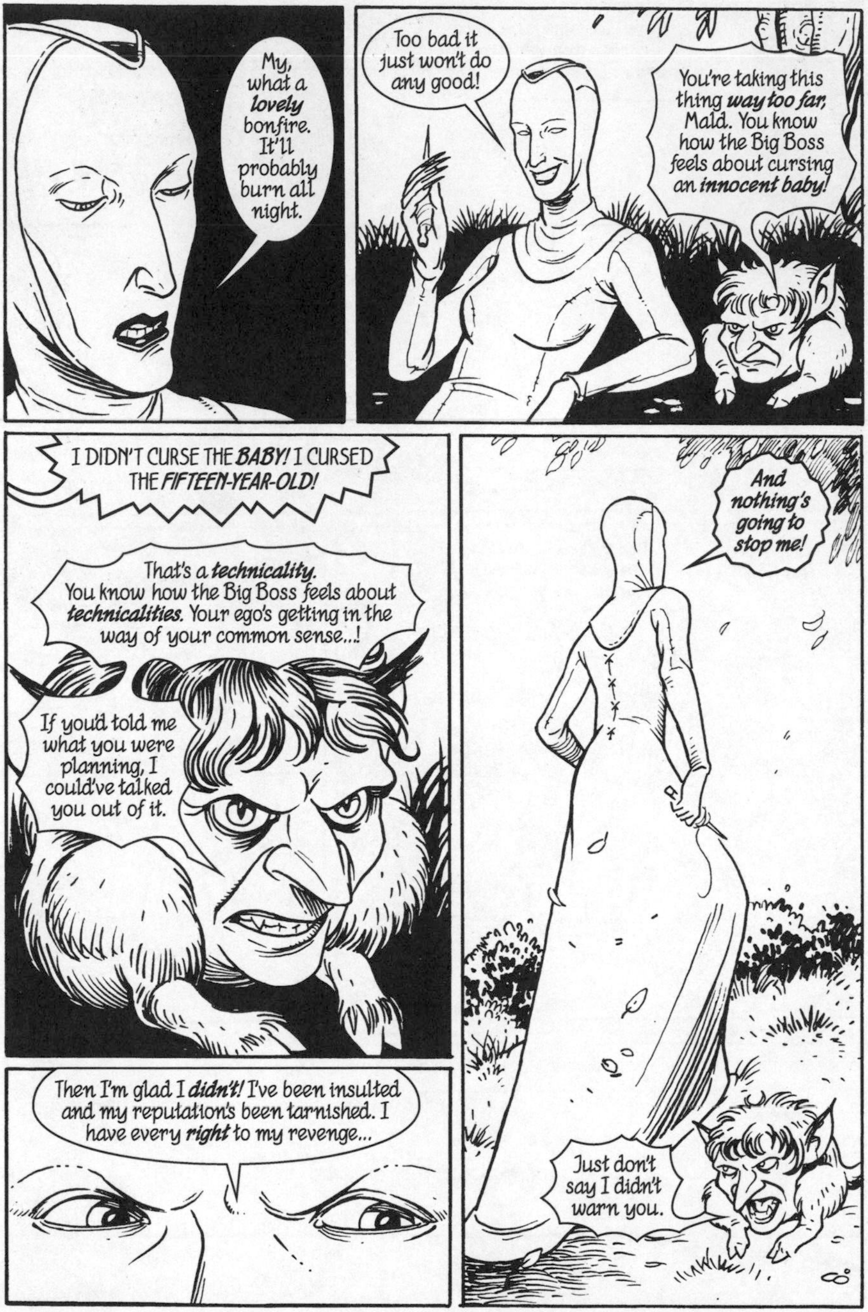
My, what a **lovely** bonfire. It'll probably burn all night.
Too bad it just won't do any good!
You're taking this thing **way too far,** Mald. You know how the Big Boss feels about cursing an **innocent baby!**
I DIDN'T CURSE THE **BABY!** I CURSED THE **FIFTEEN-YEAR-OLD!**
That's a **technicality.** You know how the Big Boss feels about **technicalities.** Your ego's getting in the way of your common sense...!
If you'd told me what you were planning, I could've talked you out of it.
Then I'm glad I **didn't!** I've been insulted and my reputation's been tarnished. I have every **right** to my revenge...
And nothing's going to stop me!
Just don't say I didn't warn you.

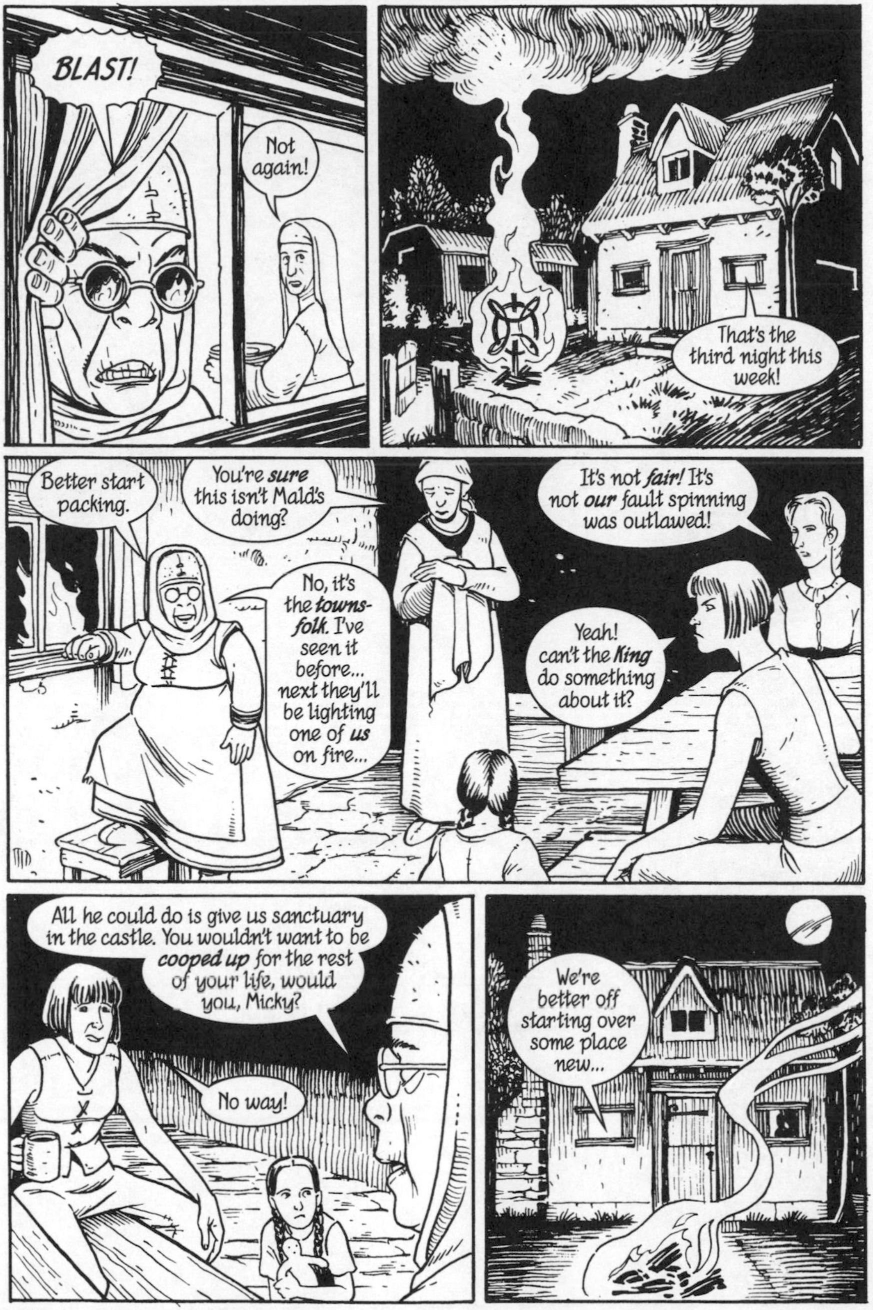
BLAST!
Not again!
That's the third night this week!
Better start packing.
You're sure this isn't Mald's doing?
No, it's the towns-folk. I've seen it before... next they'll be lighting one of us on fire...
It's not fair! It's not our fault spinning was outlawed!
Yeah! can't the King do something about it?
All he could do is give us sanctuary in the castle. You wouldn't want to be cooped up for the rest of your life, would you, Micky?
No way!
We're better off starting over some place new...

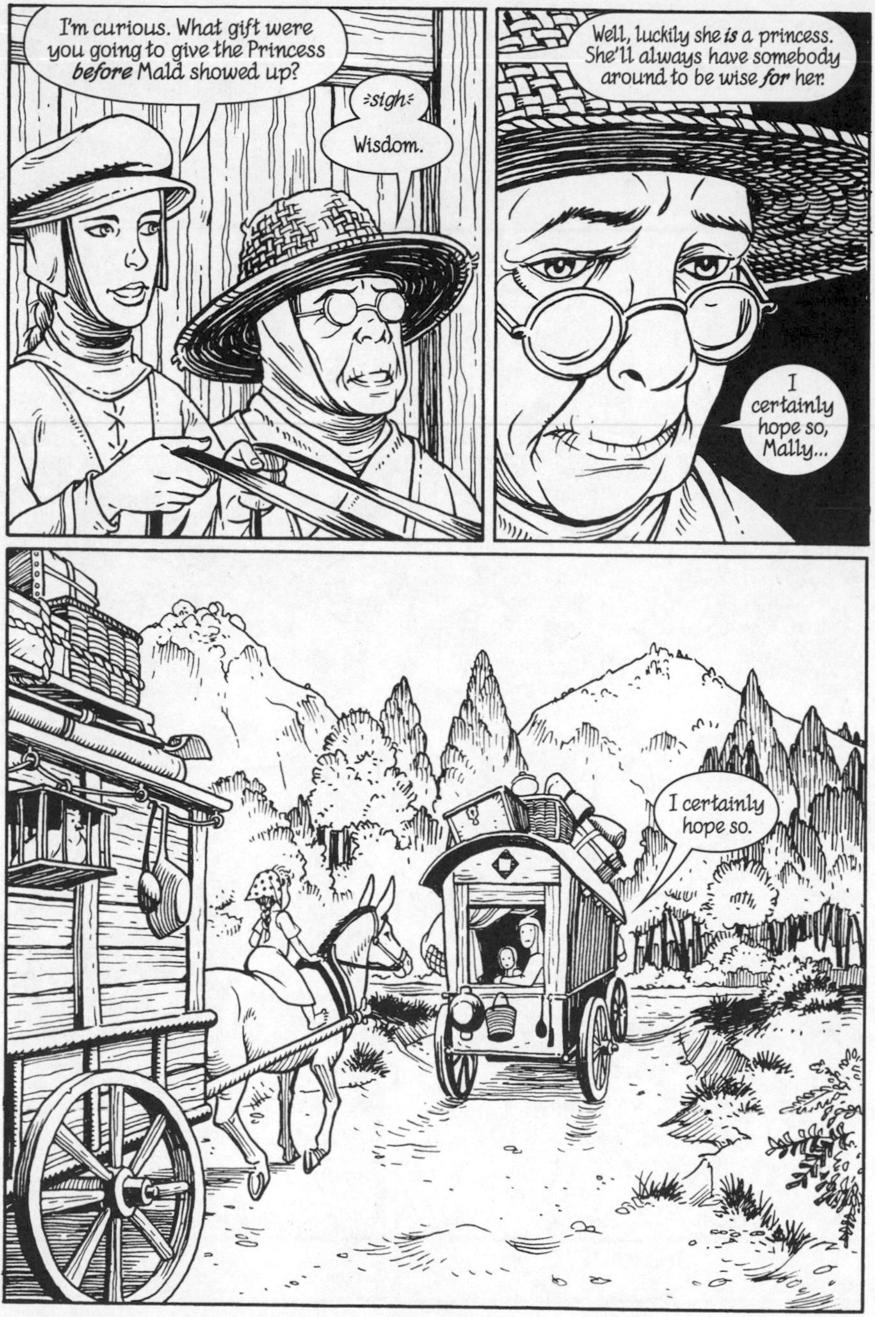
I'm curious. What gift were you going to give the Princess *before* Mald showed up?
⁼sigh⁼
Wisdom.
Well, luckily she *is* a princess. She'll always have somebody around to be wise *for* her.
I certainly hope so, Mally...
I certainly hope so.

Chapter 2.

· THE CURSE OF BRAMBLY HEDGE PT. 2 ·

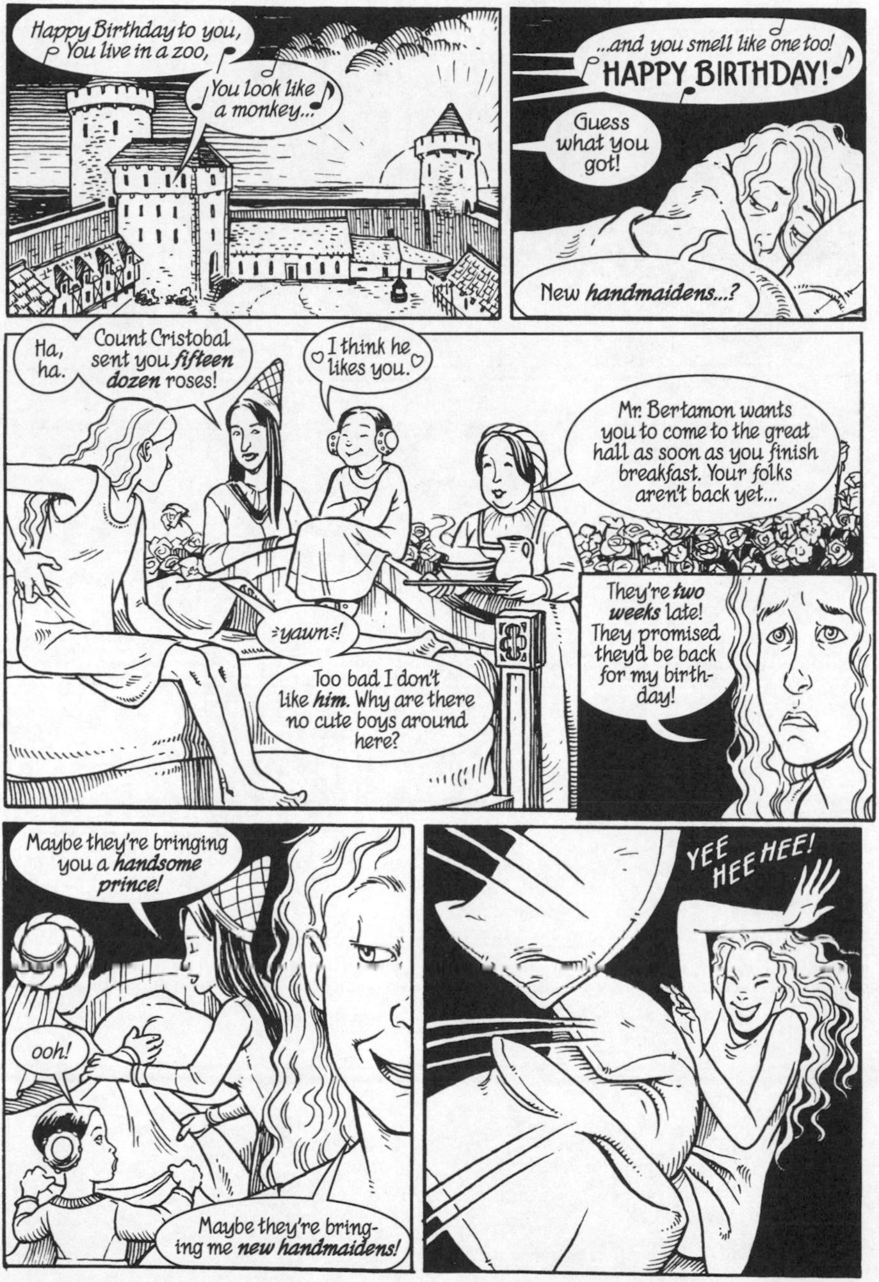
Happy Birthday to you, You live in a zoo,
You look like a monkey...
...and you smell like one too!
HAPPY BIRTHDAY!
Guess what you got!
New handmaidens...?
Ha, ha.
Count Cristobal sent you fifteen dozen roses!
I think he likes you.
Mr. Bertamon wants you to come to the great hall as soon as you finish breakfast. Your folks aren't back yet...
yawn!
Too bad I don't like him. Why are there no cute boys around here?
They're two weeks late! They promised they'd be back for my birthday!
Maybe they're bringing you a handsome prince!
ooh!
Maybe they're bringing me new handmaidens!
YEE HEE HEE!

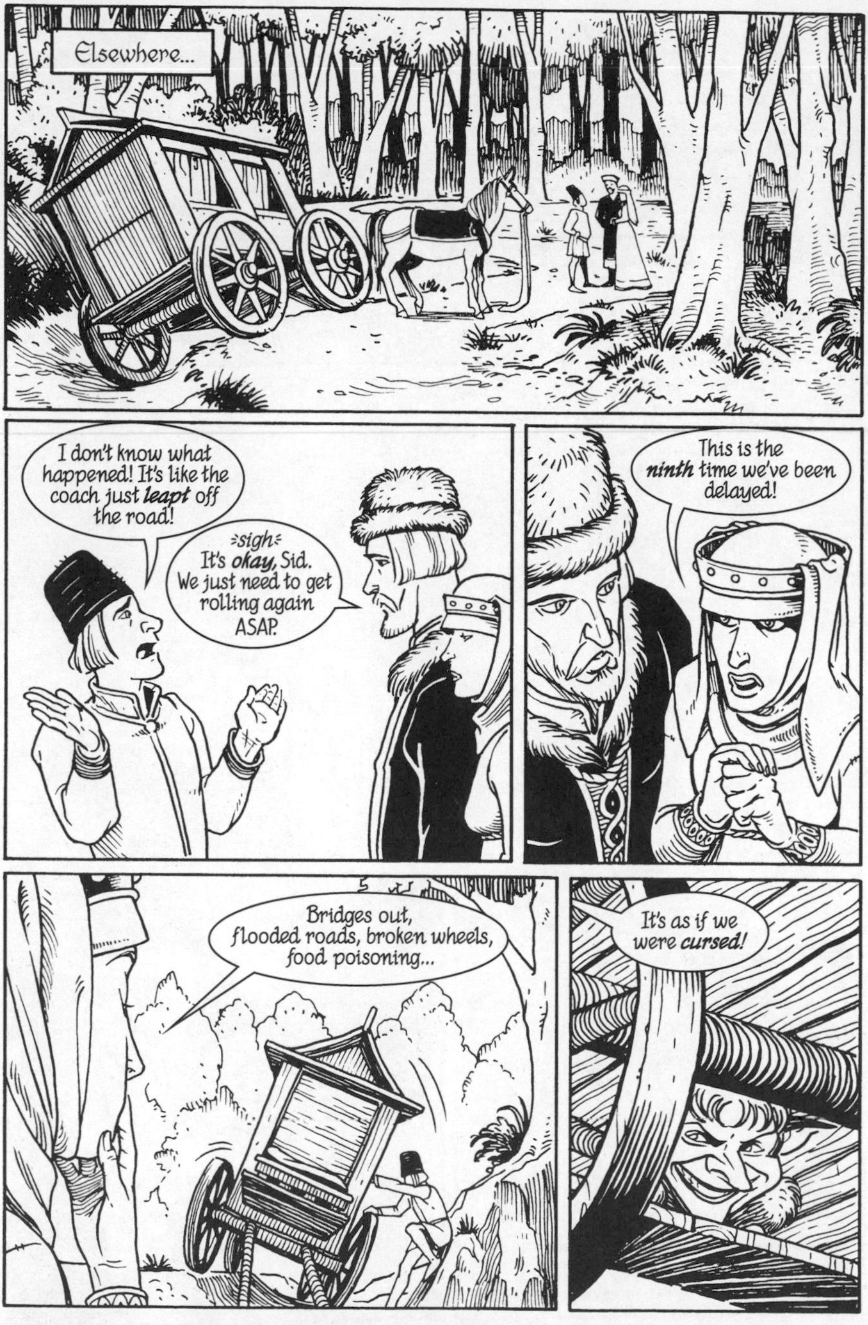
Elsewhere...
I don't know what happened! It's like the coach just *leapt* off the road!
sigh It's *okay,* Sid. We just need to get rolling again ASAP.
This is the *ninth* time we've been delayed!
Bridges out, flooded roads, broken wheels, food poisoning...
It's as if we were *cursed!*

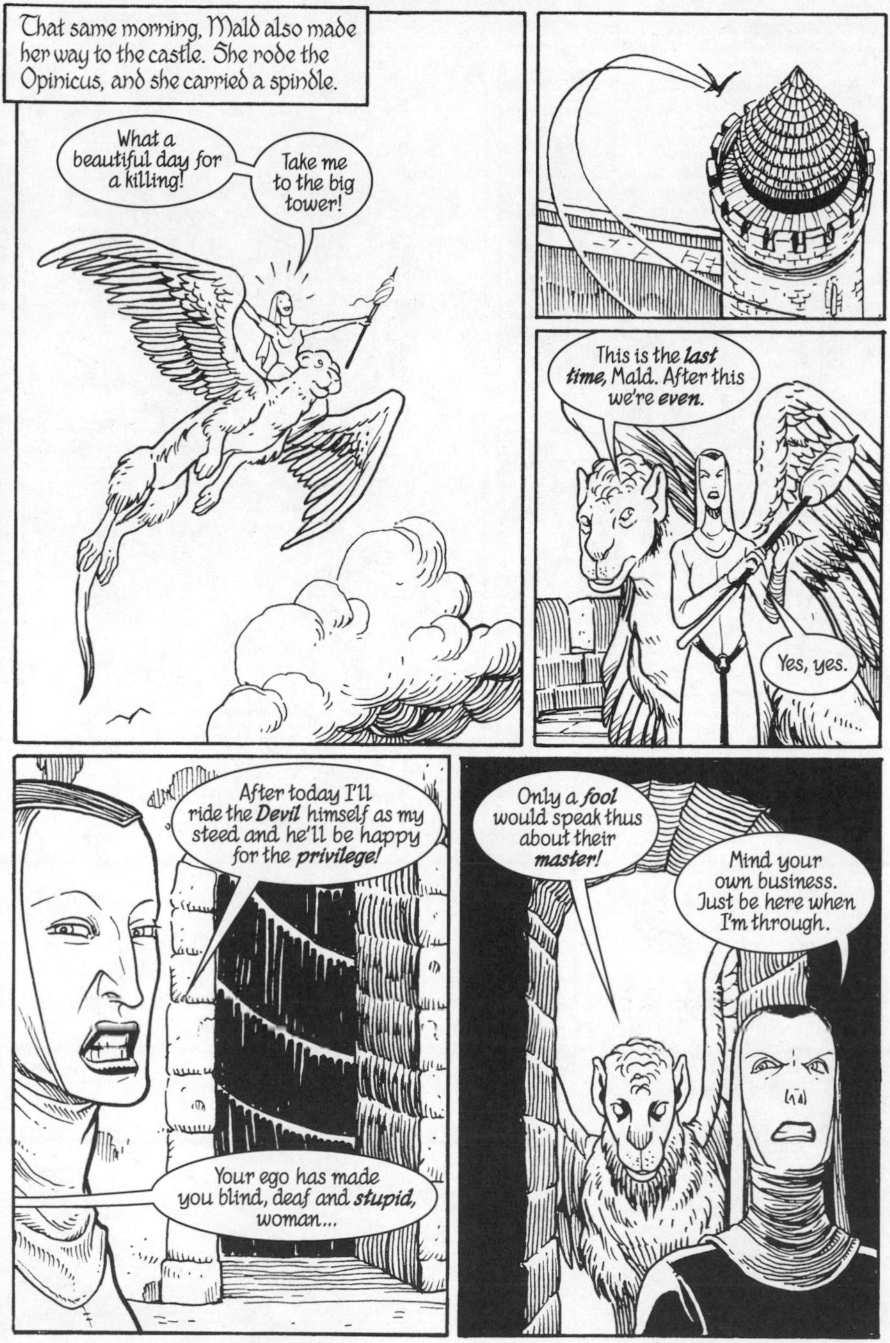
That same morning, Mald also made her way to the castle. She rode the Opinicus, and she carried a spindle.
What a beautiful day for a killing!
Take me to the big tower!
This is the last time, Mald. After this we're even.
Yes, yes.
After today I'll ride the Devil himself as my steed and he'll be happy for the privilege!
Your ego has made you blind, deaf and stupid, woman...
Only a fool would speak thus about their master!
Mind your own business. Just be here when I'm through.

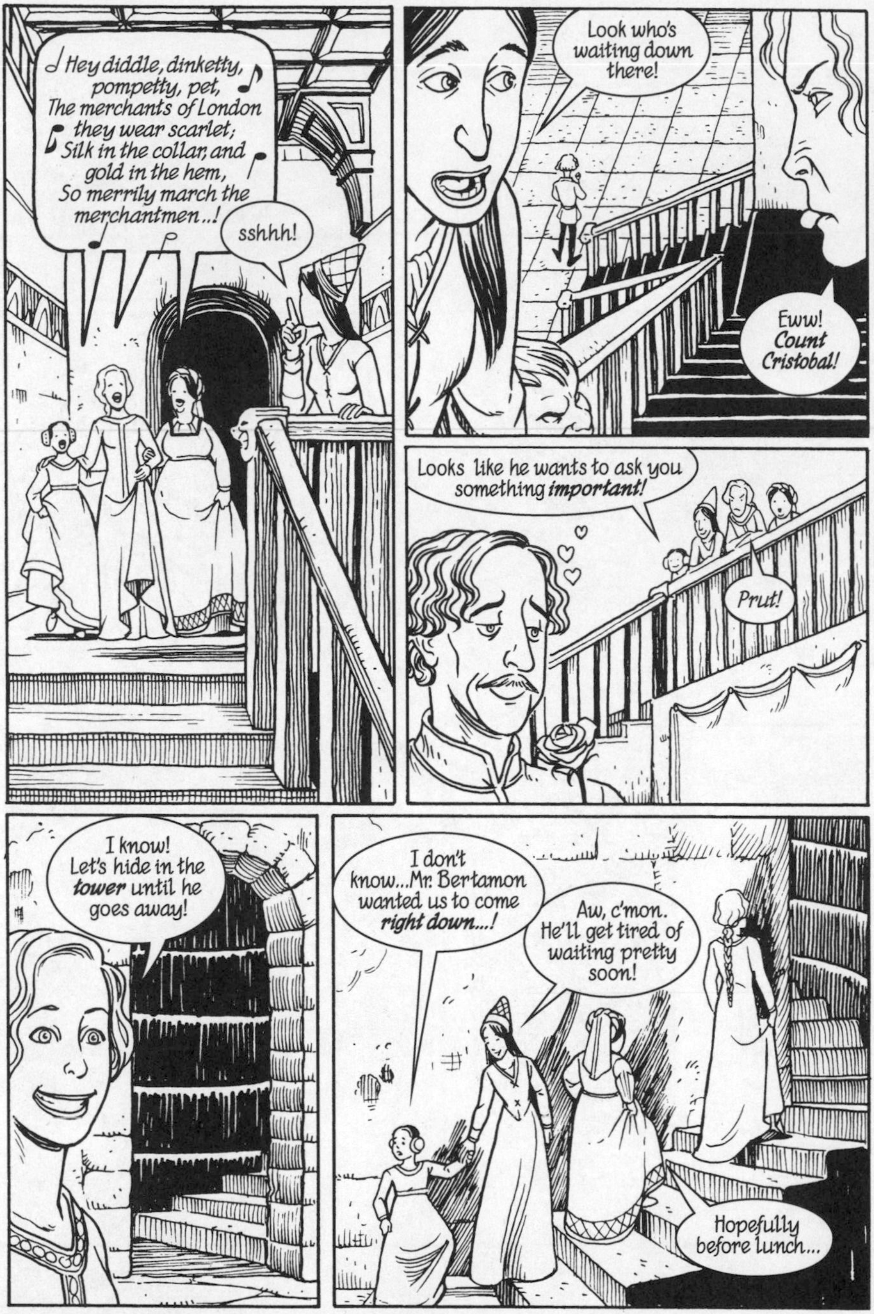
Hey diddle, dinketty, pompetty, pet, The merchants of London they wear scarlet; Silk in the collar, and gold in the hem, So merrily march the merchantmen...!
sshhh!
Look who's waiting down there!
Eww! Count Cristobal!
Looks like he wants to ask you something important!
Prut!
I know! Let's hide in the tower until he goes away!
I don't know...Mr. Bertamon wanted us to come right down...!
Aw, c'mon. He'll get tired of waiting pretty soon!
Hopefully before lunch...

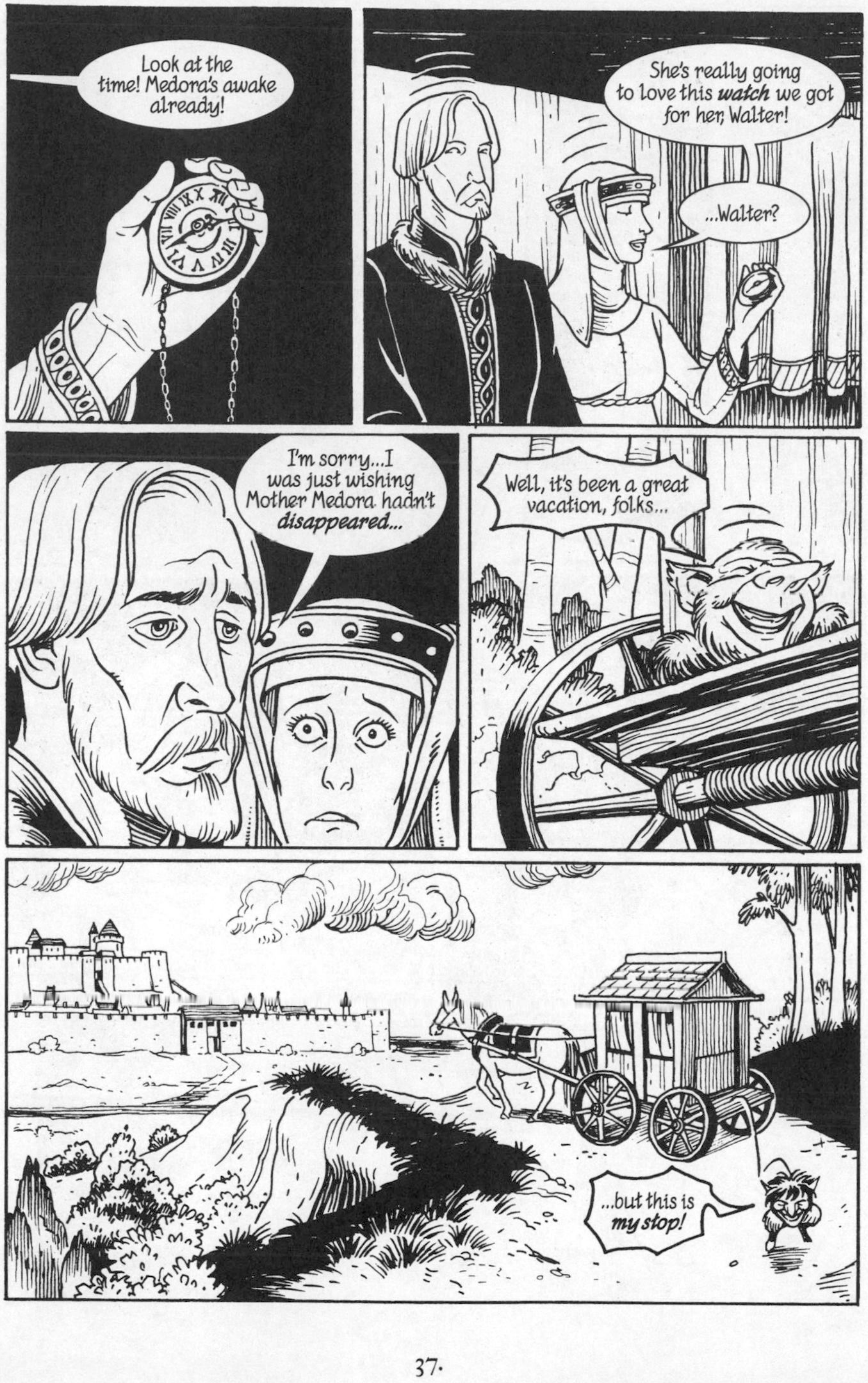
Look at the time! Medora's awake already!
She's really going to love this *watch* we got for her, Walter!
...Walter?
I'm sorry...I was just wishing Mother Medora hadn't *disappeared*...
Well, it's been a great vacation, folks...
...but this is *my stop!*

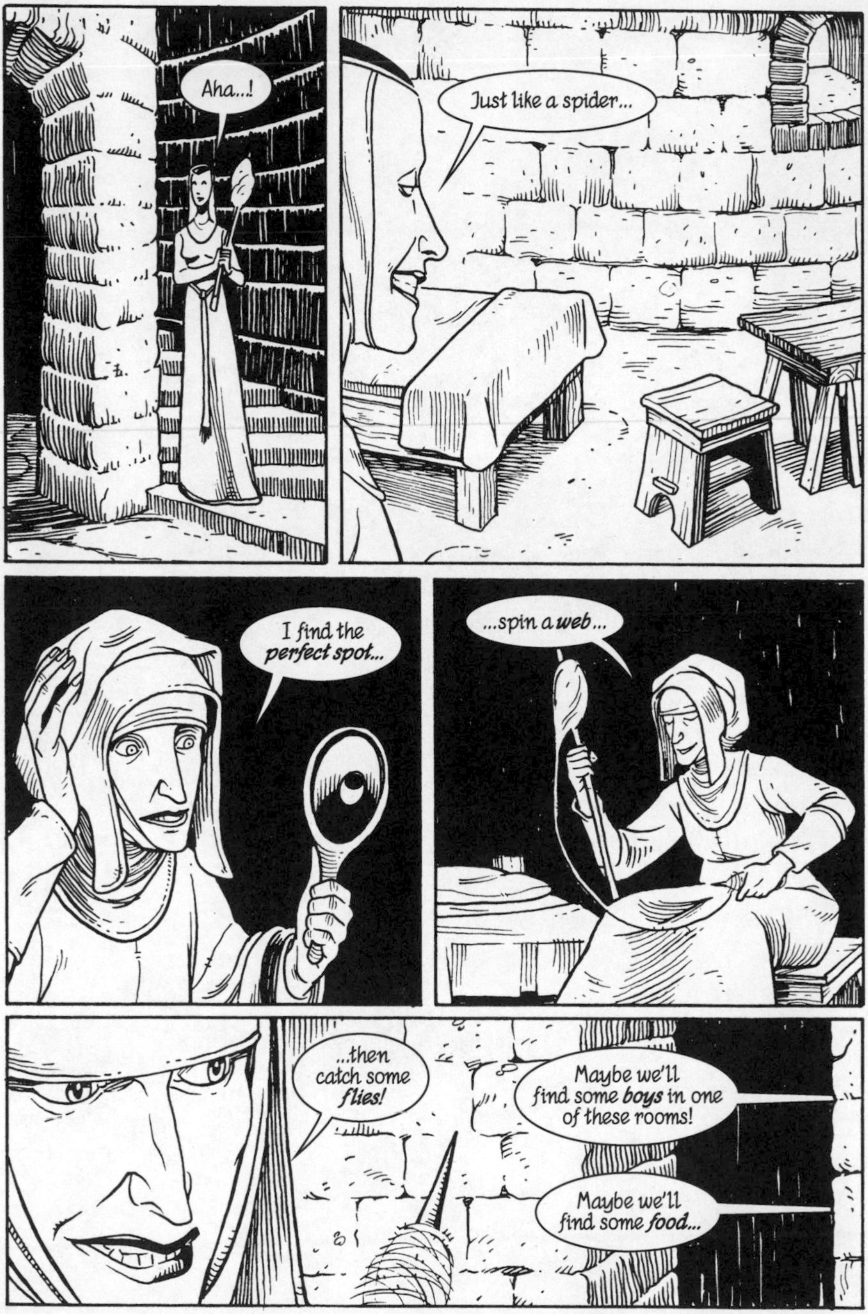
Aha...!
Just like a spider...
I find the *perfect spot*...
...spin a *web*...
...then catch some *flies!*
Maybe we'll find some *boys* in one of these rooms!
Maybe we'll find some *food*...

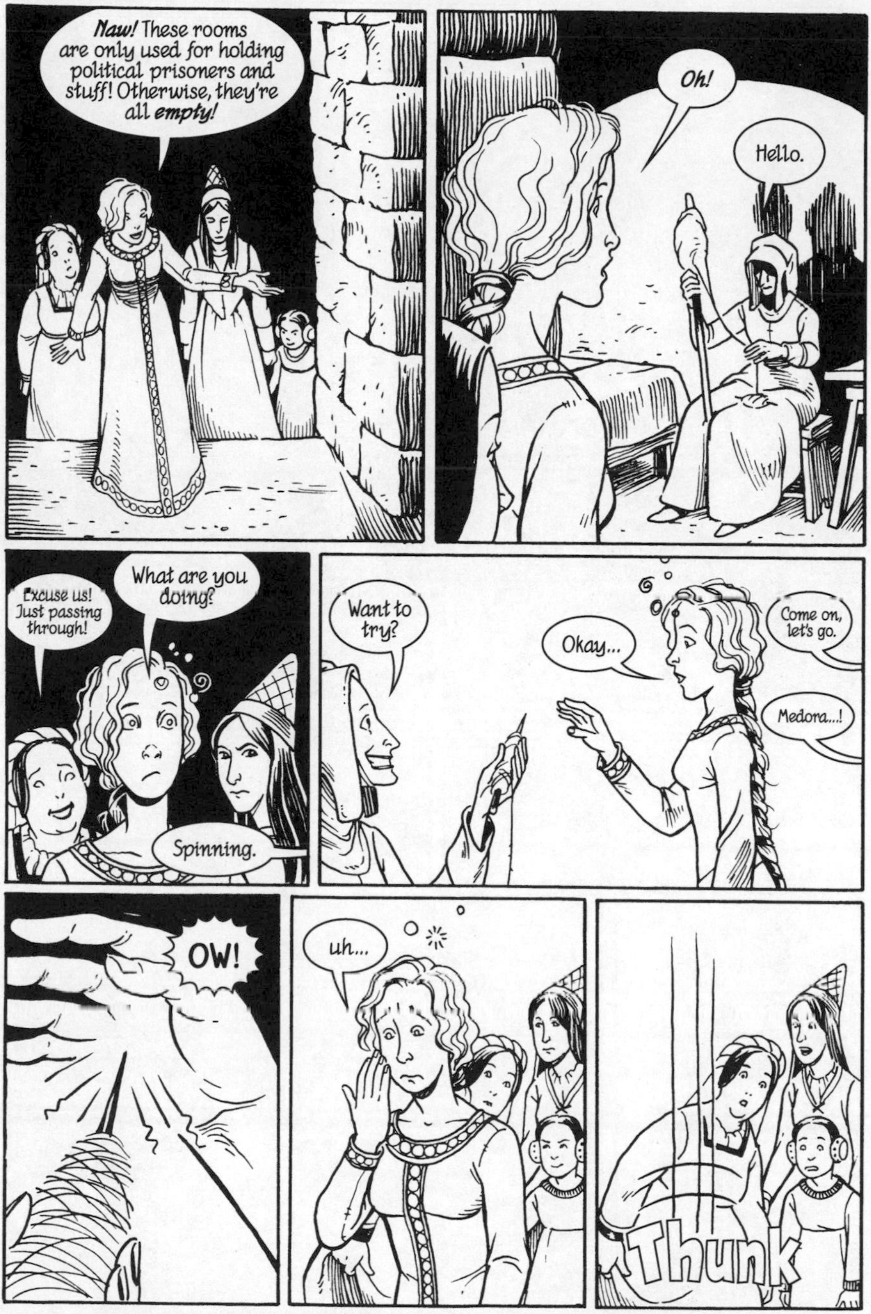
Naw! These rooms are only used for holding political prisoners and stuff! Otherwise, they're all ***empty!***
Oh!
Hello.
Excuse us! Just passing through!
What are you doing?
Spinning.
Want to try?
Okay...
Come on, let's go.
Medora...!
OW!
uh...
Thunk

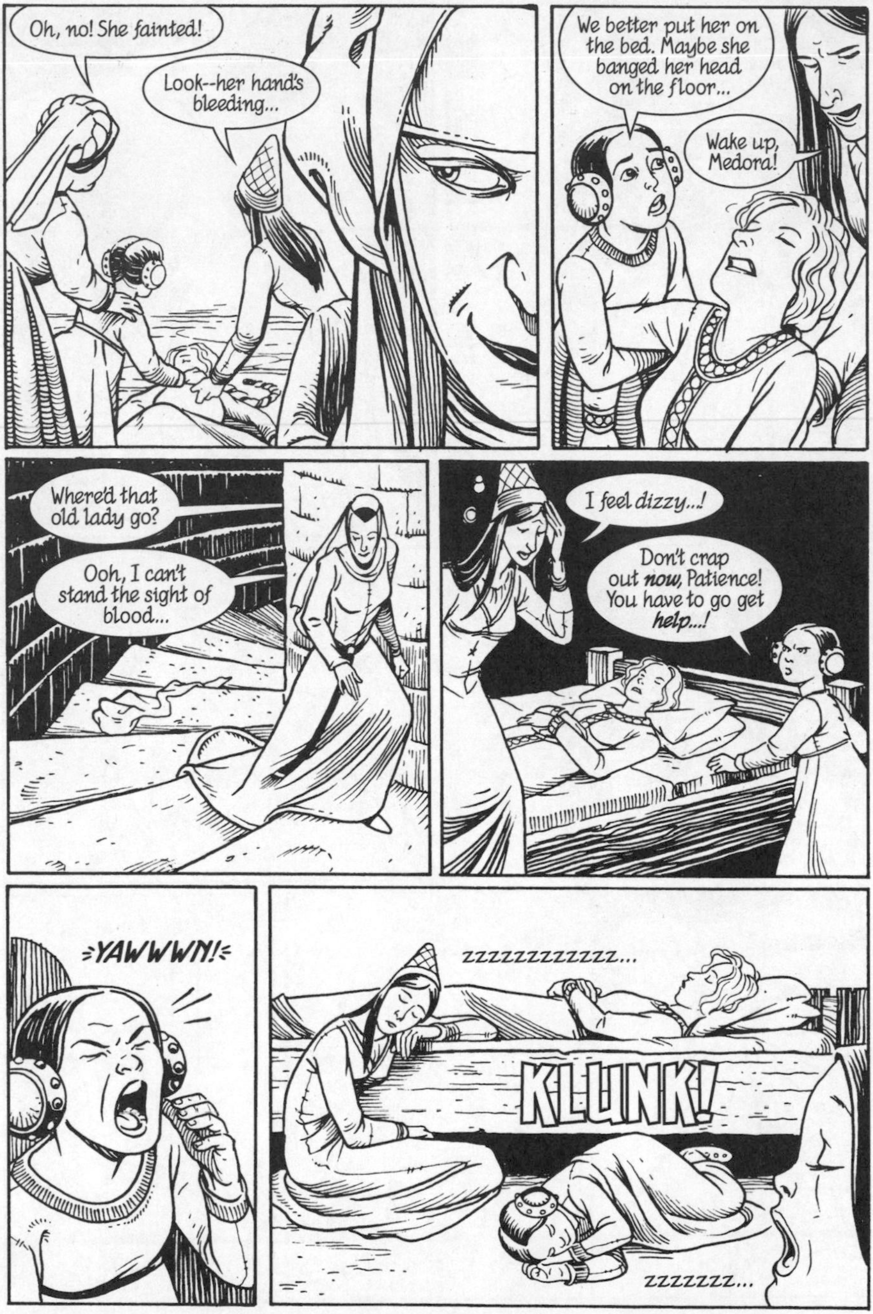
Oh, no! She fainted!
Look--her hand's bleeding...
We better put her on the bed. Maybe she banged her head on the floor...
Wake up, Medora!
Where'd that old lady go?
Ooh, I can't stand the sight of blood...
I feel dizzy...!
Don't crap out *now,* Patience! You have to go get *help...!*
YAWWWN!
zzzzzzzzzzz...
KLUNK!
zzzzzz...

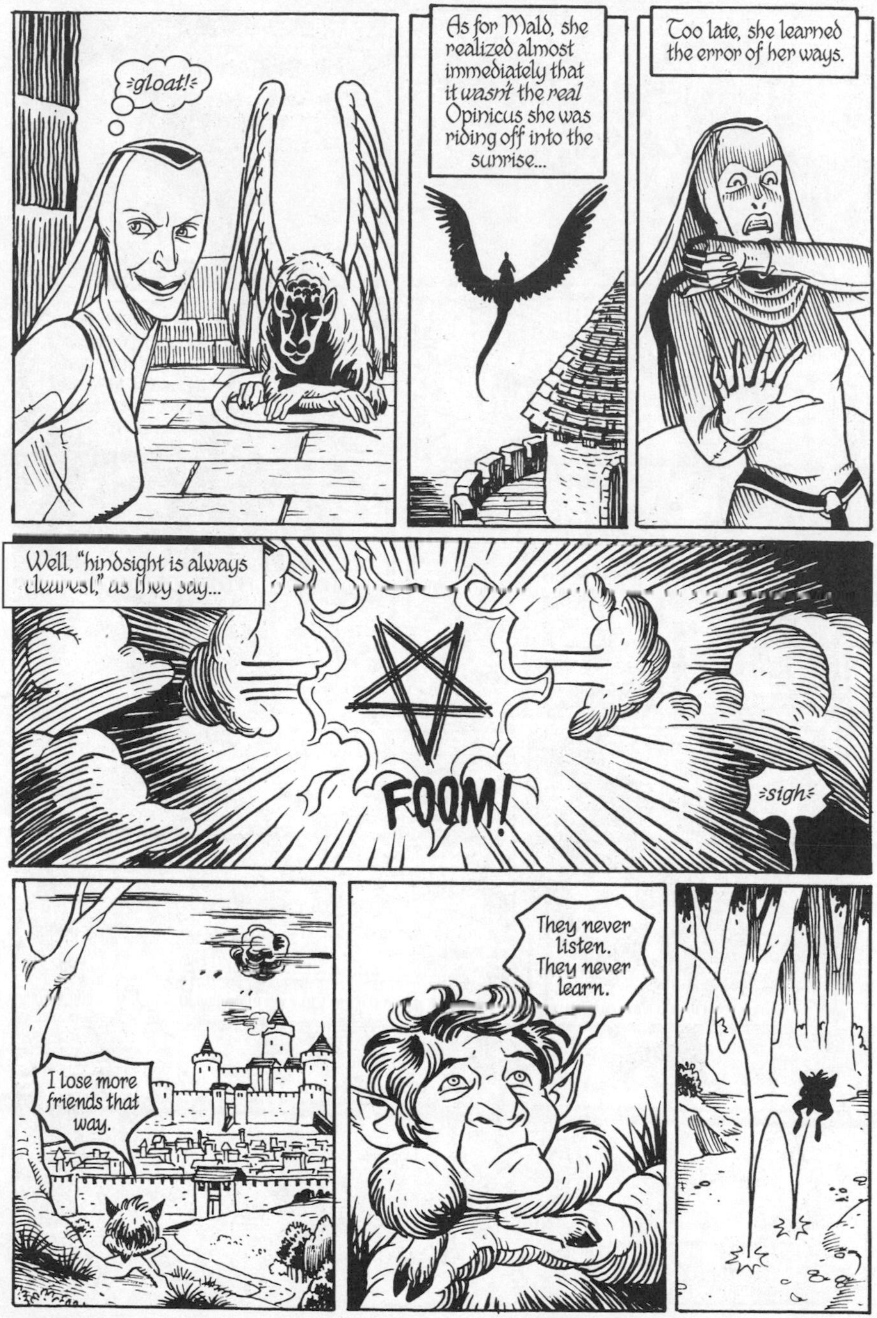

=gloat!=
As for Mald, she realized almost immediately that it *wasn't* the *real* Opinicus she was riding off into the sunrise...
Too late, she learned the error of her ways.
Well, "hindsight is always clearest," as they say...
FOOM!
=sigh=
I lose more friends that way.
They never listen. They never learn.

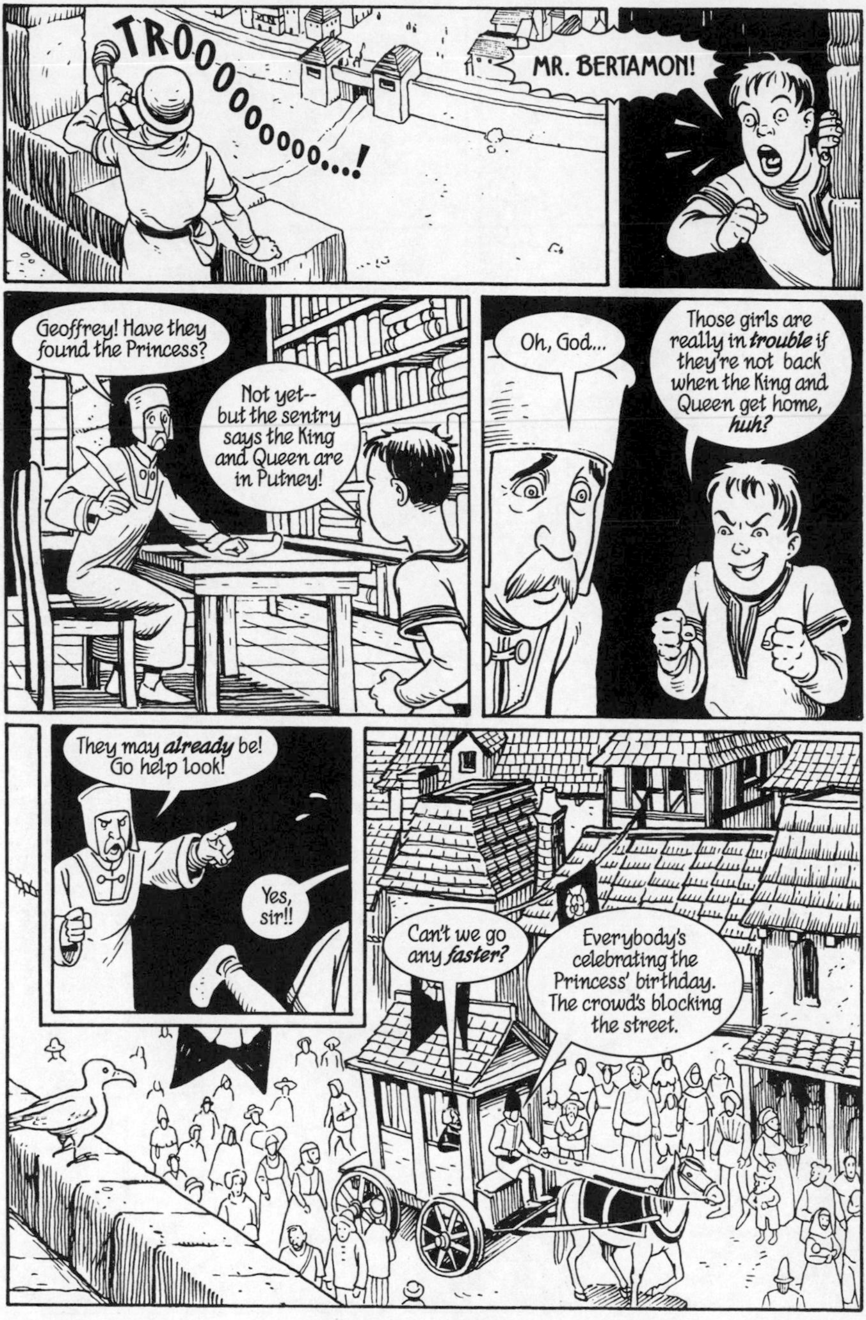
TROOOOOOOOOOO...!
MR. BERTAMON!
Geoffrey! Have they found the Princess?
Not yet-- but the sentry says the King and Queen are in Putney!
Oh, God...
Those girls are really in *trouble* if they're not back when the King and Queen get home, *huh?*
They may *already* be! Go help look!
Yes, sir!!
Can't we go any *faster?*
Everybody's celebrating the Princess' birthday. The crowd's blocking the street.

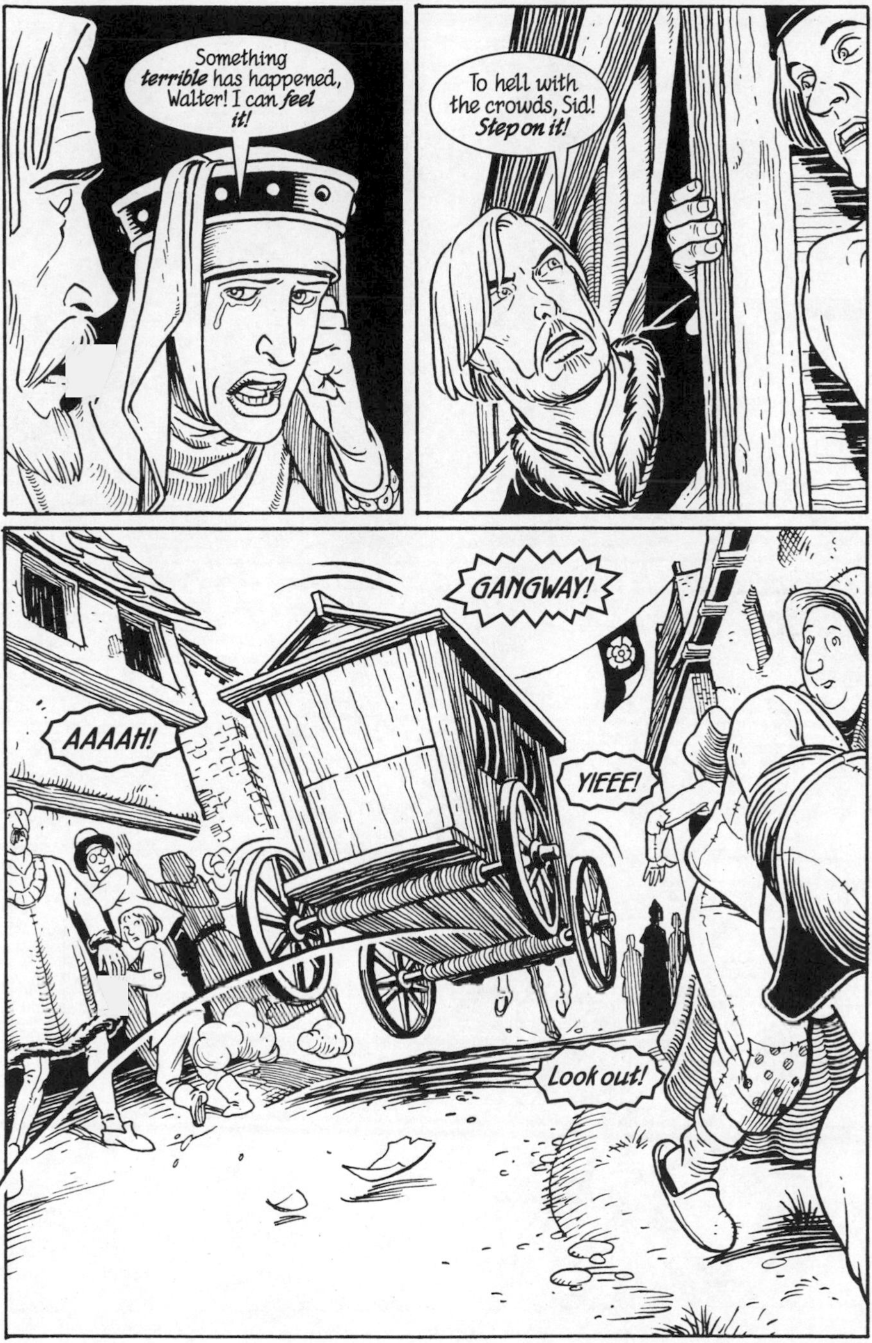
Something terrible has happened, Walter! I can feel it!
To hell with the crowds, Sid! Step on it!
GANGWAY!
AAAAH!
YIEEE!
Look out!

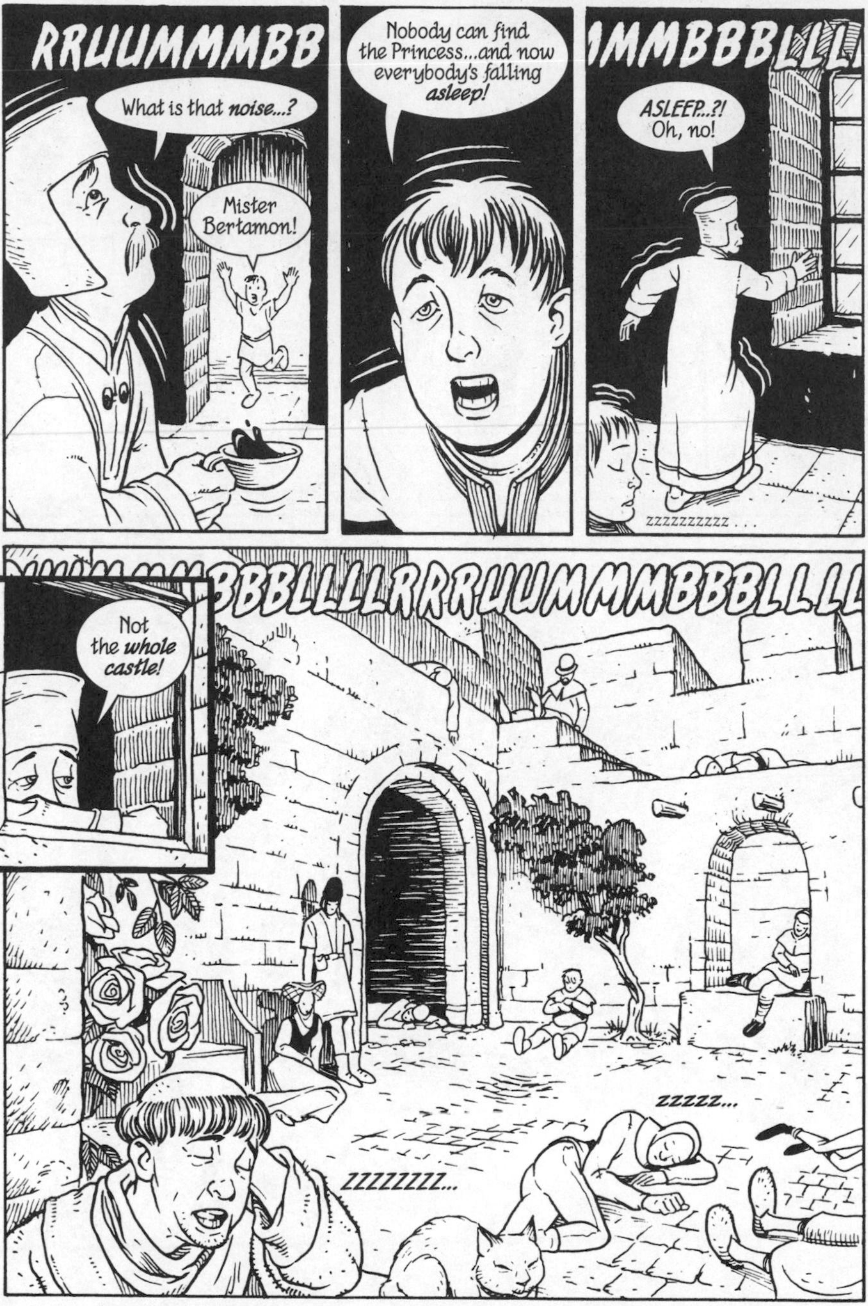
RRUUMMMMBB
What is that *noise*...?
Mister Bertamon!
Nobody can find the Princess...and now everybody's falling *asleep!*
IMMBBBLLL
ASLEEP...?! Oh, no!
ZZZZZZZZZZ . . .
BBBLLLLRRRUUMMMMBBBLLLL
Not the *whole castle!*
ZZZZZ...
ZZZZZZZ...

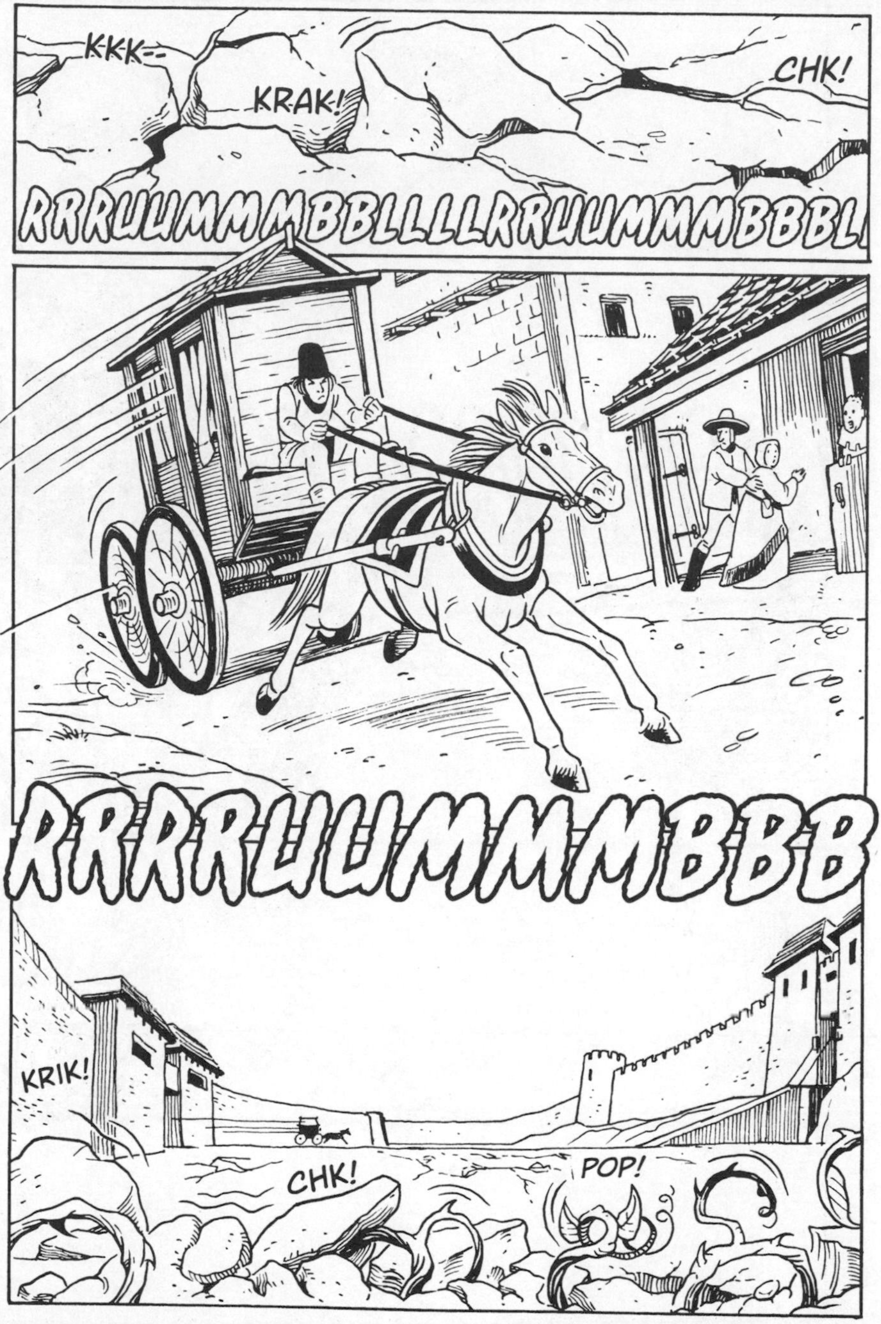
K-K-K--
KRAK!
CHK!
RRRUUMMMBBLLLLRRUUMMMBBBL
RRRRUUMMMMBBB
KRIK!
CHK!
POP!

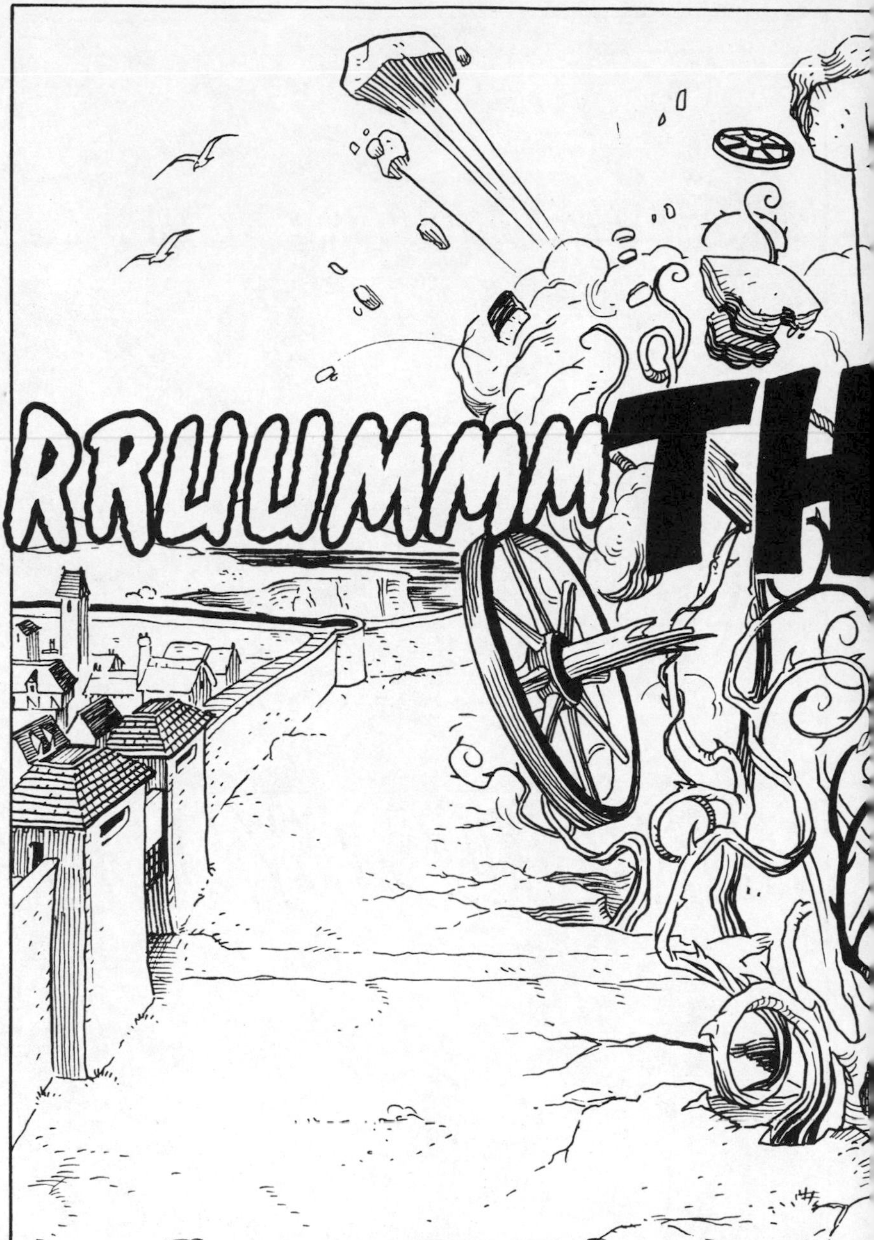
RRUUMMM
TH

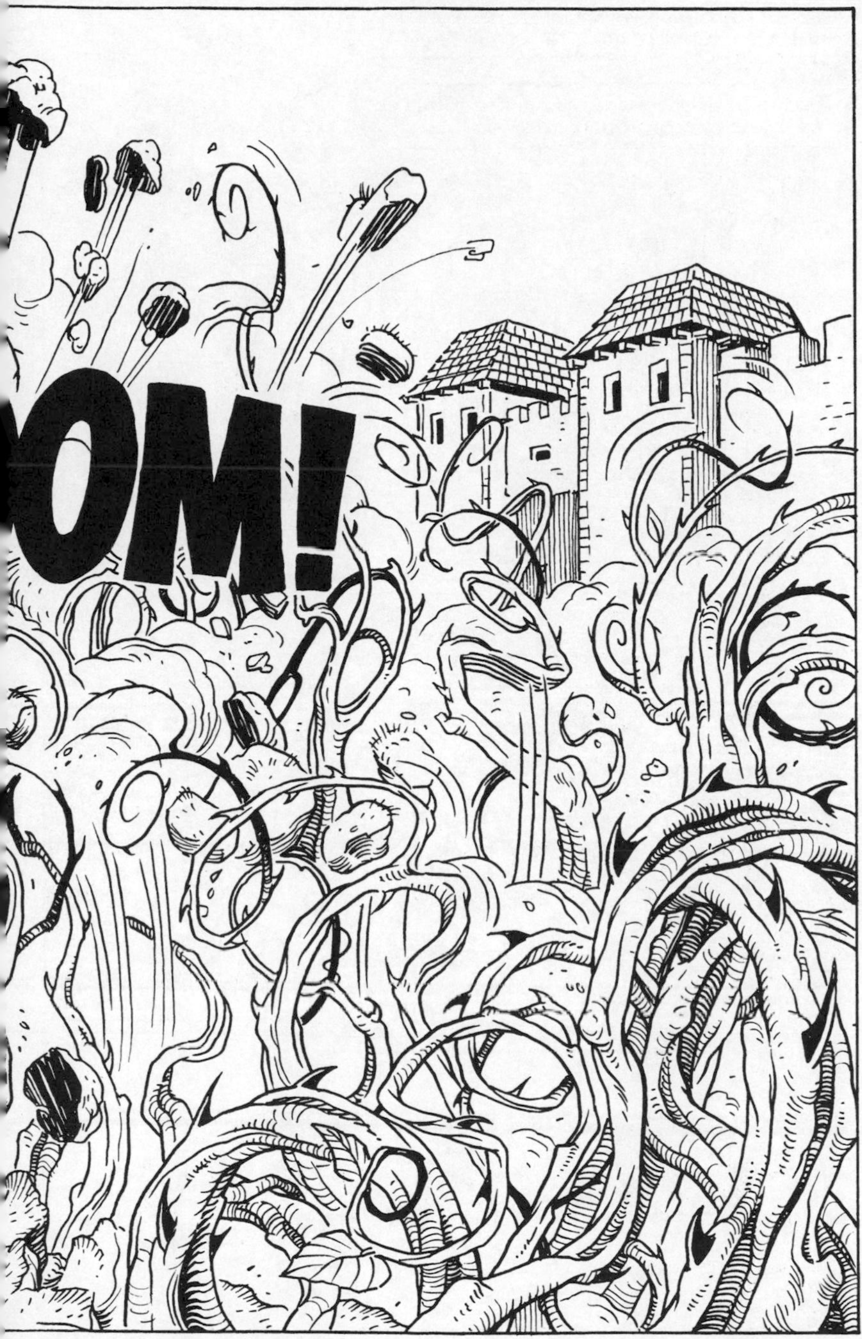
OM!

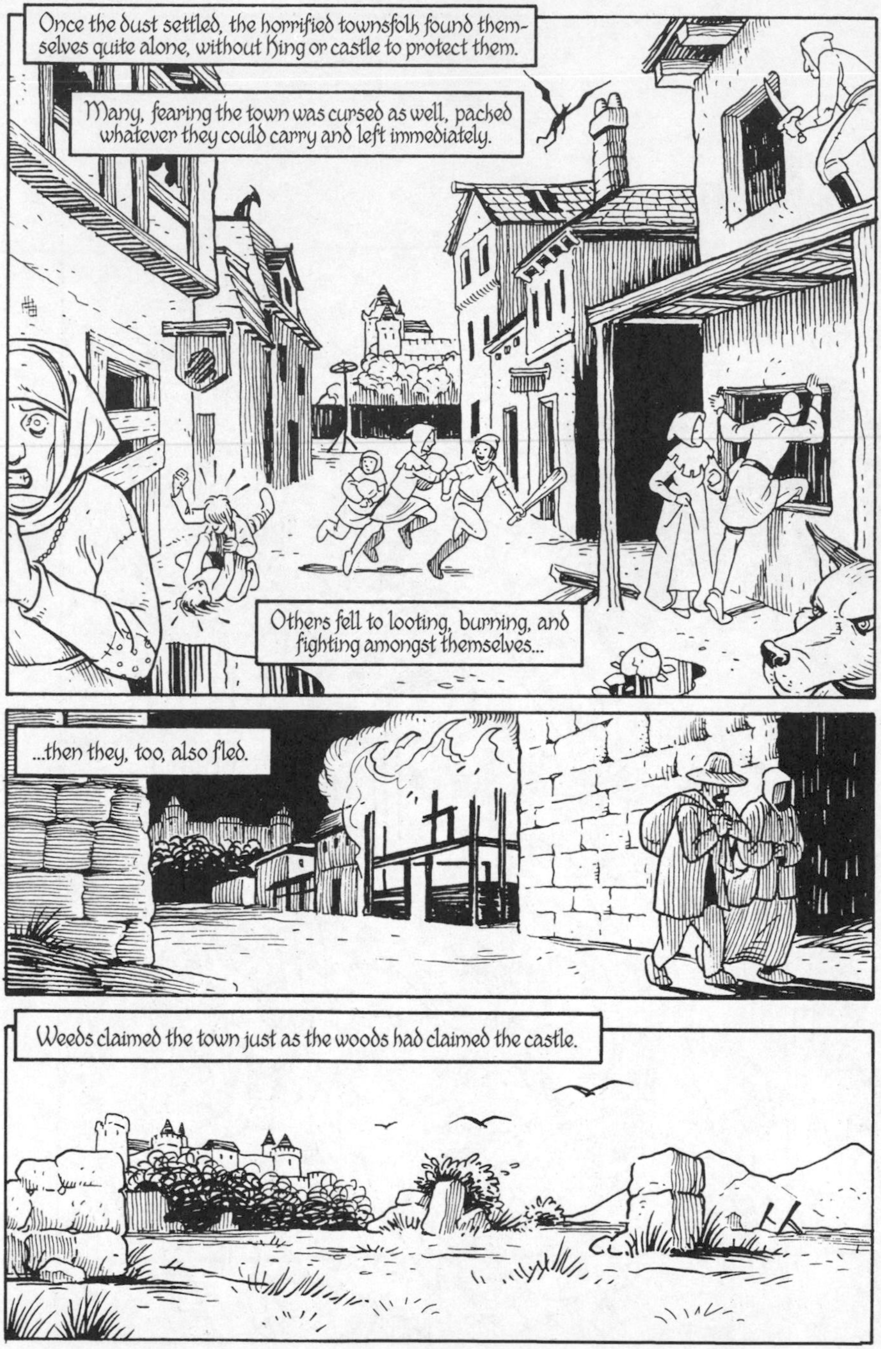
Once the dust settled, the horrified townsfolk found themselves quite alone, without King or castle to protect them.
Many, fearing the town was cursed as well, packed whatever they could carry and left immediately.
Others fell to looting, burning, and fighting amongst themselves...
...then they, too, also fled.
Weeds claimed the town just as the woods had claimed the castle.

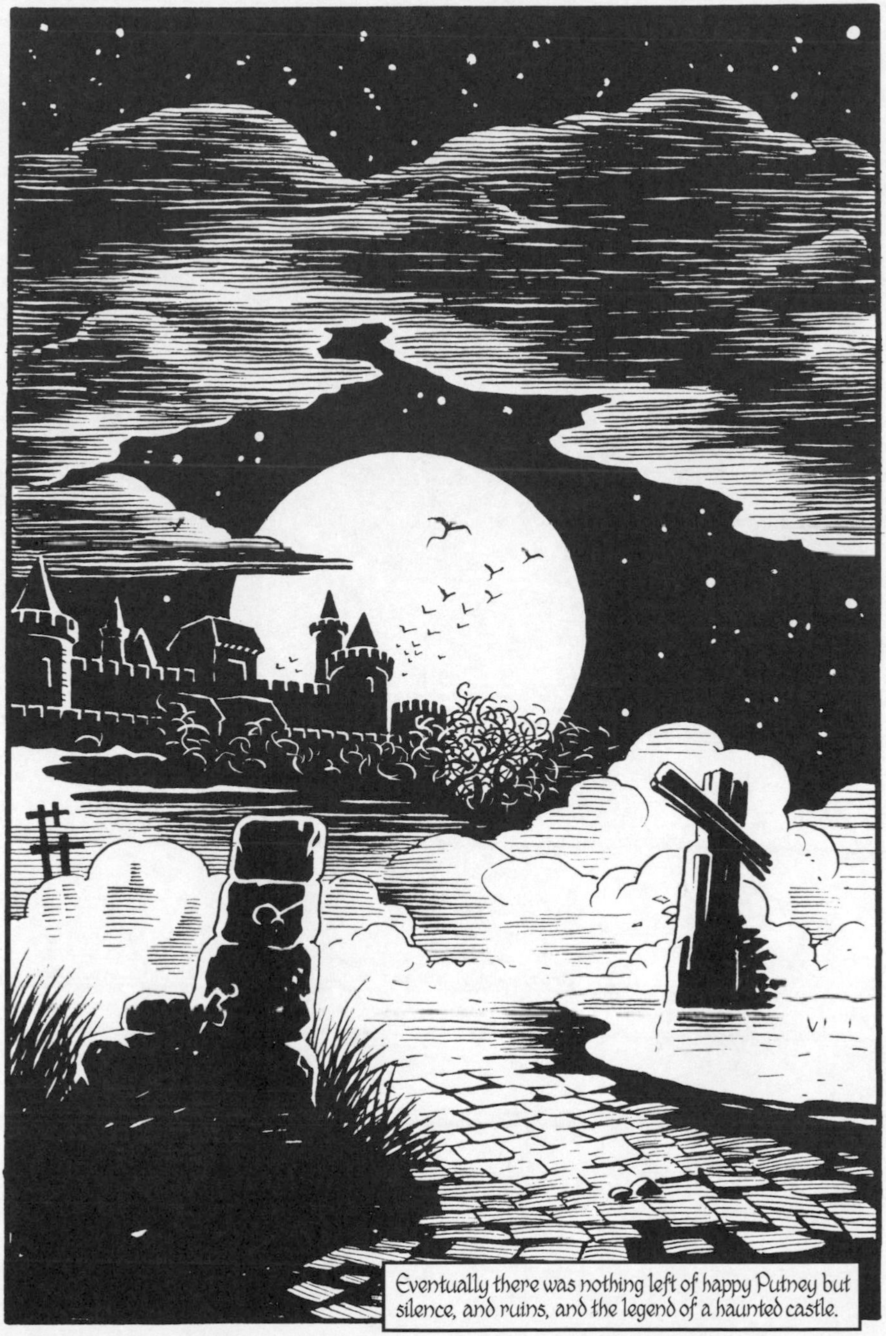
Eventually there was nothing left of happy Putney but silence, and ruins, and the legend of a haunted castle.

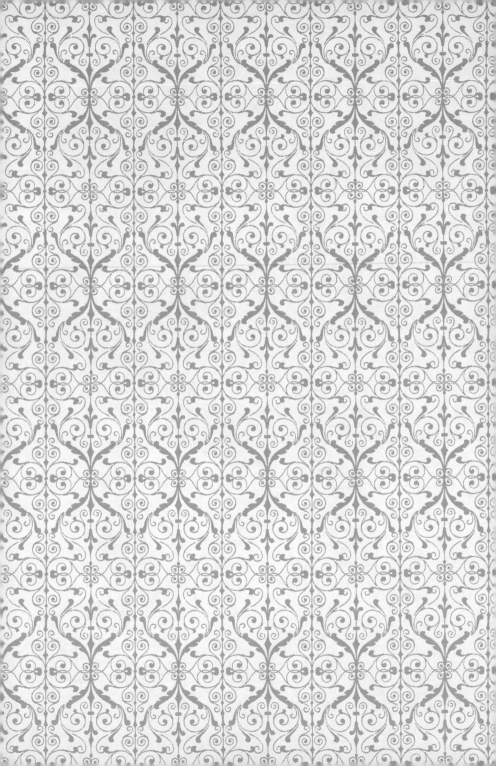

Chapter 3.

· THE CURSE OF BRAMBLY HEDGE PT. 3 ·

A century passed, just like that.

A young prince traveling through a neighboring land heard an old man tell the story of the Brambly Hedge, and how the castle behind it held a wonderful princess, "waiting for the arrival of a brave prince to break the spell she was under."

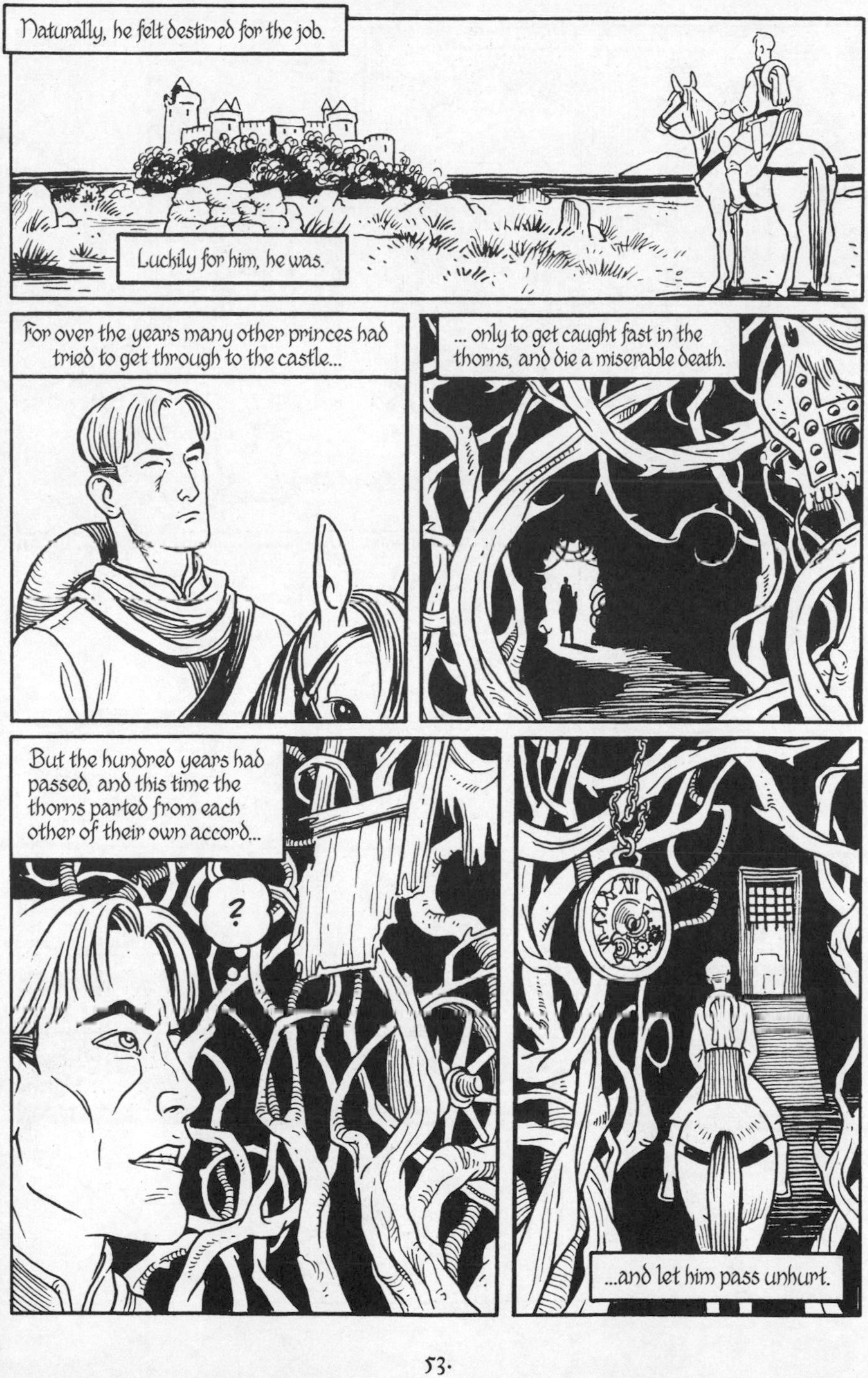
Naturally, he felt destined for the job.
Luckily for him, he was.
For over the years many other princes had tried to get through to the castle...
... only to get caught fast in the thorns, and die a miserable death.
But the hundred years had passed, and this time the thorns parted from each other of their own accord...
?
...and let him pass unhurt.

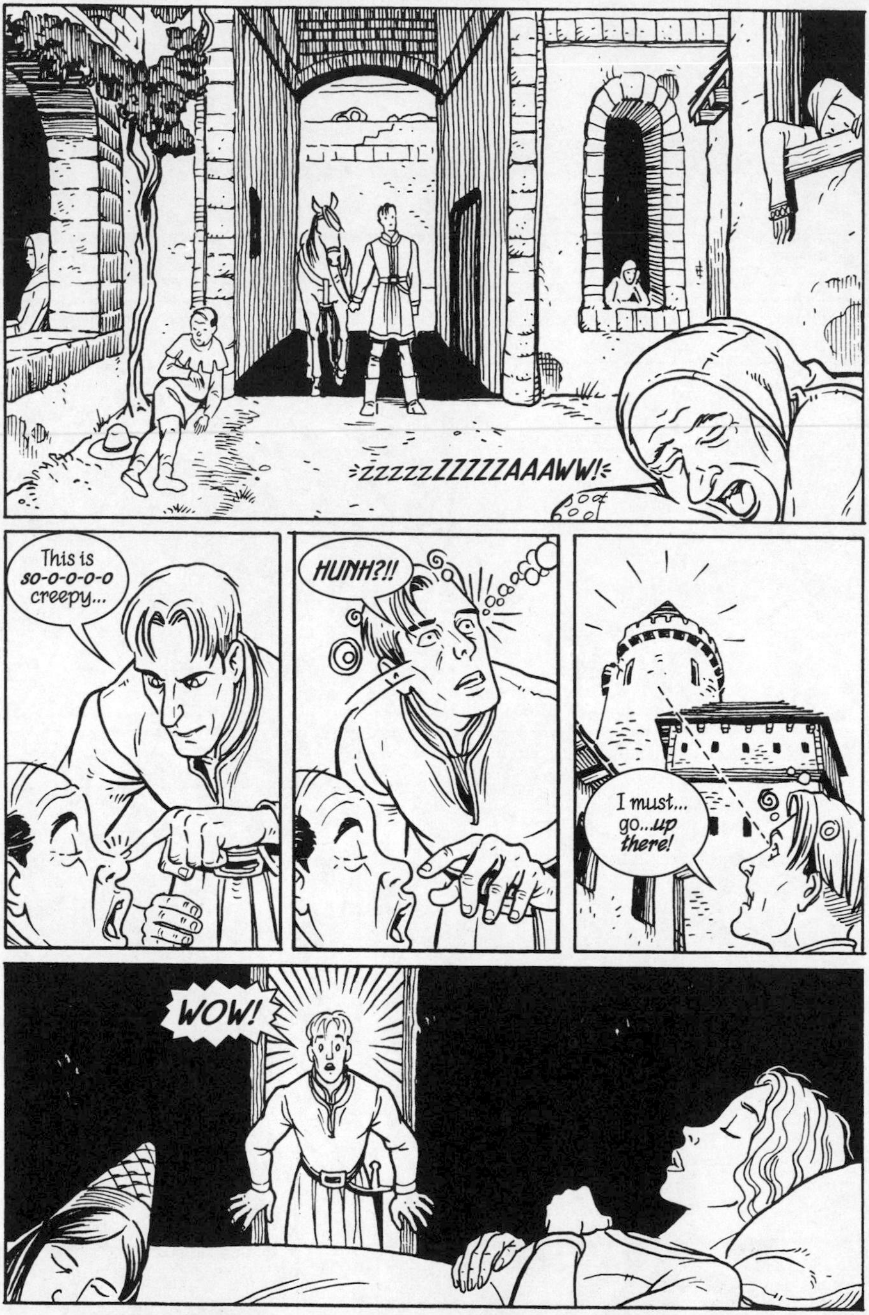
zzzzzZZZZZAAAWW!
This is so-o-o-o-o creepy...
HUNH?!!
I must... go...up there!
WOW!

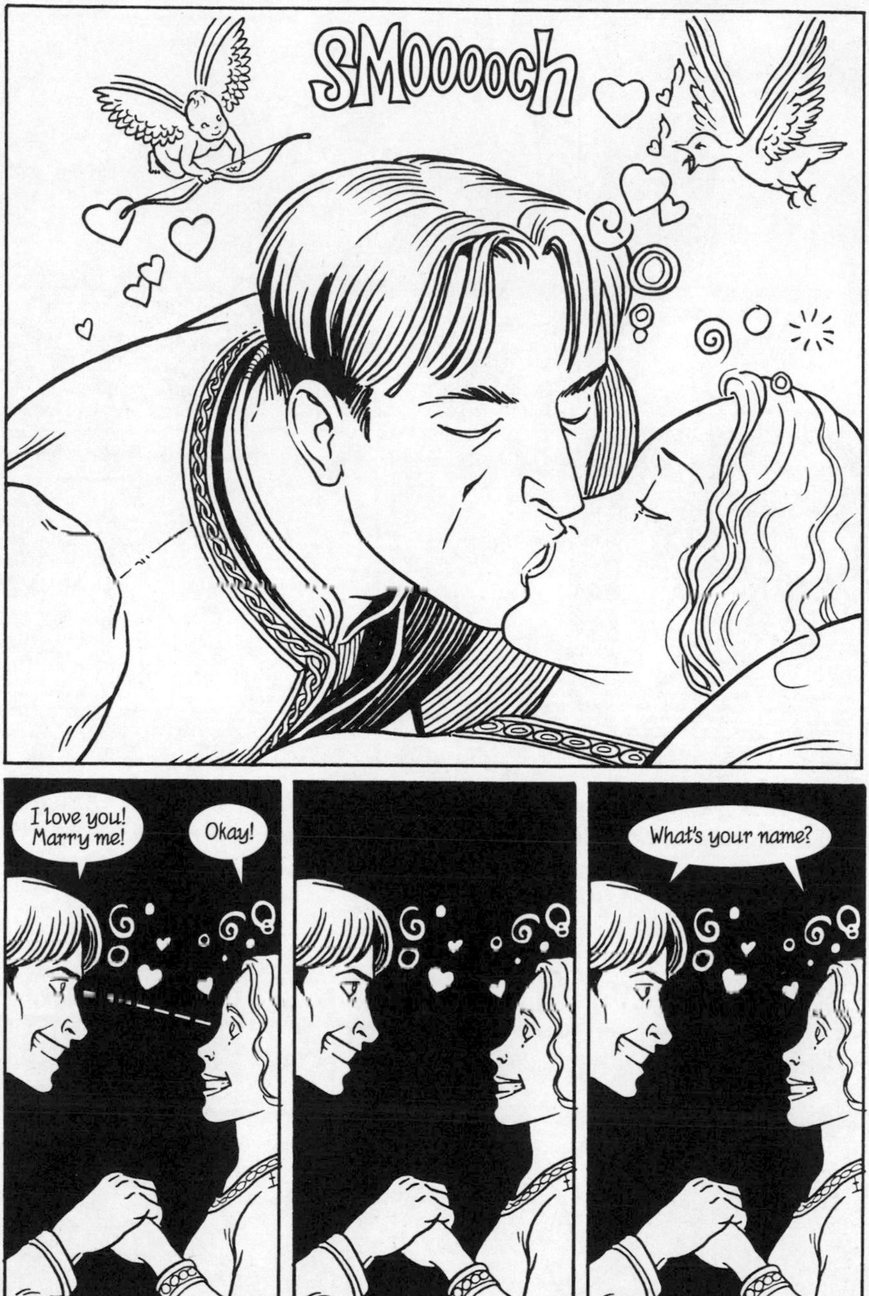
SMOOoooch
I love you! Marry me!
Okay!
What's your name?

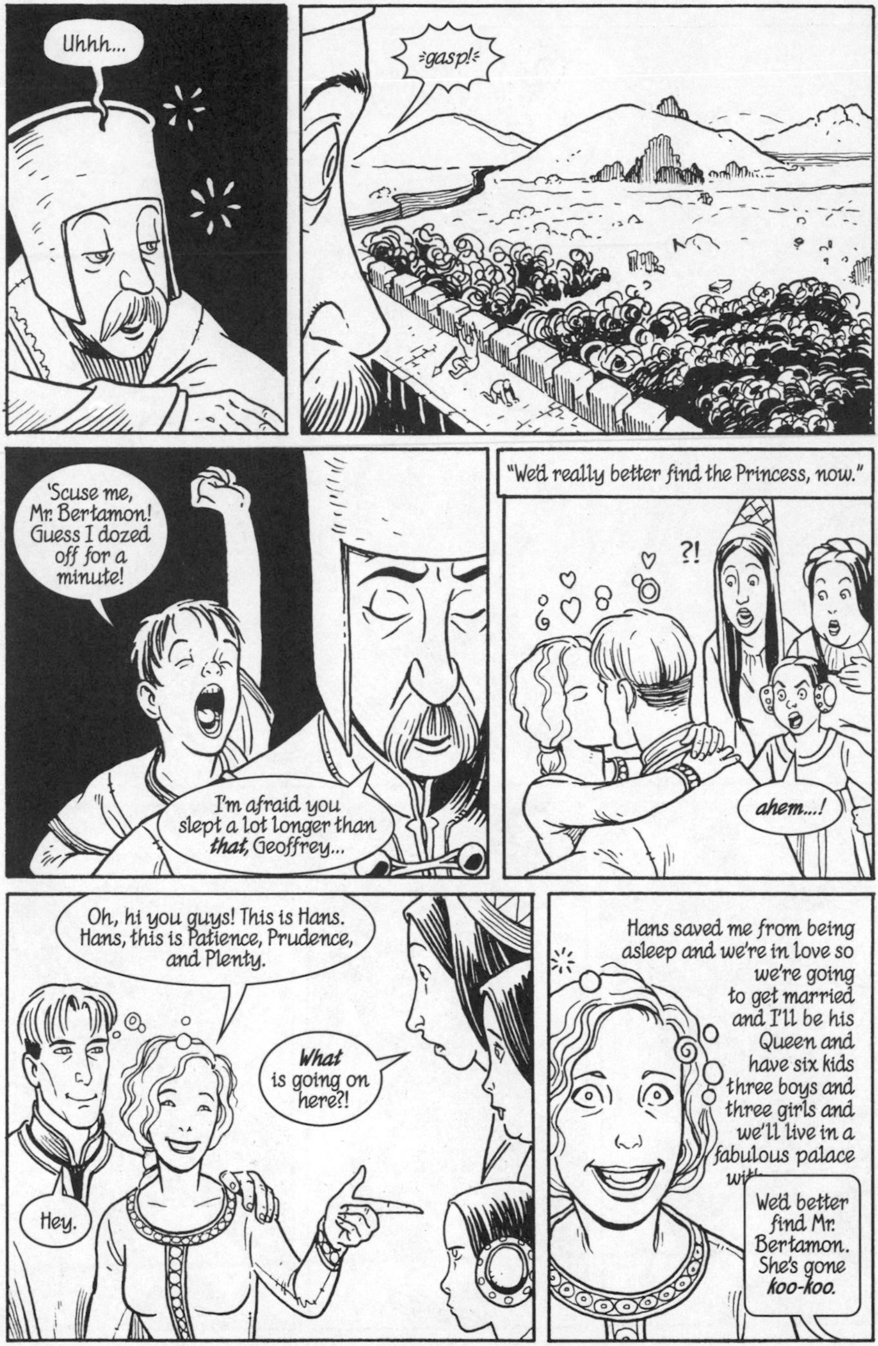
Uhhh...
gasp!
'Scuse me, Mr. Bertamon! Guess I dozed off for a minute!
I'm afraid you slept a lot longer than *that*, Geoffrey...
"We'd really better find the Princess, now."
?!
ahem...!
Oh, hi you guys! This is Hans. Hans, this is Patience, Prudence, and Plenty.
Hey.
What is going on here?!
Hans saved me from being asleep and we're in love so we're going to get married and I'll be his Queen and have six kids three boys and three girls and we'll live in a fabulous palace
We'd better find Mr. Bertamon. She's gone *koo-koo.*

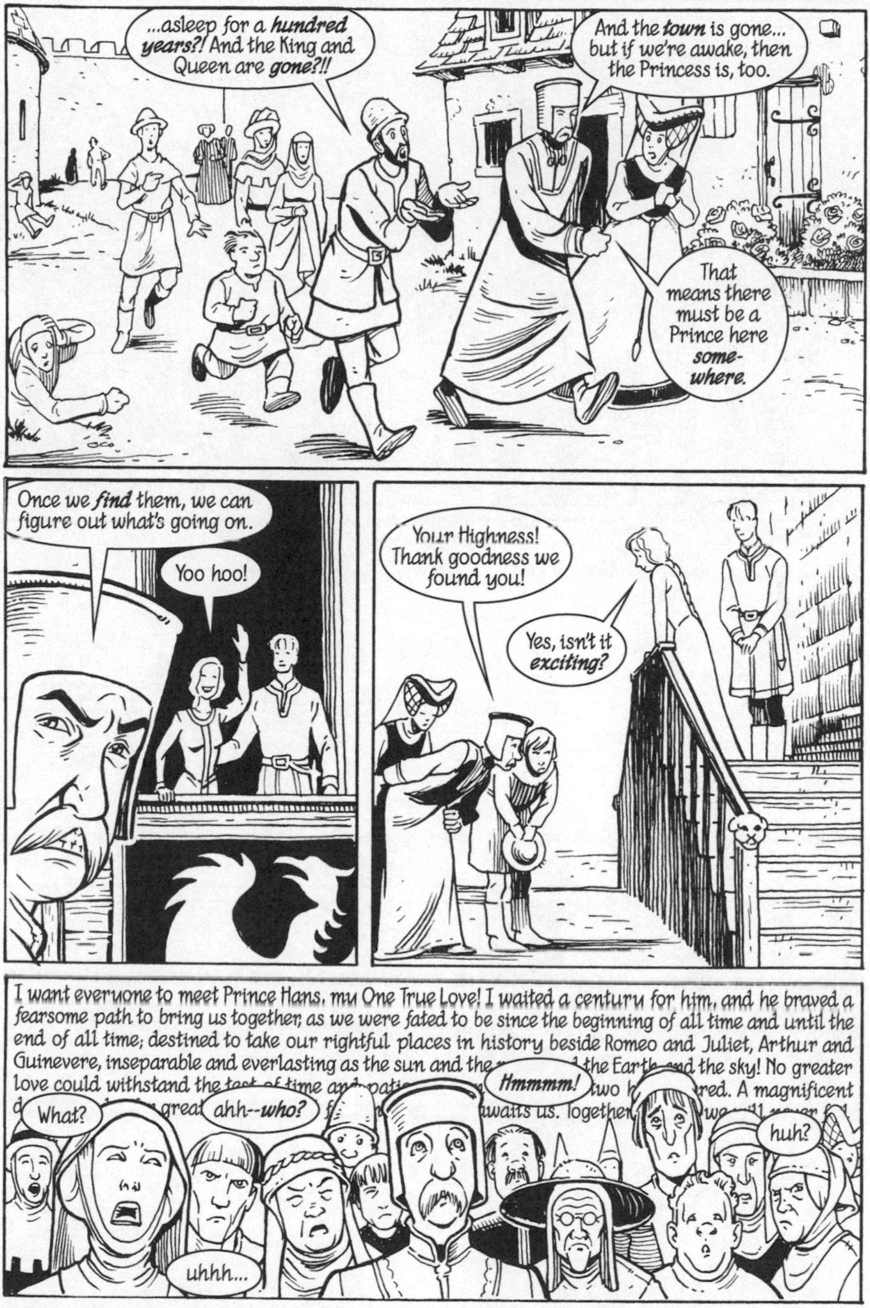
...asleep for a **hundred years?!** And the King and Queen are **gone?!!**
And the **town** is gone... but if we're awake, then the Princess is, too.
That means there must be a Prince here **some-where.**
Once we **find** them, we can figure out what's going on.
Yoo hoo!
Your Highness! Thank goodness we found you!
Yes, isn't it **exciting?**
I want everyone to meet Prince Hans, my One True Love! I waited a century for him, and he braved a fearsome path to bring us together, as we were fated to be since the beginning of all time and until the end of all time; destined to take our rightful places in history beside Romeo and Juliet, Arthur and Guinevere, inseparable and everlasting as the sun and the
the Earth
the sky! No greater love could withstand the
time
two
red. A magnificent
great
awaits us. Together
What?
ahh--**who?**
Hmmmm!
huh?
uhhh...

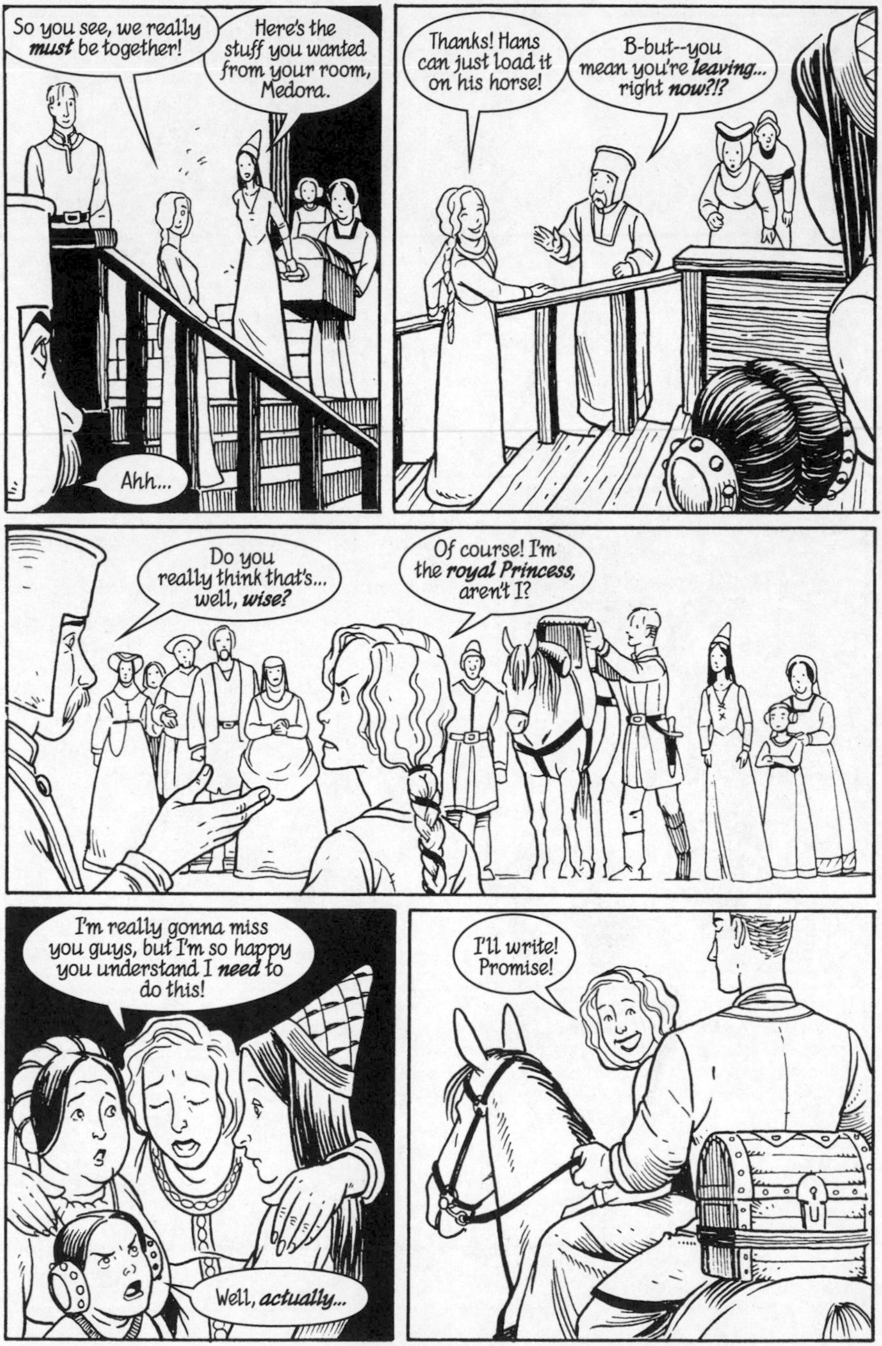
So you see, we really *must* be together!
Here's the stuff you wanted from your room, Medora.
Ahh...
Thanks! Hans can just load it on his horse!
B-but--you mean you're *leaving...* right *now?!?*
Do you really think that's... well, *wise?*
Of course! I'm the *royal Princess,* aren't I?
I'm really gonna miss you guys, but I'm so happy you understand I *need* to do this!
Well, *actually...*
I'll write! Promise!

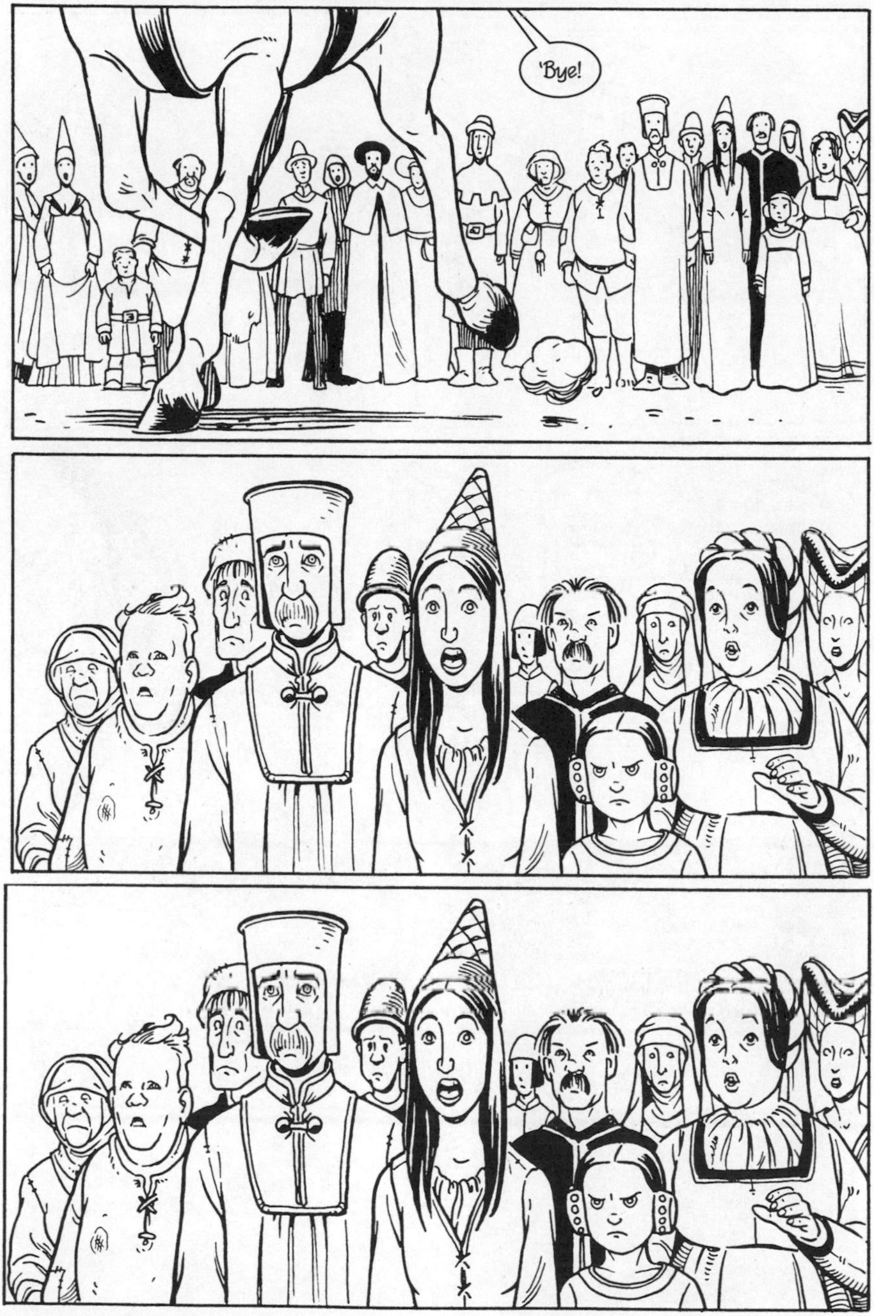
'Bye!

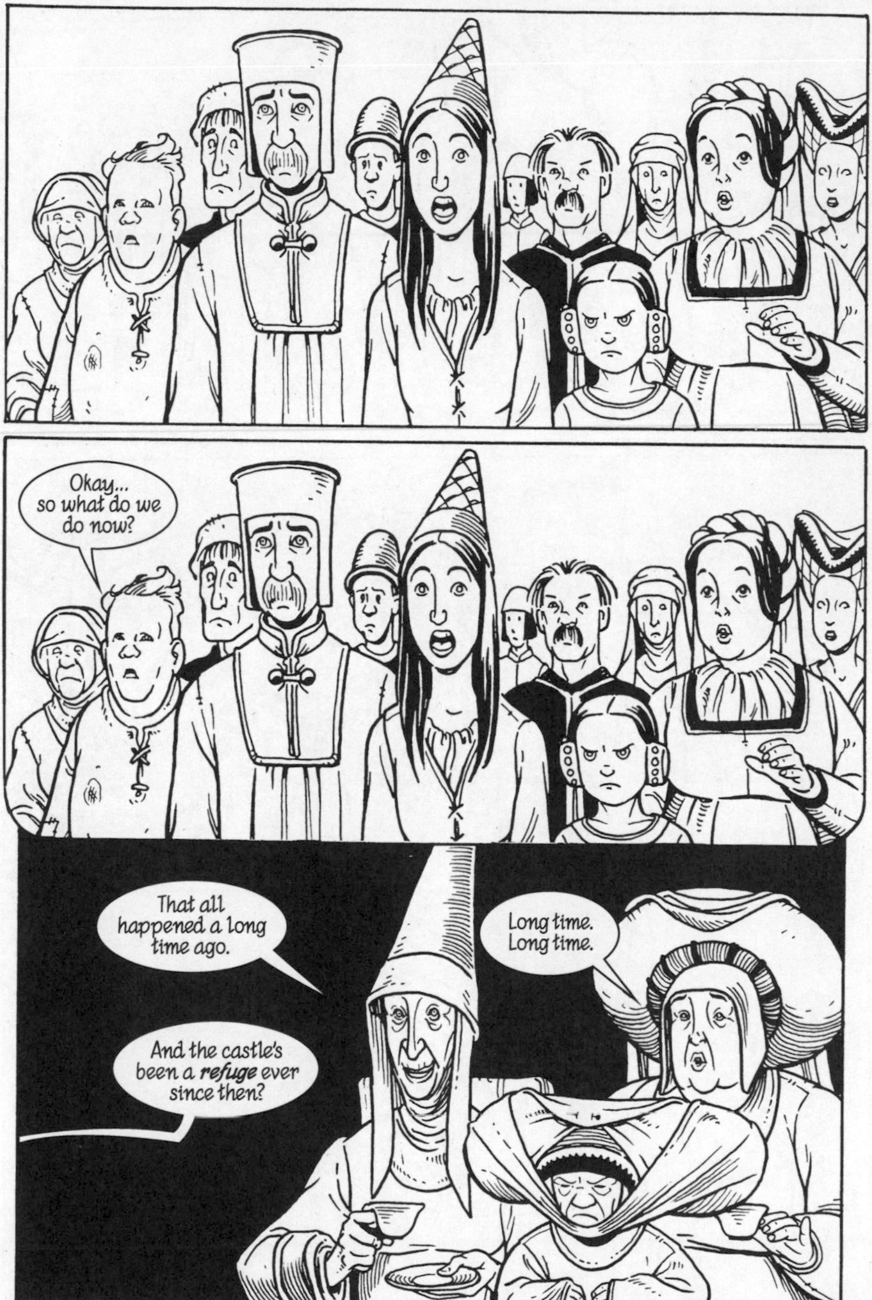
Okay...
so what do we do now?
That all happened a long time ago.
Long time. Long time.
And the castle's been a *refuge* ever since then?

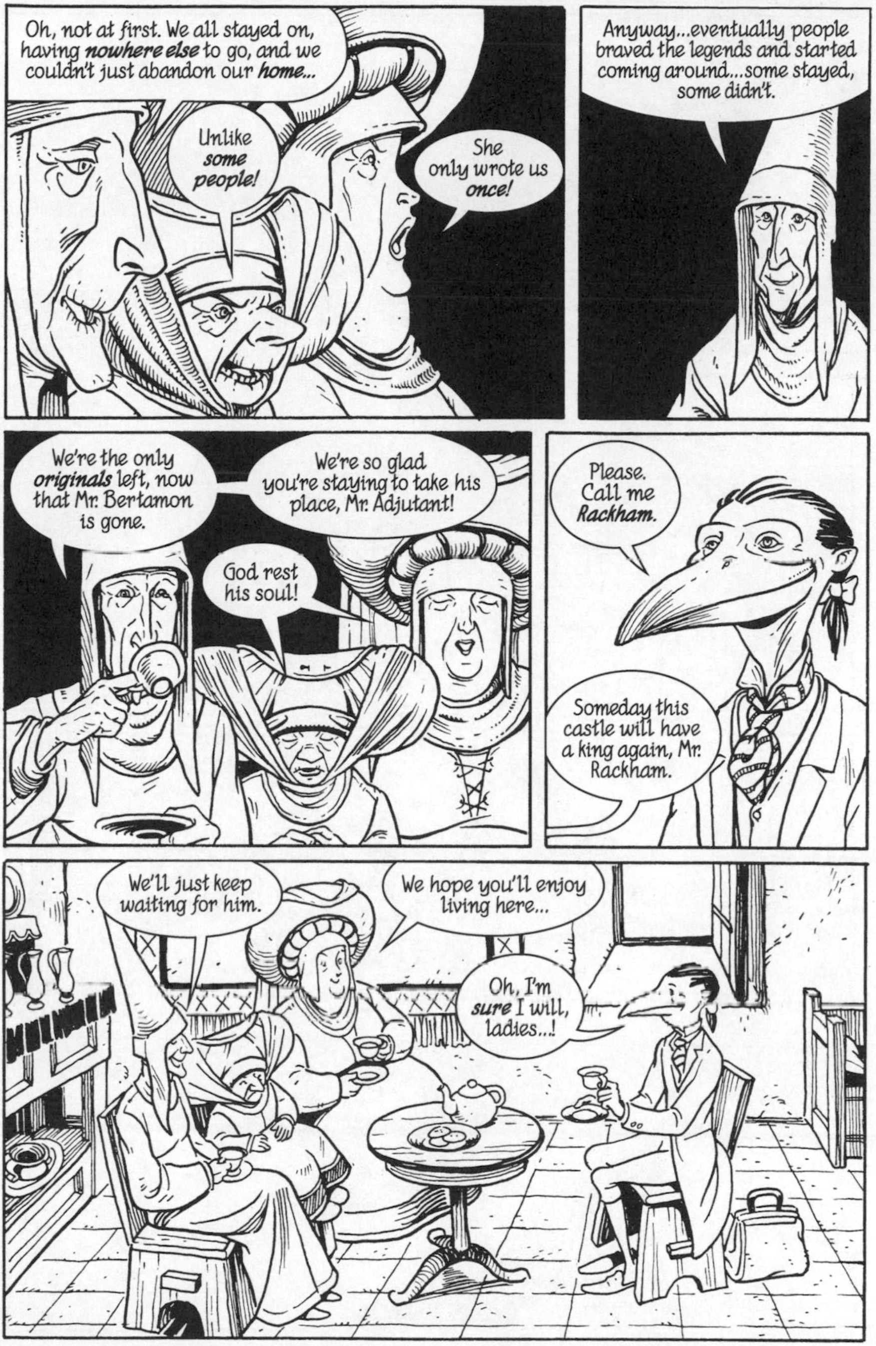
Oh, not at first. We all stayed on, having **nowhere else** to go, and we couldn't just abandon our **home...**
Unlike **some people!**
She only wrote us **once!**
Anyway...eventually people braved the legends and started coming around...some stayed, some didn't.
We're the only **originals** left, now that Mr. Bertamon is gone.
We're so glad you're staying to take his place, Mr. Adjutant!
God rest his soul!
Please. Call me **Rackham**.
Someday this castle will have a king again, Mr. Rackham.
We'll just keep waiting for him.
We hope you'll enjoy living here...
Oh, I'm **sure** I will, ladies...!

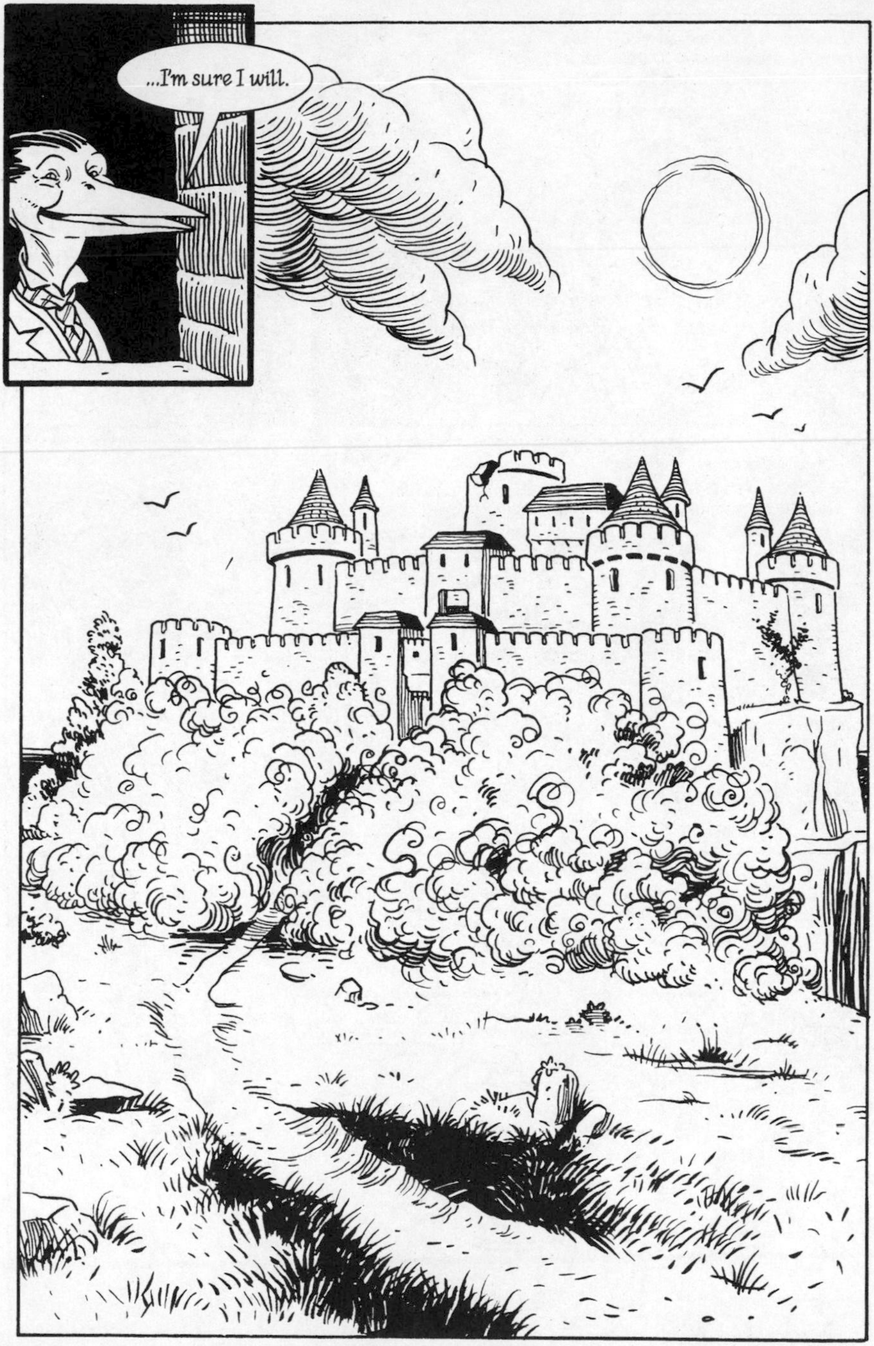
...I'm sure I will.

Chapter 4.

· BAHTALO DROM ·

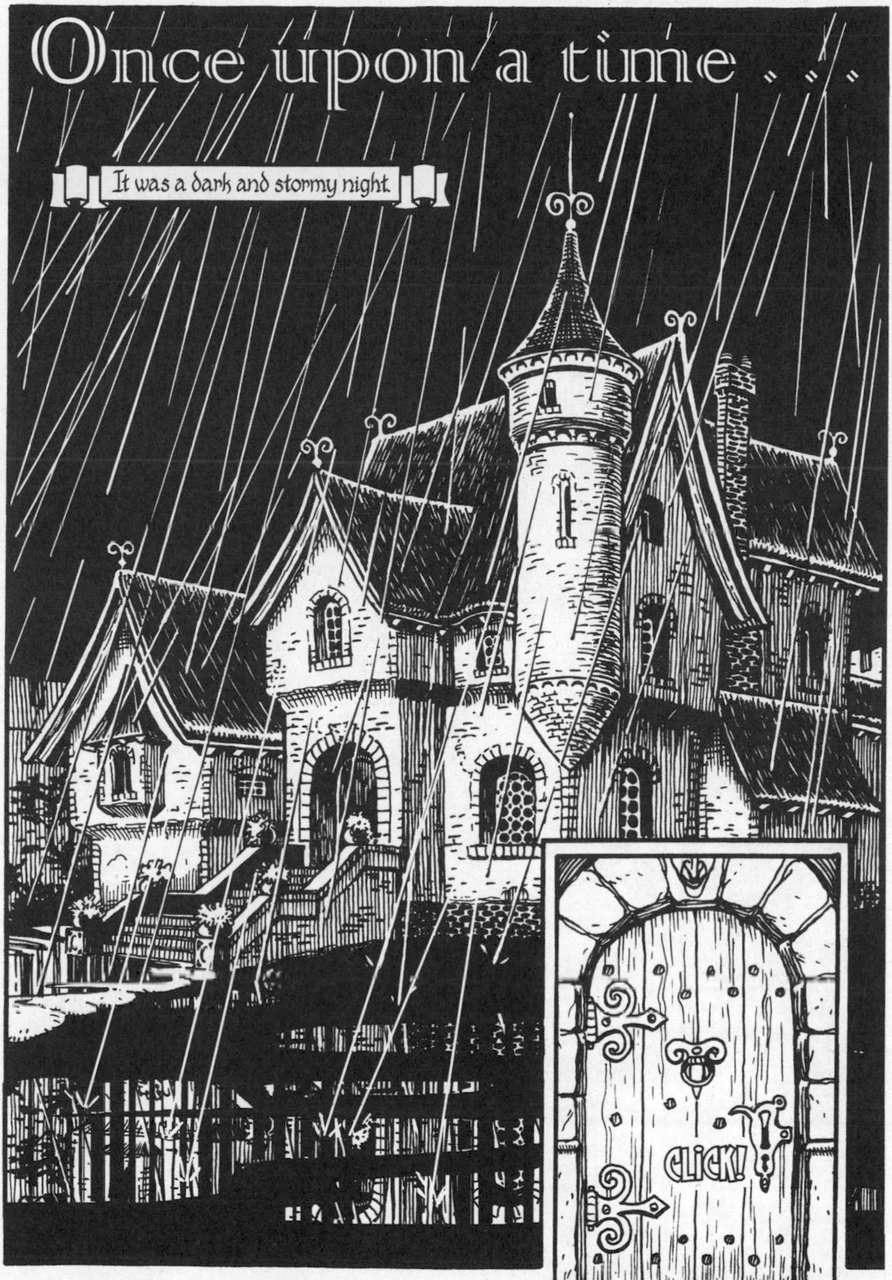
Once upon a time . . .
It was a dark and stormy night.
CLICK!

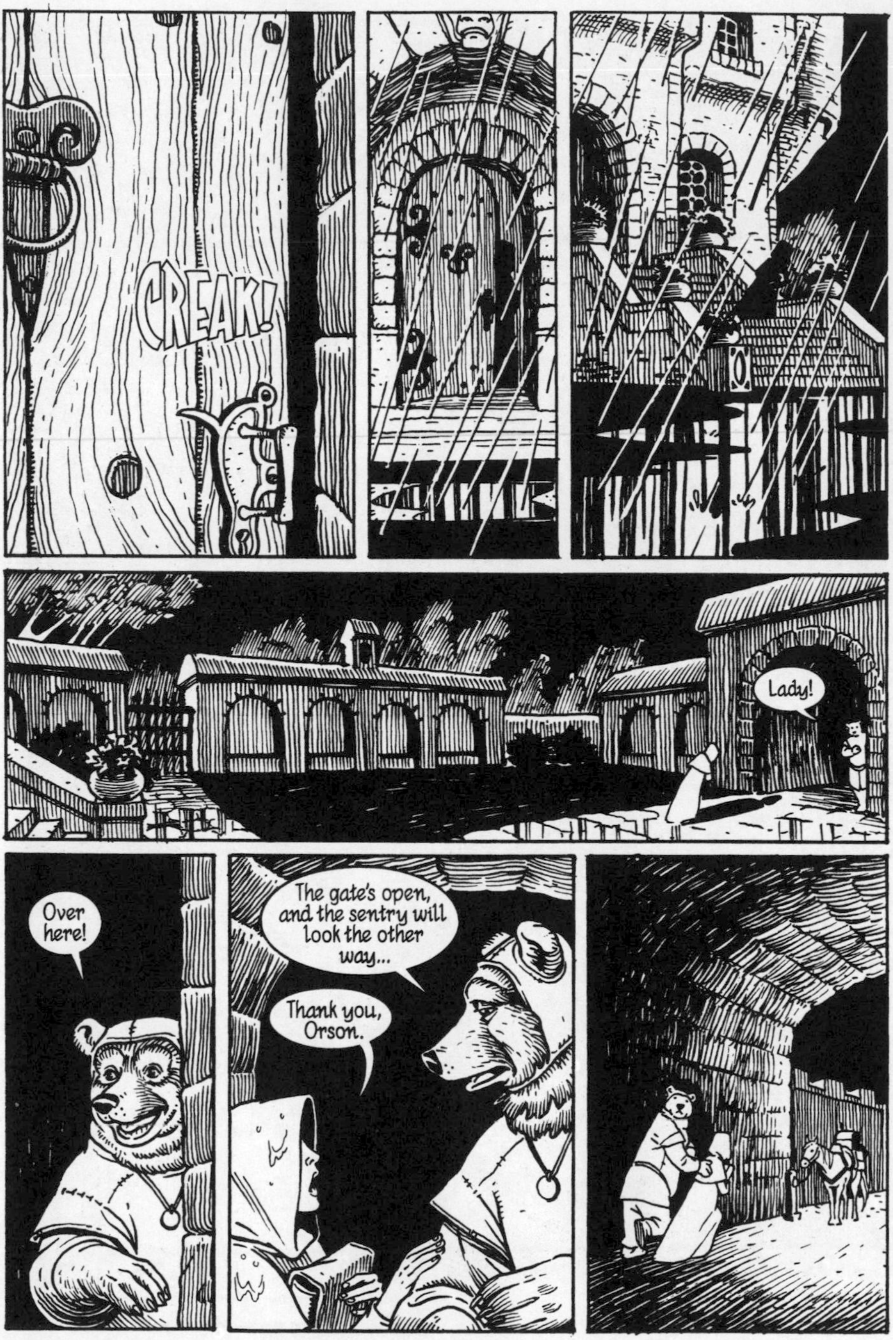
CREAK!
Lady!
Over here!
The gate's open, and the sentry will look the other way...
Thank you, Orson.

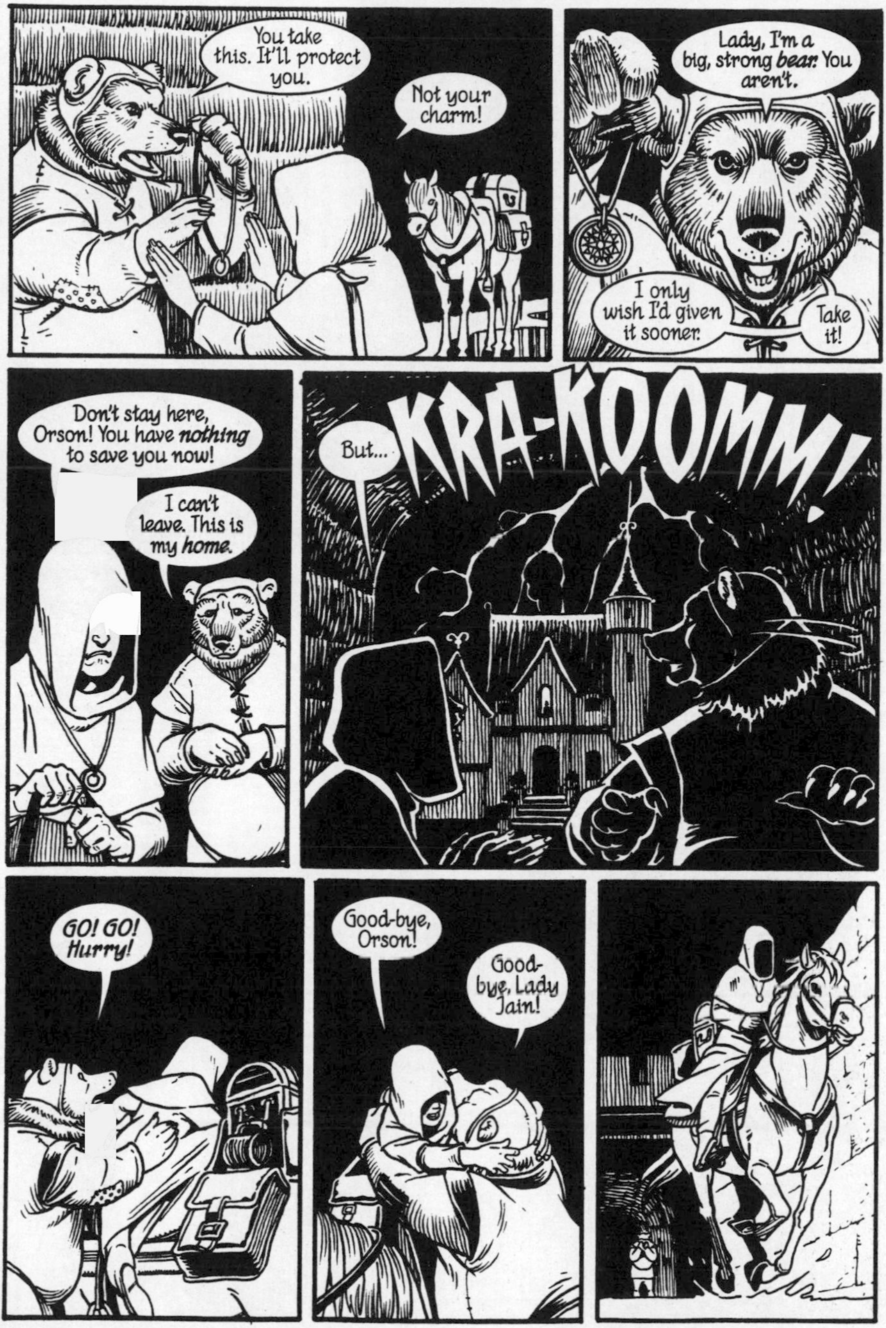
You take this. It'll protect you.
Not your charm!
Lady, I'm a big, strong *bear.* You aren't.
I only wish I'd given it sooner.
Take it!
Don't stay here, Orson! You have *nothing* to save you now!
I can't leave. This is my *home.*
But...
KRA-KOOMM!
GO! GO! Hurry!
Good-bye, Orson!
Good-bye, Lady Jain!

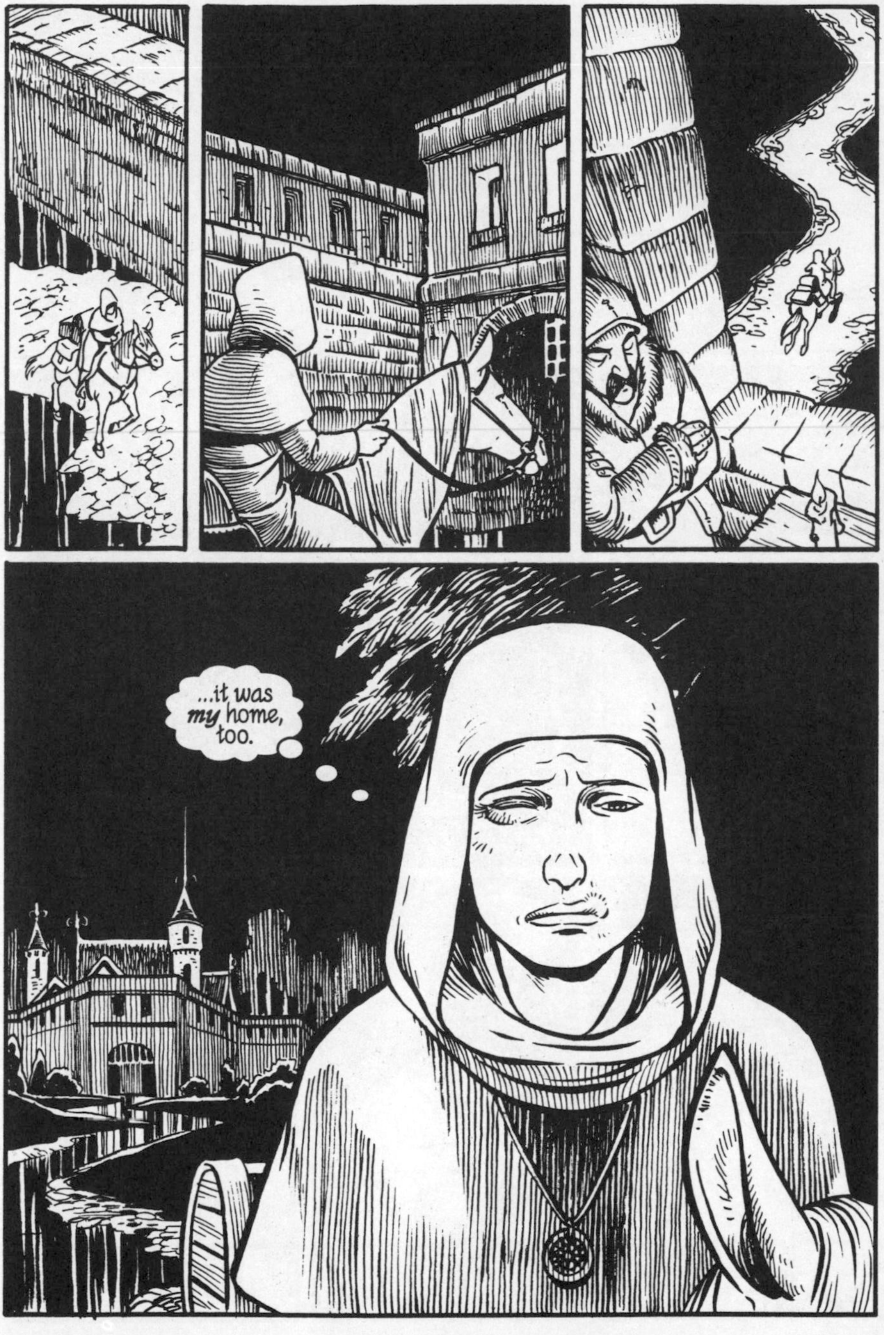
...it was *my* home, too.

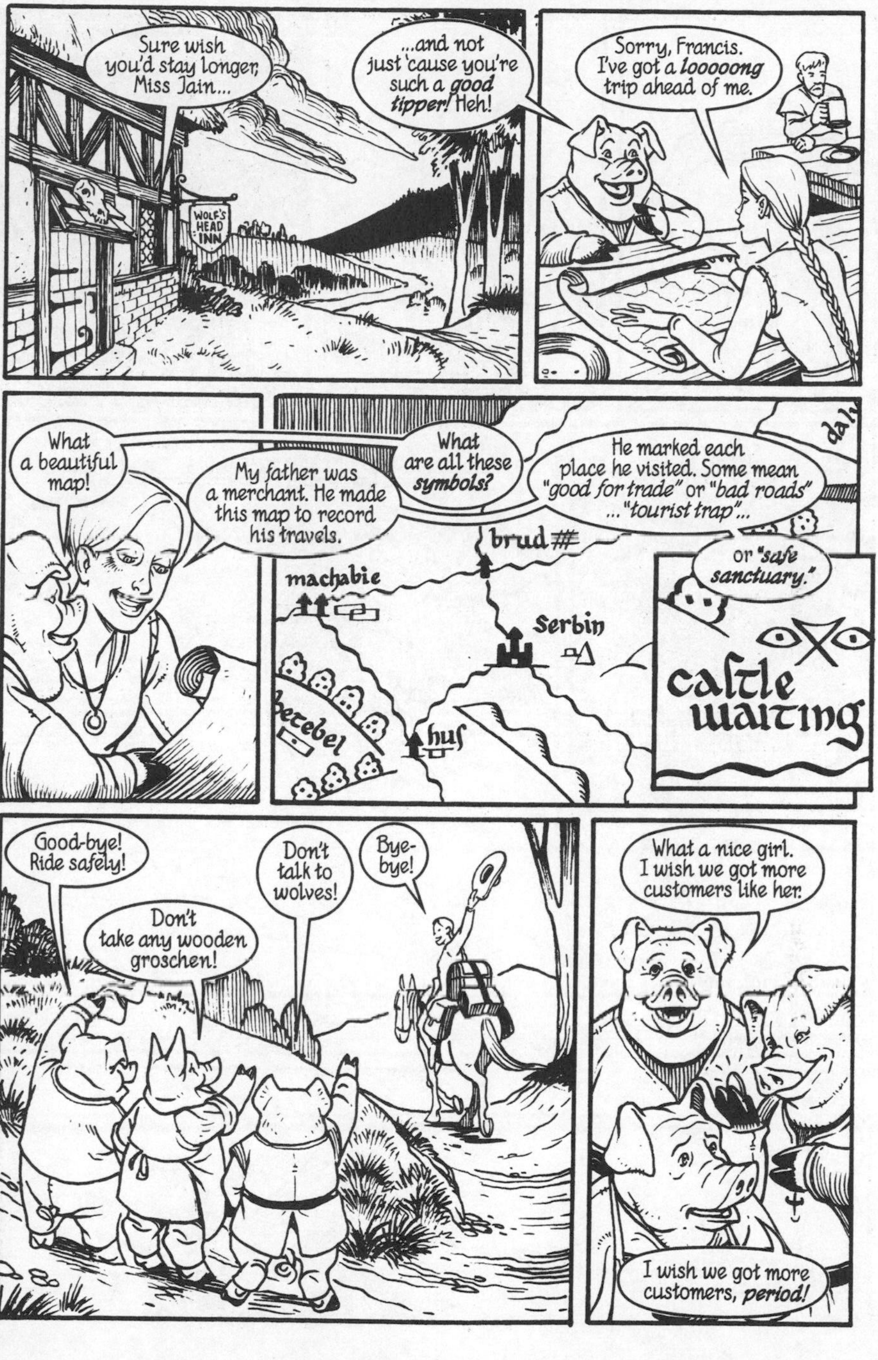
Sure wish you'd stay longer, Miss Jain...
...and not just 'cause you're such a *good tipper!* Heh!
WOLF'S HEAD INN
Sorry, Francis. I've got a ***looooong*** trip ahead of me.
What a beautiful map!
My father was a merchant. He made this map to record his travels.
What are all these ***symbols?***
He marked each place he visited. Some mean *"good for trade"* or *"bad roads"* ... *"tourist trap"*...
or ***"safe sanctuary."***
brud
machabie
Serbin
castle waiting
Good-bye! Ride safely!
Don't take any wooden groschen!
Don't talk to wolves!
Bye-bye!
What a nice girl. I wish we got more customers like her.
I wish we got more customers, ***period!***

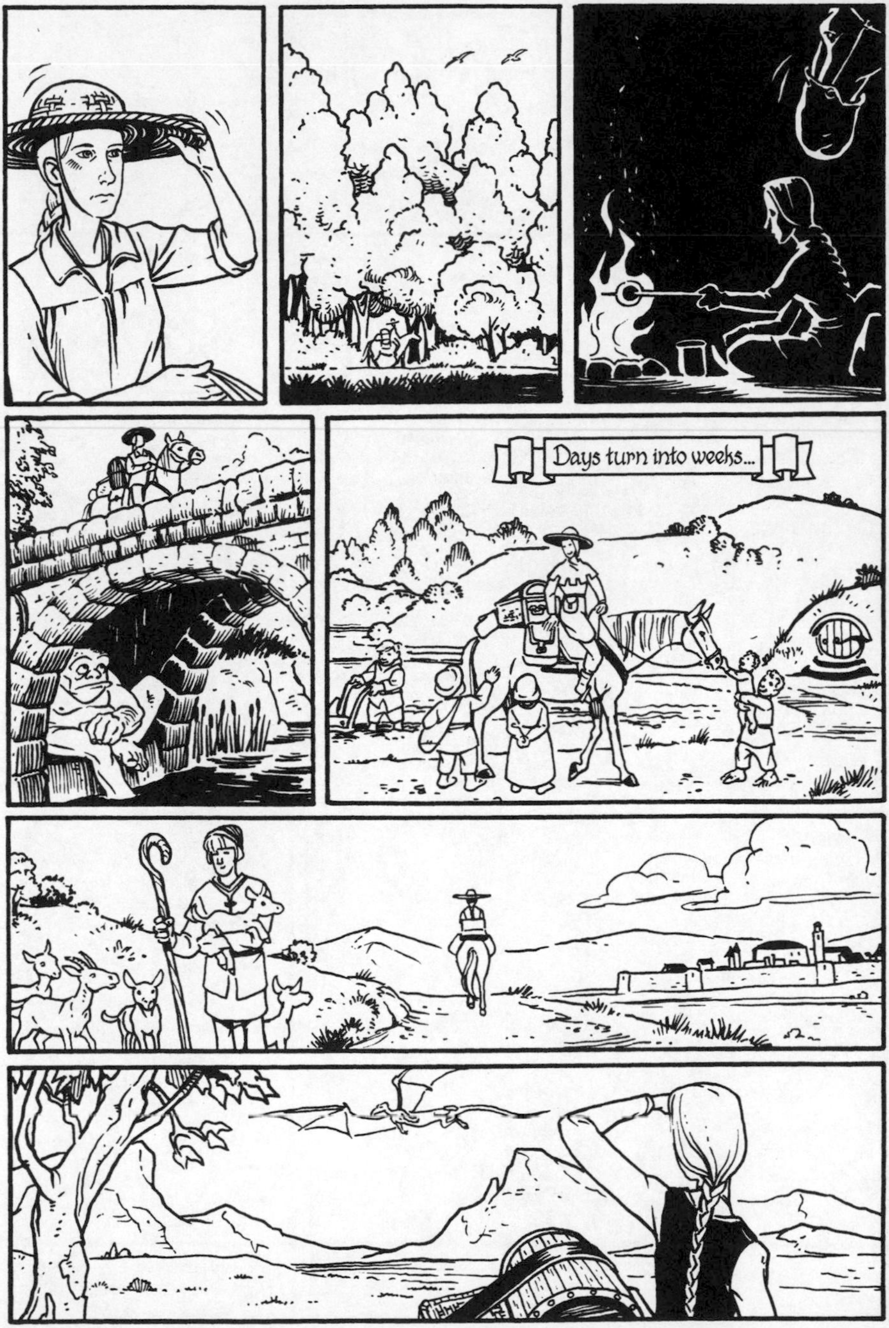
Days turn into weeks...

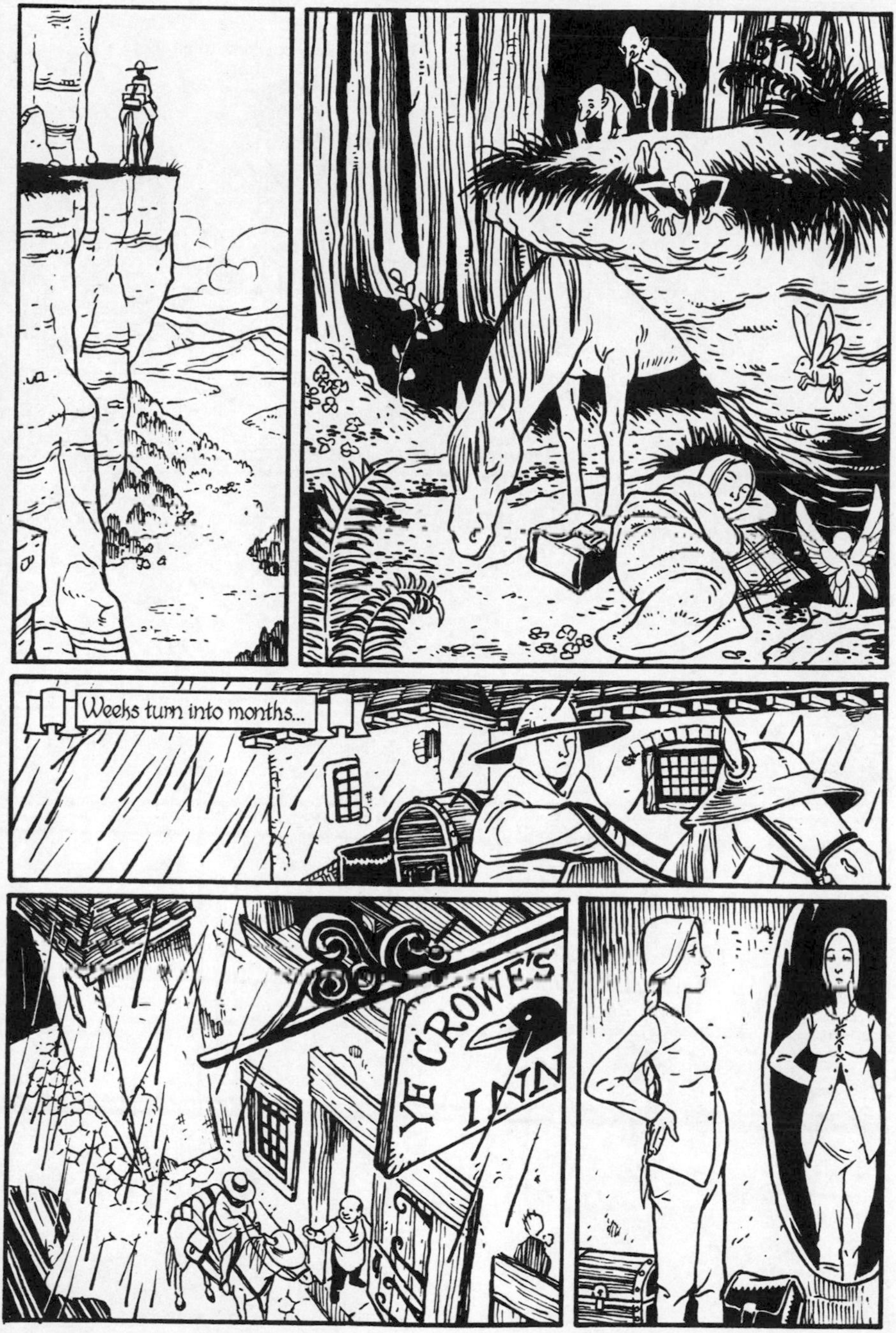
Weeks turn into months...
YE CROWE'S INN

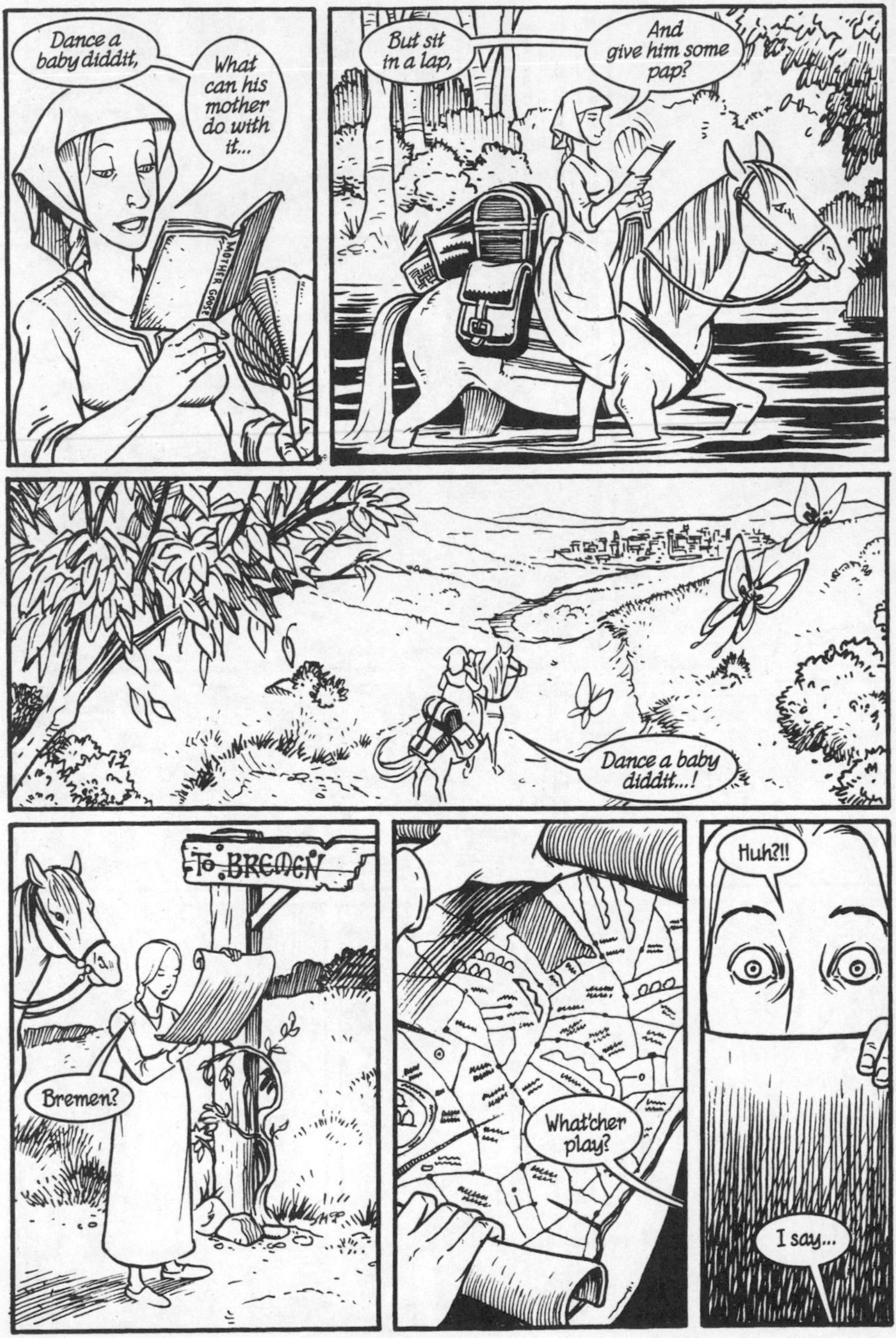
Dance a baby diddit,
What can his mother do with it...
MOTHER GOOSE
But sit in a lap,
And give him some pap?
Dance a baby diddit...!
TO BREMEN
Bremen?
What'cher play?
Huh?!!
I say...

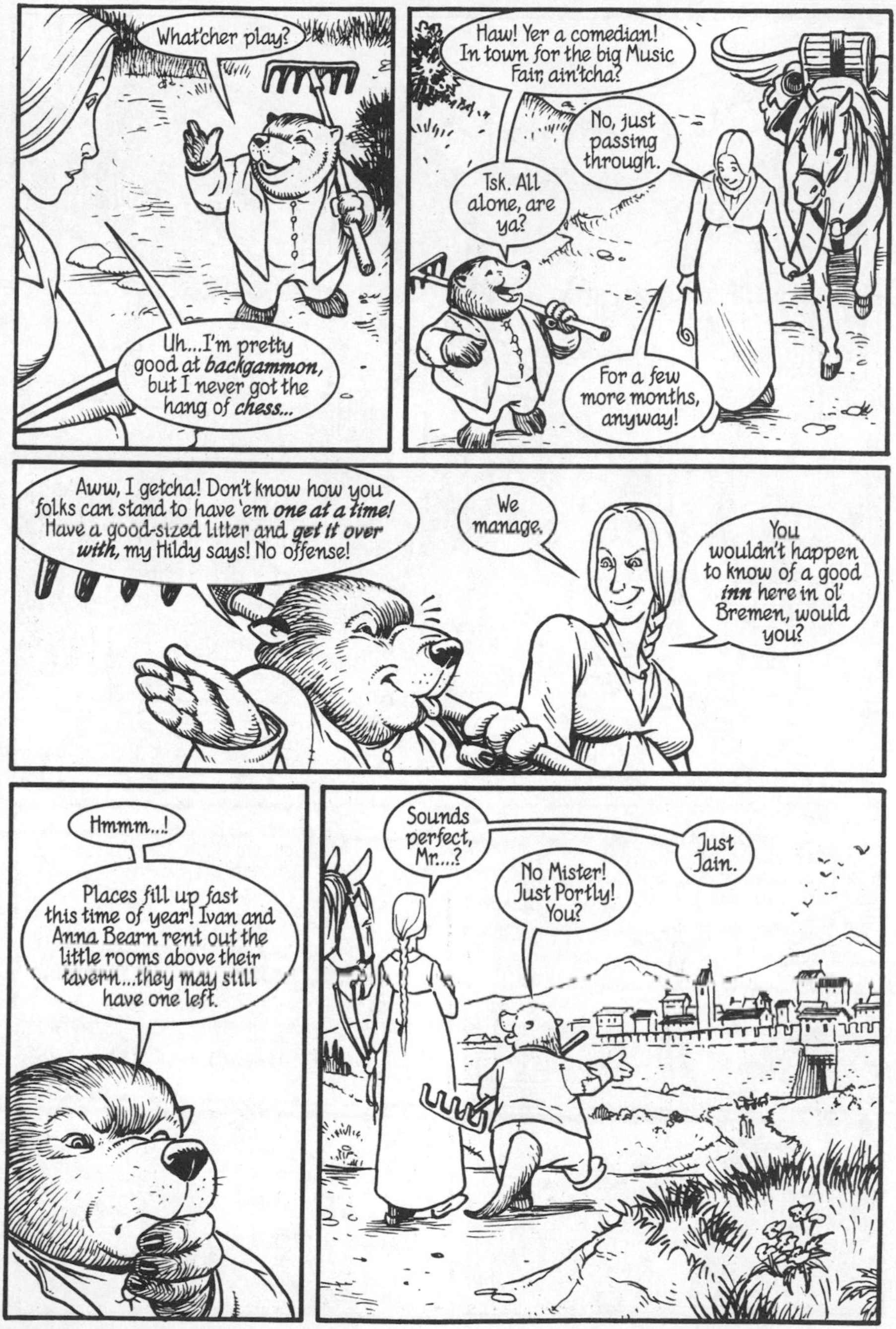
What'cher play?
Uh...I'm pretty good at *backgammon*, but I never got the hang of *chess*...
Haw! Yer a comedian! In town for the big Music Fair, ain'tcha?
No, just passing through.
Tsk. All alone, are ya?
For a few more months, anyway!
Aww, I getcha! Don't know how you folks can stand to have 'em *one at a time!* Have a good-sized litter and *get it over with,* my Hildy says! No offense!
We manage.
You wouldn't happen to know of a good *inn* here in ol' Bremen, would you?
Hmmm...!
Places fill up fast this time of year! Ivan and Anna Bearn rent out the little rooms above their tavern...they may still have one left.
Sounds perfect, Mr....?
No Mister! Just Portly! You?
Just Jain.

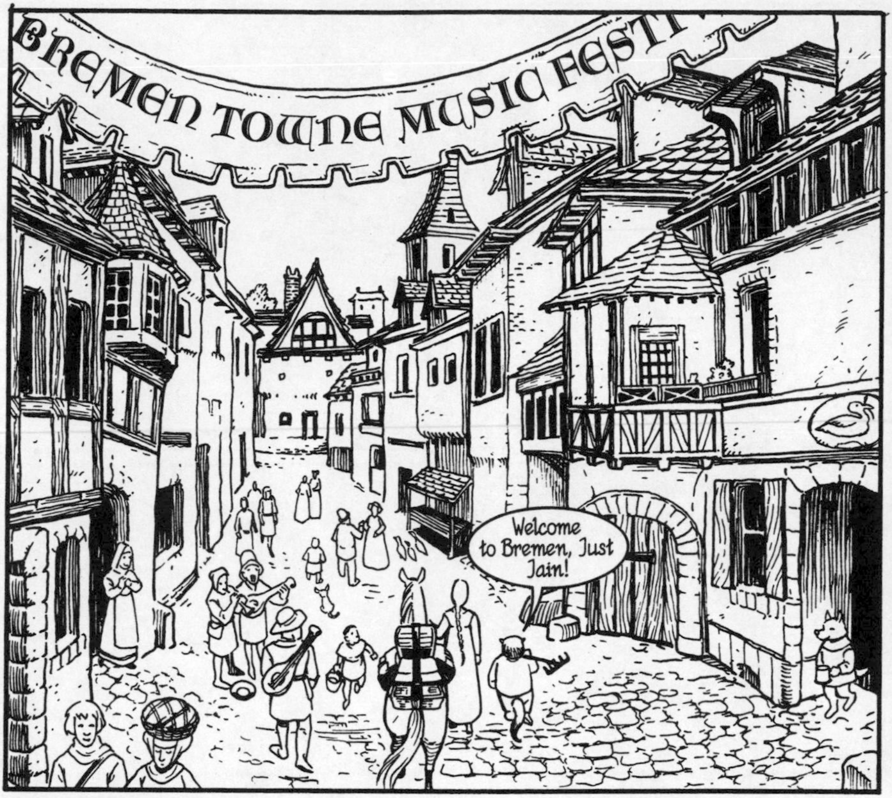
BREMEN TOWNE MUSIC FESTI
Welcome to Bremen, Just Jain!

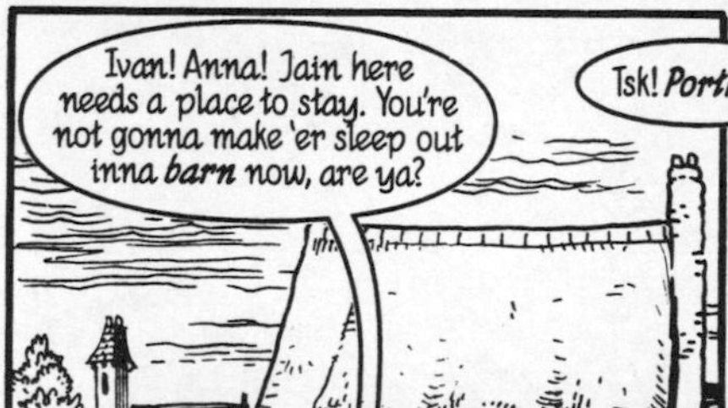
Ivan! Anna! Jain here needs a place to stay. You're not gonna make 'er sleep out inna *barn* now, are ya?
BEARN'S

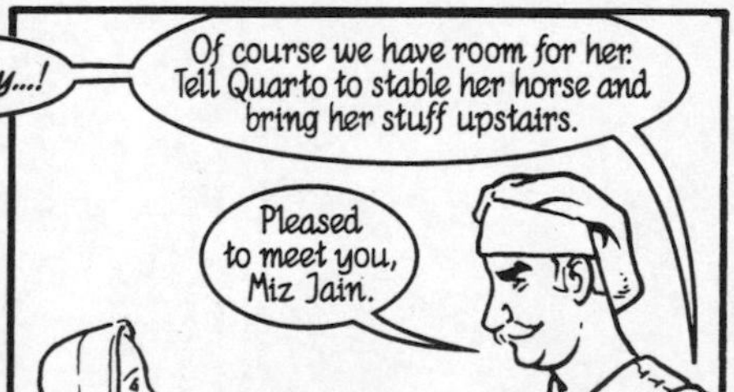
Tsk! *Portly...!*
Of course we have room for her. Tell Quarto to stable her horse and bring her stuff upstairs.
Pleased to meet you, Miz Jain.
Likewise!

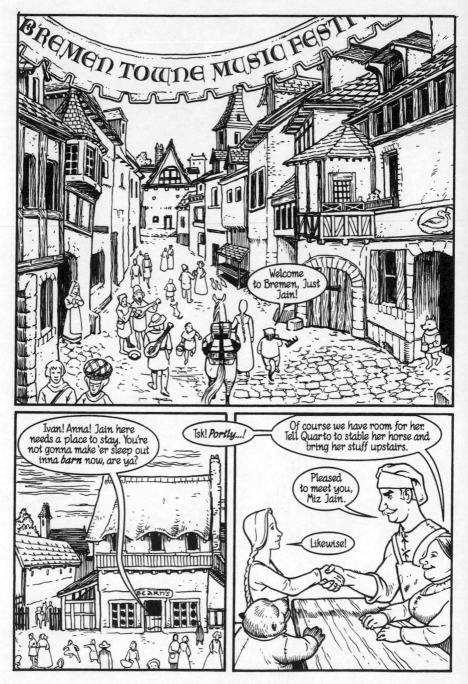

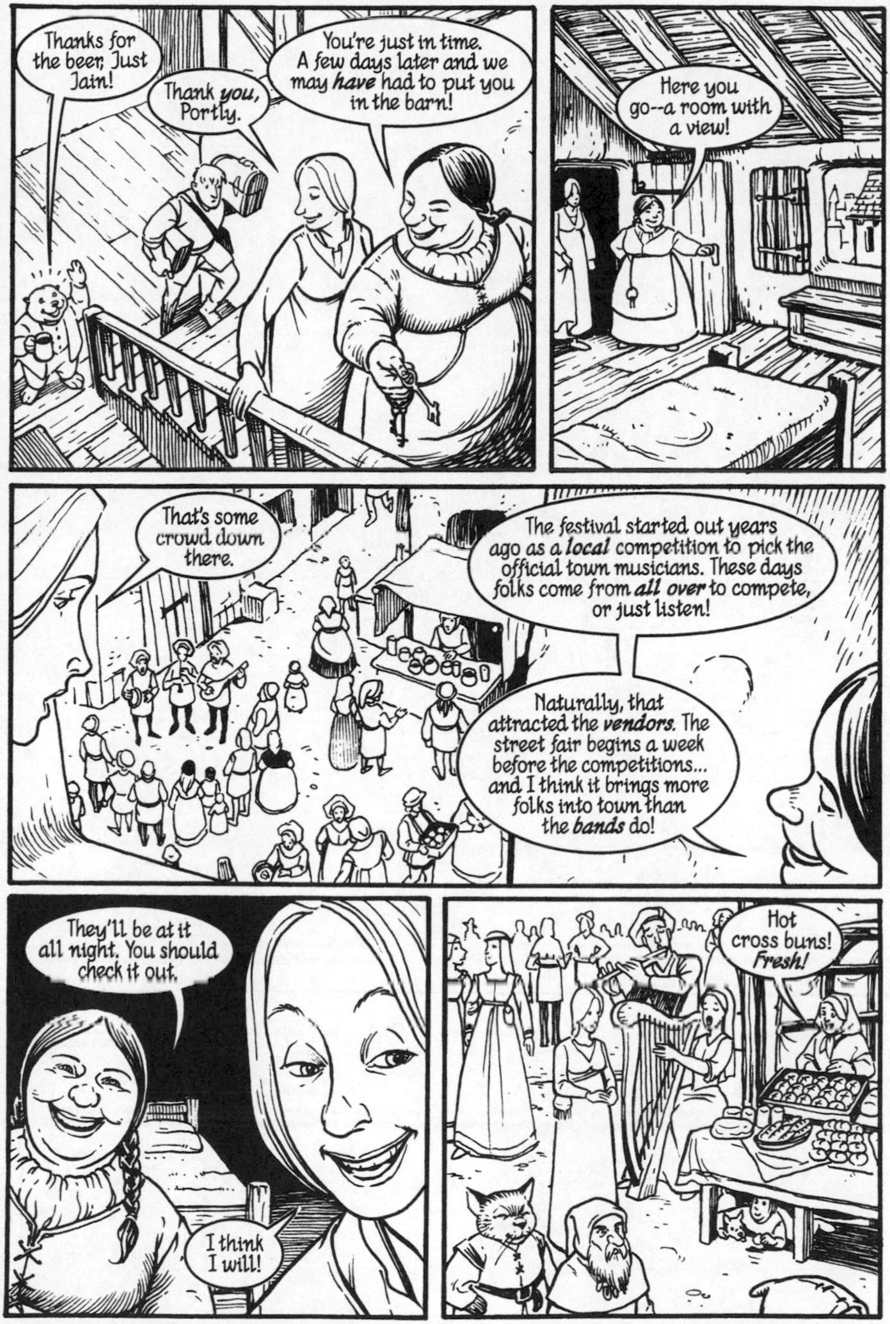
Thanks for the beer, Just Jain!
Thank *you*, Portly.
You're just in time. A few days later and we may ***have*** had to put you in the barn!
Here you go--a room with a view!
That's some crowd down there.
The festival started out years ago as a ***local*** competition to pick the official town musicians. These days folks come from ***all over*** to compete, or just listen!
Naturally, that attracted the ***vendors***. The street fair begins a week before the competitions... and I think it brings more folks into town than the ***bands*** do!
They'll be at it all night. You should check it out.
I think I will!
Hot cross buns! ***Fresh!***

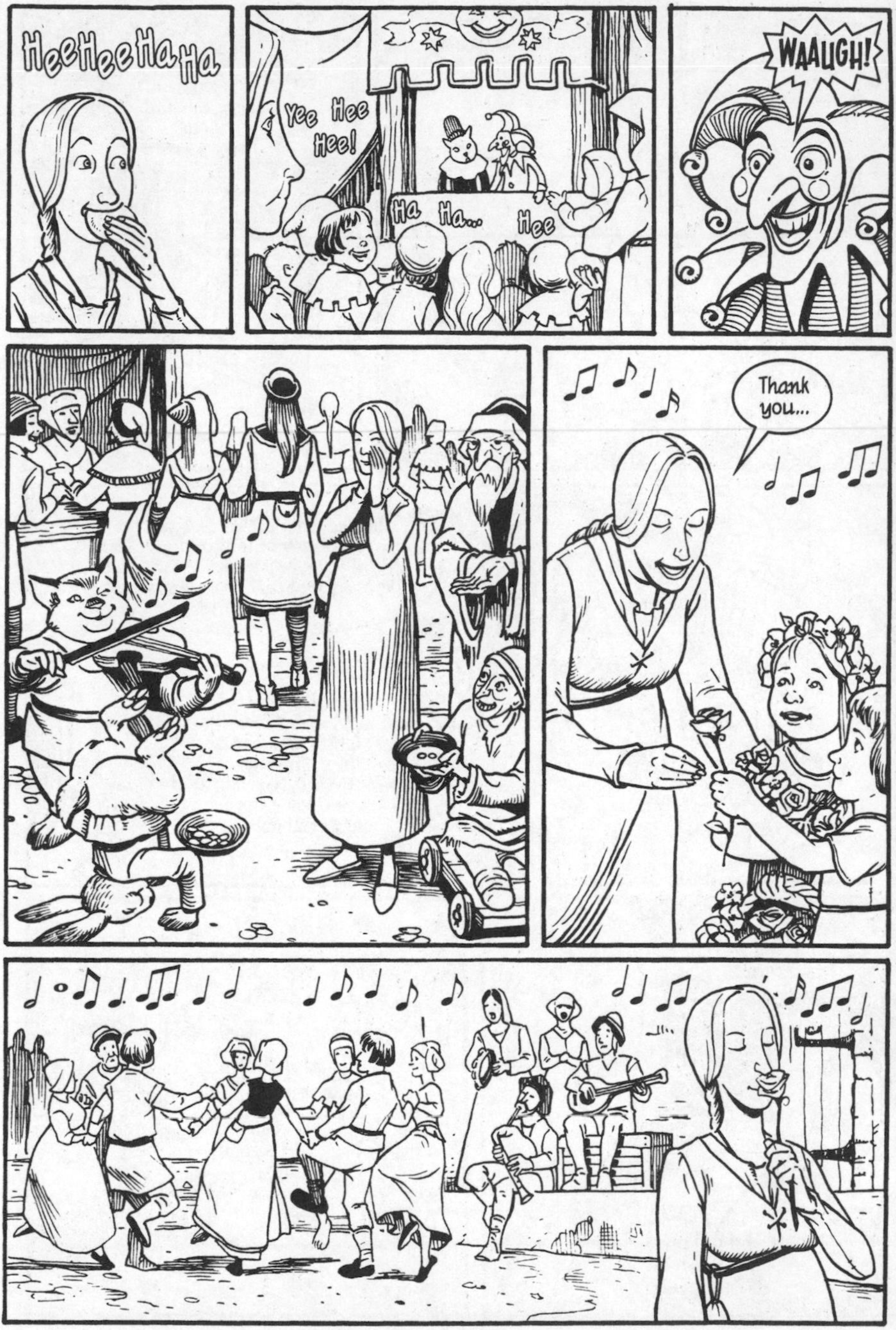
HeeHeeHaHa Ha
Yee Hee Hee!
Ha Ha... Hee
WAAUGH!
Thank you...

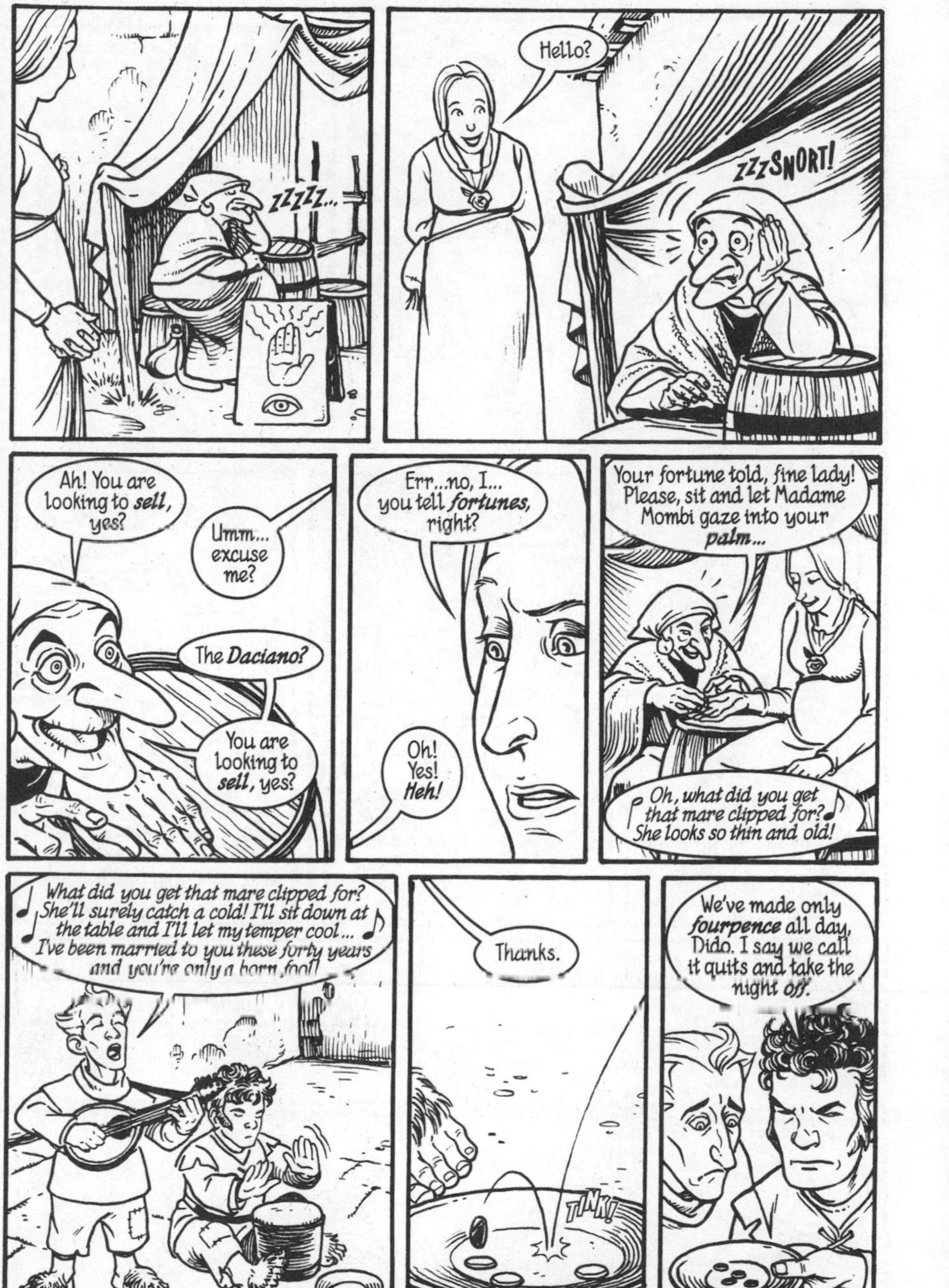
ZZZZZ...
Hello?
ZZZSNORT!
Ah! You are looking to *sell*, yes?
Umm... excuse me?
The *Daciano?*
You are looking to *sell*, yes?
Err...no, I... you tell *fortunes*, right?
Oh! Yes! *Heh!*
Your fortune told, fine lady! Please, sit and let Madame Mombi gaze into your *palm*...
♪ Oh, what did you get that mare clipped for? She looks so thin and old! ♪
♪ What did you get that mare clipped for? She'll surely catch a cold! I'll sit down at the table and I'll let my temper cool... I've been married to you these forty years and you're only a born fool! ♪
Thanks.
TINK!
We've made only *fourpence* all day, Dido. I say we call it quits and take the night *off*.

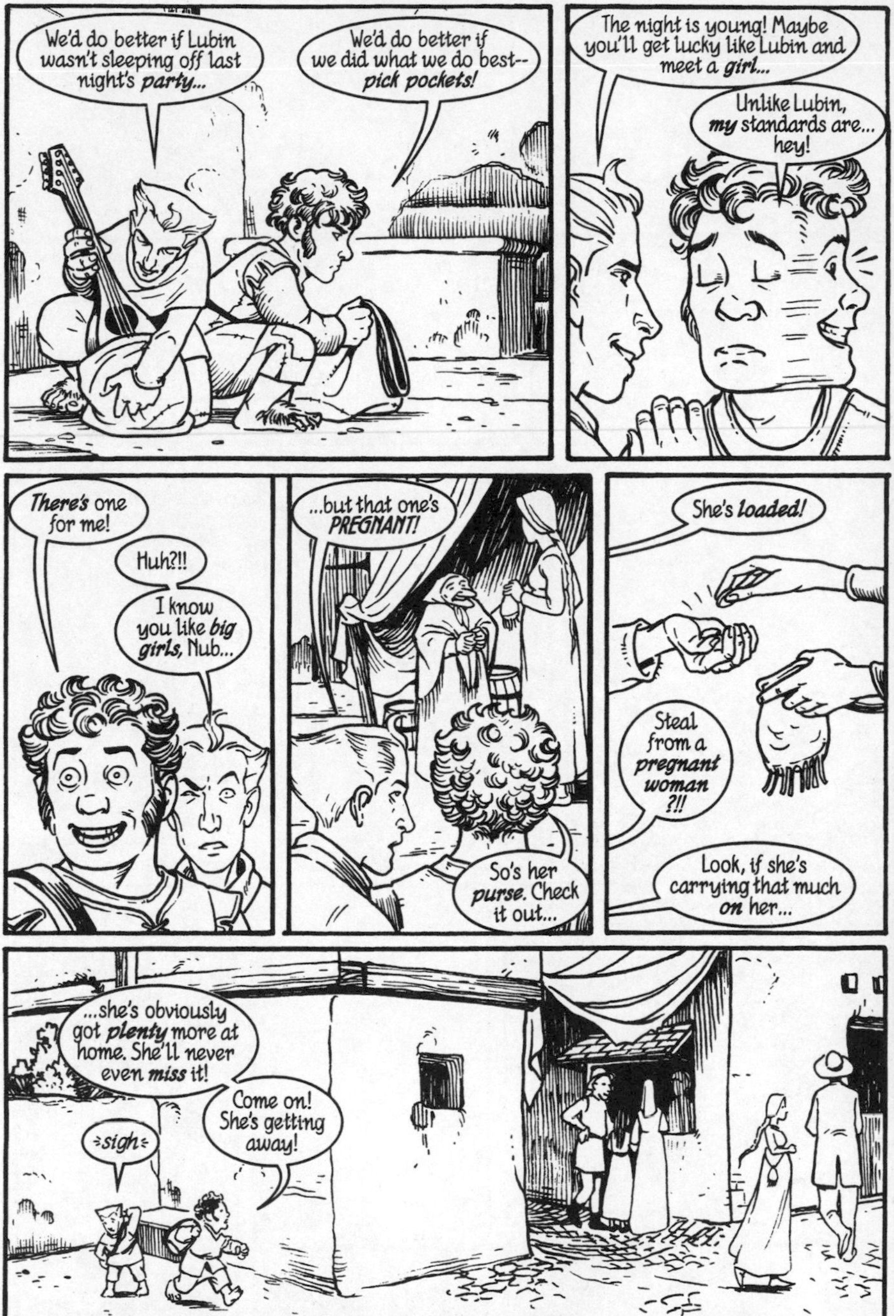
We'd do better if Lubin wasn't sleeping off last night's *party*...
We'd do better if we did what we do best-- *pick pockets!*
The night is young! Maybe you'll get lucky like Lubin and meet a *girl*...
Unlike Lubin, *my* standards are... hey!
There's one for me!
Huh?!!
I know you like *big girls*, Nub...
...but that one's *PREGNANT!*
So's her *purse*. Check it out...
She's *loaded!*
Steal from a *pregnant woman* ?!!
Look, if she's carrying that much *on* her...
...she's obviously got *plenty* more at home. She'll never even *miss* it!
Come on! She's getting away!
sigh

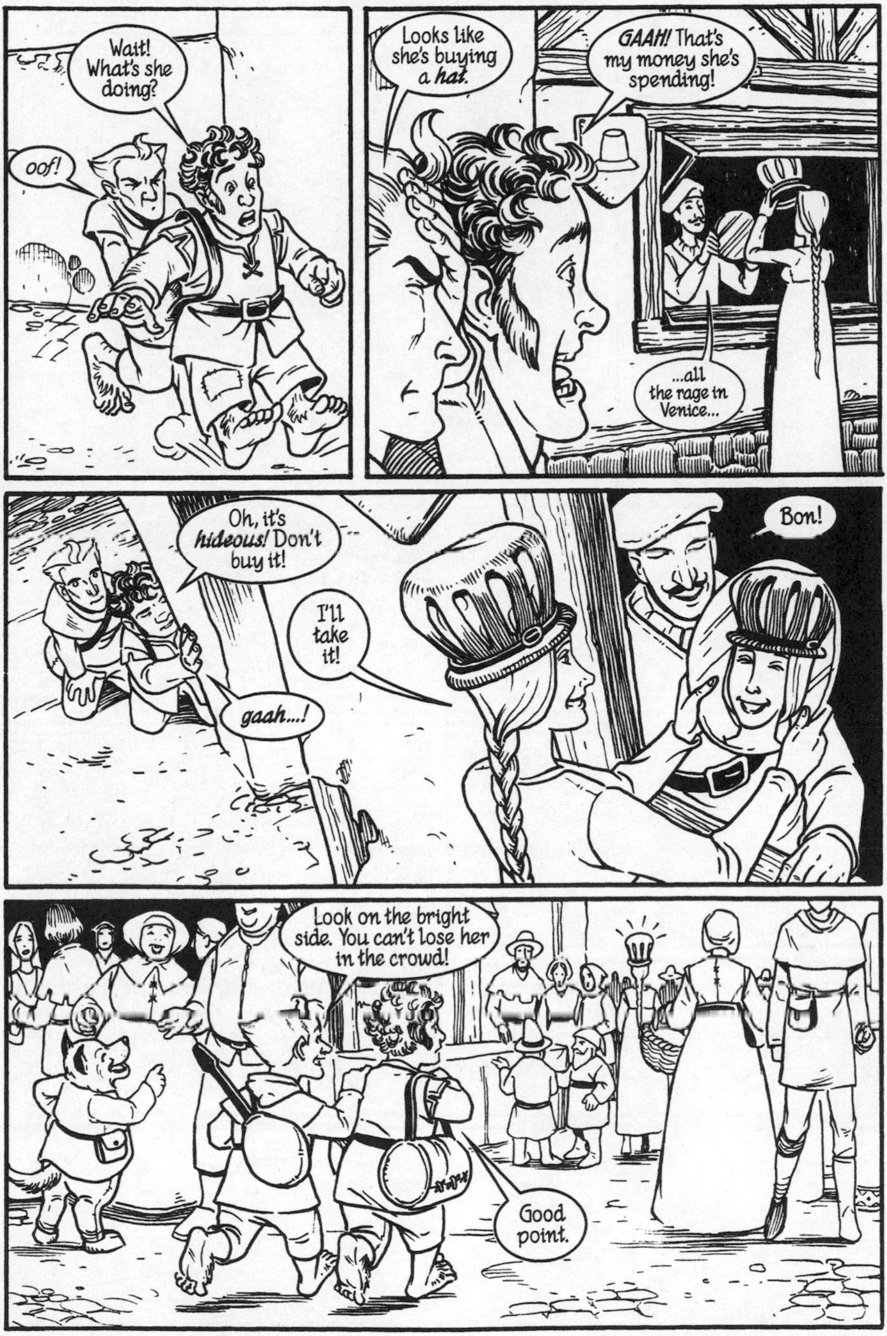
Wait! What's she doing?
oof!
Looks like she's buying a *hat.*
GAAH! That's my money she's spending!
...all the rage in Venice...
Oh, it's *hideous!* Don't buy it!
I'll take it!
gaah...!
Bon!
Look on the bright side. You can't lose her in the crowd!
Good point.

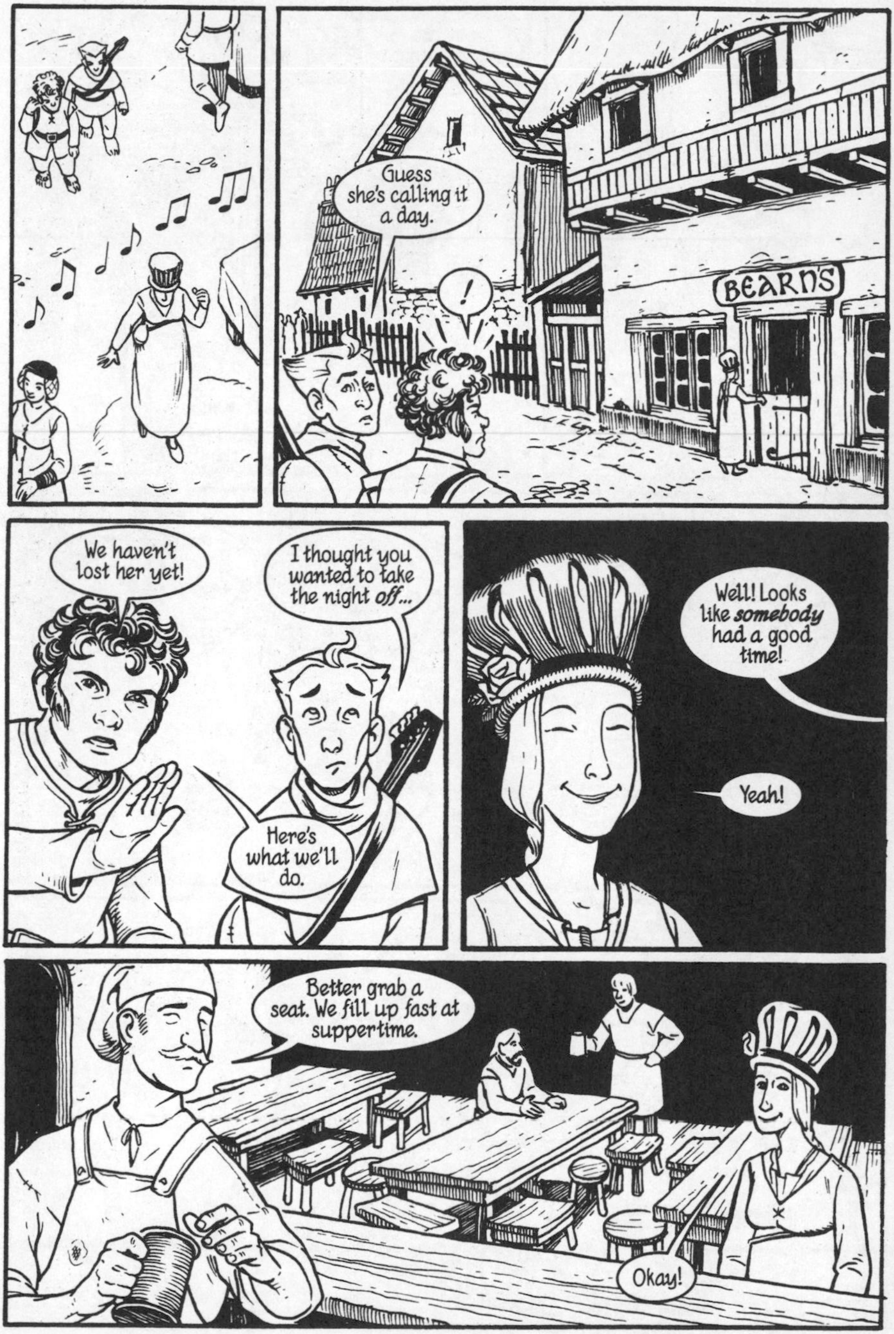
Guess she's calling it a day.
!
BEARNS
We haven't lost her yet!
I thought you wanted to take the night *off*...
Here's what we'll do.
Well! Looks like ***somebody*** had a good time!
Yeah!
Better grab a seat. We fill up fast at suppertime.
Okay!

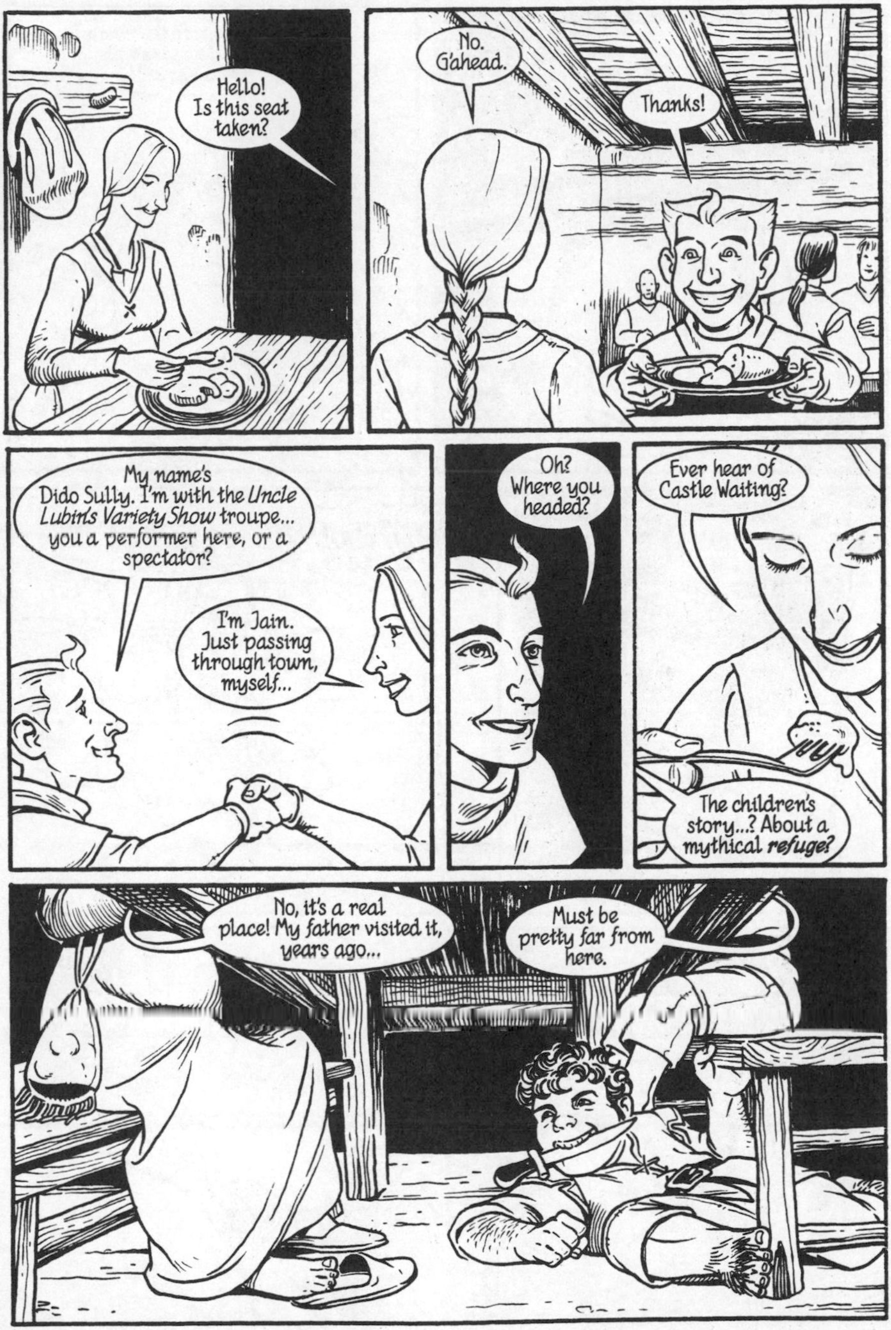
Hello! Is this seat taken?
No. G'ahead.
Thanks!
My name's Dido Sully. I'm with the *Uncle Lubin's Variety Show* troupe... you a performer here, or a spectator?
I'm Jain. Just passing through town, myself...
Oh? Where you headed?
Ever hear of Castle Waiting?
The children's story...? About a mythical *refuge*?
No, it's a real place! My father visited it, years ago...
Must be pretty far from here.

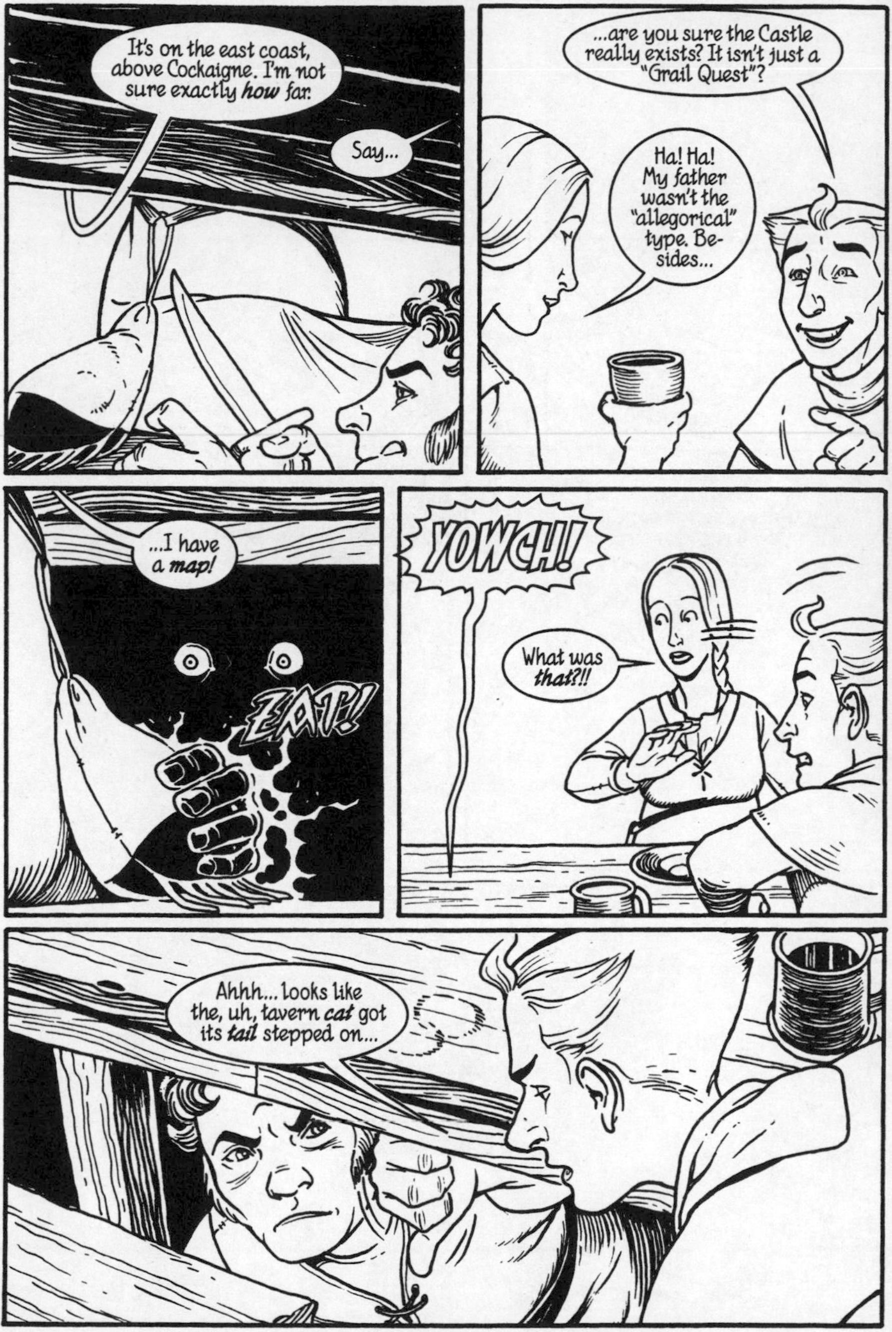
It's on the east coast, above Cockaigne. I'm not sure exactly *how* far.
Say...
...are you sure the Castle really exists? It isn't just a "Grail Quest"?
Ha! Ha! My father wasn't the "allegorical" type. Be-sides...
...I have a *map!*
ZAT!
YOWCH!
What was *that?!!*
Ahhh... looks like the, uh, tavern *cat* got its *tail* stepped on...

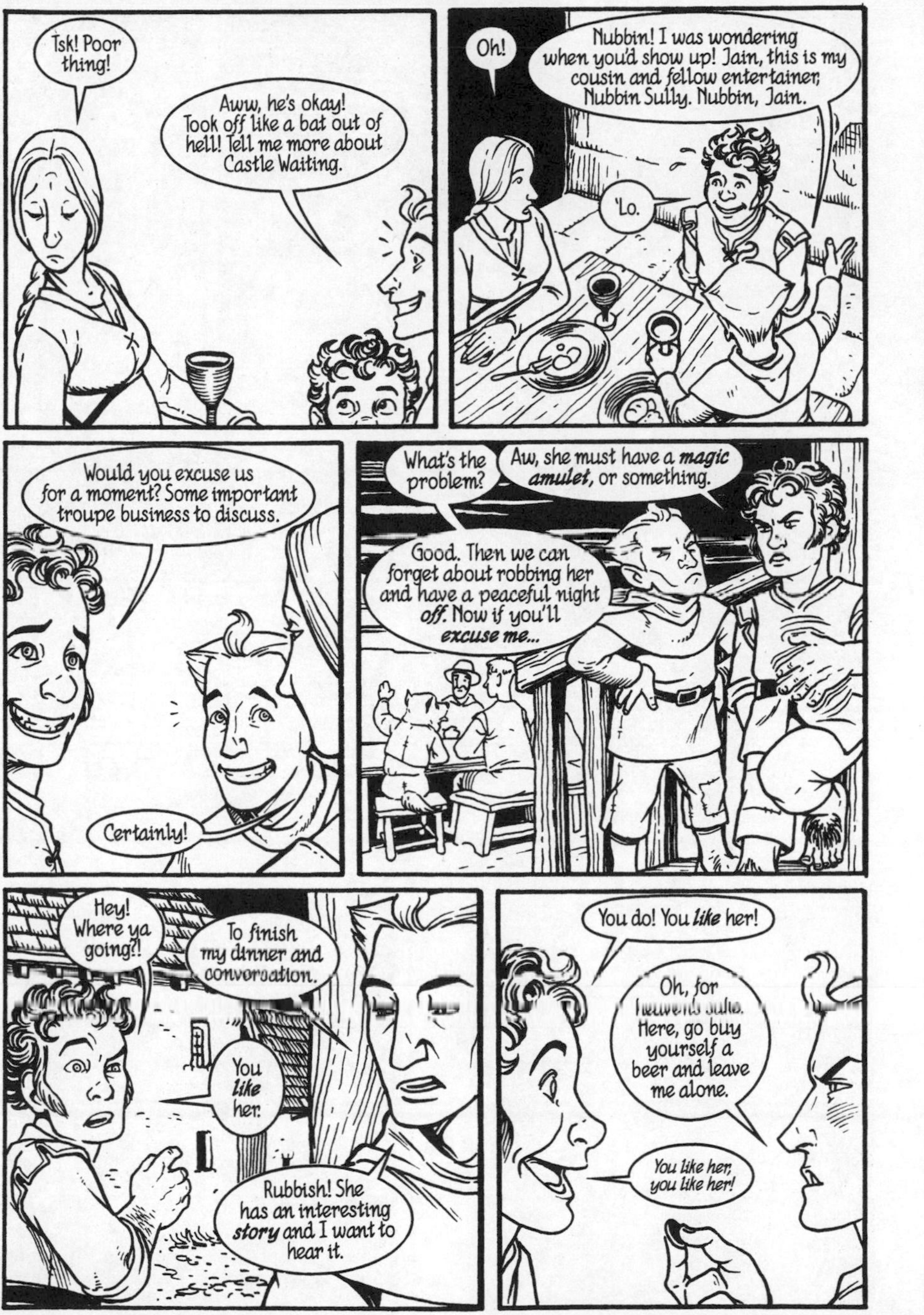
Tsk! Poor thing!
Aww, he's okay! Took off like a bat out of hell! Tell me more about Castle Waiting.
Oh!
Nubbin! I was wondering when you'd show up! Jain, this is my cousin and fellow entertainer, Nubbin Sully. Nubbin, Jain.
'Lo.
Would you excuse us for a moment? Some important troupe business to discuss.
Certainly!
What's the problem?
Aw, she must have a *magic amulet*, or something.
Good. Then we can forget about robbing her and have a peaceful night *off*. Now if you'll *excuse me...*
Hey! Where ya going?!
To finish my dinner and conversation.
You *like* her.
Rubbish! She has an interesting *story* and I want to hear it.
You do! You *like* her!
Oh, for heaven's sake. Here, go buy yourself a beer and leave me alone.
You like her, you like her!

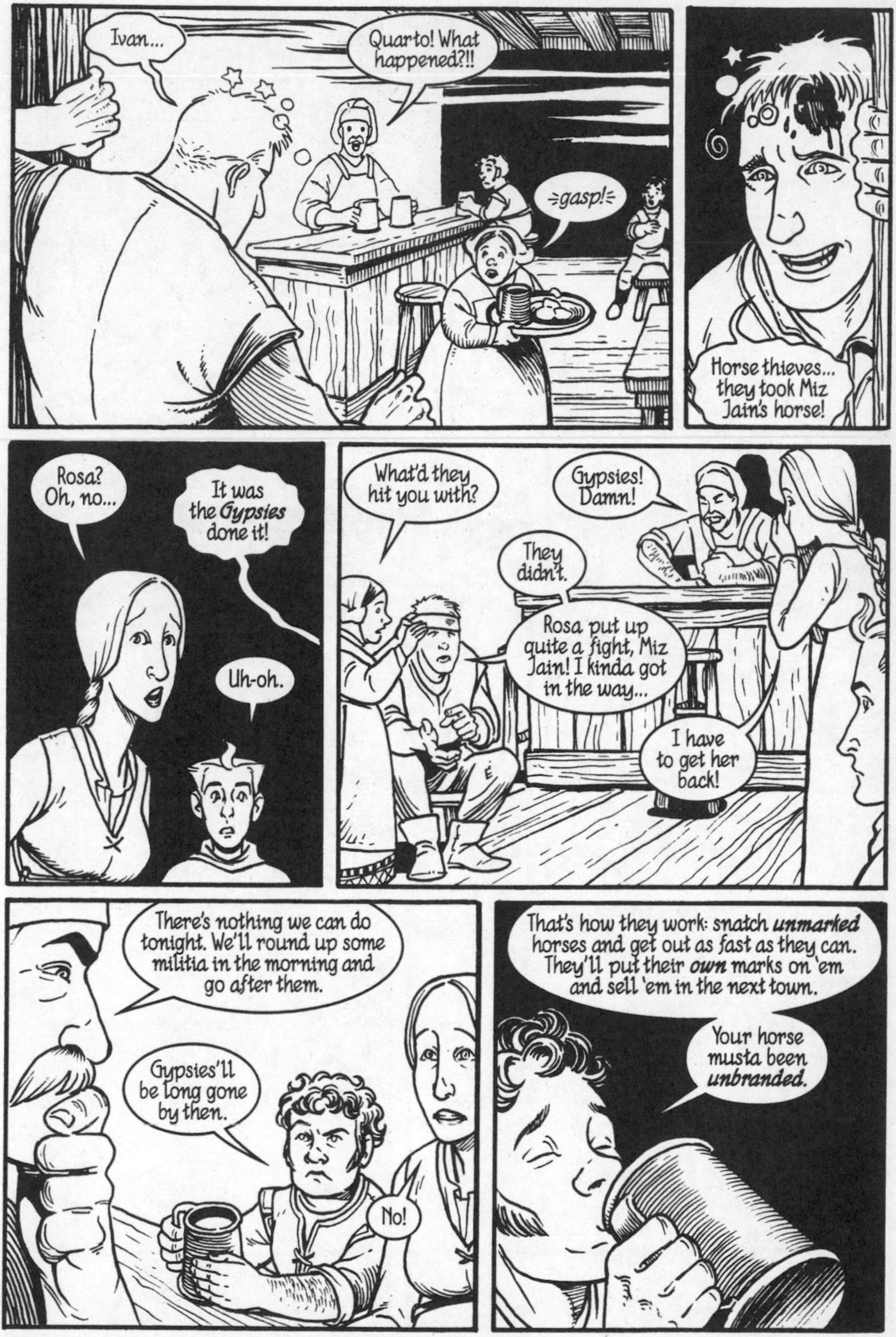
Ivan...
Quarto! What happened?!!
=gasp!=
Horse thieves... they took Miz Jain's horse!
Rosa? Oh, no...
It was the *Gypsies* done it!
Uh-oh.
What'd they hit you with?
Gypsies! Damn!
They didn't.
Rosa put up quite a fight, Miz Jain! I kinda got in the way...
I have to get her back!
There's nothing we can do tonight. We'll round up some militia in the morning and go after them.
Gypsies'll be long gone by then.
No!
That's how they work: snatch ***unmarked*** horses and get out as fast as they can. They'll put their ***own*** marks on 'em and sell 'em in the next town.
Your horse musta been ***unbranded***.

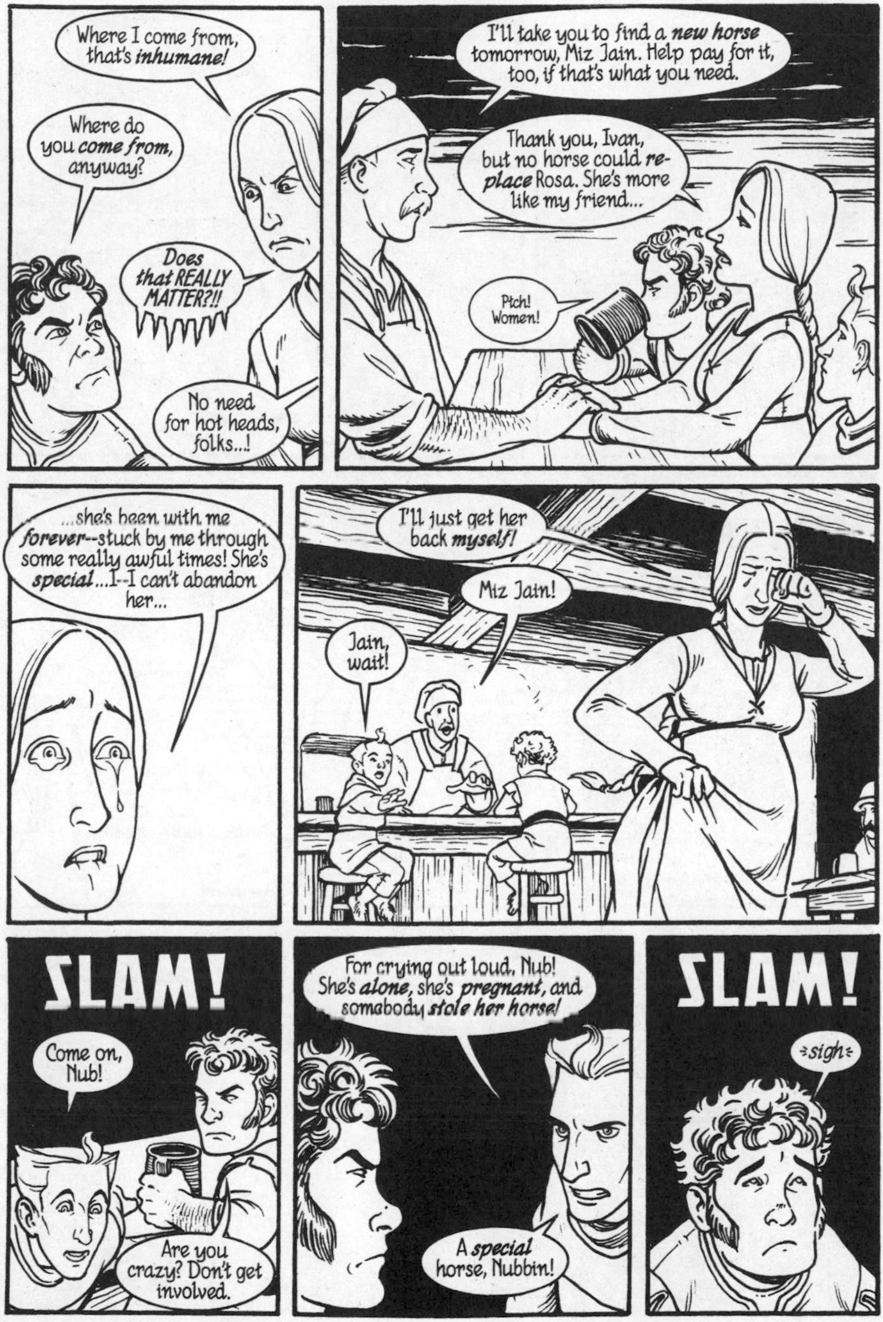
Where I come from, that's *inhumane!*
Where do you *come from,* anyway?
Does that REALLY MATTER?!!
No need for hot heads, folks...!
I'll take you to find a *new horse* tomorrow, Miz Jain. Help pay for it, too, if that's what you need.
Thank you, Ivan, but no horse could *re-place* Rosa. She's more like my friend...
Ptch! Women!
...she's been with me *forever*--stuck by me through some really awful times! She's *special*...I--I can't abandon her...
I'll just get her back *myself!*
Miz Jain!
Jain, wait!
SLAM!
Come on, Nub!
Are you crazy? Don't get involved.
For crying out loud, Nub! She's *alone*, she's *pregnant*, and somebody *stole her horse!*
A *special* horse, Nubbin!
SLAM!
sigh

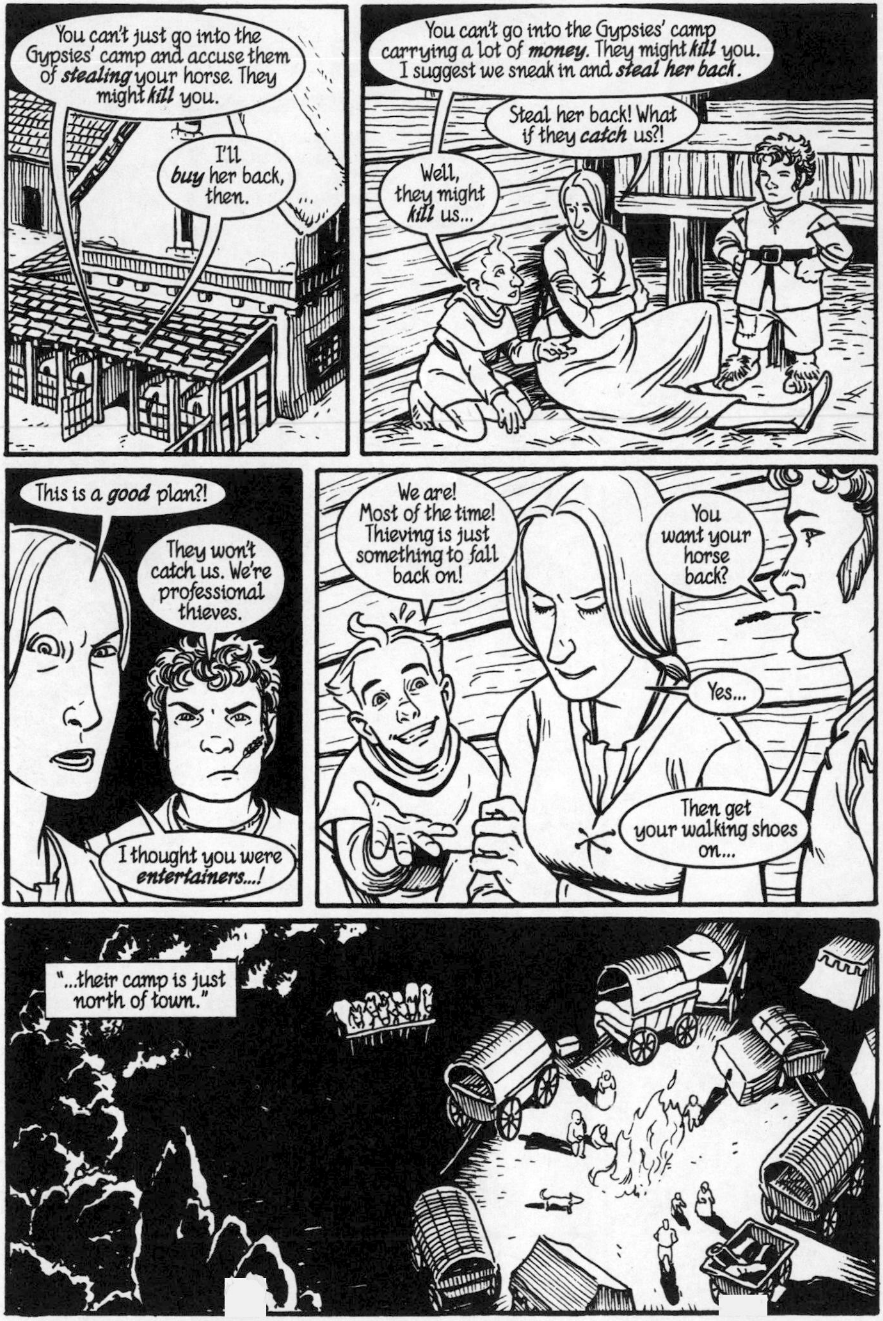
You can't just go into the Gypsies' camp and accuse them of *stealing* your horse. They might *kill* you.
I'll *buy* her back, then.
You can't go into the Gypsies' camp carrying a lot of *money*. They might *kill* you. I suggest we sneak in and *steal her back*.
Steal her back! What if they *catch* us?!
Well, they might *kill* us...
This is a *good* plan?!
They won't catch us. We're professional thieves.
I thought you were *entertainers*...!
We are! Most of the time! Thieving is just something to fall back on!
You want your horse back?
Yes...
Then get your walking shoes on...
"...their camp is just north of town."

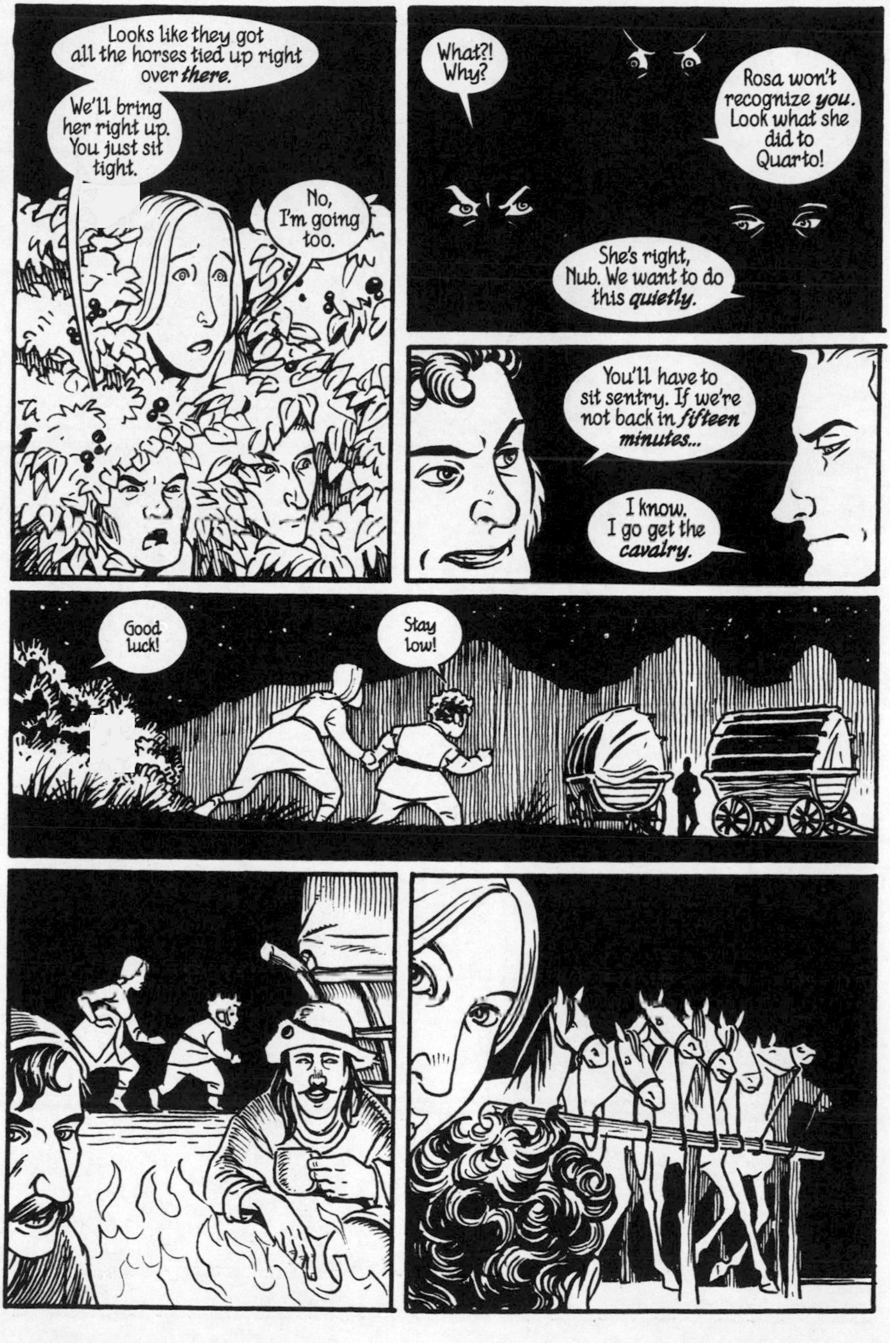
Looks like they got all the horses tied up right over *there.*
We'll bring her right up. You just sit tight.
No, I'm going too.
What?! Why?
Rosa won't recognize *you*. Look what she did to Quarto!
She's right, Nub. We want to do this *quietly.*
You'll have to sit sentry. If we're not back in *fifteen minutes...*
I know. I go get the *cavalry.*
Good luck!
Stay low!

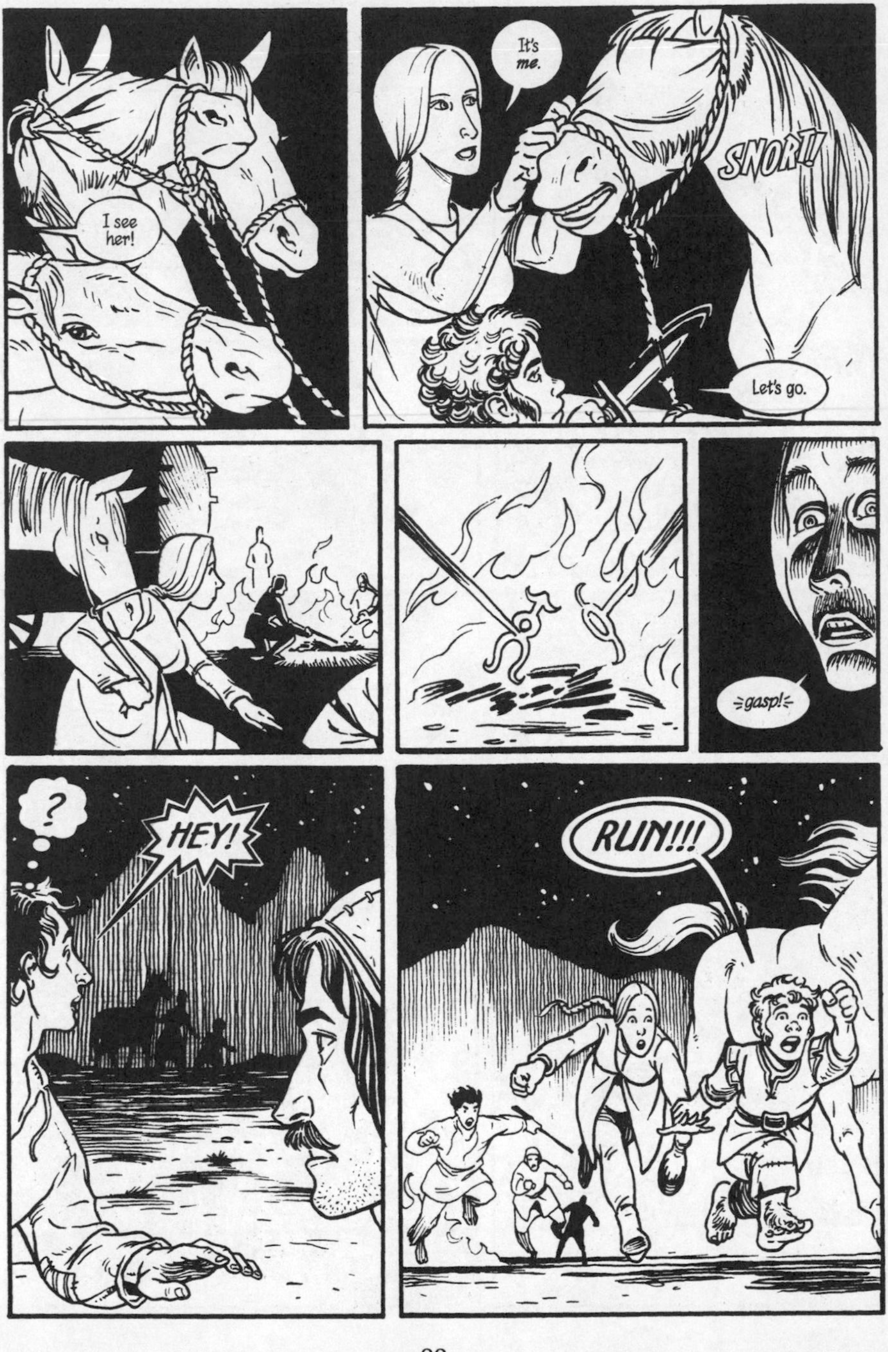
I see her!
It's me.
SNORT!
Let's go.
gasp!
?
HEY!
RUN!!!

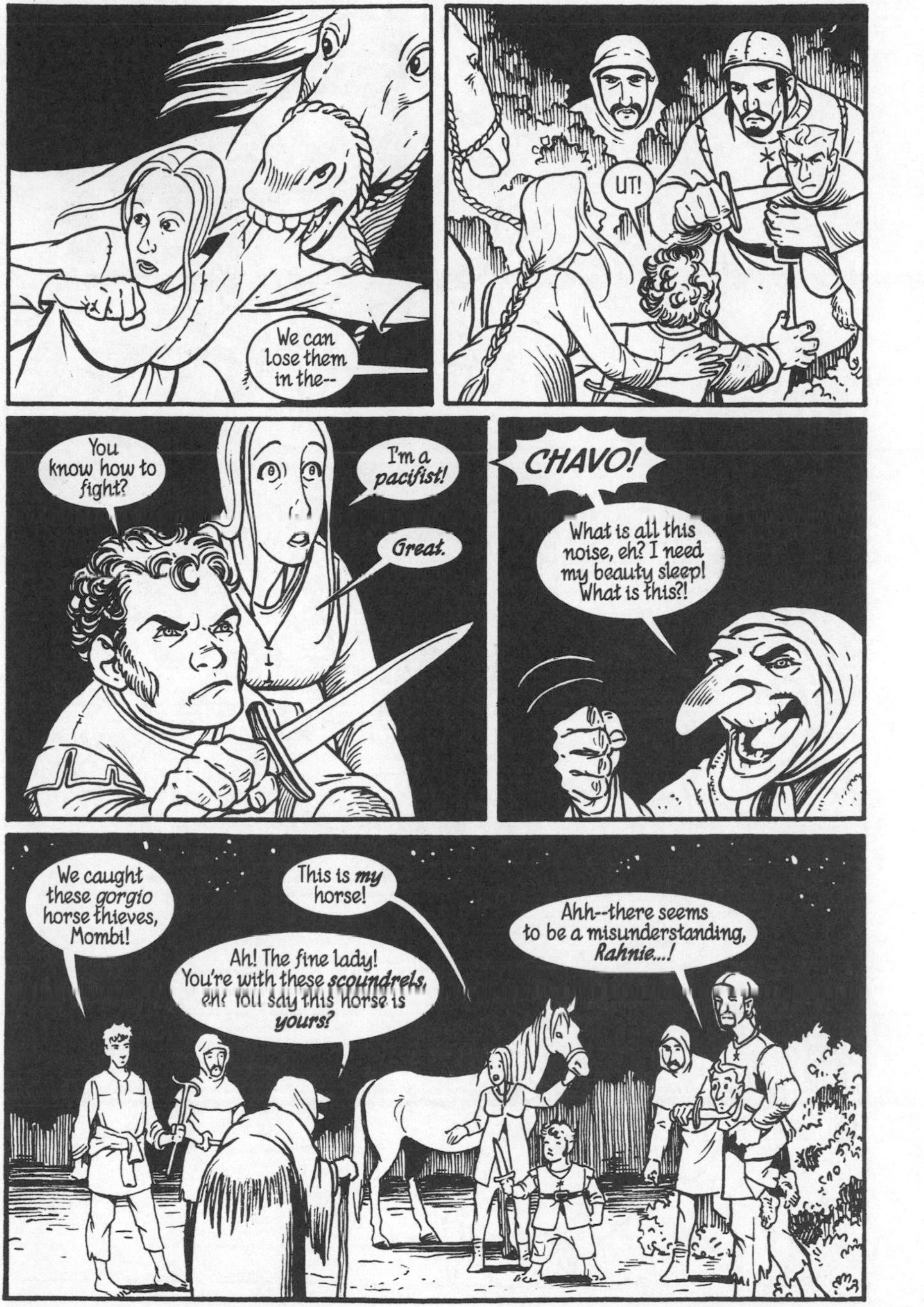
We can lose them in the--
UT!
You know how to fight?
I'm a *pacifist!*
Great.
CHAVO!
What is all this noise, eh? I need my beauty sleep! What is this?!
We caught these *gorgio* horse thieves, Mombi!
This is *my* horse!
Ah! The fine lady! You're with these *scoundrels,* eh? You say this horse is *yours?*
Ahh--there seems to be a misunderstanding, *Rahnie...!*

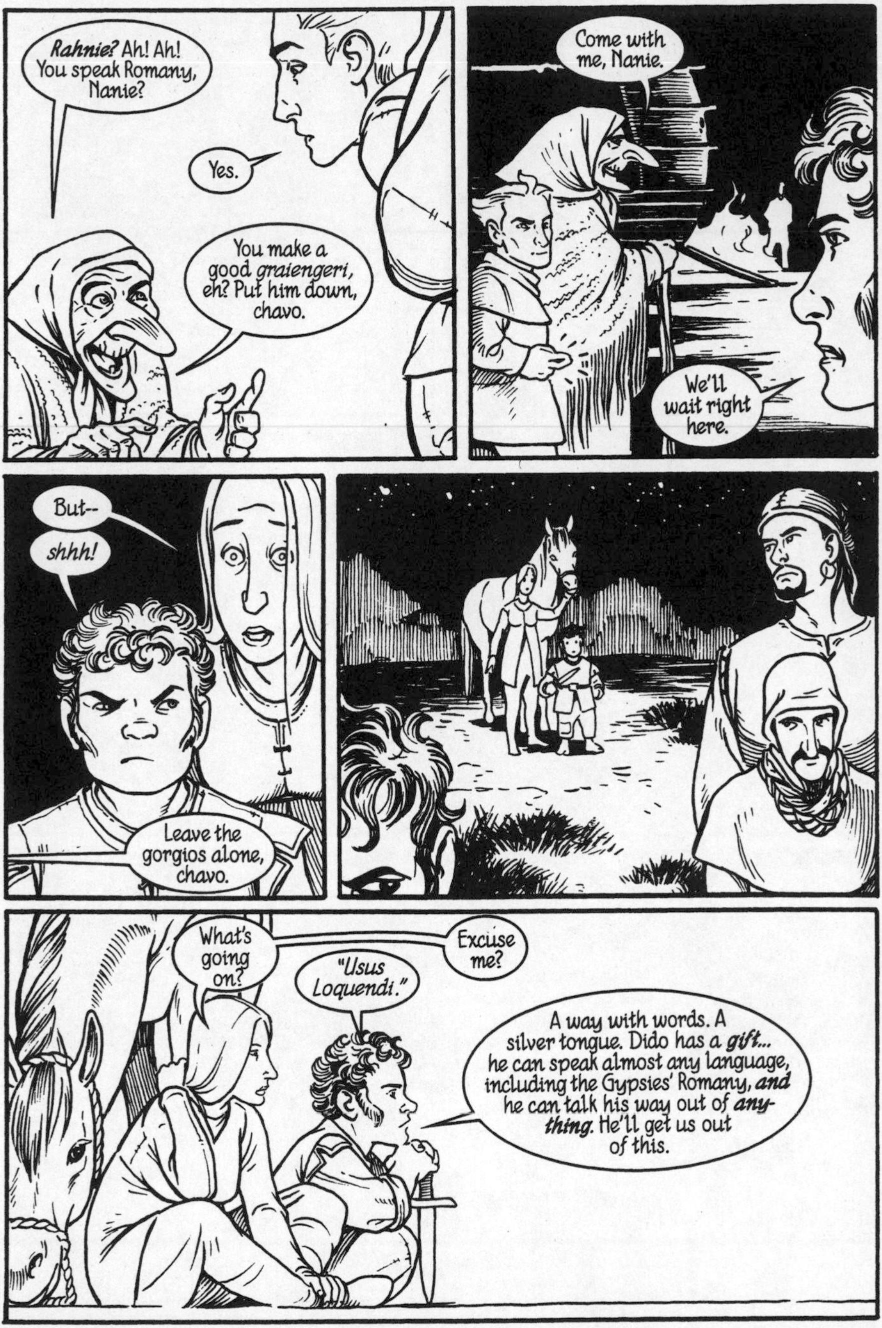
Rahnie? Ah! Ah! You speak Romany, Nanie?
Yes.
You make a good *graiengeri*, eh? Put him down, chavo.
Come with me, Nanie.
We'll wait right here.
But--
shhh!
Leave the gorgios alone, chavo.
What's going on?
"Usus Loquendi."
Excuse me?
A way with words. A silver tongue. Dido has a ***gift...*** he can speak almost any language, including the Gypsies' Romany, ***and*** he can talk his way out of ***any-thing***. He'll get us out of this.

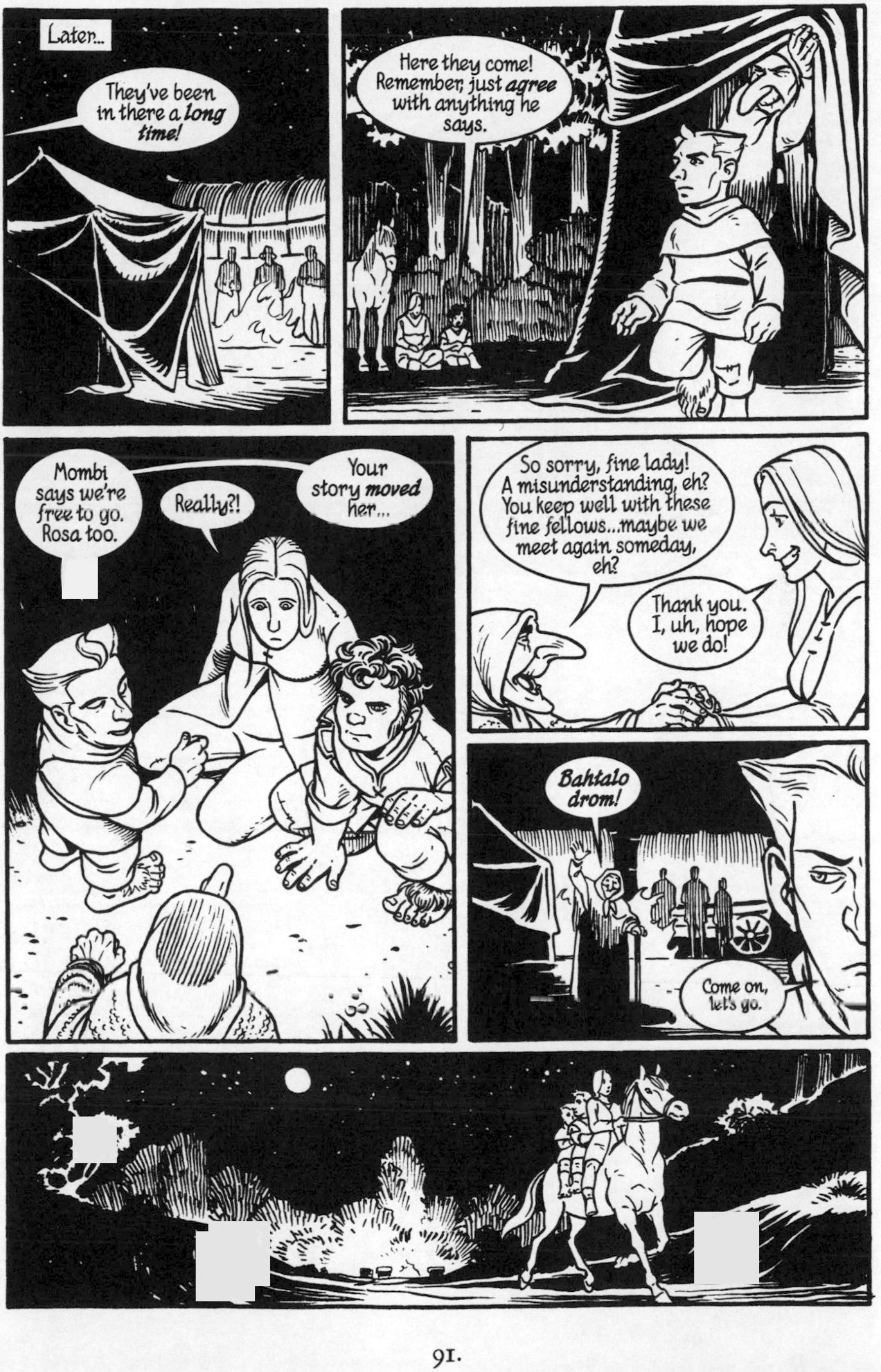
Later...
They've been in there a *long time!*
Here they come! Remember, just *agree* with anything he says.
Mombi says we're free to go. Rosa too.
Really?!
Your story *moved* her...
So sorry, fine lady! A misunderstanding, eh? You keep well with these fine fellows...maybe we meet again someday, eh?
Thank you. I, uh, hope we do!
Bahtalo drom!
Come on, let's go.

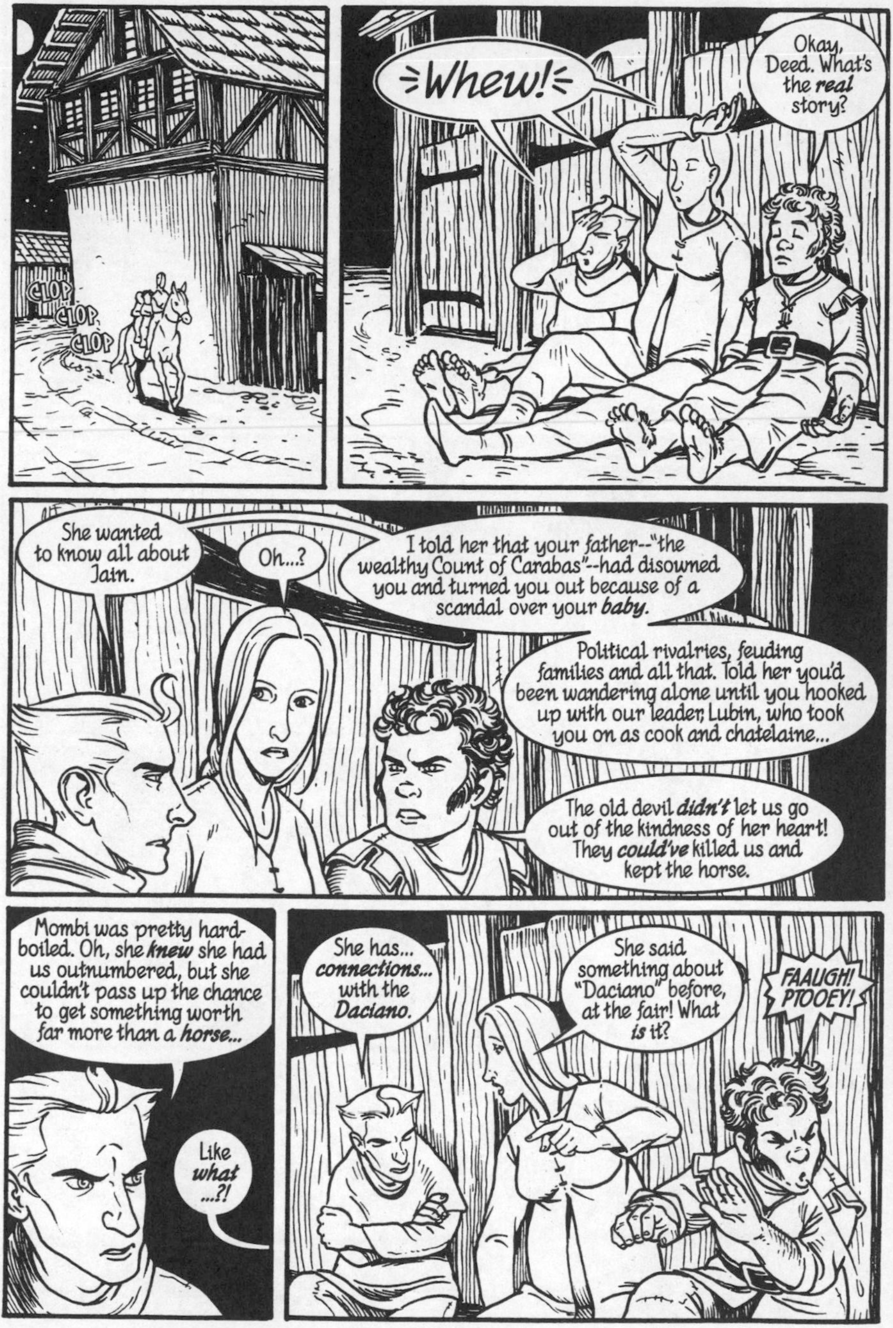

CLOP
CLOP
CLOP
Whew!
Okay, Deed. What's the *real* story?
She wanted to know all about Jain.
Oh...?
I told her that your father--"the wealthy Count of Carabas"--had disowned you and turned you out because of a scandal over your *baby*.
Political rivalries, feuding families and all that. Told her you'd been wandering alone until you hooked up with our leader, Lubin, who took you on as cook and chatelaine...
The old devil *didn't* let us go out of the kindness of her heart! They *could've* killed us and kept the horse.
Mombi was pretty hard-boiled. Oh, she *knew* she had us outnumbered, but she couldn't pass up the chance to get something worth far more than a *horse*...
Like *what* ...?!
She has... *connections*... with the *Daciano*.
She said something about "Daciano" before, at the fair! What *is* it?
FAAUGH! PTOOEY!

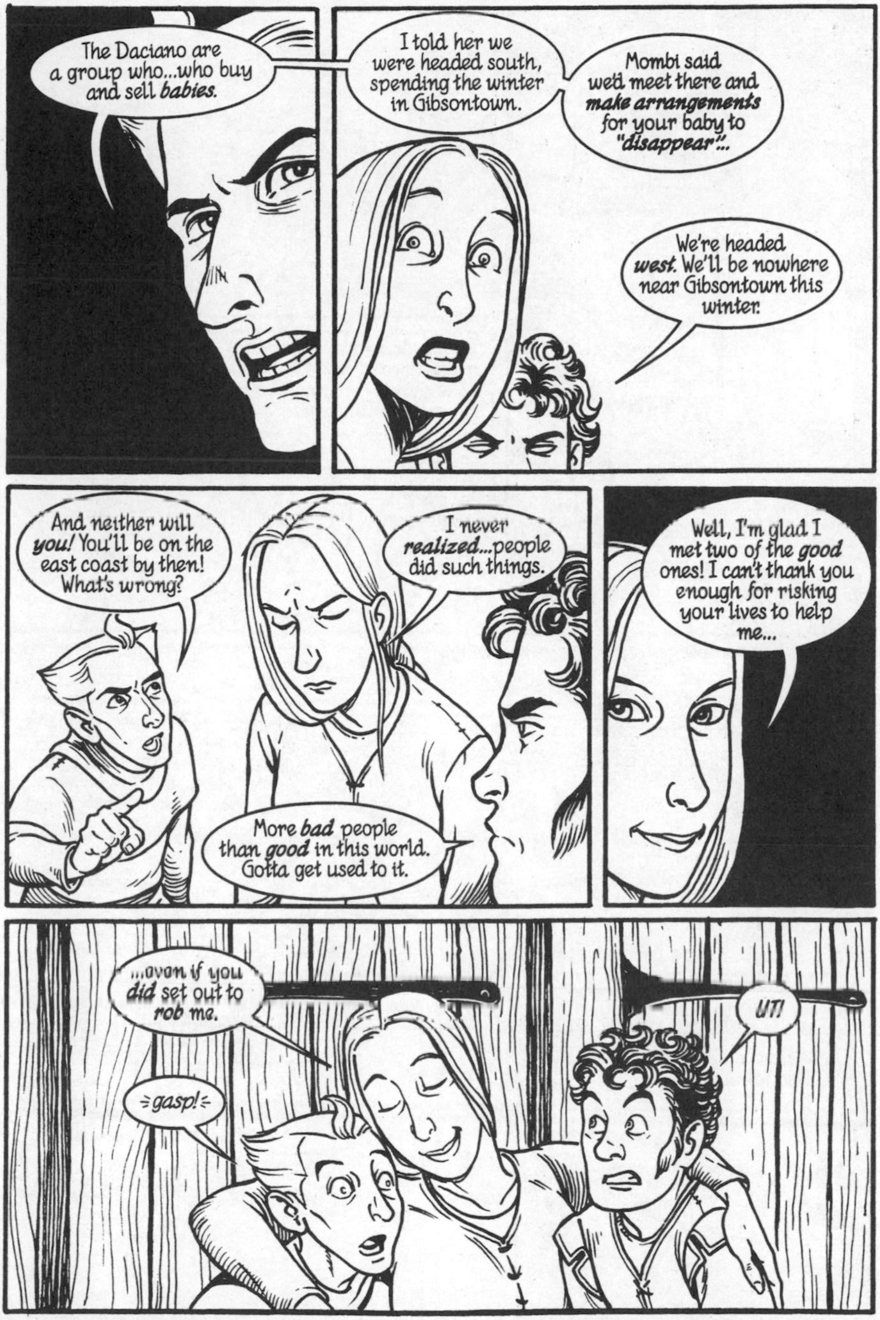
The Daciano are a group who...who buy and sell *babies.*
I told her we were headed south, spending the winter in Gibsontown.
Mombi said we'd meet there and ***make arrangements*** for your baby to ***"disappear"...***
We're headed ***west.*** We'll be nowhere near Gibsontown this winter.
And neither will ***you!*** You'll be on the east coast by then! What's wrong?
I never ***realized...*** people did such things.
More ***bad*** people than ***good*** in this world. Gotta get used to it.
Well, I'm glad I met two of the ***good*** ones! I can't thank you enough for risking your lives to help me...
...even if you ***did*** set out to ***rob*** me.
UT!
gasp!

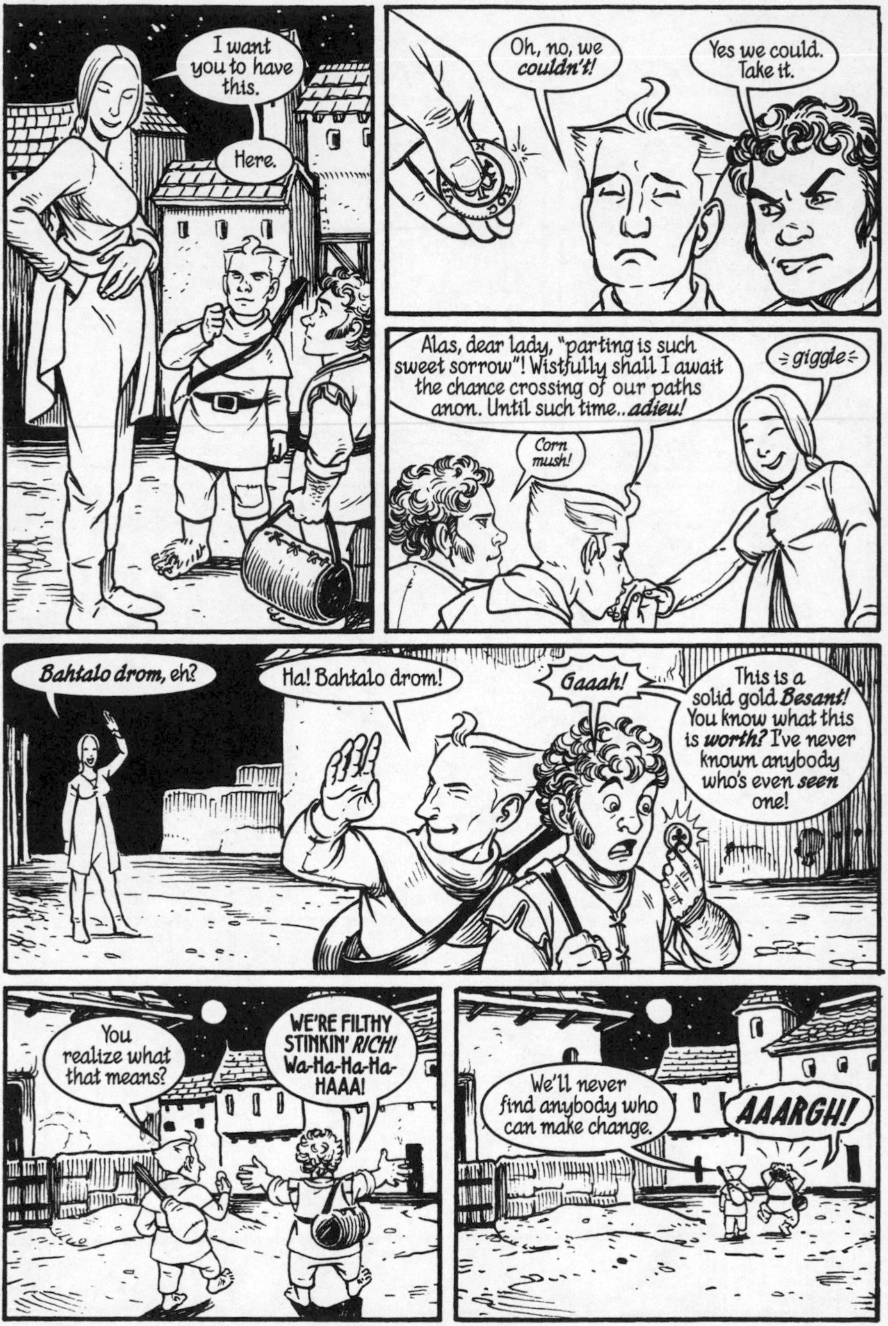
I want you to have this.
Here.
Oh, no, we *couldn't!*
Yes we could. Take it.
Alas, dear lady, "parting is such sweet sorrow"! Wistfully shall I await the chance crossing of our paths anon. Until such time... *adieu!*
Corn mush!
giggle
Bahtalo drom, eh?
Ha! Bahtalo drom!
Gaaah!
This is a solid gold *Besant!* You know what this is *worth?* I've never known anybody who's even *seen* one!
You realize what that means?
WE'RE FILTHY STINKIN' *RICH!* Wa-Ha-Ha-Ha-HAAA!
We'll never find anybody who can make change.
AAARGH!

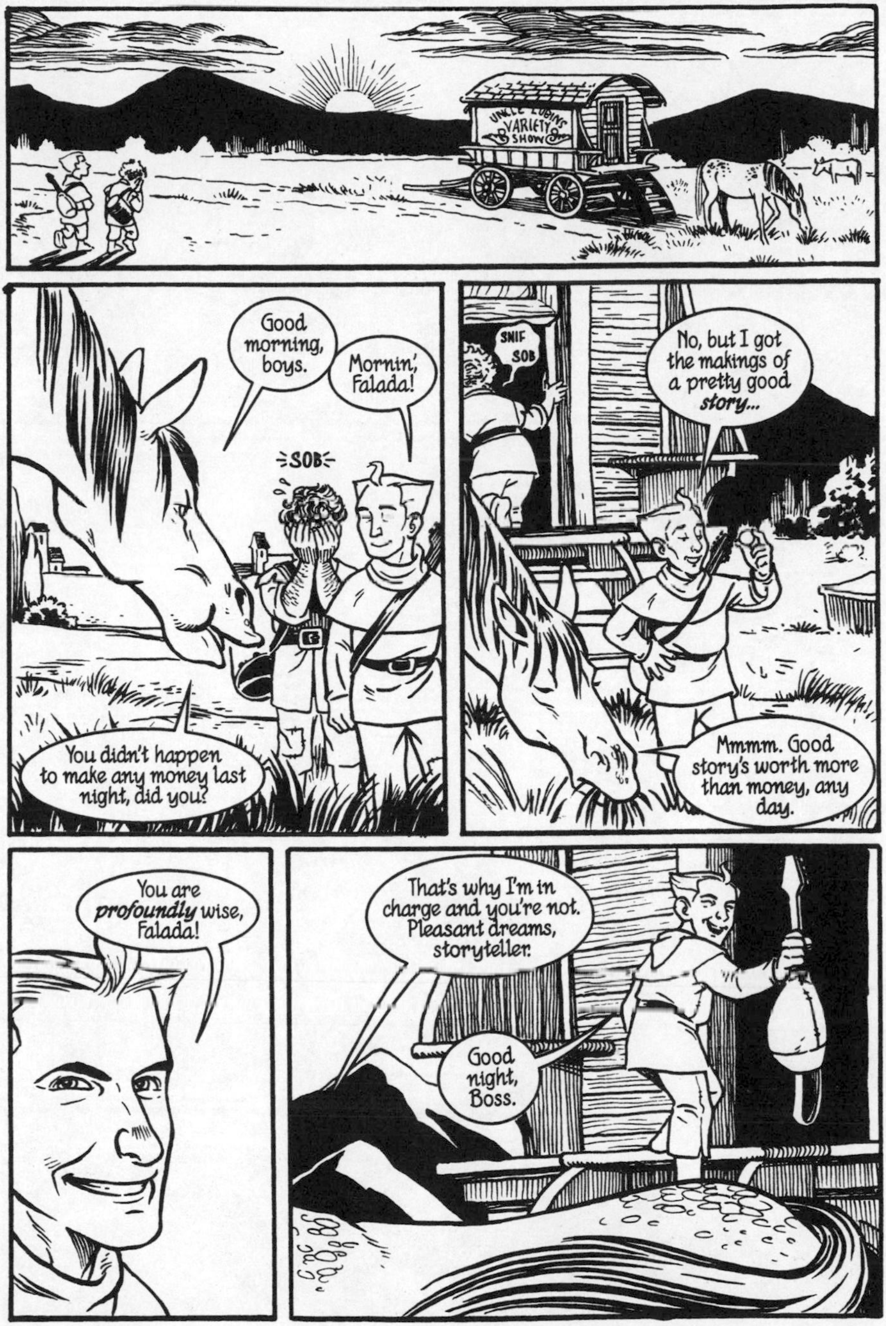
UNCLE LUBIN'S
VARIETY
SHOW
Good morning, boys.
Mornin', Falada!
SOB
You didn't happen to make any money last night, did you?
SNIF
SOB
No, but I got the makings of a pretty good *story...*
Mmmm. Good story's worth more than money, any day.
You are *profoundly* wise, Falada!
That's why I'm in charge and you're not. Pleasant dreams, storyteller.
Good night, Boss.

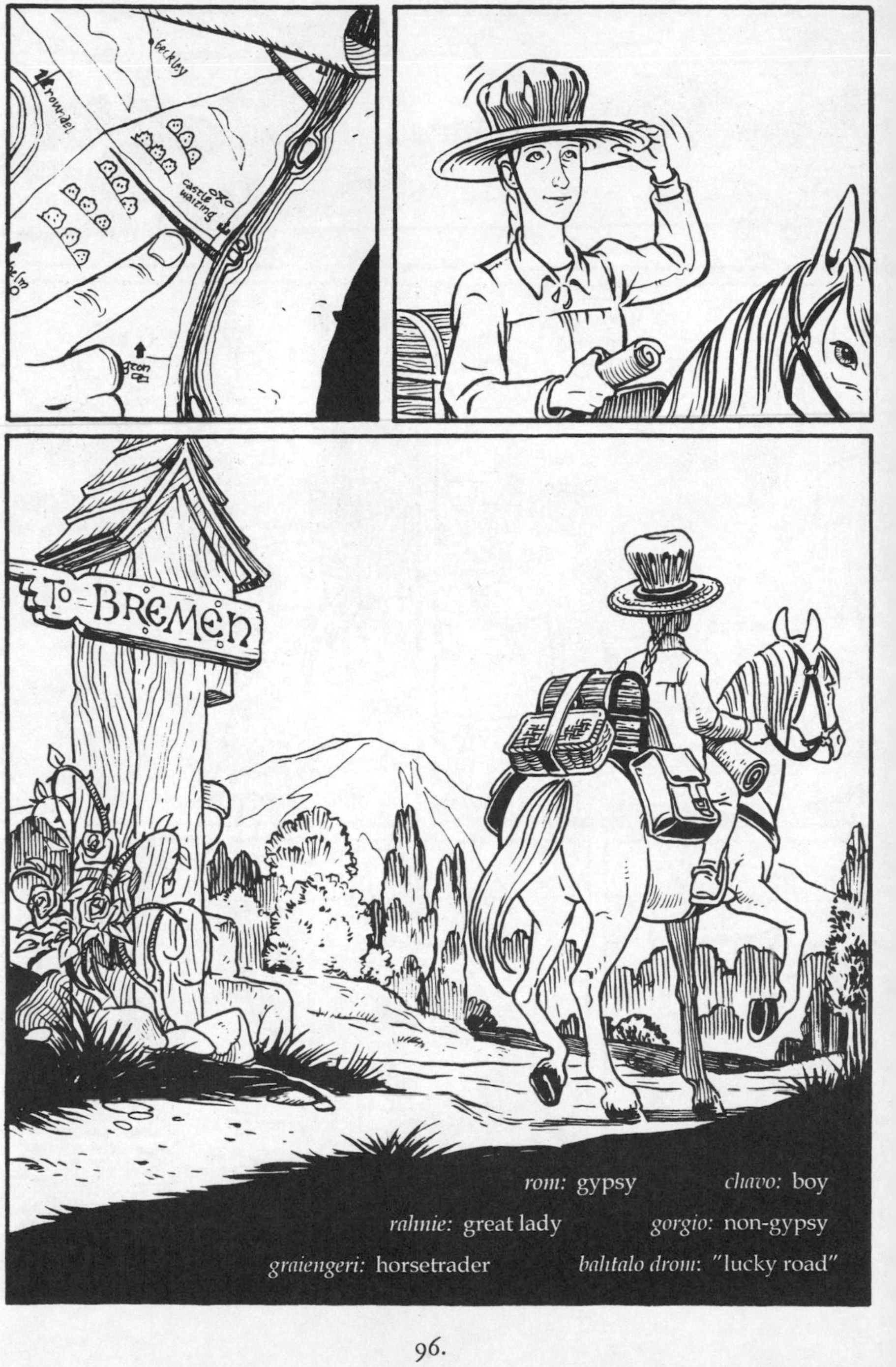
beckley
castle waiting
To BREMEN
rom: gypsy
chavo: boy
rahnie: great lady
gorgio: non-gypsy
graiengeri: horsetrader
bahtalo drom: "lucky road"

Chapter 5.

· YOUR CASTLE IS YOUR HOME ·

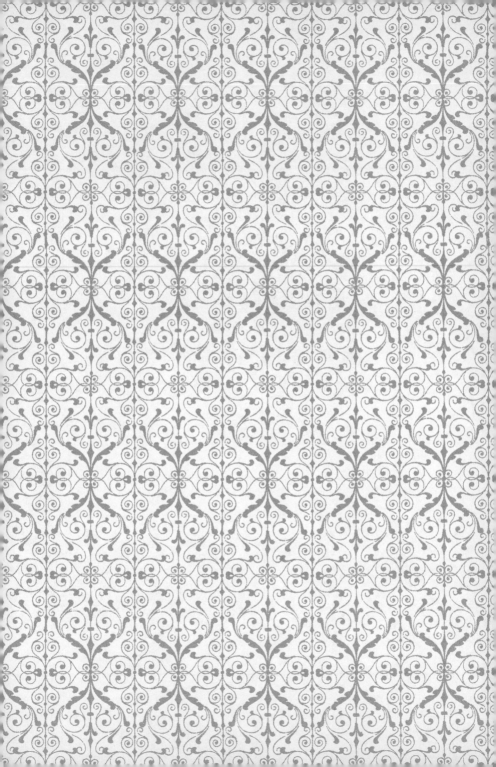

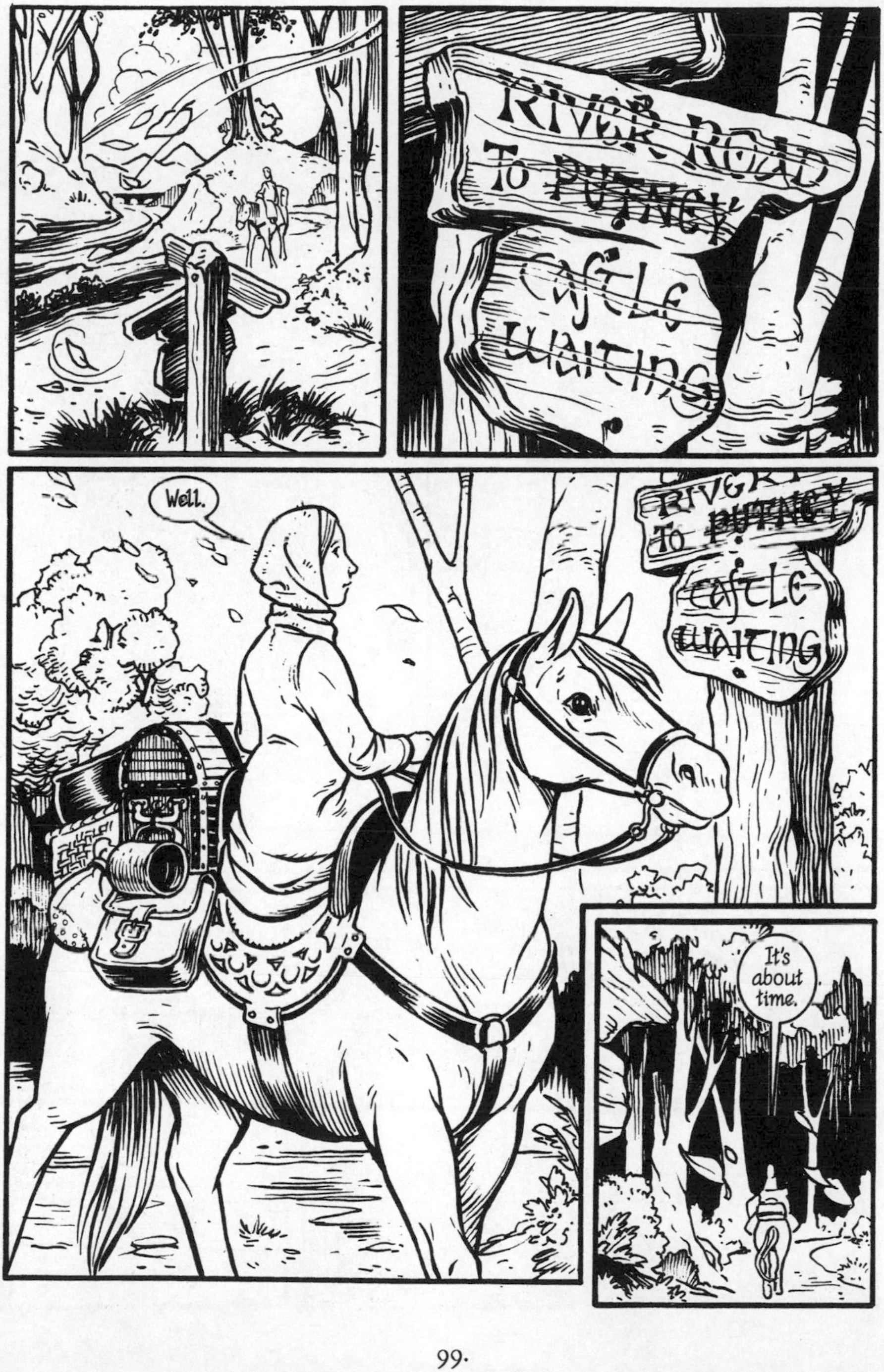
RIVER ROAD
TO PUTNEY
CASTLE
WAITING
Well.
RIVER
TO PUTNEY
CASTLE
WAITING
It's about time.

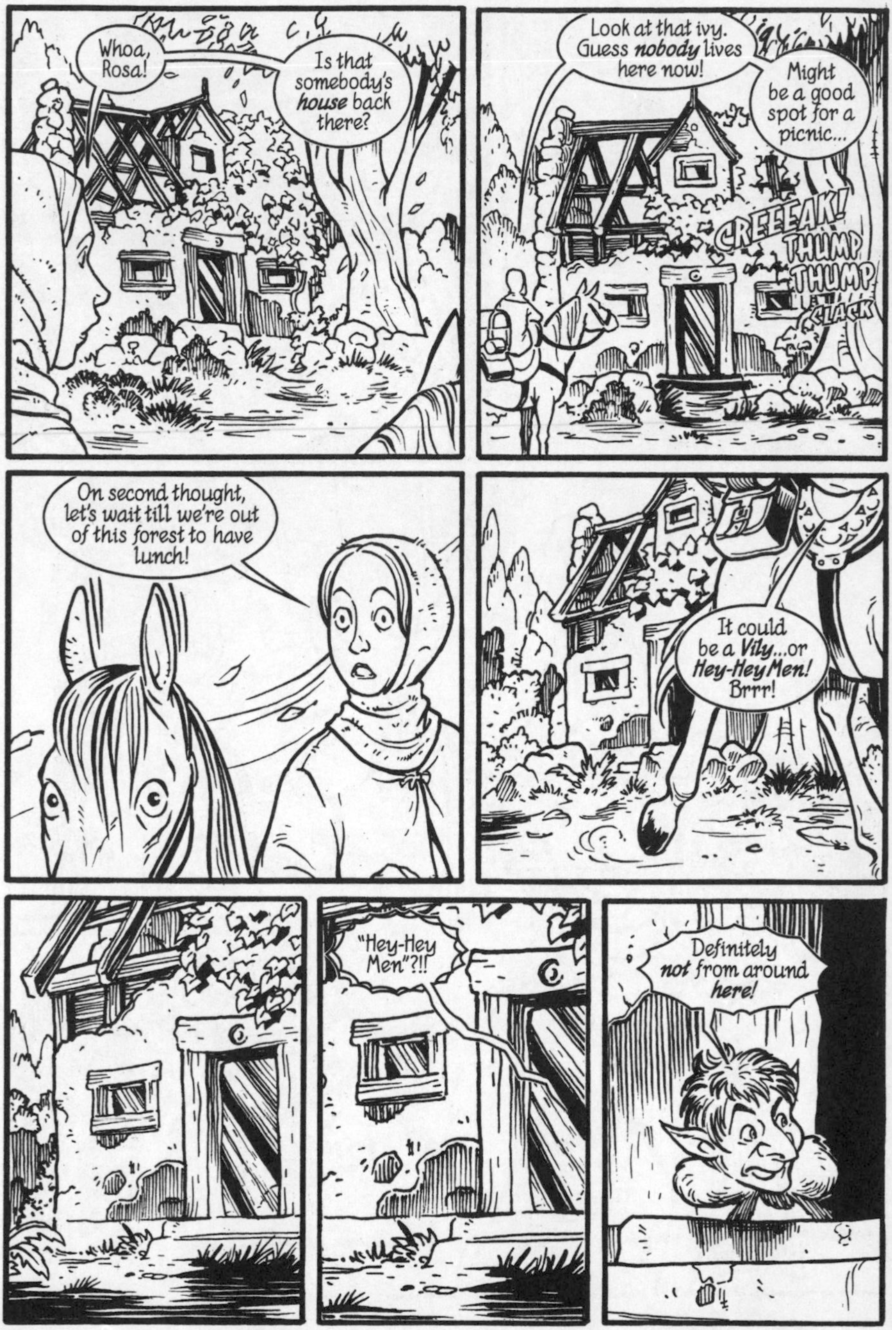
Whoa, Rosa!
Is that somebody's **house** back there?
Look at that ivy. Guess **nobody** lives here now!
Might be a good spot for a picnic...
CREEEAK!
THUMP
THUMP
CLACK
On second thought, let's wait till we're out of this forest to have lunch!
It could be a **Vily**...or **Hey-Hey Men!** Brrr!
"Hey-Hey Men"?!!
Definitely **not** from around **here!**

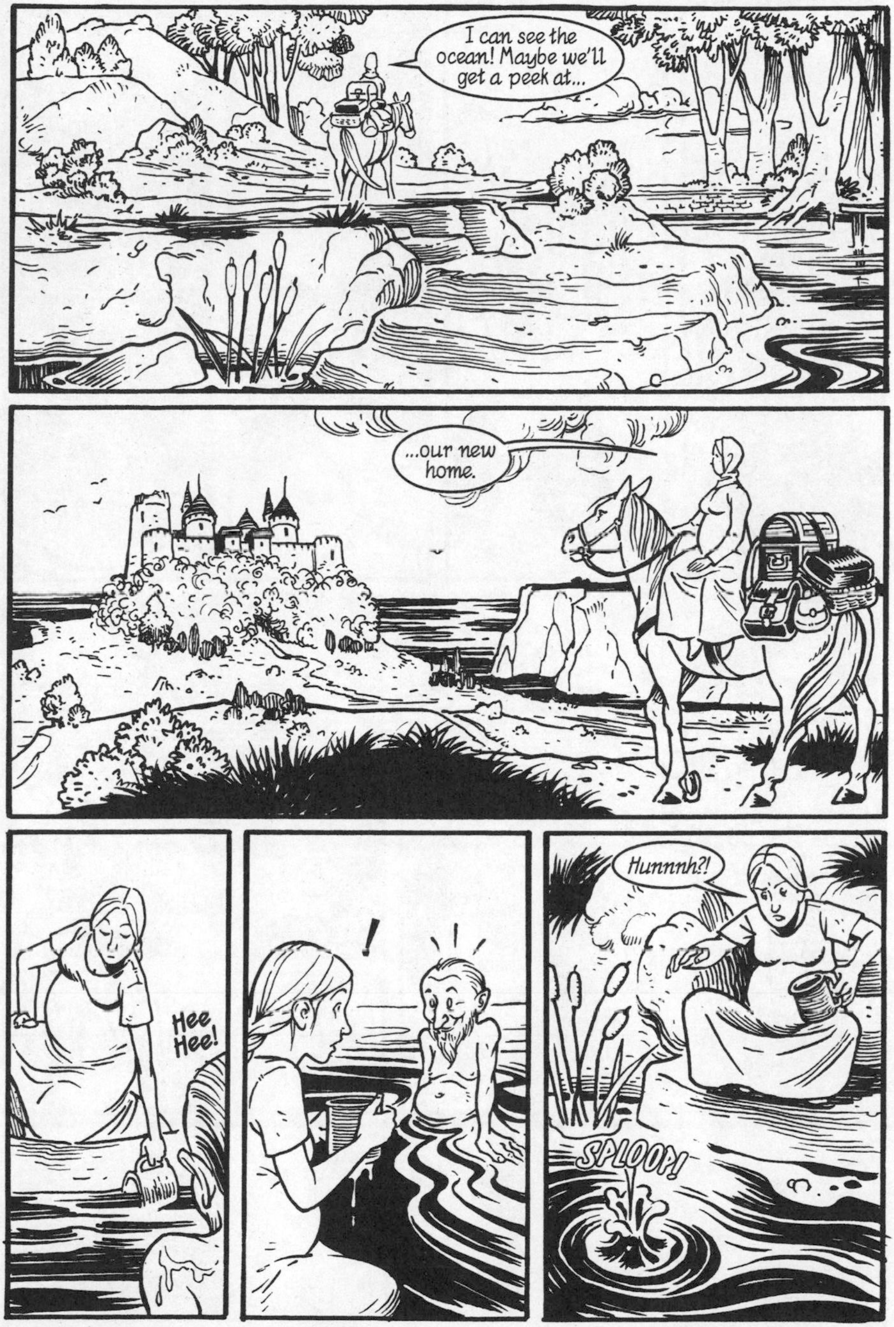
I can see the ocean! Maybe we'll get a peek at...
...our new home.
Hee Hee!
!
Hunnnh?!
SPLOOP!

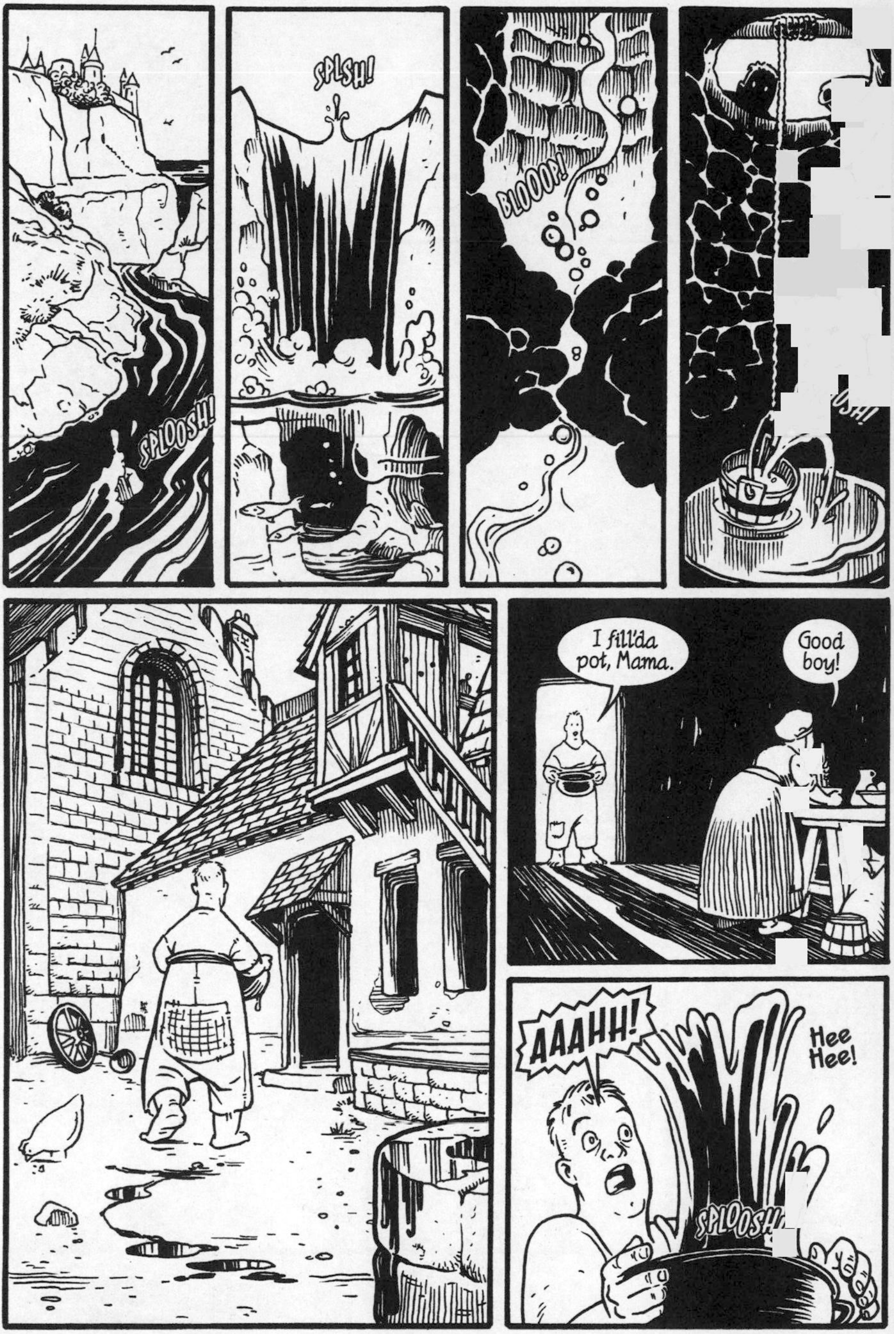
SPLOOSH!
SPLSH!
BLOOOP!
I fill'da pot, Mama.
Good boy!
AAAHH!
Hee Hee!
SPLOOSH

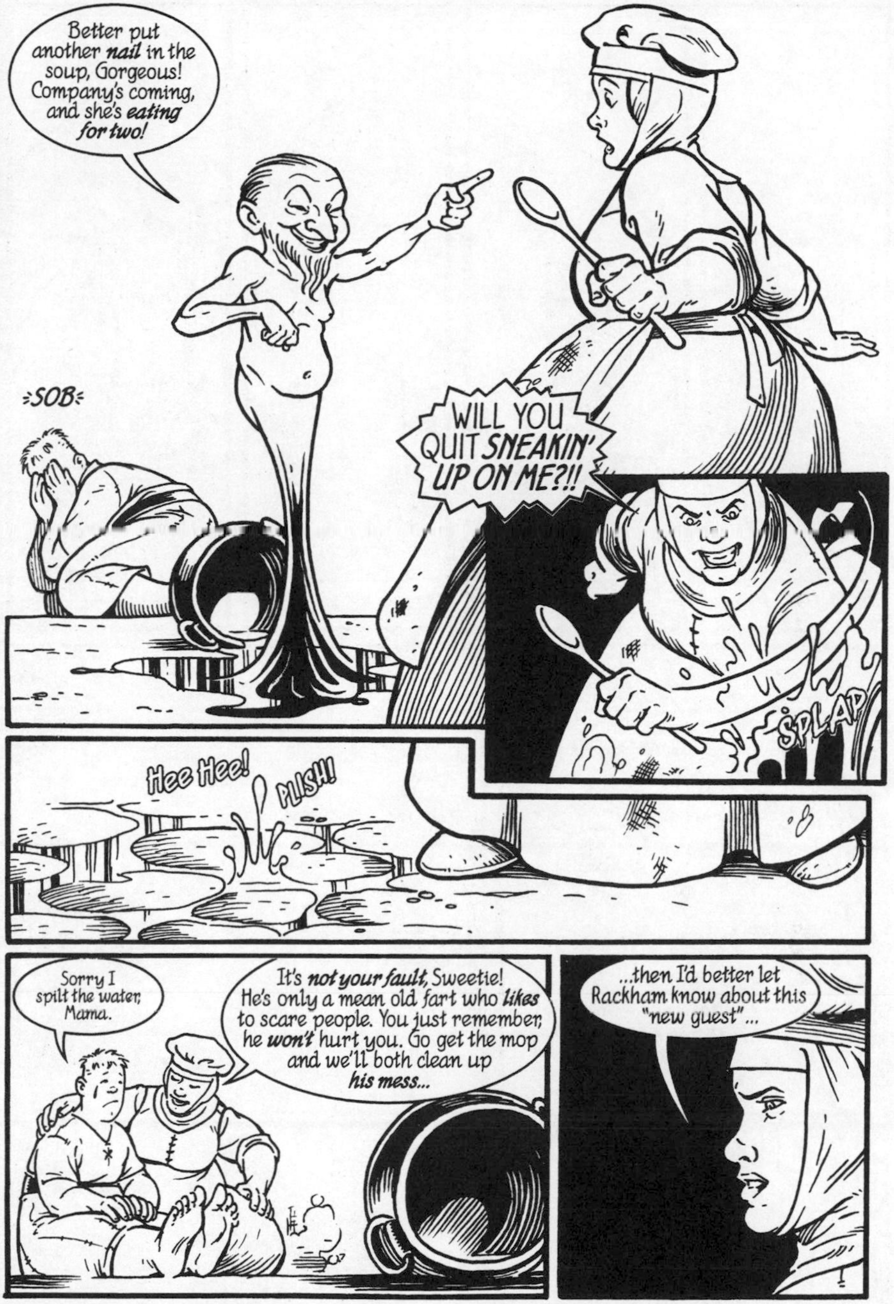
Better put another nail in the soup, Gorgeous! Company's coming, and she's eating for two!
SOB
WILL YOU QUIT SNEAKIN' UP ON ME?!!
SPLAP
Hee Hee!
PLISH!
Sorry I spilt the water, Mama.
It's not your fault, Sweetie! He's only a mean old fart who likes to scare people. You just remember, he won't hurt you. Go get the mop and we'll both clean up his mess...
...then I'd better let Rackham know about this "new guest"...

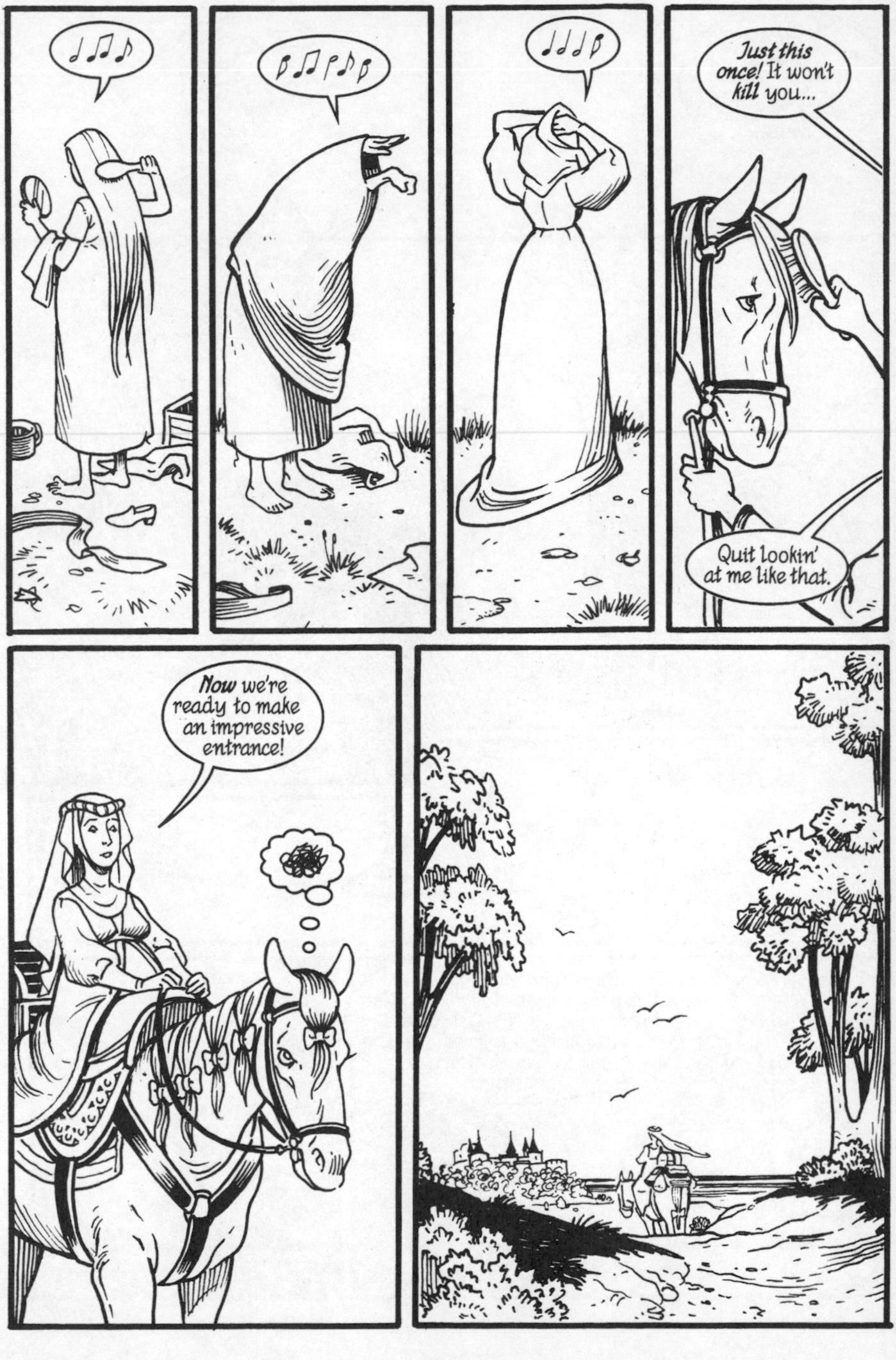
Just this once! It won't kill you...
Quit lookin' at me like that.
Now we're ready to make an impressive entrance!

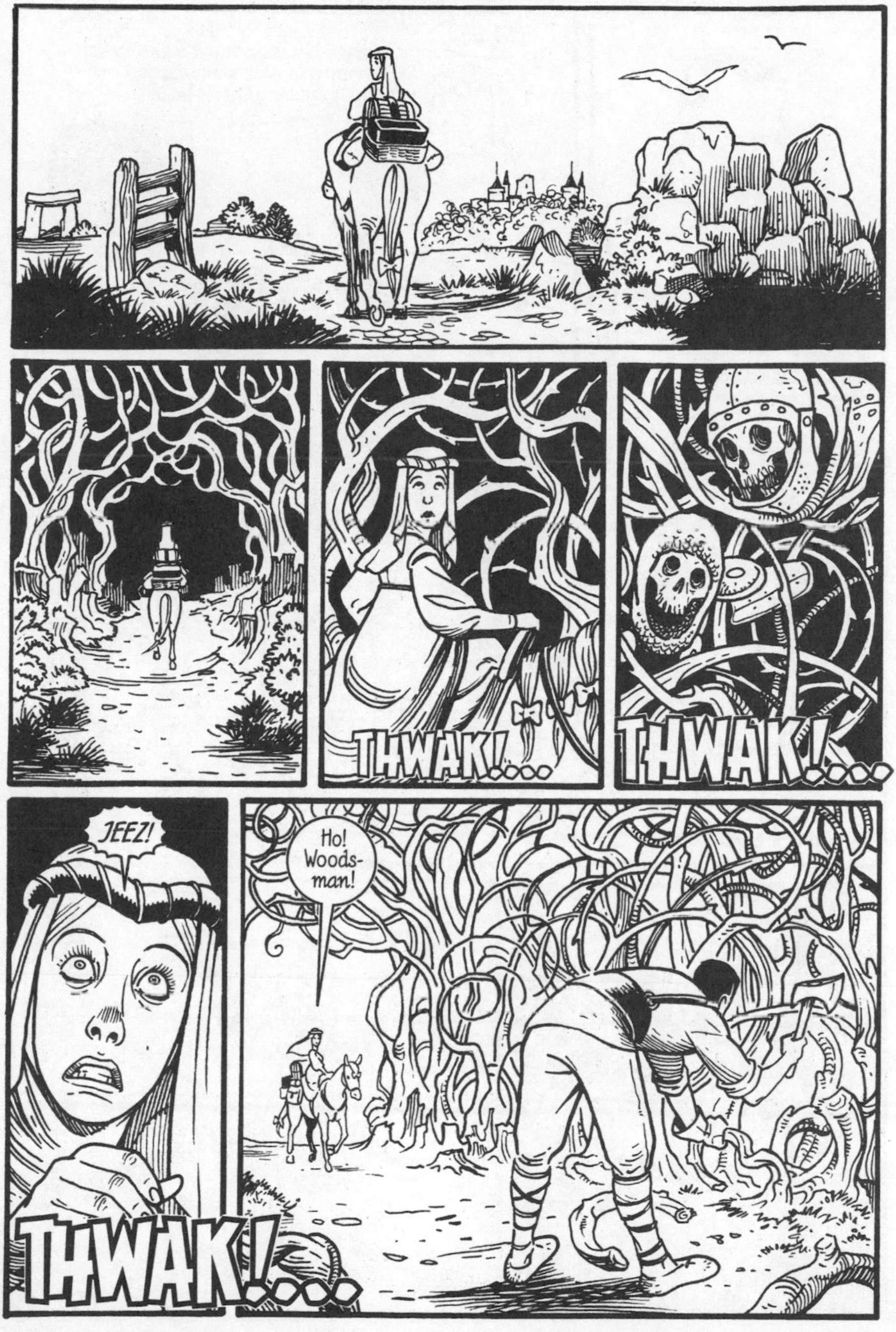
THWAK!....
THWAK!....
JEEZ!
THWAK!....
Ho! Woods-man!

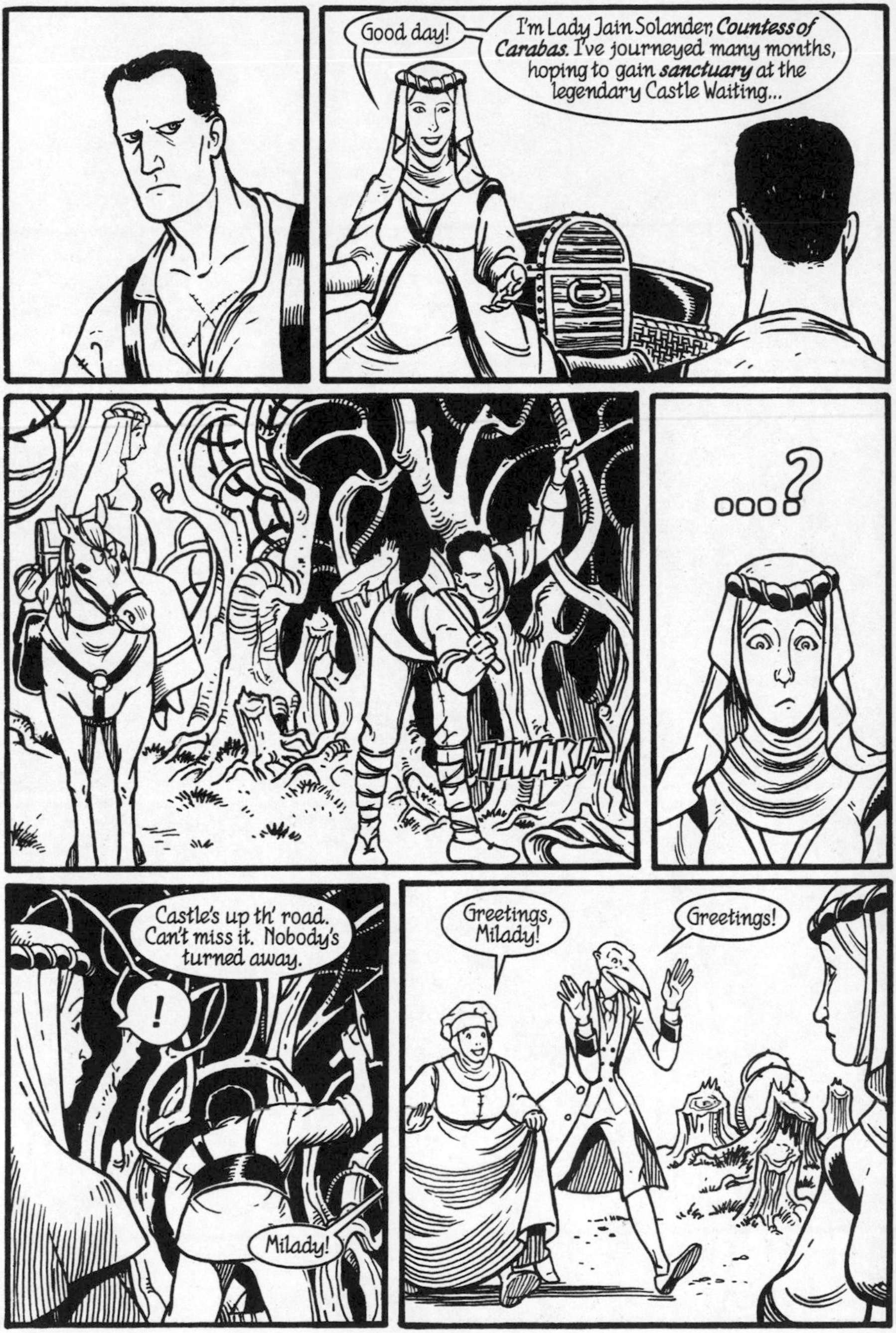
Good day!
I'm Lady Jain Solander, Countess of Carabas. I've journeyed many months, hoping to gain sanctuary at the legendary Castle Waiting...
THWAK!
ooo?
Castle's up th' road. Can't miss it. Nobody's turned away.
!
Milady!
Greetings, Milady!
Greetings!

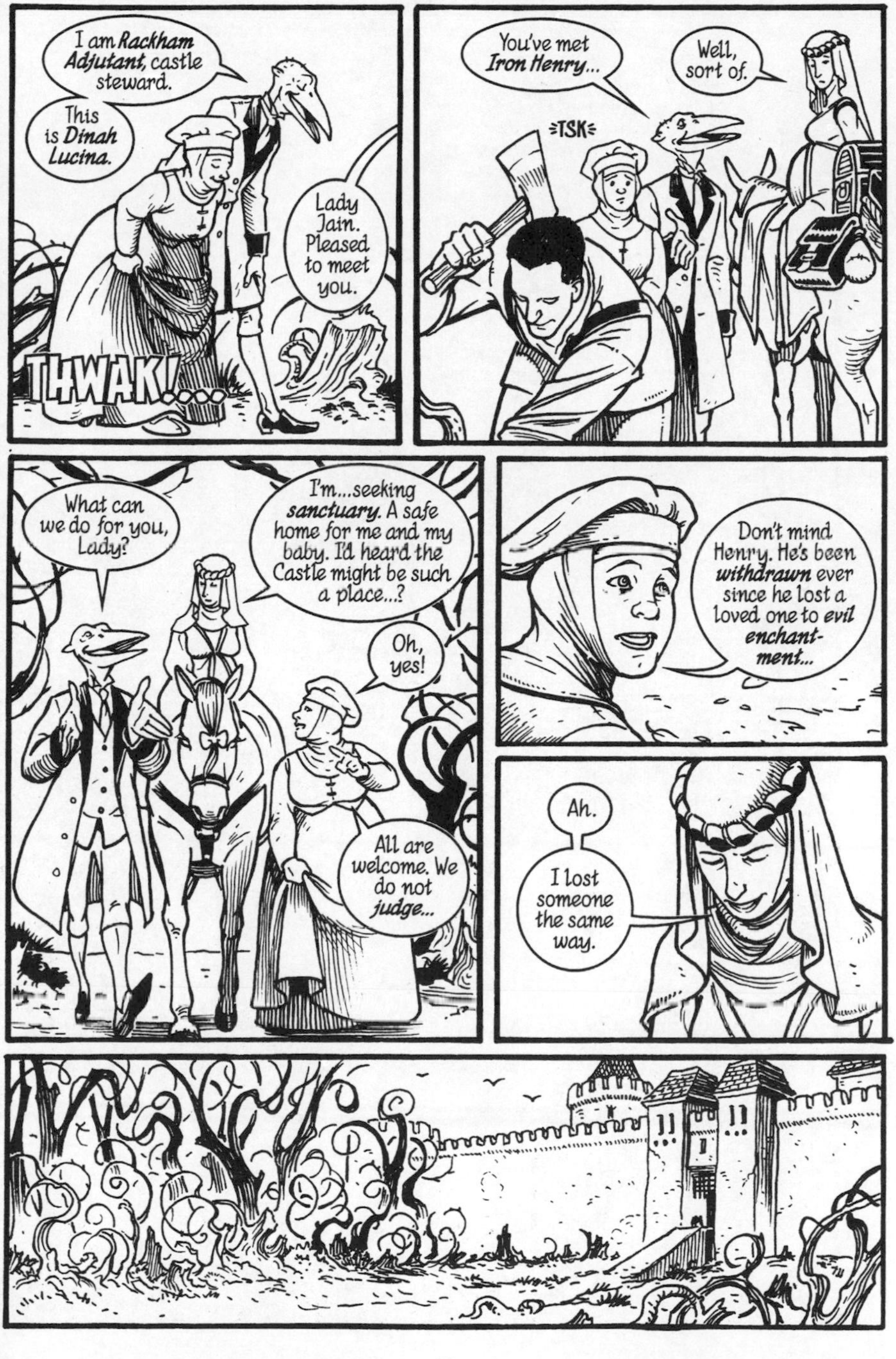
I am Rackham Adjutant, castle steward.
This is Dinah Lucina.
Lady Jain. Pleased to meet you.
THWAK!....
You've met Iron Henry...
Well, sort of.
TSK
What can we do for you, Lady?
I'm...seeking sanctuary. A safe home for me and my baby. I'd heard the Castle might be such a place...?
Oh, yes!
All are welcome. We do not judge...
Don't mind Henry. He's been withdrawn ever since he lost a loved one to evil enchantment...
Ah.
I lost someone the same way.

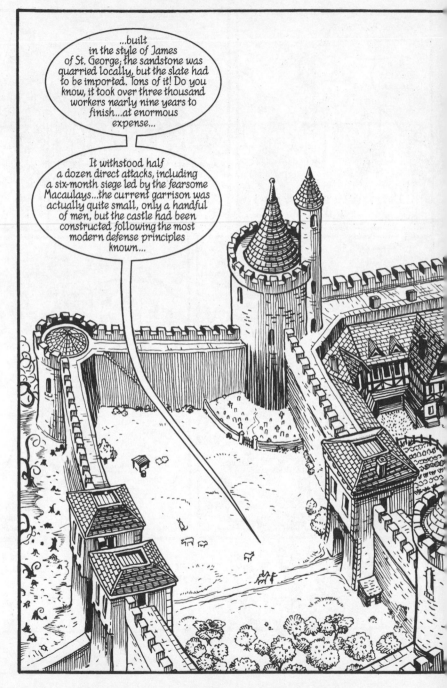

...built in the style of James of St. George; the sandstone was quarried locally, but the slate had to be imported. Tons of it! Do you know, it took over three thousand workers nearly nine years to finish....at enormous expense...

It withstood half a dozen direct attacks, including a six-month siege led by the fearsome Macaulays...the current garrison was actually quite small, only a handful of men, but the castle had been constructed following the most modern defense principles known...

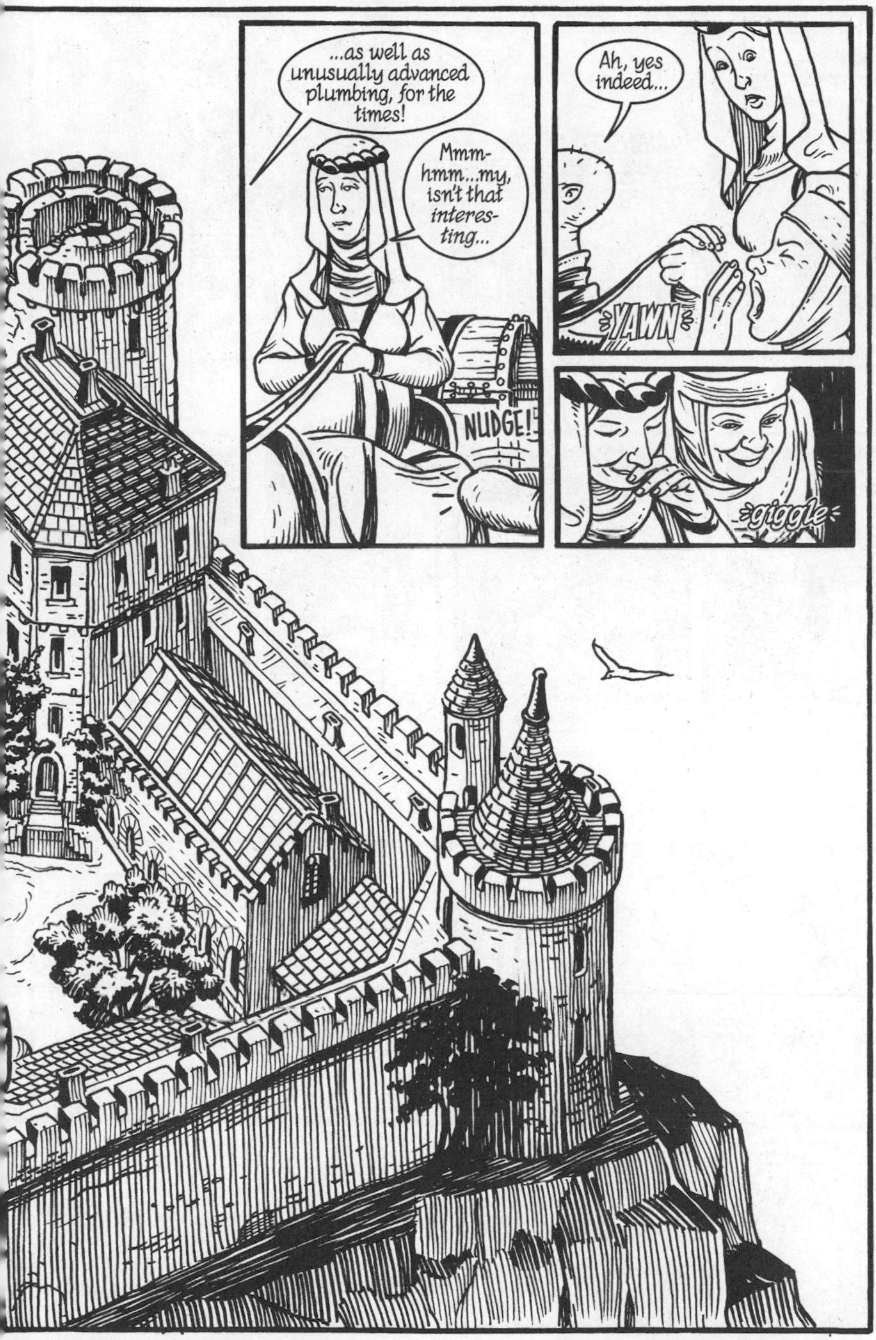
...as well as unusually advanced plumbing, for the times!
Mmm-hmm...my, isn't that interes-ting...
NUDGE!
Ah, yes indeed...
YAWN
giggle

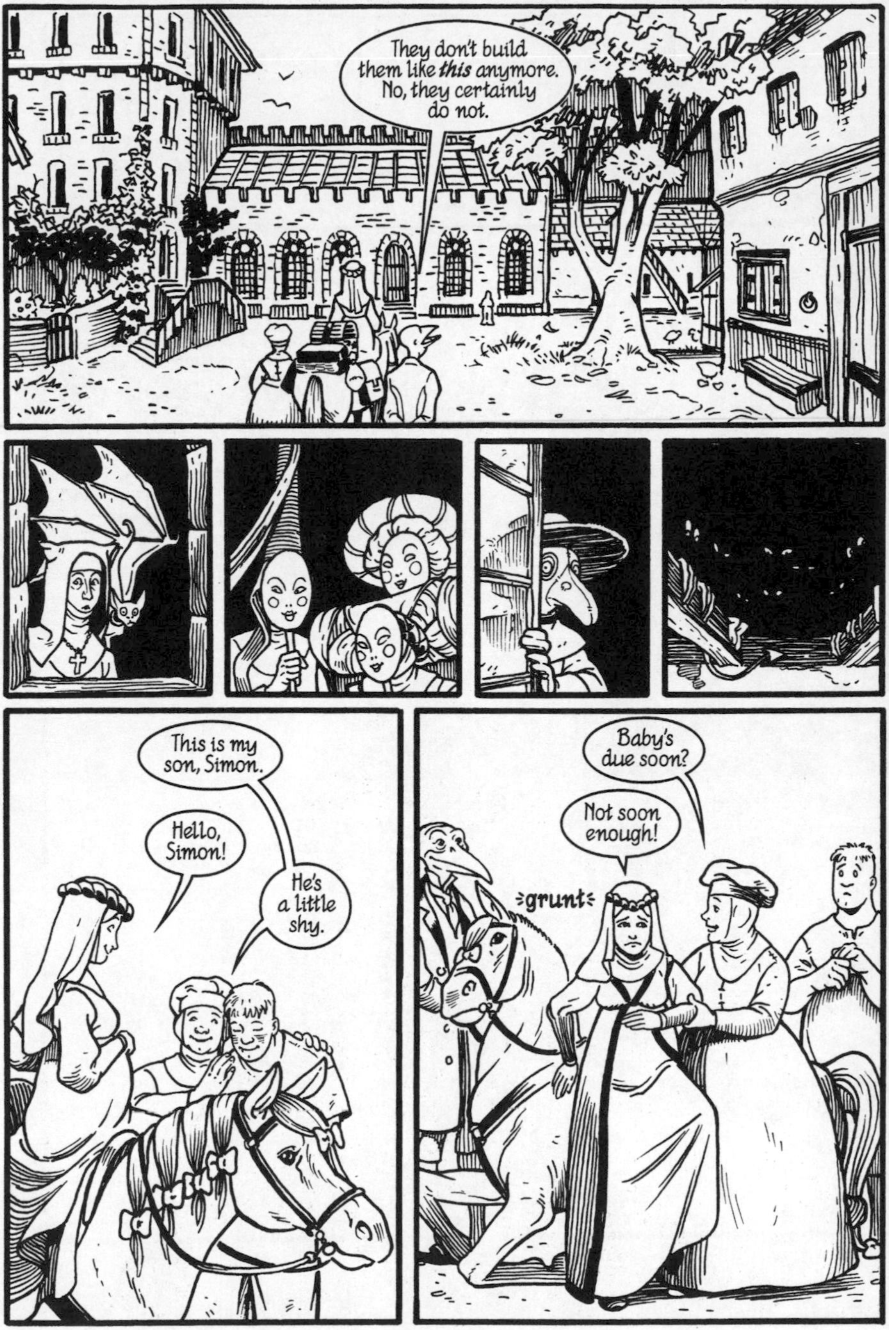
They don't build them like *this* anymore. No, they certainly do not.
This is my son, Simon.
Hello, Simon!
He's a little shy.
Baby's due soon?
Not soon enough!
grunt

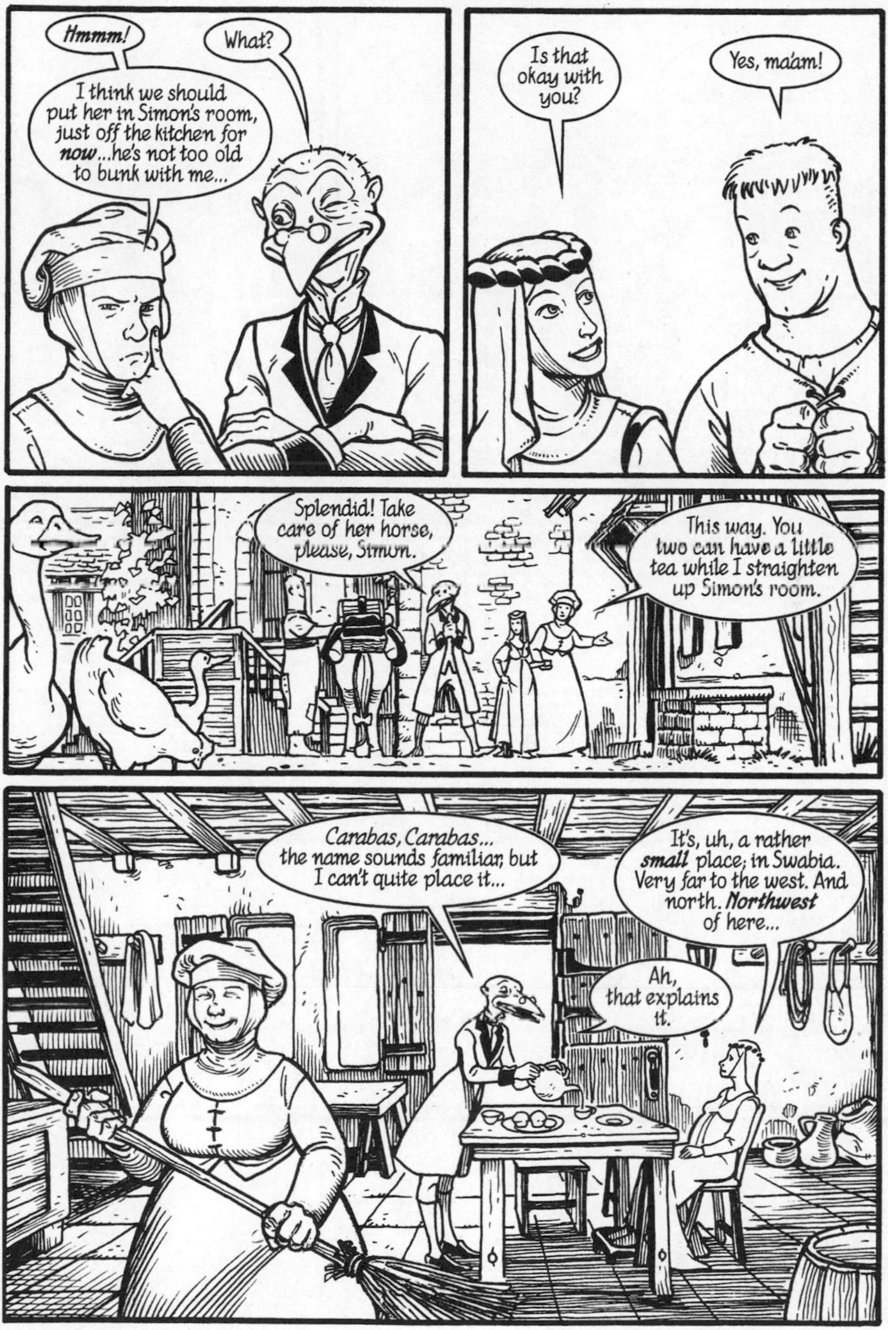
Hmmm!
What?
I think we should put her in Simon's room, just off the kitchen for now...he's not too old to bunk with me...
Is that okay with you?
Yes, ma'am!
Splendid! Take care of her horse, please, Simon.
This way. You two can have a little tea while I straighten up Simon's room.
Carabas, Carabas... the name sounds familiar, but I can't quite place it...
It's, uh, a rather small place; in Swabia. Very far to the west. And north. Northwest of here...
Ah, that explains it.

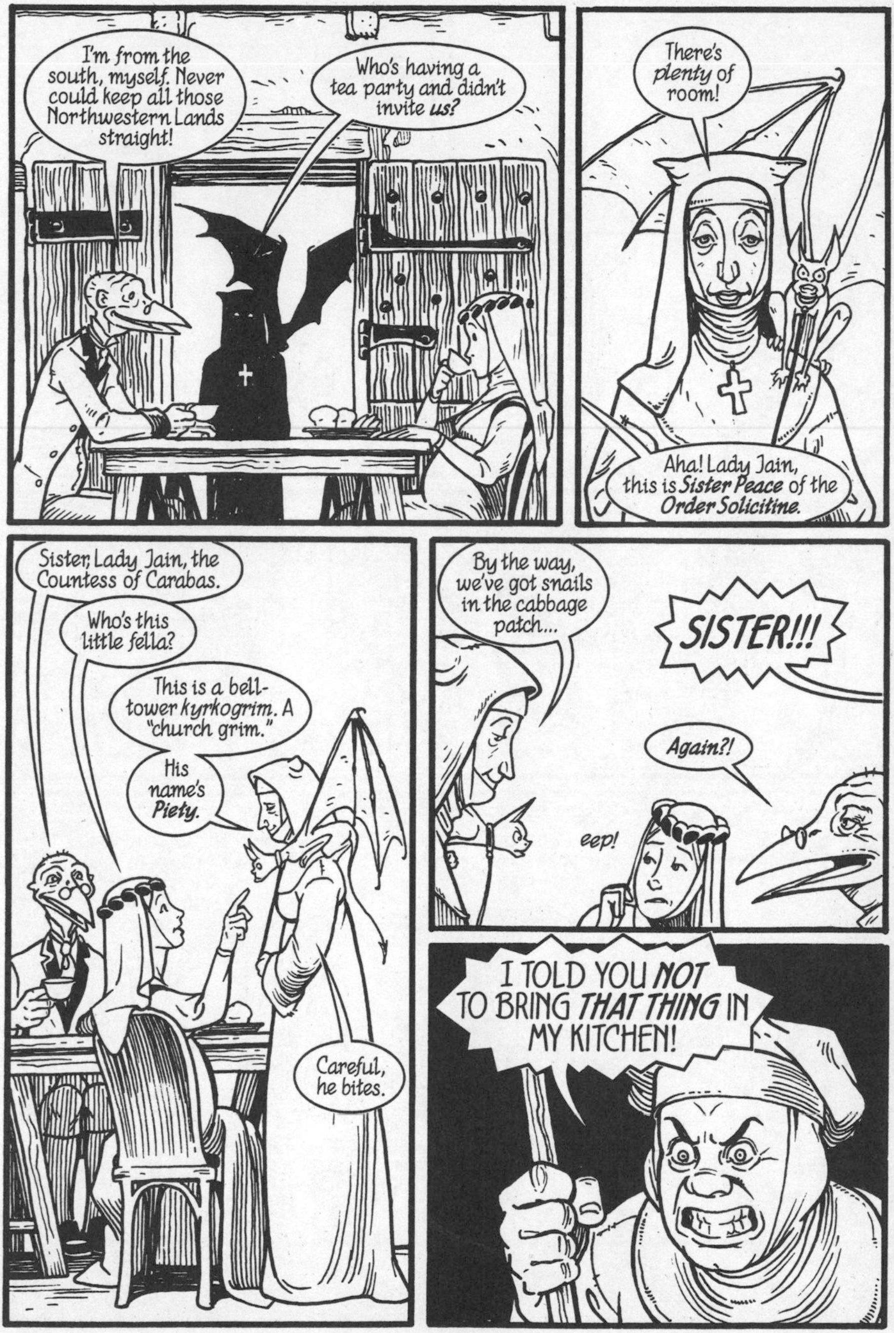
I'm from the south, myself. Never could keep all those Northwestern Lands straight!
Who's having a tea party and didn't invite *us?*
There's *plenty* of room!
Aha! Lady Jain, this is *Sister Peace* of the *Order Solicitine.*
Sister, Lady Jain, the Countess of Carabas.
Who's this little fella?
This is a bell-tower *kyrkogrim*. A "church grim."
His name's *Piety.*
Careful, he bites.
By the way, we've got snails in the cabbage patch...
SISTER!!!
Again?!
eep!
I TOLD YOU *NOT* TO BRING *THAT THING* IN MY KITCHEN!

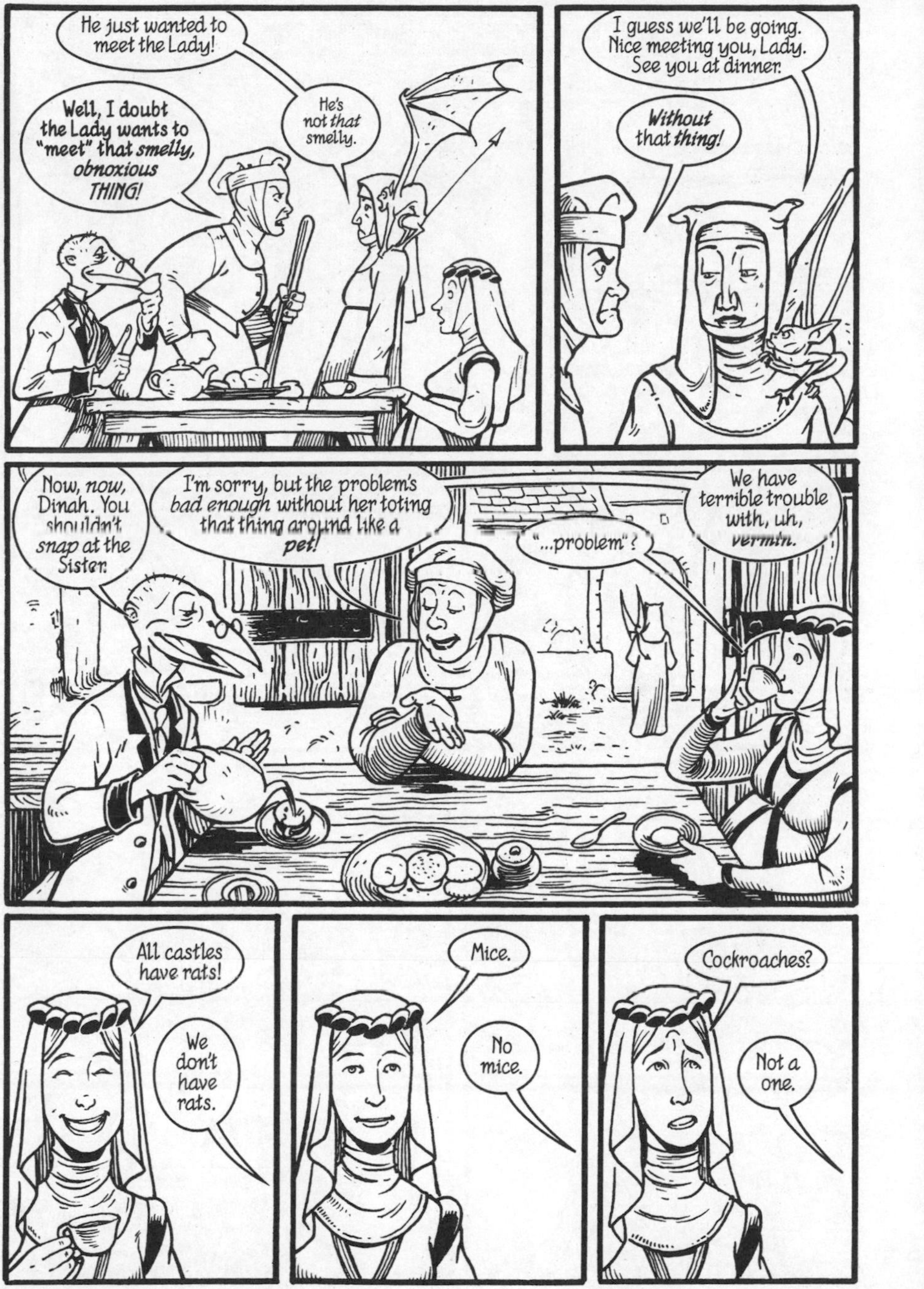
He just wanted to meet the Lady!
Well, I doubt the Lady wants to "meet" that smelly, obnoxious THING!
He's not that smelly.
I guess we'll be going. Nice meeting you, Lady. See you at dinner.
Without that thing!
Now, now, Dinah. You shouldn't snap at the Sister.
I'm sorry, but the problem's bad enough without her toting that thing around like a pet!
"...problem"?
We have terrible trouble with, uh, vermin.
All castles have rats!
We don't have rats.
Mice.
No mice.
Cockroaches?
Not a one.

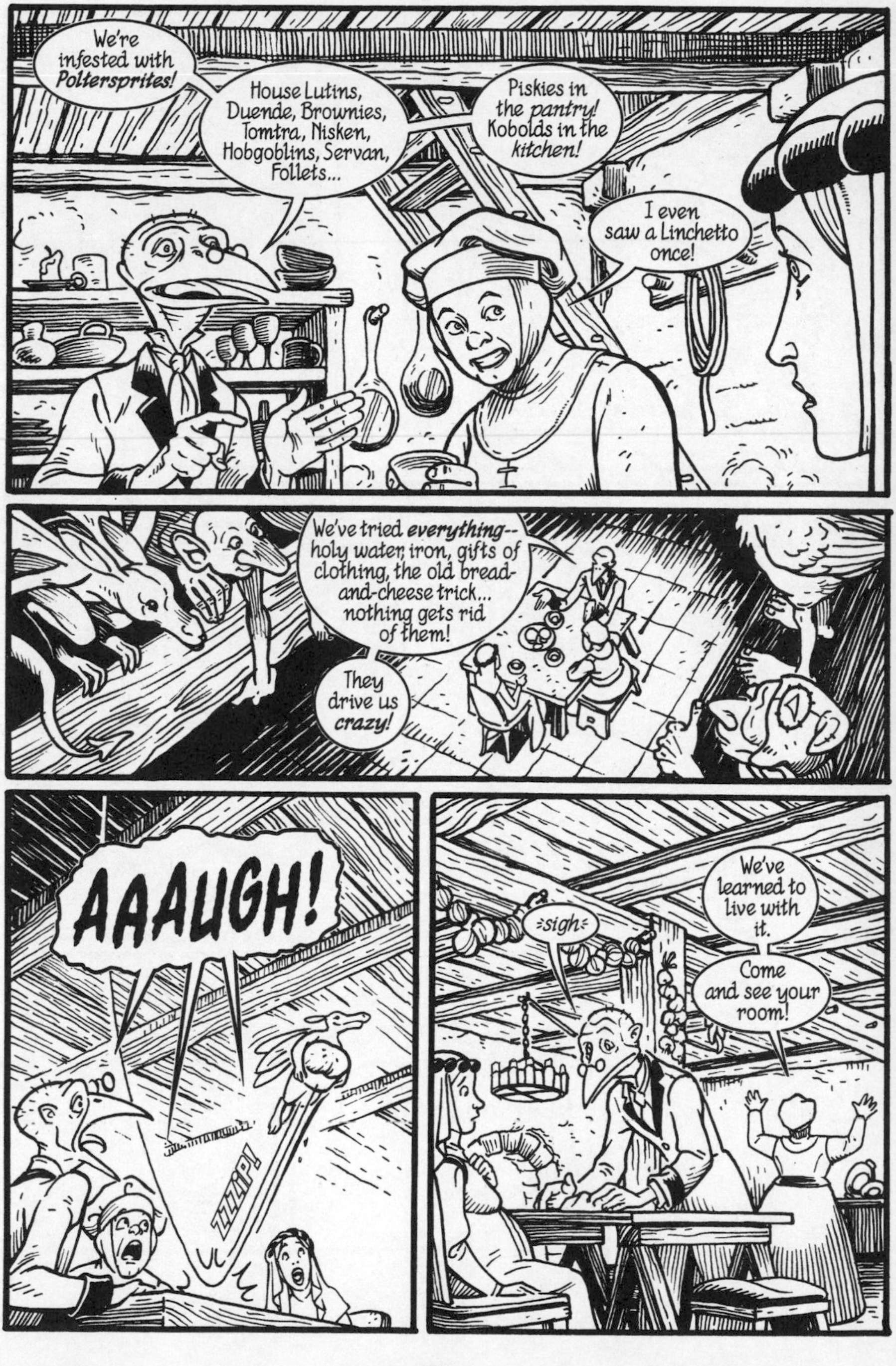
We're infested with *Poltersprites!*
House Lutins, Duende, Brownies, Tomtra, Nisken, Hobgoblins, Servan, Follets...
Piskies in the *pantry!* Kobolds in the *kitchen!*
I even saw a Linchetto once!
We've tried ***everything***-- holy water, iron, gifts of clothing, the old bread-and-cheese trick... nothing gets rid of them!
They drive us ***crazy!***
AAAUGH!
ZZZIP!
sigh
We've learned to live with it.
Come and see your room!

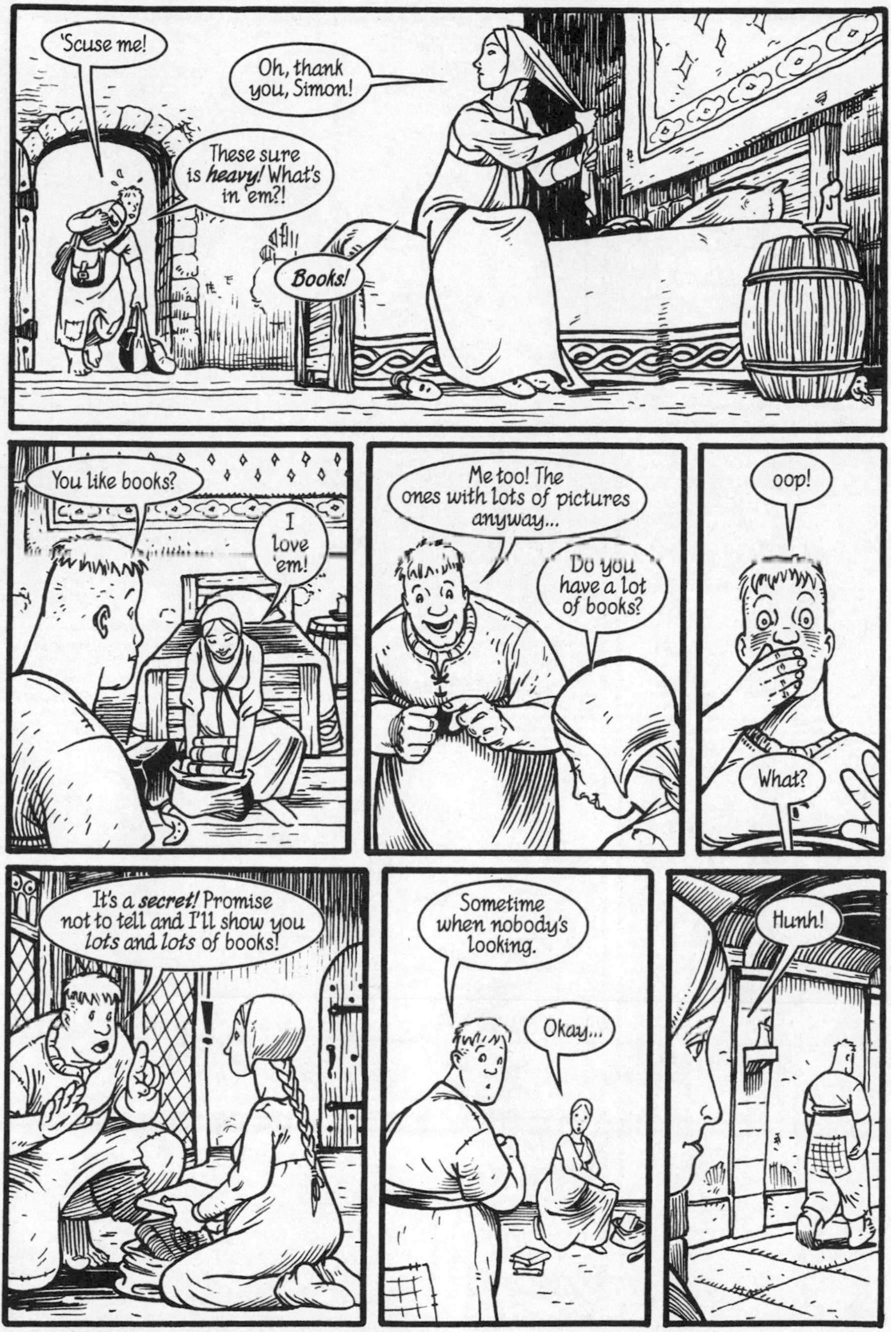

'Scuse me!
Oh, thank you, Simon!
These sure is *heavy!* What's in 'em?!
Books!
You like books?
I love 'em!
Me too! The ones with lots of pictures anyway...
Do you have a lot of books?
oop!
What?
It's a *secret!* Promise not to tell and I'll show you *lots and lots* of books!
Sometime when nobody's looking.
Okay...
Hunh!

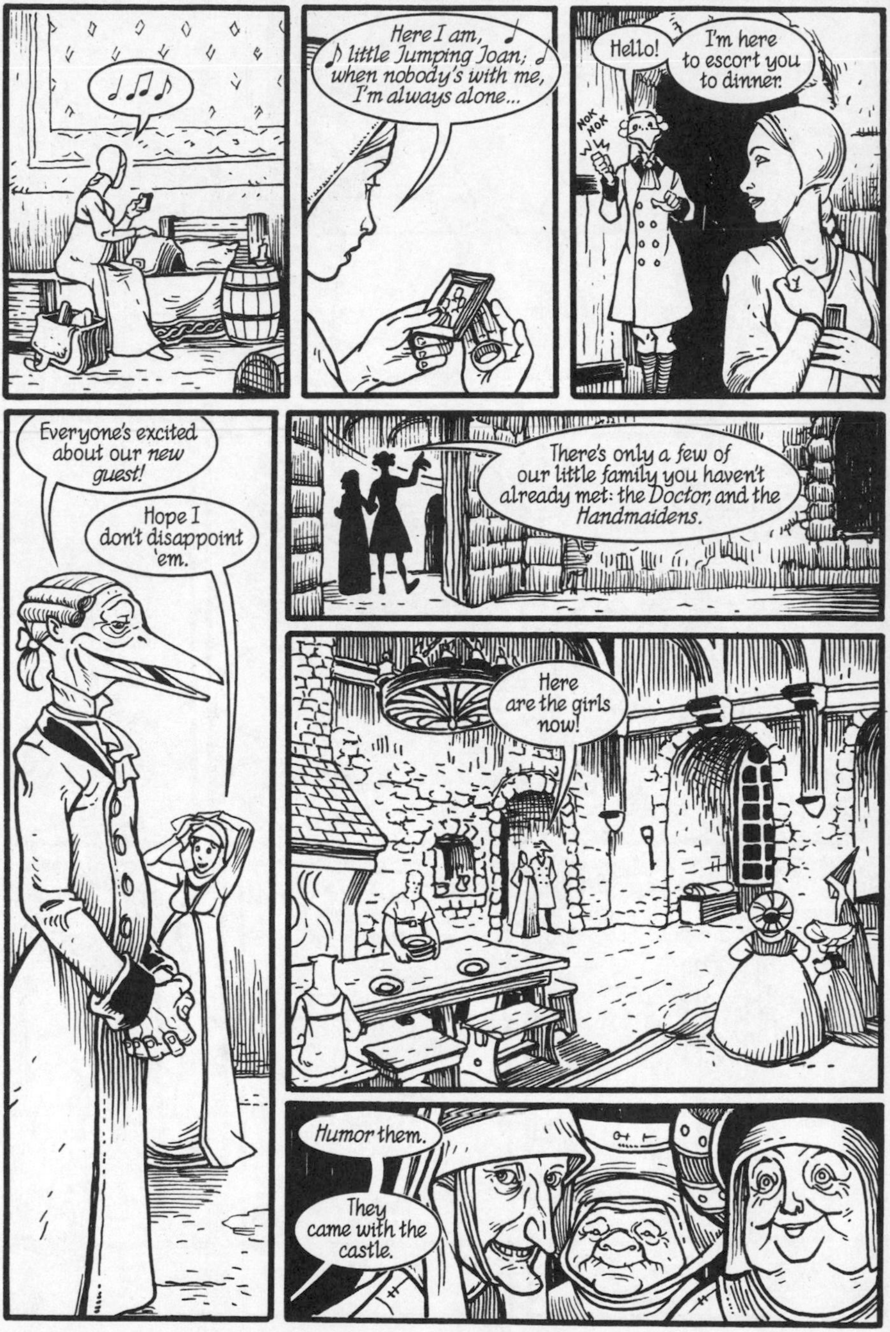
♩♫♪
Here I am, little Jumping Joan; when nobody's with me, I'm always alone...
NOK NOK
Hello!
I'm here to escort you to dinner.
Everyone's excited about our *new guest!*
Hope I don't disappoint 'em.
There's only a few of our little family you haven't already met: the *Doctor,* and the *Handmaidens.*
Here are the girls now!
Humor them.
They came with the castle.

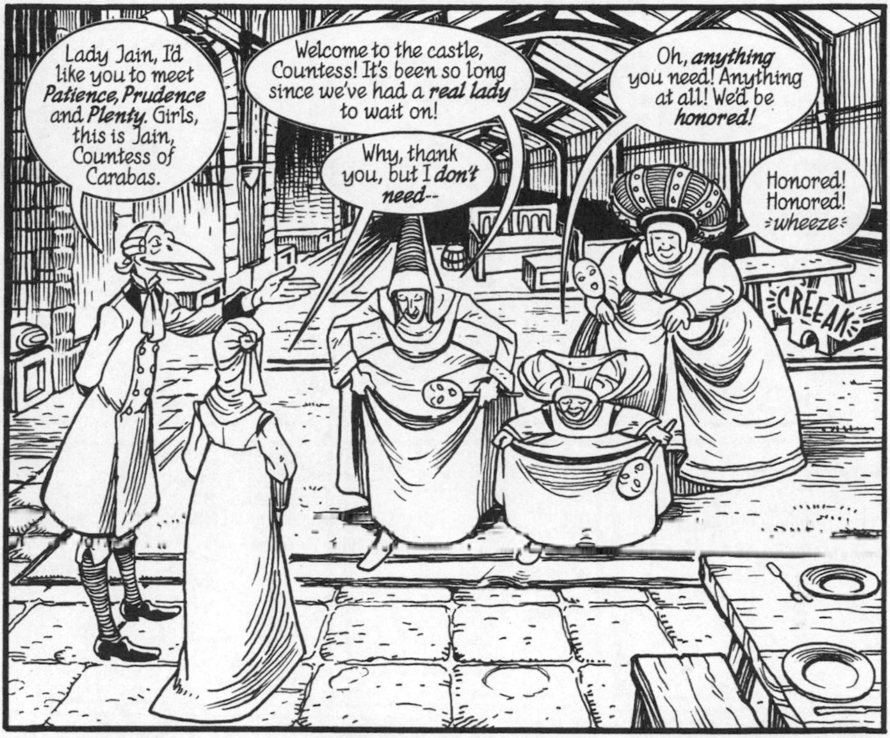
Lady Jain, I'd like you to meet **Patience, Prudence** and **Plenty**. Girls, this is Jain, Countess of Carabas.
Welcome to the castle, Countess! It's been so long since we've had a **real lady** to wait on!
Why, thank you, but I **don't need--**
Oh, **anything** you need! Anything at all! We'd be **honored!**
Honored! Honored! *wheeze*
CREEAK

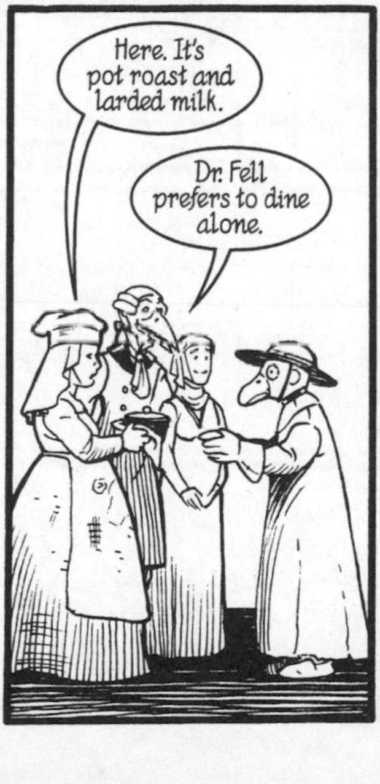
Here. It's pot roast and larded milk.
Dr. Fell prefers to dine alone.

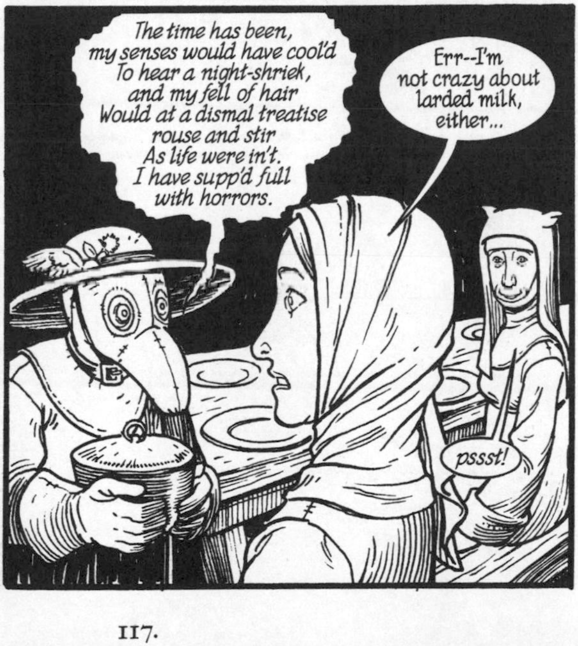
The time has been, my senses would have cool'd To hear a night-shriek, and my fell of hair Would at a dismal treatise rouse and stir As life were in't. I have supp'd full with horrors.
Err--I'm not crazy about larded milk, either...
pssst!

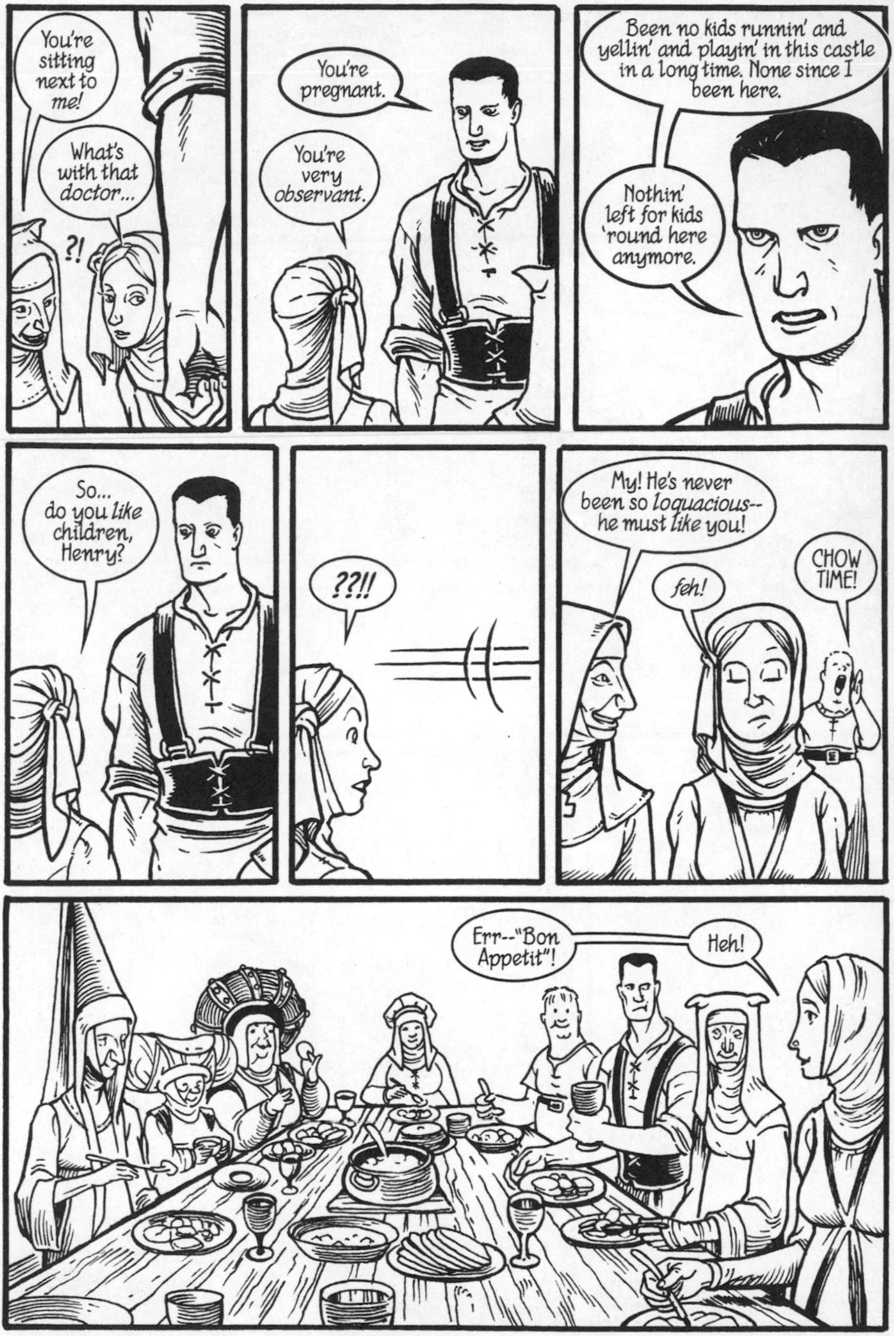
You're sitting next to me!
What's with that doctor...
?!
You're pregnant.
You're very observant.
Been no kids runnin' and yellin' and playin' in this castle in a long time. None since I been here.
Nothin' left for kids 'round here anymore.
So... do you like children, Henry?
??!!
My! He's never been so loquacious-- he must like you!
feh!
CHOW TIME!
Err--"Bon Appetit"!
Heh!

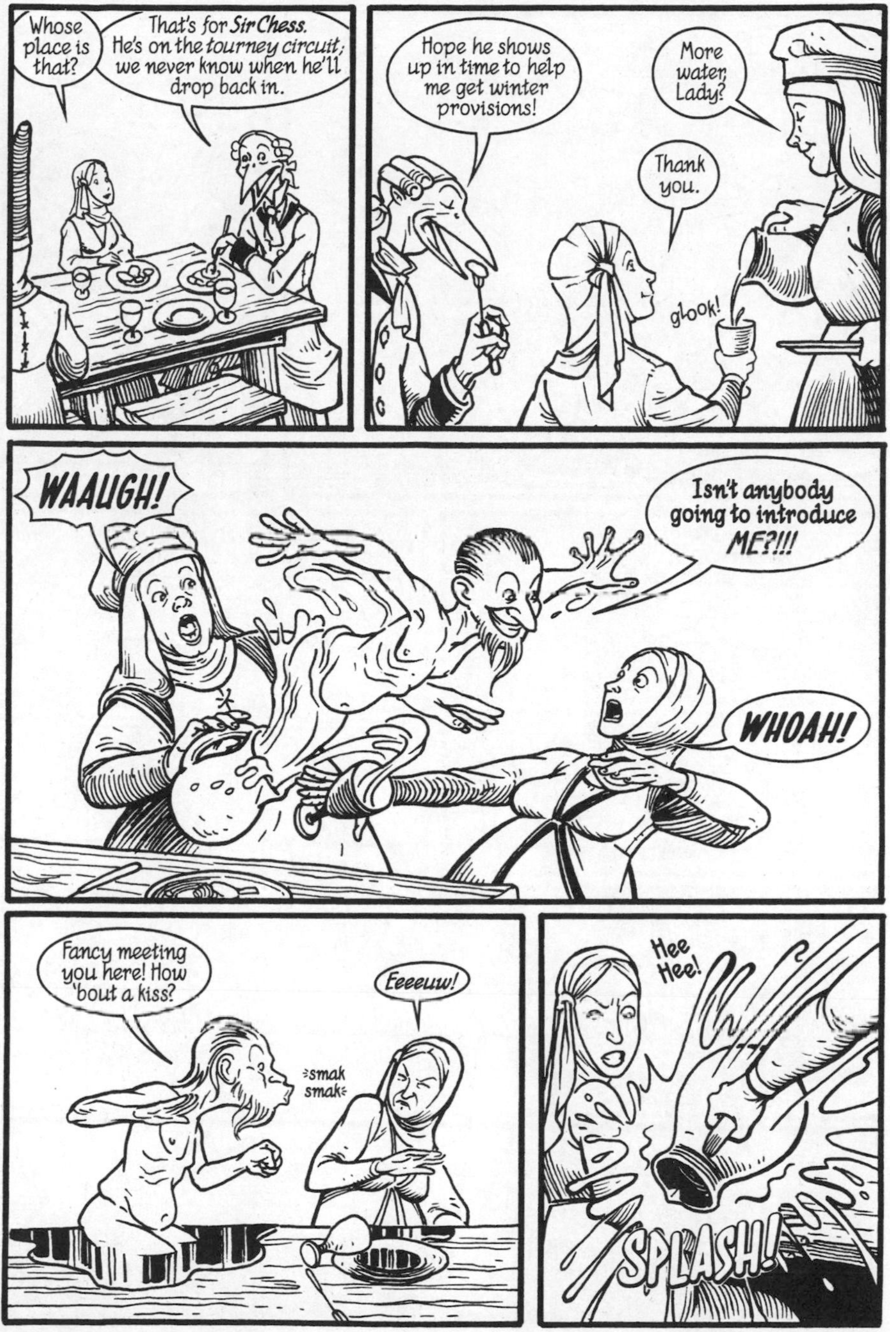
Whose place is that?
That's for Sir Chess. He's on the tourney circuit; we never know when he'll drop back in.
Hope he shows up in time to help me get winter provisions!
More water, Lady?
Thank you.
glook!
WAAUGH!
Isn't anybody going to introduce ME?!!!
WHOAH!
Fancy meeting you here! How 'bout a kiss?
Eeeeuw!
smak smak
Hee Hee!
SPLASH!

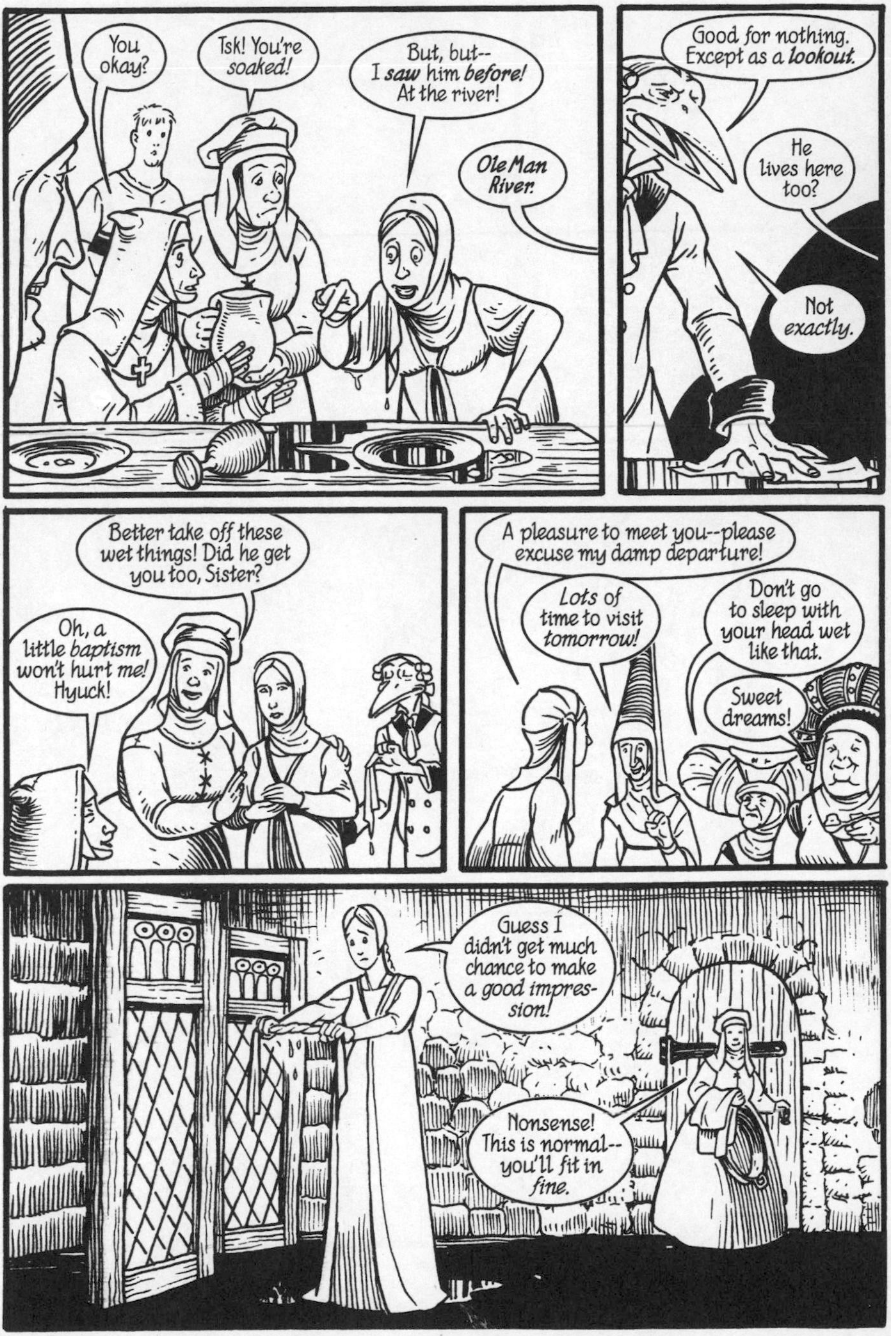
You okay?
Tsk! You're *soaked!*
But, but-- I *saw* him *before!* At the river!
Ole Man River.
Good for nothing. Except as a *lookout.*
He lives here too?
Not *exactly.*
Better take off these wet things! Did he get you too, Sister?
Oh, a little *baptism* won't hurt me! Hyuck!
A pleasure to meet you--please excuse my damp departure!
Lots of time to visit *tomorrow!*
Don't go to sleep with your head wet like that.
Sweet dreams!
Guess I didn't get much chance to make a *good impression!*
Nonsense! This is normal-- you'll *fit* in *fine.*

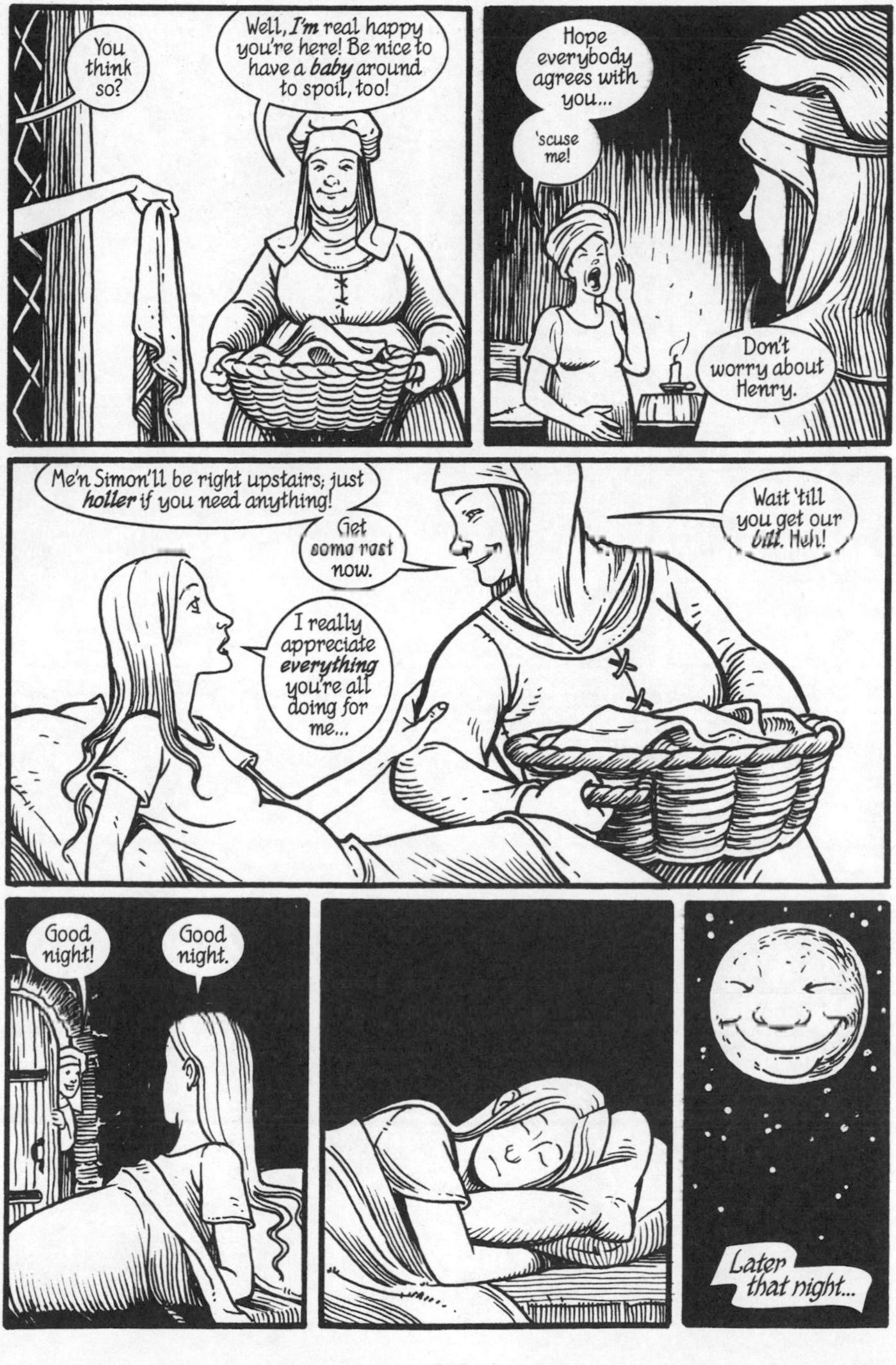

You think so?
Well, *I'm* real happy you're here! Be nice to have a ***baby*** around to spoil, too!
Hope everybody agrees with you...
'scuse me!
Don't worry about Henry.
Me'n Simon'll be right upstairs; just ***holler*** if you need anything!
Get some rest now.
Wait 'till you get our ***bill***. Heh!
I really appreciate ***everything*** you're all doing for me...
Good night!
Good night.
Later that night...

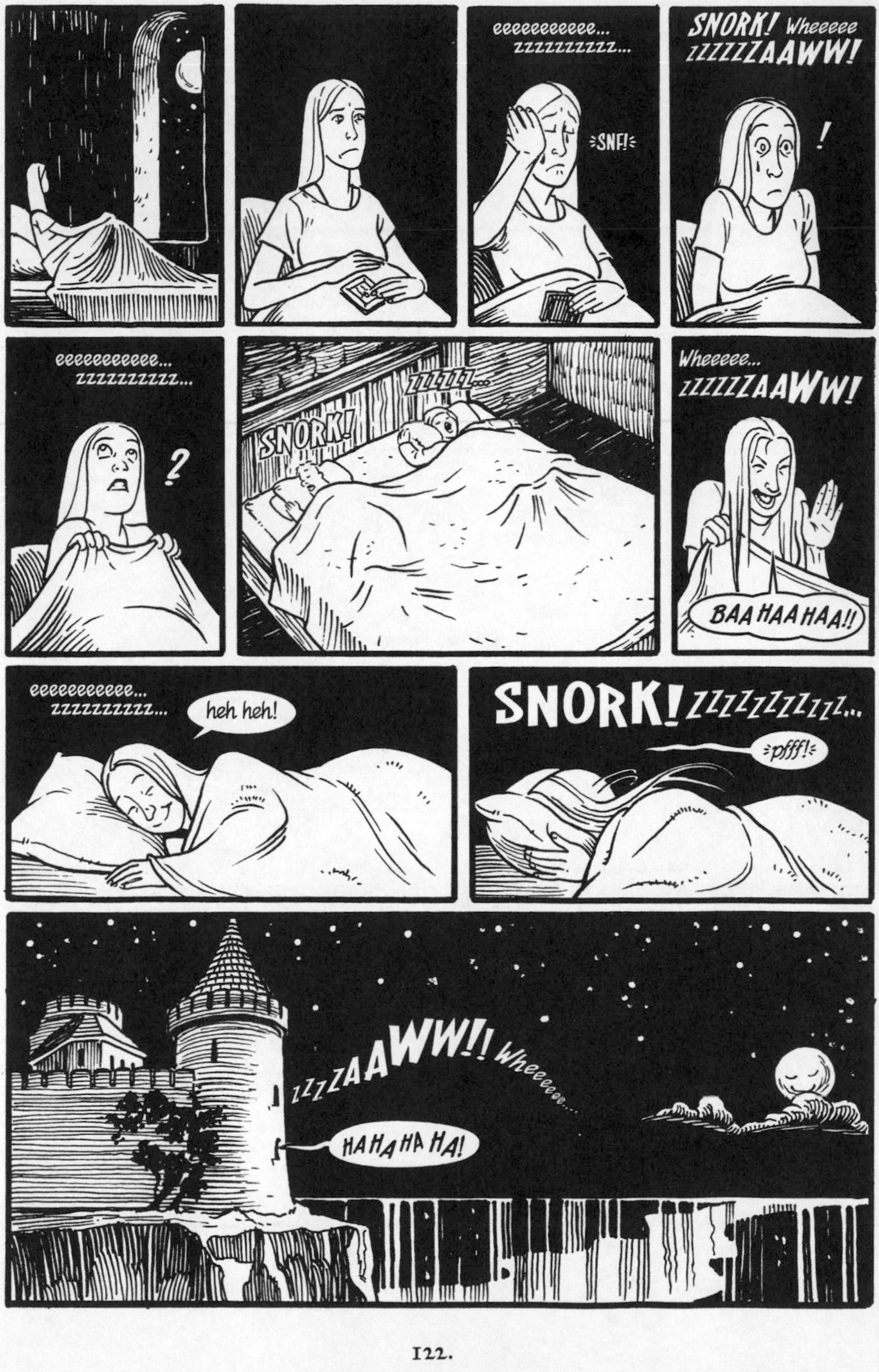
eeeeeeeeeee...
zzzzzzzzzz...
SNF!
SNORK! Wheeeee
zzzzzZAAWW!
!
eeeeeeeeeee...
zzzzzzzzzz...
?
ZZZZZZ...
SNORK!
Wheeeee...
zzzzzZAAWW!
BAA HAA HAA!!
eeeeeeeeeee...
zzzzzzzzzz...
heh heh!
SNORK! ZZZZZZZZZZZ...
pfff!
zzzzZAAWW!! Wheeeeee...
HA HA HA HA!

Chapter 6.

· LABORS OF LOVE ·

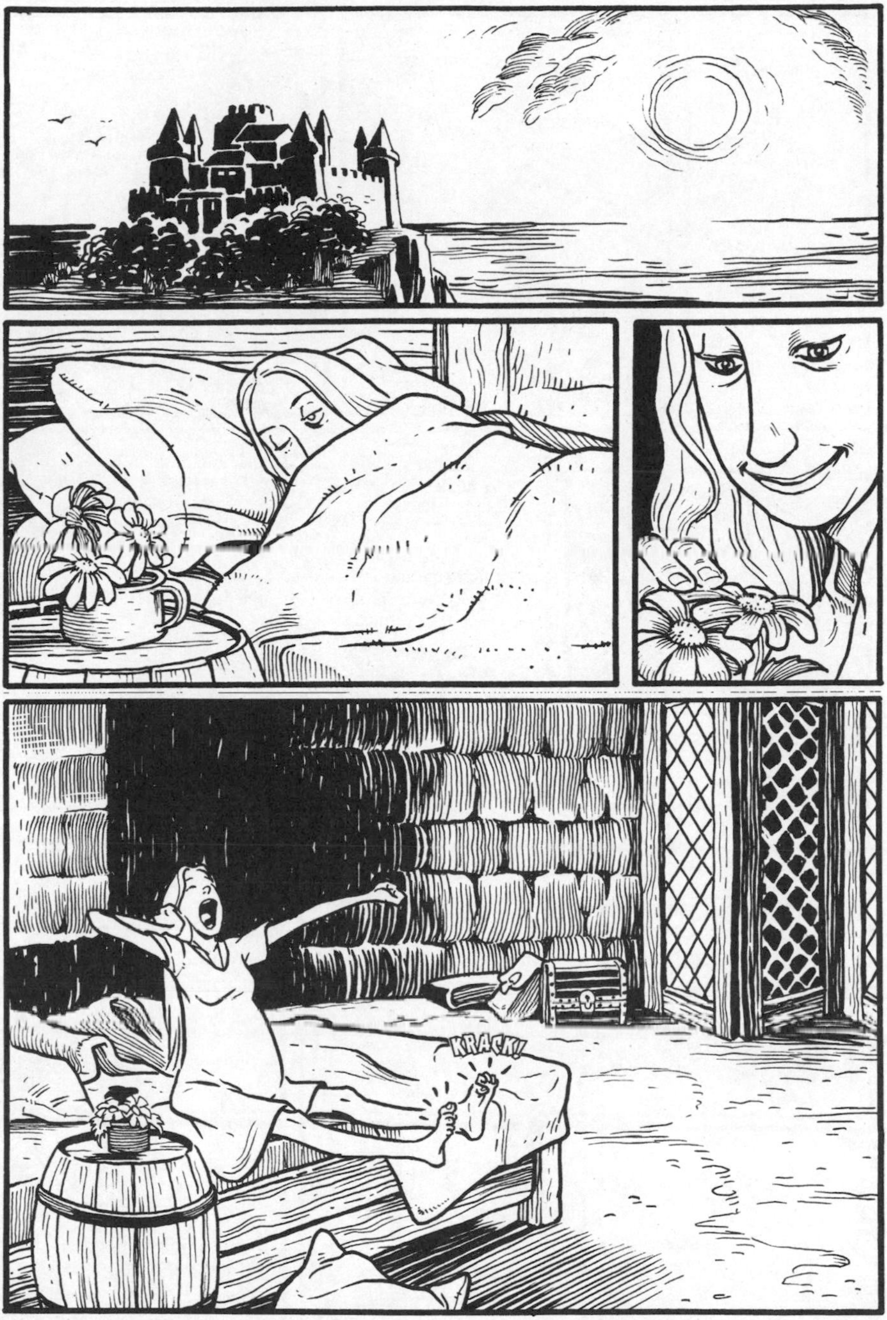
KRACK!

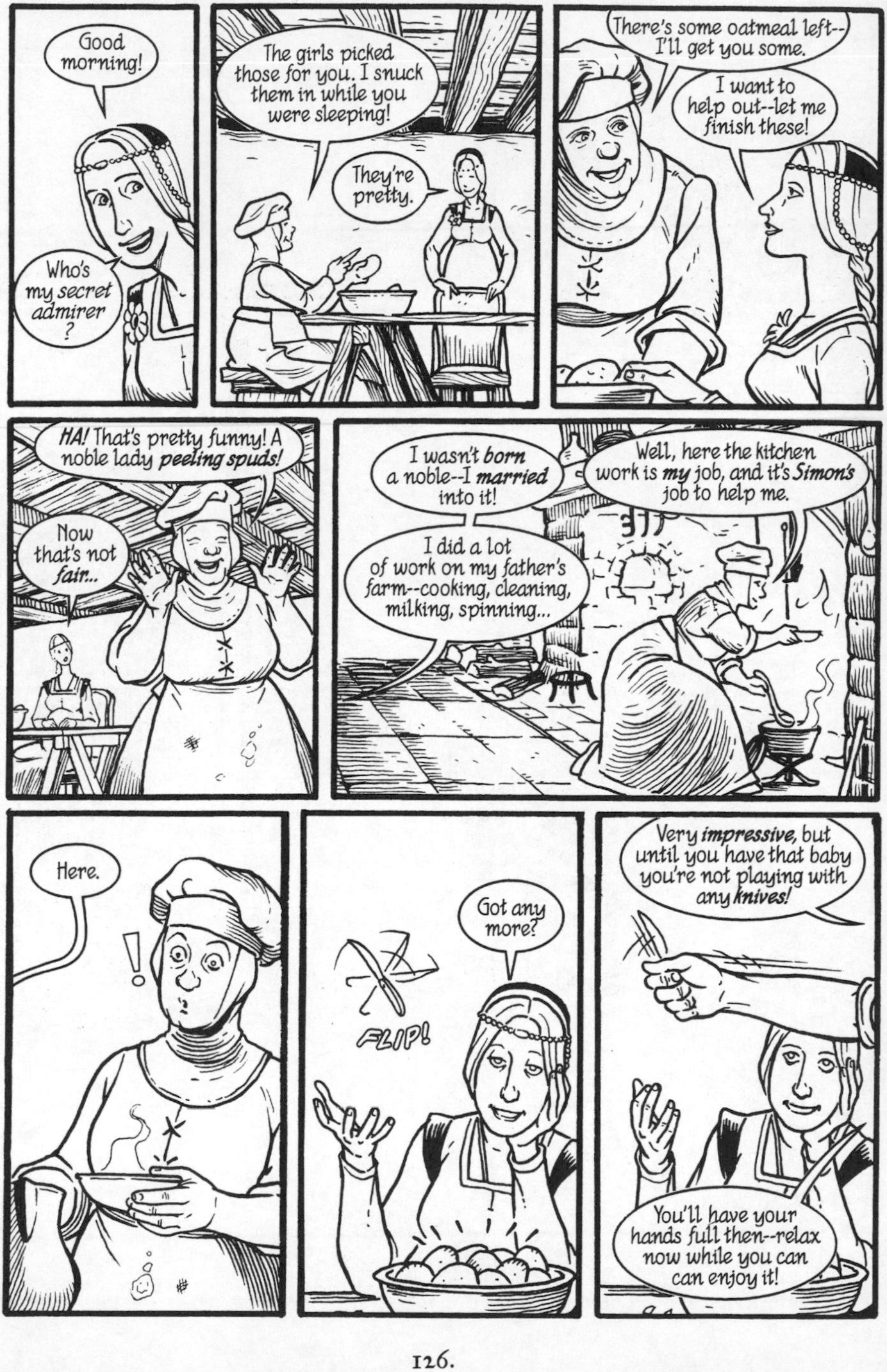
Good morning!
Who's my *secret admirer* ?
The girls picked those for you. I snuck them in while you were sleeping!
They're pretty.
There's some oatmeal left-- I'll get you some.
I want to help out--let me finish these!
HA! That's pretty funny! A noble lady *peeling spuds!*
Now that's not *fair...*
I wasn't *born* a noble--I *married* into it!
I did a lot of work on my father's farm--cooking, cleaning, milking, spinning...
Well, here the kitchen work is *my* job, and it's *Simon's* job to help me.
Here.
!
FLIP!
Got any more?
Very *impressive,* but until you have that baby you're not playing with any *knives!*
You'll have your hands full then--relax now while you can can enjoy it!

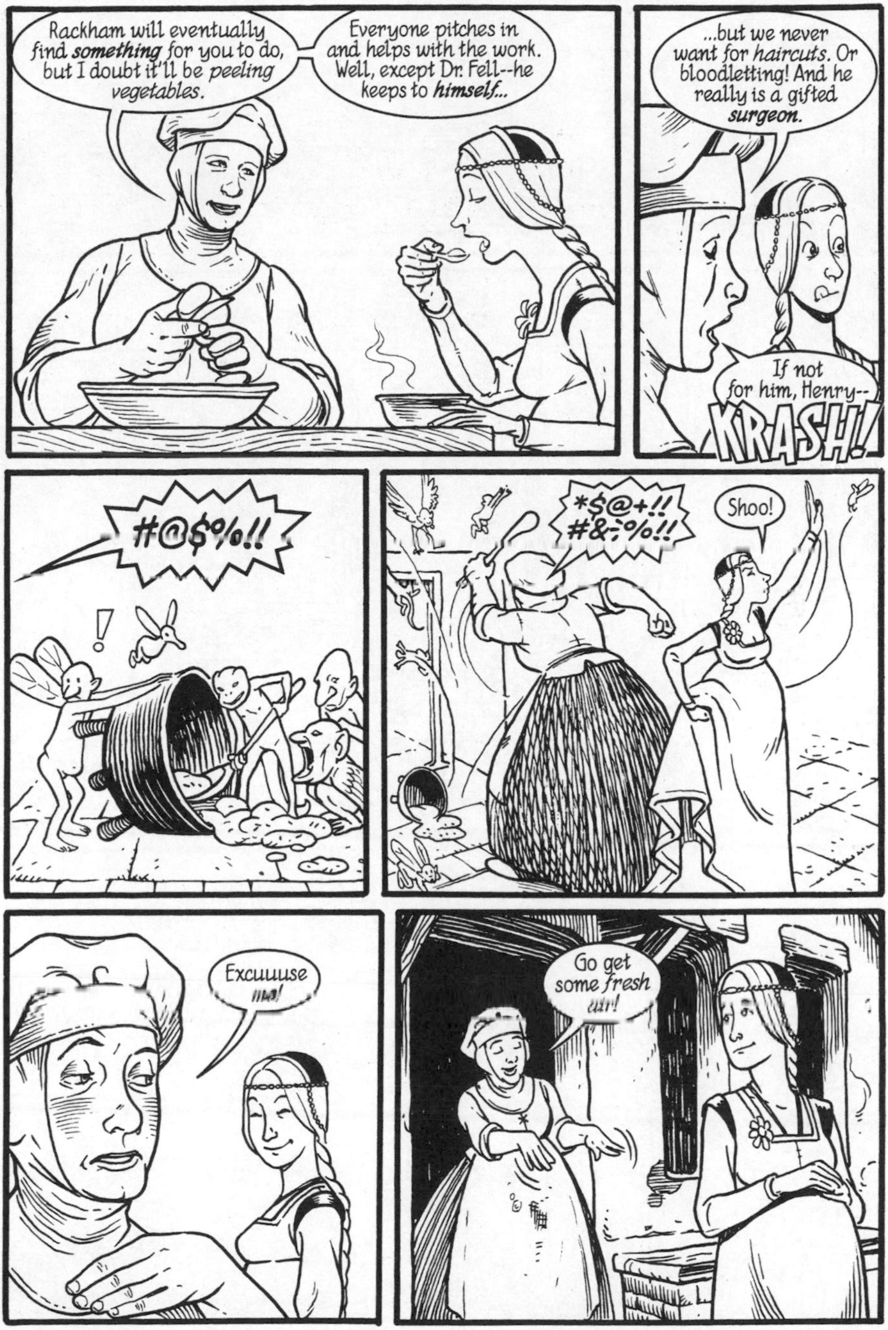
Rackham will eventually find something for you to do, but I doubt it'll be peeling vegetables.
Everyone pitches in and helps with the work. Well, except Dr. Fell--he keeps to himself...
...but we never want for haircuts. Or bloodletting! And he really is a gifted surgeon.
If not for him, Henry--
KRASH!
#@$%!!
!
*$@+!! #&;%!!
Shoo!
Excuuuse
Go get some fresh

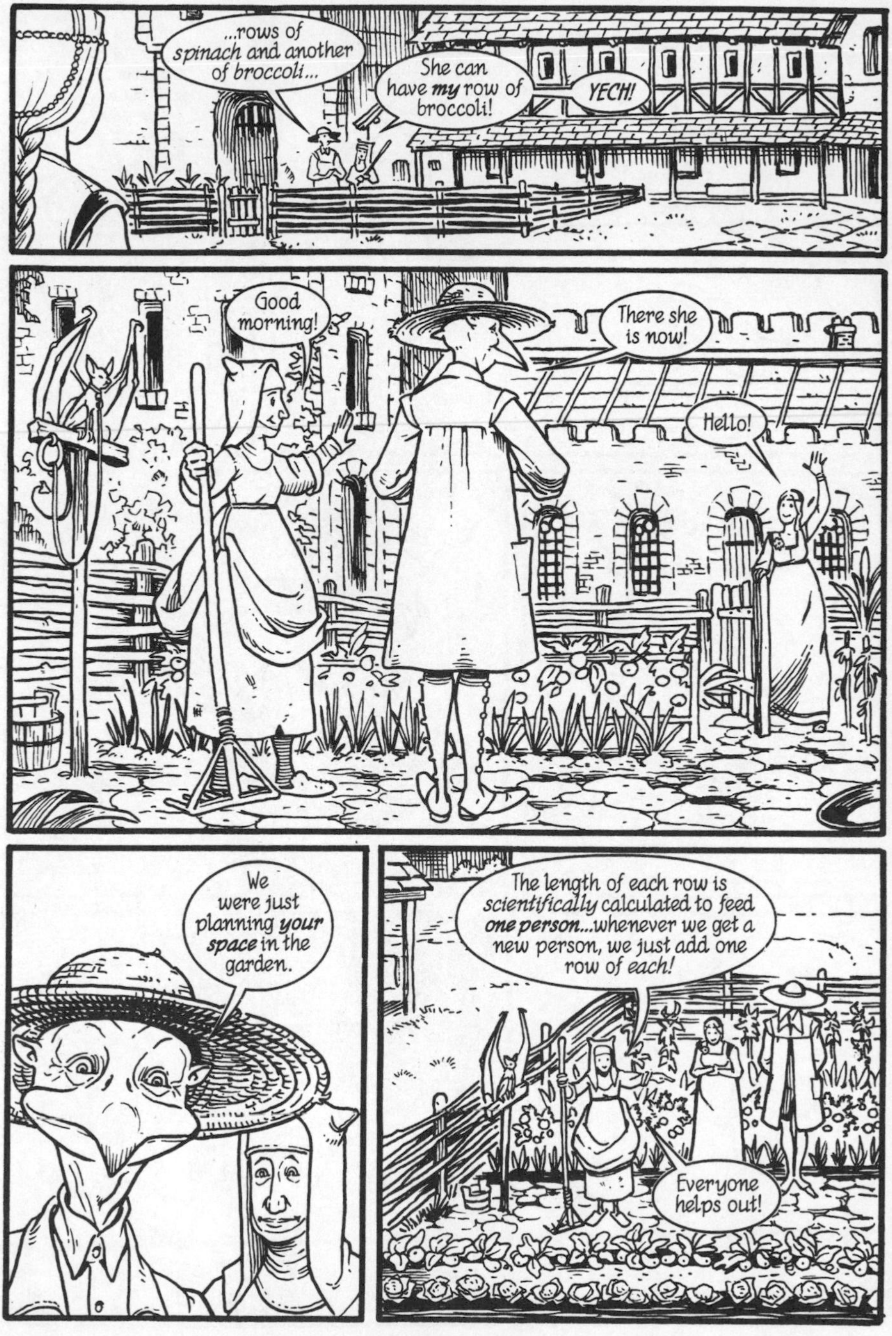
...rows of *spinach* and another of *broccoli*...
She can have ***my*** row of broccoli!
YECH!
Good morning!
There she is now!
Hello!
We were just planning ***your space*** in the garden.
The length of each row is *scientifically* calculated to feed ***one person***...whenever we get a new person, we just add one row of *each!*
Everyone helps out!

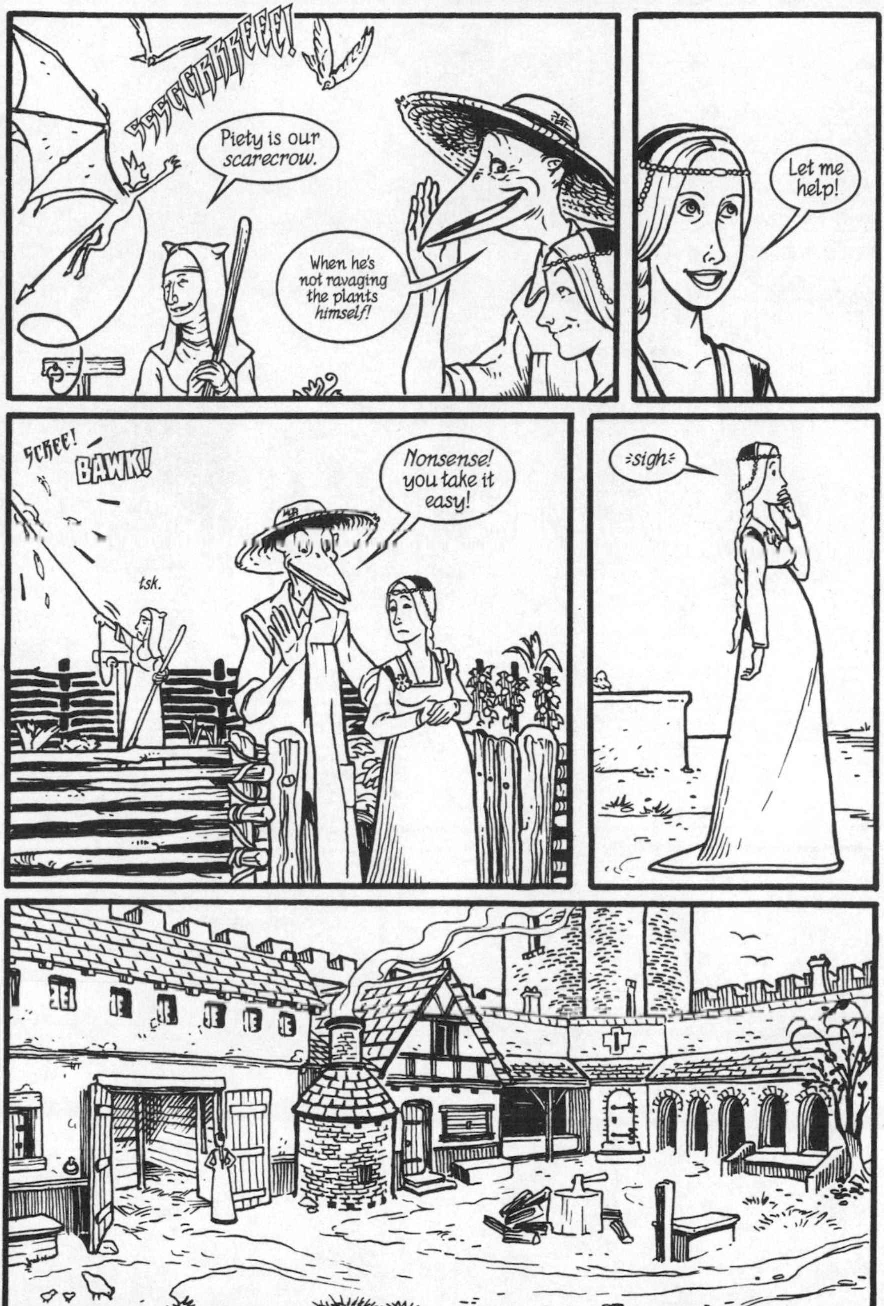
SSSGRKREEE!
Piety is our scarecrow.
When he's not ravaging the plants himself!
Let me help!
SCREE!
BAWK!
Nonsense! you take it easy!
tsk.
sigh

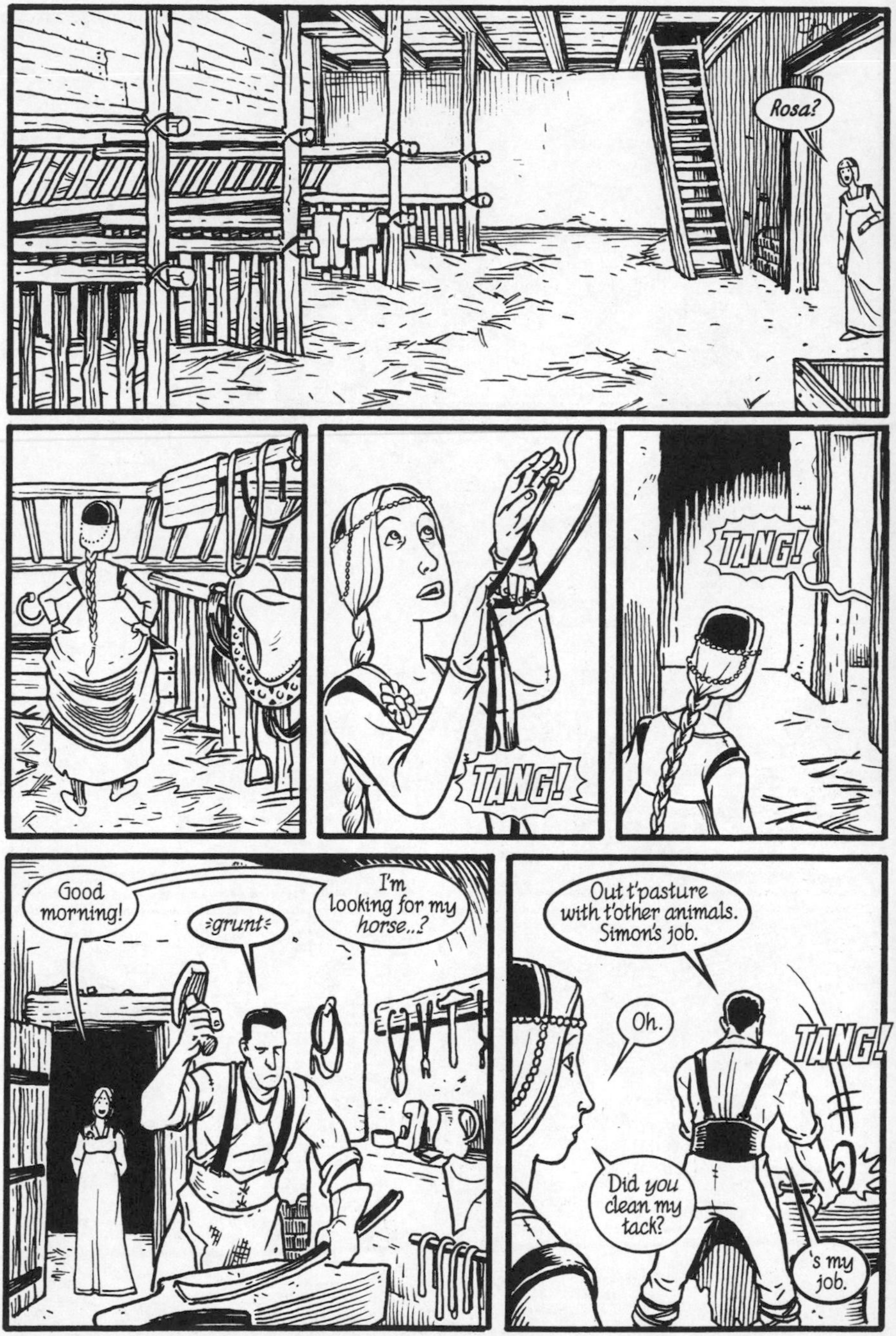
Rosa?
TANG!
TANG!
Good morning!
I'm looking for my horse...?
grunt
Out t'pasture with t'other animals. Simon's job.
Oh.
TANG!
Did *you* clean my tack?
's my job.

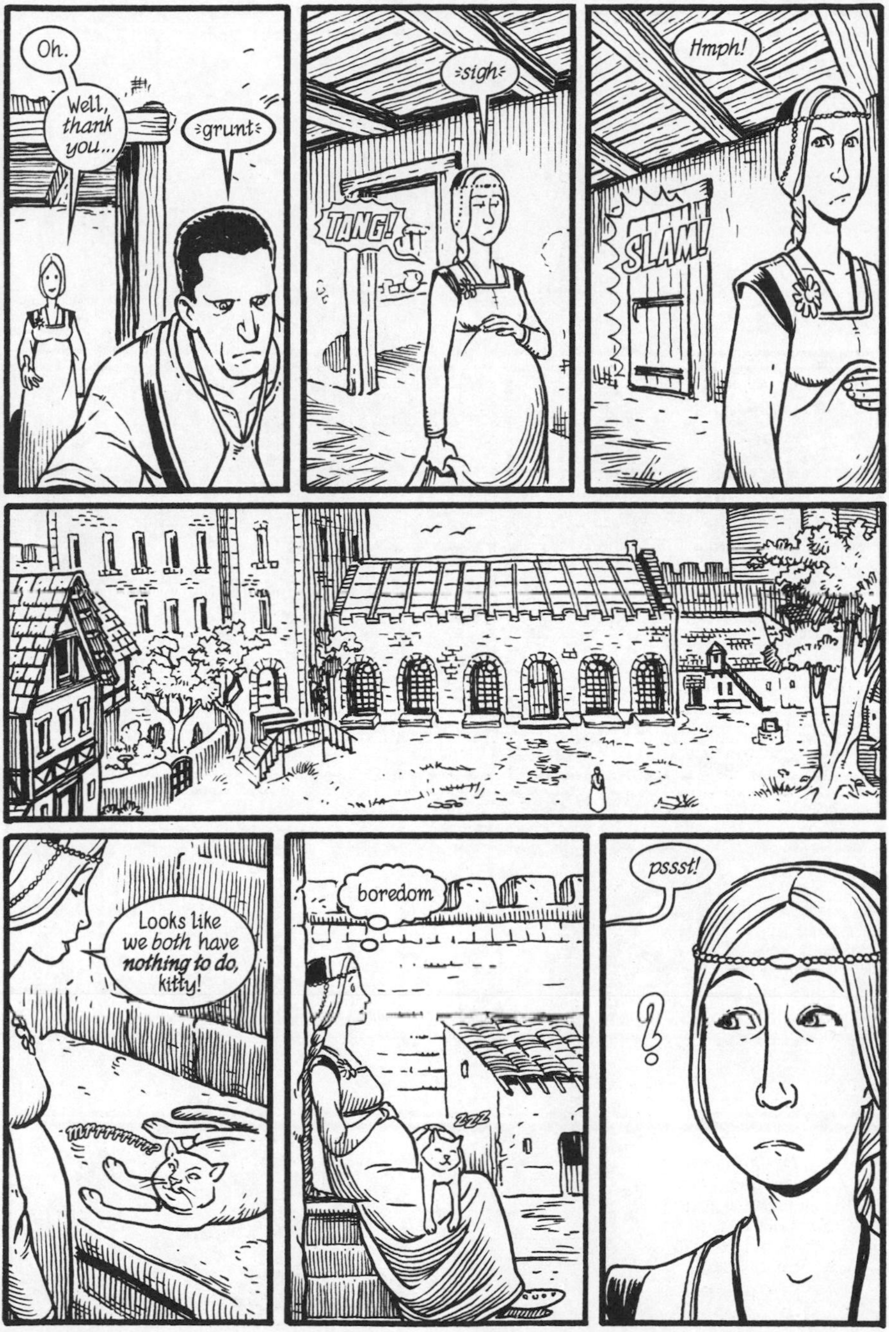
Oh.
Well, thank you...
grunt
TANG!
sigh
SLAM!
Hmph!
Looks like we both have *nothing to do,* kitty!
mrrrrrrrr?
boredom
zzz
pssst!
?

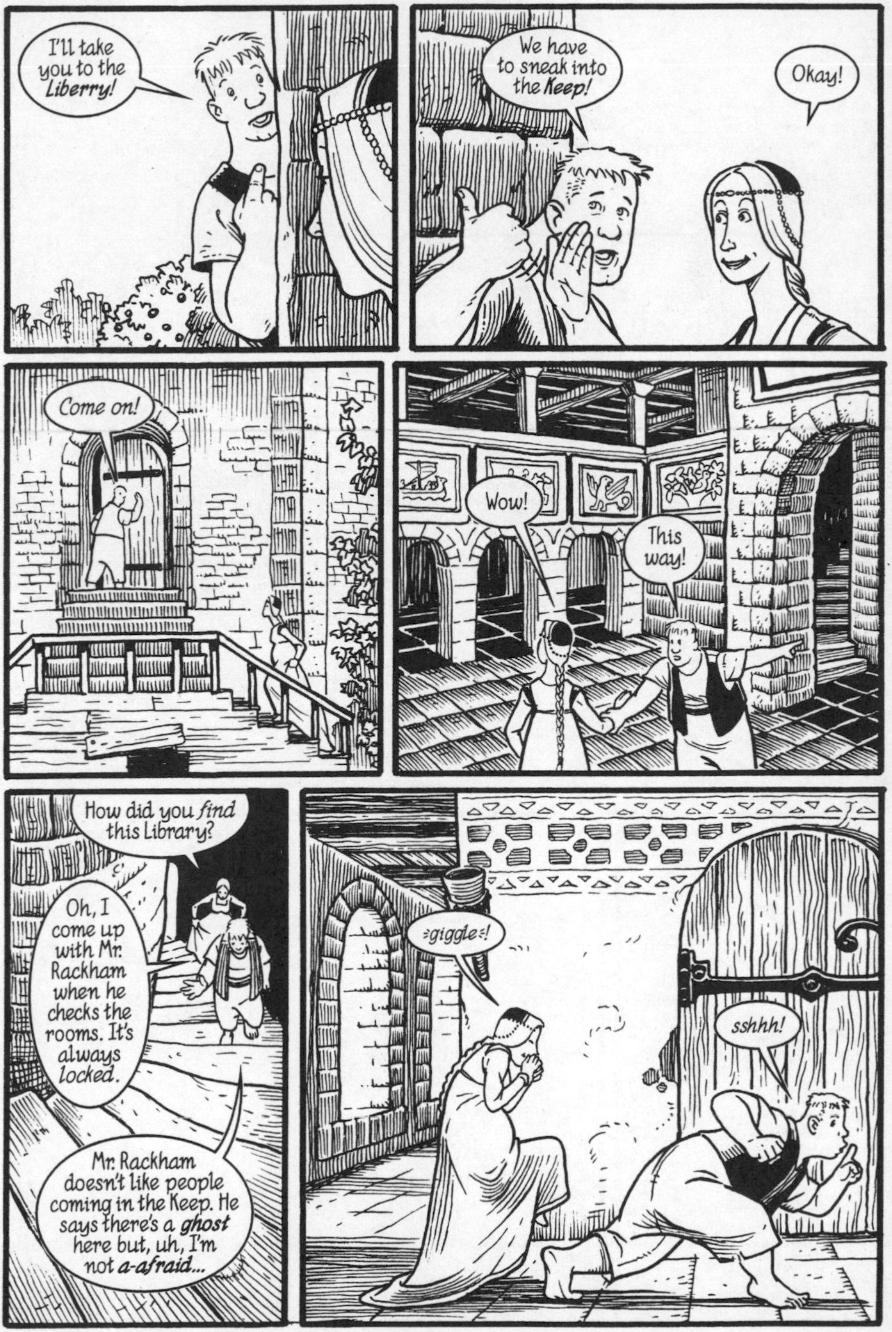
I'll take you to the *Liberry!*
We have to sneak into the *Keep!*
Okay!
Come on!
Wow!
This way!
How did you *find* this Library?
Oh, I come up with Mr. Rackham when he checks the rooms. It's always *locked.*
Mr. Rackham doesn't like people coming in the Keep. He says there's a ***ghost*** here but, uh, I'm not ***a-afraid...***
giggle!
sshhh!

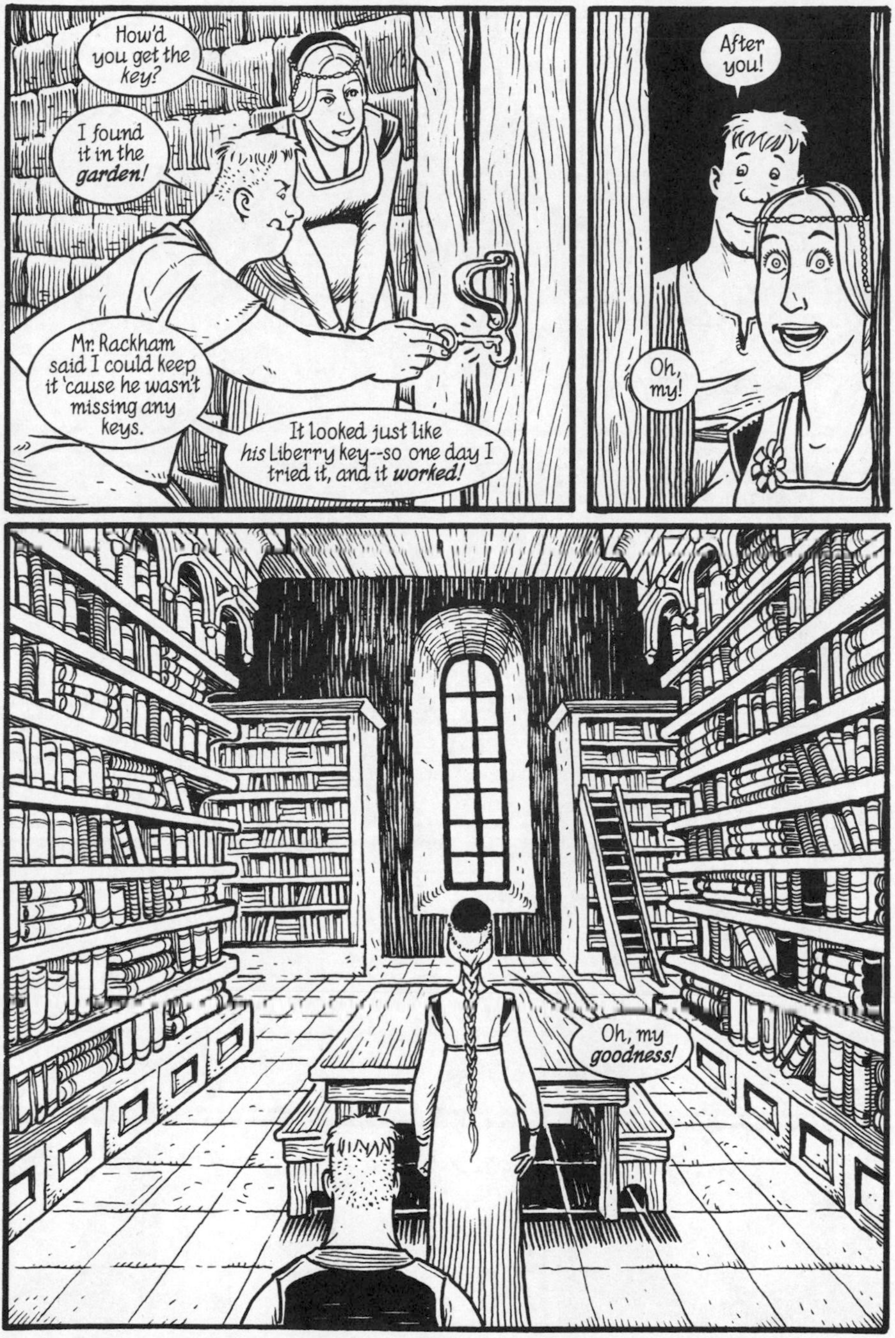
How'd you get the key?
I found it in the *garden!*
Mr. Rackham said I could keep it 'cause he wasn't missing any keys.
It looked just like *his* Liberry key--so one day I tried it, and it *worked!*
After you!
Oh, my!
Oh, my *goodness!*

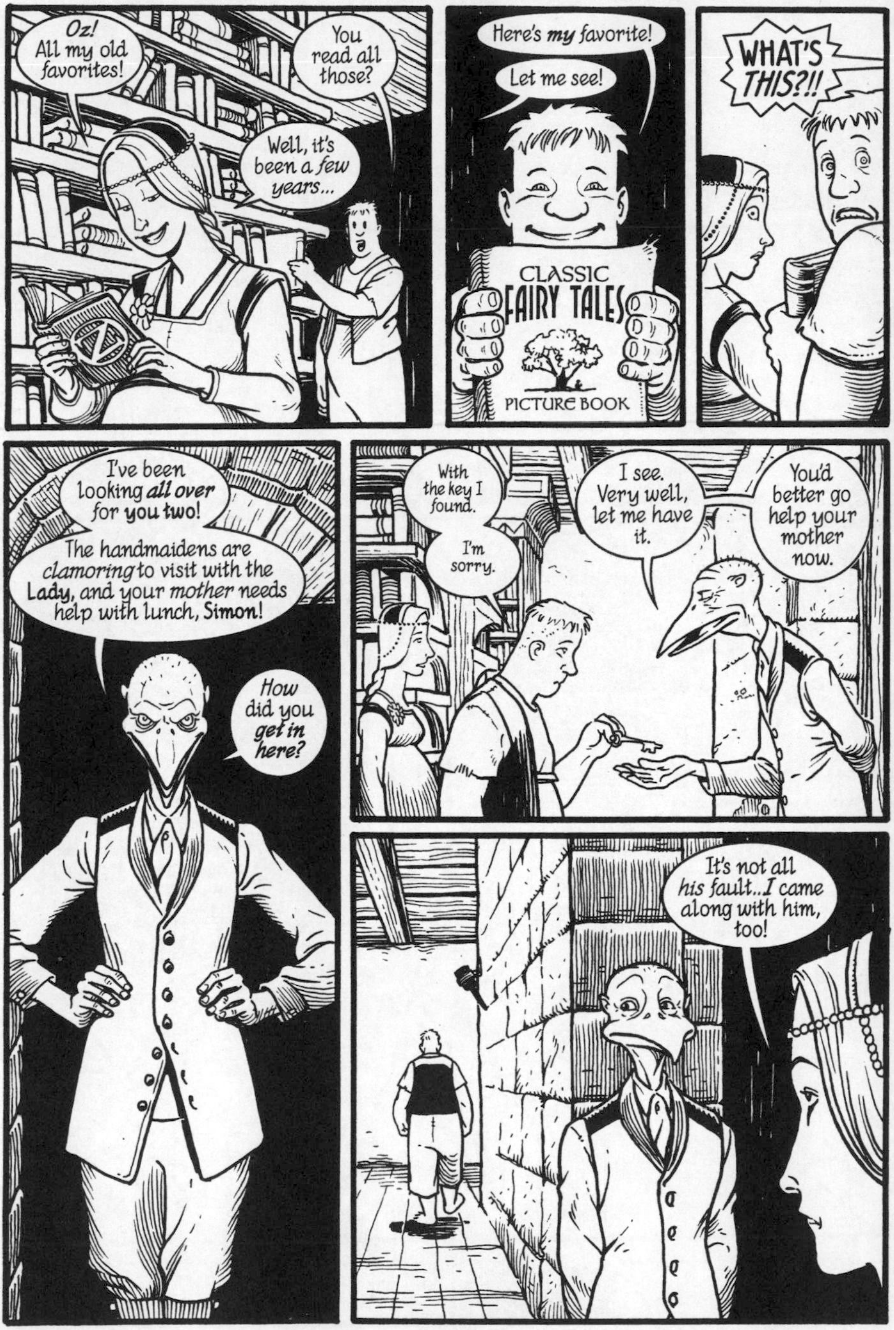

Oz! All my old favorites!
You read all those?
Well, it's been a few years...
Here's my favorite!
Let me see!
CLASSIC FAIRY TALES
PICTURE BOOK
WHAT'S THIS?!!
I've been looking all over for you two!
The handmaidens are clamoring to visit with the Lady, and your mother needs help with lunch, Simon!
How did you get in here?
With the key I found.
I'm sorry.
I see. Very well, let me have it.
You'd better go help your mother now.
It's not all his fault...I came along with him, too!

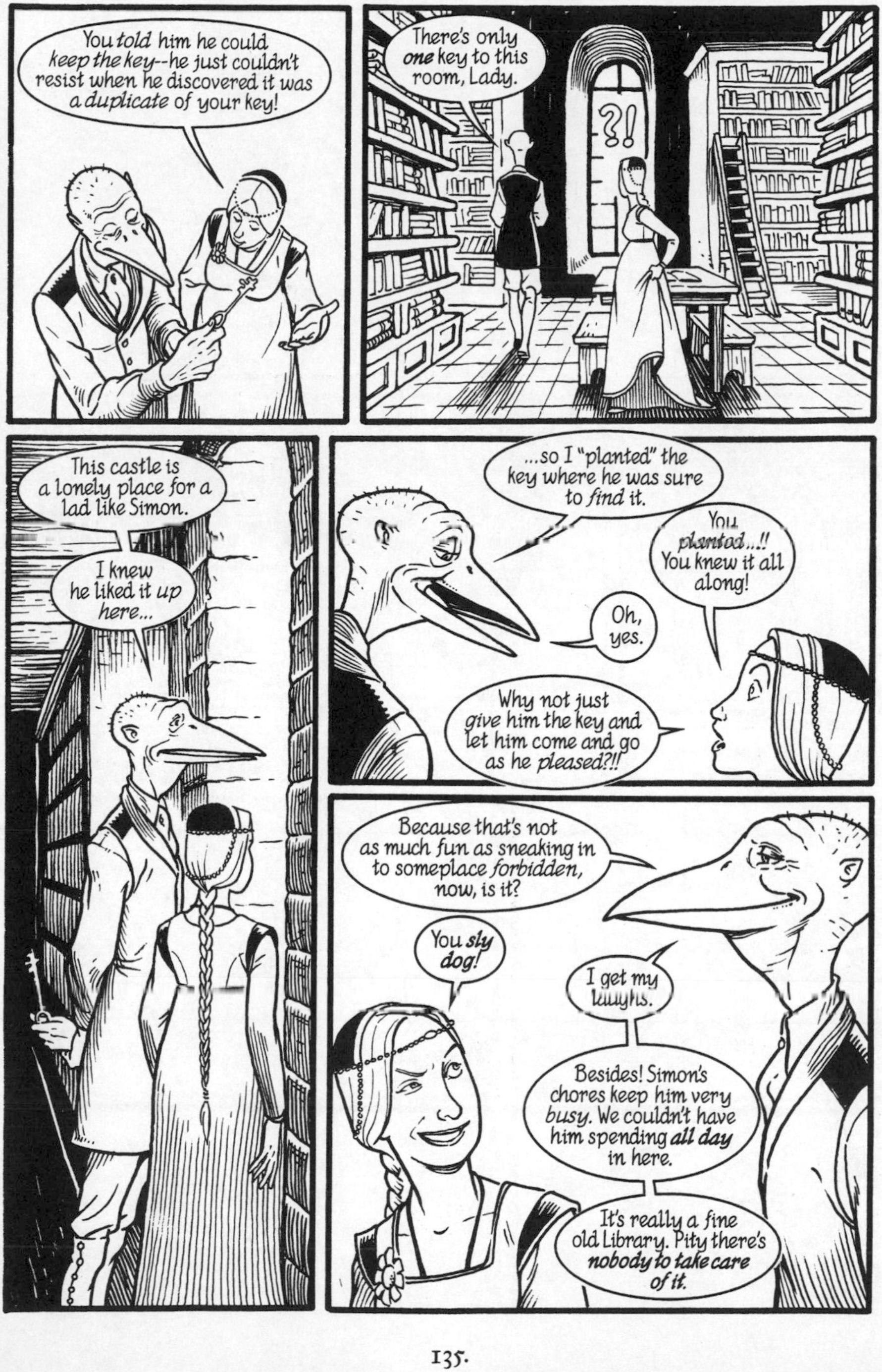
You *told* him he could *keep the key*--he just couldn't resist when he discovered it was a *duplicate* of your key!
There's only **one** key to this room, Lady.
?!
This castle is a lonely place for a lad like Simon.
I knew he liked it *up here*...
...so I "planted" the key where he was sure to *find* it.
You *planted*...!! You knew it all along!
Oh, yes.
Why not just *give* him the key and let him come and go as he *pleased*?!!
Because that's not as much fun as sneaking in to someplace *forbidden*, now, is it?
You ***sly dog!***
I get my laughs.
Besides! Simon's chores keep him very *busy*. We couldn't have him spending ***all day*** in here.
It's really a fine old Library. Pity there's ***nobody to take care of it.***

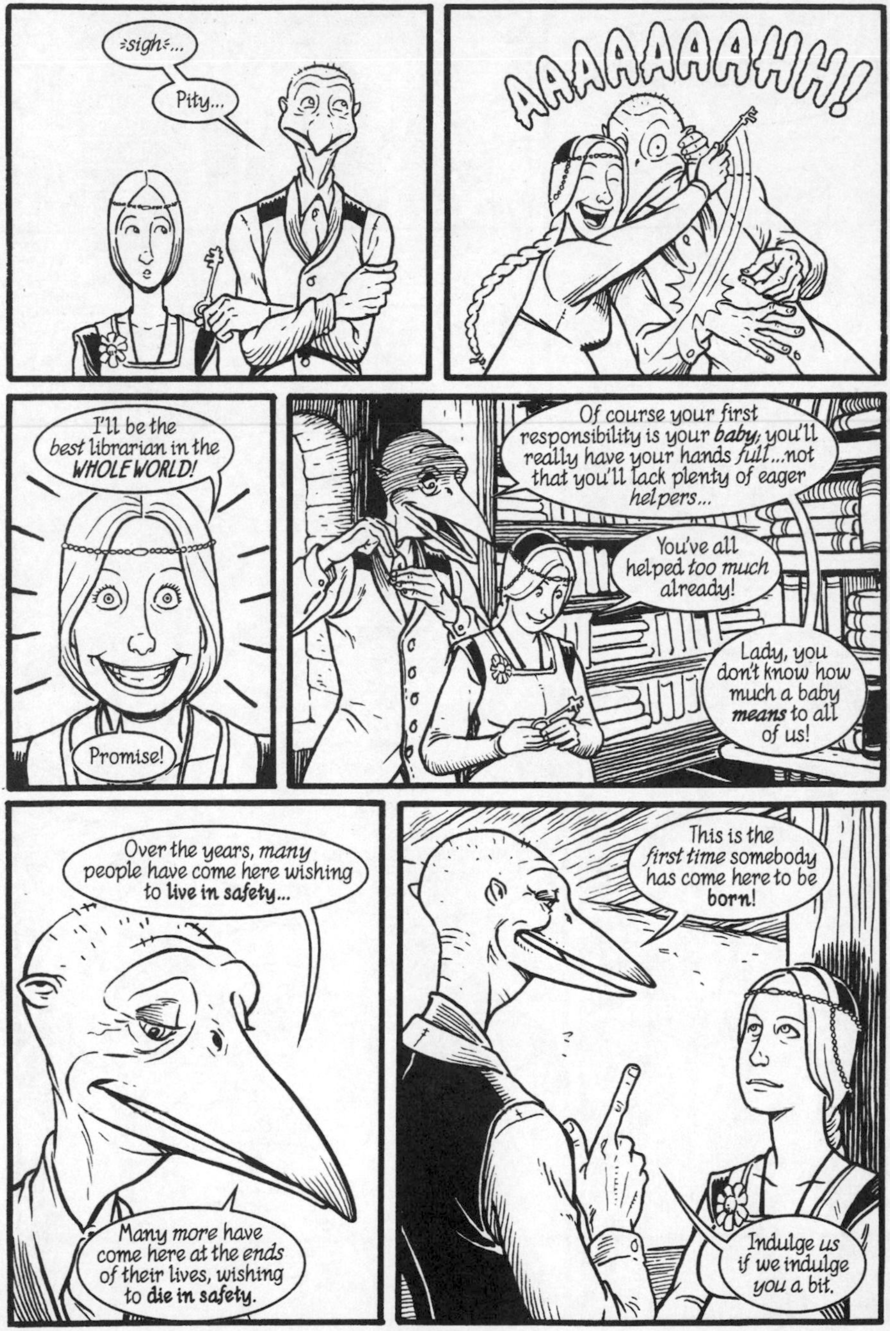

sigh...
Pity...
AAAAAAAHH!
I'll be the *best* librarian in the **WHOLE WORLD!**
Promise!
Of course your first responsibility is your ***baby;*** you'll really have your hands *full*...not that you'll lack plenty of eager *helpers*...
You've all helped *too much* already!
Lady, you don't know how much a baby ***means*** to all of us!
Over the years, *many* people have come here wishing to **live in safety**...
Many *more* have come here at the *ends* of their lives, wishing to **die in safety**.
This is the *first time* somebody has come here to be **born**!
Indulge *us* if we indulge *you* a bit.

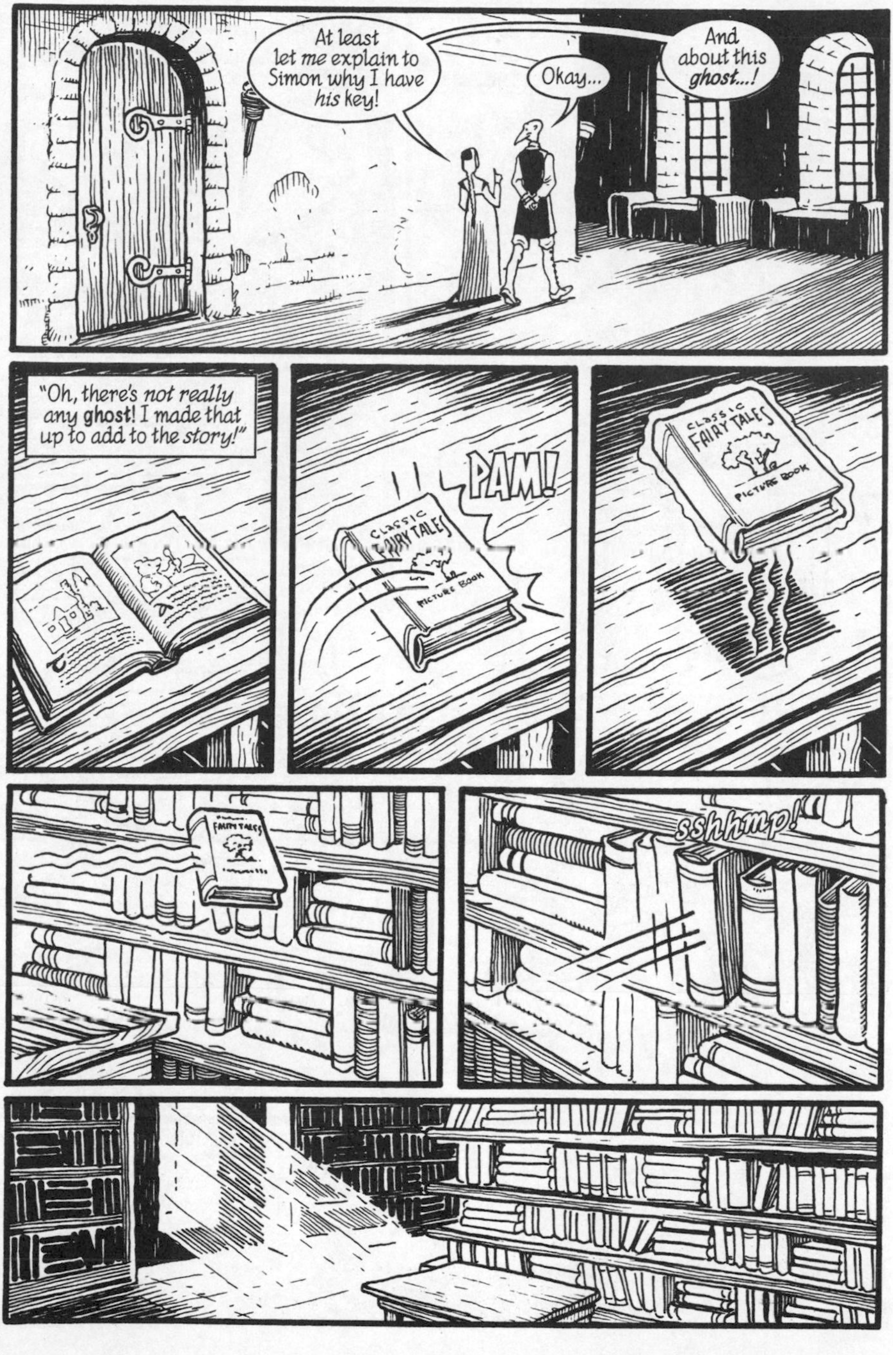
At least let me explain to Simon why I have his key!
Okay...
And about this ghost...!
"Oh, there's not really any ghost! I made that up to add to the story!"
PAM!
CLASSIC FAIRY TALES
PICTURE BOOK
CLASSIC FAIRY TALES
PICTURE BOOK
FAIRY TALES
sshhmp!

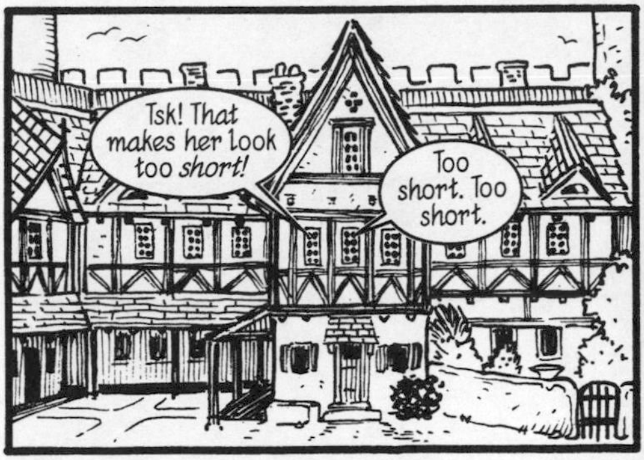
Tsk! That makes her look too *short!*
Too short. Too short.

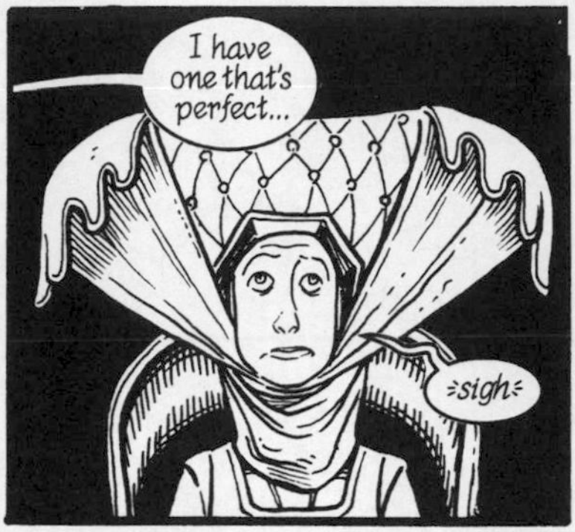
I have one that's perfect...
sigh

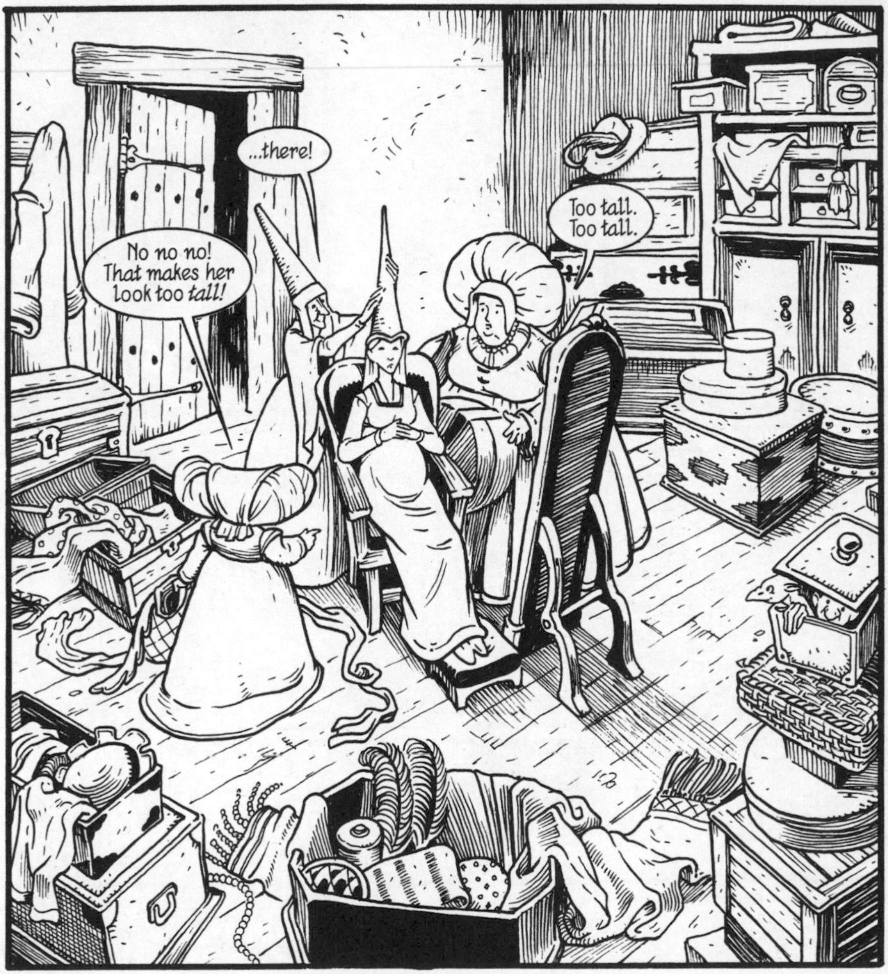
...there!
No no no! That makes her look too *tall!*
Too tall. Too tall.

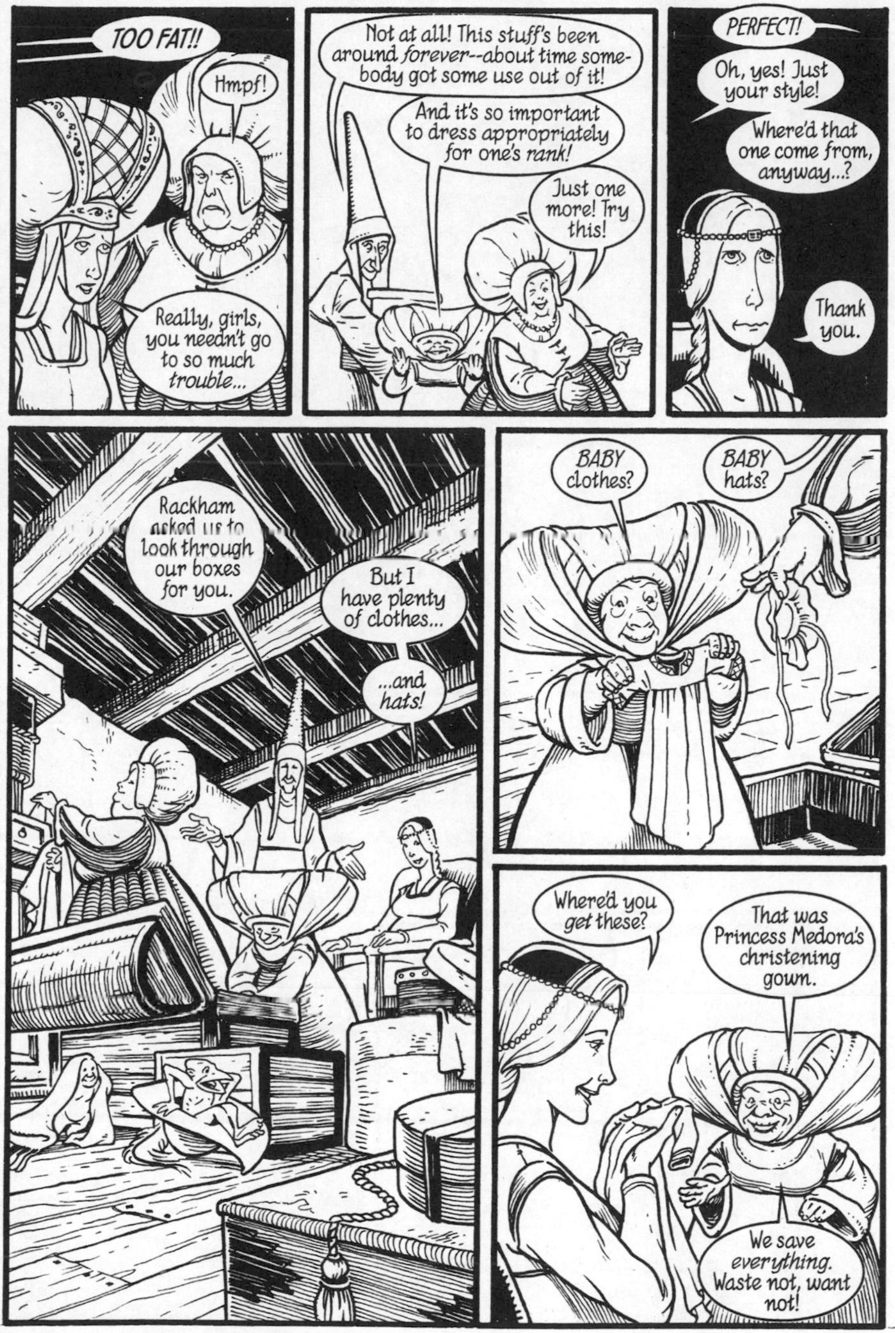
TOO FAT!!
Hmpf!
Really, girls, you needn't go to so much *trouble*...
Not at all! This stuff's been around *forever*--about time somebody got some use out of it!
And it's so important to dress appropriately for one's *rank!*
Just one more! Try this!
PERFECT!
Oh, yes! Just your style!
Where'd that one come from, anyway...?
Thank you.
Rackham asked us to look through our boxes for you.
But I have plenty of clothes...
...and *hats!*
BABY clothes?
BABY hats?
Where'd you *get* these?
That was Princess Medora's christening gown.
We save *everything.* Waste not, want not!

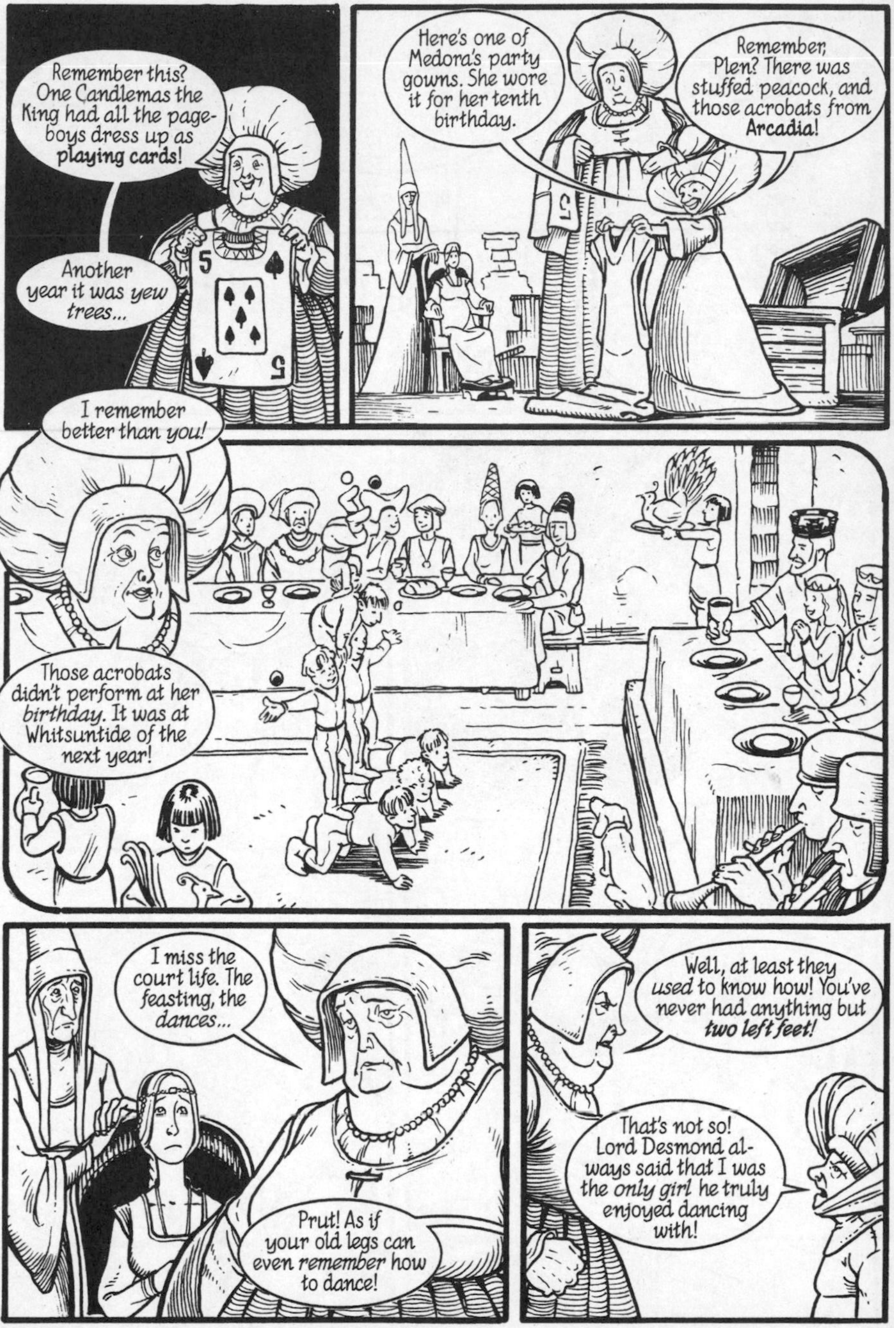
Remember this? One Candlemas the King had all the page-boys dress up as **playing cards**!
Another year it was *yew trees*...
Here's one of Medora's party gowns. She wore it for her tenth birthday.
Remember, Plen? There was stuffed peacock, and those acrobats from **Arcadia**!
I remember better than *you*!
Those acrobats didn't perform at her *birthday*. It was at Whitsuntide of the next year!
I miss the court life. The feasting, the *dances*...
Prut! As if your old legs can even *remember* how to dance!
Well, at least they *used* to know how! You've never had anything but ***two left feet!***
That's not so! Lord Desmond always said that I was the *only girl* he truly enjoyed dancing with!

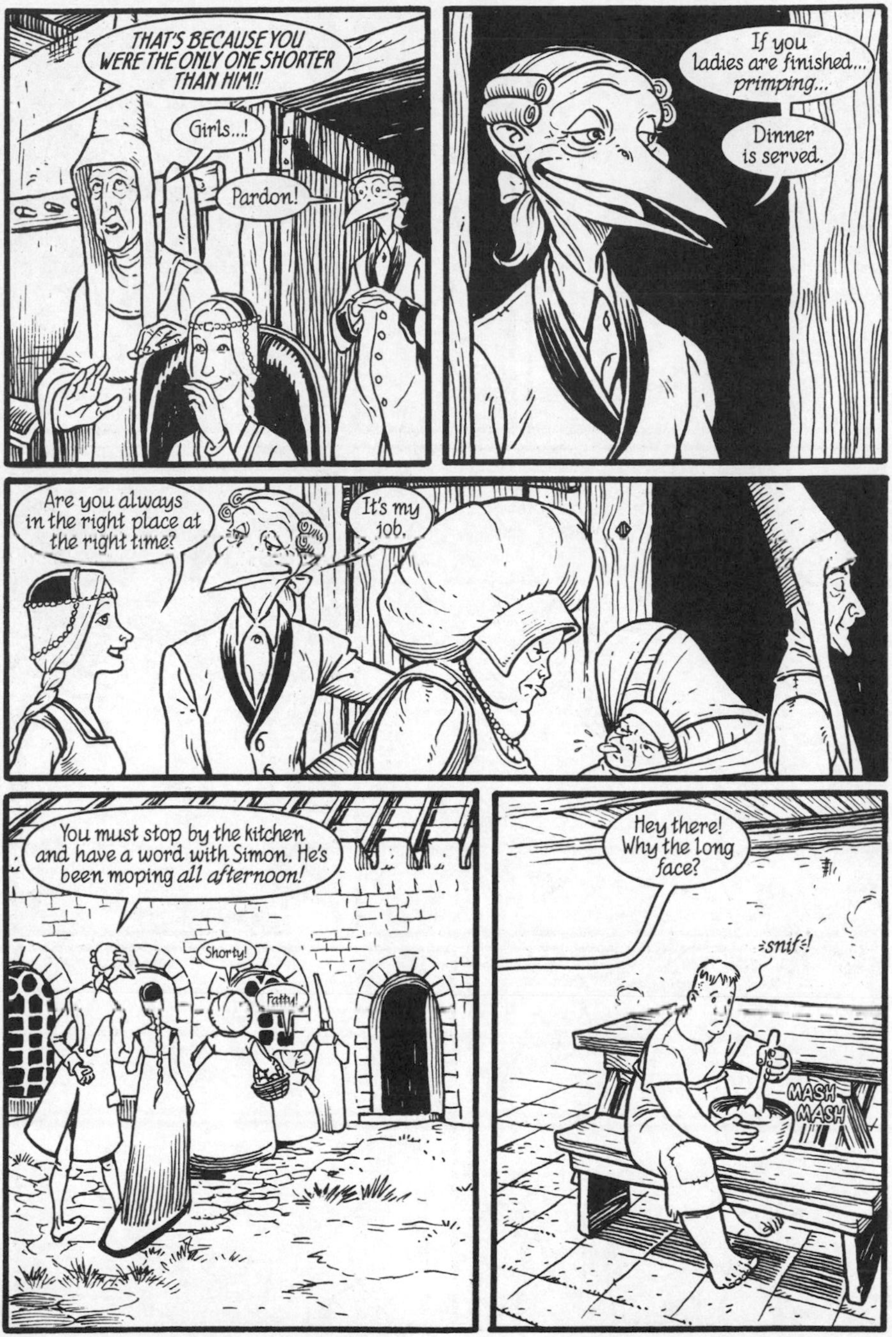
THAT'S BECAUSE YOU WERE THE ONLY ONE SHORTER THAN HIM!!
Girls...!
Pardon!
If you ladies are finished... primping...
Dinner is served.
Are you always in the right place at the right time?
It's my job.
You must stop by the kitchen and have a word with Simon. He's been moping all afternoon!
Shorty!
Fatty!
Hey there! Why the long face?
snif!
MASH
MASH

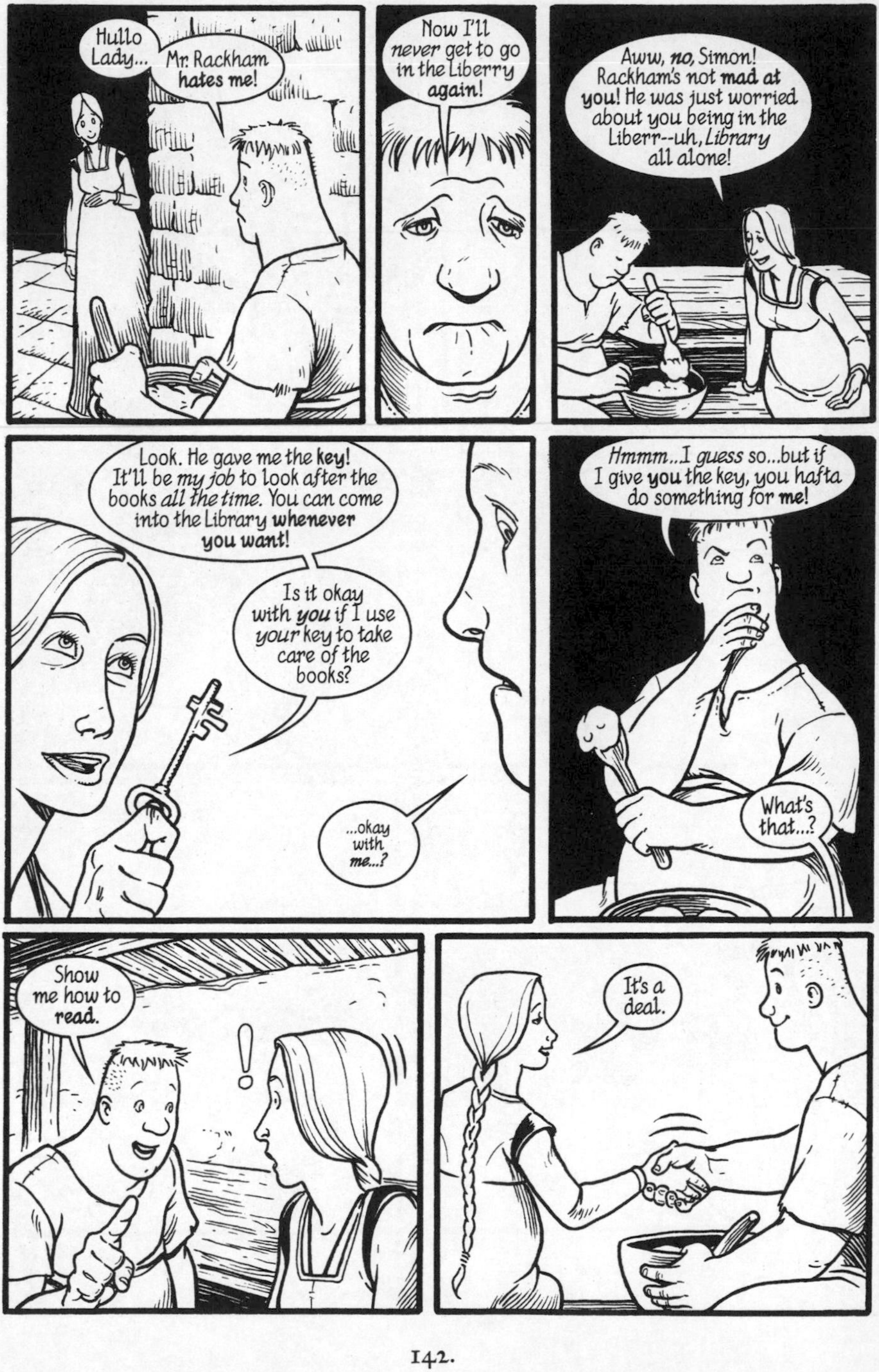
Hullo Lady...
Mr. Rackham hates me!
Now I'll never get to go in the Liberry again!
Aww, no, Simon! Rackham's not mad at you! He was just worried about you being in the Liberr--uh, Library all alone!
Look. He gave me the key! It'll be my job to look after the books all the time. You can come into the Library whenever you want!
Is it okay with you if I use your key to take care of the books?
...okay with me...?
Hmmm...I guess so...but if I give you the key, you hafta do something for me!
What's that...?
Show me how to read.
!
It's a deal.

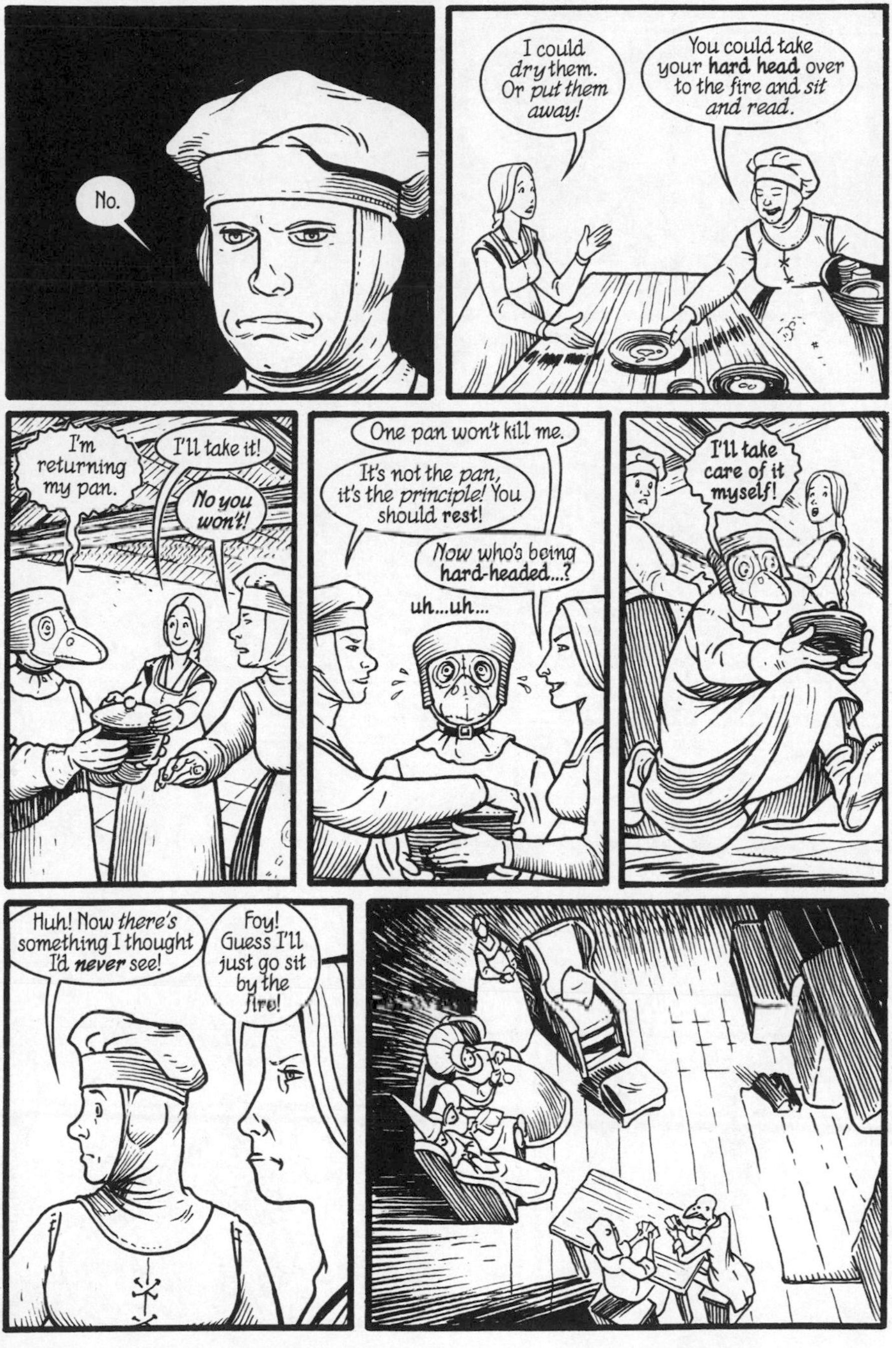
No.
I could dry them. Or put them away!
You could take your **hard head** over to the fire and *sit* and read.
I'm returning my pan.
I'll take it!
No you won't!
One pan won't kill me.
It's not the *pan*, it's the *principle!* You should **rest**!
Now who's being **hard-headed...?**
uh...uh...
I'll take care of it myself!
Huh! Now *there's* something I thought I'd ***never*** see!
Foy! Guess I'll just go sit by the fire!

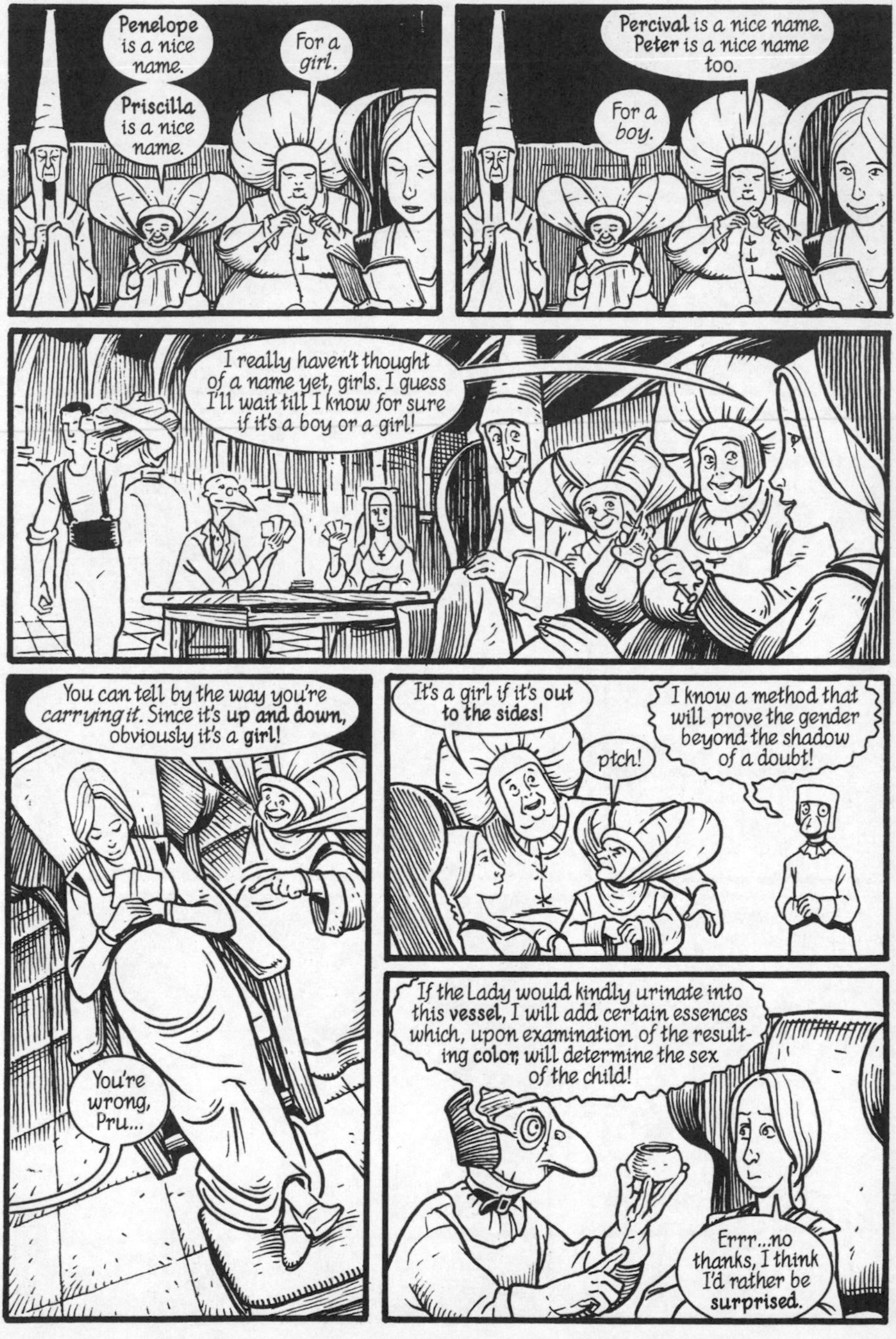

Penelope is a nice name.
Priscilla is a nice name.
For a girl.
Percival is a nice name. Peter is a nice name too.
For a boy.
I really haven't thought of a name yet, girls. I guess I'll wait till I know for sure if it's a boy or a girl!
You can tell by the way you're carrying it. Since it's up and down, obviously it's a girl!
You're wrong, Pru...
It's a girl if it's out to the sides!
ptch!
I know a method that will prove the gender beyond the shadow of a doubt!
If the Lady would kindly urinate into this vessel, I will add certain essences which, upon examination of the resulting color, will determine the sex of the child!
Errr...no thanks, I think I'd rather be surprised.

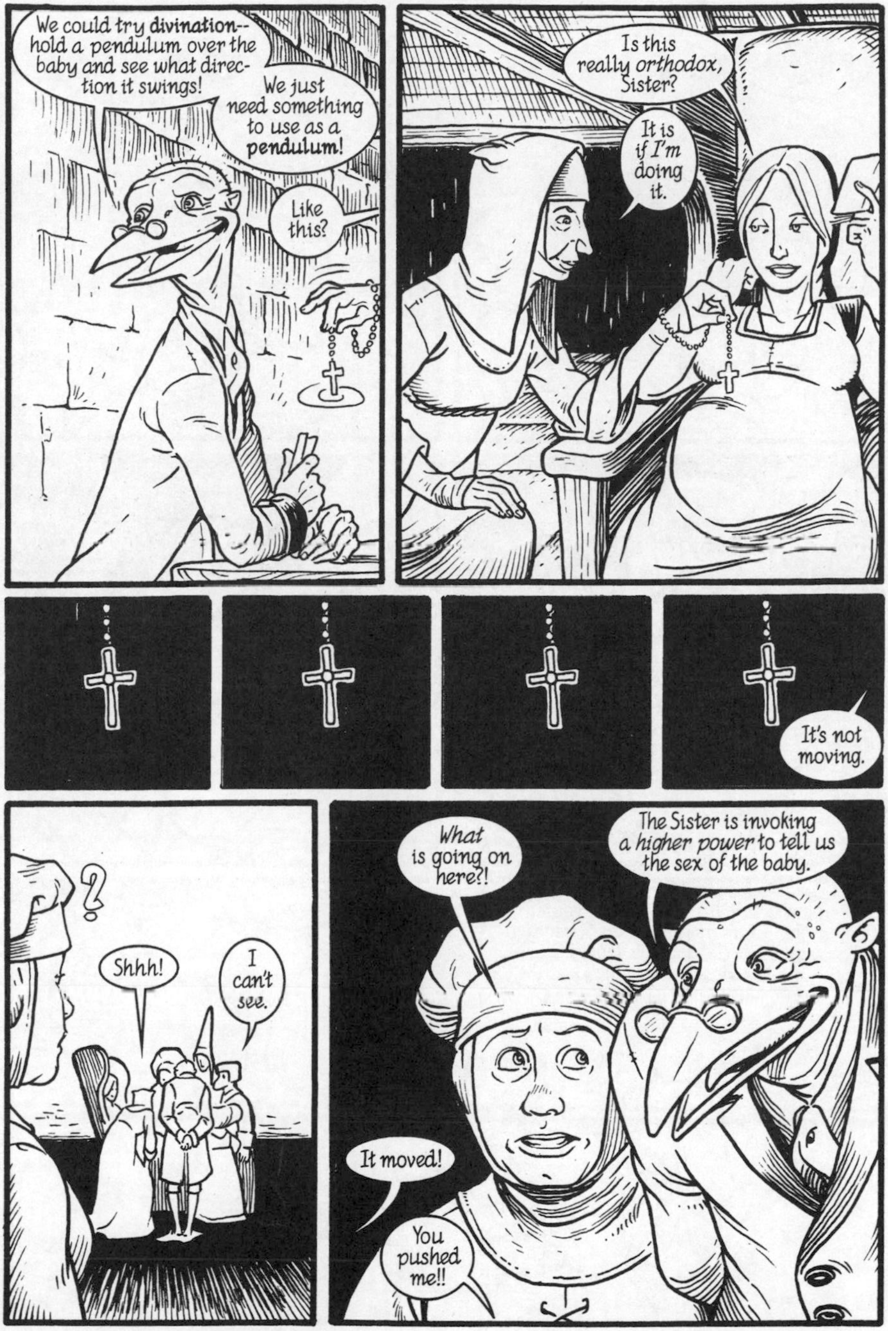
We could try divination--hold a pendulum over the baby and see what direction it swings!
We just need something to use as a pendulum!
Like this?
Is this really orthodox, Sister?
It is if I'm doing it.
It's not moving.
?
Shhh!
I can't see.
What is going on here?!
The Sister is invoking a higher power to tell us the sex of the baby.
It moved!
You pushed me!!

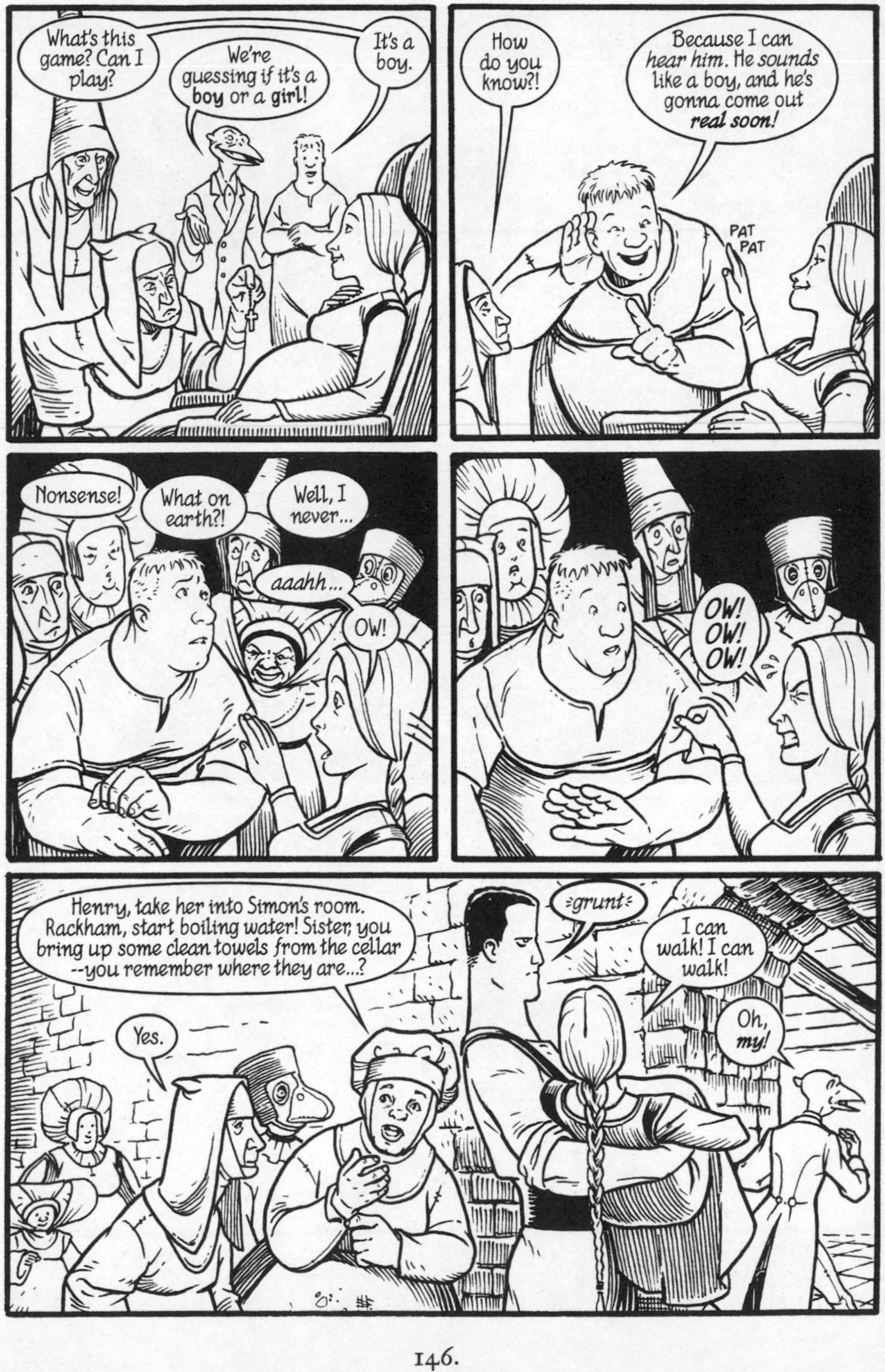
What's this game? Can I play?
We're guessing if it's a **boy** or a **girl**!
It's a boy.
How do you know?!
Because I can *hear him*. He *sounds* like a boy, and he's gonna come out ***real soon!***
PAT PAT
Nonsense!
What on earth?!
Well, I never...
aaahh...
OW!
OW! OW! OW!
Henry, take her into Simon's room. Rackham, start boiling water! Sister, you bring up some clean towels from the cellar --you remember where they are...?
Yes.
grunt
I can walk! I can walk!
Oh, ***my!***

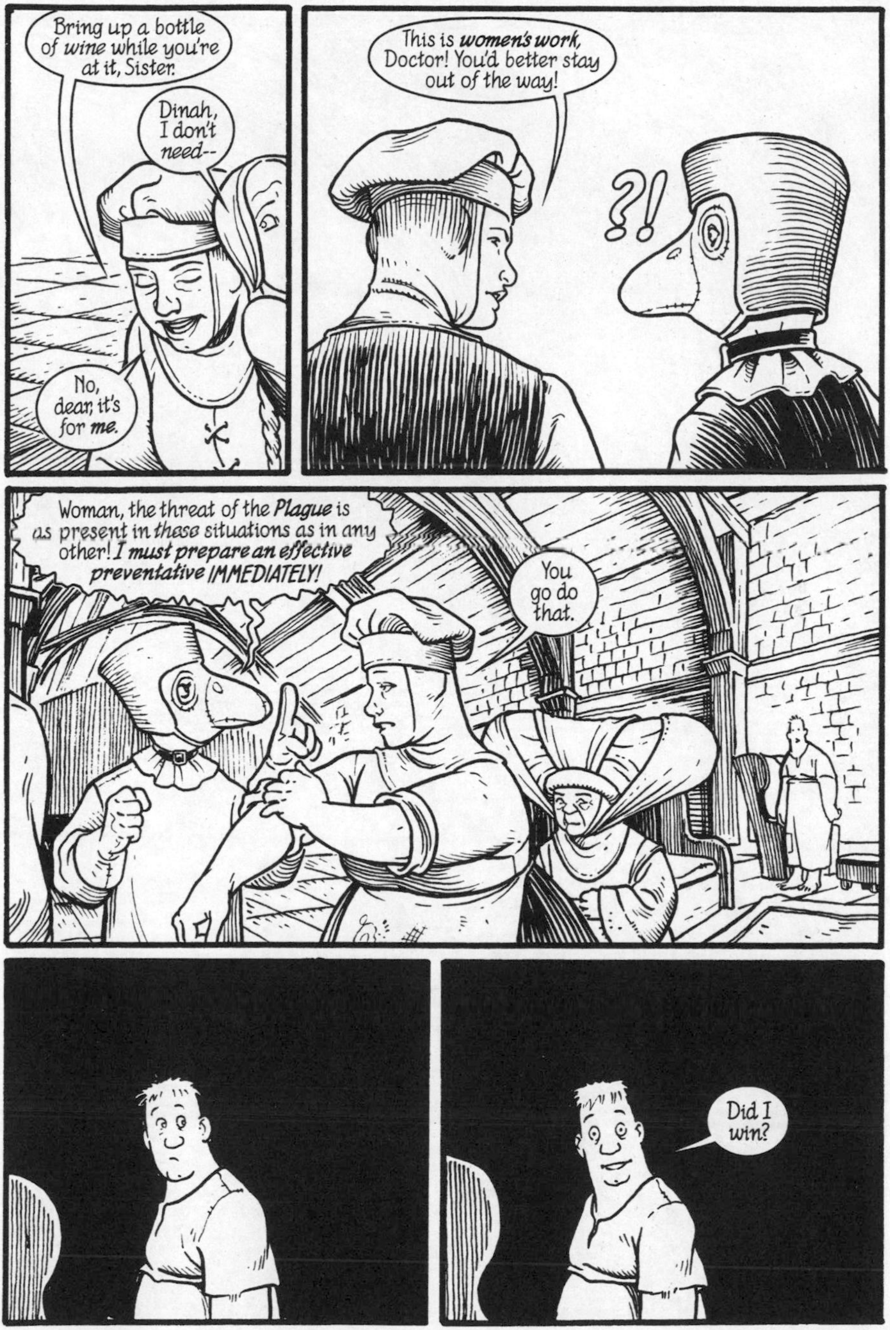
Bring up a bottle of *wine* while you're at it, Sister.
Dinah, I don't need--
No, dear, it's for *me*.
This is ***women's work,*** Doctor! You'd better stay out of the way!
?!
Woman, the threat of the *Plague* is as present in *these* situations as in any other! ***I must prepare an effective preventative IMMEDIATELY!***
You go do that.
Did I win?

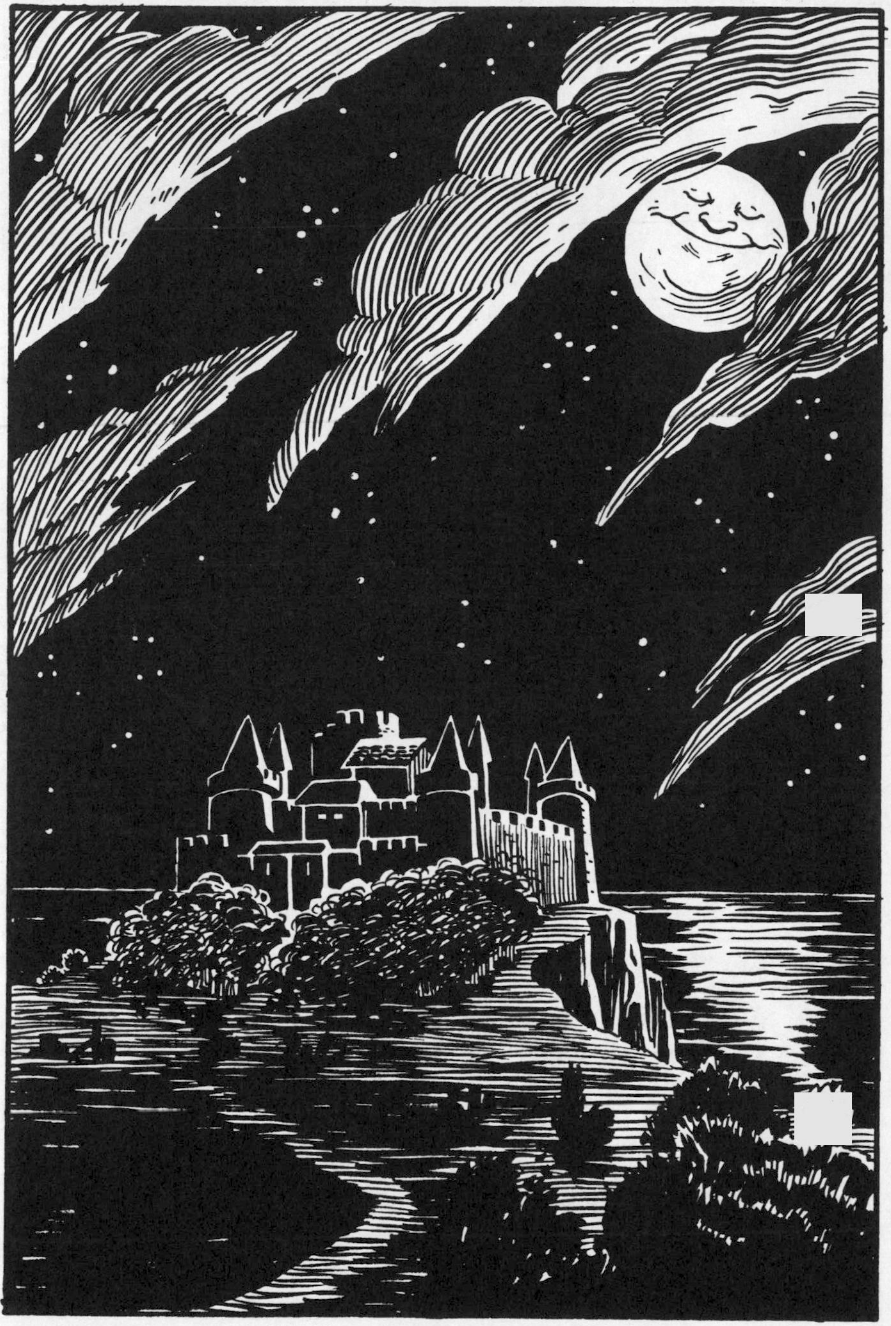

Chapter 7.

· THE CAGED HEART ·

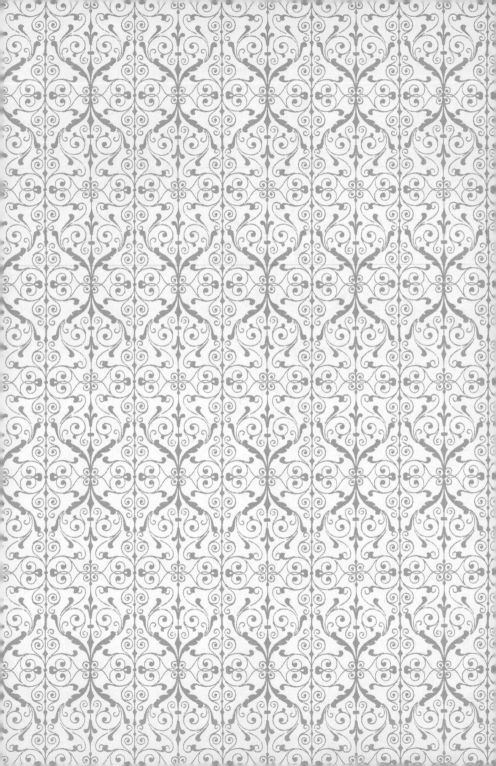

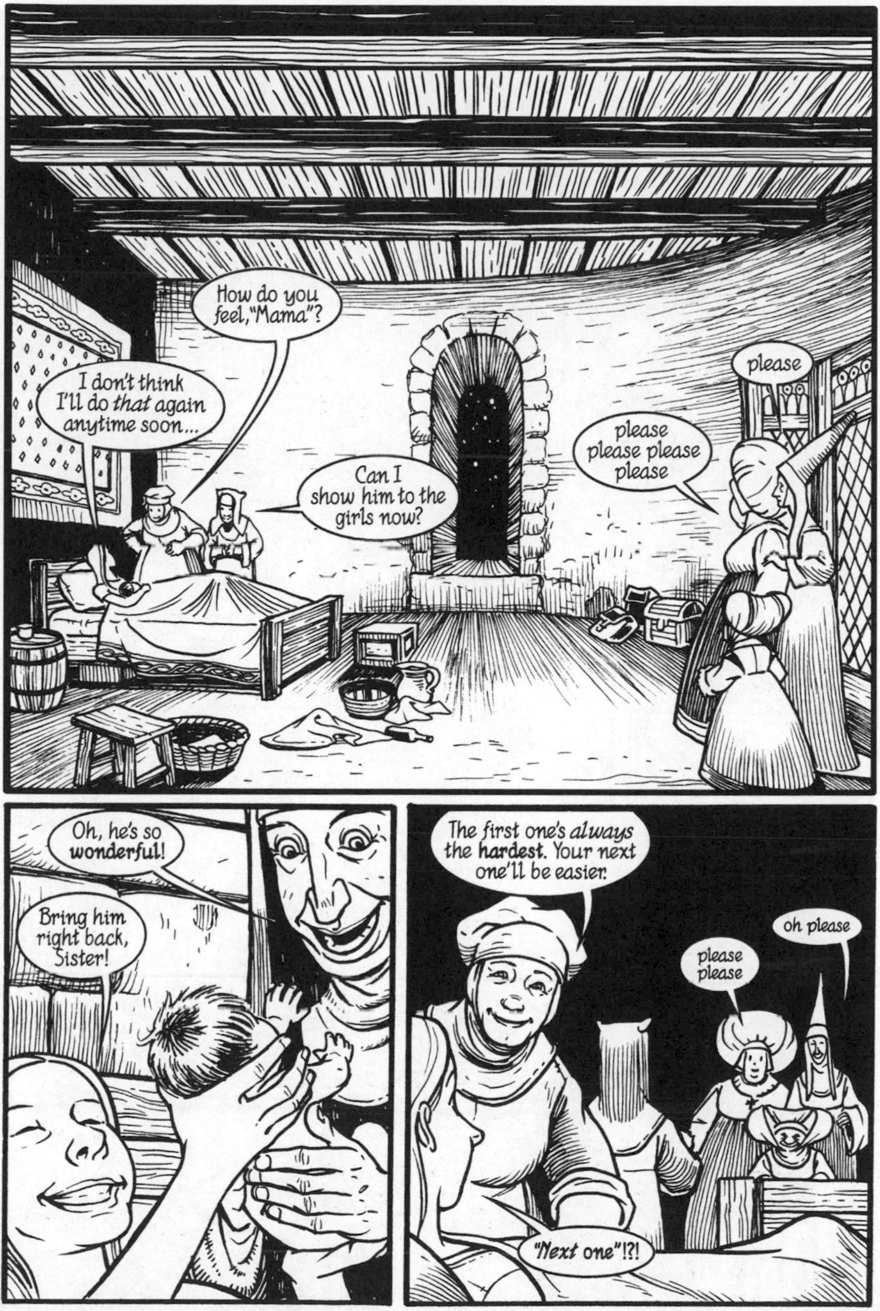
I don't think I'll do *that* again anytime soon...
How do you feel, "Mama"?
Can I show him to the girls now?
please please please please
please
Oh, he's so **wonderful**!
Bring him right back, Sister!
The first one's *always* the **hardest**. Your next one'll be easier.
oh please
please please
"*Next* one"!?!

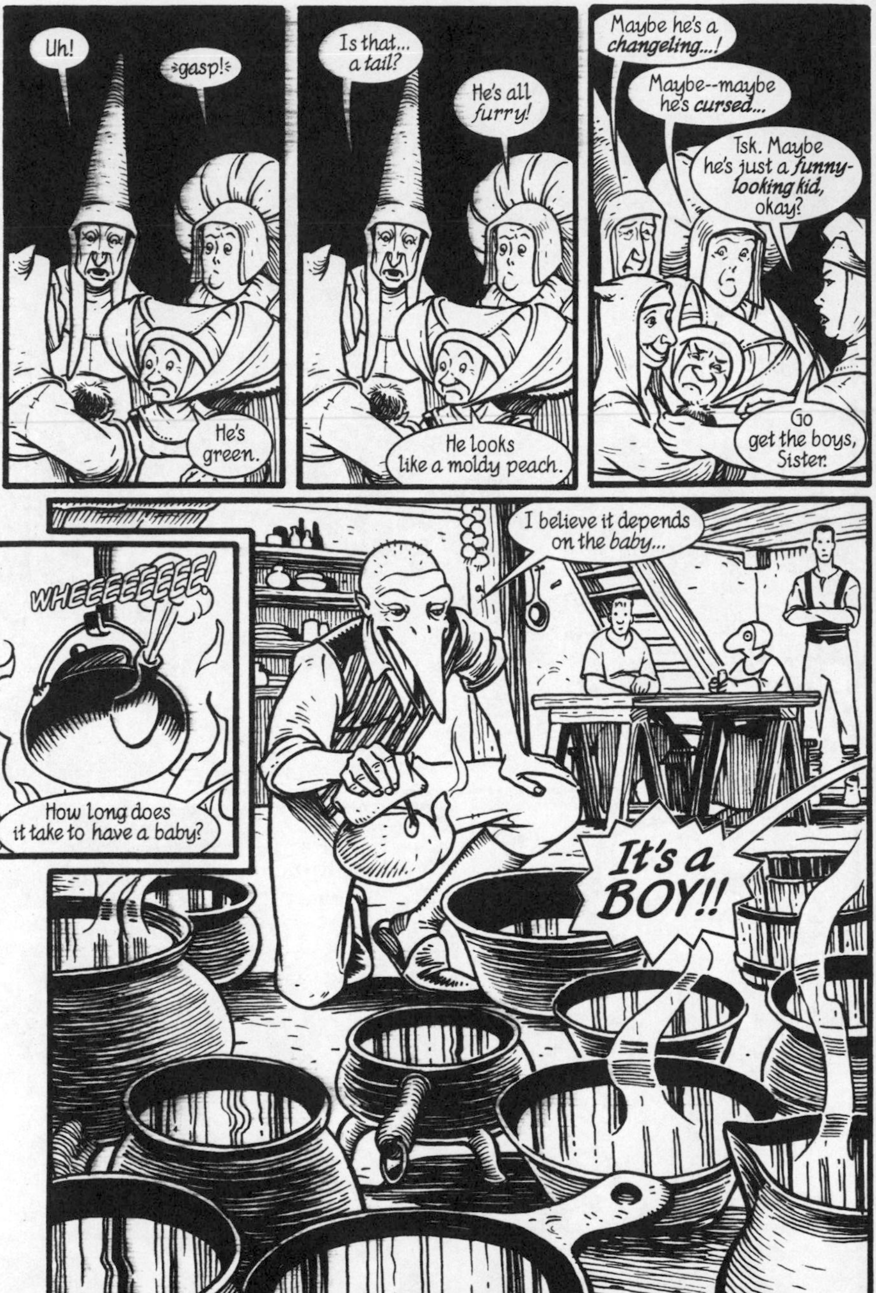
Uh!
gasp!
He's green.
Is that... a tail?
He's all furry!
He looks like a moldy peach.
Maybe he's a changeling...!
Maybe--maybe he's cursed...
Tsk. Maybe he's just a funny-looking kid, okay?
Go get the boys, Sister.
WHEEEEEEEEE!
How long does it take to have a baby?
I believe it depends on the baby...
It's a BOY!!

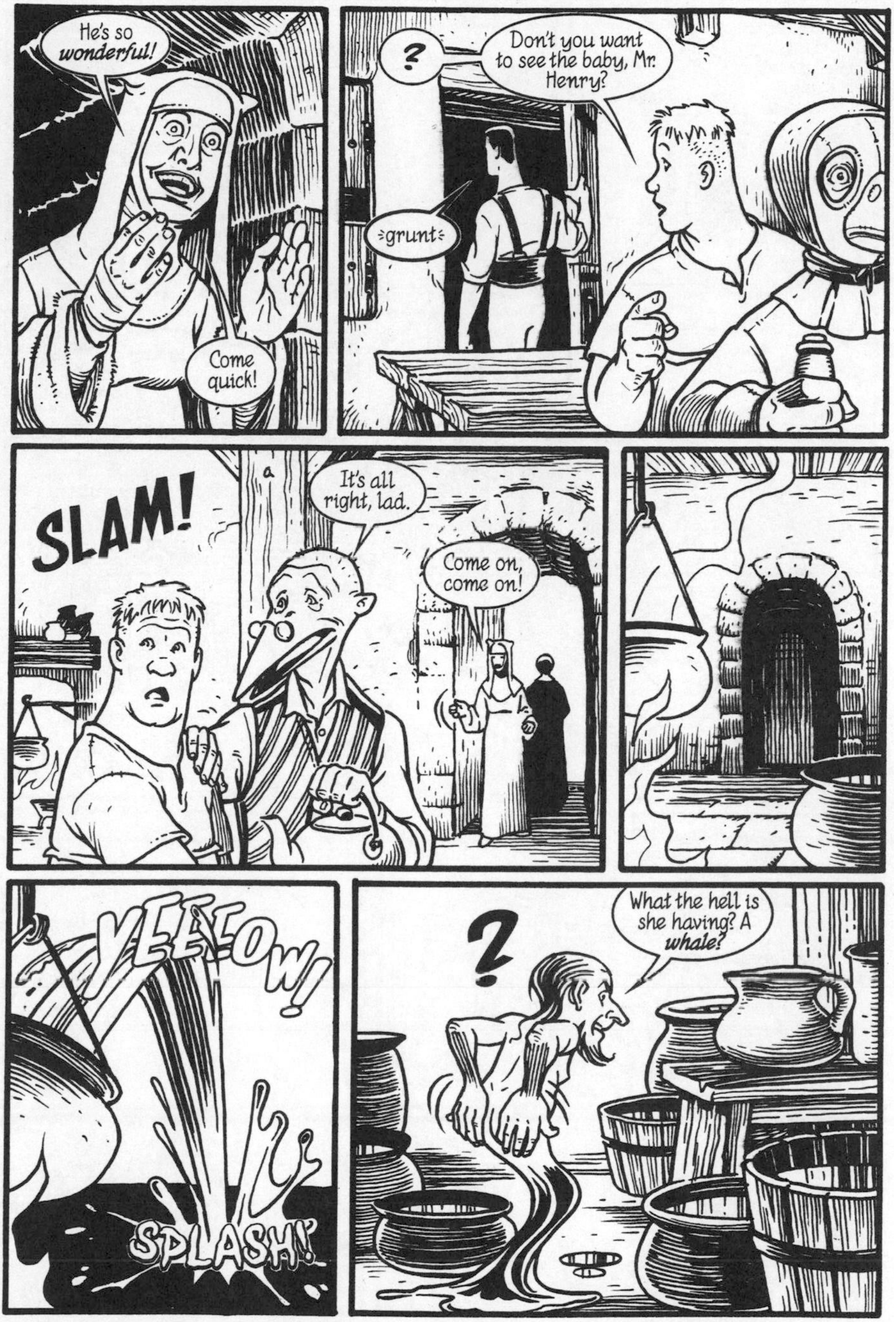
He's so *wonderful!*
Come quick!
?
Don't you want to see the baby, Mr. Henry?
grunt
SLAM!
It's all right, lad.
Come on, come on!
YEEEOW!
SPLASH!
?
What the hell is she having? A *whale?*

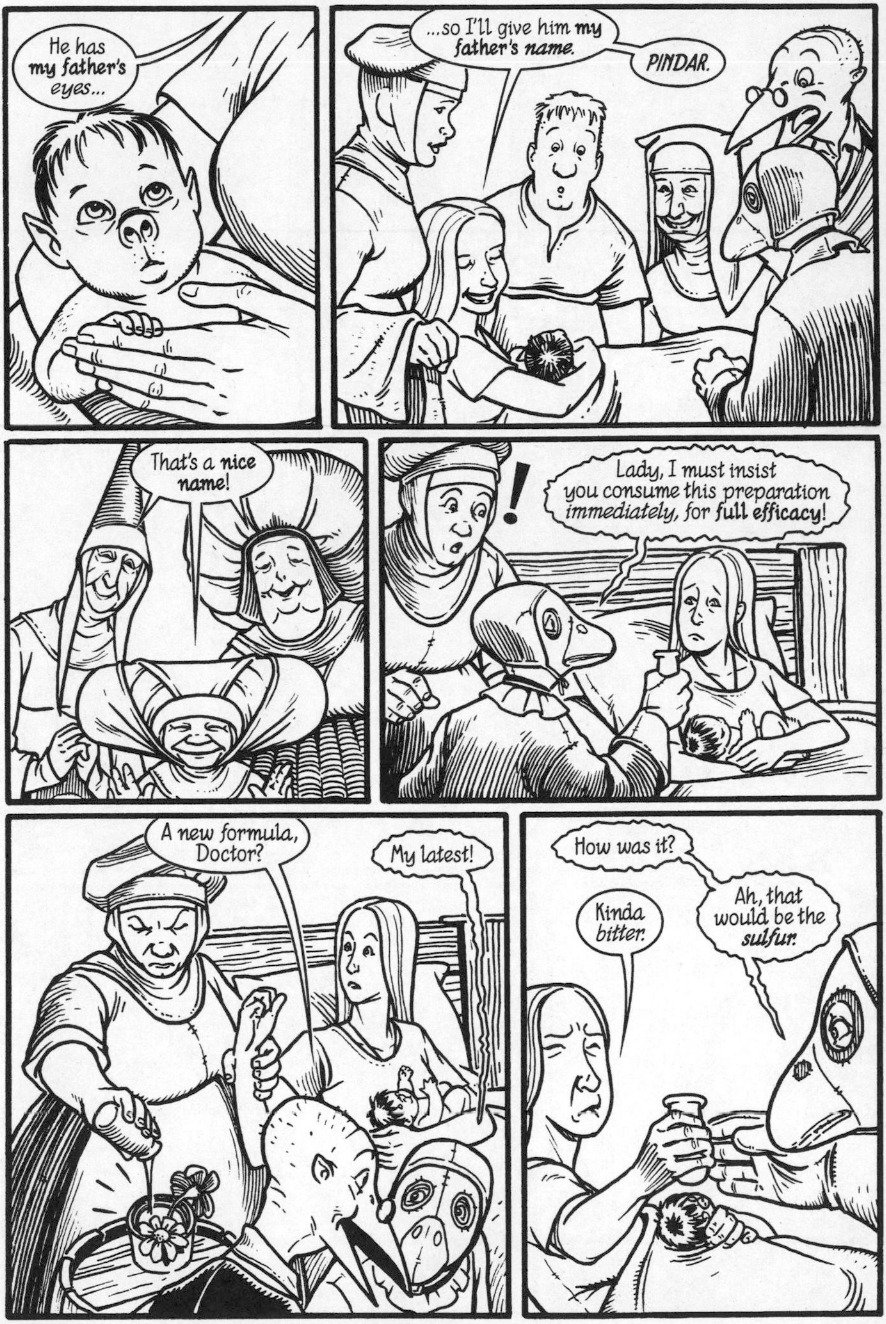
He has **my father's** *eyes...*
...so I'll give him **my father's *name*.**
PINDAR.
That's a **nice name**!
!
Lady, I must insist you consume this preparation *immediately*, for **full efficacy**!
A new *formula*, Doctor?
My latest!
How was it?
Kinda *bitter.*
Ah, that would be the ***sulfur.***

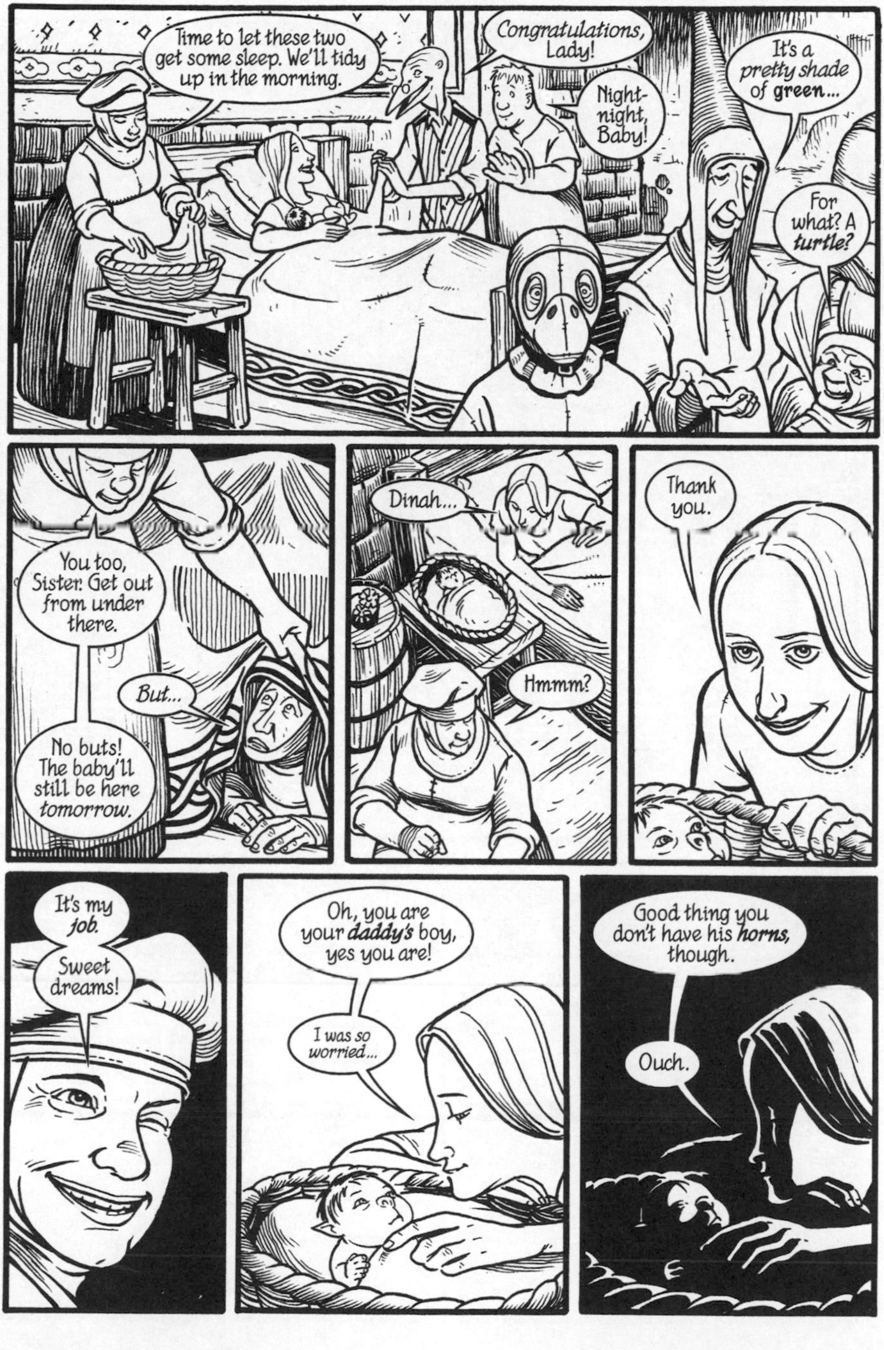
Time to let these two get some sleep. We'll tidy up in the morning.
Congratulations, Lady!
Night-night, Baby!
It's a pretty shade of green...
For what? A turtle?
You too, Sister. Get out from under there.
But...
No buts! The baby'll still be here tomorrow.
Dinah...
Hmmm?
Thank you.
It's my job.
Sweet dreams!
Oh, you are your daddy's boy, yes you are!
I was so worried...
Good thing you don't have his horns, though.
Ouch.

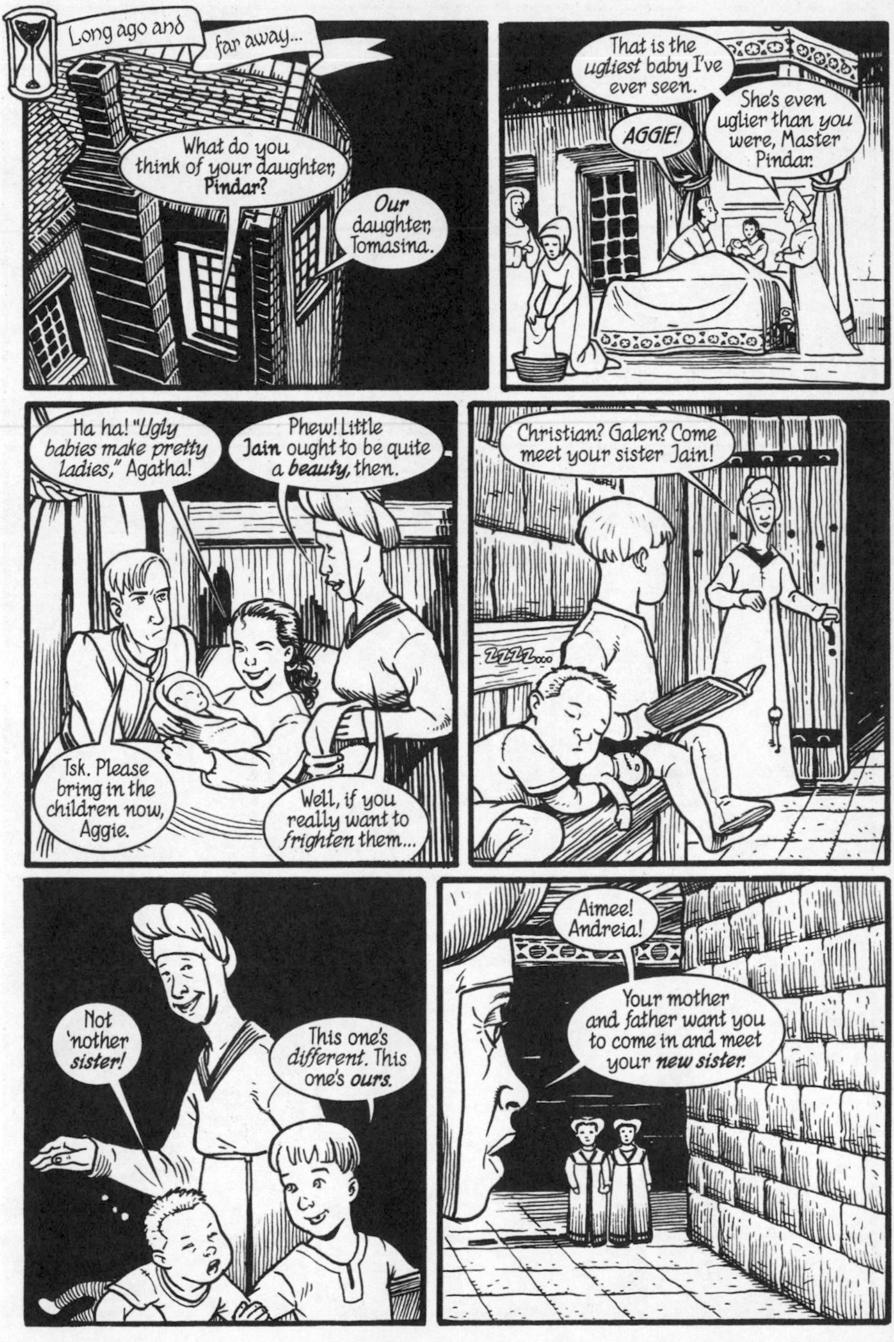
Long ago and
far away...
What do you think of your daughter, Pindar?
Our daughter, Tomasina.
That is the ugliest baby I've ever seen.
AGGIE!
She's even uglier than you were, Master Pindar.
Ha ha! "Ugly babies make pretty ladies," Agatha!
Phew! Little Jain ought to be quite a beauty, then.
Tsk. Please bring in the children now, Aggie.
Well, if you really want to frighten them...
Christian? Galen? Come meet your sister Jain!
ZZZZ...
Not 'nother sister!
This one's different. This one's ours.
Aimee! Andreia!
Your mother and father want you to come in and meet your new sister.

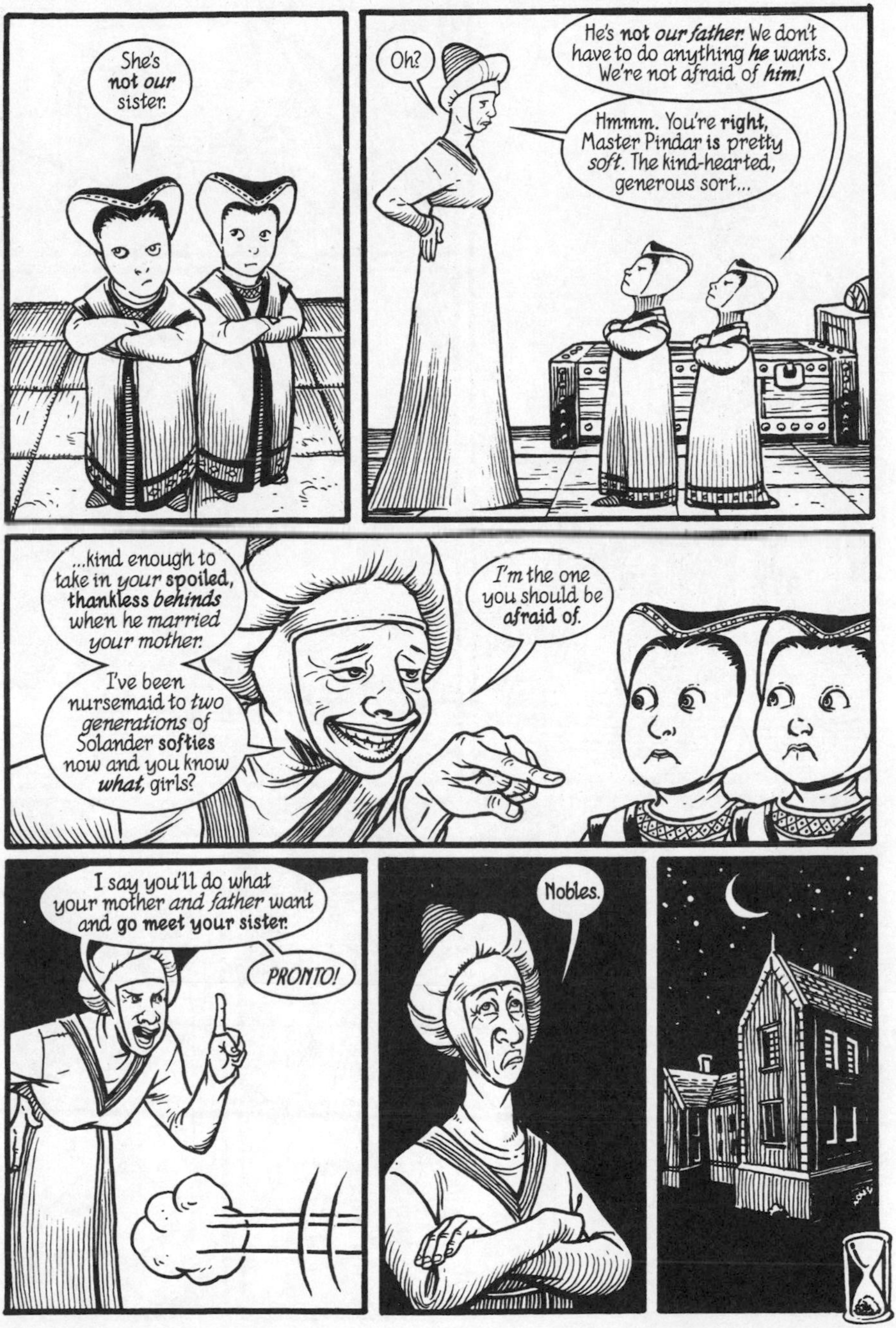
She's **not our** sister.
Oh?
He's **not *our father*.** We don't have to do anything ***he*** wants. We're not afraid of ***him!***
Hmmm. You're **right,** Master Pindar is pretty *soft*. The kind-hearted, generous sort...
...kind enough to take in *your* **spoiled, thankless *behinds*** when he *married your mother.*
I've been nursemaid to *two generations* of Solander **softies** now and you know ***what,*** girls?
I'm the one you should be **afraid of.**
I say you'll do what your mother *and father* want and **go meet your sister.**
PRONTO!
Nobles.

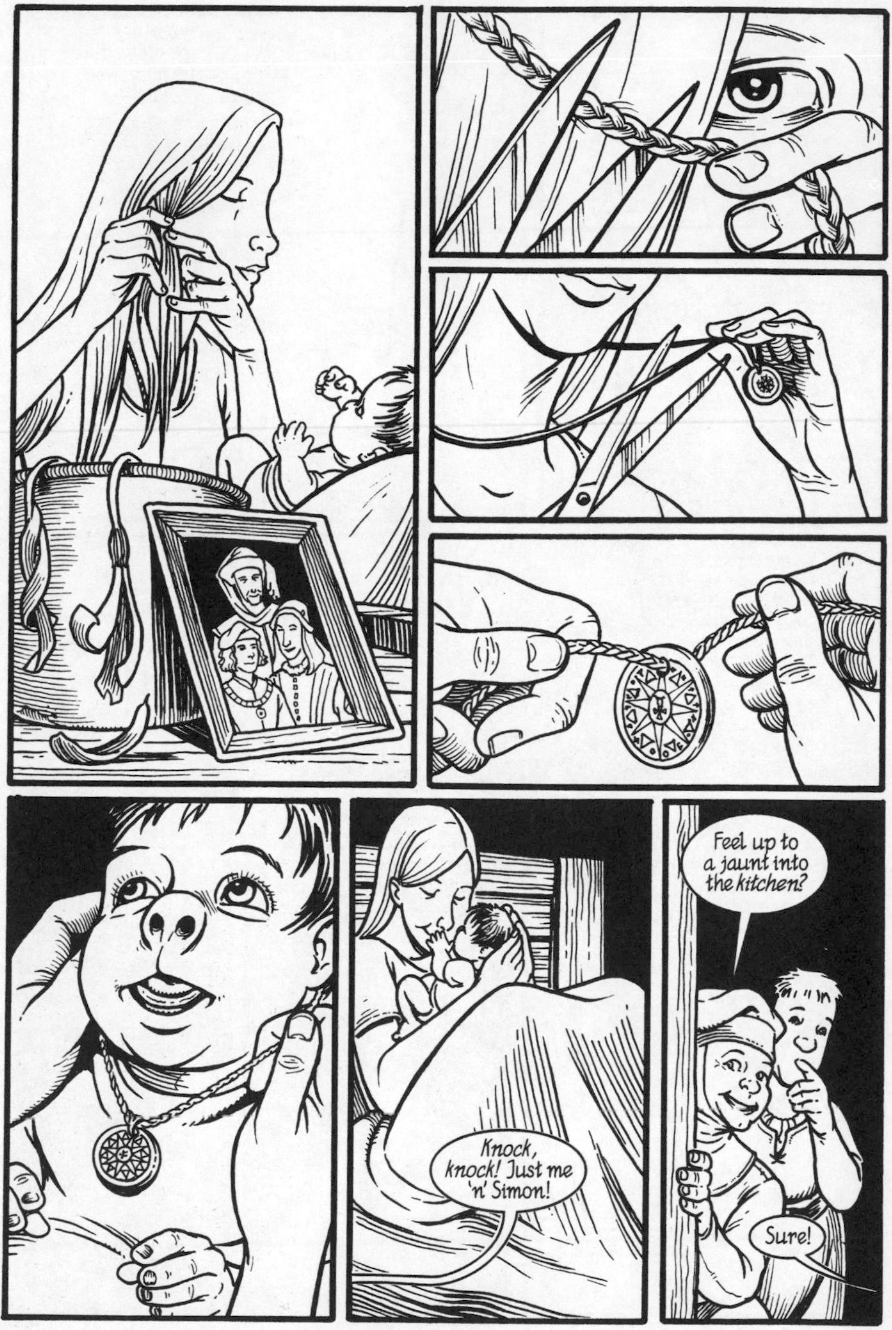
Knock, knock! Just me 'n' Simon!
Feel up to a jaunt into the *kitchen*?
Sure!

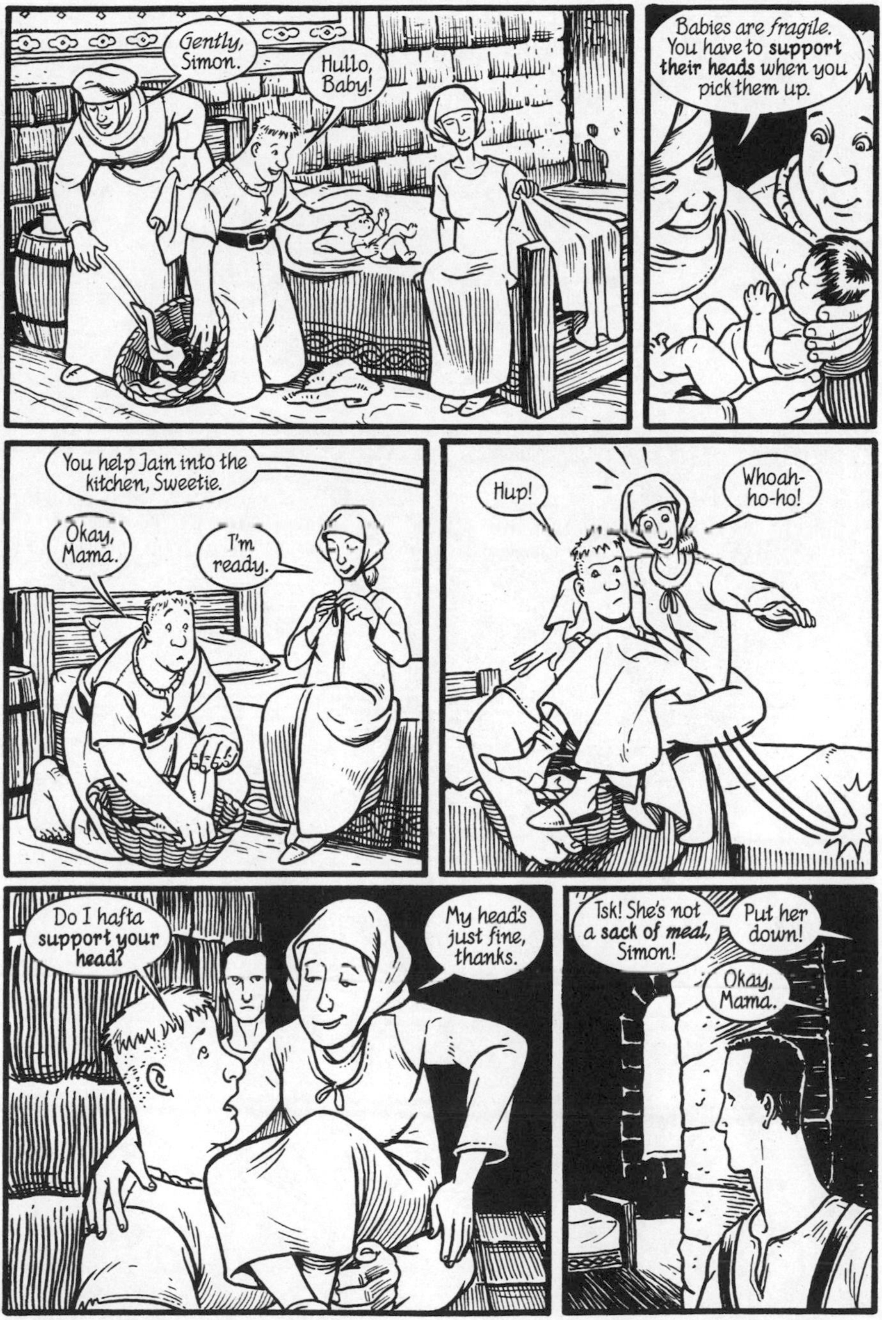
Gently, Simon.
Hullo, Baby!
Babies are *fragile*. You have to **support their heads** when you pick them up.
You help Jain into the kitchen, Sweetie.
Okay, Mama.
I'm ready.
Hup!
Whoah-ho-ho!
Do I hafta **support your head?**
My head's just fine, thanks.
Tsk! She's not a **sack of *meal***, Simon!
Put her down!
Okay, Mama.

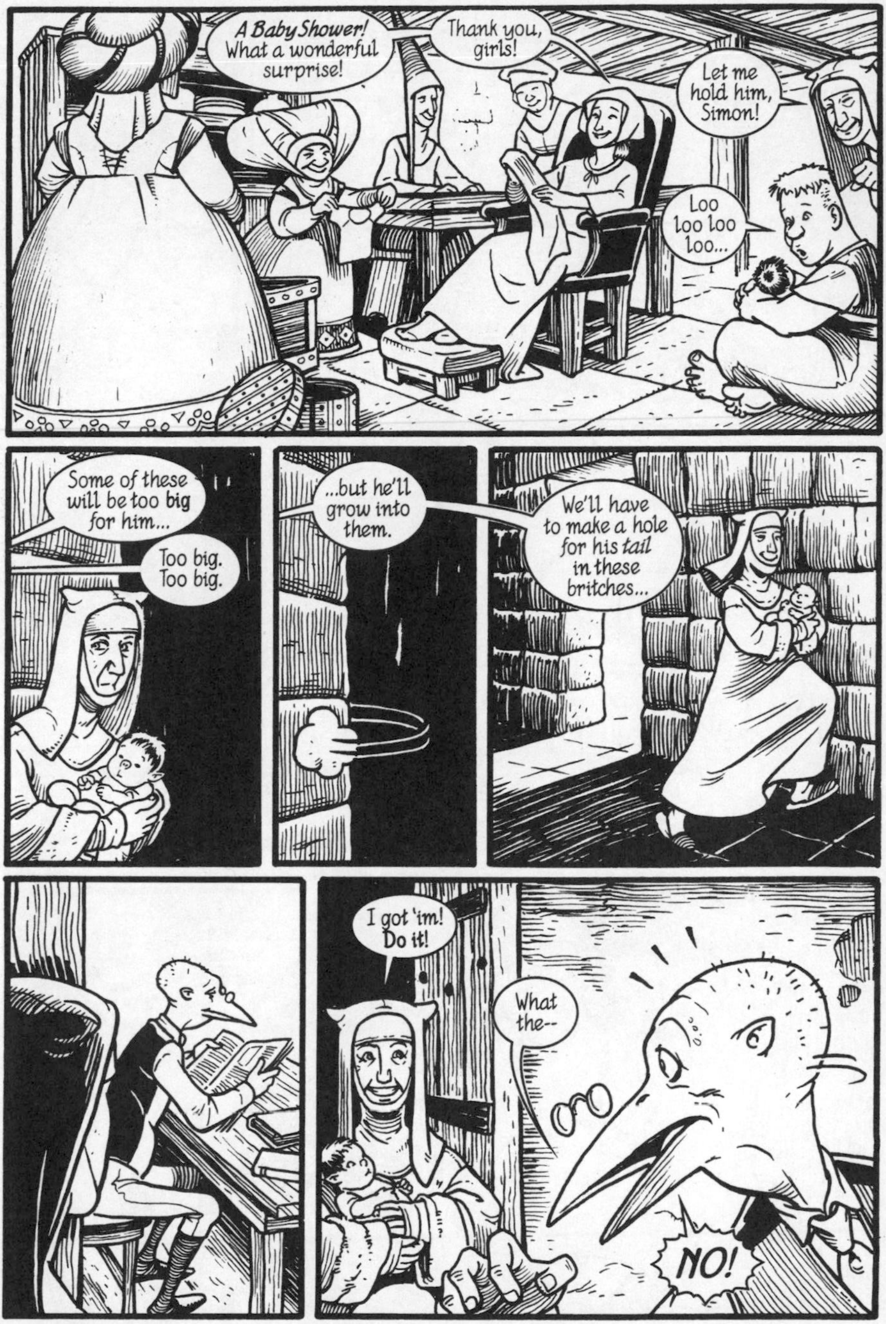
A Baby Shower! What a wonderful surprise!
Thank you, girls!
Let me hold him, Simon!
Loo loo loo loo...
Some of these will be too big for him...
Too big. Too big.
...but he'll grow into them.
We'll have to make a hole for his tail in these britches...
I got 'im! Do it!
What the--
NO!

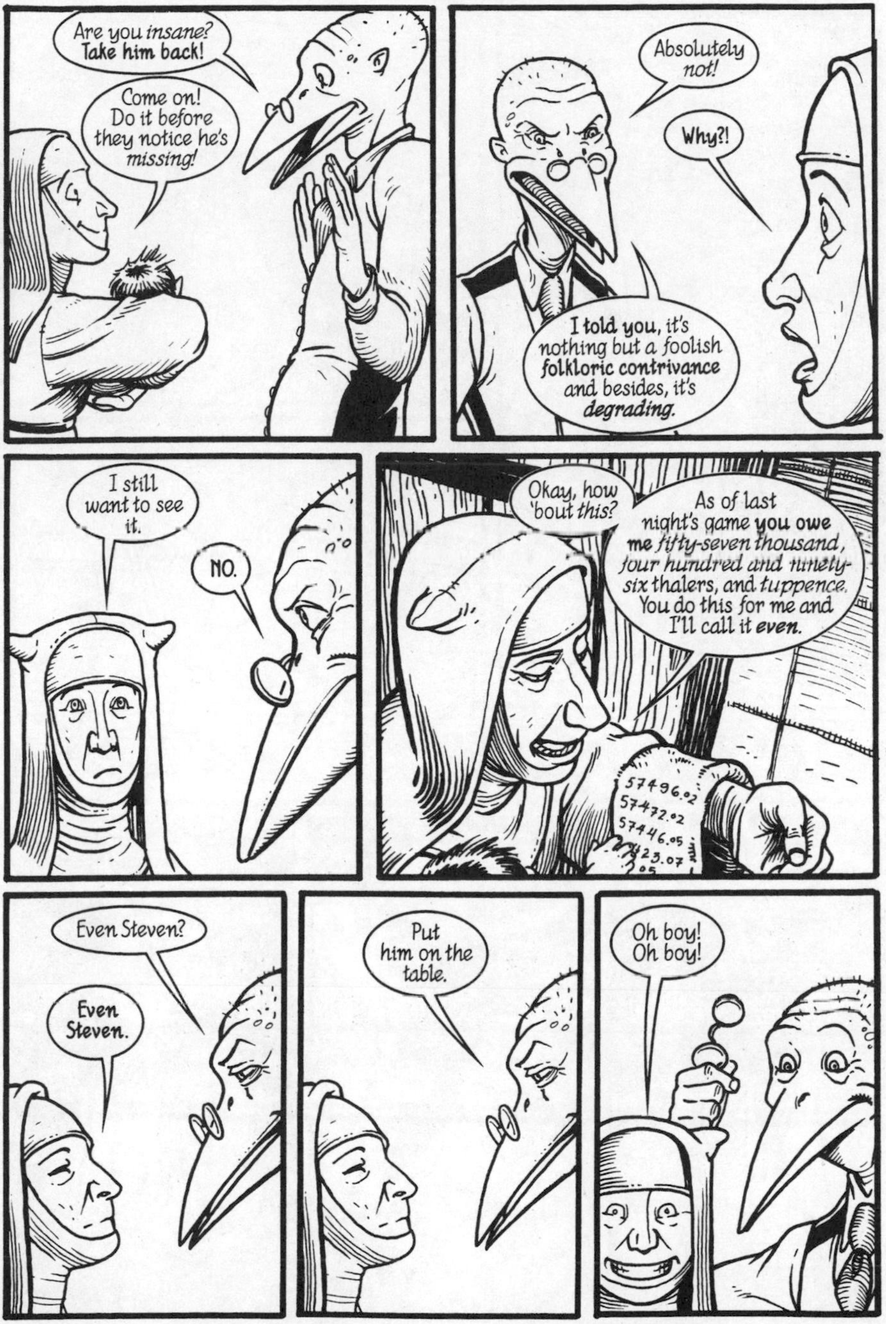
Are you *insane?* **Take him back!**
Come on! Do it before they notice he's *missing!*
Absolutely *not!*
Why?!
I told you, it's nothing but a foolish **folkloric contrivance** and besides, it's *degrading.*
I still want to see it.
NO.
Okay, how 'bout *this?*
As of last night's game **you owe me** *fifty-seven thousand, four hundred and ninety-six* thalers, and *tuppence.* You do this for me and I'll call it **even.**
57496.02
57472.02
57446.05
Even Steven?
Even Steven.
Put him on the table.
Oh boy! Oh boy!

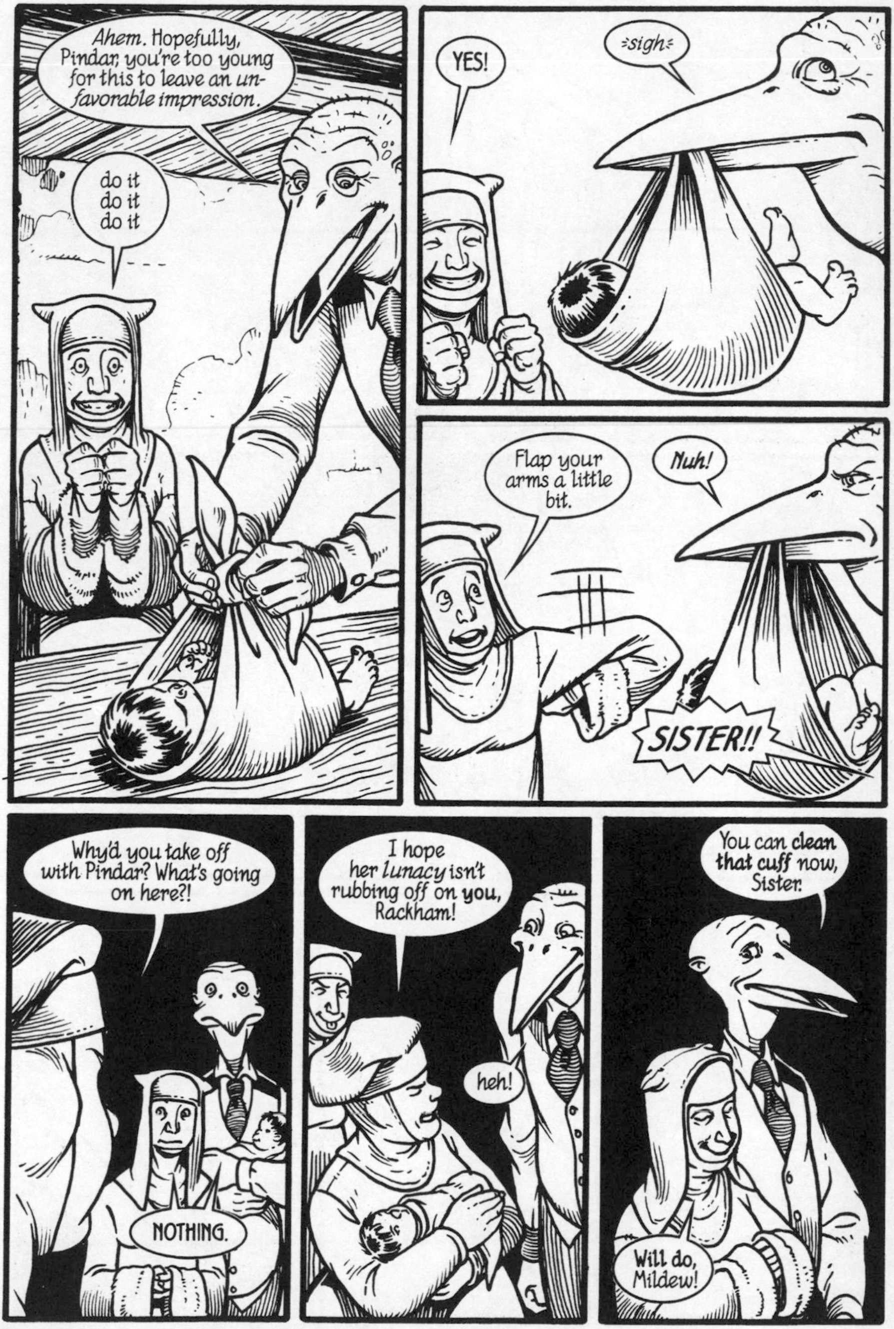
Ahem. Hopefully, Pindar, you're too young for this to leave an unfavorable impression.
do it do it do it
YES!
sigh
Flap your arms a little bit.
Nuh!
SISTER!!
Why'd you take off with Pindar? What's going on here?!
NOTHING.
I hope her lunacy isn't rubbing off on you, Rackham!
heh!
You can clean that cuff now, Sister.
Will do, Mildew!

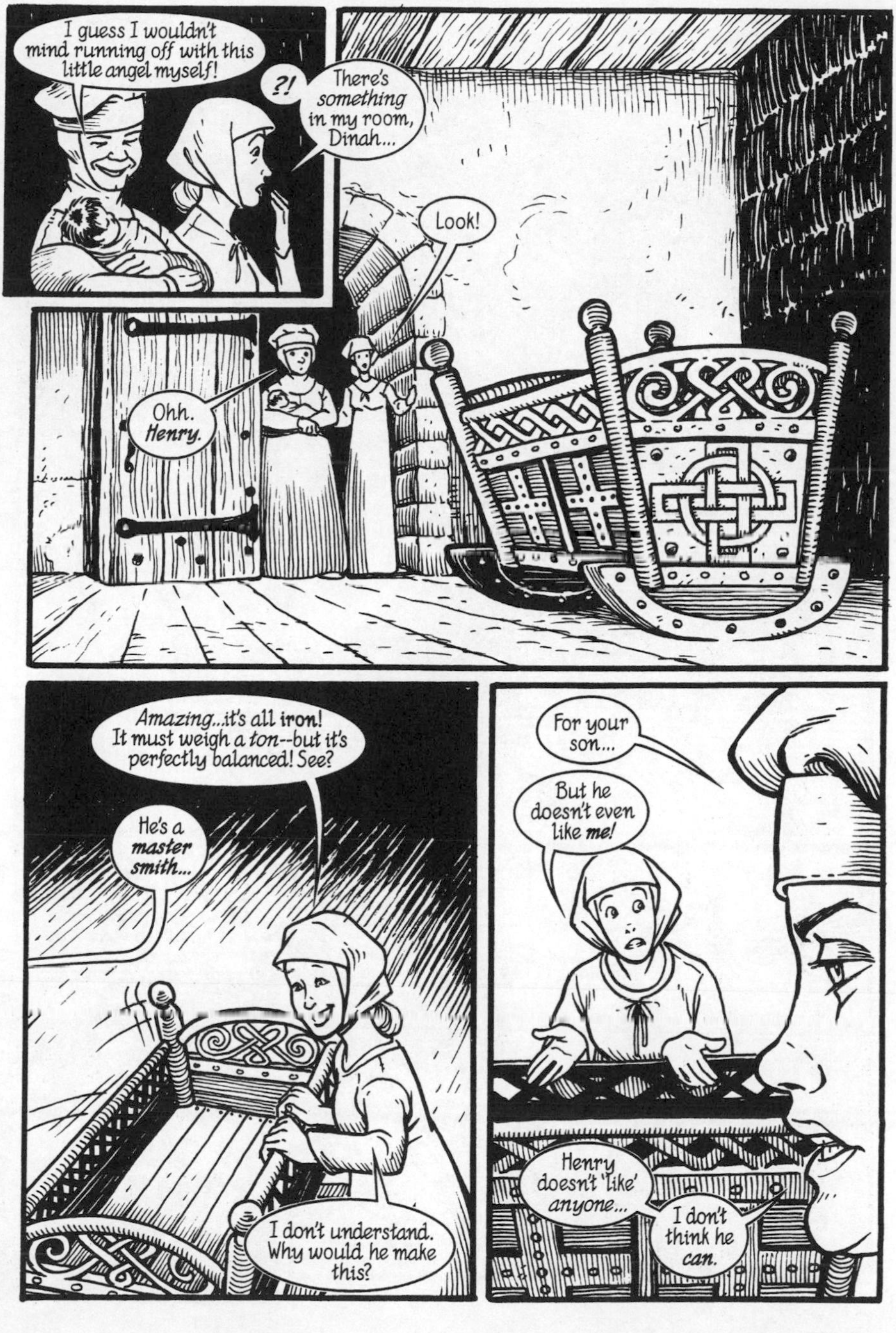
I guess I wouldn't mind running off with this little angel myself!
?!
There's *something* in my room, Dinah...
Look!
Ohh. *Henry.*
Amazing...it's all **iron**! It must weigh a *ton*--but it's perfectly balanced! See?
He's a ***master smith...***
I don't understand. Why would he make this?
For your son...
But he doesn't even like ***me!***
Henry doesn't 'like' *anyone*...
I don't think he ***can.***

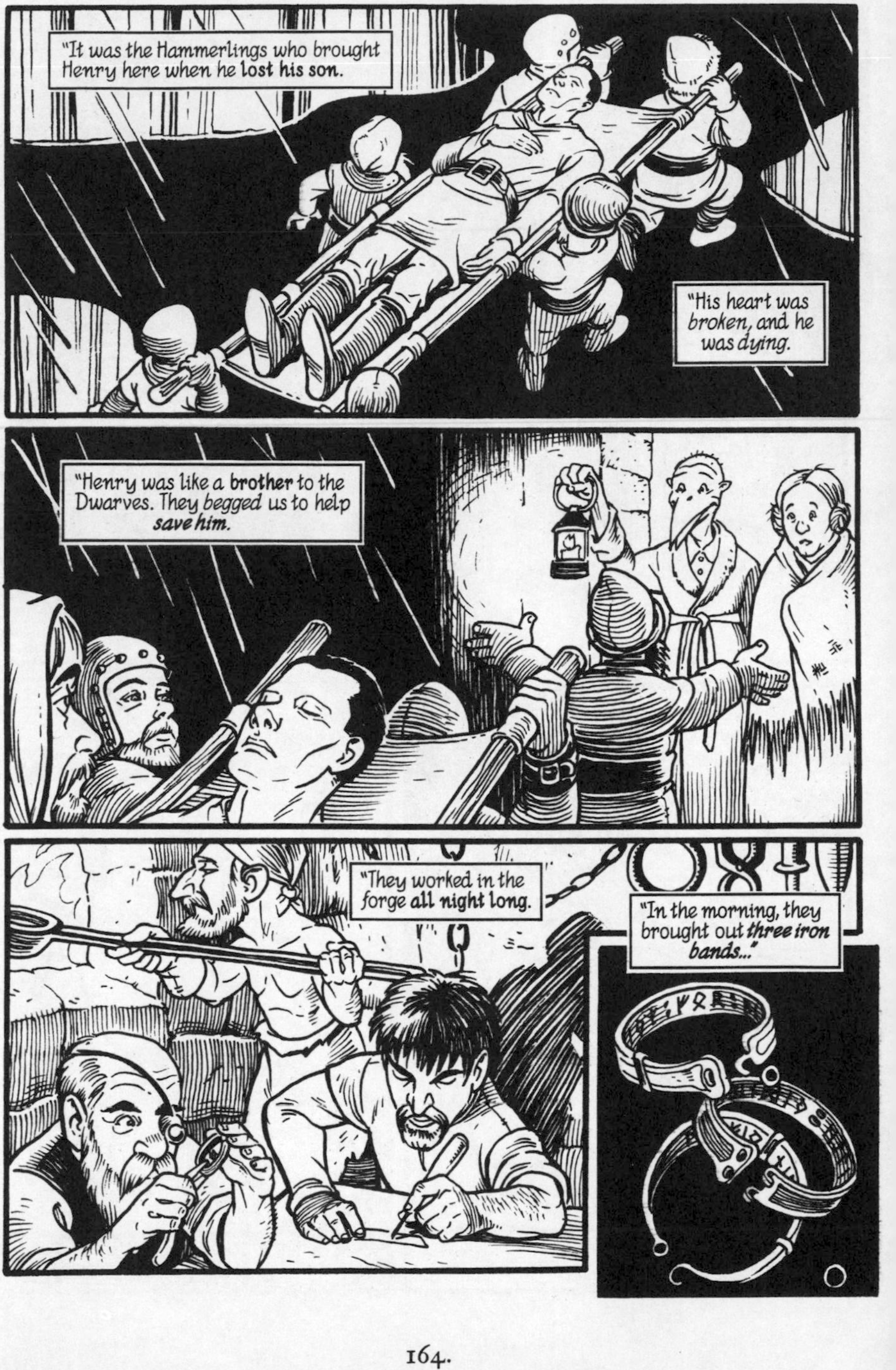
"It was the Hammerlings who brought Henry here when he lost his son.
"His heart was broken, and he was dying.
"Henry was like a brother to the Dwarves. They begged us to help save him.
"They worked in the forge all night long.
"In the morning, they brought out three iron bands..."

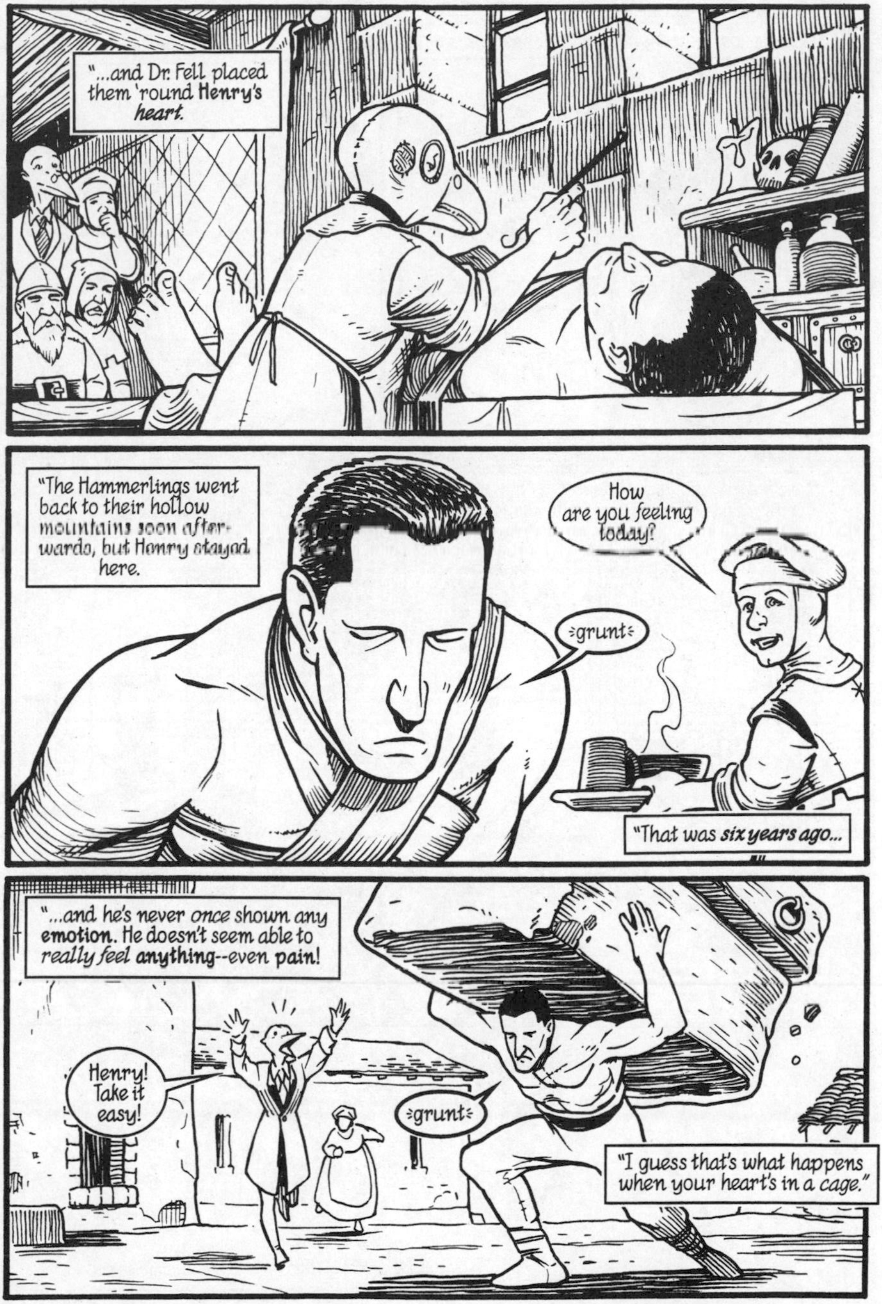
"...and Dr. Fell placed them 'round Henry's *heart.*
"The Hammerlings went back to their hollow mountains soon after-wards, but Henry stayed here.
How are you feeling today?
grunt
"That was *six years ago...*
"...and he's never *once* shown any **emotion**. He doesn't seem able to *really feel* **anything**--even pain!
Henry! Take it easy!
grunt
"I guess that's what happens when your heart's in a *cage.*"

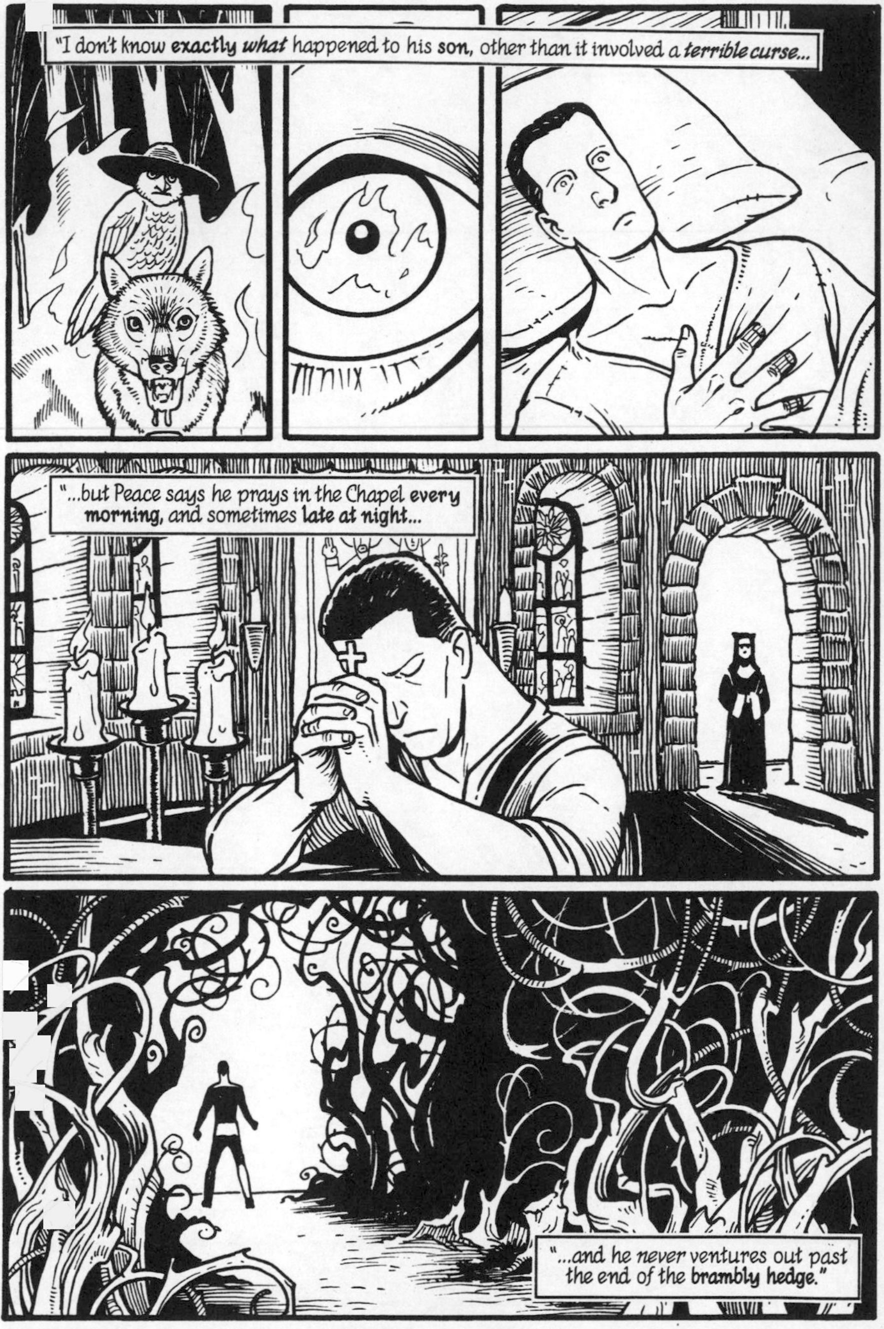
"I don't know exactly what happened to his son, other than it involved a terrible curse...
"...but Peace says he prays in the Chapel every morning, and sometimes late at night...
"...and he never ventures out past the end of the brambly hedge."

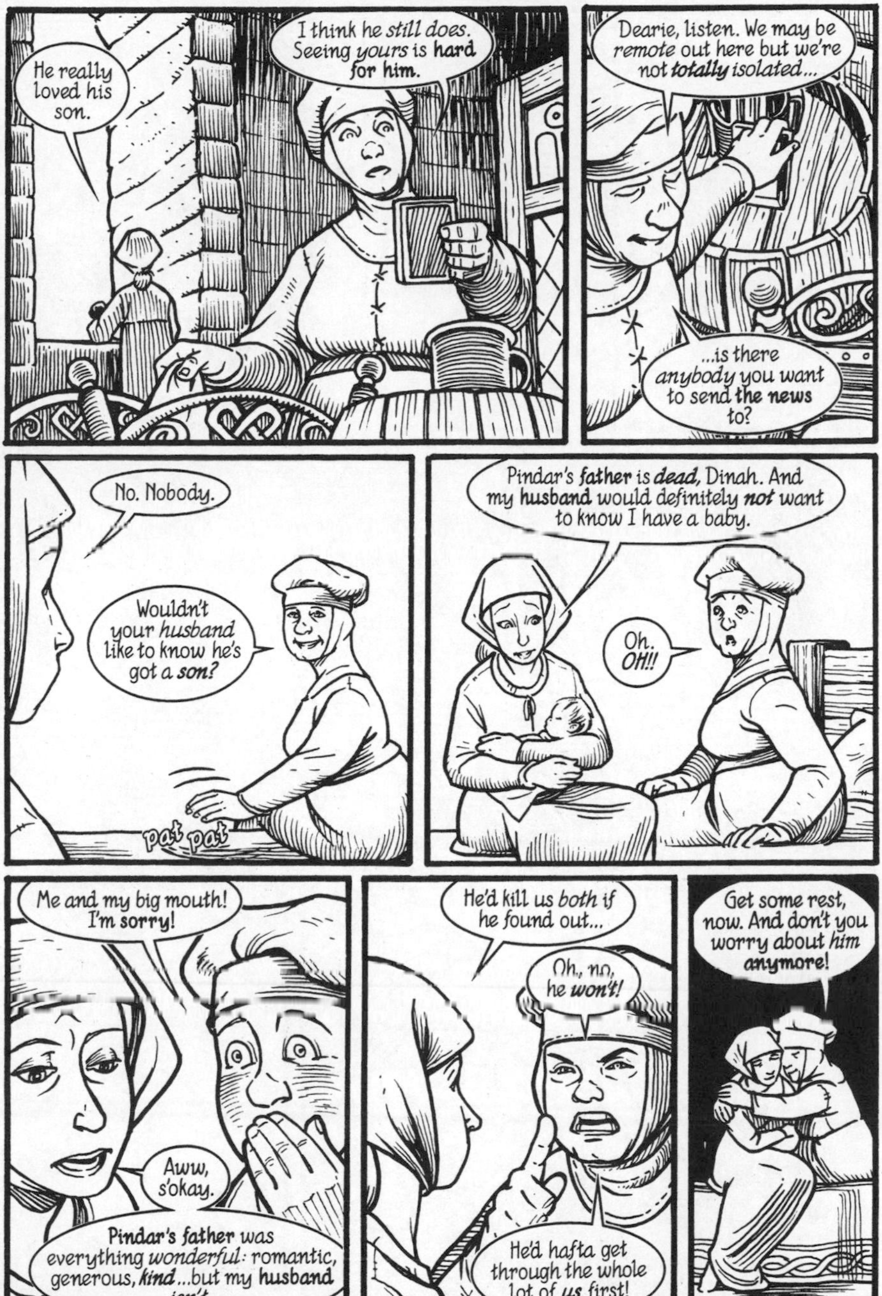
He really loved his son.
I think he *still does*. Seeing *yours* is **hard for him.**
Dearie, listen. We may be *remote* out here but we're not ***totally*** *isolated*...
...is there *anybody* you want to send **the news** to?
No. Nobody.
Wouldn't your *husband* like to know he's got a ***son?***
pat pat
Pindar's ***father*** is ***dead***, Dinah. And my **husband** would definitely ***not*** want to know I have a baby.
Oh. *OH!!*
Me and my big mouth! I'm **sorry**!
Aww, s'okay.
Pindar's *father* was everything *wonderful*: romantic, generous, ***kind***...but my **husband** *isn't*.
He'd kill us *both* if he found out...
Oh, no, he ***won't!***
He'd hafta get through the whole lot of ***us*** first!
Get some rest, now. And don't you worry about *him* **anymore**!

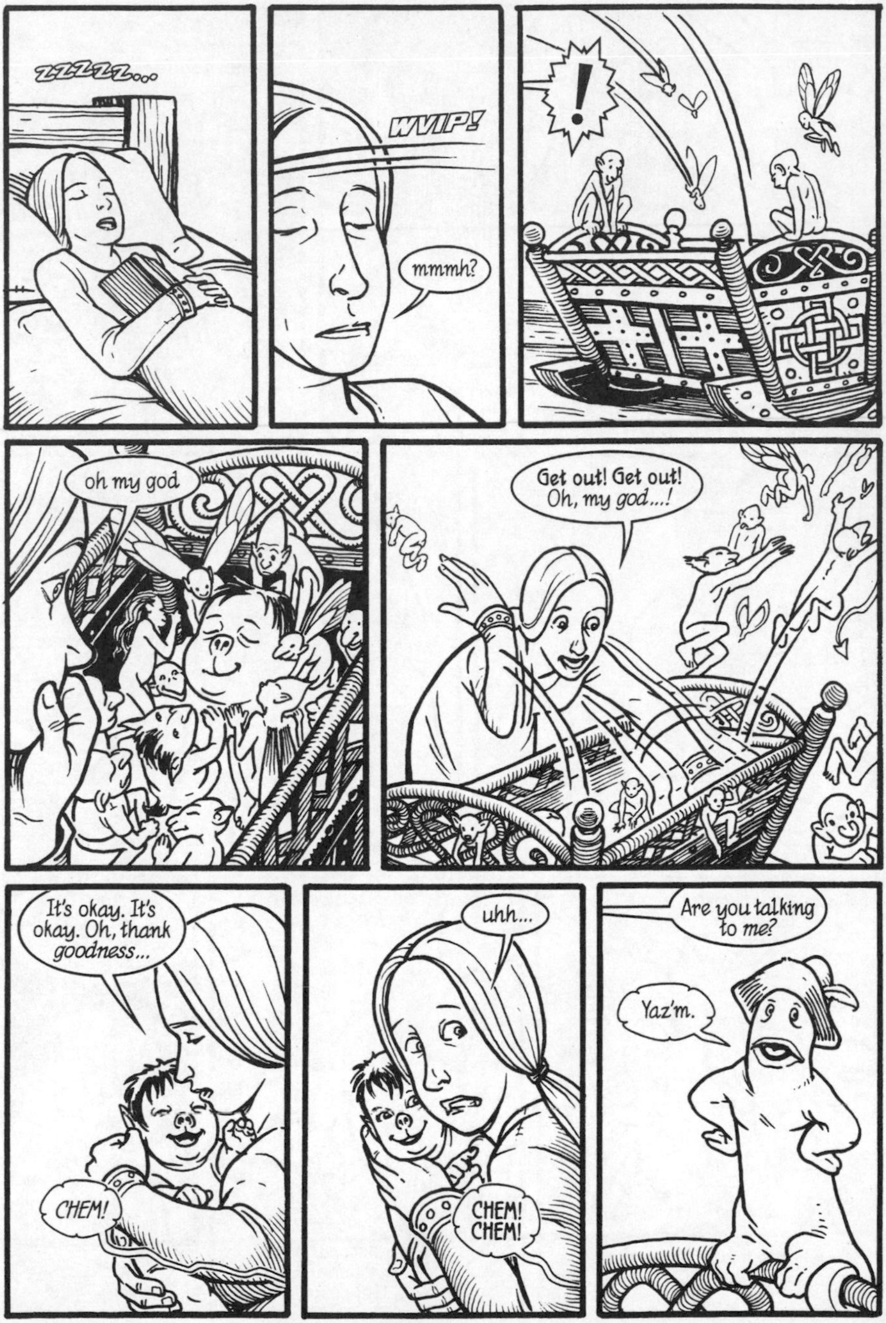
ZZZZZ...
WVIP!
mmmh?
!
oh my god
Get out! Get out!
Oh, my god...!
It's okay. It's okay. Oh, thank goodness...
CHEM!
uhh...
CHEM! CHEM!
Are you talking to me?
Yaz'm.

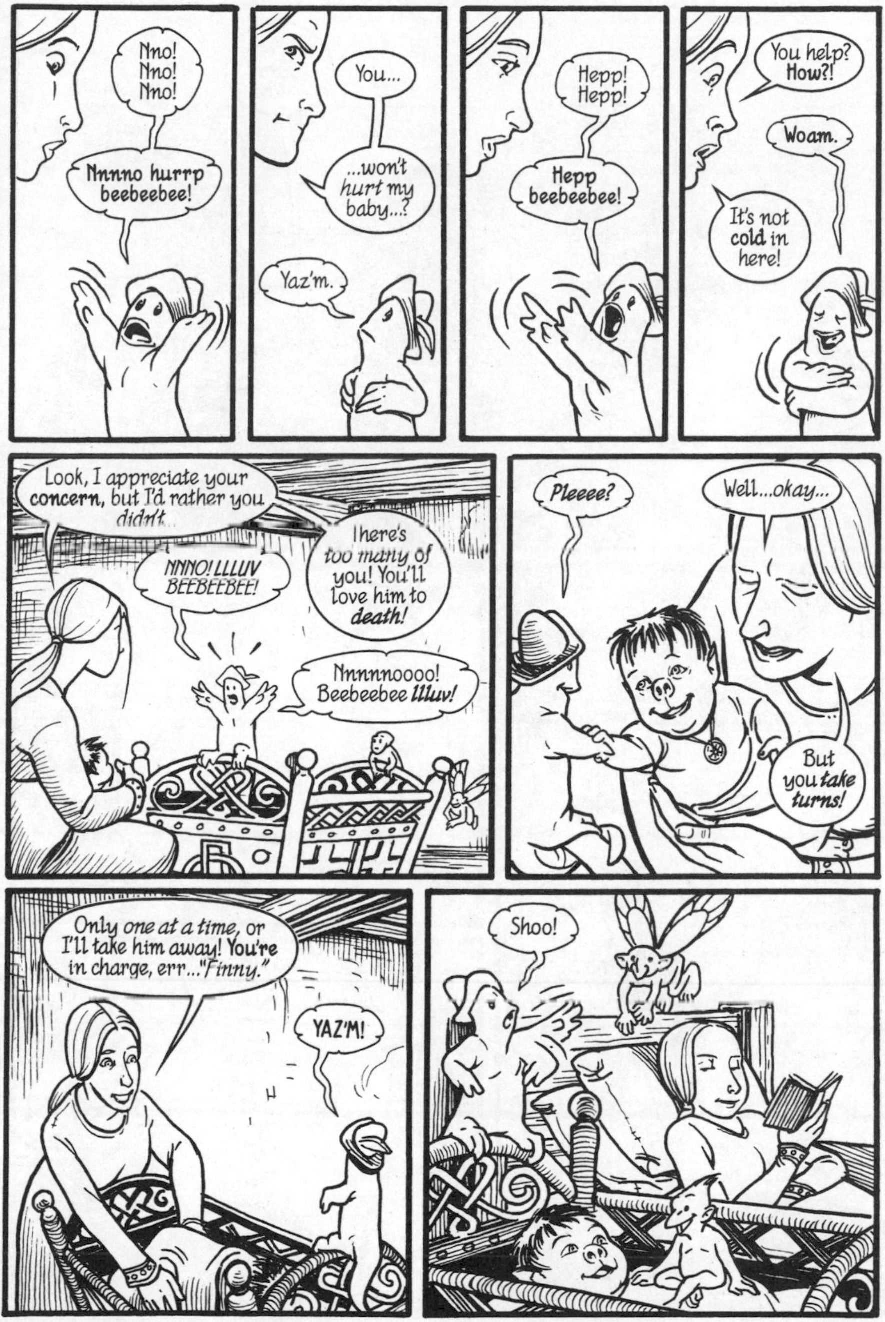
Nno! Nno! Nno!
Nnnno hurrp beebeebee!
You...
...won't hurt my baby...?
Yaz'm.
Hepp! Hepp!
Hepp beebeebee!
You help? How?!
Woam.
It's not cold in here!
Look, I appreciate your concern, but I'd rather you didn't...
NNNO! LLLUV BEEBEEBEE!
There's too many of you! You'll love him to death!
Nnnnnoooo! Beebeebee llluv!
Pleeee?
Well...okay...
But you take turns!
Only one at a time, or I'll take him away! You're in charge, err..."Finny."
YAZ'M!
Shoo!

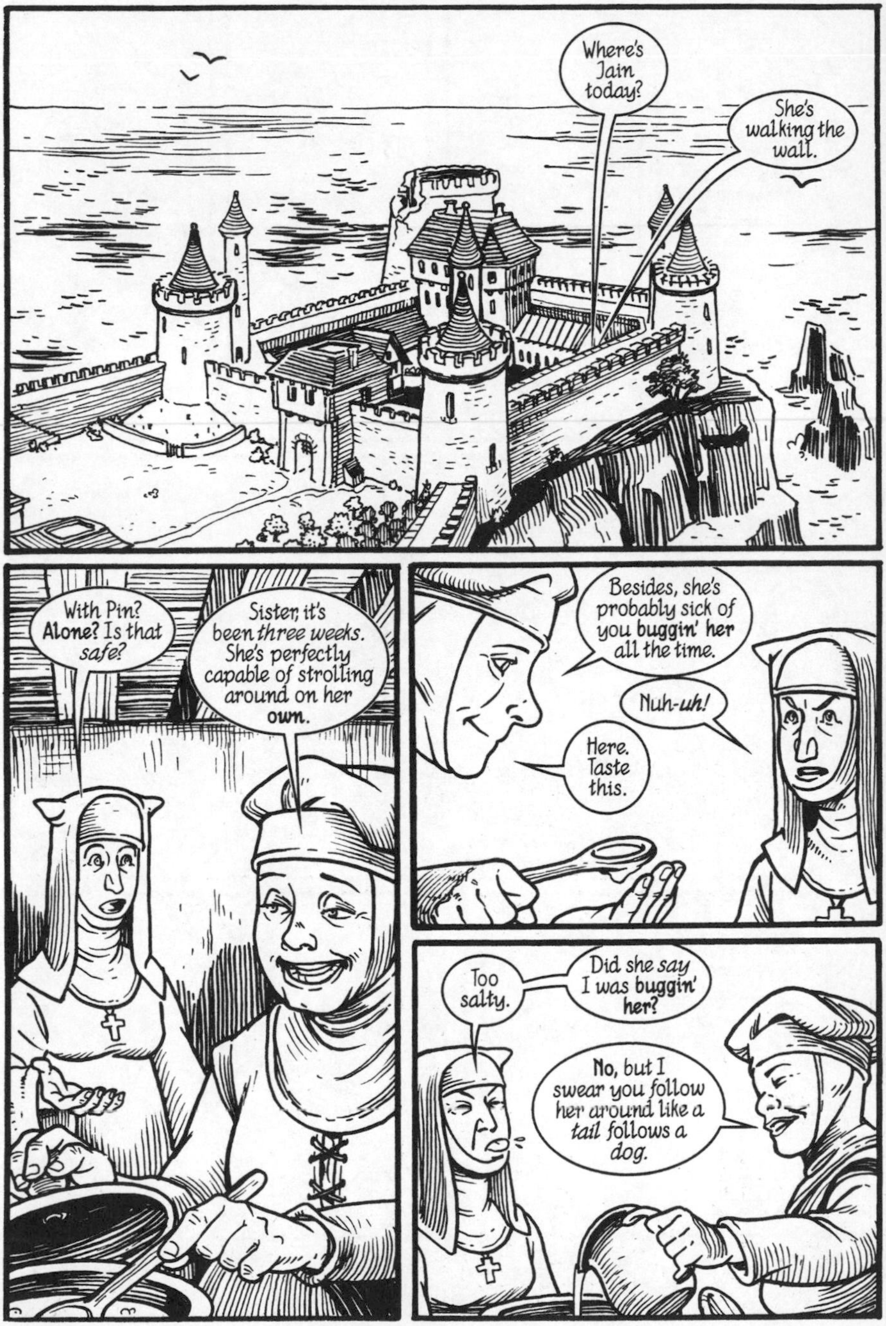
Where's Jain today?
She's walking the wall.
With Pin? Alone? Is that safe?
Sister, it's been three weeks. She's perfectly capable of strolling around on her own.
Besides, she's probably sick of you buggin' her all the time.
Nuh-uh!
Here. Taste this.
Too salty.
Did she say I was buggin' her?
No, but I swear you follow her around like a tail follows a dog.

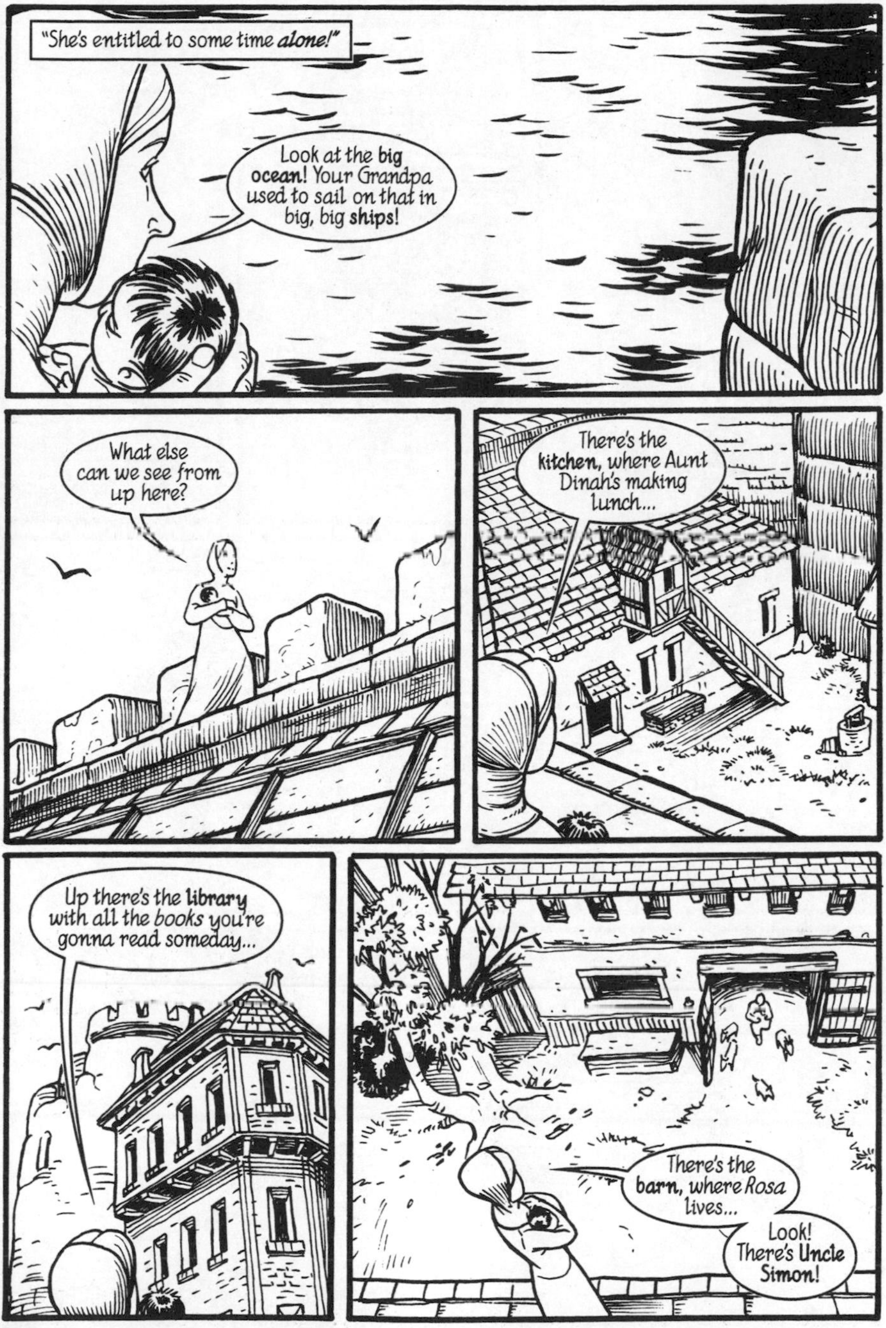
"She's entitled to some time alone!"
Look at the big ocean! Your Grandpa used to sail on that in big, big ships!
What else can we see from up here?
There's the kitchen, where Aunt Dinah's making lunch...
Up there's the library with all the books you're gonna read someday...
There's the barn, where Rosa lives...
Look! There's Uncle Simon!

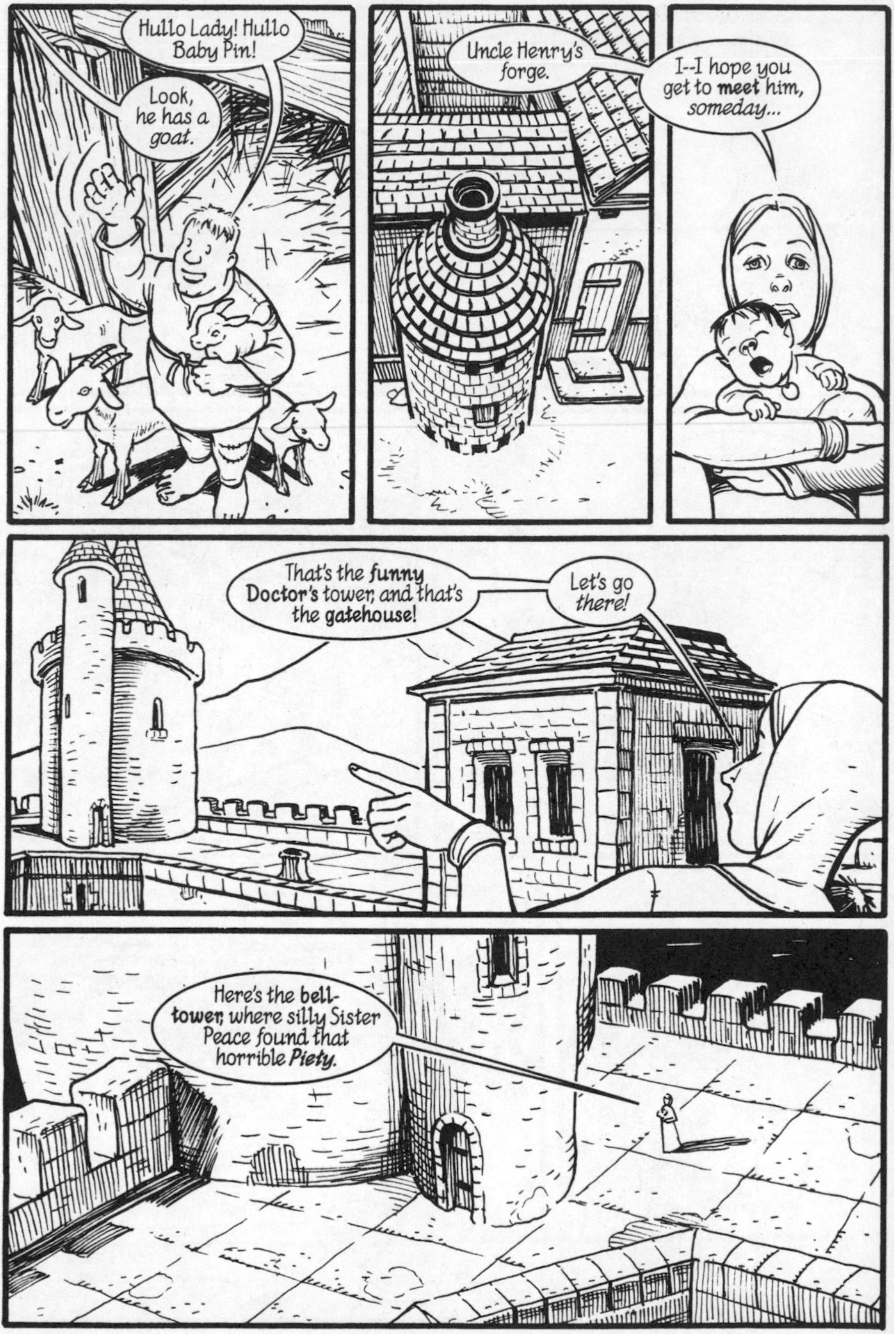
Hullo Lady! Hullo Baby Pin!
Look, he has a goat.
Uncle Henry's forge.
I--I hope you get to **meet** him, *someday...*
That's the **funny Doctor's** tower, and that's the **gatehouse!**
Let's go *there!*
Here's the **bell-tower,** where silly Sister Peace found that horrible *Piety.*

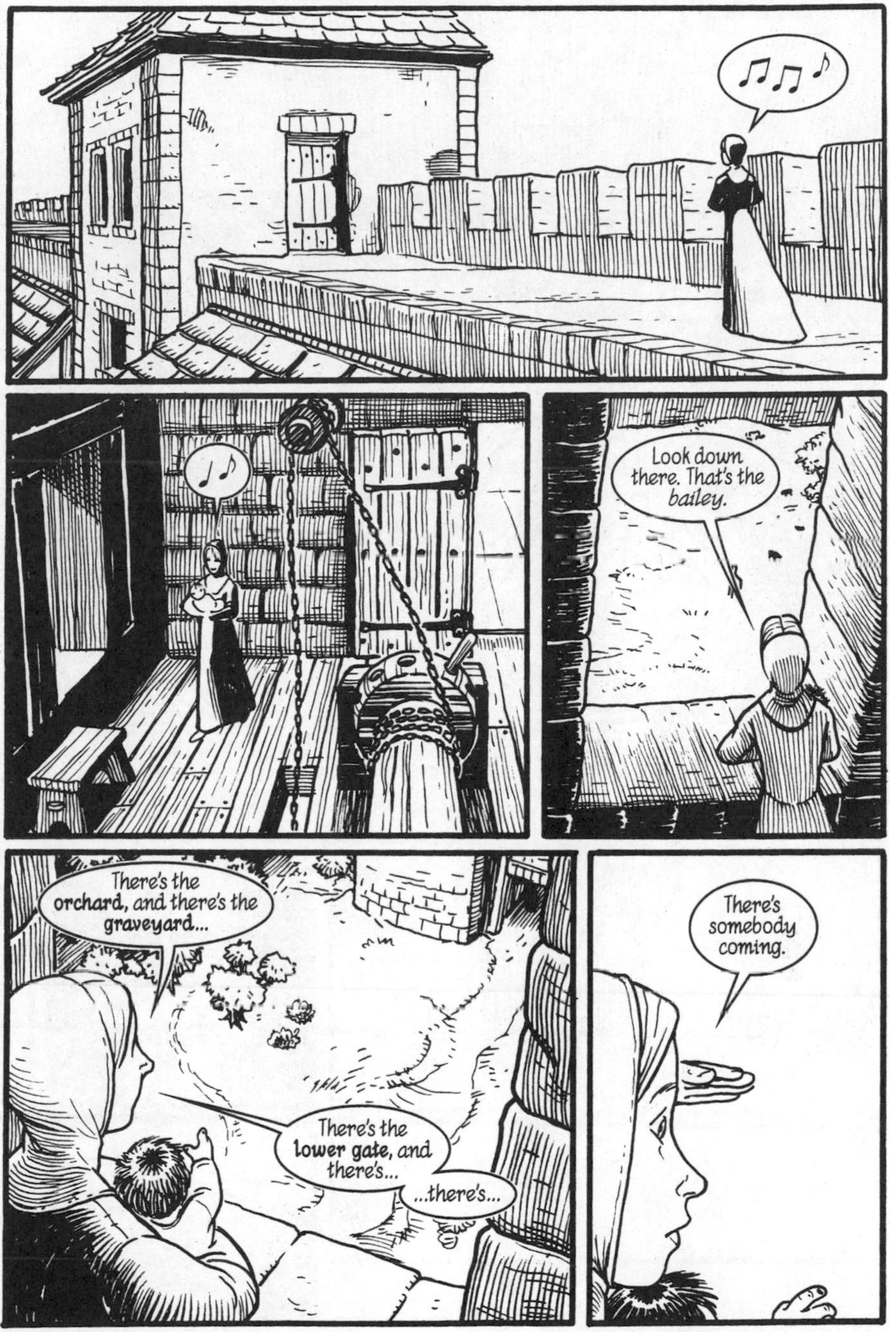
Look down there. That's the *bailey.*
There's the **orchard**, and there's the **graveyard**...
There's the **lower gate**, and there's...
...there's...
There's somebody coming.

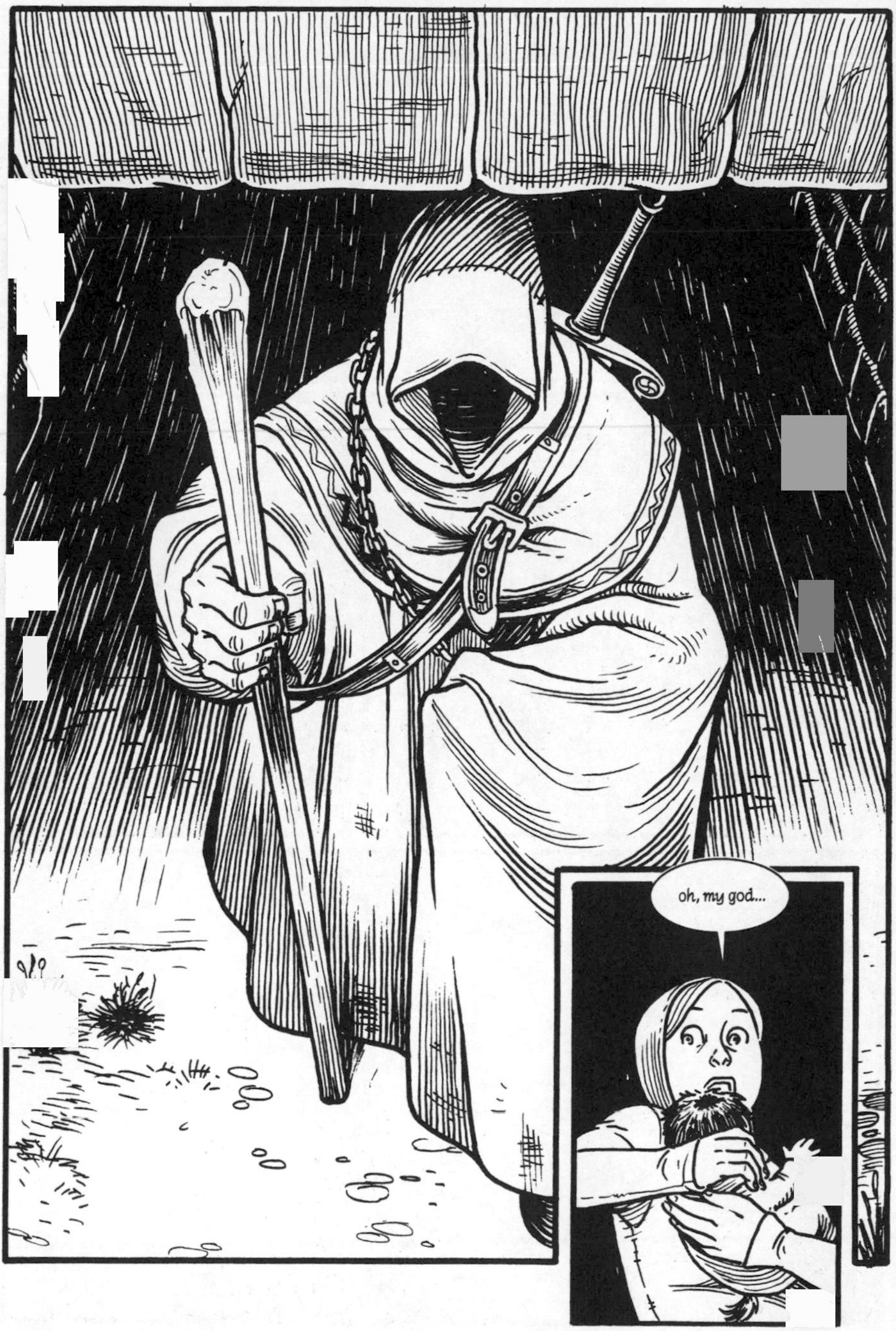
oh, my god...

Chapter 8.

· CAVALIER ·

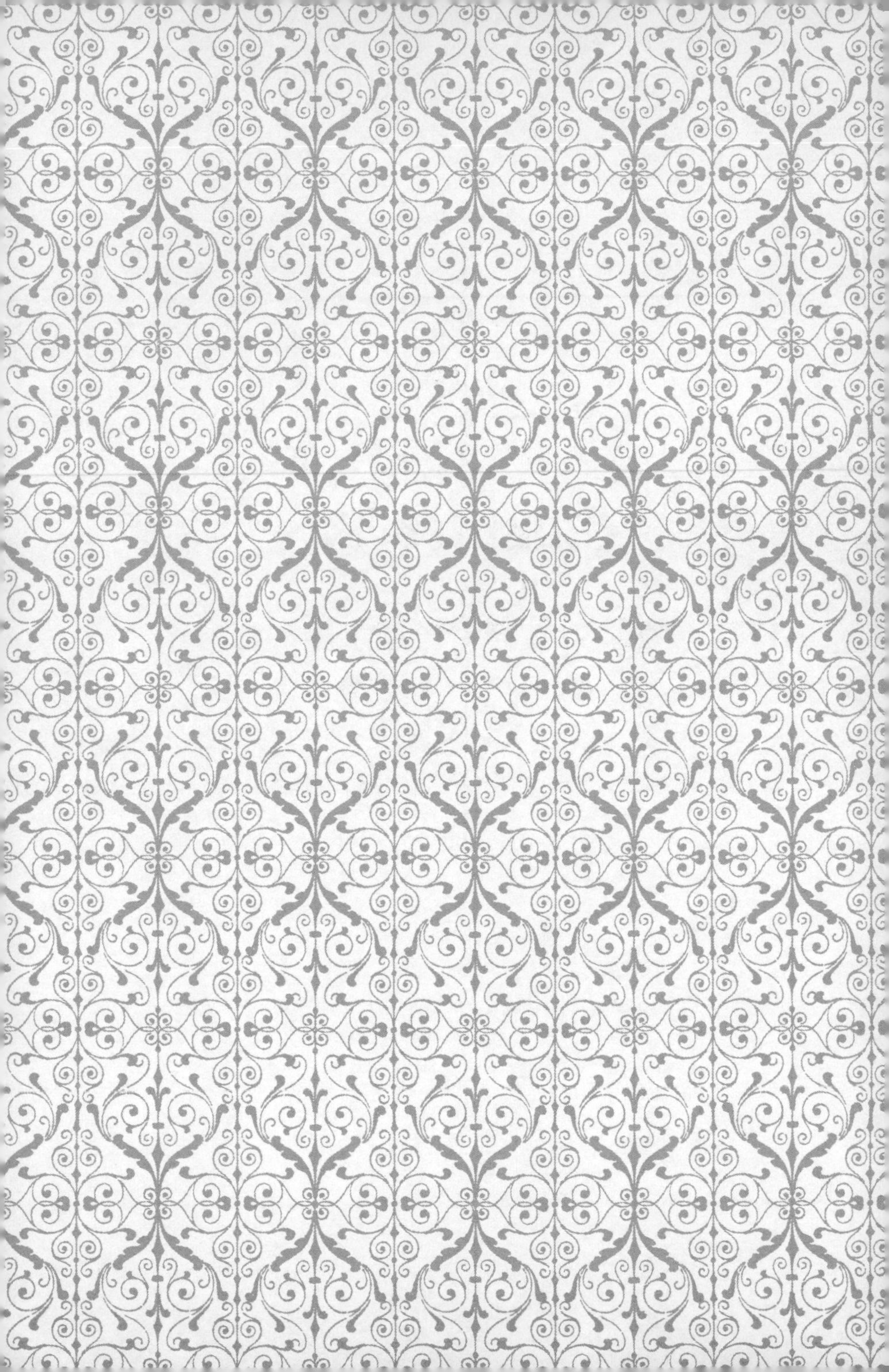

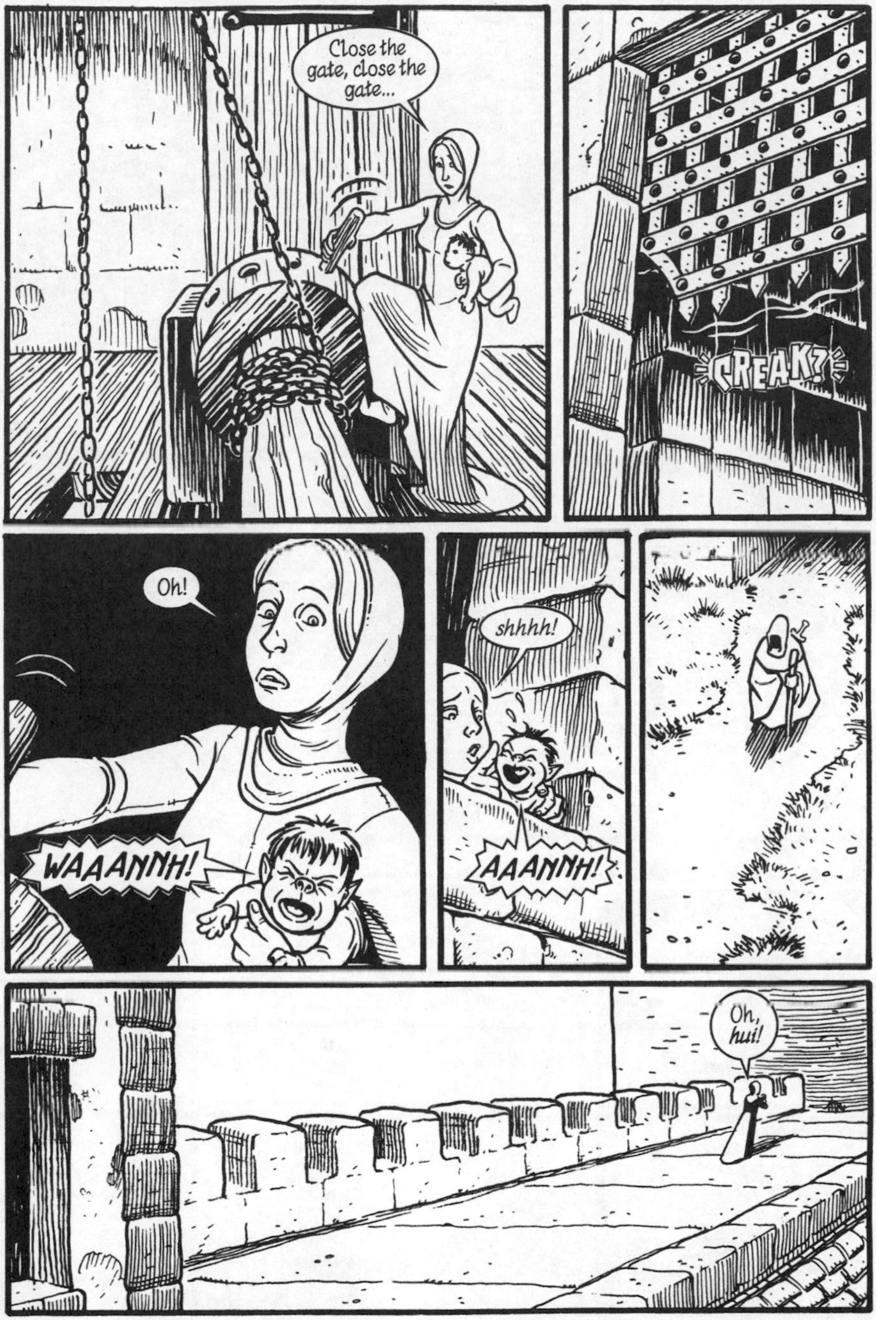
Close the gate, close the gate...
CREAK?
Oh!
WAAANNH!
shhhh!
AAANNH!
Oh, hui!

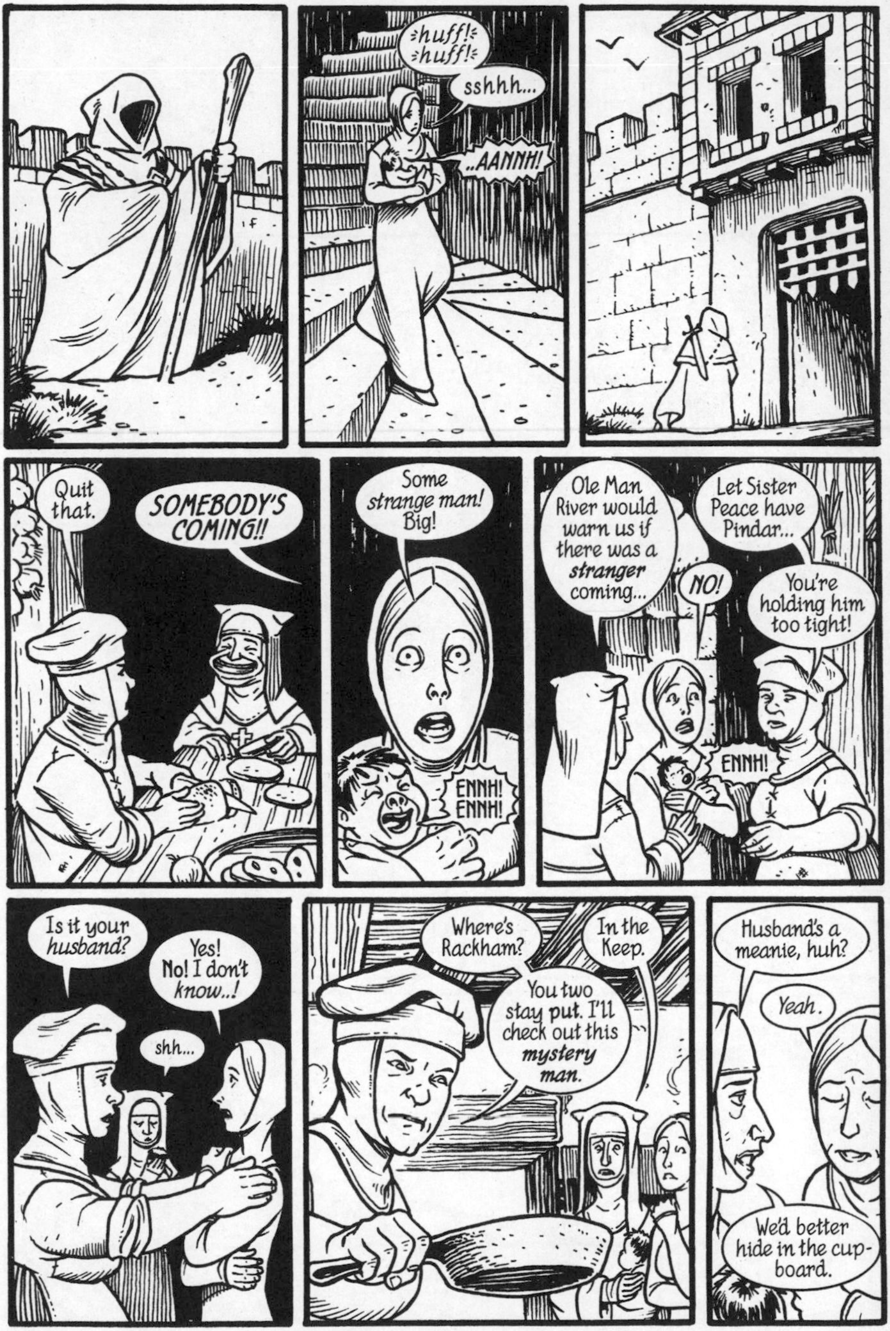
huff! huff!
sshhh...
..AANNH!
Quit that.
SOMEBODY'S COMING!!
Some strange man! Big!
ENNH! ENNH!
Ole Man River would warn us if there was a stranger coming...
NO!
Let Sister Peace have Pindar...
You're holding him too tight!
ENNH!
Is it your husband?
Yes! No! I don't know..!
shh...
Where's Rackham?
In the Keep.
You two stay put. I'll check out this mystery man.
Husband's a meanie, huh?
Yeah.
We'd better hide in the cupboard.

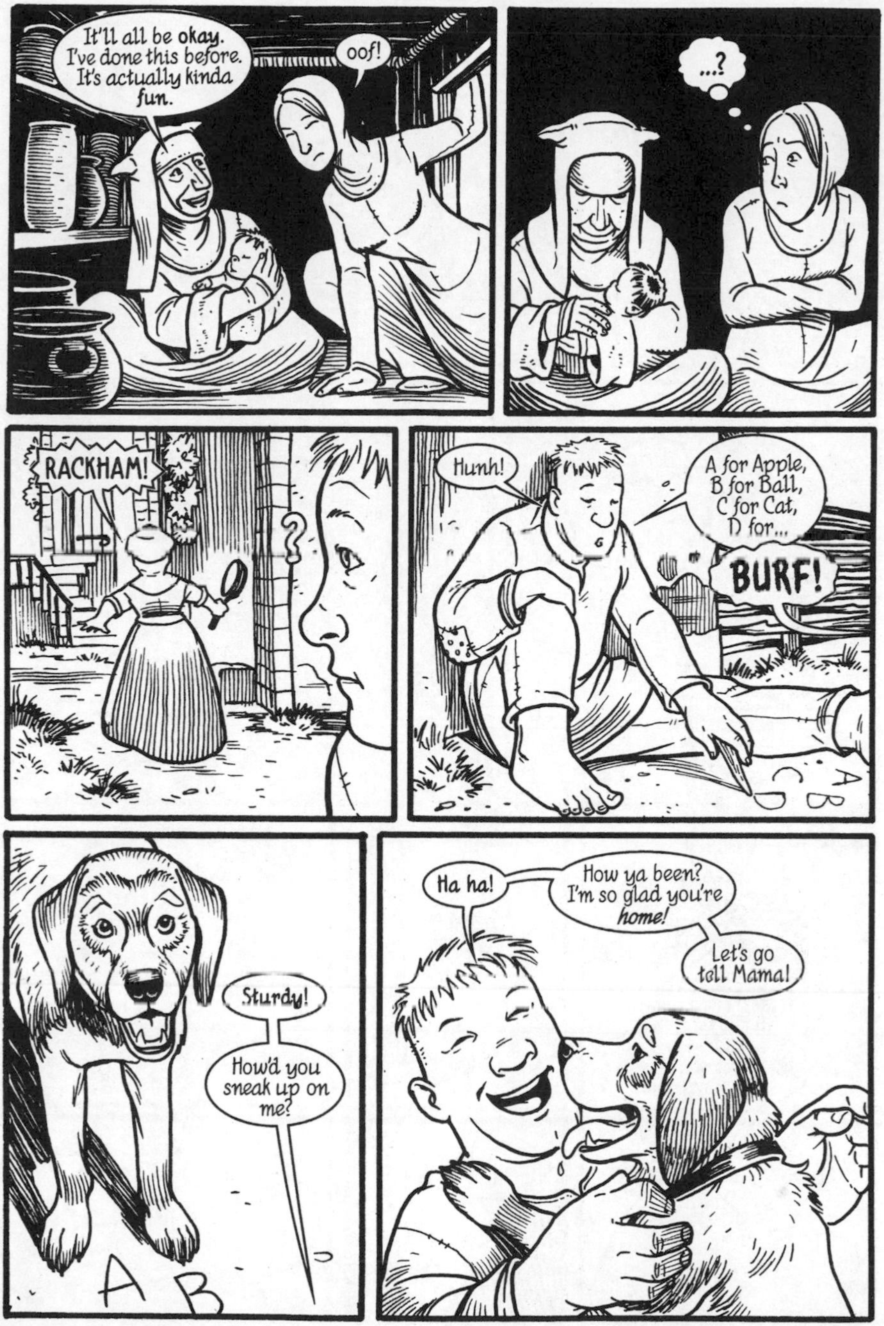
It'll all be okay. I've done this before. It's actually kinda fun.
oof!
...?
RACKHAM!
?
Hunh!
A for Apple, B for Ball, C for Cat, D for...
BURF!
Sturdy!
How'd you sneak up on me?
Ha ha!
How ya been? I'm so glad you're home!
Let's go tell Mama!

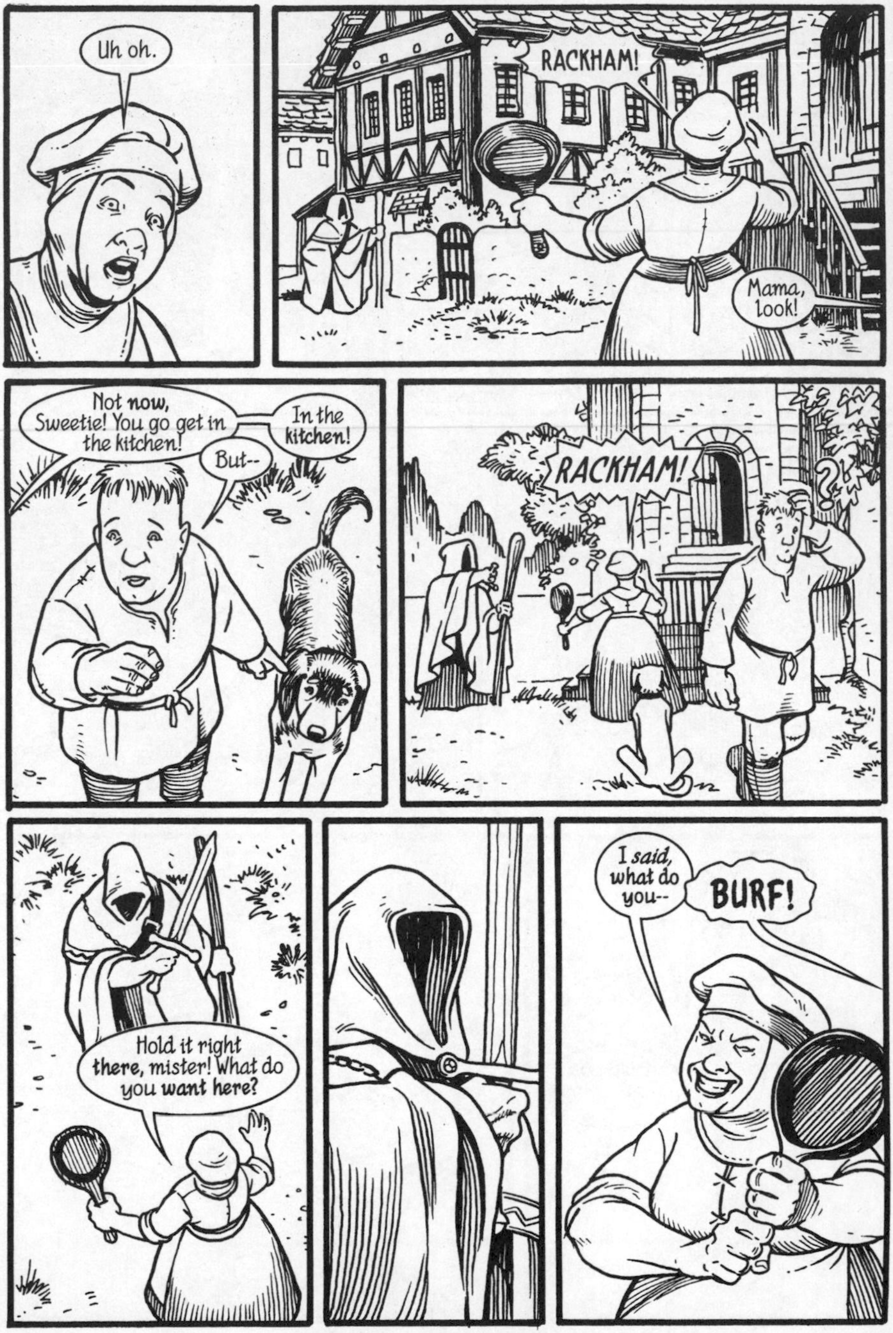
Uh oh.
RACKHAM!
Mama, look!
Not now, Sweetie! You go get in the kitchen!
In the kitchen!
But--
RACKHAM!
?
Hold it right there, mister! What do you want here?
I said, what do you--
BURF!

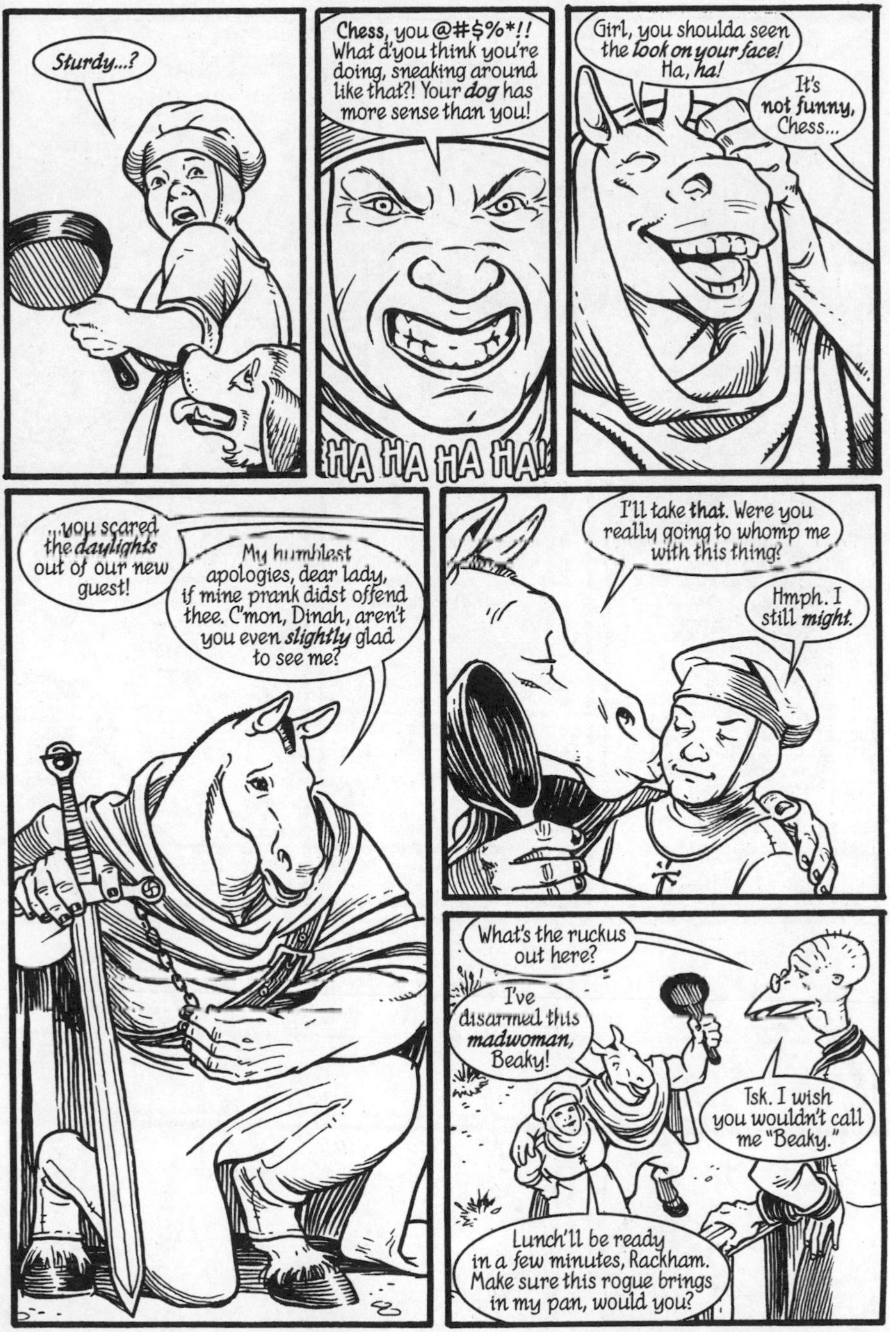
Sturdy...?
Chess, you @#$%*!! What d'you think you're doing, sneaking around like that?! Your dog has more sense than you!
HA HA HA HA!
Girl, you shoulda seen the look on your face! Ha, ha!
It's not funny, Chess...
...you scared the daylights out of our new guest!
My humblest apologies, dear lady, if mine prank didst offend thee. C'mon, Dinah, aren't you even slightly glad to see me?
I'll take that. Were you really going to whomp me with this thing?
Hmph. I still might.
What's the ruckus out here?
I've disarmed this madwoman, Beaky!
Tsk. I wish you wouldn't call me "Beaky."
Lunch'll be ready in a few minutes, Rackham. Make sure this rogue brings in my pan, would you?

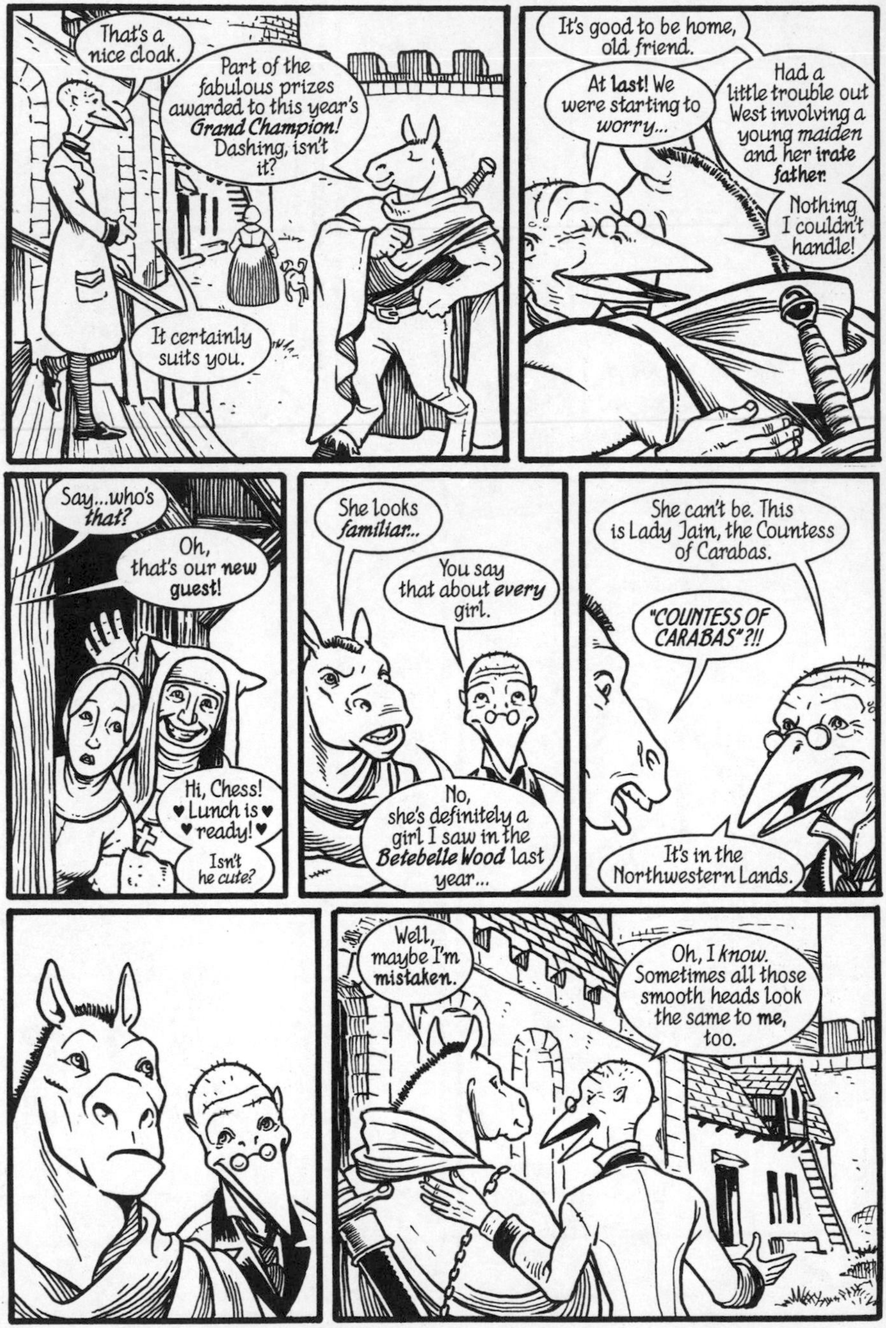
That's a nice cloak.
Part of the fabulous prizes awarded to this year's *Grand Champion!* Dashing, isn't it?
It certainly suits you.
It's good to be home, old friend.
At **last!** We were starting to *worry...*
Had a little trouble out West involving a young *maiden* and her **irate father.**
Nothing I couldn't handle!
Say...who's *that?*
Oh, that's our **new guest!**
Hi, Chess! ♥ Lunch is ♥ ♥ ready! ♥
Isn't he cute?
She looks *familiar...*
You say that about **every** girl.
No, she's definitely a girl I saw in the ***Betebelle Wood*** last year...
She can't be. This is Lady Jain, the Countess of Carabas.
"COUNTESS OF CARABAS"?!!
It's in the Northwestern Lands.
Well, maybe I'm **mistaken.**
Oh, I *know.* Sometimes all those smooth heads look the same to **me,** too.

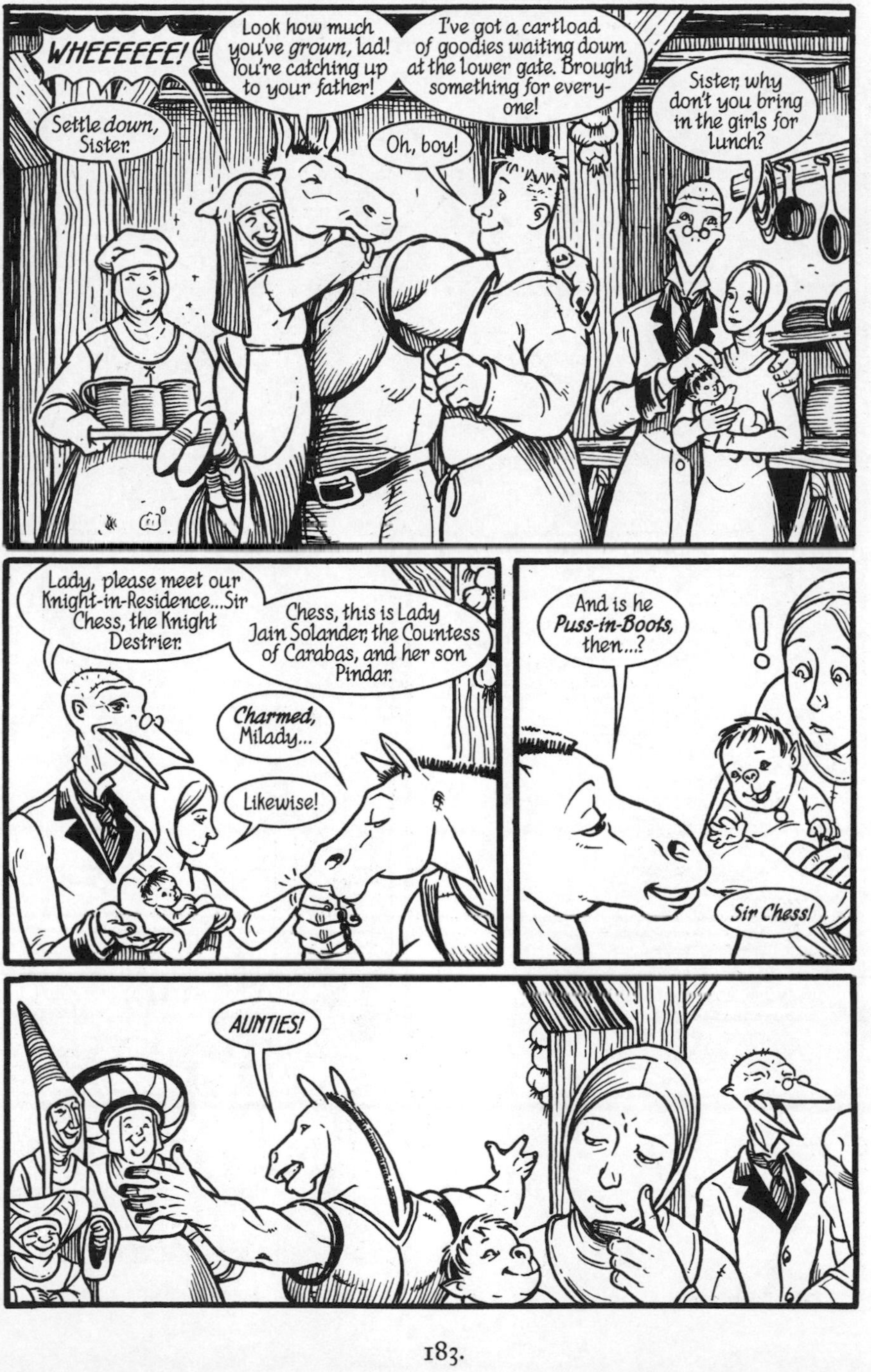
WHEEEEEEE!
Look how much you've *grown*, lad! You're catching up to your father!
I've got a cartload of goodies waiting down at the lower gate. Brought something for every-one!
Settle down, Sister.
Oh, boy!
Sister, why don't you bring in the girls for lunch?
Lady, please meet our Knight-in-Residence...Sir Chess, the Knight Destrier.
Chess, this is Lady Jain Solander, the Countess of Carabas, and her son Pindar.
Charmed, Milady...
Likewise!
And is he *Puss-in-Boots*, then...?
!
Sir Chess!
AUNTIES!

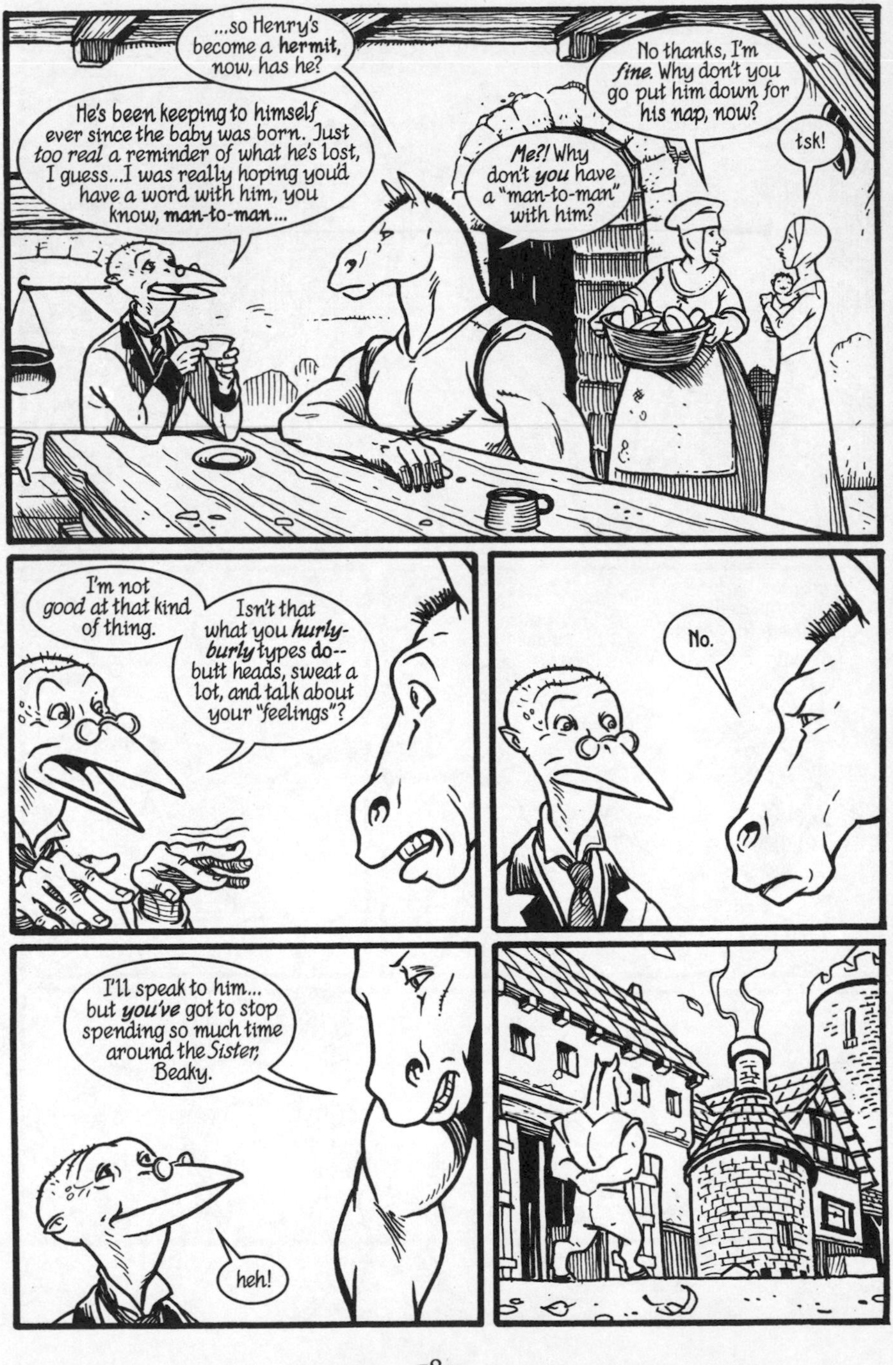
...so Henry's become a **hermit**, now, has he?
He's been keeping to himself ever since the baby was born. Just *too real* a reminder of what he's lost, I guess...I was really hoping you'd have a word with him, you know, **man-to-man**...
Me?! Why don't **you** have a "man-to-man" with him?
No thanks, I'm *fine*. Why don't you go put him down for his nap, now?
tsk!
I'm not *good* at that kind of thing.
Isn't that what you ***hurly-burly*** types do-- butt heads, sweat a lot, and talk about your "*feelings*"?
No.
I'll speak to him... but ***you've*** got to stop spending so much time around the *Sister*, Beaky.
heh!

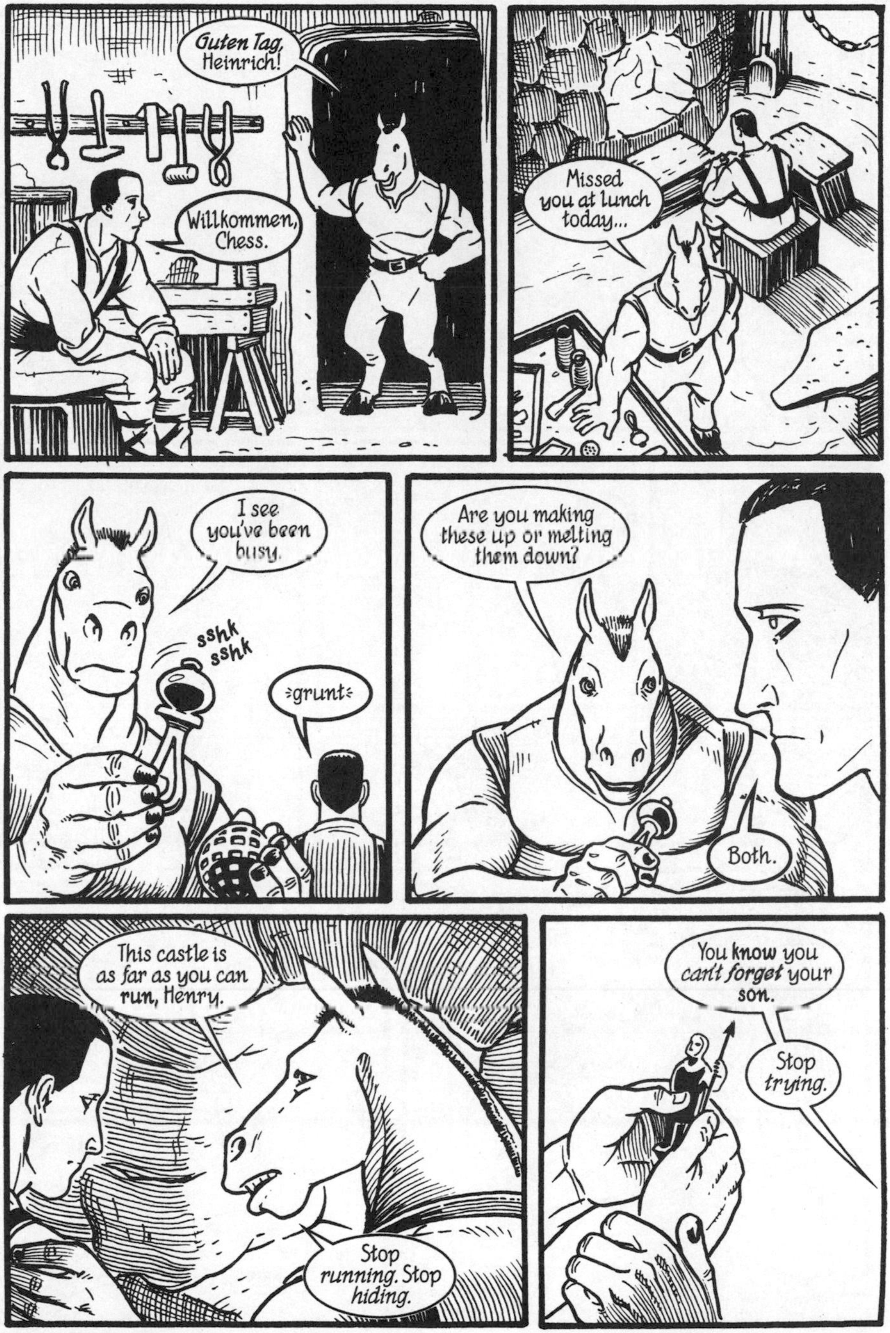
Guten Tag, Heinrich!
Willkommen, Chess.
Missed you at lunch today...
I see you've been busy.
sshk sshk
grunt
Are you making these up or melting them down?
Both.
This castle is as far as you can run, Henry.
Stop running. Stop hiding.
You know you can't forget your son.
Stop trying.

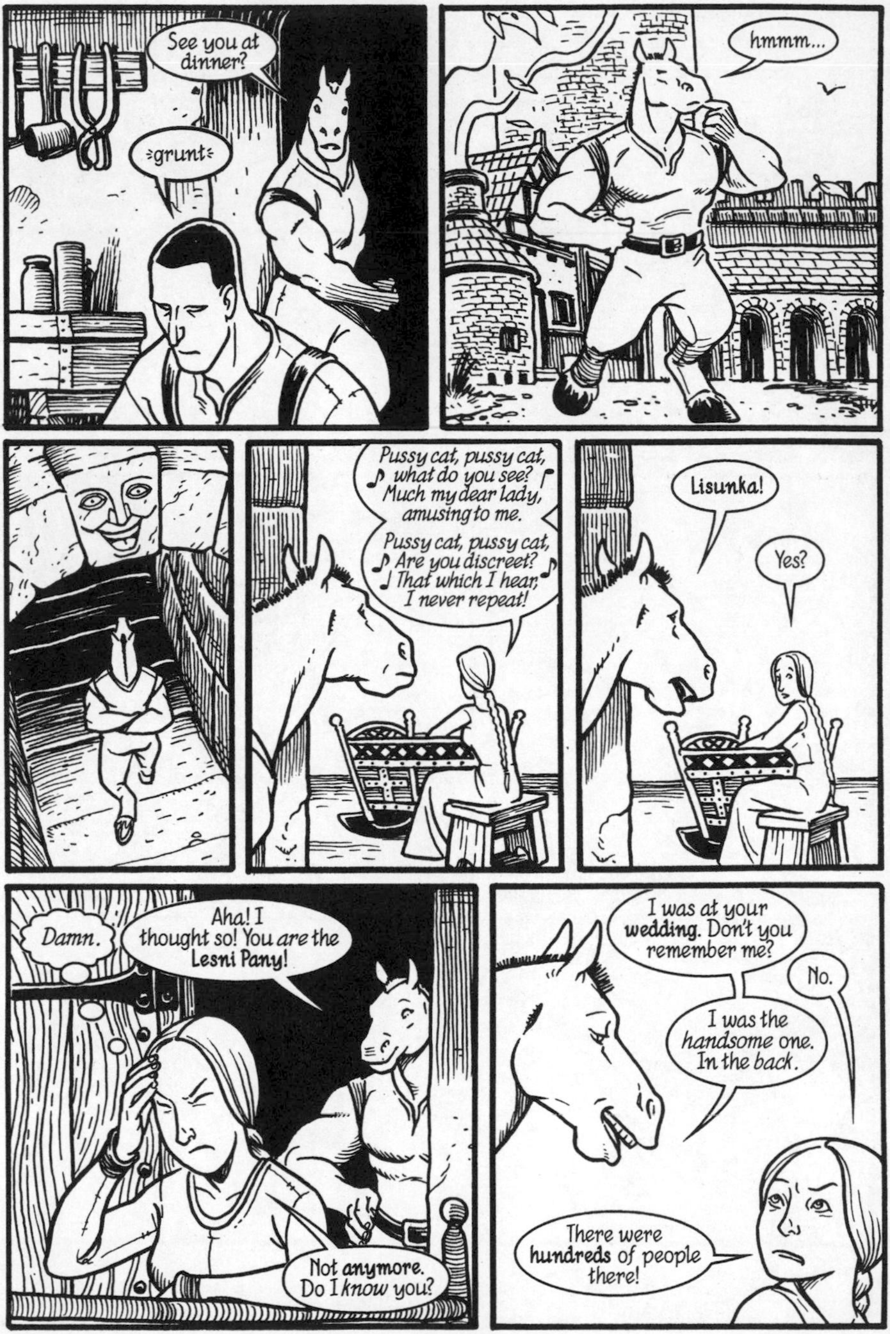
See you at dinner?
grunt
hmmm...
Pussy cat, pussy cat, what do you see? Much my dear lady, amusing to me.
Pussy cat, pussy cat, Are you discreet? That which I hear, I never repeat!
Lisunka!
Yes?
Damn.
Aha! I thought so! You *are* the **Lesni Pany**!
Not **anymore**. Do I *know* you?
I was at your **wedding**. Don't you remember me?
No.
I was the *handsome* one. In the *back*.
There were **hundreds** of people there!

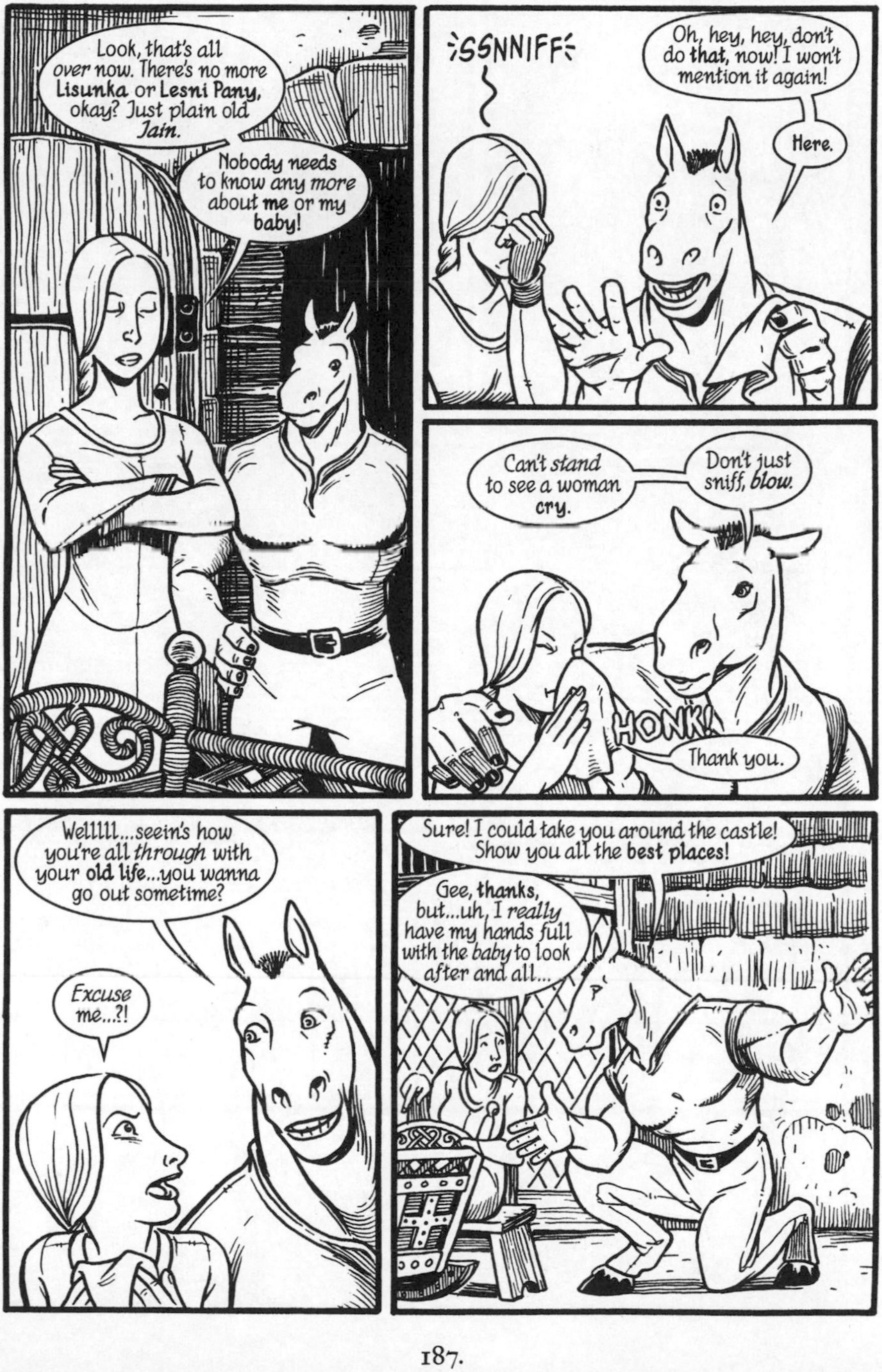
Look, that's all over now. There's no more **Lisunka** or **Lesni Pany,** okay? Just plain old *Jain.*
Nobody **needs** to know *any more* about **me** or my **baby!**
SSNNIFF
Oh, hey, hey, don't do **that,** now! I won't mention it again!
Here.
Can't *stand* to see a woman **cry.**
Don't just sniff, *blow.*
HONK!
Thank you.
Wellllll...seein's how you're all *through* with your **old life**...you wanna go out sometime?
Excuse me...?!
Sure! I could take you around the castle! Show you all the **best places!**
Gee, **thanks,** but...uh, I *really* have my hands full with the *baby* to look after and all...

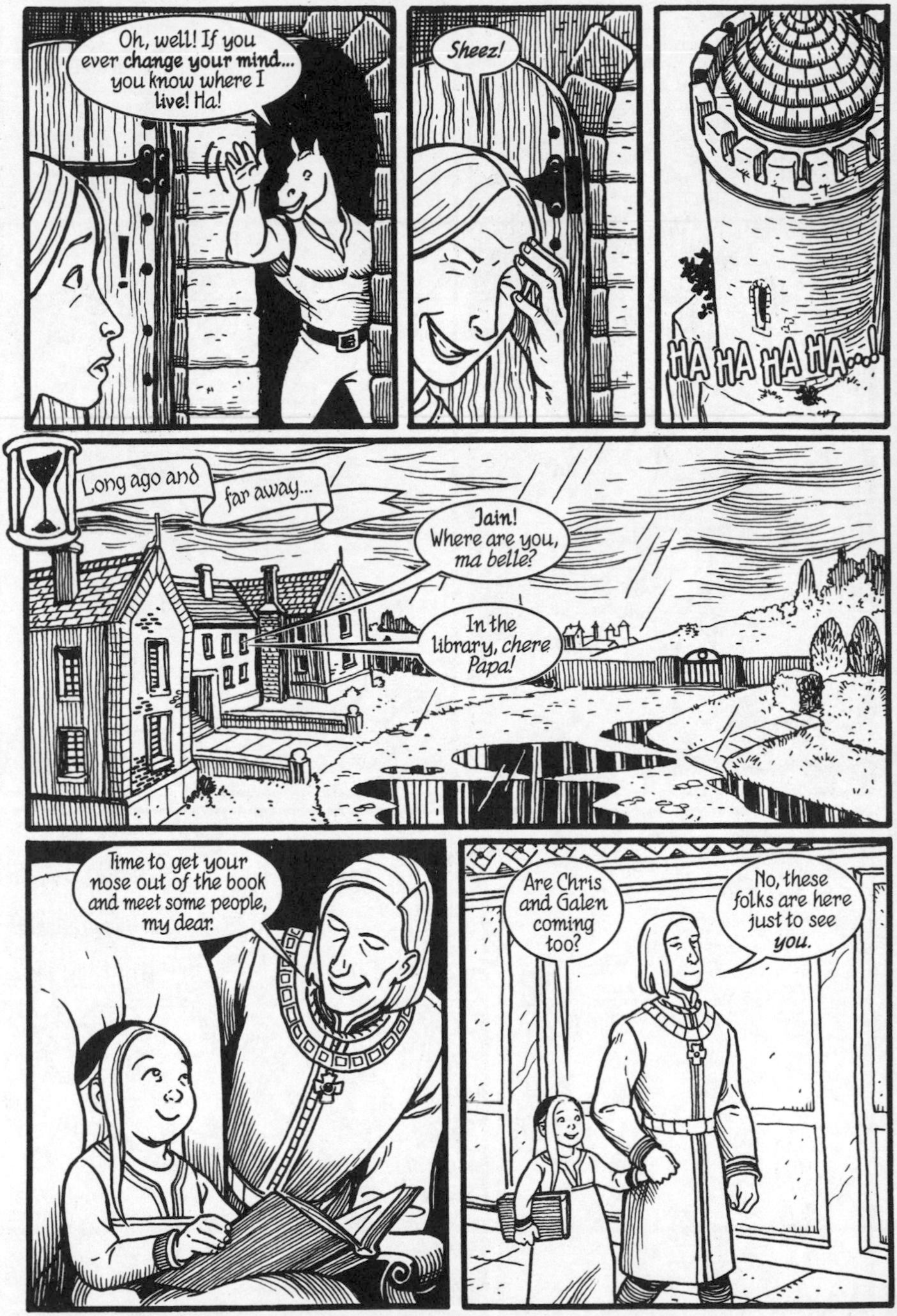
Oh, well! If you ever change your mind... you know where I live! Ha!
!
Sheez!
HA HA HA HA...!
Long ago and
far away...
Jain! Where are you, ma belle?
In the library, chere Papa!
Time to get your nose out of the book and meet some people, my dear.
Are Chris and Galen coming too?
No, these folks are here just to see you.

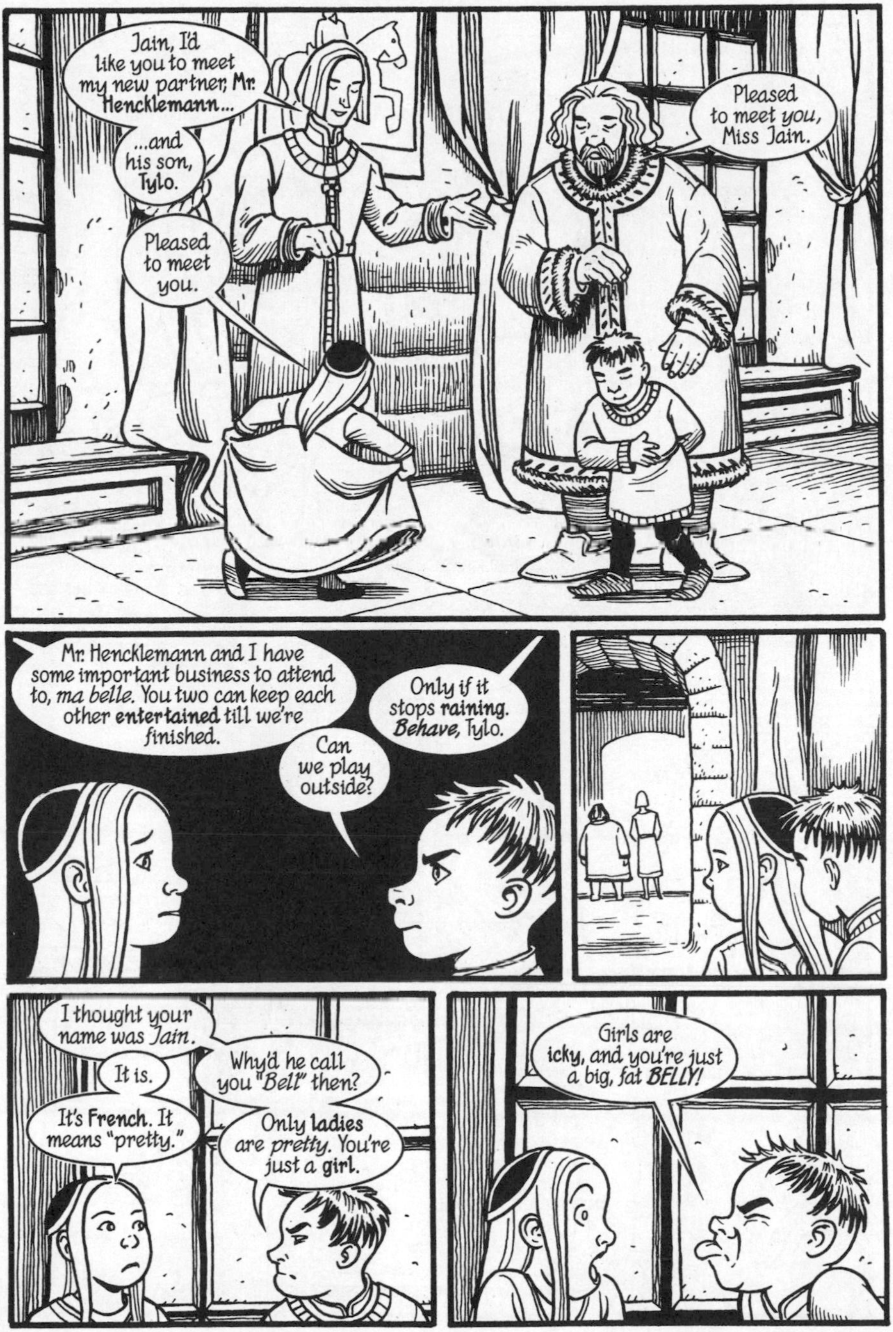
Jain, I'd like you to meet my new partner, Mr. Hencklemann...
...and his son, Tylo.
Pleased to meet you, Miss Jain.
Pleased to meet you.
Mr. Hencklemann and I have some important business to attend to, *ma belle*. You two can keep each other **entertained** till we're finished.
Can we play outside?
Only if it stops **raining**. ***Behave***, Tylo.
I thought your name was *Jain*.
It is.
Why'd he call you "*Bell*" then?
It's **French**. It means "pretty."
Only **ladies** are *pretty*. You're just a **girl**.
Girls are **icky**, and you're just a big, fat ***BELLY!***

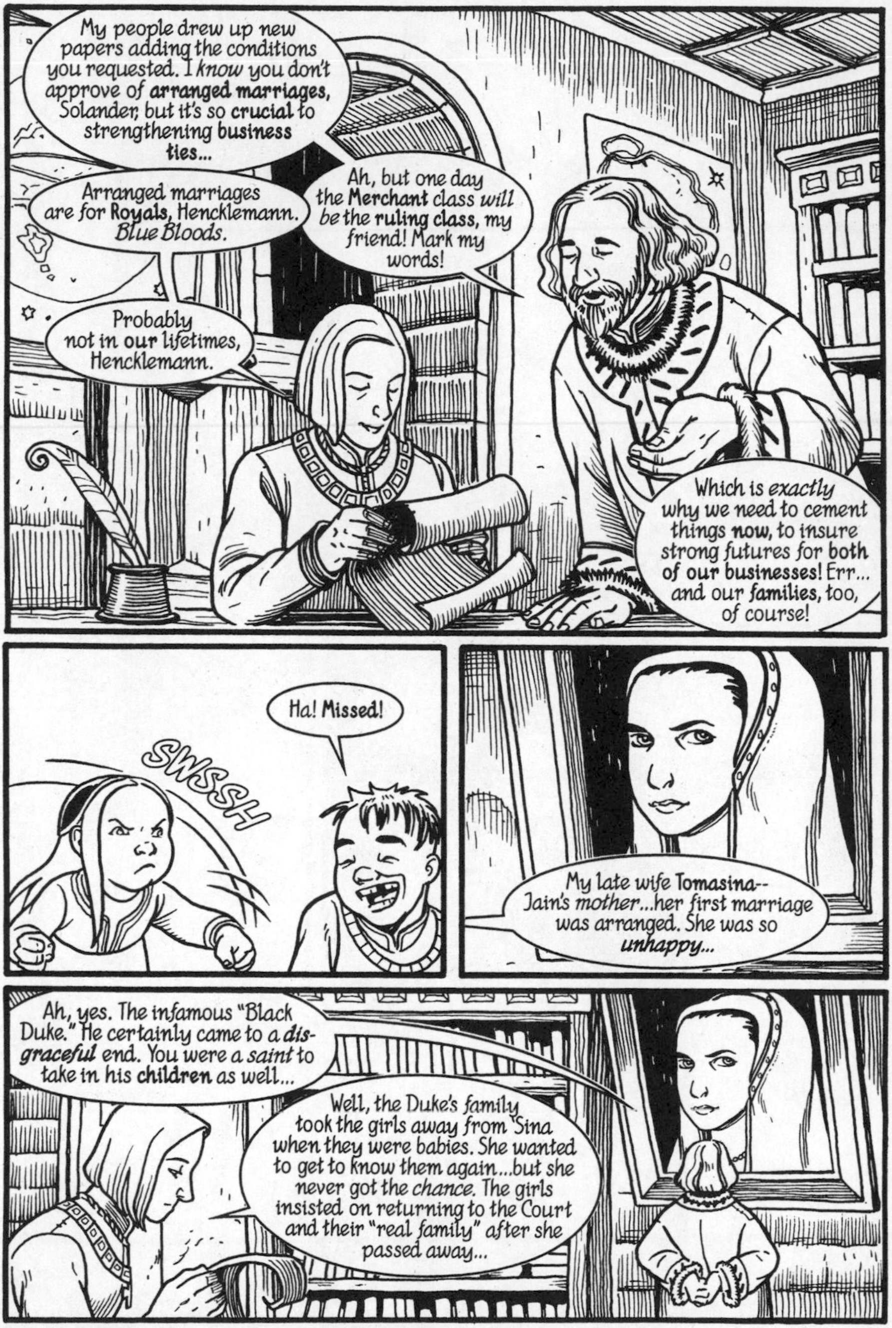
My people drew up new papers adding the conditions you requested. I *know* you don't approve of **arranged marriages**, Solander, but it's so **crucial** to strengthening **business ties...**
Arranged marriages are for **Royals**, Hencklemann. *Blue Bloods*.
Ah, but one day the **Merchant** class *will* be the **ruling class**, my friend! Mark my words!
Probably not in **our** lifetimes, Hencklemann.
Which is *exactly* why we need to cement things **now**, to insure strong futures for **both of our businesses**! Err... and our **families**, too, of course!
SWSSH
Ha! **Missed!**
My late wife **Tomasina**-- Jain's *mother*...her first marriage was arranged. She was so ***unhappy...***
Ah, yes. The infamous "Black Duke." He certainly came to a ***dis-graceful*** end. You were a *saint* to take in his **children** as well...
Well, the Duke's *family* took the girls away from 'Sina when they were babies. She wanted to get to know them again...but she never got the *chance*. The girls insisted on returning to the Court and their *"real family"* after she passed away...

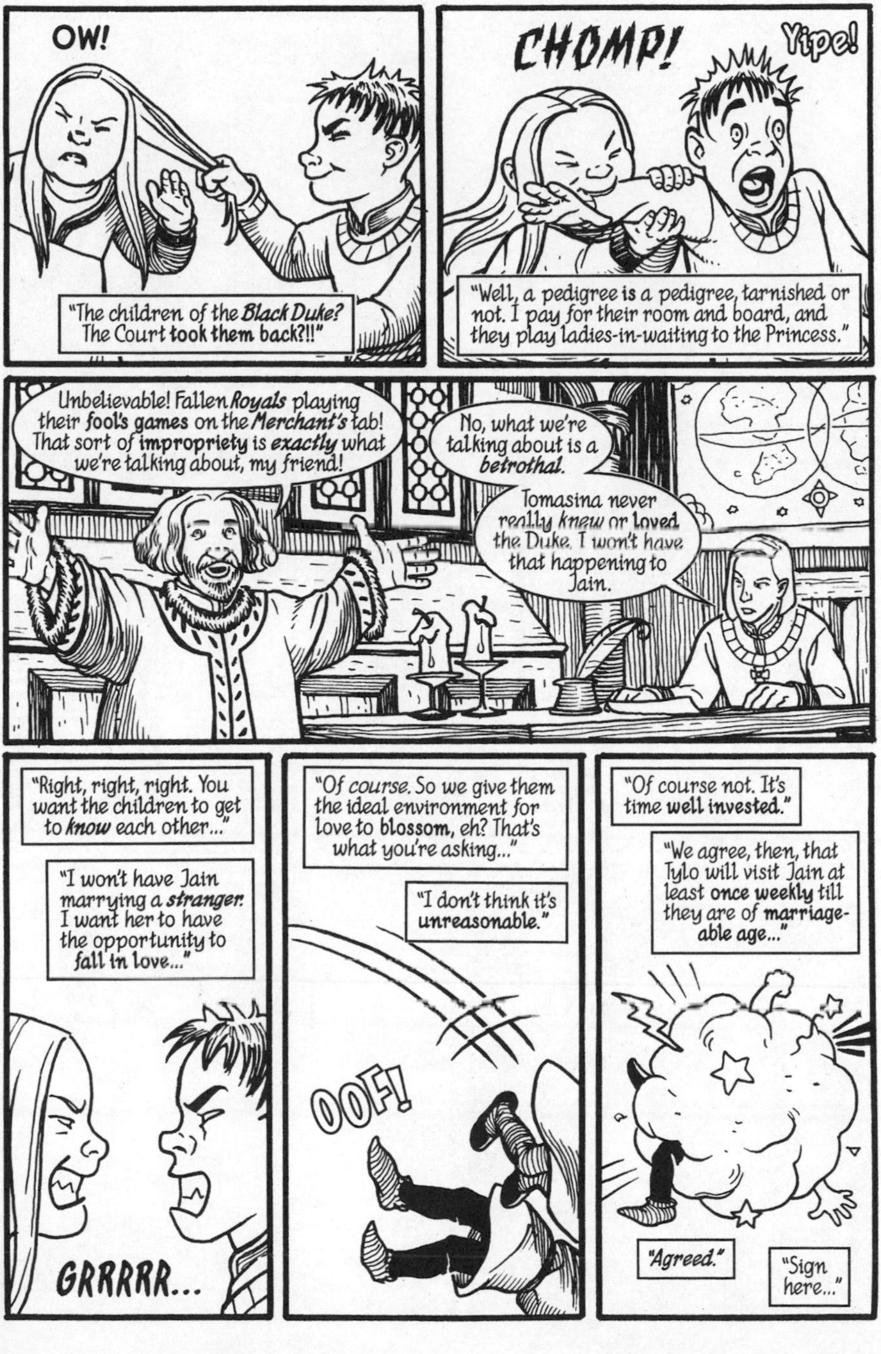
OW!
"The children of the Black Duke? The Court took them back?!!"
CHOMP!
Yipe!
"Well, a pedigree is a pedigree, tarnished or not. I pay for their room and board, and they play ladies-in-waiting to the Princess."
Unbelievable! Fallen Royals playing their fool's games on the Merchant's tab! That sort of impropriety is exactly what we're talking about, my friend!
No, what we're talking about is a betrothal.
Tomasina never really knew or loved the Duke. I won't have that happening to Jain.
"Right, right, right. You want the children to get to know each other..."
"I won't have Jain marrying a stranger. I want her to have the opportunity to fall in love..."
GRRRRR...
"Of course. So we give them the ideal environment for love to blossom, eh? That's what you're asking..."
"I don't think it's unreasonable."
OOF!
"Of course not. It's time well invested."
"We agree, then, that Tylo will visit Jain at least once weekly till they are of marriage-able age..."
"Agreed."
"Sign here..."

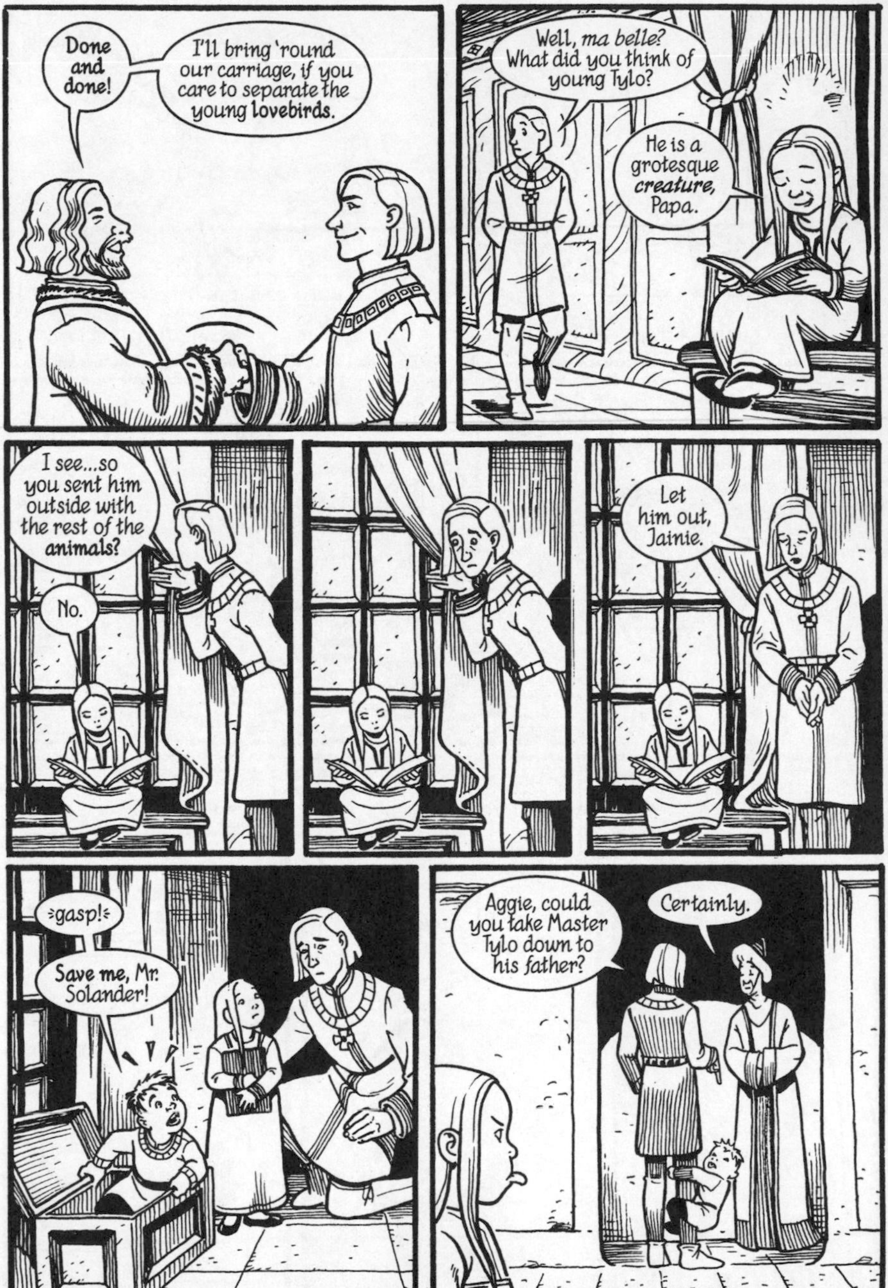
Done and done!
I'll bring 'round our carriage, if you care to separate the young **lovebirds**.
Well, *ma belle?* What did you think of young Tylo?
He is a grotesque ***creature,*** Papa.
I see...so you sent him outside with the rest of the **animals?**
No.
Let him out, Jainie.
gasp!
Save me, Mr. Solander!
Aggie, could you take Master Tylo down to his father?
Certainly.

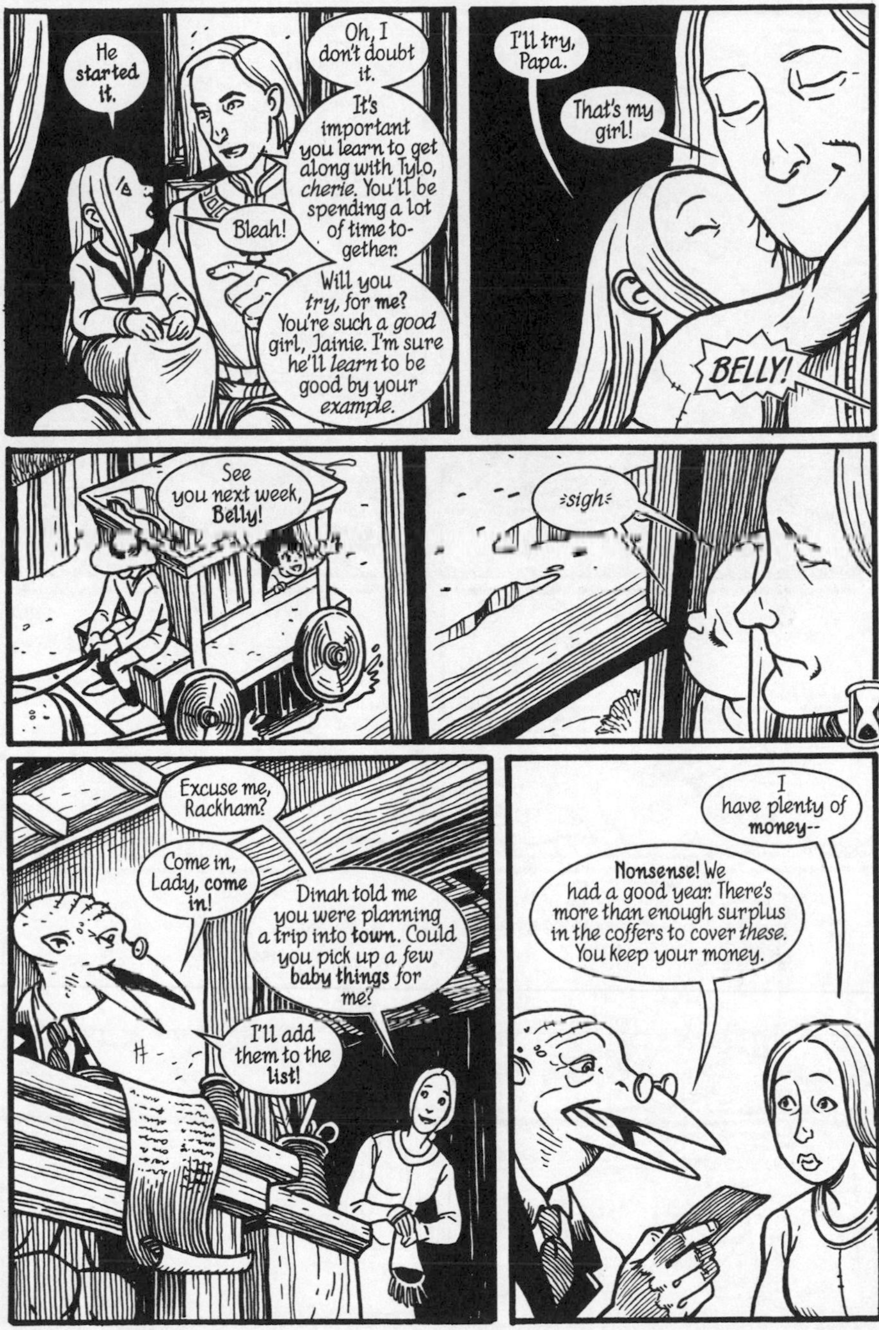
He started it.
Oh, I don't doubt it.
It's important you learn to get along with Tylo, *cherie*. You'll be spending a lot of time together.
Bleah!
Will you *try*, for me? You're such a *good* girl, Jainie. I'm sure he'll *learn* to be good by your *example*.
I'll try, Papa.
That's my girl!
BELLY!
See you next week, **Belly!**
sigh
Excuse me, Rackham?
Come in, Lady, **come in!**
Dinah told me you were planning a trip into **town**. Could you pick up a few **baby things** for me?
I'll add them to the **list!**
I have plenty of **money**--
Nonsense! We had a good year. There's more than enough surplus in the coffers to cover *these*. You keep your money.

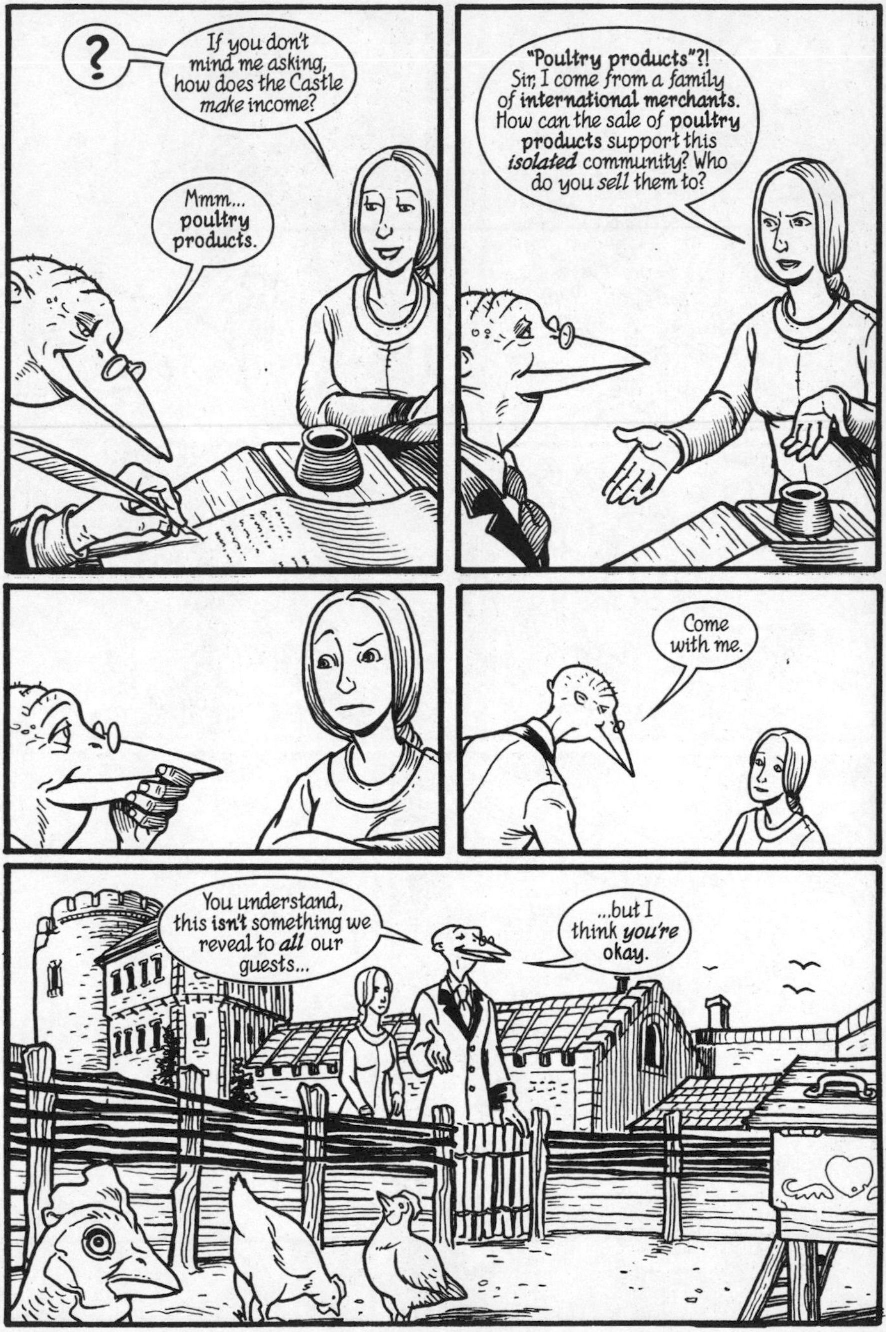
?
If you don't mind me asking, how does the Castle *make* income?
Mmm... **poultry products.**
"**Poultry products**"?! Sir, I come from a family of **international merchants.** How can the sale of **poultry products** support this *isolated* community? Who do you *sell* them to?
Come with me.
You understand, this **isn't** something we reveal to *all* our guests...
...but I think *you're* okay.

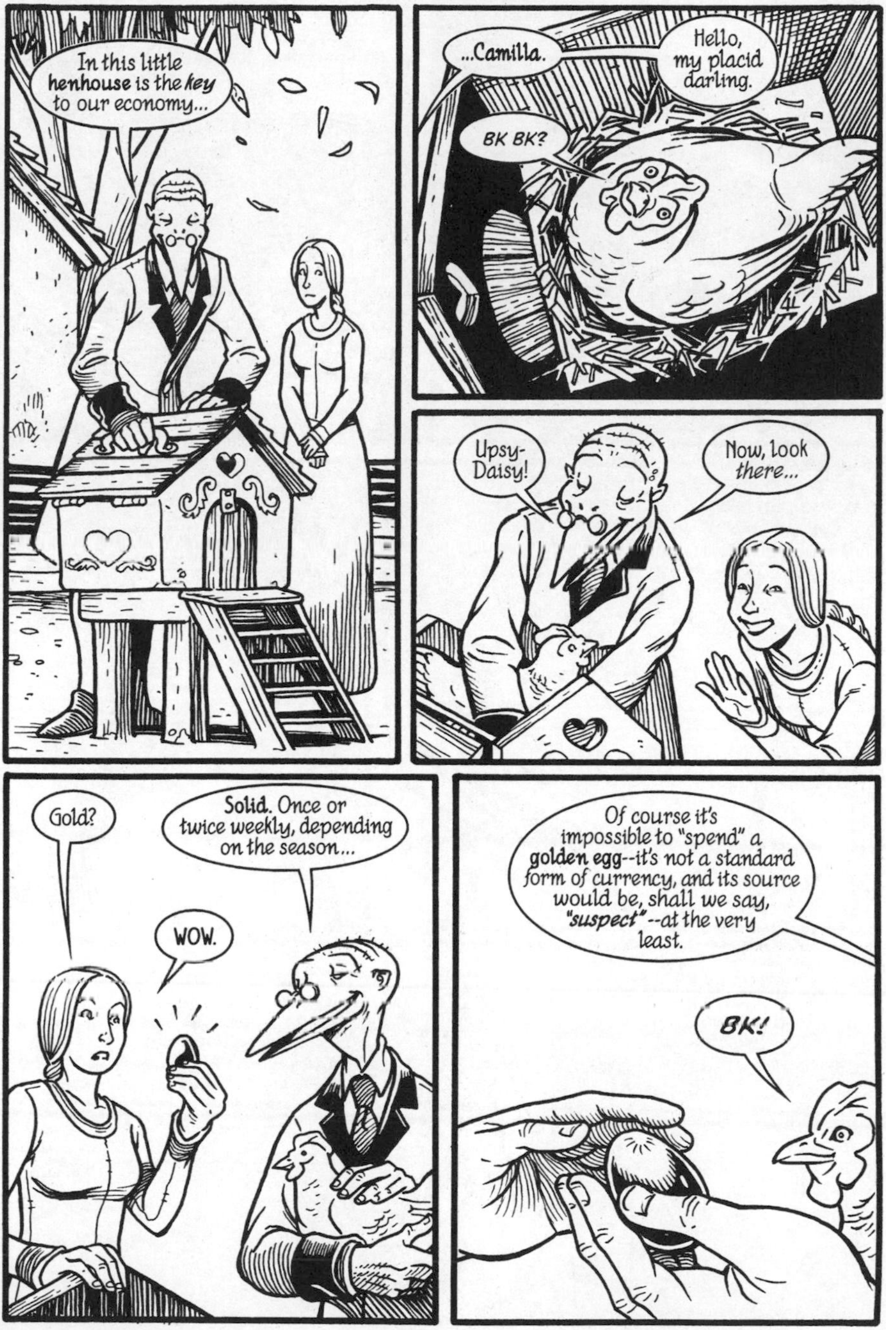
In this little **henhouse** is the *key* to our economy...
...Camilla.
Hello, my placid darling.
BK BK?
Upsy-Daisy!
Now, look *there*...
Gold?
Solid. Once or twice weekly, depending on the season...
WOW.
Of course it's impossible to "spend" a **golden egg**--it's not a standard form of currency, and its source would be, shall we say, *"suspect"*--at the very least.
BK!

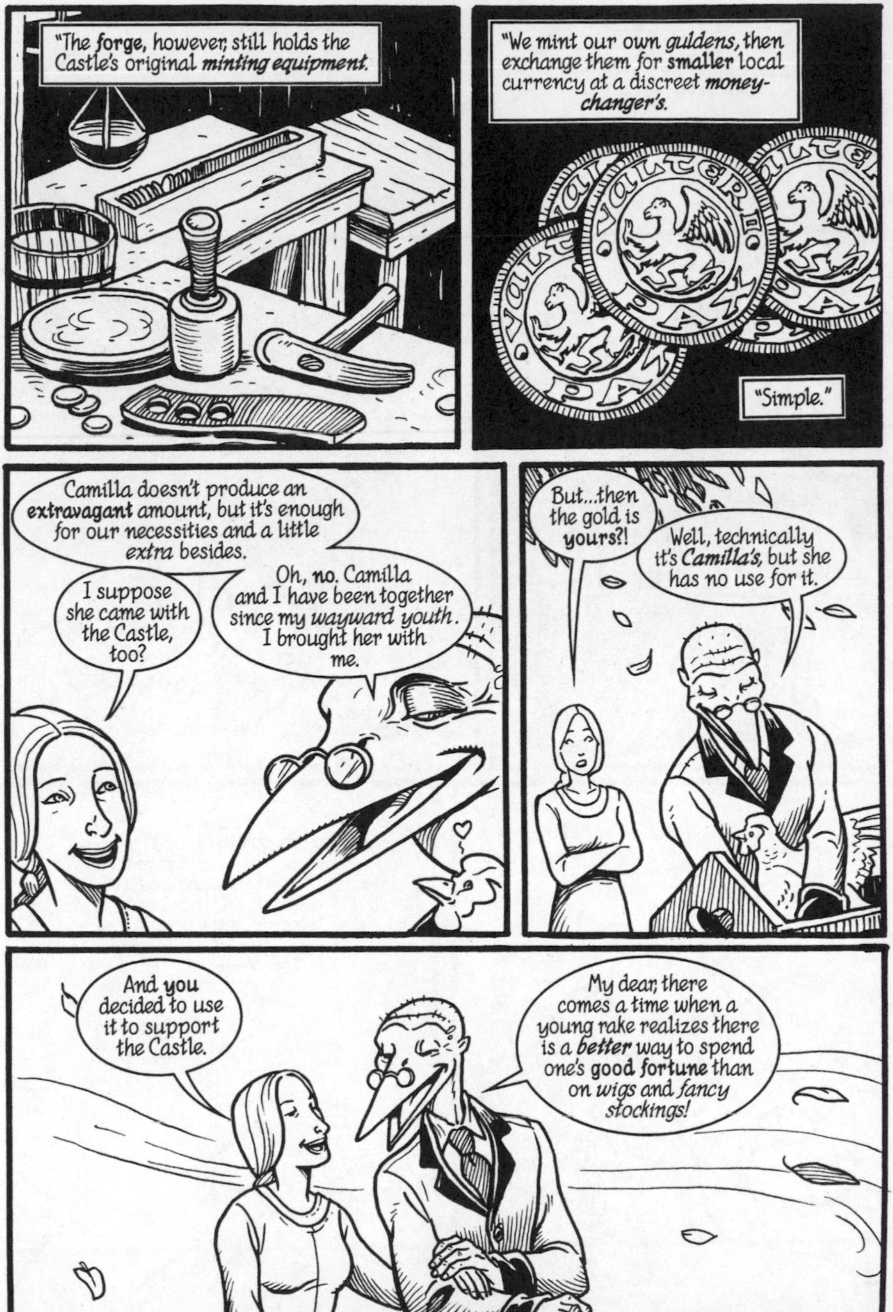

"The forge, however, still holds the Castle's original minting equipment.
"We mint our own guldens, then exchange them for smaller local currency at a discreet money-changer's.
"Simple."
Camilla doesn't produce an extravagant amount, but it's enough for our necessities and a little extra besides.
I suppose she came with the Castle, too?
Oh, no. Camilla and I have been together since my wayward youth. I brought her with me.
But...then the gold is yours?!
Well, technically it's Camilla's, but she has no use for it.
And you decided to use it to support the Castle.
My dear, there comes a time when a young rake realizes there is a better way to spend one's good fortune than on wigs and fancy stockings!

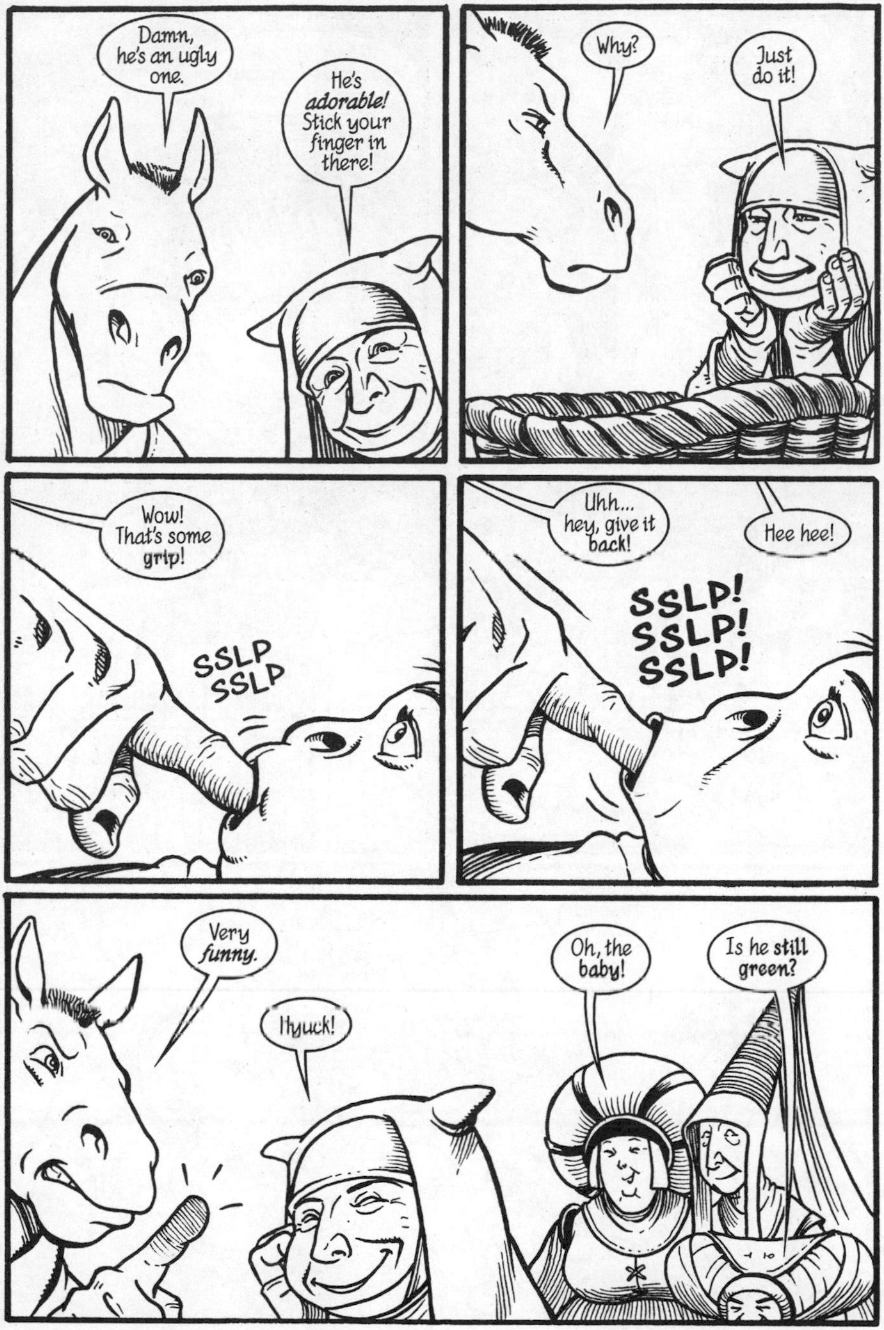
Damn, he's an ugly one.
He's *adorable!* Stick your finger in there!
Why?
Just do it!
Wow! That's some **grip!**
SSLP SSLP
Uhh... hey, give it back!
Hee hee!
SSLP! SSLP! SSLP!
Very *funny.*
Hyuck!
Oh, the baby!
Is he **still green?**

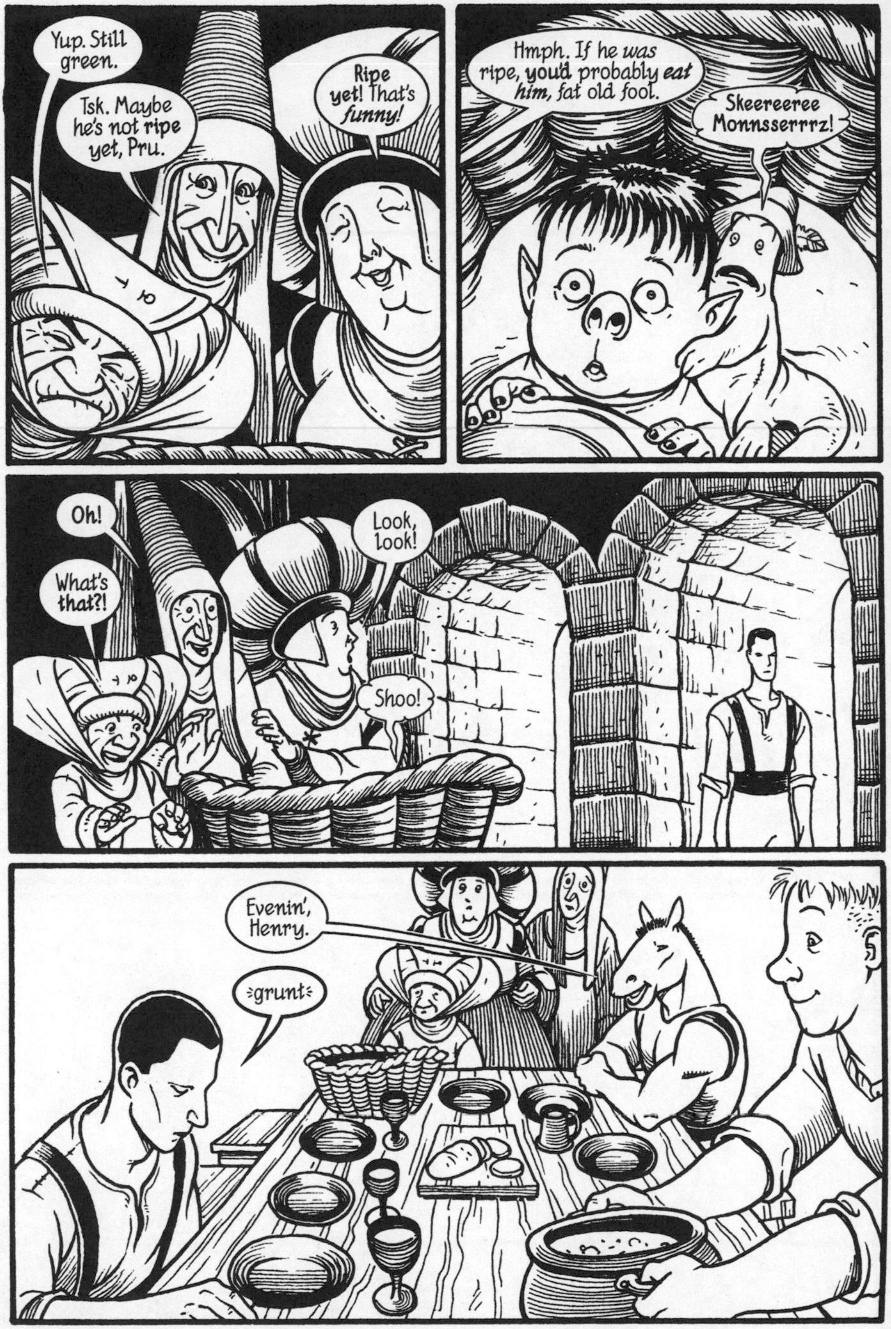
Yup. Still green.
Tsk. Maybe he's not ripe yet, Pru.
Ripe yet! That's *funny!*
Hmph. If he *was* ripe, **you'd** probably ***eat him,*** fat old fool.
Skeereeree Monnsserrrz!
Oh!
What's **that?!**
Look, look!
Shoo!
Evenin', Henry.
=grunt=

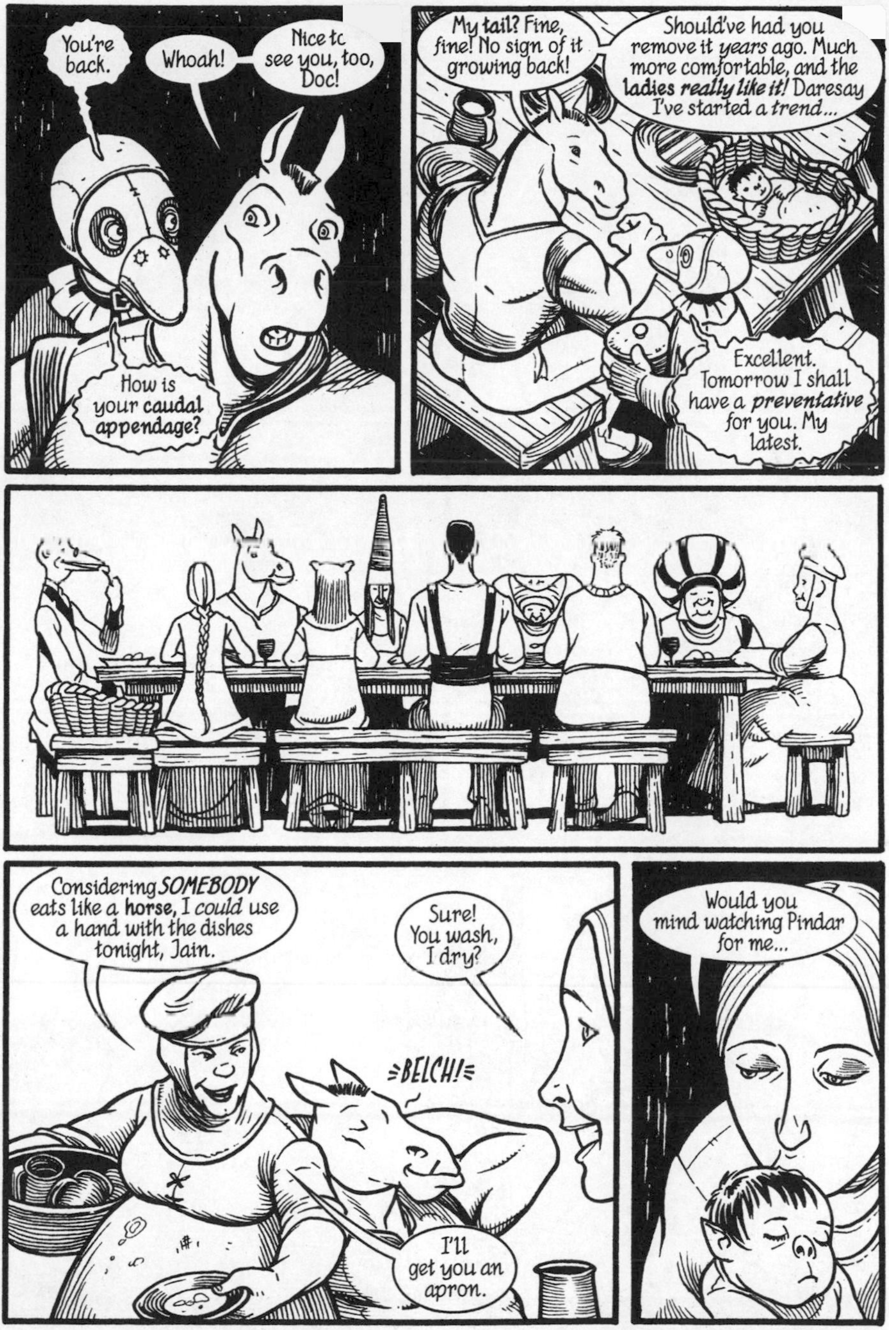
You're back.
Whoah!
Nice to see you, too, Doc!
How is your caudal appendage?
My tail? Fine, fine! No sign of it growing back!
Should've had you remove it years ago. Much more comfortable, and the ladies really like it! Daresay I've started a trend...
Excellent. Tomorrow I shall have a preventative for you. My latest.
Considering SOMEBODY eats like a horse, I could use a hand with the dishes tonight, Jain.
Sure! You wash, I dry?
BELCH!
I'll get you an apron.
Would you mind watching Pindar for me...

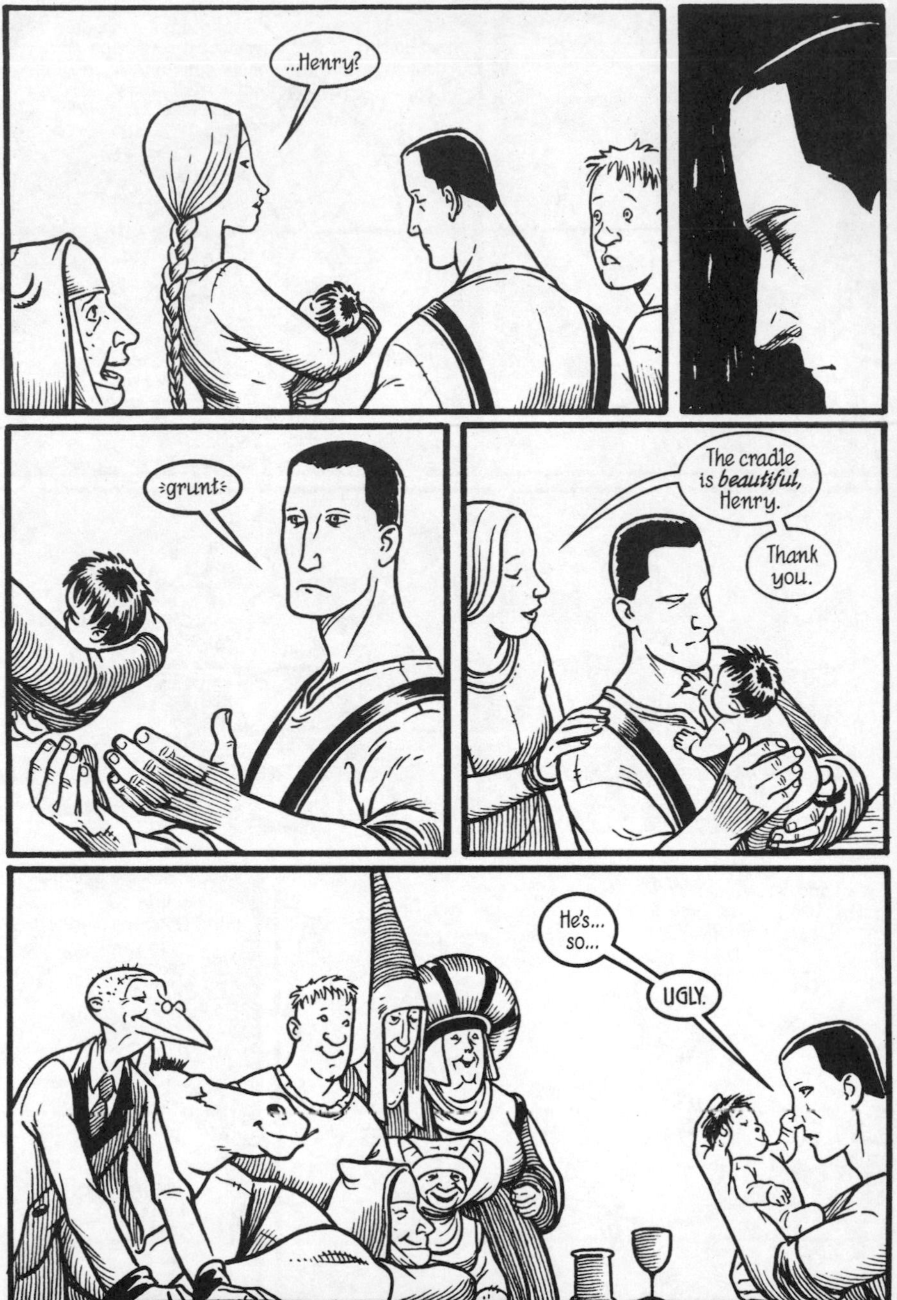
...Henry?
grunt
The cradle is *beautiful,* Henry.
Thank you.
He's... so...
UGLY.

Chapter 9.

· CITY MOUSE, COUNTRY MOUSE PT. I ·

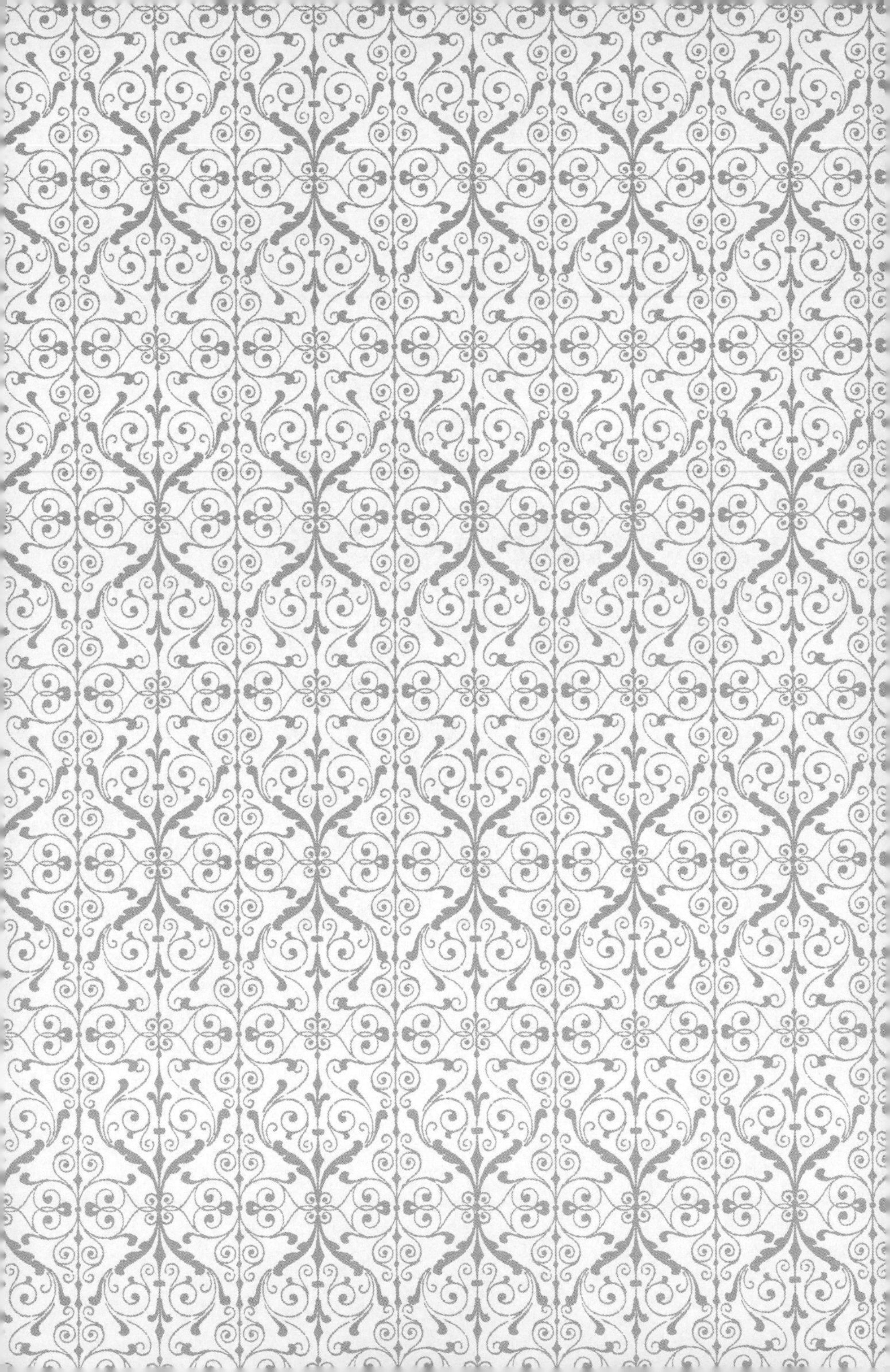

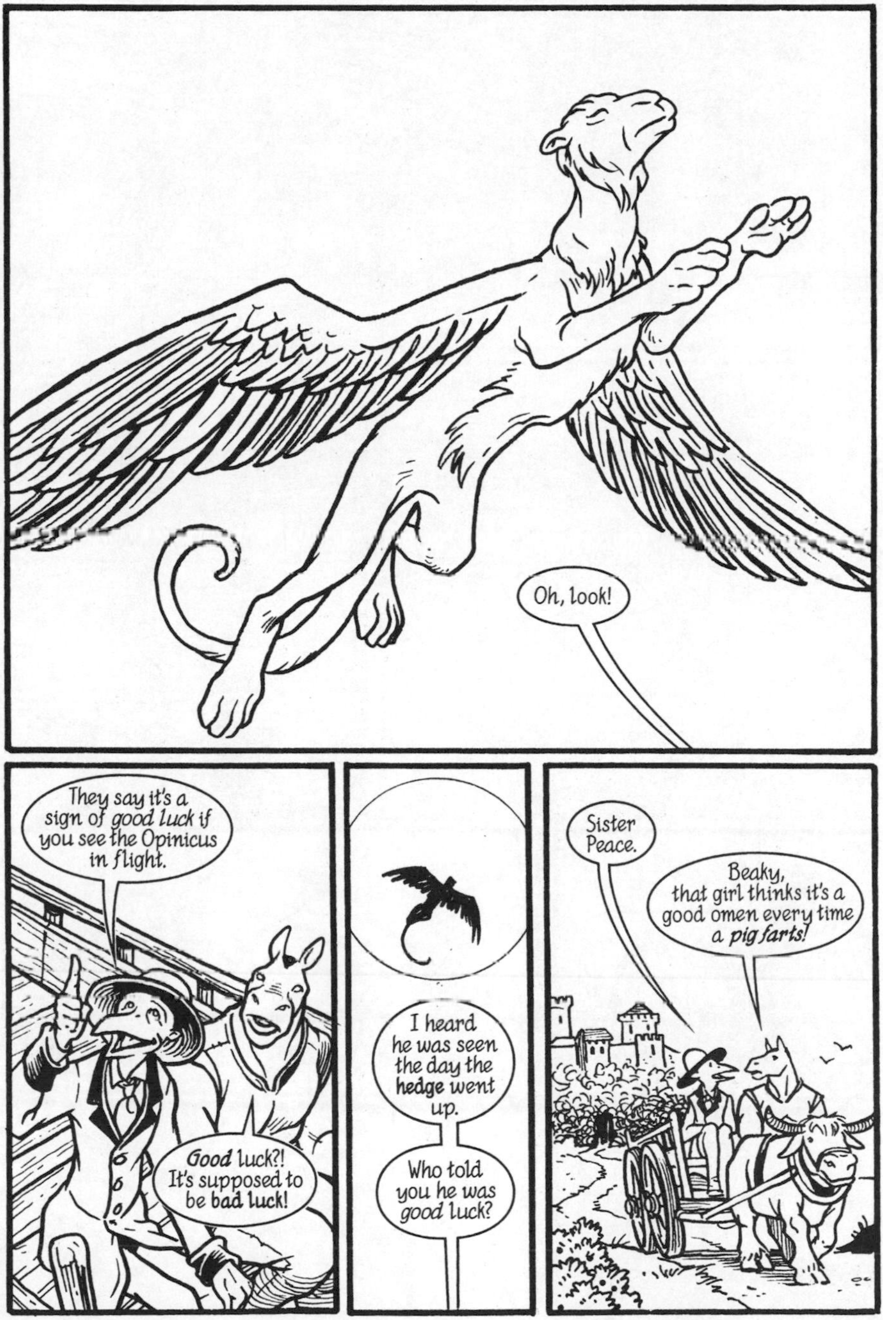

Oh, look!
They say it's a sign of *good luck* if you see the Opinicus in flight.
Good luck?! It's supposed to be **bad luck**!
I heard he was seen the day the **hedge** went up.
Who told you he was *good* luck?
Sister Peace.
Beaky, that girl thinks it's a good omen every time a ***pig farts!***

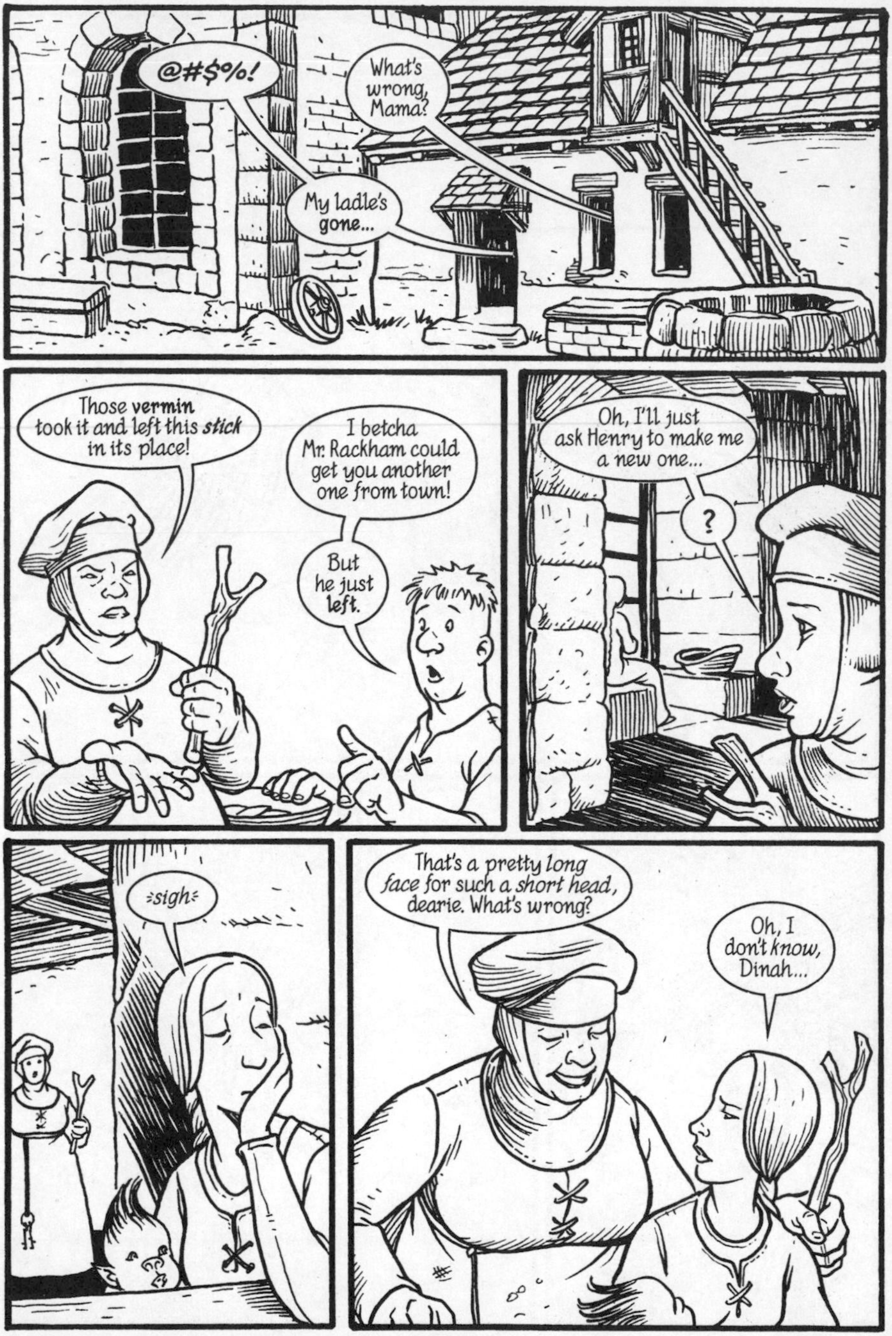
@#$%!
What's wrong, Mama?
My ladle's gone...
Those vermin took it and left this stick in its place!
I betcha Mr. Rackham could get you another one from town!
But he just left.
Oh, I'll just ask Henry to make me a new one...
?
sigh
That's a pretty long face for such a short head, dearie. What's wrong?
Oh, I don't know, Dinah...

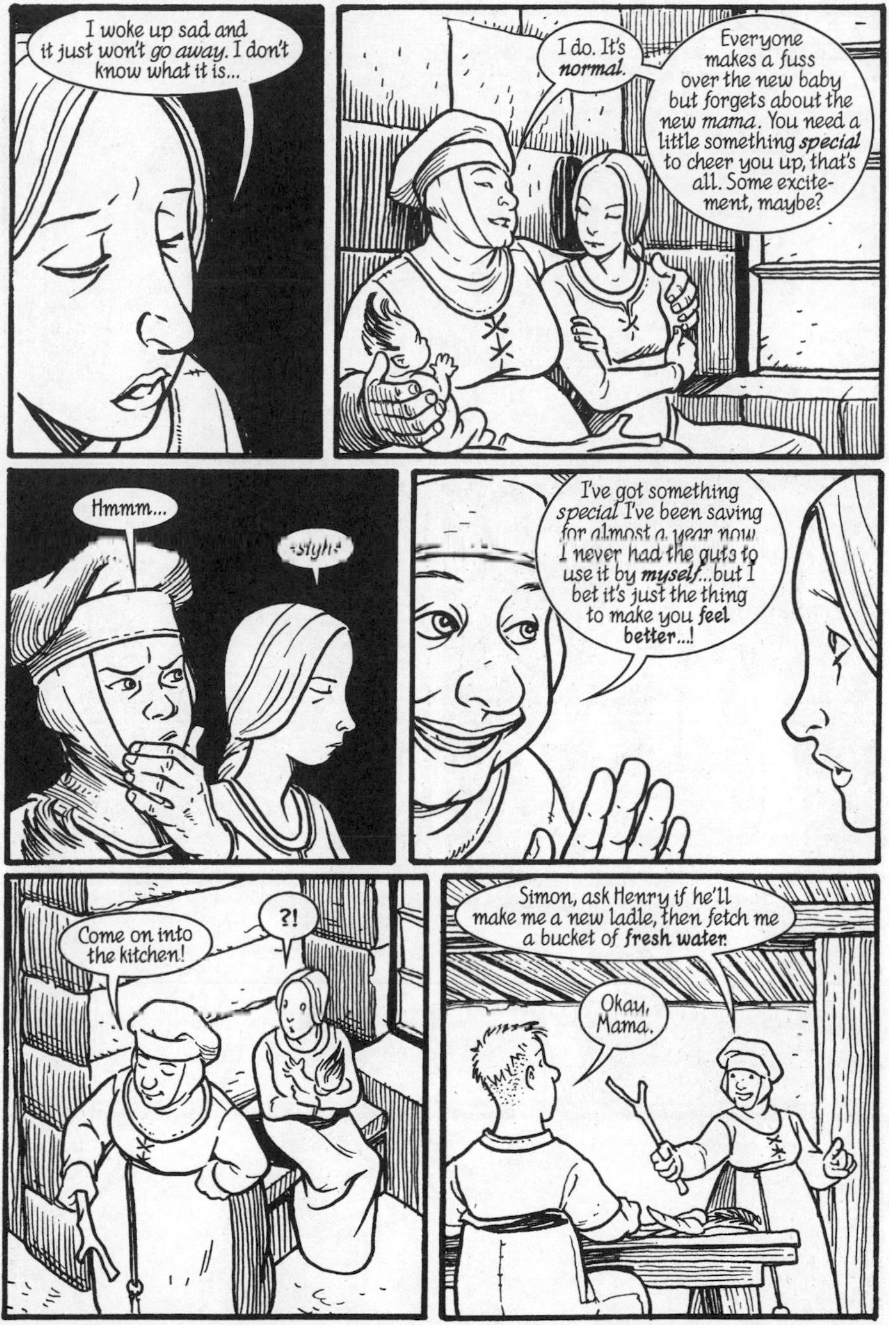
I woke up sad and it just won't *go away*. I don't know what it is...
I do. It's *normal*.
Everyone makes a fuss over the new baby but forgets about the new *mama*. You need a little something *special* to cheer you up, that's all. Some excitement, maybe?
Hmmm...
I've got something *special* I've been saving for almost a year now. I never had the guts to use it by *myself*...but I bet it's just the thing to make you **feel better**...!
Come on into the kitchen!
?!
Simon, ask Henry if he'll make me a new ladle, then fetch me a bucket of **fresh water**.
Okay, Mama.

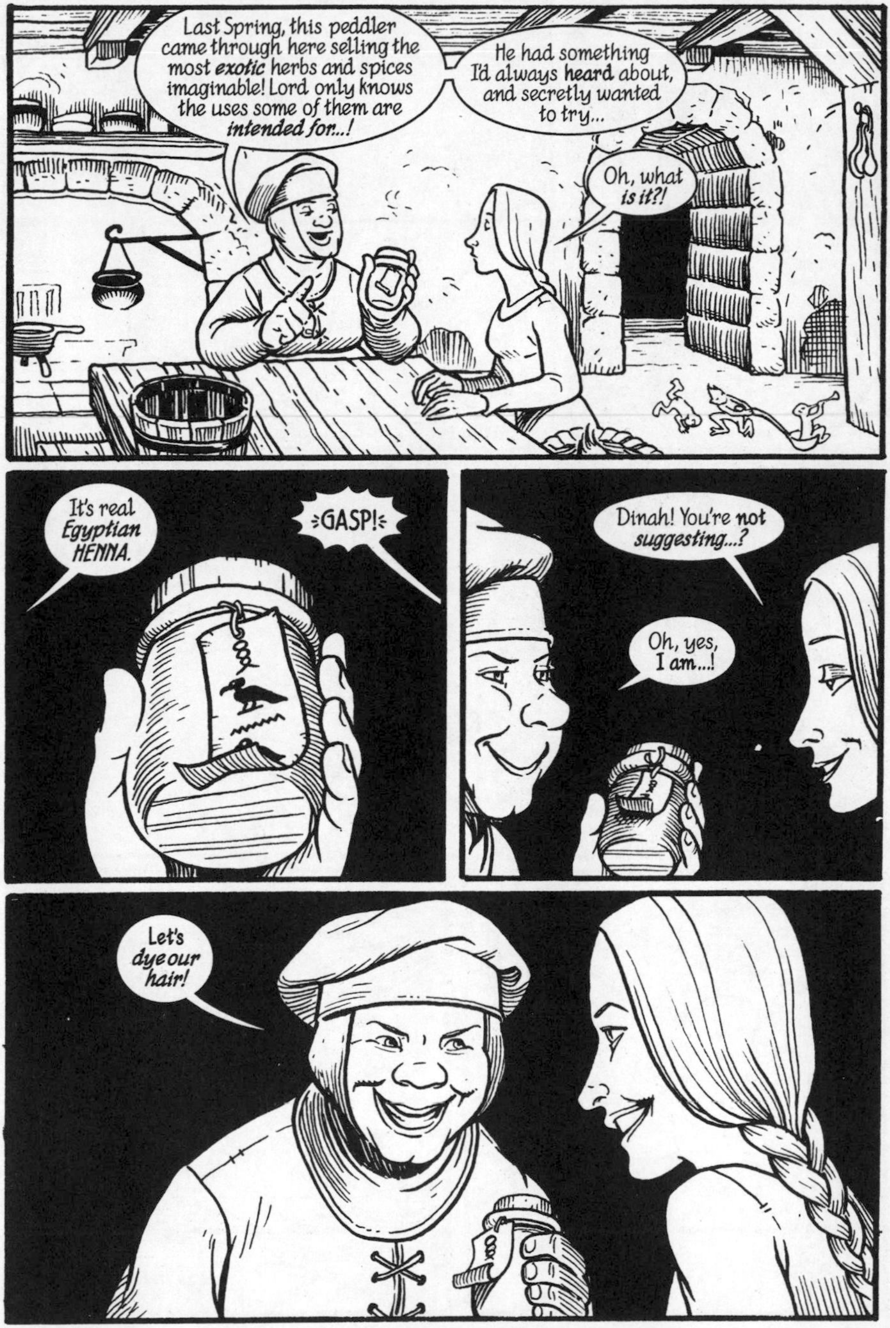
Last Spring, this peddler came through here selling the most *exotic* herbs and spices imaginable! Lord only knows the uses some of them are *intended for*...!
He had something I'd always **heard** about, and secretly wanted to try...
Oh, what *is it?!*
It's real *Egyptian HENNA.*
GASP!
Dinah! You're **not** *suggesting...?*
Oh, yes, I am...!
Let's *dye our hair!*

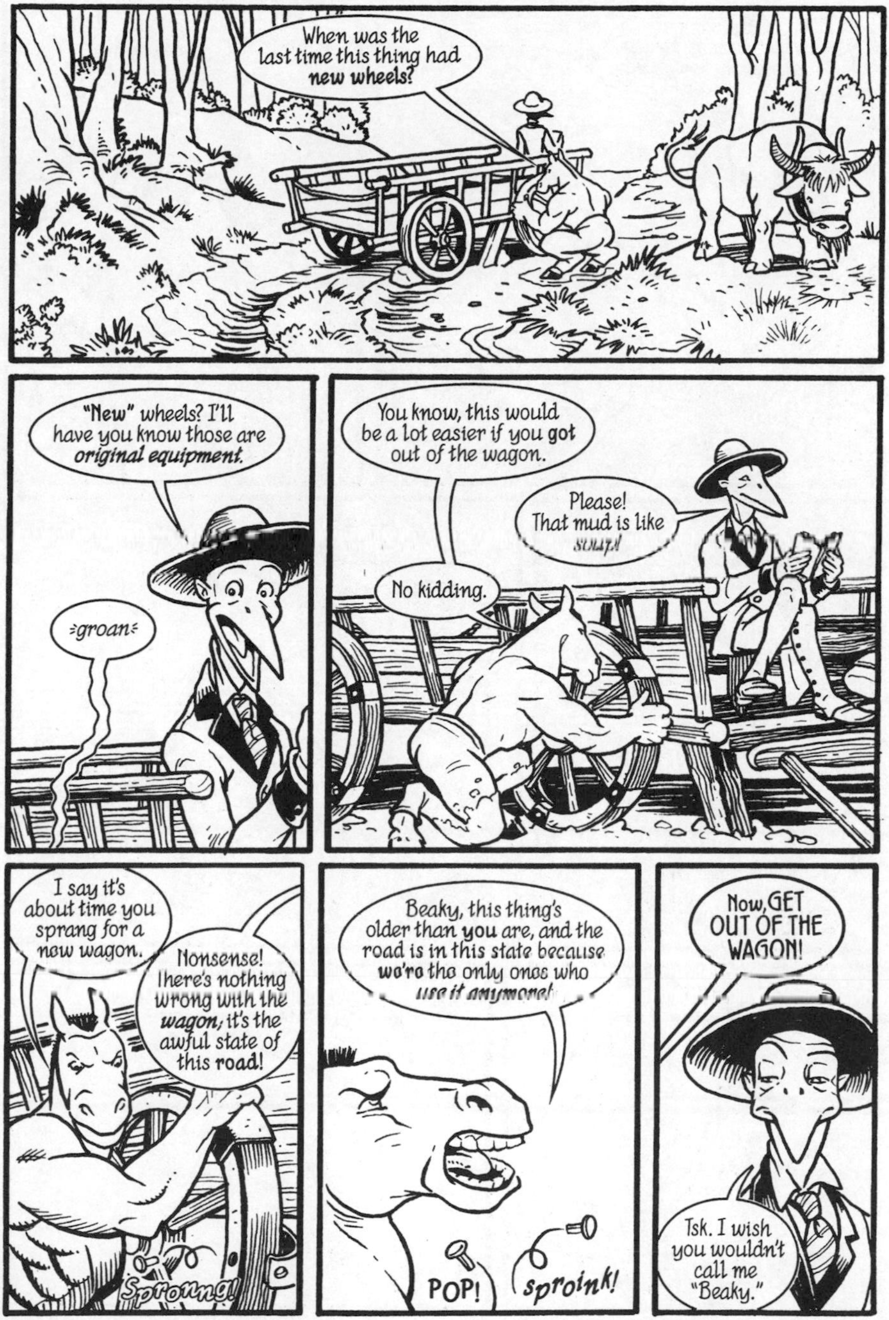
When was the last time this thing had new wheels?
"New" wheels? I'll have you know those are original equipment.
groan
You know, this would be a lot easier if you got out of the wagon.
Please! That mud is like soup!
No kidding.
I say it's about time you sprang for a new wagon.
Nonsense! There's nothing wrong with the wagon; it's the awful state of this road!
Sproinng!
Beaky, this thing's older than you are, and the road is in this state because we're the only ones who use it anymore!
POP!
sproink!
Now, GET OUT OF THE WAGON!
Tsk. I wish you wouldn't call me "Beaky."

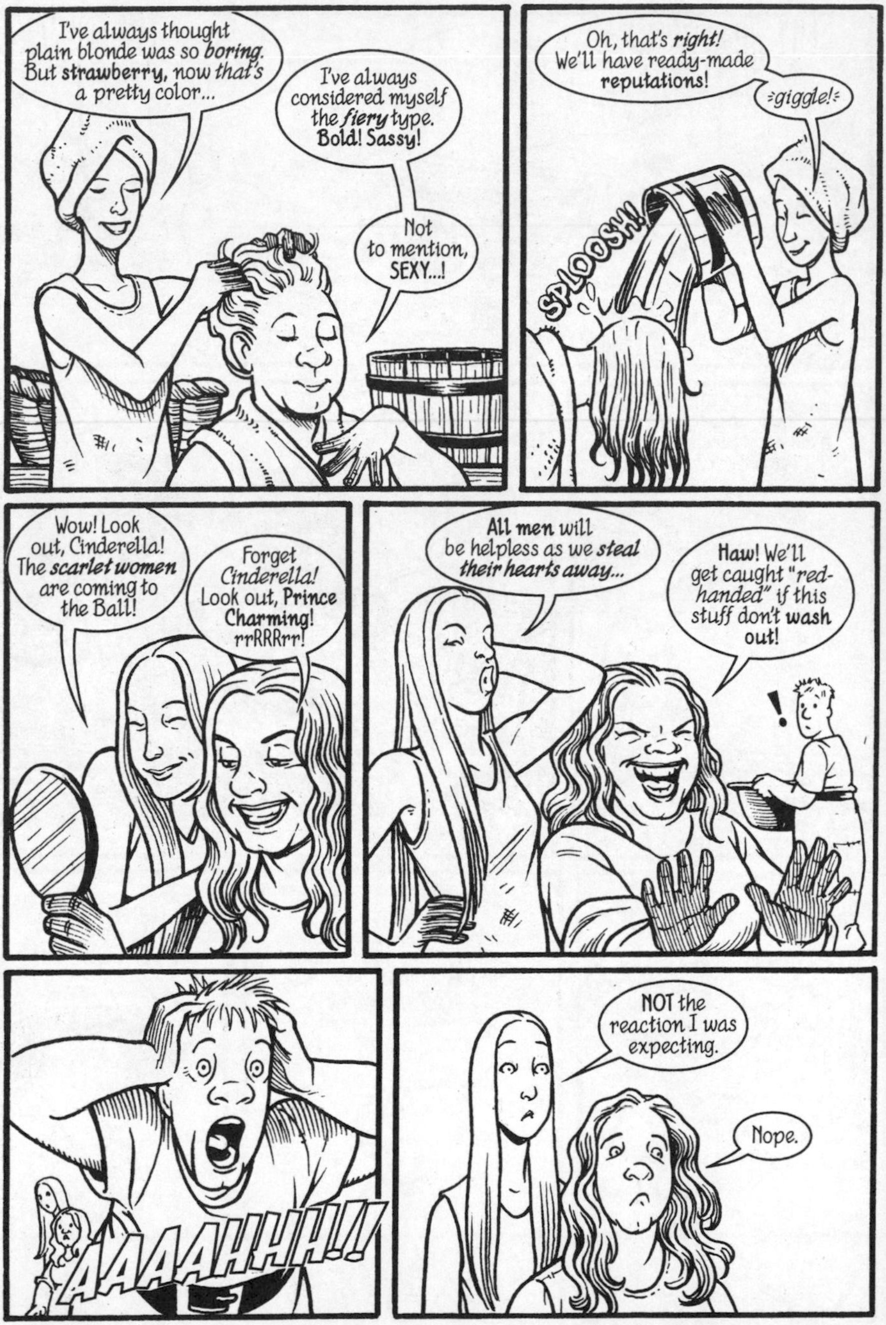
I've always thought plain blonde was so boring. But strawberry, now that's a pretty color...
I've always considered myself the fiery type. Bold! Sassy!
Not to mention, SEXY...!
Oh, that's right! We'll have ready-made reputations!
giggle!
SPLOOSH!
Wow! Look out, Cinderella! The scarlet women are coming to the Ball!
Forget Cinderella! Look out, Prince Charming! rrRRRrr!
All men will be helpless as we steal their hearts away...
Haw! We'll get caught "red-handed" if this stuff don't wash out!
!
AAAAAHHHH!!
NOT the reaction I was expecting.
Nope.

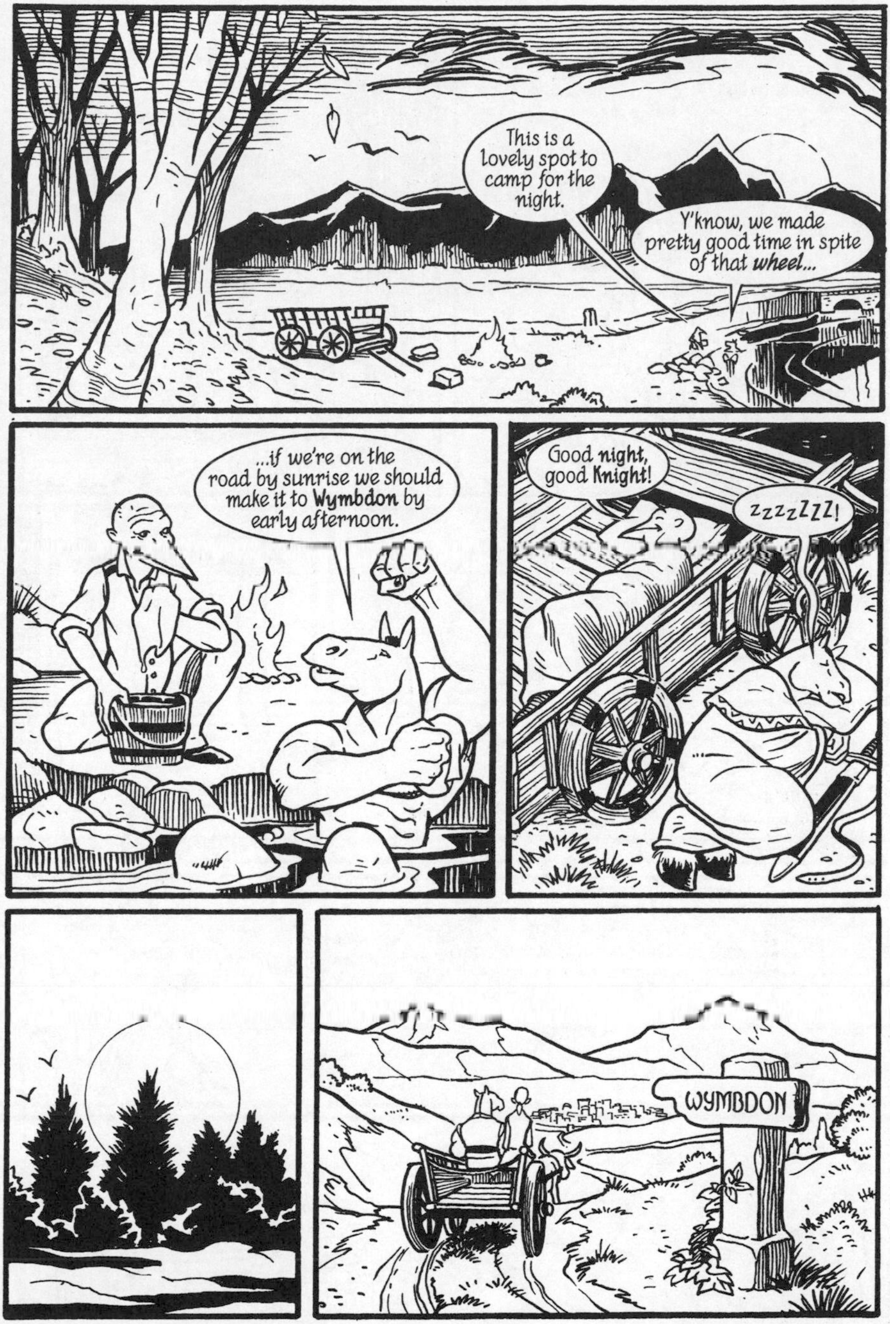
This is a lovely spot to camp for the night.
Y'know, we made pretty good time in spite of that *wheel*...
...if we're on the road by sunrise we should make it to **Wymbdon** by early afternoon.
Good **night**, good **Knight**!
zzzzZZZ!
WYMBDON

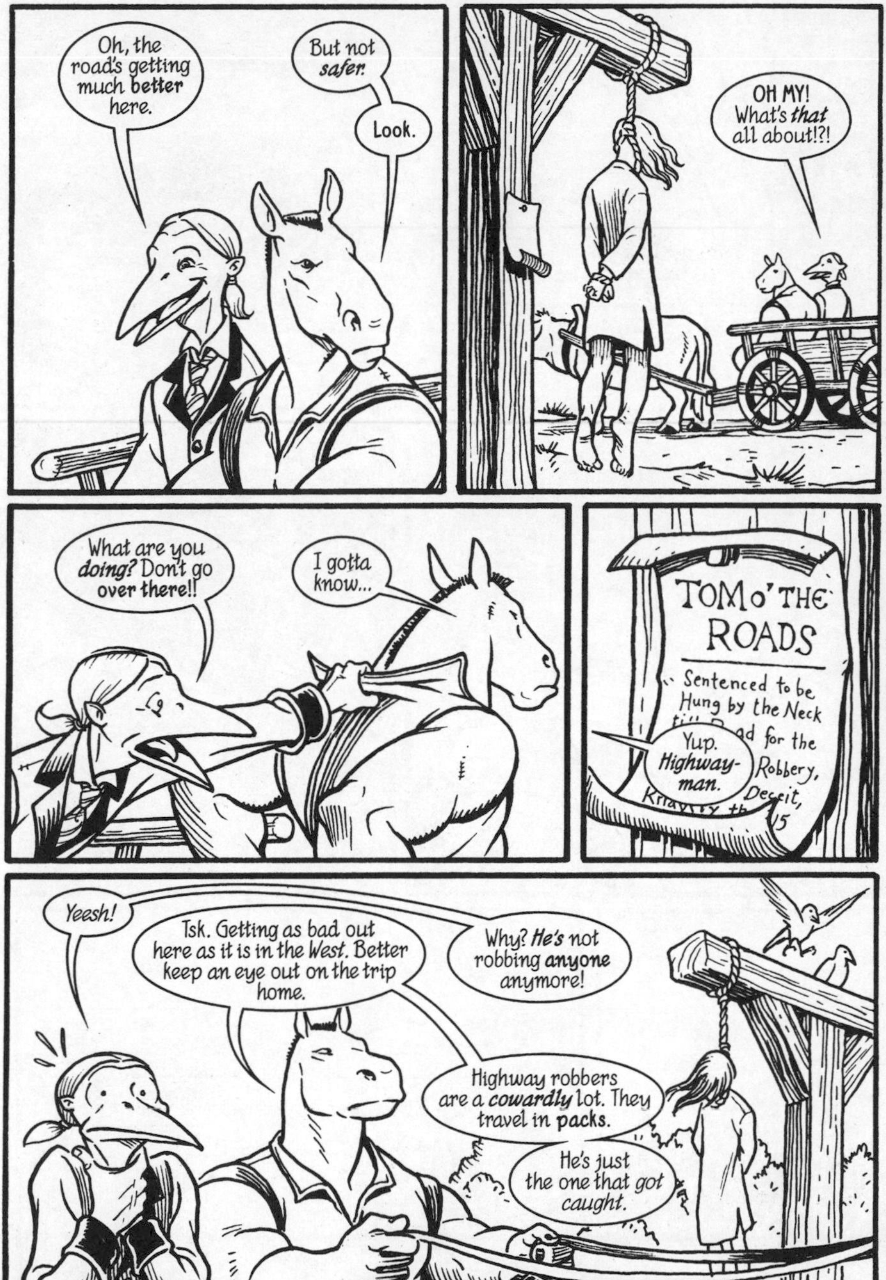
Oh, the road's getting much better here.
But not safer.
Look.
OH MY! What's that all about!?!
What are you doing? Don't go over there!!
I gotta know...
TOM o' THE ROADS
Sentenced to be Hung by the Neck
Robbery,
Deceit,
Yup. Highwayman.
Yeesh!
Tsk. Getting as bad out here as it is in the West. Better keep an eye out on the trip home.
Why? He's not robbing anyone anymore!
Highway robbers are a cowardly lot. They travel in packs.
He's just the one that got caught.

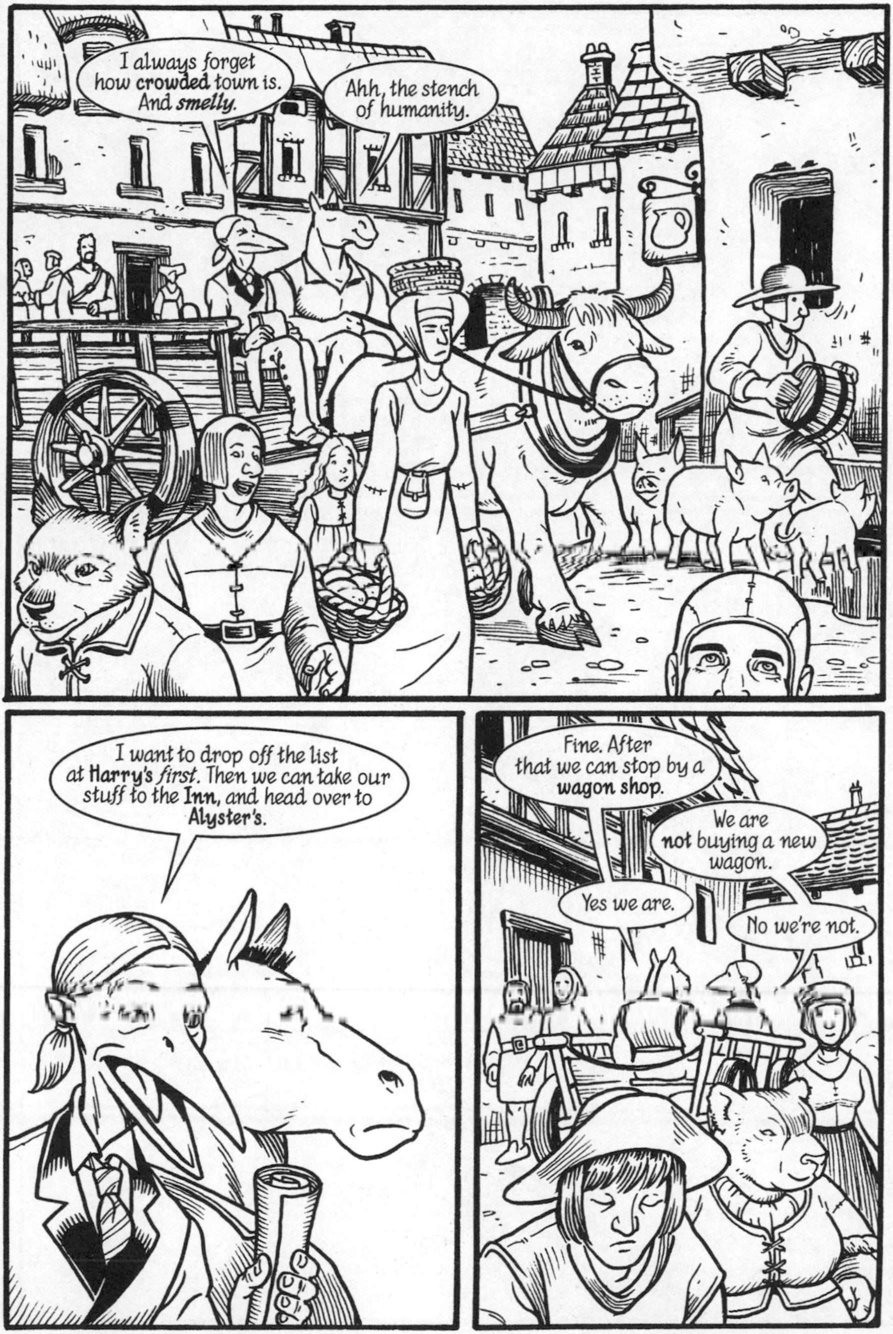
I always forget how crowded town is. And smelly.
Ahh, the stench of humanity.
I want to drop off the list at Harry's first. Then we can take our stuff to the Inn, and head over to Alyster's.
Fine. After that we can stop by a wagon shop.
We are not buying a new wagon.
Yes we are.
No we're not.

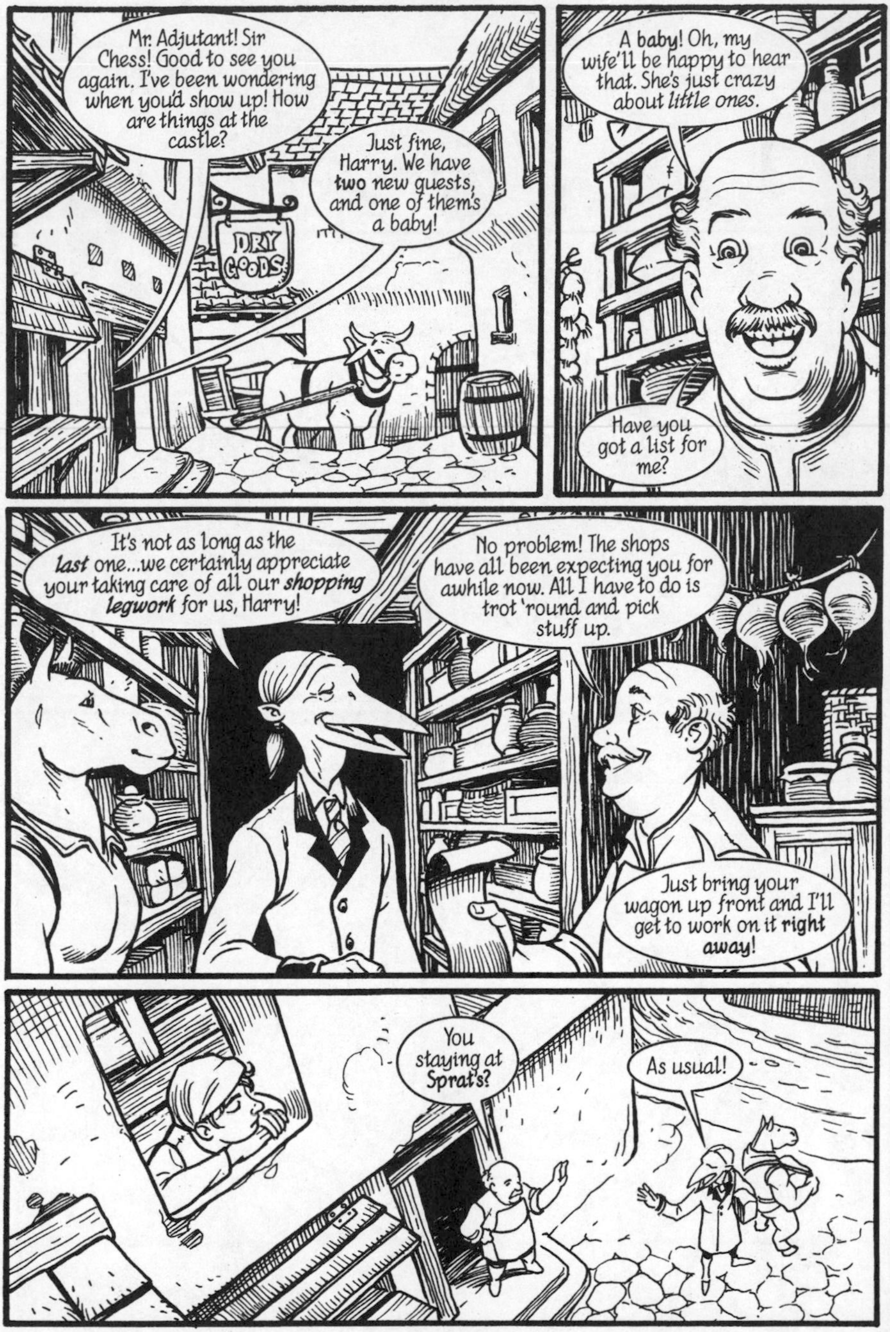
Mr. Adjutant! Sir Chess! Good to see you again. I've been wondering when you'd show up! How are things at the castle?
Just fine, Harry. We have **two** new guests, and one of them's a baby!
DRY GOODS
A **baby**! Oh, my wife'll be happy to hear that. She's just crazy about *little ones*.
Have you got a list for me?
It's not as long as the *last* one...we certainly appreciate your taking care of all our *shopping legwork* for us, Harry!
No problem! The shops have all been expecting you for awhile now. All I have to do is trot 'round and pick stuff up.
Just bring your wagon up front and I'll get to work on it **right away**!
You staying at **Sprat's**?
As usual!

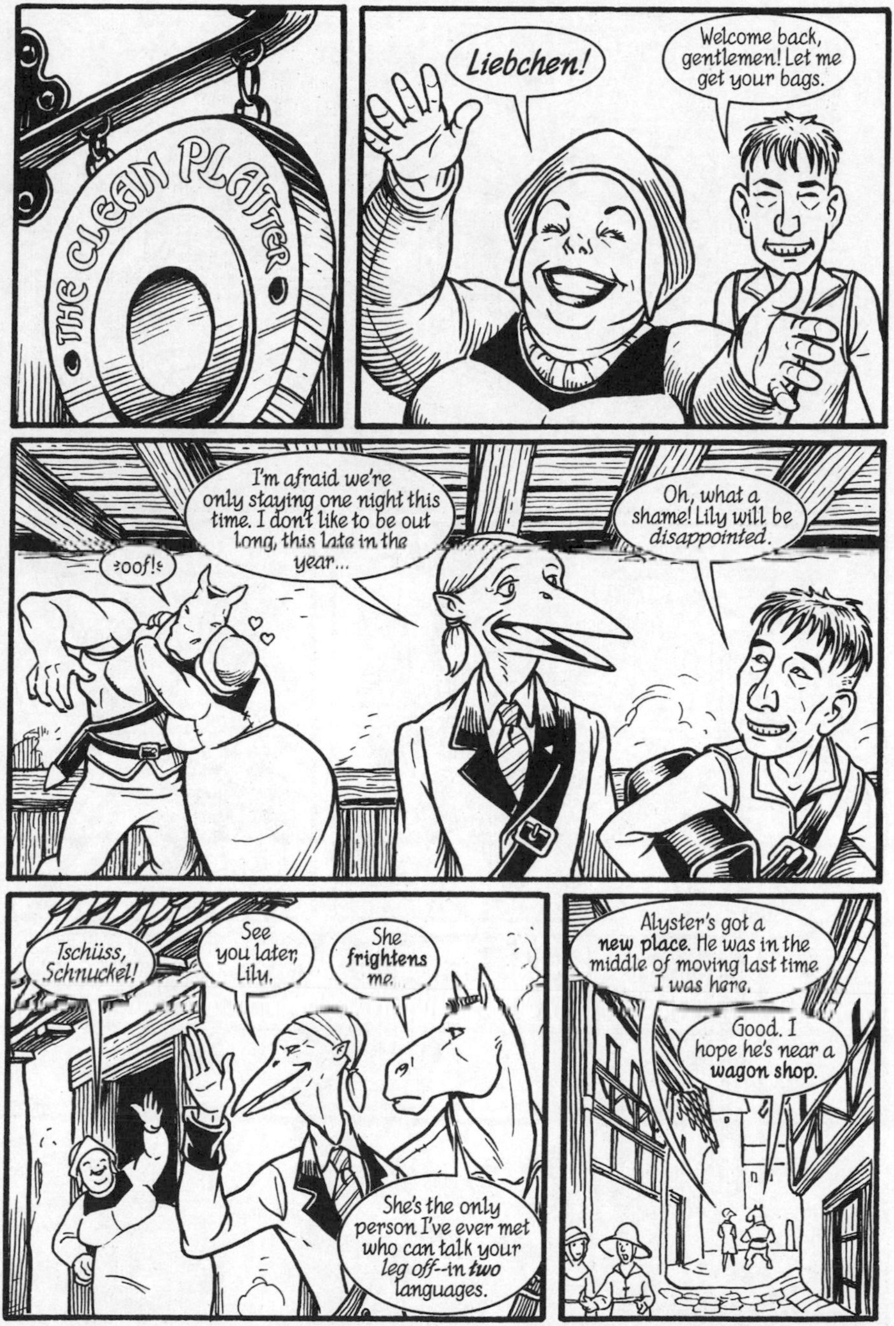
THE CLEAN PLATTER
Liebchen!
Welcome back, gentlemen! Let me get your bags.
I'm afraid we're only staying one night this time. I don't like to be out long, this late in the year...
oof!
Oh, what a shame! Lily will be disappointed.
Tschüss, Schnuckel!
See you later, Lily.
She frightens me.
She's the only person I've ever met who can talk your leg off--in two languages.
Alyster's got a new place. He was in the middle of moving last time I was here.
Good. I hope he's near a wagon shop.

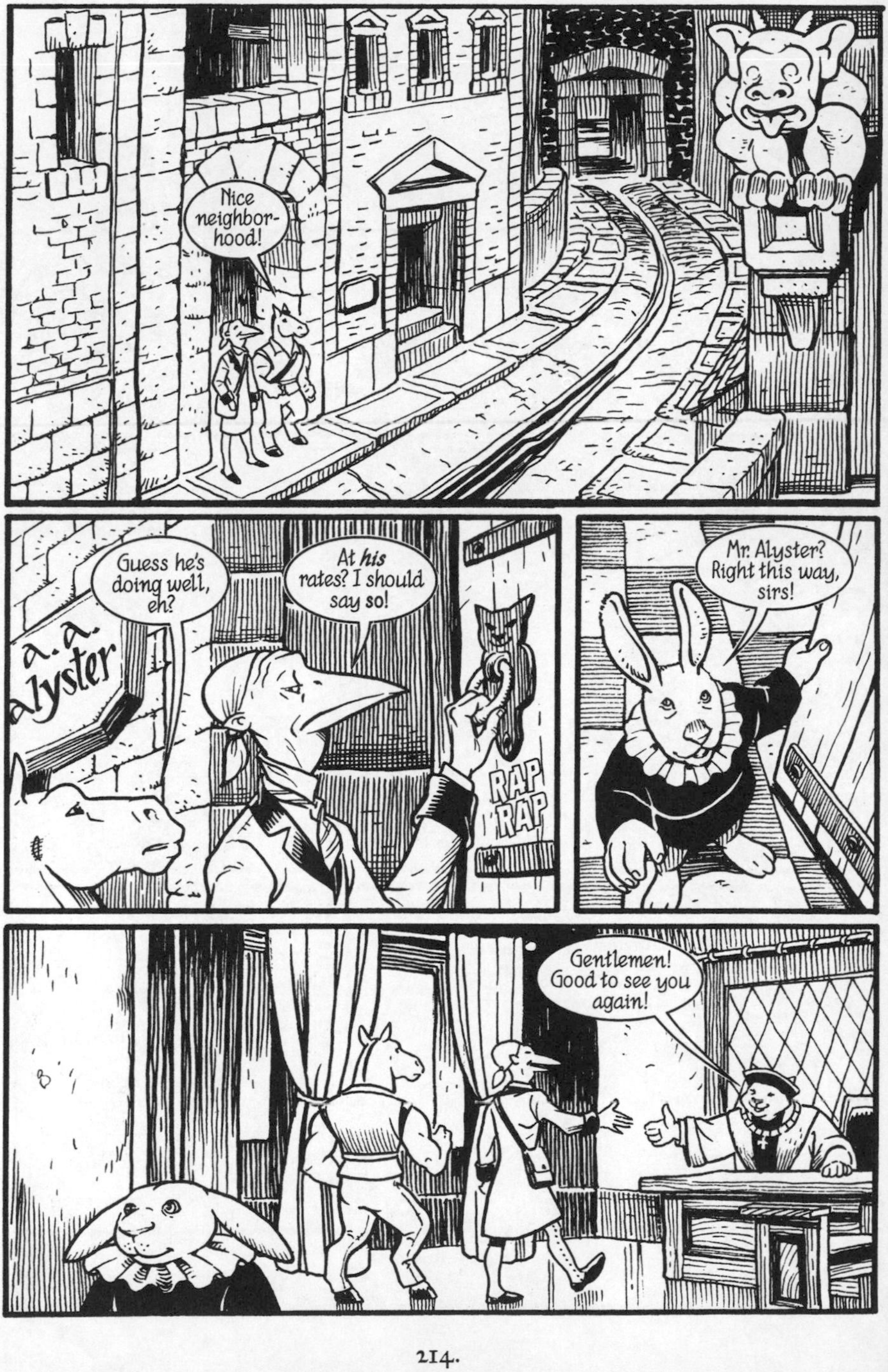
Nice neighbor-hood!
Guess he's doing well, eh?
At *his* rates? I should say so!
a. a. Alyster
RAP RAP
Mr. Alyster? Right this way, sirs!
Gentlemen! Good to see you again!

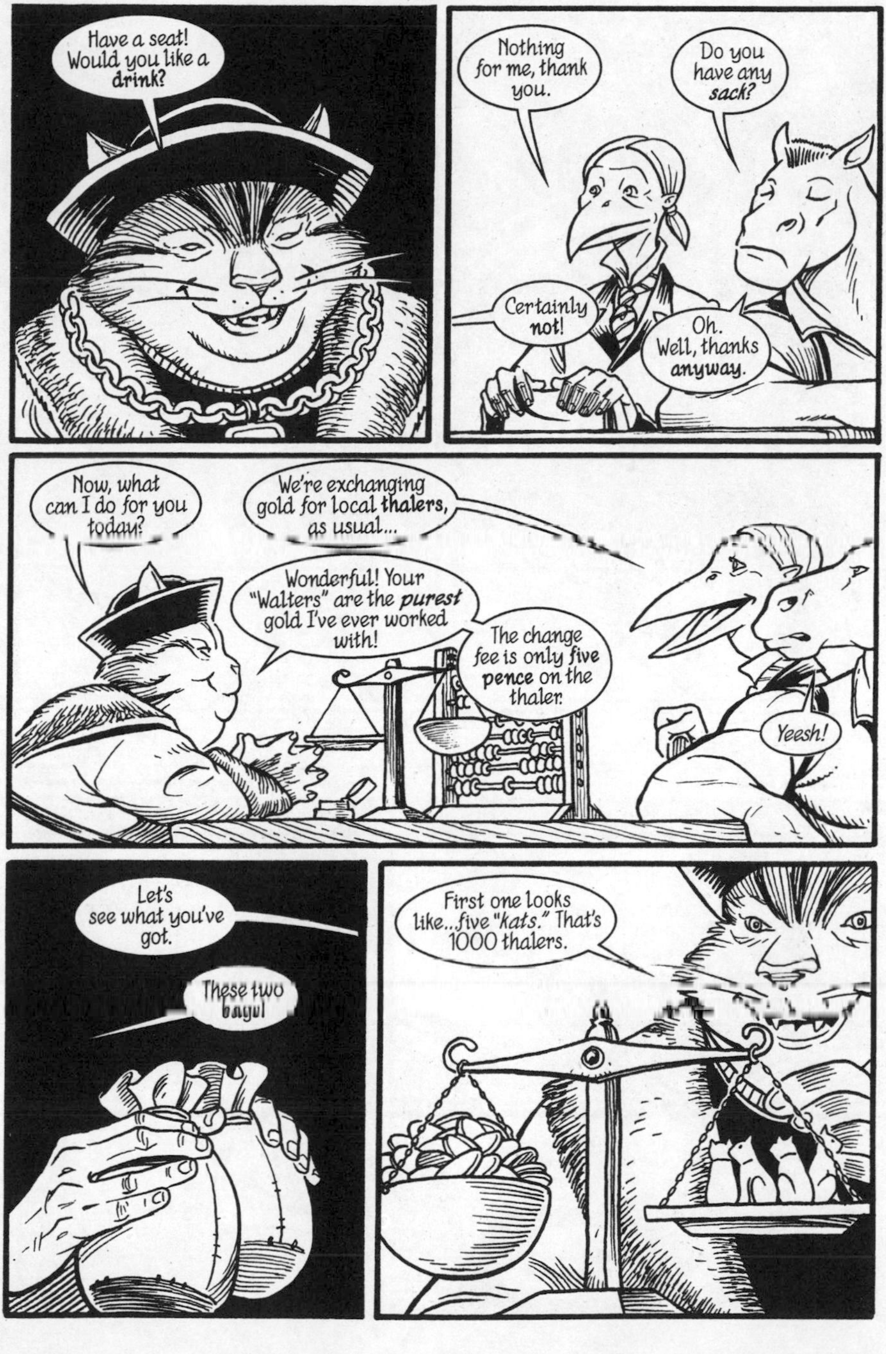
Have a seat! Would you like a **drink?**
Nothing for me, thank you.
Do you have any *sack?*
Certainly **not!**
Oh. Well, thanks **anyway.**
Now, what can I do for you today?
We're exchanging gold for local **thalers**, as usual...
Wonderful! Your "Walters" are the ***purest*** gold I've ever worked with!
The change fee is only **five pence** on the thaler.
Yeesh!
Let's see what you've got.
These two bags!
First one looks like... five "*kats.*" That's 1000 thalers.

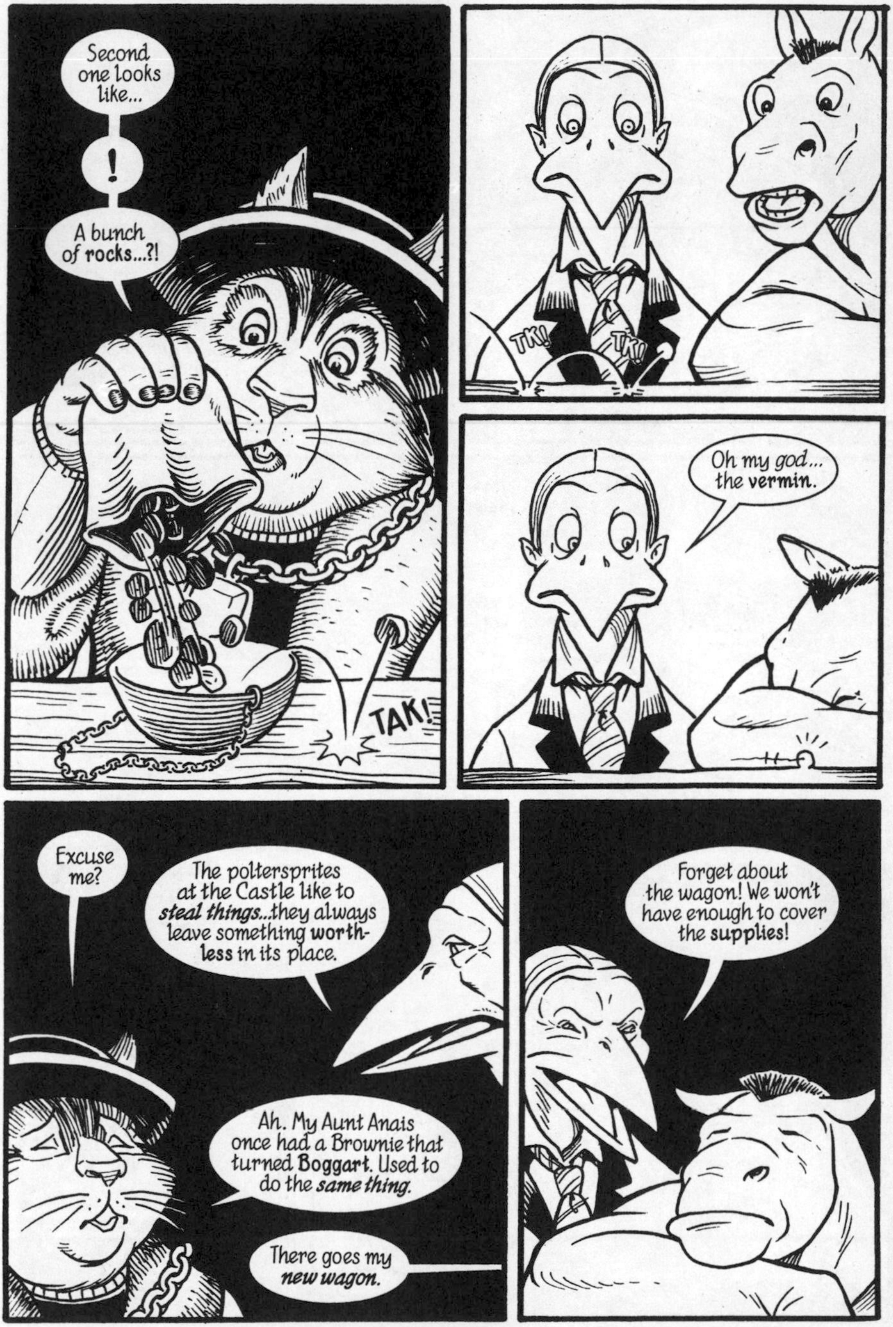
Second one looks like...
!
A bunch of rocks...?!
TAK!
TK!
TK!
Oh my god... the vermin.
Excuse me?
The poltersprites at the Castle like to steal things...they always leave something worthless in its place.
Ah. My Aunt Anais once had a Brownie that turned Boggart. Used to do the same thing.
There goes my new wagon.
Forget about the wagon! We won't have enough to cover the supplies!

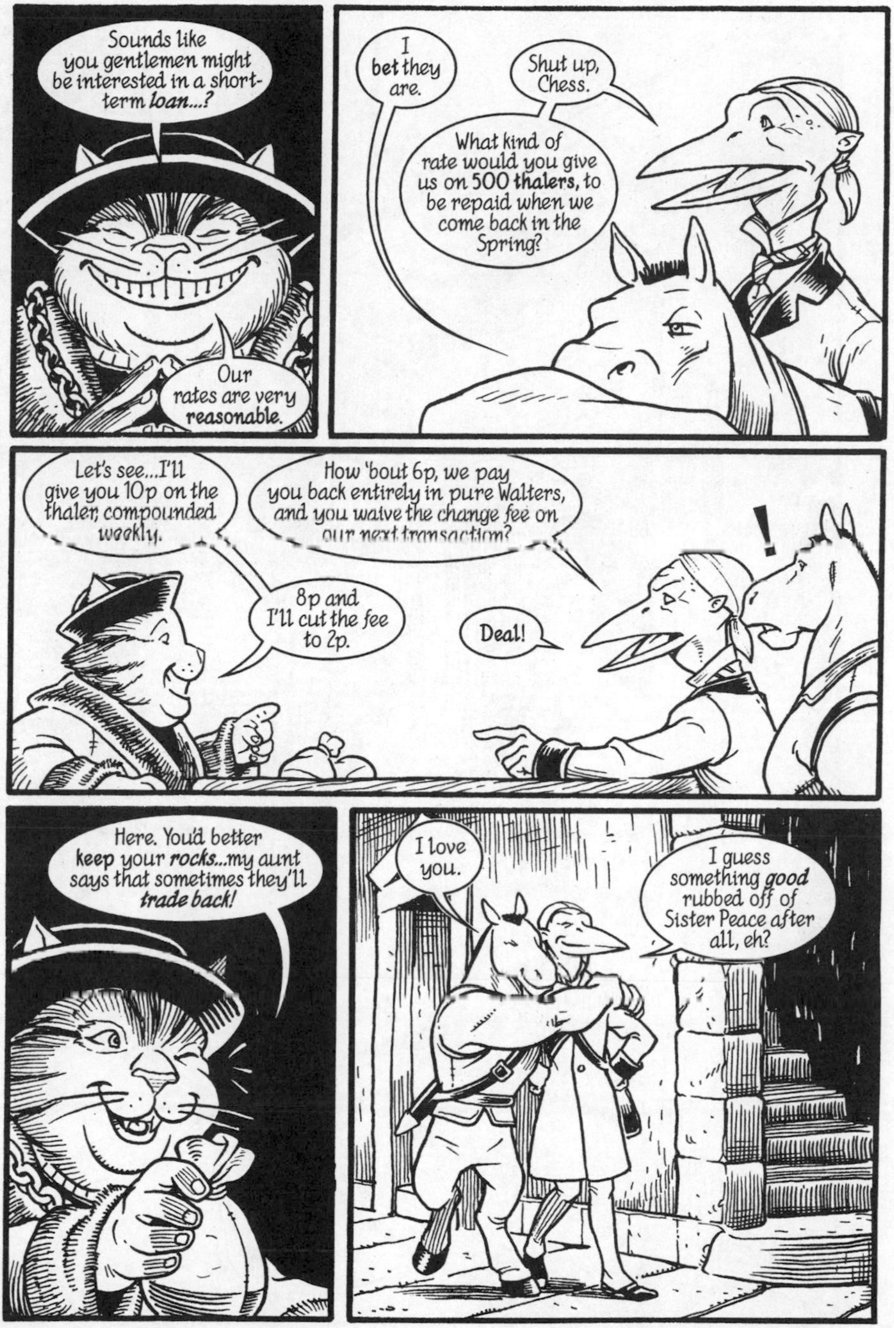
Sounds like you gentlemen might be interested in a short-term *loan*...?
Our rates are very **reasonable**.
I **bet** they are.
Shut up, Chess.
What kind of rate would you give us on **500 thalers**, to be repaid when we come back in the Spring?
Let's see...I'll give you 10p on the thaler, compounded weekly.
How 'bout 6p, we pay you back entirely in pure Walters, and you waive the change fee on our next transaction?
!
8p and I'll cut the fee to 2p.
Deal!
Here. You'd better **keep your *rocks*...**my aunt says that sometimes they'll ***trade back!***
I love you.
I guess something ***good*** rubbed off of Sister Peace after all, eh?

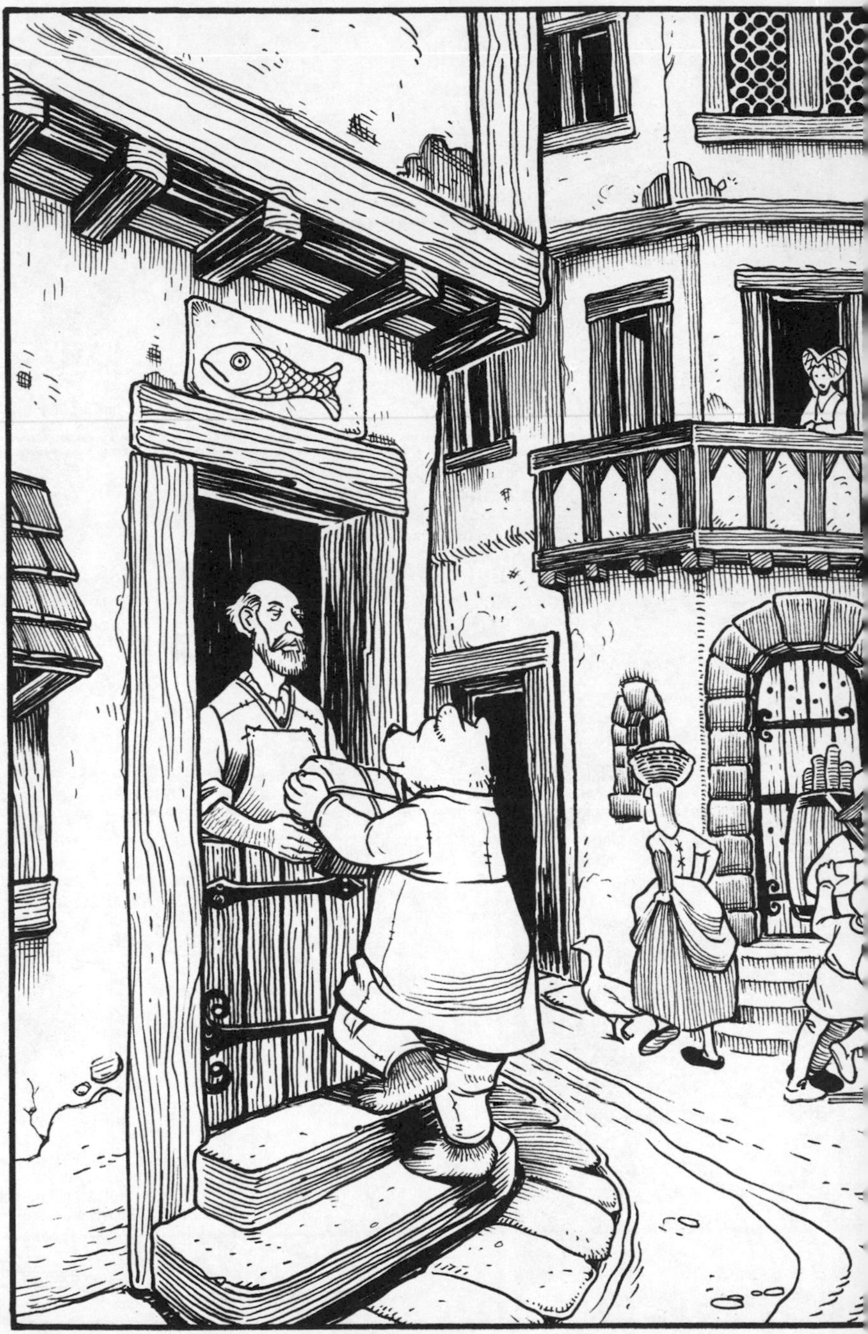

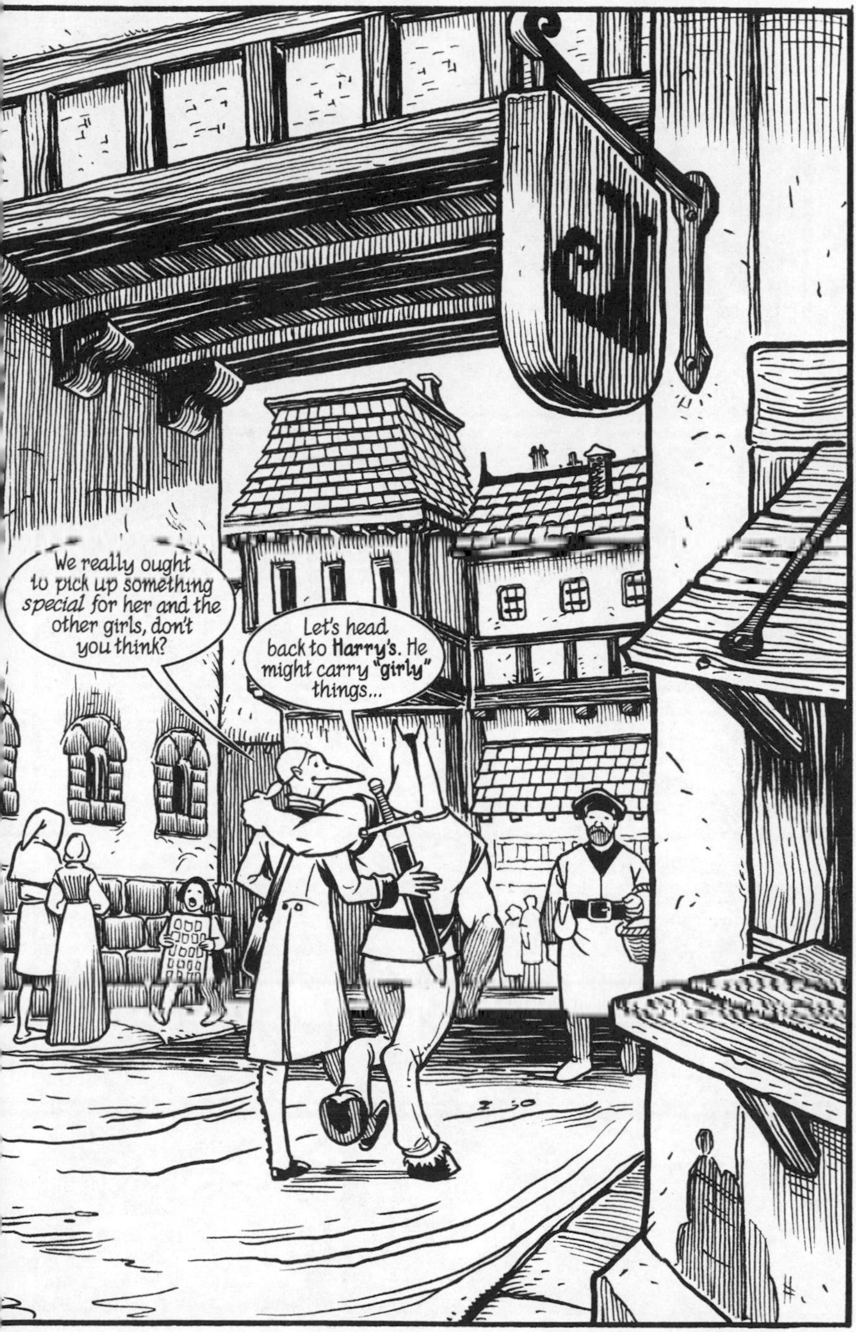

We really ought to pick up something *special* for her and the other girls, don't you think?
Let's head back to **Harry's**. He might carry **"girly"** things...

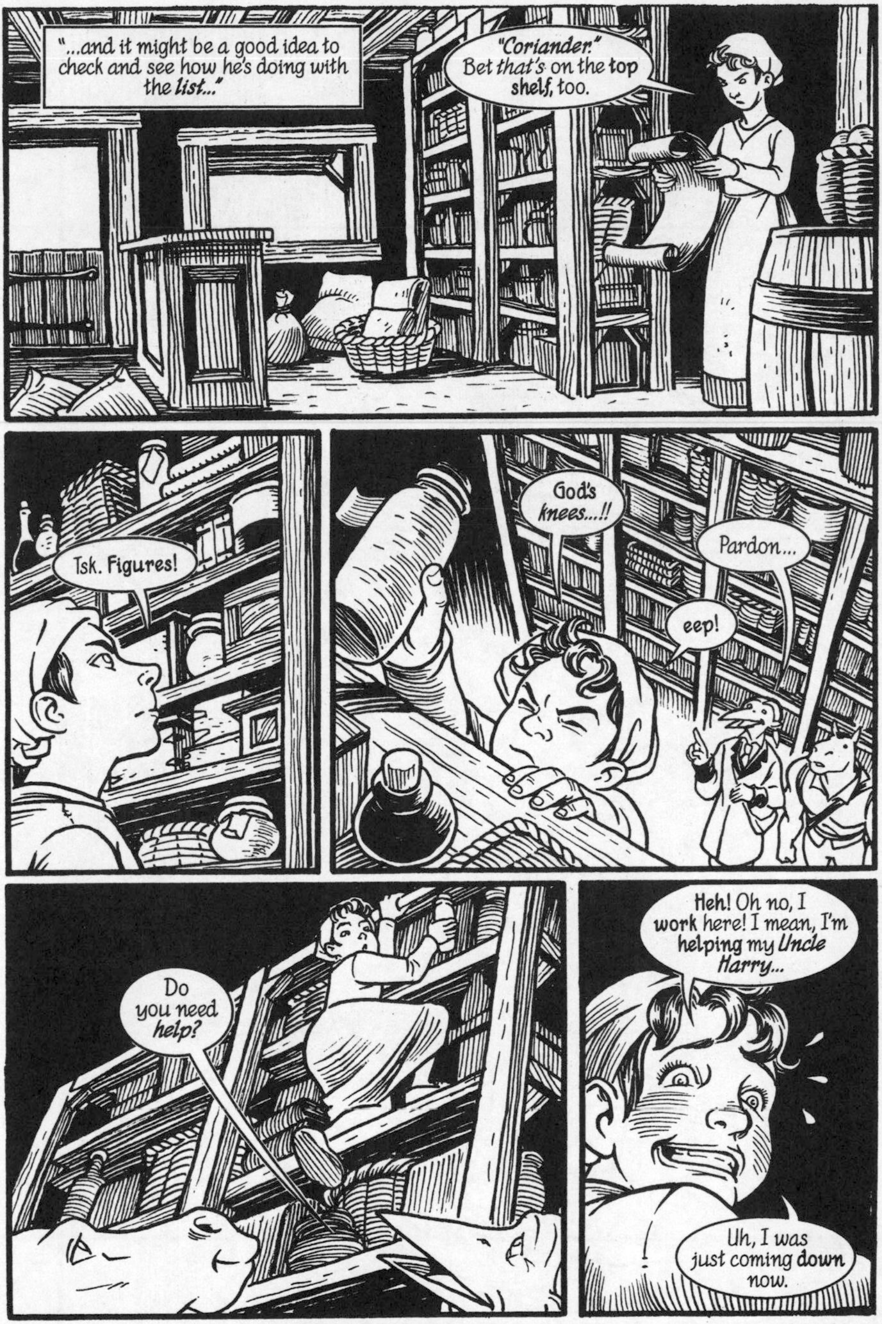
"...and it might be a good idea to check and see how he's doing with the *list*..."
"Coriander." Bet *that's* on the **top shelf,** too.
Tsk. Figures!
God's *knees*...!!
Pardon...
eep!
Do you need *help?*
Heh! Oh no, I *work* here! I mean, I'm helping my *Uncle Harry*...
Uh, I was just coming **down** now.

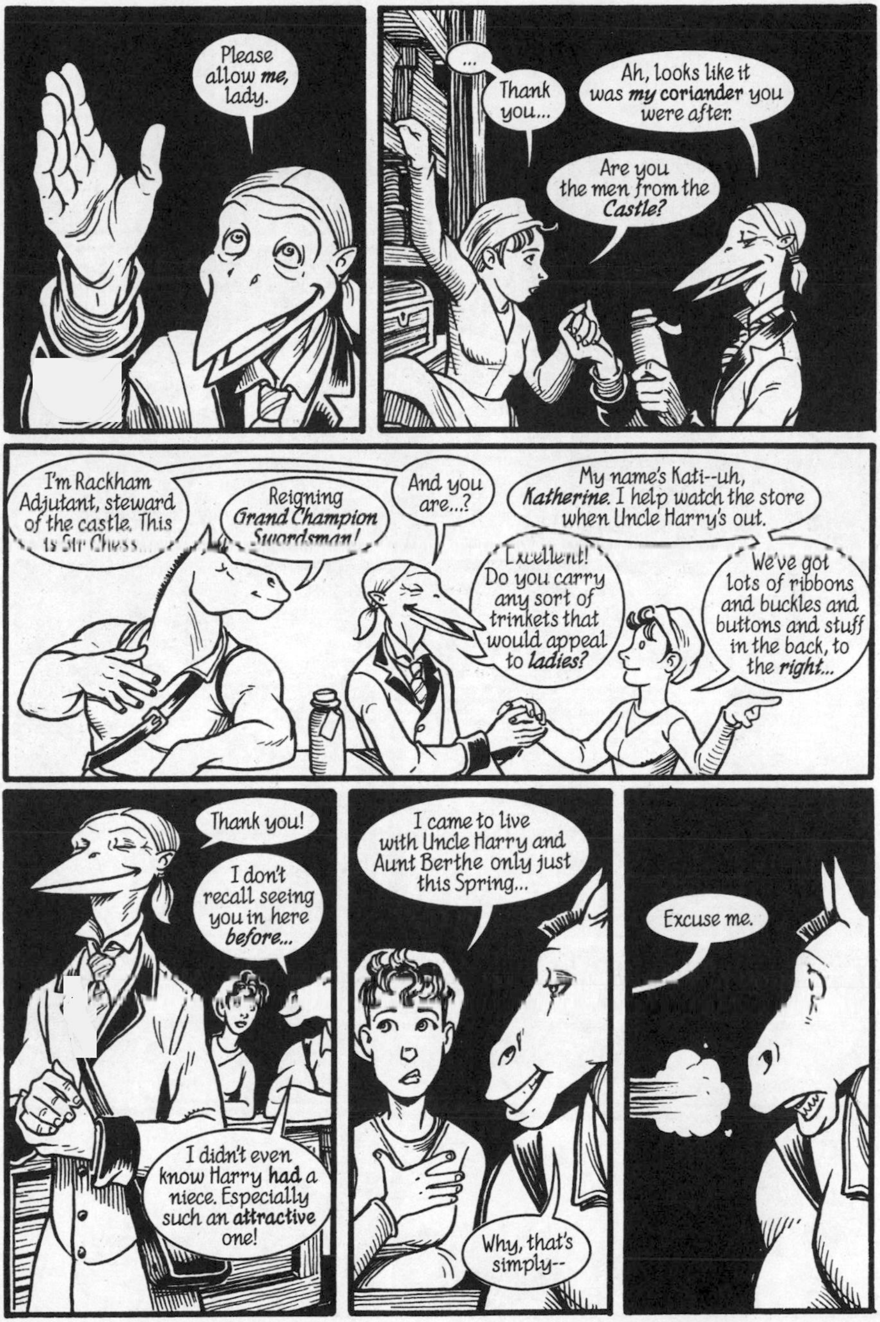
Please allow **me,** lady.
...
Thank you...
Ah, looks like it was **my coriander** you were after.
Are you the men from the ***Castle?***
I'm Rackham Adjutant, steward of the castle. This is Sir Chess...
Reigning ***Grand Champion Swordsman!***
And you are...?
My name's Kati--uh, ***Katherine.*** I help watch the store when Uncle Harry's out.
Excellent! Do you carry any sort of trinkets that would appeal to ***ladies?***
We've got lots of ribbons and buckles and buttons and stuff in the back, to the ***right...***
Thank you!
I don't recall seeing you in here ***before...***
I didn't even know Harry **had** a niece. Especially such an **attractive** one!
I came to live with Uncle Harry and Aunt Berthe only just this Spring...
Why, that's simply--
Excuse me.

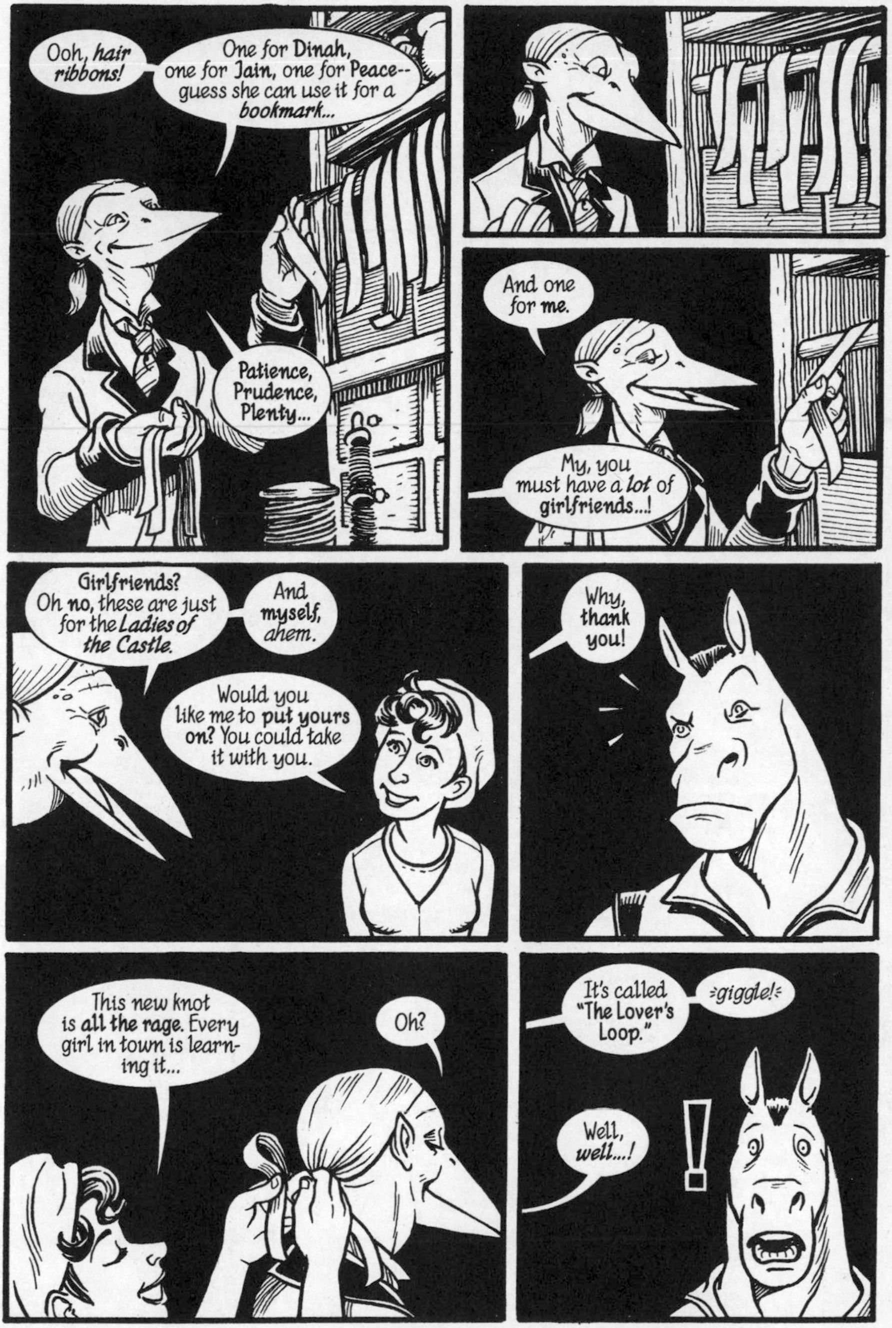
Ooh, *hair ribbons!*
One for **Dinah**, one for **Jain**, one for **Peace**-- guess she can use it for a *bookmark...*
Patience, Prudence, Plenty...
And one for **me**.
My, you must have a *lot* of **girlfriends...!**
Girlfriends? Oh **no**, these are just for the *Ladies of the Castle.*
And **myself**, *ahem.*
Would you like me to **put yours on?** You could take it with you.
Why, **thank you!**
This new knot is **all the rage**. Every girl in town is learning it...
Oh?
It's called **"The Lover's Loop."**
giggle!
Well, ***well...!***
!

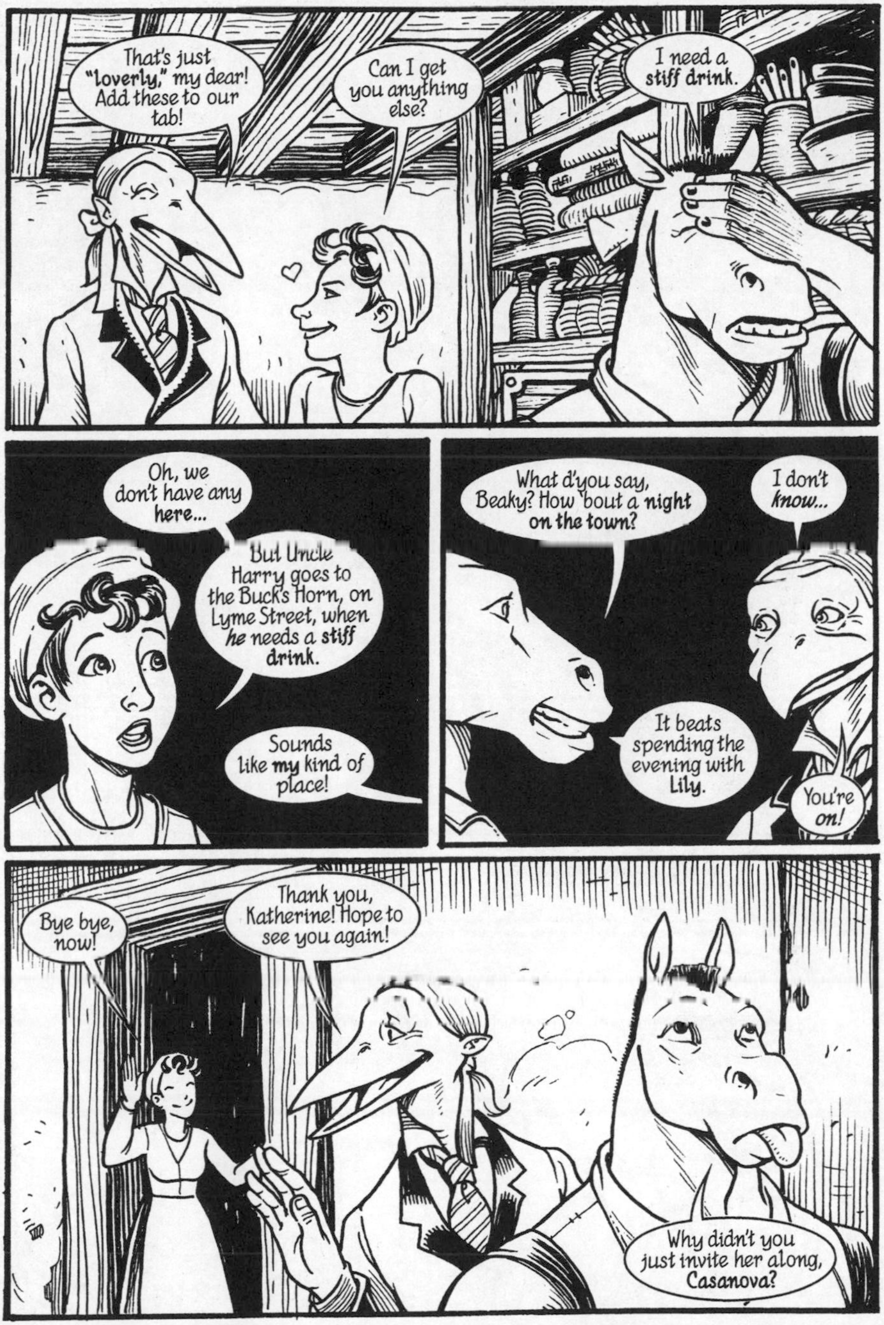
That's just "loverly," my dear! Add these to our tab!
Can I get you anything else?
I need a stiff drink.
Oh, we don't have any here...
But Uncle Harry goes to the Buck's Horn, on Lyme Street, when he needs a stiff drink.
Sounds like my kind of place!
What d'you say, Beaky? How 'bout a night on the town?
I don't know...
It beats spending the evening with Lily.
You're on!
Bye bye, now!
Thank you, Katherine! Hope to see you again!
Why didn't you just invite her along, Casanova?

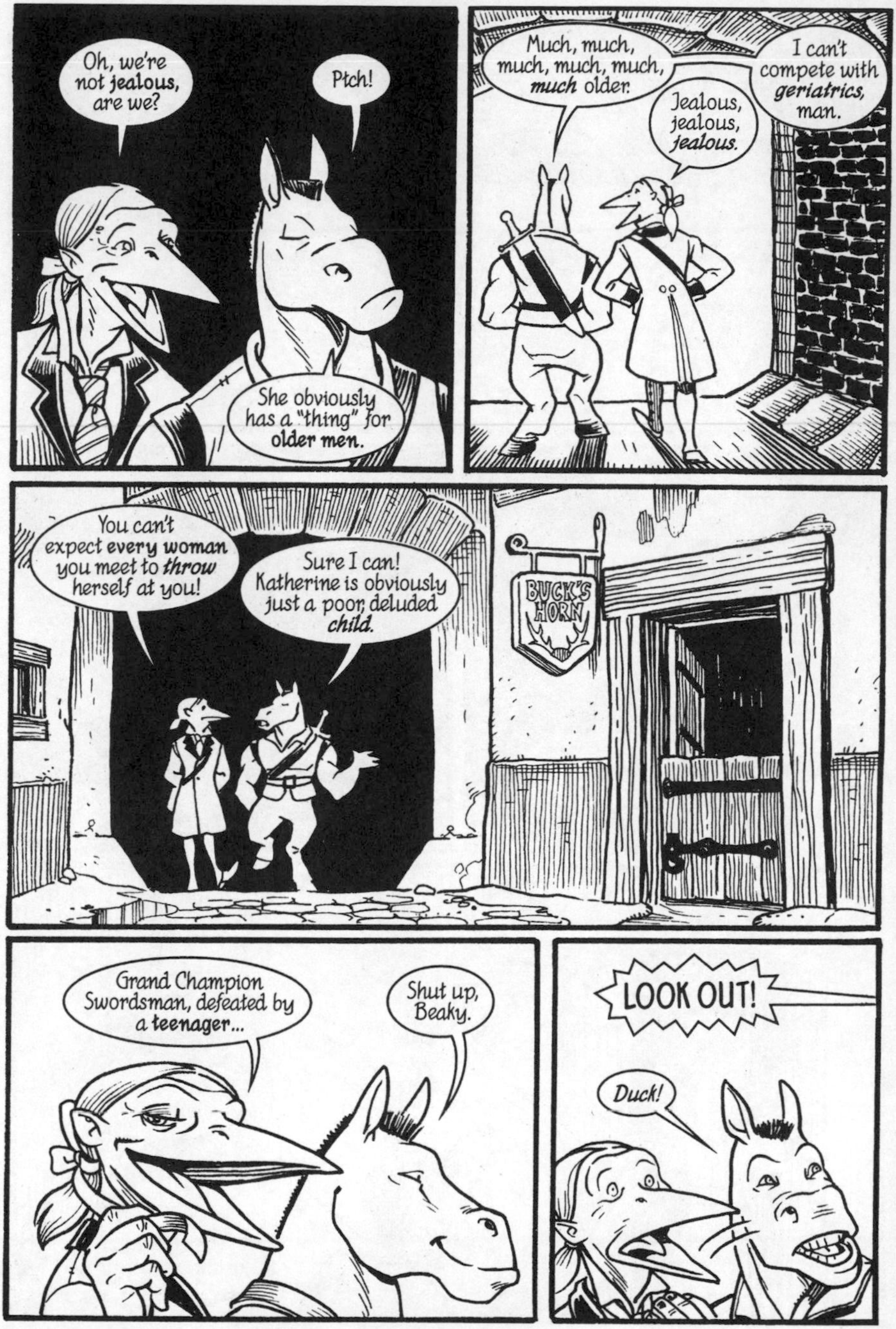
Oh, we're not jealous, are we?
Ptch!
She obviously has a "thing" for older men.
Much, much, much, much, much, much older.
Jealous, jealous, jealous.
I can't compete with geriatrics, man.
You can't expect every woman you meet to throw herself at you!
Sure I can! Katherine is obviously just a poor, deluded child.
BUCK'S HORN
Grand Champion Swordsman, defeated by a teenager...
Shut up, Beaky.
LOOK OUT!
Duck!

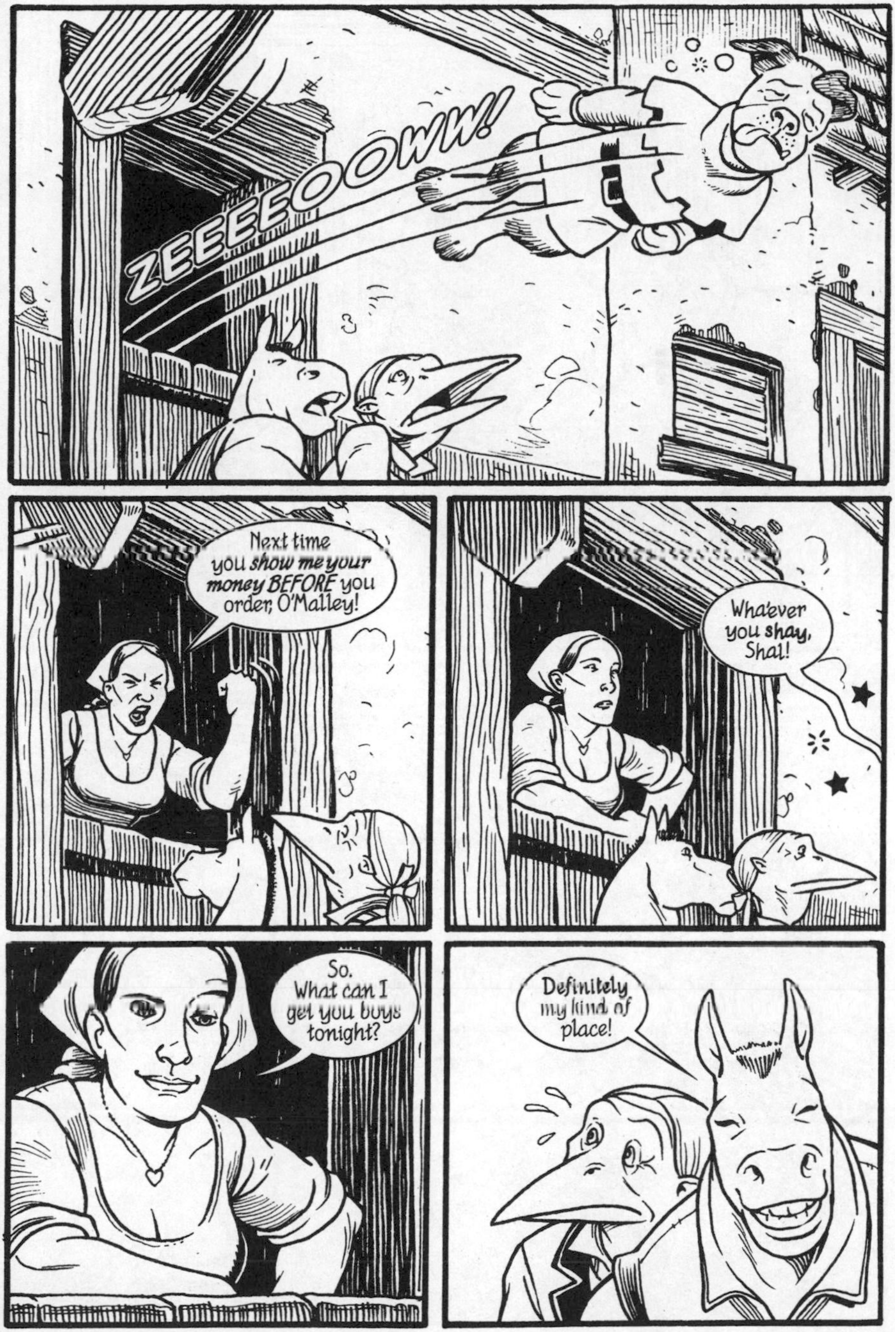
ZEEEEOOOWW!
Next time you show me your money BEFORE you order, O'Malley!
Wha'ever you shay, Shal!
So. What can I get you boys tonight?
Definitely my kind of place!

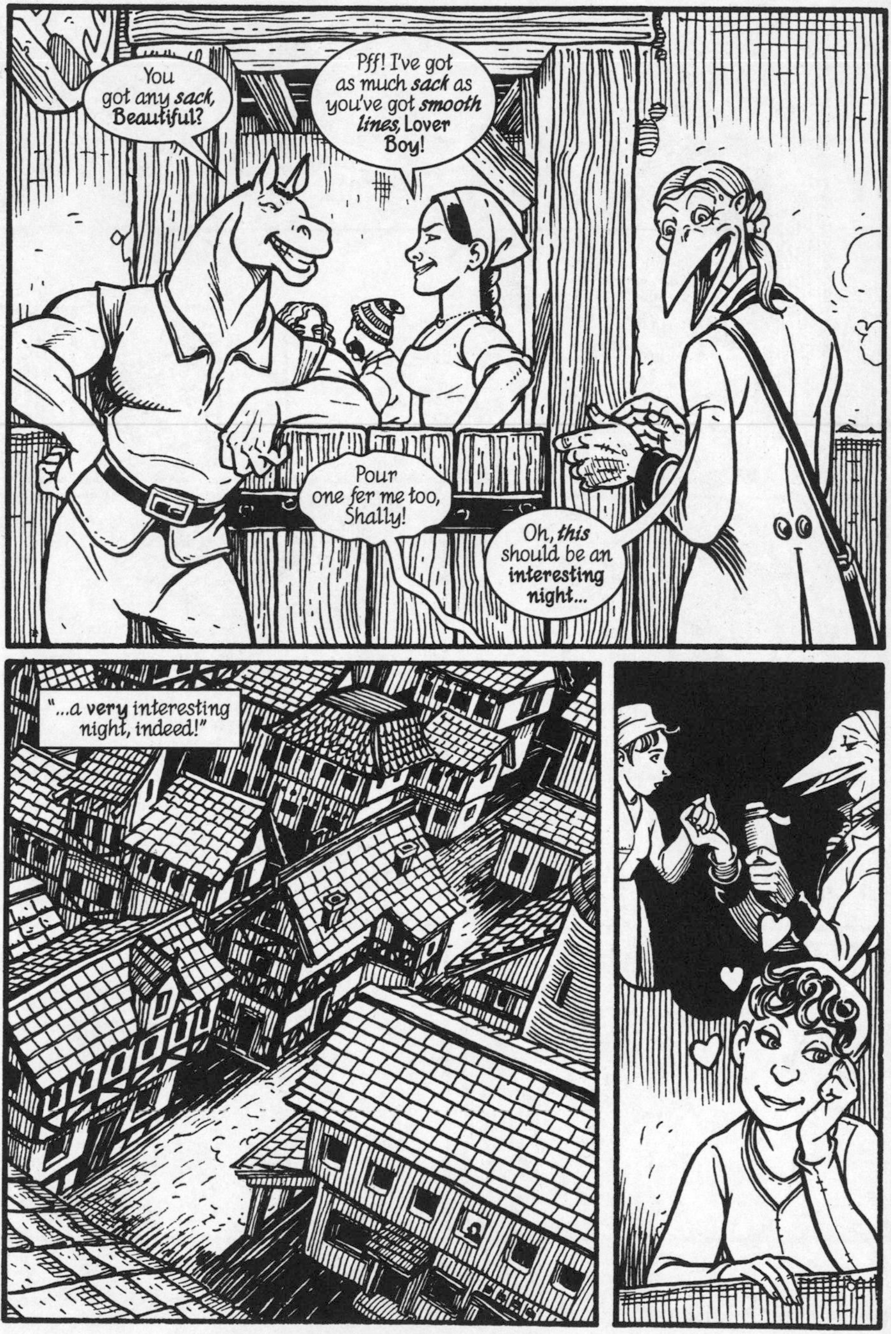

You got any sack, Beautiful?
Pff! I've got as much sack as you've got smooth lines, Lover Boy!
Pour one fer me too, Shally!
Oh, this should be an interesting night...
"...a very interesting night, indeed!"

Chapter 10.

CITY MOUSE, COUNTRY MOUSE PT. 2.

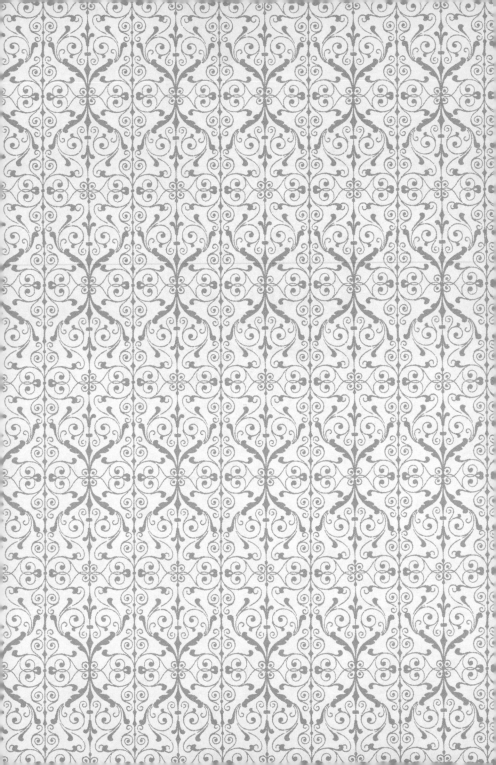

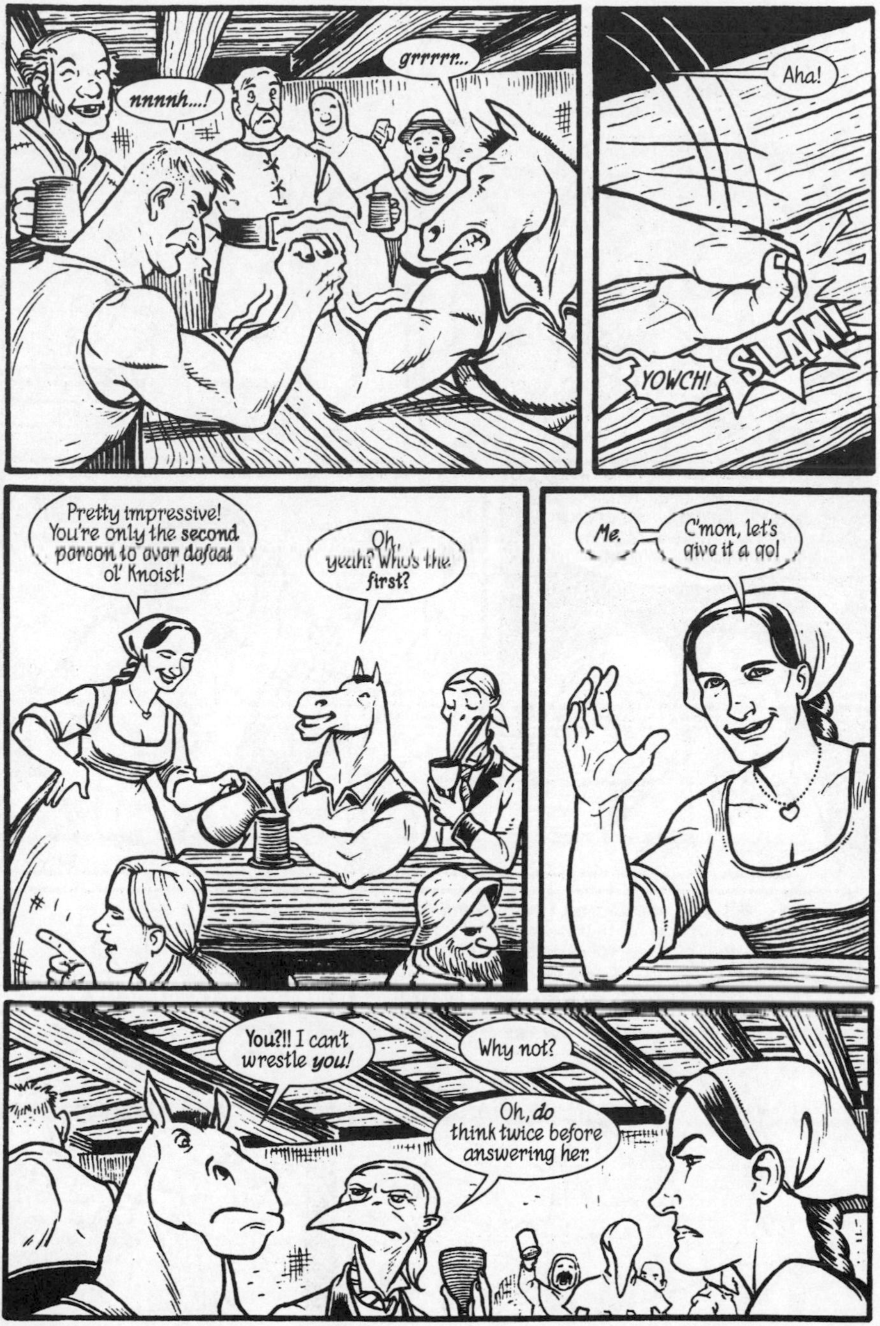
nnnnh...!
grrrrr...
Aha!
YOWCH!
SLAM!
Pretty impressive! You're only the second person to ever defeat ol' Kneist!
Oh, yeah? Who's the first?
Me.
C'mon, let's give it a go!
You?!! I can't wrestle you!
Why not?
Oh, do think twice before answering her.

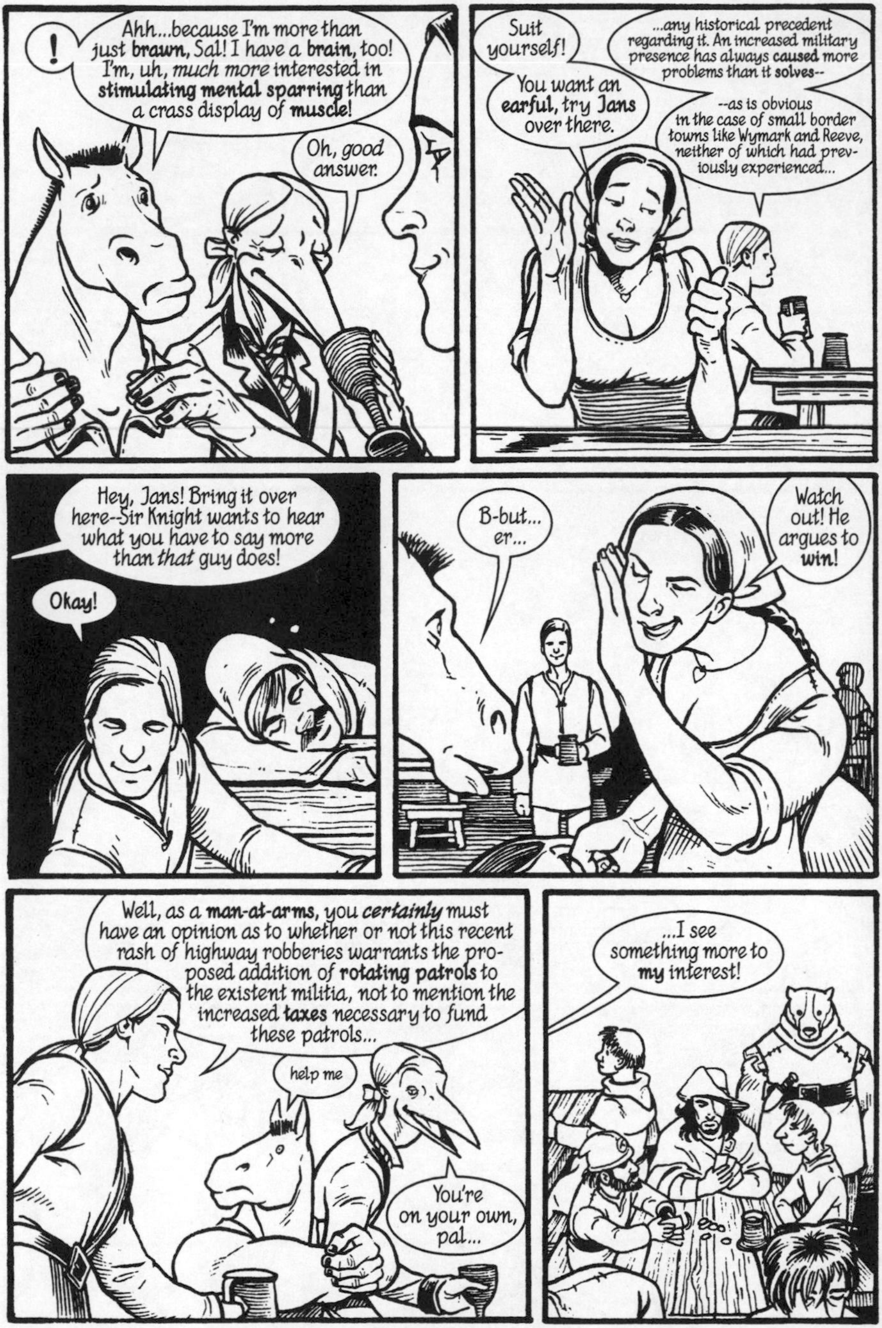
!
Ahh...because I'm more than just **brawn**, Sal! I have a **brain**, too! I'm, uh, *much more* interested in **stimulating mental sparring** than a crass display of **muscle**!
Oh, *good* answer.
Suit yourself!
You want an **earful**, try **Jans** over there.
...any historical precedent regarding it. An increased military presence has always **caused** more problems than it **solves**--
--as is obvious in the case of small border towns like Wymark and Reeve, neither of which had previously experienced...
Hey, Jans! Bring it over here--Sir Knight wants to hear what you have to say more than *that* guy does!
Okay!
B-but... er...
Watch out! He argues to **win**!
Well, as a **man-at-arms**, you ***certainly*** must have an opinion as to whether or not this recent rash of highway robberies warrants the proposed addition of **rotating patrols** to the existent militia, not to mention the increased **taxes** necessary to fund these patrols...
help me
You're on your own, pal...
...I see something more to **my** interest!

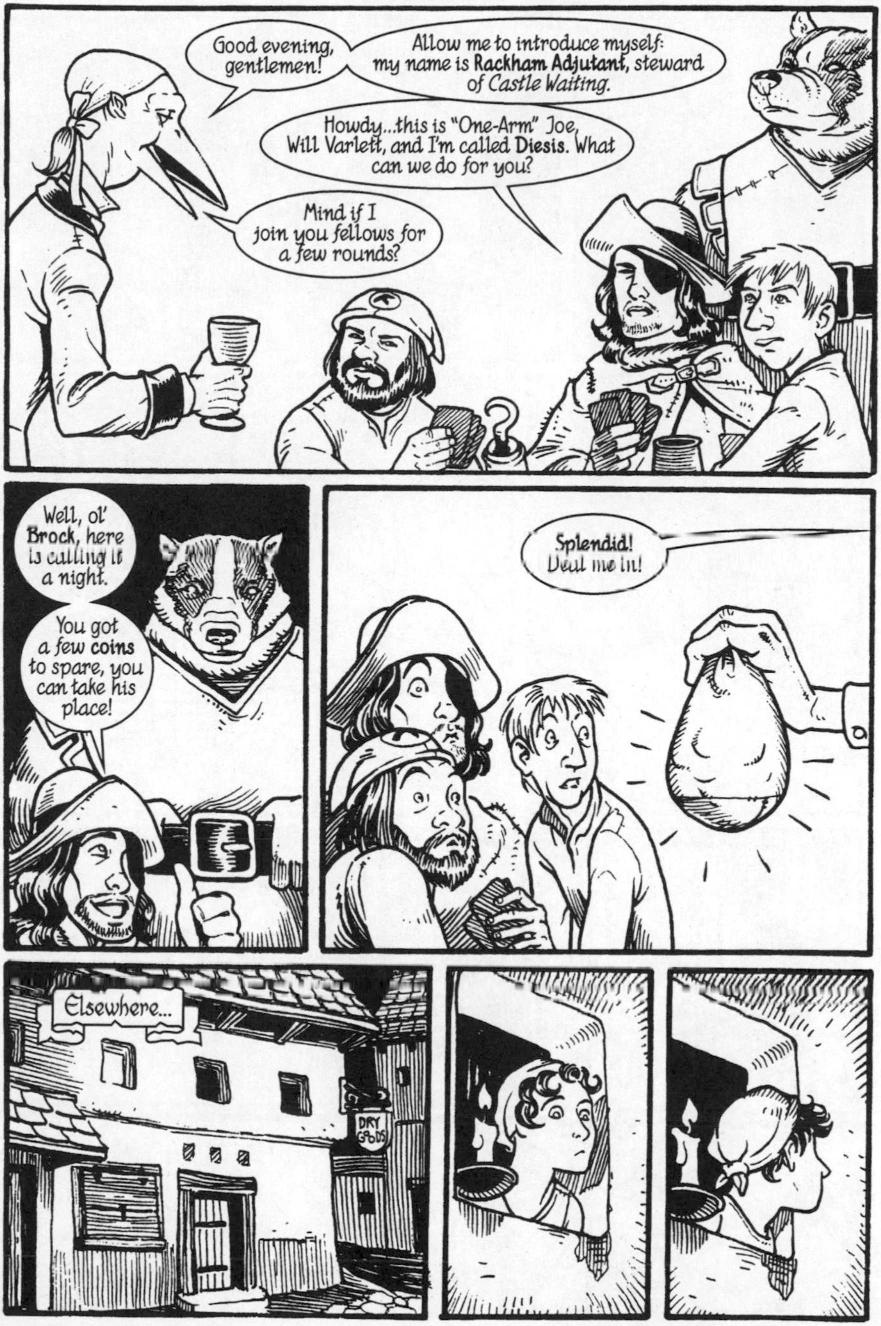
Good evening, gentlemen!
Allow me to introduce myself: my name is **Rackham Adjutant**, steward of *Castle Waiting*.
Howdy...this is "One-Arm" Joe, Will Varlett, and I'm called **Diesis**. What can we do for you?
Mind if I join you fellows for a few rounds?
Well, ol' **Brock**, here is calling it a night.
You got a few **coins** to spare, you can take his place!
Splendid! Deal me in!
Elsewhere...
DRY GOODS

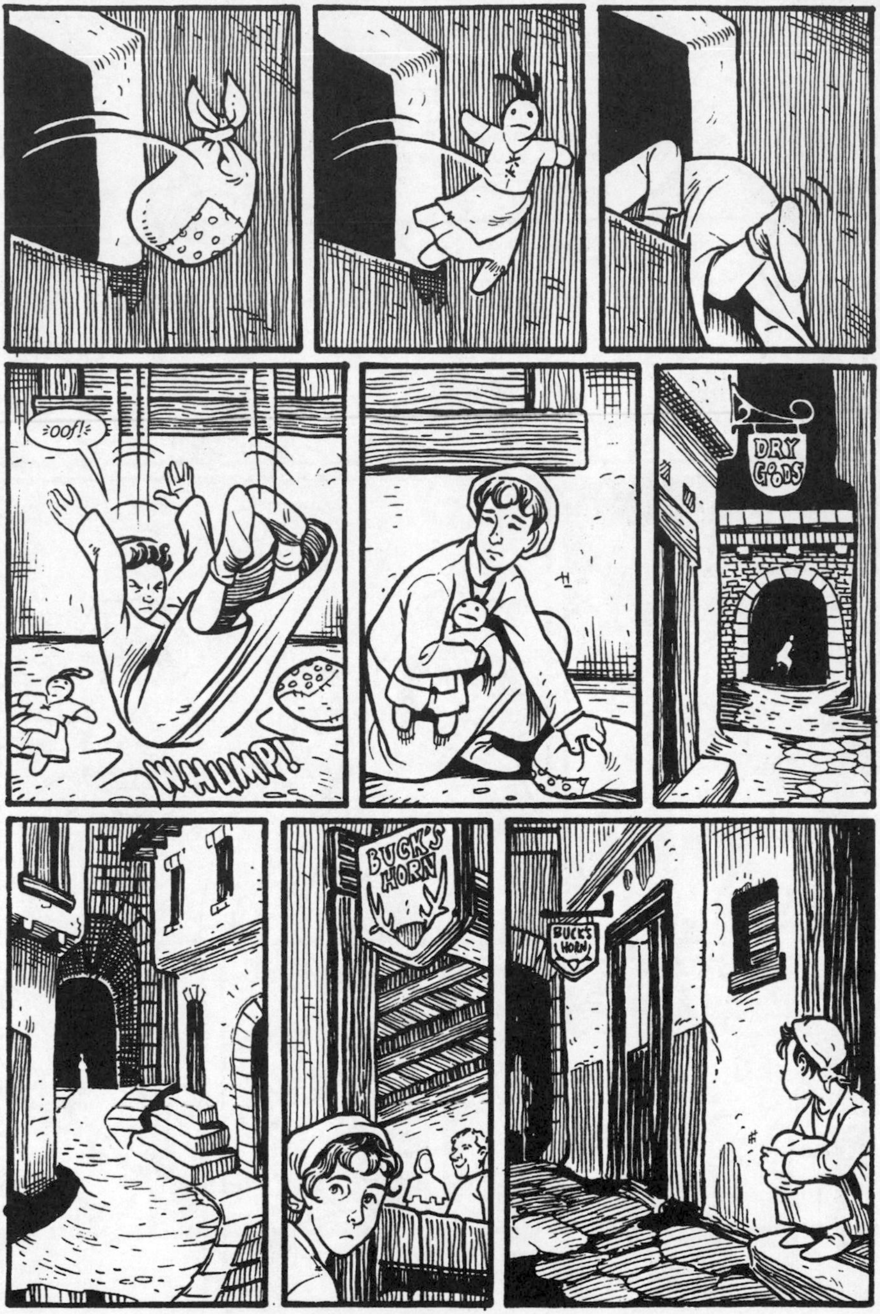
oof!
WHUMP!
DRY GOODS
BUCK'S HORN
BUCK'S HORN

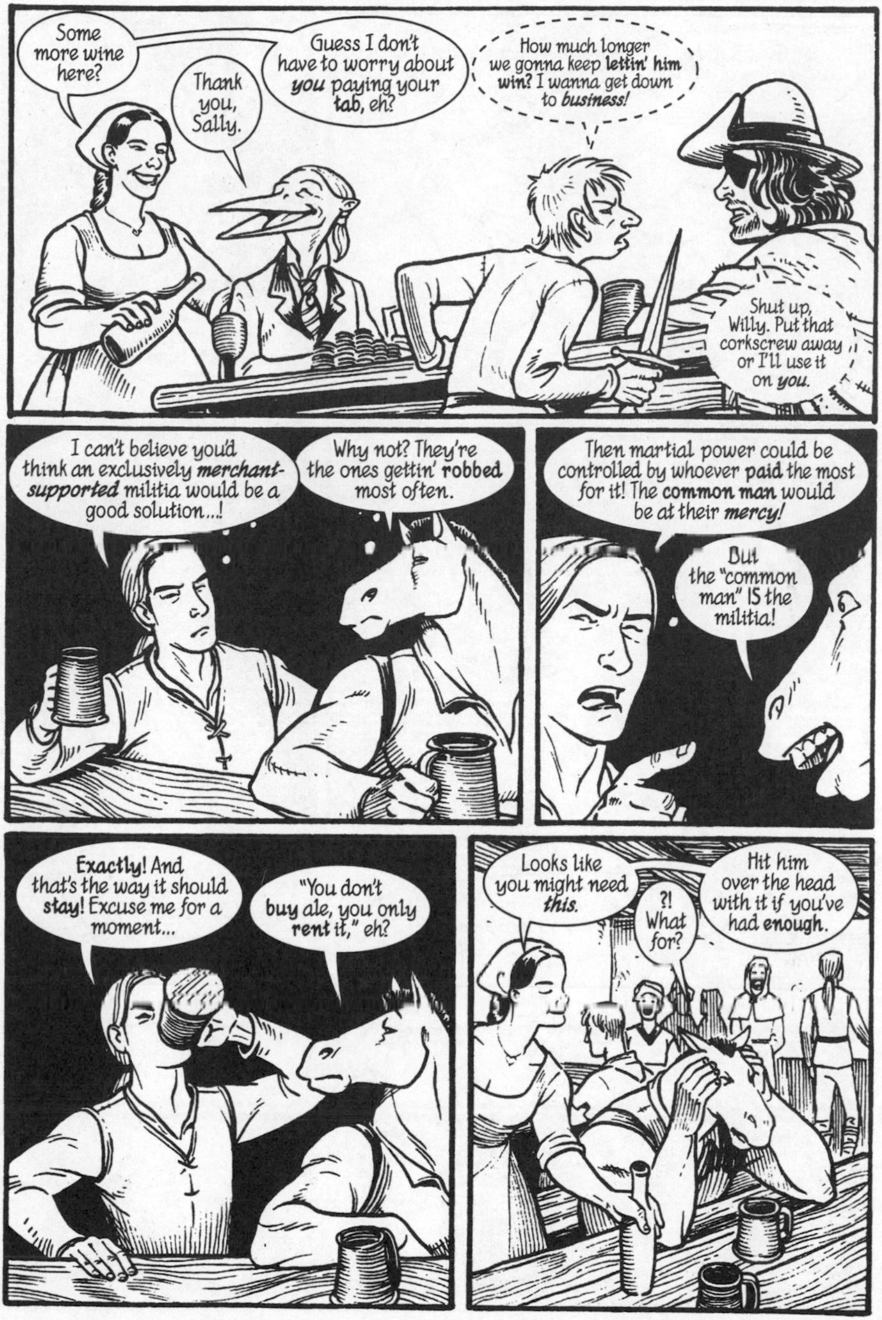
Some more wine here?
Thank you, Sally.
Guess I don't have to worry about *you* paying your **tab**, eh?
How much longer we gonna keep **lettin' him win?** I wanna get down to ***business!***
Shut up, Willy. Put that corkscrew away or I'll use it on ***you***.
I can't believe you'd think an exclusively ***merchant-supported*** militia would be a good solution...!
Why not? They're the ones gettin' **robbed** most often.
Then martial power could be controlled by whoever **paid** the most for it! The **common man** would be at their ***mercy!***
But the "common man" IS the militia!
Exactly! And that's the way it should **stay!** Excuse me for a moment...
"You don't **buy** ale, you only **rent** it," eh?
Looks like you might need ***this***.
?! What for?
Hit him over the head with it if you've had **enough**.

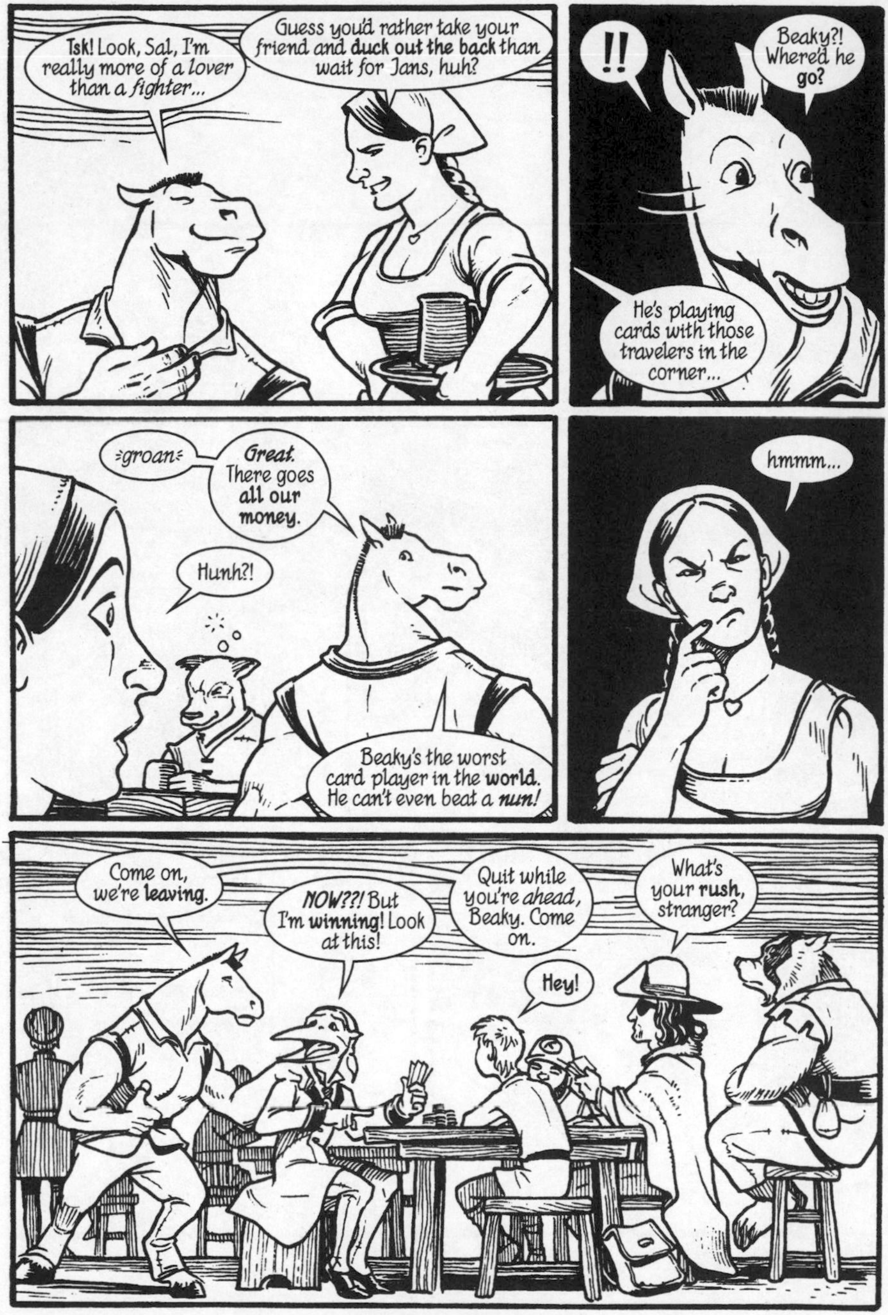
Tsk! Look, Sal, I'm really more of a *lover* than a *fighter*...
Guess you'd rather take your friend and **duck out the back** than wait for Jans, huh?
!!
Beaky?! Where'd he **go?**
He's playing cards with those travelers in the corner...
⁼groan⁼
Great. There goes **all our money.**
Hunh?!
Beaky's the worst card player in the **world**. He can't even beat a ***nun!***
hmmm...
Come on, we're **leaving**.
NOW??! But I'm **winning**! Look at this!
Quit while you're *ahead*, Beaky. Come on.
Hey!
What's your **rush**, stranger?

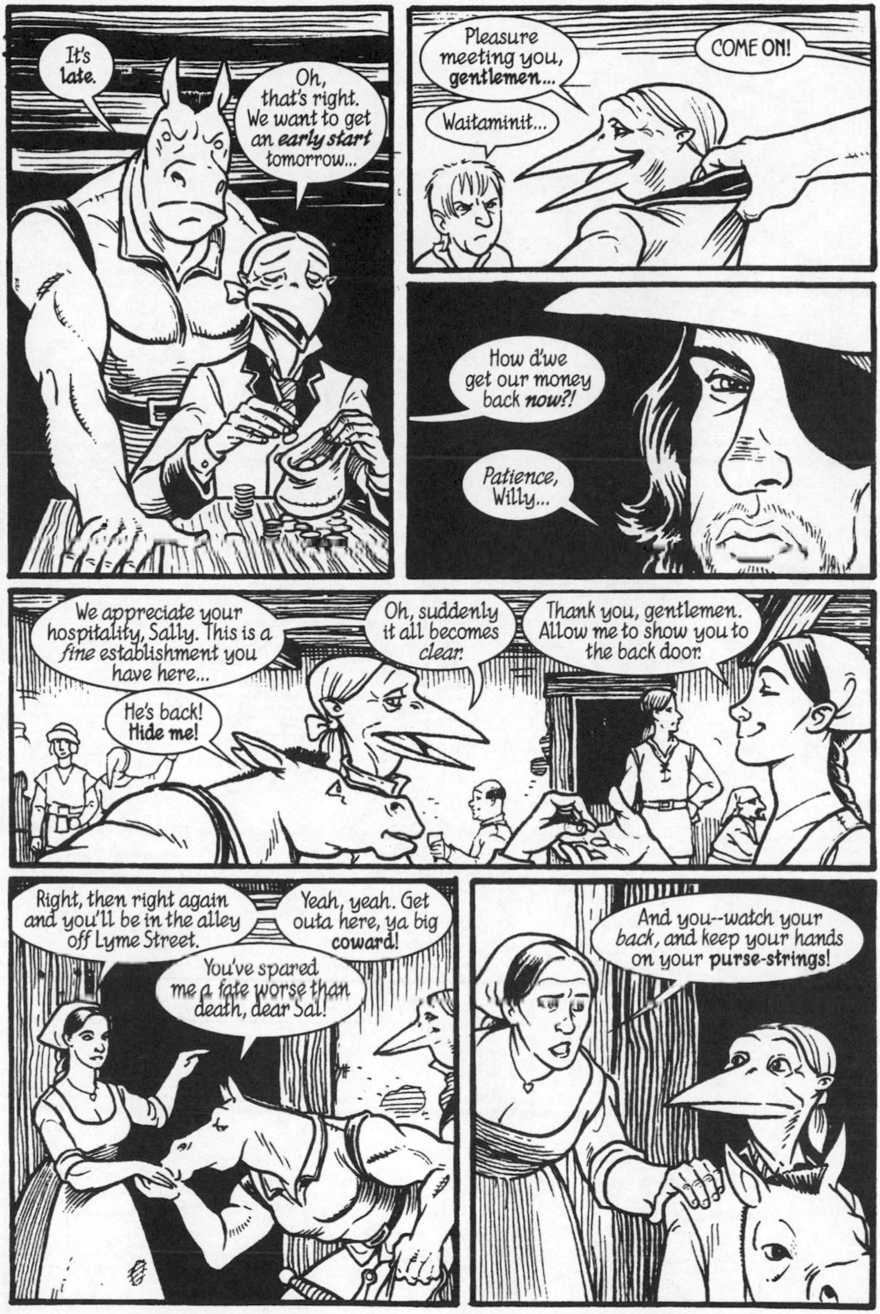
It's late.
Oh, that's right. We want to get an early start tomorrow...
Pleasure meeting you, gentlemen...
COME ON!
Waitaminit...
How d'we get our money back now?!
Patience, Willy...
We appreciate your hospitality, Sally. This is a fine establishment you have here...
He's back! Hide me!
Oh, suddenly it all becomes clear.
Thank you, gentlemen. Allow me to show you to the back door.
Right, then right again and you'll be in the alley off Lyme Street.
Yeah, yeah. Get outa here, ya big coward!
You've spared me a fate worse than death, dear Sal!
And you--watch your back, and keep your hands on your purse-strings!

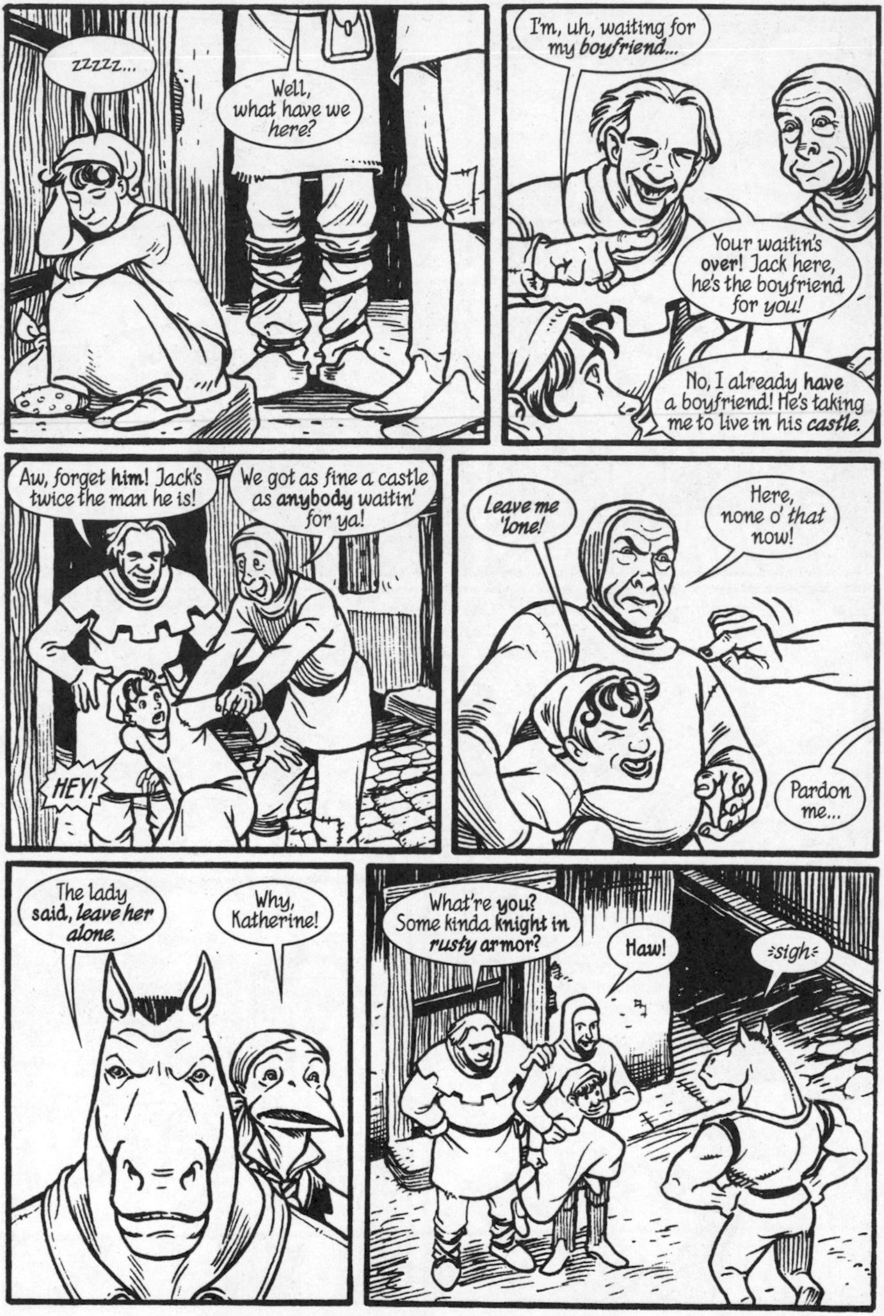
zzzzz...
Well, what have we here?
I'm, uh, waiting for my boyfriend...
Your waitin's over! Jack here, he's the boyfriend for you!
No, I already have a boyfriend! He's taking me to live in his castle.
Aw, forget him! Jack's twice the man he is!
We got as fine a castle as anybody waitin' for ya!
HEY!
Leave me 'lone!
Here, none o' that now!
Pardon me...
The lady said, leave her alone.
Why, Katherine!
What're you? Some kinda knight in rusty armor?
Haw!
sigh

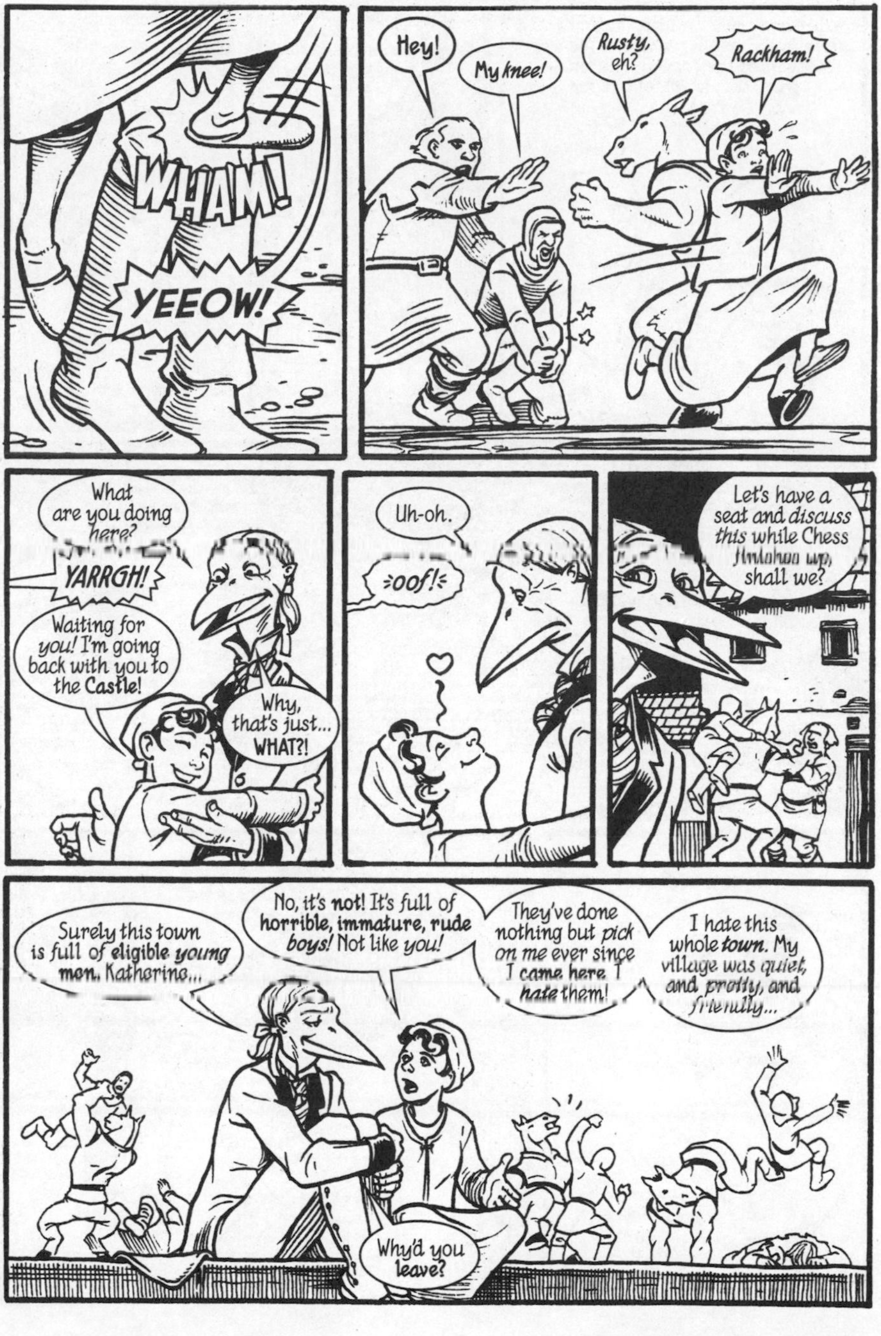
WHAM!
YEEOW!
Hey!
My knee!
Rusty, eh?
Rackham!
What are you doing here?
YARRGH!
Waiting for you! I'm going back with you to the Castle!
Why, that's just... WHAT?!
Uh-oh.
oof!
Let's have a seat and discuss this while Chess
shall we?
Surely this town is full of eligible young men, Katherine...
No, it's not! It's full of horrible, immature, rude boys! Not like you!
They've done nothing but pick on me ever since I came here. I hate them!
I hate this whole town. My village was quiet, and pretty, and friendly...
Why'd you leave?

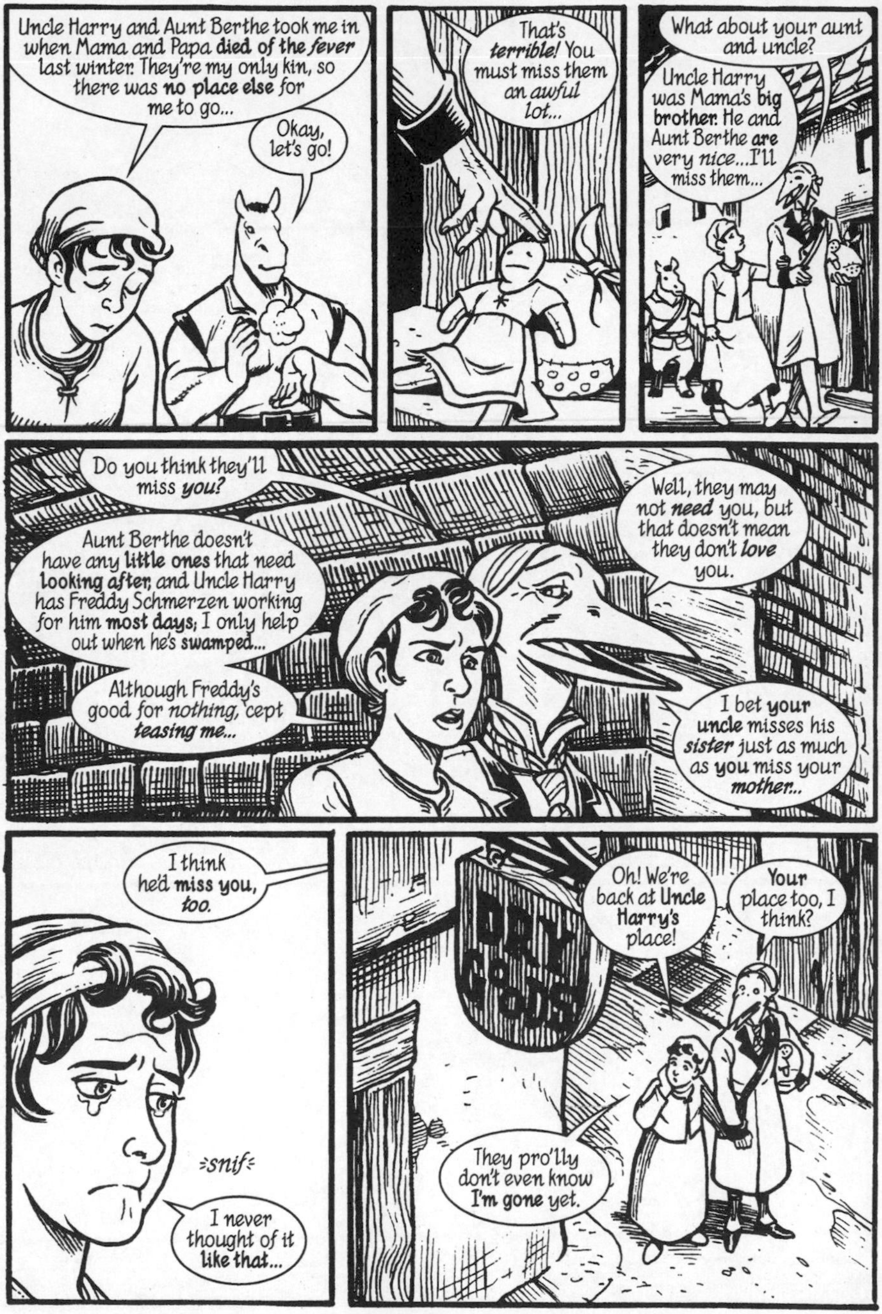
Uncle Harry and Aunt Berthe took me in when Mama and Papa died of the fever last winter. They're my only kin, so there was no place else for me to go...
Okay, let's go!
That's terrible! You must miss them an awful lot...
What about your aunt and uncle?
Uncle Harry was Mama's big brother. He and Aunt Berthe are very nice...I'll miss them...
Do you think they'll miss you?
Aunt Berthe doesn't have any little ones that need looking after, and Uncle Harry has Freddy Schmerzen working for him most days; I only help out when he's swamped...
Although Freddy's good for nothing, 'cept teasing me...
Well, they may not need you, but that doesn't mean they don't love you.
I bet your uncle misses his sister just as much as you miss your mother...
I think he'd miss you, too.
snif
I never thought of it like that...
DRY GOODS
Oh! We're back at Uncle Harry's place!
Your place too, I think?
They pro'lly don't even know I'm gone yet.

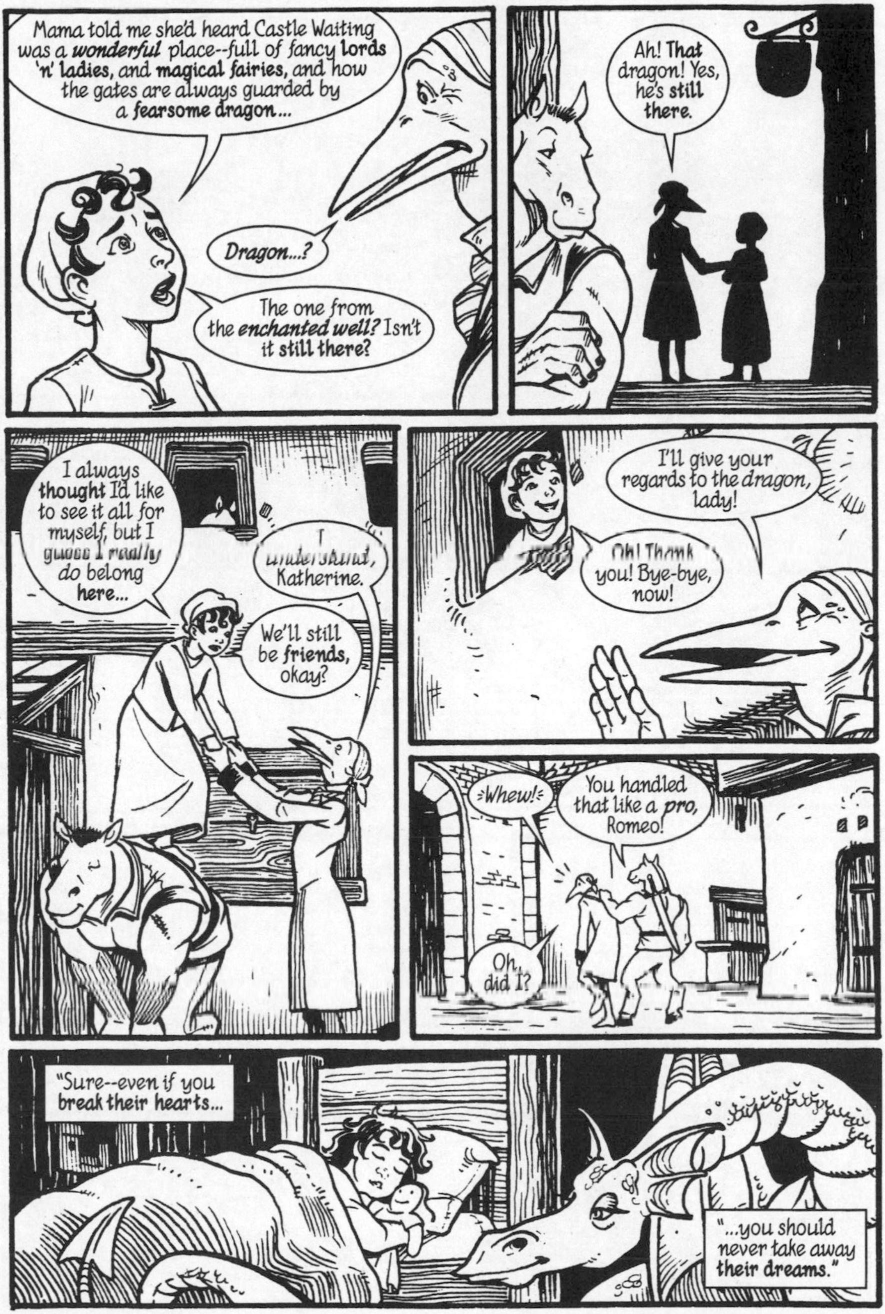
Mama told me she'd heard Castle Waiting was a wonderful place--full of fancy lords 'n' ladies, and magical fairies, and how the gates are always guarded by a fearsome dragon...
Dragon...?
The one from the enchanted well? Isn't it still there?
Ah! That dragon! Yes, he's still there.
I always thought I'd like to see it all for myself, but I guess I really do belong here...
I understand, Katherine.
We'll still be friends, okay?
I'll give your regards to the dragon, lady!
Oh! Thank you! Bye-bye, now!
Whew!
You handled that like a pro, Romeo!
Oh, did I?
"Sure--even if you break their hearts...
"...you should never take away their dreams."

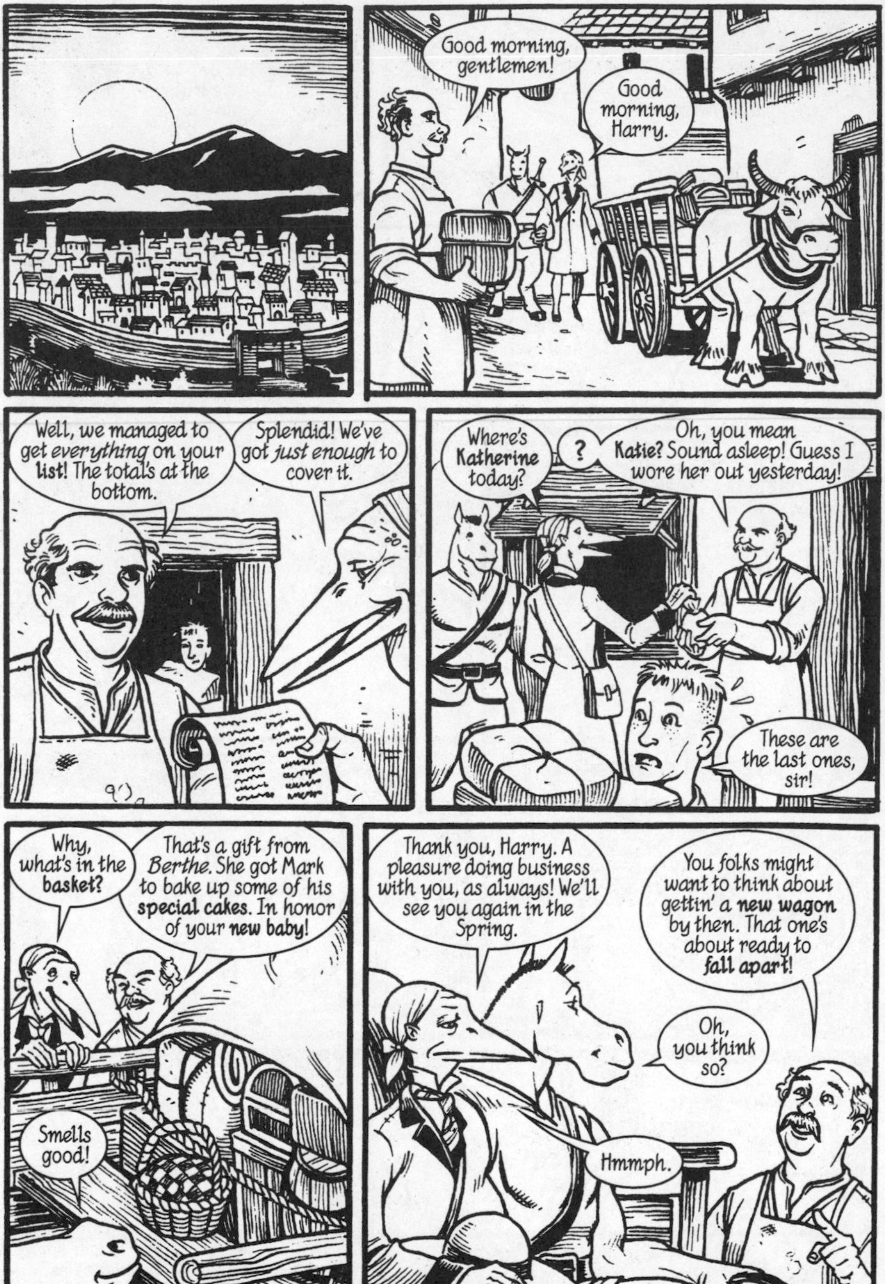
Good morning, gentlemen!
Good morning, Harry.
Well, we managed to get *everything* on your **list**! The total's at the bottom.
Splendid! We've got *just enough* to cover it.
Where's **Katherine** today?
?
Oh, you mean **Katie**? Sound asleep! Guess I wore her out yesterday!
These are the last ones, sir!
Why, what's in the **basket?**
That's a gift from *Berthe*. She got Mark to bake up some of his **special cakes**. In honor of your **new baby**!
Smells good!
Thank you, Harry. A pleasure doing business with you, as always! We'll see you again in the Spring.
You folks might want to think about gettin' a **new wagon** by then. That one's about ready to **fall apart**!
Oh, you think so?
Hmmph.

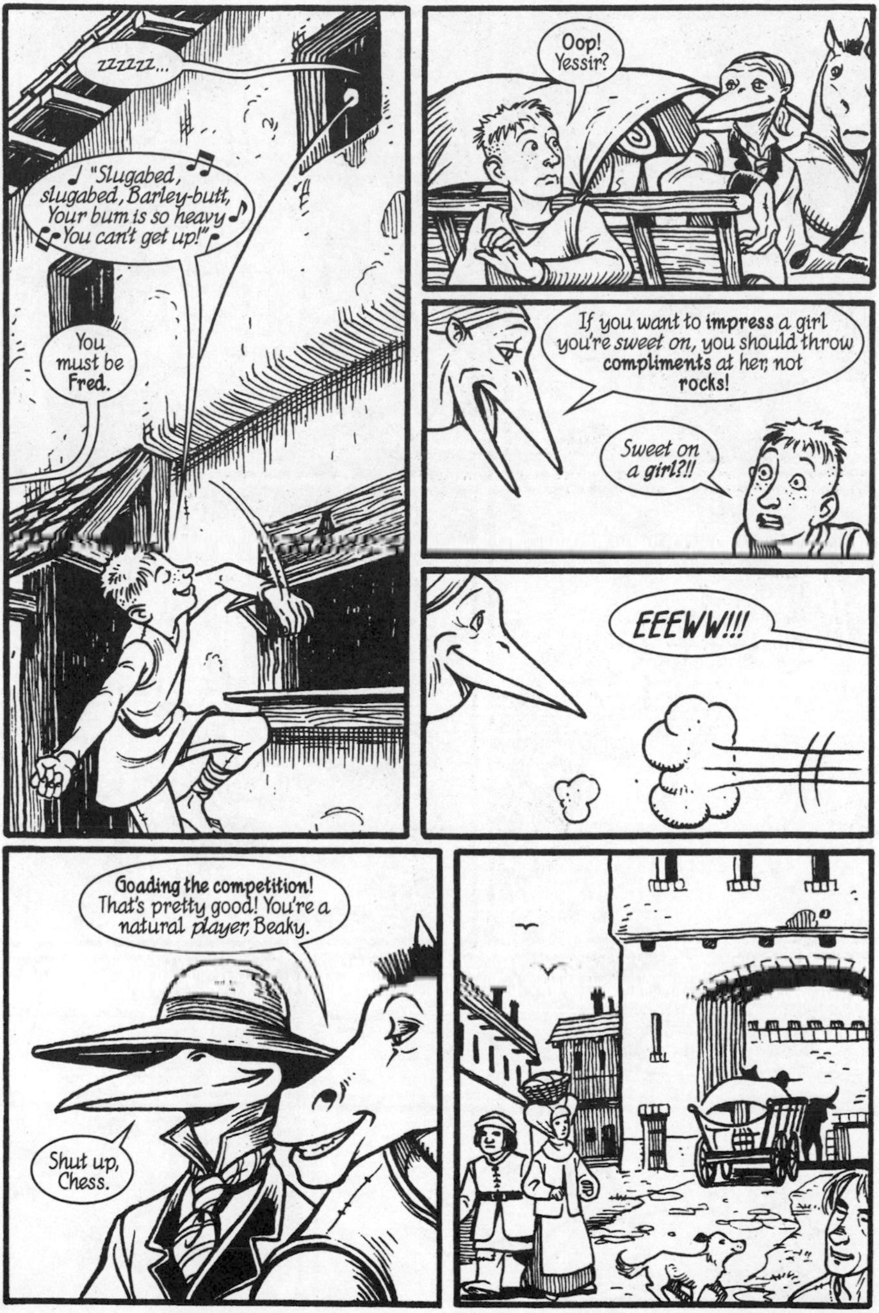
zzzzzz...
"Slugabed, slugabed, Barley-butt, Your bum is so heavy You can't get up!"
You must be Fred.
Oop! Yessir?
If you want to impress a girl you're sweet on, you should throw compliments at her, not rocks!
Sweet on a girl?!!
EEEWW!!!
Goading the competition! That's pretty good! You're a natural player, Beaky.
Shut up, Chess.

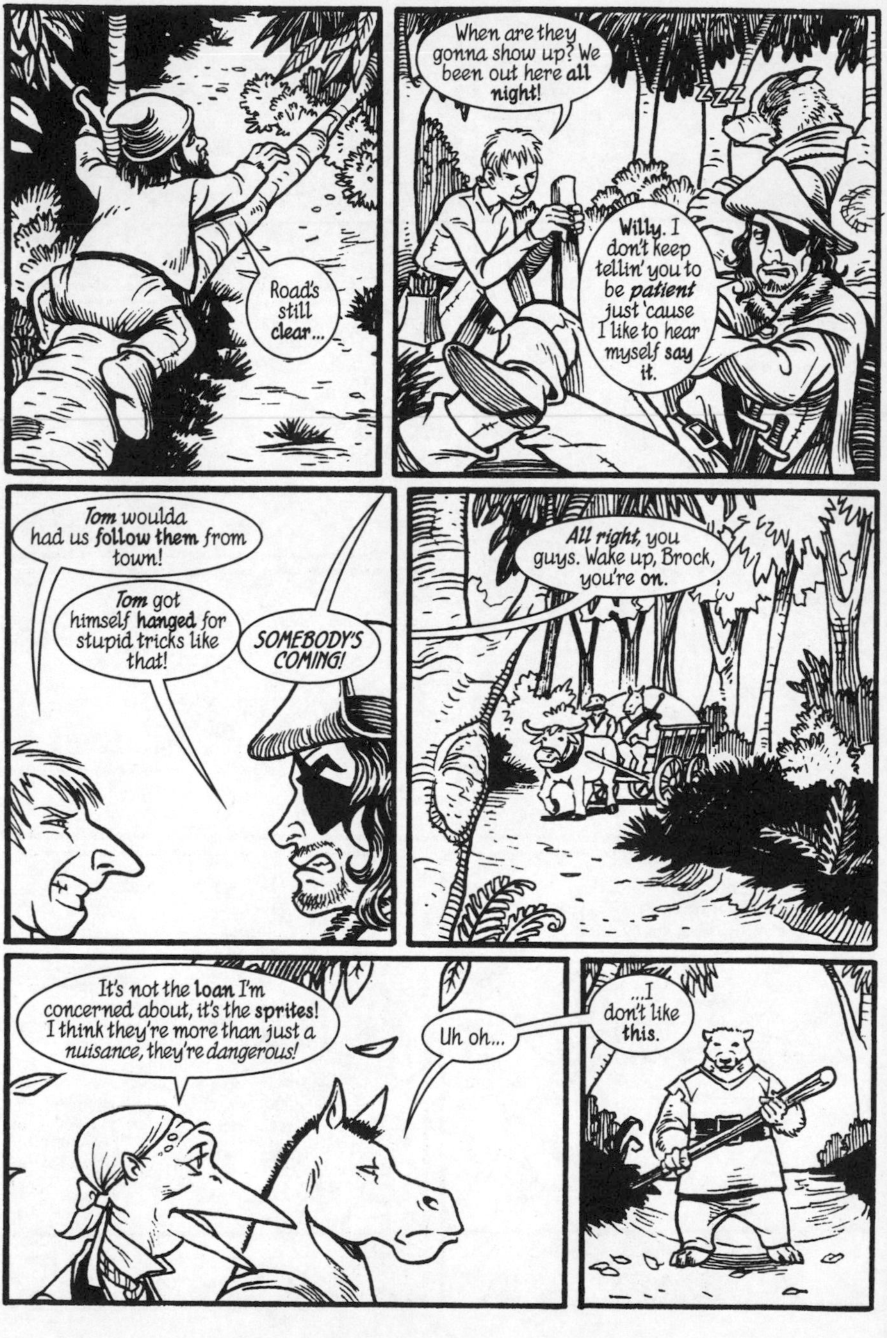
Road's still clear...
When are they gonna show up? We been out here all night!
Willy. I don't keep tellin' you to be patient just 'cause I like to hear myself say it.
Tom woulda had us follow them from town!
Tom got himself hanged for stupid tricks like that!
SOMEBODY'S COMING!
All right, you guys. Wake up, Brock, you're on.
It's not the loan I'm concerned about, it's the sprites! I think they're more than just a nuisance, they're dangerous!
Uh oh...
...I don't like this.

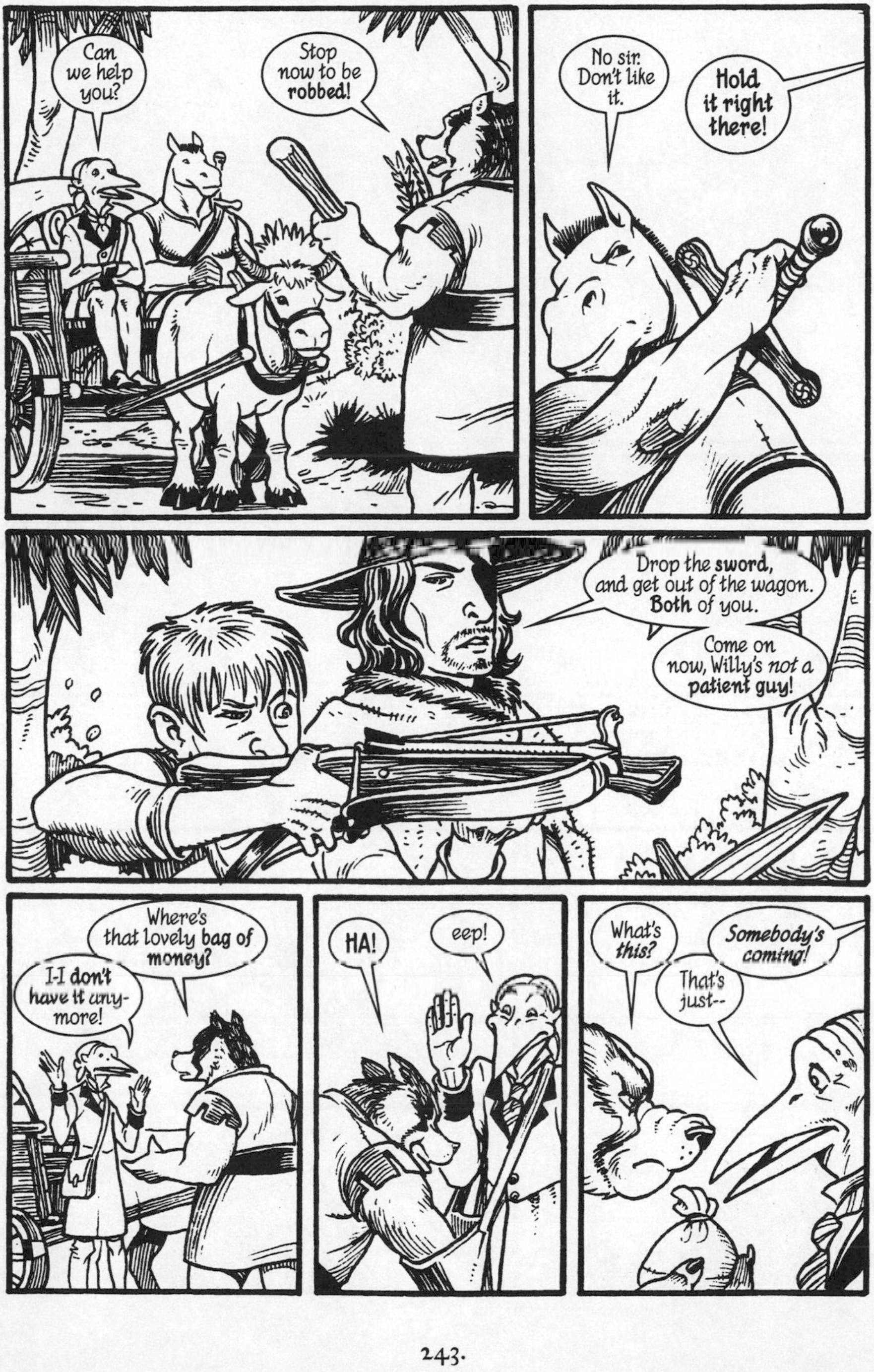
Can we help you?
Stop now to be robbed!
No sir. Don't like it.
Hold it right there!
Drop the sword, and get out of the wagon. Both of you.
Come on now, Willy's not a patient guy!
Where's that lovely bag of money?
I-I don't have it any-more!
HA!
eep!
What's this?
That's just--
Somebody's coming!

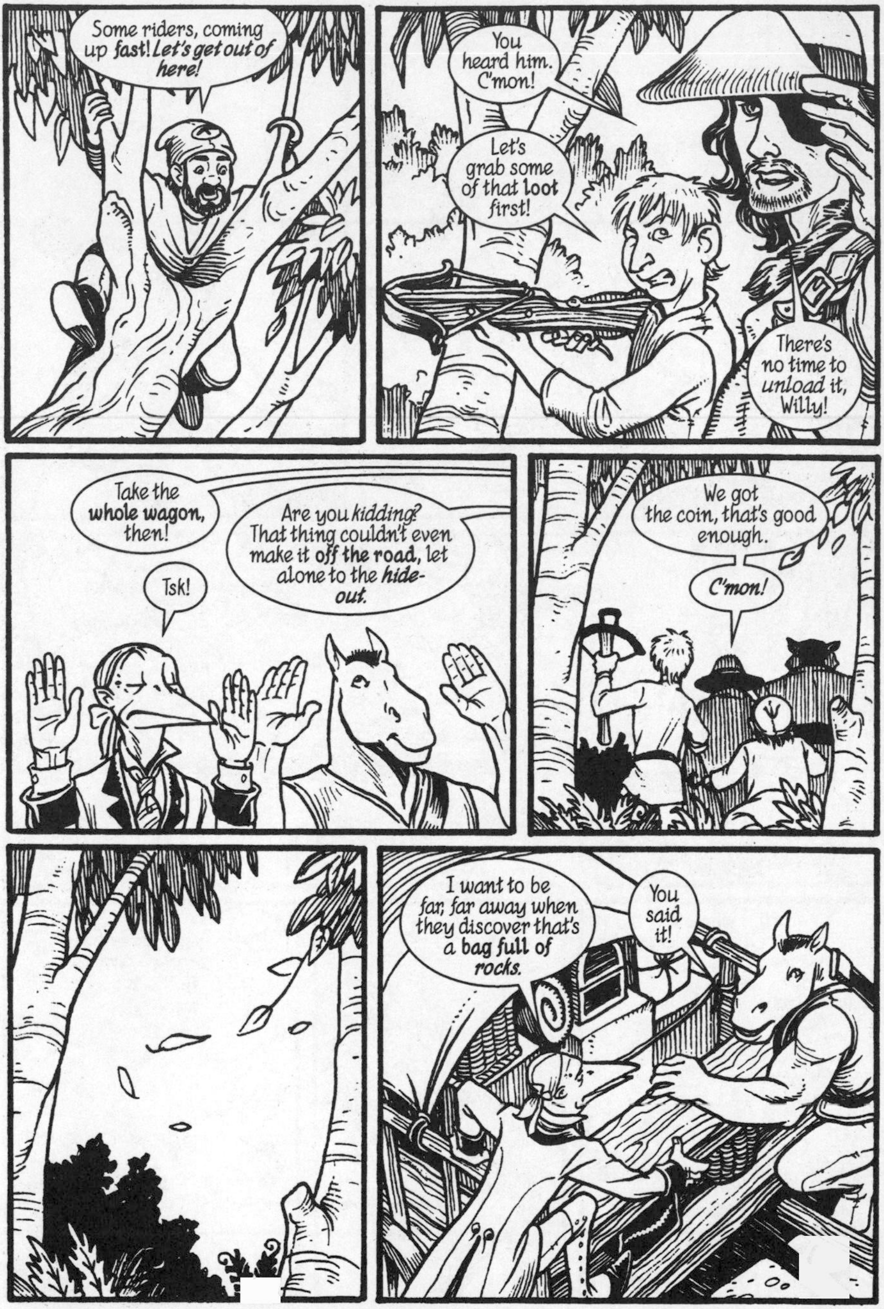
Some riders, coming up fast! Let's get out of here!
You heard him. C'mon!
Let's grab some of that loot first!
There's no time to unload it, Willy!
Take the whole wagon, then!
Tsk!
Are you kidding? That thing couldn't even make it off the road, let alone to the hide-out.
We got the coin, that's good enough.
C'mon!
I want to be far, far away when they discover that's a bag full of rocks.
You said it!

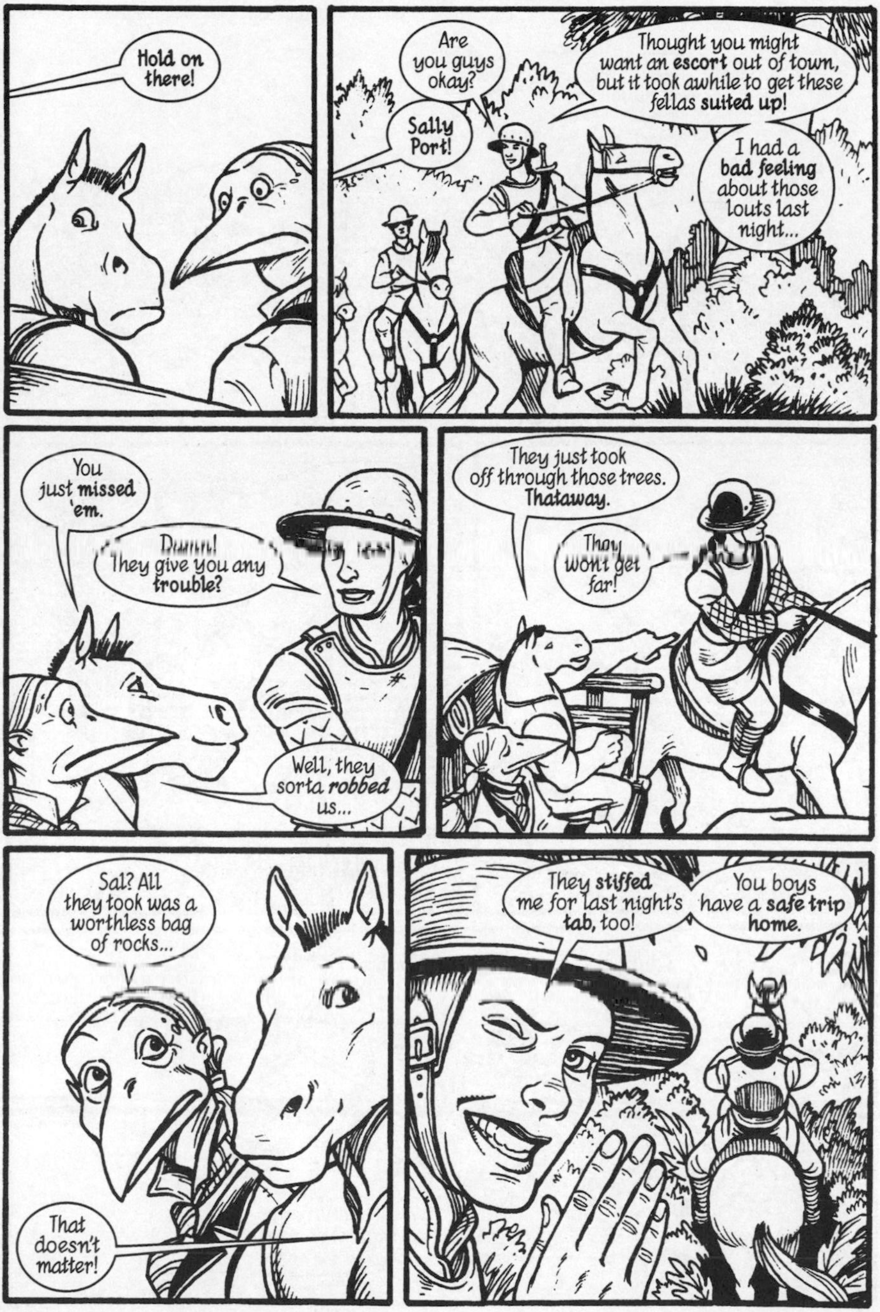
Hold on there!
Sally Port!
Are you guys okay?
Thought you might want an escort out of town, but it took awhile to get these fellas suited up!
I had a bad feeling about those louts last night...
You just missed 'em.
Damn! They give you any trouble?
Well, they sorta robbed us...
They just took off through those trees. Thataway.
They won't get far!
Sal? All they took was a worthless bag of rocks...
That doesn't matter!
They stiffed me for last night's tab, too!
You boys have a safe trip home.

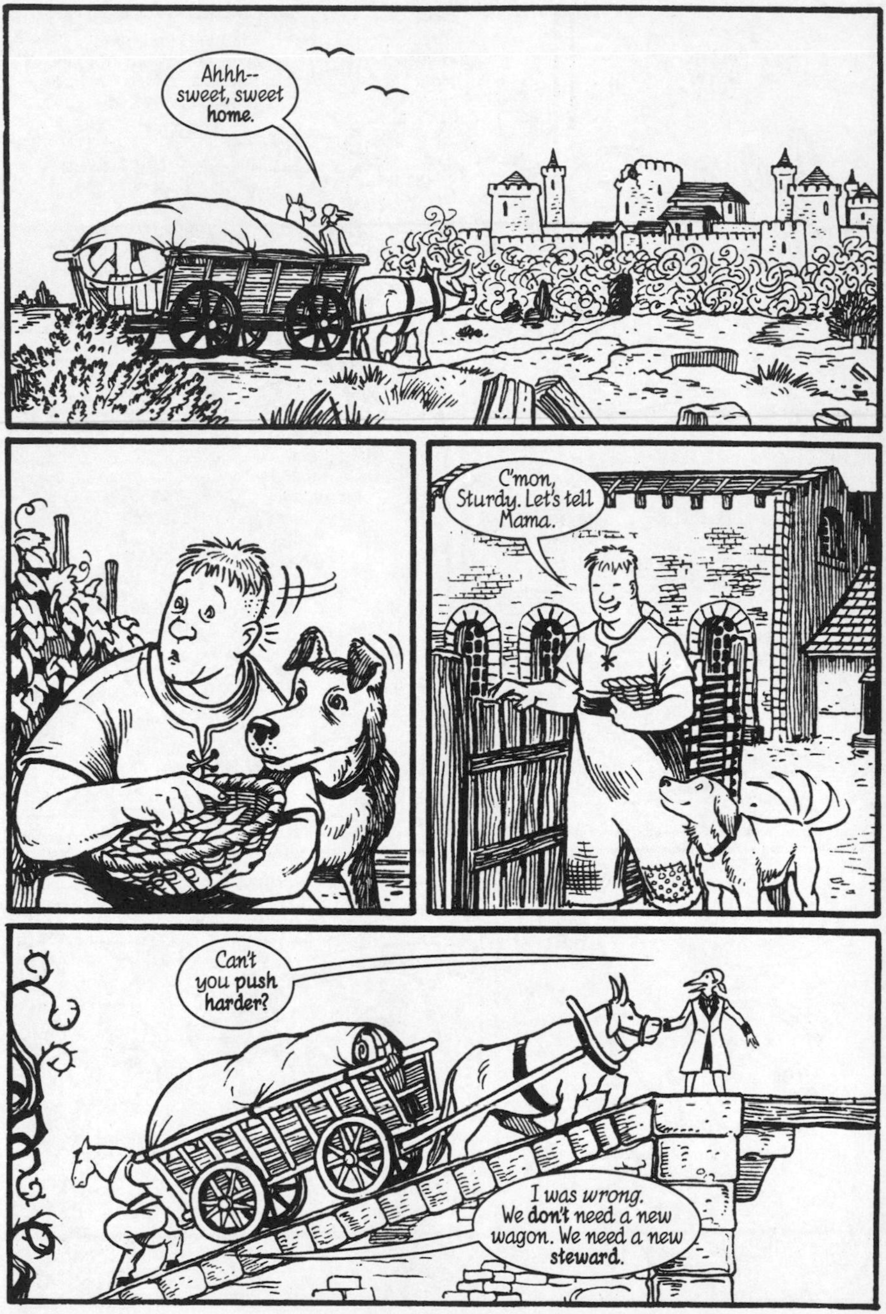
Ahhh-- sweet, sweet **home.**
C'mon, Sturdy. Let's tell Mama.
Can't you **push harder?**
I was *wrong.* We **don't** need a new wagon. We need a new **steward.**

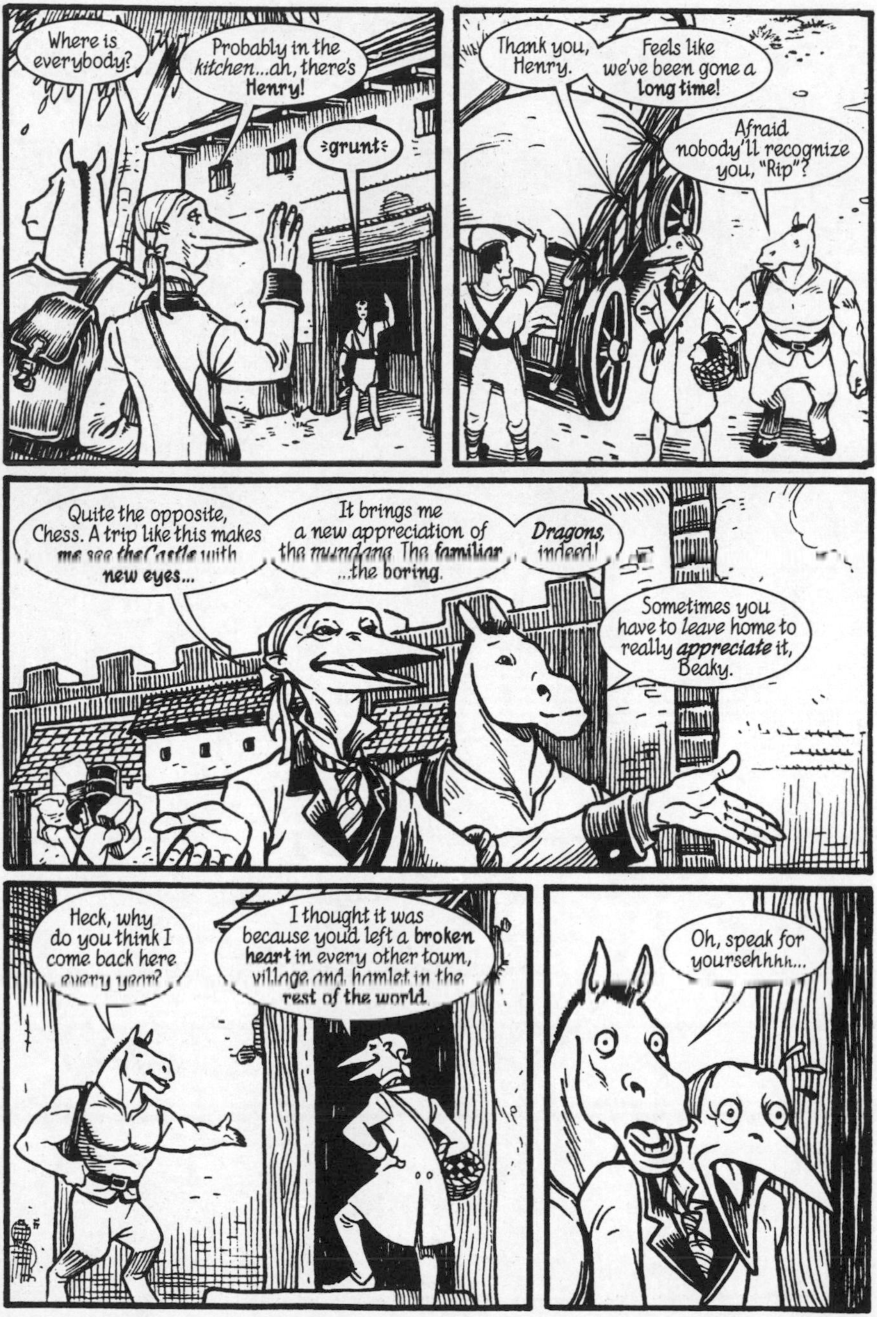
Where is everybody?
Probably in the kitchen...ah, there's Henry!
grunt
Thank you, Henry.
Feels like we've been gone a long time!
Afraid nobody'll recognize you, "Rip"?
Quite the opposite, Chess. A trip like this makes me see the Castle with new eyes...
It brings me a new appreciation of the mundane. The familiar ...the boring.
Dragons, indeed!
Sometimes you have to leave home to really appreciate it, Beaky.
Heck, why do you think I come back here every year?
I thought it was because you'd left a broken heart in every other town, village and hamlet in the rest of the world.
Oh, speak for yoursehhhh...

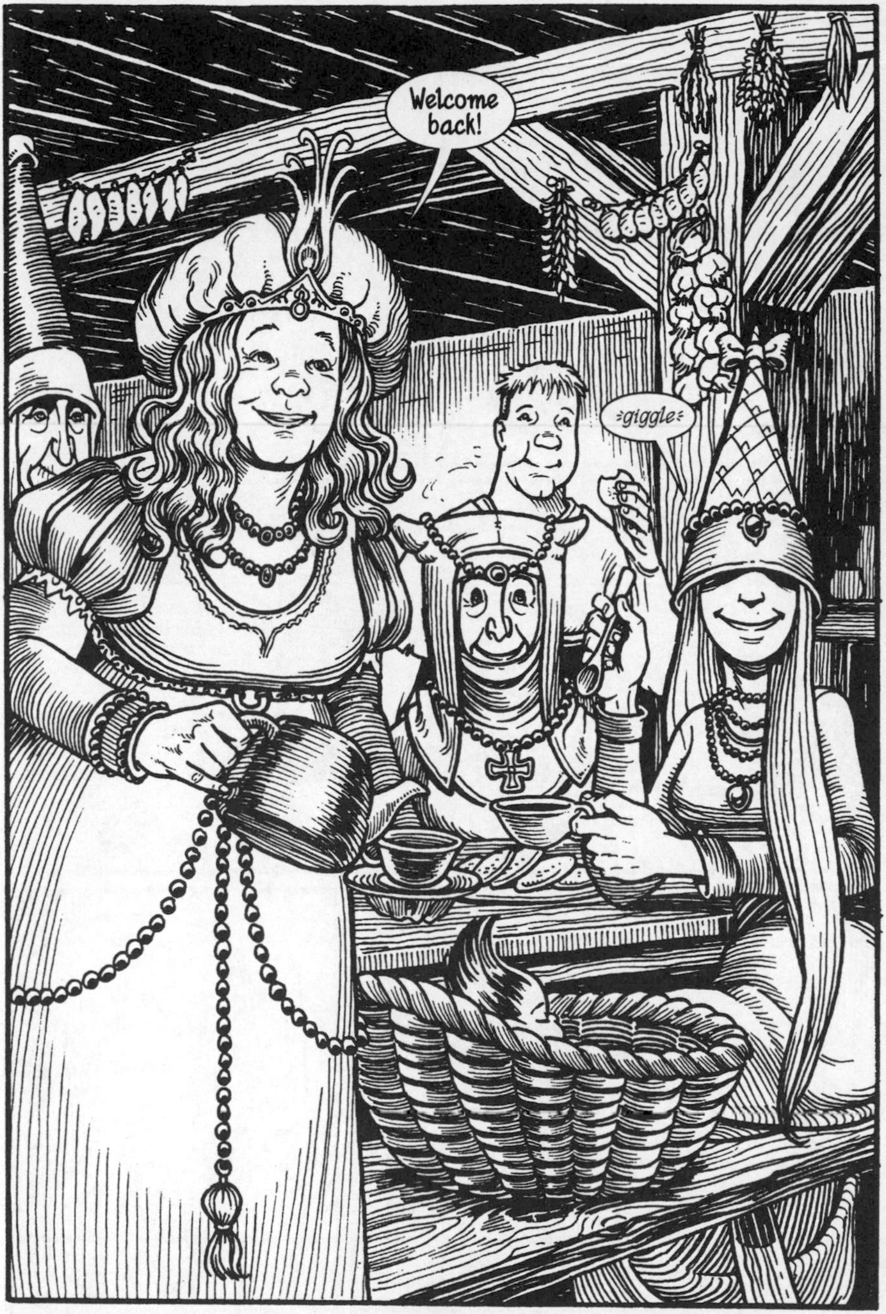
Welcome back!
giggle

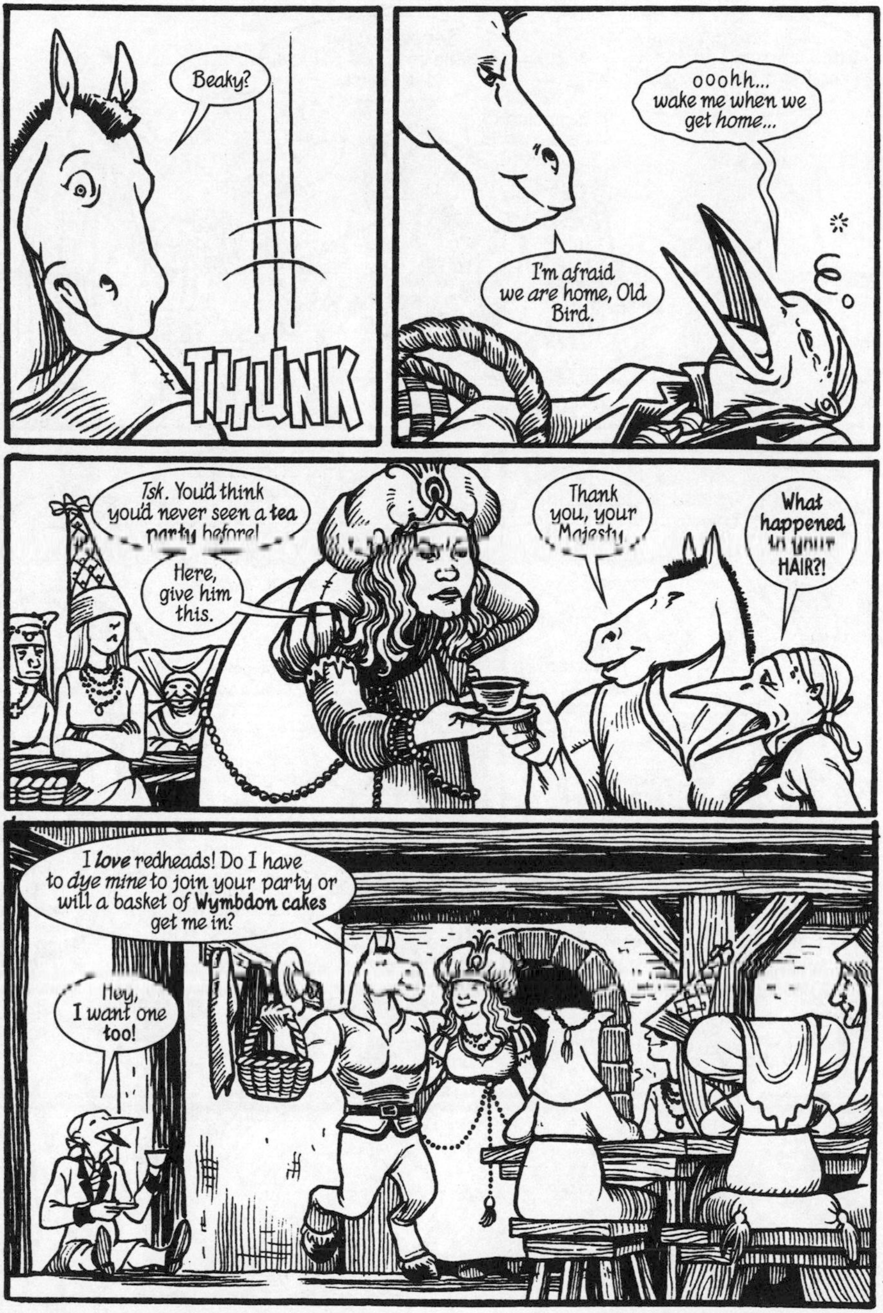
Beaky?
THUNK
ooohh... wake me when we get home...
I'm afraid we are home, Old Bird.
Tsk. You'd think you'd never seen a tea party before!
Here, give him this.
Thank you, your Majesty.
What happened to your HAIR?!
I love redheads! Do I have to dye mine to join your party or will a basket of Wymbdon cakes get me in?
Hey, I want one too!

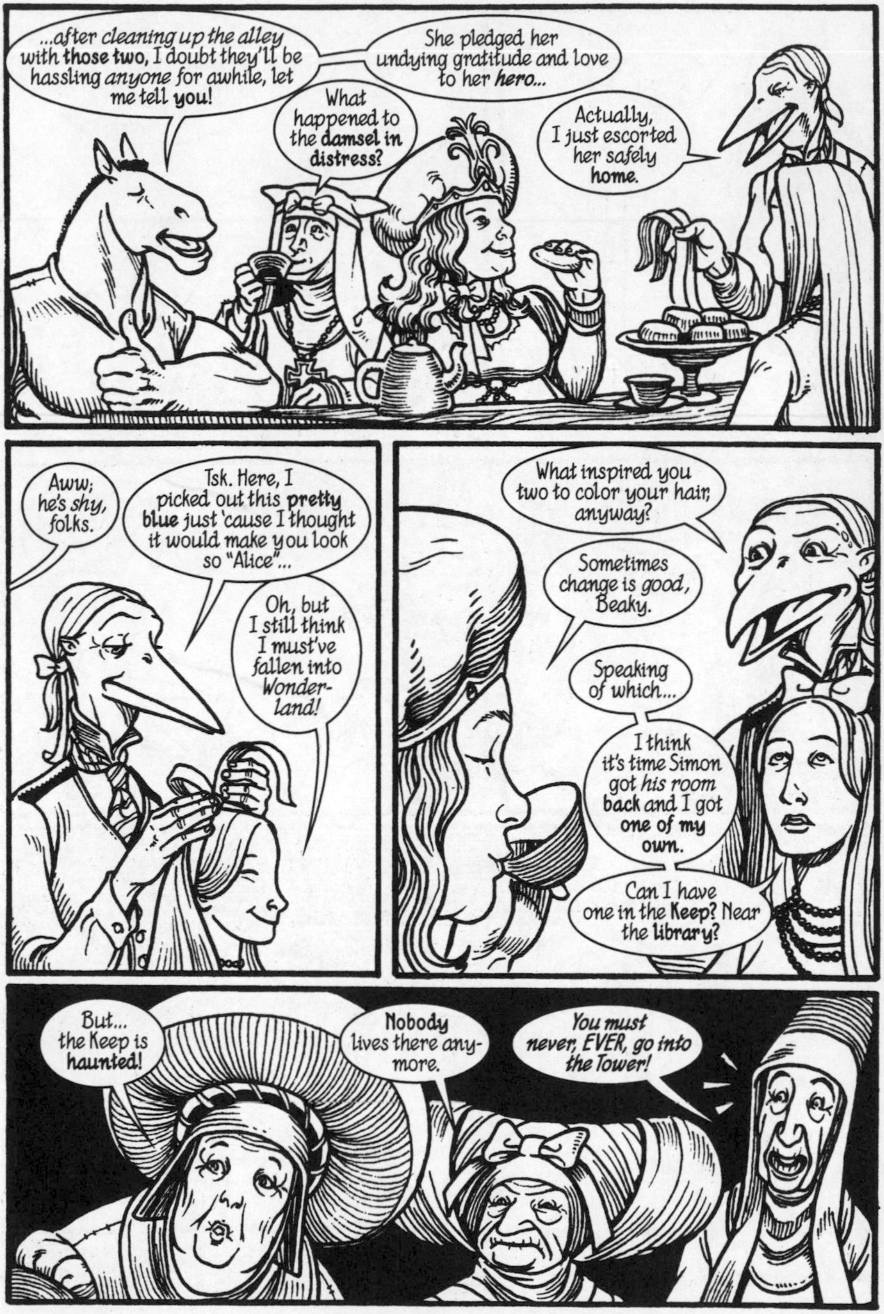
...after cleaning up the alley with those two, I doubt they'll be hassling anyone for awhile, let me tell you!
She pledged her undying gratitude and love to her hero...
What happened to the damsel in distress?
Actually, I just escorted her safely home.
Aww; he's shy, folks.
Tsk. Here, I picked out this pretty blue just 'cause I thought it would make you look so "Alice"...
Oh, but I still think I must've fallen into Wonder-land!
What inspired you two to color your hair, anyway?
Sometimes change is good, Beaky.
Speaking of which...
I think it's time Simon got his room back and I got one of my own.
Can I have one in the Keep? Near the library?
But... the Keep is haunted!
Nobody lives there any-more.
You must never, EVER, go into the Tower!

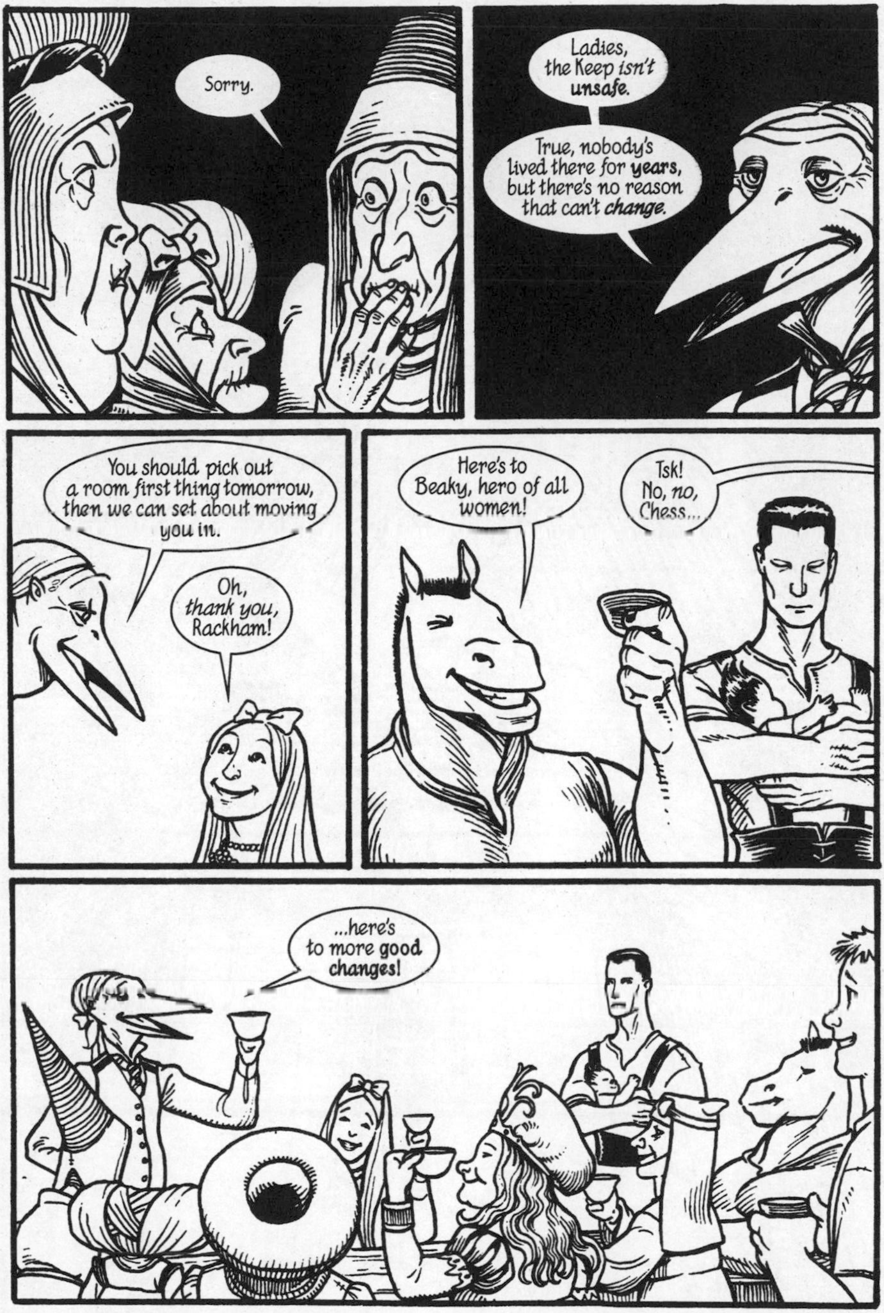
Sorry.
Ladies, the Keep isn't unsafe.
True, nobody's lived there for years, but there's no reason that can't change.
You should pick out a room first thing tomorrow, then we can set about moving you in.
Oh, thank you, Rackham!
Here's to Beaky, hero of all women!
Tsk! No, no, Chess...
...here's to more good changes!

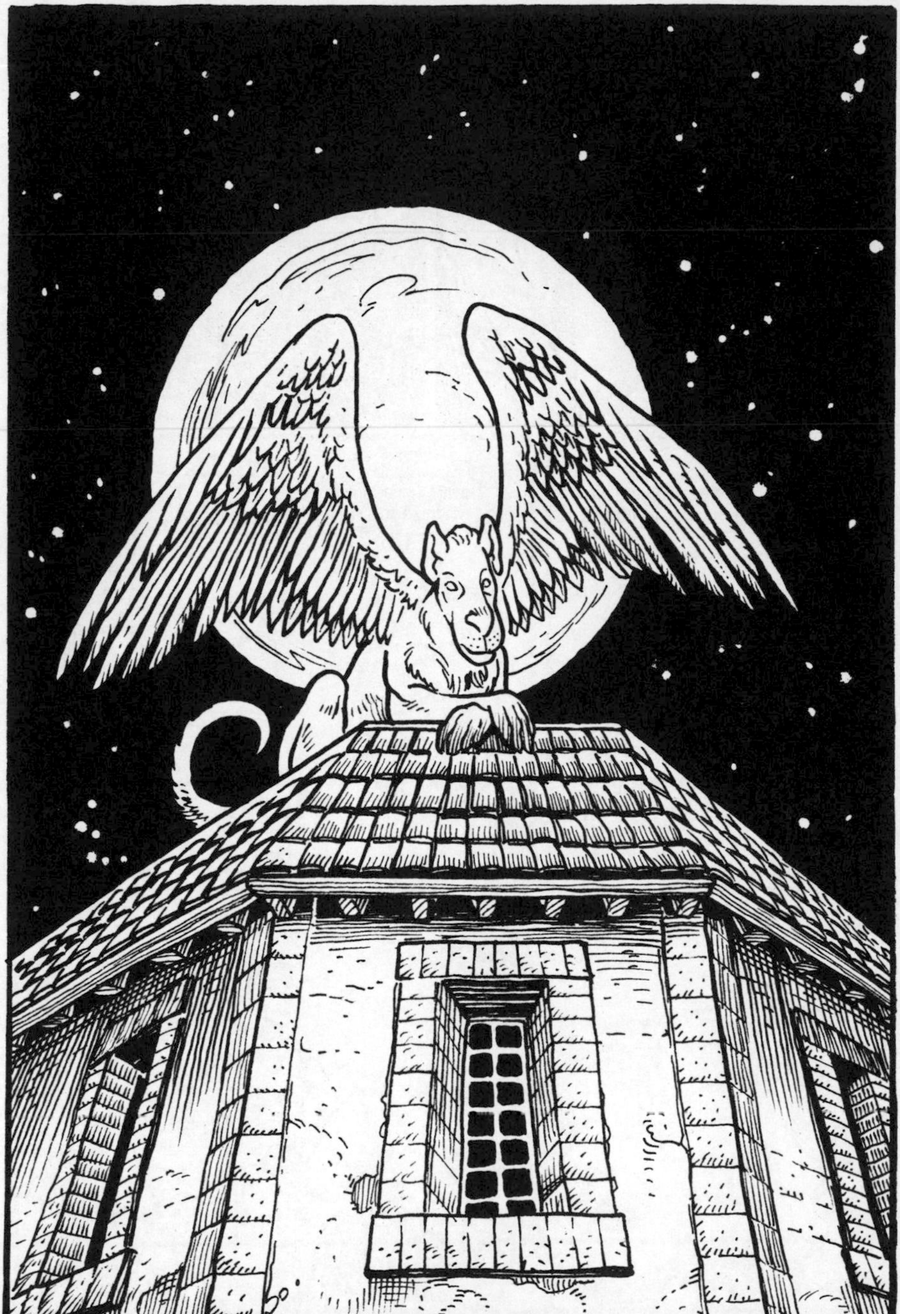

Chapter 11.

· HOOK, LINE, AND SINKER ·

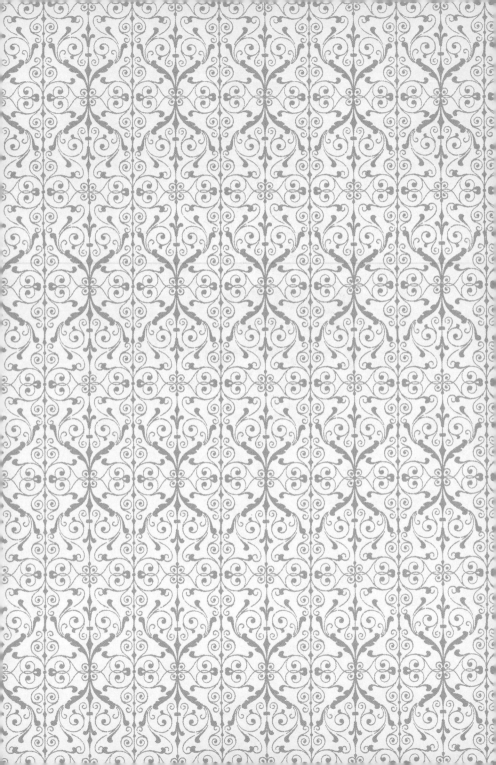

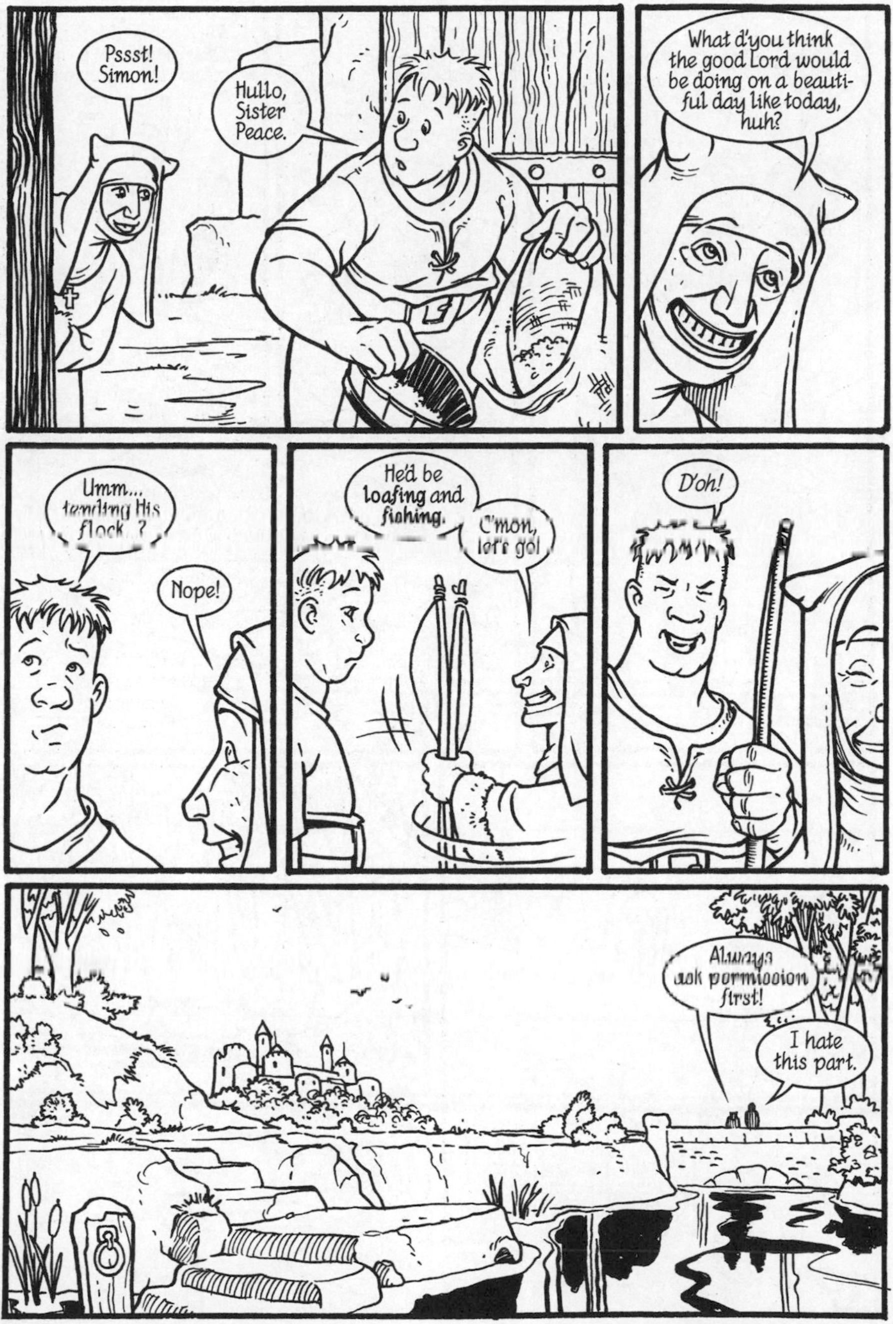
Pssst! Simon!
Hullo, Sister Peace.
What d'you think the good Lord would be doing on a beautiful day like today, huh?
Umm... tending His flock..?
Nope!
He'd be loafing and fishing.
C'mon, let's go!
D'oh!
Always ask permission first!
I hate this part.

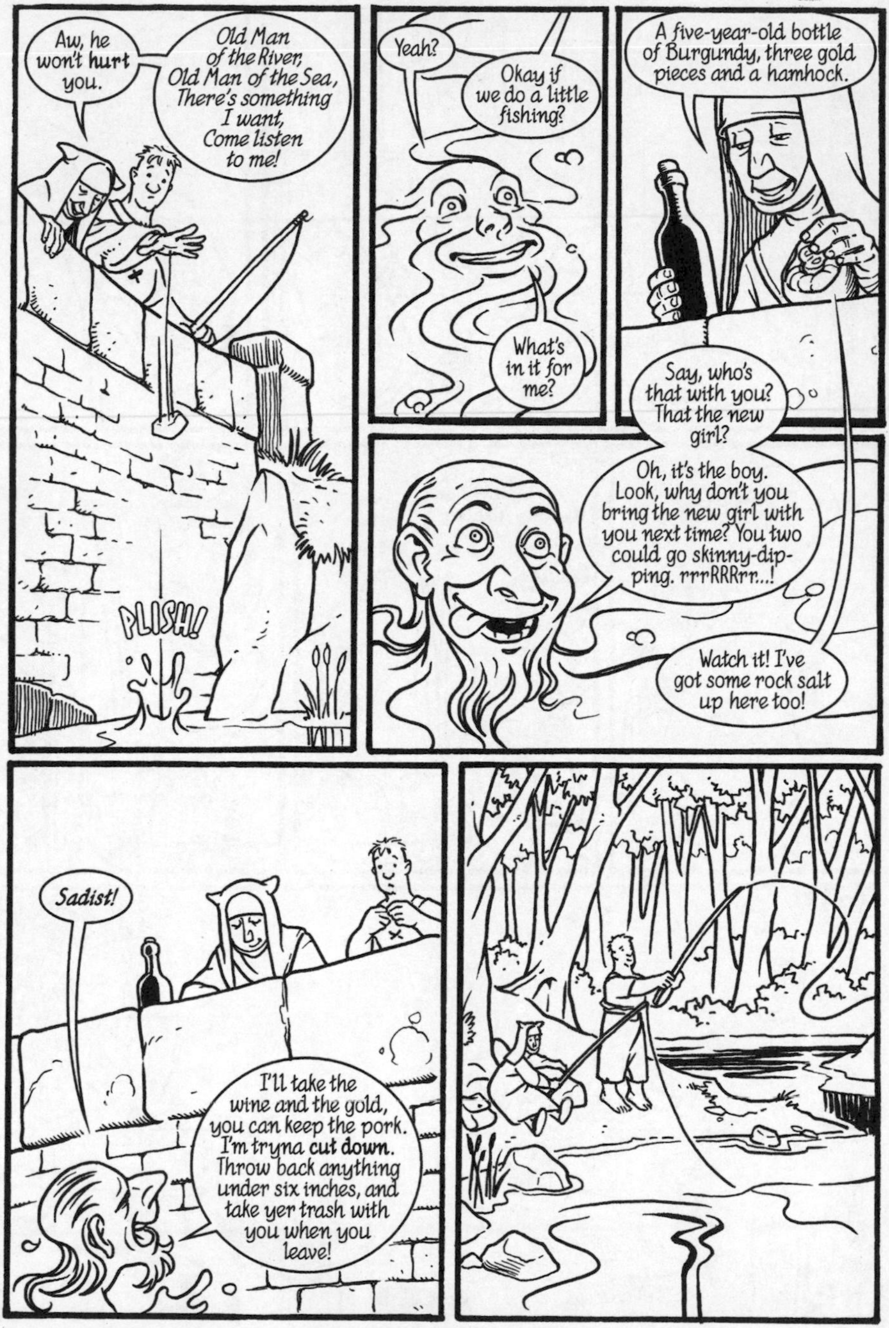
Aw, he won't **hurt** you.
Old Man of the River, Old Man of the Sea, There's something I want, Come listen to me!
PLISH!
Yeah?
Okay if we do a little fishing?
What's in it for me?
A five-year-old bottle of Burgundy, three gold pieces and a hamhock.
Say, who's that with you? That the new girl?
Oh, it's the boy. Look, why don't you bring the new girl with you next time? You two could go skinny-dip-ping. rrrRRRrr...!
Watch it! I've got some rock salt up here too!
Sadist!
I'll take the wine and the gold, you can keep the pork. I'm tryna **cut down**. Throw back anything under six inches, and take yer trash with you when you leave!

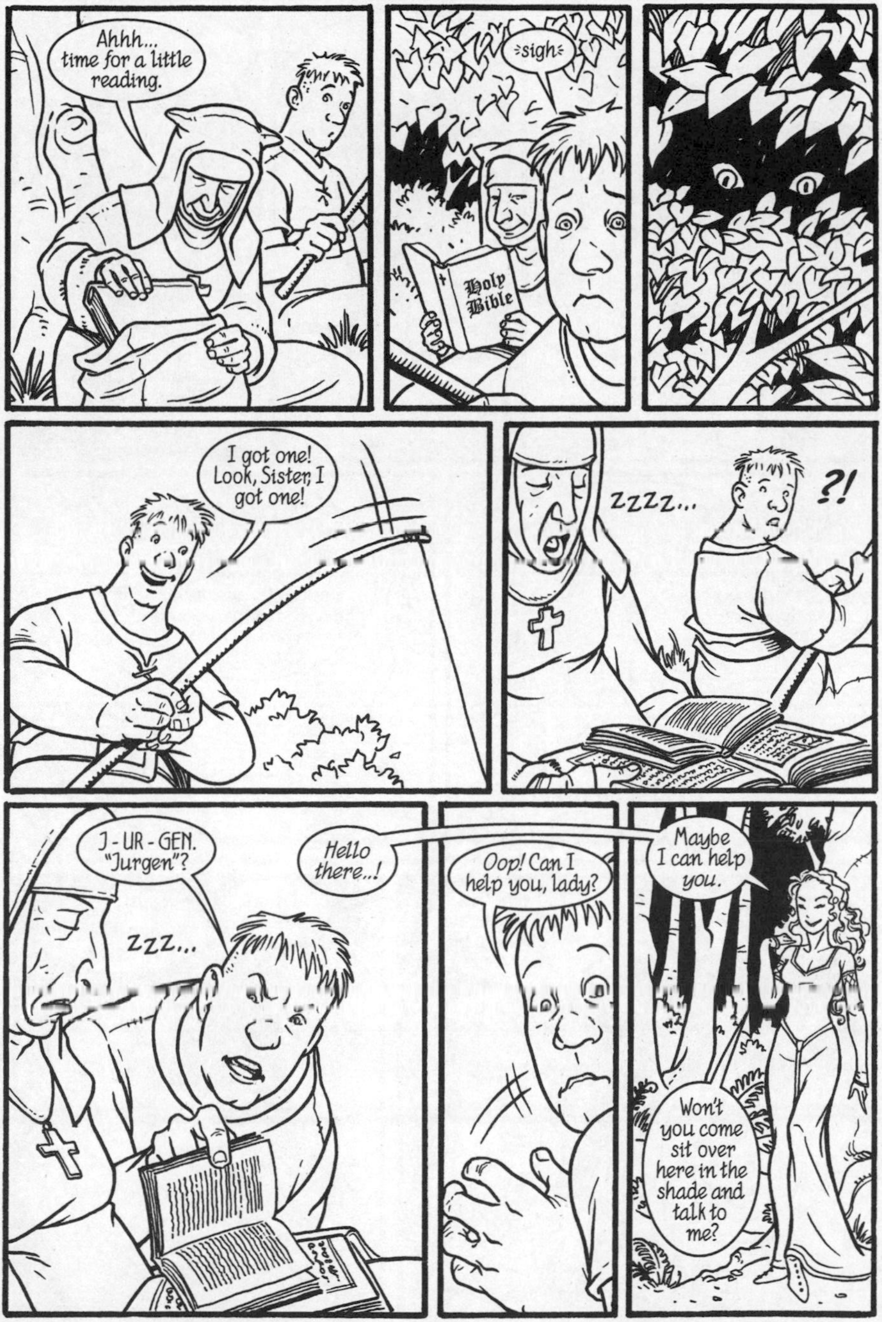
Ahhh... time for a little reading.
sigh
Holy Bible
I got one! Look, Sister, I got one!
ZZZZ...
?!
J - UR - GEN. "Jurgen"?
ZZZ...
Hello there...!
Oop! Can I help you, lady?
Maybe I can help you.
Won't you come sit over here in the shade and talk to me?

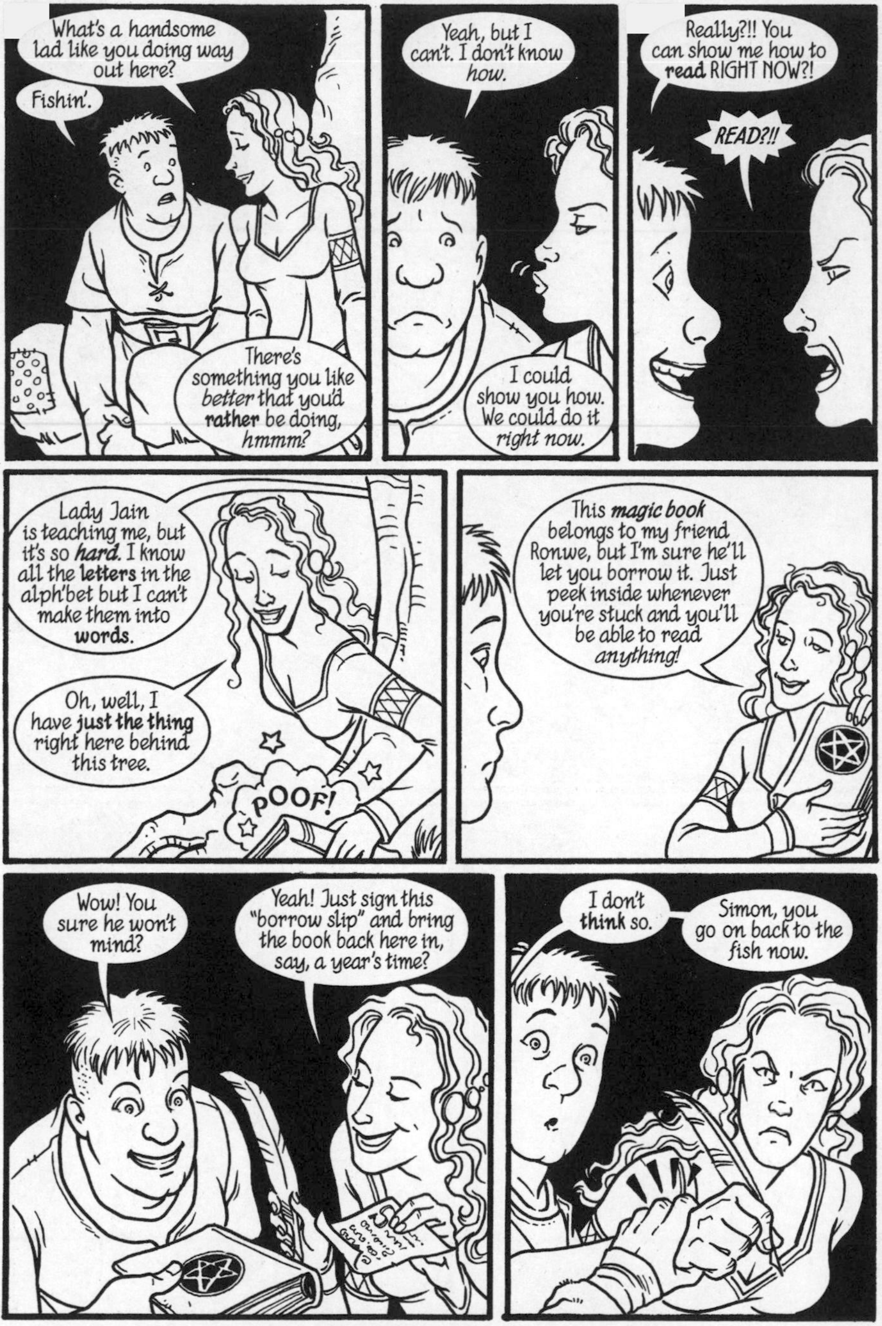
What's a handsome lad like you doing way out here?
Fishin'.
There's something you like better that you'd rather be doing, hmmm?
Yeah, but I can't. I don't know how.
I could show you how. We could do it right now.
Really?!! You can show me how to read RIGHT NOW?!
READ?!!
Lady Jain is teaching me, but it's so hard. I know all the letters in the alph'bet but I can't make them into words.
Oh, well, I have just the thing right here behind this tree.
POOF!
This magic book belongs to my friend Ronwe, but I'm sure he'll let you borrow it. Just peek inside whenever you're stuck and you'll be able to read anything!
Wow! You sure he won't mind?
Yeah! Just sign this "borrow slip" and bring the book back here in, say, a year's time?
I don't think so.
Simon, you go on back to the fish now.

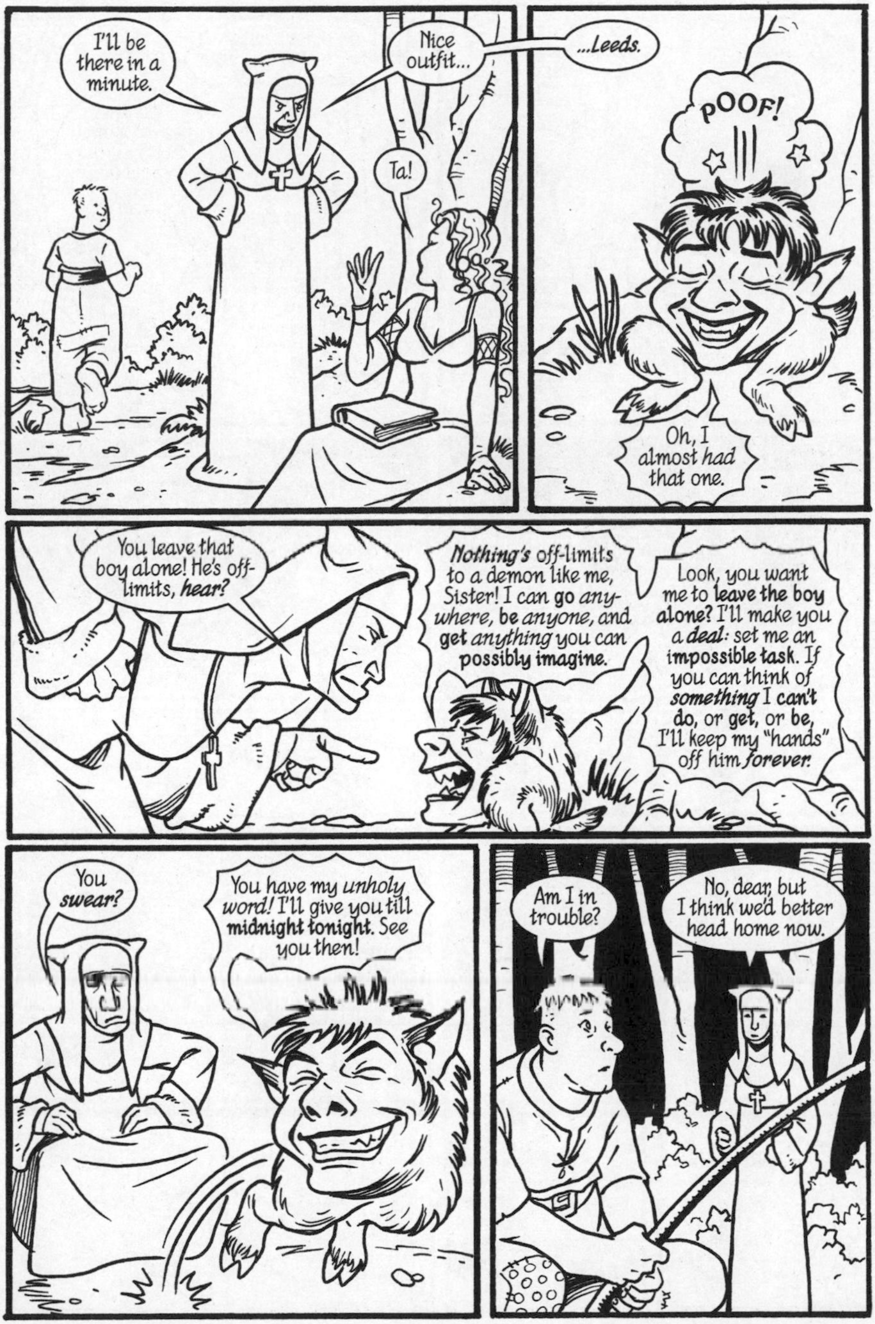
I'll be there in a minute.
Nice outfit...
...Leeds.
Ta!
POOF!
Oh, I almost had that one.
You leave that boy alone! He's off-limits, hear?
Nothing's off-limits to a demon like me, Sister! I can go anywhere, be anyone, and get anything you can possibly imagine.
Look, you want me to leave the boy alone? I'll make you a deal: set me an impossible task. If you can think of something I can't do, or get, or be, I'll keep my "hands" off him forever.
You swear?
You have my unholy word! I'll give you till midnight tonight. See you then!
Am I in trouble?
No, dear, but I think we'd better head home now.

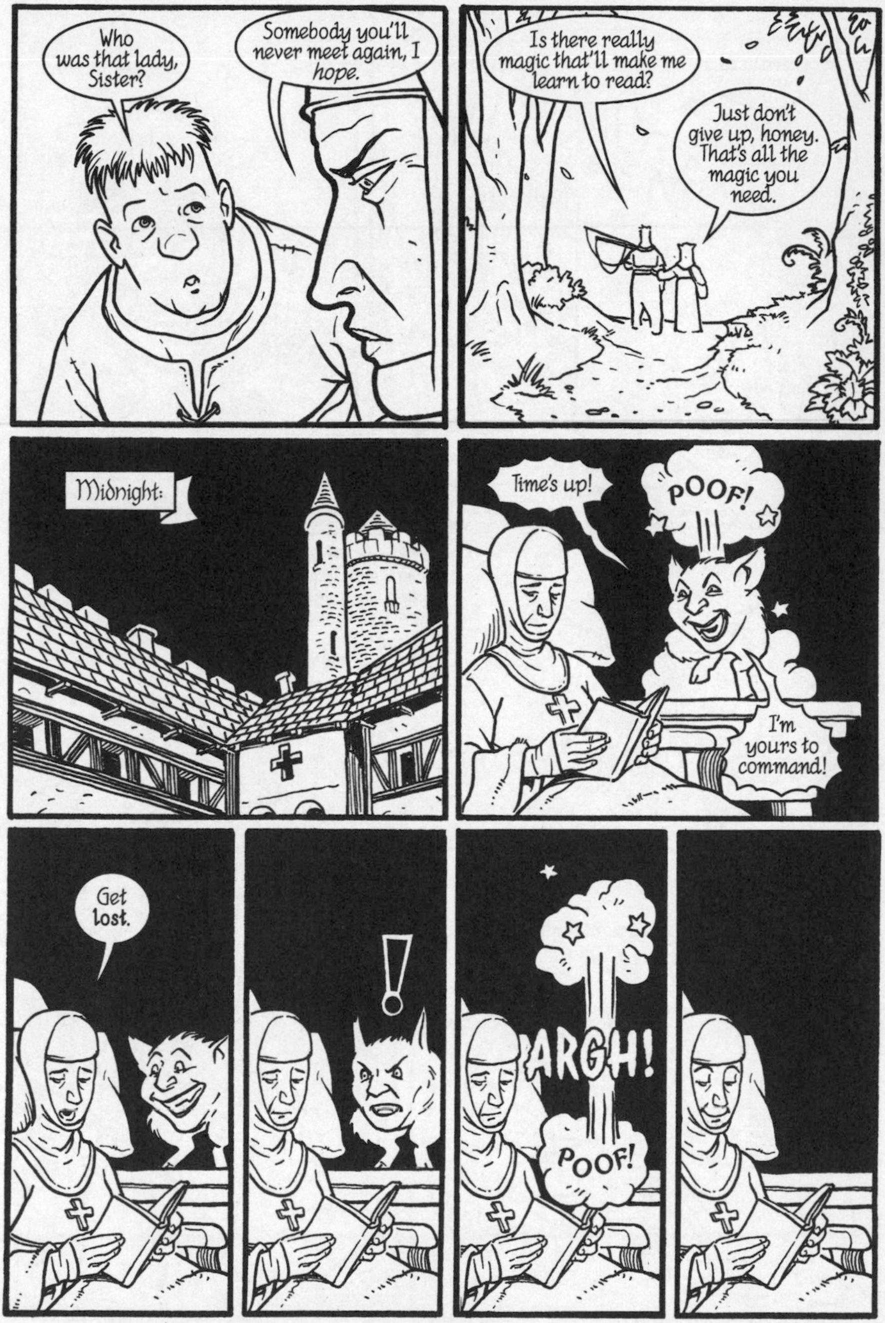
Who was that lady, Sister?
Somebody you'll never meet again, I *hope*.
Is there really magic that'll make me learn to read?
Just don't give up, honey. That's all the magic you need.
Midnight:
Time's up!
POOF!
I'm yours to command!
Get lost.
!
ARGH!
POOF!

Chapter 12.

· SWEET TEMPTATIONS ·

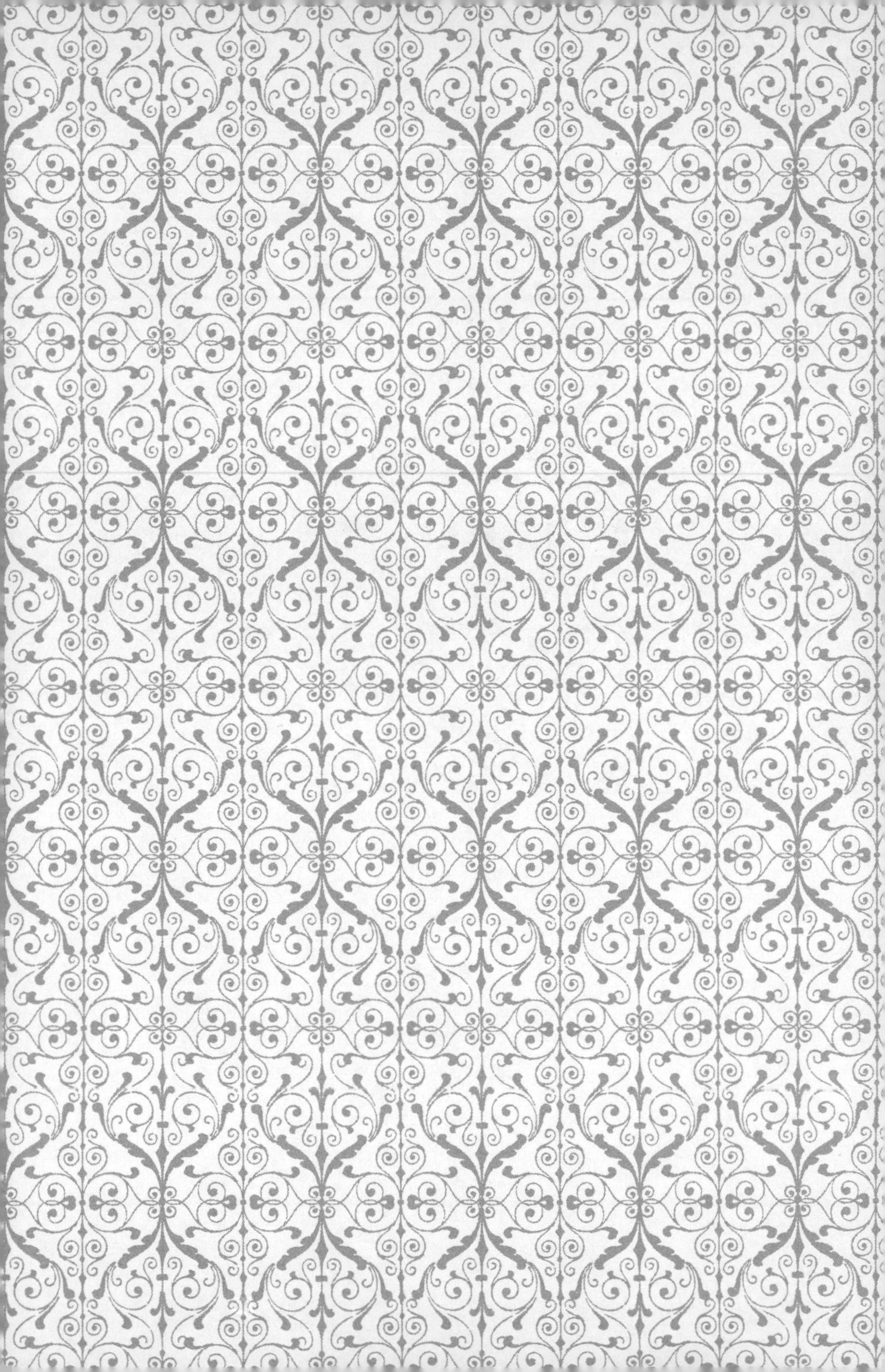

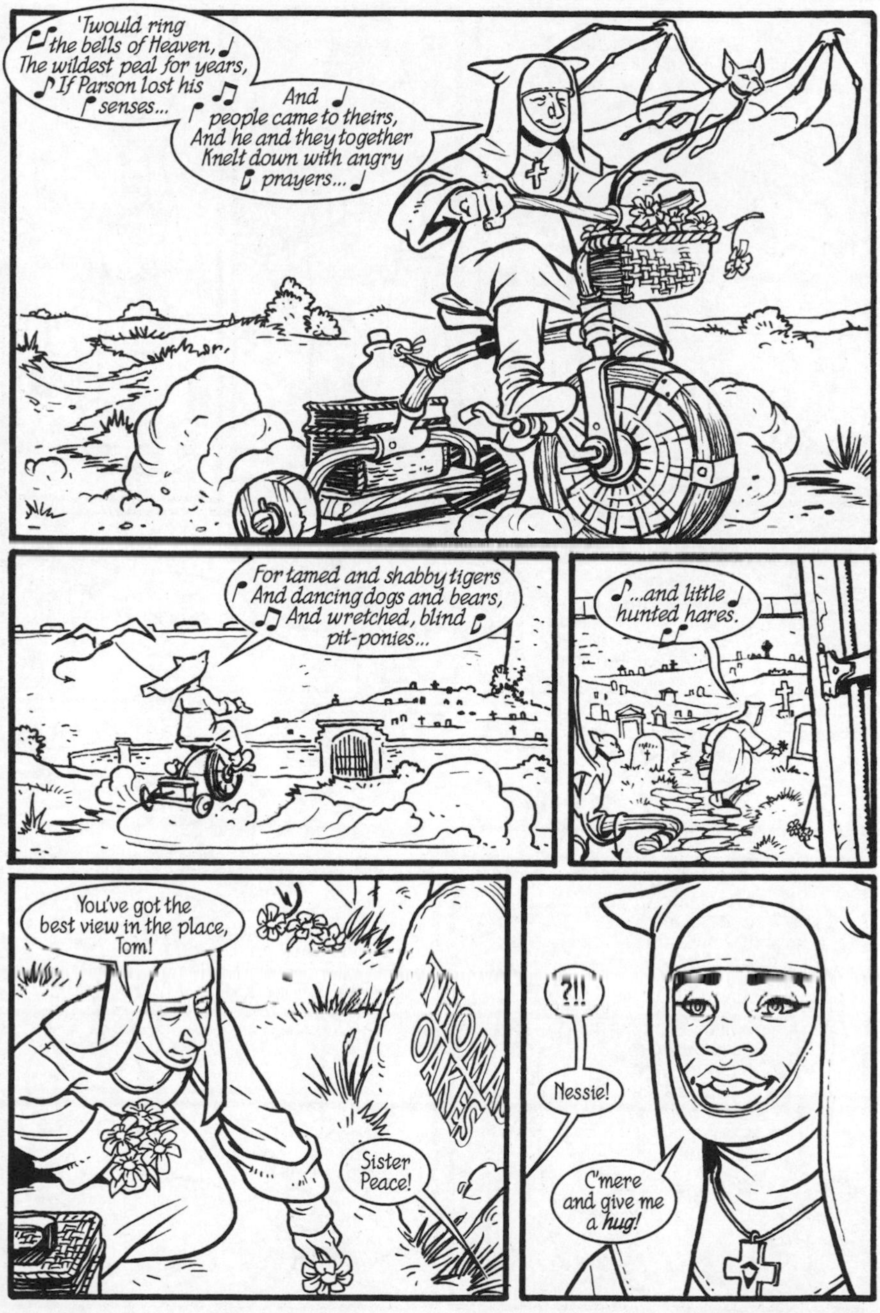
'Twould ring the bells of Heaven, The wildest peal for years, If Parson lost his senses...
And people came to theirs, And he and they together Knelt down with angry prayers...
For tamed and shabby tigers And dancing dogs and bears, And wretched, blind pit-ponies...
...and little hunted hares.
You've got the best view in the place, Tom!
THOMA
OAKES
Sister Peace!
?!!
Nessie!
C'mere and give me a hug!

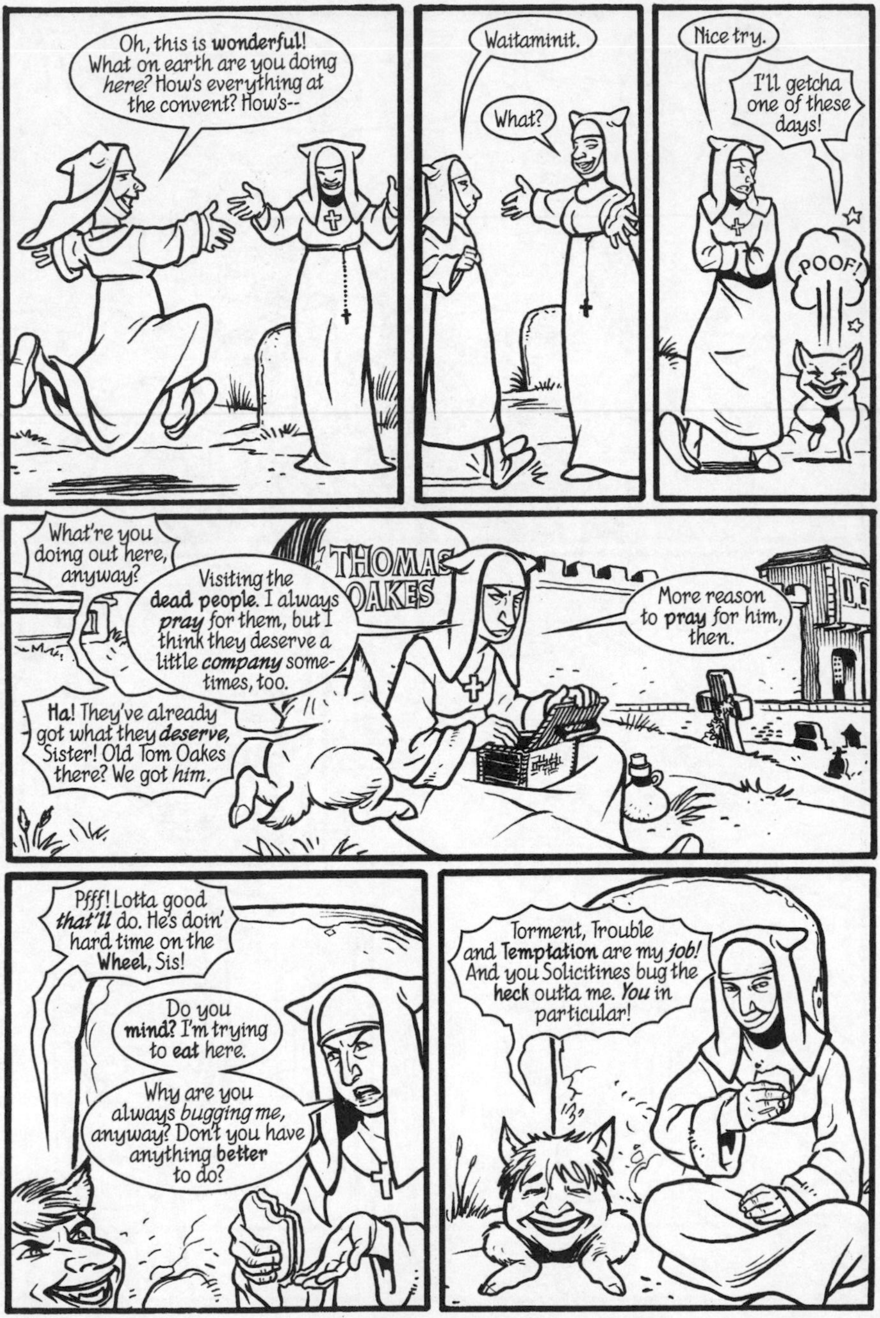

Oh, this is **wonderful**! What on earth are you doing *here*? How's everything at the convent? How's--
Waitaminit.
What?
Nice try.
I'll getcha one of these days!
POOF!
What're you doing out here, anyway?
Visiting the **dead people**. I always *pray* for them, but I think they deserve a little *company* sometimes, too.
THOMAS OAKES
Ha! They've already got what they *deserve*, Sister! Old Tom Oakes there? We got *him*.
More reason to **pray** for him, then.
Pfff! Lotta good *that'll* do. He's doin' hard time on the **Wheel**, Sis!
Do you **mind?** I'm trying to **eat** here.
Why are you always *bugging me*, anyway? Don't you have anything **better** to do?
Torment, Trouble and **Temptation** are my *job!* And you Solicitines bug the **heck** outta me. ***You*** in particular!

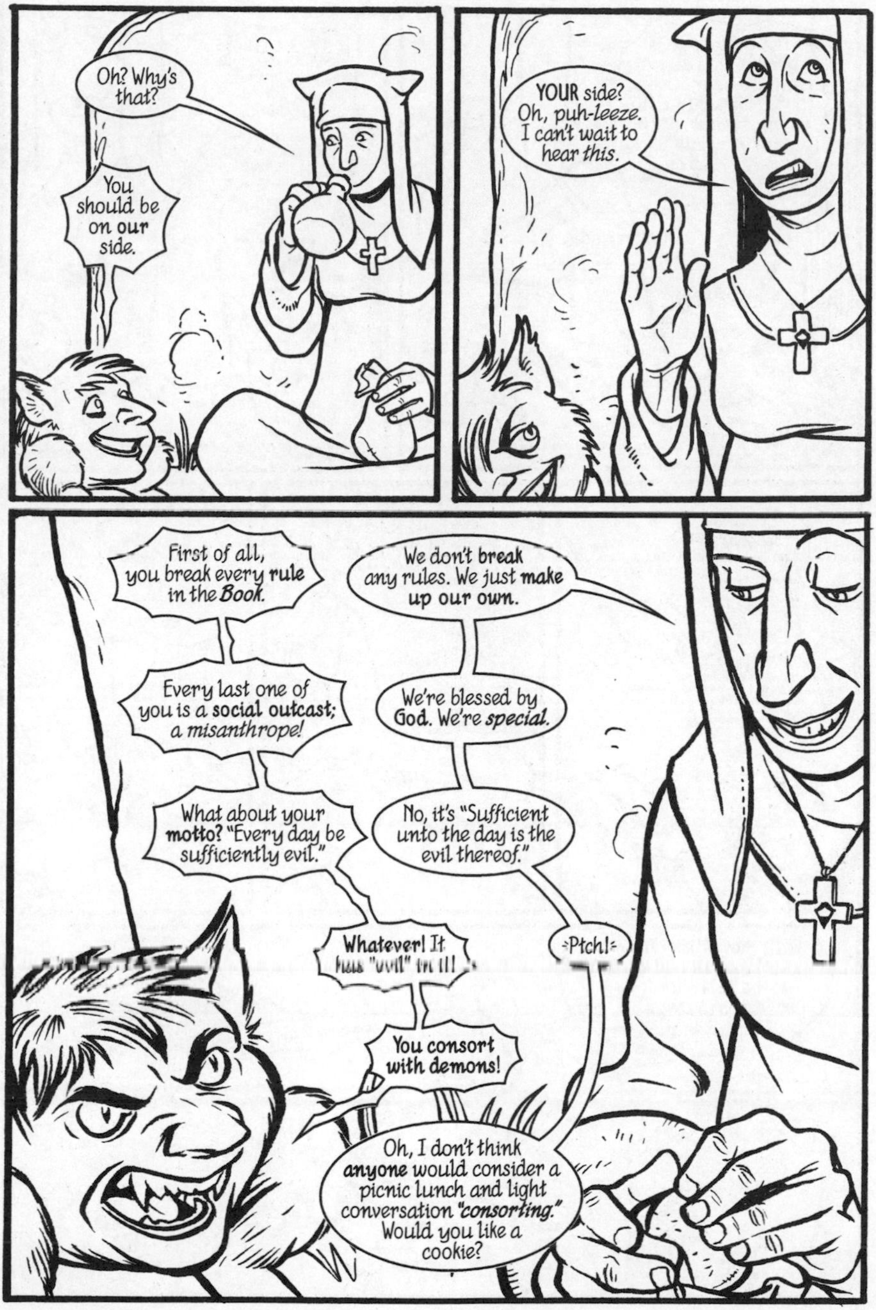
Oh? Why's that?
You should be on our side.
YOUR side? Oh, puh-leeze. I can't wait to hear this.
First of all, you break every rule in the Book.
We don't break any rules. We just make up our own.
Every last one of you is a social outcast; a misanthrope!
We're blessed by God. We're special.
What about your motto? "Every day be sufficiently evil."
No, it's "Sufficient unto the day is the evil thereof."
Whatever! It
-Ptch!-
You consort with demons!
Oh, I don't think anyone would consider a picnic lunch and light conversation "consorting." Would you like a cookie?

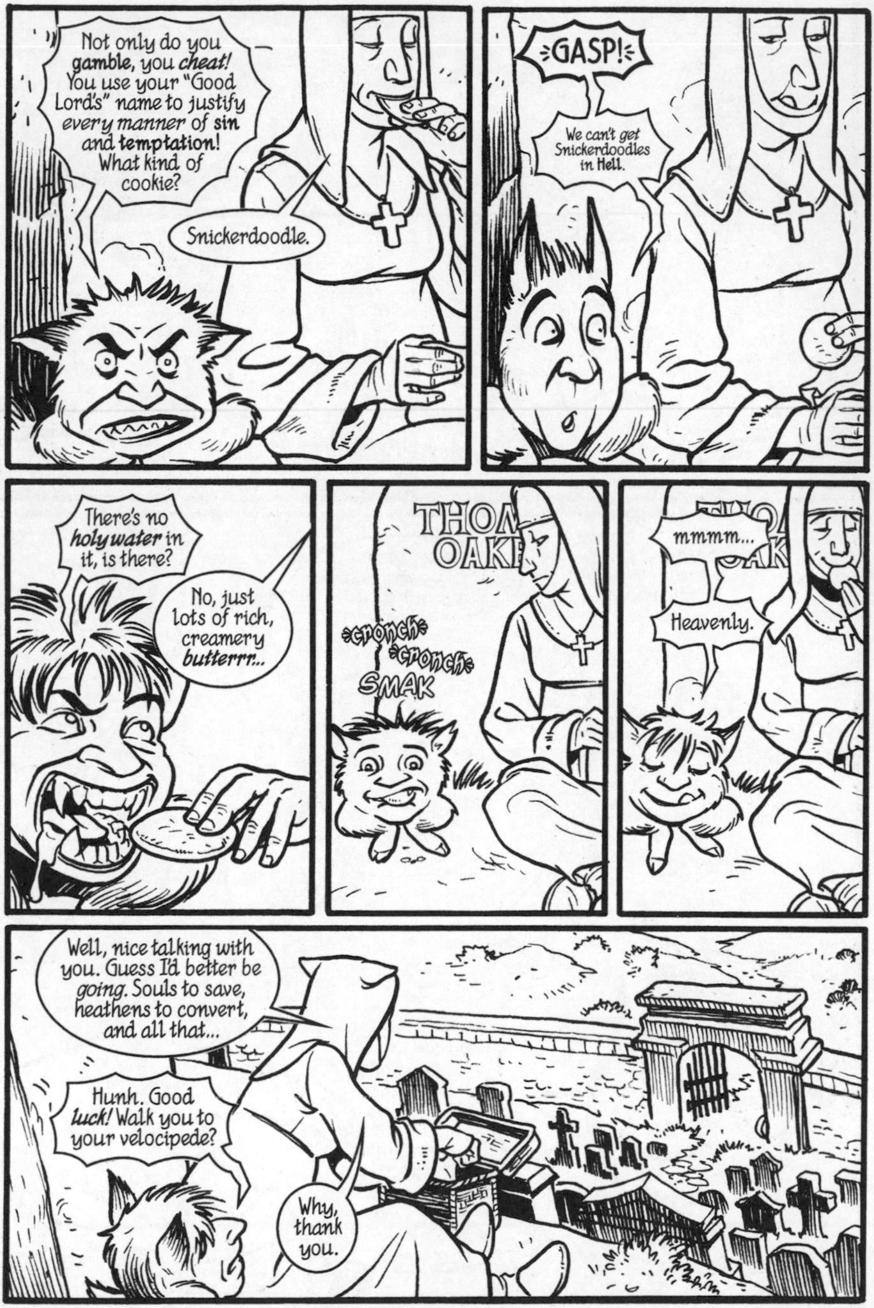
Not only do you gamble, you cheat! You use your "Good Lord's" name to justify every manner of sin and temptation! What kind of cookie?
Snickerdoodle.
GASP!
We can't get Snickerdoodles in Hell.
There's no holy water in it, is there?
No, just lots of rich, creamery butterrr...
THOM
OAK
cronch cronch
SMAK
mmmm...
Heavenly.
Well, nice talking with you. Guess I'd better be going. Souls to save, heathens to convert, and all that...
Hunh. Good luck! Walk you to your velocipede?
Why, thank you.

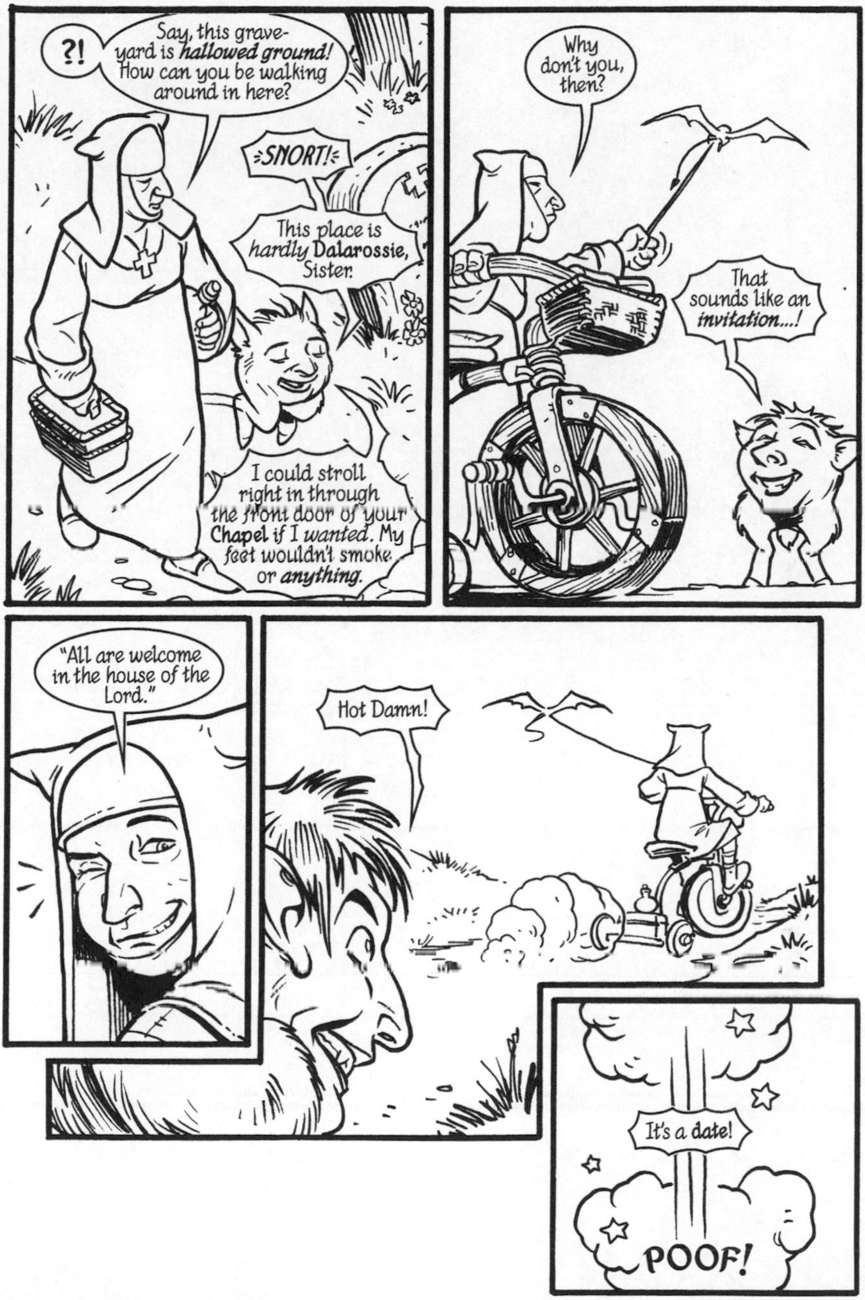
?!
Say, this graveyard is hallowed ground! How can you be walking around in here?
SNORT!
This place is hardly Dalarossie, Sister.
I could stroll right in through the front door of your Chapel if I wanted. My feet wouldn't smoke or anything.
Why don't you, then?
That sounds like an invitation...!
"All are welcome in the house of the Lord."
Hot Damn!
It's a date!
POOF!

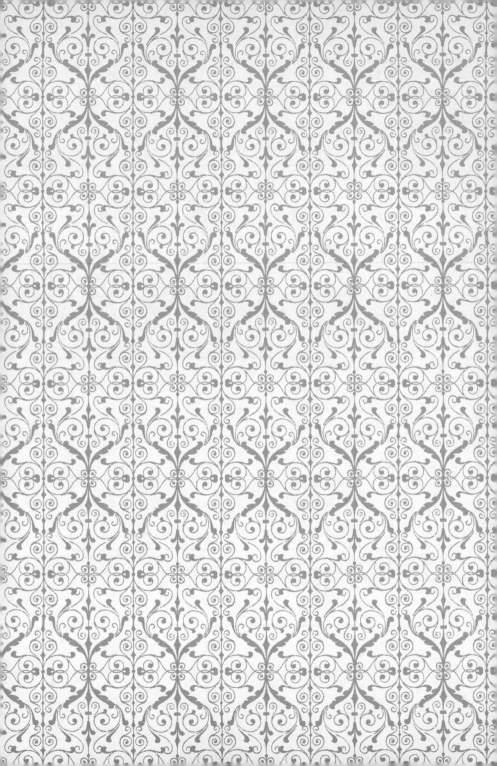

Chapter 13.

· SOLICITINE PT. I ·

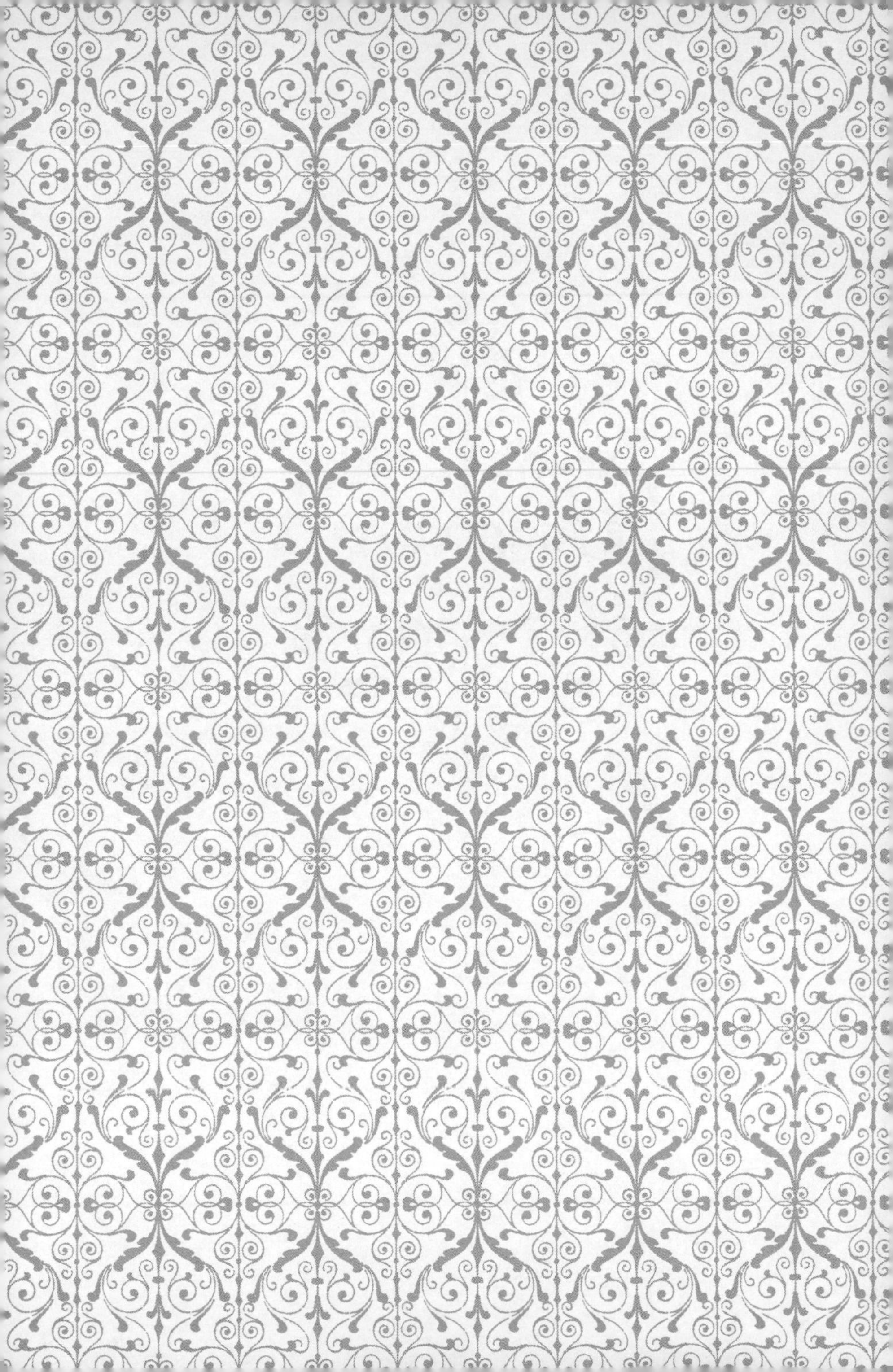

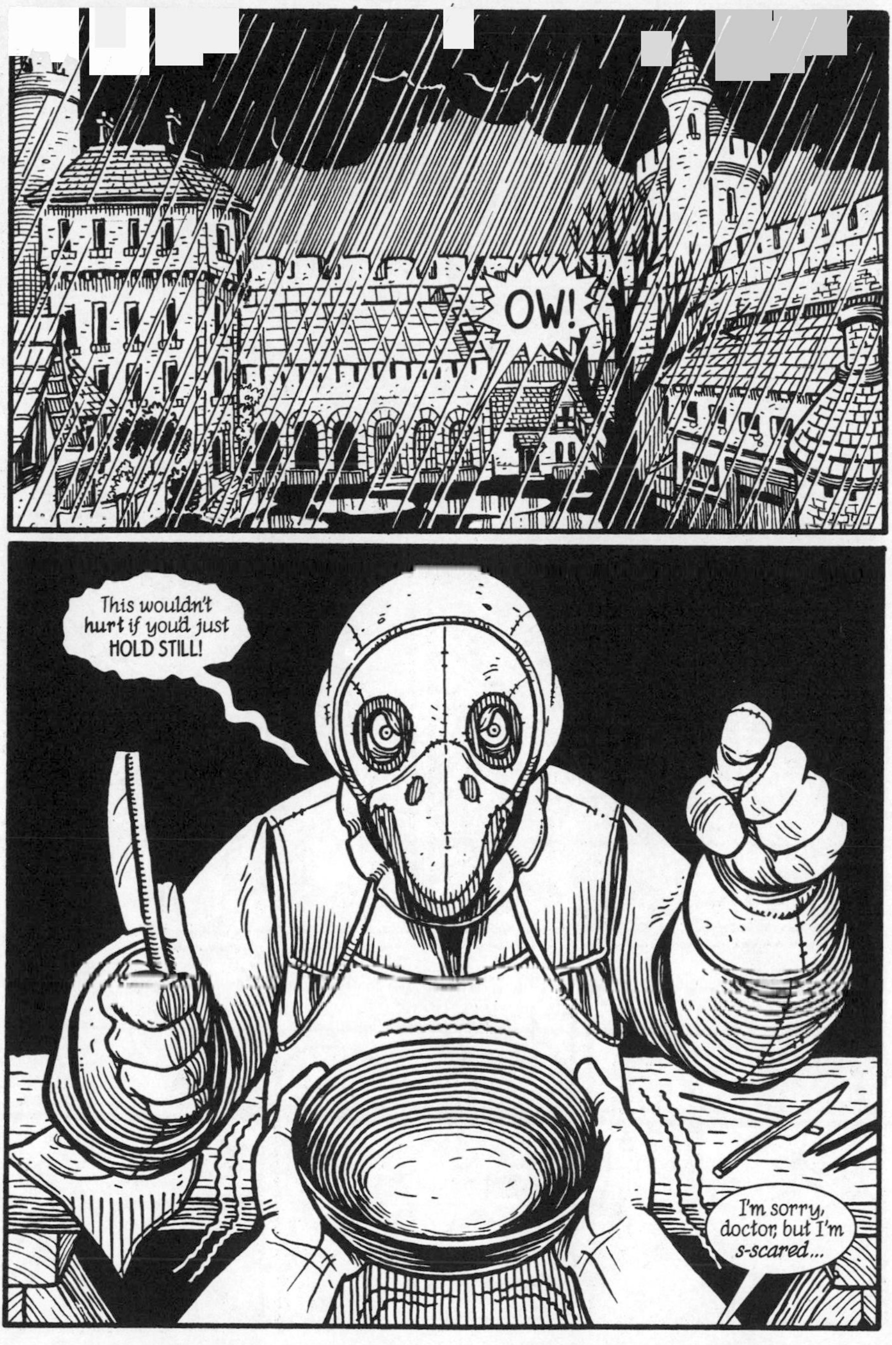
OW!
This wouldn't hurt if you'd just HOLD STILL!
I'm sorry, doctor, but I'm s-scared...

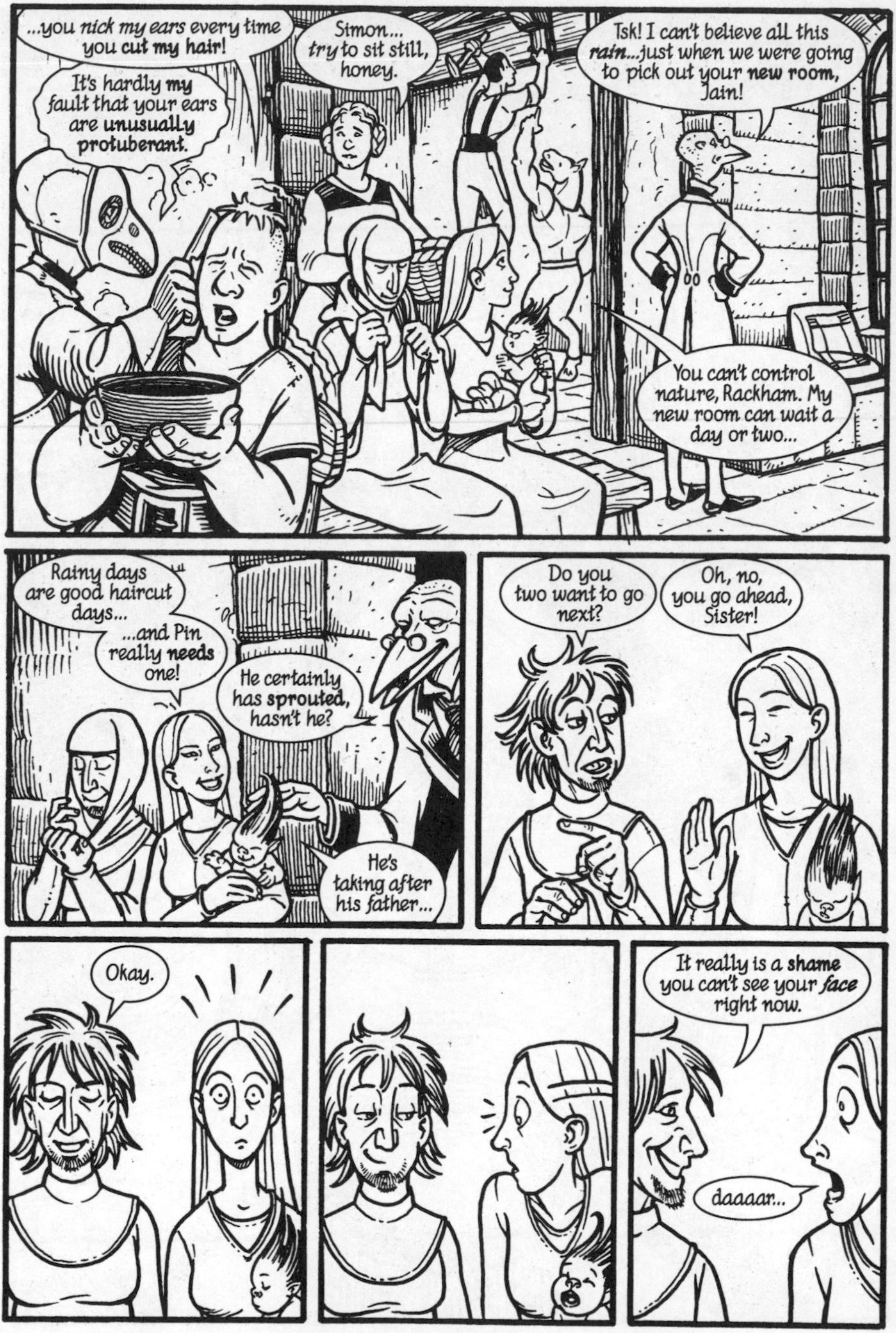
...you *nick my ears* every time you **cut my hair**!
It's hardly **my** fault that your ears are **unusually protuberant**.
Simon... *try* to sit still, honey.
Tsk! I can't believe all this ***rain***...just when we were going to pick out your **new room**, Jain!
You can't control nature, Rackham. My new room can wait a day or two...
Rainy days are good haircut days...
...and Pin really **needs** one!
He certainly has **sprouted**, hasn't he?
He's taking after his father...
Do you two want to go next?
Oh, no, you go ahead, Sister!
Okay.
It really is a **shame** you can't see your ***face*** right now.
daaaar...

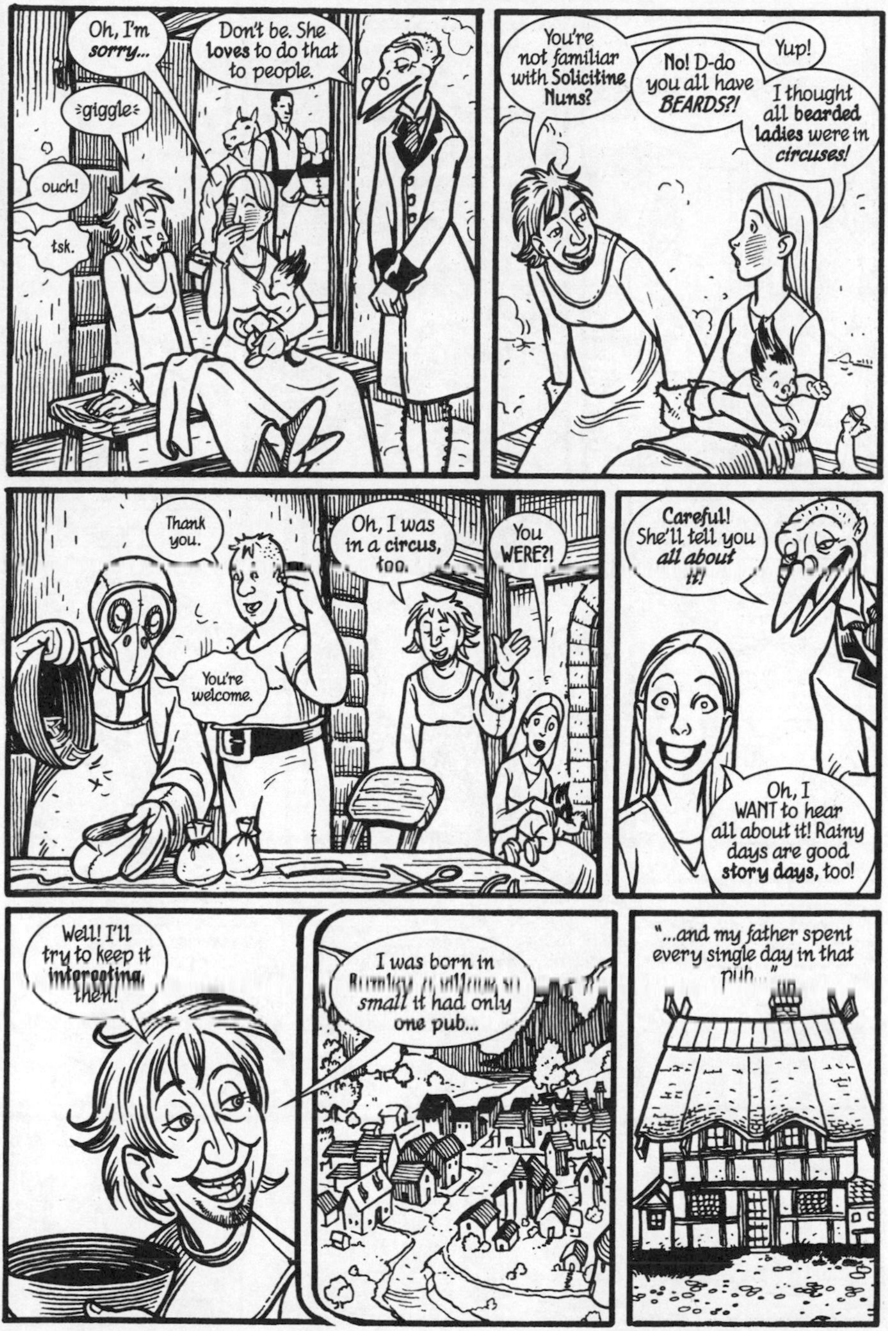
Oh, I'm *sorry*...
Don't be. She **loves** to do that to people.
giggle
ouch!
tsk.
You're *not familiar* with Solicitine Nuns?
No! D-do you all have ***BEARDS?!***
Yup!
I thought all **bearded ladies** were in ***circuses!***
Thank you.
You're welcome.
Oh, I was in a **circus**, too.
You WERE?!
Careful! She'll tell you ***all about it!***
Oh, I WANT to hear all about it! Rainy days are good **story days**, too!
Well! I'll try to keep it
then!
I was born in
small it had only one pub...
"...and my father spent every single day in that pub..."

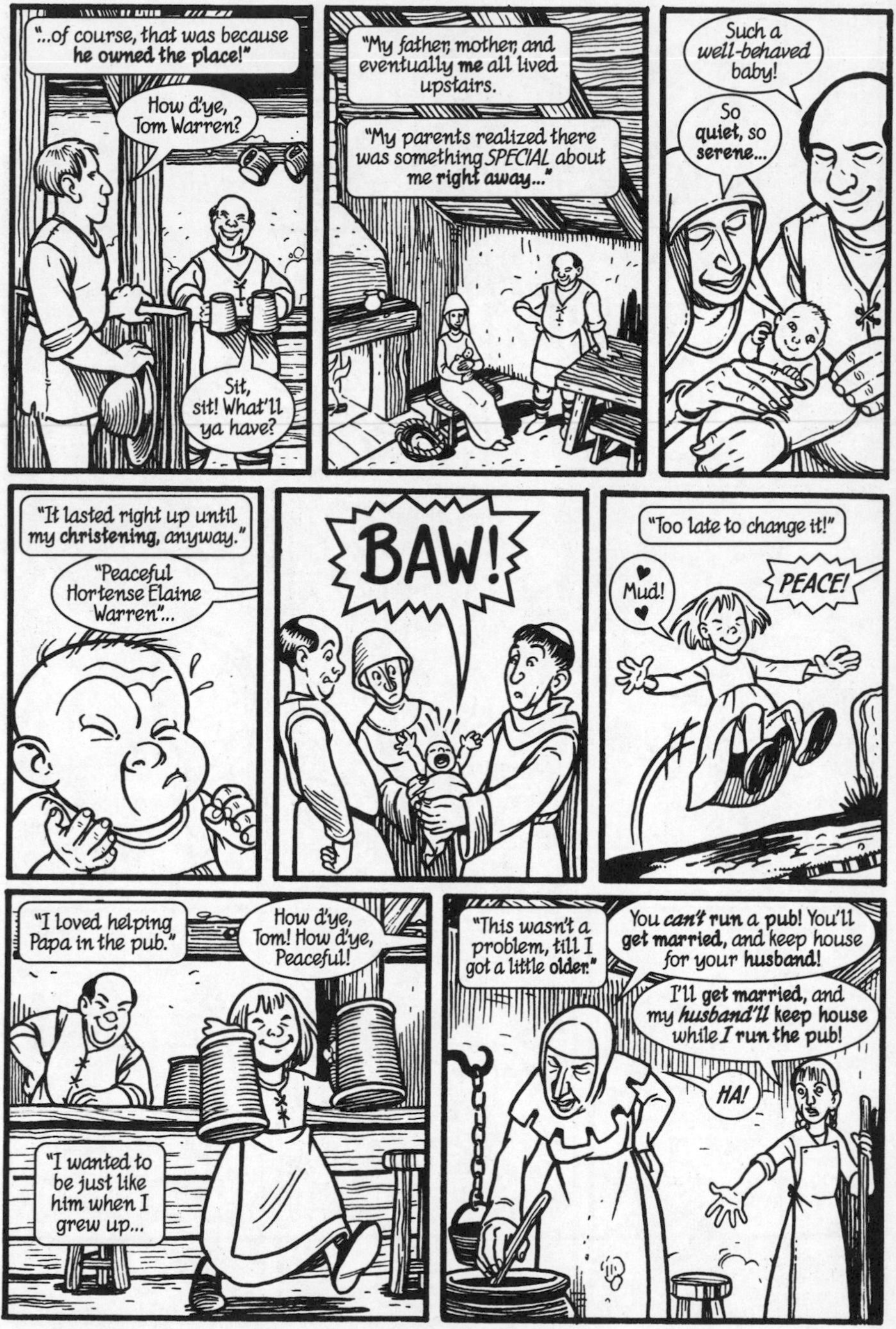
"...of course, that was because **he owned the place!**"
How d'ye, Tom Warren?
Sit, sit! What'll ya have?
"My *father,* mother, and eventually **me** all lived upstairs.
"My parents realized there was something *SPECIAL* about me **right away...**"
Such a *well-behaved* baby!
So **quiet,** so **serene...**
"It lasted right up until my **christening,** anyway."
"Peaceful Hortense Elaine Warren"...
BAW!
"Too late to change it!"
Mud!
PEACE!
"I loved helping Papa in the pub."
How d'ye, Tom! How d'ye, Peaceful!
"I wanted to be just like him when I grew up...
"This wasn't a problem, till I got a little **older.**"
You ***can't* run** a pub! You'll **get married,** and keep house for your **husband!**
I'll **get married,** and my ***husband'll*** **keep house** while ***I*** **run the pub!**
HA!

"Papa always managed to smooth things over with Mama, but I knew it wouldn't last forever."

You know there's **no harm** in letting Peace help me out in the pub.

And what better place for her to **meet a husband**?

She'll have to face reality *someday*, Tom!

"He was right about **meeting men**. Every guy in town came into Papa's place, not to mention the occasional travelers...

"They all *liked* talking to me, too...

"...but it was always about their **wife or girlfriend problems**!"

Well, you know Alf, if I were Meggy, I'd be expecting a humble apology and a bunch of flowers after you pulled a bone headed thing like that!

You think...?

"Even though I didn't land a *boyfriend*, I was certainly the **most popular girl in town**!

"Then one day it just **appeared**, out of the blue..."

Peach fuzz...?!

"Mama was *horrified*; no matter how often I shaved, it *grew right back again*! She was sure my life was ruined."

You'll never marry!

Hmmm....!

Hey Peaceful-- you growin' a beard?

Looks like it, Alf!

Humh! That's *unusual*, ain't it?

Sure is! What'll you have?

The regular.

"And after the initial surprise, the guys in the pub treated me no differently than before."

275.

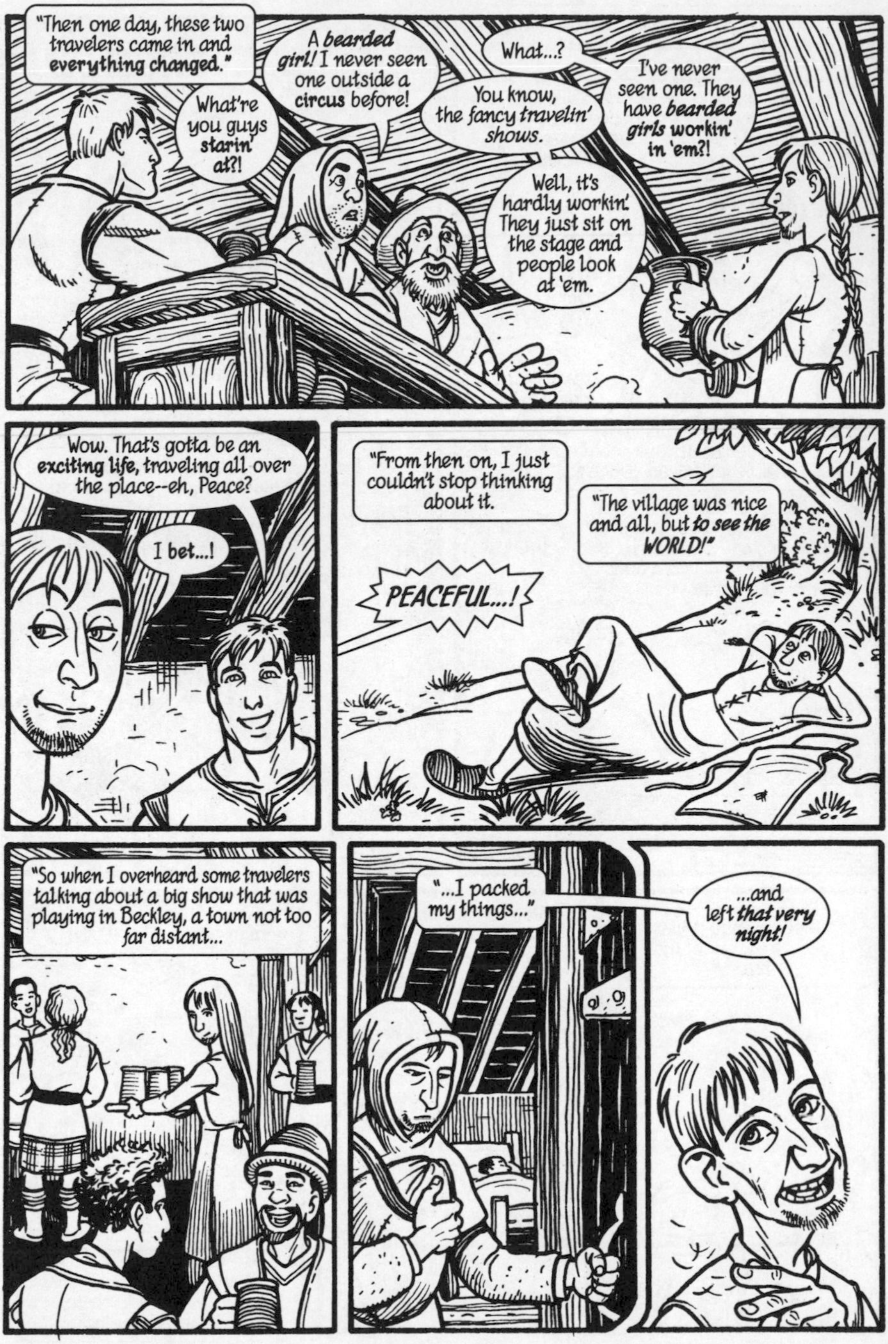
"Then one day, these two travelers came in and **everything changed.**"
What're you guys *starin' at?!*
A *bearded girl!* I never seen one outside a **circus** before!
What...?
You know, the *fancy travelin'* shows.
I've never seen one. They have *bearded girls* workin' in 'em?!
Well, it's hardly workin'. They just sit on the stage and people look at 'em.
Wow. That's gotta be an **exciting life**, traveling all over the place--eh, Peace?
I bet...!
"From then on, I just couldn't stop thinking about it.
"The village was nice and all, but *to see the WORLD!*"
PEACEFUL...!
"So when I overheard some travelers talking about a big show that was playing in Beckley, a town not too far distant...
"...I packed my things..."
...and left *that very night!*

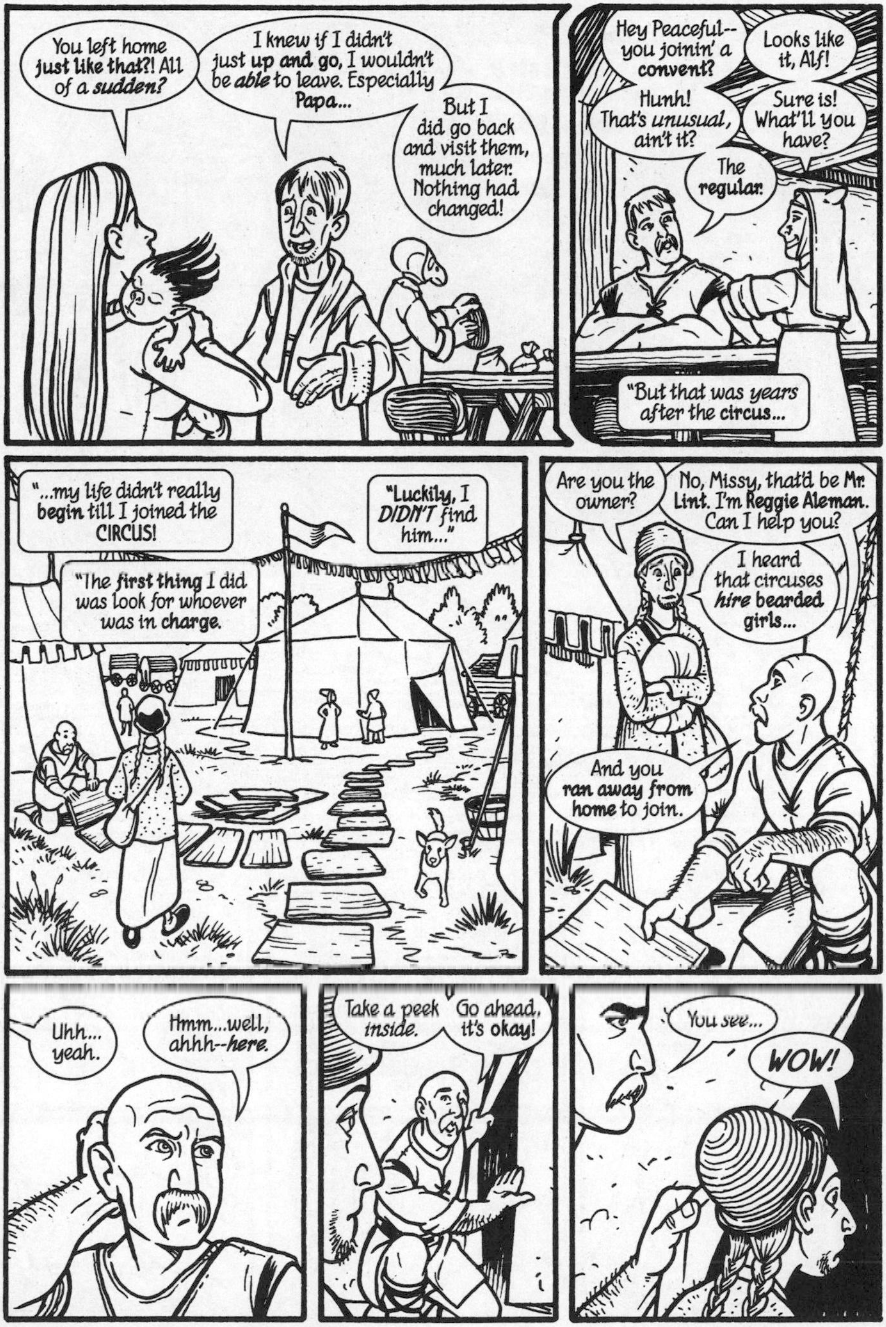
You left home just like that?! All of a sudden?
I knew if I didn't just up and go, I wouldn't be able to leave. Especially Papa...
But I did go back and visit them, much later. Nothing had changed!
Hey Peaceful-- you joinin' a convent?
Looks like it, Alf!
Hunh! That's unusual, ain't it?
Sure is! What'll you have?
The regular.
"But that was years after the circus...
"...my life didn't really begin till I joined the CIRCUS!
"Luckily, I DIDN'T find him..."
"The first thing I did was look for whoever was in charge.
Are you the owner?
No, Missy, that'd be Mr. Lint. I'm Reggie Aleman. Can I help you?
I heard that circuses hire bearded girls...
And you ran away from home to join.
Uhh... yeah.
Hmm...well, ahhh--here.
Take a peek inside.
Go ahead, it's okay!
You see...
WOW!

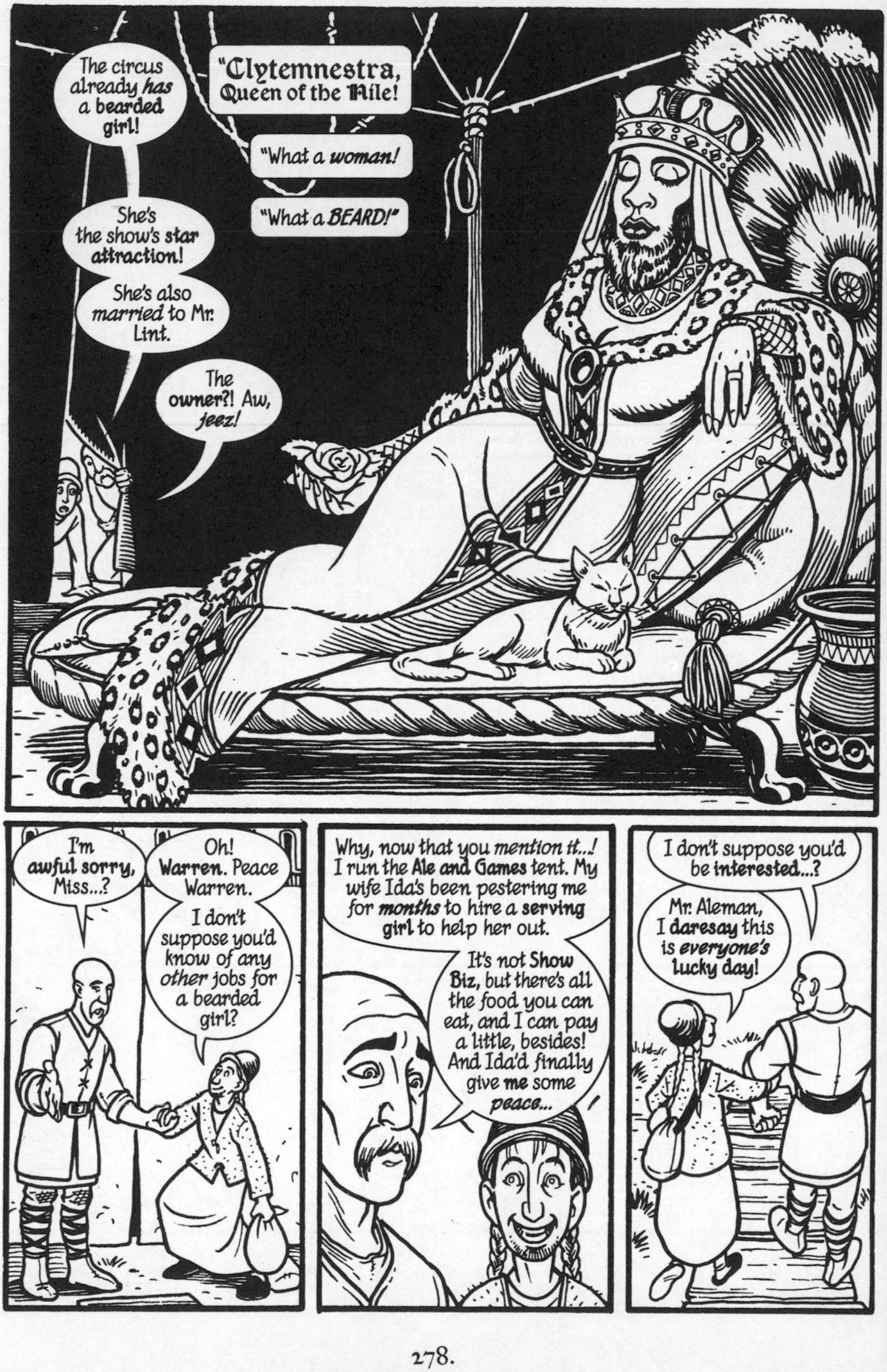
The circus already has a bearded girl!
"Clytemnestra, Queen of the Nile!
"What a woman!
"What a BEARD!"
She's the show's star attraction!
She's also married to Mr. Lint.
The owner?! Aw, jeez!
I'm awful sorry, Miss...?
Oh! Warren. Peace Warren.
I don't suppose you'd know of any other jobs for a bearded girl?
Why, now that you mention it...! I run the Ale and Games tent. My wife Ida's been pestering me for months to hire a serving girl to help her out.
It's not Show Biz, but there's all the food you can eat, and I can pay a little, besides! And Ida'd finally give me some peace...
I don't suppose you'd be interested...?
Mr. Aleman, I daresay this is everyone's lucky day!

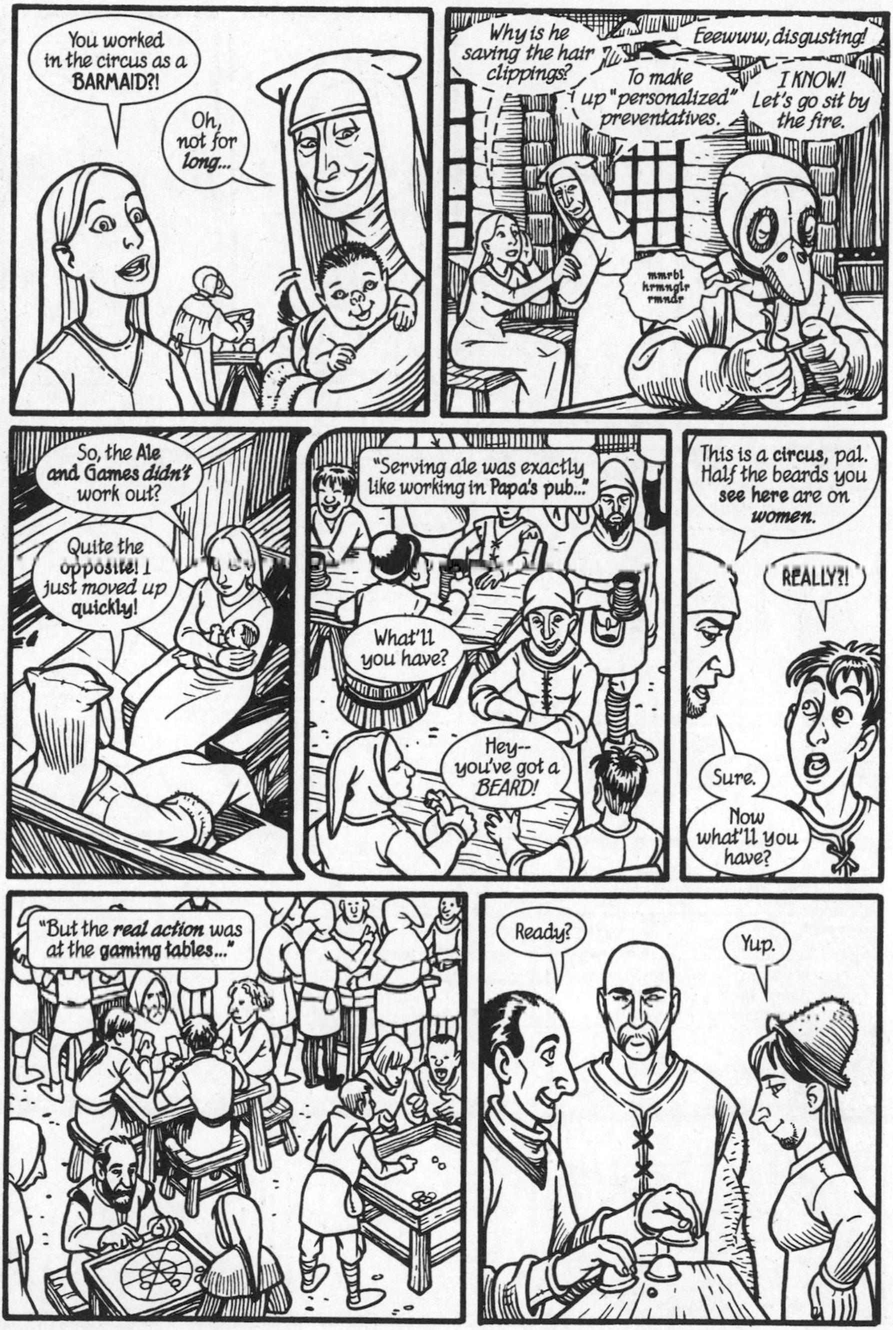
You worked in the circus as a BARMAID?!
Oh, not for long...
Why is he saving the hair clippings?
Eeewww, disgusting!
To make up "personalized" preventatives.
I KNOW! Let's go sit by the fire.
mmrbl hrmnglr rmndr
So, the Ale and Games didn't work out?
Quite the opposite! I just moved up quickly!
"Serving ale was exactly like working in Papa's pub..."
What'll you have?
Hey-- you've got a BEARD!
This is a circus, pal. Half the beards you see here are on women.
REALLY?!
Sure.
Now what'll you have?
"But the real action was at the gaming tables..."
Ready?
Yup.

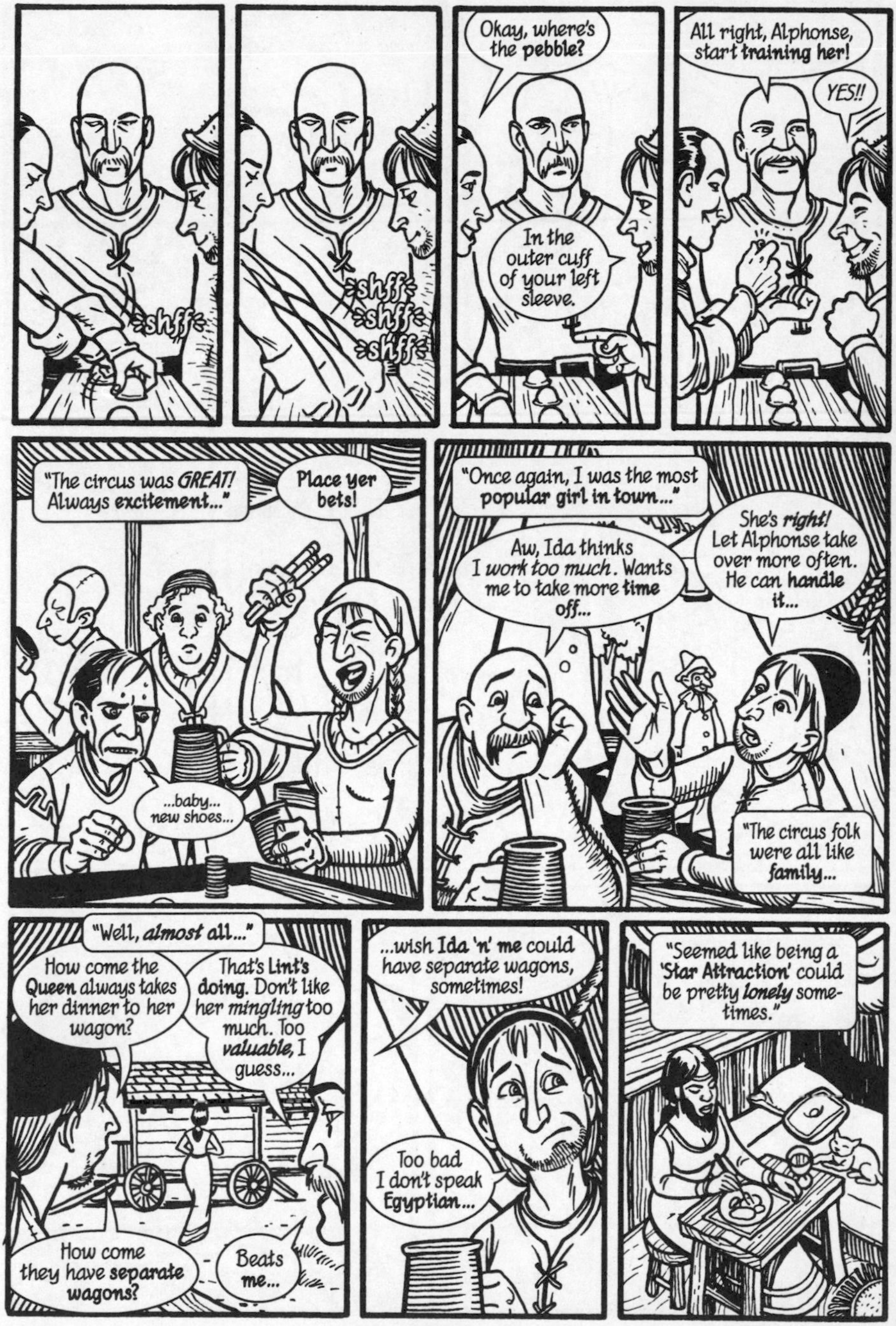
shff
shff
shff
shff
Okay, where's the pebble?
In the outer cuff of your left sleeve.
All right, Alphonse, start training her!
YES!!
"The circus was GREAT! Always excitement..."
Place yer bets!
...baby... new shoes...
"Once again, I was the most popular girl in town..."
Aw, Ida thinks I work too much. Wants me to take more time off...
She's right! Let Alphonse take over more often. He can handle it...
"The circus folk were all like family...
"Well, almost all..."
How come the Queen always takes her dinner to her wagon?
That's Lint's doing. Don't like her mingling too much. Too valuable, I guess...
How come they have separate wagons?
Beats me...
...wish Ida 'n' me could have separate wagons, sometimes!
Too bad I don't speak Egyptian...
"Seemed like being a 'Star Attraction' could be pretty lonely sometimes."

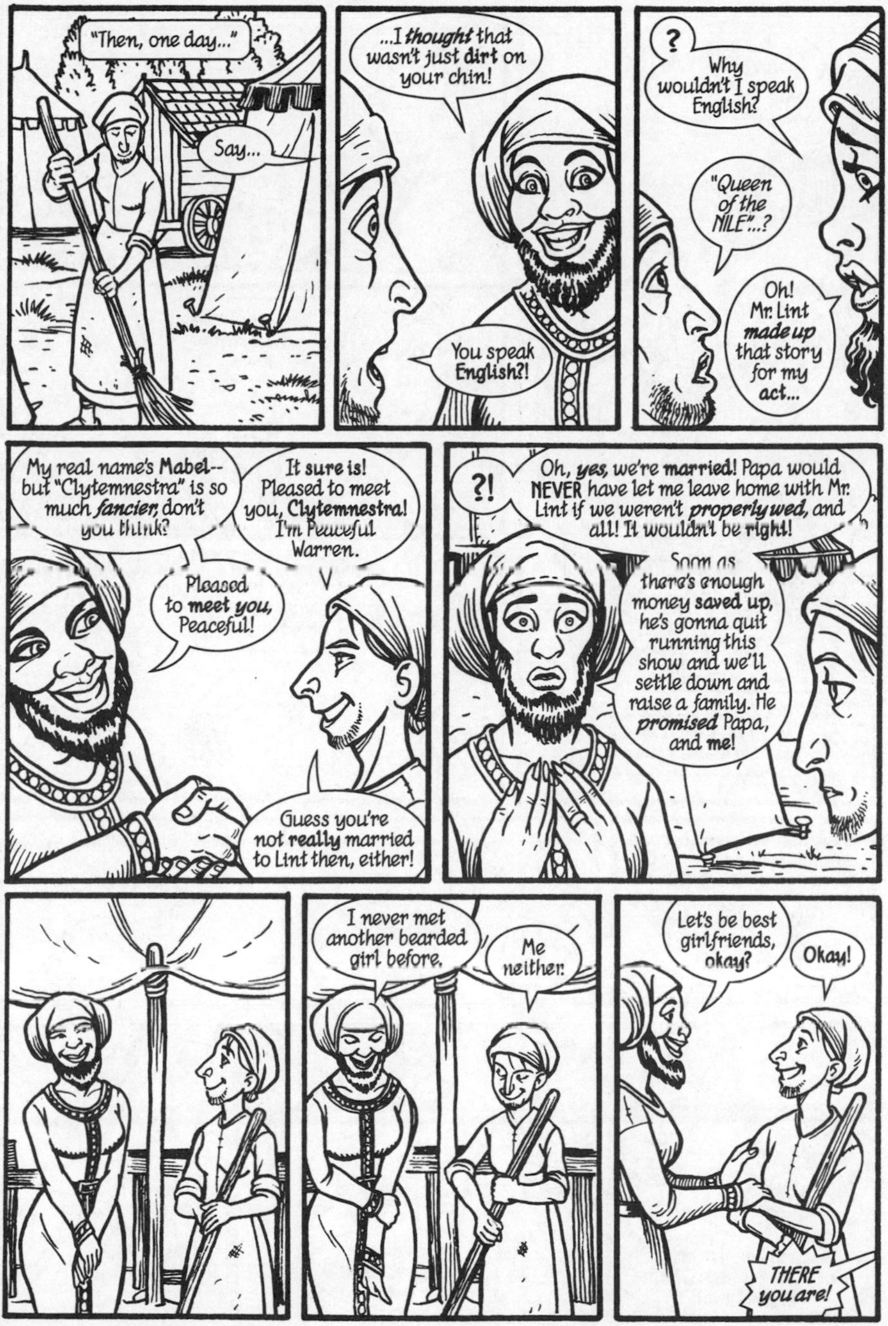
"Then, one day..."
Say...
...I thought that wasn't just dirt on your chin!
You speak English?!
?
Why wouldn't I speak English?
"Queen of the NILE"...?
Oh! Mr. Lint made up that story for my act...
My real name's Mabel-- but "Clytemnestra" is so much fancier, don't you think?
It sure is! Pleased to meet you, Clytemnestra! I'm Peaceful Warren.
Pleased to meet you, Peaceful!
Guess you're not really married to Lint then, either!
?!
Oh, yes, we're married! Papa would NEVER have let me leave home with Mr. Lint if we weren't properly wed, and all! It wouldn't be right!
Soon as there's enough money saved up, he's gonna quit running this show and we'll settle down and raise a family. He promised Papa, and me!
I never met another bearded girl before.
Me neither.
Let's be best girlfriends, okay?
Okay!
THERE you are!

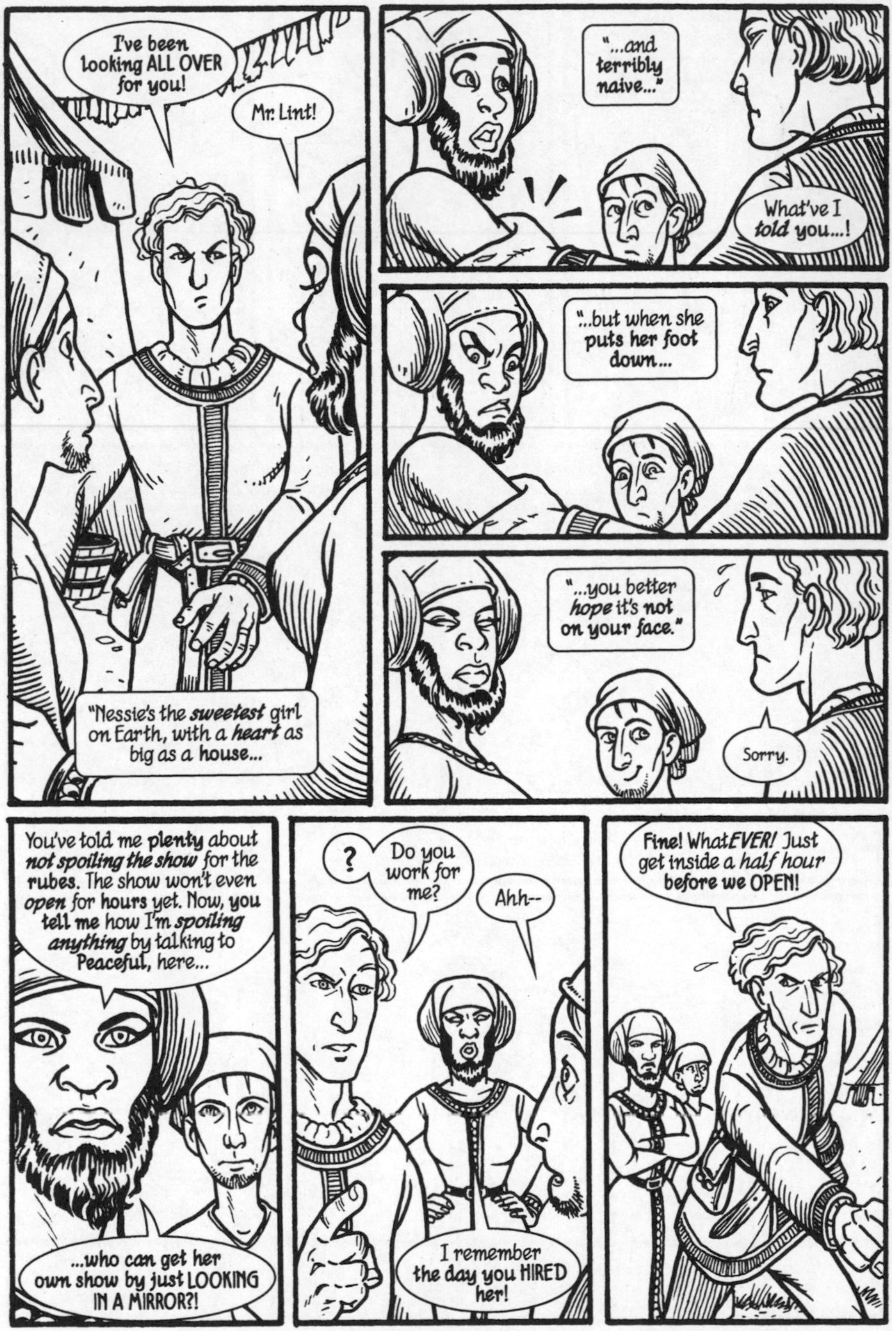
I've been looking ALL OVER for you!
Mr. Lint!
"Nessie's the *sweetest* girl on Earth, with a *heart* as big as a house...
"...and terribly naive..."
What've I *told* you...!
"...but when she puts her foot down...
"...you better *hope* it's not on your face."
Sorry.
You've told me **plenty** about ***not spoiling the show*** for the rubes. The show won't even ***open*** for hours yet. Now, you tell me how I'm ***spoiling anything*** by talking to Peaceful, here...
...who can get her own show by just LOOKING IN A MIRROR?!
?
Do you work for me?
Ahh--
I remember the day you HIRED her!
Fine! What*EVER!* Just get inside a *half hour* before we OPEN!

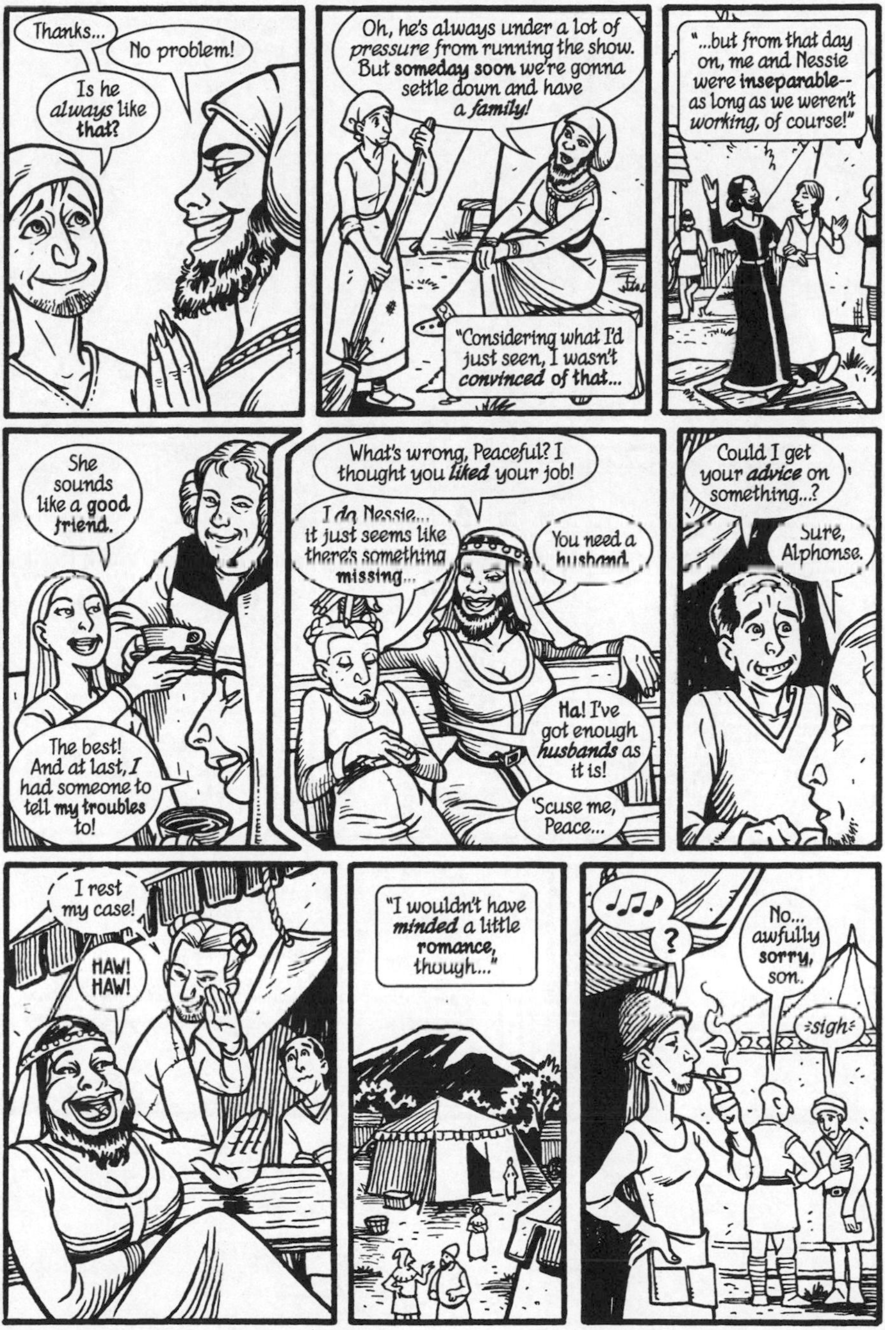
Thanks...
No problem!
Is he always like that?
Oh, he's always under a lot of pressure from running the show. But someday soon we're gonna settle down and have a family!
"Considering what I'd just seen, I wasn't convinced of that...
"...but from that day on, me and Nessie were inseparable--as long as we weren't working, of course!"
She sounds like a good friend.
The best! And at last, I had someone to tell my troubles to!
What's wrong, Peaceful? I thought you liked your job!
I do, Nessie... it just seems like there's something missing...
You need a husband.
Ha! I've got enough husbands as it is!
'Scuse me, Peace...
Could I get your advice on something...?
Sure, Alphonse.
I rest my case!
HAW! HAW!
"I wouldn't have minded a little romance, though..."
?
No... awfully sorry, son.
sigh

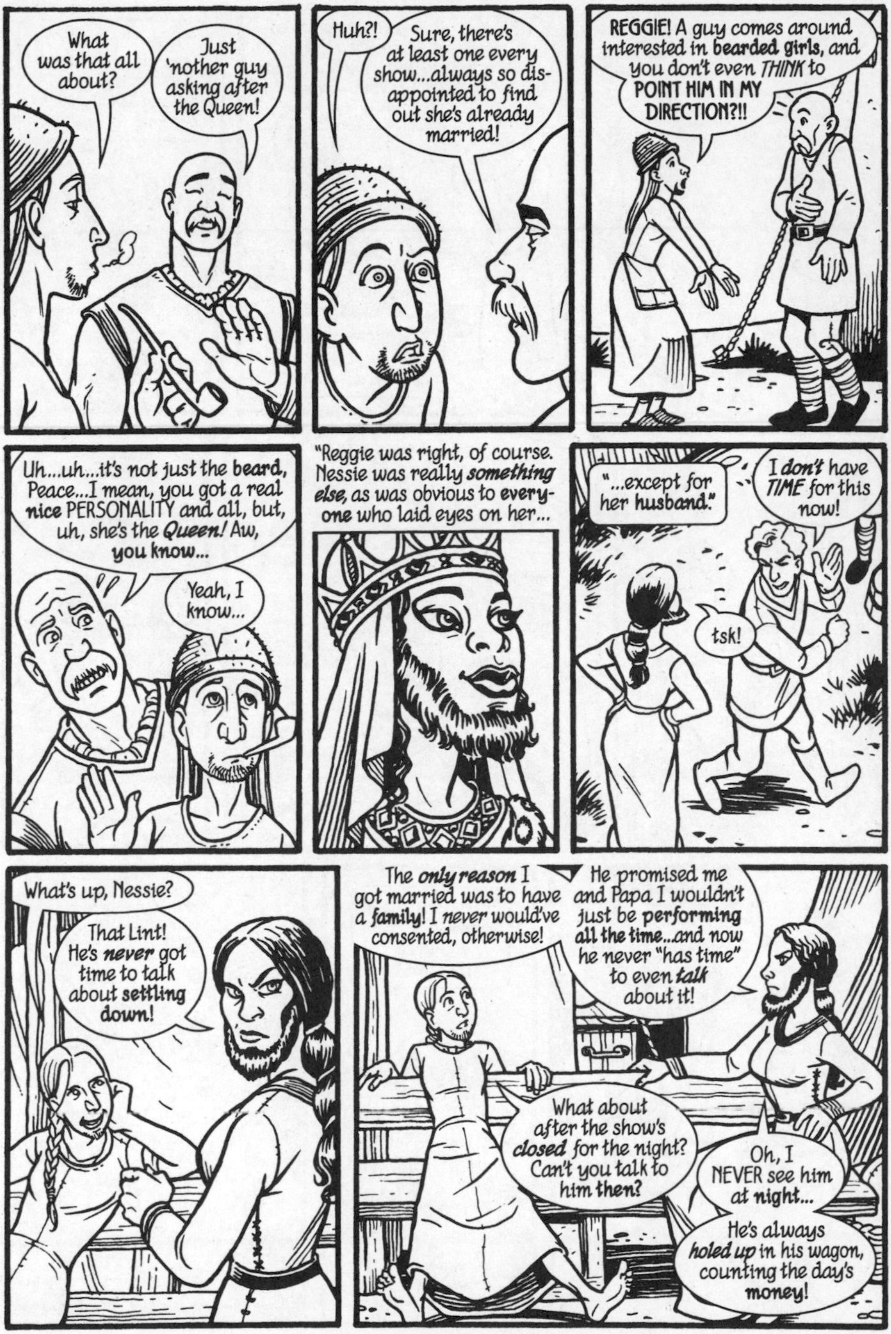
What was that all about?
Just 'nother guy asking after the Queen!
Huh?!
Sure, there's at least one every show...always so dis-appointed to find out she's already married!
REGGIE! A guy comes around interested in bearded girls, and you don't even THINK to POINT HIM IN MY DIRECTION?!!
Uh...uh...it's not just the beard, Peace...I mean, you got a real nice PERSONALITY and all, but, uh, she's the Queen! Aw, you know...
Yeah, I know...
"Reggie was right, of course. Nessie was really something else, as was obvious to every-one who laid eyes on her...
"...except for her husband."
I don't have TIME for this now!
tsk!
What's up, Nessie?
That Lint! He's never got time to talk about settling down!
The only reason I got married was to have a family! I never would've consented, otherwise!
He promised me and Papa I wouldn't just be performing all the time...and now he never "has time" to even talk about it!
What about after the show's closed for the night? Can't you talk to him then?
Oh, I NEVER see him at night...
He's always holed up in his wagon, counting the day's money!

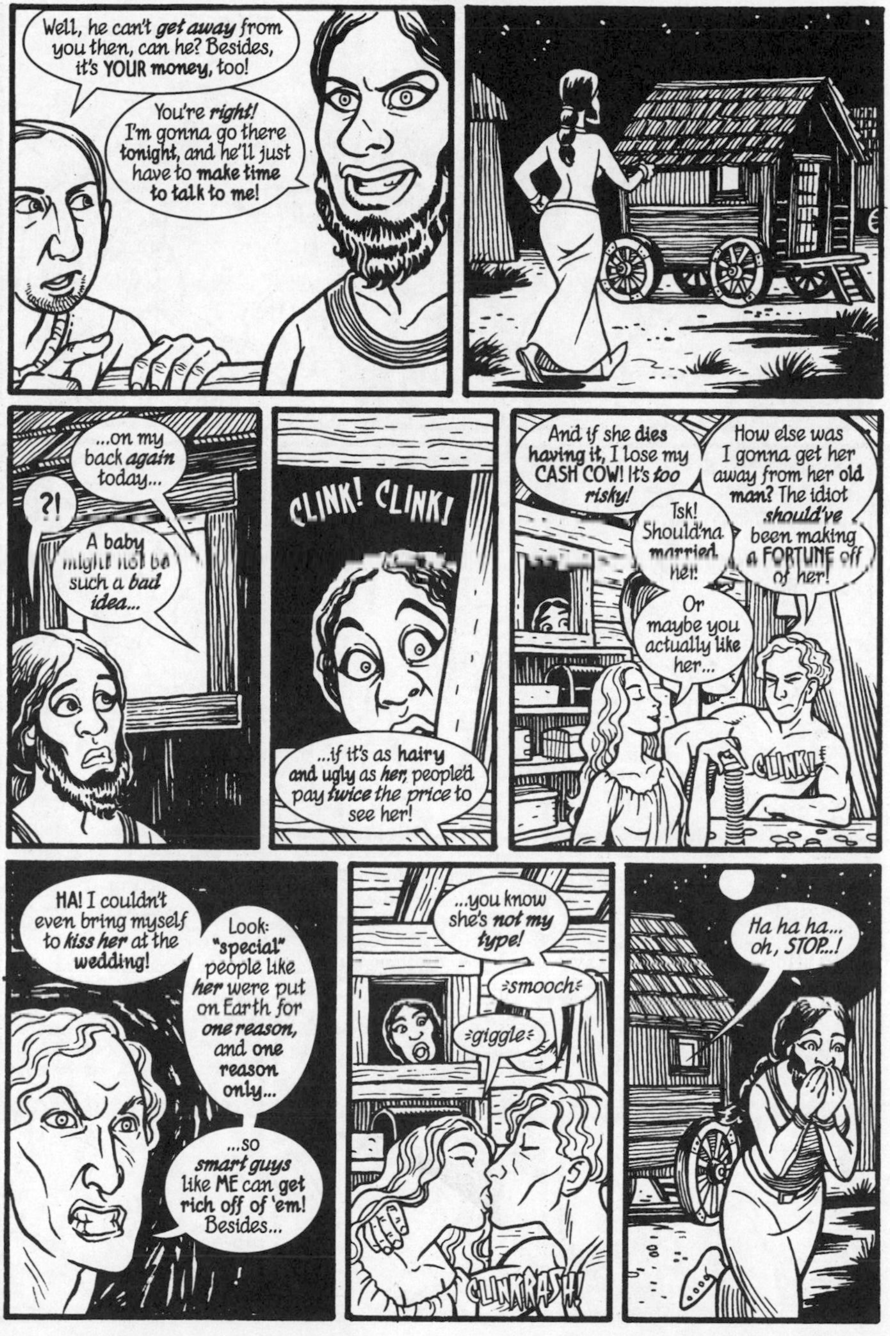
Well, he can't get away from you then, can he? Besides, it's YOUR money, too!
You're right! I'm gonna go there tonight, and he'll just have to make time to talk to me!
...on my back again today...
?!
A baby might not be such a bad idea...
CLINK! CLINK!
...if it's as hairy and ugly as her, people'd pay twice the price to see her!
And if she dies having it, I lose my CASH COW! It's too risky!
How else was I gonna get her away from her old man? The idiot should've been making a FORTUNE off of her!
Tsk! Should'na married her!
Or maybe you actually like her...
CLINK!
HA! I couldn't even bring myself to kiss her at the wedding!
Look: "special" people like her were put on Earth for one reason, and one reason only...
...so smart guys like ME can get rich off of 'em! Besides...
...you know she's not my type!
smooch
giggle
CLINKRASH!
Ha ha ha... oh, STOP...!

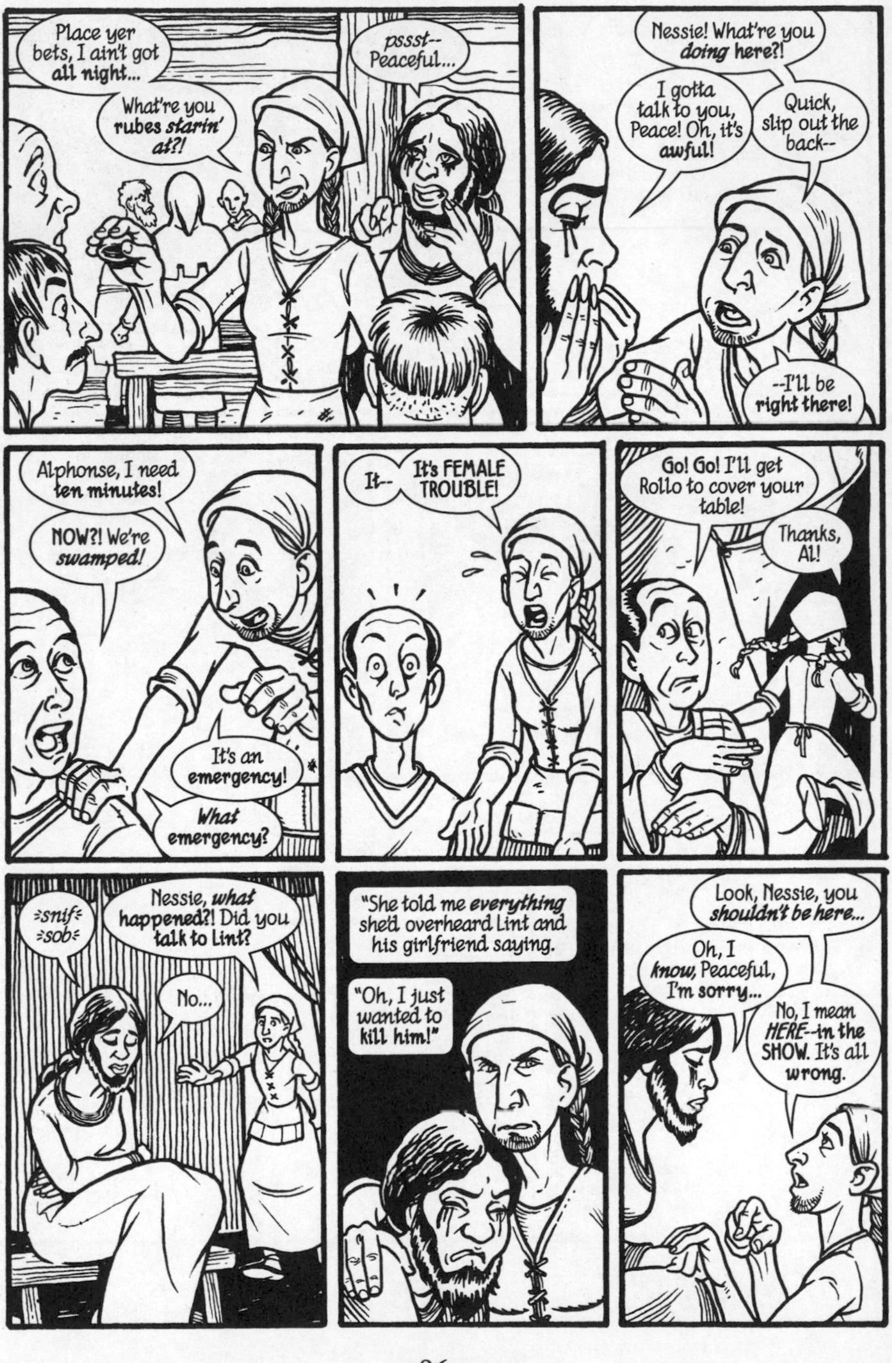
Place yer bets, I ain't got **all night...**
What're you **rubes *starin'* at?!**
pssst-- Peaceful...
Nessie! What're you ***doing* here?!**
I gotta talk to you, Peace! Oh, it's **awful!**
Quick, slip out the back--
--I'll be **right there!**
Alphonse, I need **ten minutes!**
NOW?! We're ***swamped!***
It's an **emergency!**
***What* emergency?**
It--
It's FEMALE TROUBLE!
Go! Go! I'll get Rollo to cover your table!
Thanks, Al!
≈snif≈
≈sob≈
Nessie, ***what* happened?!** Did you **talk to Lint?**
No...
"She told me ***everything*** she'd overheard Lint and his girlfriend saying.
"Oh, I just wanted to **kill him!"**
Look, Nessie, you ***shouldn't be here...***
Oh, I ***know,*** Peaceful, **I'm sorry...**
No, I mean ***HERE***--in the SHOW. It's all **wrong.**

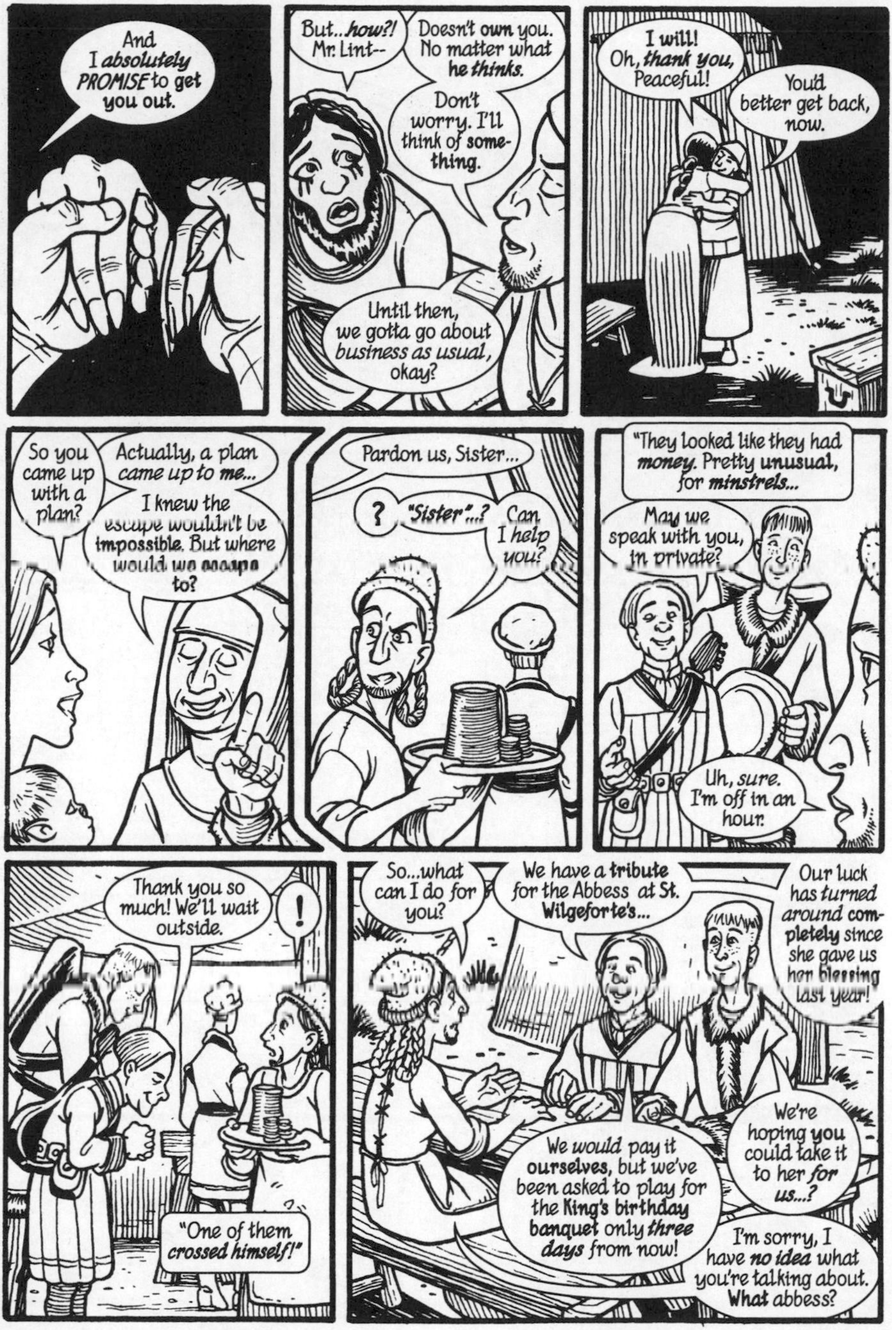

And I absolutely PROMISE to get you out.
But...how?! Mr. Lint--
Doesn't own you. No matter what he thinks.
Don't worry. I'll think of something.
Until then, we gotta go about business as usual, okay?
I will! Oh, thank you, Peaceful!
You'd better get back, now.
So you came up with a plan?
Actually, a plan came up to me...
I knew the escape wouldn't be impossible. But where would we escape to?
Pardon us, Sister...
?
"Sister"...?
Can I help you?
"They looked like they had money. Pretty unusual, for minstrels...
May we speak with you, in private?
Uh, sure. I'm off in an hour.
Thank you so much! We'll wait outside.
!
"One of them crossed himself!"
So...what can I do for you?
We have a tribute for the Abbess at St. Wilgeforte's...
Our luck has turned around completely since she gave us her blessing last year!
We would pay it ourselves, but we've been asked to play for the King's birthday banquet only three days from now!
We're hoping you could take it to her for us...?
I'm sorry, I have no idea what you're talking about. What abbess?

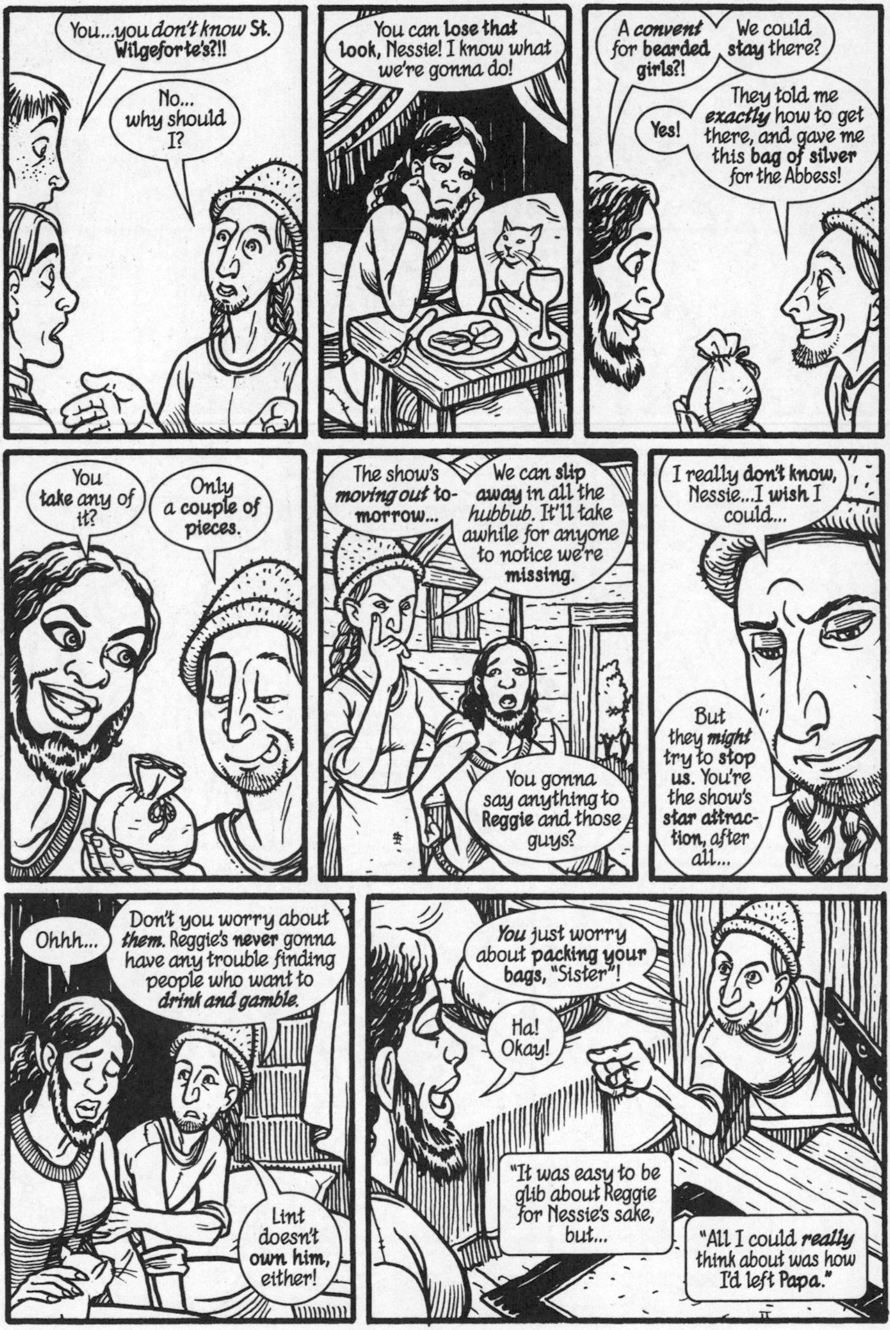
You...you *don't know* St. Wilgeforte's?!!
No... why should I?
You can **lose that look**, Nessie! I know what we're gonna do!
A *convent* for **bearded girls**?!
We could **stay** there?
Yes!
They told me *exactly* how to get there, and gave me this **bag of silver** for the Abbess!
You **take** any of it?
Only a **couple of pieces**.
The show's *moving out* to-morrow...
We can **slip away** in all the *hubbub*. It'll take awhile for anyone to notice we're **missing**.
You gonna say anything to Reggie and those guys?
I really **don't know**, Nessie...I **wish** I could...
But they *might* try to **stop** us. You're the show's **star attraction**, after all...
Ohhh...
Don't you worry about *them*. Reggie's **never** gonna have any trouble finding people who want to *drink and gamble*.
Lint doesn't **own him**, either!
You just worry about **packing your bags**, "Sister"!
Ha! Okay!
"It was easy to be glib about Reggie for Nessie's sake, but...
"All I could *really* think about was how I'd left **Papa**."

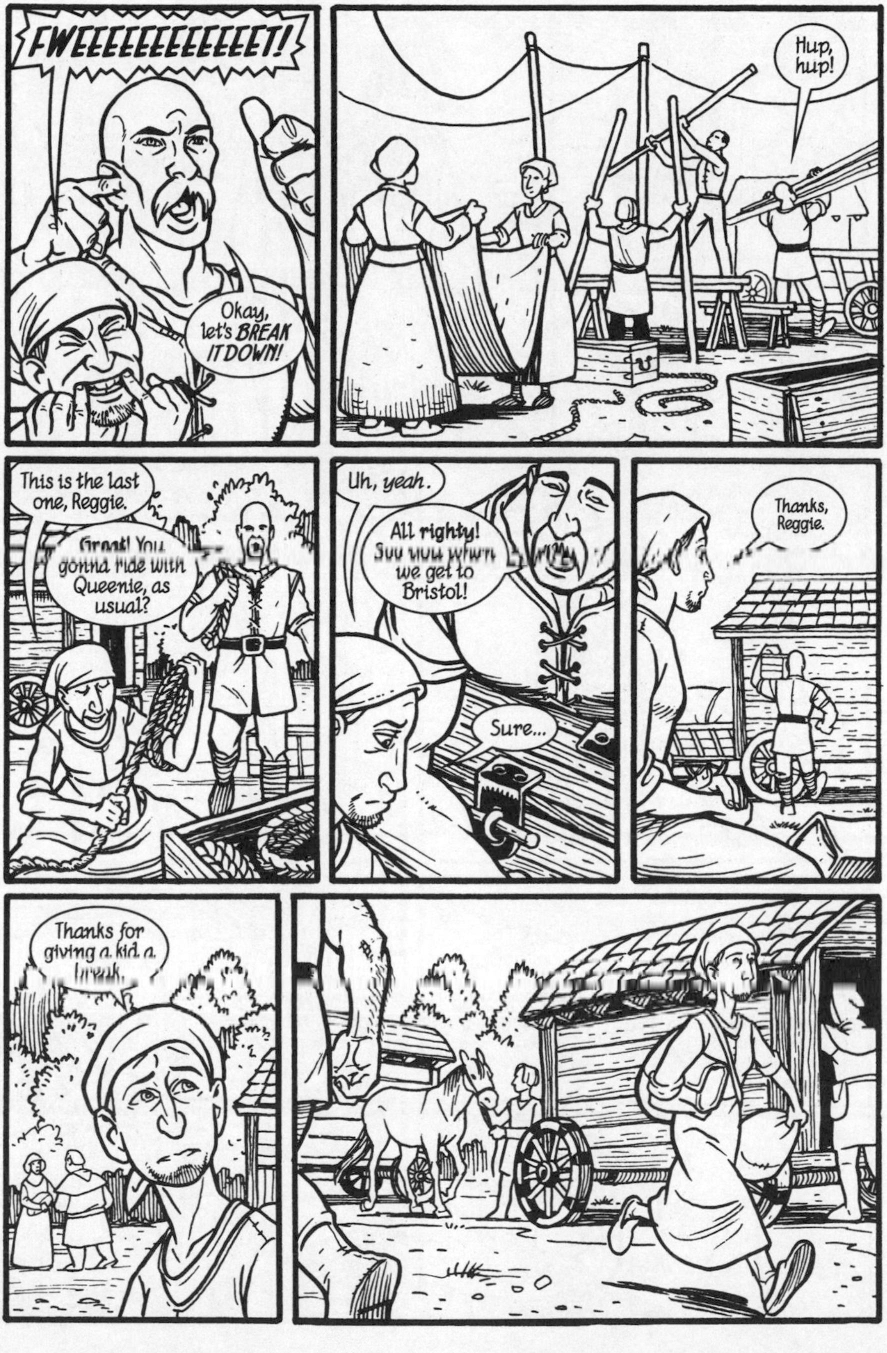
FWEEEEEEEEEEEEEET!
Okay, let's BREAK IT DOWN!
Hup, hup!
This is the last one, Reggie.
Great! You gonna ride with Queenie, as usual?
Uh, yeah.
All righty! See you when we get to Bristol!
Sure...
Thanks, Reggie.
Thanks for giving a kid a break.

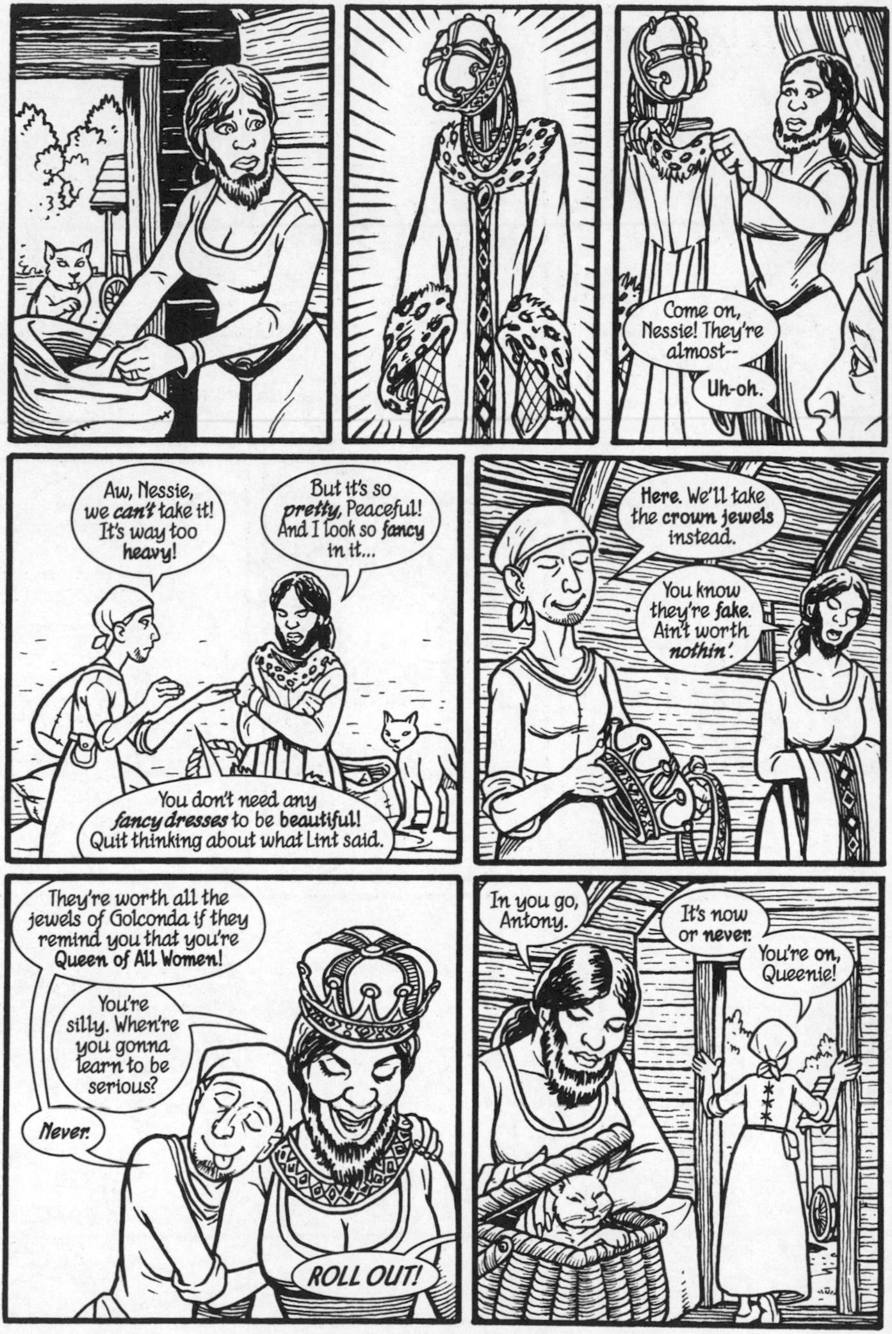
Come on, Nessie! They're almost--
Uh-oh.
Aw, Nessie, we can't take it! It's way too heavy!
But it's so pretty, Peaceful! And I look so fancy in it...
You don't need any fancy dresses to be beautiful! Quit thinking about what Lint said.
Here. We'll take the crown jewels instead.
You know they're fake. Ain't worth nothin'.
They're worth all the jewels of Golconda if they remind you that you're Queen of All Women!
You're silly. When're you gonna learn to be serious?
Never.
ROLL OUT!
In you go, Antony.
It's now or never.
You're on, Queenie!

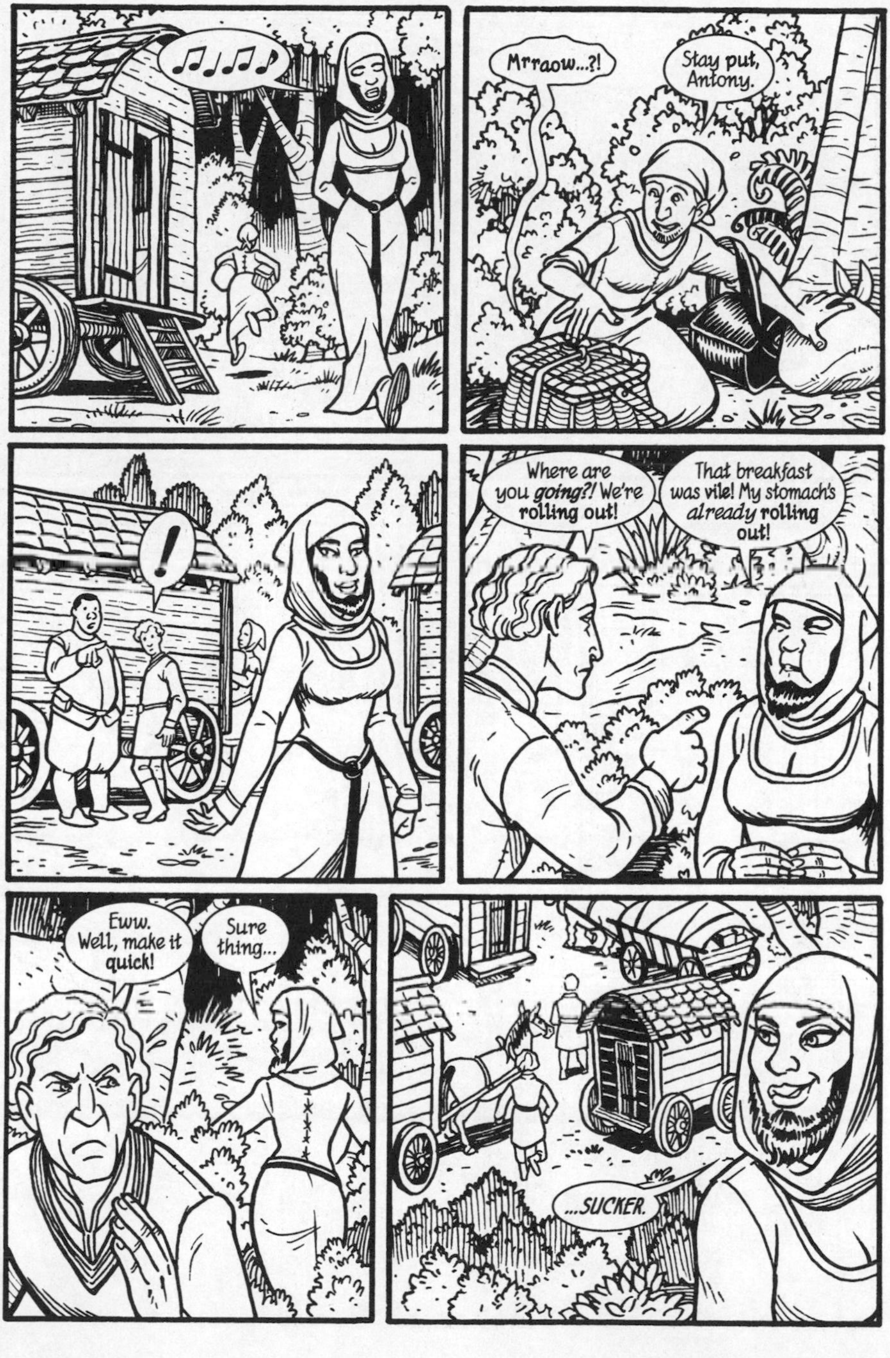
♫♩♫♪
Mrraow...?!
Stay put, Antony.
Where are you *going?!* We're **rolling out!**
That breakfast was vile! My stomach's *already* **rolling out!**
Eww. Well, make it **quick!**
Sure thing...
...SUCKER.

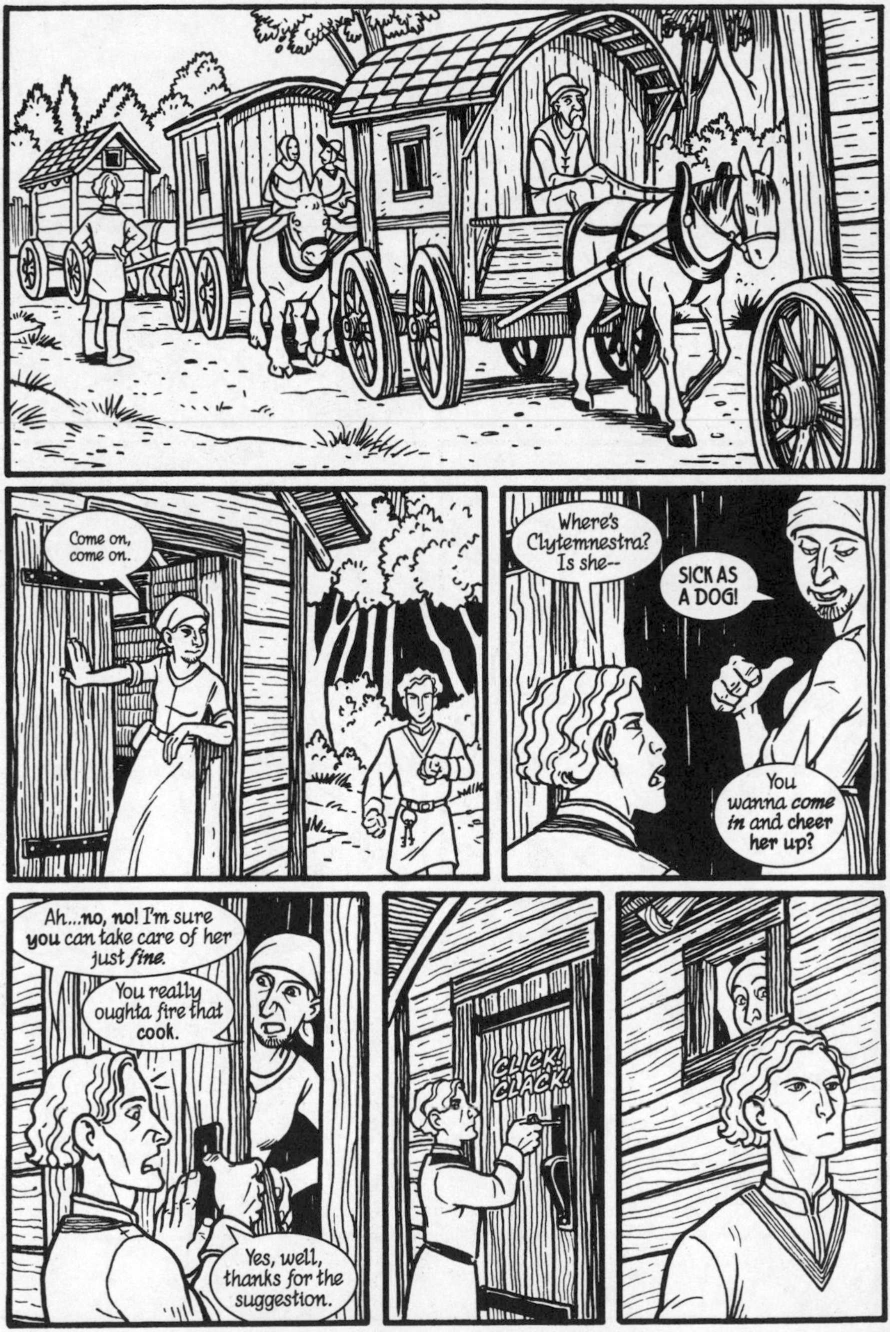
Come on, come on.
Where's Clytemnestra? Is she--
SICK AS A DOG!
You wanna *come in* and cheer her up?
Ah...**no, no!** I'm sure **you** can take care of her just ***fine***.
You really oughta fire that cook.
Yes, well, thanks for the suggestion.
CLICK! CLACK!

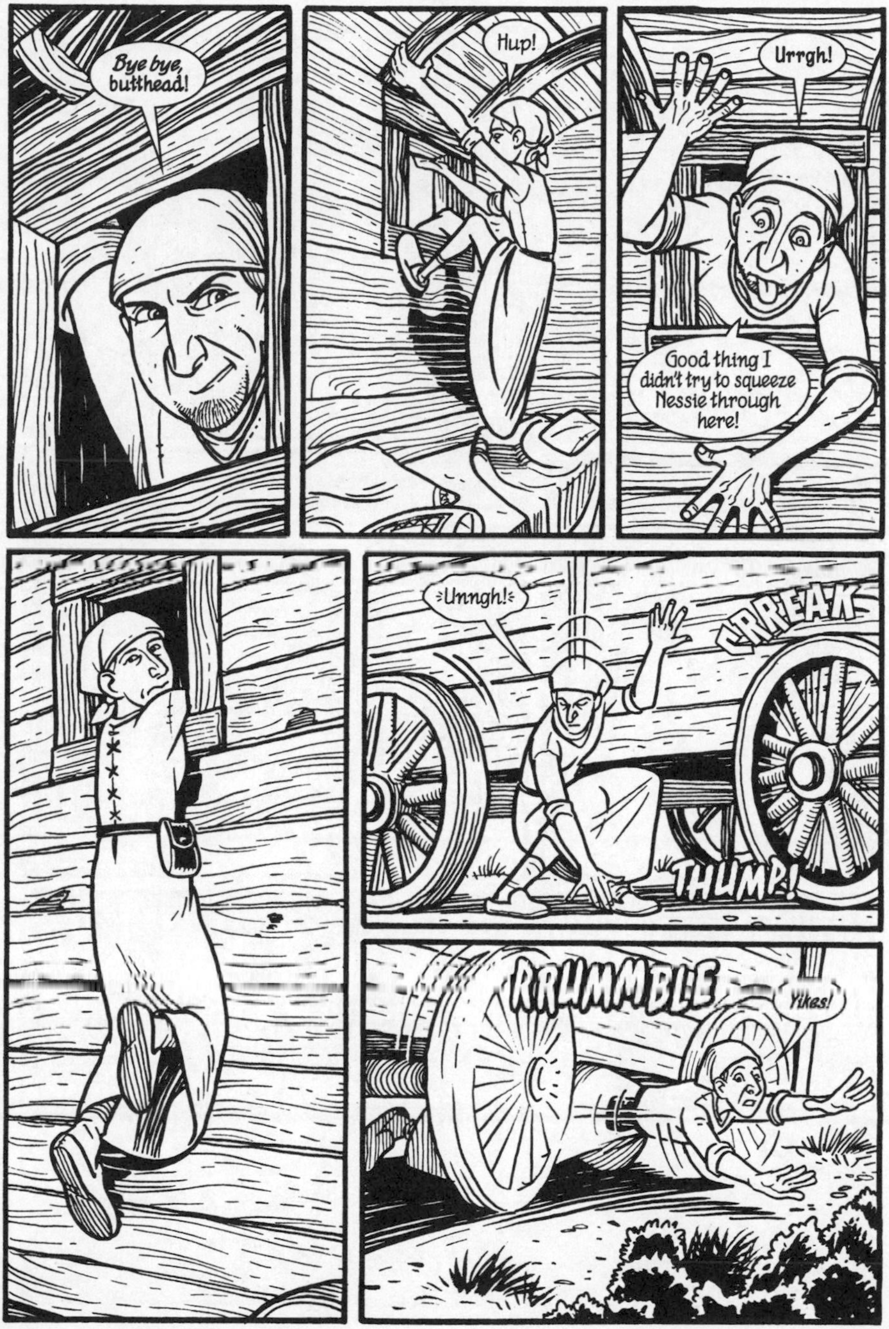
Bye bye, butthead!
Hup!
Urrgh!
Good thing I didn't try to squeeze Nessie through here!
Unngh!
CRREAK
THUMP!
RRUMMBLE
Yikes!

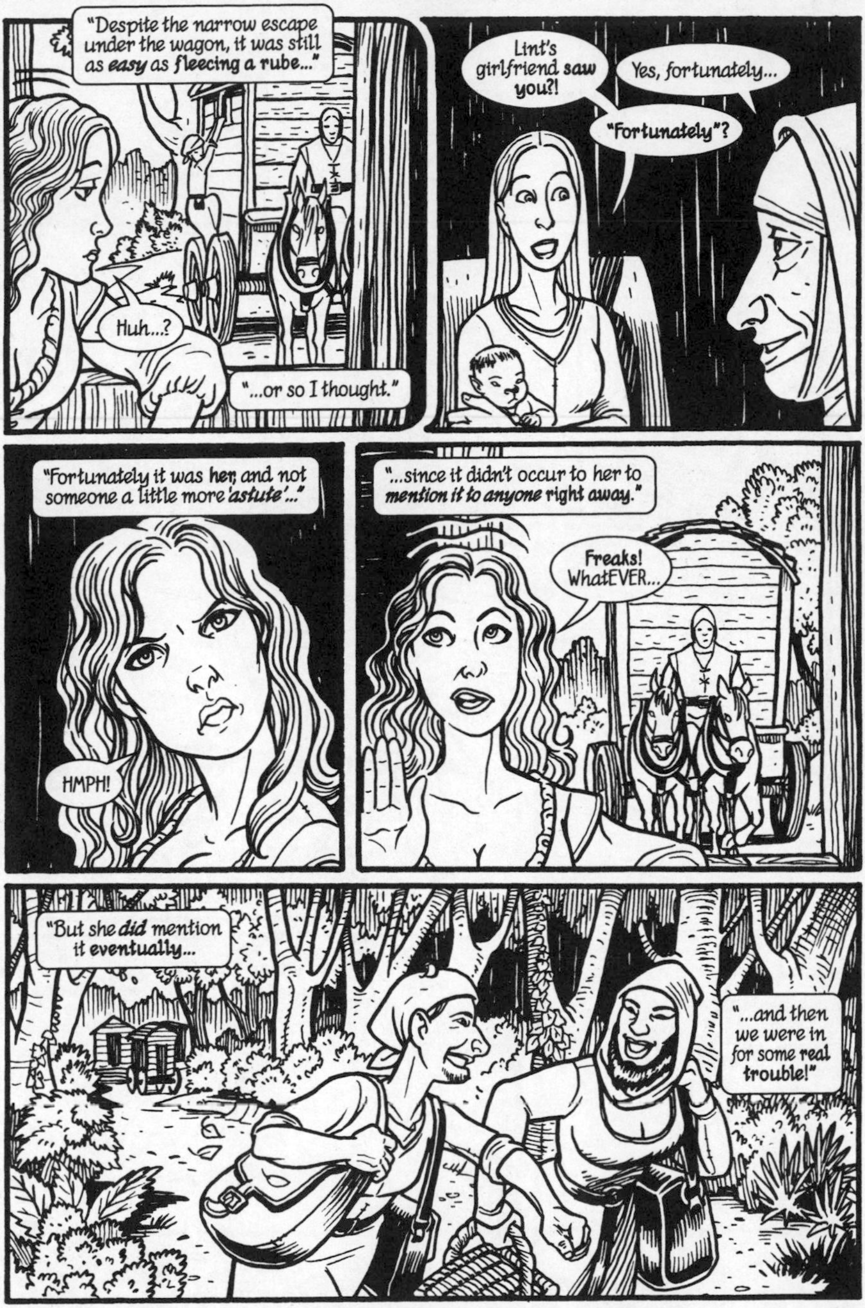
"Despite the narrow escape under the wagon, it was still as *easy* as **fleecing a rube**..."
Huh...?
"...or so I thought."
Lint's girlfriend **saw** you?!
Yes, fortunately...
"**Fortunately**"?
"Fortunately it was **her**, and not someone a little more '*astute*'..."
HMPH!
"...since it didn't occur to her to ***mention it to anyone*** right away."
Freaks! WhatEVER...
"But she ***did*** mention it **eventually**...
"...and then we were in for some real **trouble**!"

Chapter 14.

· SOLICITINE PT. 2 ·

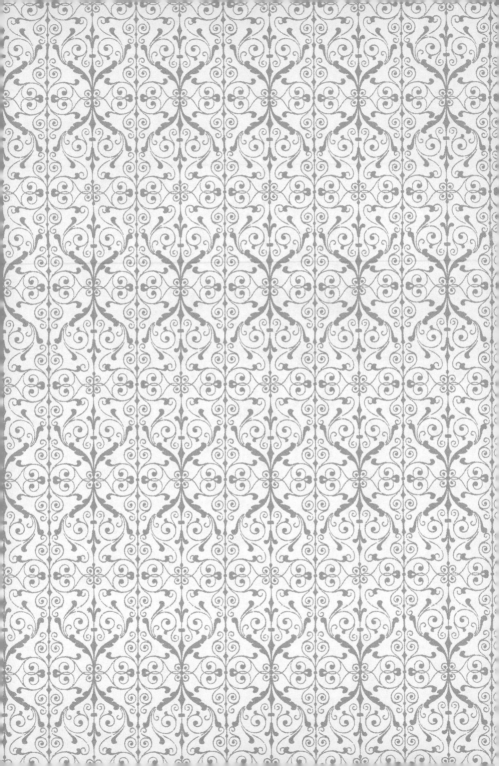

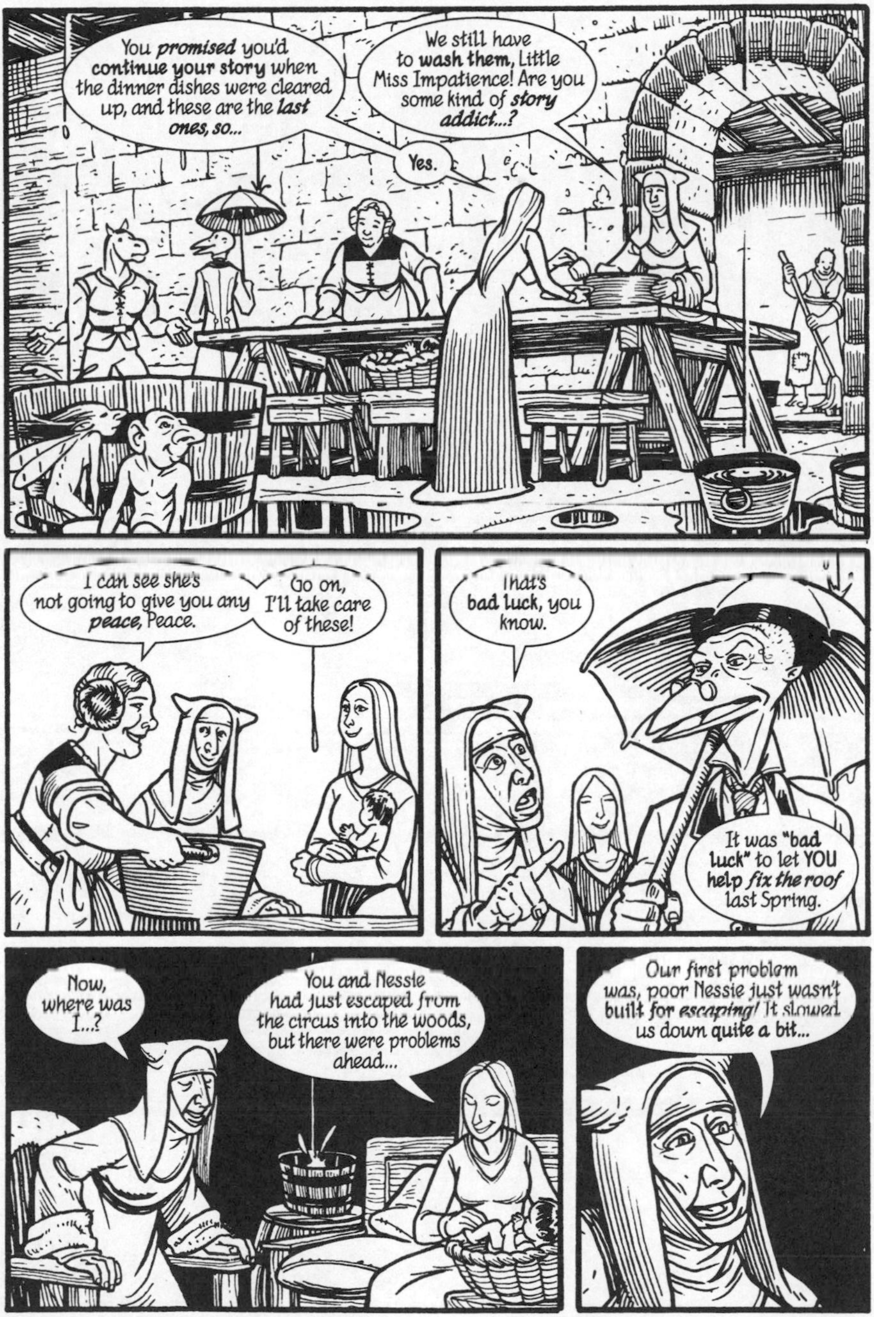
You *promised* you'd **continue your story** when the dinner dishes were cleared up, and these are the ***last ones***, so...
We still have to **wash them**, Little Miss Impatience! Are you some kind of ***story addict***...?
Yes.
I can see she's not going to give you any *peace*, Peace.
Go on, I'll take care of these!
That's **bad luck**, you know.
It was "**bad luck**" to let YOU help ***fix the roof*** last Spring.
Now, where was I...?
You and Nessie had just escaped from the circus into the woods, but there were problems ahead...
Our first problem was, poor Nessie just wasn't **built** for ***escaping***! It slowed us down **quite a bit**...

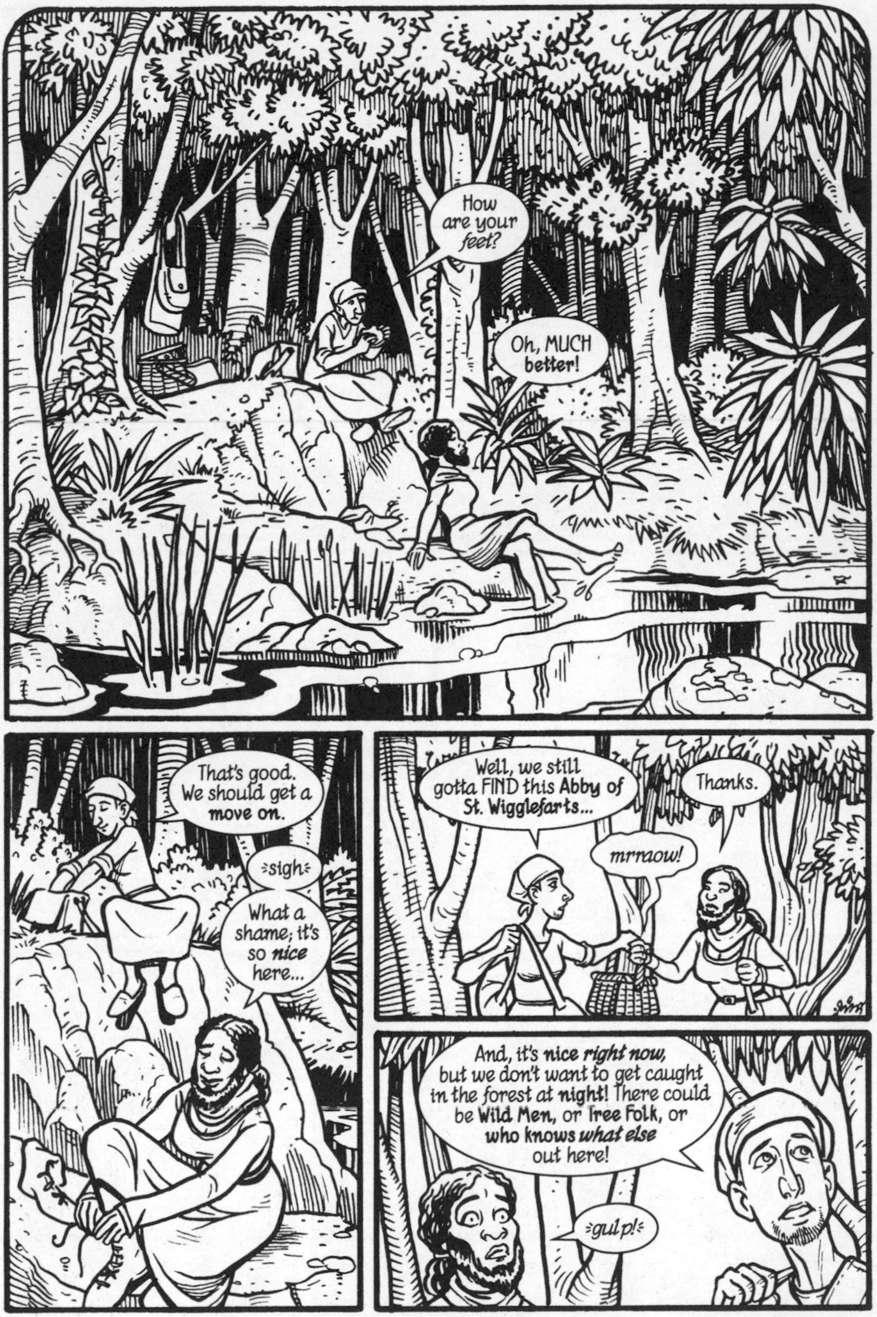
How are your feet?
Oh, MUCH better!
That's good. We should get a move on.
sigh
What a shame; it's so nice here...
Well, we still gotta FIND this Abby of St. Wigglefarts...
Thanks.
mrraow!
And, it's nice right now, but we don't want to get caught in the forest at night! There could be Wild Men, or Tree Folk, or who knows what else out here!
gulp!

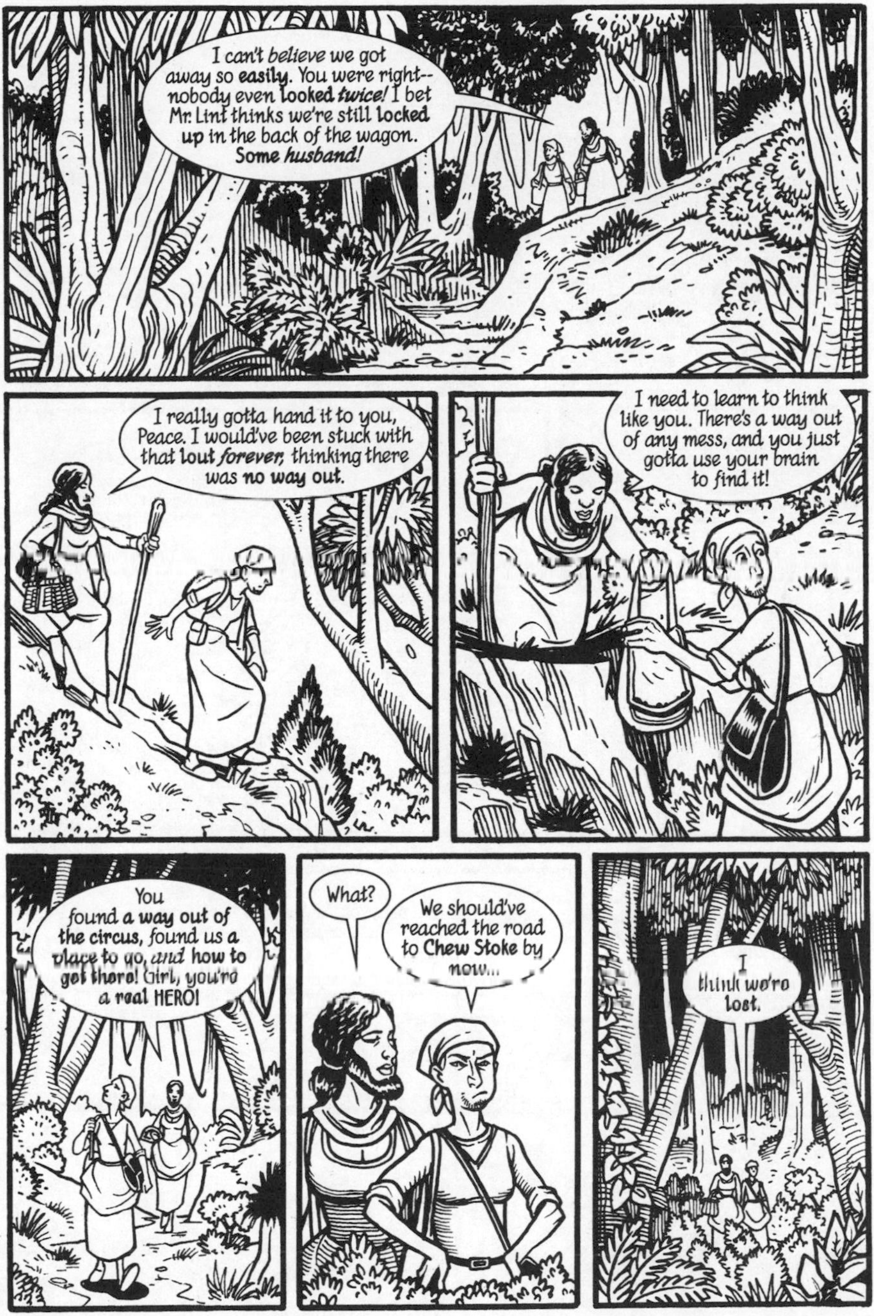
I can't believe we got away so easily. You were right-- nobody even looked twice! I bet Mr. Lint thinks we're still locked up in the back of the wagon. Some husband!
I really gotta hand it to you, Peace. I would've been stuck with that lout forever, thinking there was no way out.
I need to learn to think like you. There's a way out of any mess, and you just gotta use your brain to find it!
You found a way out of the circus, found us a place to go, and how to get there! Girl, you're a real HERO!
What?
We should've reached the road to Chew Stoke by now...
I think we're lost.

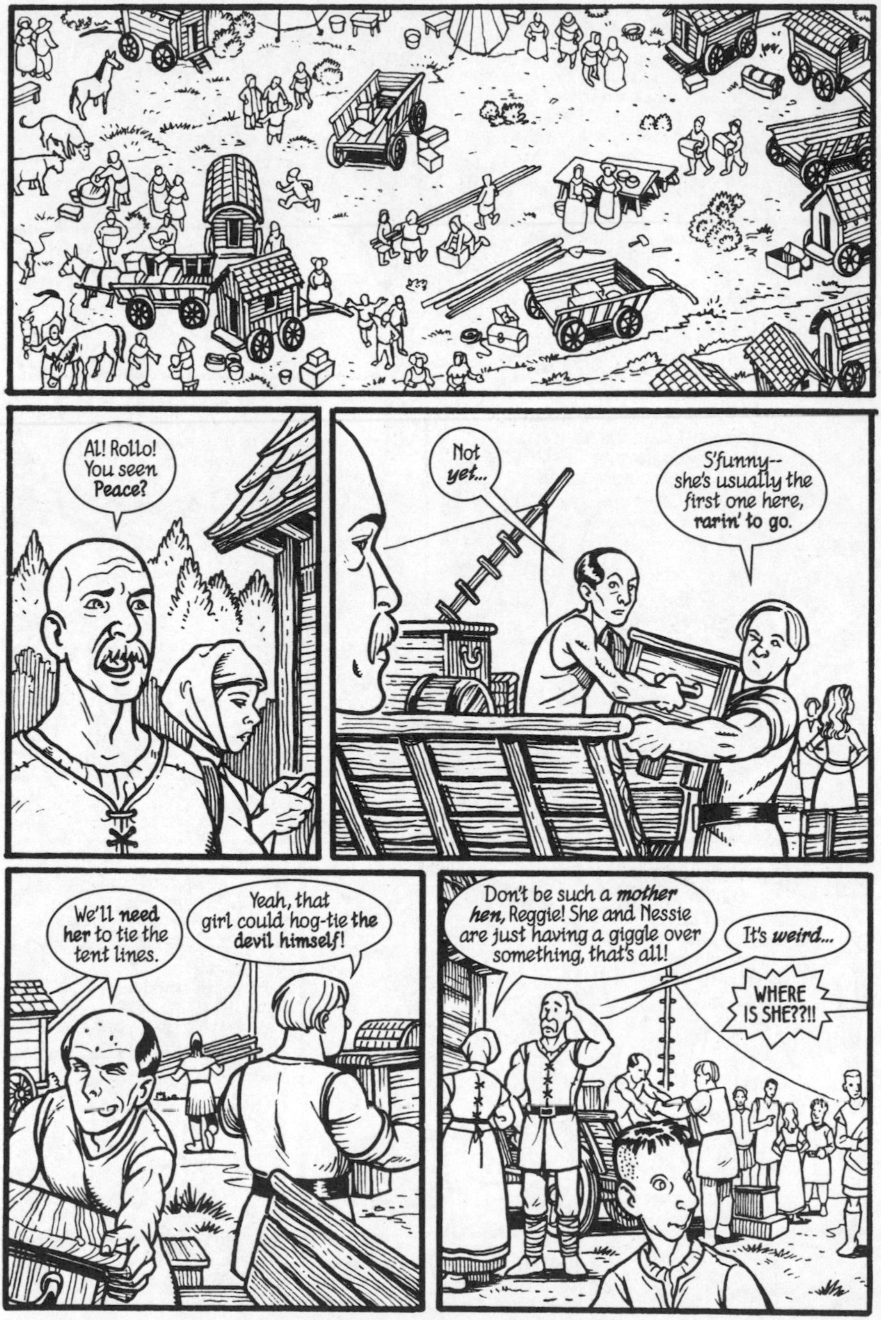
Al! Rollo! You seen Peace?
Not yet...
S'funny-- she's usually the first one here, rarin' to go.
We'll need her to tie the tent lines.
Yeah, that girl could hog-tie the devil himself!
Don't be such a mother hen, Reggie! She and Nessie are just having a giggle over something, that's all!
It's weird...
WHERE IS SHE??!!

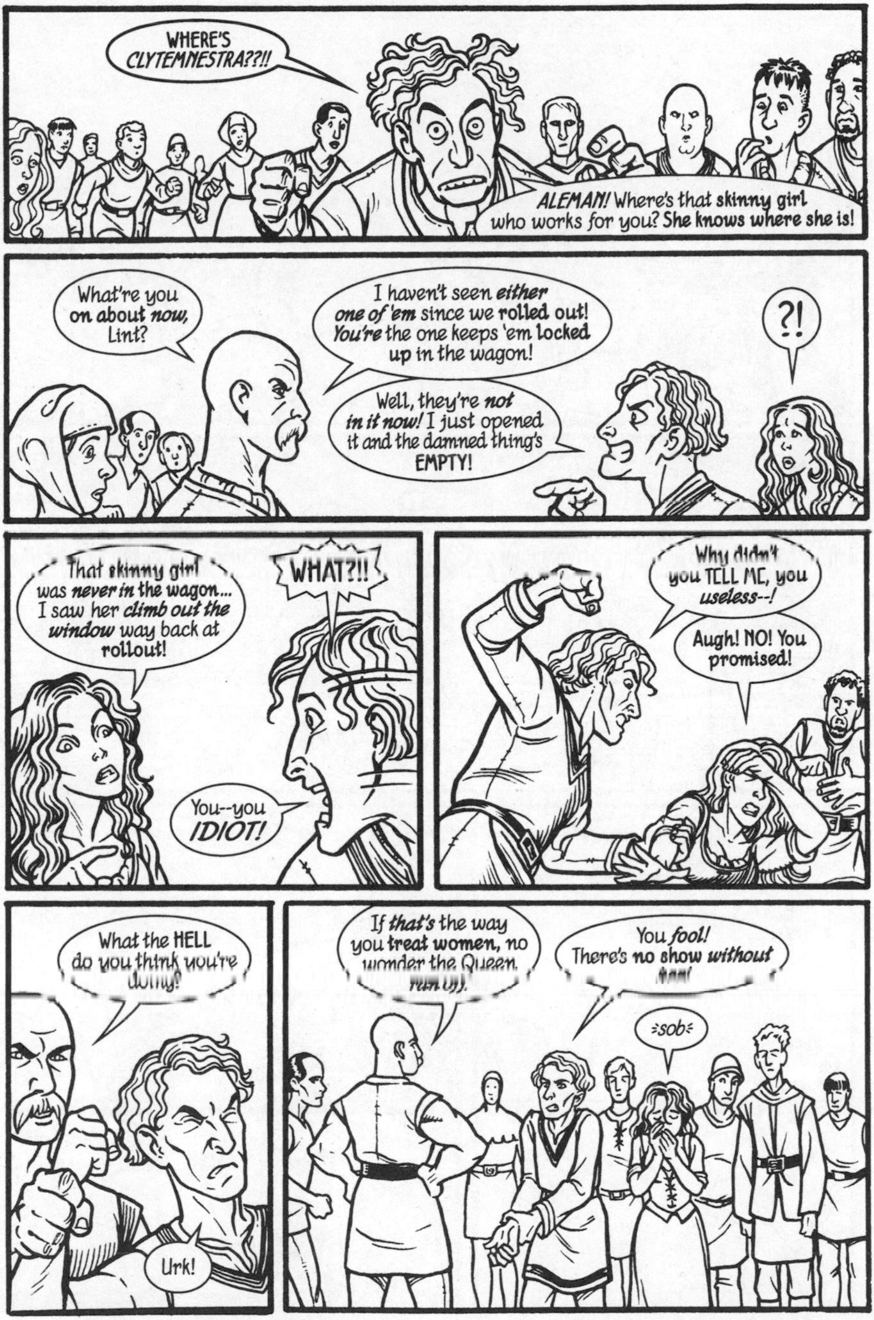
WHERE'S CLYTEMNESTRA??!!
ALEMAN! Where's that skinny girl who works for you? She knows where she is!
What're you on about now, Lint?
I haven't seen either one of 'em since we rolled out! You're the one keeps 'em locked up in the wagon!
Well, they're not in it now! I just opened it and the damned thing's EMPTY!
?!
That skinny girl was never in the wagon... I saw her climb out the window way back at rollout!
WHAT?!!
You--you IDIOT!
Why didn't you TELL ME, you useless--!
Augh! NO! You promised!
What the HELL do you think you're doing?
Urk!
If that's the way you treat women, no wonder the Queen ran off.
You fool! There's no show without
sob

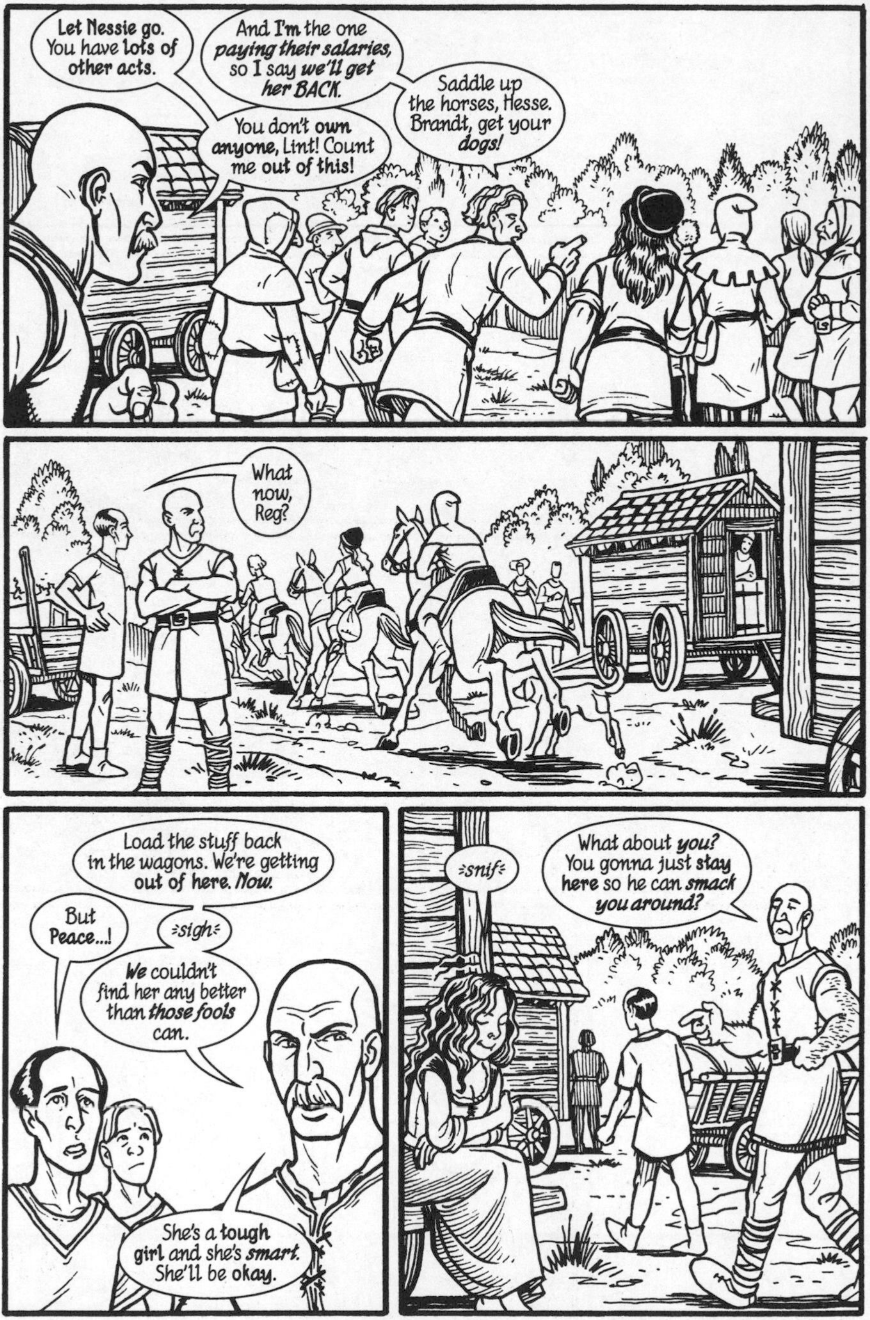
Let Nessie go. You have lots of other acts.
And I'm the one paying their salaries, so I say we'll get her BACK.
You don't own anyone, Lint! Count me out of this!
Saddle up the horses, Hesse. Brandt, get your dogs!
What now, Reg?
Load the stuff back in the wagons. We're getting out of here. Now.
But Peace...!
sigh
We couldn't find her any better than those fools can.
She's a tough girl and she's smart. She'll be okay.
snif
What about you? You gonna just stay here so he can smack you around?

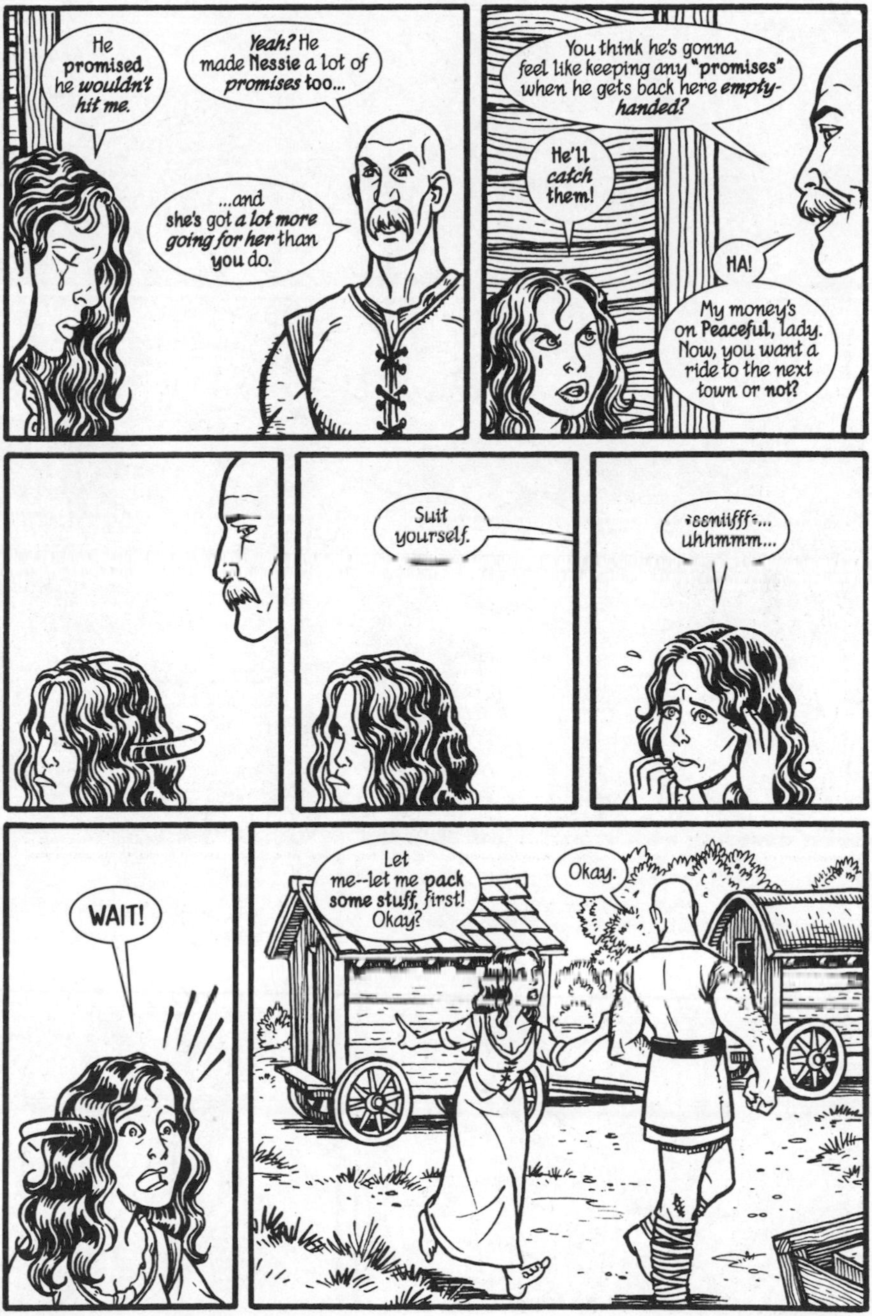
He promised he wouldn't hit me.
Yeah? He made Nessie a lot of promises too...
...and she's got a lot more going for her than you do.
You think he's gonna feel like keeping any "promises" when he gets back here empty-handed?
He'll catch them!
HA!
My money's on Peaceful, lady. Now, you want a ride to the next town or not?
Suit yourself.
snifff... uhhmmm...
WAIT!
Let me--let me pack some stuff, first! Okay?
Okay.

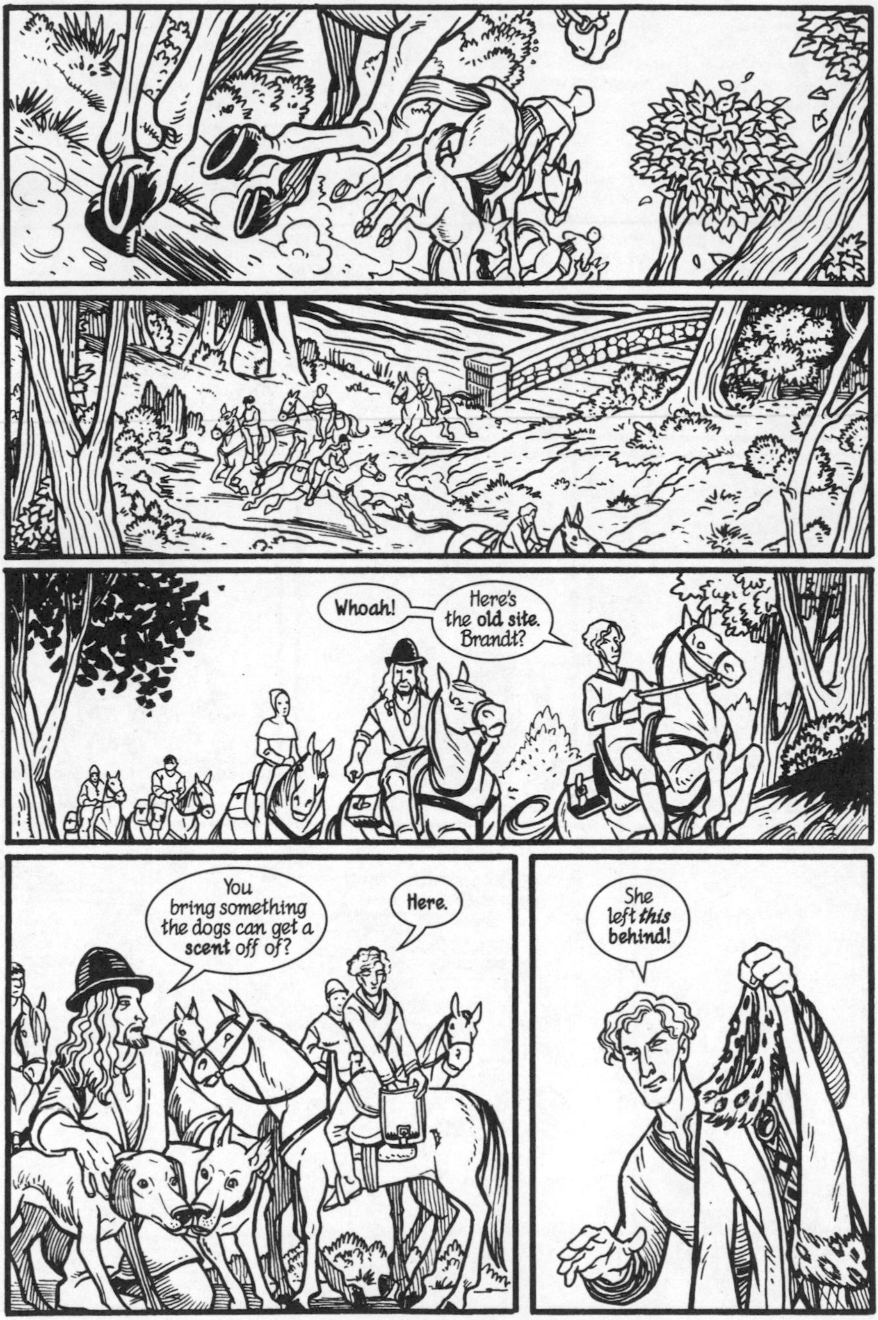
Whoah!
Here's the old site. Brandt?
You bring something the dogs can get a scent off of?
Here.
She left this behind!

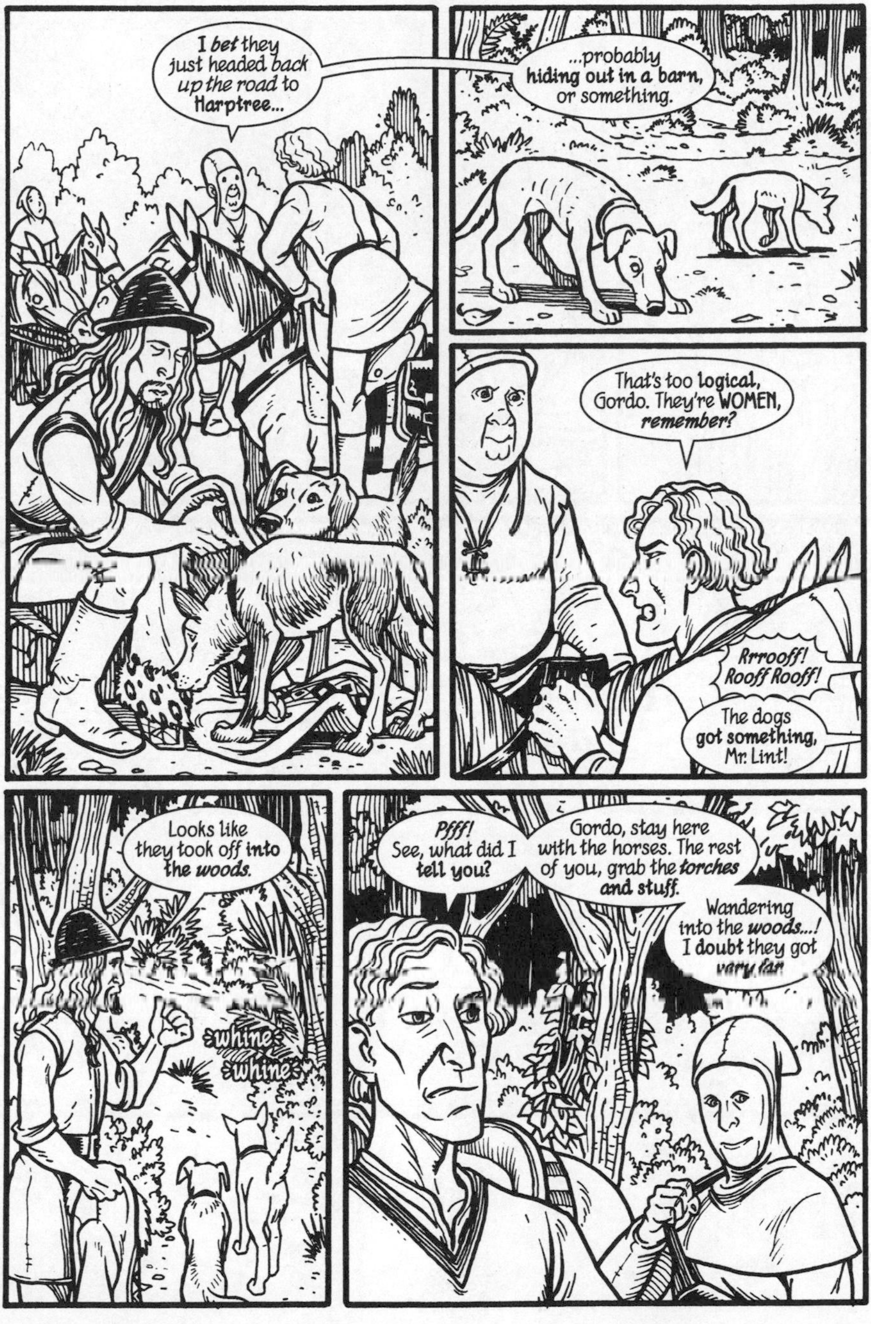
I bet they just headed back up the road to Harptree...
...probably hiding out in a barn, or something.
That's too logical, Gordo. They're WOMEN, remember?
Rrrooff! Rooff Rooff!
The dogs got something, Mr. Lint!
Looks like they took off into the woods.
whine
whine
Pfff! See, what did I tell you?
Gordo, stay here with the horses. The rest of you, grab the torches and stuff.
Wandering into the woods...! I doubt they got very far

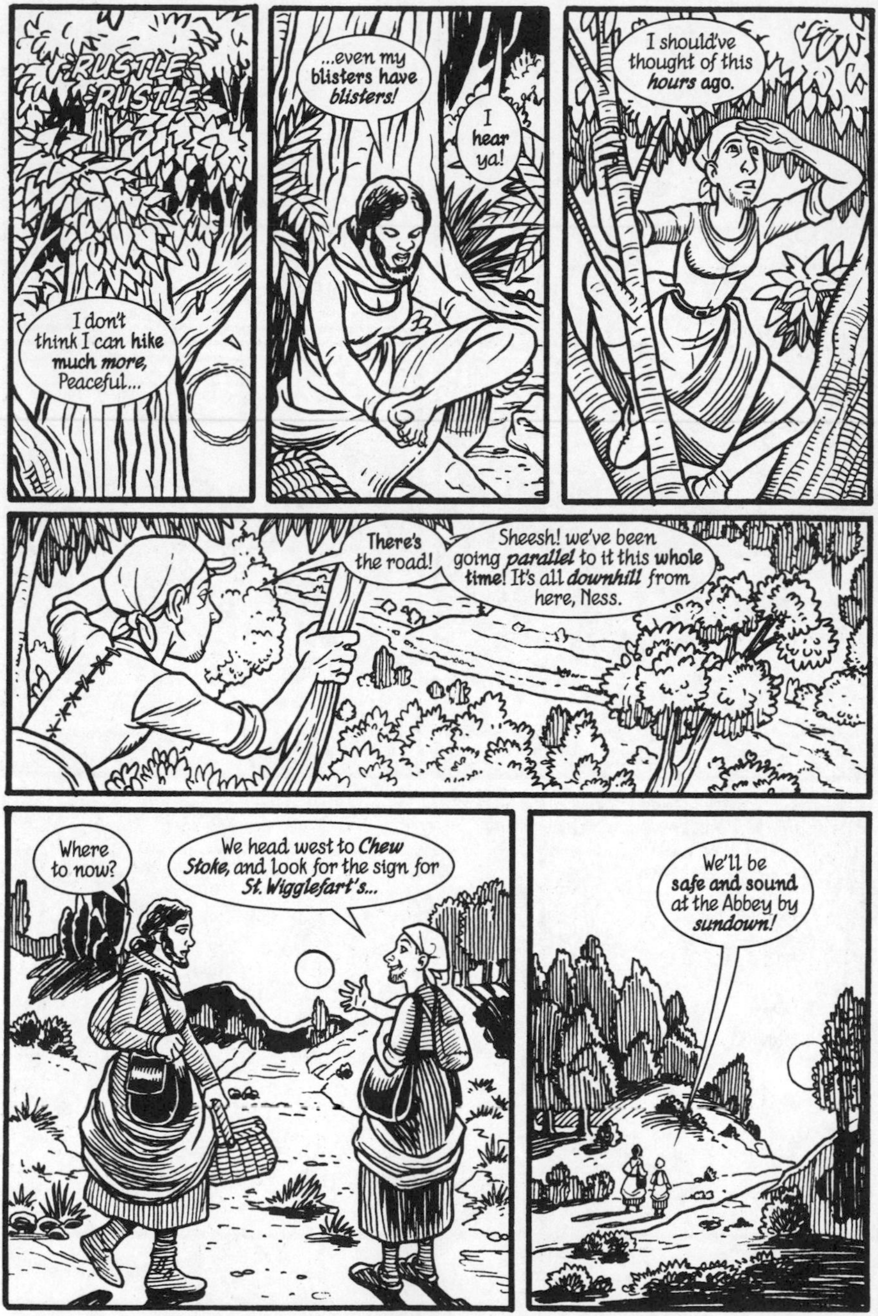
RUSTLE RUSTLE
I don't think I can hike much more, Peaceful...
...even my blisters have blisters!
I hear ya!
I should've thought of this hours ago.
There's the road!
Sheesh! we've been going parallel to it this whole time! It's all downhill from here, Ness.
Where to now?
We head west to Chew Stoke, and look for the sign for St. Wigglefart's...
We'll be safe and sound at the Abbey by sundown!

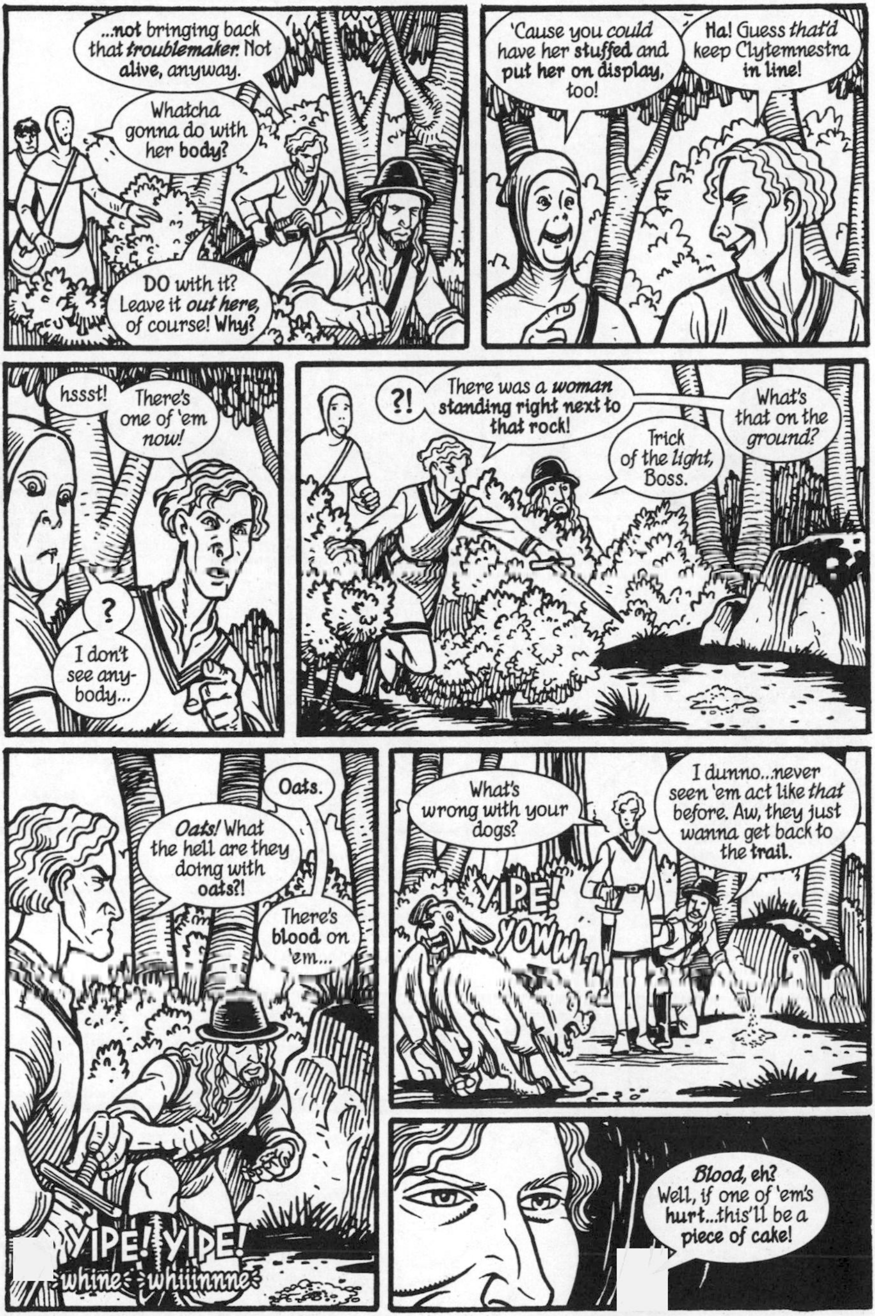
...not bringing back that troublemaker. Not alive, anyway.
Whatcha gonna do with her body?
DO with it? Leave it out here, of course! Why?
'Cause you could have her stuffed and put her on display, too!
Ha! Guess that'd keep Clytemnestra in line!
hssst!
There's one of 'em now!
?
I don't see any-body...
?!
There was a woman standing right next to that rock!
Trick of the light, Boss.
What's that on the ground?
Oats.
Oats! What the hell are they doing with oats?!
There's blood on 'em....
YIPE! YIPE!
whine whiiinnne
What's wrong with your dogs?
I dunno...never seen 'em act like that before. Aw, they just wanna get back to the trail.
YIPE!
YOWW!
Blood, eh? Well, if one of 'em's hurt...this'll be a piece of cake!

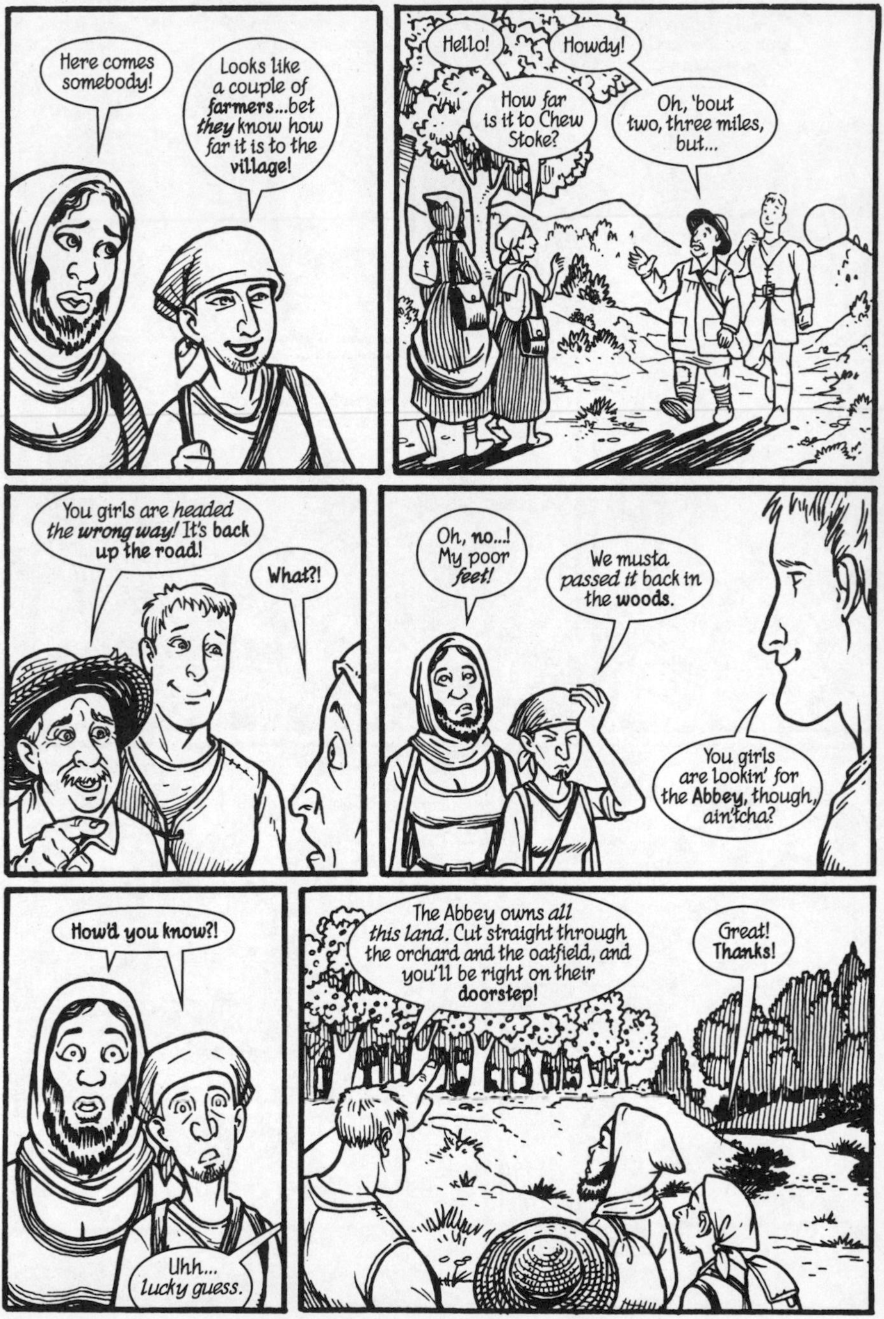
Here comes somebody!
Looks like a couple of **farmers**...bet ***they*** know how far it is to the **village**!
Hello!
Howdy!
How far is it to Chew Stoke?
Oh, 'bout two, three miles, but...
You girls are *headed the **wrong** way!* It's back up the road!
What?!
Oh, **no**...! My poor ***feet!***
We musta *passed it* back in the **woods.**
You girls are lookin' for the **Abbey**, though, ain'tcha?
How'd you know?!
Uhh... *lucky guess.*
The Abbey owns *all this land.* Cut straight through the orchard and the oatfield, and you'll be right on their **doorstep!**
Great! **Thanks!**

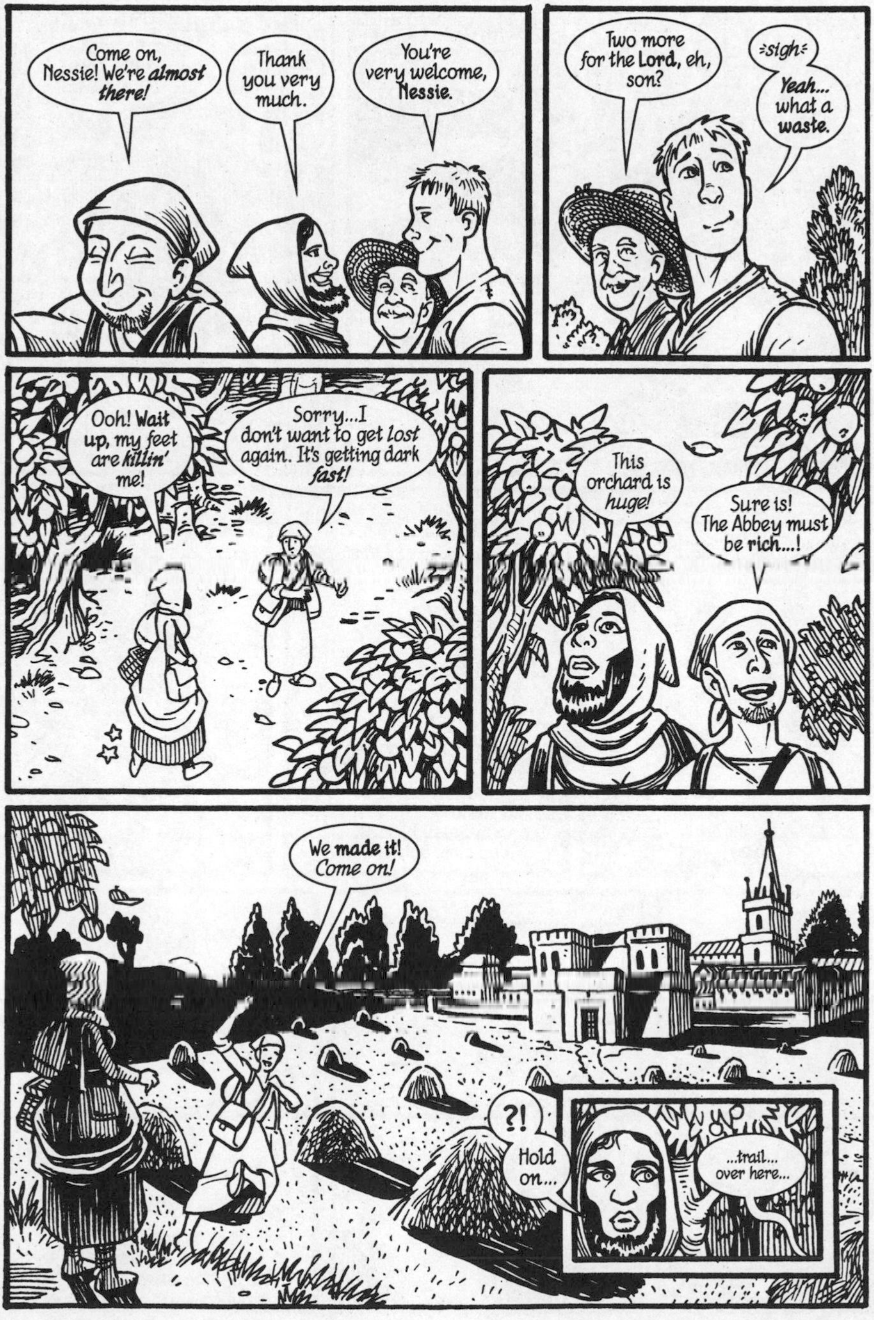
Come on, Nessie! We're *almost there!*
Thank you very much.
You're very welcome, Nessie.
Two more for the Lord, eh, son?
sigh
Yeah... what a waste.
Ooh! Wait up, my feet are *killin'* me!
Sorry...I don't want to get *lost* again. It's getting dark *fast!*
This orchard is *huge!*
Sure is! The Abbey must be rich...!
We made it! Come on!
?!
Hold on...
...trail... over here...

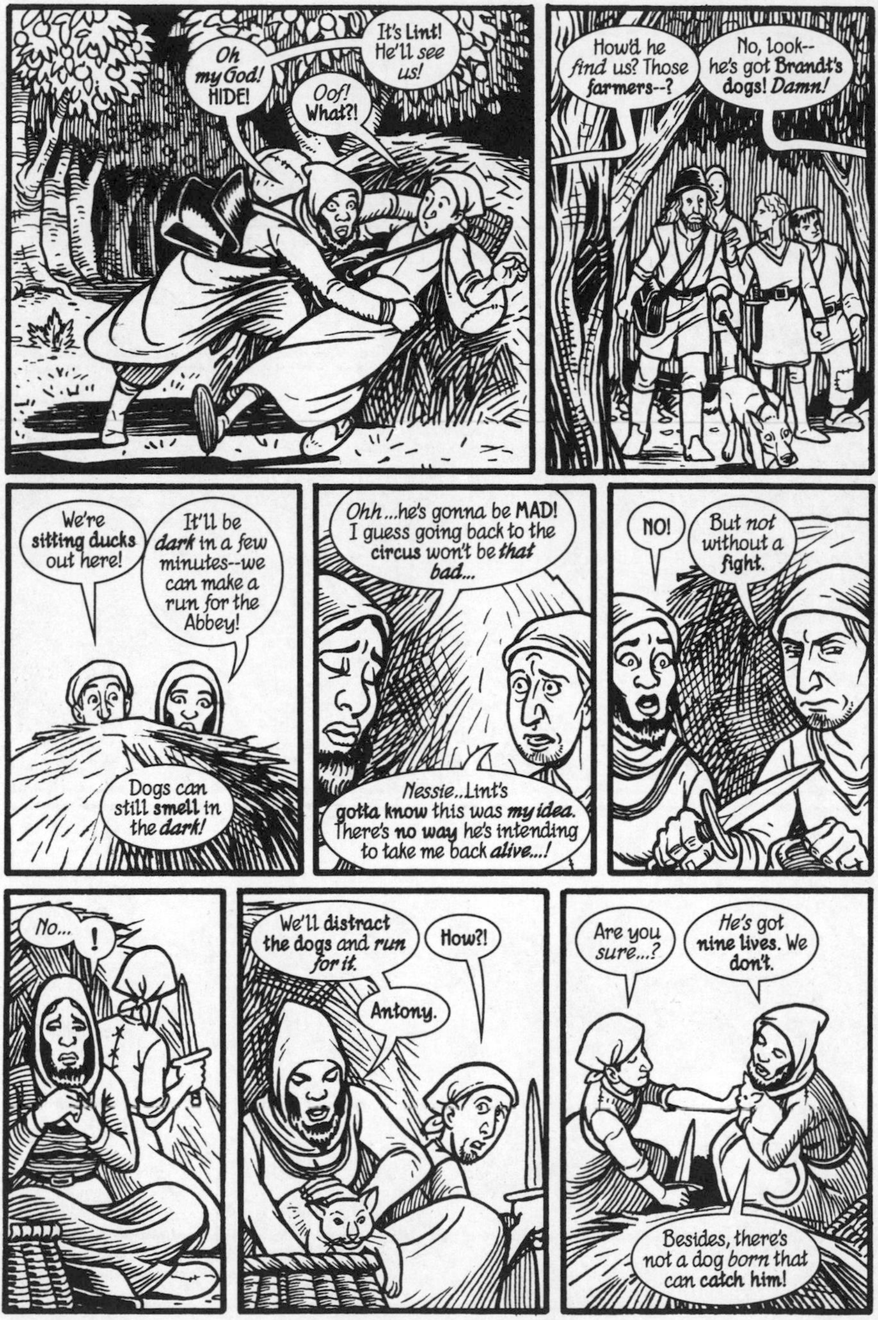
Oh my God! HIDE!
It's Lint! He'll see us!
Oof! What?!
How'd he find us? Those farmers--?
No, look-- he's got Brandt's dogs! Damn!
We're sitting ducks out here!
It'll be dark in a few minutes--we can make a run for the Abbey!
Dogs can still smell in the dark!
Ohh...he's gonna be MAD! I guess going back to the circus won't be that bad...
Nessie...Lint's gotta know this was my idea. There's no way he's intending to take me back alive...!
NO!
But not without a fight.
No...
!
We'll distract the dogs and run for it.
How?!
Antony.
Are you sure...?
He's got nine lives. We don't.
Besides, there's not a dog born that can catch him!

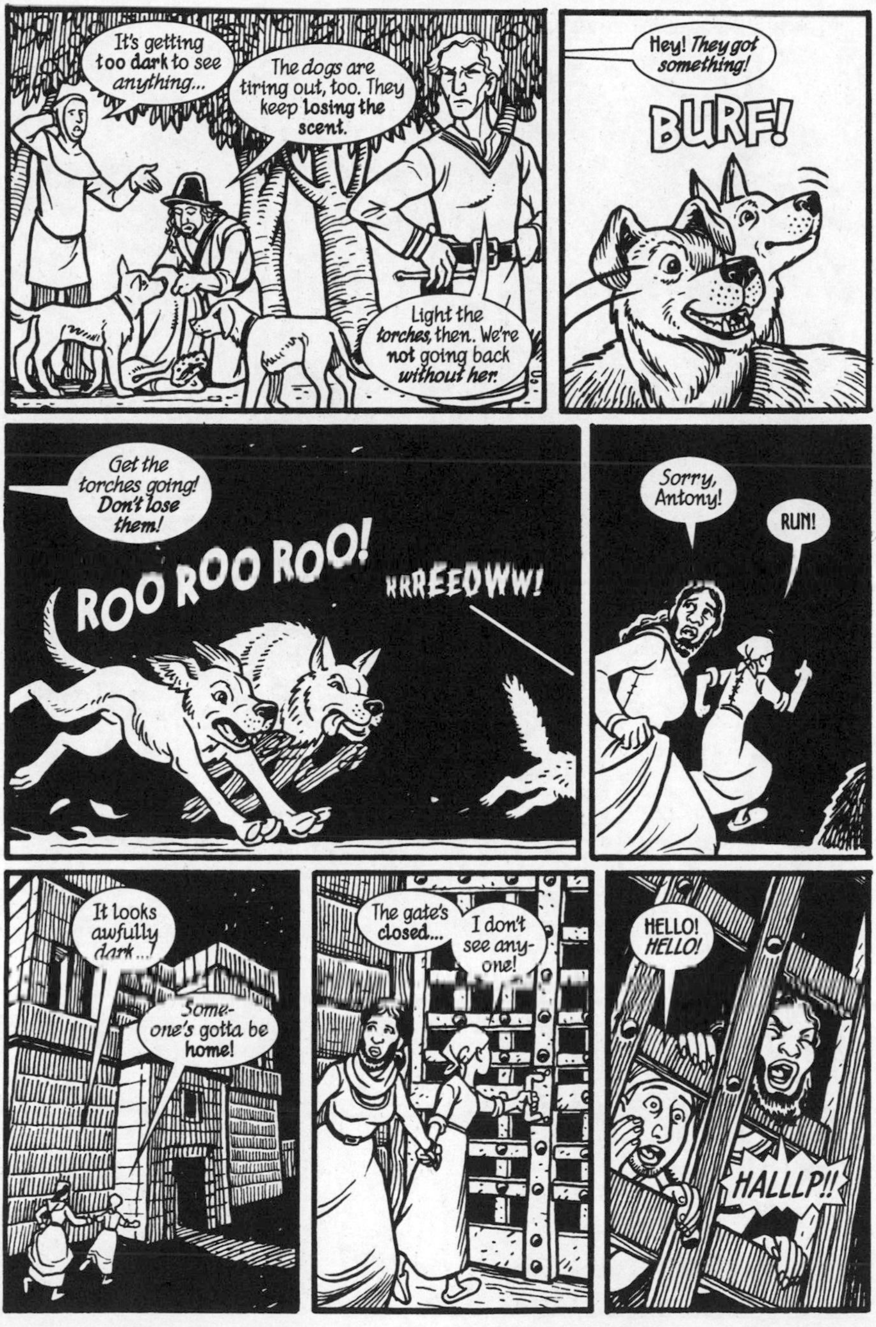
It's getting too dark to see anything...
The dogs are tiring out, too. They keep losing the scent.
Light the torches, then. We're not going back without her.
Hey! They got something!
BURF!
Get the torches going! Don't lose them!
ROO ROO ROO!
HRREEOWW!
Sorry, Antony!
RUN!
It looks awfully dark...
Some-one's gotta be home!
The gate's closed...
I don't see any-one!
HELLO! HELLO!
HALLLP!!

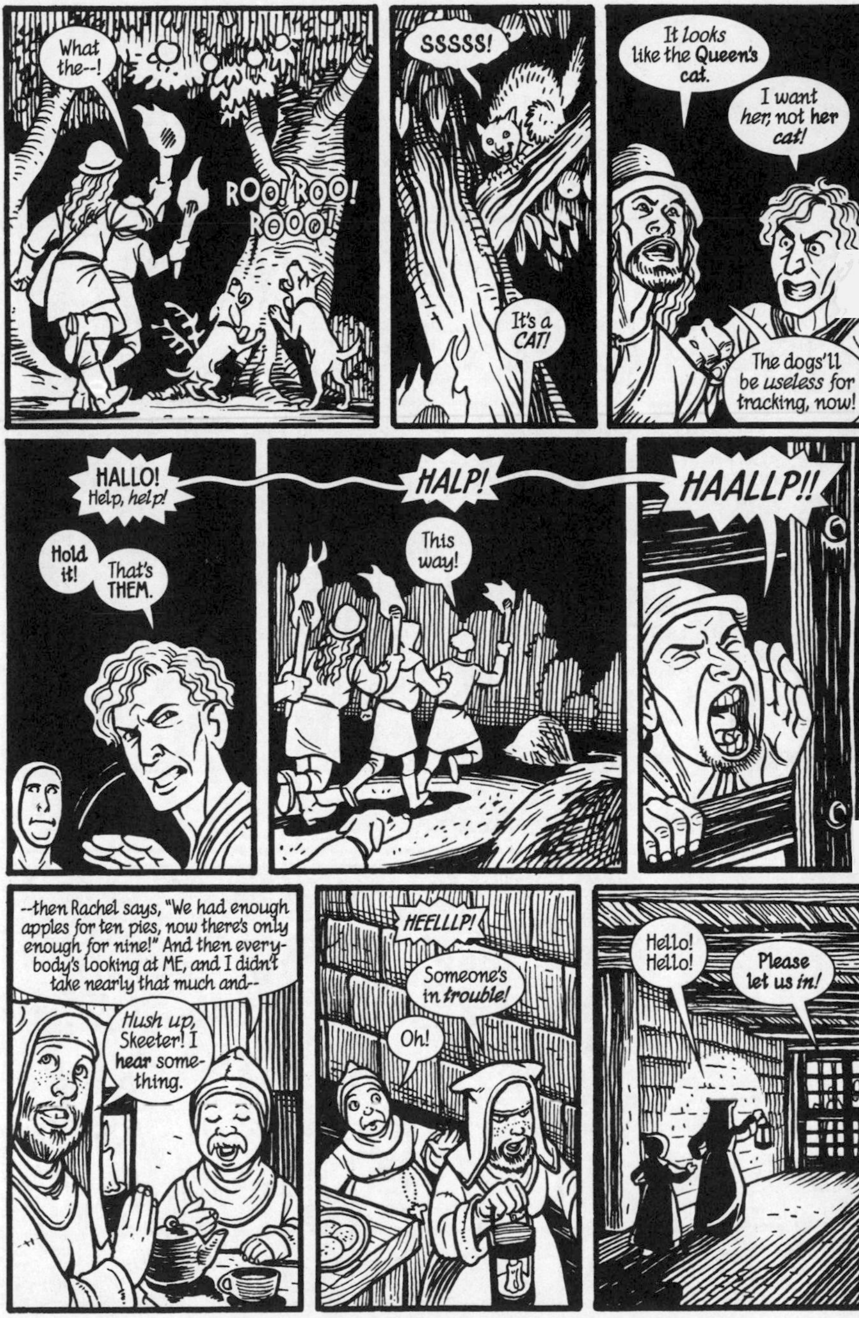
What the--!
ROO! ROO! ROOO!
SSSSS!
It's a CAT!
It looks like the Queen's cat.
I want her, not her cat!
The dogs'll be useless for tracking, now!
HALLO! Help, help!
HALP!
HAALLP!!
Hold it!
That's THEM.
This way!
--then Rachel says, "We had enough apples for ten pies, now there's only enough for nine!" And then everybody's looking at ME, and I didn't take nearly that much and--
Hush up, Skeeter! I hear something.
HEELLLP!
Someone's in trouble!
Oh!
Hello! Hello!
Please let us in!

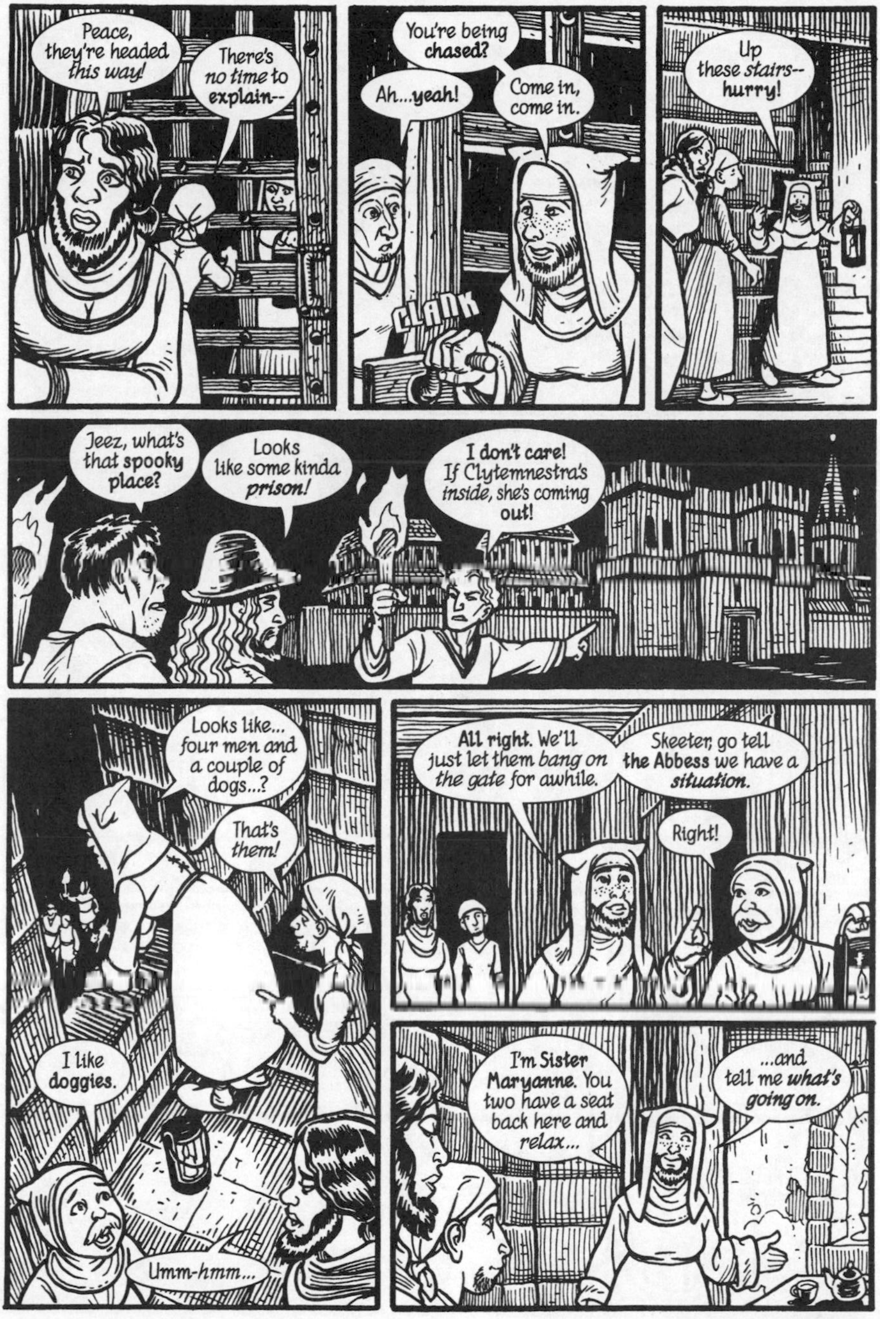

Peace, they're headed *this way!*
There's *no time* to **explain--**
You're being **chased?**
Ah...**yeah!**
Come in, come in.
CLANK
Up these *stairs*-- **hurry!**
Jeez, what's that **spooky** place?
Looks like some kinda *prison!*
I don't care! If Clytemnestra's *inside*, she's coming **out!**
Looks like... four men and a couple of dogs...?
That's *them!*
I like **doggies.**
Umm-*hmm*...
All right. We'll just let them *bang on the gate* for awhile.
Skeeter, go tell **the Abbess** we have a ***situation.***
Right!
I'm Sister **Maryanne.** You two have a seat back here and *relax...*
...and tell me ***what's going on.***

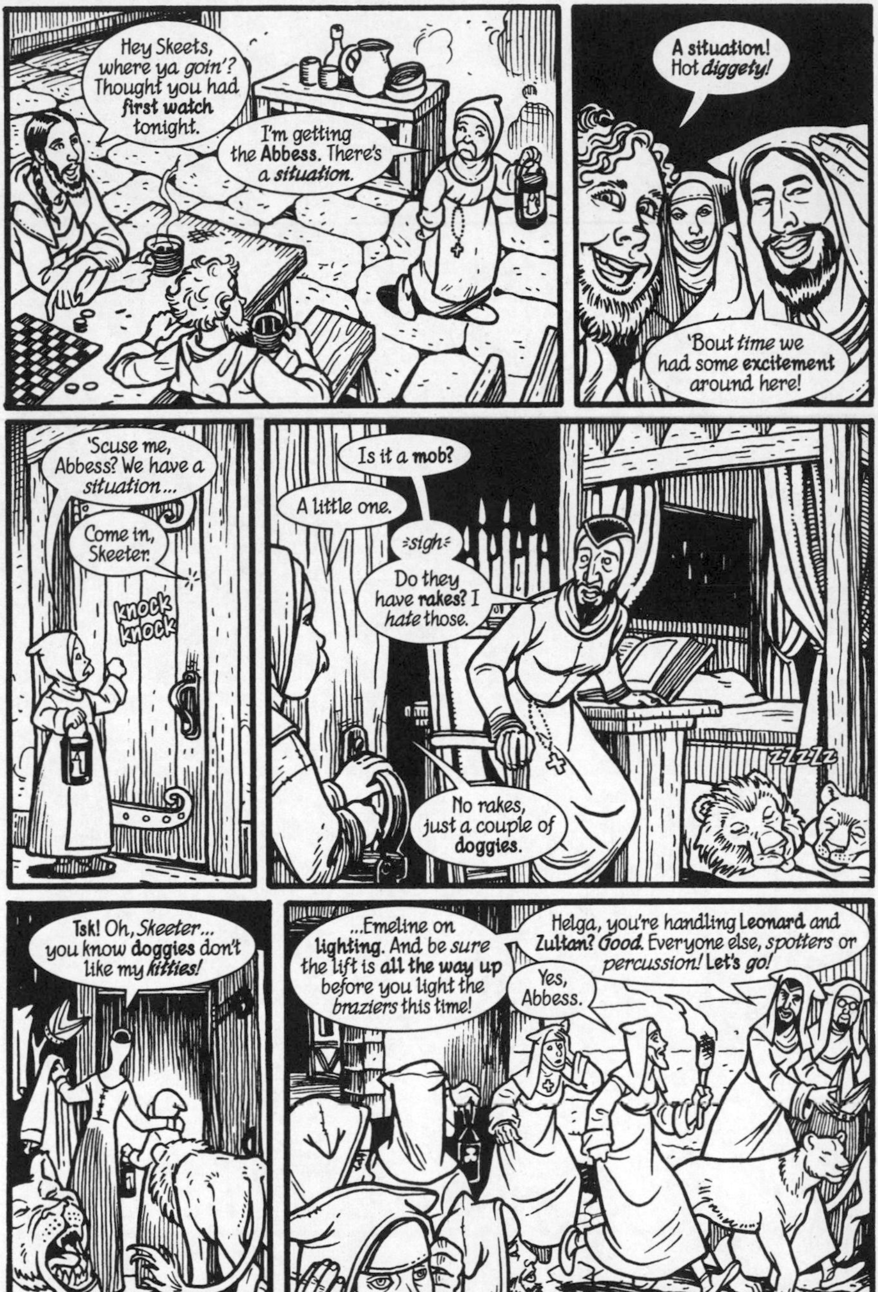
Hey Skeets, where ya goin'? Thought you had first watch tonight.
I'm getting the Abbess. There's a situation.
A situation! Hot diggety!
'Bout time we had some excitement around here!
'Scuse me, Abbess? We have a situation...
Come in, Skeeter.
knock knock
Is it a mob?
A little one.
sigh
Do they have rakes? I hate those.
No rakes, just a couple of doggies.
zzzzz
Tsk! Oh, Skeeter... you know doggies don't like my kitties!
...Emeline on lighting. And be sure the lift is all the way up before you light the braziers this time!
Helga, you're handling Leonard and Zultan? Good. Everyone else, spotters or percussion! Let's go!
Yes, Abbess.

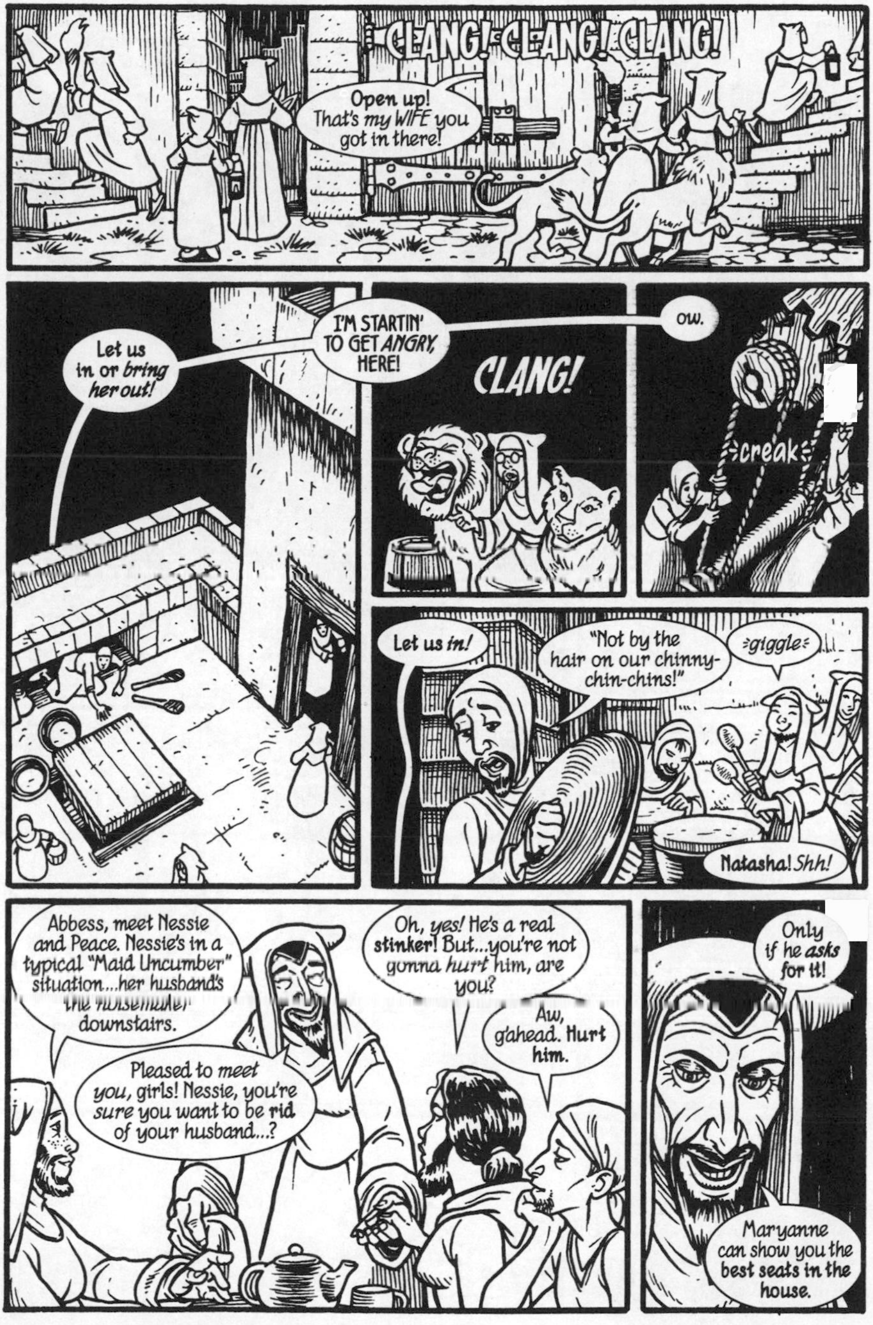
CLANG! CLANG! CLANG!
Open up! That's my *WIFE* you got in there!
Let us in or *bring* her out!
I'M STARTIN' TO GET *ANGRY*, HERE!
OW.
CLANG!
creak
Let us *in*!
"Not by the hair on our chinny-chin-chins!"
giggle
Natasha! *Shh!*
Abbess, meet Nessie and Peace. Nessie's in a typical "Maid Uncumber" situation...her husband's
downstairs.
Pleased to *meet you*, girls! Nessie, you're *sure* you want to be rid of your husband...?
Oh, *yes!* He's a real **stinker**! But...you're not gonna *hurt* him, are you?
Aw, g'ahead. **Hurt him.**
Only if he *asks* for it!
Maryanne can show you the **best seats in the house.**

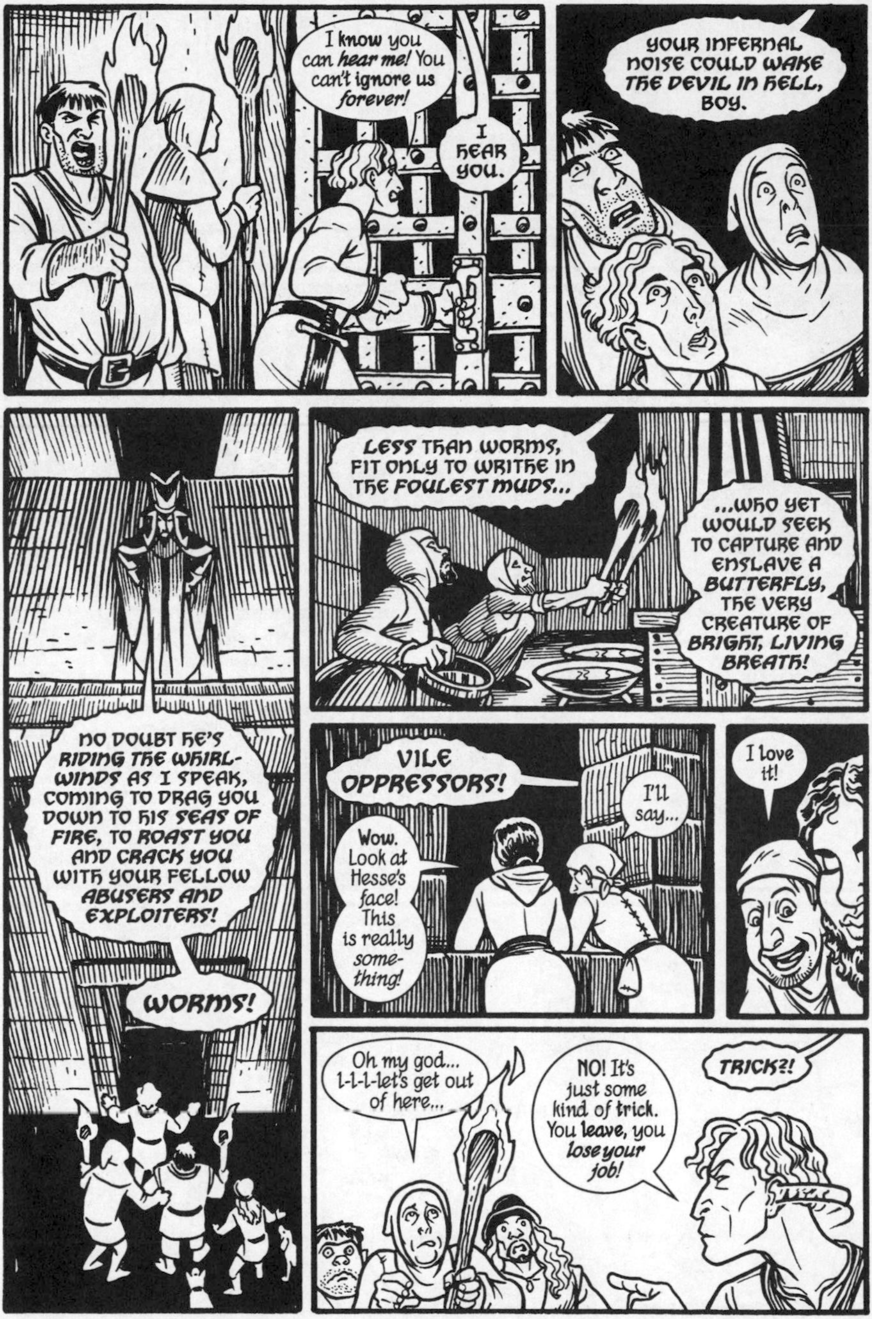
I know you can hear me! You can't ignore us forever!
I HEAR YOU.
YOUR INFERNAL NOISE COULD WAKE THE DEVIL IN HELL, BOY.
NO DOUBT HE'S RIDING THE WHIRL-WINDS AS I SPEAK, COMING TO DRAG YOU DOWN TO HIS SEAS OF FIRE, TO ROAST YOU AND CRACK YOU WITH YOUR FELLOW ABUSERS AND EXPLOITERS!
WORMS!
LESS THAN WORMS, FIT ONLY TO WRITHE IN THE FOULEST MUDS...
...WHO YET WOULD SEEK TO CAPTURE AND ENSLAVE A BUTTERFLY, THE VERY CREATURE OF BRIGHT, LIVING BREATH!
VILE OPPRESSORS!
I'll say...
Wow. Look at Hesse's face! This is really some-thing!
I love it!
Oh my god... l-l-l-let's get out of here...
NO! It's just some kind of trick. You leave, you lose your job!
TRICK?!

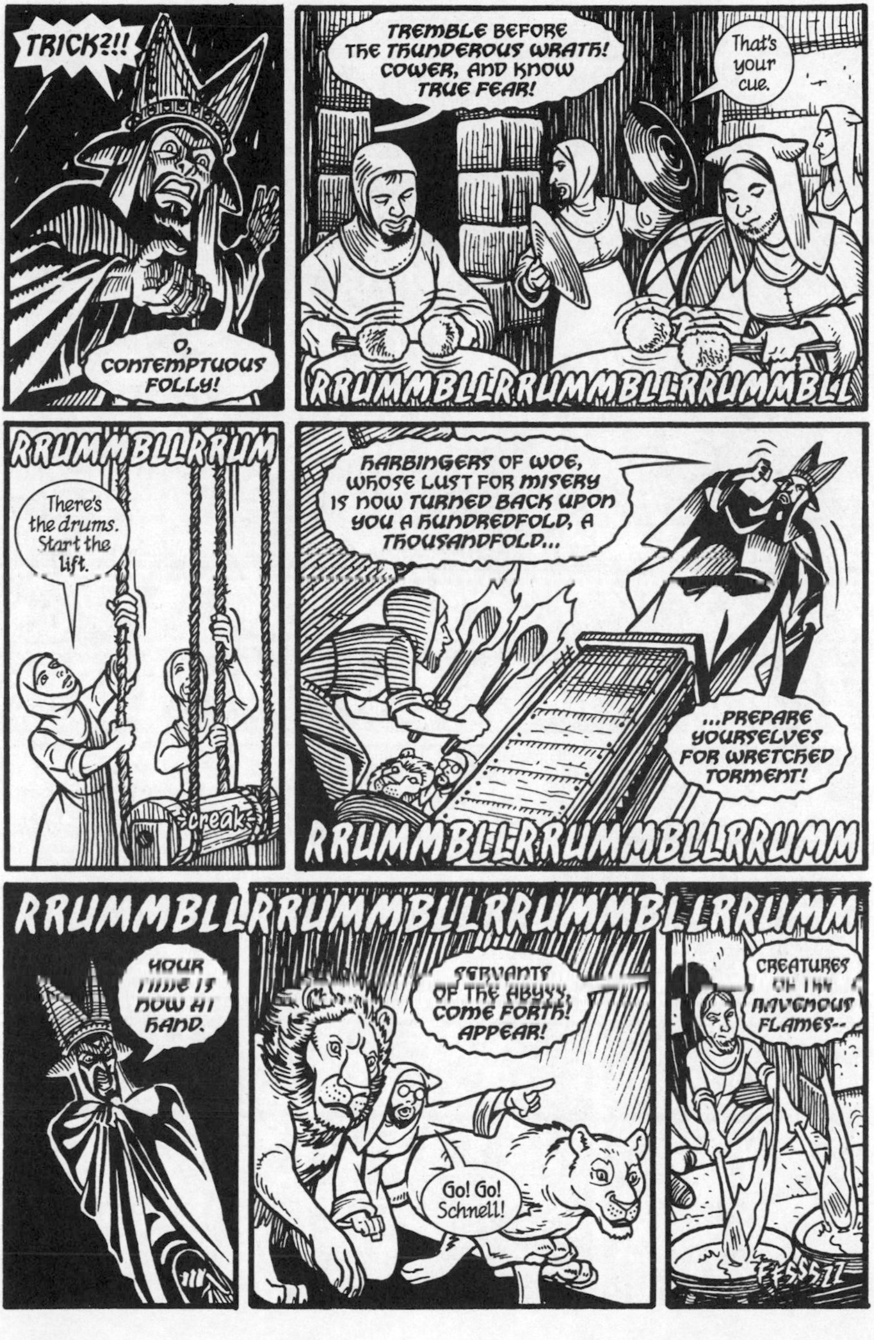
TRICK?!!
O, CONTEMPTUOUS FOLLY!
TREMBLE BEFORE THE THUNDEROUS WRATH! COWER, AND KNOW TRUE FEAR!
That's your cue.
RRUMMBLLRRUMMBLLRRUMMBLL
RRUMMBLLRRUM
There's the drums. Start the lift.
creak
HARBINGERS OF WOE, WHOSE LUST FOR MISERY IS NOW TURNED BACK UPON YOU A HUNDREDFOLD, A THOUSANDFOLD...
...PREPARE YOURSELVES FOR WRETCHED TORMENT!
RRUMMBLLRRUMMBLLRRUMM
RRUMMBLLRRUMMBLLRRUMMBLLRRUMM
YOUR TIME IS NOW AT HAND.
SERVANTS OF THE ABYSS, COME FORTH! APPEAR!
Go! Go! Schnell!
CREATURES OF THE RAVENOUS FLAMES--
FFSSSZZ

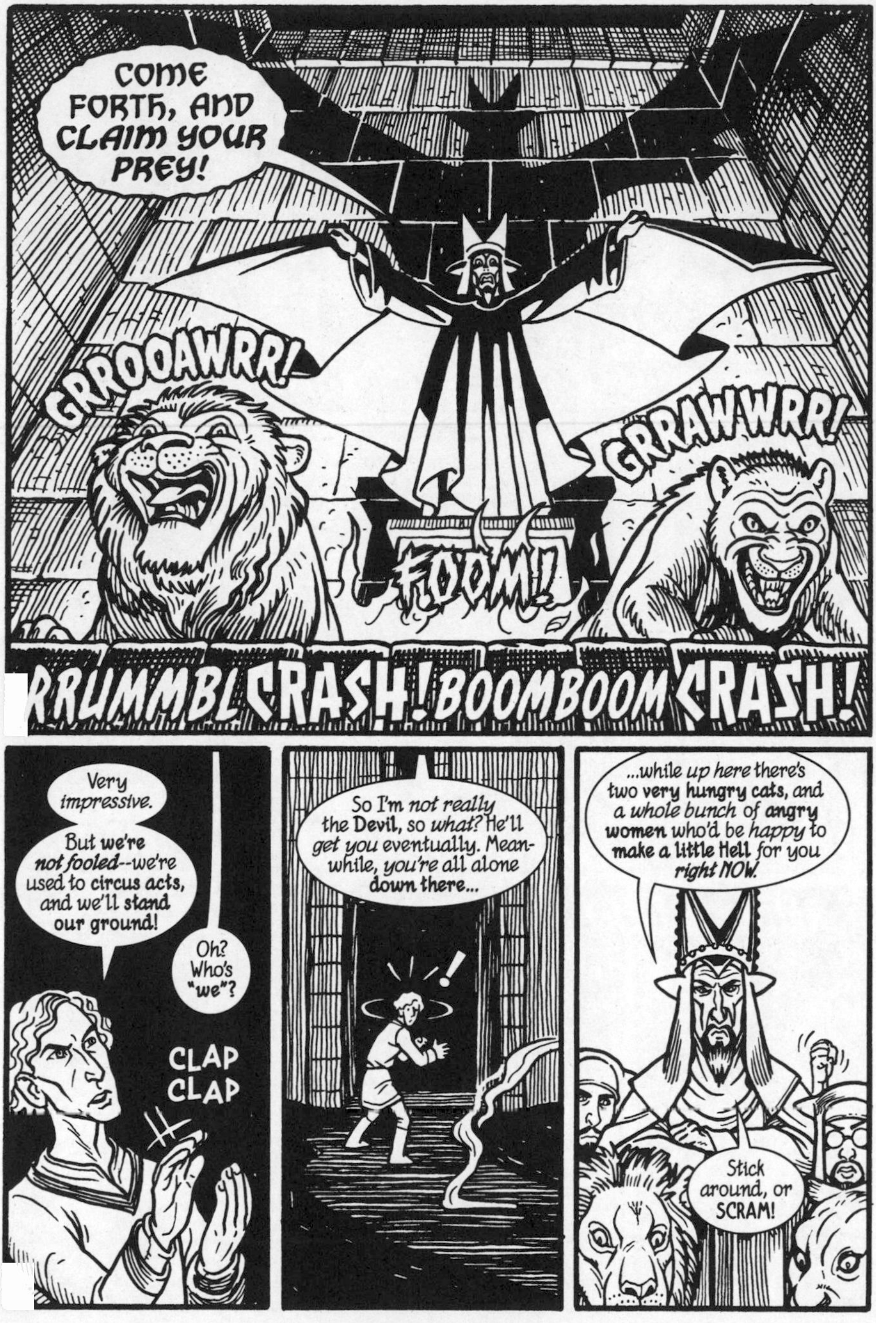
COME FORTH, AND CLAIM YOUR PREY!
GRROOAWRR!
GRRAWWRR!
FOOM!
RRUMMBL CRASH! BOOMBOOM CRASH!
Very impressive.
But we're not fooled--we're used to circus acts, and we'll stand our ground!
Oh? Who's "we"?
CLAP CLAP
So I'm not really the Devil, so what? He'll get you eventually. Meanwhile, you're all alone down there...
...while up here there's two very hungry cats, and a whole bunch of angry women who'd be happy to make a little Hell for you right NOW.
Stick around, or SCRAM!

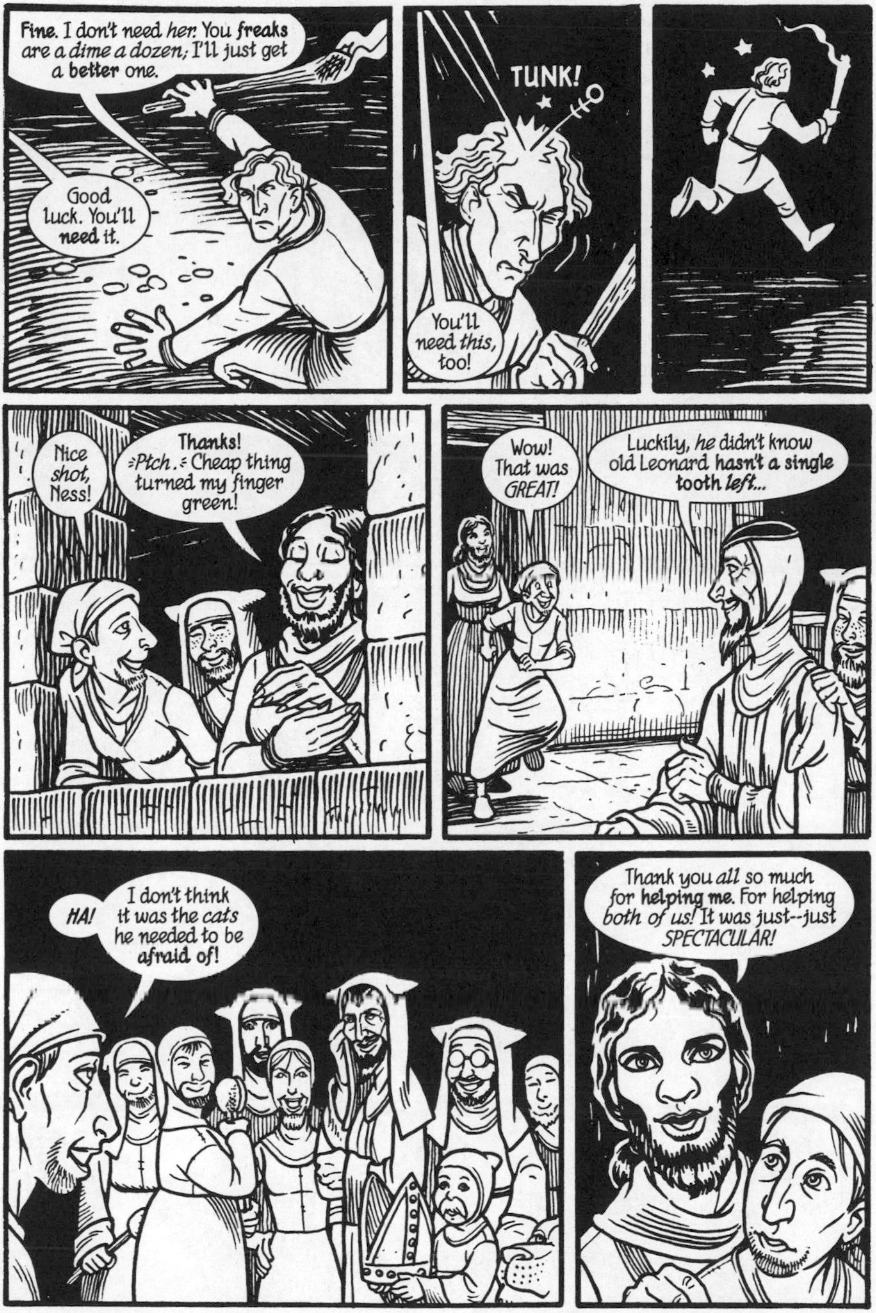
Fine. I don't need her. You freaks are a dime a dozen; I'll just get a better one.
Good luck. You'll need it.
TUNK!
You'll need this, too!
Nice shot, Ness!
Thanks! ≈Ptch.≈ Cheap thing turned my finger green!
Wow! That was GREAT!
Luckily, he didn't know old Leonard hasn't a single tooth left...
HA!
I don't think it was the cats he needed to be afraid of!
Thank you all so much for helping me. For helping both of us! It was just--just SPECTACULAR!

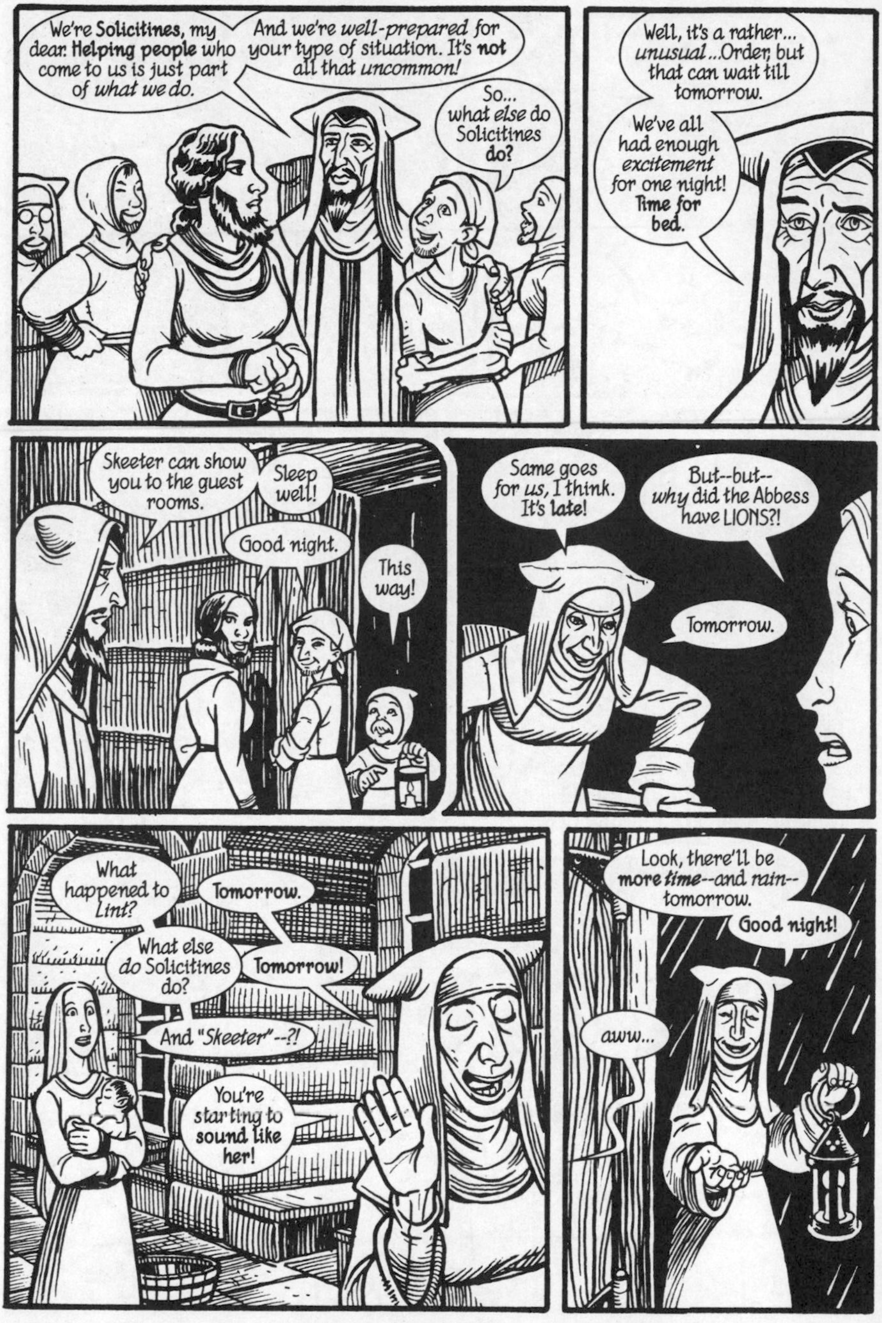

We're Solicitines, my dear. Helping people who come to us is just part of what we do.
And we're well-prepared for your type of situation. It's not all that uncommon!
So... what else do Solicitines do?
Well, it's a rather... unusual...Order, but that can wait till tomorrow.
We've all had enough excitement for one night! Time for bed.
Skeeter can show you to the guest rooms.
Sleep well!
Good night.
This way!
Same goes for us, I think. It's late!
But--but-- why did the Abbess have LIONS?!
Tomorrow.
What happened to Lint?
Tomorrow.
What else do Solicitines do?
Tomorrow!
And "Skeeter"--?!
You're starting to sound like her!
Look, there'll be more time--and rain-- tomorrow.
Good night!
aww...

Chapter 15.

· SOLICITINE PT. 3 ·

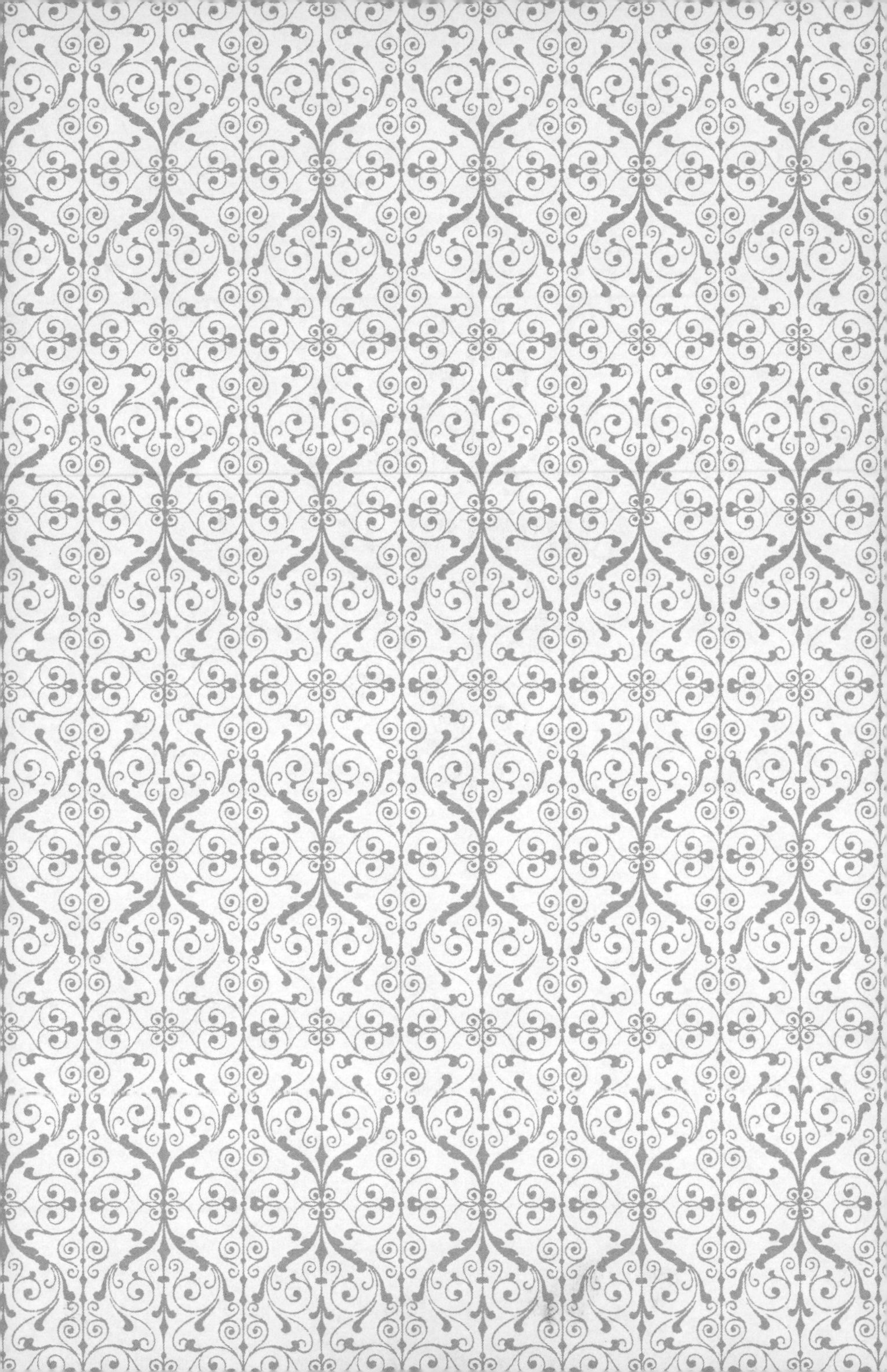

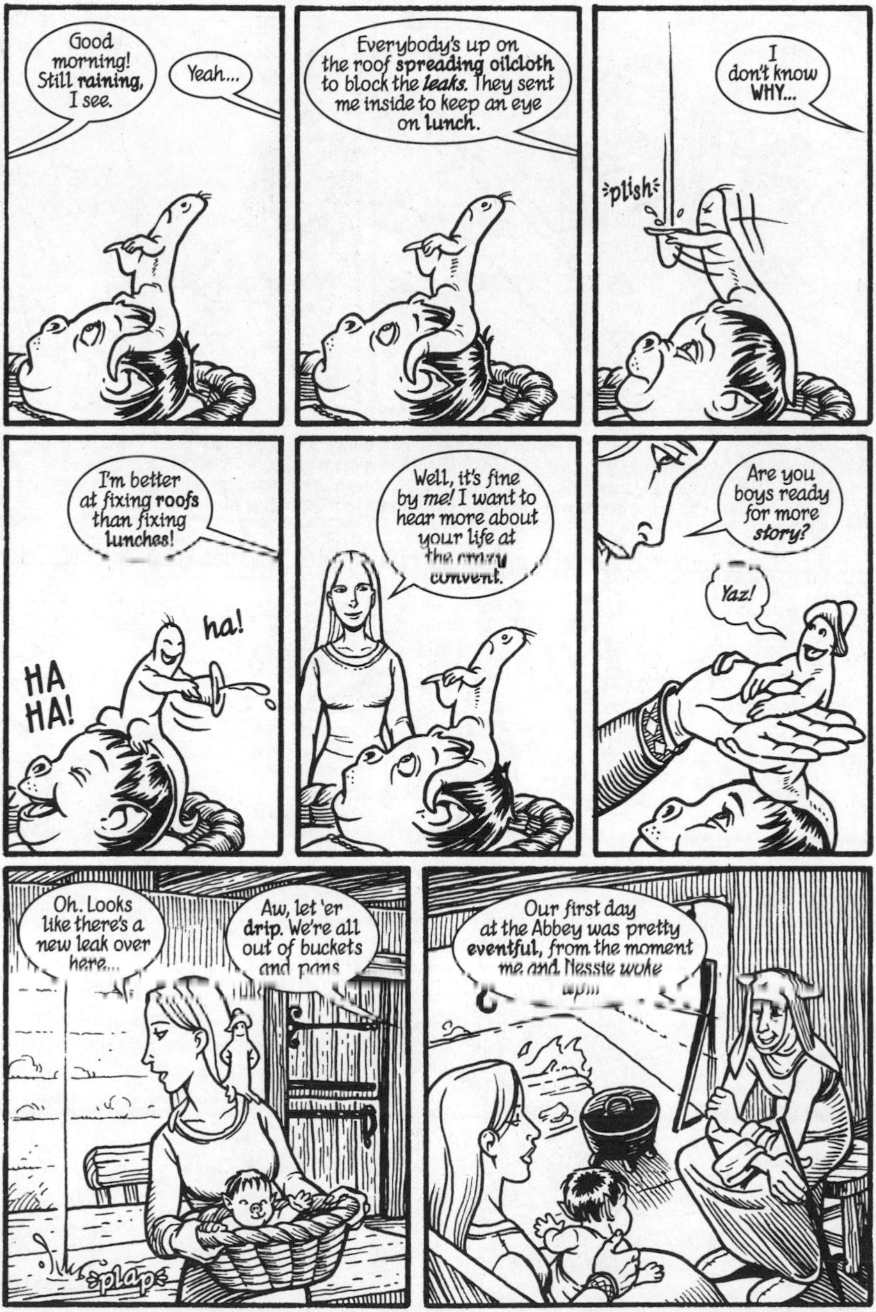
Good morning! Still raining, I see.
Yeah...
Everybody's up on the roof spreading oilcloth to block the leaks. They sent me inside to keep an eye on lunch.
I don't know WHY...
plish
I'm better at fixing roofs than fixing lunches!
ha!
HA HA!
Well, it's fine by me! I want to hear more about your life at the crazy convent.
Are you boys ready for more story?
Yaz!
Oh. Looks like there's a new leak over here...
Aw, let 'er drip. We're all out of buckets and pans.
plap
Our first day at the Abbey was pretty eventful, from the moment me and Nessie woke up!!

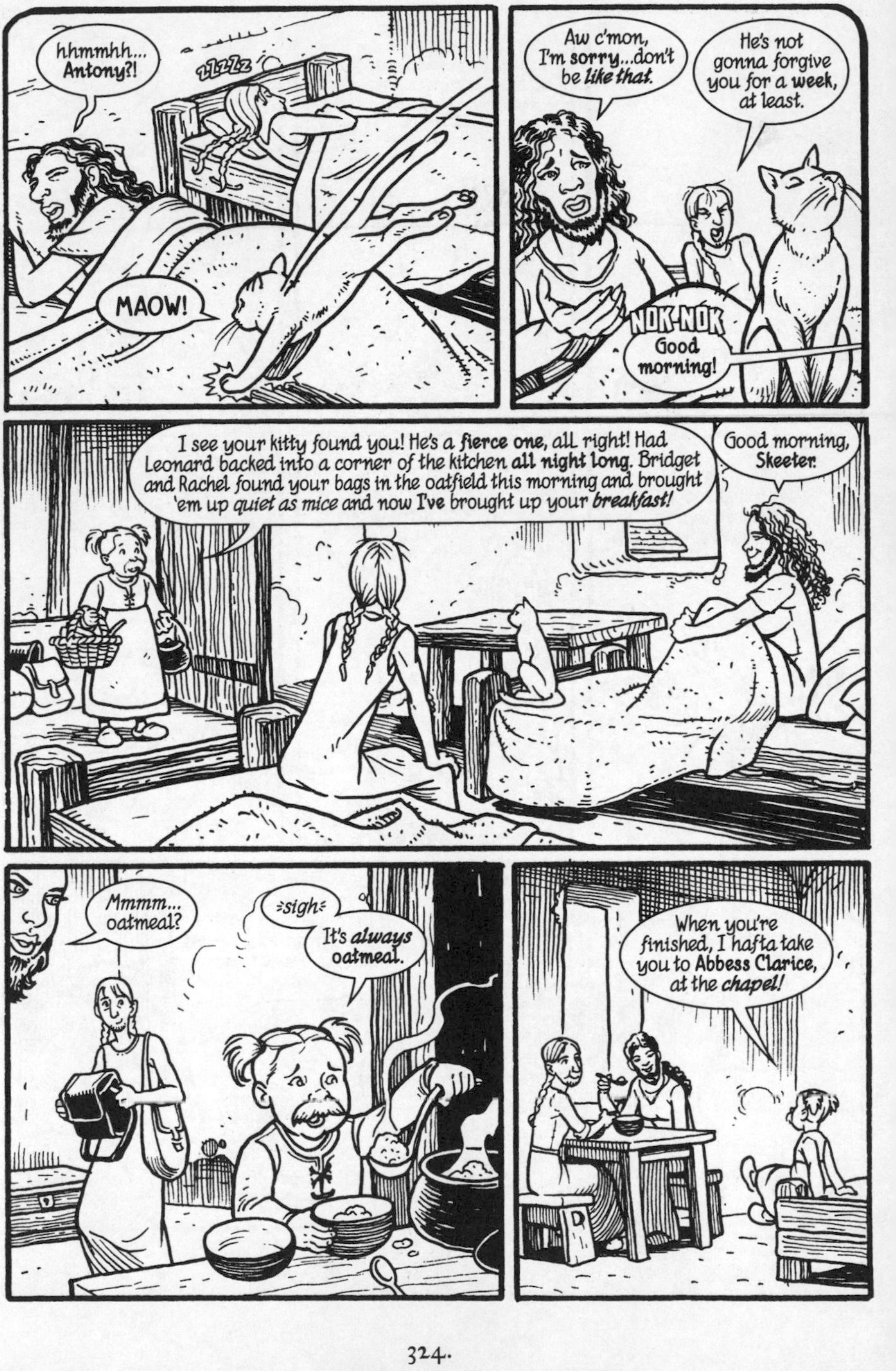
hhmmhh... Antony?!
zzzz
MAOW!
Aw c'mon, I'm sorry...don't be like that.
He's not gonna forgive you for a week, at least.
NOK-NOK
Good morning!
I see your kitty found you! He's a fierce one, all right! Had Leonard backed into a corner of the kitchen all night long. Bridget and Rachel found your bags in the oatfield this morning and brought 'em up quiet as mice and now I've brought up your breakfast!
Good morning, Skeeter.
Mmmm... oatmeal?
sigh
It's always oatmeal.
When you're finished, I hafta take you to Abbess Clarice, at the chapel!

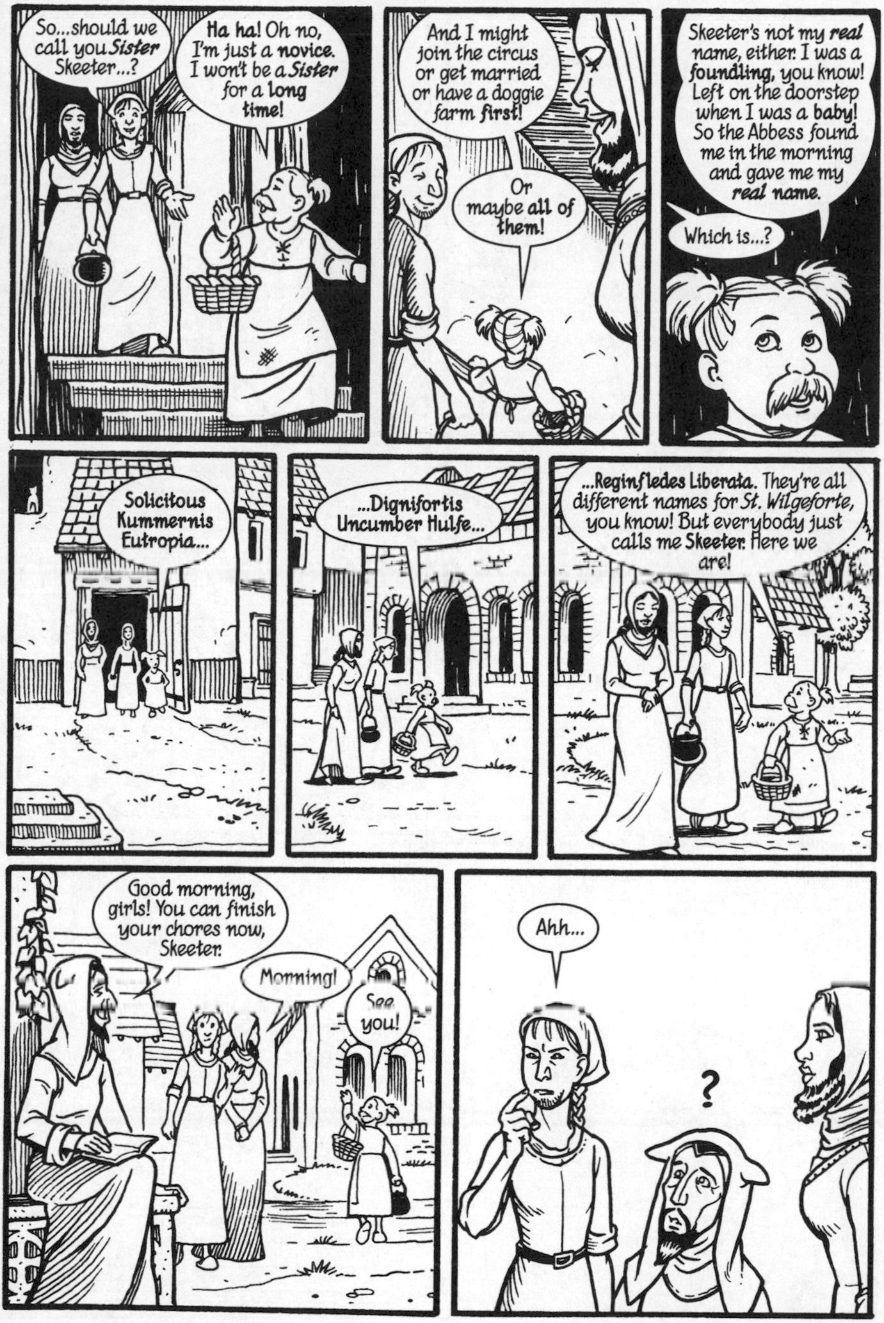

So...should we call you *Sister* Skeeter...?
Ha ha! Oh no, I'm just a **novice**. I won't be a *Sister* for a **long time!**
And I might join the circus or get married or have a doggie farm *first!*
Or maybe **all** of **them!**
Skeeter's not my *real* name, either. I was a **foundling**, you know! Left on the doorstep when I was a **baby!** So the Abbess found me in the morning and gave me my *real name.*
Which is...?
Solicitous Kummernis Eutropia....
...Dignifortis Uncumber Hulfe...
...Reginfledes Liberata. They're all different names for *St. Wilgeforte*, you know! But everybody just calls me **Skeeter**. Here we are!
Good morning, girls! You can finish your chores now, Skeeter.
Morning!
See you!
Ahh...
?

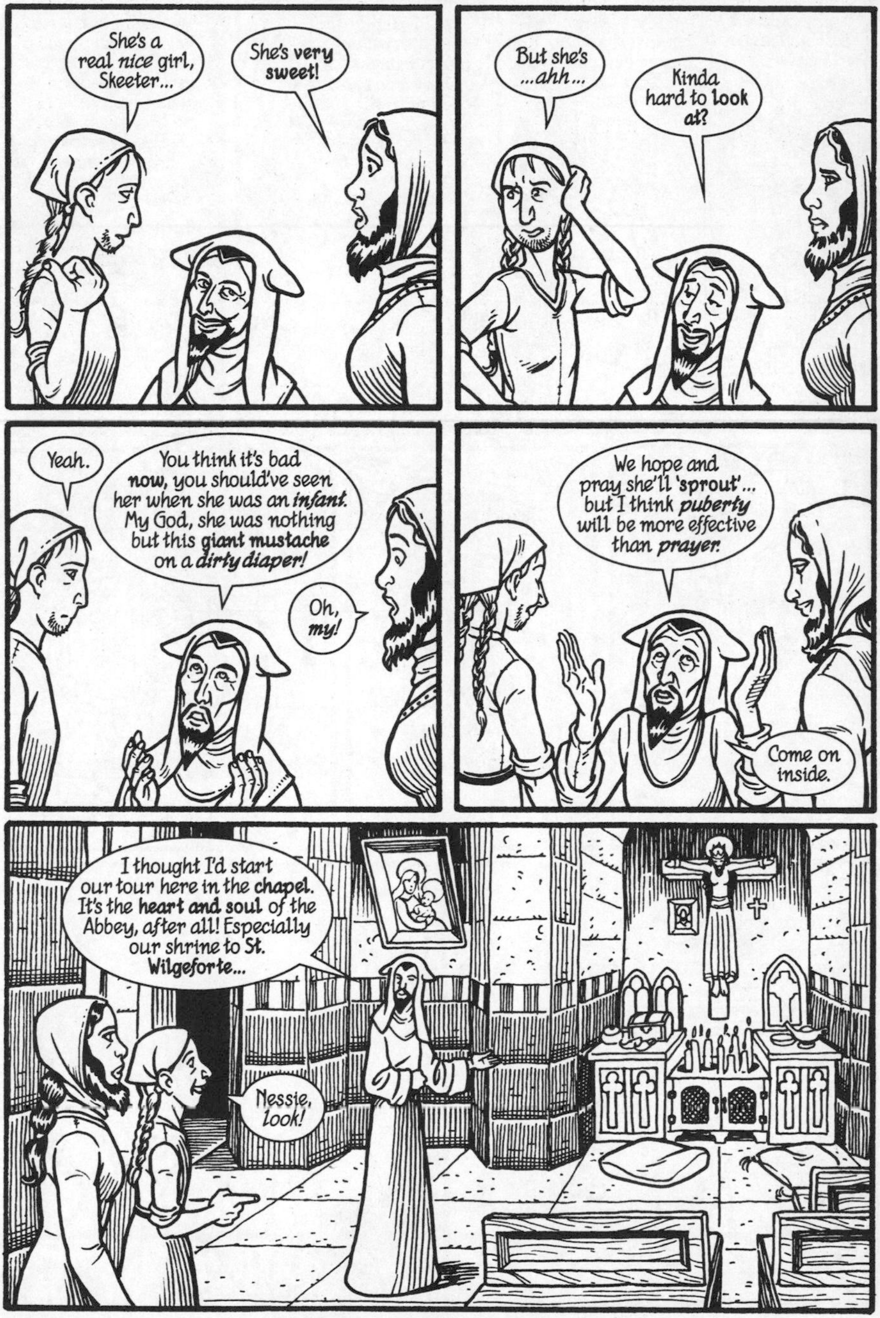
She's a real *nice* girl, Skeeter...
She's **very sweet!**
But she's ...*ahh*...
Kinda hard to look at?
Yeah.
You think it's bad **now**, you should've seen her when she was an *infant*. My God, she was nothing but this **giant mustache** on a *dirty diaper!*
Oh, *my!*
We hope and pray she'll **'sprout'**... but I think *puberty* will be more effective than *prayer.*
Come on inside.
I thought I'd start our tour here in the **chapel**. It's the **heart and soul** of the Abbey, *after all!* Especially our shrine to St. **Wilgeforte...**
Nessie, *look!*

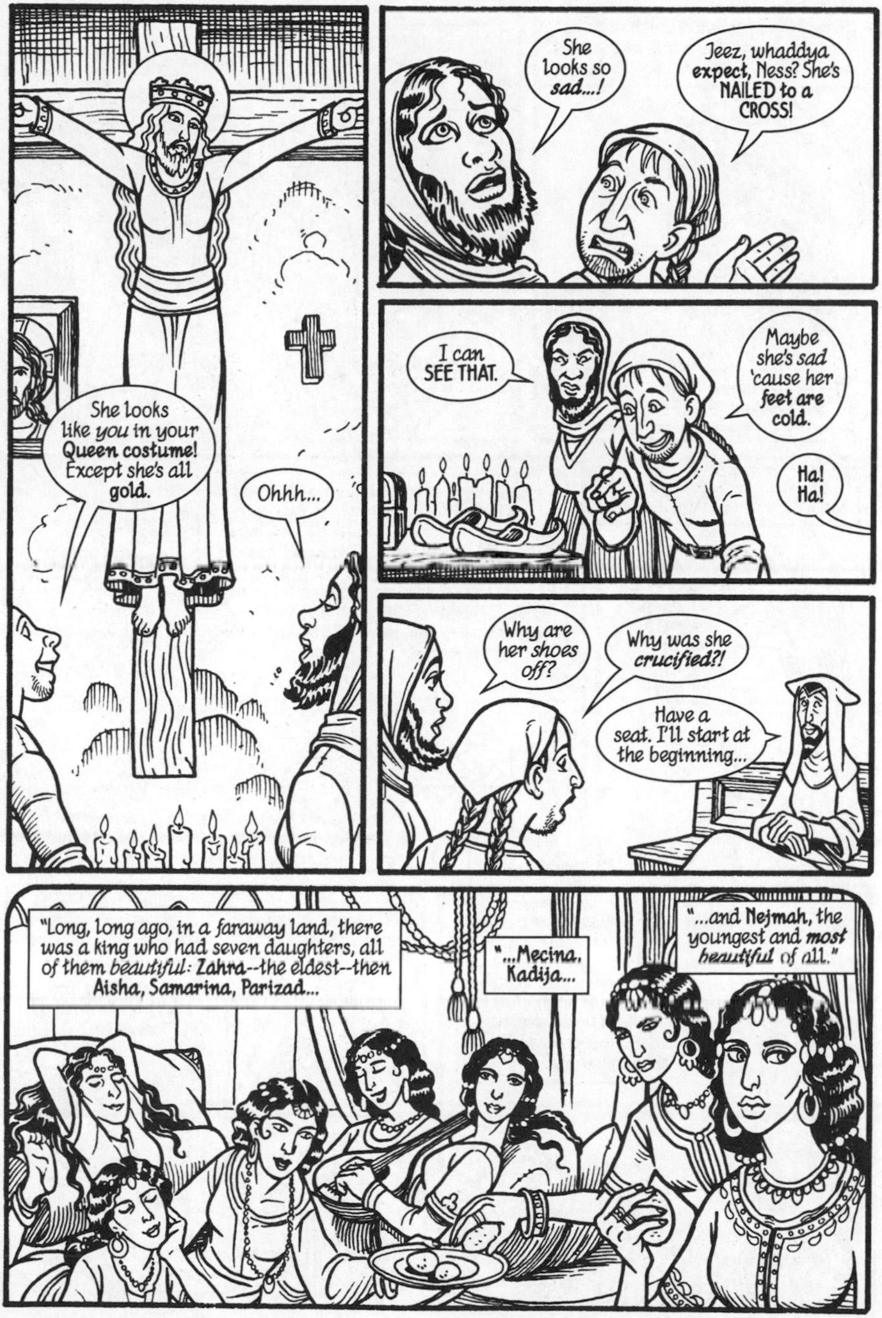
She looks like *you* in your **Queen costume!** Except she's all **gold.**
Ohhh...
She looks so *sad*...!
Jeez, whaddya **expect,** Ness? She's **NAILED to a CROSS!**
I can **SEE THAT.**
Maybe she's *sad* 'cause her **feet are cold.**
Ha! Ha!
Why are her shoes off?
Why was she *crucified?!*
Have a seat. I'll start at the beginning...
"Long, long ago, in a *faraway* land, there was a king who had seven daughters, all of them *beautiful*: **Zahra**--the eldest--then **Aisha, Samarina, Parizad...**
"...**Mecina, Kadija...**
"...and **Nejmah,** the youngest and *most beautiful* of all."

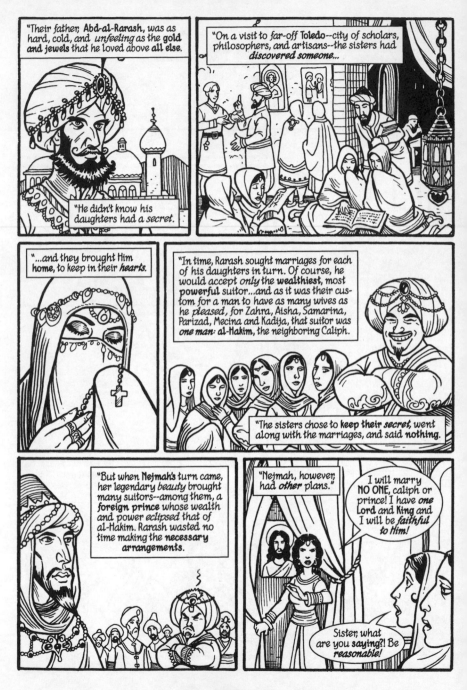

"Their father, Abd-al-Rarash, was as hard, cold, and *unfeeling* as the gold and jewels that he loved above all else.

"He didn't know his daughters had a *secret*.

"On a visit to *far-off* **Toledo**--city of scholars, philosophers, and artisans--the sisters had *discovered someone...*

"...and they brought Him home, to keep in their *hearts*.

"In time, Rarash sought marriages for each of his daughters in turn. Of course, he would accept *only* the **wealthiest**, most **powerful** suitor...and as it was their custom for a man to have as many wives as he *pleased*, for Zahra, Aisha, Samarina, Parizad, Mecina and Kadija, that suitor was *one man*: al-Hakim, the neighboring Caliph.

"The sisters chose to **keep their** *secret*, went along with the marriages, and said nothing.

"But when **Nejmah's** turn came, her legendary *beauty* brought many suitors--among them, a **foreign prince** whose wealth and power *eclipsed* that of al-Hakim. Rarash wasted no time making the **necessary arrangements**.

"**Nejmah**, however, had *other* plans."

I will marry NO ONE, caliph or prince! I have **one** Lord and King and I will be *faithful to Him!*

Sister, what are you *saying*?! Be *reasonable!*

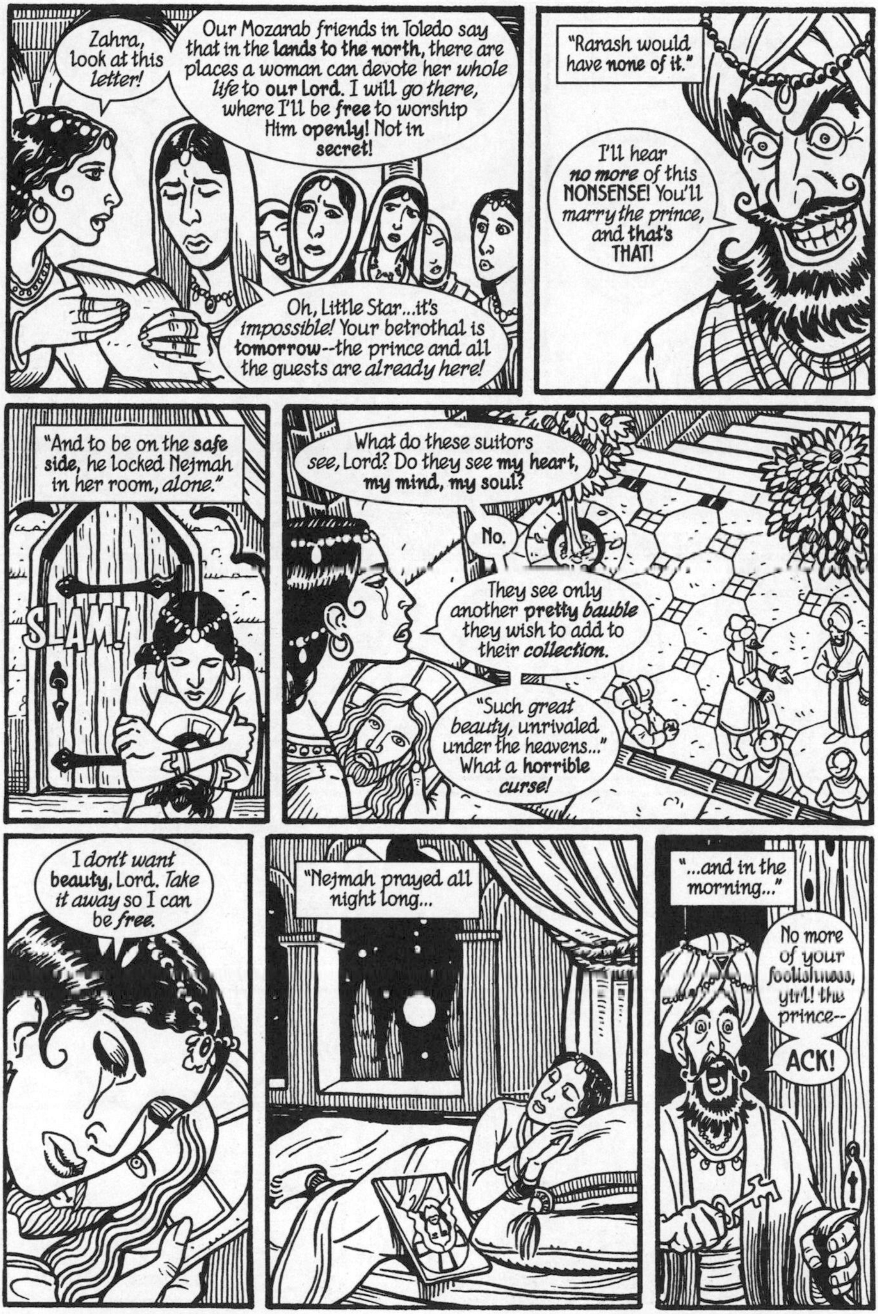
Zahra, look at this letter!
Our Mozarab friends in Toledo say that in the lands to the north, there are places a woman can devote her whole life to our Lord. I will go there, where I'll be free to worship Him openly! Not in secret!
Oh, Little Star...it's impossible! Your betrothal is tomorrow--the prince and all the guests are already here!
"Rarash would have none of it."
I'll hear no more of this NONSENSE! You'll marry the prince, and that's THAT!
"And to be on the safe side, he locked Nejmah in her room, alone."
SLAM!
What do these suitors see, Lord? Do they see my heart, my mind, my soul?
No.
They see only another pretty bauble they wish to add to their collection.
"Such great beauty, unrivaled under the heavens..." What a horrible curse!
I don't want beauty, Lord. Take it away so I can be free.
"Nejmah prayed all night long...
"...and in the morning..."
No more of your foolishness, girl! the prince--
ACK!

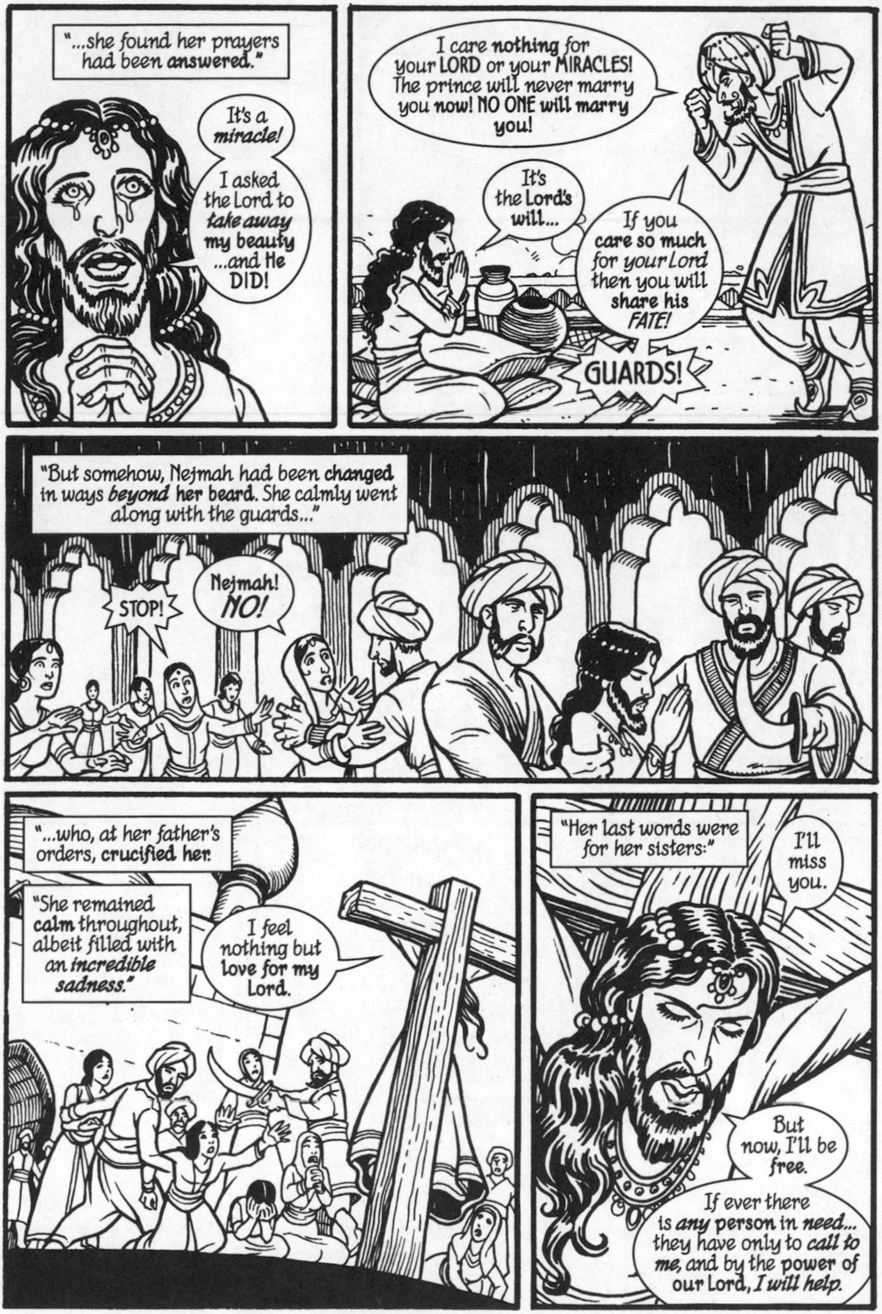
"...she found her prayers had been **answered.**"
It's a ***miracle!***
I asked the Lord to ***take away*** **my beauty** ...and He **DID!**
I care **nothing** for your **LORD** or your **MIRACLES!** The prince will never marry you **now! NO ONE will marry** you!
It's the Lord's will...
If you **care so much** for *your Lord* then you will **share his** *FATE!*
GUARDS!
"But somehow, Nejmah had been **changed** in ways ***beyond*** **her beard.** She calmly went along with the guards..."
STOP!
Nejmah! *NO!*
"...who, at her father's orders, **crucified** her.
"She remained **calm** throughout, albeit filled with an ***incredible sadness.***"
I feel **nothing** but **love for my** Lord.
"Her last words were for her sisters:"
I'll miss you.
But now, I'll be **free.**
If ever there is ***any*** **person** in ***need...*** they have only to ***call to me,*** and by the **power** of **our Lord,** ***I will help.***

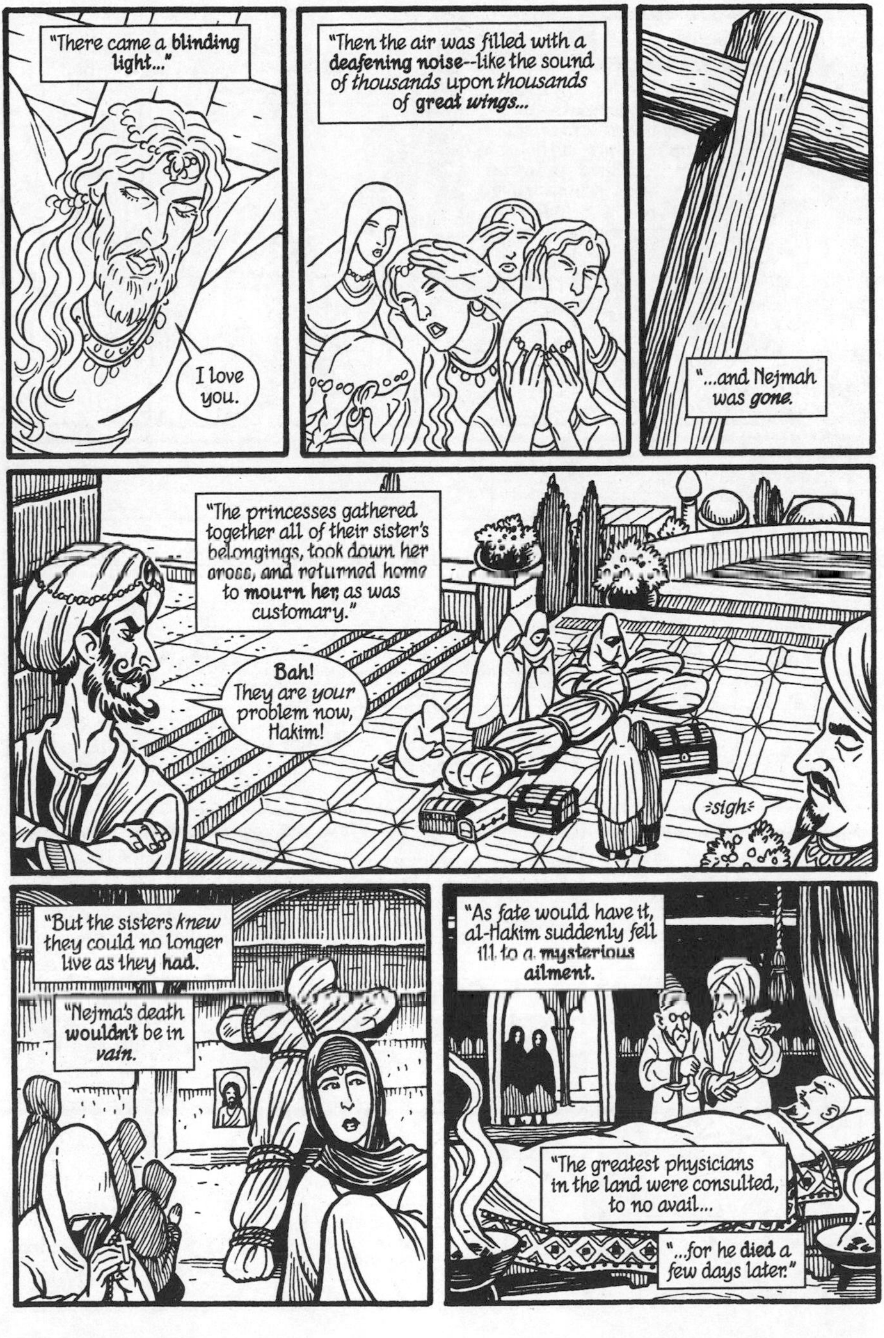
"There came a **blinding light...**"
I love you.
"Then the air was filled with a **deafening noise**--like the sound of *thousands* upon *thousands* of **great wings...**
"...and Nejmah was *gone*.
"The princesses gathered together all of their sister's belongings, took down her cross, and returned home to **mourn her,** as was customary."
Bah! They are *your* problem now, Hakim!
sigh
"But the sisters *knew* they could no longer live as they **had**.
"Nejma's death **wouldn't** be in *vain*.
"As *fate* would have it, al-Hakim suddenly fell ill to a **mysterious ailment**.
"The greatest physicians in the land were consulted, to no avail...
"...for he **died** a few days later."

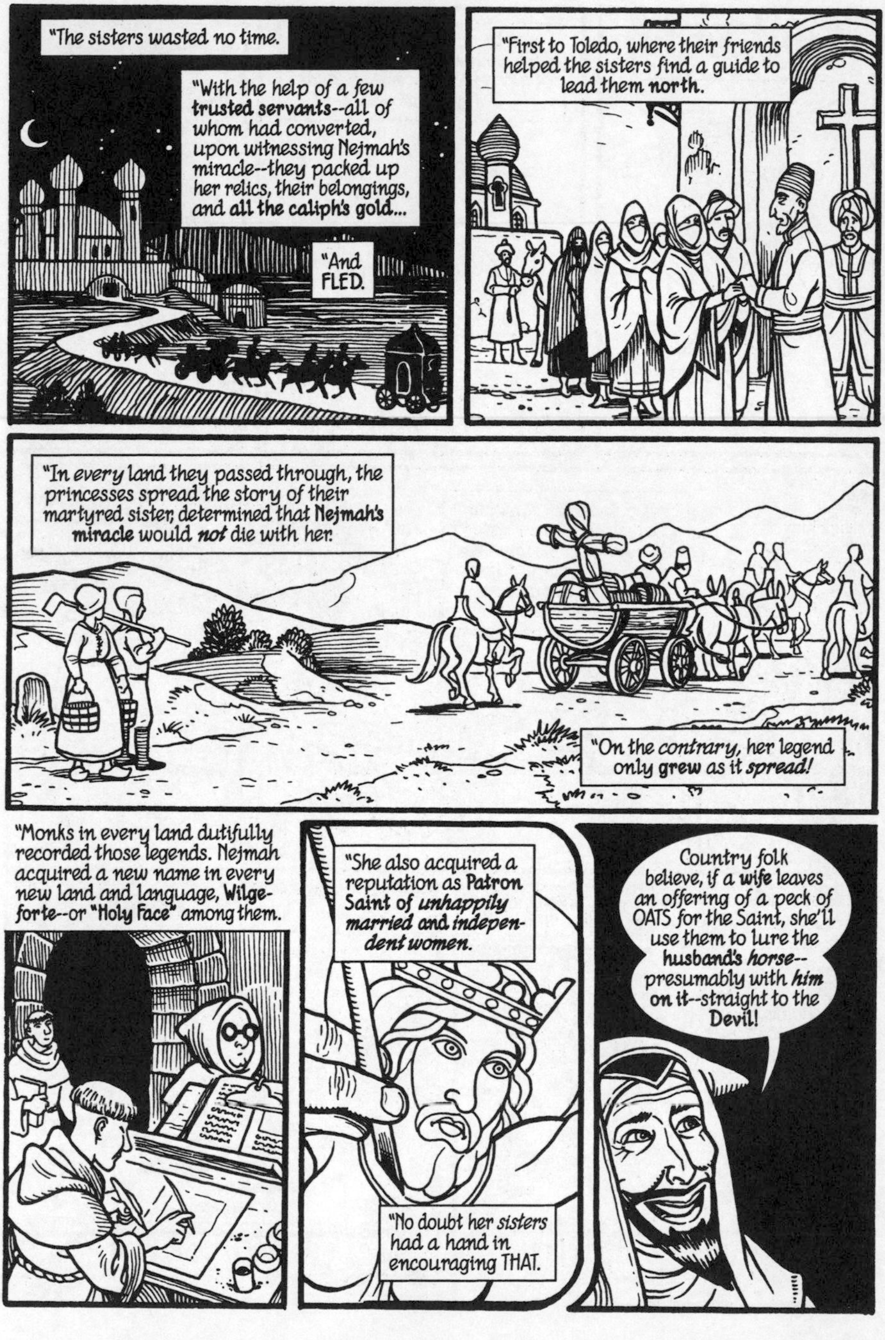
"The sisters wasted no time.
"With the help of a few trusted servants--all of whom had converted, upon witnessing Nejmah's miracle--they packed up her relics, their belongings, and all the caliph's gold...
"And FLED.
"First to Toledo, where their friends helped the sisters find a guide to lead them north.
"In every land they passed through, the princesses spread the story of their martyred sister, determined that Nejmah's miracle would not die with her.
"On the contrary, her legend only grew as it spread!
"Monks in every land dutifully recorded those legends. Nejmah acquired a new name in every new land and language, Wilgeforte--or "Holy Face" among them.
"She also acquired a reputation as Patron Saint of unhappily married and independent women.
"No doubt her sisters had a hand in encouraging THAT.
Country folk believe, if a wife leaves an offering of a peck of OATS for the Saint, she'll use them to lure the husband's horse--presumably with him on it--straight to the Devil!

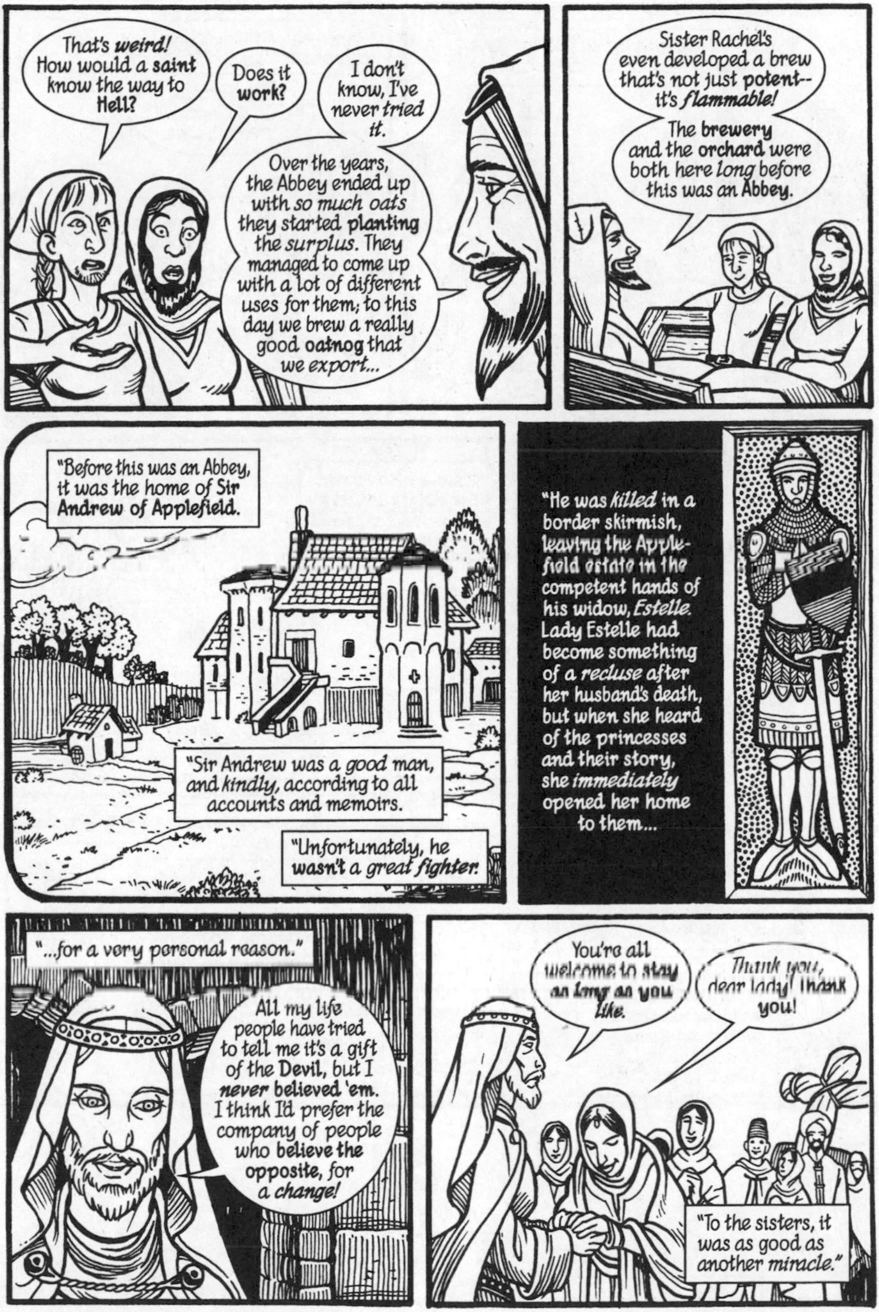
That's weird! How would a saint know the way to Hell?
Does it work?
I don't know, I've never tried it.
Over the years, the Abbey ended up with so much oats they started planting the surplus. They managed to come up with a lot of different uses for them; to this day we brew a really good oatnog that we export...
Sister Rachel's even developed a brew that's not just potent-- it's flammable!
The brewery and the orchard were both here long before this was an Abbey.
"Before this was an Abbey, it was the home of Sir Andrew of Applefield.
"Sir Andrew was a good man, and kindly, according to all accounts and memoirs.
"Unfortunately, he wasn't a great fighter.
"He was killed in a border skirmish, leaving the Applefield estate in the competent hands of his widow, Estelle. Lady Estelle had become something of a recluse after her husband's death, but when she heard of the princesses and their story, she immediately opened her home to them...
"...for a very personal reason."
All my life people have tried to tell me it's a gift of the Devil, but I never believed 'em. I think I'd prefer the company of people who believe the opposite, for a change!
You're all welcome to stay as long as you like.
Thank you, dear lady! Thank you!
"To the sisters, it was as good as another miracle."

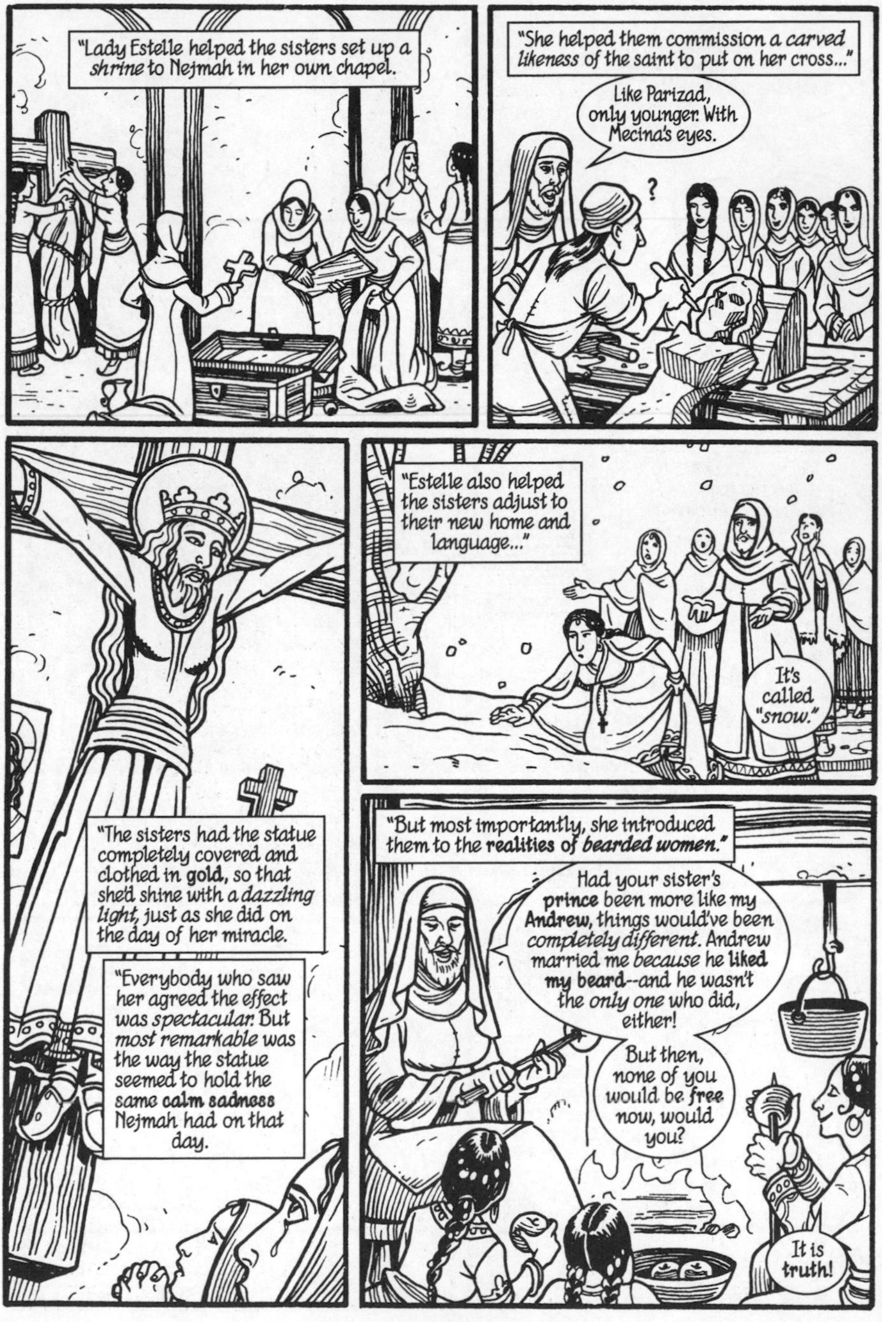
"Lady Estelle helped the sisters set up a *shrine* to Nejmah in her own chapel.
"She helped them commission a *carved likeness* of the saint to put on her cross..."
Like Parizad, only younger. With Mecina's eyes.
?
"The sisters had the statue completely covered and clothed in **gold**, so that she'd shine with a *dazzling light*, just as she did on the day of her miracle.
"Everybody who saw her agreed the effect was *spectacular*. But *most remarkable* was the way the statue seemed to hold the same **calm sadness** Nejmah had on that day.
"Estelle also helped the sisters adjust to their new home and language..."
It's called *"snow."*
"But most importantly, she introduced them to the **realities of *bearded women.***"
Had your sister's **prince** been more like my **Andrew**, things would've been *completely different*. Andrew married me *because* he **liked my beard**--and he wasn't the *only one* who did, either!
But then, none of you would be **free** now, would you?
It is **truth!**

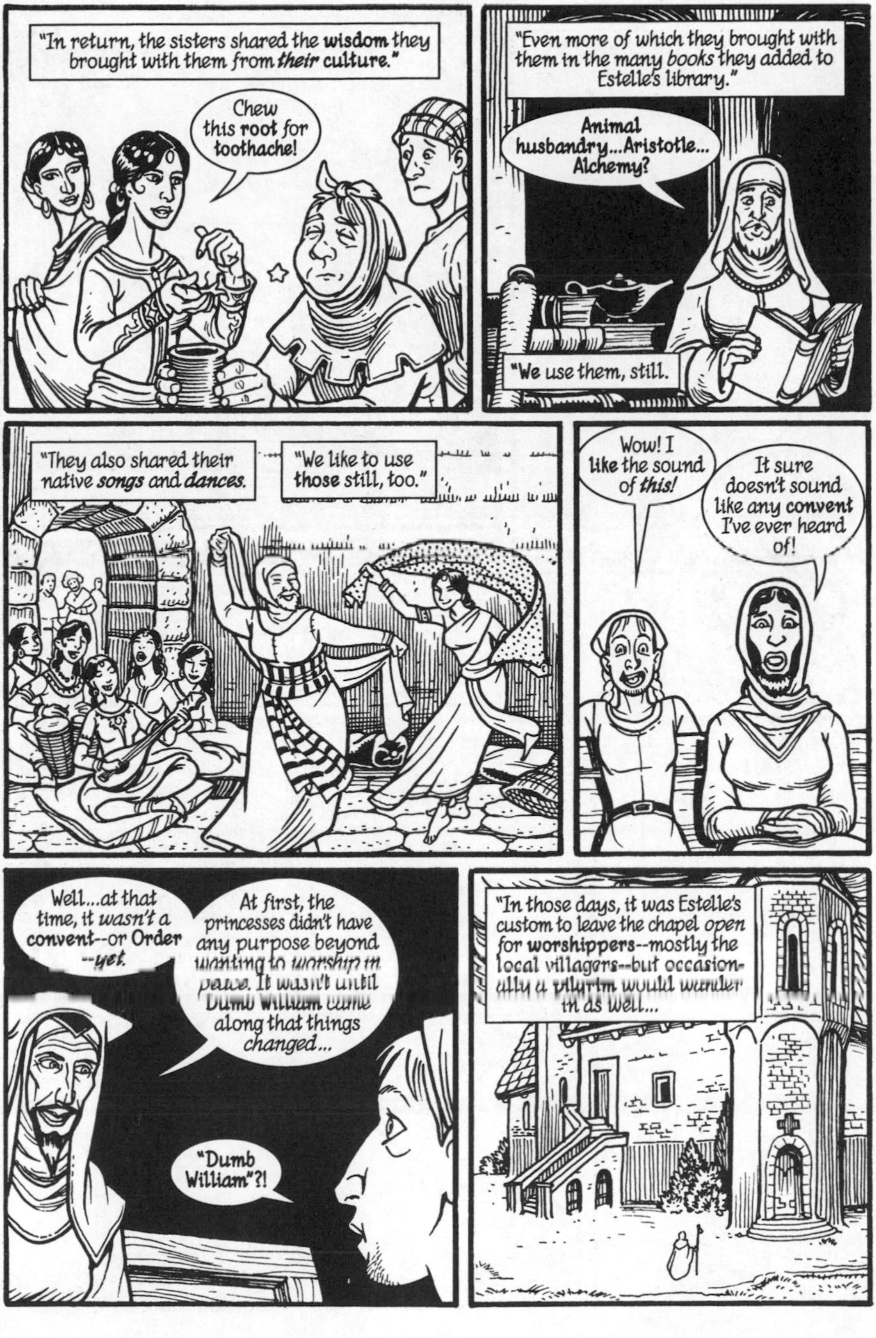
"In return, the sisters shared the wisdom they brought with them from their culture."
Chew this root for toothache!
"Even more of which they brought with them in the many books they added to Estelle's library."
Animal husbandry...Aristotle... Alchemy?
"We use them, still.
"They also shared their native songs and dances.
"We like to use those still, too."
Wow! I like the sound of this!
It sure doesn't sound like any convent I've ever heard of!
Well...at that time, it wasn't a convent--or Order --yet.
At first, the princesses didn't have any purpose beyond wanting to worship in peace. It wasn't until Dumb William came along that things changed...
"Dumb William"?!
"In those days, it was Estelle's custom to leave the chapel open for worshippers--mostly the local villagers--but occasionally a pilgrim would wander in as well...

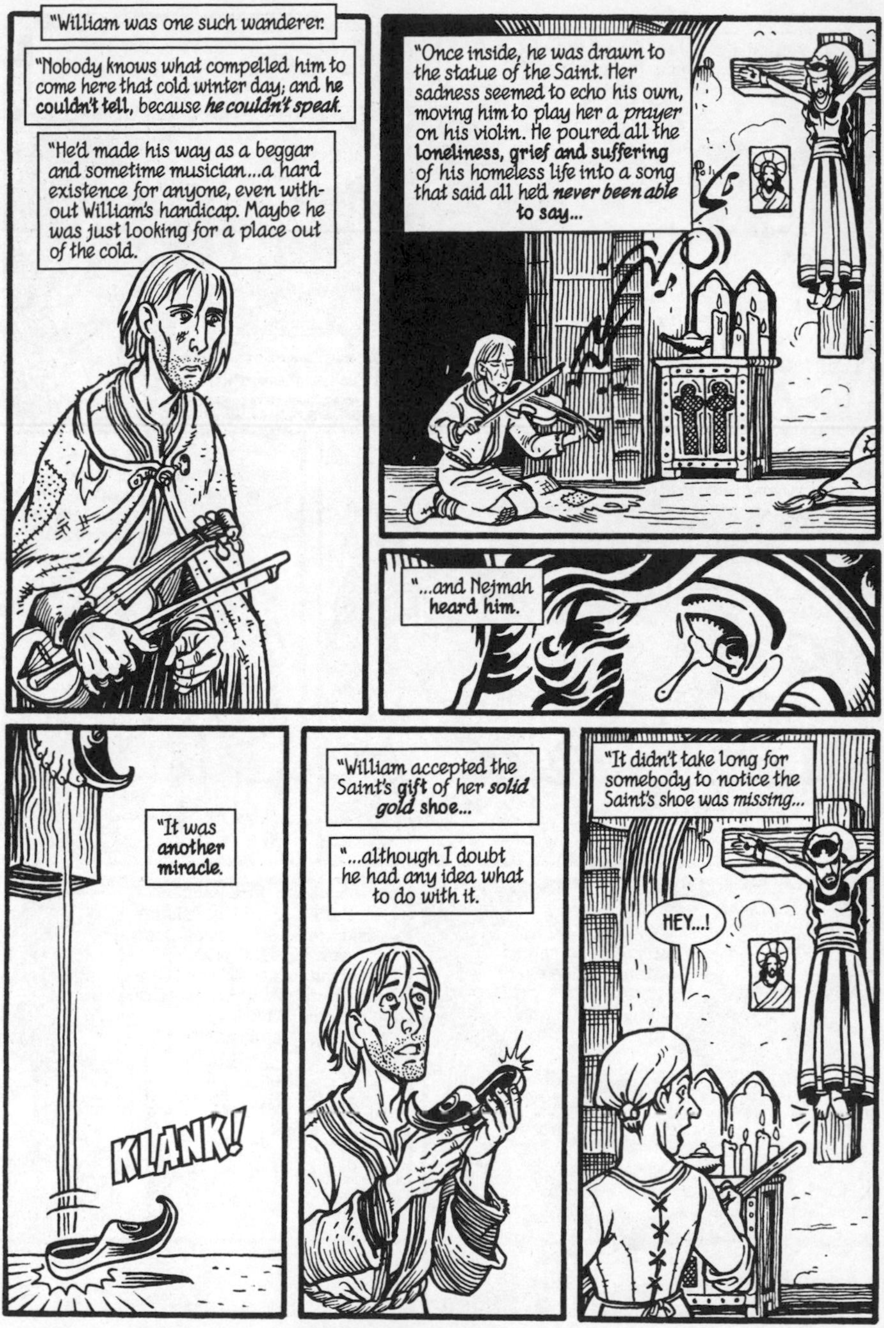
"William was one such wanderer.
"Nobody knows what compelled him to come here that cold winter day; and he couldn't tell, because he couldn't speak.
"He'd made his way as a beggar and sometime musician...a hard existence for anyone, even without William's handicap. Maybe he was just looking for a place out of the cold.
"Once inside, he was drawn to the statue of the Saint. Her sadness seemed to echo his own, moving him to play her a prayer on his violin. He poured all the loneliness, grief and suffering of his homeless life into a song that said all he'd never been able to say...
"...and Nejmah heard him.
"It was another miracle.
KLANK!
"William accepted the Saint's gift of her solid gold shoe...
"...although I doubt he had any idea what to do with it.
"It didn't take long for somebody to notice the Saint's shoe was missing...
HEY...!

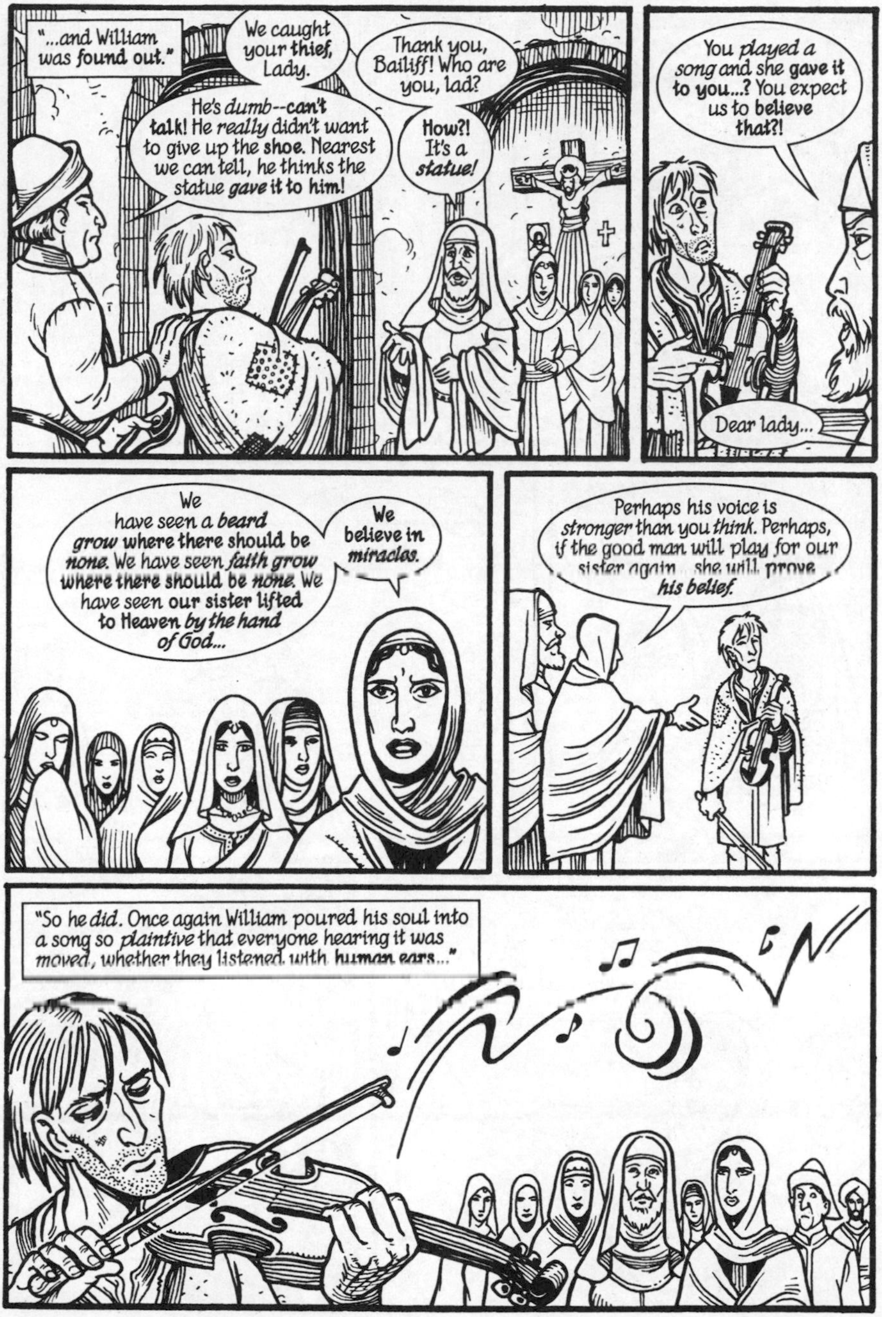
"...and William was found out."
We caught your thief, Lady.
He's dumb--can't talk! He really didn't want to give up the shoe. Nearest we can tell, he thinks the statue gave it to him!
Thank you, Bailiff! Who are you, lad?
How?! It's a statue!
You played a song and she gave it to you...? You expect us to believe that?!
Dear lady...
We have seen a beard grow where there should be none. We have seen faith grow where there should be none. We have seen our sister lifted to Heaven by the hand of God...
We believe in miracles.
Perhaps his voice is stronger than you think. Perhaps, if the good man will play for our sister again, she will prove his belief.
"So he did. Once again William poured his soul into a song so plaintive that everyone hearing it was moved, whether they listened with human ears..."

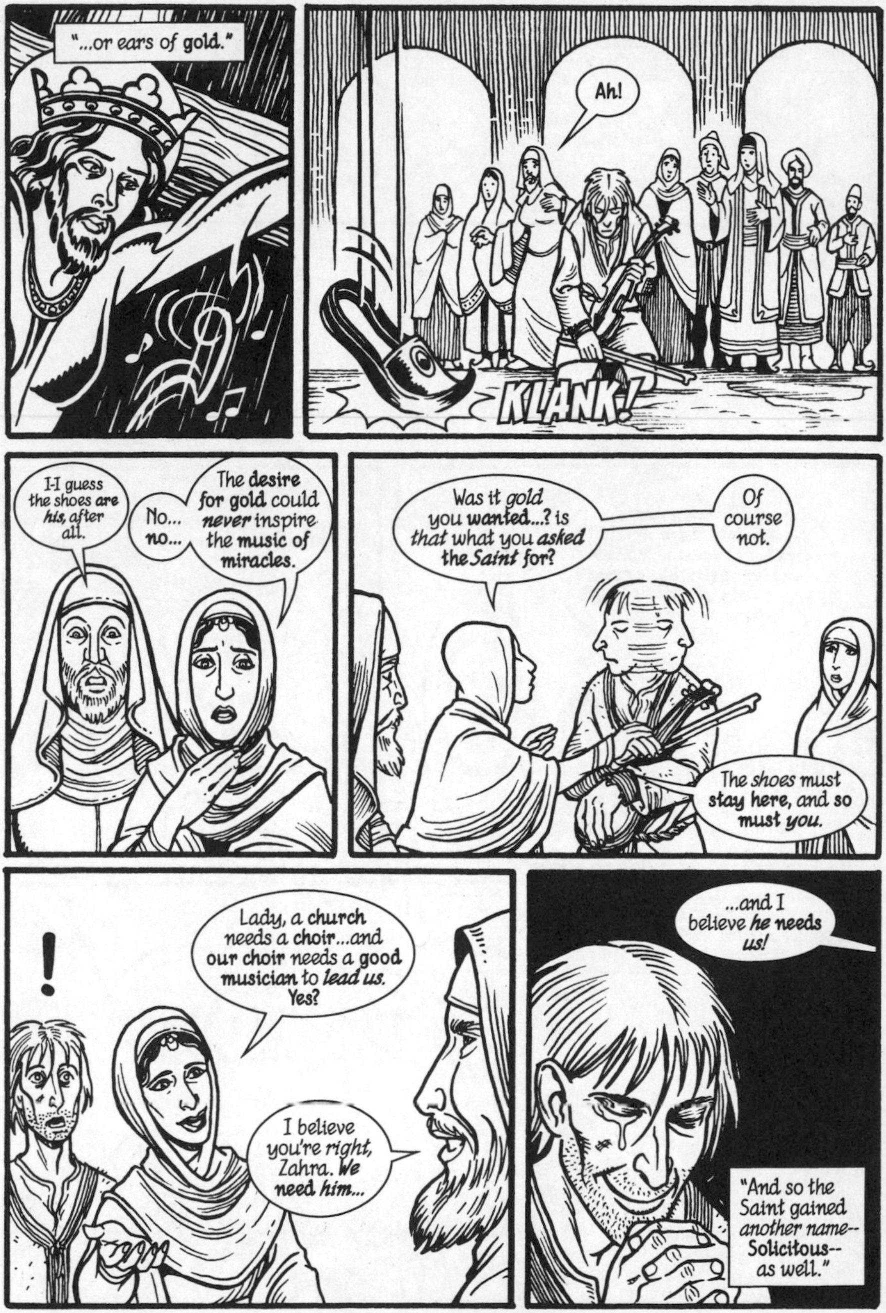
"...or ears of gold."
Ah!
KLANK!
I-I guess the shoes are his, after all.
No... no...
The desire for gold could never inspire the music of miracles.
Was it gold you wanted...? is that what you asked the Saint for?
Of course not.
The shoes must stay here, and so must you.
!
Lady, a church needs a choir...and our choir needs a good musician to lead us. Yes?
I believe you're right, Zahra. We need him...
...and I believe he needs us!
"And so the Saint gained another name-- Solicitous-- as well."

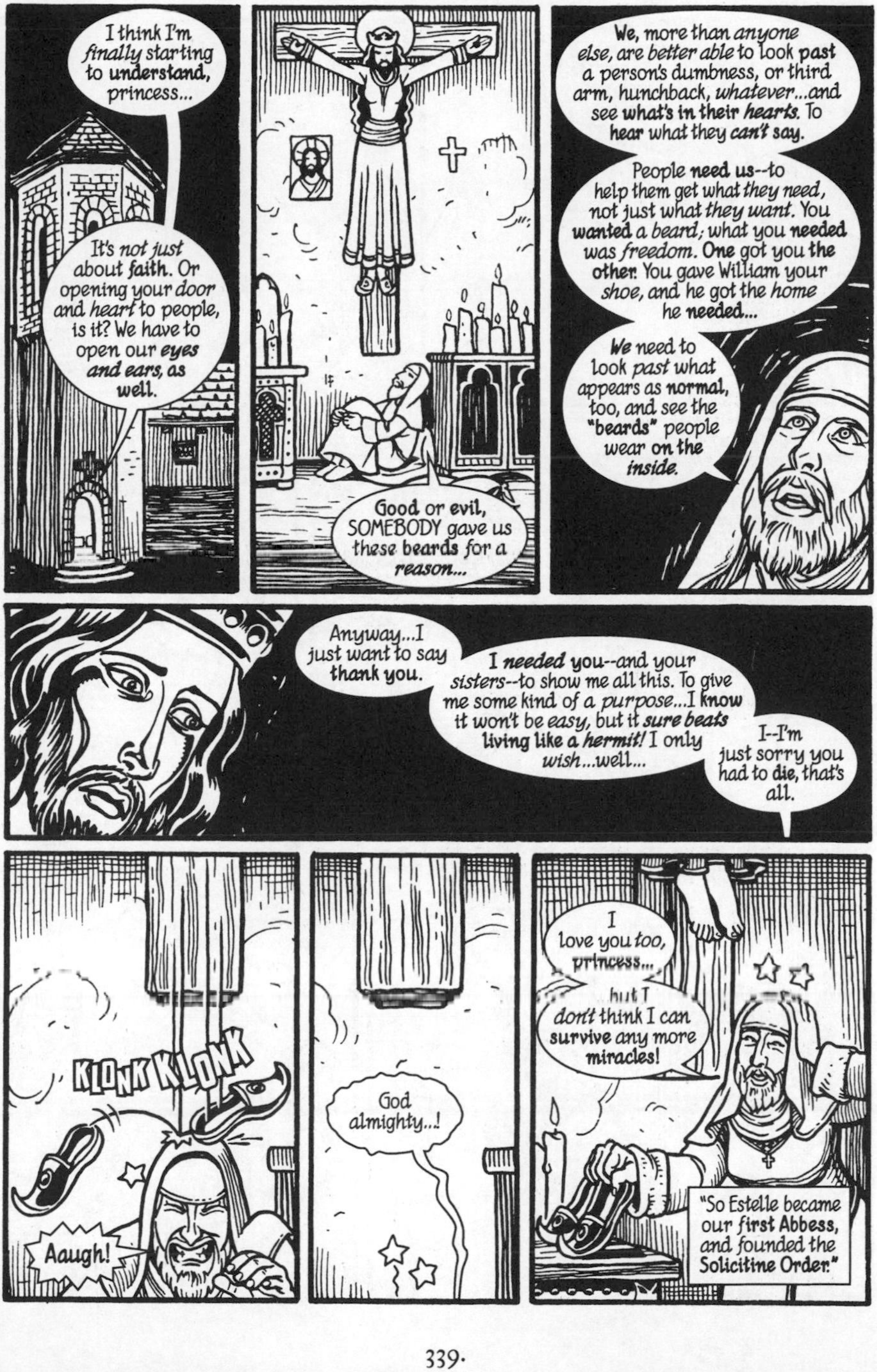
I think I'm finally starting to understand, princess...
It's not just about faith. Or opening your door and heart to people, is it? We have to open our eyes and ears, as well.
Good or evil, SOMEBODY gave us these beards for a reason...
We, more than anyone else, are better able to look past a person's dumbness, or third arm, hunchback, whatever...and see what's in their hearts. To hear what they can't say.
People need us--to help them get what they need, not just what they want. You wanted a beard; what you needed was freedom. One got you the other. You gave William your shoe, and he got the home he needed...
We need to look past what appears as normal, too, and see the "beards" people wear on the inside.
Anyway...I just want to say thank you.
I needed you--and your sisters--to show me all this. To give me some kind of a purpose...I know it won't be easy, but it sure beats living like a hermit! I only wish...well...
I--I'm just sorry you had to die, that's all.
KLONK KLONK
Aaugh!
God almighty...!
I love you too, princess...
...but I don't think I can survive any more miracles!
"So Estelle became our first Abbess, and founded the Solicitine Order."

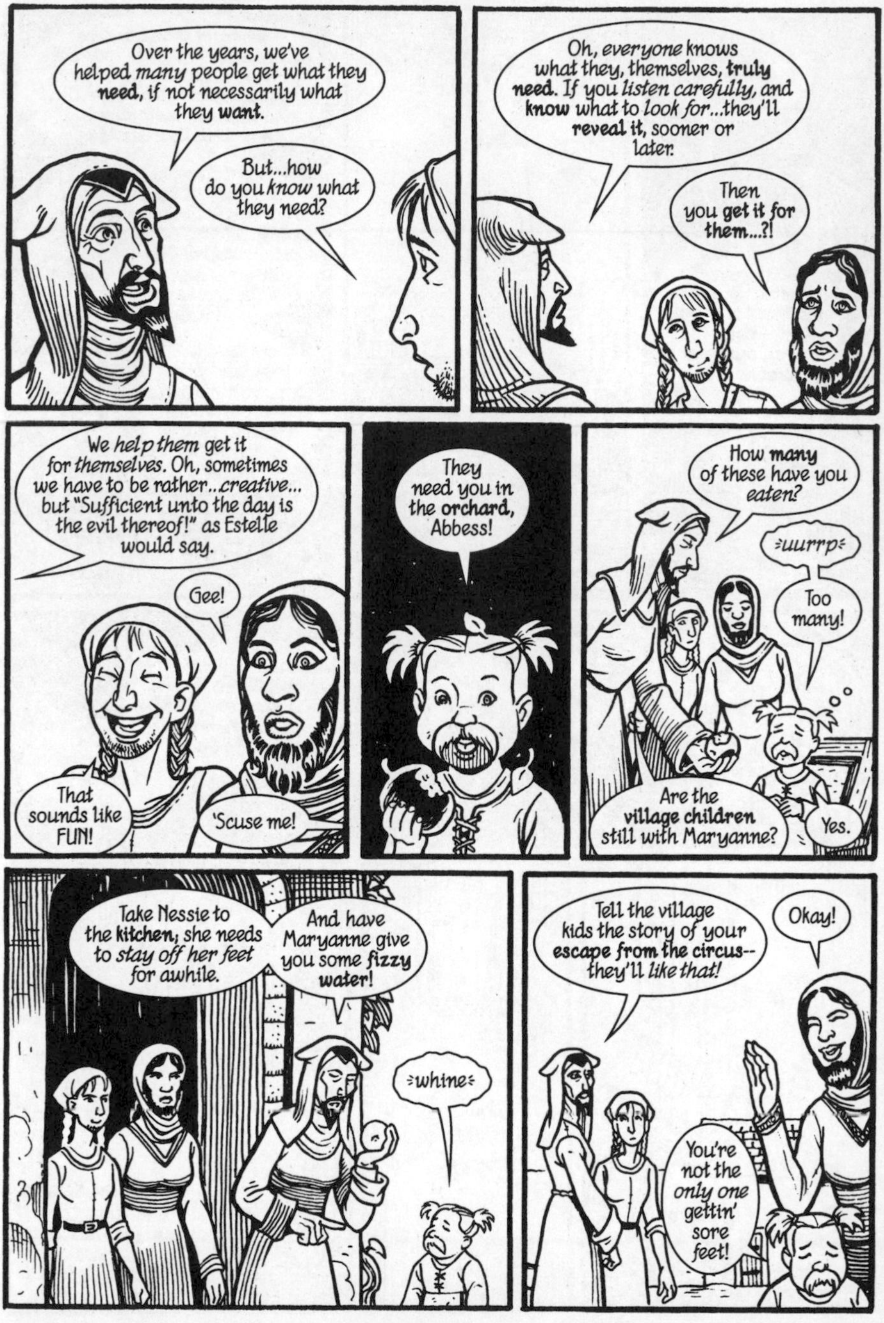
Over the years, we've helped *many* people get what they **need**, if not necessarily what they **want**.
But...how do you *know* what they need?
Oh, *everyone* knows what they, themselves, **truly need**. If you *listen carefully*, and **know** *what to* *look for*...they'll **reveal it**, sooner or later.
Then you **get it for them**...?!
We *help them* get it for *themselves*. Oh, sometimes we have to be rather...*creative*... but "Sufficient unto the day is the evil thereof!" as Estelle would say.
Gee!
That sounds like FUN!
'Scuse me!
They need you in the **orchard**, Abbess!
How **many** of these have you *eaten*?
uurrp
Too many!
Are the **village children** still with Maryanne?
Yes.
Take Nessie to the **kitchen**; she needs to *stay off her feet* for awhile.
And have Maryanne give you some **fizzy water**!
whine
Tell the village kids the story of your **escape from the circus**-- they'll *like that!*
Okay!
You're not the *only one* gettin' sore feet!

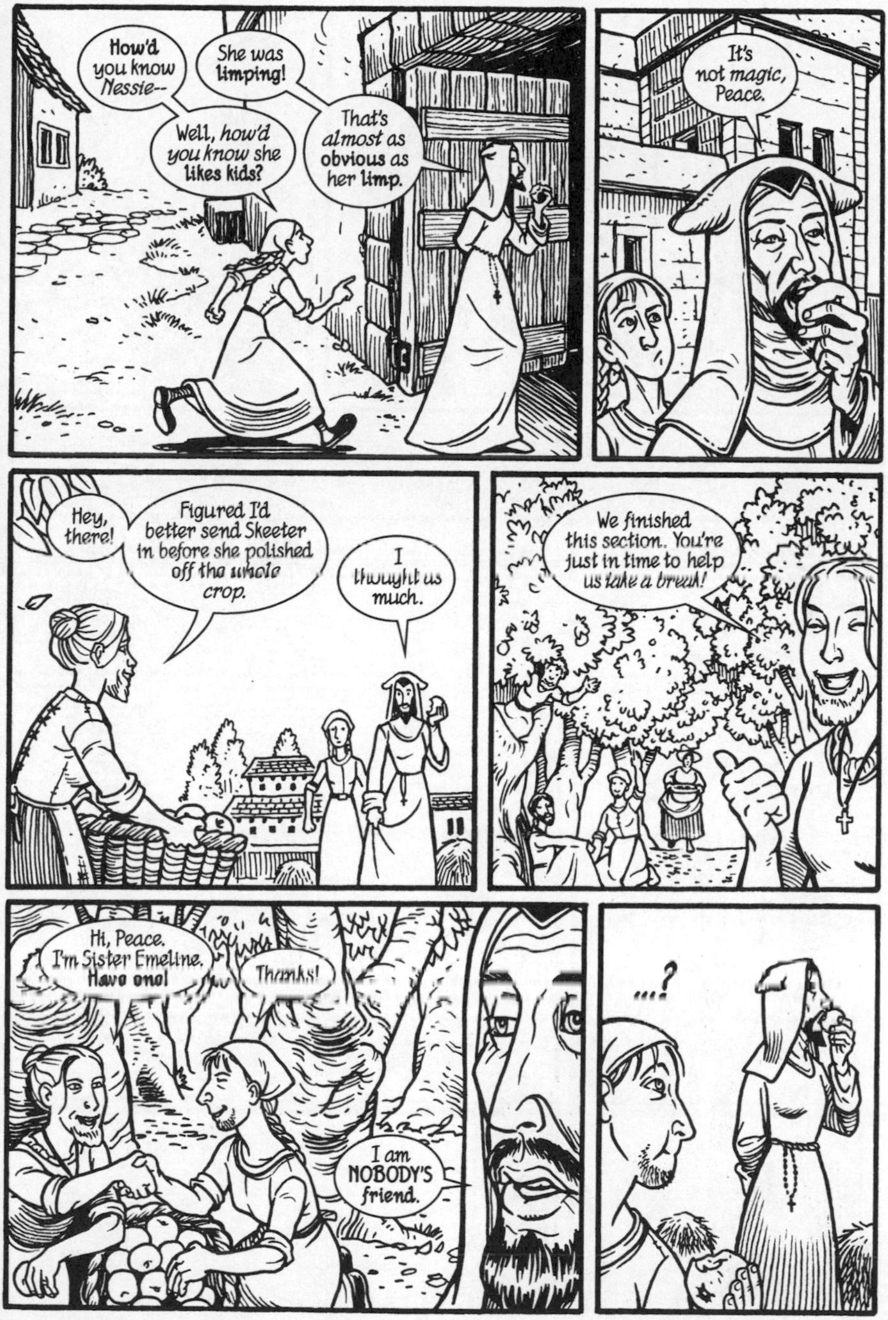
How'd you know Nessie--
She was limping!
Well, how'd you know she likes kids?
That's almost as obvious as her limp.
It's not magic, Peace.
Hey, there!
Figured I'd better send Skeeter in before she polished off the whole crop.
I thought as much.
We finished this section. You're just in time to help us take a break!
Hi, Peace. I'm Sister Emeline. Have one!
Thanks!
I am NOBODY'S friend.
...?

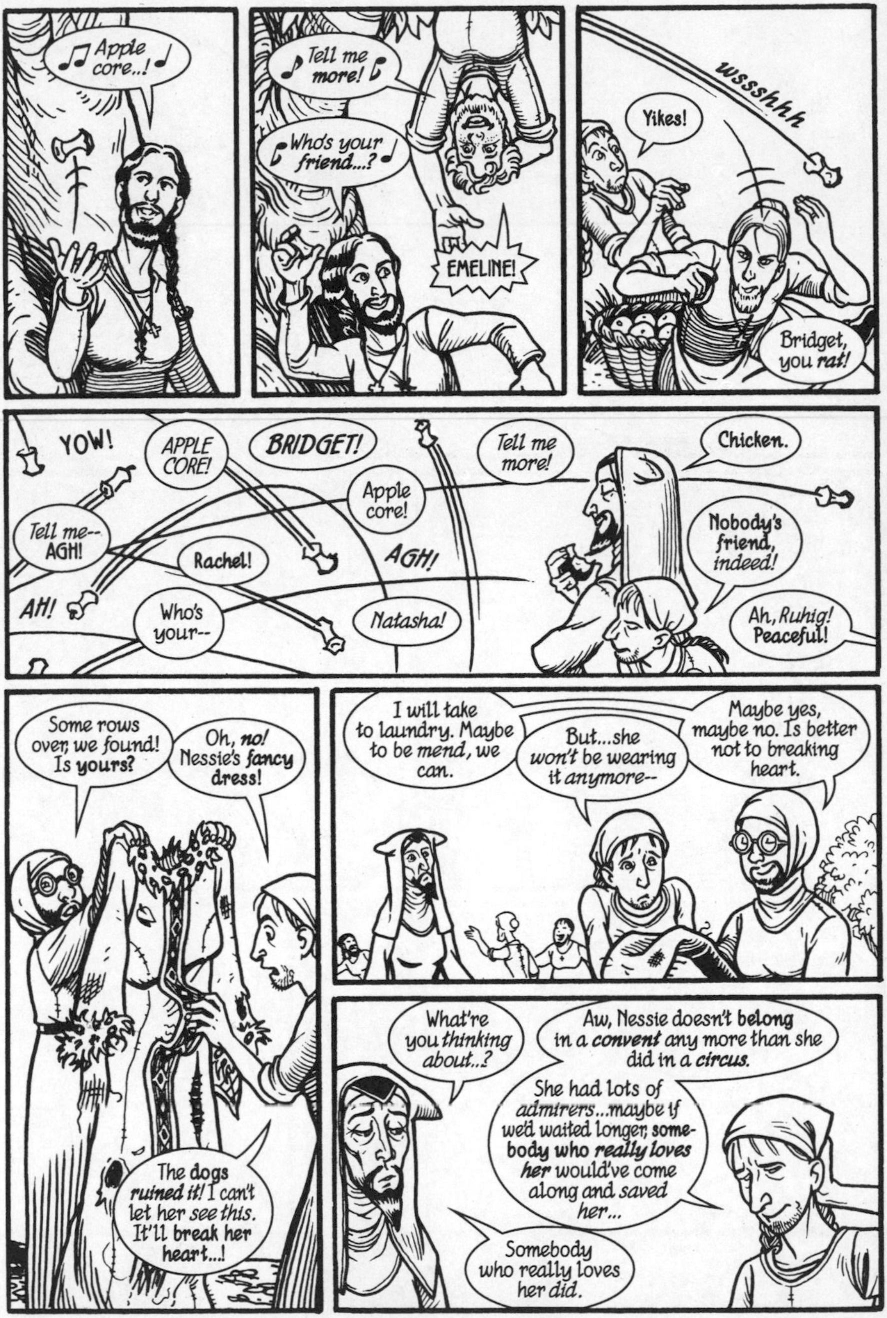

♫ Apple core...! ♩
♪ Tell me more! ♫
♫ Who's your friend...? ♩
EMELINE!
wssshhh
Yikes!
Bridget, you rat!
YOW!
APPLE CORE!
BRIDGET!
Tell me more!
Chicken.
Apple core!
Tell me-- AGH!
Nobody's friend, indeed!
Rachel!
AGH!
AH!
Who's your--
Natasha!
Ah, Ruhig! Peaceful!
Some rows over, we found! Is yours?
Oh, no! Nessie's fancy dress!
The dogs ruined it! I can't let her see this. It'll break her heart...!
I will take to laundry. Maybe to be mend, we can.
But...she won't be wearing it anymore--
Maybe yes, maybe no. Is better not to breaking heart.
What're you thinking about...?
Aw, Nessie doesn't belong in a convent any more than she did in a circus.
She had lots of admirers...maybe if we'd waited longer, somebody who really loves her would've come along and saved her...
Somebody who really loves her did.

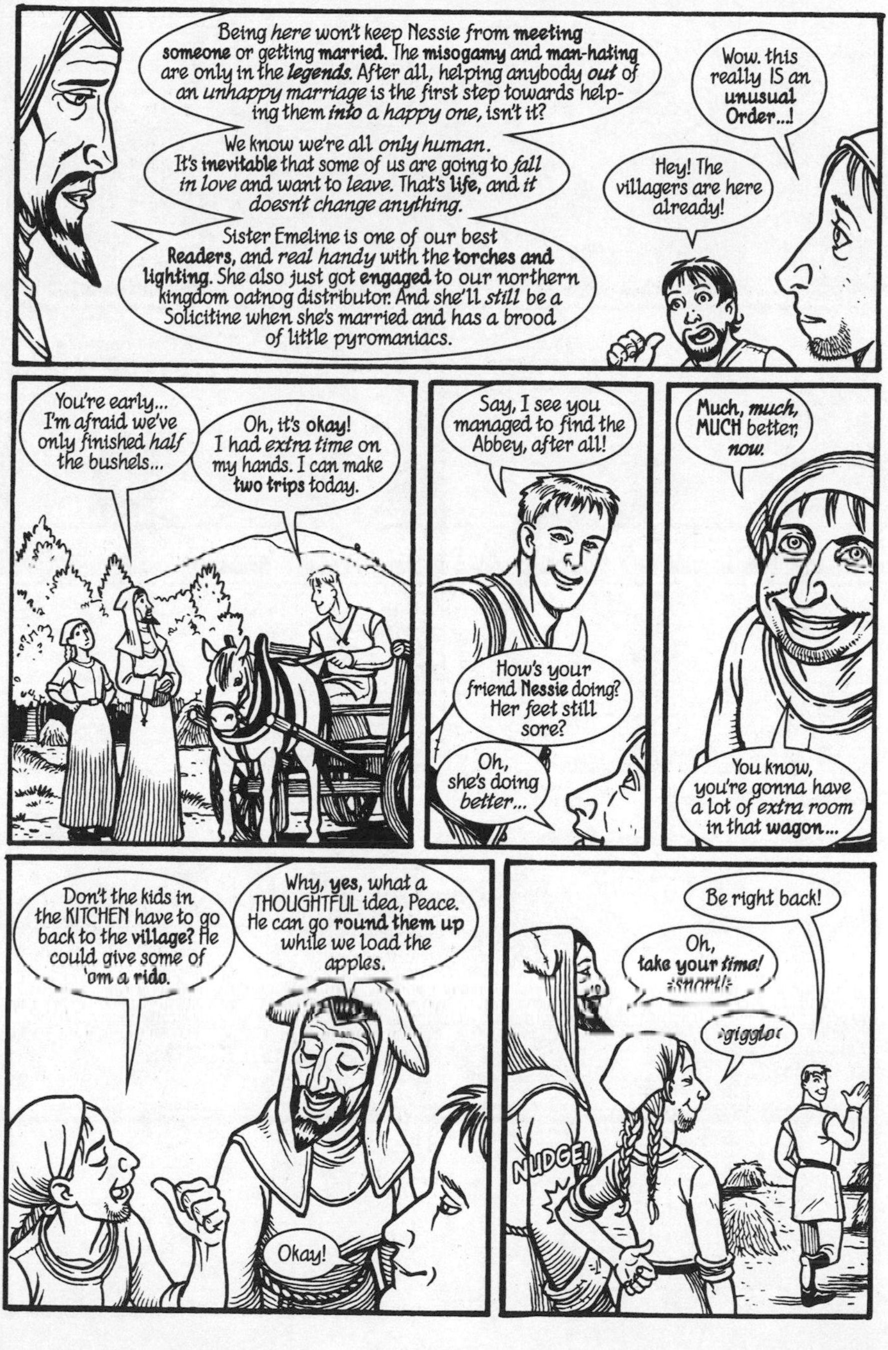
Being here won't keep Nessie from meeting someone or getting married. The misogamy and man-hating are only in the legends. After all, helping anybody out of an unhappy marriage is the first step towards helping them into a happy one, isn't it?
We know we're all only human. It's inevitable that some of us are going to fall in love and want to leave. That's life, and it doesn't change anything.
Sister Emeline is one of our best Readers, and real handy with the torches and lighting. She also just got engaged to our northern kingdom oatnog distributor. And she'll still be a Solicitine when she's married and has a brood of little pyromaniacs.
Wow. this really IS an unusual Order...!
Hey! The villagers are here already!
You're early... I'm afraid we've only finished half the bushels...
Oh, it's okay! I had extra time on my hands. I can make two trips today.
Say, I see you managed to find the Abbey, after all!
How's your friend Nessie doing? Her feet still sore?
Oh, she's doing better...
Much, much, MUCH better, now.
You know, you're gonna have a lot of extra room in that wagon....
Don't the kids in the KITCHEN have to go back to the village? He could give some of 'em a ride.
Why, yes, what a THOUGHTFUL idea, Peace. He can go round them up while we load the apples.
Okay!
Be right back!
Oh, take your time!
:giggle:
NUDGE!

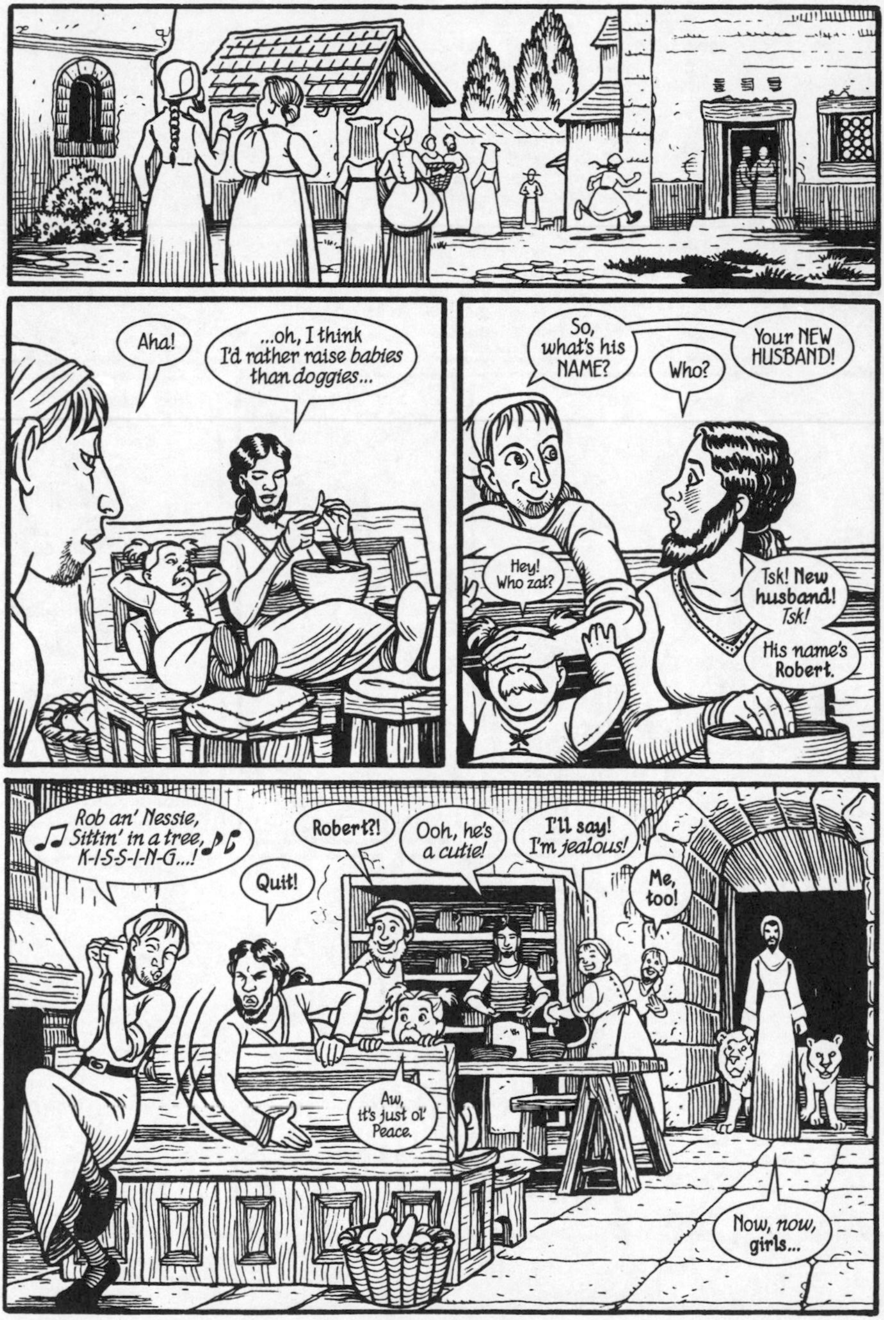
Aha!
...oh, I think I'd rather raise babies than doggies...
So, what's his NAME?
Who?
Your NEW HUSBAND!
Hey! Who zat?
Tsk! New husband! Tsk!
His name's Robert.
Rob an' Nessie, Sittin' in a tree, K-I-S-S-I-N-G...!
Quit!
Robert?!
Ooh, he's a cutie!
I'll say! I'm jealous!
Me, too!
Aw, it's just ol' Peace.
Now, now, girls...

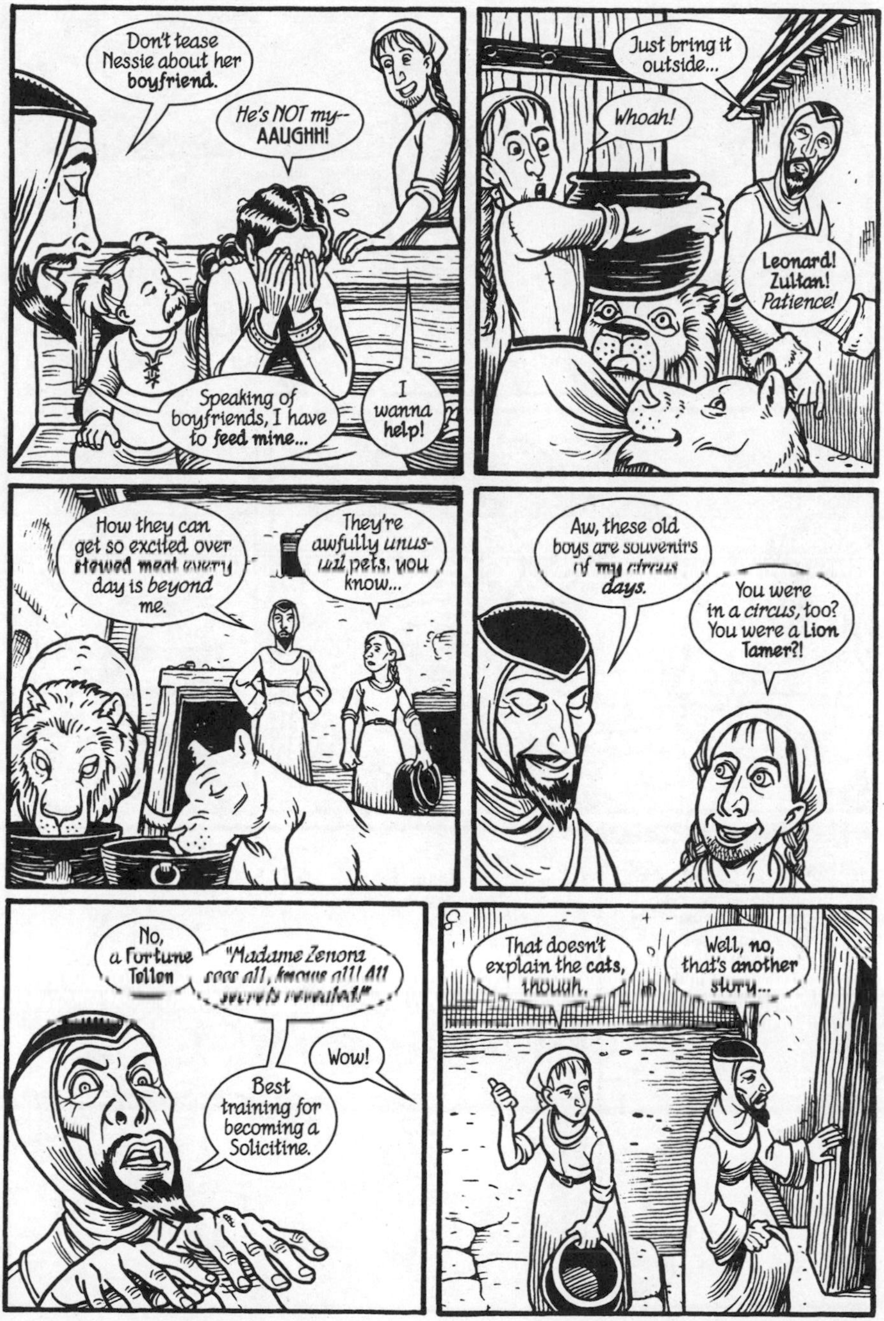
Don't tease Nessie about her **boyfriend.**
He's *NOT* my-- **AAUGHH!**
Speaking of boyfriends, I have to ***feed mine...***
I wanna **help!**
Just bring it outside...
Whoah!
Leonard! Zultan! *Patience!*
How they can get so excited over stewed meat every day is *beyond* me.
They're awfully *unusual* pets, you know...
Aw, these old boys are souvenirs of my *circus days.*
You were in a *circus,* too? You were a **Lion Tamer?!**
No, a Fortune Teller
"Madame Zenona sees all, knows all! All secrets revealed!"
Best training for becoming a Solicitine.
Wow!
That doesn't explain the cats, though.
Well, no, that's **another** story...

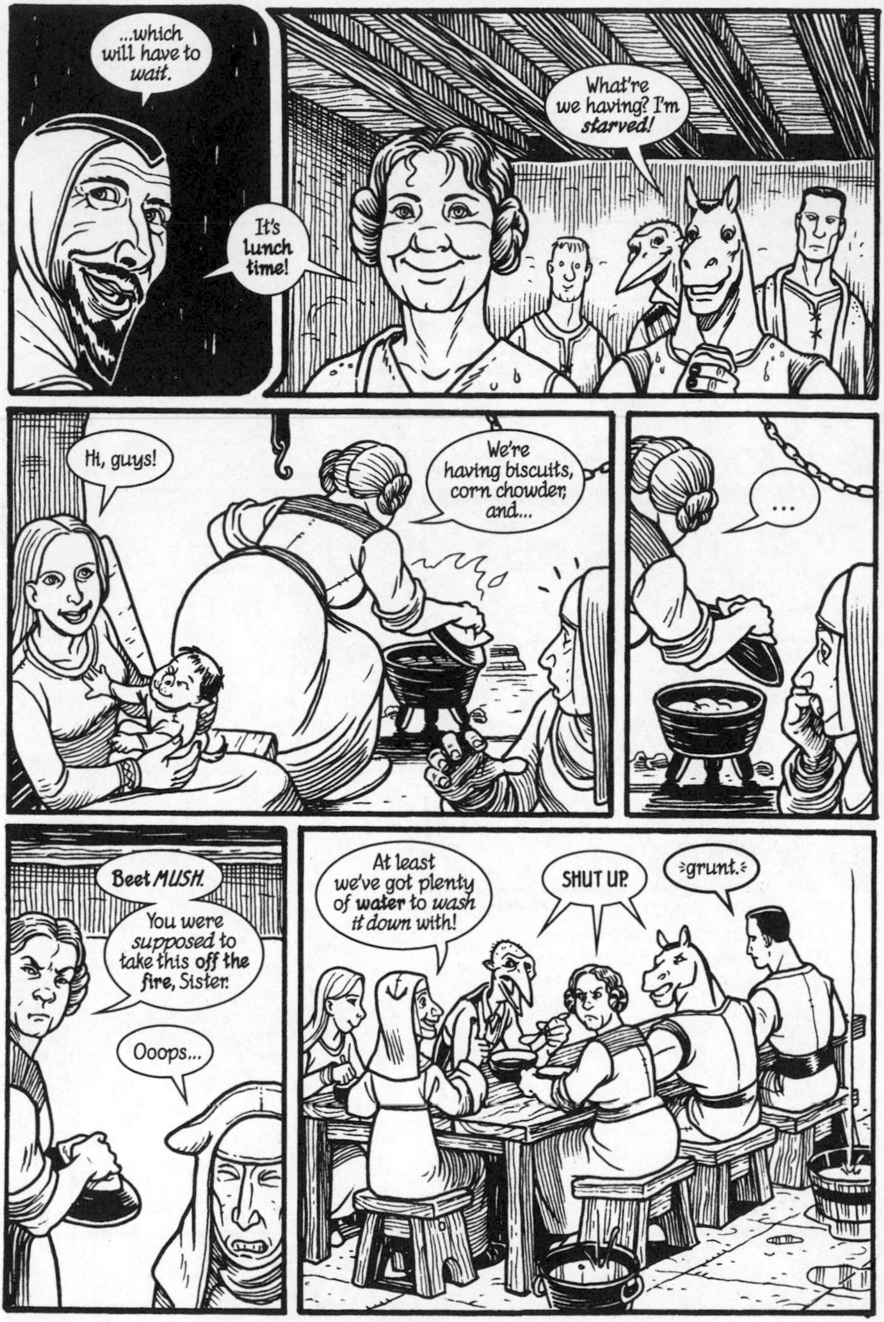
...which will have to *wait*.
It's **lunch time!**
What're we having? I'm ***starved!***
Hi, guys!
We're having biscuits, corn chowder, and...
...
Beet *MUSH.*
You were *supposed* to take this **off the fire**, Sister.
Ooops...
At least we've got plenty of **water** to *wash it down* with!
SHUT UP.
grunt.

Chapter 16.

· SOLICITINE PT. 4 ·

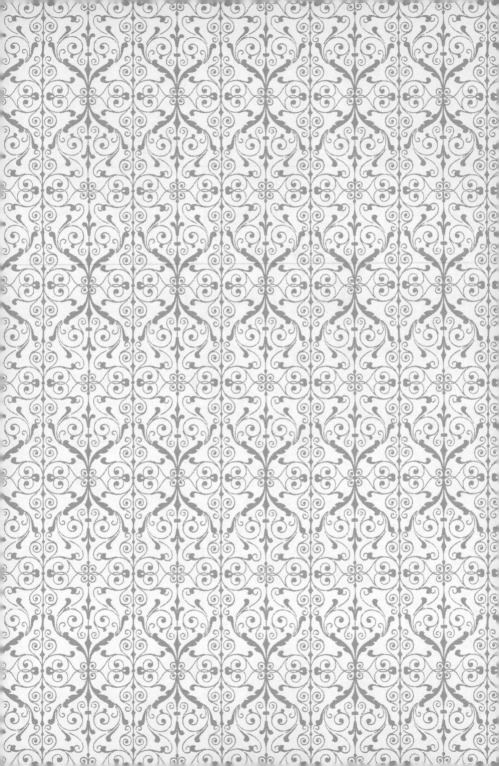

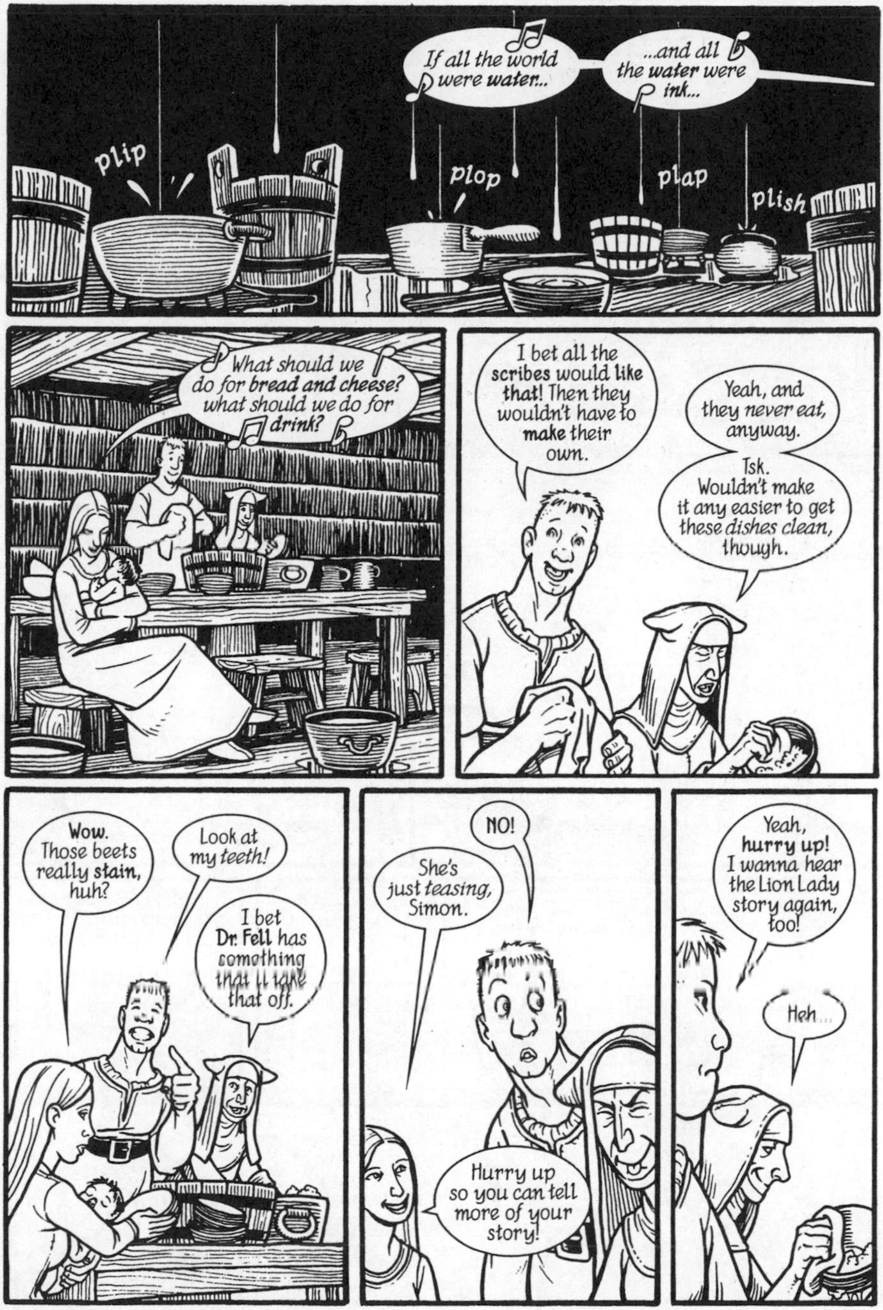
plip
plop
plap
plish
If all the world were water...
...and all the water were ink...
What should we do for bread and cheese? what should we do for drink?
I bet all the scribes would like that! Then they wouldn't have to make their own.
Yeah, and they never eat, anyway.
Tsk. Wouldn't make it any easier to get these dishes clean, though.
Wow. Those beets really stain, huh?
Look at my teeth!
I bet Dr. Fell has something that'll take that off.
She's just teasing, Simon.
NO!
Hurry up so you can tell more of your story!
Yeah, hurry up! I wanna hear the Lion Lady story again, too!
Heh...

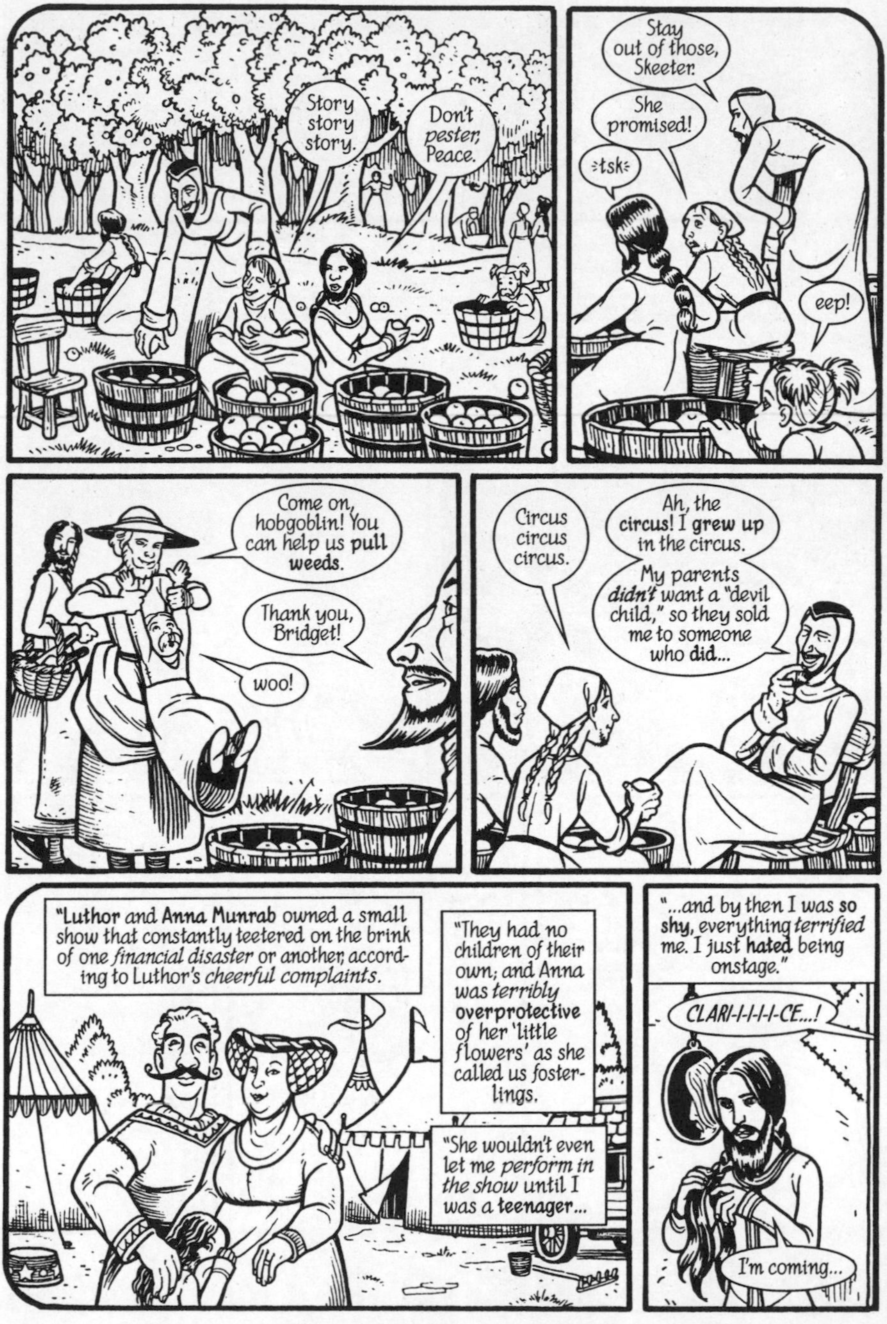
Story story story.
Don't *pester*, Peace.
Stay out of those, Skeeter.
She promised!
tsk
eep!
Come on, hobgoblin! You can help us **pull weeds**.
Thank you, Bridget!
woo!
Circus circus circus.
Ah, the **circus**! I **grew up** in the circus.
My parents ***didn't*** want a "devil child," so they sold me to someone who **did**...
"**Luthor** and **Anna Munrab** owned a small show that constantly teetered on the brink of one *financial disaster* or another, according to Luthor's *cheerful complaints*.
"They had no children of their own; and Anna was *terribly* **overprotective** of her 'little flowers' as she called us fosterlings.
"She wouldn't even let me *perform in the show* until I was a **teenager**...
"...and by then I was **so shy**, everything *terrified* me. I just **hated** being onstage."
CLARI-I-I-I-CE...!
I'm coming...

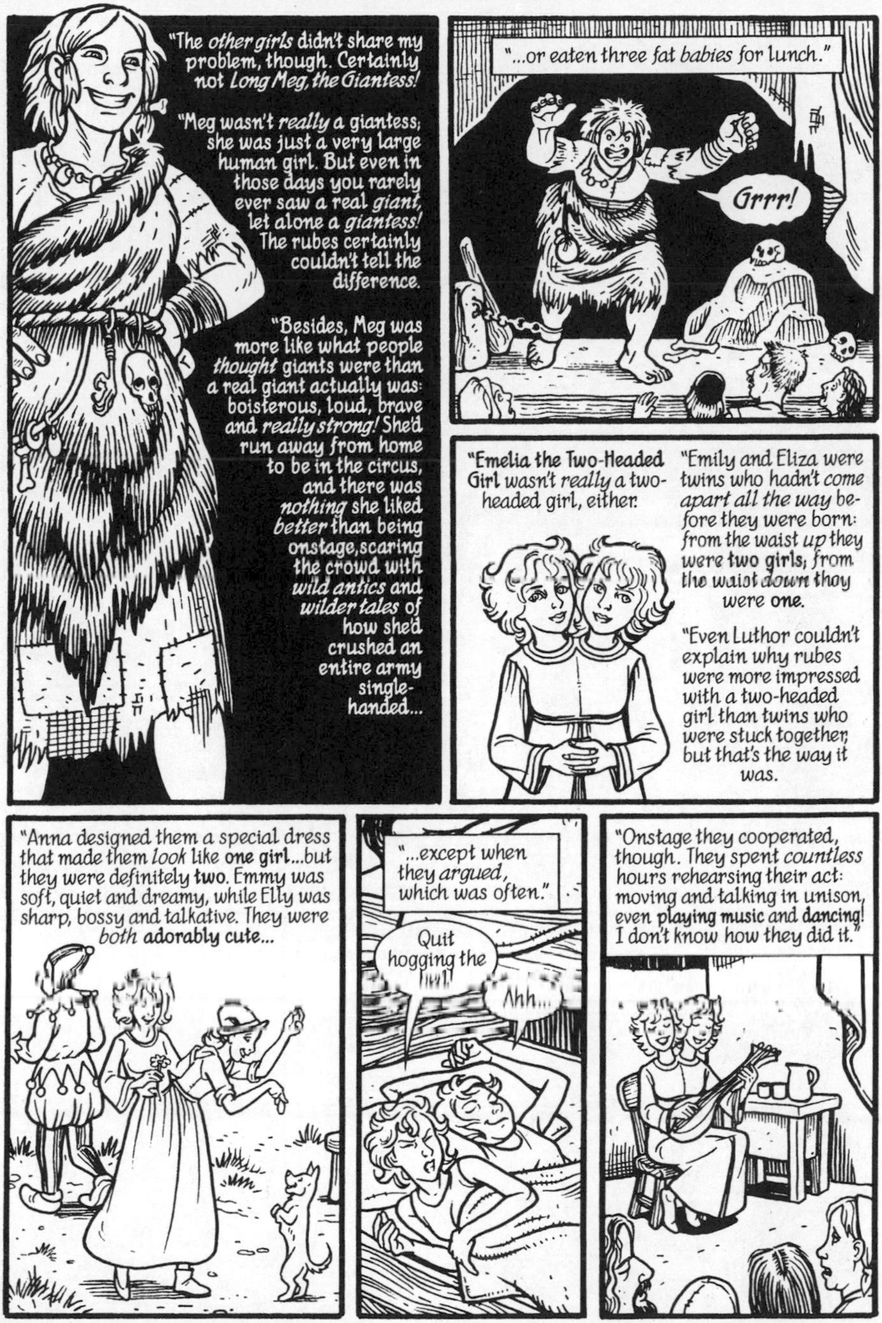
"The other girls didn't share my problem, though. Certainly not Long Meg, the Giantess!
"Meg wasn't really a giantess; she was just a very large human girl. But even in those days you rarely ever saw a real giant, let alone a giantess! The rubes certainly couldn't tell the difference.
"Besides, Meg was more like what people thought giants were than a real giant actually was: boisterous, loud, brave and really strong! She'd run away from home to be in the circus, and there was nothing she liked better than being onstage, scaring the crowd with wild antics and wilder tales of how she'd crushed an entire army single-handed...
"...or eaten three fat babies for lunch."
Grrr!
"Emelia the Two-Headed Girl wasn't really a two-headed girl, either.
"Emily and Eliza were twins who hadn't come apart all the way before they were born: from the waist up they were two girls; from the waist down they were one.
"Even Luthor couldn't explain why rubes were more impressed with a two-headed girl than twins who were stuck together, but that's the way it was.
"Anna designed them a special dress that made them look like one girl...but they were definitely two. Emmy was soft, quiet and dreamy, while Elly was sharp, bossy and talkative. They were both adorably cute...
"...except when they argued, which was often."
Quit hogging the
Ahh...
"Onstage they cooperated, though. They spent countless hours rehearsing their act: moving and talking in unison, even playing music and dancing! I don't know how they did it."

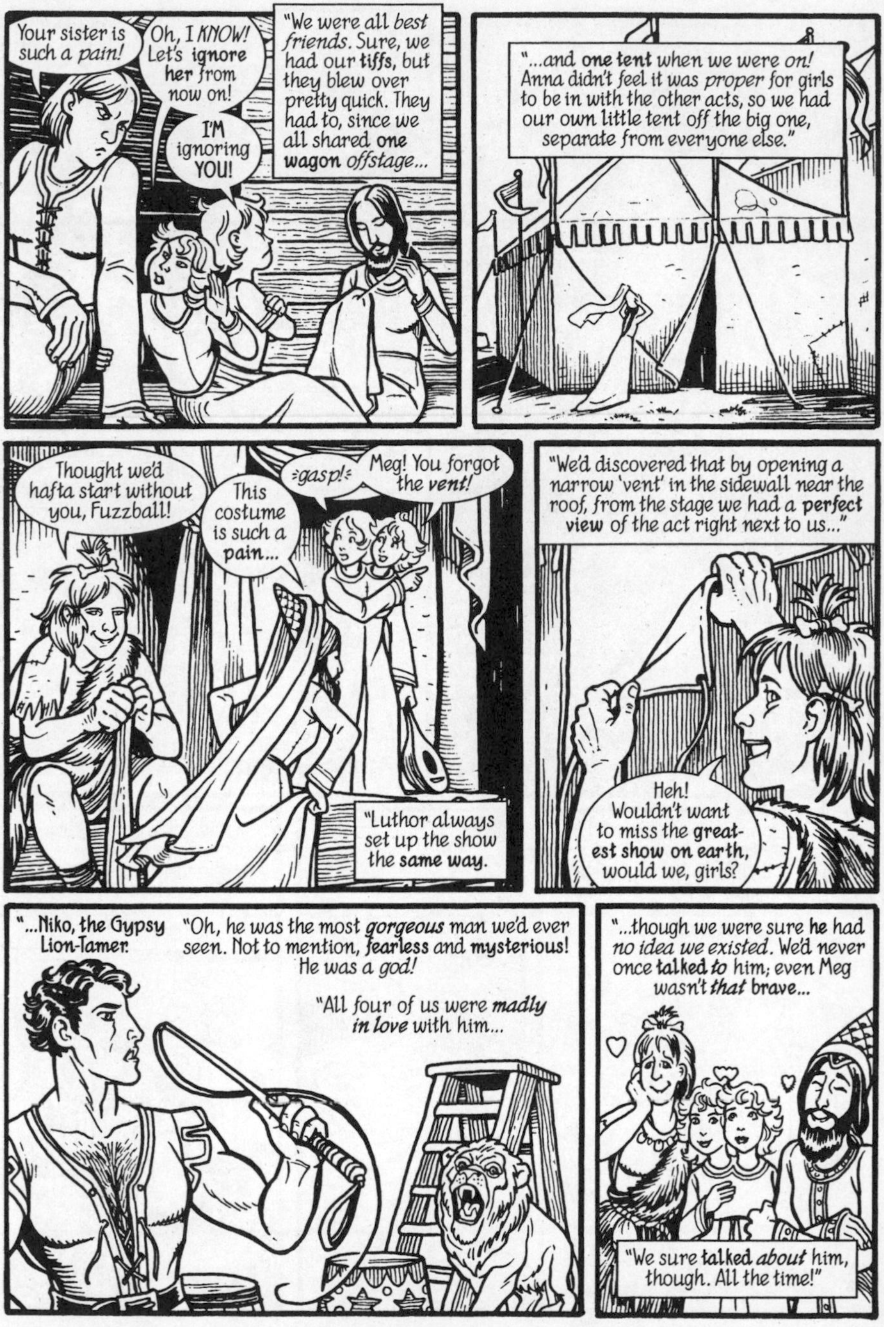
Your sister is such a pain!
Oh, I KNOW! Let's ignore her from now on!
I'M ignoring YOU!
"We were all best friends. Sure, we had our tiffs, but they blew over pretty quick. They had to, since we all shared one wagon offstage...
"...and one tent when we were on! Anna didn't feel it was proper for girls to be in with the other acts, so we had our own little tent off the big one, separate from everyone else."
Thought we'd hafta start without you, Fuzzball!
This costume is such a pain...
gasp!
Meg! You forgot the vent!
"Luthor always set up the show the same way.
"We'd discovered that by opening a narrow 'vent' in the sidewall near the roof, from the stage we had a perfect view of the act right next to us..."
Heh! Wouldn't want to miss the greatest show on earth, would we, girls?
"...Niko, the Gypsy Lion-Tamer.
"Oh, he was the most gorgeous man we'd ever seen. Not to mention, fearless and mysterious! He was a god!
"All four of us were madly in love with him...
"...though we were sure he had no idea we existed. We'd never once talked to him; even Meg wasn't that brave...
"We sure talked about him, though. All the time!"

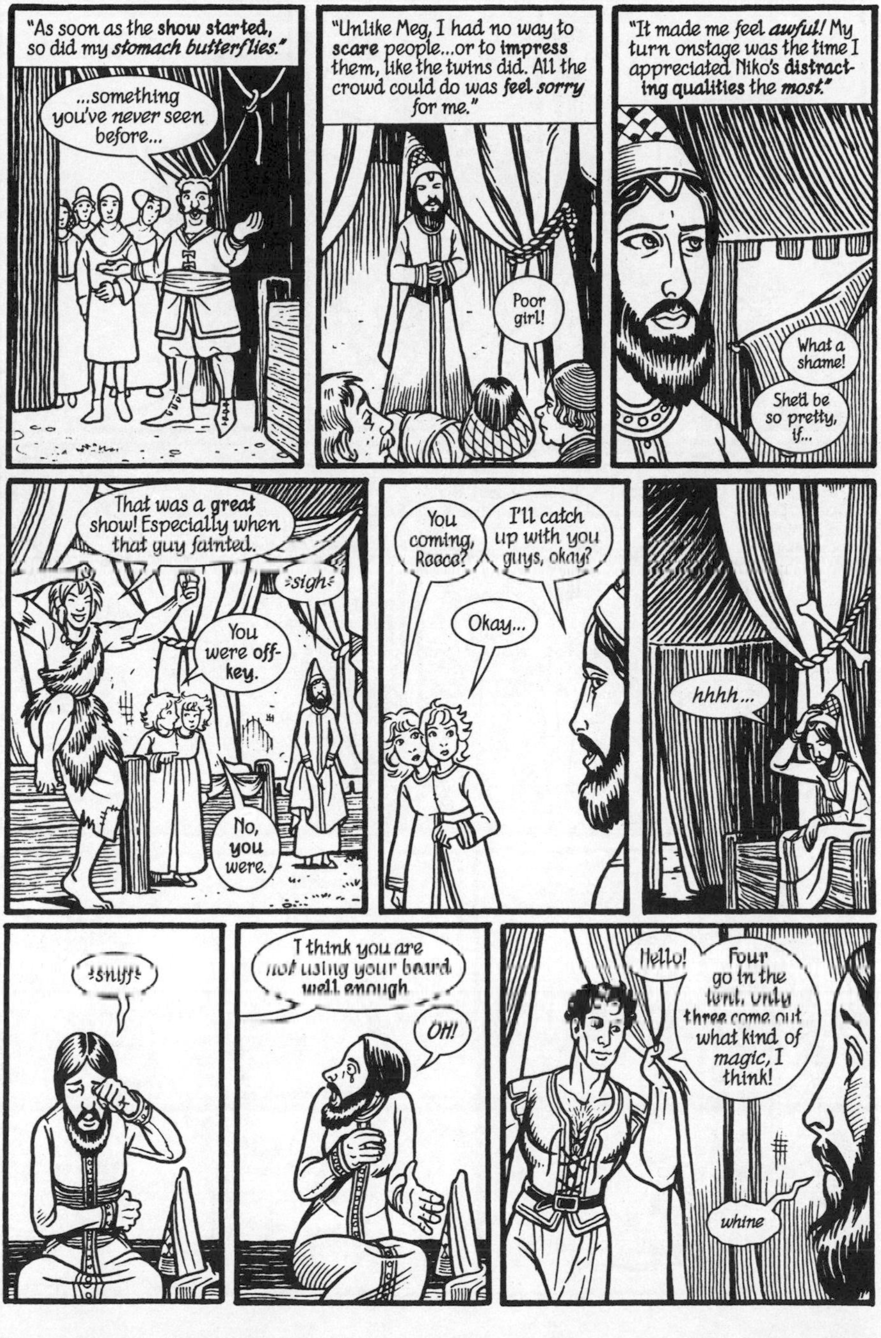
"As soon as the show started, so did my stomach butterflies."
...something you've never seen before...
"Unlike Meg, I had no way to scare people...or to impress them, like the twins did. All the crowd could do was feel sorry for me."
Poor girl!
"It made me feel awful! My turn onstage was the time I appreciated Niko's distracting qualities the most."
What a shame!
She'd be so pretty, if...
That was a great show! Especially when that guy fainted.
≈sigh≈
You were off-key.
No, you were.
You coming, Reece?
I'll catch up with you guys, okay?
Okay...
hhhh...
≈sniff≈
I think you are not using your beard well enough.
OH!
Hello!
Four go in the tent. Only three come out what kind of magic, I think!
whine

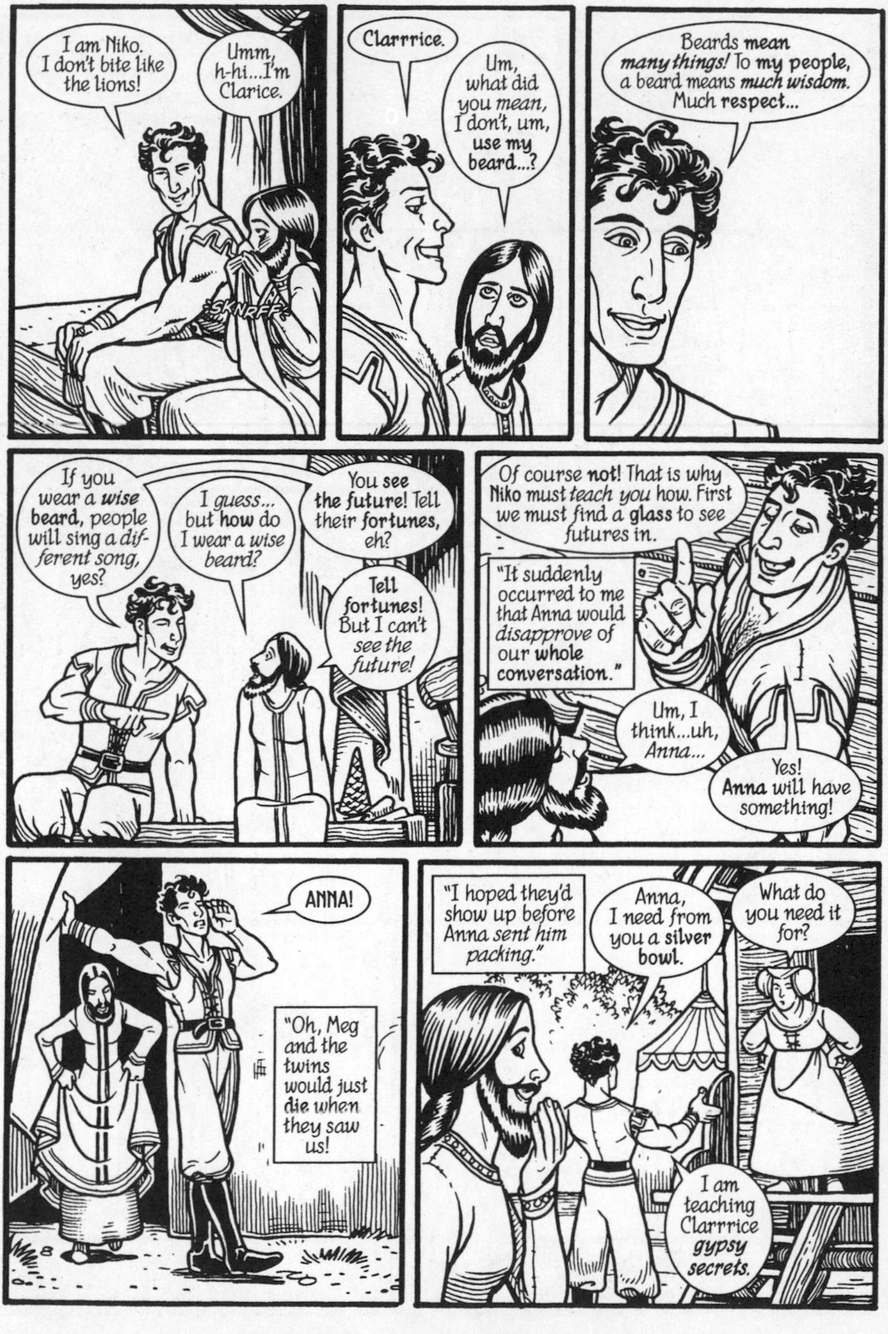
I am Niko. I don't bite like the lions!
Umm, h-hi...I'm Clarice.
SKNRFF
Clarrrice.
Um, what did you *mean*, I don't, um, **use my beard**...?
Beards **mean** ***many things!*** To **my people**, a beard means ***much wisdom***. Much **respect**...
If you wear a ***wise* beard**, people will sing a *different song*, yes?
I *guess*... but **how** do I wear a *wise* beard?
You **see the future**! Tell their **fortunes**, eh?
Tell fortunes! But I can't *see the future!*
Of course **not**! That is why Niko must *teach you* how. First we must find a **glass** to see futures in.
"It suddenly occurred to me that Anna would *disapprove* of our **whole conversation**."
Um, I think...uh, Anna...
Yes! **Anna** will have something!
ANNA!
"Oh, Meg and the twins would just **die** when they saw us!"
"I hoped they'd show up before Anna *sent him packing*."
Anna, I need from you a **silver bowl**.
What do you need it for?
I am teaching Clarrrice ***gypsy secrets***.

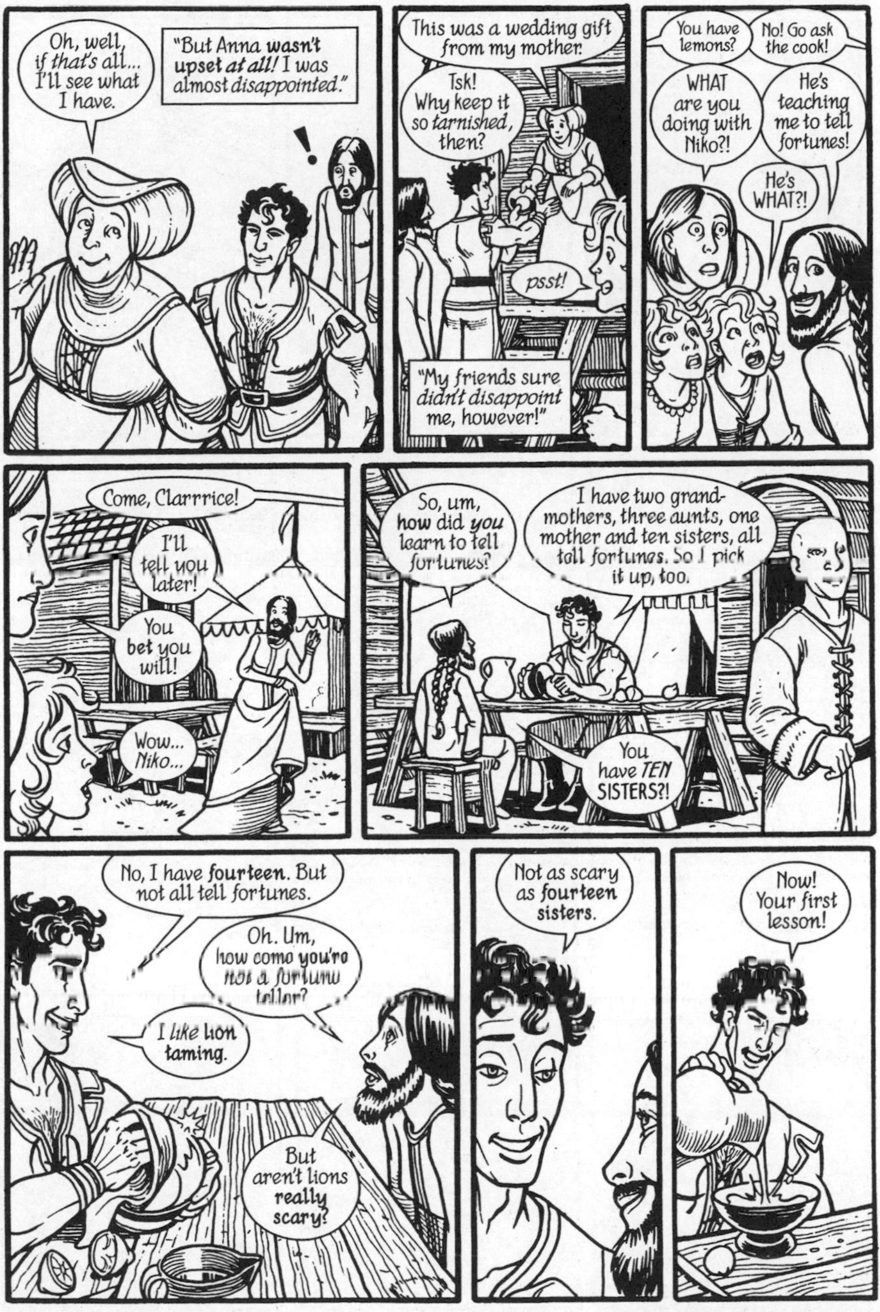
Oh, well, if that's all... I'll see what I have.
"But Anna wasn't upset at all! I was almost disappointed."
!
This was a wedding gift from my mother.
Tsk! Why keep it so tarnished, then?
psst!
"My friends sure didn't disappoint me, however!"
You have lemons?
No! Go ask the cook!
WHAT are you doing with Niko?!
He's teaching me to tell fortunes!
He's WHAT?!
Come, Clarrrice!
I'll tell you later!
You bet you will!
Wow... Niko...
So, um, how did you learn to tell fortunes?
I have two grandmothers, three aunts, one mother and ten sisters, all tell fortunes. So I pick it up, too.
You have TEN SISTERS?!
No, I have fourteen. But not all tell fortunes.
Oh. Um, how come you're not a fortune teller?
I like lion taming.
But aren't lions really scary?
Not as scary as fourteen sisters.
Now! Your first lesson!

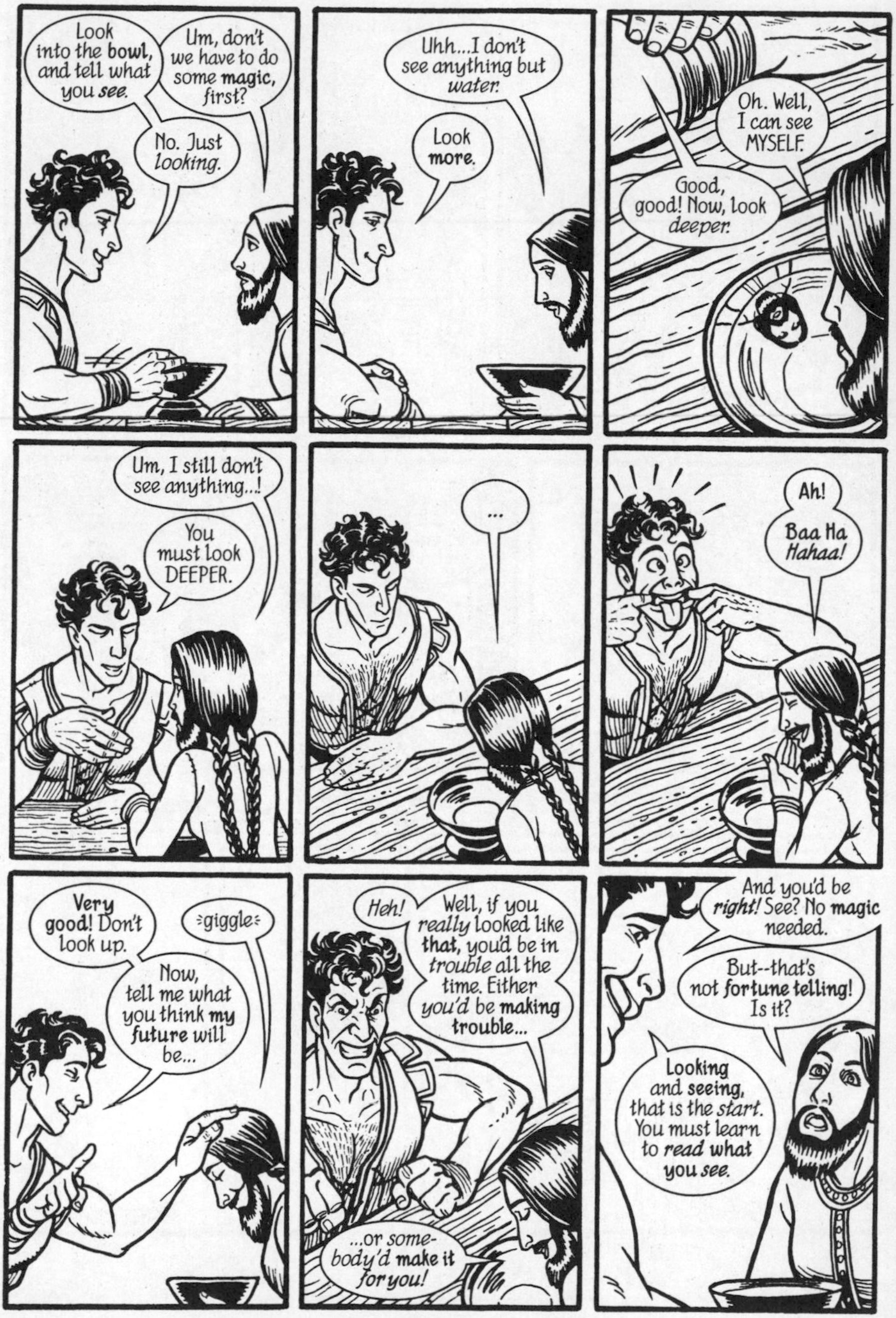
Look into the bowl, and tell what you see.
Um, don't we have to do some magic, first?
No. Just looking.
Uhh...I don't see anything but water.
Look more.
Oh. Well, I can see MYSELF.
Good, good! Now, look deeper.
Um, I still don't see anything...!
You must look DEEPER.
...
Ah!
Baa Ha Hahaa!
Very good! Don't look up.
giggle
Now, tell me what you think my future will be...
Heh!
Well, if you really looked like that, you'd be in trouble all the time. Either you'd be making trouble...
...or somebody'd make it for you!
And you'd be right! See? No magic needed.
But--that's not fortune telling! Is it?
Looking and seeing, that is the start. You must learn to read what you see.

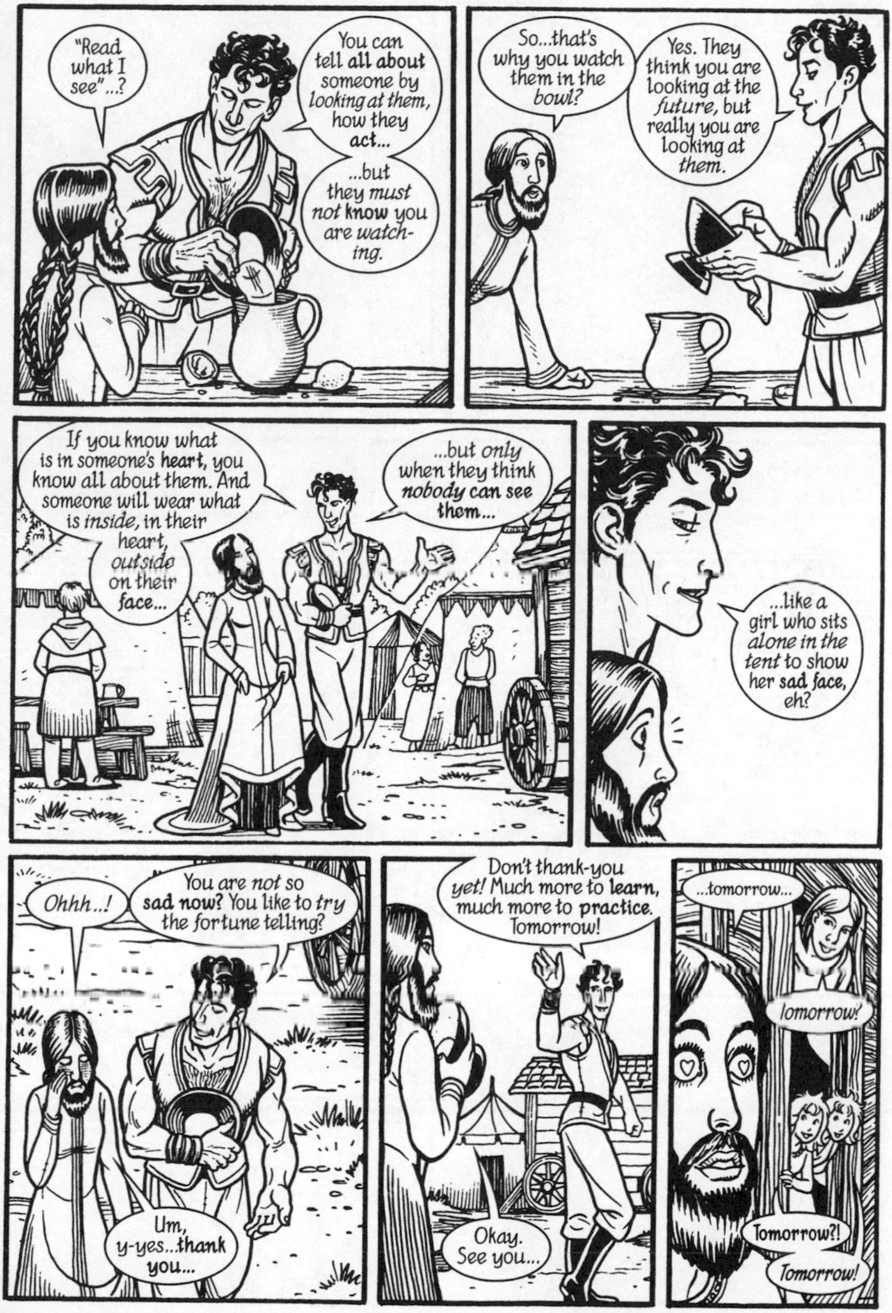
"Read what I see"...?
You can tell all about someone by looking at them, how they act...
...but they must not know you are watching.
So...that's why you watch them in the bowl?
Yes. They think you are looking at the future, but really you are looking at them.
If you know what is in someone's heart, you know all about them. And someone will wear what is inside, in their heart, outside on their face...
...but only when they think nobody can see them...
...like a girl who sits alone in the tent to show her sad face, eh?
Ohhh..!
You are not so sad now? You like to try the fortune telling?
Um, y-yes...thank you...
Don't thank-you yet! Much more to learn, much more to practice. Tomorrow!
Okay. See you...
...tomorrow...
Tomorrow!
Tomorrow?!
Tomorrow!

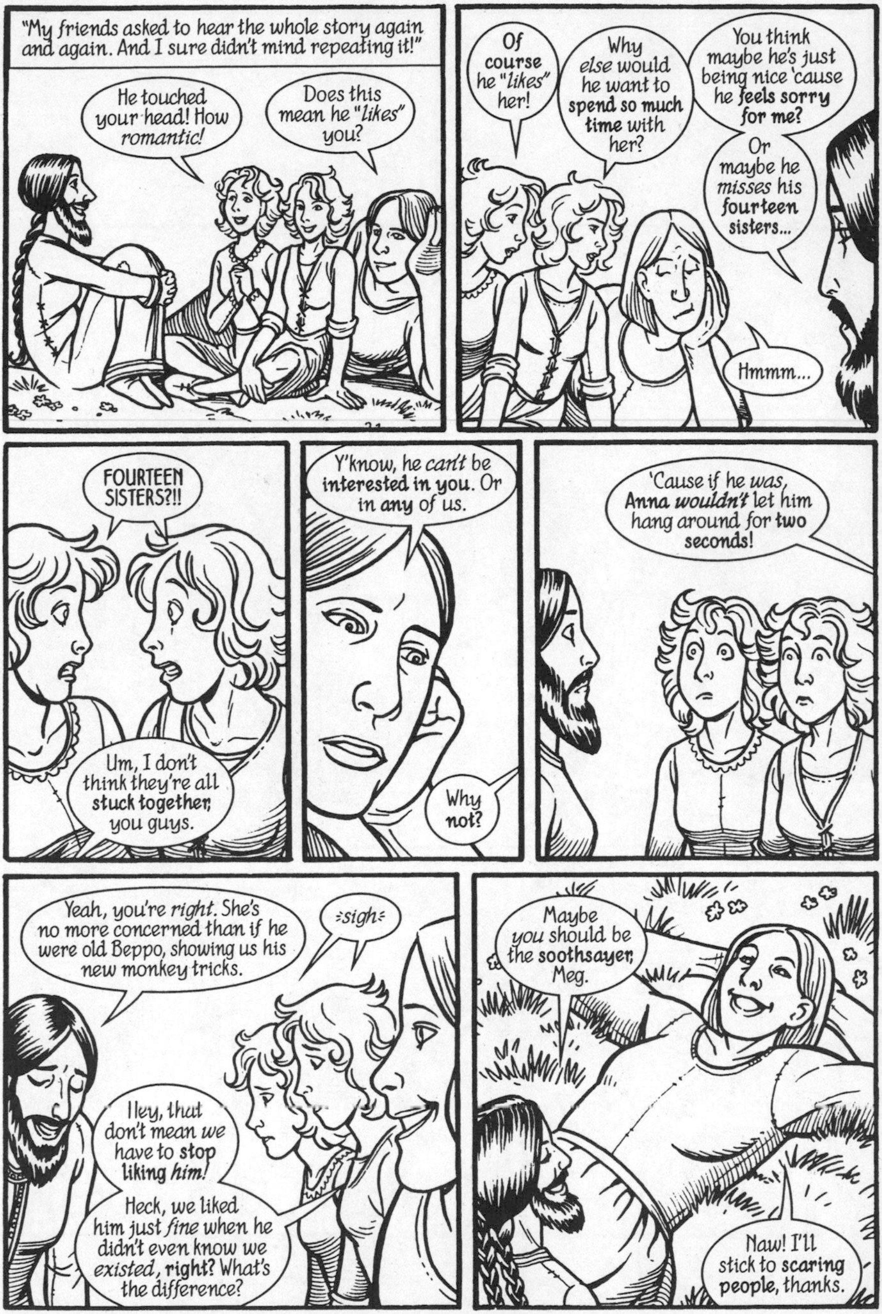
"My friends asked to hear the whole story again and again. And I sure didn't mind repeating it!"
He touched your head! How *romantic!*
Does this mean he "*likes*" you?
Of **course** he "*likes*" her!
Why *else* would he want to **spend so much time** with her?
You think maybe he's just being nice 'cause he **feels sorry for me?**
Or maybe he *misses* his **fourteen** sisters...
Hmmm...
FOURTEEN SISTERS?!!
Um, I don't think they're all **stuck together,** you guys.
Y'know, he *can't* be **interested in you**. Or in **any** of us.
Why **not?**
'Cause if he *was*, **Anna *wouldn't*** let him hang around for **two seconds!**
Yeah, you're *right*. She's no more concerned than if he were old Beppo, showing us his new monkey tricks.
sigh
Hey, that don't mean *we* have to **stop liking *him!***
Heck, we liked him just *fine* when he didn't even know we *existed*, **right?** What's the difference?
Maybe *you* should be the **soothsayer,** Meg.
Naw! I'll stick to **scaring** people, thanks.

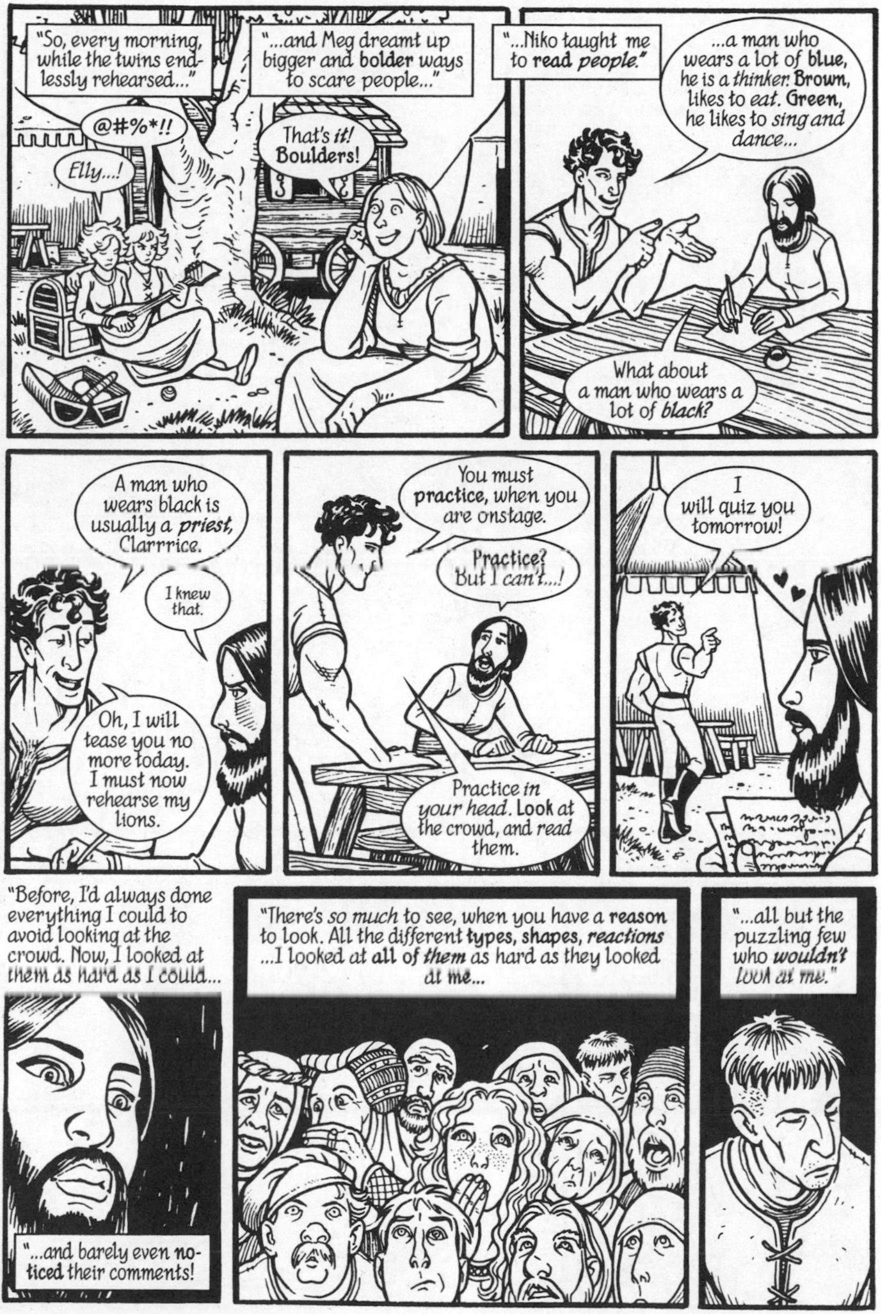
"So, every morning, while the twins endlessly rehearsed..."
@#%*!!
Elly...!
"...and Meg dreamt up bigger and bolder ways to scare people..."
That's it! Boulders!
"...Niko taught me to read people."
...a man who wears a lot of blue, he is a thinker. Brown, likes to eat. Green, he likes to sing and dance...
What about a man who wears a lot of black?
A man who wears black is usually a priest, Clarrrice.
I knew that.
Oh, I will tease you no more today. I must now rehearse my lions.
You must practice, when you are onstage.
Practice? But I can't...!
Practice in your head. Look at the crowd, and read them.
I will quiz you tomorrow!
"Before, I'd always done everything I could to avoid looking at the crowd. Now, I looked at them as hard as I could...
"...and barely even noticed their comments!
"There's so much to see, when you have a reason to look. All the different types, shapes, reactions ...I looked at all of them as hard as they looked at me...
"...all but the puzzling few who wouldn't look at me."

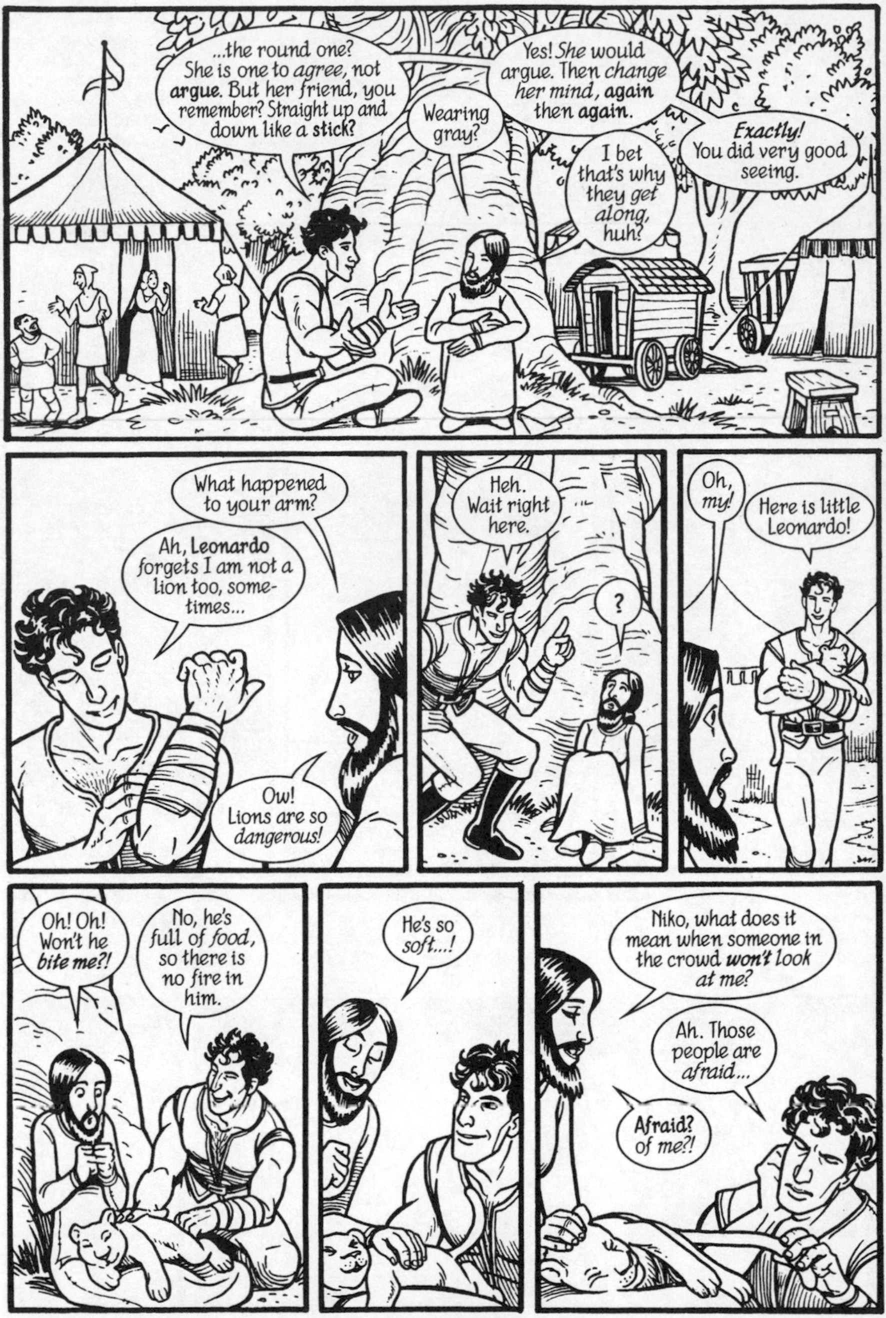

...the round one? She is one to *agree*, not **argue**. But her friend, you remember? Straight up and down like a **stick**?
Wearing gray?
Yes! *She* would argue. Then *change her mind*, **again** then **again**.
I bet that's why they *get along*, huh?
Exactly! You did very good seeing.
What happened to your arm?
Ah, **Leonardo** forgets I am not a lion too, sometimes...
Ow! Lions are so *dangerous!*
Heh. Wait right here.
?
Oh, *my!*
Here is little Leonardo!
Oh! Oh! Won't he ***bite me?!***
No, he's full of *food*, so there is no fire in him.
He's so *soft*...!
Niko, what does it mean when someone in the crowd ***won't*** *look at me?*
Ah. Those people are *afraid*...
Afraid? *of me?!*

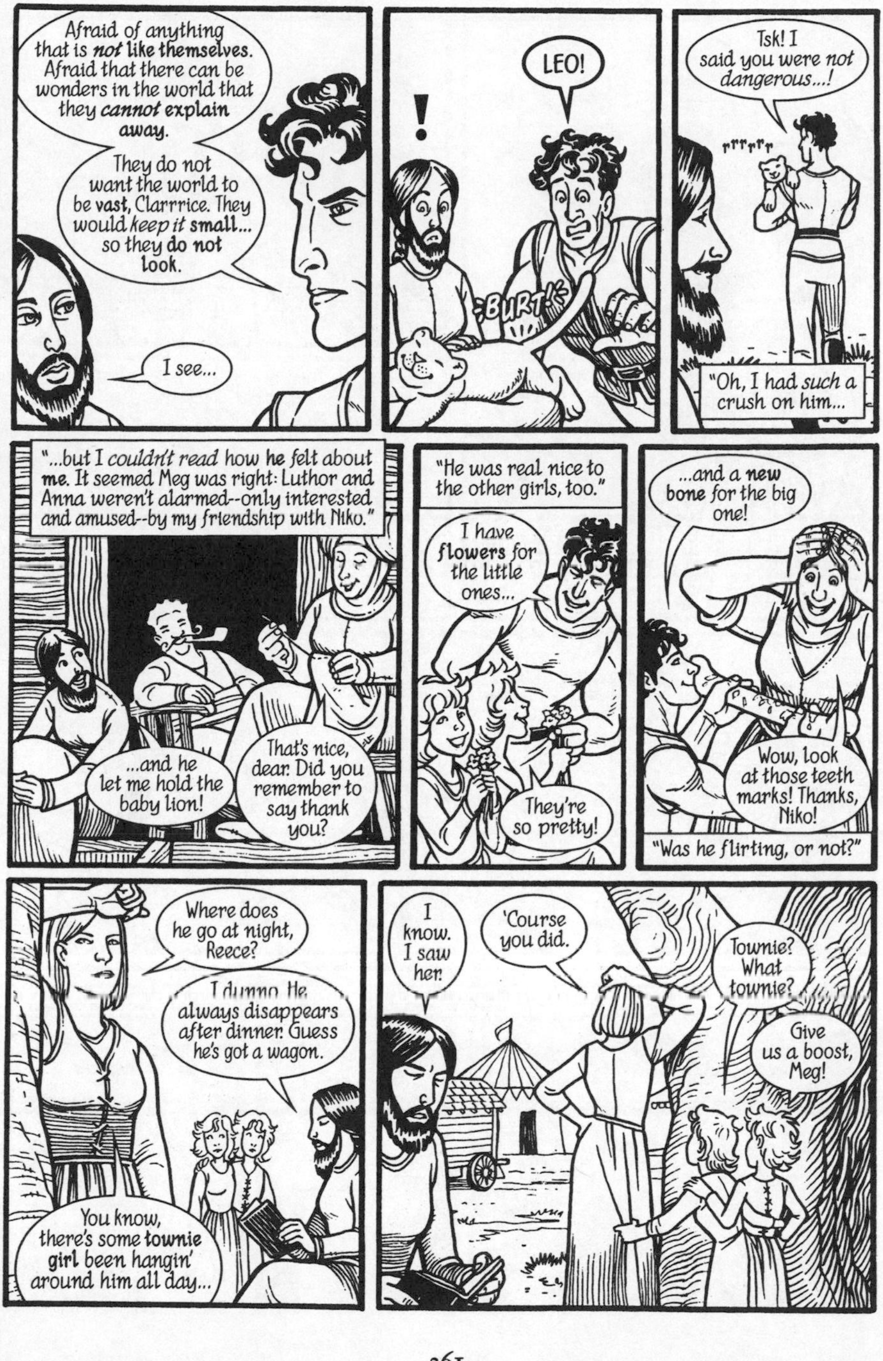
Afraid of anything that is **not like themselves.** Afraid that there can be wonders in the world that they ***cannot* explain away.**
They do not want the world to be **vast,** Clarrrice. They would *keep it* **small...** so they **do not** look.
I see...
!
LEO!
BURT!
Tsk! I said you were *not dangerous...!*
rrrrrr
"Oh, I had *such* a crush on him...
"...but I *couldn't read* how **he** felt about **me.** It seemed Meg was right: Luthor and Anna weren't alarmed--only interested and amused--by my friendship with Niko."
...and he let me hold the baby lion!
That's nice, dear. Did you remember to say thank you?
"He was real nice to the other girls, too."
I have **flowers** for the little ones...
They're so pretty!
...and a **new bone** for the big one!
Wow, look at those teeth marks! Thanks, Niko!
"Was he flirting, or not?"
Where does he go at night, Reece?
I dunno. He always disappears after dinner. Guess he's got a wagon.
You know, there's some **townie girl** been hangin' around him all day...
I know. I saw her.
'Course you did.
Townie? What townie?
Give us a boost, Meg!

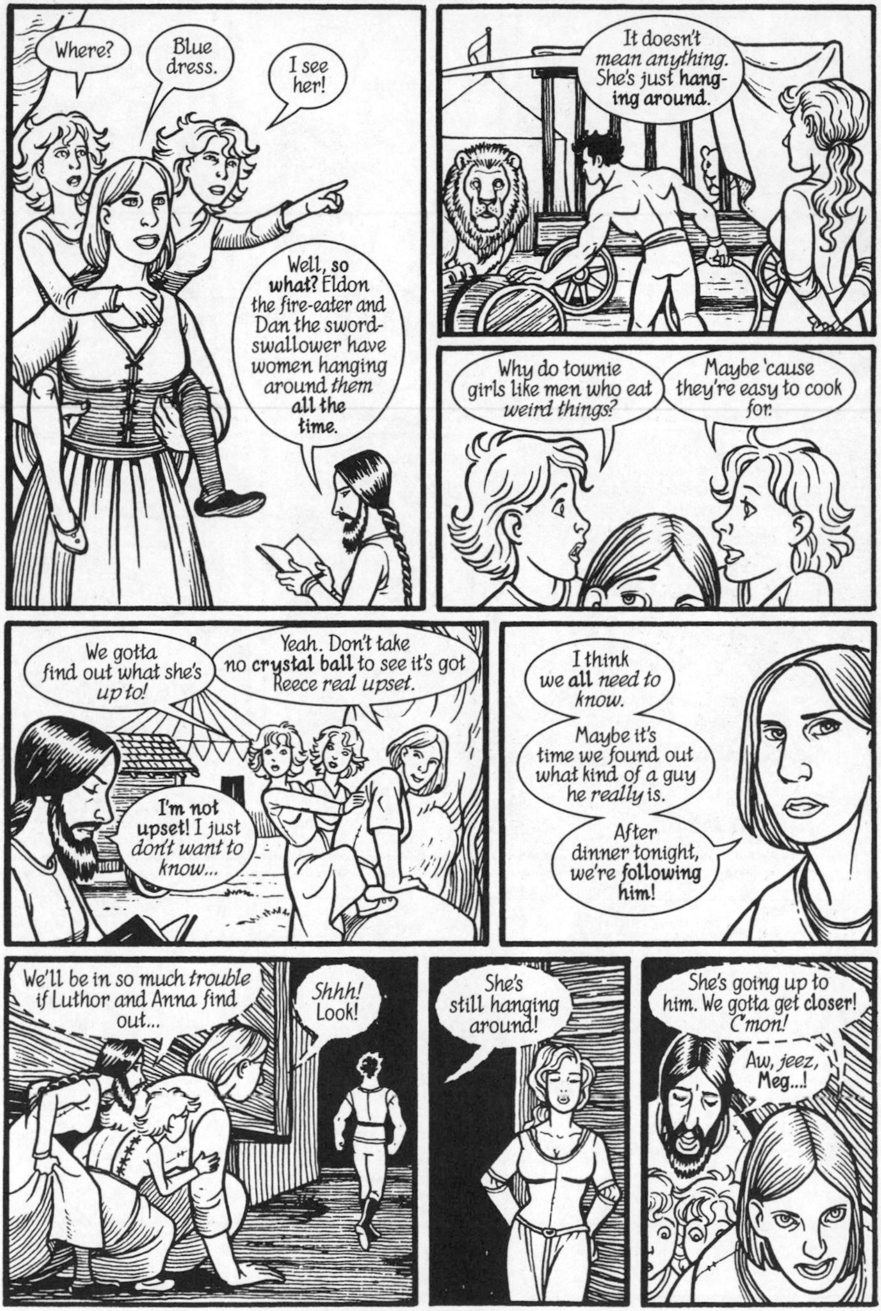
Where?
Blue dress.
I see her!
Well, so what? Eldon the fire-eater and Dan the sword-swallower have women hanging around them all the time.
It doesn't mean anything. She's just hanging around.
Why do townie girls like men who eat weird things?
Maybe 'cause they're easy to cook for.
We gotta find out what she's up to!
Yeah. Don't take no crystal ball to see it's got Reece real upset.
I'm not upset! I just don't want to know...
I think we all need to know.
Maybe it's time we found out what kind of a guy he really is.
After dinner tonight, we're following him!
We'll be in so much trouble if Luthor and Anna find out...
Shhh! Look!
She's still hanging around!
She's going up to him. We gotta get closer! C'mon!
Aw, jeez, Meg...!

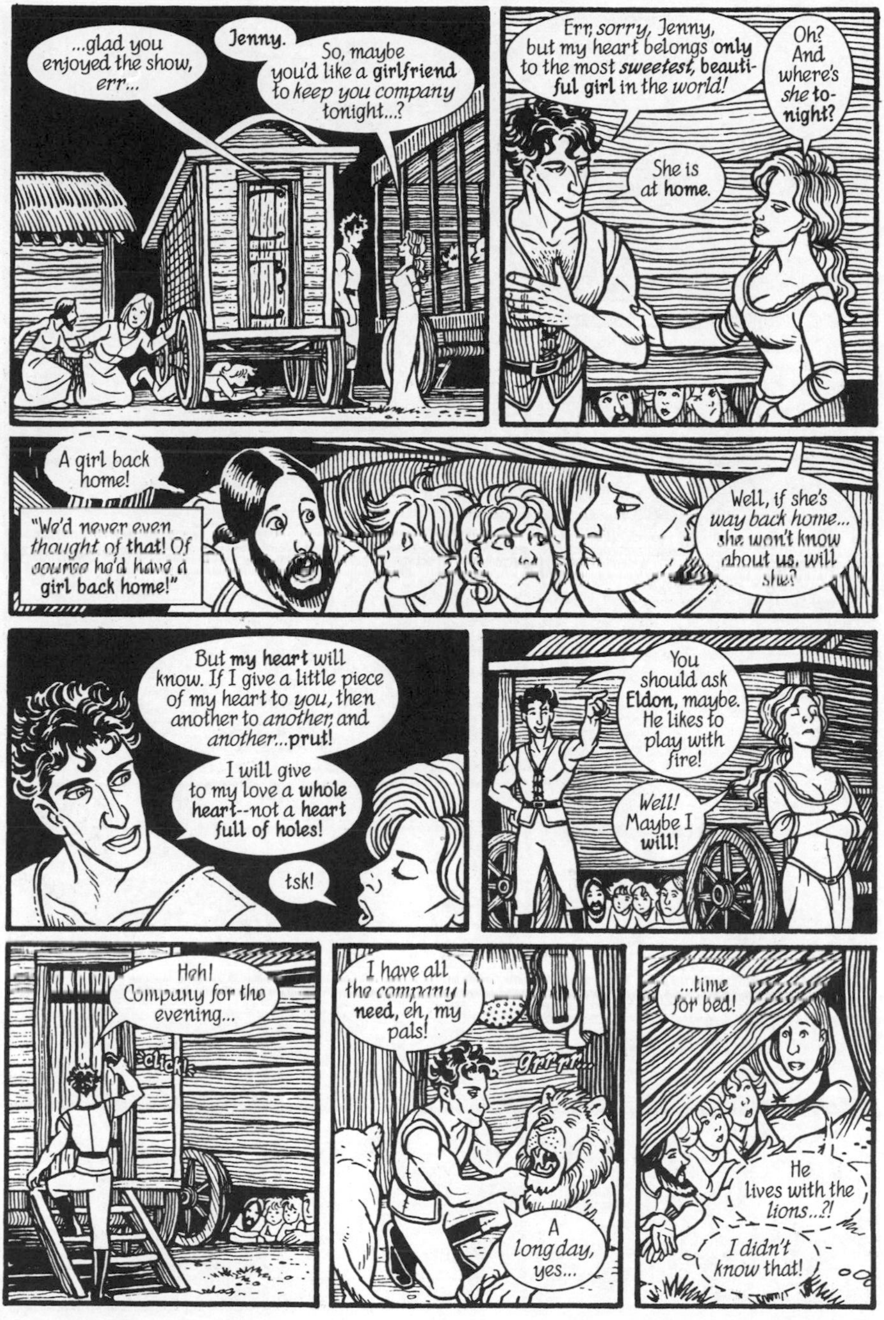
...glad you enjoyed the show, err...
Jenny.
So, maybe you'd like a **girlfriend** to *keep you company* tonight...?
Err, *sorry*, Jenny, but my heart belongs **only** to the most ***sweetest***, **beautiful girl** in the *world*!
Oh? And where's *she* **tonight?**
She is at **home**.
A girl back home!
"We'd never even *thought* of **that**! Of course he'd have a **girl back home!**"
Well, if she's *way back home*... she won't know about **us**, will she?
But **my heart** will know. If I give a little piece of my heart to *you*, then another to *another*, and *another*...**prut!**
I will give to my love a **whole heart**--not a **heart full of holes!**
tsk!
You should ask **Eldon**, maybe. He likes to play with fire!
Well! Maybe I **will!**
Heh! Company for the evening...
CLICK!
I have all the *company* I **need**, eh, my pals!
Grrrrr...
A long day, yes...
...time for bed!
He lives with the *lions*...?!
I didn't know that!

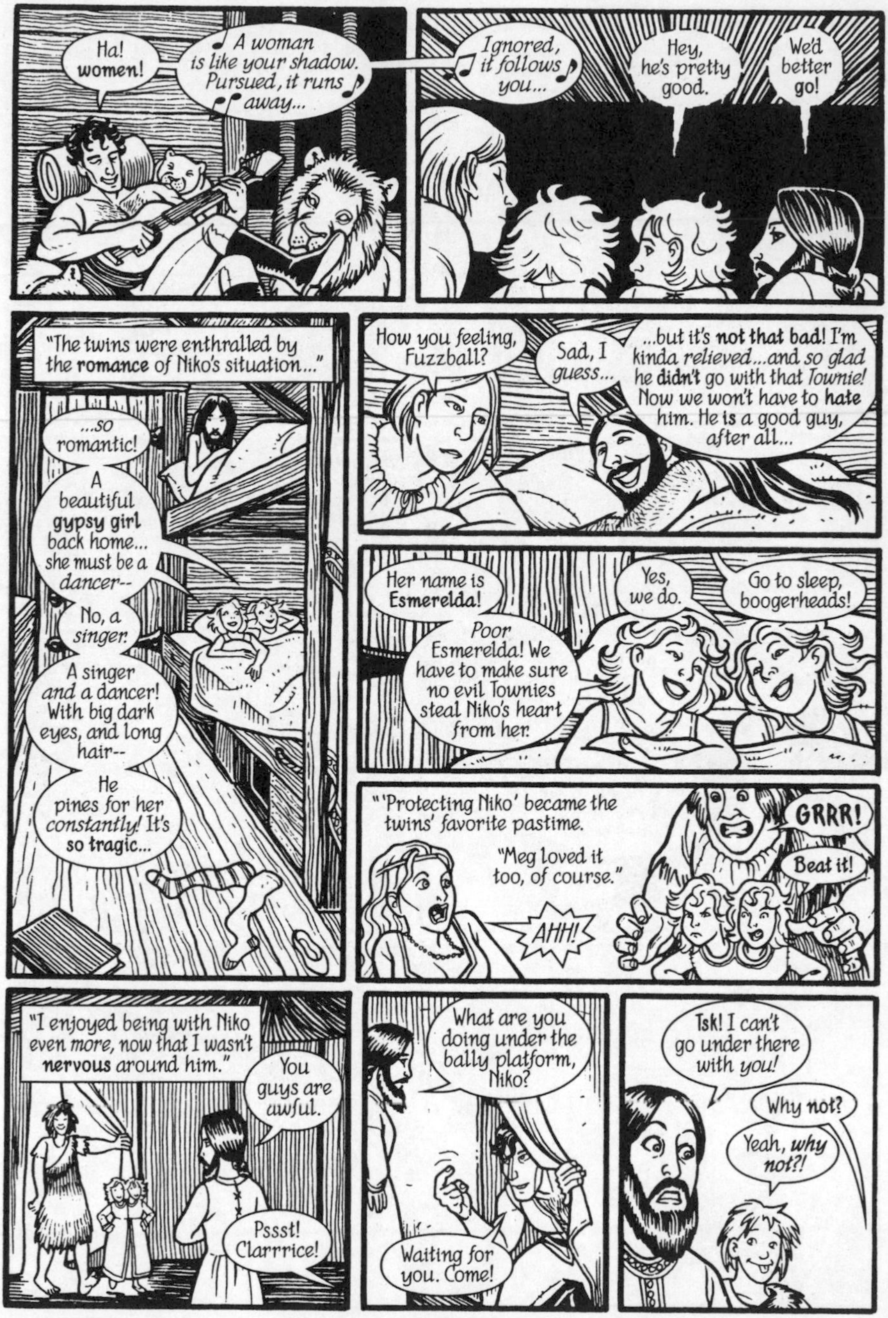
Ha! **women!**
A woman is like your shadow. Pursued, it runs away...
Ignored, it follows you...
Hey, he's pretty good.
We'd better **go!**
"The twins were enthralled by the **romance** of Niko's situation..."
...so romantic!
A beautiful **gypsy girl** back home... she must be a *dancer*--
No, a *singer.*
A singer *and* a dancer! With big dark eyes, and long hair--
He pines for her *constantly!* It's **so tragic...**
How you feeling, Fuzzball?
Sad, I *guess...*
...but it's **not that bad!** I'm kinda *relieved*...and so glad he **didn't** go with that *Townie!* Now we won't have to **hate** him. He **is** a good guy, after all...
Her name is **Esmerelda!**
Poor Esmerelda! We have to make sure no evil Townies steal Niko's heart from her.
Yes, we do.
Go to sleep, boogerheads!
"'Protecting Niko' became the twins' favorite pastime.
"Meg loved it too, of course."
AHH!
GRRR!
Beat it!
"I enjoyed being with Niko even *more*, now that I wasn't **nervous** around him."
You guys are *awful.*
Pssst! Clarrrice!
What are you doing under the bally platform, Niko?
Waiting for you. Come!
Tsk! I can't go under there with *you!*
Why **not?**
Yeah, ***why not?!***

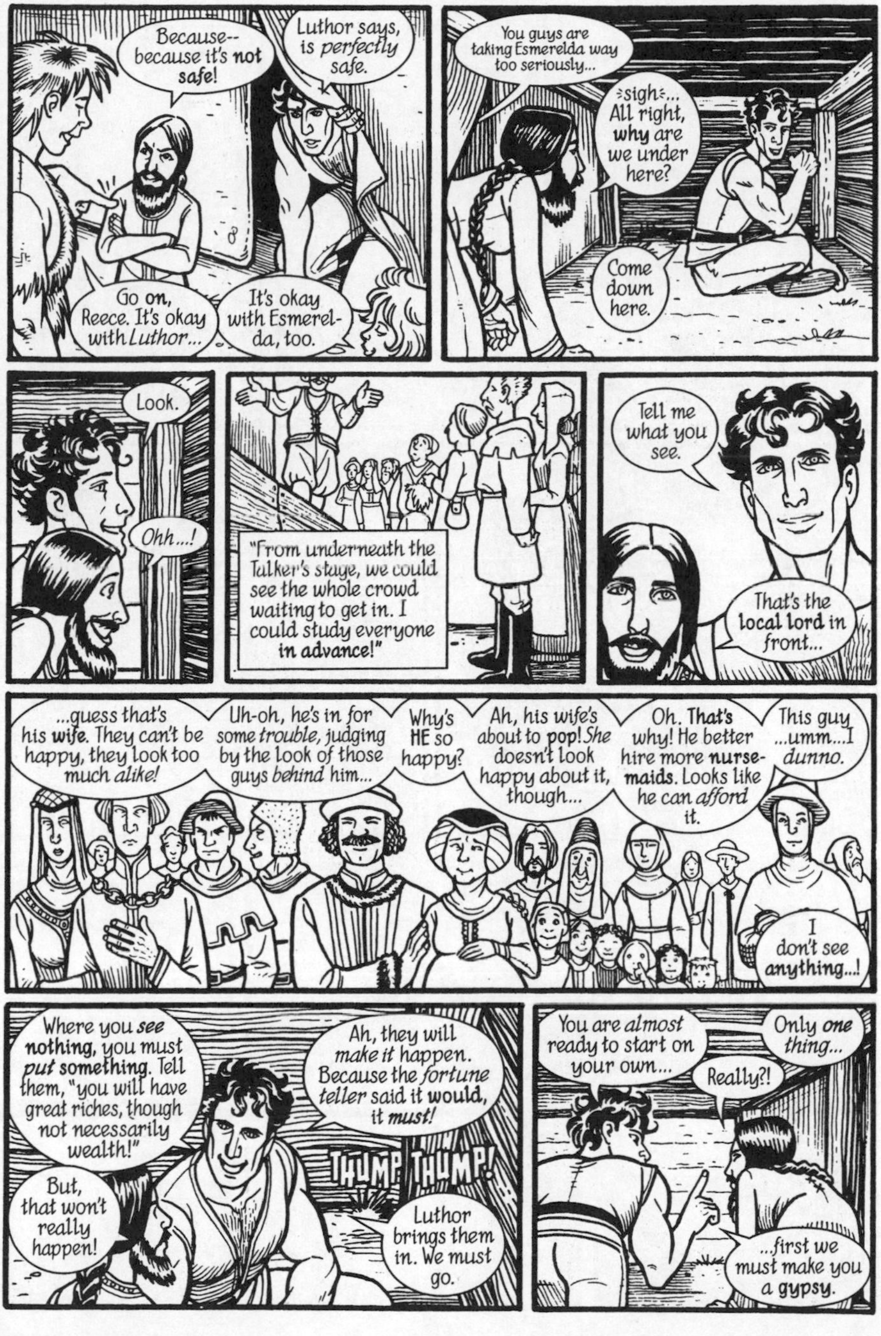
Because--
because it's **not** **safe**!
Luthor says, is *perfectly* safe.
Go **on**, Reece. It's okay with *Luthor*...
It's okay with Esmerelda, too.
You guys are taking Esmerelda way too seriously...
sigh... All right, **why** are we under here?
Come down here.
Look.
Ohh...!
"From underneath the Talker's stage, we could see the whole crowd waiting to get in. I could study everyone **in advance**!"
Tell me what you see.
That's the **local lord** in front...
...guess that's his **wife**. They can't be happy, they look too much *alike!*
Uh-oh, he's in for some *trouble*, judging by the look of those guys *behind* him...
Why's **HE** so happy?
Ah, his wife's about to **pop**! *She* doesn't look happy about it, though...
Oh. **That's** why! He better hire more **nurse-maids**. Looks like he can *afford* it.
This guy ...umm...I *dunno.*
I don't see **anything**...!
Where you *see* **nothing**, you must *put* **something**. Tell them, "you will have great riches, though not necessarily wealth!"
But, that won't really happen!
Ah, they will *make it* happen. Because the *fortune teller* said it **would**, it *must!*
THUMP THUMP!
Luthor brings them in. We must go.
You are *almost* ready to start on your own...
Really?!
Only *one* thing...
...first we must make you a **gypsy**.

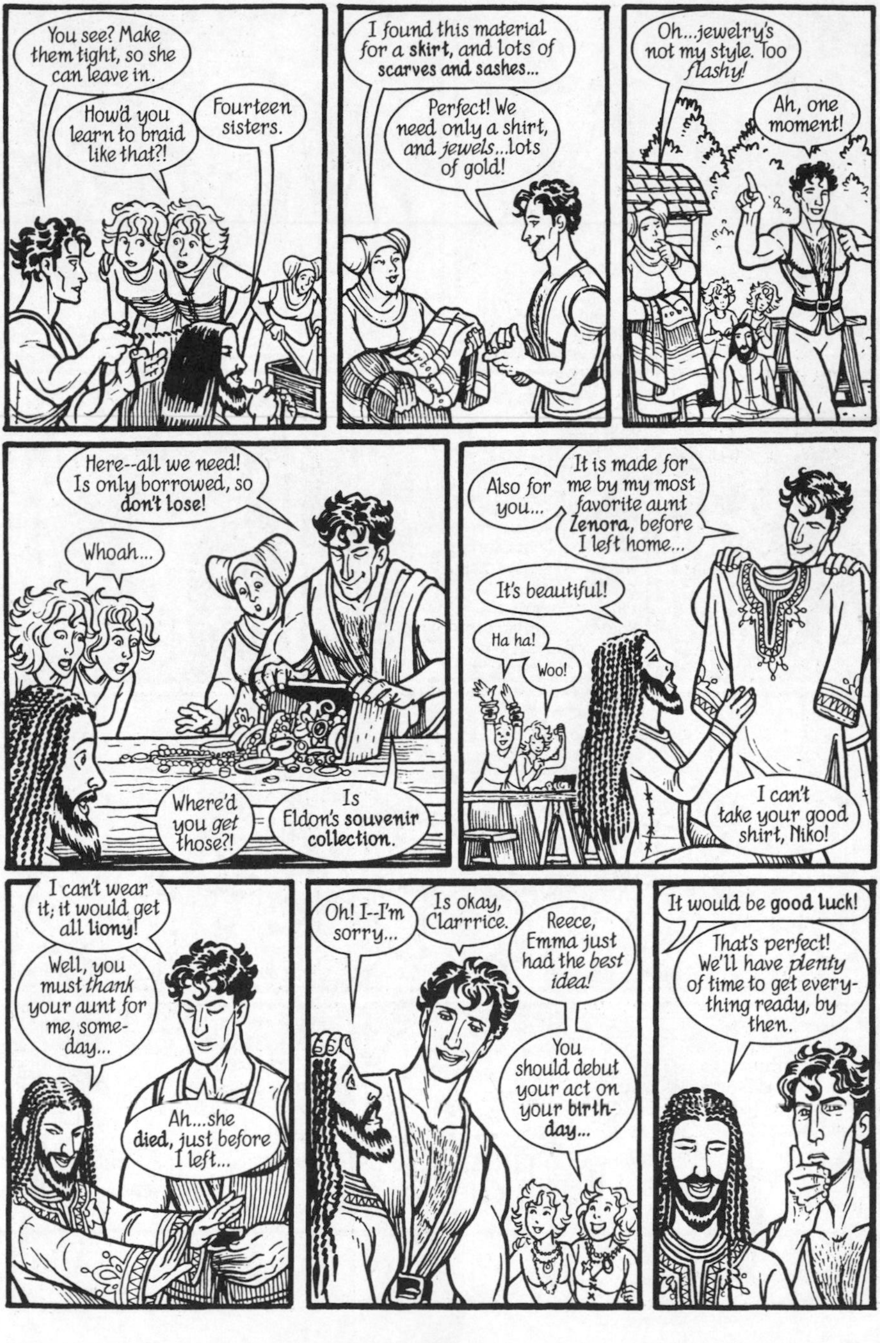

You see? Make them tight, so she can leave in.
How'd you learn to braid like that?!
Fourteen sisters.
I found this material for a skirt, and lots of scarves and sashes...
Perfect! We need only a shirt, and jewels...lots of gold!
Oh...jewelry's not my style. Too flashy!
Ah, one moment!
Here--all we need! Is only borrowed, so don't lose!
Whoah...
Where'd you get those?!
Is Eldon's souvenir collection.
Also for you...
It is made for me by my most favorite aunt Zenora, before I left home...
It's beautiful!
Ha ha!
Woo!
I can't take your good shirt, Niko!
I can't wear it; it would get all liony!
Well, you must thank your aunt for me, someday...
Ah...she died, just before I left...
Oh! I--I'm sorry...
Is okay, Clarrrice.
Reece, Emma just had the best idea!
You should debut your act on your birthday...
It would be good luck!
That's perfect! We'll have plenty of time to get everything ready, by then.

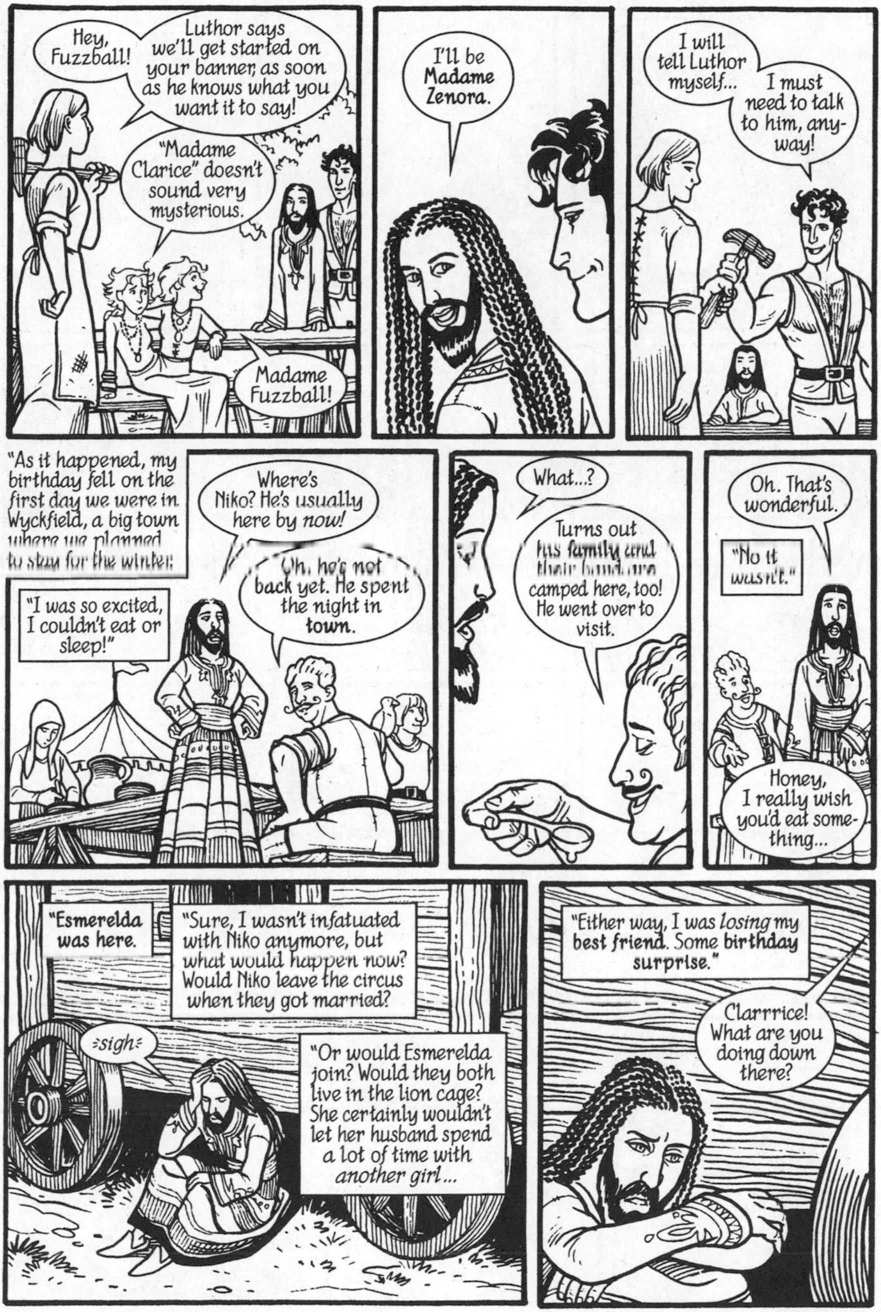
Hey, Fuzzball!
Luthor says we'll get started on your banner, as soon as he knows what you want it to say!
"Madame Clarice" doesn't sound very mysterious.
Madame Fuzzball!
I'll be **Madame Zenora**.
I will tell Luthor myself...
I must need to talk to him, any-way!
"As it happened, my birthday fell on the first day we were in Wyckfield, a big town where we planned to stay for the winter.
"I was so excited, I couldn't eat or sleep!"
Where's Niko? He's usually here by *now!*
Oh, he's not back yet. He spent the night in **town**.
What...?
Turns out his **family** and their band are camped here, too! He went over to visit.
Oh. That's wonderful.
"No it wasn't."
Honey, I really wish you'd eat some-thing...
"Esmerelda was here.
"Sure, I wasn't infatuated with Niko anymore, but what would happen now? Would Niko leave the circus when they got married?
sigh
"Or would Esmerelda join? Would they both live in the lion cage? She certainly wouldn't let her husband spend a lot of time with *another girl*...
"Either way, I was *losing* my **best friend**. Some **birthday surprise**."
Clarrrice! What are you doing down there?

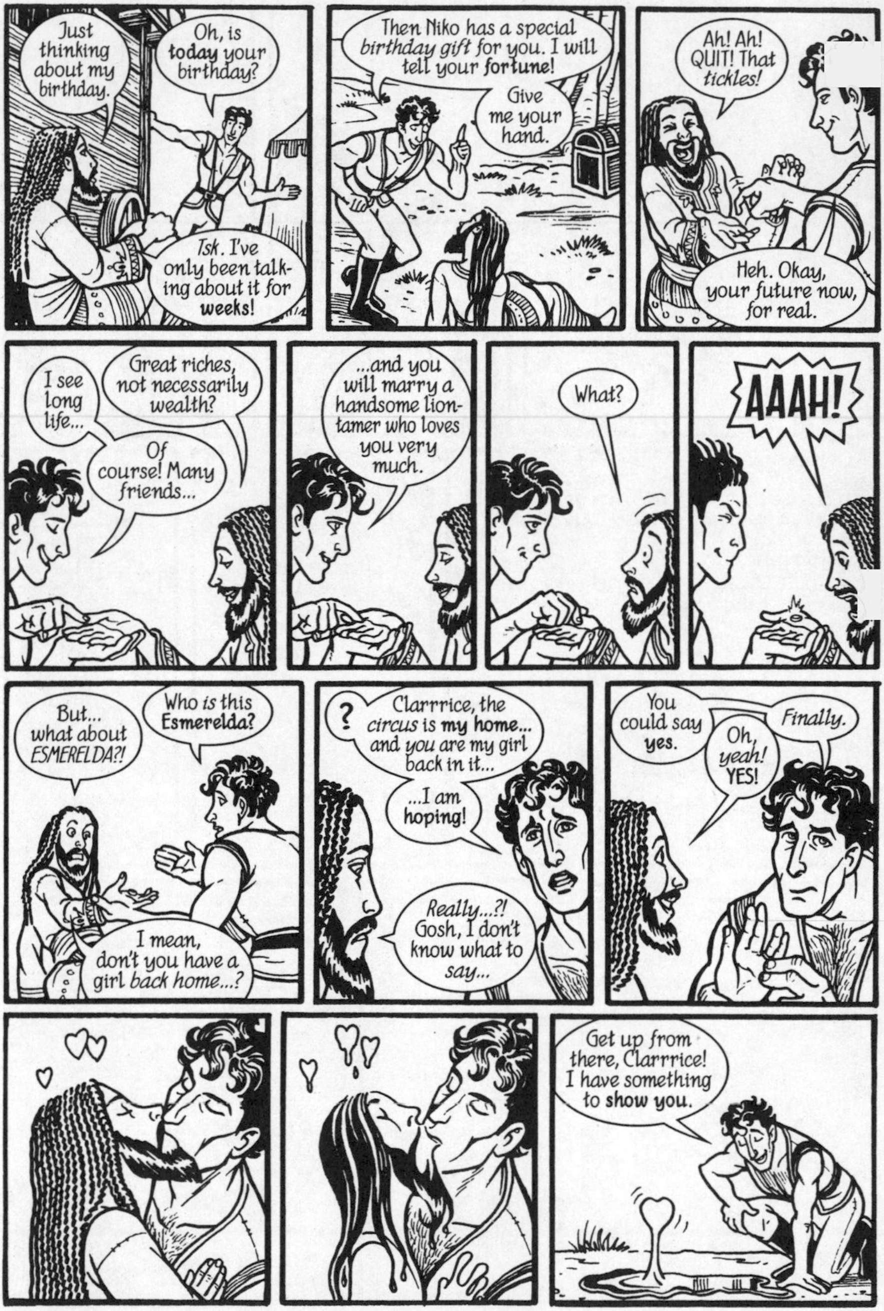
Just thinking about my birthday.
Oh, is **today** your birthday?
Tsk. I've only been talking about it for **weeks**!
Then Niko has a special *birthday gift* for you. I will tell your **fortune**!
Give me your hand.
Ah! Ah! QUIT! That *tickles*!
Heh. Okay, your future now, for real.
I see long life...
Great riches, not necessarily wealth?
Of course! Many friends...
...and you will marry a handsome lion-tamer who loves you very much.
What?
AAAH!
But... what about *ESMERELDA*?!
Who *is* this **Esmerelda?**
I mean, don't you have a girl *back home*...?
?
Clarrrice, the *circus* is **my home...** and *you* are my girl back in it...
...I am **hoping**!
Really...?! Gosh, I don't know what to *say*...
You could say **yes**.
Oh, *yeah!* YES!
Finally.
Get up *from* there, Clarrrice! I have something to **show you**.

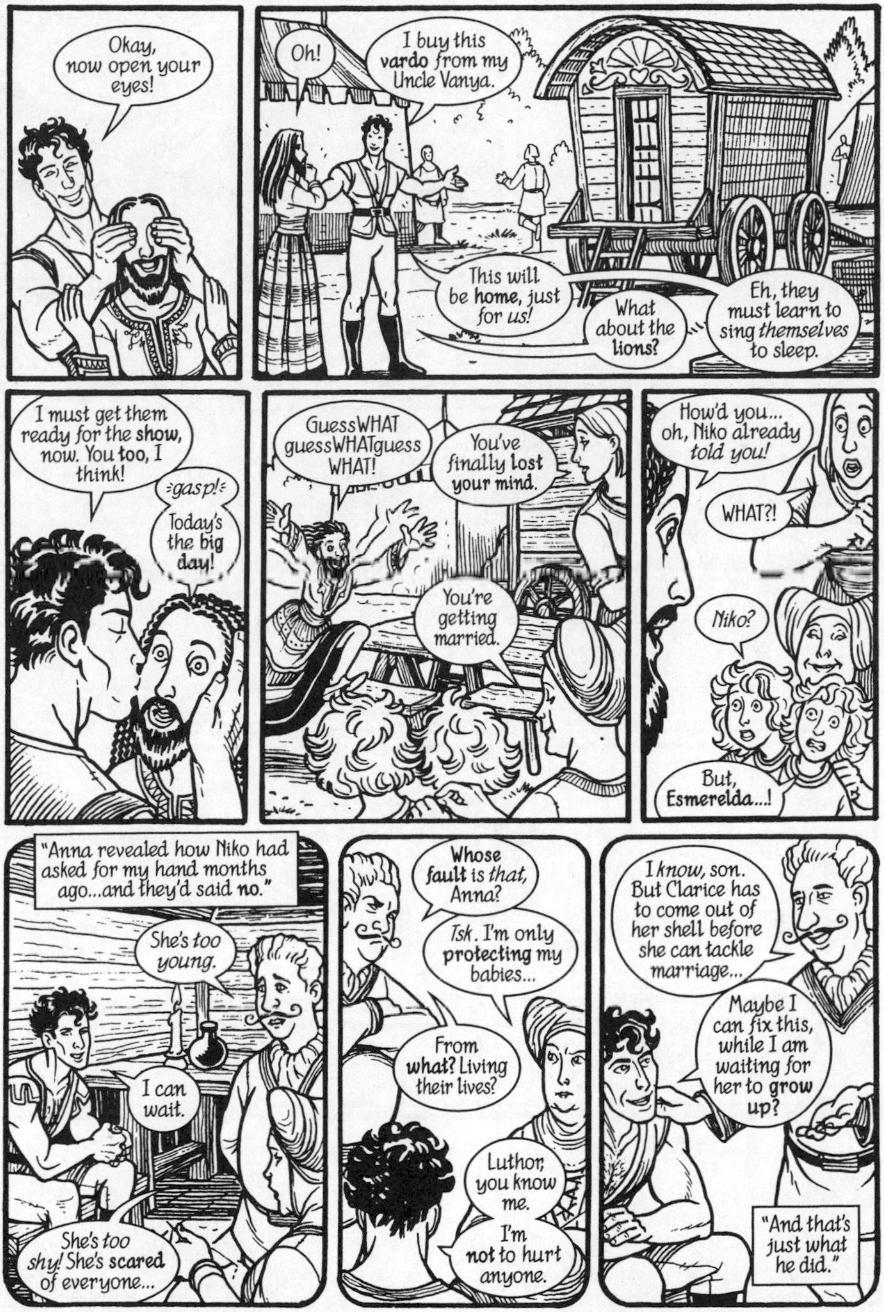
Okay, now open your eyes!
Oh!
I buy this vardo from my Uncle Vanya.
This will be home, just for us!
What about the lions?
Eh, they must learn to sing themselves to sleep.
I must get them ready for the show, now. You too, I think!
gasp!
Today's the big day!
GuessWHAT guessWHATguess WHAT!
You've finally lost your mind.
You're getting married.
How'd you... oh, Niko already told you!
WHAT?!
Niko?
But, Esmerelda...!
"Anna revealed how Niko had asked for my hand months ago...and they'd said no."
She's too young.
I can wait.
She's too shy! She's scared of everyone...
Whose fault is that, Anna?
Tsk. I'm only protecting my babies...
From what? Living their lives?
Luthor, you know me.
I'm not to hurt anyone.
I know, son. But Clarice has to come out of her shell before she can tackle marriage...
Maybe I can fix this, while I am waiting for her to grow up?
"And that's just what he did."

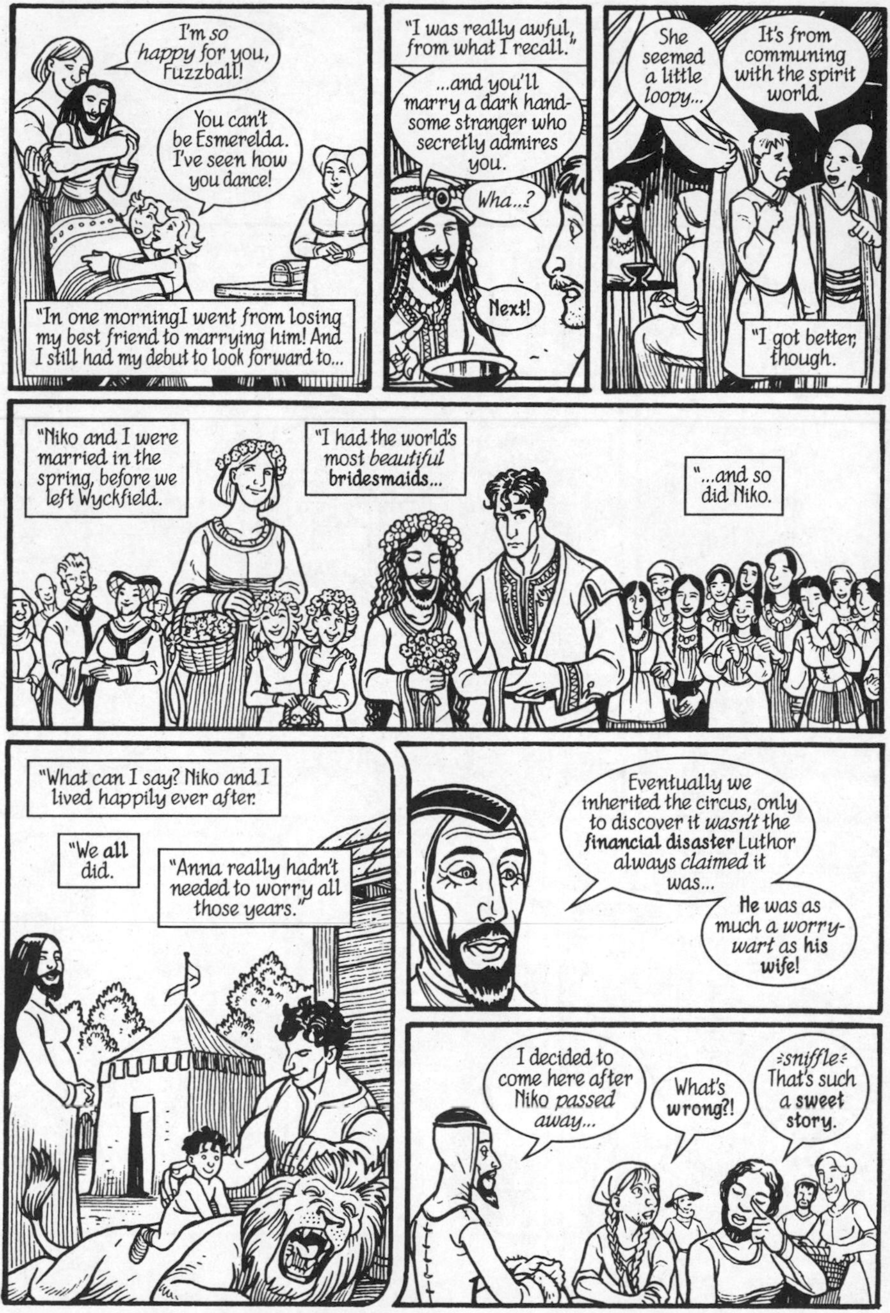
I'm so happy for you, Fuzzball!
You can't be Esmerelda. I've seen how you dance!
"In one morning I went from losing my best friend to marrying him! And I still had my debut to look forward to...
"I was really awful, from what I recall."
...and you'll marry a dark handsome stranger who secretly admires you.
Wha...?
Next!
She seemed a little loopy...
It's from communing with the spirit world.
"I got better, though.
"Niko and I were married in the spring, before we left Wyckfield.
"I had the world's most beautiful bridesmaids...
"...and so did Niko.
"What can I say? Niko and I lived happily ever after.
"We all did.
"Anna really hadn't needed to worry all those years."
Eventually we inherited the circus, only to discover it wasn't the financial disaster Luthor always claimed it was...
He was as much a worry-wart as his wife!
I decided to come here after Niko passed away...
What's wrong?!
sniffle That's such a sweet story.

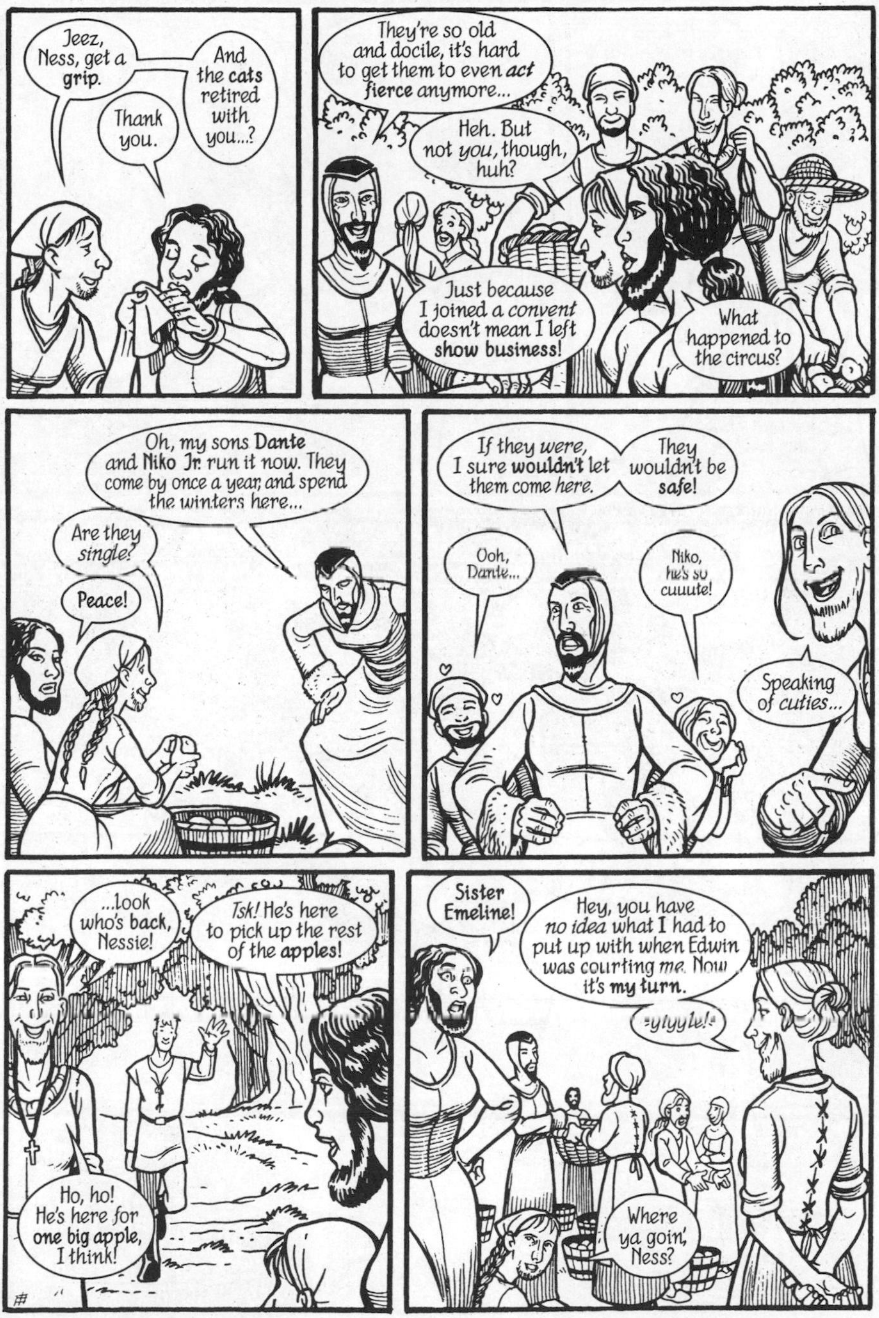
Jeez, Ness, get a **grip**.
And the **cats** retired with you...?
Thank you.
They're so old and docile, it's hard to get them to even *act* **fierce** anymore...
Heh. But not *you*, though, huh?
Just because I joined a *convent* doesn't mean I left **show business**!
What happened to the circus?
Oh, my sons **Dante** and **Niko Jr.** run it now. They come by once a year, and spend the winters here...
Are they *single?*
Peace!
If they *were*, I sure **wouldn't** let them come *here*.
They wouldn't be **safe**!
Ooh, Dante...
Niko, he's so cuuute!
Speaking of *cuties*...
...look who's **back**, Nessie!
Tsk! He's here to pick up the rest of the **apples**!
Ho, ho! He's here for **one big apple**, I think!
Sister Emeline!
Hey, you have *no idea* what I had to put up with when Edwin was courting *me*. Now it's **my turn**.
giggle!
Where ya goin', Ness?

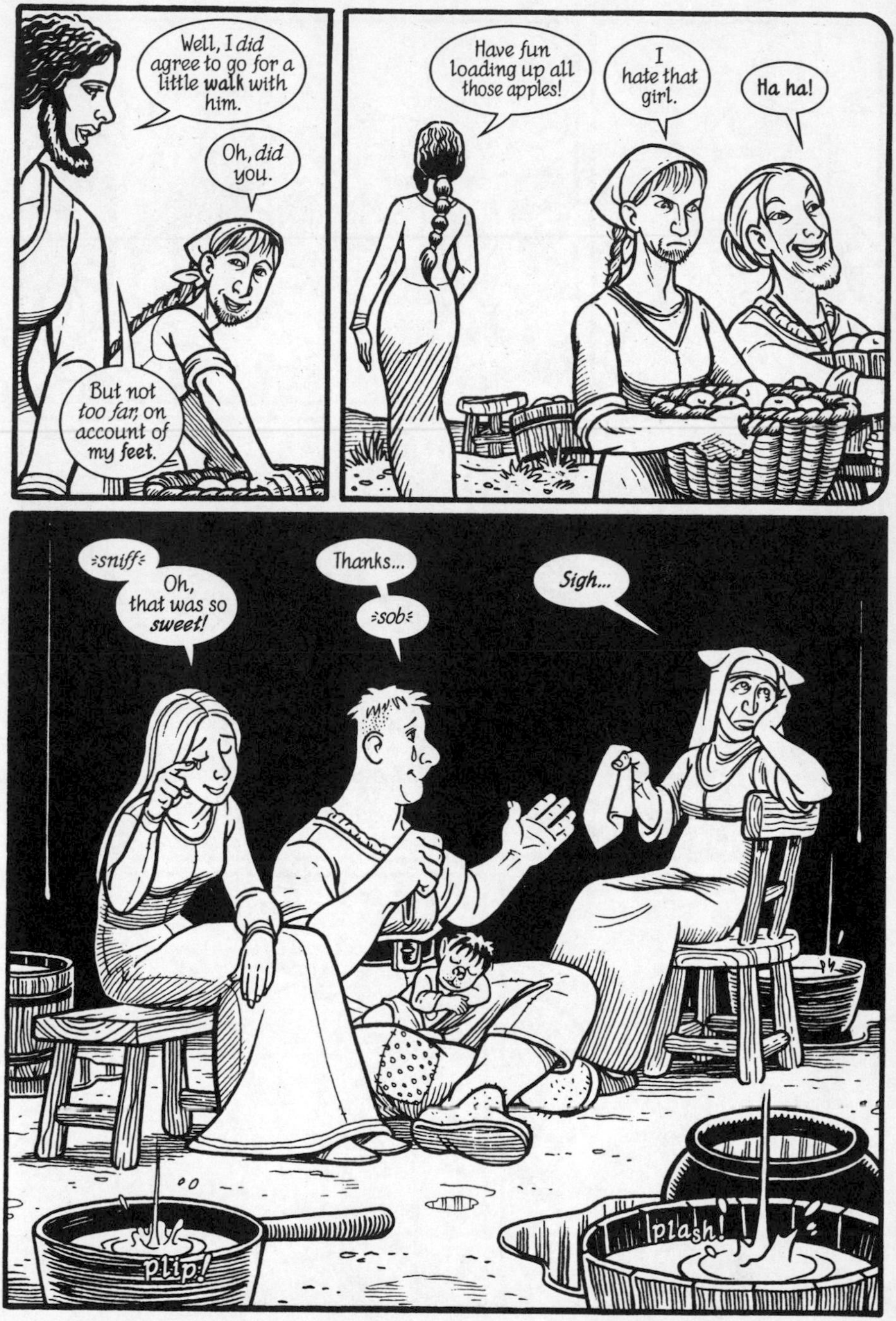
Well, I *did* agree to go for a little **walk** with him.
Oh, *did* you.
But not *too far*, on account of my **feet**.
Have fun loading up all those apples!
I hate that girl.
Ha ha!
sniff
Oh, that was so **sweet!**
Thanks...
sob
Sigh...
plip!
plash!

Chapter 17.

· SOLICITINE PT. 5 ·

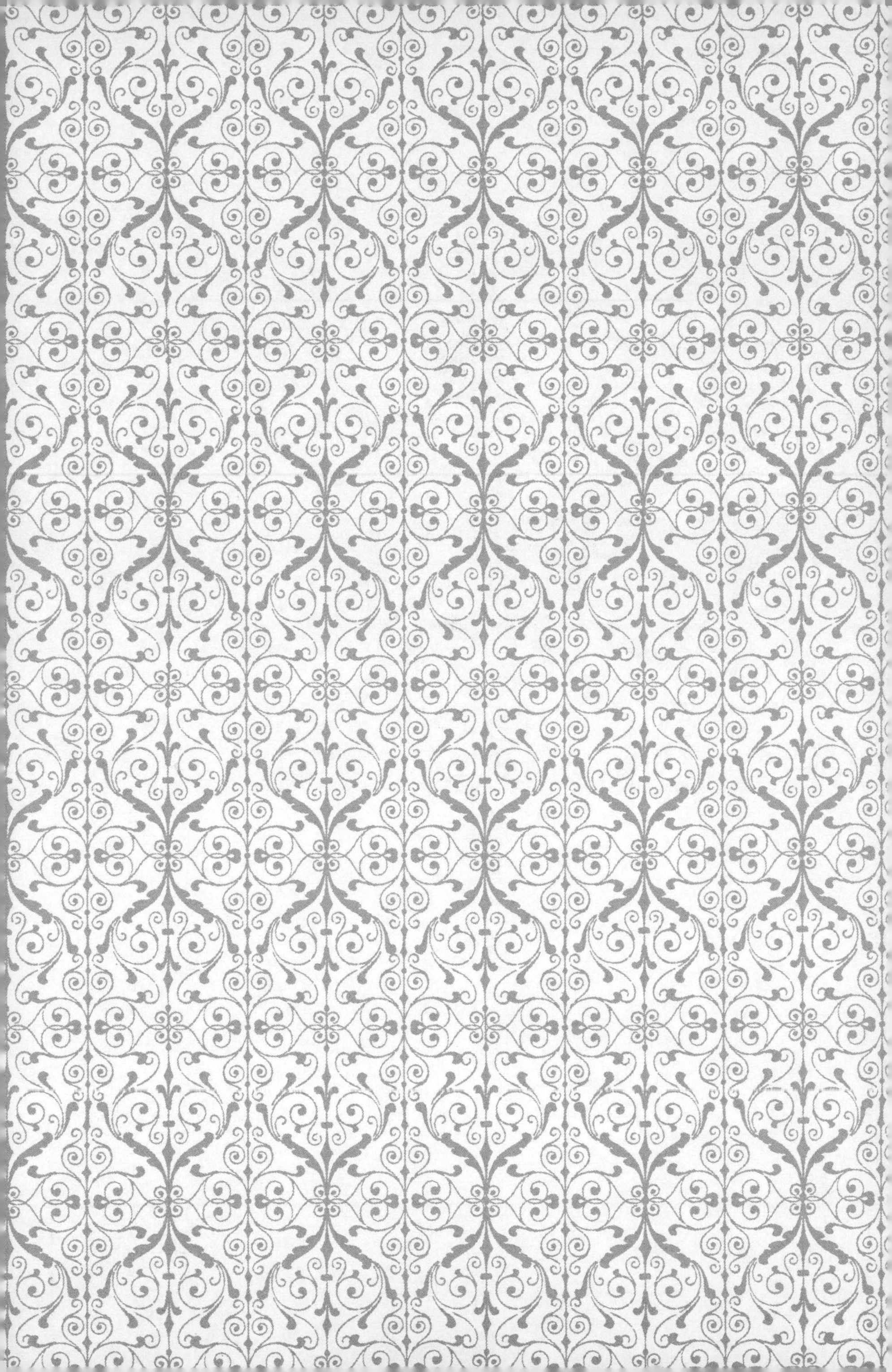

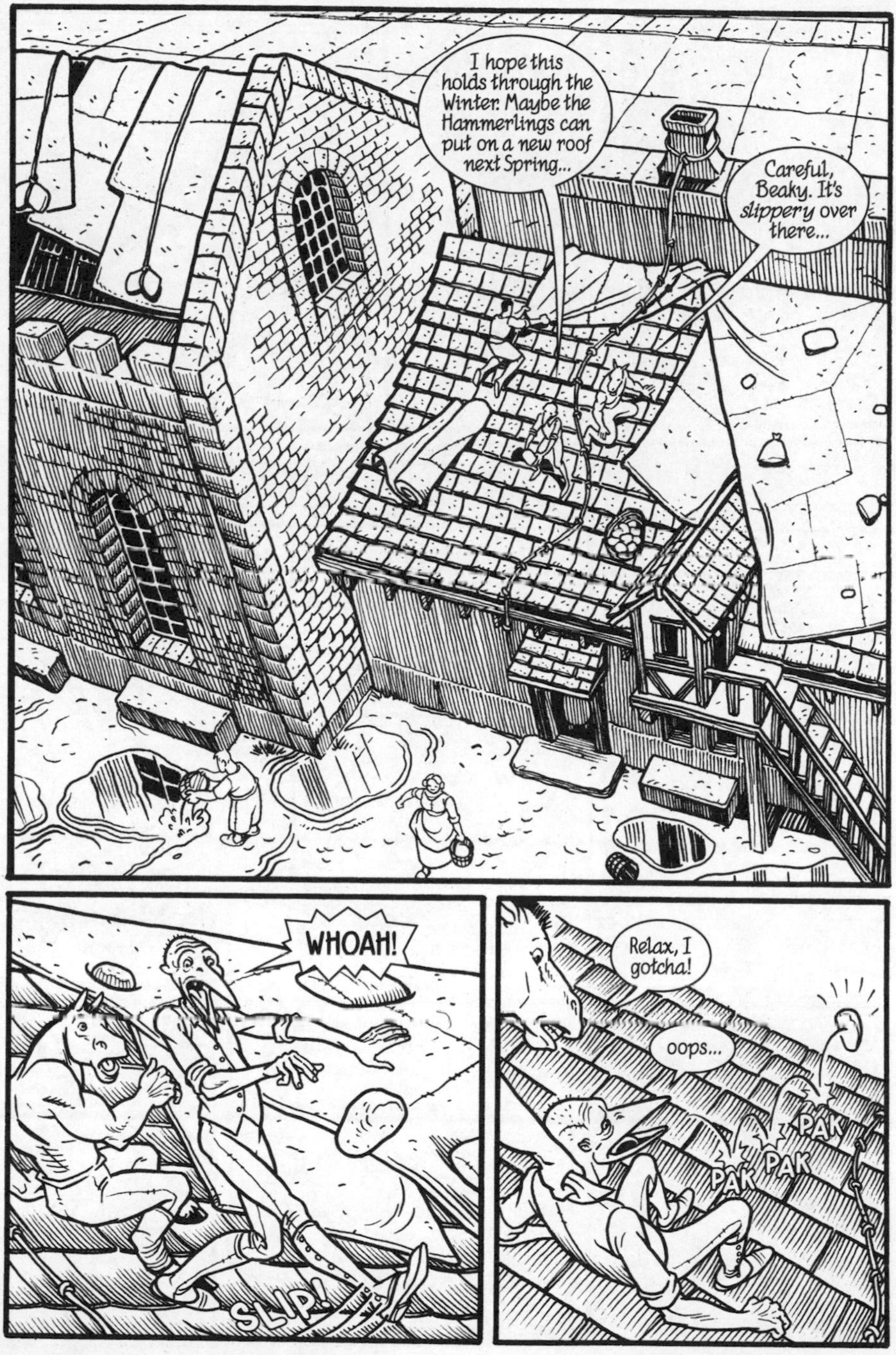
I hope this holds through the Winter. Maybe the Hammerlings can put on a new roof next Spring...
Careful, Beaky. It's slippery over there...
WHOAH!
SLIP!
Relax, I gotcha!
oops...
PAK
PAK
PAK

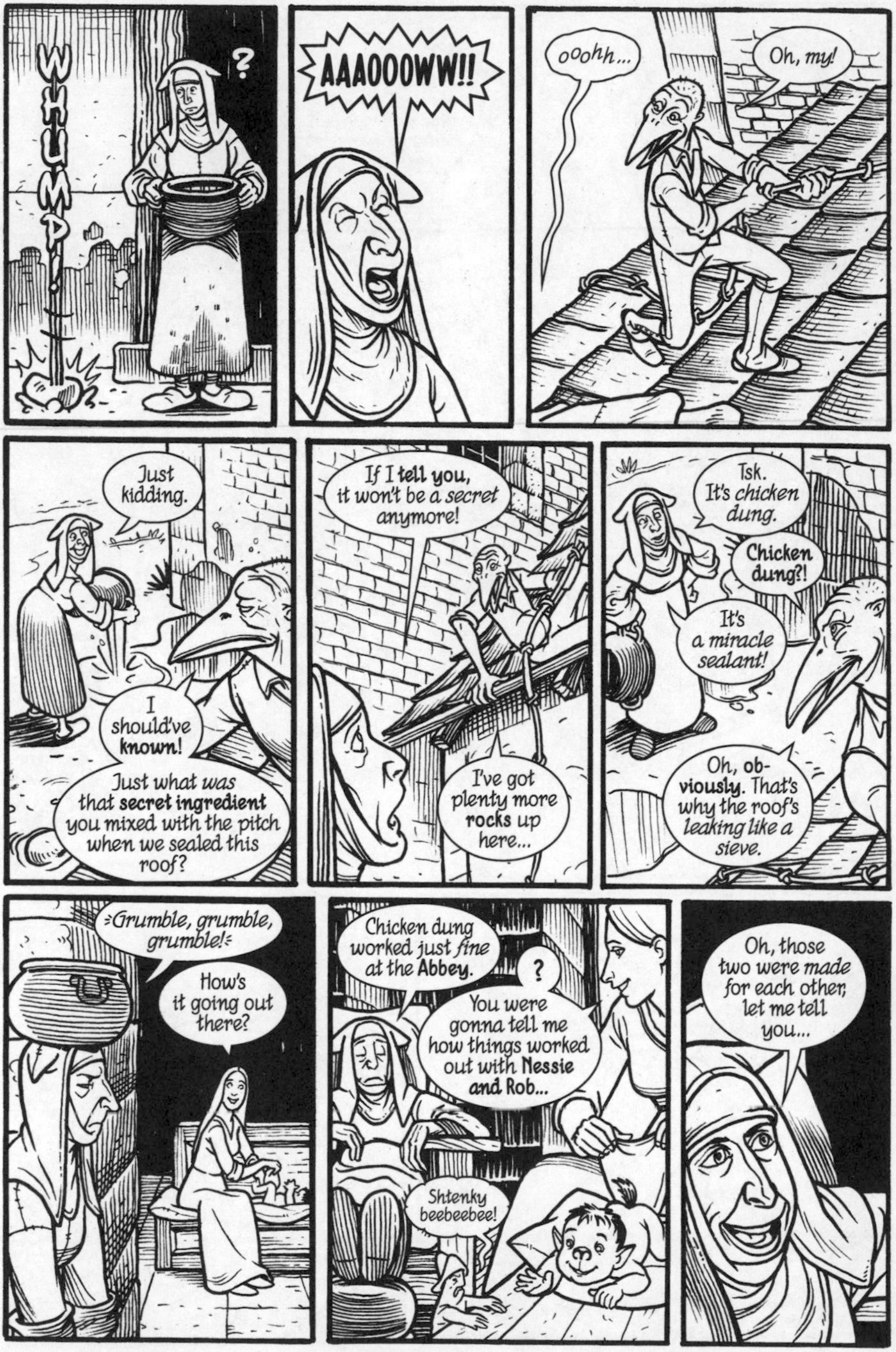
WHUMP!
?
AAAOOOWW!!
ooohh...
Oh, my!
Just kidding.
I should've **known**!
Just what *was* that **secret ingredient** you mixed with the pitch when we sealed this roof?
If I **tell you**, it won't be a *secret* anymore!
I've got plenty more **rocks** up here...
Tsk. It's *chicken dung*.
Chicken dung?!
It's *a miracle sealant!*
Oh, **ob- viously**. That's why the roof's *leaking like a sieve*.
Grumble, grumble, grumble!
How's it going out there?
Chicken dung worked just *fine* at the **Abbey**.
?
You were gonna tell me how things worked out with **Nessie and Rob...**
Shtenky beebeebee!
Oh, those two were *made* for each other, let me tell you...

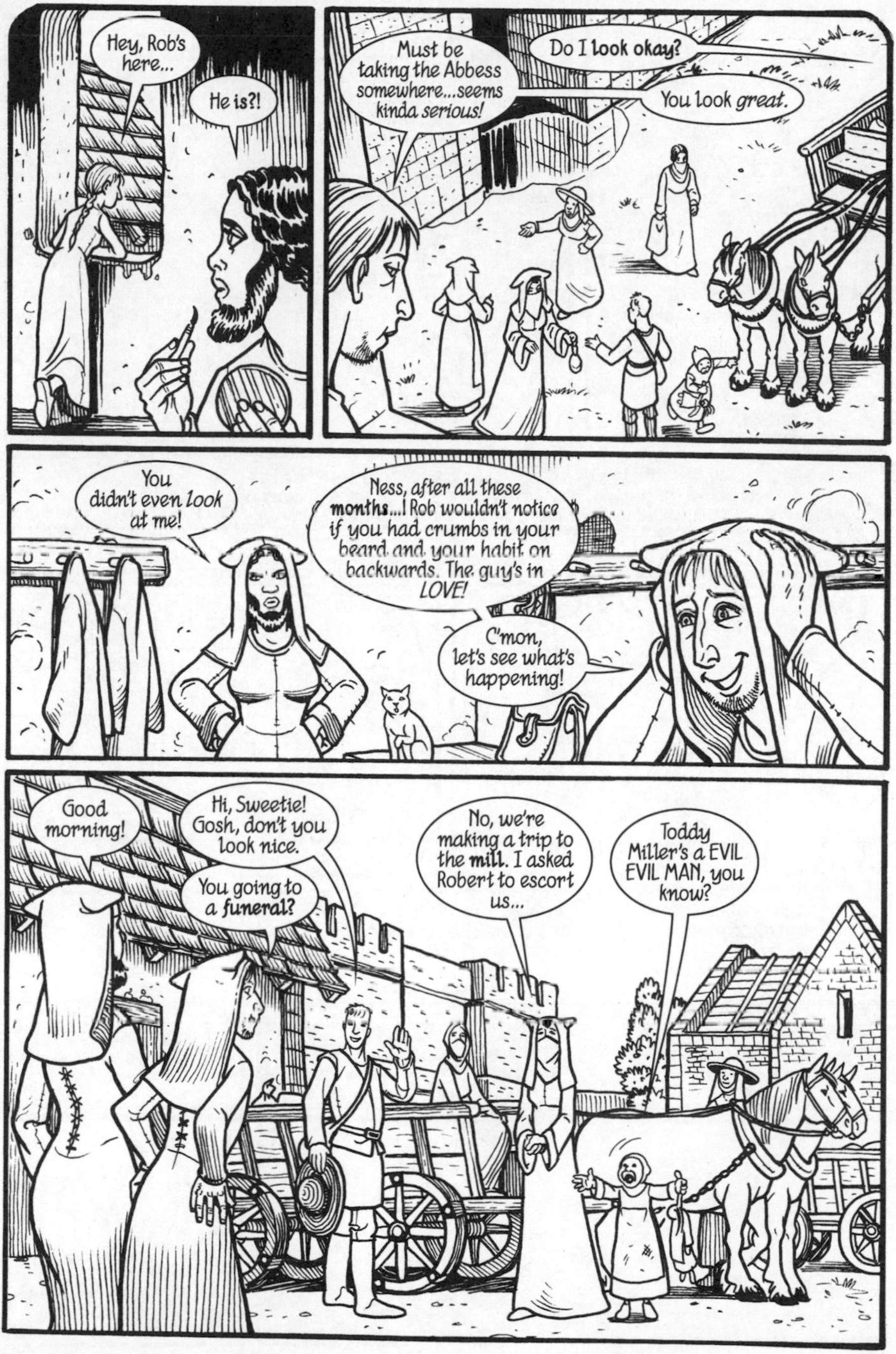
Hey, Rob's here...
He is?!
Must be taking the Abbess somewhere...seems kinda serious!
Do I look okay?
You look great.
You didn't even look at me!
Ness, after all these months...I Rob wouldn't notice if you had crumbs in your beard and your habit on backwards. The guy's in LOVE!
C'mon, let's see what's happening!
Good morning!
Hi, Sweetie! Gosh, don't you look nice.
You going to a funeral?
No, we're making a trip to the mill. I asked Robert to escort us...
Toddy Miller's a EVIL EVIL MAN, you know?

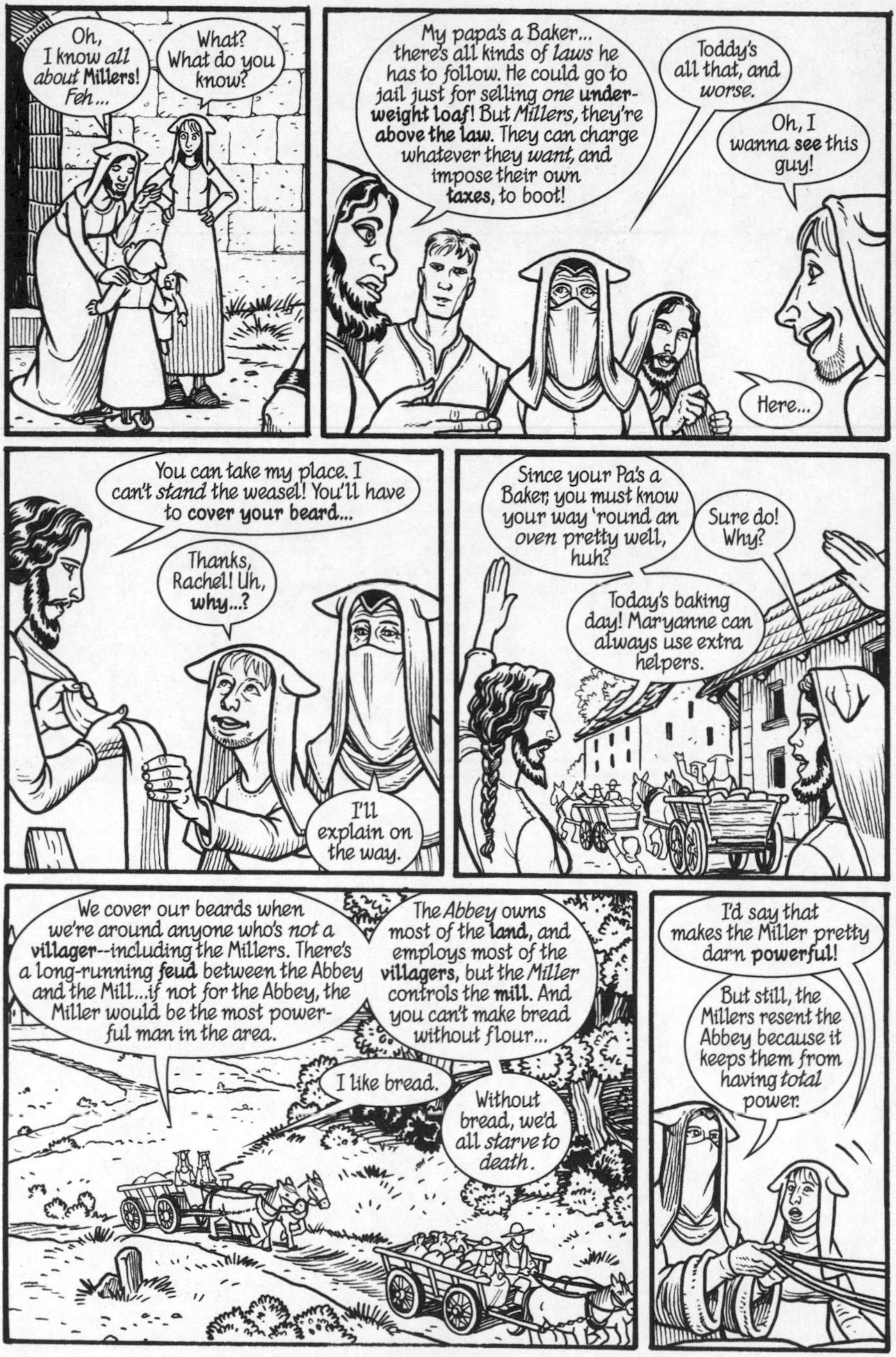
Oh, I know *all about* **Millers!** *Feh...*
What? What do you know?
My papa's a Baker... there's all kinds of *laws* he has to follow. He could go to jail just for selling *one* **under-weight loaf!** But *Millers,* they're **above the law.** They can charge whatever they *want,* and impose their own **taxes,** to boot!
Toddy's all that, and *worse.*
Oh, I wanna **see** this guy!
Here...
You can take my place. I can't *stand* the weasel! You'll have to **cover your beard...**
Thanks, Rachel! Uh, **why...?**
I'll explain on the way.
Since your Pa's a Baker, you must know your way 'round an *oven* pretty well, huh?
Sure do! Why?
Today's baking day! Maryanne can always use extra helpers.
We cover our beards when we're around anyone who's *not* a **villager**--including the Millers. There's a long-running **feud** between the Abbey and the Mill...*if* not for the Abbey, the Miller would be the most power-ful man in the area.
The *Abbey* owns most of the **land,** and employs most of the **villagers,** but the *Miller* controls the **mill.** And you can't make bread without flour...
I like bread.
Without bread, we'd all *starve* to *death.*
I'd say that makes the Miller pretty darn **powerful!**
But still, the Millers resent the Abbey because it keeps them from having *total* power.

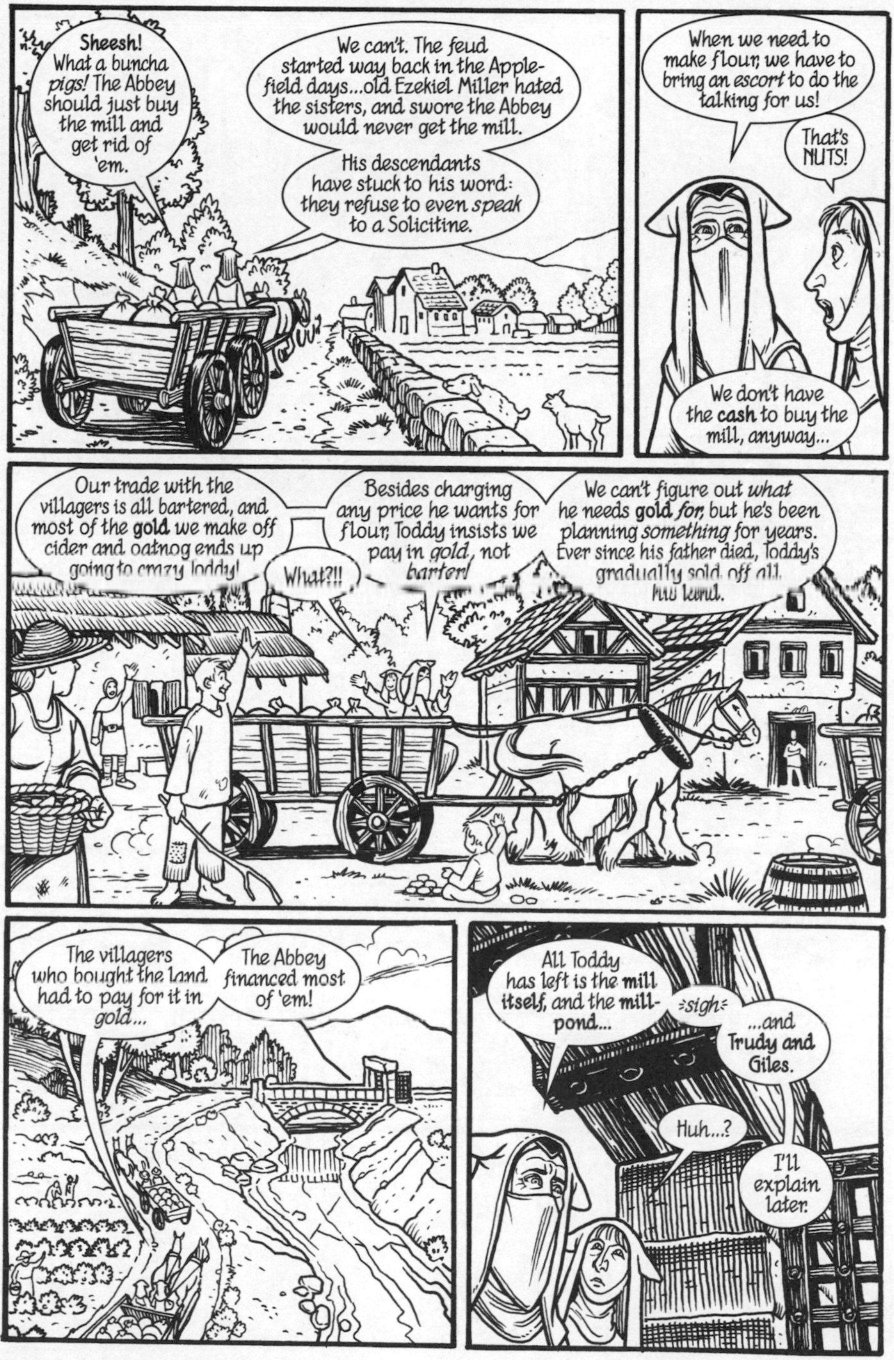
Sheesh! What a buncha pigs! The Abbey should just buy the mill and get rid of 'em.
We can't. The feud started way back in the Applefield days...old Ezekiel Miller hated the sisters, and swore the Abbey would never get the mill.
His descendants have stuck to his word: they refuse to even speak to a Solicitine.
When we need to make flour, we have to bring an escort to do the talking for us!
That's NUTS!
We don't have the cash to buy the mill, anyway...
Our trade with the villagers is all bartered, and most of the gold we make off cider and oatnog ends up going to crazy Toddy!
What?!!
Besides charging any price he wants for flour, Toddy insists we pay in gold, not barter!
We can't figure out what he needs gold for, but he's been planning something for years. Ever since his father died, Toddy's gradually sold off all his land.
The villagers who bought the land had to pay for it in gold...
The Abbey financed most of 'em!
All Toddy has left is the mill itself, and the mill-pond...
sigh
...and Trudy and Giles.
Huh...?
I'll explain later.

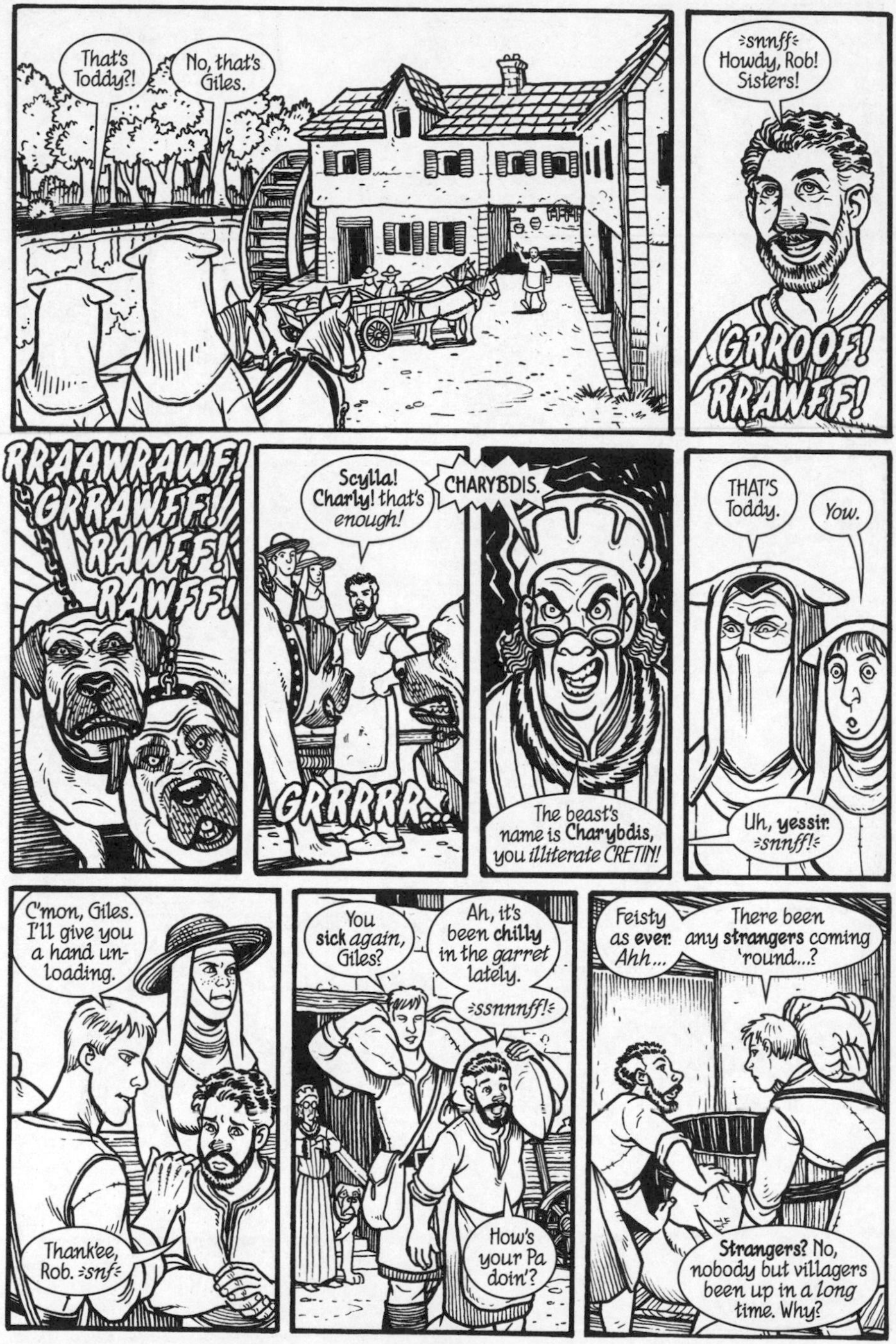
That's Toddy?!
No, that's Giles.
≈snnff≈ Howdy, Rob! Sisters!
GRROOF! RRAWFF!
RRAAWRAWF! GRRAWFF! RAWFF! RAWFF!
Scylla! Charly! that's enough!
CHARYBDIS.
GRRRRRR...
The beast's name is Charybdis, you illiterate CRETIN!
THAT'S Toddy.
You.
Uh, yessir. ≈snnff!≈
C'mon, Giles. I'll give you a hand unloading.
Thank'ee, Rob. ≈snf≈
You sick again, Giles?
Ah, it's been chilly in the garret lately.
≈ssnnnff!≈
How's your Pa doin'?
Feisty as ever. Ahh...
There been any strangers coming 'round...?
Strangers? No, nobody but villagers been up in a long time. Why?

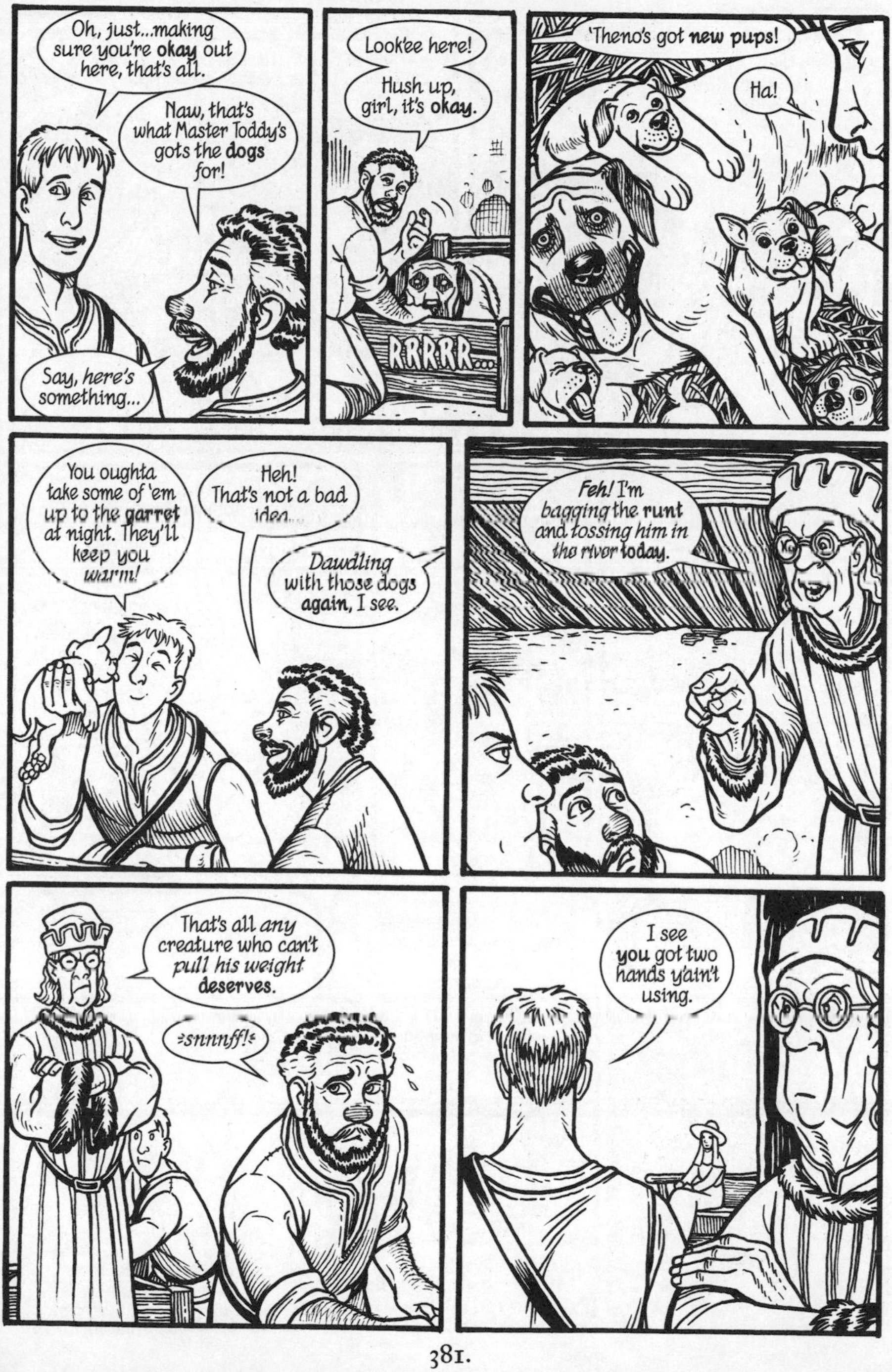
Oh, just...making sure you're **okay** out here, that's all.
Naw, that's what Master Toddy's gots the **dogs** for!
Say, *here's* something...
Look'ee here!
Hush up, girl, it's **okay**.
RRRRR...
'Theno's got **new pups**!
Ha!
You oughta take some of 'em up to the **garret** at night. They'll keep you *warm*!
Heh! That's not a bad idea...
Dawdling with those dogs **again**, I see.
Feh! I'm *bagging* the **runt** and *tossing* him in the river **today**.
That's all *any* creature who can't *pull his weight* **deserves**.
≈snnnff!≈
I see **you** got two hands y'ain't using.

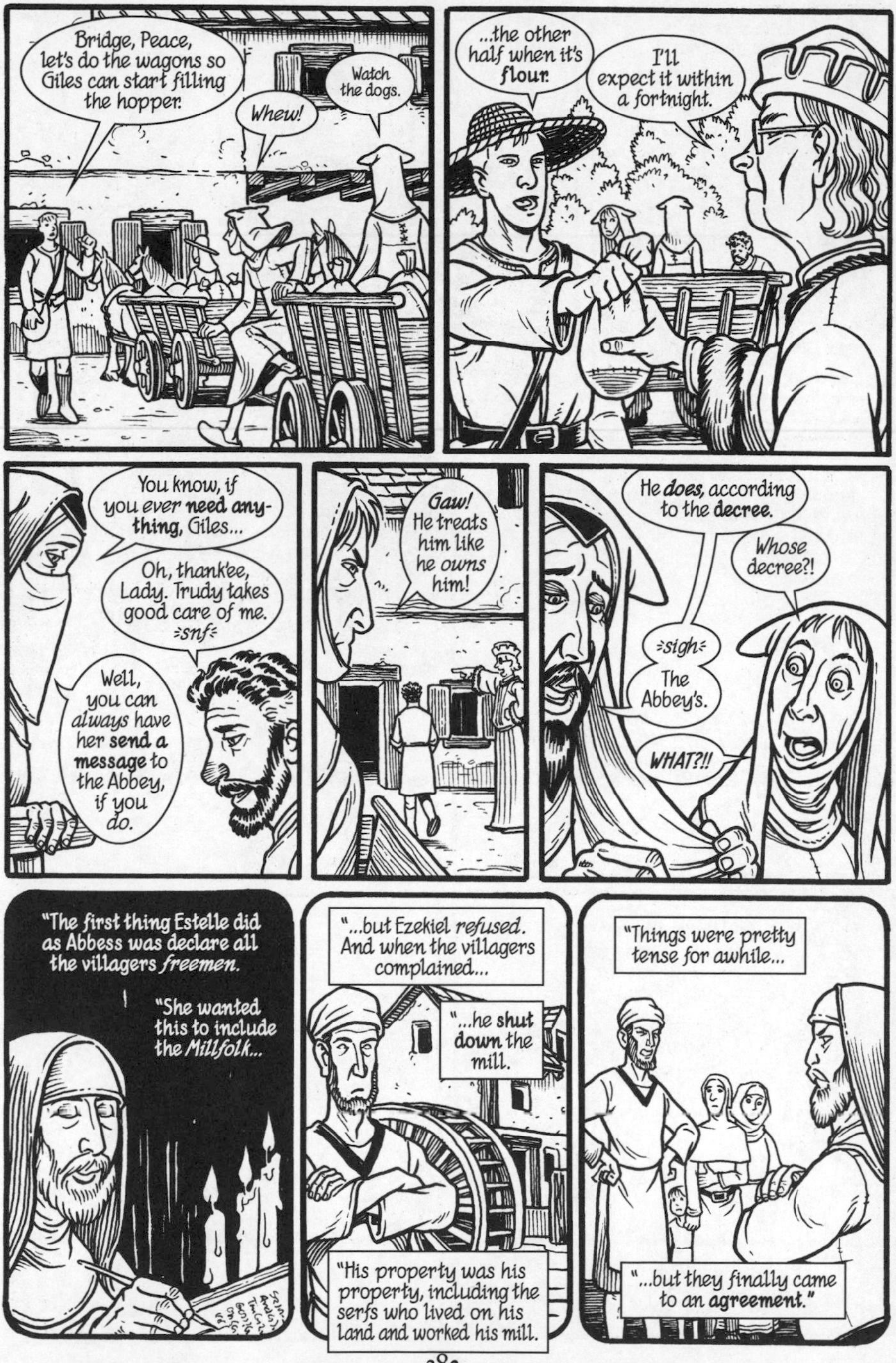
Bridge, Peace, let's do the wagons so Giles can start filling the hopper.
Whew!
Watch the dogs.
...the other half when it's **flour.**
I'll expect it within a fortnight.
You know, if you *ever* **need anything,** Giles...
Oh, thank'ee, Lady. Trudy takes good care of me.
snf
Well, you can *always* have her **send a message** to the Abbey, if you *do.*
Gaw! He treats him like he *owns* him!
He ***does,*** according to the **decree.**
Whose decree?!
sigh
The Abbey's.
WHAT?!!
"The first thing Estelle did as Abbess was declare all the villagers *freemen.*
"She wanted this to include the *Millfolk*...
"...but Ezekiel *refused.* And when the villagers complained...
"...he **shut down** the mill.
"His property was his property, including the serfs who lived on his land and worked his mill.
"Things were pretty tense for awhile...
"...but they finally came to an **agreement.**"

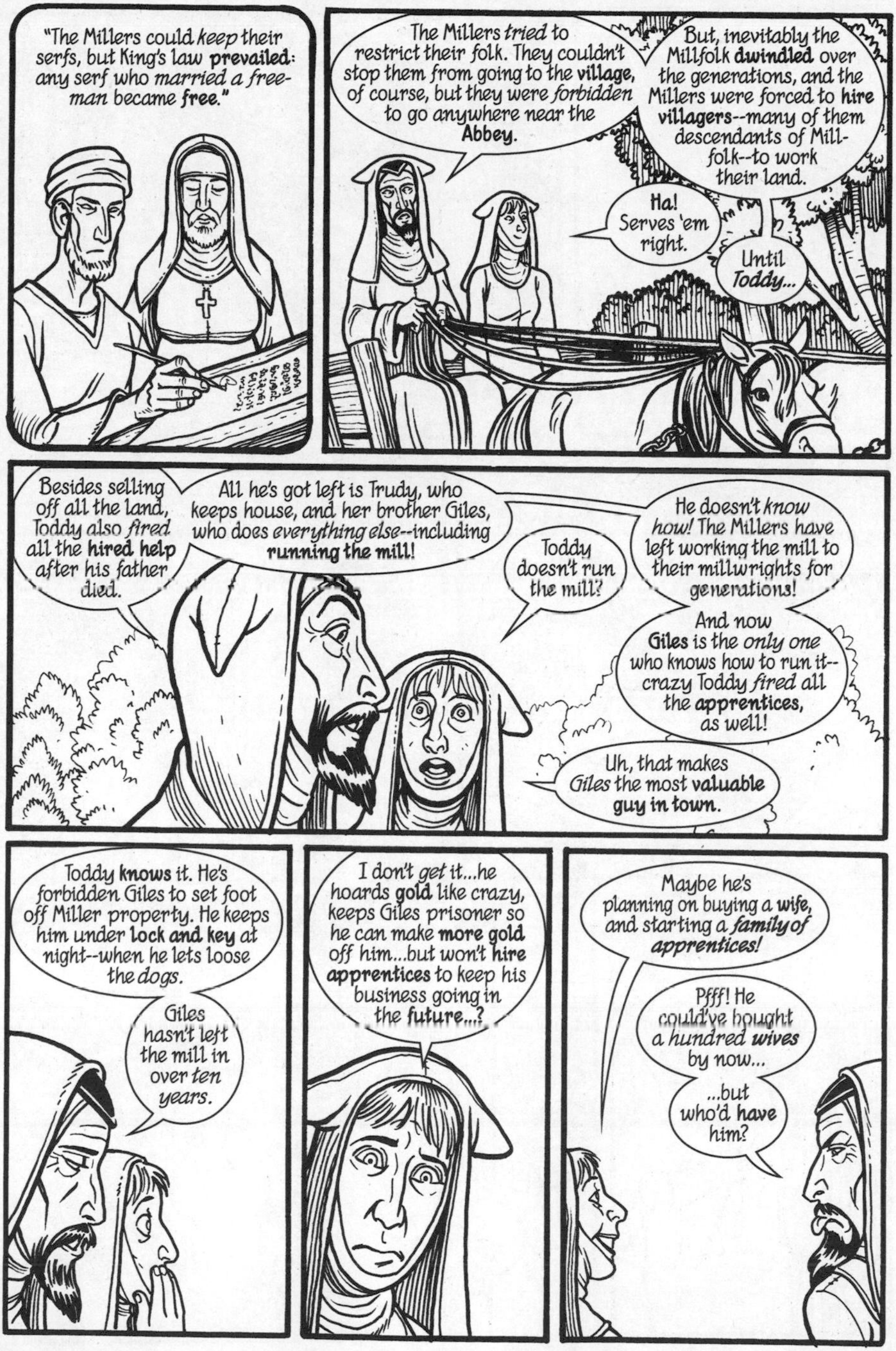
"The Millers could *keep* their serfs, but King's law **prevailed**: any serf who *married a free-man* became **free**."
The Millers *tried* to restrict their folk. They couldn't stop them from going to the **village**, of course, but they were *forbidden* to go anywhere near the **Abbey**.
But, inevitably the Millfolk **dwindled** over the generations, and the Millers were forced to **hire villagers**--many of them descendants of Mill-folk--to work their land.
Ha! Serves 'em right.
Until *Toddy...*
Besides selling off all the land, Toddy also *fired* all the **hired help** after his father died.
All he's got left is Trudy, who keeps house, and her brother Giles, who does *everything else*--including **running the mill**!
Toddy doesn't run the mill?
He doesn't *know how!* The Millers have left working the mill to their millwrights for generations!
And now **Giles** is the *only one* who knows how to run it--crazy Toddy *fired* all the **apprentices**, as well!
Uh, that makes *Giles* the most **valuable guy in town**.
Toddy **knows** it. He's forbidden Giles to set foot off Miller property. He keeps him under **lock and key** at night--when he lets loose the *dogs*.
Giles hasn't left the mill in over *ten years*.
I don't *get* it...he hoards **gold** like crazy, keeps Giles prisoner so he can make **more gold** off him...but won't **hire apprentices** to keep his business going in the **future**...?
Maybe he's planning on buying a **wife**, and starting a ***family* of *apprentices!***
Pfff! He could've bought *a hundred* **wives** by now...
...but who'd **have** him?

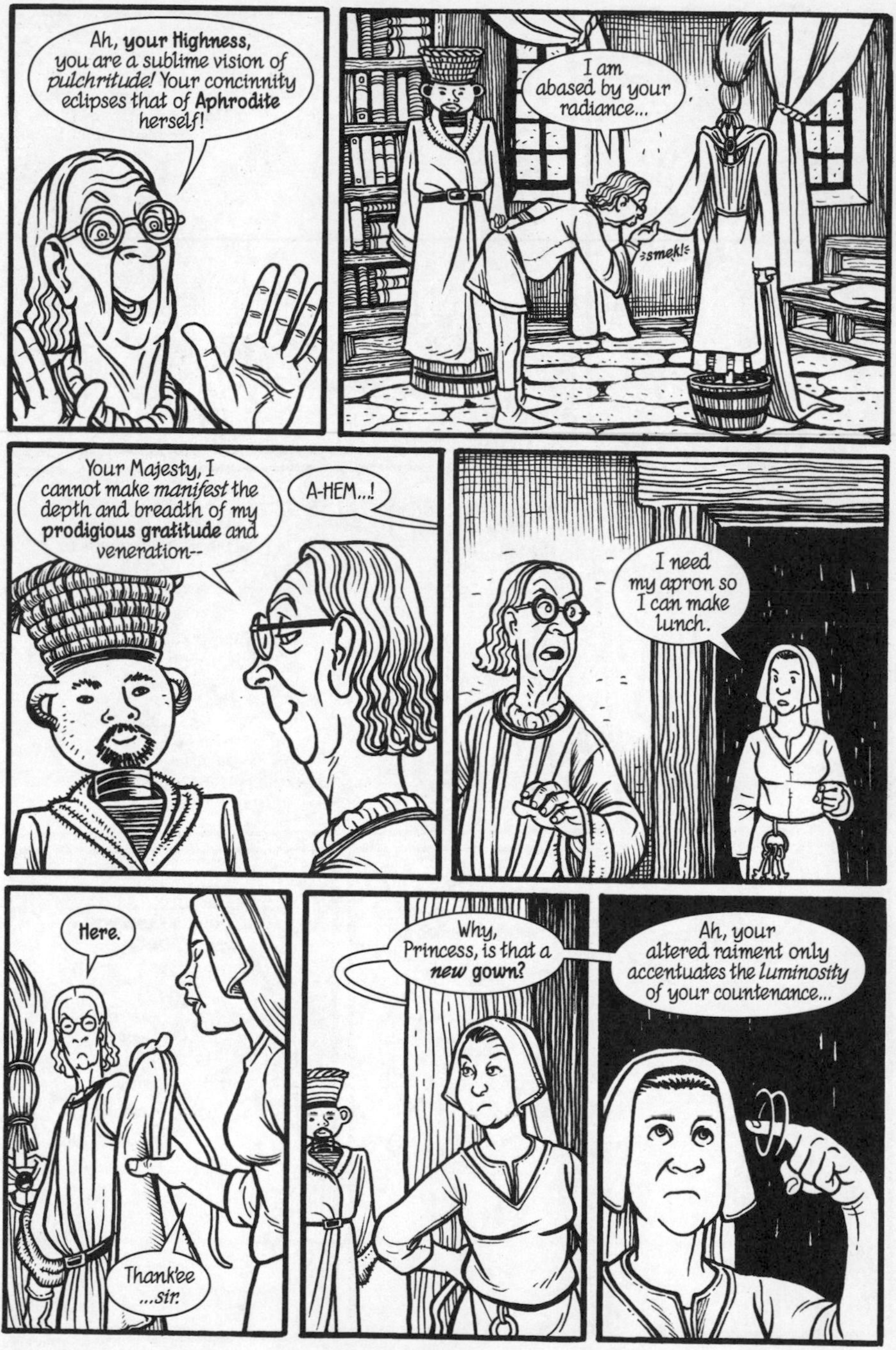
Ah, **your Highness**, you are a sublime vision of *pulchritude!* Your concinnity eclipses that of **Aphrodite** herself!
I am abased by your radiance...
smek!
Your Majesty, I cannot make *manifest* the depth and breadth of my **prodigious gratitude** and veneration--
A-HEM...!
I need my apron so I can make lunch.
Here.
Thank'ee ...*sir.*
Why, Princess, is that a ***new* gown?**
Ah, your altered raiment only accentuates the *luminosity* of your countenance...

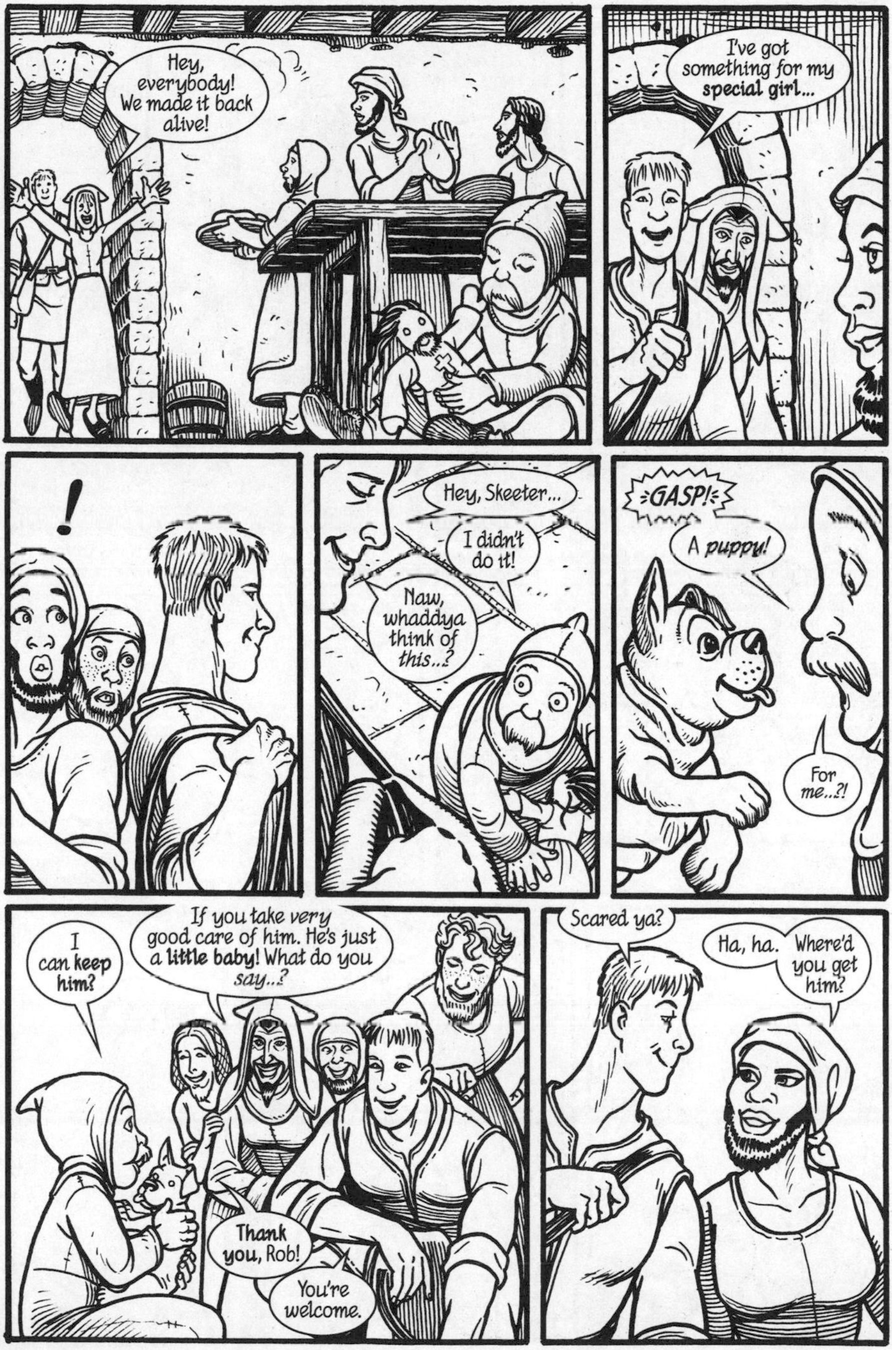
Hey, everybody! We made it back alive!
I've got something for my special girl...
!
Hey, Skeeter...
I didn't do it!
Naw, whaddya think of this...?
GASP!
A puppy!
For me...?!
I can keep him?
If you take very good care of him. He's just a little baby! What do you say...?
Thank you, Rob!
You're welcome.
Scared ya?
Ha, ha.
Where'd you get him?

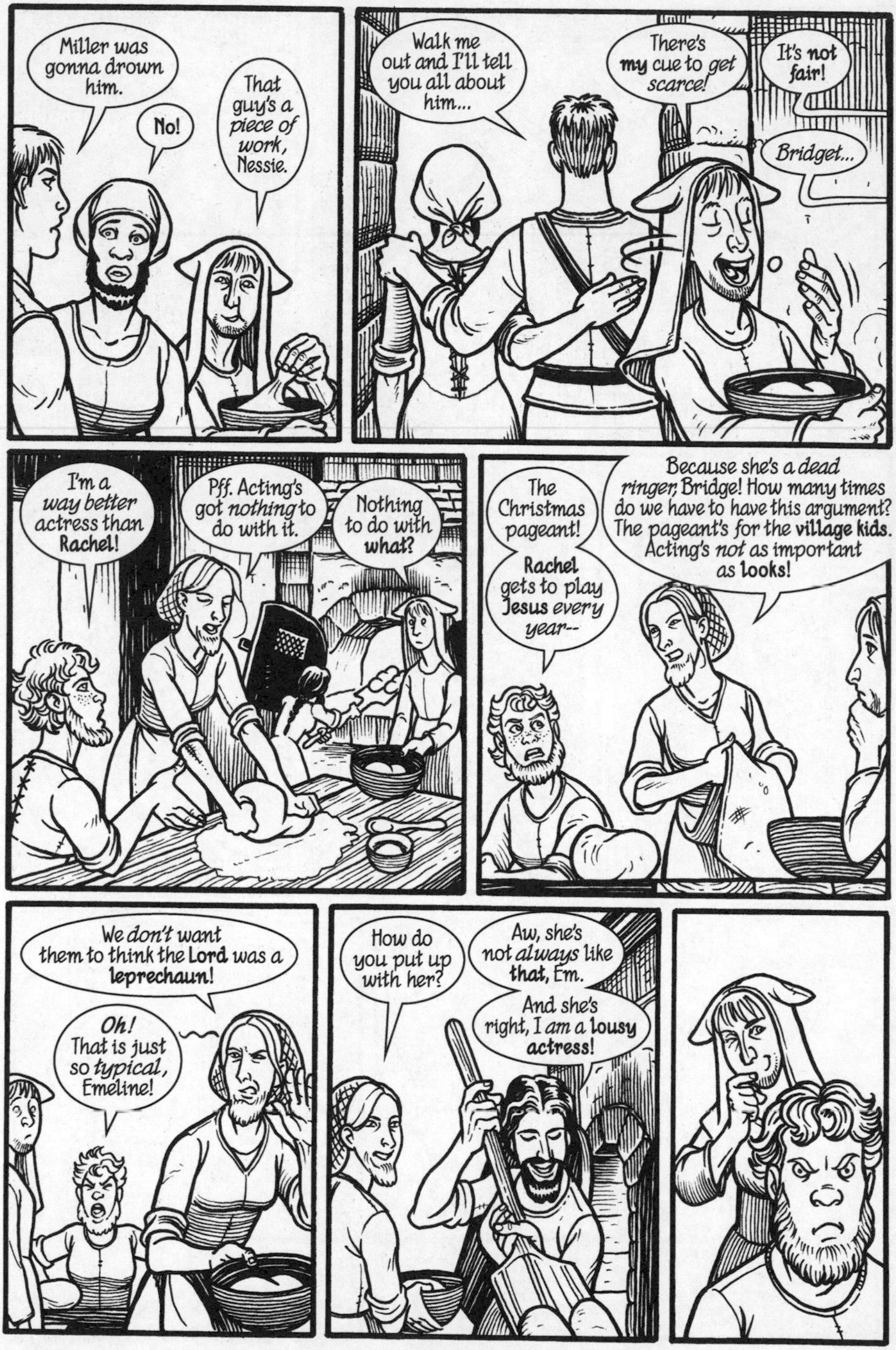
Miller was gonna drown him.
No!
That guy's a *piece of work*, Nessie.
Walk me out and I'll tell you all about him...
There's **my** cue to *get scarce*!
It's **not fair**!
Bridget...
I'm a *way better* actress than **Rachel**!
Pff. Acting's got *nothing* to do with it.
Nothing to do with **what**?
The Christmas pageant!
Rachel gets to play **Jesus** *every year*--
Because she's a *dead ringer*, Bridge! How many times do we have to have this argument? The pageant's *for* the **village kids**. Acting's *not* as important as **looks**!
We *don't want* them to think the **Lord** was a **leprechaun**!
Oh! That is just so *typical*, Emeline!
How do you put up with her?
Aw, she's not *always* like **that**, Em.
And she's right, I *am* a **lousy actress**!

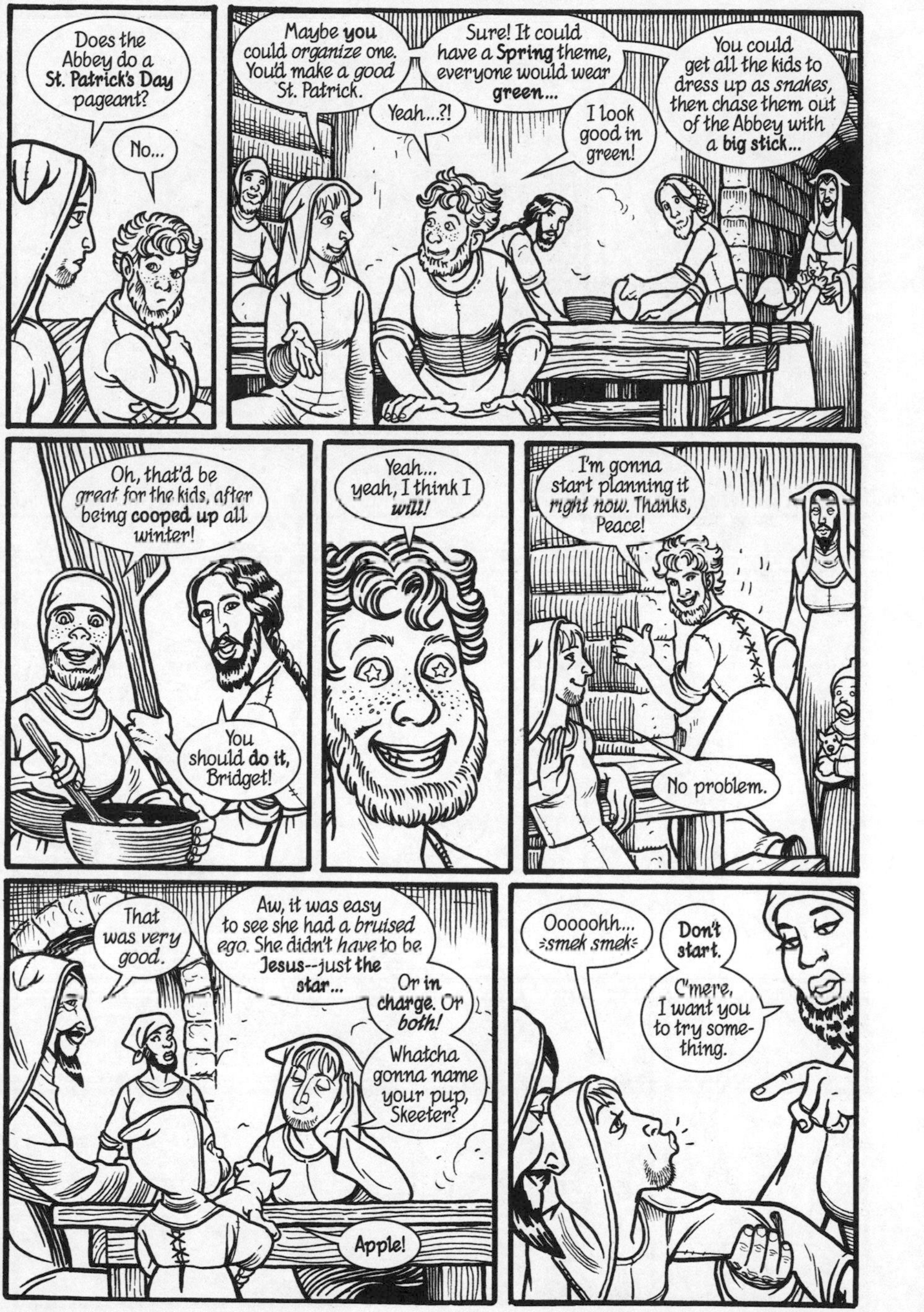

Does the Abbey do a St. Patrick's Day pageant?
No...
Maybe you could organize one. You'd make a good St. Patrick.
Yeah...?!
Sure! It could have a Spring theme, everyone would wear green...
I look good in green!
You could get all the kids to dress up as snakes, then chase them out of the Abbey with a big stick...
Oh, that'd be great for the kids, after being cooped up all winter!
You should do it, Bridget!
Yeah... yeah, I think I will!
I'm gonna start planning it right now. Thanks, Peace!
No problem.
That was very good.
Aw, it was easy to see she had a bruised ego. She didn't have to be Jesus--just the star...
Or in charge. Or both!
Whatcha gonna name your pup, Skeeter?
Apple!
Ooooohh... ~smek smek~
Don't start.
C'mere, I want you to try some-thing.

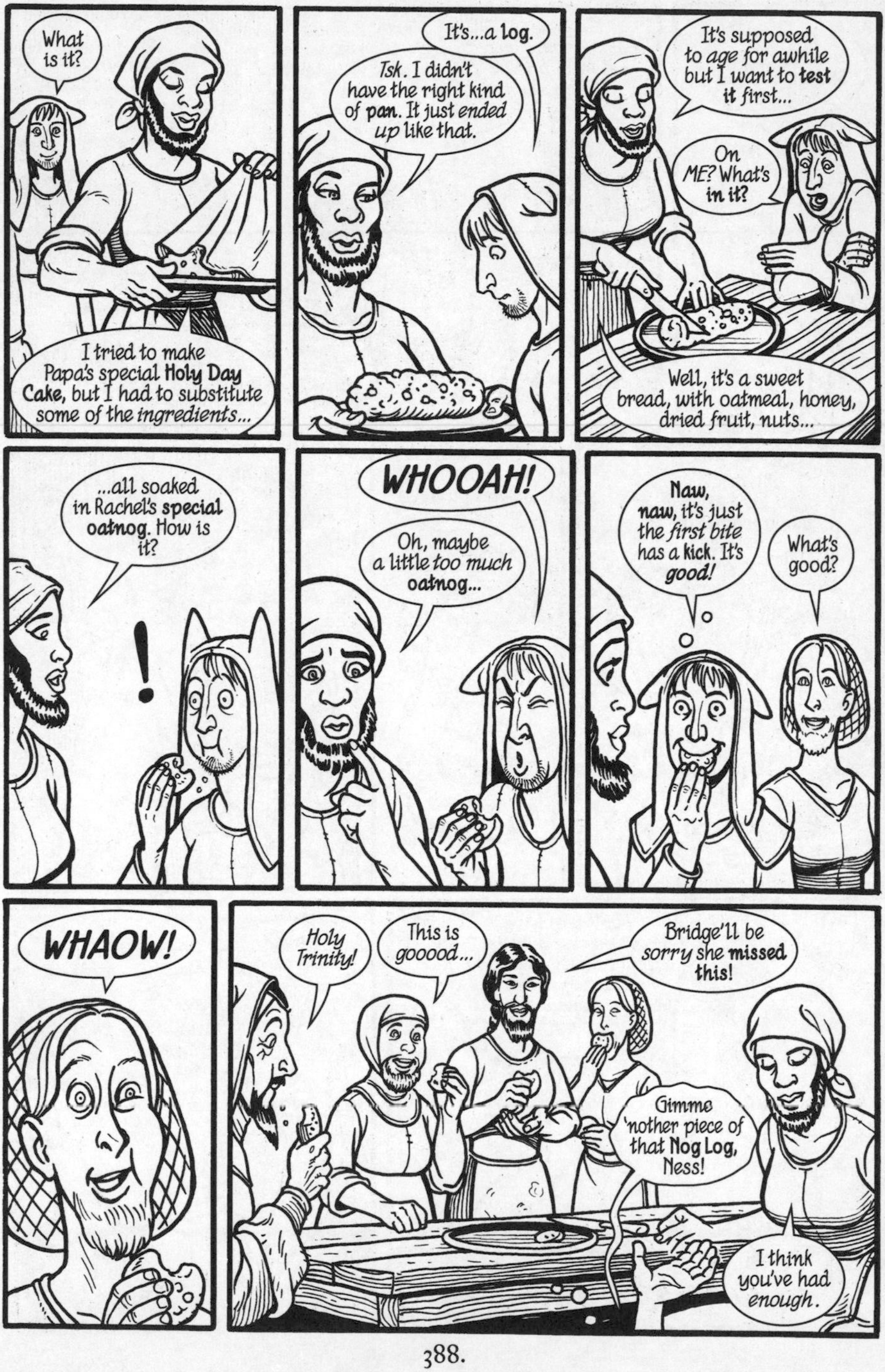
What is it?
I tried to make Papa's special Holy Day Cake, but I had to substitute some of the ingredients...
It's...a log.
Tsk. I didn't have the right kind of pan. It just ended up like that.
It's supposed to age for awhile but I want to test it first...
On ME? What's in it?
Well, it's a sweet bread, with oatmeal, honey, dried fruit, nuts...
...all soaked in Rachel's special oatnog. How is it?
!
WHOOAH!
Oh, maybe a little too much oatnog...
Naw, naw, it's just the first bite has a kick. It's good!
What's good?
WHAOW!
Holy Trinity!
This is gooood...
Bridge'll be sorry she missed this!
Gimme 'nother piece of that Nog Log, Ness!
I think you've had enough.

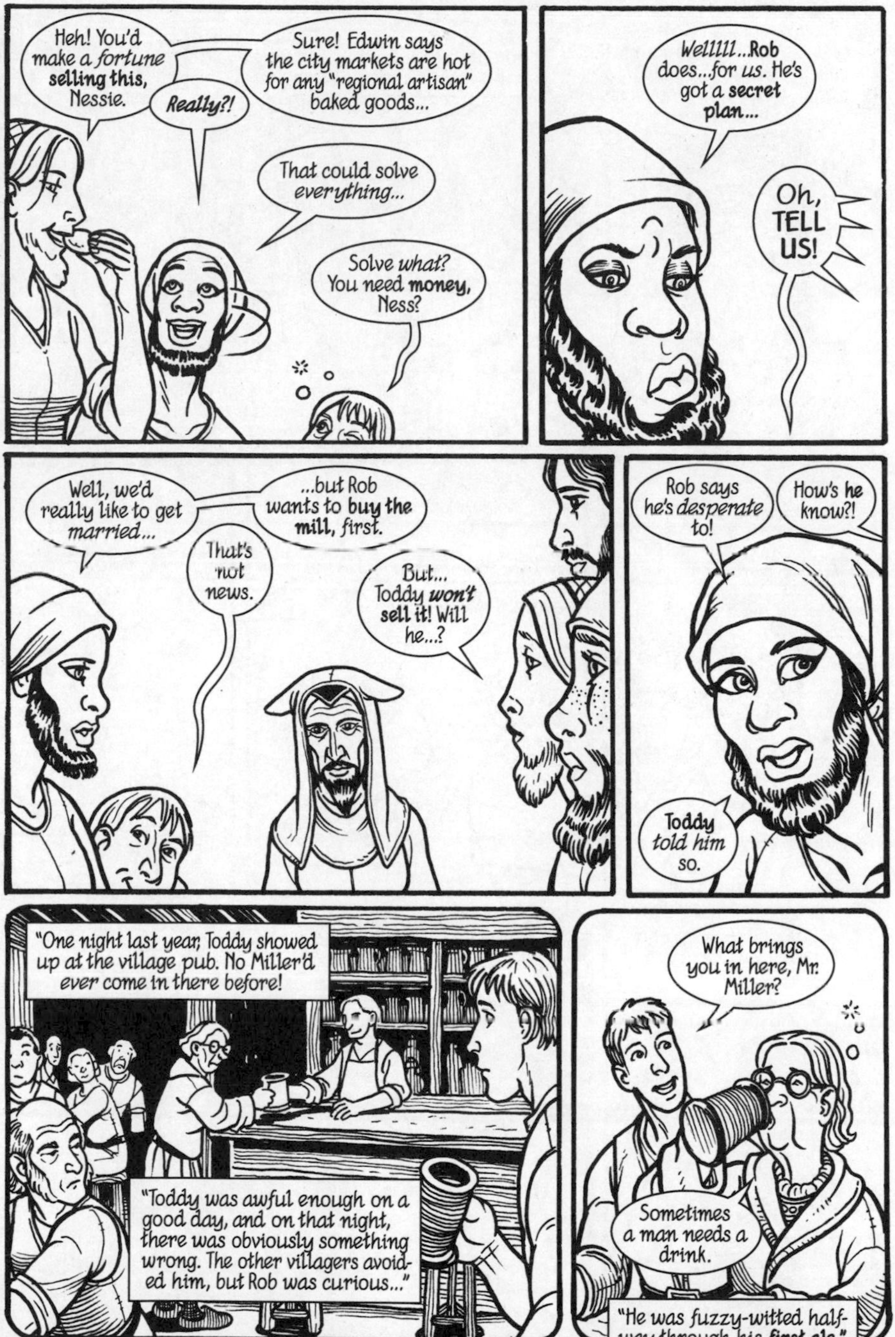
Heh! You'd make a *fortune* **selling this,** Nessie.
Sure! Edwin says the city markets are hot for any "regional artisan" baked goods...
Really?!
That could solve *everything...*
Solve *what?* You need **money,** Ness?
Welllll...**Rob** does...*for us.* He's got a **secret plan...**
Oh, TELL US!
Well, we'd really like to get *married...*
...but Rob wants to **buy the mill,** *first.*
That's *not* news.
But... Toddy ***won't*** **sell it!** Will he...?
Rob says he's *desperate* to!
How's he know?!
Toddy *told him* so.
"One night last year, Toddy showed up at the village pub. No Miller'd *ever* come in there before!
"Toddy was awful enough on a good day, and on that night, there was obviously something wrong. The other villagers avoided him, but Rob was curious..."
What brings you in here, Mr. Miller?
Sometimes a man needs a drink.
"He was fuzzy-witted halfway through his **first ale.**"

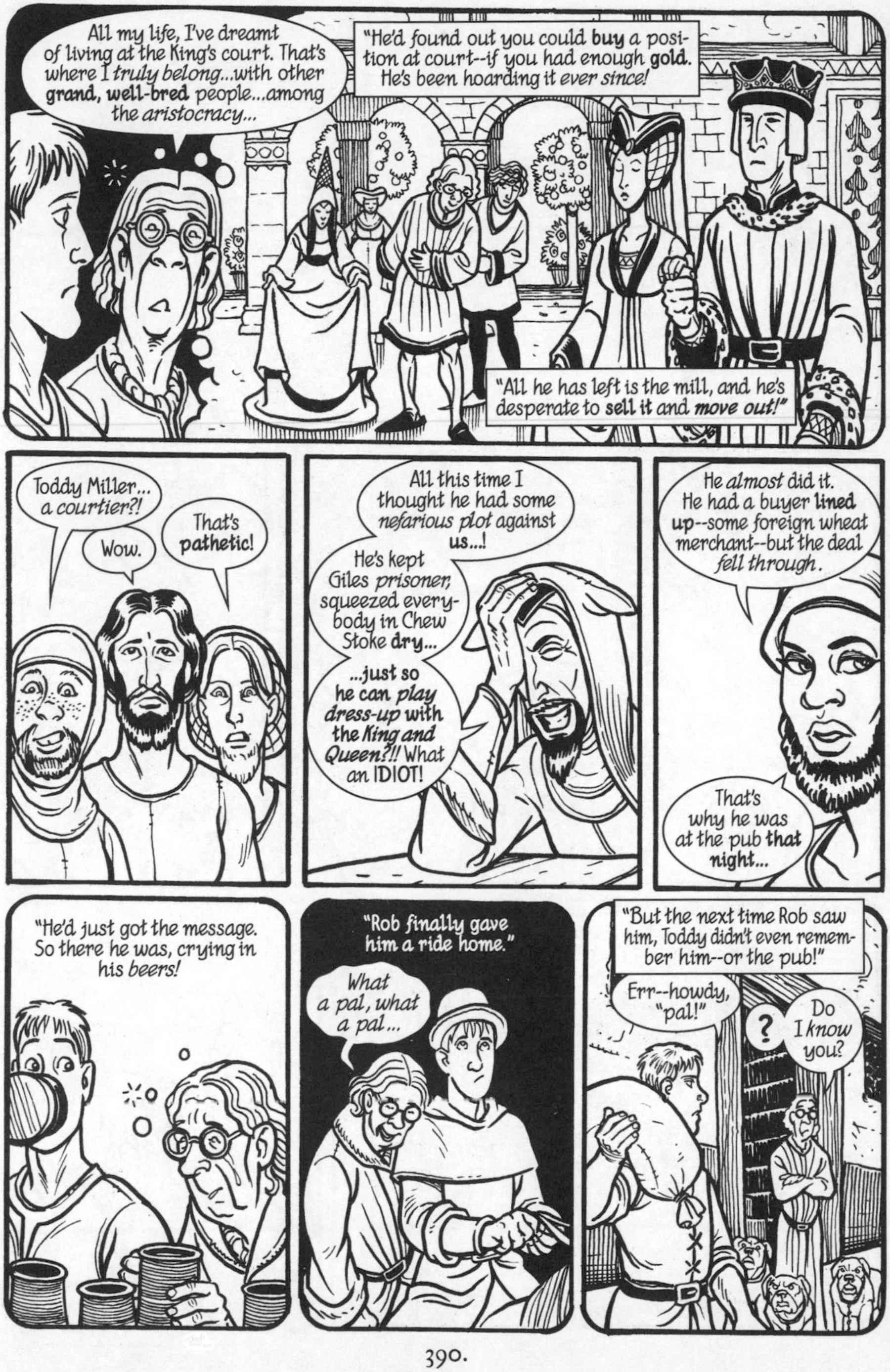
All my life, I've dreamt of living at the King's court. That's where I *truly belong*...with other **grand, well-bred** people...among the *aristocracy*...
"He'd found out you could **buy** a position at court--if you had enough **gold**. He's been hoarding it *ever since!*
"All he has left is the mill, and he's desperate to **sell it** and ***move out!"***
Toddy Miller... *a courtier?!*
Wow.
That's **pathetic!**
All this time I thought he had some *nefarious plot* against **us**...!
He's kept Giles *prisoner,* squeezed everybody in Chew Stoke **dry**...
...just so he can *play dress-up* with the *King and Queen?!!* What an IDIOT!
He *almost* did it. He had a buyer **lined up**--some foreign wheat merchant--but the deal *fell through*.
That's why he was at the pub **that night...**
"He'd just got the message. So there he was, crying in his *beers!*
"Rob finally gave him a ride home."
What a pal, what a pal...
"But the next time Rob saw him, Toddy didn't even remember him--or the pub!"
Err--howdy, "pal!"
?
Do I *know* you?

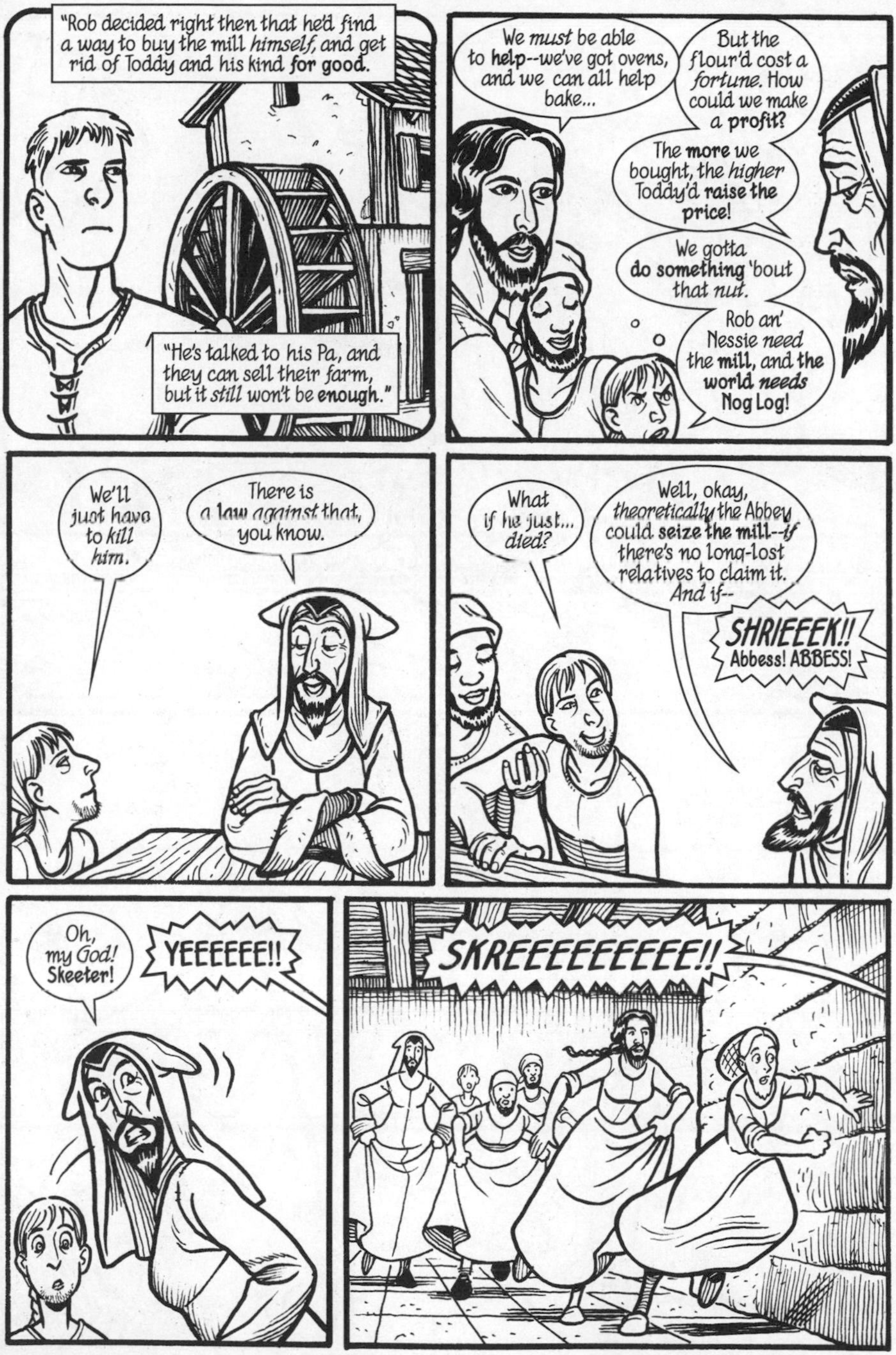
"Rob decided right then that he'd find a way to buy the mill himself, and get rid of Toddy and his kind for good.
"He's talked to his Pa, and they can sell their farm, but it still won't be enough."
We must be able to help--we've got ovens, and we can all help bake...
But the flour'd cost a fortune. How could we make a profit?
The more we bought, the higher Toddy'd raise the price!
We gotta do something 'bout that nut.
Rob an' Nessie need the mill, and the world needs Nog Log!
We'll just have to kill him.
There is a law against that, you know.
What if he just... died?
Well, okay, theoretically the Abbey could seize the mill--if there's no long-lost relatives to claim it. And if--
SHRIEEEK!! Abbess! ABBESS!
Oh, my God! Skeeter!
YEEEEEE!!
SKREEEEEEEEEE!!

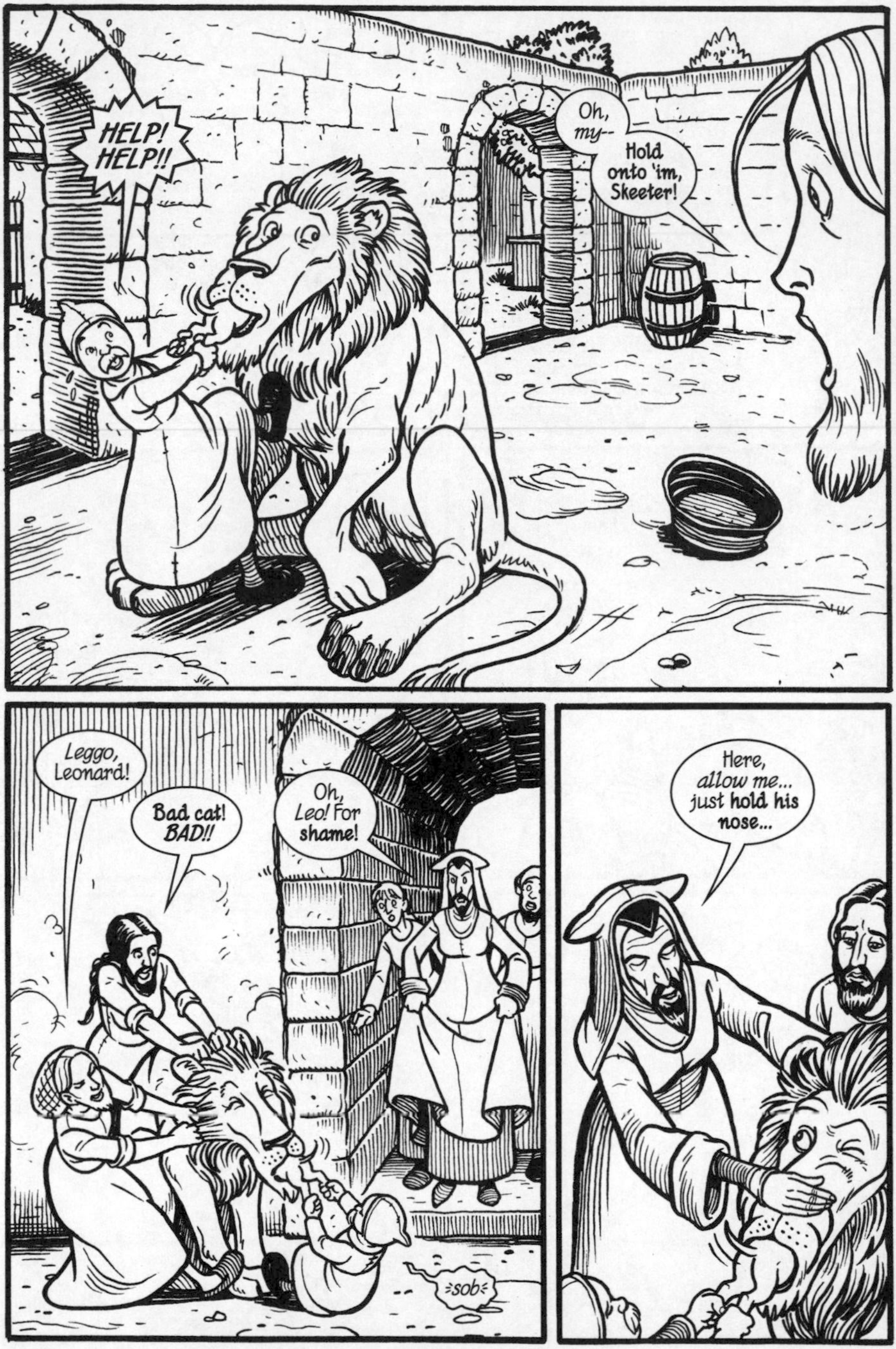
HELP! HELP!!
Oh, my--
Hold onto 'im, Skeeter!
Leggo, Leonard!
Bad cat! BAD!!
Oh, Leo! For shame!
sob
Here, allow me... just hold his nose...

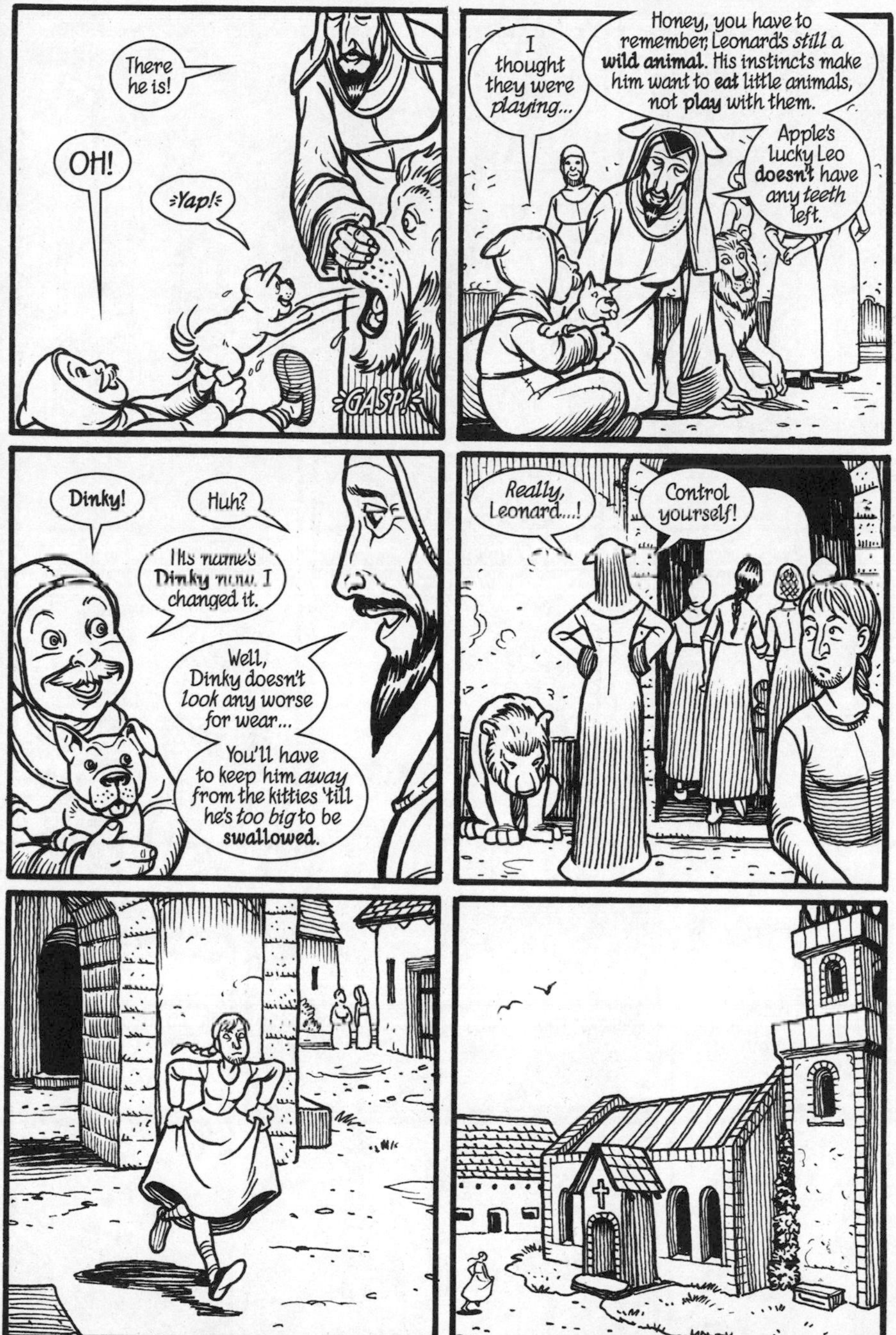
There he is!
OH!
Yap!
GASP!
I thought they were playing...
Honey, you have to remember, Leonard's still a wild animal. His instincts make him want to eat little animals, not play with them.
Apple's lucky Leo doesn't have any teeth left.
Dinky!
Huh?
His name's Dinky now. I changed it.
Well, Dinky doesn't look any worse for wear...
You'll have to keep him away from the kitties 'till he's too big to be swallowed.
Really, Leonard...!
Control yourself!

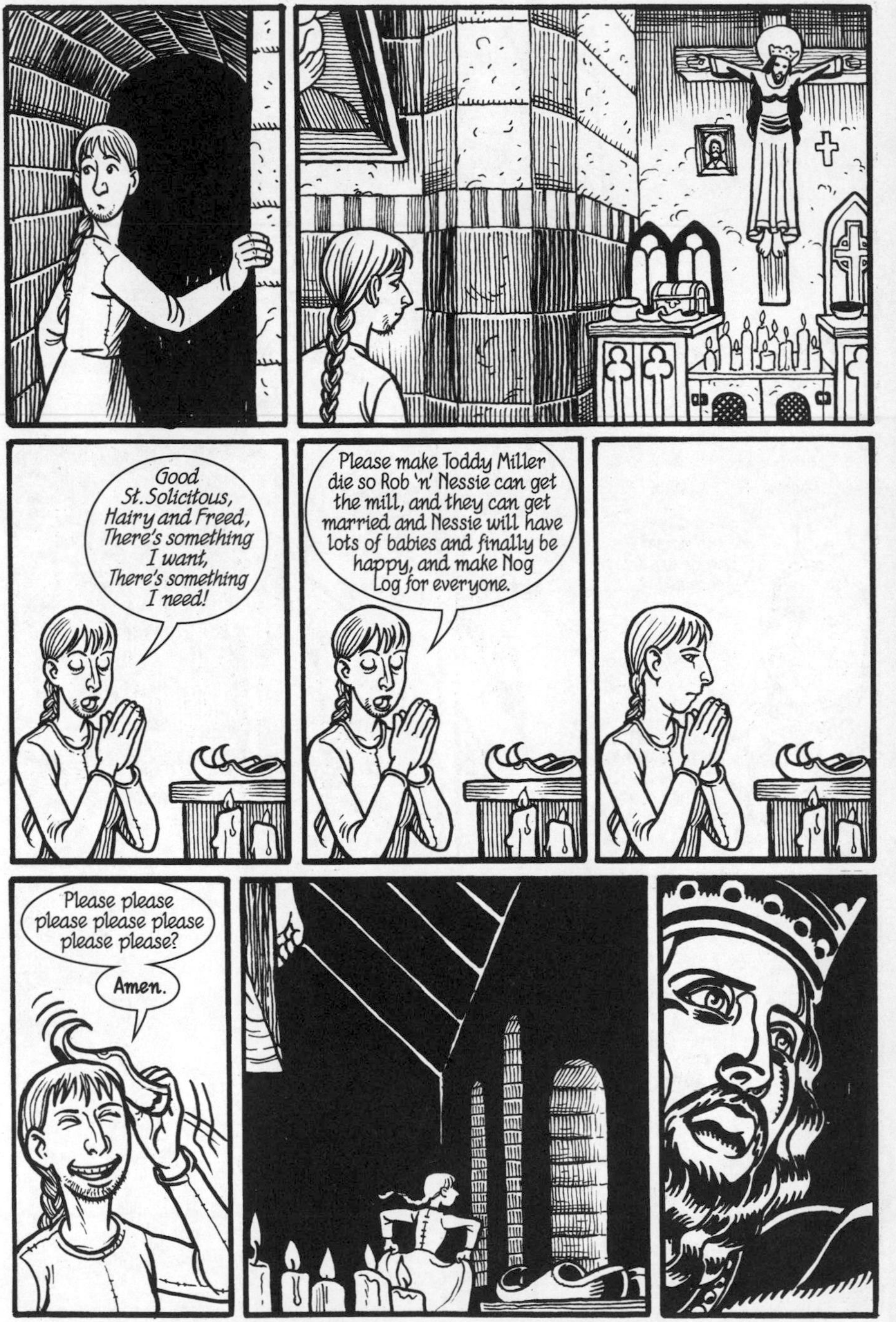
Good St. Solicitous, Hairy and Freed, There's something I want, There's something I need!
Please make Toddy Miller die so Rob 'n' Nessie can get the mill, and they can get married and Nessie will have lots of babies and finally be happy, and make Nog Log for everyone.
Please please please please please please please?
Amen.

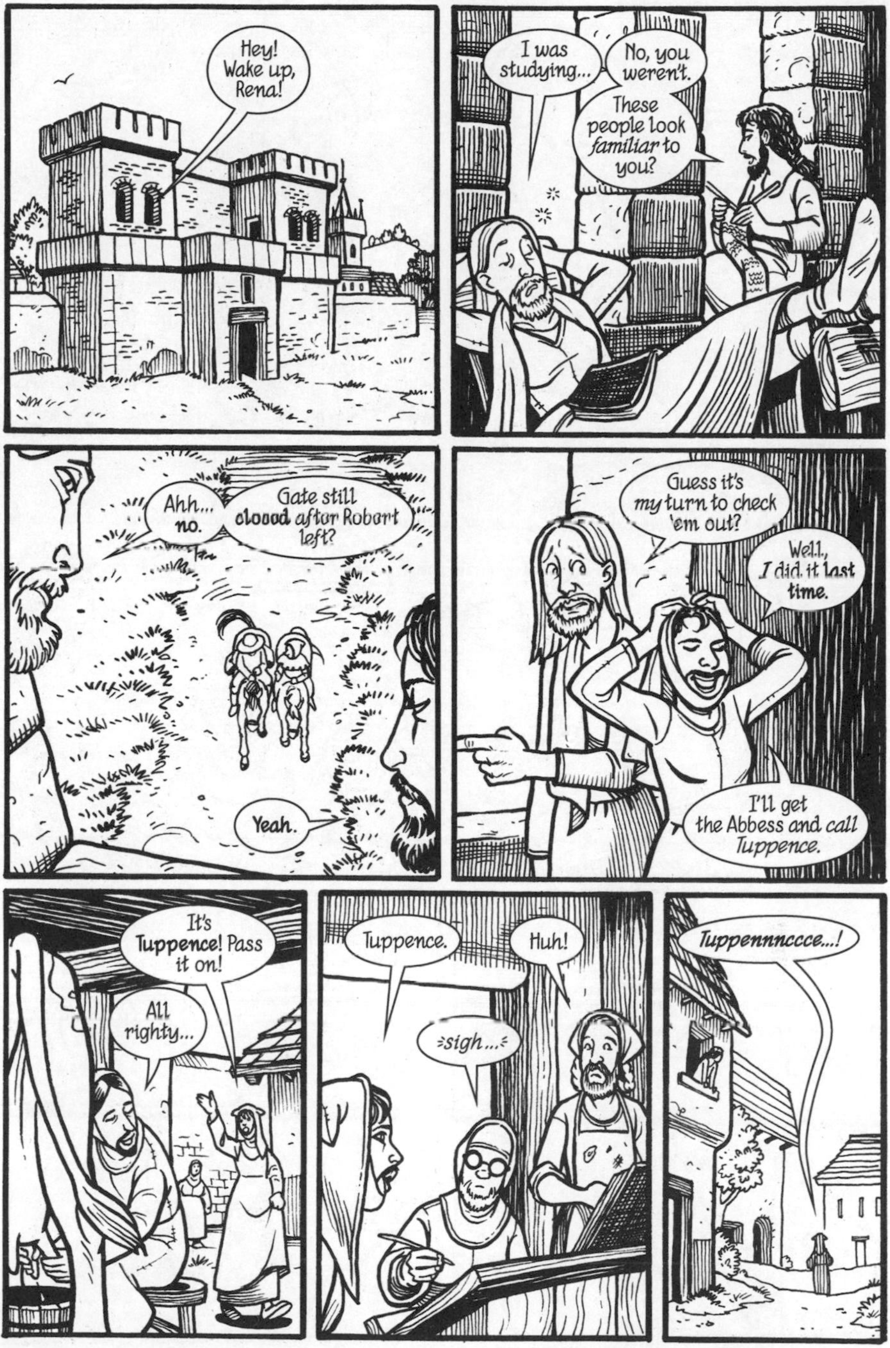
Hey! Wake up, Rena!
I was studying...
No, you weren't.
These people look *familiar* to you?
Ahh... **no.**
Gate still **closed** after Robert left?
Yeah.
Guess it's *my* turn to check 'em out?
Well, *I* did it **last time.**
I'll get the Abbess and call *Tuppence.*
It's **Tuppence!** Pass it on!
All righty...
Tuppence.
Huh!
sigh...
Tuppennnccce...!

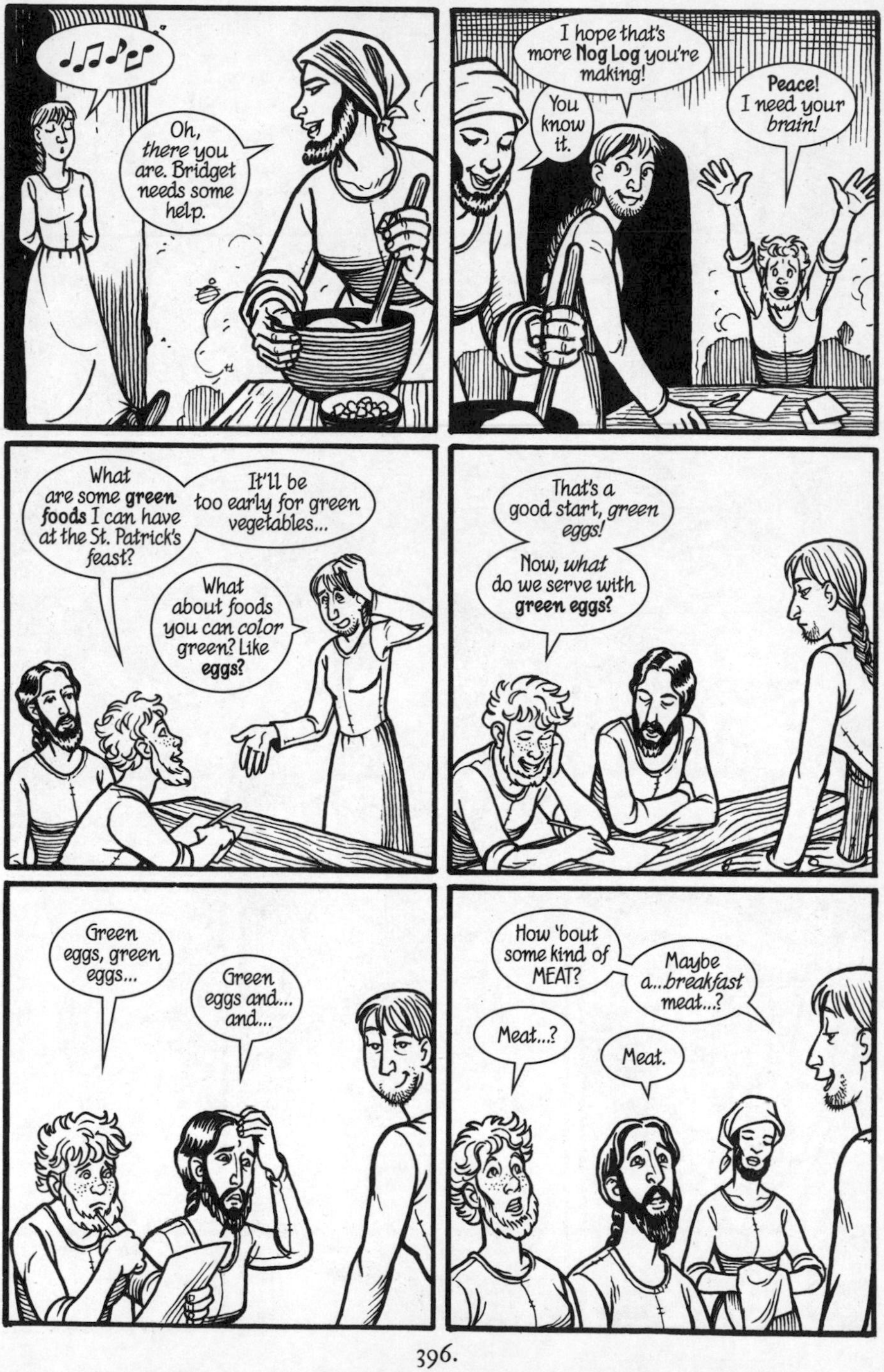
♩♫♪♫
Oh, *there you* are. Bridget needs some help.
I hope that's more **Nog Log** you're making!
You know it.
Peace! I need your *brain!*
What are some **green foods** I can have at the St. Patrick's feast?
It'll be too early for green vegetables...
What about foods you can *color* green? Like **eggs?**
That's a good start, *green eggs!*
Now, *what* do we serve with **green eggs?**
Green eggs, green eggs...
Green eggs and... and...
How 'bout some kind of MEAT?
Maybe a...*breakfast* meat...?
Meat...?
Meat.

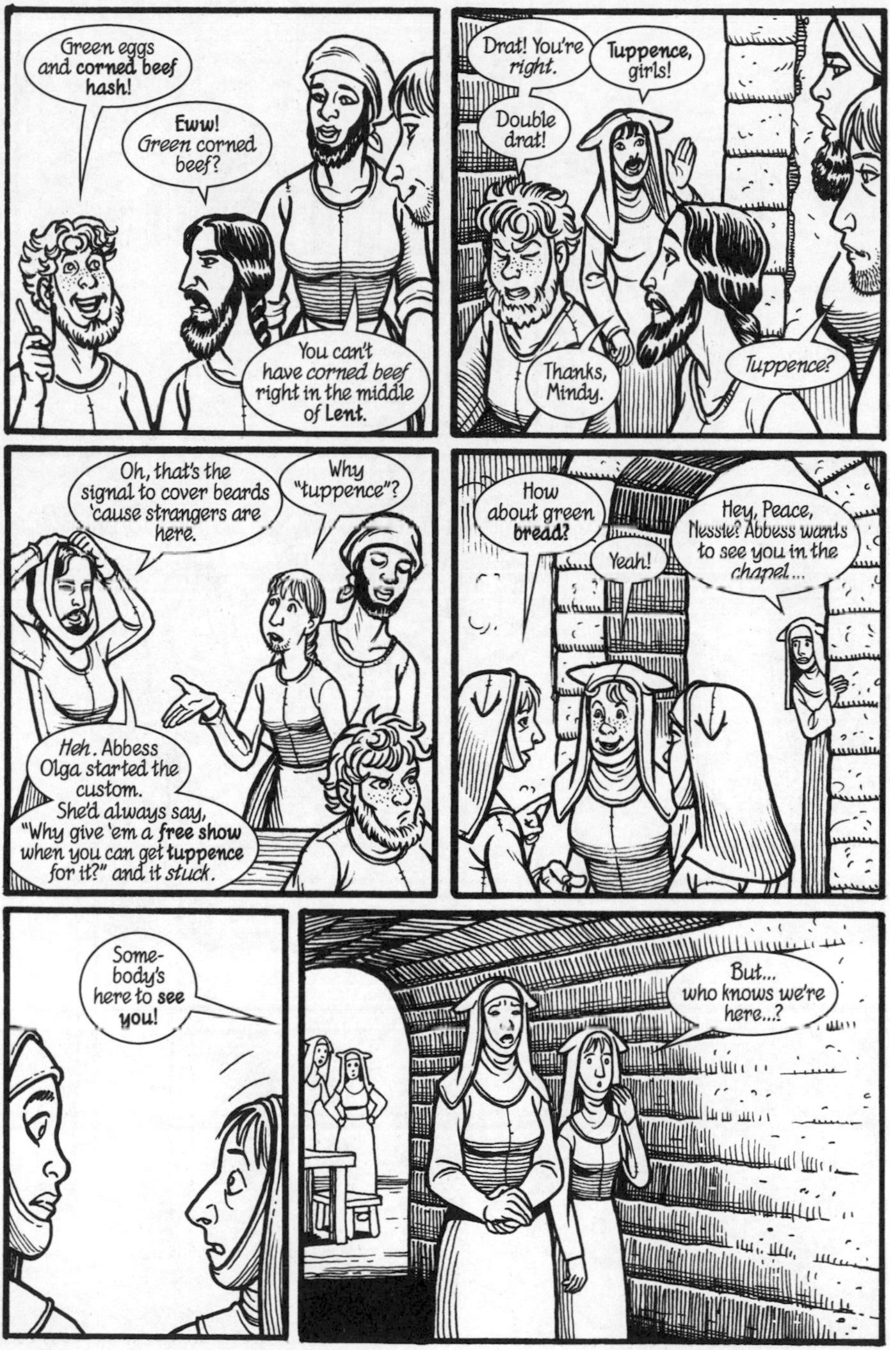
Green eggs and corned beef hash!
Eww! Green corned beef?
You can't have corned beef right in the middle of Lent.
Drat! You're right.
Tuppence, girls!
Double drat!
Thanks, Mindy.
Tuppence?
Oh, that's the signal to cover beards 'cause strangers are here.
Why "tuppence"?
Heh. Abbess Olga started the custom.
She'd always say, "Why give 'em a free show when you can get tuppence for it?" and it stuck.
How about green bread?
Yeah!
Hey, Peace, Nessie? Abbess wants to see you in the chapel...
Some-body's here to see you!
But... who knows we're here...?

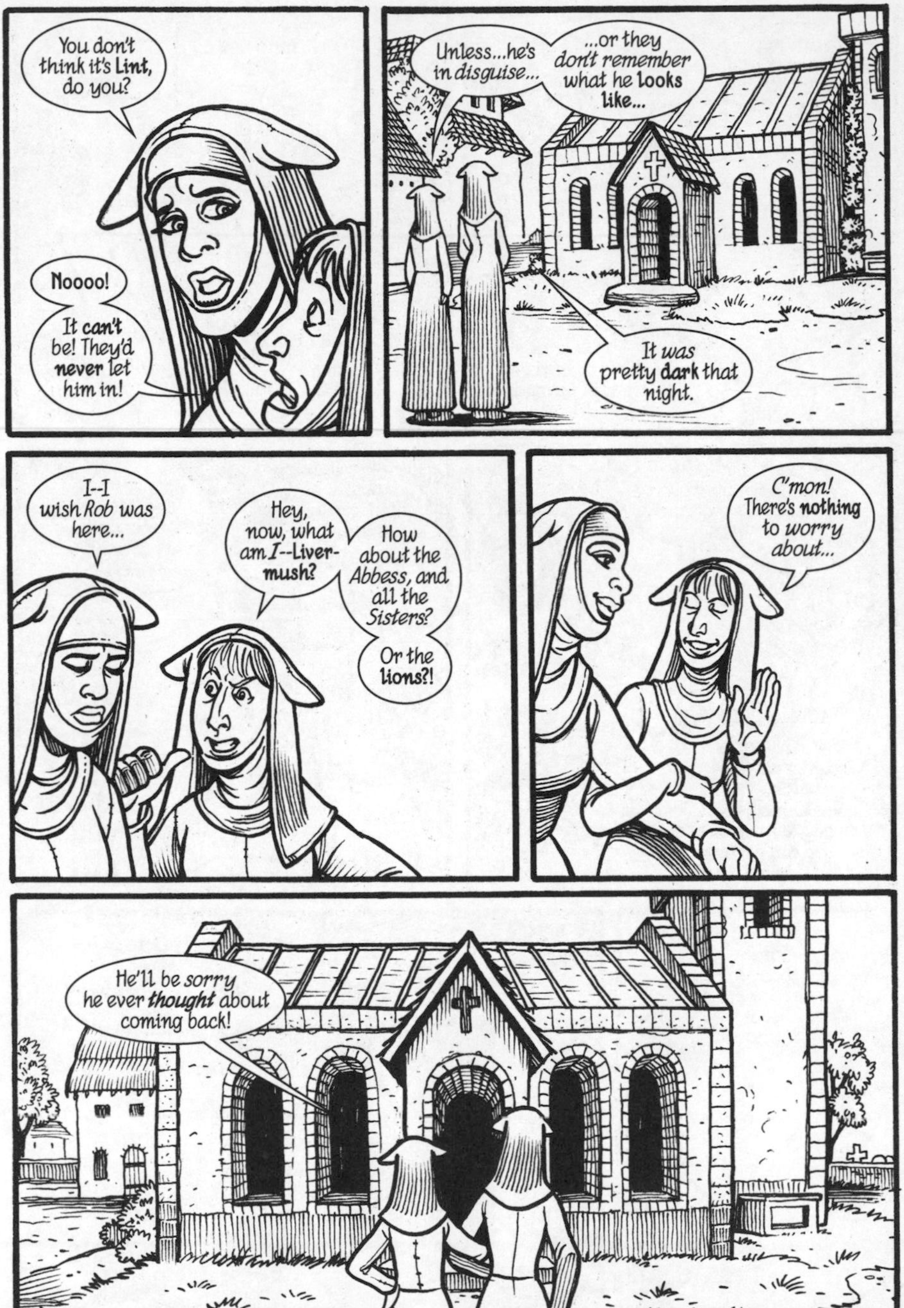
You don't think it's Lint, do you?
Noooo!
It can't be! They'd never let him in!
Unless...he's in disguise...
...or they don't remember what he looks like...
It was pretty dark that night.
I--I wish Rob was here...
Hey, now, what am I--Liver-mush?
How about the Abbess, and all the Sisters?
Or the lions?!
C'mon! There's nothing to worry about...
He'll be sorry he ever thought about coming back!

Chapter 18.

· SOLICITINE PT. 6 ·

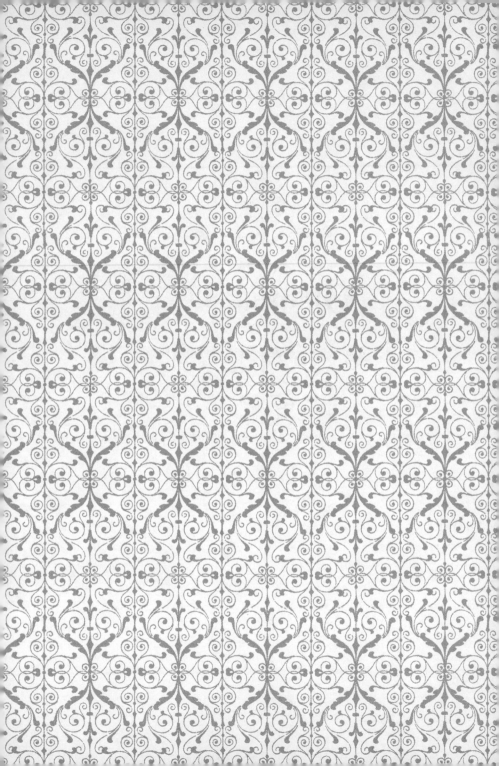

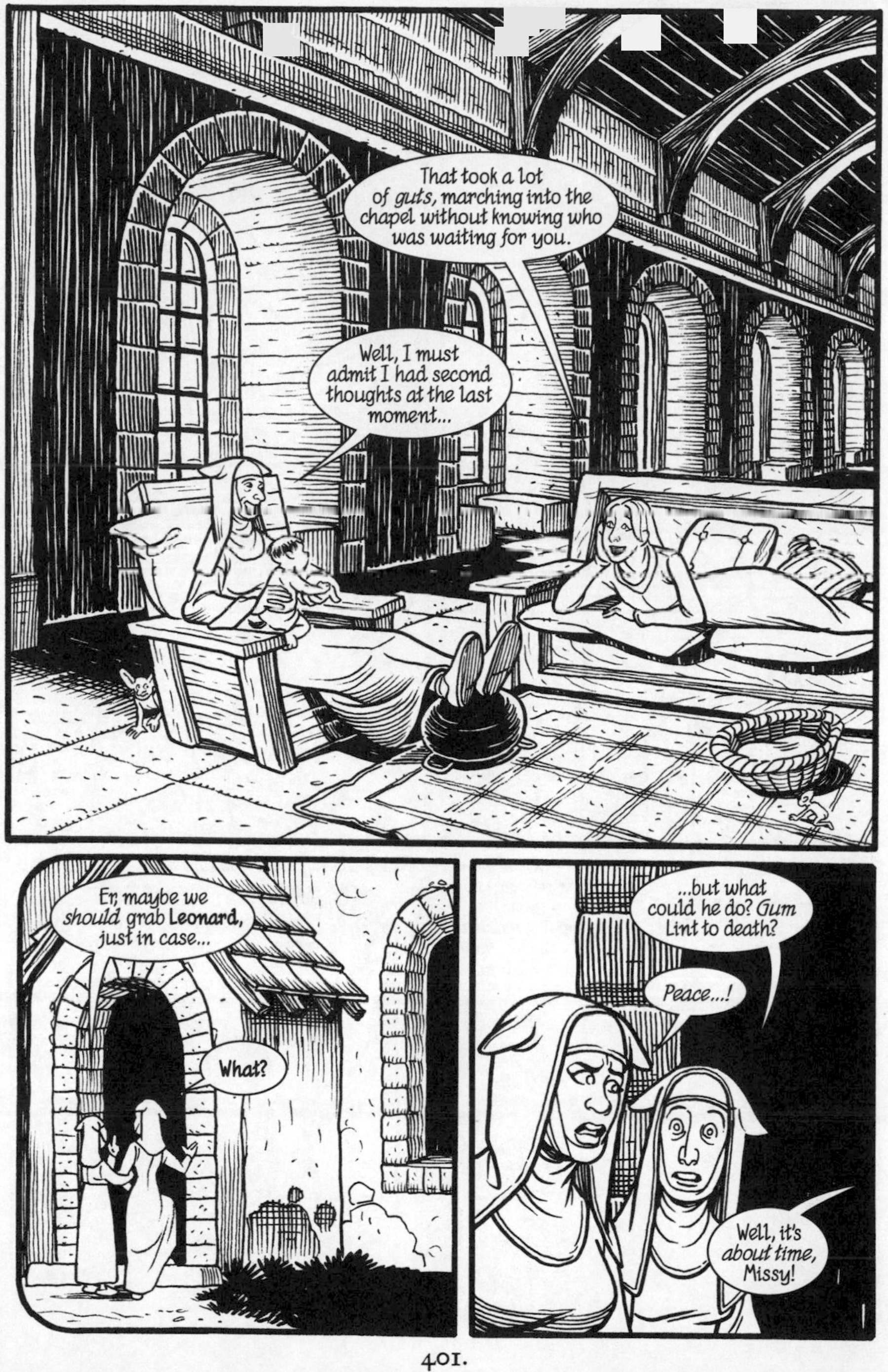
That took a lot of *guts*, marching into the chapel without knowing who was waiting for you.
Well, I must admit I had second thoughts at the last moment...
Er, maybe we *should* grab **Leonard**, just in case...
What?
...but what could he do? *Gum* Lint to death?
Peace...!
Well, it's *about time*, Missy!

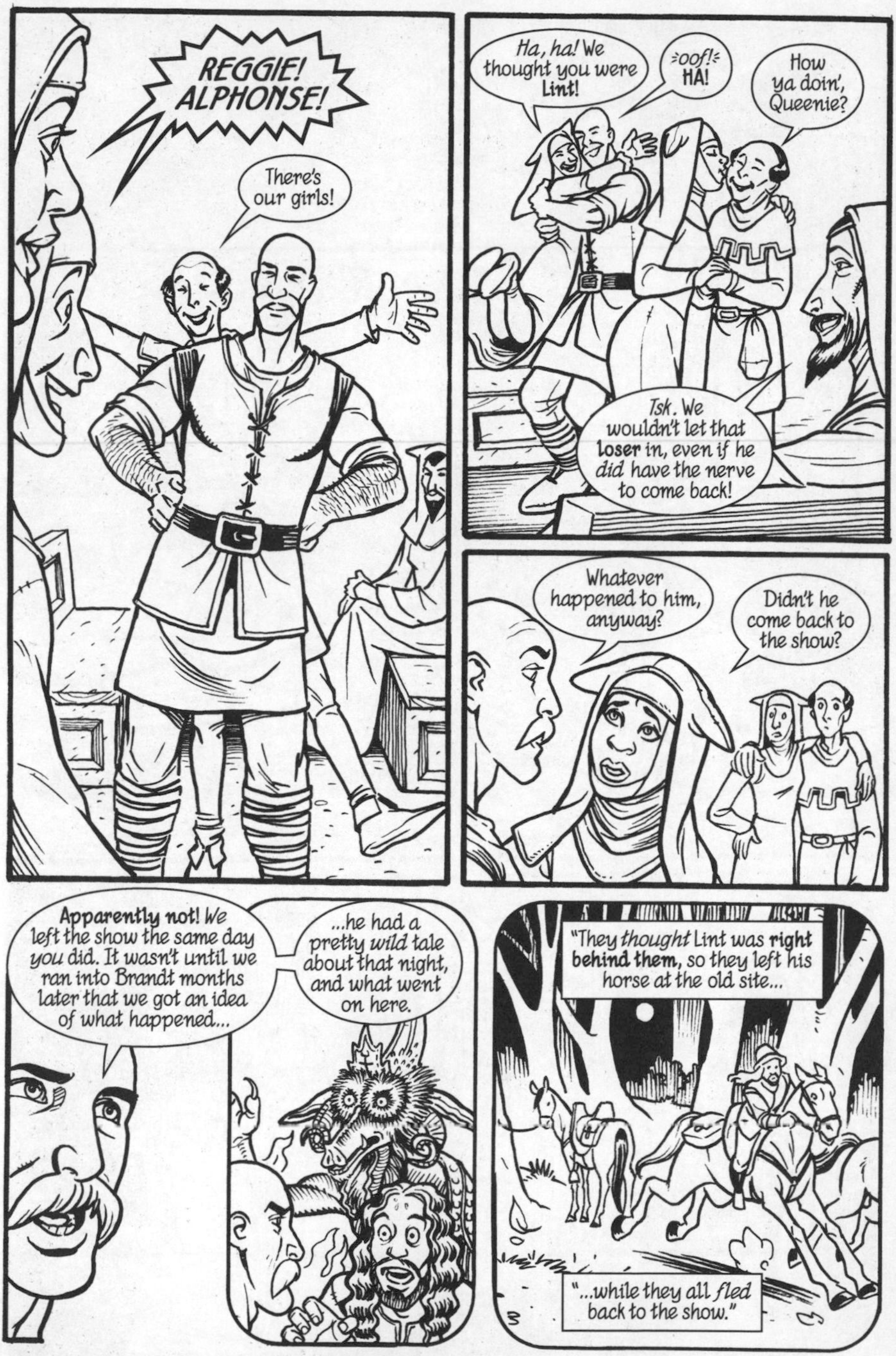
REGGIE! ALPHONSE!
There's our girls!
Ha, ha! We thought you were Lint!
oof! HA!
How ya doin', Queenie?
Tsk. We wouldn't let that loser in, even if he did have the nerve to come back!
Whatever happened to him, anyway?
Didn't he come back to the show?
Apparently not! We left the show the same day you did. It wasn't until we ran into Brandt months later that we got an idea of what happened...
...he had a pretty wild tale about that night, and what went on here.
"They thought Lint was right behind them, so they left his horse at the old site...
"...while they all fled back to the show."

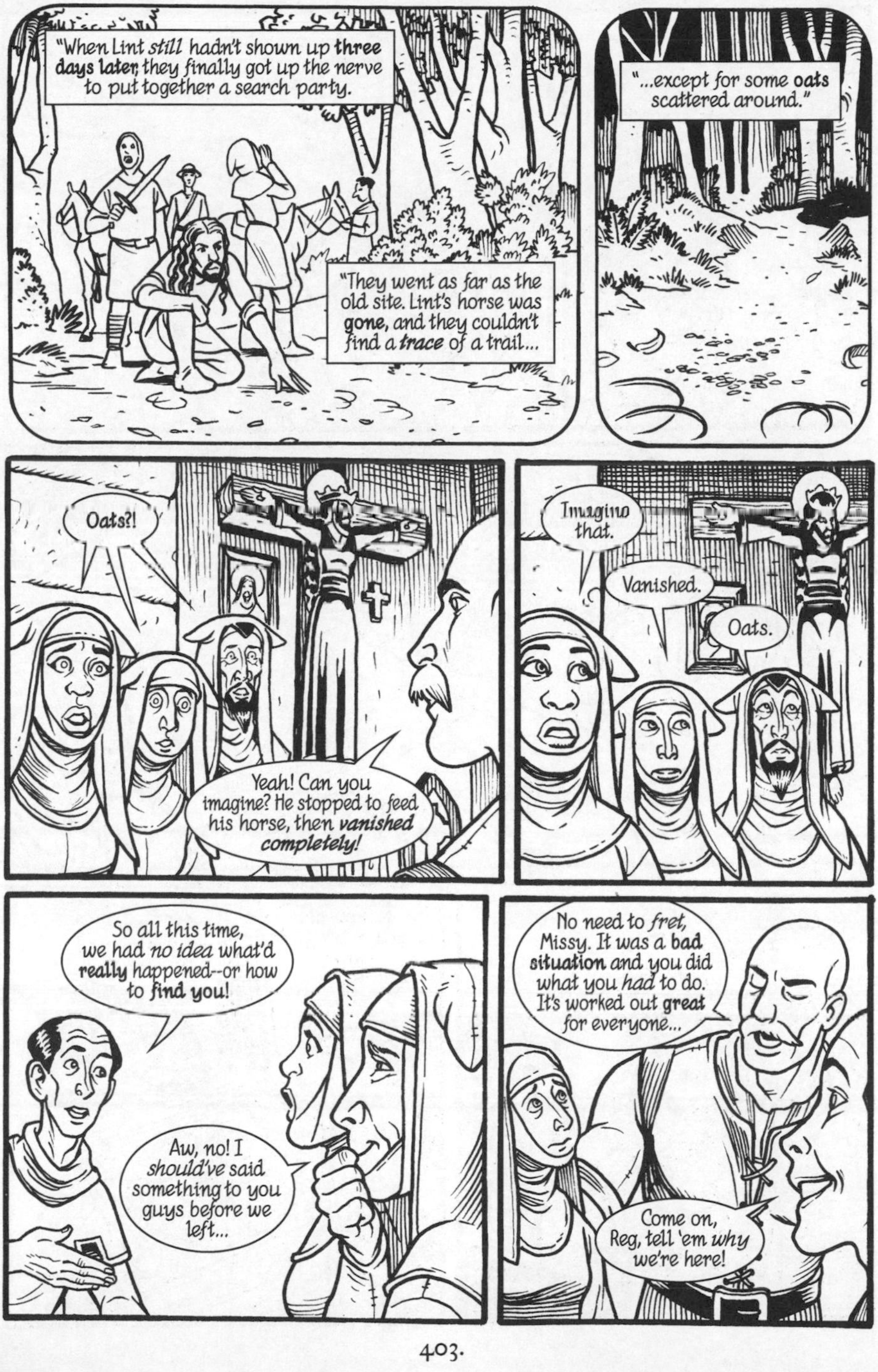
"When Lint still hadn't shown up three days later, they finally got up the nerve to put together a search party.
"They went as far as the old site. Lint's horse was gone, and they couldn't find a trace of a trail...
"...except for some oats scattered around."
Oats?!
Yeah! Can you imagine? He stopped to feed his horse, then vanished completely!
Imagine that.
Vanished.
Oats.
So all this time, we had no idea what'd really happened--or how to find you!
Aw, no! I should've said something to you guys before we left...
No need to fret, Missy. It was a bad situation and you did what you had to do. It's worked out great for everyone...
Come on, Reg, tell 'em why we're here!

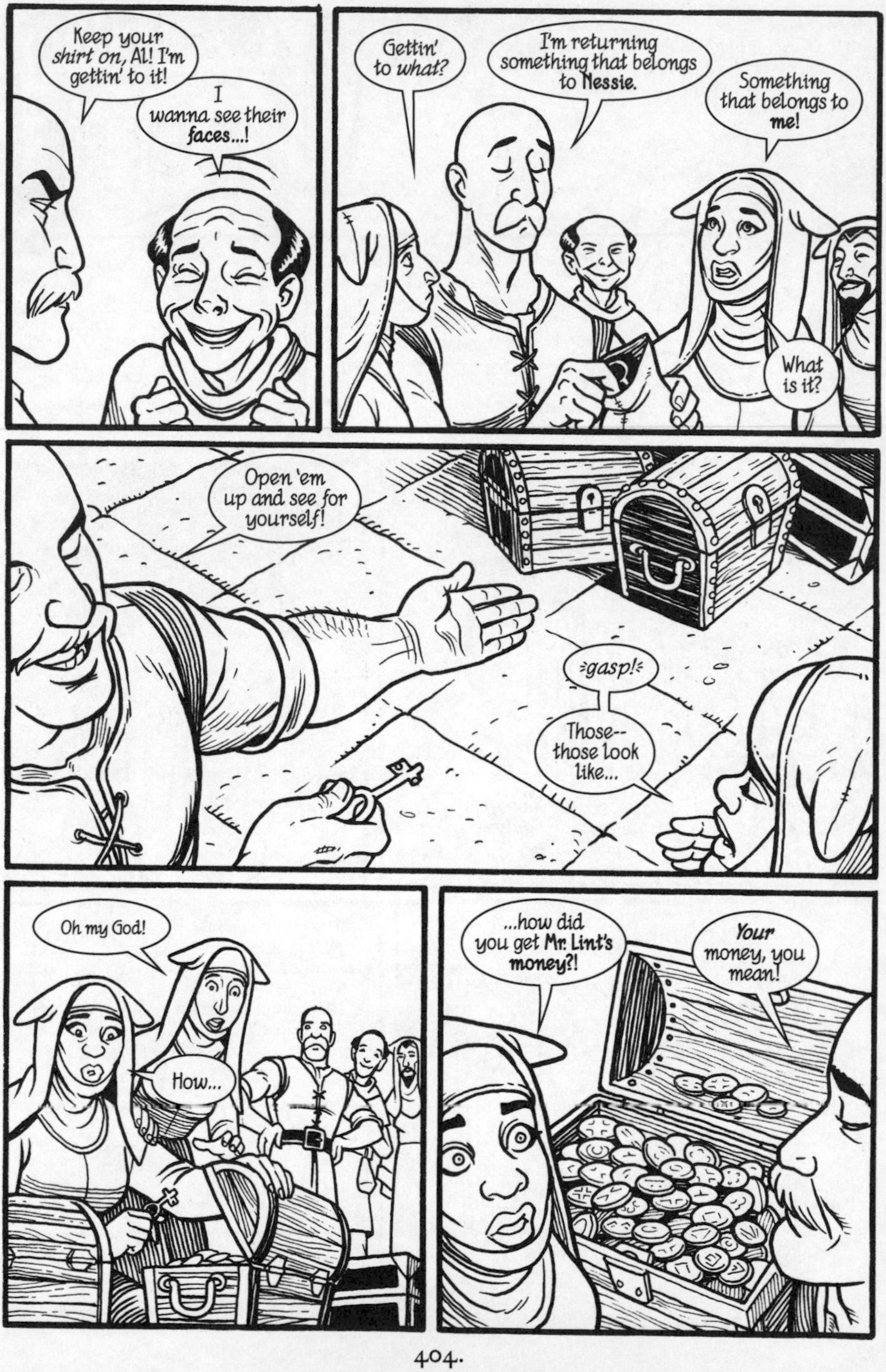
Keep your *shirt on*, Al! I'm gettin' to it!
I wanna see their **faces**...!
Gettin' to *what*?
I'm returning something that belongs to **Nessie**.
Something that belongs to **me**!
What is it?
Open 'em up and see for yourself!
gasp!
Those-- those look like...
Oh my God!
How...
...how did you get **Mr. Lint's money**?!
Your money, you mean!

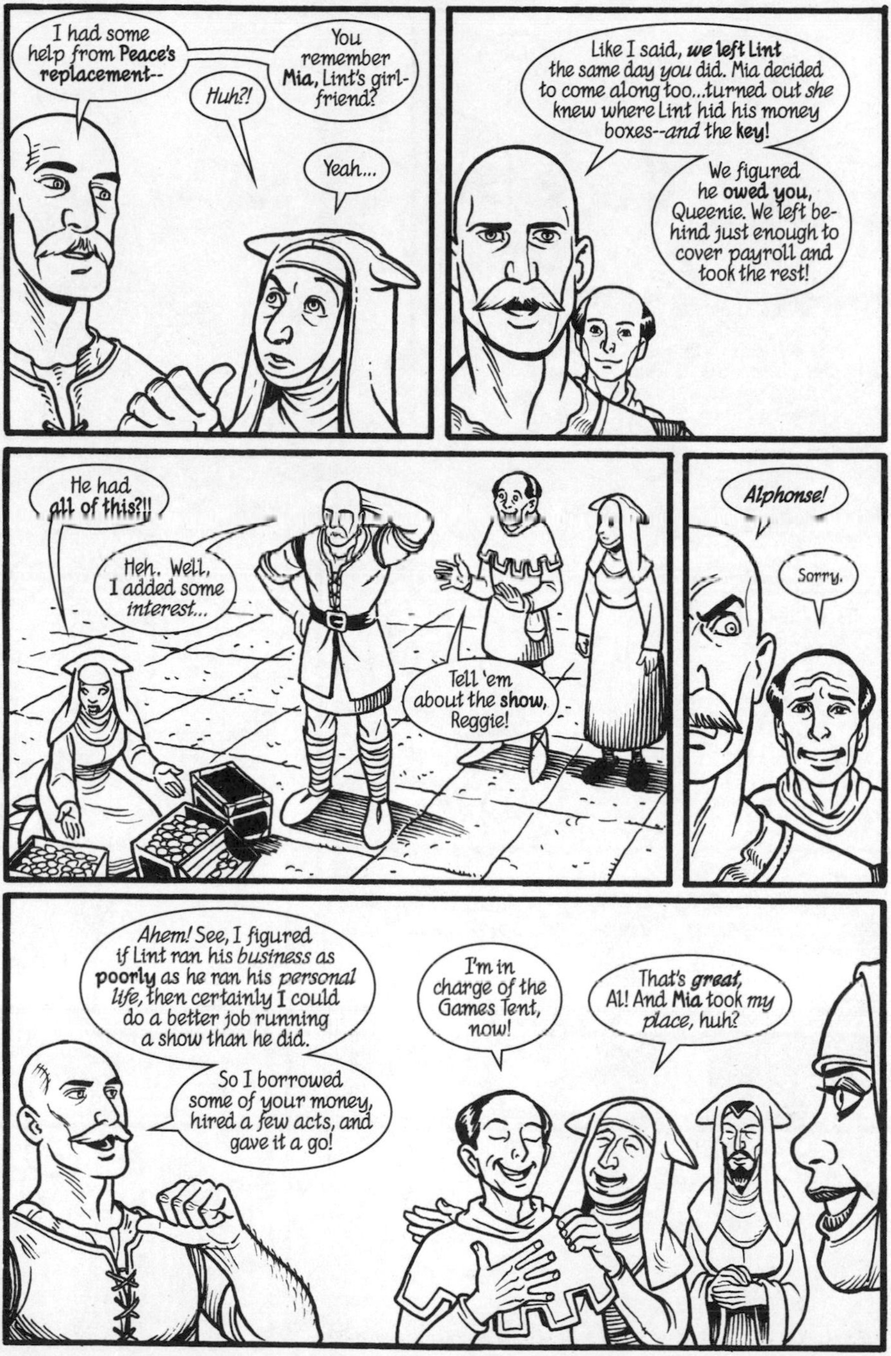
I had some help from Peace's replacement--
You remember Mia, Lint's girl-friend?
Huh?!
Yeah...
Like I said, we left Lint the same day you did. Mia decided to come along too...turned out she knew where Lint hid his money boxes--and the key!
We figured he owed you, Queenie. We left be-hind just enough to cover payroll and took the rest!
He had all of this?!!
Heh. Well, I added some interest...
Tell 'em about the show, Reggie!
Alphonse!
Sorry.
Ahem! See, I figured if Lint ran his business as poorly as he ran his personal life, then certainly I could do a better job running a show than he did.
So I borrowed some of your money, hired a few acts, and gave it a go!
I'm in charge of the Games Tent, now!
That's great, Al! And Mia took my place, huh?

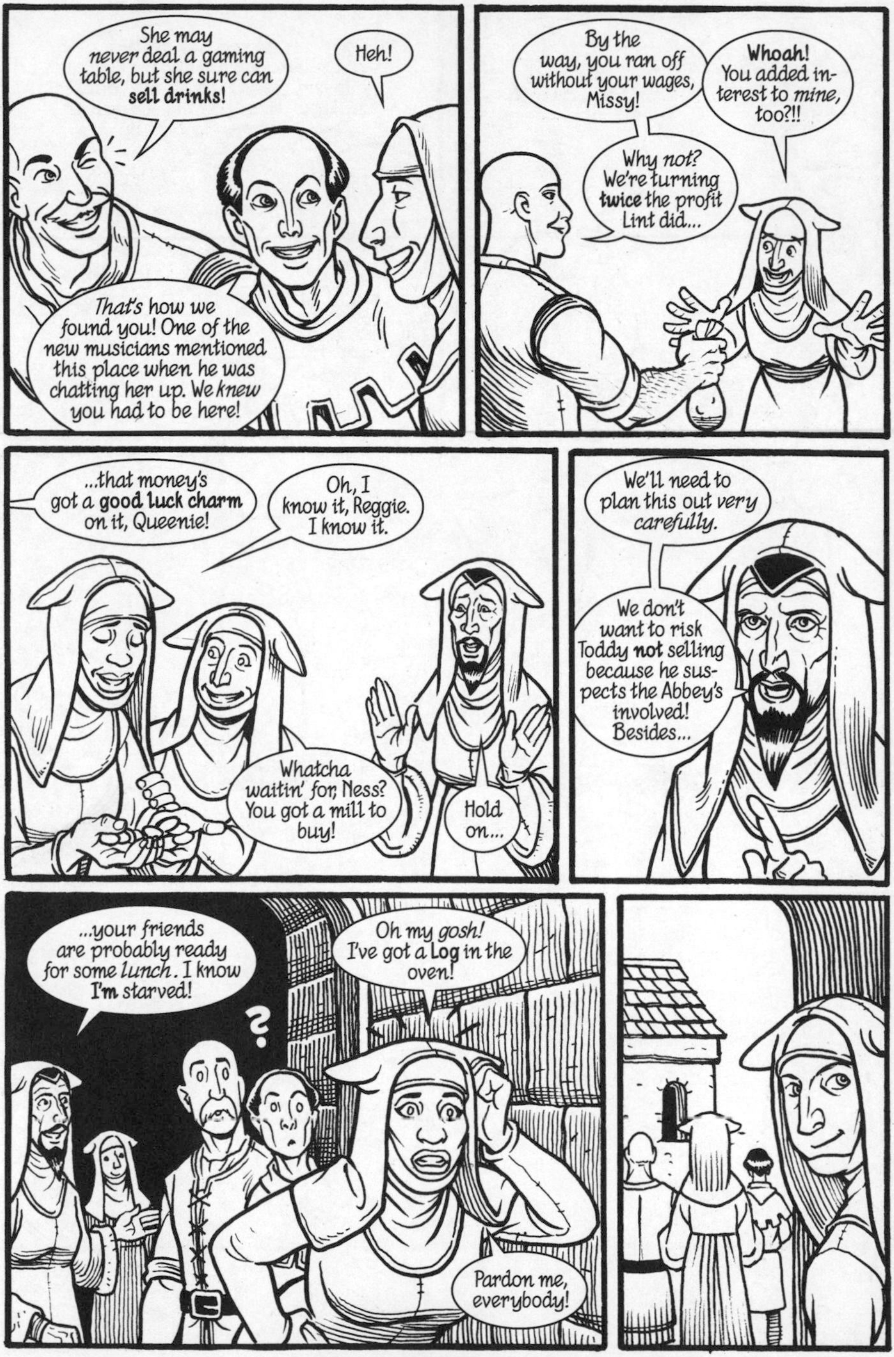

She may *never* deal a gaming table, but she sure can **sell drinks**!
Heh!
That's how we found you! One of the new musicians mentioned this place when he was chatting her up. We *knew* you had to be here!
By the way, you ran off without your wages, Missy!
Why *not*? We're turning **twice** the profit Lint did...
Whoah! You added interest to *mine*, too?!!
...that money's got a **good luck charm** on it, Queenie!
Oh, I know it, Reggie. I know it.
Whatcha waitin' for, Ness? You got a mill to buy!
Hold on...
We'll need to plan this out *very carefully*.
We don't want to risk Toddy **not** selling because he suspects the Abbey's involved! Besides...
...your friends are probably ready for some *lunch*. I know **I'm** starved!
?
Oh my *gosh*! I've got a **Log** in the oven!
Pardon me, everybody!

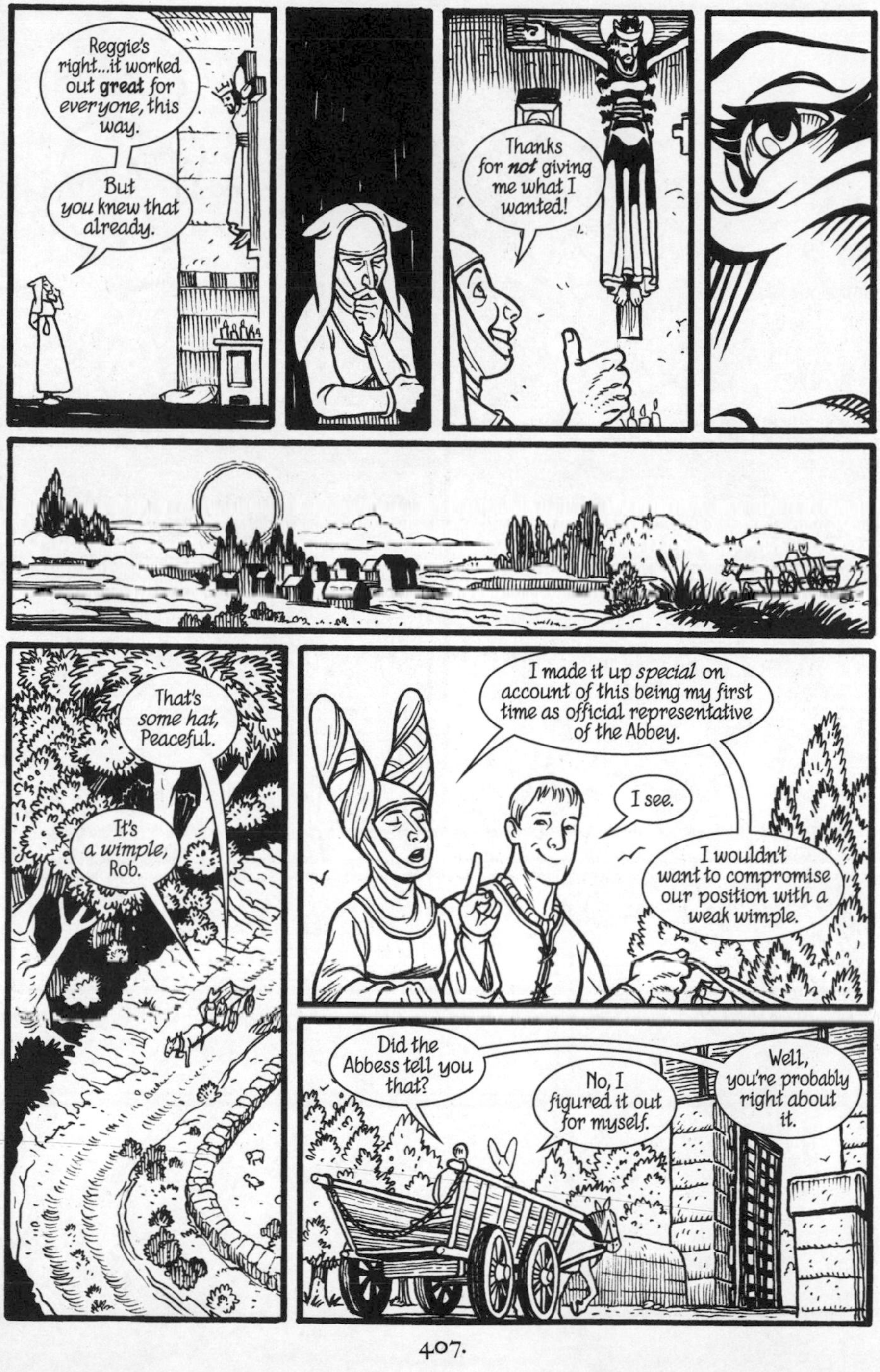
Reggie's right...it worked out **great** for everyone, this way.
But you knew that already.
Thanks for ***not*** giving me what I wanted!
That's *some hat*, Peaceful.
It's *a wimple*, Rob.
I made it up *special* on account of this being my first time as official representative of the Abbey.
I see.
I wouldn't want to compromise our position with a weak wimple.
Did the Abbess tell you that?
No, I figured it out for myself.
Well, you're probably right about it.

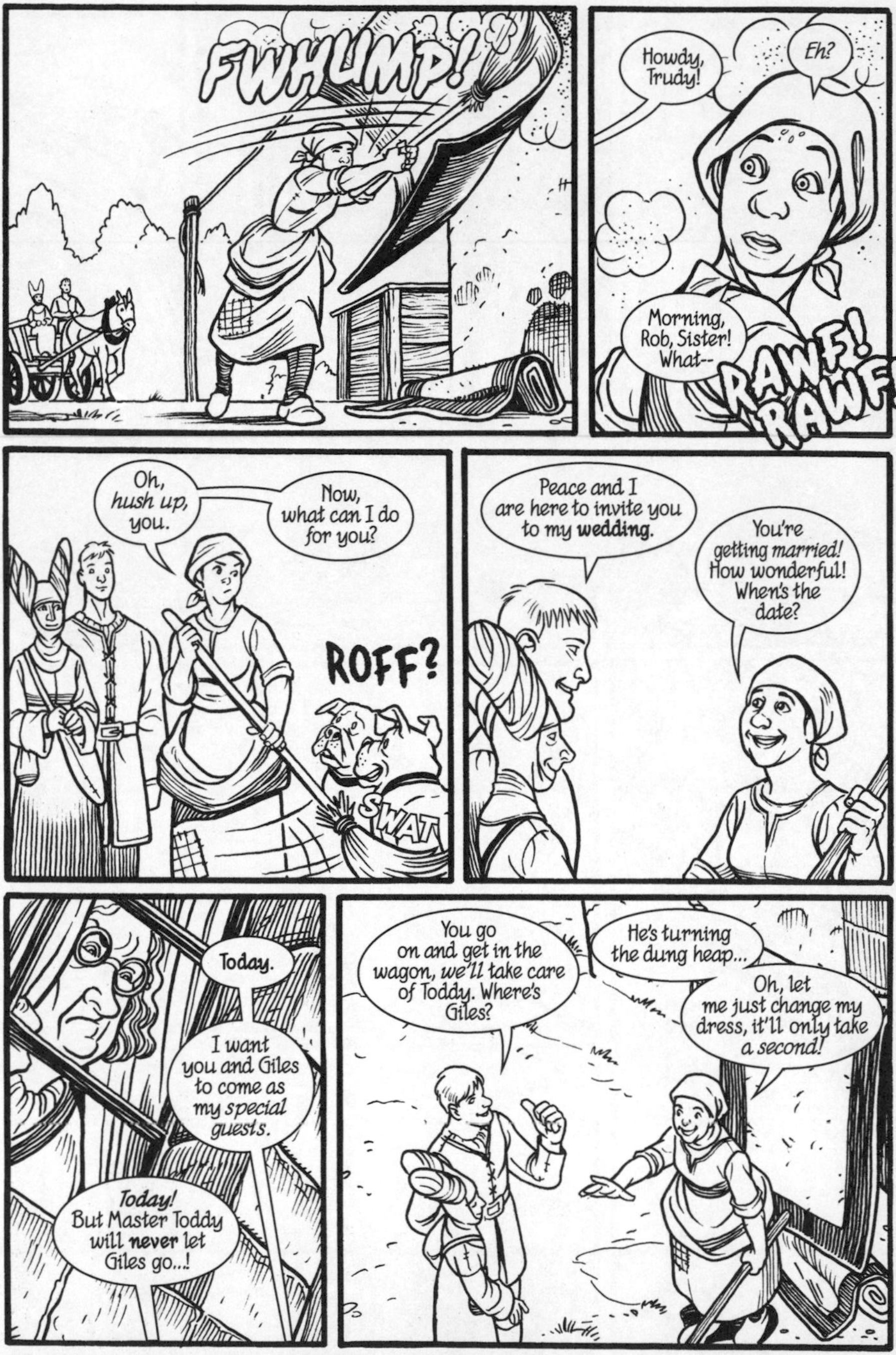
FWHUMP!
Howdy, Trudy!
Eh?
Morning, Rob, Sister! What--
RAWF! RAWF!
Oh, *hush up,* you.
Now, what can I do for you?
ROFF?
SWAT
Peace and I are here to invite you to my **wedding**.
You're getting *married!* How wonderful! When's the date?
Today.
I want you and Giles to come as my *special guests.*
Today! But Master Toddy will **never** let Giles go...!
You go on and get in the wagon, *we'll* take care of Toddy. Where's Giles?
He's turning the dung heap...
Oh, let me just change my dress, it'll only take a *second!*

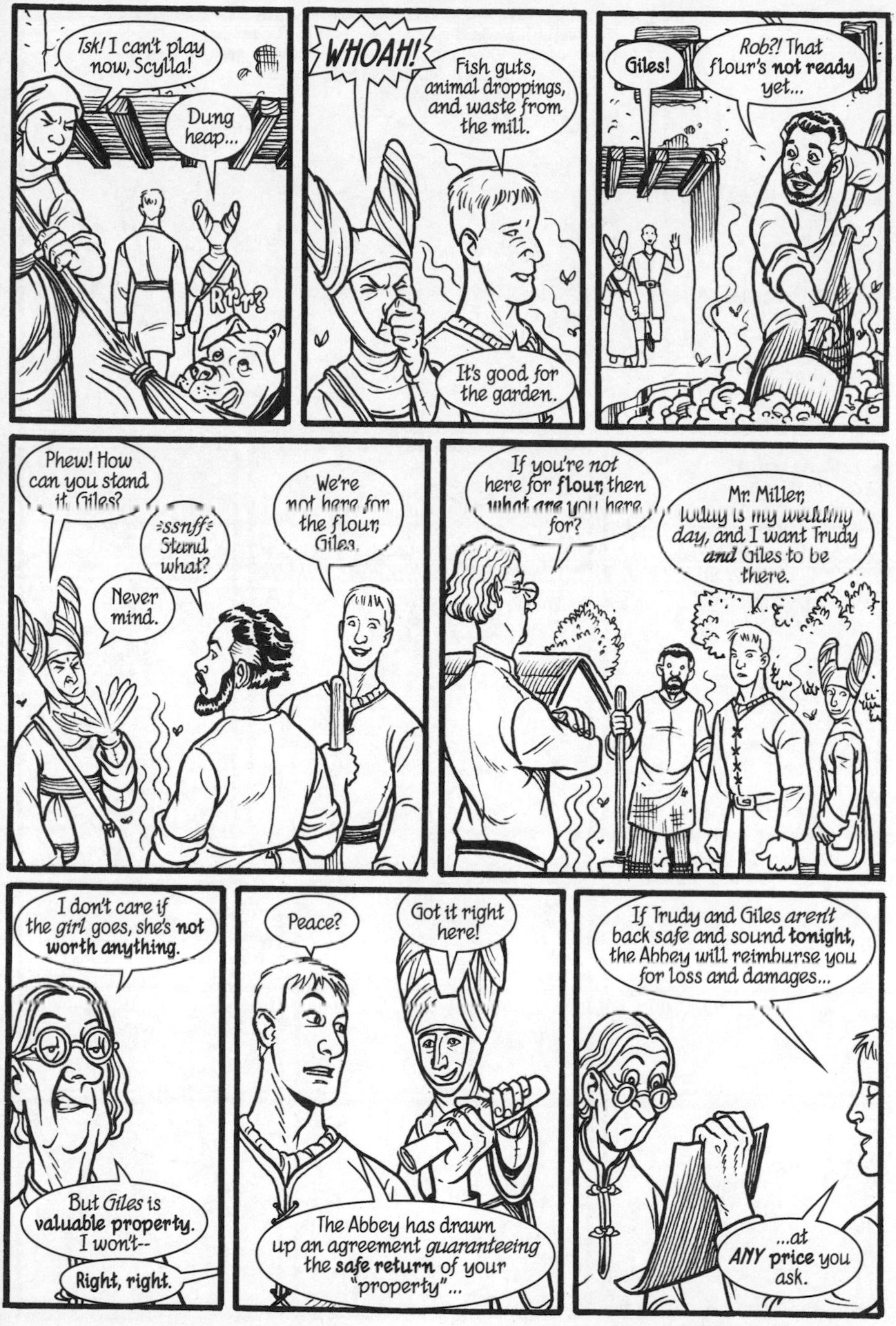
Tsk! I can't play now, Scylla!
Dung heap...
Rrr?
WHOAH!
Fish guts, animal droppings, and waste from the mill.
It's good for the garden.
Giles!
Rob?! That flour's not ready yet...
Phew! How can you stand it, Giles?
ssnff Stand what?
Never mind.
We're not here for the flour, Giles.
If you're not here for flour, then what are you here for?
Mr. Miller, today is my wedding day, and I want Trudy and Giles to be there.
I don't care if the girl goes, she's not worth anything.
But Giles is valuable property. I won't--
Right, right.
Peace?
Got it right here!
The Abbey has drawn up an agreement guaranteeing the safe return of your "property"...
If Trudy and Giles aren't back safe and sound tonight, the Abbey will reimburse you for loss and damages...
...at ANY price you ask.

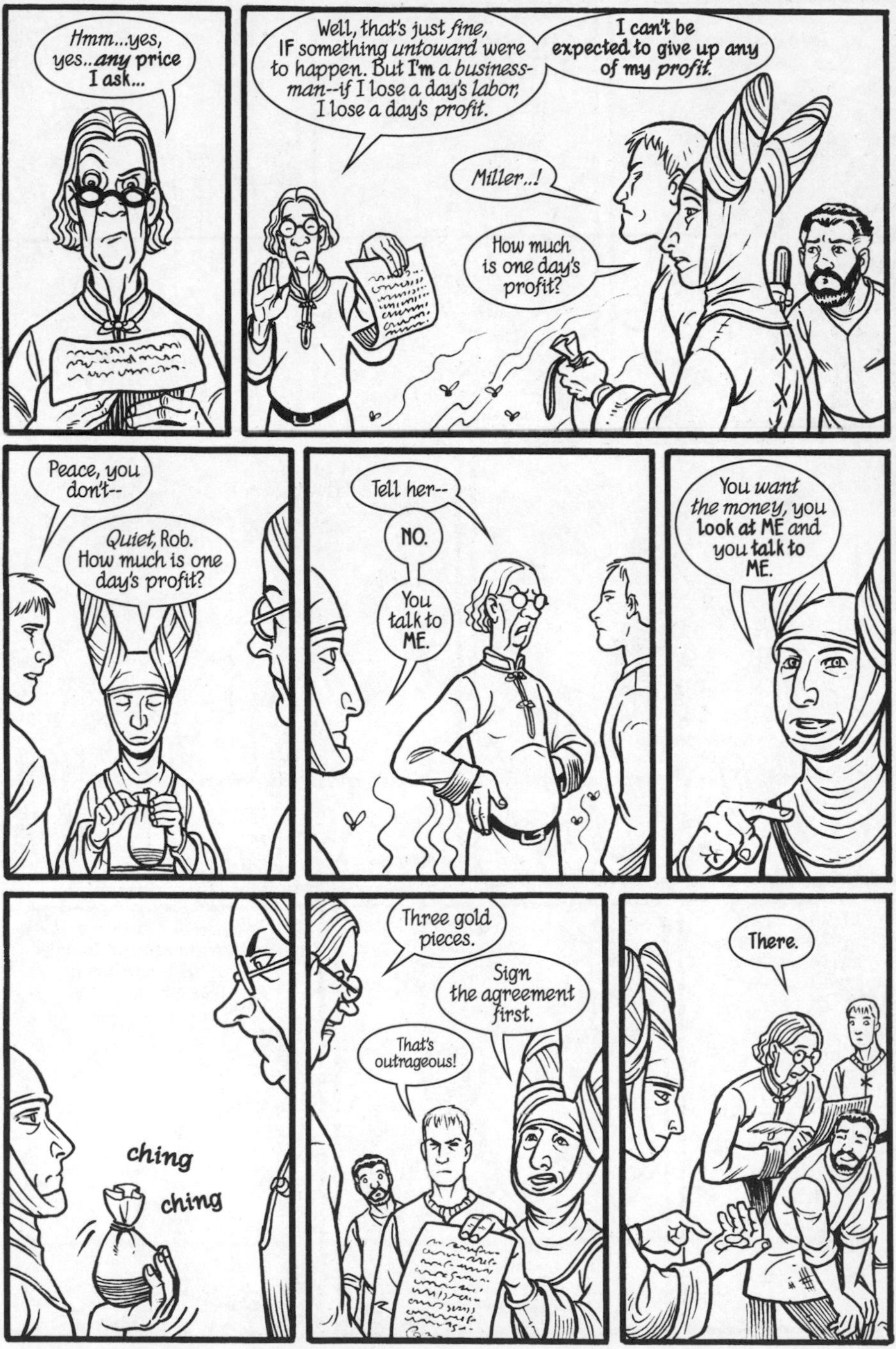
Hmm...yes, yes..*any* price I ask...
Well, that's just *fine*, IF something *untoward* were to happen. But **I'm** a *business-man*--if I lose a day's *labor*, I lose a day's *profit*.
I can't be expected to give up any of my *profit*.
Miller..!
How much is one day's profit?
Peace, you don't--
Quiet, Rob. How much is one day's profit?
Tell her--
NO.
You talk to ME.
You *want the money*, you **look at ME** and you **talk to ME.**
ching
ching
Three gold pieces.
Sign the agreement first.
That's outrageous!
There.

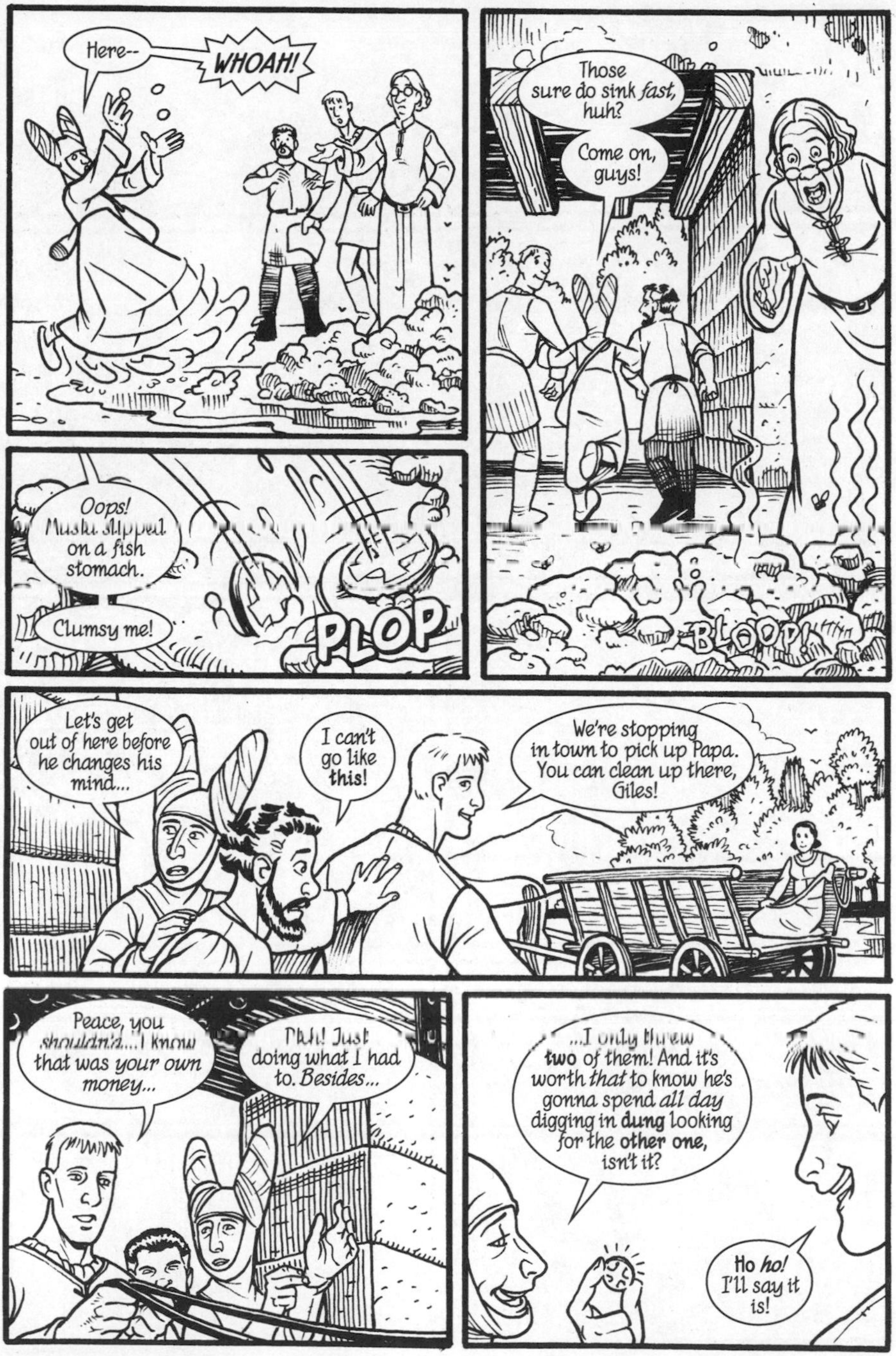
Here--
WHOAH!
Those sure do sink *fast*, huh?
Come on, guys!
Oops!
slipped
on a fish stomach.
Clumsy me!
PLOP
BLOOP!
Let's get out of here before he changes his mind...
I can't go like **this**!
We're stopping in town to pick up Papa. You can clean up there, Giles!
Peace, you
that was *your own* money...
Just
doing what I had to. *Besides*...
...I only threw
two of them! And it's worth *that* to know he's gonna spend *all day* digging in **dung** looking for the **other one**, isn't it?
Ho *ho*! I'll say it is!

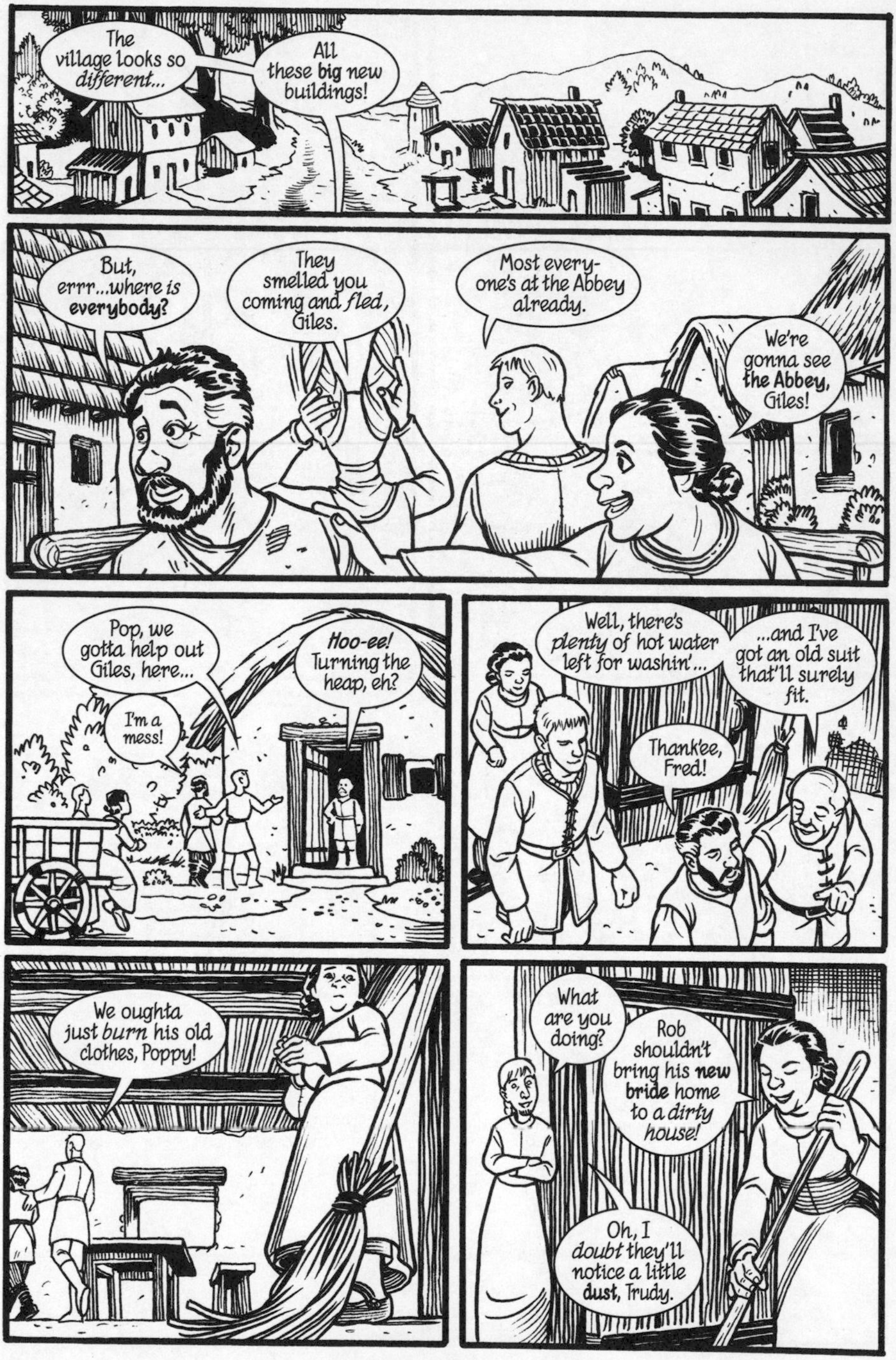
The village looks so *different*...
All these **big new** buildings!
But, errr...where *is* **everybody?**
They smelled you coming and *fled*, Giles.
Most every-one's at the Abbey already.
We're gonna see **the Abbey,** Giles!
Pop, we gotta help out Giles, here...
I'm a mess!
Hoo-ee! Turning the heap, eh?
Well, there's *plenty* of hot water left for washin'...
...and I've got an old suit that'll surely fit.
Thank'ee, Fred!
We oughta just *burn* his old clothes, Poppy!
What are you doing?
Rob shouldn't bring his **new bride** home to a *dirty house!*
Oh, I *doubt* they'll notice a little **dust**, Trudy.

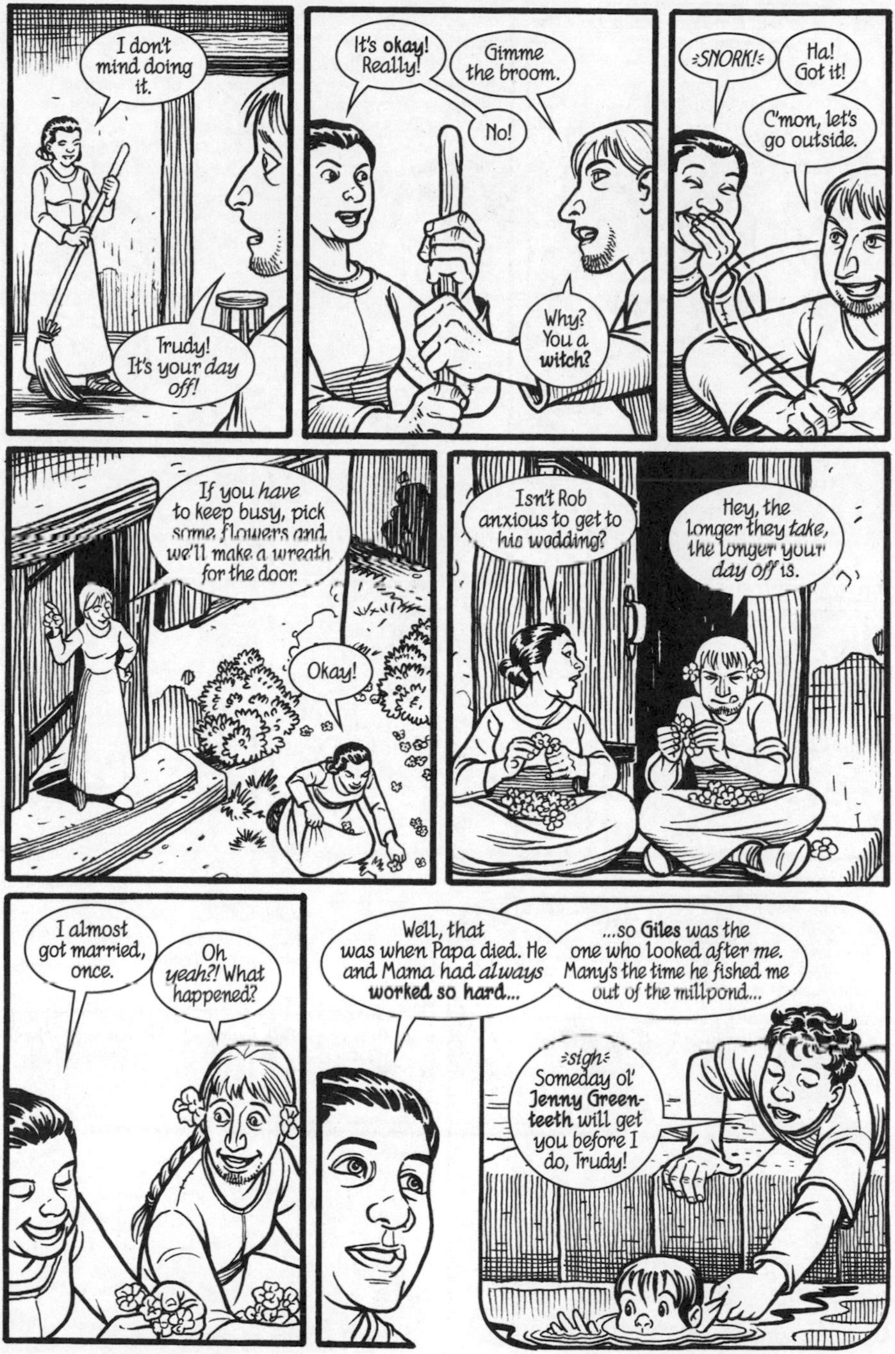

I don't mind doing it.
Trudy! It's your *day off*!
It's **okay**! Really!
Gimme the broom.
No!
Why? You a **witch**?
SNORK!
Ha! Got it!
C'mon, let's go outside.
If you *have* to keep busy, pick some *flowers* and we'll make a wreath for the door.
Okay!
Isn't Rob anxious to get to his wedding?
Hey, the longer they *take*, the longer your *day off* is.
I almost got married, once.
Oh *yeah?!* What happened?
Well, that was when Papa died. He and Mama had *always* **worked so hard**...
...so **Giles** was the one who looked after *me*. Many's the time he fished me out of the millpond...
sigh Someday ol' **Jenny Greenteeth** will get you before I do, Trudy!

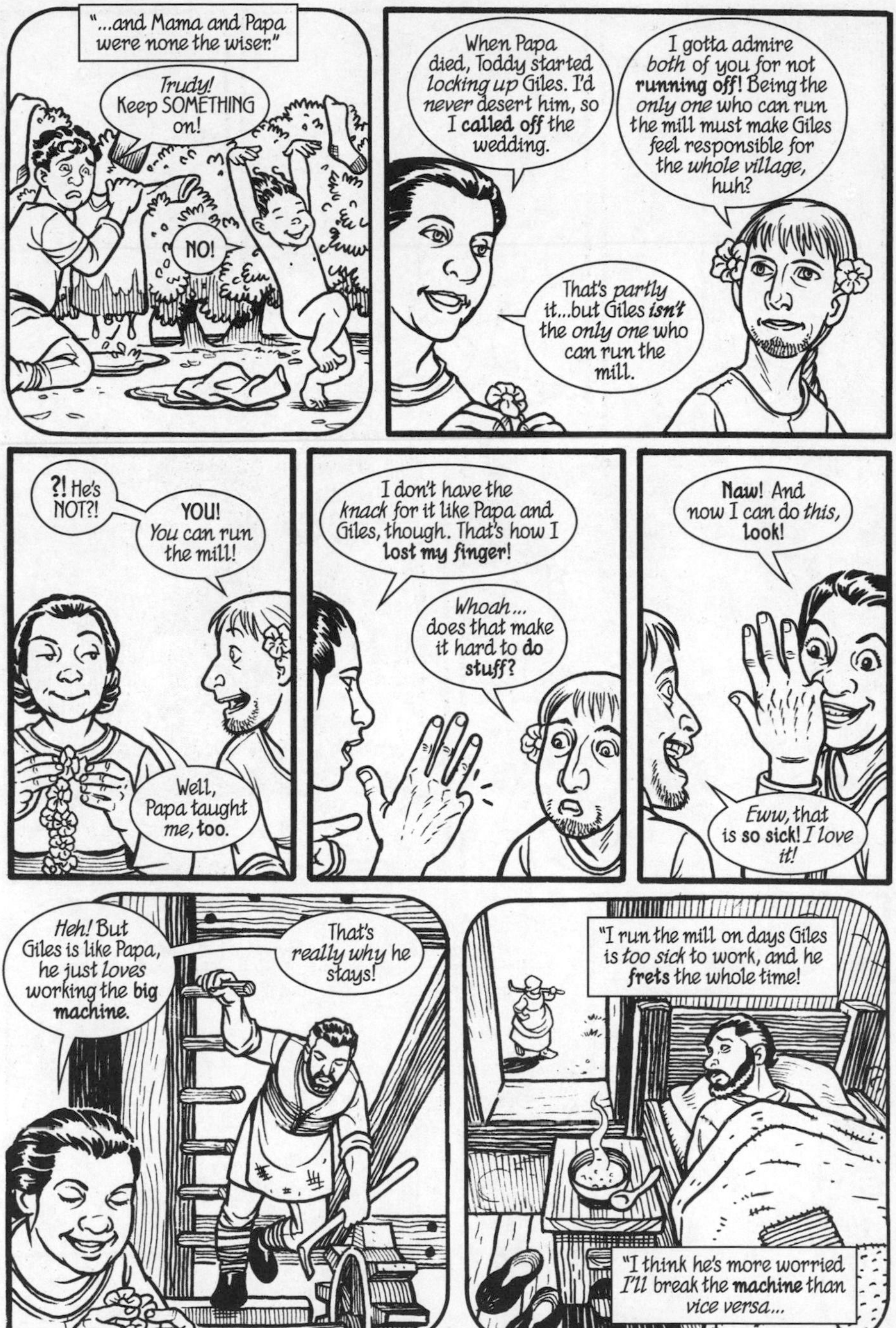
"...and Mama and Papa were none the wiser."
Trudy! Keep SOMETHING on!
NO!
When Papa died, Toddy started locking up Giles. I'd never desert him, so I called off the wedding.
I gotta admire both of you for not running off! Being the only one who can run the mill must make Giles feel responsible for the whole village, huh?
That's partly it...but Giles isn't the only one who can run the mill.
?! He's NOT?!
YOU! You can run the mill!
Well, Papa taught me, too.
I don't have the knack for it like Papa and Giles, though. That's how I lost my finger!
Whoah... does that make it hard to do stuff?
Naw! And now I can do this, look!
Eww, that is so sick! I love it!
Heh! But Giles is like Papa, he just loves working the big machine.
That's really why he stays!
"I run the mill on days Giles is too sick to work, and he frets the whole time!
"I think he's more worried I'll break the machine than vice versa...

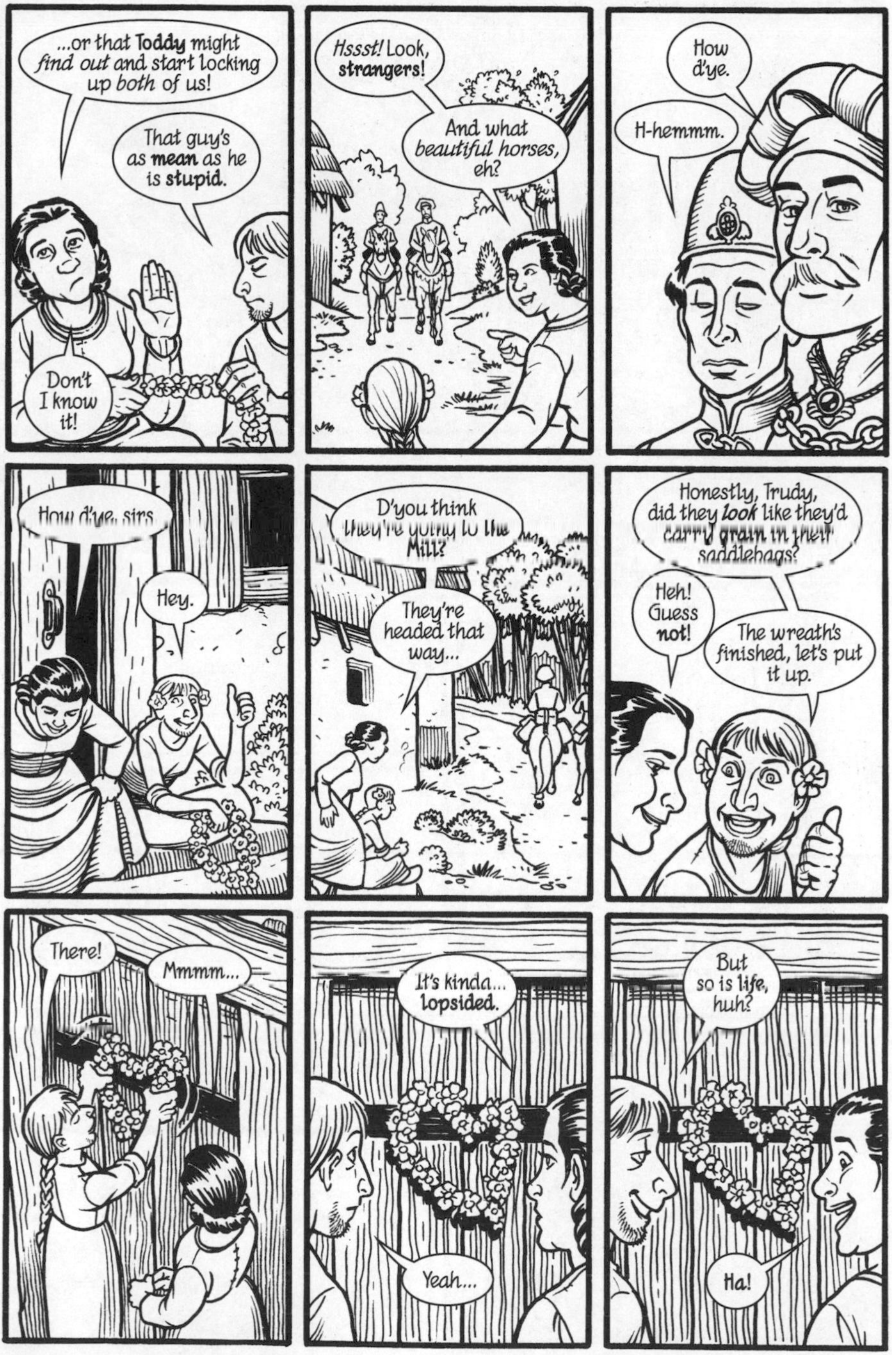
...or that **Toddy** might *find out* and start locking up *both* of us!
That guy's as **mean** as he is **stupid**.
Don't I know it!
Hssst! Look, **strangers**!
And what *beautiful horses*, eh?
How d'ye.
H-hemmm.
How d'ye, sirs.
Hey.
D'you think they're going to the Mill?
They're headed that way...
Honestly, Trudy, did they *look* like they'd carry grain in their saddlebags?
Heh! Guess **not**!
The wreath's finished, let's put it up.
There!
Mmmm...
It's kinda... **lopsided**.
Yeah...
But so is **life**, huh?
Ha!

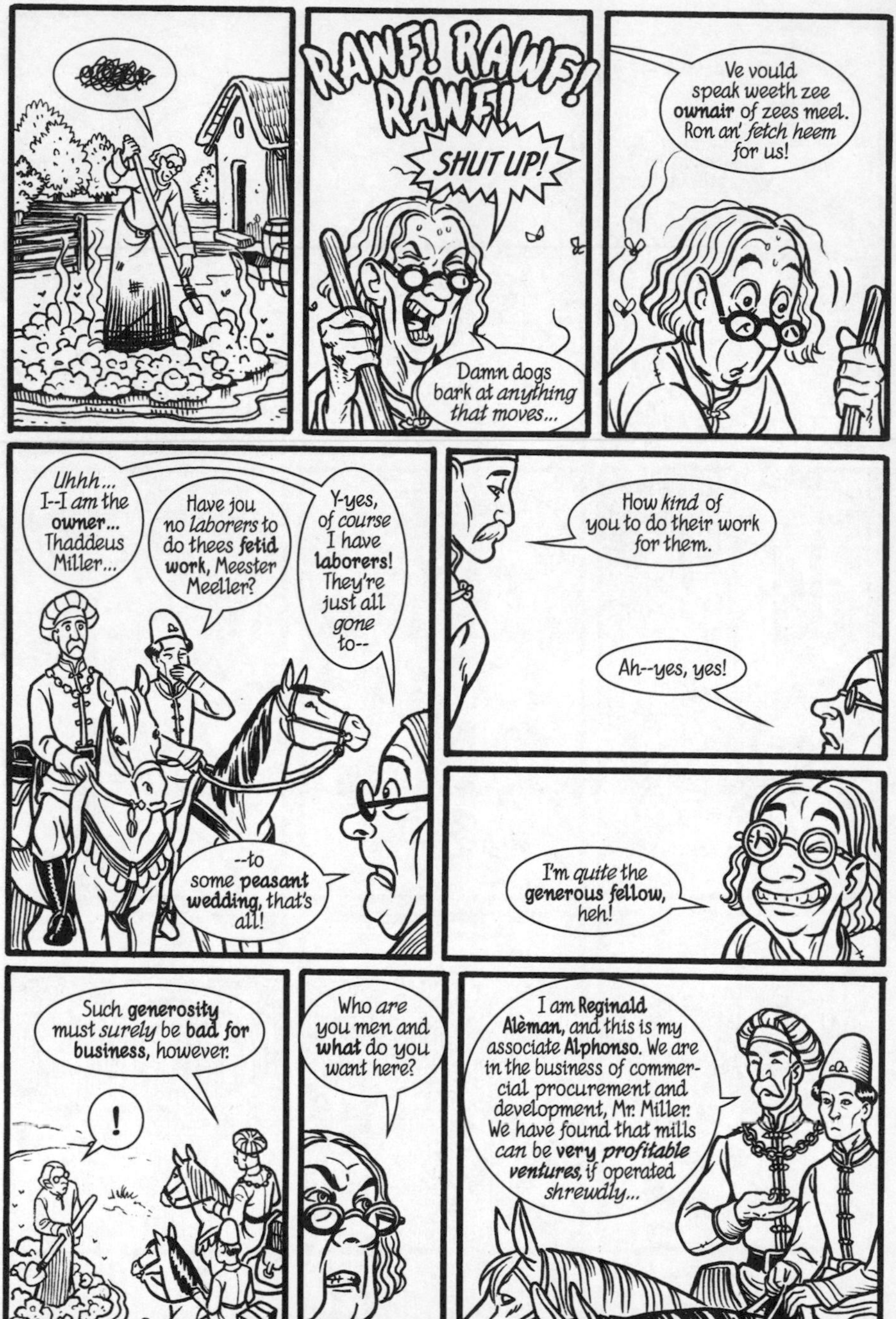
RAWF! RAWF! RAWF!
SHUT UP!
Damn dogs bark at *anything* that moves...
Ve vould speak weeth zee **ownair** of zees meel. Ron an' *fetch heem* for us!
Uhhh... I--I *am* the **owner...** Thaddeus Miller...
Have jou no *laborers* to do thees **fetid work**, Meester Meeller?
Y-yes, of *course* I have **laborers**! They're just all *gone* to--
--to some **peasant wedding**, that's all!
How *kind* of you to do their work for them.
Ah--yes, yes!
I'm *quite* the **generous fellow**, heh!
Such **generosity** must *surely* be **bad for business**, however.
!
Who *are* you men and **what** do you want here?
I am **Reginald Alèman**, and this is my associate **Alphonso**. We are in the business of commercial procurement and development, Mr. Miller. We have found that mills *can* be ***very profitable ventures***, if operated *shrewdly*...

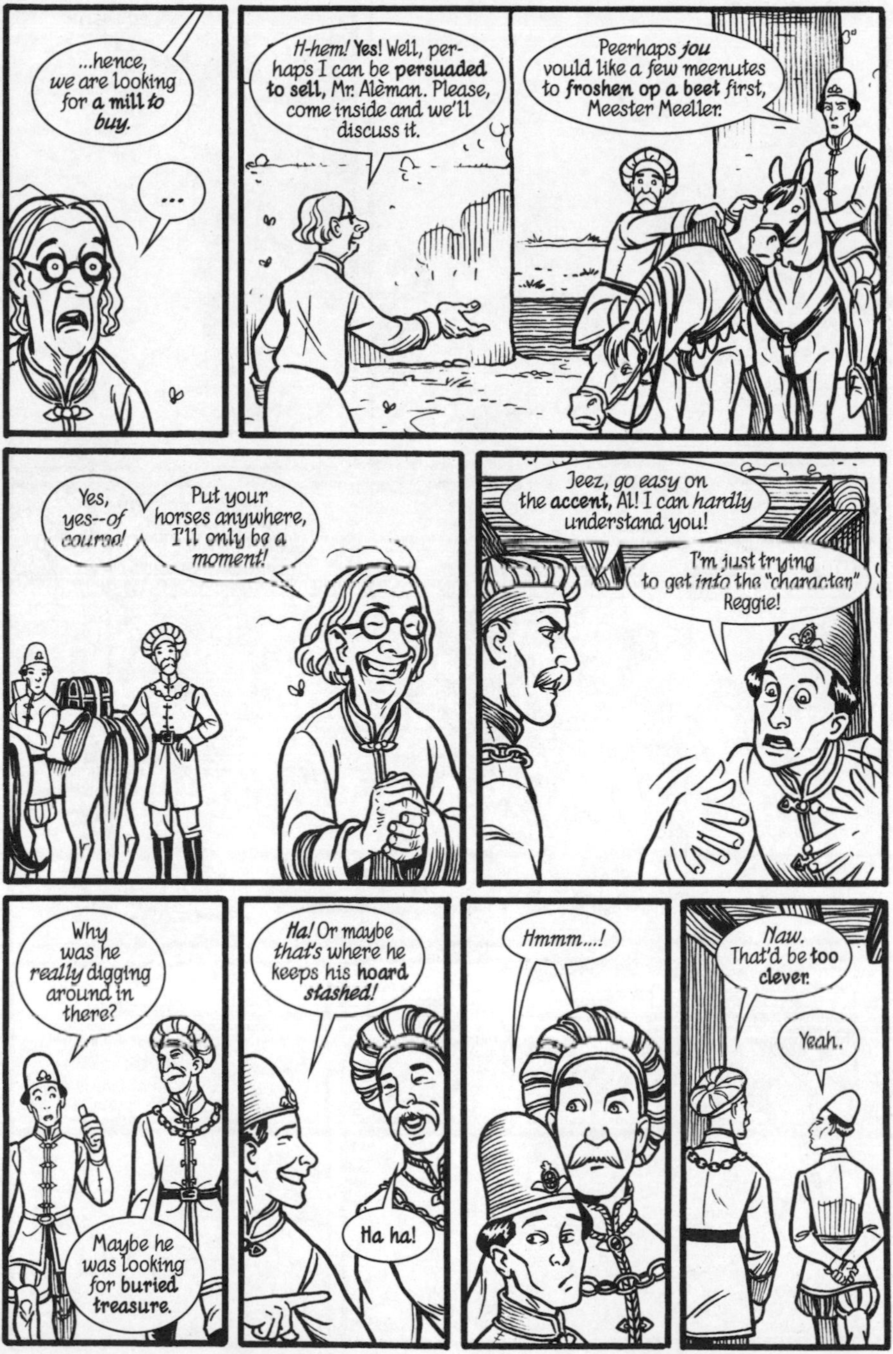
...hence, we are looking for **a mill to buy.**
...
H-hem! **Yes!** Well, perhaps I can be **persuaded to sell,** Mr. Alèman. Please, come inside and we'll discuss it.
Peerhaps ***jou*** vould like a few meenutes to **froshen op a beet** first, Meester Meeller.
Yes, yes--*of course!*
Put your horses anywhere, I'll only be a *moment!*
Jeez, *go easy* on the **accent,** Al! I can *hardly* understand you!
I'm just trying to get *into* the "character" Reggie!
Why was he *really* digging around in there?
Maybe he was looking for **buried treasure.**
Ha! Or maybe *that's* where he keeps his **hoard *stashed!***
Ha ha!
Hmmm...!
Naw. That'd be **too clever.**
Yeah.

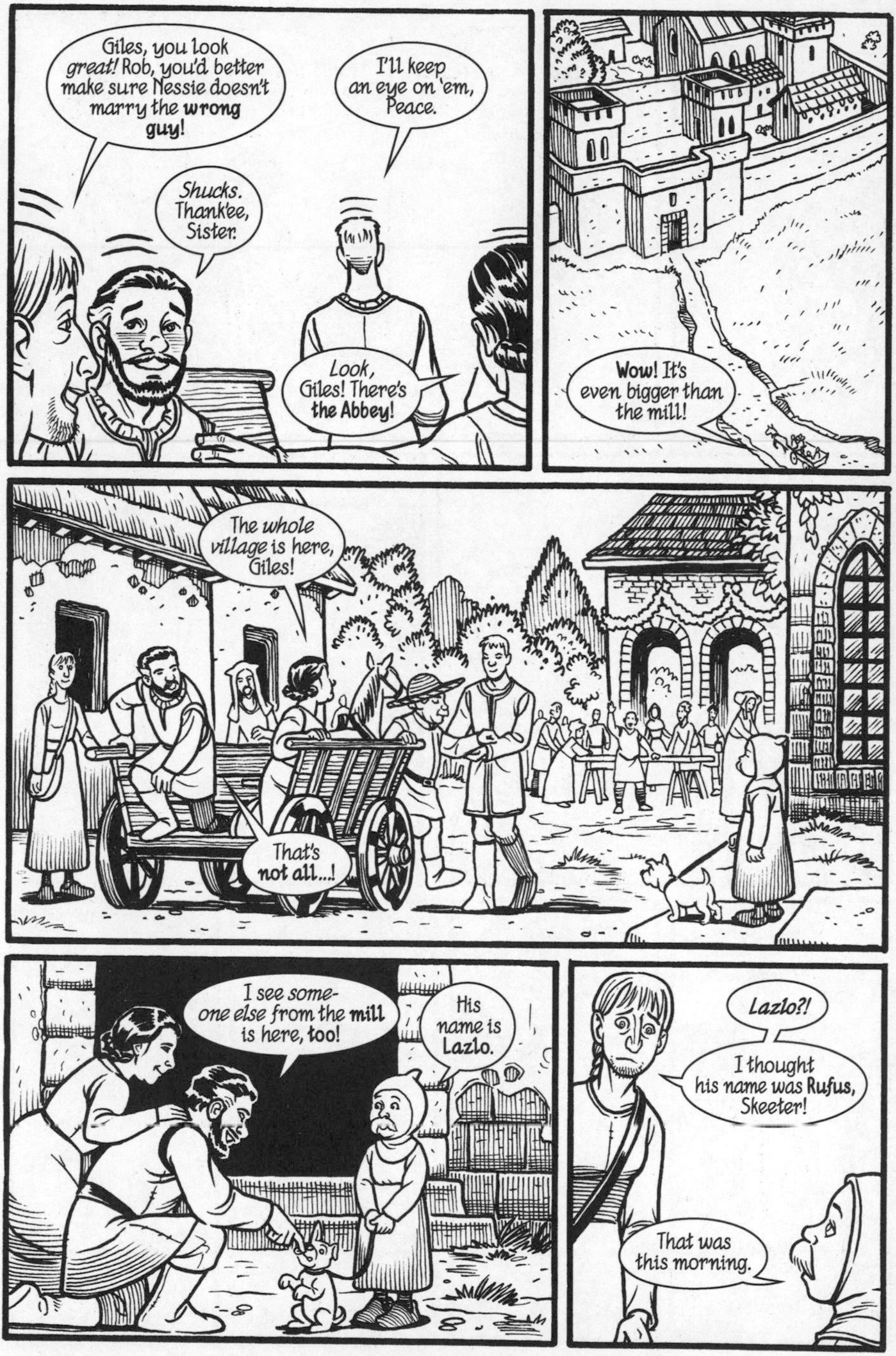
Giles, you look great! Rob, you'd better make sure Nessie doesn't marry the wrong guy!
Shucks. Thank'ee, Sister.
I'll keep an eye on 'em, Peace.
Look, Giles! There's the Abbey!
Wow! It's even bigger than the mill!
The whole village is here, Giles!
That's not all...!
I see some-one else from the mill is here, too!
His name is Lazlo.
Lazlo?!
I thought his name was Rufus, Skeeter!
That was this morning.

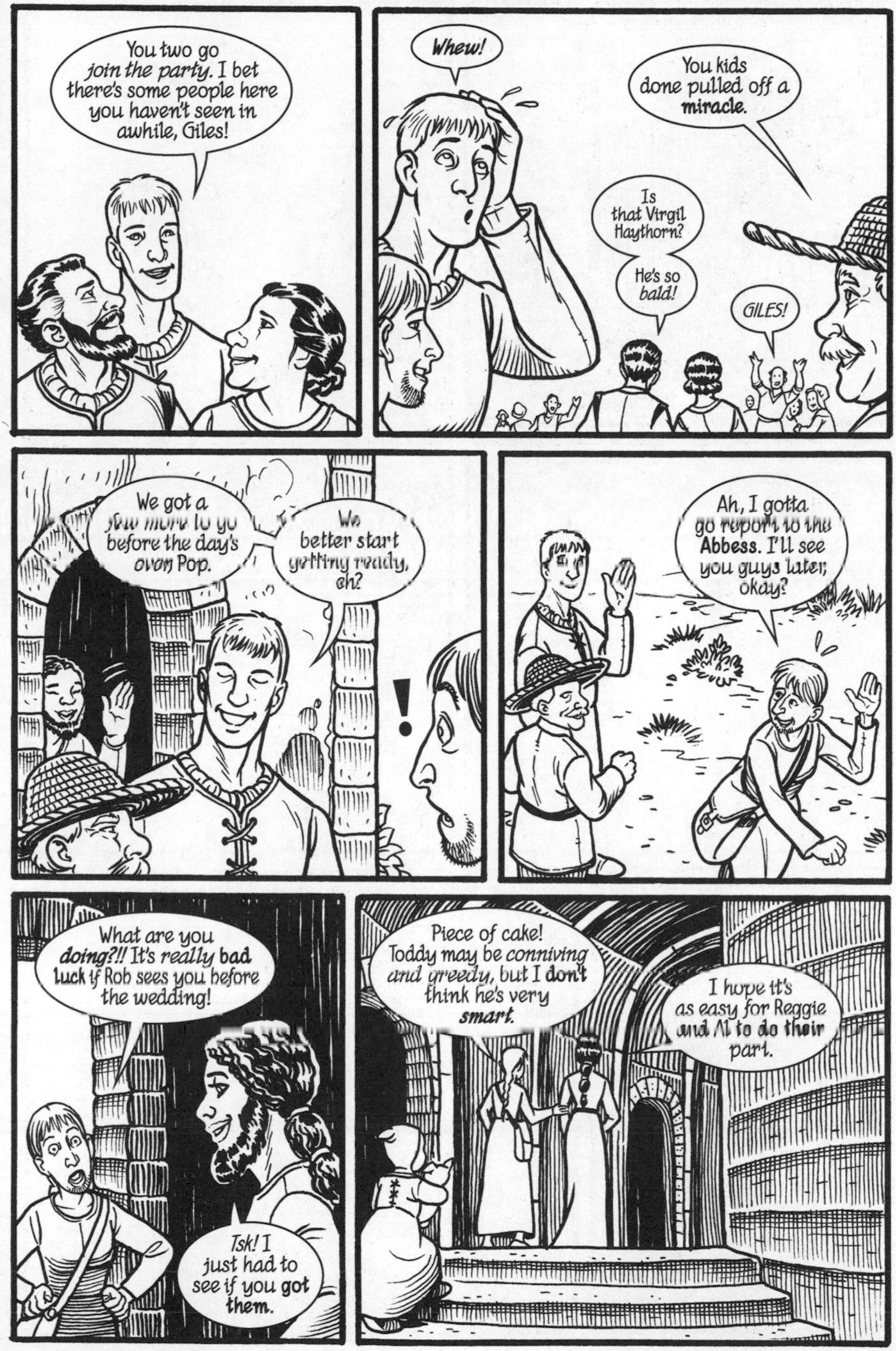
You two go *join the party*. I bet there's some people here you haven't seen in awhile, Giles!
Whew!
You kids done pulled off a **miracle**.
Is that Virgil Haythorn?
He's so *bald!*
GILES!
We got a *few more to go* before the day's *over* Pop.
We better start getting ready, eh?
!
Ah, I gotta go report to the **Abbess**. I'll see you guys later, okay?
What are you *doing?!!* It's *really* **bad luck** if Rob sees you before the wedding!
Tsk! I just had to see if you **got them**.
Piece of cake! Toddy may be *conniving and greedy*, but I **don't** think he's very ***smart***.
I hope it's as easy for Reggie **and Al to do their** part.

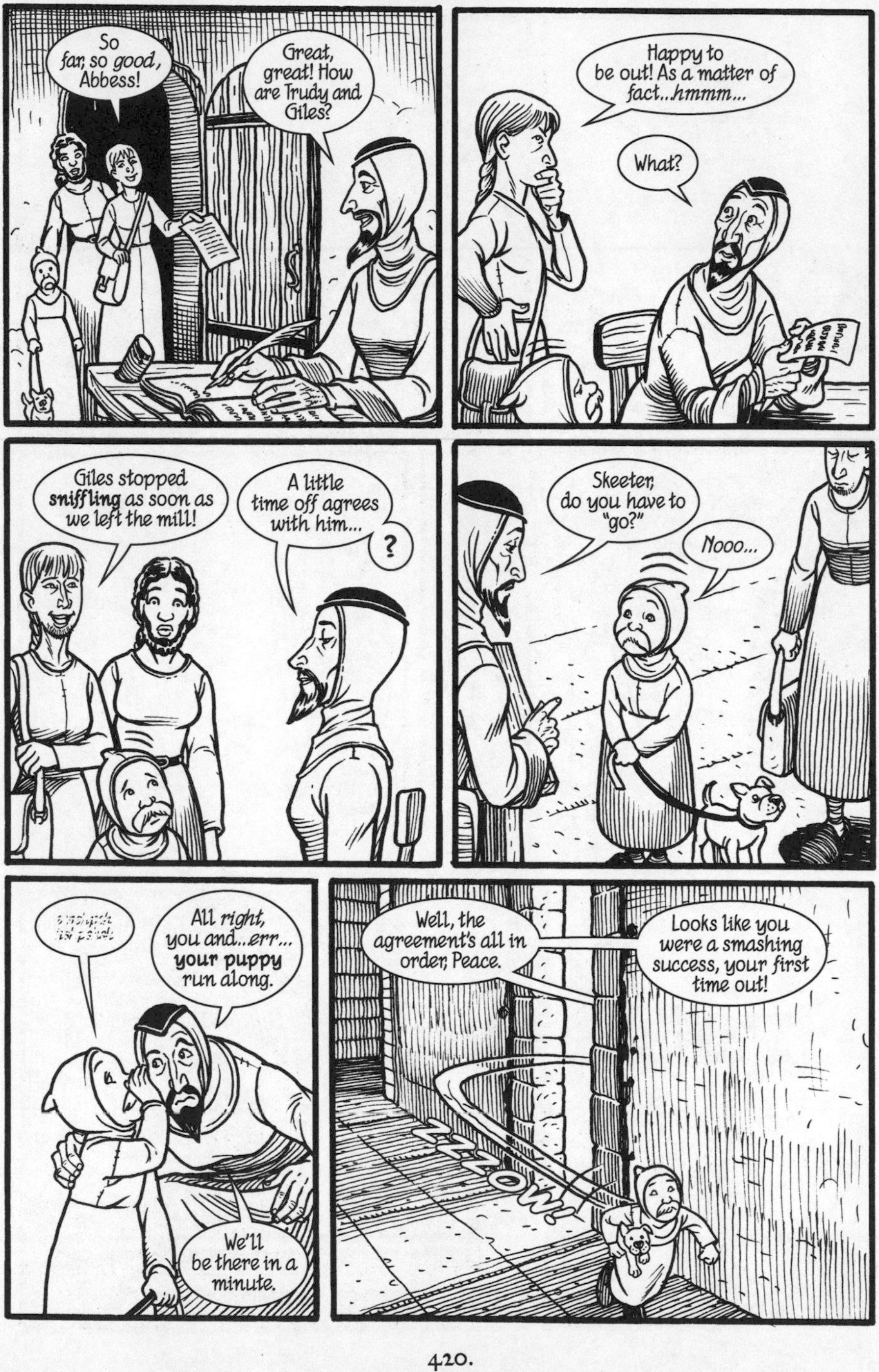
So far, so *good*, Abbess!
Great, great! How are Trudy and Giles?
Happy to be out! As a matter of fact...*hmmm*...
What?
Giles stopped **sniffling** as soon as we left the mill!
A little time off agrees with him...
?
Skeeter, do you have to "go?"
Nooo...
All *right*, you and...*err*... **your puppy** run along.
We'll be there in a minute.
Well, the agreement's all in order, Peace.
Looks like you were a smashing success, your first time out!
ZZZOW!

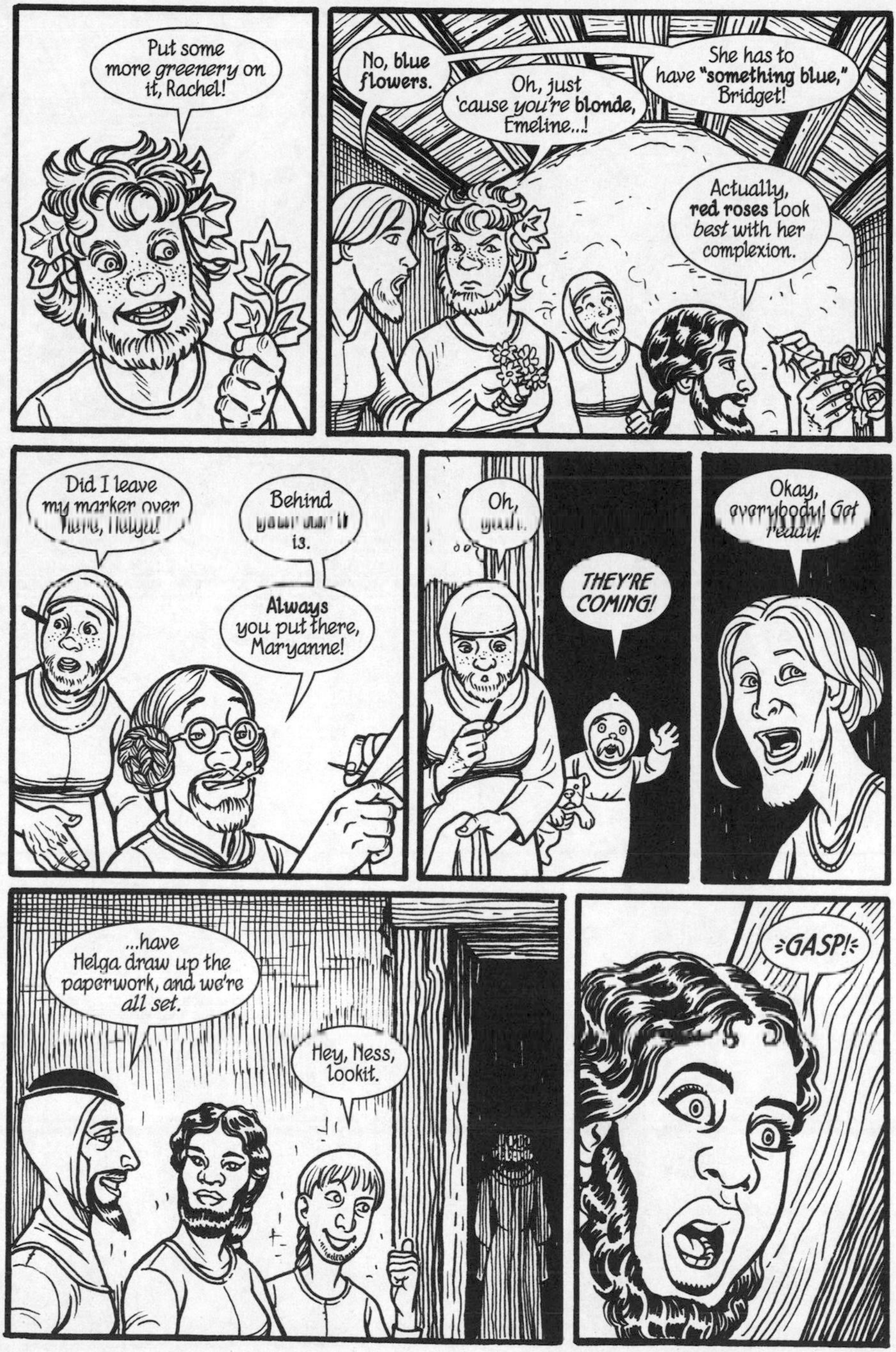
Put some more *greenery* on it, Rachel!
No, **blue flowers.**
Oh, just 'cause *you're* **blonde**, Emeline...!
She has to have **"something blue,"** Bridget!
Actually, **red roses** look *best* with her complexion.
Did I leave my marker over here, Helga!
Behind
is.
Always you put there, Maryanne!
Oh,
THEY'RE COMING!
Okay, everybody! Get ready!
...have Helga draw up the paperwork, and we're *all set.*
Hey, Ness, lookit.
GASP!

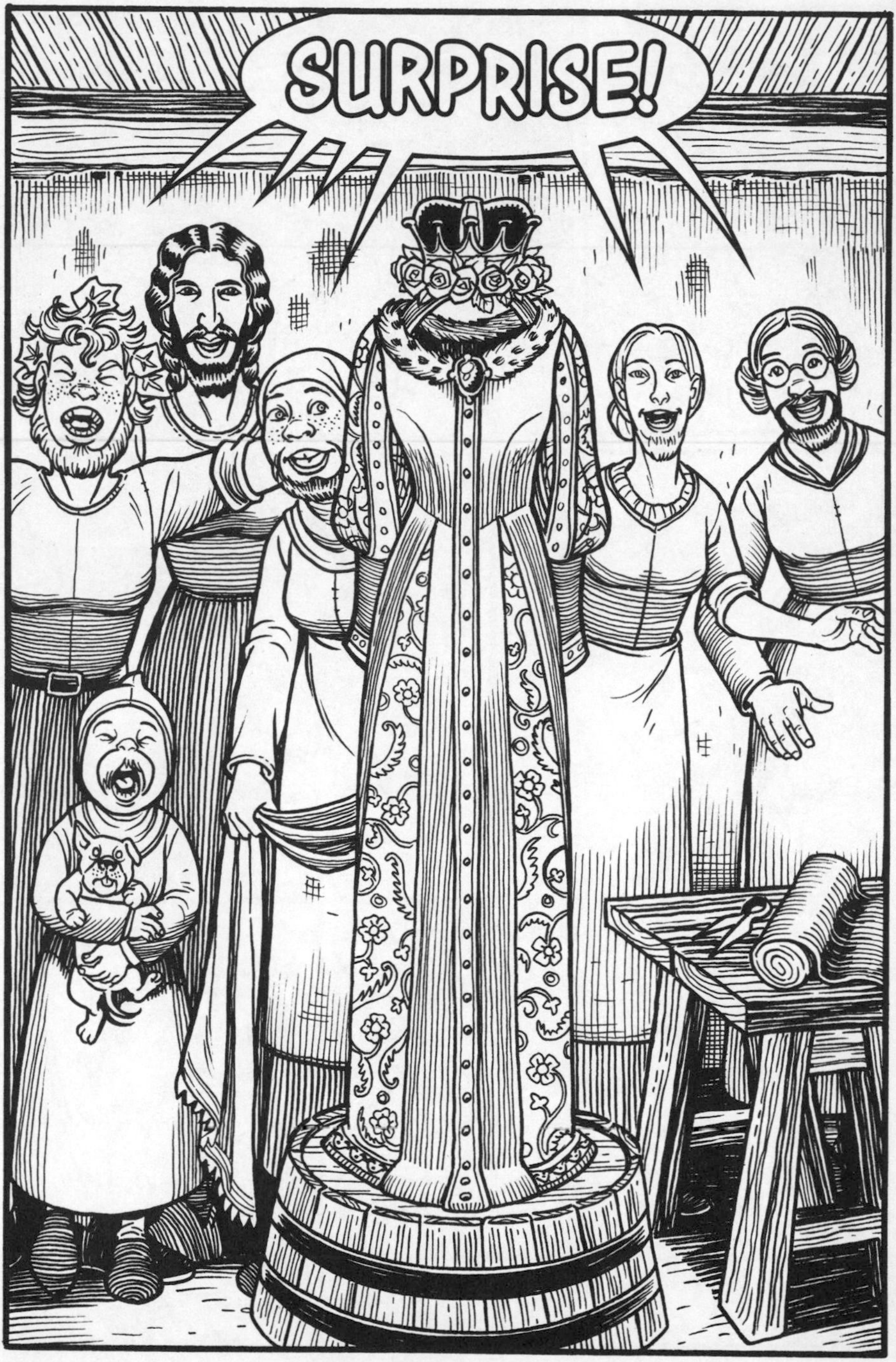
SURPRISE!

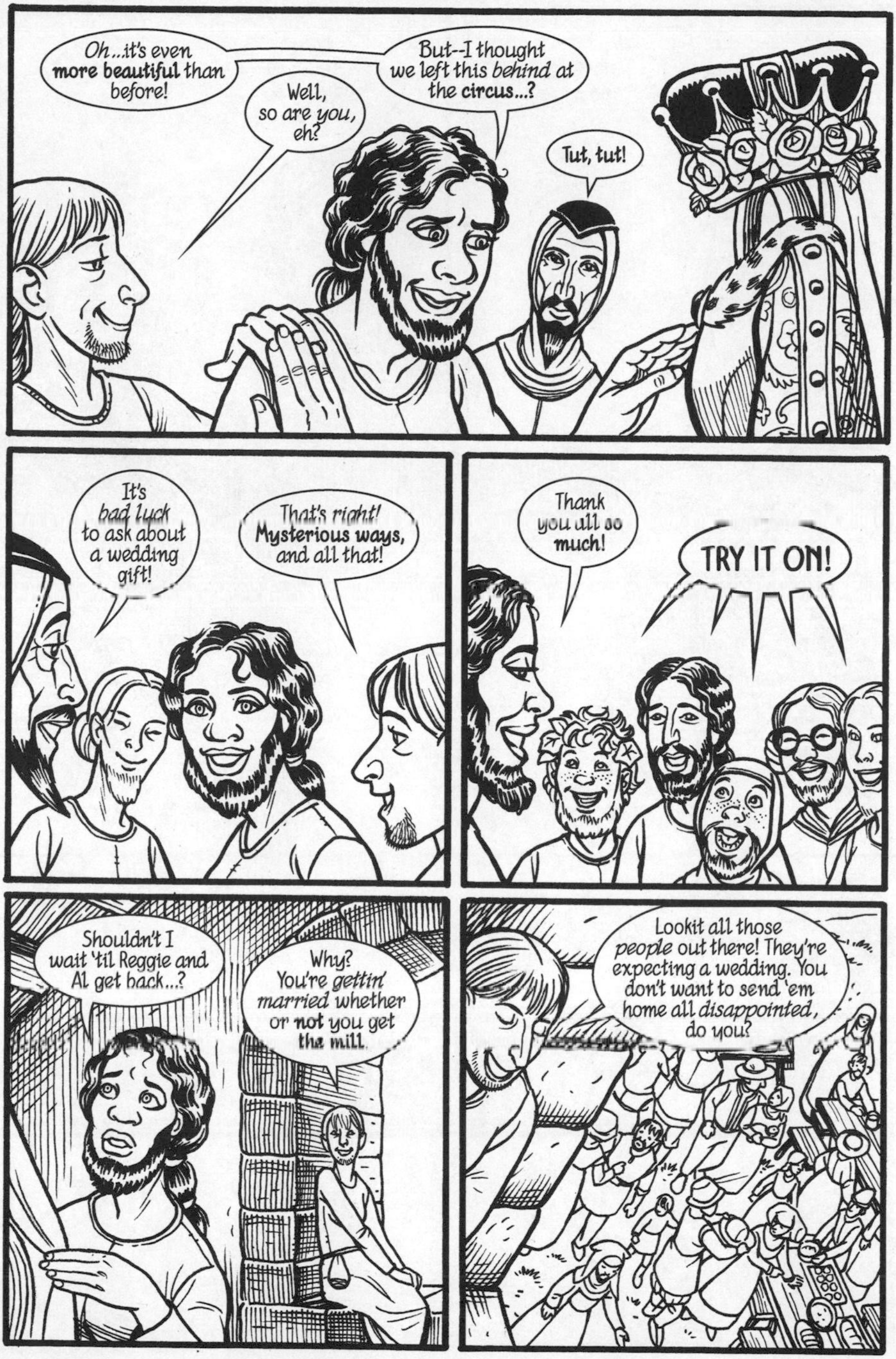
Oh...it's even **more beautiful** than before!
Well, so are *you*, eh?
But--I thought we left this *behind* at the **circus**...?
Tut, tut!
It's *bad luck* to ask about a wedding gift!
That's *right!* **Mysterious ways,** and all that!
Thank you all so **much!**
TRY IT ON!
Shouldn't I wait 'til Reggie and Al get back...?
Why? You're *gettin' married* whether or **not** you get **the mill**.
Lookit all those *people* out there! They're expecting a wedding. You don't want to send 'em home all *disappointed*, do you?

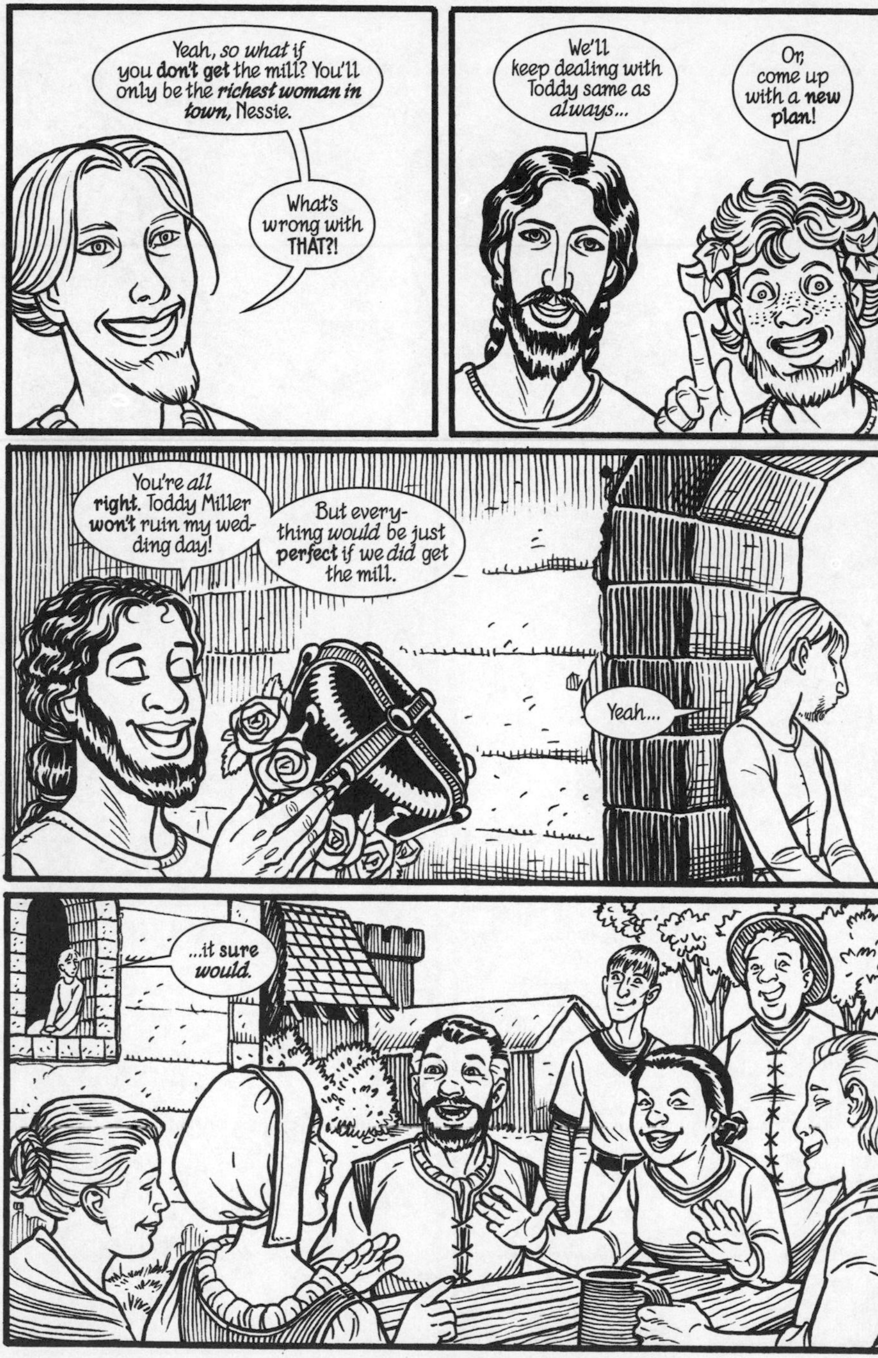
Yeah, so *what* if you **don't get** the mill? You'll only be the ***richest woman in town,*** Nessie.
What's wrong with **THAT?!**
We'll keep dealing with Toddy same as *always*...
Or, come up with a **new plan!**
You're *all* **right**. Toddy Miller **won't** ruin my wedding day!
But everything *would* be just **perfect** if we *did* get the mill.
Yeah...
...it sure ***would.***

Chapter 19.

· SOLICITINE PT. 7 ·

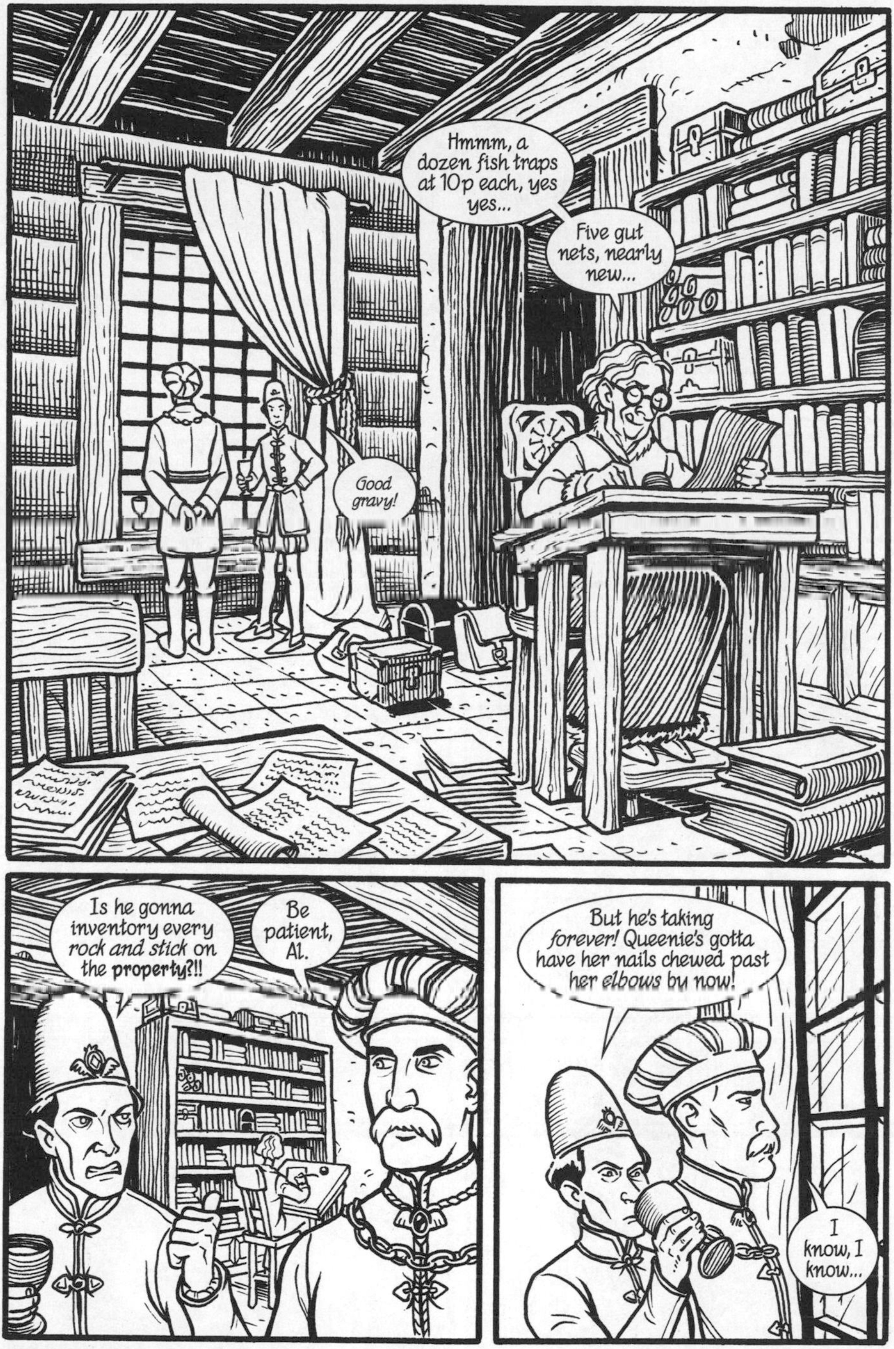
Hmmm, a dozen fish traps at 10p each, yes yes...
Five gut nets, nearly new...
Good gravy!
Is he gonna inventory every *rock and stick* on the **property?!!**
Be patient, Al.
But he's taking *forever!* Queenie's gotta have her nails chewed past her *elbows* by now!
I know, I know...

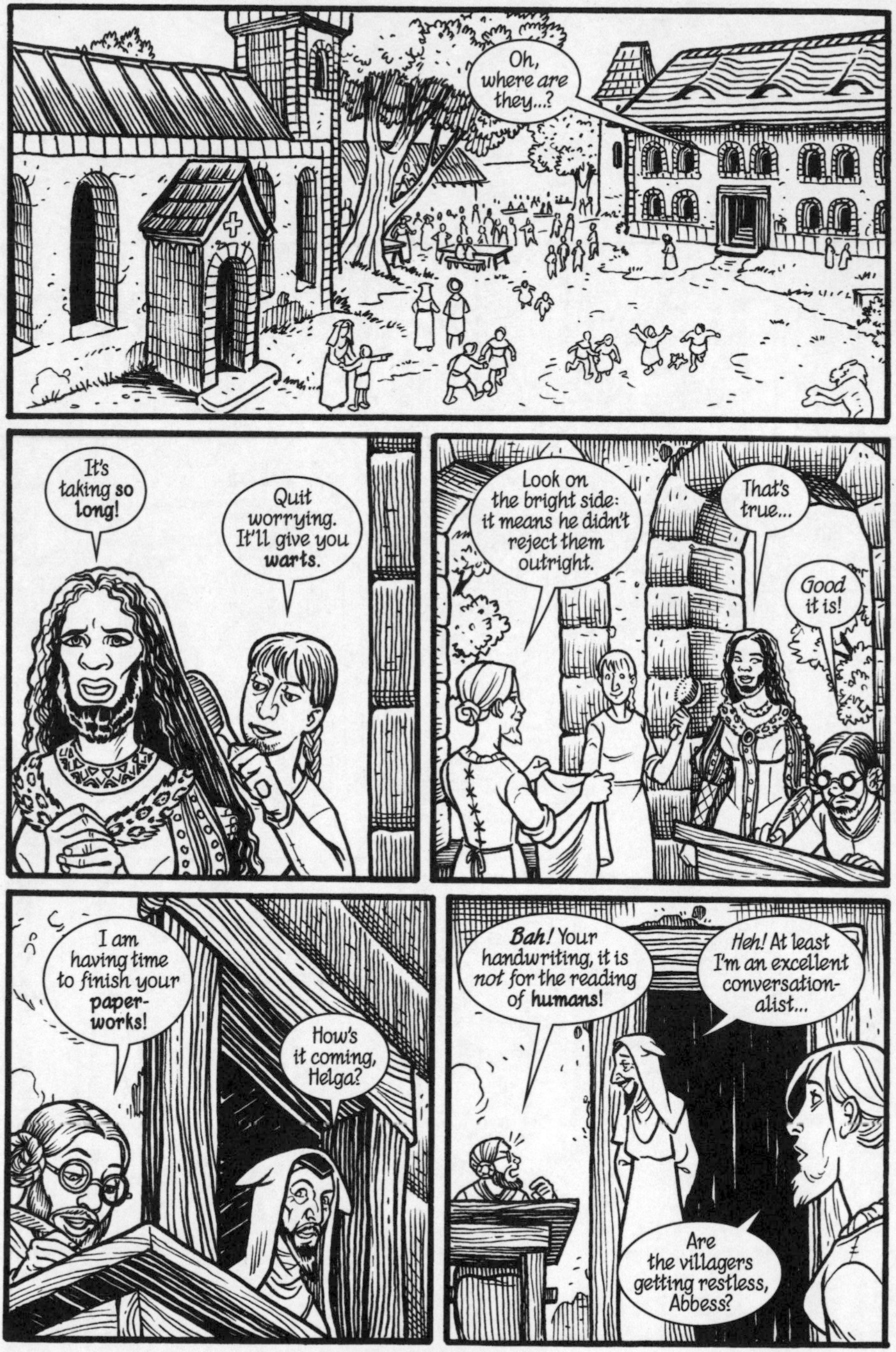
Oh, where are they...?
It's taking so long!
Quit worrying. It'll give you warts.
Look on the bright side: it means he didn't reject them outright.
That's true...
Good it is!
I am having time to finish your paper-works!
How's it coming, Helga?
Bah! Your handwriting, it is not for the reading of humans!
Heh! At least I'm an excellent conversation-alist...
Are the villagers getting restless, Abbess?

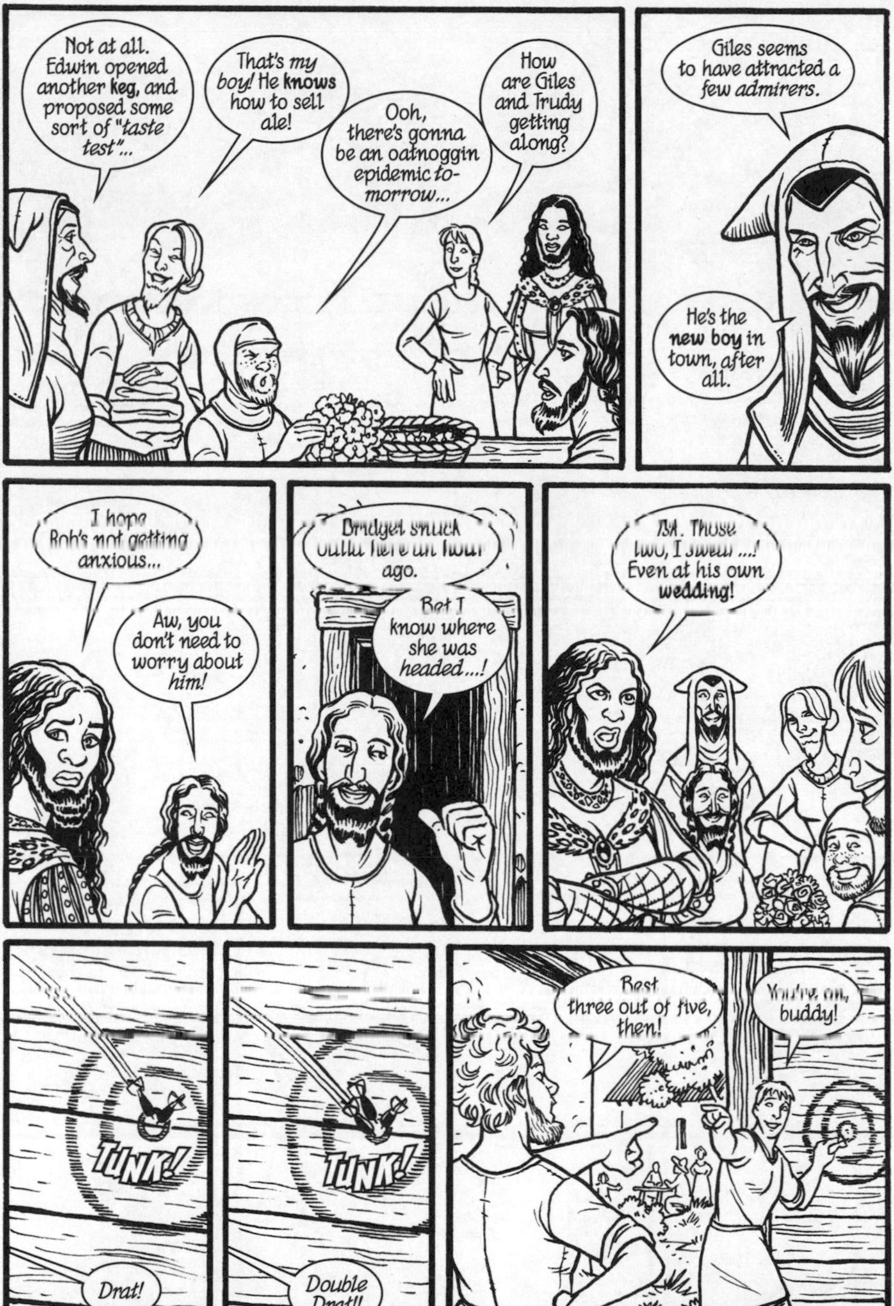
Not at all. Edwin opened another **keg**, and proposed some sort of "*taste test*"...
That's *my boy!* He **knows** how to sell ale!
Ooh, there's gonna be an oatnoggin epidemic *to-morrow*...
How are Giles and Trudy getting along?
Giles seems to have attracted a few *admirers*.
He's the **new boy** in town, *after* all.
I hope Rob's not getting anxious...
Aw, you don't need to worry about him!
Bridget snuck outta here an hour ago.
Bet I know where she was *headed*...!
Tsk. Those two, I swear...! Even at his own **wedding!**
TUNK!
Drat!
TUNK!
Double Drat!!
Best three out of five, then!
You're on, buddy!

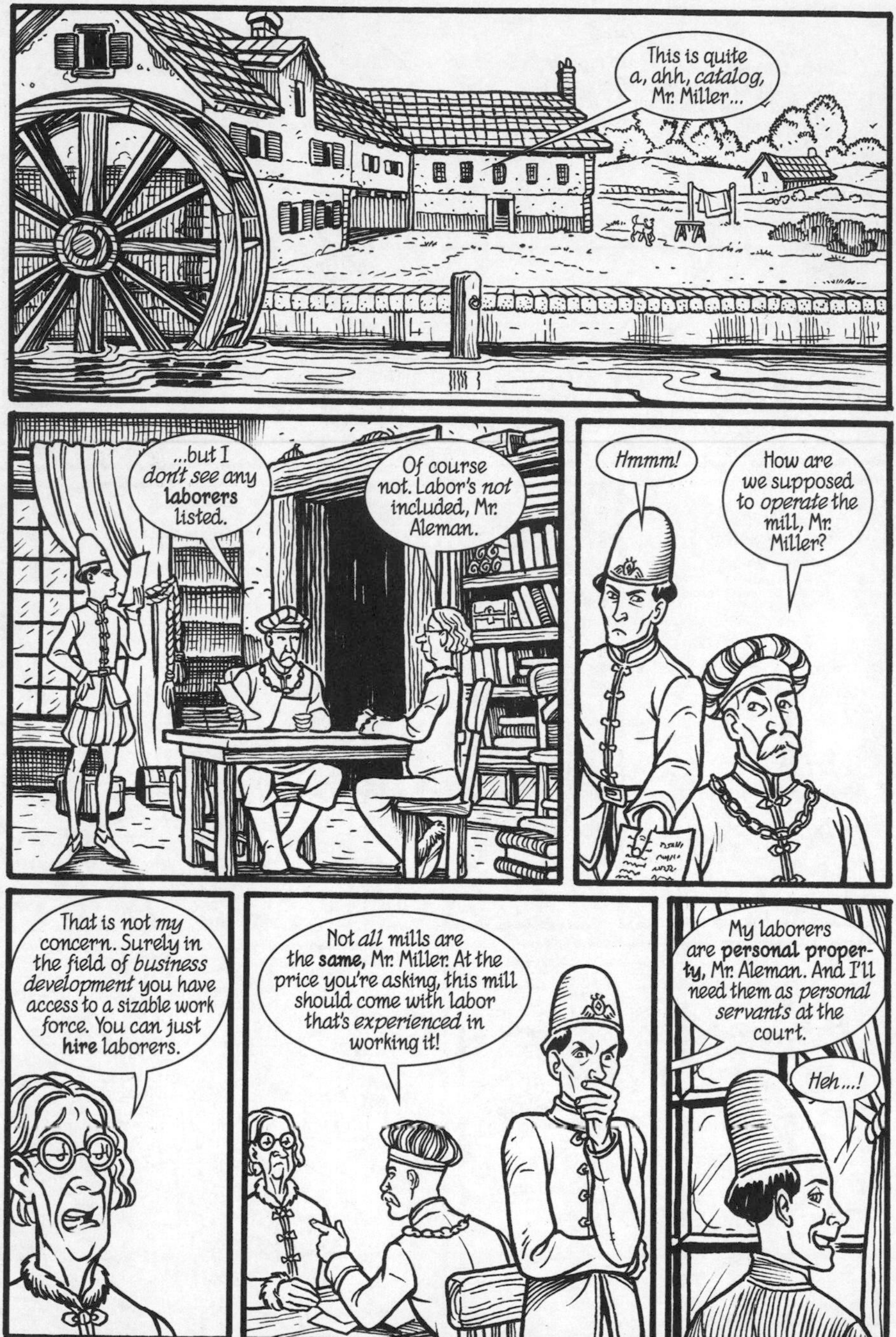
This is quite a, ahh, *catalog*, Mr. Miller...
...but I *don't see* any **laborers** listed.
Of course not. Labor's *not* included, Mr. Aleman.
Hmmm!
How are we supposed to *operate* the mill, Mr. Miller?
That is not *my* concern. Surely in the field of *business development* you have access to a sizable work force. You can just **hire** laborers.
Not *all* mills are the **same**, Mr. Miller. At the price you're asking, this mill should come with labor that's *experienced* in working it!
My laborers are **personal property**, Mr. Aleman. And I'll need them as *personal servants* at the court.
Heh...!

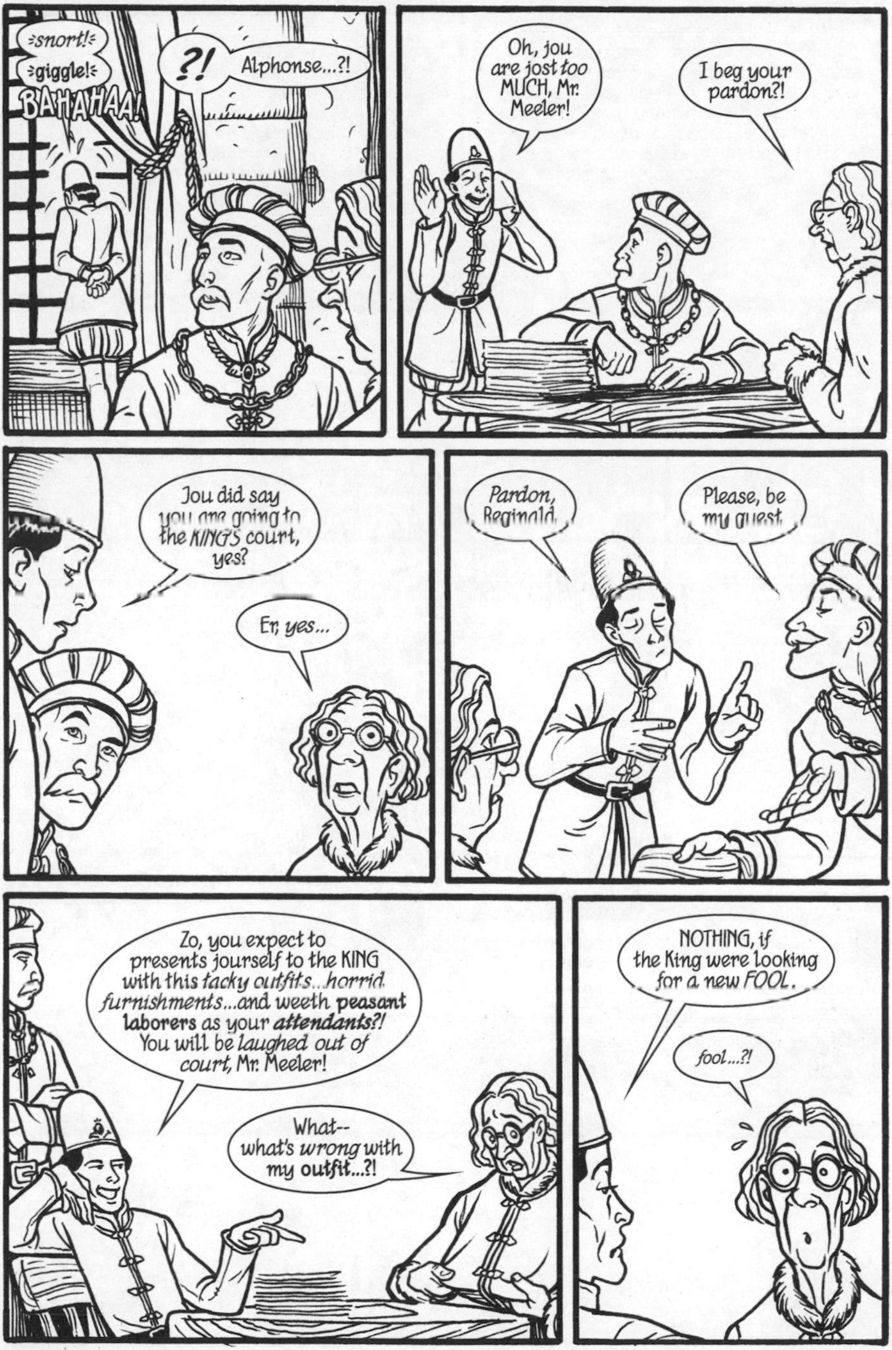
snort!
giggle!
BAHAHAA!
?!
Alphonse...?!
Oh, jou are jost too MUCH, Mr. Meeler!
I beg your pardon?!
Jou did say you are going to the KING'S court, yes?
Er, yes...
Pardon, Reginald.
Please, be my guest.
Zo, you expect to presents jourself to the KING with this tacky outfits...horrid furnishments...and weeth peasant laborers as your attendants?! You will be laughed out of court, Mr. Meeler!
What-- what's wrong with my outfit...?!
NOTHING, if the King were looking for a new FOOL.
fool...?!

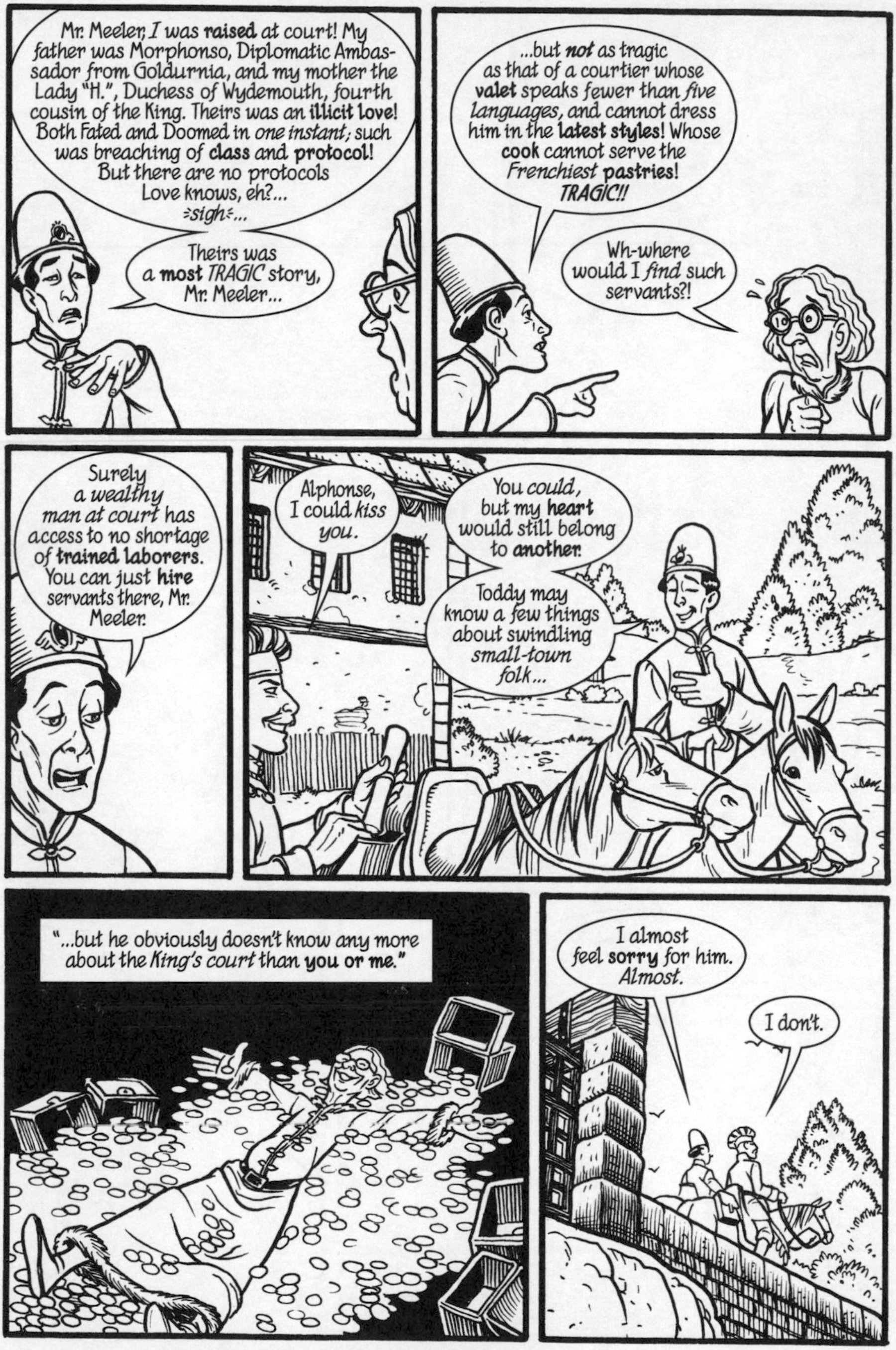
Mr. Meeler, I was raised at court! My father was Morphonso, Diplomatic Ambassador from Goldurnia, and my mother the Lady "H.", Duchess of Wydemouth, fourth cousin of the King. Theirs was an illicit love! Both Fated and Doomed in one instant; such was breaching of class and protocol! But there are no protocols Love knows, eh?... sigh...
Theirs was a most TRAGIC story, Mr. Meeler...
...but not as tragic as that of a courtier whose valet speaks fewer than five languages, and cannot dress him in the latest styles! Whose cook cannot serve the Frenchiest pastries! TRAGIC!!
Wh-where would I find such servants?!
Surely a wealthy man at court has access to no shortage of trained laborers. You can just hire servants there, Mr. Meeler.
Alphonse, I could kiss you.
You could, but my heart would still belong to another.
Toddy may know a few things about swindling small-town folk...
"...but he obviously doesn't know any more about the King's court than you or me."
I almost feel sorry for him. Almost.
I don't.

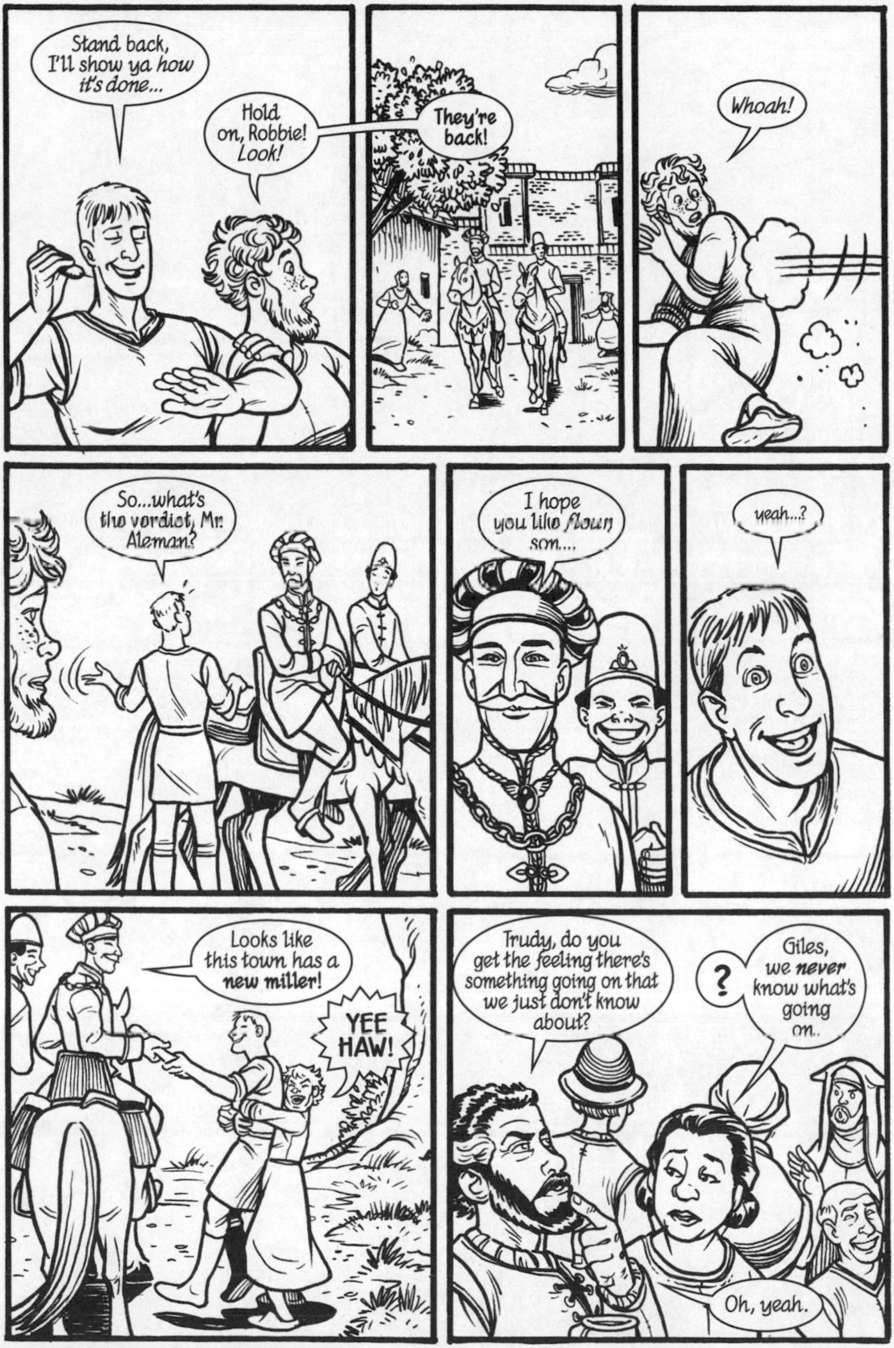
Stand back, I'll show ya how it's done...
Hold on, Robbie! Look!
They're back!
Whoah!
So...what's the verdict, Mr. Aleman?
I hope you like flour, son....
yeah...?
Looks like this town has a new miller!
YEE HAW!
Trudy, do you get the feeling there's something going on that we just don't know about?
?
Giles, we never know what's going on.
Oh, yeah.

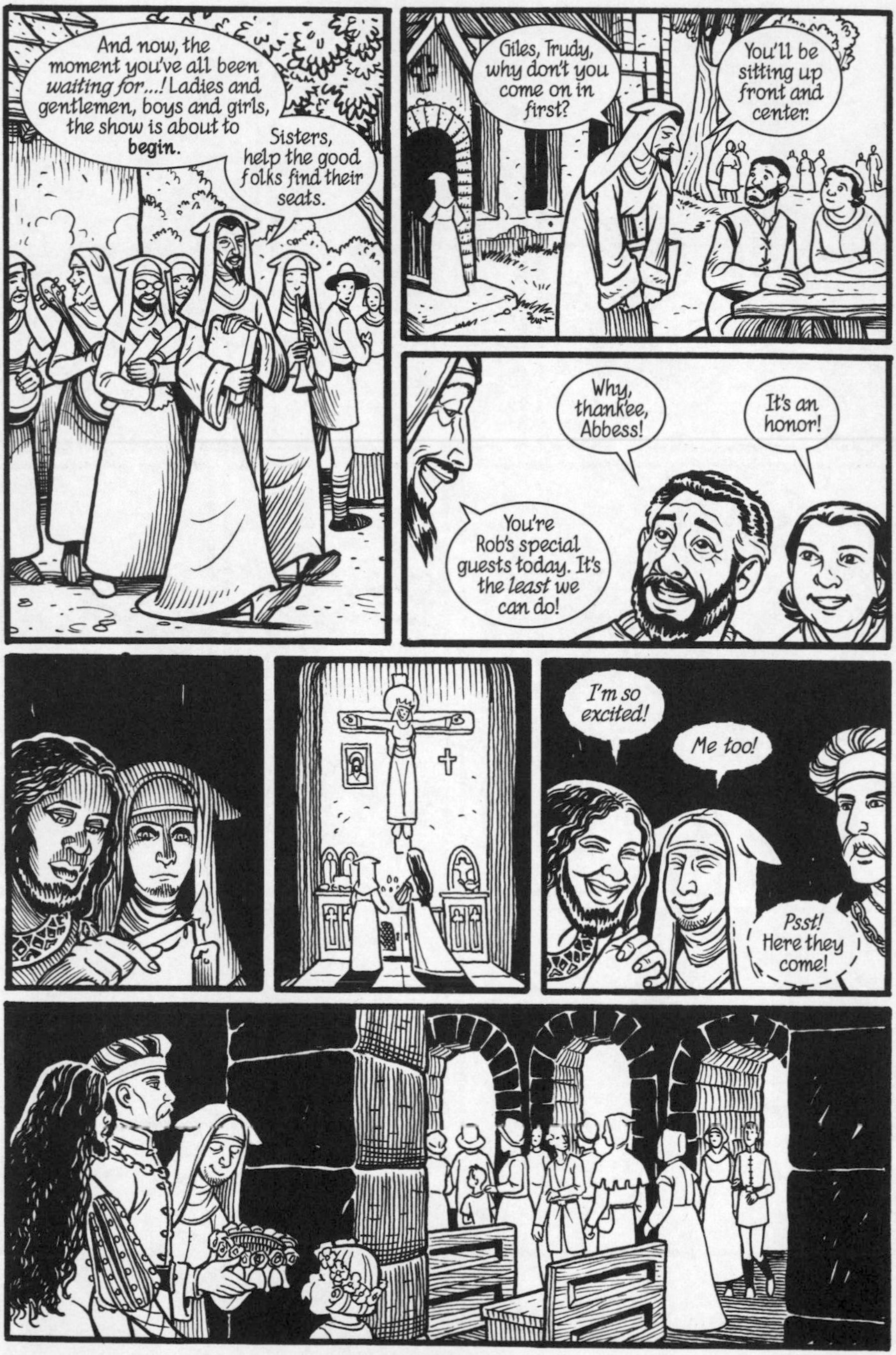
And now, the moment you've all been *waiting for...!* Ladies and gentlemen, boys and girls, the show is about to **begin.**
Sisters, help the good folks find their seats.
Giles, Trudy, why don't you come on in first?
You'll be sitting up front and center.
Why, thank'ee, Abbess!
It's an honor!
You're Rob's special guests today. It's the *least* we can do!
I'm so excited!
Me too!
Psst! Here they come!

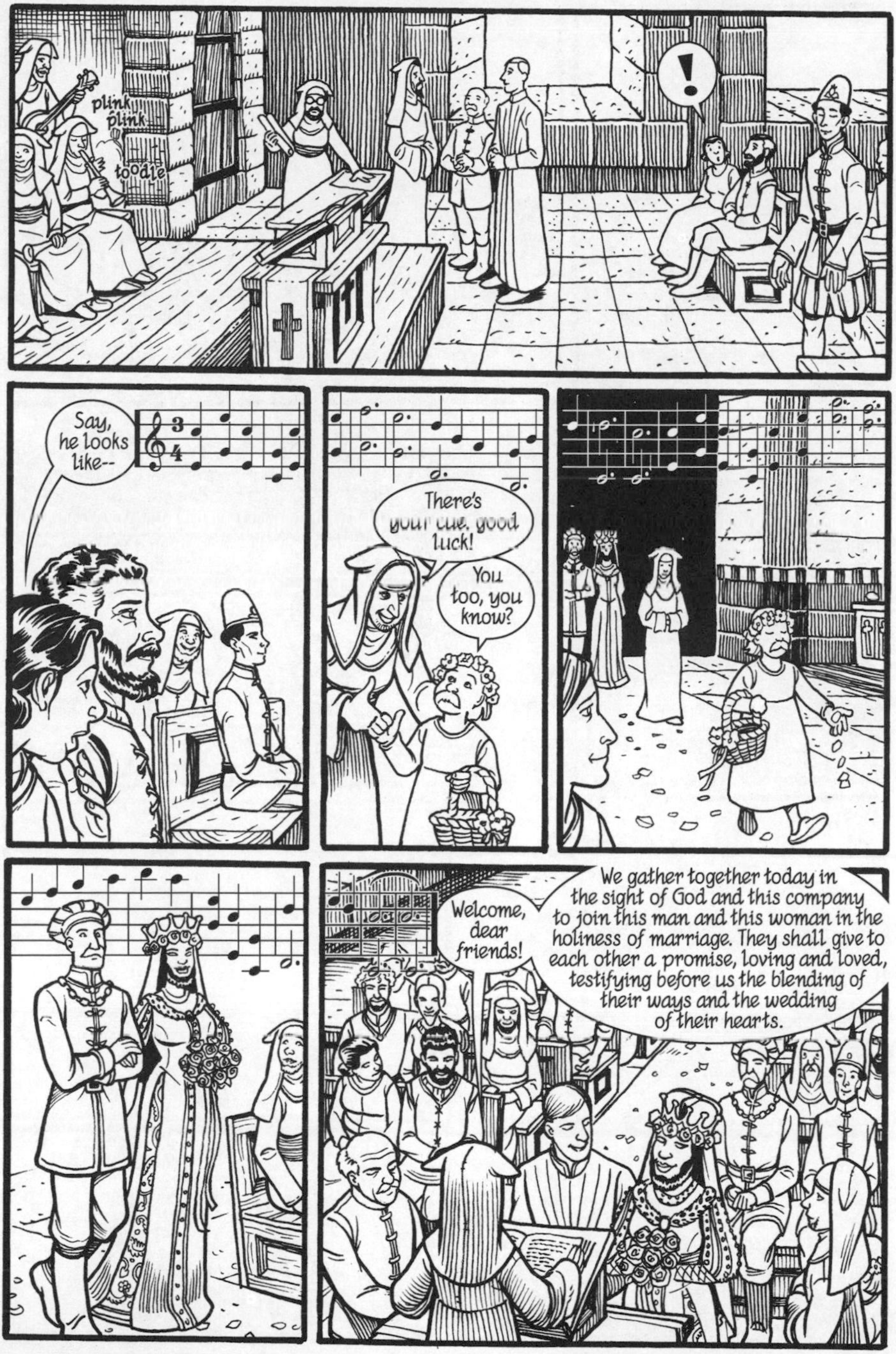
plink
plink
toodle
!
Say, he looks like--
There's your cue, good luck!
You too, you know?
Welcome, dear friends!
We gather together today in the sight of God and this company to join this man and this woman in the holiness of marriage. They shall give to each other a promise, loving and loved, testifying before us the blending of their ways and the wedding of their hearts.

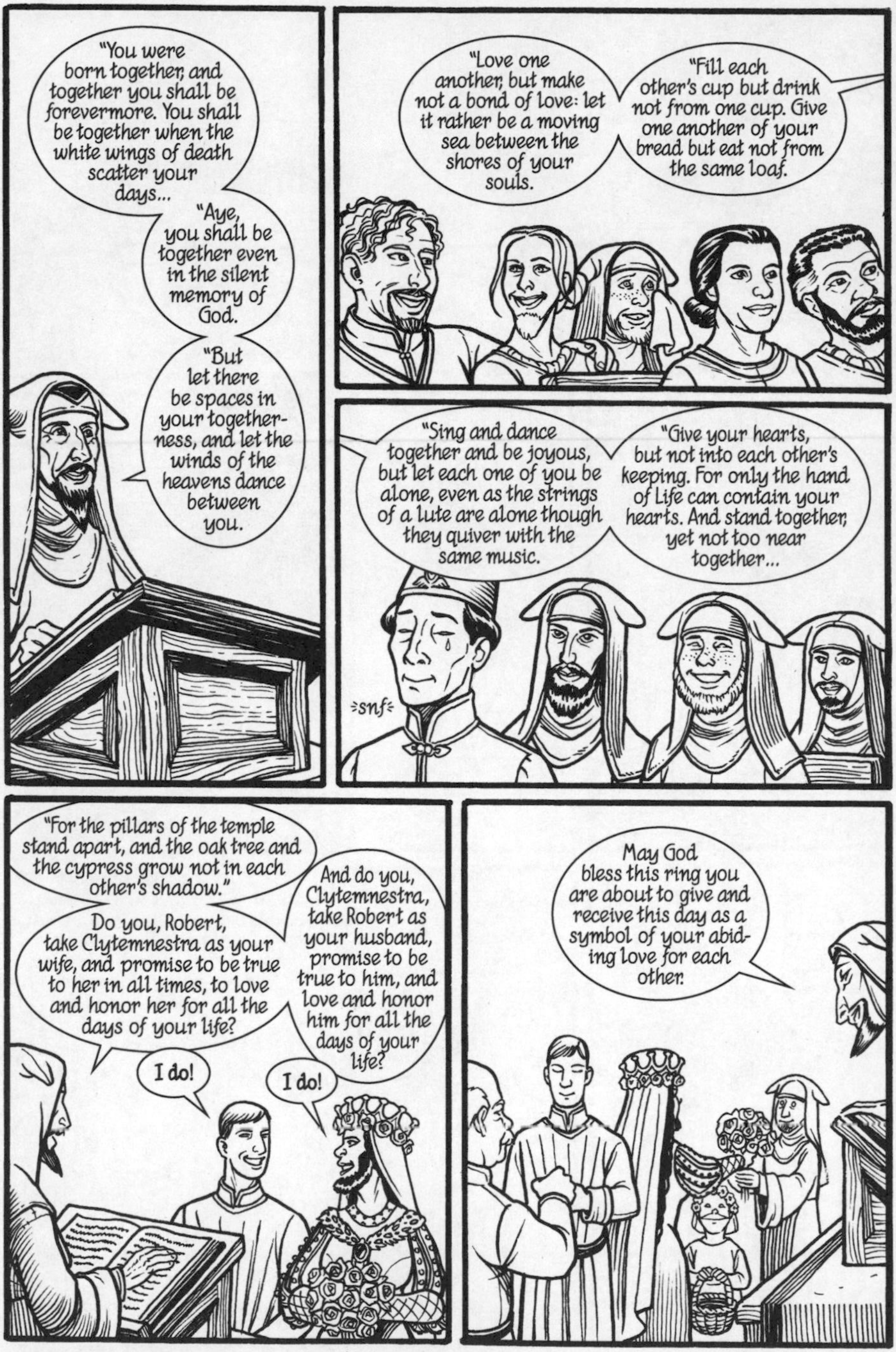
"You were born together, and together you shall be forevermore. You shall be together when the white wings of death scatter your days...
"Aye, you shall be together even in the silent memory of God.
"But let there be spaces in your togetherness, and let the winds of the heavens dance between you.
"Love one another, but make not a bond of love: let it rather be a moving sea between the shores of your souls.
"Fill each other's cup but drink not from one cup. Give one another of your bread but eat not from the same loaf.
"Sing and dance together and be joyous, but let each one of you be alone, even as the strings of a lute are alone though they quiver with the same music.
"Give your hearts, but not into each other's keeping. For only the hand of Life can contain your hearts. And stand together, yet not too near together...
snf
"For the pillars of the temple stand apart, and the oak tree and the cypress grow not in each other's shadow."
Do you, Robert, take Clytemnestra as your wife, and promise to be true to her in all times, to love and honor her for all the days of your life?
I do!
And do you, Clytemnestra, take Robert as your husband, promise to be true to him, and love and honor him for all the days of your life?
I do!
May God bless this ring you are about to give and receive this day as a symbol of your abiding love for each other.

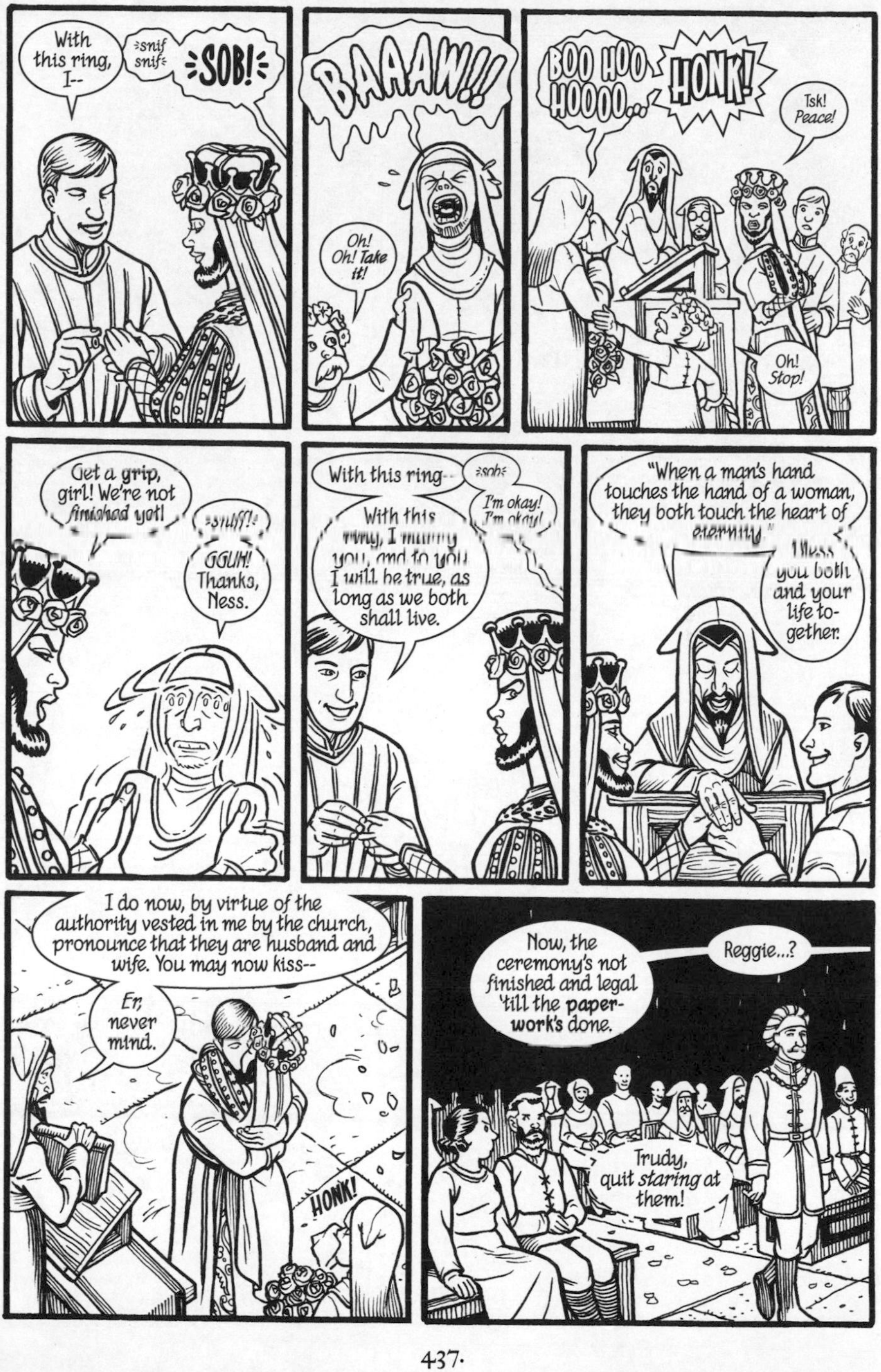
With this ring, I--
snif snif
SOB!
BAAAW!!!
Oh! Oh! Take it!
BOO HOO HOOOO...
HONK!
Tsk! Peace!
Oh! Stop!
Get a grip, girl! We're not finished yet!
sniff!
GGUH! Thanks, Ness.
With this ring--
sob
I'm okay! I'm okay!
With this ring, I marry you, and to you I will be true, as long as we both shall live.
"When a man's hand touches the hand of a woman, they both touch the heart of eternity."
Bless you both and your life together.
I do now, by virtue of the authority vested in me by the church, pronounce that they are husband and wife. You may now kiss--
Er, never mind.
HONK!
Now, the ceremony's not finished and legal 'till the paperwork's done.
Reggie...?
Trudy, quit staring at them!

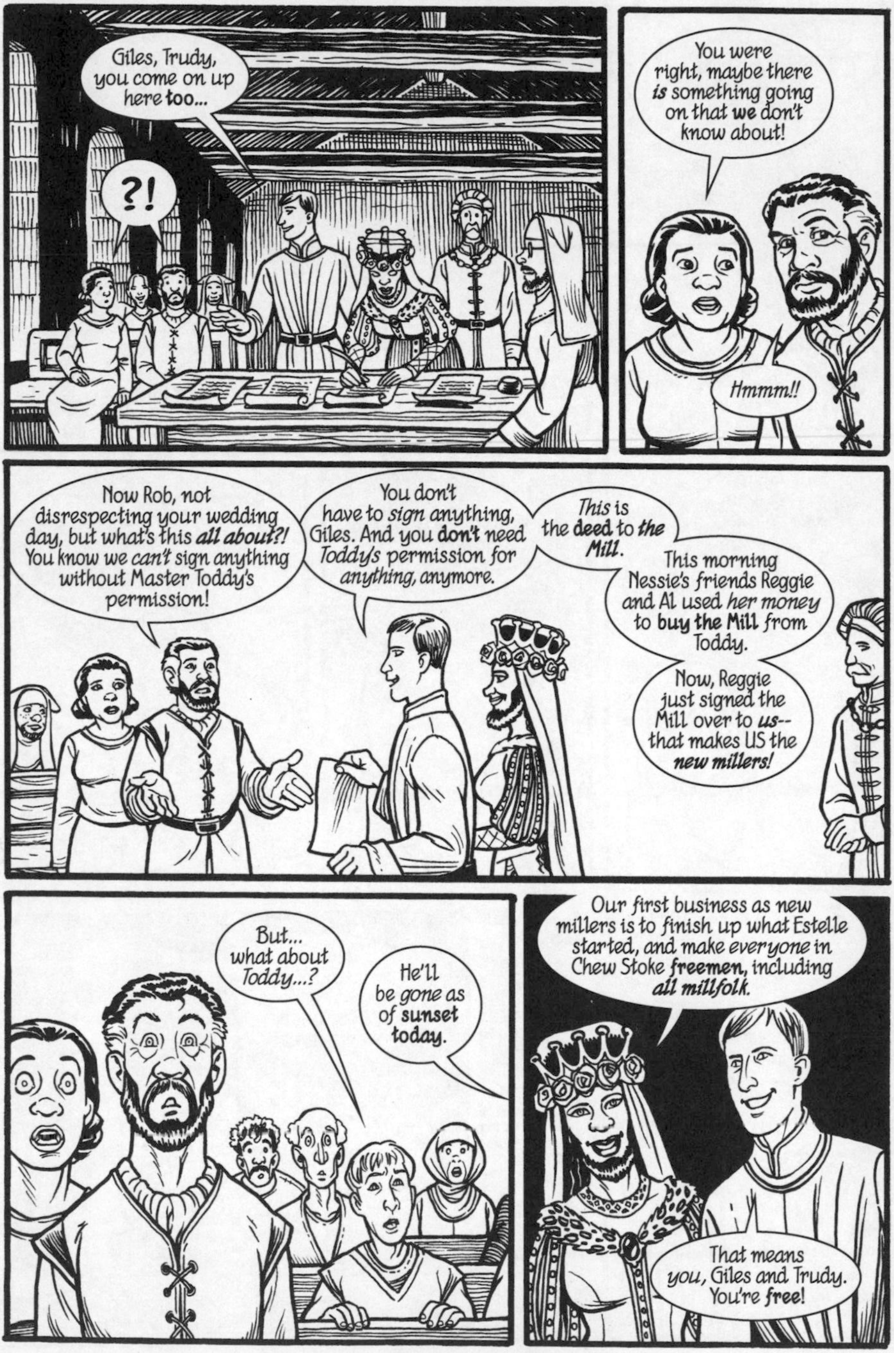
Giles, Trudy, you come on up here **too**...
?!
You were right, maybe there *is* something going on that **we** don't know about!
Hmmm!!
Now Rob, not disrespecting your wedding day, but what's this ***all about?!*** You know we *can't* sign anything without Master Toddy's permission!
You don't have to *sign* anything, Giles. And you **don't** need *Toddy's* permission for *anything*, anymore.
This is the **deed** to ***the Mill***.
This morning Nessie's friends Reggie and Al used *her money* to **buy the Mill** from Toddy.
Now, Reggie just signed the Mill over to ***us***-- that makes US the ***new millers!***
But... what about *Toddy...?*
He'll be *gone* as of **sunset today**.
Our first business as new millers is to finish up what Estelle started, and make *everyone* in Chew Stoke **freemen**, including ***all millfolk***.
That means *you*, Giles and Trudy. You're ***free!***

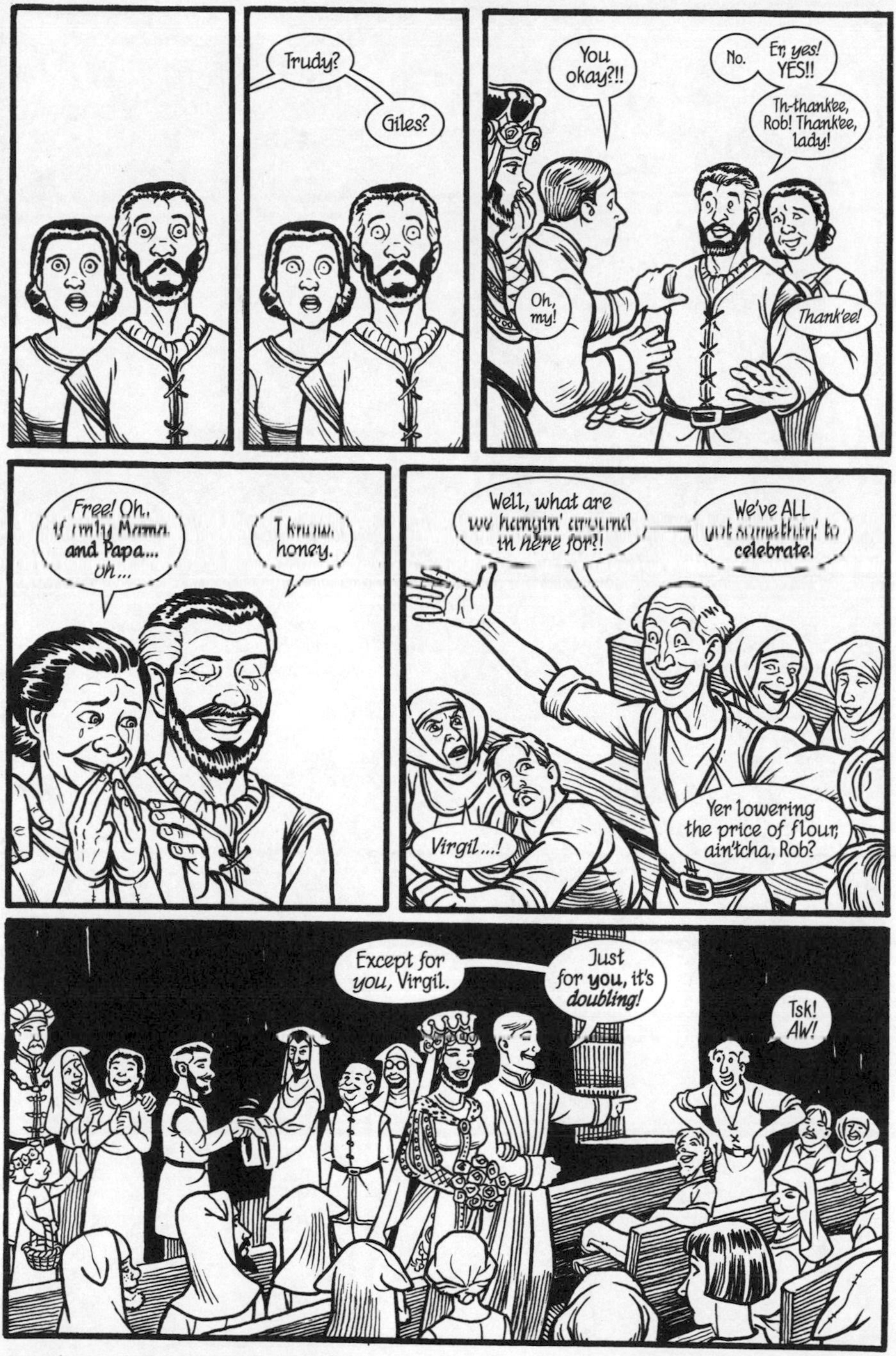
Trudy?
Giles?
You okay?!!
No.
Er, yes! YES!!
Th-thank'ee, Rob! Thank'ee, lady!
Oh, my!
Thank'ee!
Free! Oh, if only Mama and Papa... oh...
I know, honey.
Well, what are we hangin' around in here for?!
We've ALL got somethin' to celebrate!
Yer lowering the price of flour, ain'tcha, Rob?
Virgil...!
Except for you, Virgil.
Just for you, it's doubling!
Tsk! AW!

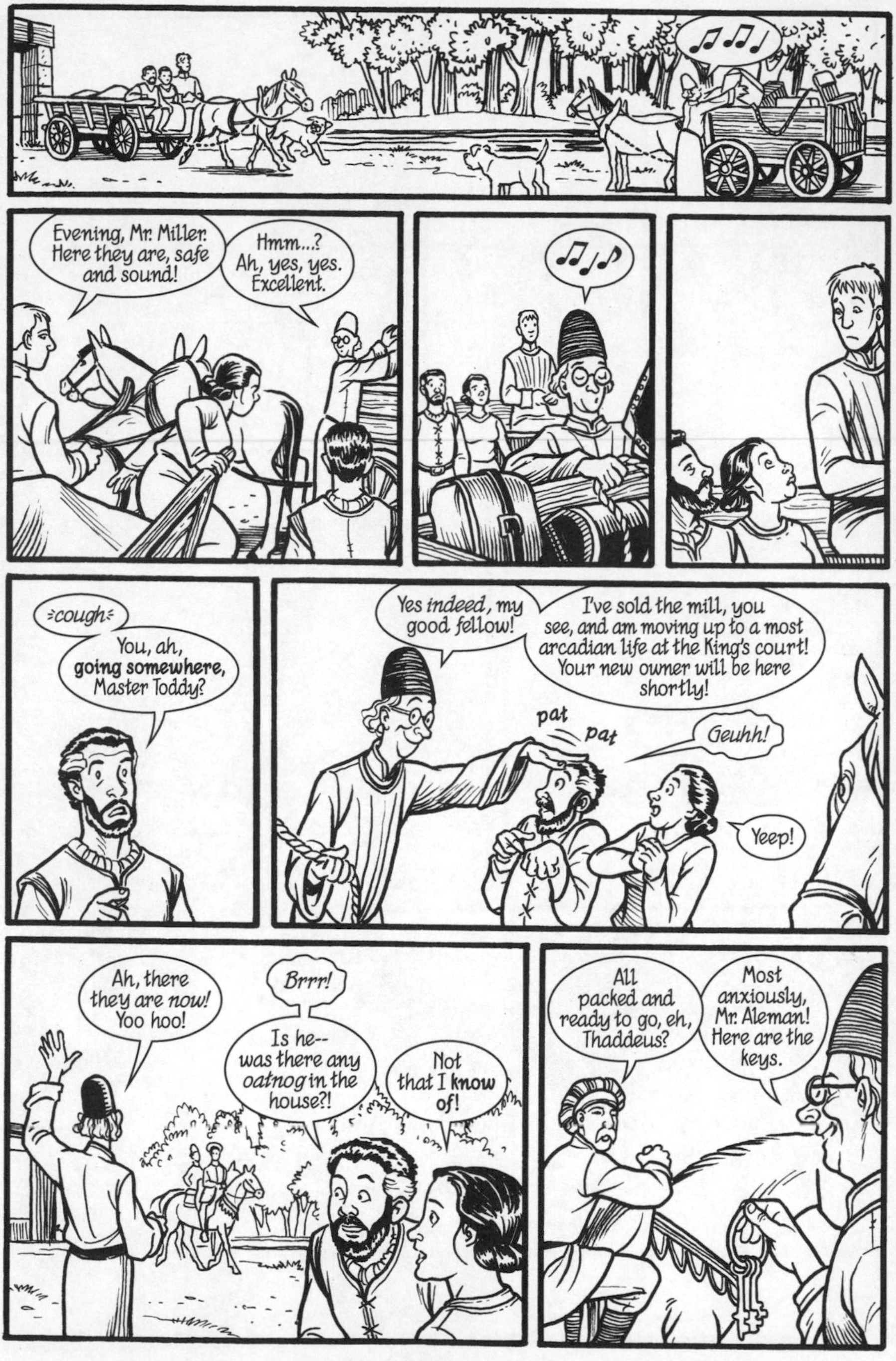
Evening, Mr. Miller. Here they are, safe and sound!
Hmm...? Ah, yes, yes. Excellent.
cough
You, ah, **going somewhere,** Master Toddy?
Yes *indeed*, my good fellow!
I've sold the mill, you see, and am moving up to a most arcadian life at the King's court! Your new owner will be here shortly!
pat
pat
Geuhh!
Yeep!
Ah, there they are *now*! Yoo hoo!
Brrr!
Is he-- was there any *oatnog* in the house?!
Not that I **know of**!
All packed and ready to go, eh, Thaddeus?
Most anxiously, Mr. Aleman! Here are the keys.

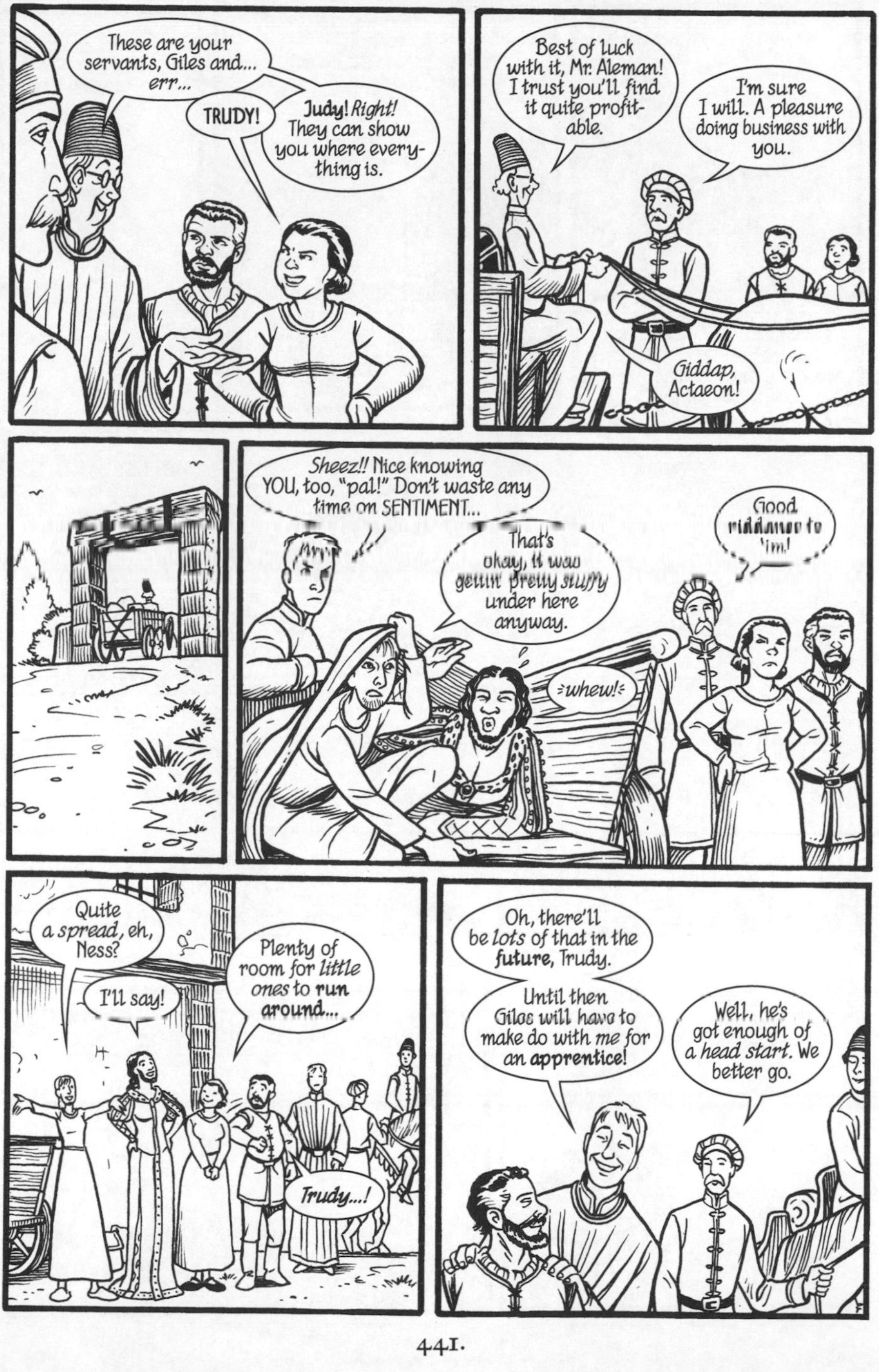
These are your servants, Giles and... err...
TRUDY!
Judy! *Right!* They can show you where every-thing is.
Best of luck with it, Mr. Aleman! I trust you'll find it quite profit-able.
I'm sure I will. A pleasure doing business with you.
Giddap, Actaeon!
Sheez!! Nice knowing YOU, too, "pal!" Don't waste any time on SENTIMENT...
That's okay, it was gettin' pretty *stuffy* under here anyway.
whew!
Good riddance to 'im!
Quite a *spread*, eh, Ness?
I'll *say!*
Plenty of room for *little ones* to **run around...**
Trudy...!
Oh, there'll be *lots* of that in the **future**, Trudy.
Until then Giles will have to make do with *me* for an **apprentice**!
Well, he's got enough of a *head start*. We better go.

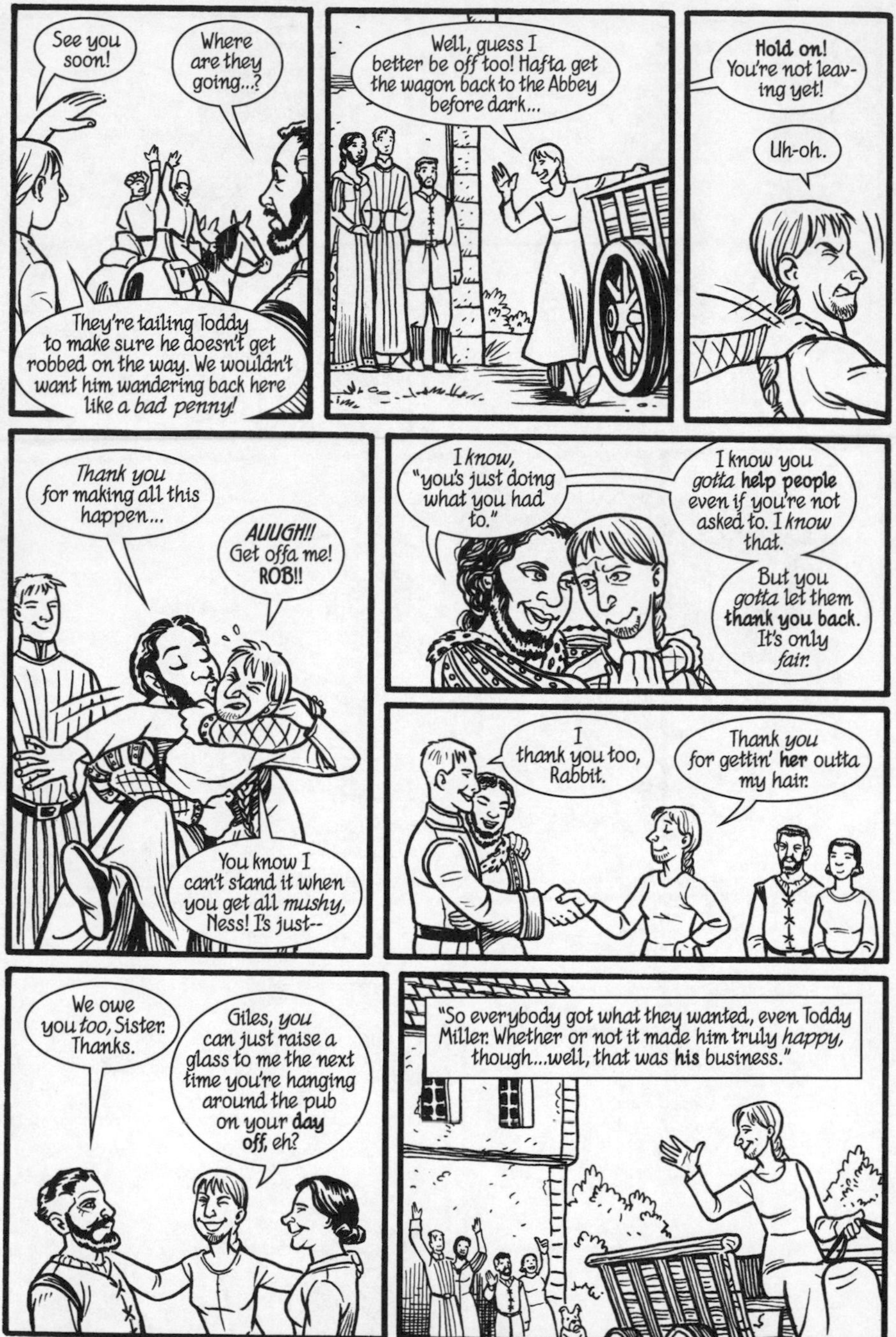
See you soon!
Where are they going...?
They're tailing Toddy to make sure he doesn't get robbed on the way. We wouldn't want him wandering back here like a *bad penny!*
Well, guess I better be off too! Hafta get the wagon back to the Abbey before dark...
Hold on! You're not leav-ing yet!
Uh-oh.
Thank you for making all this happen...
AUUGH!! Get offa me! **ROB!!**
You know I can't stand it when you get all *mushy,* Ness! I's just--
I *know,* "you's just doing what you had to."
I know you *gotta* **help people** even if you're not asked to. I *know* that.
But you *gotta* let them **thank you back.** It's only *fair.*
I thank you too, Rabbit.
Thank *you* for gettin' **her** outta my hair.
We owe you *too,* Sister. Thanks.
Giles, *you* can just raise a glass to me the next time you're hanging around the pub on your **day off,** eh?
"So everybody got what they wanted, even Toddy Miller. Whether or not it made him truly *happy,* though...well, that was **his** business."

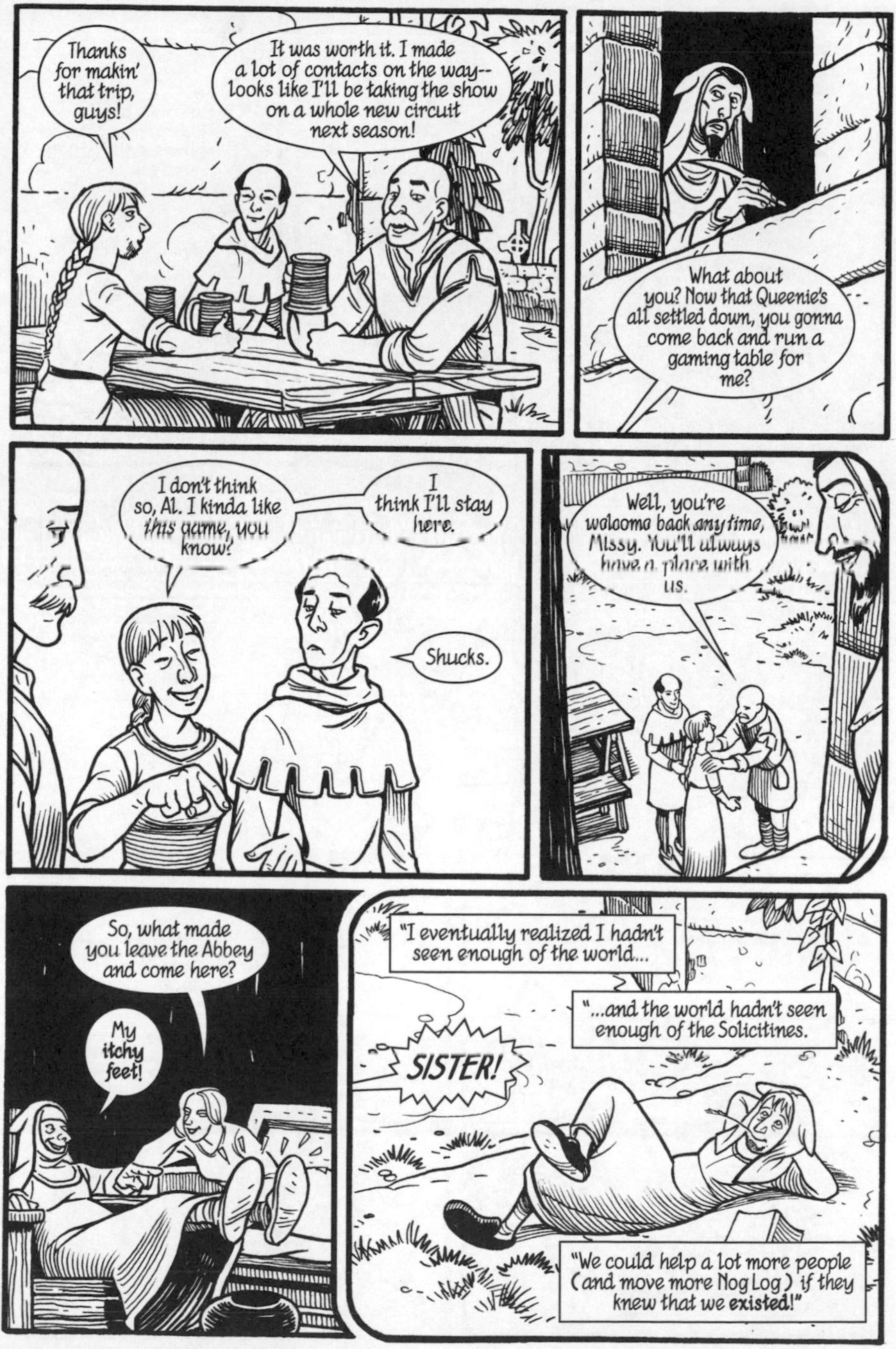
Thanks for makin' that trip, guys!
It was worth it. I made a lot of contacts on the way-- looks like I'll be taking the show on a whole new circuit next season!
What about you? Now that Queenie's all settled down, you gonna come back and run a gaming table for me?
I don't think so, Al. I kinda like this game, you know?
I think I'll stay here.
Shucks.
Well, you're welcome back any time, Missy. You'll always have a place with us.
So, what made you leave the Abbey and come here?
My itchy feet!
"I eventually realized I hadn't seen enough of the world...
"...and the world hadn't seen enough of the Solicitines.
SISTER!
"We could help a lot more people (and move more Nog Log) if they knew that we existed!"

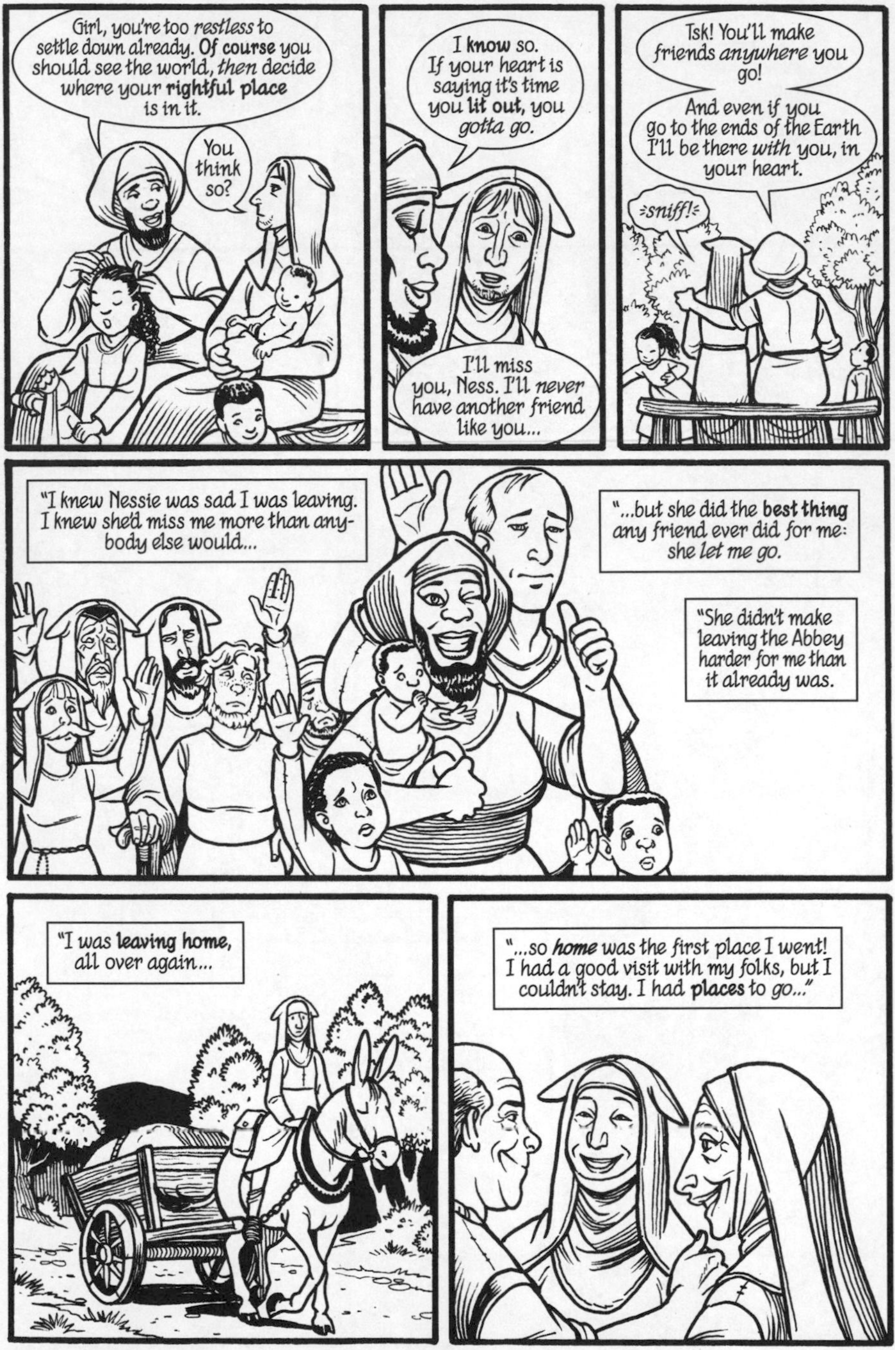
Girl, you're too *restless* to settle down already. **Of course** you should see the world, *then* decide where your **rightful place** is in it.
You think so?
I **know** so. If your heart is saying it's time you **lit out**, you *gotta go.*
I'll miss you, Ness. I'll *never* have another friend like you...
Tsk! You'll make friends *anywhere* you go!
And even if you go to the ends of the Earth I'll be there *with* you, in your heart.
sniff!
"I knew Nessie was sad I was leaving. I knew she'd miss me more than anybody else would...
"...but she did the **best thing** any friend ever did for me: she *let me go.*
"She didn't make leaving the Abbey harder for me than it already was.
"I was **leaving home**, all over again...
"...so ***home*** was the first place I went! I had a good visit with my folks, but I couldn't stay. I had **places** to *go...*"

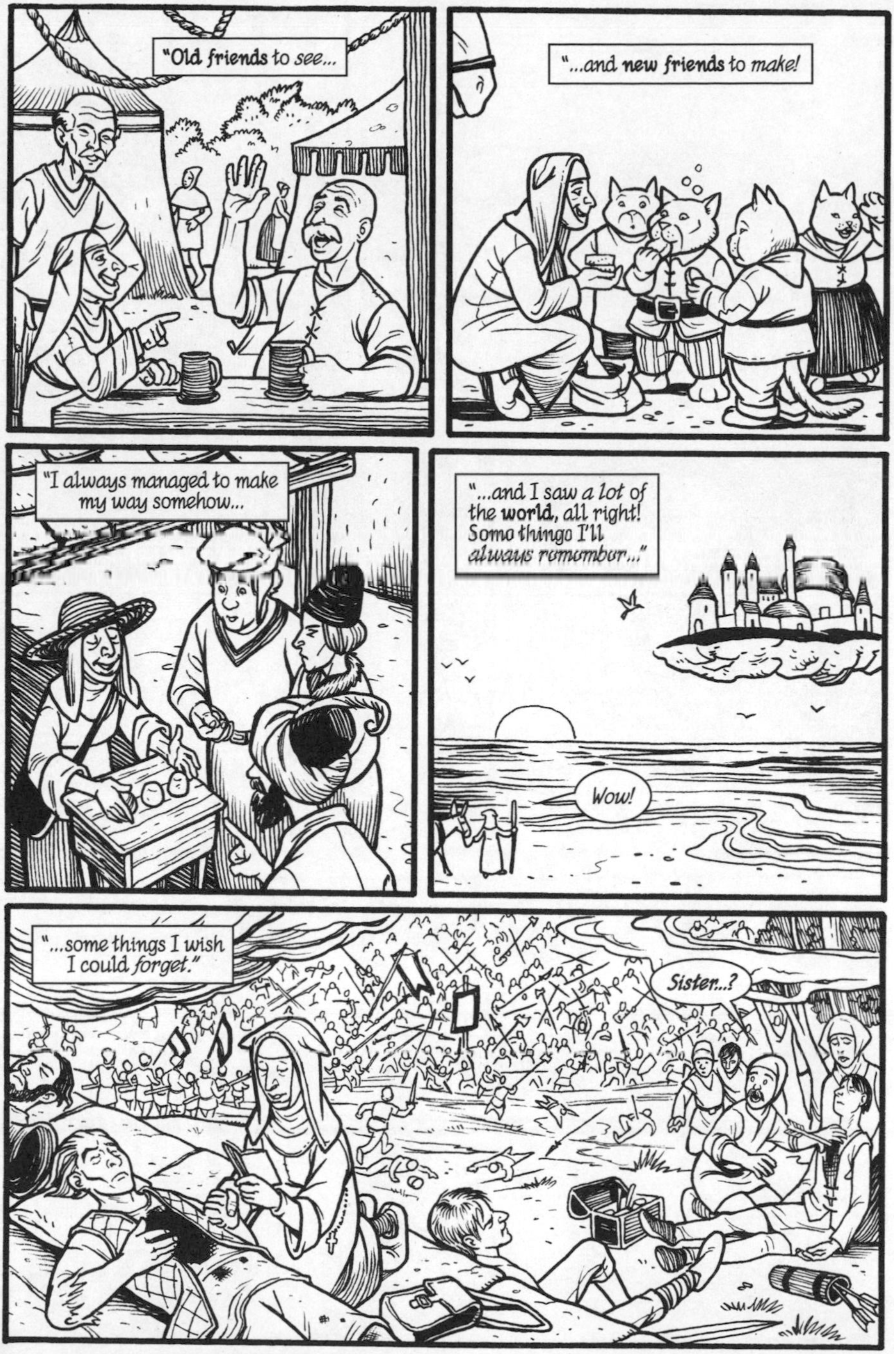
"Old friends to see...
"...and new friends to make!
"I always managed to make my way somehow...
"...and I saw a lot of the world, all right! Some things I'll always remember..."
Wow!
"...some things I wish I could forget."
Sister...?

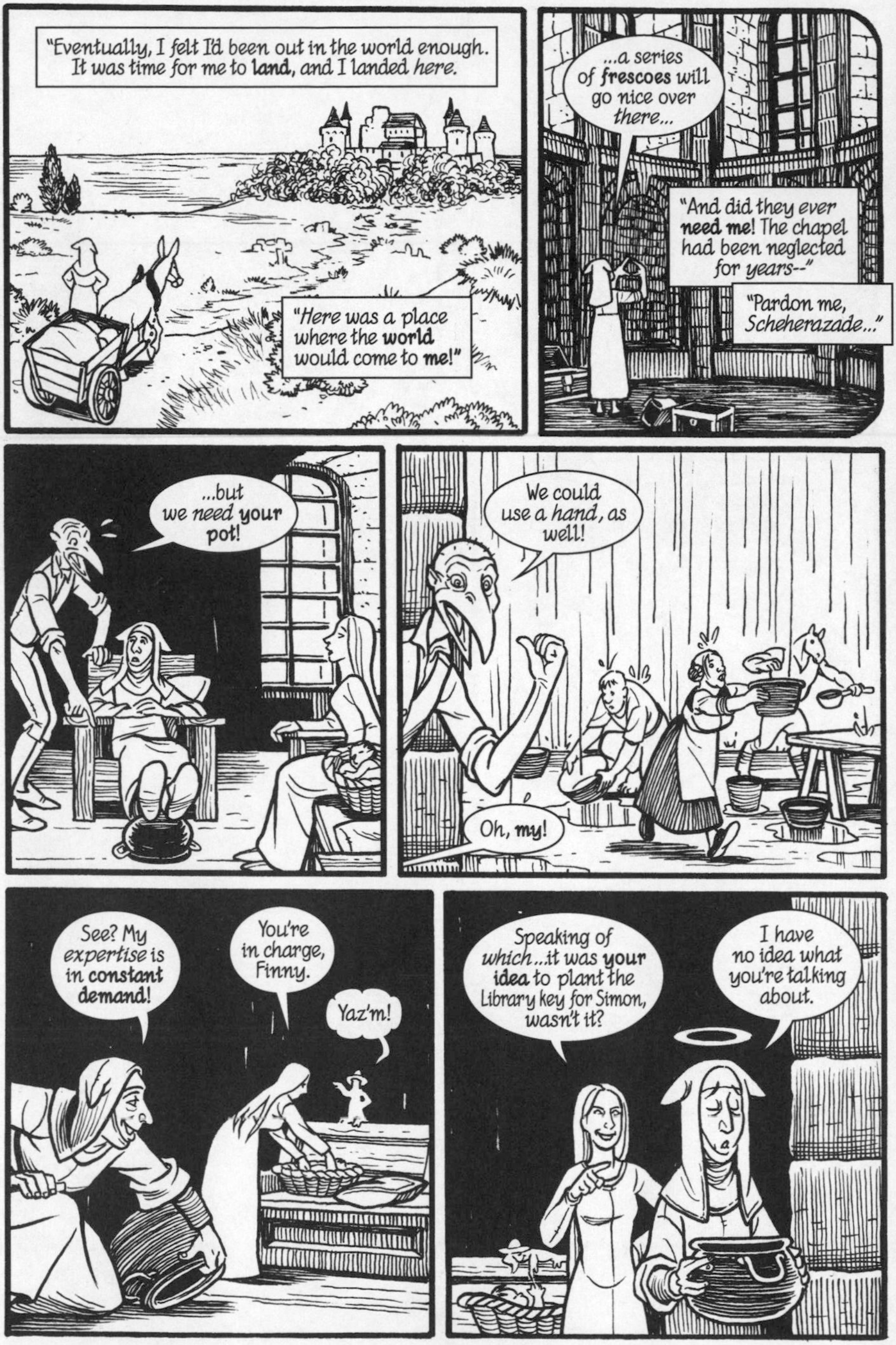
"Eventually, I felt I'd been out in the world enough. It was time for me to **land**, and I landed *here*.
"*Here* was a place where the **world** would come to **me**!"
...a series of **frescoes** will go nice over *there*...
"And did they *ever* **need me**! The chapel had been neglected for *years*--"
"Pardon me, *Scheherazade*..."
...but we *need* **your pot**!
We could use a *hand*, as well!
Oh, **my**!
See? My *expertise* is in **constant demand**!
You're in charge, Finny.
Yaz'm!
Speaking of *which*...it was **your idea** to plant the Library key for Simon, wasn't it?
I have no idea what you're talking about.

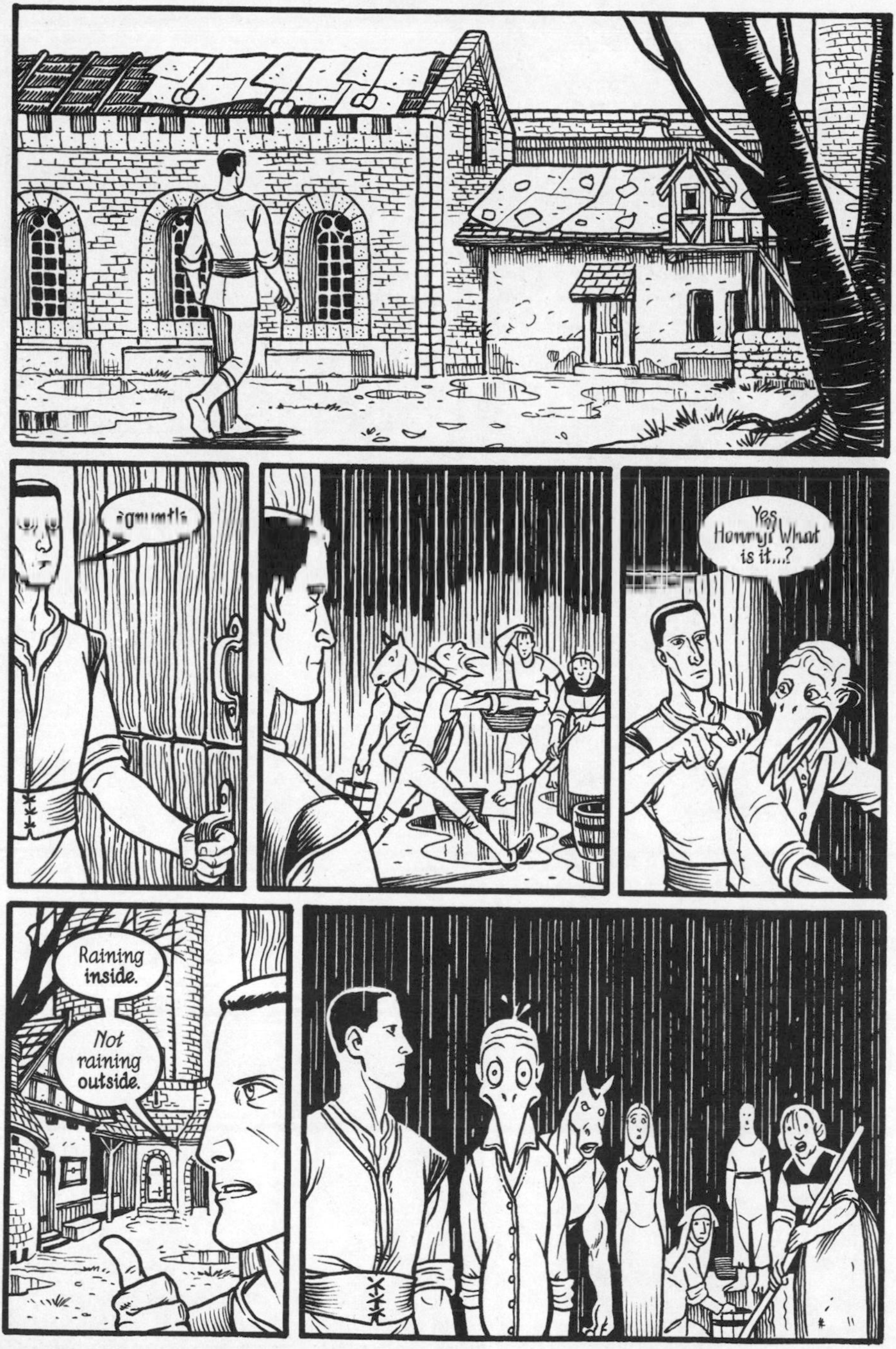
Yes, Henry? What is it...?
Raining inside.
Not raining outside.

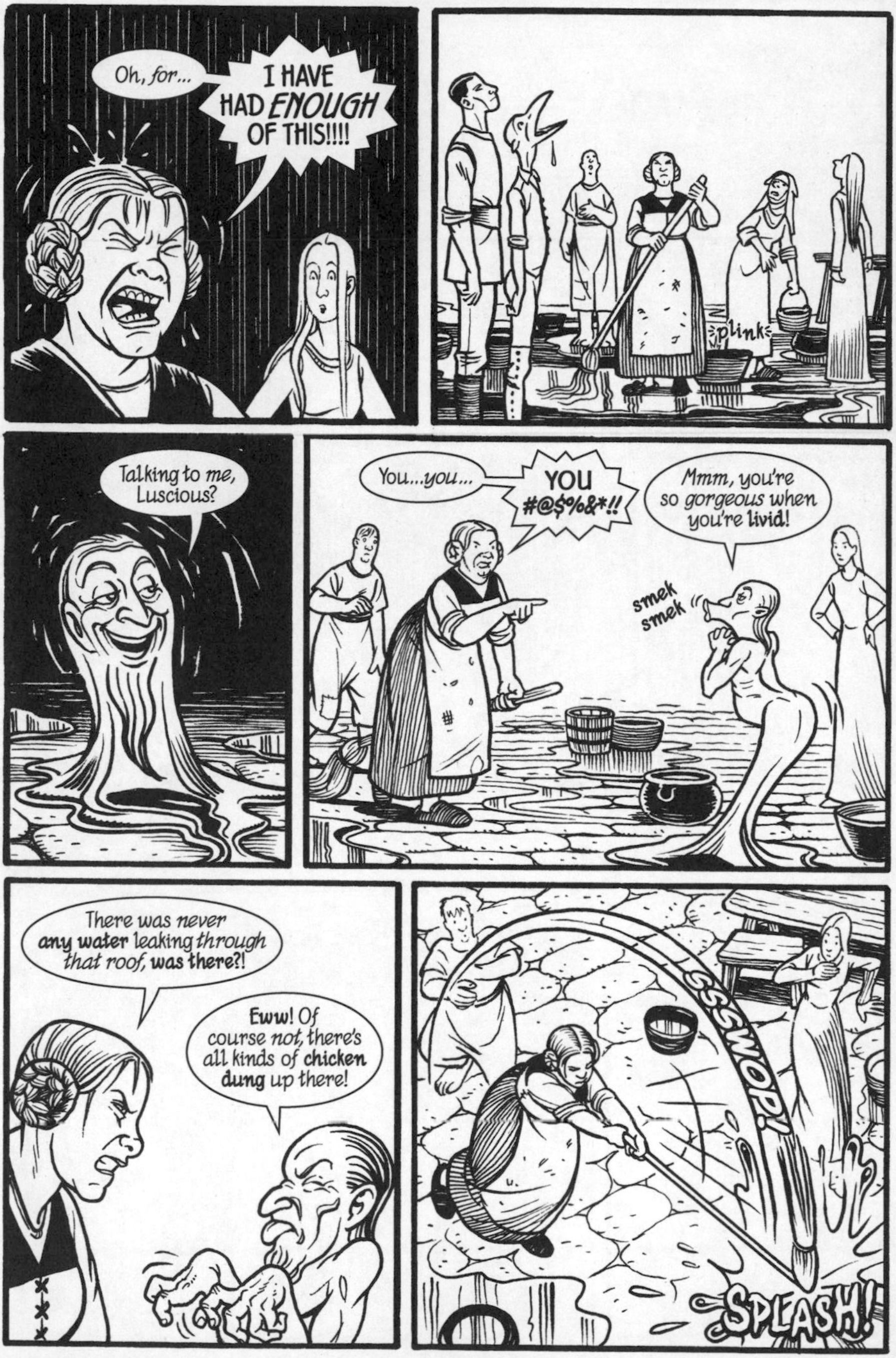
Oh, for...
I HAVE HAD ENOUGH OF THIS!!!!
plink
Talking to me, Luscious?
You...you...
YOU #@$%&*!!
Mmm, you're so gorgeous when you're livid!
smek smek
There was never any water leaking through that roof, was there?!
Eww! Of course not, there's all kinds of chicken dung up there!
SSSWOP!
SPLASH!

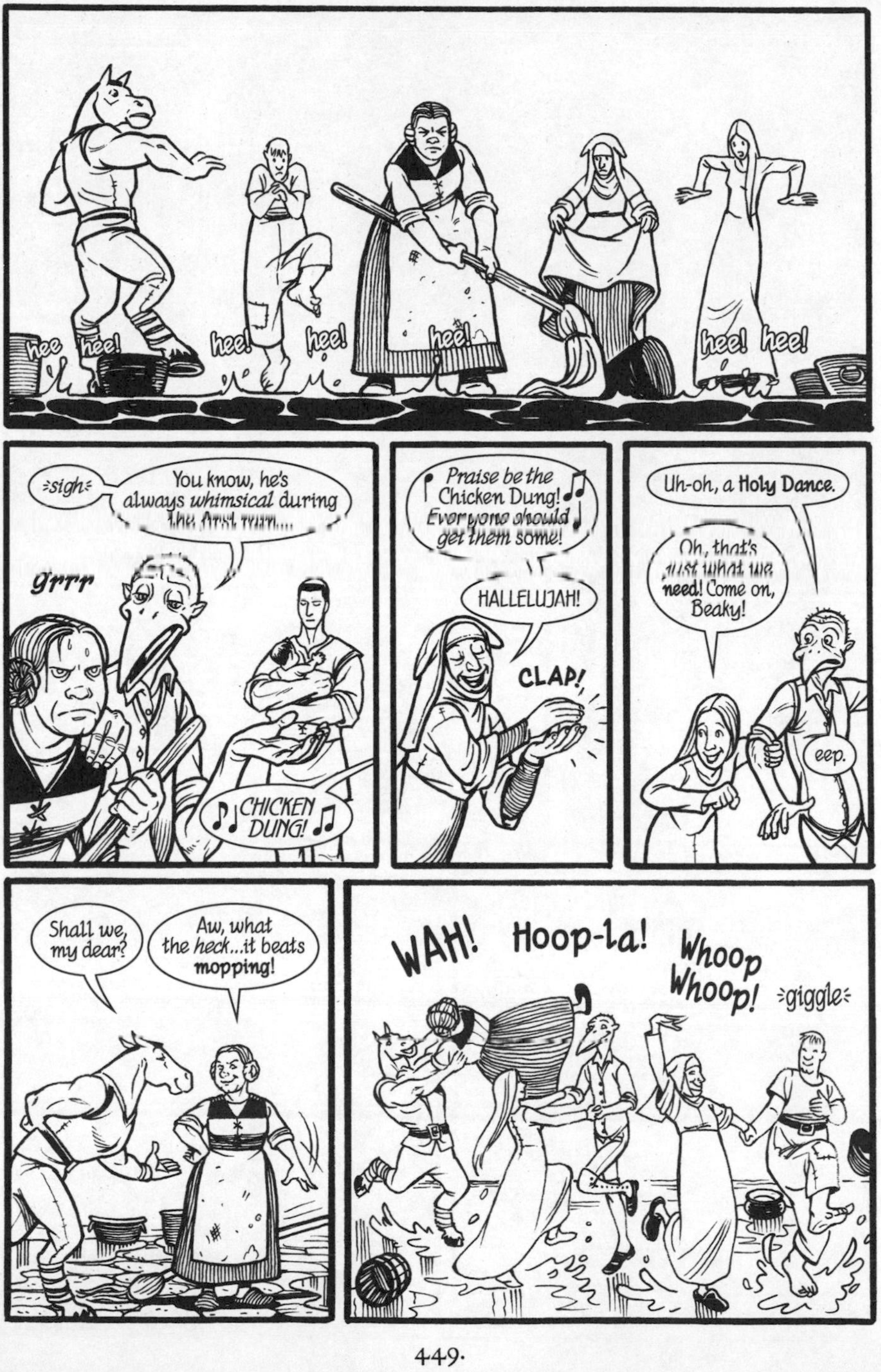
hee
hee!
hee!
hee!
hee!
hee!
hee!
sigh
You know, he's always *whimsical* during the first run...
grrr
CHICKEN DUNG!
Praise be the Chicken Dung! Everyone should get them some!
HALLELUJAH!
CLAP!
Uh-oh, a **Holy Dance.**
Oh, that's *just* what we need! Come on, Beaky!
eep.
Shall we, my dear?
Aw, what the *heck*...it beats **mopping!**
WAH!
Hoop-la!
Whoop Whoop!
giggle

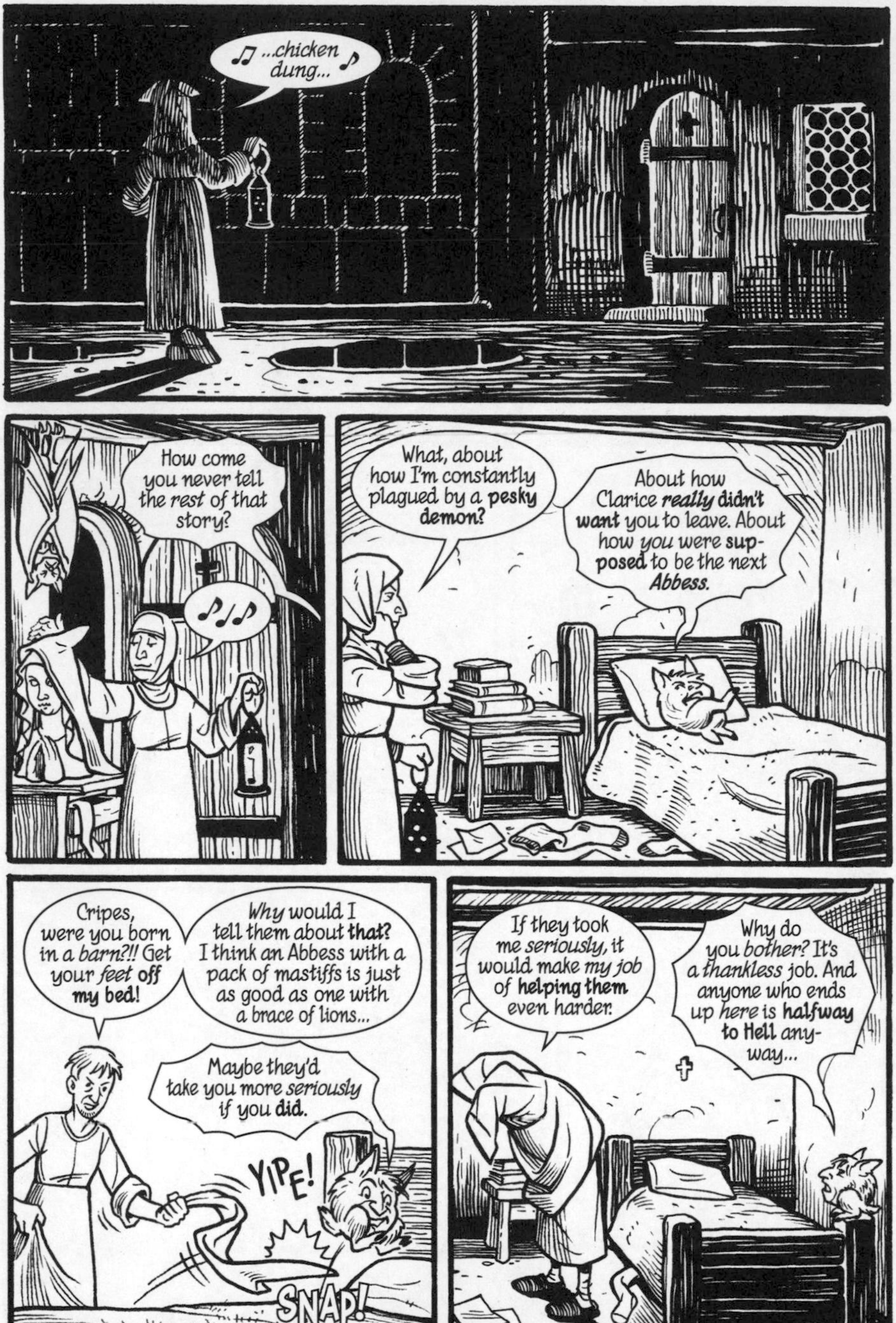
♫ ...chicken dung... ♪
How come you never tell the *rest* of that story?
♪♪♪
What, about how I'm constantly plagued by a **pesky demon?**
About how Clarice ***really* didn't want** you to leave. About how *you* were **sup-posed** to be the next ***Abbess.***
Cripes, were you born in a *barn?!!* Get your *feet* **off my bed!**
Why would I tell them about **that?** I think an Abbess with a pack of mastiffs is just as good as one with a brace of lions...
Maybe they'd take you more *seriously* if you **did.**
YIPE!
SNAP!
If they took me *seriously*, it would make *my job* of **helping them** even harder.
Why do you *bother?* It's a *thankless* job. And anyone who ends up *here* is **halfway to Hell** any-way...

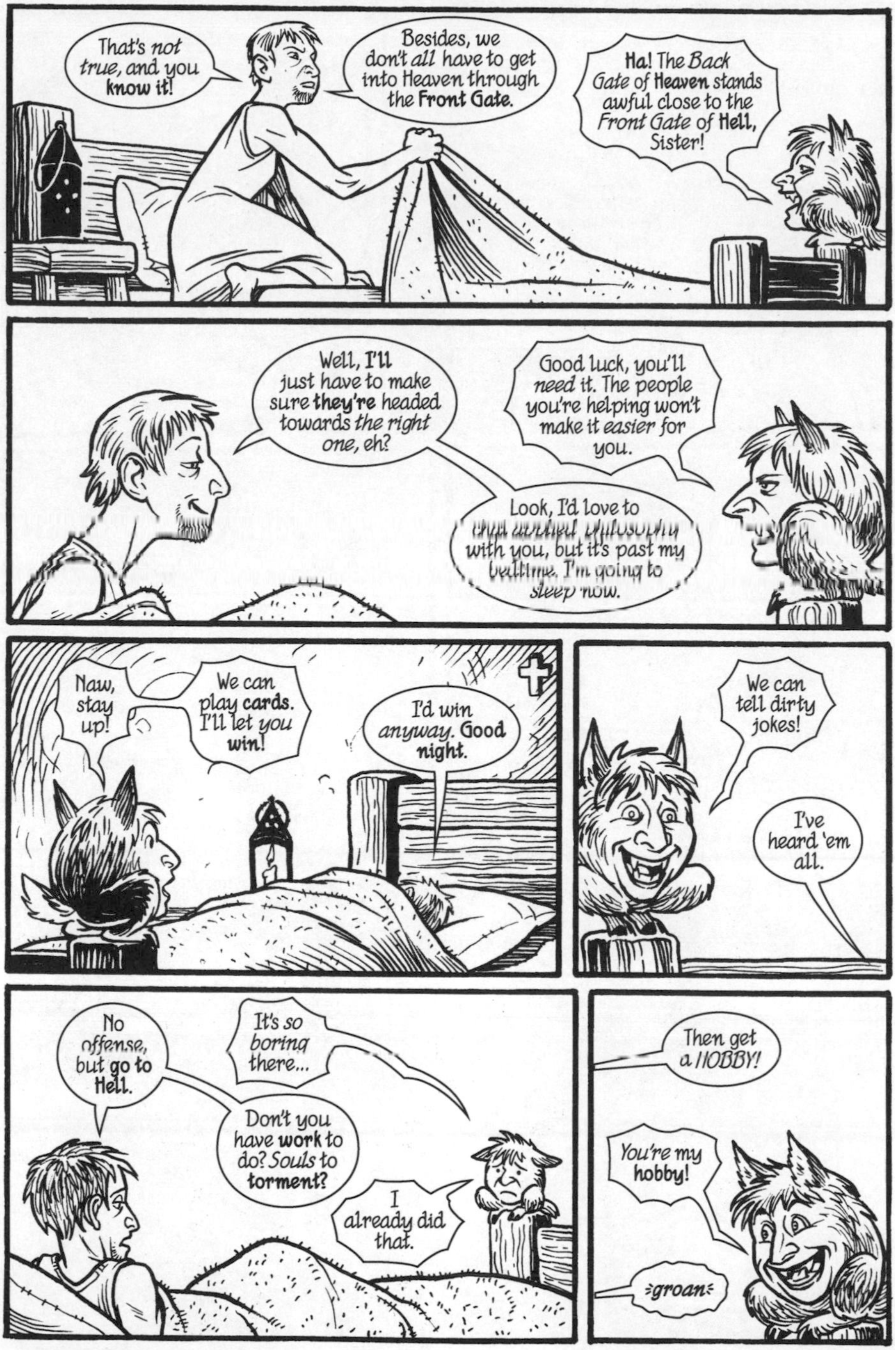
That's not true, and you know it!
Besides, we don't all have to get into Heaven through the Front Gate.
Ha! The Back Gate of Heaven stands awful close to the Front Gate of Hell, Sister!
Well, I'll just have to make sure they're headed towards the right one, eh?
Good luck, you'll need it. The people you're helping won't make it easier for you.
Look, I'd love to with you, but it's past my bedtime. I'm going to sleep now.
Naw, stay up!
We can play cards. I'll let you win!
I'd win anyway. Good night.
We can tell dirty jokes!
I've heard 'em all.
No offense, but go to Hell.
It's so boring there...
Don't you have work to do? Souls to torment?
I already did that.
Then get a HOBBY!
You're my hobby!
groan

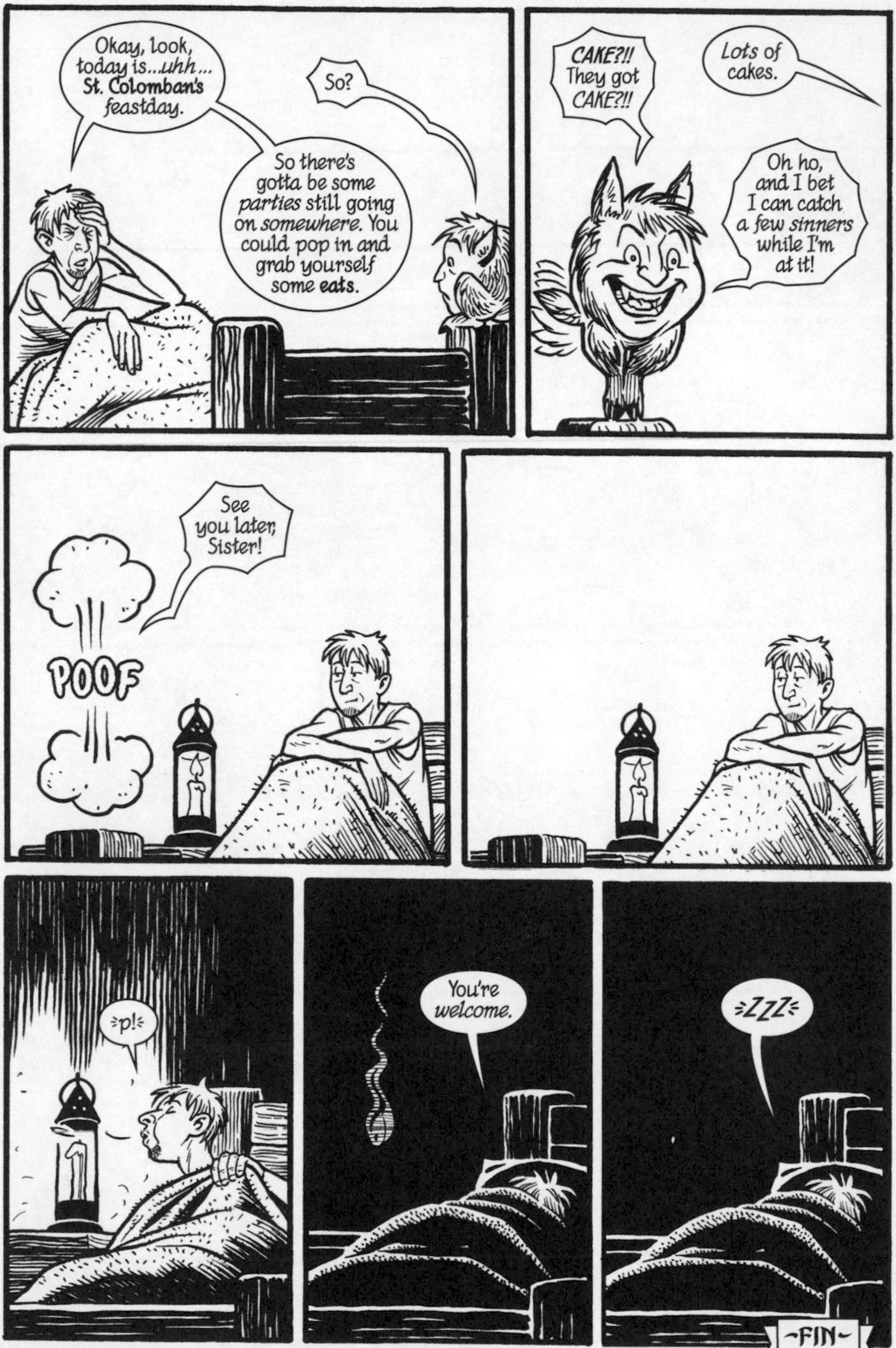
Okay, look, today is...*uhh*... **St. Colomban's** *feastday.*
So?
So there's gotta be some *parties* still going on *somewhere*. You could pop in and grab yourself some **eats**.
CAKE?!! They got *CAKE?!!*
Lots of cakes.
Oh ho, and I bet I can catch *a few sinners* while I'm at it!
See you later, Sister!
POOF
p!
You're *welcome.*
ZZZ
FIN

Epilogue.

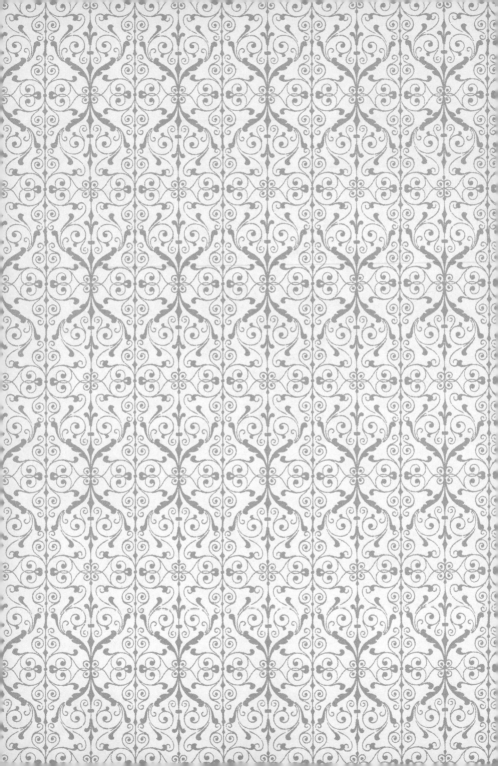

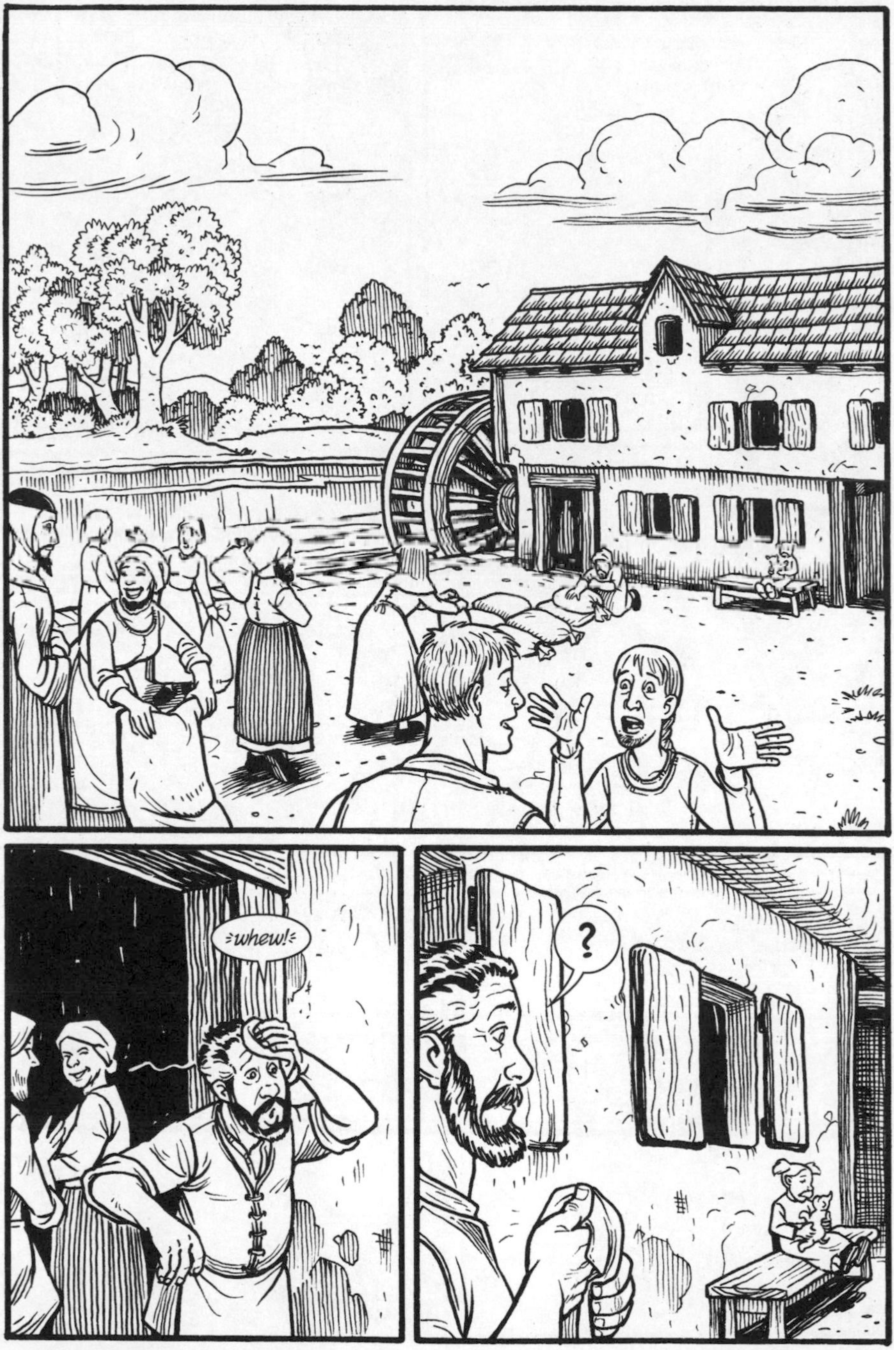
whew!
?

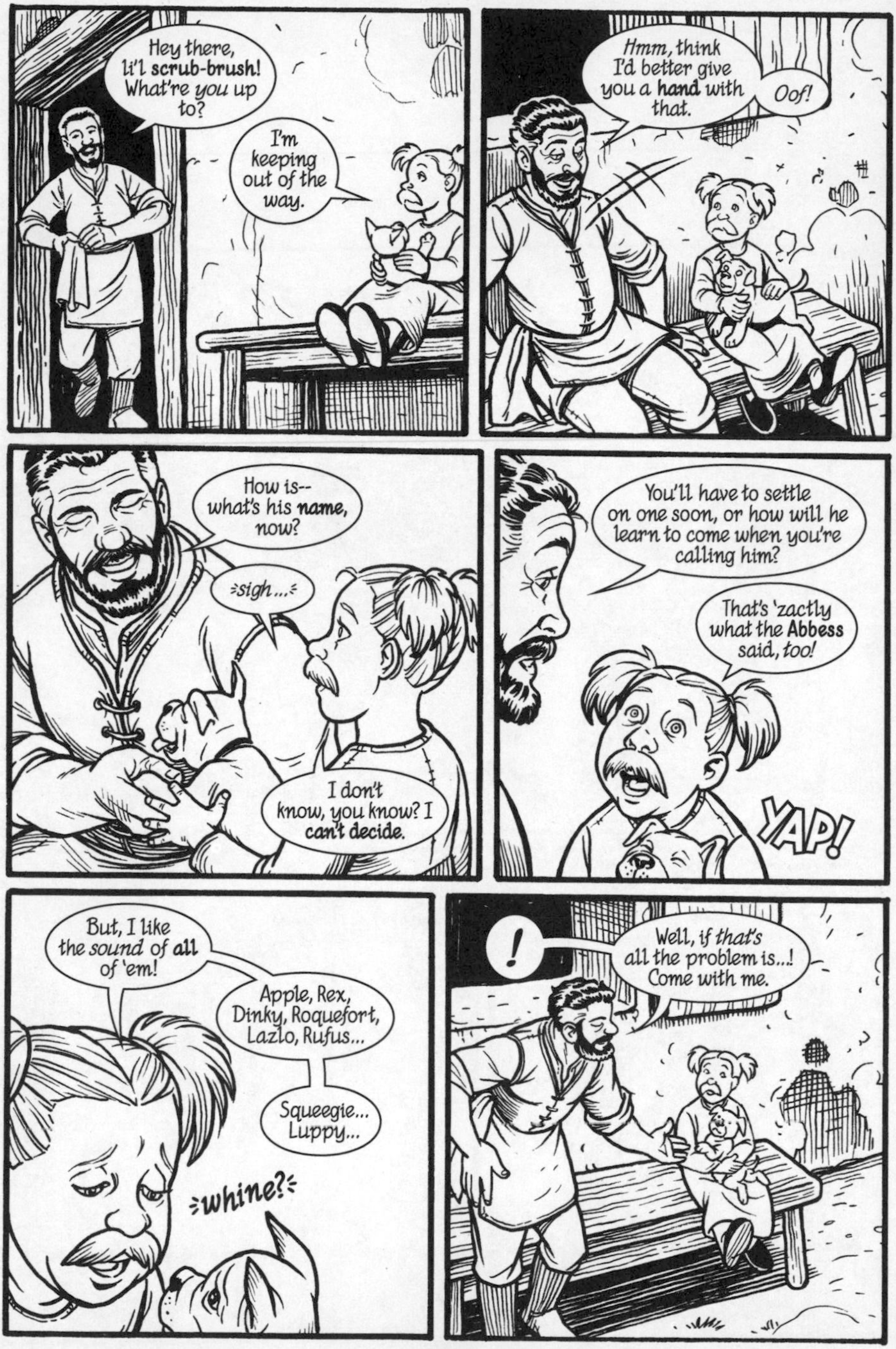
Hey there, li'l scrub-brush! What're you up to?
I'm keeping out of the way.
Hmm, think I'd better give you a hand with that.
Oof!
How is-- what's his name, now?
sigh...
I don't know, you know? I can't decide.
You'll have to settle on one soon, or how will he learn to come when you're calling him?
That's 'zactly what the Abbess said, too!
YAP!
But, I like the sound of all of 'em!
Apple, Rex, Dinky, Roquefort, Lazlo, Rufus...
Squeegie... Luppy...
whine?
!
Well, if that's all the problem is...! Come with me.

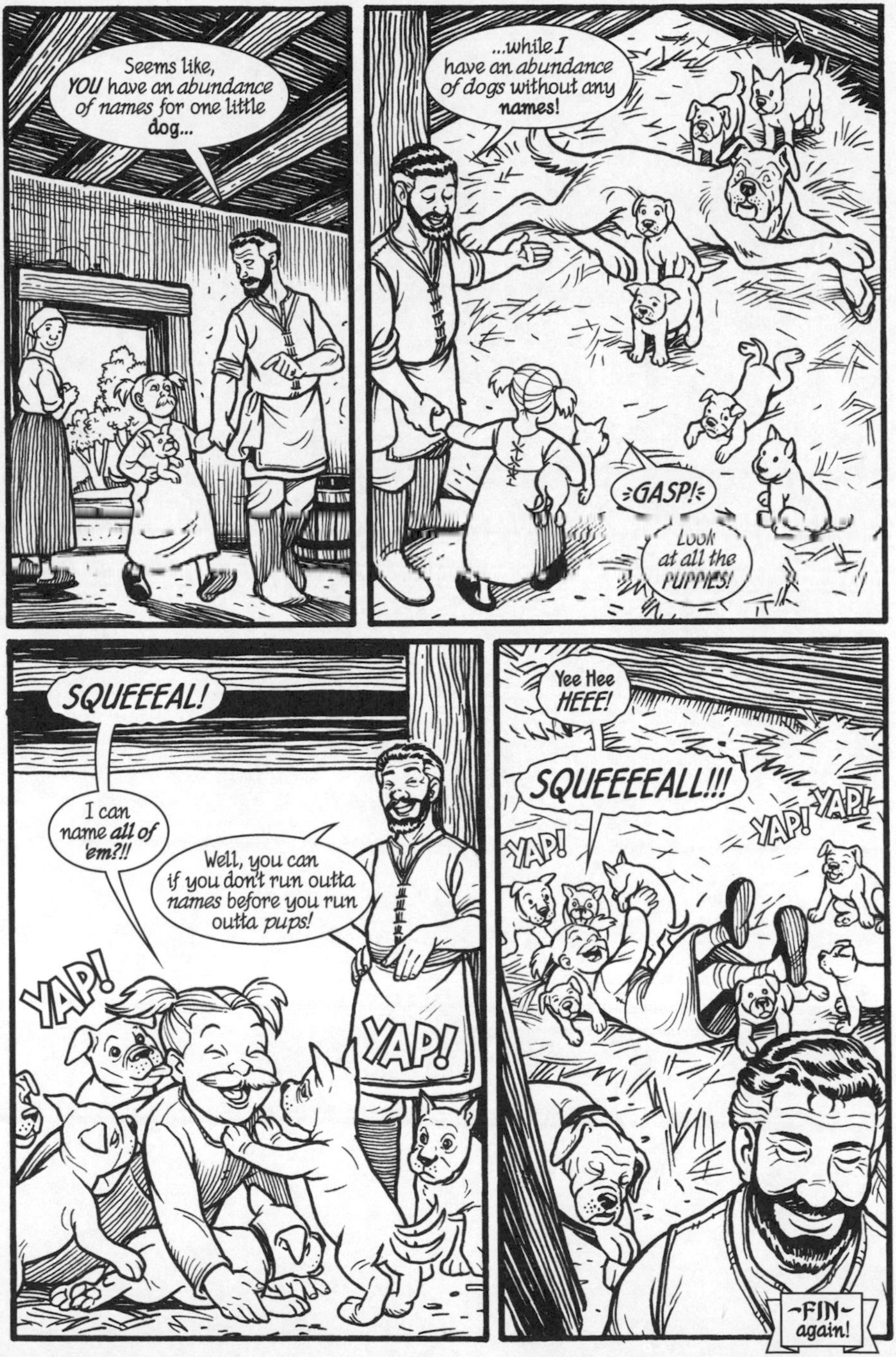

Seems like, YOU have an abundance of names for one little dog...
...while I have an abundance of dogs without any names!
GASP!
Look at all the PUPPIES!
SQUEEEAL!
I can name all of 'em?!!
Well, you can if you don't run outta names before you run outta pups!
YAP!
YAP!
Yee Hee HEEE!
SQUEEEEALL!!!
YAP!
YAP!
YAP!
-FIN- again!

EDITED BY GARY GROTH.
DESIGNED BY ADAM GRANO.
LETTERED BY TODD KLEIN.
PROMOTION BY ERIC REYNOLDS.
PUBLISHED BY GARY GROTH & KIM THOMPSON.

Castle Waiting is ™ & © Linda Medley.

Compilation copyright © 2006 Fantagraphics Books.
Introduction by Jane Yolen copyright © 2006 Jane Yolen. All
rights reserved. Permission to quote or reproduce material for
reviews must be obtained from the publisher. Fantagraphics
Books, Inc. 7563 Lake City Way, Seattle, WA 98115.

To receive a free catalogue of fine comics and books
(including the ongoing *Castle Waiting* Vol. II comic)
call 1-800-657-1100 or visit fantagraphics.com

If you'd like to buy original art from the *Castle Waiting*
series, contact Kim at kimt@fantagraphics.com

Distributed in the U.S. by W.W. Norton and Company, Inc.
Distributed in Canada by Raincoast Books
Distributed in the U.K. by Turnaround Distribution

ISBN: 978-1-56097-747-6

Fourth printing. Printed in Singapore.